Computer Information Systems

KELLY RAINER • BRAD PRINCE • HUGH J. WATSON

James Madison University
College of Business
COB 204

Wiley Custom Learning Solutions

To order books or for customer service, please call 1(800)-CALL-WILEY (225-5945).

Printed in the United States of America.

ISBN 978-1-119-19313-5
Printed and bound by Courier Digital Solutions.

10 9 8 7 6

CONTENTS

JAMES MADISON UNIVERSITY

COB 204 - COURSE LEARNING OBJECTIVES:

This course provides a broad overview of information systems used by businesses. Upon completing this course you should be able to demonstrate your ability to perform each of the actions in the bullets listed beneath each of the numbered topics:

1. **Introduction to information systems**

   o Explain the difference data versus information.

   o Explain information system concepts including input, processing, and output.

   o Describe information system components including hardware, software, databases and telecommunications.

2. **Organizational foundation of information systems**

   o Demonstrate understanding of the new role and widening scope of information systems in organizations.

   o Explain the strategic role information systems play in organizations.

   o Identify and define the major types of information systems including transaction processing systems, management information systems, decision support systems, expert systems and Enterprise Resource Planning (ERP).

   o Describe the ethical and social impact of information systems.

3. **Hardware**

   o Explain the purpose and major characteristics of the six major hardware components of an information system:

     ▪ primary memory,

     ▪ secondary storage,

     ▪ the central processing unit,

     ▪ input devices,

     ▪ output devices, and

     ▪ communication devices.

- Describe the different types of computers including

  - personal computers,

  - midrange computers,

  - mainframe computers, and

  - supercomputers.

- Explain how one would select computer hardware.

4. **Software**

  - Explain the concepts of systems software and application software.

  - Explain how one would select software.

  - Demonstrate understanding of the evolution of programming languages.

  - Use common personal productivity tools.

5. **Databases**

  - Define the data hierarchy including field, record, file and database.

  - Describe the different types of databases.

  - Explain how one would select database management software.

  - Create a database using a relational DBMS such as Access. Demonstrate the ability to create reports, queries and join two tables in the DBMS.

6. **Telecommunications**

  - Demonstrate an introductory level of knowledge about telecommunication and network components such as media, devices, software, and protocols.

  - Explain the concepts of LAN, WAN, and network topology.

  - Explain client/server systems.

7. **The Internet**

  - Explain how businesses use the Internet.

  - Describe the use of E-commerce.

  - Describe the World Wide Web and concepts such as browsers, search engines, and HTML.

- o Describe Intranets and Extranets.

- o Explain Internet privacy and security issues.

- o Use the Internet to conduct research, find information, and communicate.

- o Create a personal web page.

8. **Systems development**

- o Describe the activities that take place during each phase of the systems development life cycle.

- o Explain alternative system building approaches such as prototyping, end user development, software packages, and outsourcing.

WileyPLUS Learning Space

An easy way to help your students learn, collaborate, and grow.

Personalized Experience

Students create their own study guide while they interact with course content and work on learning activities.

Flexible Course Design

Educators can quickly organize learning activities, manage student collaboration, and customize their course—giving them full control over content as well as the amount of interactivity between students.

Clear Path to Action

With visual reports, it's easy for both students and educators to gauge problem areas and act on what's most important.

Instructor Benefits

- Assign activities and add your own materials
- Guide students through what's important in the interactive e-textbook by easily assigning specific content
- Set up and monitor collaborative learning groups
- Assess learner engagement
- Gain immediate insights to help inform teaching

Student Benefits

- Instantly know what you need to work on
- Create a personal study plan
- Assess progress along the way
- Participate in class discussions
- Remember what you have learned because you have made deeper connections to the content

e are dedicated to supporting you from idea to outcome.

WILEY

Using **WileyPLUS** with this book?
Check out **ORION**.

Whether you want to check your understanding of the material you just read or need to prepare for a test, ORION will help you use your study time most effectively.

Helping you learn by learning about you.™

Step 1 - Begin

Making it easy to figure out where to start!

First, try a few questions to get an idea of where you stand.

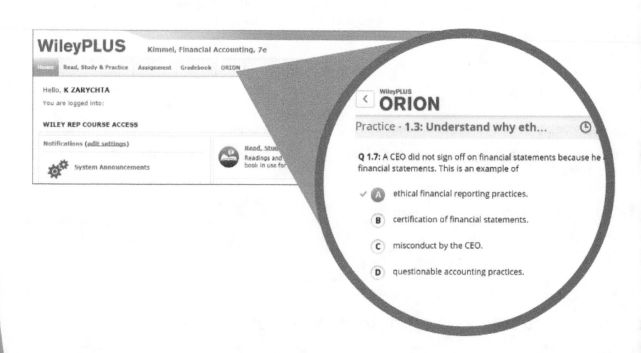

WileyPLUS   Kimmel, Financial Accounting, 7e

Home   Read, Study & Practice   Assignment   Gradebook   ORION

Hello, **K ZARYCHTA**
You are logged into:

WILEY REP COURSE ACCESS

Notifications (_edit settings_)

System Announcements

Read, Stud...
Readings and
book in use for

WileyPLUS
< ORION

Practice - 1.3: Understand why eth...

Q 1.7: A CEO did not sign off on financial statements because he
financial statements. This is an example of

✓ **A**   ethical financial reporting practices.

B   certification of financial statements.

C   misconduct by the CEO.

D   questionable accounting practices.

Step 2 - Practice

Making it easy to learn new things!

ORION gives you feedback on your performance, and you pick where to practice or study.

Ch 2: A Further Look at Financi... Practice	Proficiency	Performance
Identify the sections of a classified balance sheet.	41%	2/5
Identify tools for analyzing financial statements and ra...	65%	Study Practice
Explain the relationship between a retained earnings s...	47%	3/4
Identify and compute ratios for analyzing a company's ...	65%	5/5
Use the statement of cash flows to evaluate solvency.	31%	3/10
Explain the meaning of generally accepted accounting ...	56%	3/3
Discuss financial reporting concepts.	19%	1/7

Least Proficient Chapters

Ch 3 ▭▭▭▭ 35%
Ch 1 ▭▭▭▭ 45%

Step 3 - Maintain

Making it easy to remember everything you learn!

ORION provides a number of views into your overall proficiency so you can quickly review the things you might have forgotten before a quiz or exam.

MANAGEMENT INFORMATION SYSTEMS

Moving Business Forward

Third Edition

MANAGEMENT INFORMATION SYSTEMS

Moving Business Forward

Third Edition

Kelly Rainer
Brad Prince
Hugh Watson

with contributions by
Alina M. Chircu, Bentley University
Marco Marabelli, Bentley University

WILEY

Publisher	Don Fowley
Executive Editor	Beth Lang Golub
Senior Content Manager	Karoline Luciano
Senior Production Editor	Timothy Lindner
Senior Marketing Manager	Margaret Barrett
Marketing Assistant	Elisa Wong
Design Director	Harry Nolan
Senior Product Designer	Jenny Welter
Senior Designer	Maureen Eide
Senior Photo Editor	Lisa Gee
Cover Designer	Tom Nery
Senior Content Editor	Wendy Ashenberg
Editorial Assistant	Jayne Ziemba
Production Management Services	Thomson Digital
Cover Credit	© Click Bestsellers / Shutterstock
Icon Credits	Globe, © chudo-yudo/Shutterstock; Wave, © Litz/Shutterstock; Phone, © iQoncept/Shutterstock; Scales, © Vladstudioraw/iStockphoto; Woman with Laptop, © sbayram/iStockphoto; Happy Group, © skodonnell/iStockphoto; Mouse, © urfin/Shutterstock; Crossed Fingers, © Constantine Pankin/Shutterstock; Capitol Building, Chad Zuber / Shutterstock.

This book was set in Minion Pro 10/12 by Thomson Digital and printed and bound by Courier/Kendallville.

This book is printed on acid free paper.

Founded in 1807, John Wiley & Sons, Inc., has been a valued source of knowledge and understanding for more than 200 years, helping people around the world meet their needs and fulfill their aspirations. Our company is built on a foundation of principles that include responsibility to the communities we serve and where we live and work. In 2008, we launched a Corporate Citizenship Initiative, a global effort to address the environmental, social, economic, and ethical challenges we face in our business. Among the issues we are addressing are carbon impact, paper specifications and procurement, ethical conduct within our business and among our vendors, and community and charitable support. For more information, please visit our Web site: www.wiley.com/go/citizenship.

ISBN-13:   978-1-118-89538-2
BRV ISBN: 978-1-118-90582-1

Printed in the United States of America

10 9 8 7 6 5 4 3 2 1

To The Student

Dear Student,

Why are you here? We are not asking you a philosophical question—that is a different course. We are asking, "Why are you about to spend an entire term learning about information systems? Why are you—an accounting major, or a marketing or management major—being required to study this topic?" You may be asking, "What's in IT for me?" The short answer is that "IT's About Business," and the longer answer is the goal of this book.

Information systems are making the world a very small place and are contributing to rapidly increasing global competition. As a result, organizations are constantly trying to find ways to gain a competitive advantage—by achieving operational excellence, developing new products and services, developing new business models, providing superb customer service, improving decision making, and so on. It should be obvious, then, that an introductory course in information systems is critically important for success in your chosen career.

Rapid advances in information systems mean that, as business students, change will be the only constant you will encounter in today's dynamic digital business environment. We wrote this book for business students of all majors who will soon become business professionals. We have three goals in mind:

1. To help you be immediately successful when you join your organization
2. To help you understand the importance of information systems for individuals, organizations, and society as a whole
3. To enable you to become informed users of your organization's information systems

To accomplish these goals, we have tried to provide the essential, relevant knowledge that you need to understand to effectively use information systems in your careers.

The way we propose to do this is by keeping you *actively involved* in the material. Every section of the chapters has an activity that asks you to do something beyond just reading the textbook that will help you see why the content is useful for your future business career.

We hope you will enjoy this active approach and successfully complete the course with a richer understanding of what's in IT for you.

KELLY RAINER, BRAD PRINCE, AND HUGH WATSON

To The Instructor

Dear Instructor,

We are like you. All of us who teach the introductory course in information systems realize that it is difficult for students to understand the importance and relevance of the topics in the course. As a result, students often memorize the content just before the exam, and then forget it as soon as the exam is over. We all want to engage students at a much deeper level. We know that the best way to accomplish this objective is through *hands-on active learning,* leading to *increased student engagement* in our course content.

Accordingly, active learning and student engagement are key principles of our new book. We recognize the need to actively involve students in problem solving, creative thinking, and capitalizing on opportunities. Every section of every chapter includes extensive hands-on exercises, activities, and mini-cases. End-of-chapter material also includes exercises that require students to use software application tools. Through these activities, we enable students to understand how to *do* something with the concepts they learn, such as meet business goals using information systems, configure products, and use spreadsheets and databases to facilitate problem solving.

The preface on the next page further outlines the goals, features, and support material provided with our new text. We hope you will enjoy teaching with this approach!

KELLY RAINER, BRAD PRINCE, AND HUGH WATSON

Preface

Chapter Organization

Each chapter contains the following elements:

- **Chapter Outline:** Lists the major concepts covered in each chapter.
- **Learning Objectives:** Provide an overview of the key learning goals that students should achieve after reading the chapter.
- **Chapter-Opening Case:** A short case that focuses on a small or start-up company that is using information systems to solve a business problem. Cases in introductory information systems textbooks typically involve very large organizations. In contrast, our chapter-opening cases demonstrate that small and start-up companies also have business problems that they address using information systems. Students will see that small firms usually have to be quite creative in building and implementing IS solutions, because they do not have MIS departments or large budgets. These small-business cases also add an entrepreneurial flavor to each chapter for students who are planning to start their own businesses.
- **Apply the Concept Activities:** This book's unique pedagogical structure is designed to keep students actively engaged with the course material. Reading material in each chapter subsection is immediately followed by an "Apply the Concept" activity that is directly related to a chapter objective. These activities include links to online videos and articles and other hands-on activities that require students to immediately apply what they have learned. Via WileyPLUS, instructors can assign a section of text along with an Apply the Concept activity. Each Apply the Concept has the following elements:
  - > Background (places the activity in the context of relevant reading material)
  - > Activity (a hands-on activity that students carry out)
  - > Deliverable (various tasks for students to complete as they perform the activity)
- **IT's About Business:** Short cases that demonstrate real-world applications of IT to business. Each case is accompanied by questions relating the case to concepts covered in the chapter. Icons relate these boxes to the specific functional areas.
- **IT's Personal:** Sprinkled throughout the chapters, these short vignettes explain the relevance of MIS concepts to students' daily lives.
- **Before You Go On:** End-of-section reviews prompt students to pause and test their understanding of concepts before moving on to the next section.
- **Examples:** Interspersed throughout the text, these highlight the use (and misuse) of information systems by real-world organizations, thereby illustrating the concepts discussed in the chapter.
- **What's in IT for Me?:** A unique end-of-chapter summary that demonstrates the relevance of each key chapter topic to different functional areas, including accounting, finance, marketing, production/operations management, human resources management, and management information systems. This cross-functional focus makes the book accessible for students from any major.
- **Summary:** Keyed to the Learning Objectives listed at the beginning of the chapter, the summary enables students to review major concepts covered.
- **Discussion Questions and Problem-Solving Activities:** Provide practice through active learning. These exercises are hands-on opportunities to apply the concepts discussed in the chapter.

- **Collaboration Exercises:** Team exercises that require students to take on different functional roles and collaborate to solve business problems using Google Drive. These exercises allow students to get first-hand experience solving business problems using Cloud-based tools while also experiencing an authentic business team dynamic.

- **Closing Cases:** Each chapter concludes with two cases about business problems faced by actual companies and how they used IS to solve those issues. The cases are broken down into four parts: a description of the problem, an overview of the IS solution implemented, a presentation of the results of the implementation, and an analysis of key takeaways from the case. Each case is followed by discussion questions, so that students can further explore the concepts presented in the case.

- **Spreadsheet Activity:** Every chapter includes a hands-on spreadsheet project that requires students to practice their Excel skills within the context of the chapter material. WileyPLUS Learning Space includes an Excel Lab Manual for students who need introductory coverage or review.

- **Database Activity:** Every chapter includes a hands-on database project that requires students to practice their Access skills while using concepts learned in the chapter. WileyPLUS Learning Space includes an Access Lab Manual for students who need introductory coverage or review.

- **Internship Activity:** Every chapter includes an Internship Activity which presents a business problem found in one of four recurring industries (healthcare, banking, manufacturing, and retail.) STUDENTS are directed to various software demos that provide useful tools for addressing the business problem. Then the students must act as interns and apply the concepts they learned in the chapter to provide a solution to the business problem.

- **Glossary:** A study tool that highlights vocabulary within the chapters and facilitates studying.

Key Features

Student Engagement

As discussed in the note addressed to instructors at the beginning of this preface, one of the chief goals of this text is to engage students at a level beyond recognition of key terms. We believe the best way to achieve this goal is through hands-on, active learning that will lead to increased student engagement with the course and its content.

Accordingly, every section of every chapter provides resources that actively involve students in problem solving, creative thinking, and capitalizing on opportunities. Every chapter includes extensive hands-on exercises, activities, and mini-cases, including exercises that require students to solve business problems using Excel and Access.

Cross-Functional Approach

We emphasize the importance of information systems by calling attention in every chapter to how that chapter's topic relates to each business major. Icons guide students to relevant issues for their specific functional area—accounting (ACC), finance (FIN), marketing (MKT), operations management (OM), human resources management (HRM), and management information systems (MIS). Chapters conclude with a detailed summary (entitled 'What's in IT for Me?') of how key concepts in the chapter relate to each functional area.

Diversified and Unique Examples from Different Industries

Extensive use of vivid examples from large corporations, small businesses, and government and not-for-profit organizations enlivens the concepts from the chapter. The examples illustrate everything from the capabilities of information systems, to their cost and justification and the innovative ways that corporations are using IS in their operations. Small businesses have been included in recognition of the fact that many students will work for small-to mid-sized companies, and some will even start their own small business. In fact, some students may already be working at local businesses, and the concepts they are learning in class can be readily observed or put into practice in their part-time jobs. Each chapter constantly highlights the integral connection between business and IS. This connection is especially evident in the chapter-opening and closing cases, the "IT's About Business" boxes, and the highlighted examples.

Successes and Failures

Many textbooks present examples of the successful implementation of information systems, and our book is no exception. However, we go one step beyond by also providing numerous examples of IS failures, in the context of lessons that can be learned from such failures. Misuse of information systems can be very expensive.

Global Focus

An understanding of global competition, partnerships, and trading is essential to success in a modern business environment. Therefore, we provide a broad selection of international cases and examples. We discuss the role of information systems in facilitating export and import, the management of international companies, and electronic trading around the globe. These global examples are highlighted with the global icon.

Innovation and Creativity

In today's rapidly changing business environment, creativity and innovation are necessary for a business to operate effectively and profitably. Throughout our book, we demonstrate how information systems facilitate these processes.

Focus on Ethics

With corporate scandals appearing in the headlines almost daily, ethics and ethical questions have come to the forefront of business people's minds. In addition to devoting an entire chapter to ethics and privacy (Chapter 6), we have included examples and cases throughout the text that focus on business ethics. These examples are highlighted with the ethics icon.

What's New in the Third Edition?

- Content changes include:
  - A new section on Big Data in Chapter 3
  - Technical database material moved from Chapter 3 and expanded into new Plug IT In 3.
  - Expanded coverage of Business Processes in Chapter 2
  - A new section on Enterprise Resource Planning in Chapter 11
  - Thoroughly updated and expanded coverage of Social Computing in Chapter 8
  - All new or updated IT's About Business, chapter-opening and closing cases.
- Pedagogical changes include:
  - Revised and streamlined "Apply the Concept" activities now relate directly to chapter objectives.
  - New "Internship Activities" replace the Ruby's Club activities from previous editions. Each Internship Activity includes a software demo that requires students to apply new tools to business problems.
  - Revised "Collaboration Exercises" now each require use of Google Drive.

○ Revised and streamlined database and spreadsheet exercises for every chapter. These include references to lessons in the WileyPLUS lab manual for students who need instruction or review.

- Complete update of cases and examples including all new or updated chapter opening and closing cases and all new or updated "IT's About Business" boxes.

Online Resources

www.wiley.com/college/rainer

Our book also facilitates the teaching of an Introduction to Information Systems course by providing extensive support materials for instructors and students. Visit www.wiley.com/college/rainer to access the Student and Instructor Companion Sites.

Instructor's Manual

The *Instructor's Manual* includes a chapter overview, teaching tips and strategies, answers to all end-of-chapter questions, supplemental mini-cases with essay questions and answers, and experiential exercises that relate to particular topics. It also includes answers and solutions to all spreadsheet and database activities, along with a guide to teaching these exercises, and links to the separate Excel and Access starter and solutions files.

Test Bank

The test bank is a comprehensive resource for test questions. Each chapter contains multiple choice, true/false, short answer, and essay questions. In addition, each chapter includes "Apply Your Knowledge" questions that require more creative thought to answer. Each multiple choice and true/false question is labeled to indicate its level of difficulty: easy, medium, or hard.

The test bank is available for use in Respondus' easy-to-use software. Respondus® is a powerful tool for creating and managing exams that can be printed or published directly to Blackboard, WebCT, Desire2Learn, eCollege, ANGEL, and other learning systems. For more information on Respondus® and the Respondus Test Bank Network, please visit www.respondus.com.

Reading Quizzes

These multiple choice conceptual questions can be used by instructors to evaluate a student's understanding of the reading. They are available in Respondus, the WileyPLUS course, and the Book Companion Site.

PowerPoint Presentations

The *PowerPoint Presentations* consist of a series of slides for each chapter. The slides are designed around each chapter's content, incorporating key points from the chapter and chapter illustrations as appropriate, as well as real-life examples from the Web.

Image Library

All textbook figures are available for download from the Web site. These figures can easily be added to PowerPoint presentations.

Weekly Updates

(http://wileyinformationsystemsupdates.com)

Weekly updates, harvested from around the Internet by David Firth of the University of Montana, provide you with the latest IT news and issues. These are posted every Monday morning throughout the year at http://wileyinformationsystemsupdates.com/. They include links to current articles and videos as well as discussion questions to assign or use in class.

OfficeGrader

Office Grader™ is an Access-Based VBA Macro that enables automatic grading of Office assignments. The macros compare Office files and grade them against a master file. OfficeGrader™ is available for Word, Access, Excel, and PowerPoint for Office 2010 and 2013. For more information, contact your Wiley sales representative or visit http://www .wiley.com/college/sc/office2013/officegrader.html.

WileyPLUS Learning Space

WileyPLUS Learning Space is an easy way for students to learn, collaborate, and grow. With WileyPLUS Learning Space, students create a personalized study plan, assess progress along the way, and make deeper connections as they interact with the course material and each other. Through a combination of dynamic course materials and visual reports, this collaborative learning environment gives you and your students immediate insight into strengths and problem areas in order to act on what's most important.

- This online teaching and learning environment integrates the entire digital textbook with the most effective instructor and student resources to accommodate every learning style.
- Students achieve concept mastery in a rich, structured environment that is available 24/7.
- Instructors personalize and manage their course more effectively with assessment, assignments, grade tracking, and more. You can even add your own materials to your WileyPLUS course
- With WileyPLUS Learning Space you can identify students who are falling behind and intervene accordingly, without having to wait for them to come to office hours.
- WileyPLUS Learning Space can complement the textbook or replace the printed textbook altogether.

WileyPLUS Learning Space for Rainer MIS 3e includes the following resources to support teaching and learning:

- New author lecture videos for every section of every chapter will facilitate switch to "flipped classrooms" and/or will provide additional learning support for students.
- Orion, an adaptive, personal learning experience that helps students highlight their strengths and problems areas and navigate through their studies to get optimal results in the most efficient amount of time. (See more information below.).
- Group chat function facilitates student discussion about activities and cases.
- Complete eText allows searching across all chapters, note-taking, highlighting, and the ability to copy and paste or print key sections.
- Lab Manual for Microsoft Office 2010 and Office 2013.
- Automatically graded practice questions
- Vocabulary flash cards and quizzes
- Library of additional "IT's About Business" cases.

For more information and a demo, visit here: http://www.wiley.com/college/sc/wpls/

ORION

Included in WileyPLUS Learning Space, ORION helps gauge students' strengths and weaknesses so that instructors can tailor instruction accordingly. Instructor reports track aggregate and individual student proficiency at the objective or chapter level, to show exactly where students excel as well as the areas that need reinforcement.

Based on cognitive science, WileyPLUS with ORION is a personalized, adaptive learning experience that helps students build proficiency on topics while using their study time most effectively.

For more information and a demo, visit here: http://www.wiley.com/college/sc/oriondemo/.

WILEY Flex

In addition to WileyPLUS Learning Space, Wiley provides a wide variety of printed and electronic formats that provide many choices to your students at a wide range of price points. Contact your Wiley sales representative for more details on any of the below.

Wiley E-Text Powered by VitalSource

Wiley E-Texts are complete digital versions of the text that help students study more efficiently. Students can access content online and offline on their desktops, laptops, and mobile devices; search across the entire book content, take notes and highlight, and copy and paste or print key sections.

Wiley Binder Version

A three-hole-punched, loose-leaf version allows students to carry only the content they need, insert class notes and hand-outs, and keep all materials in one place.

Wiley Custom

This group's services allows you to adapt existing Wiley content and combine text materials, incorporate and publish your own materials, and collaborate with Wiley's team to ensure your satisfaction.

Wiley Custom Select

Wiley Custom Select allows you to build your own course materials using selected chapters of any Wiley text and your own material if desired. For more information, visit http://customselect.wiley.com.

Acknowledgments

Creating, developing, and producing a text for the introduction to information systems course is a formidable undertaking. Along the way, we were fortunate to receive continuous evaluation, criticism, and direction from many colleagues who regularly teach this course.

Special thanks to the following contributors: Ken Corley for designing the PowerPoint slides, Bob Gehling for writing test bank questions, Ranida Harris for working on the Instructor's Manual, and Carole Hollingsworth for designing Wiley PLUS activities.

Special thanks to contributors Dawna Dewire, Joan Lumpkin, Kevin Lertwachara, Roy DeJoie, and Kala Seal for working on the original Apply the Concept activities that appeared in prior editions. Thanks also to Efrem Mallach for creating the original database activities in the prior editions. Many thanks also to Alina M. Chircu and Marco Marabelli of Bentley University for developing new material that enhances our coverage of business processes and ERP. We are grateful for the dedication and creativity of all these contributors in helping us craft this new text.

We would like to thank the Wiley team: Beth Lang Golub, Executive Editor; Jayne Ziemba, Editorial Assistant; Jenny Welter, Product Designer; Wendy Ashenberg, Content Editor; and Margaret Barrett, Senior Marketing Manager. We also thank the Content Management team, including Karoline Luciano, Content Manager; Tim Lindner, Production Editor; and Faraz Sharique Ali of Thomson Digital. And thanks to Maureen Eide, Senior Designer; and Lisa Gee, Photo Editor. We would also like to thank Robert Weiss for his skillful and thorough editing of the manuscript.

Finally, we would like to acknowledge the contributions made by the individuals listed below who participated in focus groups, telesessions, surveys, chapter walkthroughs, class tests, user feedback surveys, and reviews.

KELLY RAINER
BRAD PRINCE
HUGH WATSON

Monica Adya	*Marquette University*
Lawrence Andrew	*Western Illinois University, Macomb*
Orakwue (Bay) Arinze	*Drexel University*
Laura Atkins	*James Madison University*
Nick Ball	*Brigham Young University*
Nicholas Barnes	*Nicholls College*
Susan Barzottini	*Manchester Community College*
Kristi Berg	*Minot State University*
Andy Borchers	*Lipscomb University*
David Bouchard	*Metropolitan State University*
Dave Bourgeois	*Biola University*
Mari Buche	*Michigan Tech University*
Richard Burkhard	*San Jose State University*
Ashley Bush	*Florida State University*
Frank Canovatchel	*Champlain College*
Donald Carpenter	*Mesa State College*
Teuta Cata	*Northern Kentucky University*
Wendy Ceccucci	*Quinnipiac University*
Amita Chin	*Virginia Commonwealth University*
Susan Chinn	*University of Southern ME, Portland*
Richard Christensen	*Metropolitan State University*
Dmitriy Chulkov	*Indiana University Kokomo*
Phillip Coleman	*Western Kentucky University*
Emilio Collar	*Western CT State University*
Daniel Connolly	*University of Denver*
Lee Cornell	*Minnesota State University, Mankato*
David Croasdell	*University of Nevada, Reno*
Jakov Crnkovic	*University at Albany, SUNY*
Reet Cronk	*Harding University*
Marcia Daley	*Clark, Atlanta*
Donald Danner	*San Francisco State University*
Roy DeJoie	*Purdue University*
Dawna Dewire	*Babson College*
Kevin Duffy	*Wright State University*
Lauren Eder	*Rider University*
Sean Eom	*Southeast Missouri State University*
Ahmed Eshra	*St. John's University*
Roger Finnegan	*Metropolitan State University*
Thomas Fischer	*Metropolitan State University*
Jerry Flatto	*University of Indianapolis*
Jonathan Frankel	*University of Massachusetts, Boston*
Judith Gebauer	*University of North Carolina, Wilmington*
Jennifer Gerow	*Virginia Military Institute*
Matt Graham	*University of Maine*
Katie Gray	*University of Texas, Austin*
Penelope (Sue) Greenberg	*Widener University*
Naveen Gudigantala	*University of Portland*
Saurabh Gupta	*University of North Florida*
Bernard Han	*Western Michigan University*
Hyo-Joo Han	*Georgia Southern College*
John Hagle	*Texas State Technical College*
Peter Haried	*University of Wisconsin, LaCrosse*
Ranida Harris	*Indiana University Southeast*
Roslin Hauck	*Illinois State University*
Bernd Haupt	*Penn State University*
Jun He	*University of Michigan, Dearborn*
Richard Herschel	*St. Joseph's University*
Bogdan Hoanca	*University of Alaska*
Mary Carole Hollingsworth	*Georgia Perimeter College, Clarkston Campus*
Terri Holly	*Indian River State College*
Derrick Huang	*Florida Atlantic University*
Maggie Hutchison	*Flagler College*
Mark Hwang	*Central Michigan University*
Lynn Isvik	*Upper Iowa University, Fayette*
Curtis Izen	*Baruch College, City University of New York*
Radhika Jain	*Baruch College, City University of New York*
Arpan Jani	*University of Wisconsin, River Falls*
Jonathan Jelen	*St. John's University*
Hong Jiang	*Benedict College*
Nenad Jukic	*Loyola University*
Elene Kent	*Capital University*
Stephen Klein	*Ramapo College*
Brian Kovar	*Kansas State University*
Subodha Kumar	*Texas A&M*
Diane Lending	*James Madison University*
Kevin Lertwachara	*Cal Poly San Luis Obispo*
Terry Letsche	*Wartburg College*
Victor Lipe	*Trident Tech*
Chuck Litecky	*Southern Illinois University, Carbondale*
Joan Lumpkin	*Wright State University*
Nicole Lytle	*Cal State, San Bernardino*

George Mangalaraj	*Western Illinois University*
Parand Mansouri-Rad	*University of Texas, El Paso*
Michael Martel	*Ohio University*
Nancy Martin	*Southern Illinois University, Carbondale*
Richard McMahon	*University of Houston, Downtown*
Tony McRae	*Collin College*
Vishal Midha	*University of Texas, Pan American*
Esmail Mohebbi	*University West Florida*
Luvai Motiwalla	*University Mass Online*
Mahdi Nasereddin	*Penn State, Berks*
Sandra K. Newton	*Sonoma State University*
Ann O'Brien	*University of Wisconsin, Madison*
Sungjune Park	*University of North Carolina, Charlotte*
Yang Park	*Georgia Southwestern State University*
Alan Peace	*West Virginia University*
Jacqueline Pike	*Duquesne University*
Tony Pittarese	*East Tennessee State University*
Jennifer Pitts	*Columbus State University*
Richard Platt	*University of West Florida*
Larisa Preiser	*Cal Poly Pomona*
Michelle Ramim	*Nova Southeastern University*
Alison Rampersad	*Lynn University*
Ralph Reilly	*University of Hartford*
Wes Rhea	*Kennesaw State University*
Julio Rivera	*University of Alabama, Birmingham*
Thomas Roberts	*William Patterson University*
Cynthia Ruppel	*Nova Southeastern University*
James Ryan	*Troy University*
Russell Sabadosa	*Manchester Community College*
Jim Samuel	*Baruch College, City University of New York*
Tom Sandman	*Cal State, Sacramento*
Kala Seal	*Loyola Marymount*
Tod Sedbrook	*University of Northern Colorado*
Elaine Seeman	*East Carolina University*
Richard Segall	*Arkansas State University*
Lee Sellers	*Eastern Oregon University—Mt. Hood Metro Center*
Judy Ann Serwatka	*Purdue University, North Central*
John Seydel	*Arkansas State University*
Jollean Sinclaire	*Arkansas State University*
Vivek Shah	*Texas State University, San Marcos*
Mehrdad Sharbaf	*Loyola Marymount University*
Suengjae Shin	*Mississippi State University, Meridian*
Todd Stabenow	*Hawkeye Community College*
Jo Lynne Stalnaker	*University of Wyoming*
Cynthia Stone	*Indiana University*
Nathan Stout	*University of Oklahoma*
Yi Sun	*Cal State, San Marcos*
Winston Tellis	*Fairfield University*
Doug Francis Tuggle	*Chapman University*
Wendy Urban	*Temple University*
Darlene de Vida	*Lower Columbia College*
James Villars	*Metropolitan State University*
Padmal Vitharana	*Syracuse University*
Haibo Wang	*Texas A&M International University*
Hong Wang	*North Carolina A&T State University*
June Wei	*University of West Florida*
Melody White	*University of North Texas*
Rosemary Wild	*Cal Poly San Luis Obispo*
Tom Wilder	*Cal State, Chico*
Karen Williams	*University of Texas, San Antonio*
Marie Wright	*Western Connecticut State University*
Yaquan Xu	*Virginia State University*
Benjamin Yeo	*Loyola Marymount University*
Bee Yew	*Fayetteville State University*
Jigish Zaveri	*Morgan State University*
Grace Zhang	*Augusta State University*
Wei Zhang	*University of Massachusetts, Boston*
Zuopeng Zhang	*SUNY, Plattsburgh*
Fan Zhao	*Florida Gulf Coast University*
Robert Zwick	*Yeshiva University*

Brief Contents

Contents

MANAGEMENT INFORMATION SYSTEMS

Moving Business Forward

Third Edition

HOW WE KEEP OUR URLS CURRENT:

All URLs noted in the activities in this book are "live" and accurate at the time of printing. However, due to the dynamic nature of the Internet, we know that some of these links may break over the lifetime of this book.

Therefore, our Rainer team will check all URLs every month, and replacement URLs or new activities will be provided as necessary. These will be posted on the Student Companion Site (under the link for Activity Links and Starter Files). To locate this, please visit www.wiley .com/college/rainer and click on this textbook.

If you find a broken URL . . .

- Please check the "Activity Links and Starter Files" resource first.

- If you don't see a replacement, please alert the Publisher via email at RainerMail@wiley.com. We will post new material as soon as possible.

Thanks for your understanding and help with this, and if you have suggestions for other activities or any comments about the book, please send us an email. We'd appreciate hearing from you!

—The Rainer Team at Wiley
RainerMail@wiley.com

Introduction to Information Systems

LEARNING OBJECTIVES >>>

1.1 Identify the reasons why being an informed user of information systems is important in today's world.

1.2 Describe the various types of computer-based information systems in an organization.

1.3 Discuss ways in which information technology can affect managers and nonmanagerial workers.

1.4 Identify positive and negative societal effects of the increased use of information technology.

OPENING **CASE** > AngelList Helps Entrepreneurs Build Companies

Fundraising is a difficult and time-consuming process that diverts entrepreneurs from building their companies. For decades, entrepreneurs trying to obtain funding from Silicon Valley's small, wealthy group of angel investors found the process similar to breaking into an exclusive club. They had to work with their personal networks to set up meetings with financiers and then negotiate privately, with little awareness of fair market value or better opportunities elsewhere.

To assist these individuals, AngelList (https://angel.co), founded in 2010 in San Francisco, has created an online forum where founders of early-stage companies — called *startups* — post their ideas and meet investors who fund these often risky ventures. AngelList's mission is to make startup investing transparent and efficient.

How does AngelList work? Basically, startups access the site and create profiles that list information such as their previous financial backers (if any) and the amount of capital they have already raised. They then utilize those profiles to make their "pitch" to hundreds of certified investors – financial firms as well as wealthy individuals and companies. To avoid **MKT** fraud, AngelList vets its investors by requiring them to provide a track record of their prior investments.

At the same time, it thoroughly researches any startups that they list on their Web site.

© shironosov/iStockphoto

AngelList restricts its services to startups that are trying to obtain funding for the first time. For example, the company handles the regulatory paperwork to help startups complete the relevant forms. One feature on the Web site, called "Syndicates," lets investors pool their money under the direction of a single, wealthy investor known as a "lead." Then, whenever the lead decides to back a startup, so do the other investors, or "backers." Leads set their own terms. For example, one lead investor collects a 15 percent "carry" fee from his backers, plus a portion of any positive return they receive if the startup is acquired or goes public. AngelList takes a 5 percent cut on any such paydays.

Startups such as the private taxi service Uber (www.uber.com) and babysitting-jobs Web site Urbansitter (www.urbansitter .com) have used AngelList to meet new investors and quickly finalize their funding deals. In another example, Sprig (www.eatsprig.com), a San Francisco-based dinner delivery service, raised most of the money it needed for a new kitchen in a single day on AngelList.

At the end of 2013, AngelList added startup job listings to its Web site. In addition, it was lobbying the U.S. government to further relax fundraising restrictions contained in the JOBS Act, the 2012 Federal law that lowered regulatory requirements for startups. The company's goal is for the public — rather than simply accredited investors — to use the site to provide funding for promising startups.

And the bottom line? By mid-2014, AngelList featured more than 42,000 businesses, and it had provided entrepreneurs with more than 28,000 introductions to potential investors.

Sources: Compiled from B. Stone, "The Social Network for Startups," *Bloomberg Business Week*, January 20-26, 2014; F. Lardinois, "OnTheGo Raises $700K Seed Round From Foundry Group's AngelList Syndicate and Others to Improve Smart Glasses," *TechCrunch*, January 6, 2014;

L. Rao, "Kima Ventures Will Allow Startups to Raise $150K Within 15 Days Via AngelList," *TechCrunch*, December 4, 2013; N. Hughes, "Will AngelList Help or Hurt Startup Fundraising," *Geek Wire*, October 12, 2013; A. Davidson, "Follow the Money: AngelList Has Blown Open Early-Stage Investments," *Wired*, May 17, 2013; P. Sloan, "AngelList Attacks Another Startup Pain Point: Legal Fees," *CNET News*, September 5, 2012; L. Rao, "AngelList Launches Docs to Help Startups Sign and Close Seed Rounds Online with Low Legal Fees," *TechCrunch*, September 5, 2012; www.angellist.com, accessed January 20, 2014.

Questions

1. What are the advantages offered by AngelList to entrepreneurs?

2. What are potential disadvantages that entrepreneurs might encounter by using AngelList? (*Hint:* What if you listed your company profile on AngelList and no investor provided funding?)

Introduction

Before we proceed, we need to define information technology and information systems. **Information technology (IT)** refers to any computer-based tool that people use to work with information and to support the information and information-processing needs of an organization. An **information system (IS)** collects, processes, stores, analyzes, and disseminates information for a specific purpose.

IT has far-reaching effects on individuals, organizations, and our planet. Although this text is largely devoted to the many ways in which IT has transformed modern organizations, you will also learn about the significant impacts of IT on individuals and societies, the global economy, and our physical environment. In addition, IT is making our world smaller, enabling more and more people to communicate, collaborate, and compete, thereby leveling the digital playing field.

When you graduate, you either will start your own business or you will work for an organization, whether it is public sector, private sector, for-profit, or not-for-profit. Your organization will have to survive and compete in an environment that has been radically transformed by information technology. This environment is global, massively interconnected, intensely competitive, 24/7/365, real-time, rapidly changing, and information-intensive. To compete successfully, your organization must use IT effectively.

As you read this chapter and this text, keep in mind that the information technologies you will learn about are important to businesses of all sizes. No matter what area of business you major in, what industry you work for, or the size of your company, you will benefit from learning about IT. Who knows? Maybe you will use the tools you learn about in this class to make your great idea a reality by becoming an entrepreneur and starting your own business! In fact, as you see in the chapter opening case, you can use information technology (in the form of AngelList.com) to help you raise the necessary funds to successfully grow your business.

The modern environment is intensely competitive not only for your organization, but for you as well. You must compete with human talent from around the world. Therefore, you will also have to make effective use of IT.

Accordingly, this chapter begins with a discussion of why you should become knowledgeable about IT. It also distinguishes among data, information, and knowledge, and it differentiates computer-based information systems from application programs. Finally, it considers the impacts of information systems on organizations and on society in general.

1.1 Why Should I Study Information Systems?

You are part of the most connected generation in history: You have grown up online; you are, quite literally, never out of touch; you use more information technologies (in the form of digital devices), for more tasks, and are bombarded with more information, than any generation in history. The MIT Technology Review refers to you as *Homo conexus*. Information technologies are so deeply embedded in your lives that your daily routines would be almost unrecognizable to a college student just 20 years ago.

Essentially, you practice continuous computing, surrounded by a movable information network. This network is created by constant cooperation between the digital devices you carry (for example, laptops, tablets, and smartphones); the wired and wireless networks that you access as you move about; and Web-based tools for finding information and communicating and collaborating with other people. Your network enables you to pull information about virtually anything from anywhere, at any time, and to push your own ideas back to the Web, from wherever you are, via a mobile device. Think of everything you do online, often with your smart phone: register for classes; take classes (and not just at your university); access class syllabi, information, PowerPoints, and lectures; research class papers and presentations; conduct banking; pay your bills; research, shop, and buy products from companies or other people; sell your "stuff"; search for, and apply for, jobs; make your travel reservations (hotel, airline, rental car); create your own blog and post your own podcasts and videocasts to it; design your own page on Facebook; make and upload videos to YouTube; take, edit, and print your own digital photographs; "burn" your own custom-music CDs and DVDs; use RSS feeds to create your personal electronic newspaper; text and tweet your friends and family throughout your day; send Snaps; and many other activities. (Note: If any of these terms are unfamiliar to you, don't worry. You will learn about everything mentioned here in detail later in this text.)

The Informed User—You!

So, the question is: Why you should learn about information systems and information technologies? After all, you can comfortably use a computer (or other electronic devices) to perform many activities, you have been surfing the Web for years, and you feel confident that you can manage any IT application that your organization's MIS department installs.

The answer lies in your becoming an **informed user**; that is, a person knowledgeable about information systems and information technology. There are several reasons why you should be an informed user.

In general, informed users tend to get more value from whatever technologies they use. You will enjoy many benefits from being an informed user of IT.

- First, you will benefit more from your organization's IT applications because you will understand what is "behind" those applications (see FIGURE 1.1). That is, what you see on your computer screen is brought to you by your MIS department, who are operating "behind" your screen.

- Second, you will be in a position to enhance the quality of your organization's IT applications with your input.

- Third, even as a new graduate, you will quickly be in a position to recommend—and perhaps help select—the IT applications that your organization will use.

- Fourth, being an informed user will keep you abreast of both new information technologies and rapid developments in existing technologies. Remaining "on top of things" will help you to anticipate the impacts that "new and improved" technologies will have on your organization and to make recommendations on the adoption and use of these technologies.

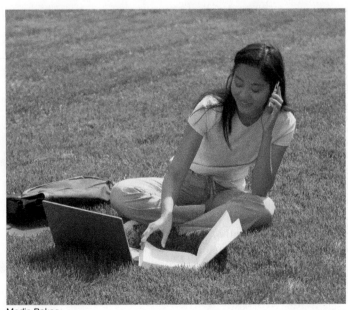

Students today are connected by many devices—almost all are wireless.

- Fifth, you will understand how using IT can improve your organization's performance and teamwork as well as your own productivity.

- Finally, if you have ideas of becoming an entrepreneur, then being an informed user will help you use IT when you start your own business.

Going further, managing the IS function within an organization is no longer the exclusive responsibility of the IS department. Rather, users now play key roles in every step of this process. The overall objective in this text is to provide you with the necessary information to contribute immediately to managing the IS function in your organization. In short, the goal is to help you become a very informed user!

© Slawomir Fajer/iStockphoto

Figure 1.1 IT skills open many doors because IT is so widely used.

IT Offers Career Opportunities

Because information technology is vital to the operation of modern businesses, it offers many employment opportunities. The demand for traditional IT staff—programmers, business analysts, systems analysts, and designers—is substantial. In addition, many well-paid jobs exist in areas such as the Internet and electronic commerce (e-commerce), mobile commerce (m-commerce), network security, telecommunications, and multimedia design.

The information systems field includes the people in various organizations who design and build information systems, the people who use those systems, and the people responsible for managing those systems. At the top of the list is the chief information officer (CIO).

The CIO is the executive who is in charge of the IS function. In most modern organizations, the CIO works with the chief executive officer (CEO), the chief financial officer (CFO), and other senior executives. Therefore, he or she actively participates in the organization's strategic planning process. In today's digital environment, the IS function has become increasingly strategic within organizations. As a result, although most CIOs still rise from the IS department, a growing number are coming up through the ranks in the business units (e.g., marketing, finance, etc.). So, regardless of your major, you could become the CIO of your organization one day. This is another reason to be an informed user of information systems!

Table 1.1 provides a list of IT jobs, along with a description of each one. For further details about careers in IT, see www.computerworld.com/careertopics/careers and www.monster.com.

Career opportunities in IS are strong and are projected to remain strong over the next ten years. In fact, the *U.S. News & World Report and Money* listed their "100 top jobs" for 2013, and *Forbes* listed its "10 top jobs" for 2013. Let's take a look at these rankings. (Note that the rankings differ because the magazines used different criteria in their research.) As you can see, jobs suited for MIS majors rank extremely high in all three lists. The magazines with their job rankings are as follows:

Forbes

#1 Software developer

#4 Systems analyst

#6 Network and systems administrator

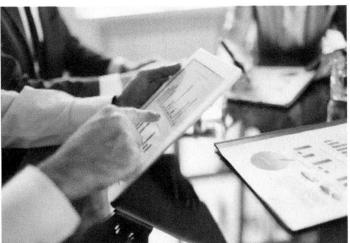

© shironosov/iStockphoto

It's not just students. Today's professionals must be able to use computing technologies to do their job.

TABLE 1.1 Information
Technology Jobs

Position	Job Description
Chief Information Officer	Highest-ranking IS manager; is responsible for all strategic planning in the organization
IS Director	Manages all systems throughout the organization and the day-to-day operations of the entire IS organization
Information Center Manager	Manages IS services such as help desks, hot lines, training, and consulting
Applications Development Manager	Coordinates and manages new systems development projects
Project Manager	Manages a particular new systems development project
Systems Manager	Manages a particular existing system
Operations Manager	Supervises the day-to-day operations of the data and/or computer center
Programming Manager	Coordinates all applications programming efforts
Systems Analyst	Interfaces between users and programmers; determines information requirements and technical specifications for new applications
Business Analyst	Focuses on designing solutions for business problems; interfaces closely with users to demonstrate how IT can be used innovatively
Systems Programmer	Creates the computer code for developing new systems software or maintaining existing systems software
Applications Programmer	Creates the computer code for developing new applications or maintaining existing applications
Emerging Technologies Manager	Forecasts technology trends; evaluates and experiments with new technologies
Network Manager	Coordinates and manages the organization's voice and data networks
Database Administrator	Manages the organization's databases and oversees the use of database-management software
Auditing or Computer Security Manager	Oversees the ethical and legal use of information systems
Webmaster	Manages the organization's World Wide Web site
Web Designer	Creates World Wide Web sites and pages

U.S. News & World Report

#4 Computer systems analyst

#6 Database administrator

#7 Software developer

#9 Web developer

#20 IT manager

Money

#3 Software architect

#5 Database administrator

#9 Software developer

#13 IT consultant

#21 Systems administrator

#28 IT business analyst

Going further, when *Forbes* identified its "15 most valuable college majors" in 2012, the list included two business majors: Management Information Systems at #8 and Finance at #14.

Not only do IS careers offer strong job growth, but the pay is excellent as well. The Bureau of Labor Statistics, an agency within the Department of Labor that is responsible for tracking and analyzing trends relating to the labor market, notes that the median salary in 2013 for "computer and information systems managers" is approximately $115,000.

Managing Information Resources

Managing information systems in modern organizations is a difficult, complex task. Several factors contribute to this complexity. First, information systems have enormous strategic value to organizations. Firms rely on them so heavily that, in some cases, when these systems are not working (even for a short time), the firm cannot function. (This situation is called "being hostage to information systems.") Second, information systems are very expensive to acquire, operate, and maintain.

A third factor contributing to the difficulty in managing information systems is the evolution of the management information systems (MIS) function within the organization. When businesses first began to use computers in the early 1950s, the MIS department "owned" the only computing resource in the organization, the mainframe. At that time, end users did not interact directly with the mainframe.

In contrast, in the modern organization, computers are located in all departments, and almost all employees use computers in their work. This situation, known as *end user computing*, has led to a partnership between the MIS department and the end users. The MIS department now acts as more of a consultant to end users, viewing them as customers. In fact, the main function of the MIS department is to use IT to solve end users' business problems.

As a result of these developments, the responsibility for managing information resources is now divided between the MIS department and the end users. This arrangement raises several important questions: Which resources are managed by whom? What is the role of the MIS department, its structure, and its place within the organization? What is the appropriate relationship between the MIS department and the end users? Regardless of who is doing what, it is essential that the MIS department and the end users work in close cooperation.

There is no standard way to divide responsibility for developing and maintaining information resources between the MIS department and the end users. Instead, that division depends on several factors: the size and nature of the organization, the amount and type of IT resources, the organization's attitudes toward computing, the attitudes of top management toward computing, the maturity level of the technology, the amount and nature of outsourced IT work, and even the countries in which the company operates. Generally speaking, the MIS department is responsible for corporate-level and shared resources, and the end users are responsible for departmental resources. Table 1.2 identifies both the traditional functions and various new, consultative functions of the MIS department.

Traditional Functions of the MIS Department

TABLE 1.2 The Changing Role of the Information Systems Department

- Managing systems development and systems project management
  - As an end user, you will have critical input into the systems development process. You will learn about systems development in Chapter 14.

- Managing computer operations, including the computer center

- Staffing, training, and developing IS skills

- Providing technical services

- Infrastructure planning, development, and control
  - As an end user, you will provide critical input about the IS infrastructure needs of your department.

New (Consultative) Functions of the MIS Department

- Initiating and designing specific strategic information systems
  - As an end user, your information needs will often mandate the development of new strategic information systems.

    You will decide which strategic systems you need (because you know your business needs better than the MIS department does), and you will provide input into developing these systems.

- Incorporating the Internet and electronic commerce into the business
  - As an end user, you will be primarily responsible for effectively using the Internet and electronic commerce in your business. You will work with the MIS department to accomplish this task.

- Managing system integration including the Internet, intranets, and extranets
  - As an end user, your business needs will determine how you want to use the Internet, your corporate intranets, and extranets to accomplish your goals. You will be primarily responsible for advising the MIS department on the most effective use of the Internet, your corporate intranets, and extranets.

- Educating the non-MIS managers about IT
  - Your department will be primarily responsible for advising the MIS department on how best to educate and train your employees about IT.

- Educating the MIS staff about the business
  - Communication between the MIS department and the business units is a two-way street. You will be responsible for educating the MIS staff on your business, its needs, and its goals.

- Partnering with business-unit executives
  - Essentially, you will be in a partnership with the MIS department. You will be responsible for seeing that this partnership is one "between equals" and ensuring its success.

- Managing outsourcing
  - Outsourcing is driven by business needs. Therefore, the outsourcing decision resides largely with the business units (i.e., with you). The MIS department, working closely with you, will advise you on technical issues such as communications bandwidth, security, etc.

- Proactively using business and technical knowledge to seed innovative ideas about IT
  - Your business needs often will drive innovative ideas about how to effectively use information systems to accomplish your goals. The best way to bring these innovative uses of IS to life is to partner closely with your MIS department. Such close partnerships have amazing synergies!

- Creating business alliances with business partners
  - The needs of your business unit will drive these alliances, typically along your supply chain. Again, your MIS department will act as your advisor on various issues, including hardware and software compatibility, implementing extranets, communications, and security.

So, where do the end users come in? Take a close look at Table 1.2. Under the traditional MIS functions, you will see two functions for which you provide vital input: managing systems development, and infrastructure planning. Under the consultative MIS functions, in contrast, you exercise the primary responsibility for each function, while the MIS department acts as your advisor. IT's About Business 1.1 illustrates how the University System of Georgia manages its IT resources across its 31 member higher-education institutions.

IT'S ABOUT BUSINESS 1.1

Information Technology Supports Students in Georgia

There are two major drivers for change in higher education: lowering costs and improving performance. Lowering costs is necessary because higher education costs have been rapidly increasing for many years, leading to concerns that higher education is out of reach for low-income families. Improving performance is necessary because there is pressure on universities to graduate more students while at the same time maintaining a high-quality educational experience. In essence, colleges and universities are under increasing pressure to accomplish more with less.

The University System of Georgia (USG; www.usg.edu) has employed cutting-edge information technologies to achieve these seemingly contradictory goals. USG is the organizational body that includes 31 public institutions of higher learning in the state of Georgia. The system, which is governed by the Georgia Board of Regents, establishes goals and dictates general policy to its member institutions.

MIS These policies require universities to deliver learning using new technologies (for example, delivering lectures via video) to stay current. In addition, university IT organizations must devise innovative strategies to reduce costs and increase efficiencies both within and among universities. This requirement has become vital as state funding shrinks and students struggle under the escalating costs of higher education. To accomplish these tasks, university IT departments have to be flexible and entrepreneurial.

The individual who bears the major responsibility for implementing these policies is Board of Regents Vice Chancellor and CIO Curtis Carver. Significantly, Carver has to collaborate with 31 independent-minded university CIOs. This position requires him to sell services. USG institutions can pursue technology contracts on their own. So, Carver looks for scenarios where 3 to 5 universities are planning to buy the same product and can consolidate their buying or centralize the service. That approach not only reduces costs, but it also helps alleviate staff shortages in some areas, such as database administration and analytics. The central IT organization's vision statement asserts, "If our customers can choose anyone to provide them IT services, they would choose us." Let's take a look at a specific example of how Carver utilized his strategy to resolve a problem.

The problem involves situations where a class is overbooked at one member university while the same class at other schools has empty seats. To manage such situations, the universities offered a number of such classes across institutions via videoconferencing, but the registration process posed a serious problem for students.

In addition to constituting a major inconvenience, overbooked classes and waiting lists can cause students to take longer to graduate, adding to their loan debt and delaying their entry into the workforce. Although a few vendors sell

software to facilitate cross-institution registration, Carver considered those products too complex and costly. As an alternative, USG system developers wrote custom computer code to handle cross-registration. This software integrated student information sys-

© Spectral-Design/iStockphoto

tems to create a total headcount of registrants in each course across all USG universities. The system provides an interface for each student that exactly resembles the user interface at his or her home institution. Therefore, if a student at Coastal Georgia University registers for a course at the University of Georgia, the system looks exactly like the Coastal Georgia system, with no need to register or pay fees to another university. Thousands of students now sign up for courses through this cross-registration system, known as the Intra-Georgia Registration Sharing System, or Ingress (not to be confused with the open-source Ingres database).

After the developers had created Ingress, Carver had to convince member universities that this system was really the way to go. University CIOs often have the option to use or not to use a shared service. As of this writing, 22 of the 31 USG universities use or are implementing Ingress. Carver takes the same approach with shared data center services, which the central group offers via a private cloud. The USG also has centralized the operation of its Desire2Learn learning management system, used by 300,000 students state-wide. Finally, Carver is exploring whether the USG can sell Ingress to other institutions.

Sources: Compiled from C. Murphy, "Chiefs of the Year," *InformationWeek*, December 16, 2013; K. Flinders, "Universities Investing in Back-Office IT Systems," *Computer Weekly*, March 2, 2012; "University IT Departments Can Drive Efficiencies and Modernisation," *The Guardian*, June, 2011; "Information Technology in Higher Education: Survey of Chief Information Officers," *The Chronicle of Higher Education*, 2010; www.usg.edu, accessed January 25, 2014.

Questions

1. Describe how the University System of Georgia manages its information resources vis-à-vis the individual universities in the system.

2. What are the advantages of central management of information systems in the University System of Georgia?

3. What are the disadvantages of central management of information systems in the University System of Georgia?

Apply The Concept 1.1

LEARNING OBJECTIVE 1.1 Identify the reasons why being an informed user of information systems is important in today's world.

STEP 1 – Background (Here is what you are learning.)

Section 1.1 discussed how businesses are utilizing modern technologies to become more productive by connecting to their customers, suppliers, partners, and other parties. Those connections, however, do not exist simply to support the businesses. Do you realize how connected *you* are? Computers and information systems have become an essential feature of our everyday lives. Most of you have a cell phone within reach and have looked at it within the past 5 minutes. No longer is a phone just a phone; rather, it is your connection to family, friends, shopping, driving directions, entertainment (games, movies, music, etc.), and much more.

When you embark on your career, you likely will have to interface with information systems to post transactions and search for or record information. Accomplishing these tasks will require you to work effectively with computers, regardless of the industry you find yourself employed in.

STEP 2 – Activity (Here is what you do.)

Visit the Web sites of three local businesses: a bank, a dentist, and a retail shop. Examine their information to see if you can determine what types of information systems they use to support their operations. It is likely that you will find some similarities and differences among the three. Also, see if they have any open positions. If they do, what technical skills do these positions require? Summarize your findings in a paragraph or two.

STEP 3 – Assignment (Here is what you turn in.)

Based on your research, identify five reasons why it is important for you to be an informed user of information technology. Reference your summarized findings to support your reasoning. Submit this list to your instructor, but also keep it in mind. You have just looked into the real world (your local world, in fact) and identified a reason for taking this course!

1.2 Overview of Computer-Based Information Systems

Organizations refer to their management information systems functional area by several names, including the MIS Department, the Information Systems (IS) Department, the Information Technology Department, and the Information Services Department. Regardless of the name, however, this functional area deals with the planning for—and the development, management, and use of—information technology tools to help people perform all the tasks related to information processing and management. Recall that information technology relates to any computer-based tool that people use to work with information and to support the information and information-processing needs of an organization.

As previously stated, an information system collects, processes, stores, analyzes, and disseminates information for a specific purpose. The purpose of information systems has been defined as getting the right information to the right people, at the right time, in the right amount, and in the right format. Because information systems are intended to supply useful information, we need to differentiate between information and two closely related terms: data and knowledge (see FIGURE 1.2).

Data items refer to an elementary description of things, events, activities, and transactions that are recorded, classified, and stored but are not organized to convey any specific meaning. Data items can be numbers, letters, figures, sounds, and images. Examples of data items are collections of numbers (e.g., 3.11, 2.96, 3.95, 1.99, 2.08) and characters (e.g., B, A, C, A, B, D, F, C).

© creischl/iStockphoto
Data

Exactostock/SuperStock
Information

© TPopova/iStockphoto
Knowledge

Figure 1.2 Binary Code, the foundation of information and knowledge, is the key to making complex decisions.

Information refers to data that have been organized so that they have meaning and value to the recipient. For example, a grade point average (GPA) by itself is data, but a student's name coupled with his or her GPA is information. The recipient interprets the meaning and draws conclusions and implications from the information. Consider the examples of data provided in the preceding paragraph. Within the context of a university, the numbers could be grade point averages, and the letters could be grades in an Introduction to MIS class.

Knowledge consists of data and/or information that have been organized and processed to convey understanding, experience, accumulated learning, and expertise as they apply to a current business problem. For example, suppose that a company recruiting at your school has found over time that students with grade point averages over 3.0 have experienced the greatest success in its management program. Based on this accumulated knowledge, that company may decide to interview only those students with GPAs over 3.0. This example presents an example of knowledge because the company utilizes information—GPAs—to address a business problem—hiring successful employees. As you can see from this example, organizational knowledge, which reflects the experience and expertise of many people, has great value to all employees.

Consider this example:

Data	Information	Knowledge
[No context]	[University context]	
3.16	3.16 + John Jones = GPA	* Job prospects
2.92	2.92 + Sue Smith = GPA	* Graduate school prospects
1.39	1.39 + Kyle Owens = GPA	* Scholarship prospects
3.95	3.95 + Tom Elias = GPA	

Data	Information	Knowledge
[No context]	[Professional baseball pitcher context]	
3.16	3.16 + Ken Rice = ERA	
2.92	2.92 + Ed Dyas = ERA	* Keep pitcher, trade pitcher, or send pitcher to minor leagues
1.39	1.39 + Hugh Carr = ERA	* Salary/contract negotiations
3.95	3.95 + Nick Ford = ERA	

GPA = grade point average (higher is better)
ERA = earned run average (lower is better); ERA is the number of runs per nine innings that a pitcher surrenders.

You see that the same data items, with no context, can mean entirely different things in different contexts.

Now that you have a clearer understanding of data, information, and knowledge, let's shift our focus to computer-based information systems. As you have seen, these systems process data into information and knowledge that you can use.

A **computer-based information system (CBIS)** is an information system that uses computer technology to perform some or all of its intended tasks. Although not all information systems are computerized, today most are. For this reason the term "information system" is typically used synonymously with "computer-based information system." The basic components of computer-based information systems are listed below. The first four are called **information technology components**. FIGURE 1.3 illustrates how these four components interact to form a CBIS.

- **Hardware** consists of devices such as the processor, monitor, keyboard, and printer. Together, these devices accept, process, and display data and information.
- **Software** is a program or collection of programs that enable the hardware to process data.
- A **database** is a collection of related files or tables containing data.
- A **network** is a connecting system (wireline or wireless) that permits different computers to share resources.

Figure 1.3 It takes technology (hardware, software, databses, and networks) with appropriate procedures to make a CBIS useful for people.

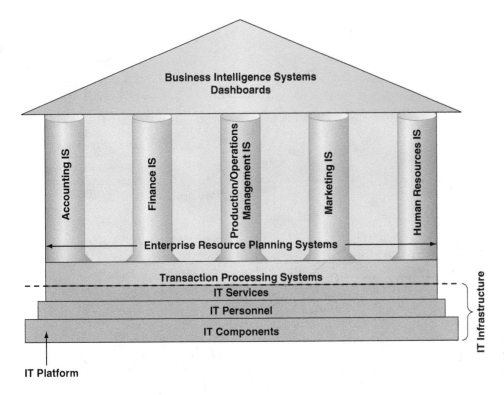

IT Platform

Figure 1.4 Information technology inside your organization.

- **Procedures** are the instructions for combining the above components to process information and generate the desired output.
- *People* are those individuals who use the hardware and software, interface with it, or utilize its output.

FIGURE 1.4 illustrates how these components are integrated to form the wide variety of information systems found within an organization. Starting at the bottom of the figure, you see that the IT components of hardware, software, networks (wireline and wireless), and databases form the **information technology platform**. IT personnel use these components to develop information systems, oversee security and risk, and manage data. These activities cumulatively are called **information technology services**. The IT components plus IT services comprise the organization's **information technology infrastructure**. At the top of the pyramid are the various organizational information systems.

Computer-based information systems have many capabilities. Table 1.3 summarizes the most important ones.

Information systems perform these various tasks via a wide spectrum of applications. An **application** (or **app**) is a computer program designed to support a specific task or business process. (A synonymous term is *application program*.) Each functional area or department within a business organization uses dozens of application programs. For instance, the human resources department sometimes uses one application for screening job applicants and another for monitoring employee turnover. The collection of application programs in a

TABLE 1.3 Major Capabilities of Information Systems

Perform high-speed, high-volume numerical computations.
Provide fast, accurate communication and collaboration within and among organizations.
Store huge amounts of information in an easy-to-access, yet small space.
Allow quick and inexpensive access to vast amounts of information, worldwide.
Interpret vast amounts of data quickly and efficiently.
Automate both semiautomatic business processes and manual tasks.

Figure 1.5 Information systems that function among multiple organizations.

single department is usually referred to as a *departmental information system* (also known as a *functional area information system*). For example, the collection of application programs in the human resources area is called the *human resources information system* (*HRIS*). There are collections of application programs—that is, departmental information systems—in the other functional areas as well, such as accounting, finance, marketing, and production/operations.

Types of Computer-Based Information Systems

© Sonda Dawes/The Image Works

Modern organizations employ many different types of information systems. FIGURE 1.4 illustrates the different types of information systems that function *within* a single organization, and FIGURE 1.5 shows the different types of information systems that function *among* multiple organizations. You will study transaction processing systems, management information systems, and enterprise resource planning systems in Chapter 11. You will learn about customer relationship management (CRM) systems in Chapter 12 and supply chain management (SCM) systems in Chapter 13.

In the next section you will learn about the numerous and diverse types of information systems employed by modern organizations. You will also read about the types of support these systems provide.

Breadth of Support of Information Systems. Certain information systems support parts of organizations, others support entire organizations, and still others support groups of organizations. This section addresses all of these systems.

Recall that each department or functional area within an organization has its own collection of application programs, or information systems. These **functional area information systems (FAISs)** are supporting pillars for the information systems located at the top of FIGURE 1.4, namely, business intelligence systems and dashboards. As the name suggests, each FAIS supports a particular functional area within the organization. Examples are accounting IS, finance IS, production/operations management (POM) IS, marketing IS, and human resources IS.

Consider these examples of IT systems in the various functional areas of an organization. In finance and accounting, managers use IT systems to forecast revenues and business activity, to determine the best sources and uses of funds, and to perform audits to ensure that the organization is fundamentally sound and that all financial reports and documents are accurate.

In sales and marketing, managers use information technology to perform the following functions:

- *Product analysis:* developing new goods and services
- *Site analysis:* determining the best location for production and distribution facilities
- *Promotion analysis:* identifying the best advertising channels
- *Price analysis:* setting product prices to obtain the highest total revenues

Marketing managers also use IT to manage their relationships with their customers. In *manufacturing*, managers use IT to process customer orders, develop production schedules, control inventory levels, and monitor product quality. They also use IT to design and manufacture products. These processes are called *computer-assisted design (CAD)* and *computer-assisted manufacturing (CAM)*.

Managers in *human resources* use IT to manage the recruiting process, analyze and screen job applicants, and hire new employees. They also employ IT to help employees manage their careers, to administer performance tests to employees, and to monitor employee productivity. Finally, they rely on IT to manage compensation and benefits packages.

Two information systems support the entire organization: enterprise resource planning systems and transaction processing systems. **Enterprise resource planning (ERP) systems** are designed to correct a lack of communication among the functional area ISs. For this reason FIGURE 1.4 shows ERP systems spanning the FAISs. ERP systems were an important innovation because the various functional area ISs were often developed as standalone systems and did not communicate effectively (if at all) with one another. ERP systems resolve this problem by tightly integrating the functional area ISs via a common database. In doing so, they enhance communications among the functional areas of an organization. For this reason, experts credit ERP systems with greatly increasing organizational productivity.

A **transaction processing system** (TPS) supports the monitoring, collection, storage, and processing of data from the organization's basic business transactions, each of which generates data. When you are checking out at Walmart, for example, a transaction occurs each time the cashier swipes an item across the bar code reader. Significantly, within an organization, different functions or departments can define a transaction differently. In accounting, for example, a transaction is anything that changes a firm's chart of accounts. The information system definition of a transaction is broader: A transaction is anything that changes the firm's database. The chart of accounts is only part of the firm's database. Consider a scenario in which a student transfers from one section of an Introduction to MIS course to another section. This move would be a transaction to the university's information system, but not to the university's accounting department (the tuition would not change).

The TPS collects data continuously, typically in *real time*—that is, as soon as the data are generated—and it provides the input data for the corporate databases. TPSs are considered critical to the success of any enterprise because they support core operations. Significantly, nearly all ERP systems are also TPSs, but not all TPSs are ERP systems. In fact, modern ERP systems incorporate many functions that previously were handled by the organization's functional area information systems. You study both TPSs and ERP systems in detail in Chapter 11.

ERP systems and TPSs function primarily within a single organization. Information systems that connect two or more organizations are referred to as **interorganizational information systems (IOSs)**. IOSs support many interorganizational operations, of which *supply chain management* is the best known. An organization's **supply chain** is the flow of materials, information, money, and services from suppliers of raw materials through factories and warehouses to the end customers.

Note that the supply chain in FIGURE 1.5 shows physical flows, information flows, and financial flows. Digitizable products are those that can be represented in electronic form, such as music and software. Information flows, financial flows, and digitizable products go through the Internet, whereas physical products are shipped. For example, when you order a computer from *www.dell.com*, your information goes to Dell via the Internet. When your transaction is completed (that is, your credit card is approved and your order is processed), Dell ships your computer to you. (We discuss supply chains in more detail in Chapter 13.)

Electronic commerce (e-commerce) systems are another type of interorganizational information system. These systems enable organizations to conduct transactions, called business-to-business (B2B) electronic commerce, and customers to conduct transactions with businesses, called business-to-consumer (B2C) electronic commerce. E-commerce systems typically are Internet-based. FIGURE 1.5 illustrates B2B and B2C electronic commerce. Electronic commerce systems are so important that we discuss them in detail in Chapter 9, with additional examples interspersed throughout the text.

Support for Organizational Employees. So far, you have concentrated on information systems that support specific functional areas and operations. Now you will learn about information systems that typically support particular employees within the organization.

Clerical workers, who support managers at all levels of the organization, include bookkeepers, secretaries, electronic file clerks, and insurance claim processors. *Lower-level managers* handle the day-to-day operations of the organization, making routine decisions such as assigning tasks to employees and placing purchase orders. *Middle managers* make tactical decisions, which deal with activities such as short-term planning, organizing, and control.

Knowledge workers are professional employees such as financial and marketing analysts, engineers, lawyers, and accountants. All knowledge workers are experts in a particular subject area. They create information and knowledge, which they integrate into the business. Knowledge workers, in turn, act as advisors to middle managers and executives. Finally, *executives* make decisions that deal with situations that can significantly change the manner in which business is done. Examples of executive decisions are introducing a new product line, acquiring other businesses, and relocating operations to a foreign country.

Office automation systems (OASs) typically support the clerical staff, lower and middle managers, and knowledge workers. These employees use OASs to develop documents (word processing and desktop publishing software), schedule resources (electronic calendars), and communicate (e-mail, voice mail, videoconferencing, and groupware).

Functional area information systems summarize data and prepare reports, primarily for middle managers, but sometimes for lower-level managers as well. Because these reports typically concern a specific functional area, report generators (RPGs) are an important type of functional area IS.

Business intelligence (BI) systems provide computer-based support for complex, nonroutine decisions, primarily for middle managers and knowledge workers. (They also support lower-level managers, but to a lesser extent.) These systems are typically used with a data warehouse, and they enable users to perform their own data analysis. You learn about BI systems in Chapter 5.

Expert systems (ES) attempt to duplicate the work of human experts by applying reasoning capabilities, knowledge, and expertise within a specific domain. They have become valuable in many application areas, primarily but not exclusively areas involving decision making. For example, navigation systems use rules to select routes, but we do not typically think of these systems as expert systems. Significantly, expert systems can operate as standalone systems or be embedded in other applications. We examine ESs in greater detail in Plug IT In 5.

Dashboards (also called **digital dashboards**) are a special form of IS that support all managers of the organization. They provide rapid access to timely information and direct access to structured information in the form of reports. Dashboards that are tailored to the information needs of executives are called *executive dashboards*. Chapter 5 provides a thorough discussion of dashboards.

Table 1.4 provides an overview of the different types of information systems used by organizations.

Type of System	Function	Example
Functional area IS	Supports the activities within specific functional area.	System for processing payroll
Transaction processing system	Processes transaction data from terminal	Walmart checkout point-of-sale business events.
Enterprise resource planning	Integrates all functional areas of the organization.	Oracle, SAP system
Office automation system	Supports daily work activities of individuals and groups.	Microsoft® Office
Management information system	Produces reports summarized from transaction data, usually in one functional area.	Report on total sales for each customer
Decision support system	Provides access to data and analysis tools.	"What-if" analysis of changes in budget
Expert system	Mimics human expert in a particular area and makes decisions.	Credit card approval analysis
Executive dashboard	Presents structured, summarized information about aspects of business important to executives.	Status of sales by product
Supply chain management system	Manages flows of products, services, and information among organizations.	Walmart Retail Link system connecting suppliers to Walmart
Electronic commerce system	Enables transactions among organizations and between organizations and customers.	www.dell.com

TABLE 1.4 Types of Organizational Information Systems

Apply The Concept 1.2

LEARNING OBJECTIVE 1.2 Classify the activities supported by various types of computer-based information systems in an organization.

STEP 1 – Background

Section 1.2 discussed the various functional areas in which you most likely will be employed and the different IS that support them. It should be no surprise that these are the majors you can choose from in most colleges of business. The four major functional areas are marketing/sales, finance/accounting, manufacturing, and human resources. Often, these areas will use the same database and networks within a company, but they will use them to support their specific needs. This activity will help you develop a solid understanding of the role of IS within the different functional areas.

STEP 2 – Activity

Review the section material that describes the major functions of the four major functional areas. Then, review the basic functions of the following types of information systems: transaction processing, management information, and decision support. After you have acquired a solid understanding of the functional areas and information systems that support them, you are ready to move forward with the activity!

BEFORE YOU GO ON....

1. What is a computer-based information system?
2. Describe the components of computer-based information systems.
3. What is an application program?
4. Explain how information systems provide support for knowledge workers.
5. As we move up the organization's hierarchy from clerical workers to executives, how does the type of support provided by information systems change?

Create a table like the one shown below, and classify the activities supported by various types of computer-based information systems. To assist you, we have pre-filled one item in each type of system. After you complete your chart, submit it to your professor.

	Transaction Processing	Management Information System	Decision Support System
Marketing/Sales	Enter Sales Data		
Accounting/Finance			
Human Resources			Comply with EEOC
Manufacturing		Inventory Reporting	

1.3 How Does IT Impact Organizations?

Throughout this text you will encounter numerous examples of how IT affects various types of organizations. This section provides an overview of the impact of IT on modern organizations. As you read this section you will learn how IT will affect you as well.

IT Reduces the Number of Middle Managers

IT makes managers more productive, and it increases the number of employees who can report to a single manager. Thus, IT ultimately decreases the number of managers and experts. It is reasonable to assume, therefore, that in coming years organizations will have fewer managerial levels and fewer staff and line managers. If this trend materializes, promotional opportunities will decrease, making promotions much more competitive. Bottom line: Pay attention in school!

IT Changes the Manager's Job

One of the most important tasks of managers is making decisions. A major consequence of IT has been to change the manner in which managers make their decisions. In this way, IT ultimately has changed managers' jobs.

IT often provides managers with near-real-time information, meaning that managers have less time to make decisions, making their jobs even more stressful. Fortunately, IT also provides many tools—for example, business analytics applications such as dashboards, search engines, and intranets—to help managers handle the volumes of information they must deal with on an ongoing basis.

So far in this section, we have been focusing on managers in general. Now, let's focus on you. Due to advances in IT, you will increasingly supervise employees and teams who are geographically dispersed. Employees can work from anywhere at any time, and teams can consist of employees who are literally dispersed throughout the world. Information technologies such as telepresence systems (discussed in Chapter 4) can help you manage these employees even though you do not often see them face-to-face. For these employees, electronic or "remote" supervision will become the norm. Remote supervision places greater emphasis on completed work and less emphasis on personal contacts and office politics. You will have to reassure your employees that they are valued members of the organization, thereby diminishing any feelings they might have of being isolated and "out of the loop."

Will IT Eliminate Jobs?

One major concern of every employee, part-time or full-time, is job security. Relentless cost-cutting measures in modern organizations often lead to large-scale layoffs. Put simply, organizations are responding to today's highly competitive environment by doing more with less. Regardless of your position, then, you consistently will have to add value to your organization and to make certain that your superiors are aware of this value.

Many companies have responded to difficult economic times, increased global competition, demands for customization, and increased consumer sophistication by increasing their investments in IT. In fact, as computers continue to advance in terms of intelligence and capabilities, the competitive advantage of replacing people with machines is increasing rapidly. This process frequently leads to layoffs. At the same time, however, IT creates entirely new categories of jobs, such as electronic medical record keeping and nanotechnology.

IT Impacts Employees at Work

Many people have experienced a loss of identity because of computerization. They feel like "just another number" because computers reduce or eliminate the human element present in noncomputerized systems.

The Internet threatens to exert an even more isolating influence than have computers and television. Encouraging people to work and shop from their living rooms could produce some unfortunate psychological effects, such as depression and loneliness.

IT Impacts Employees' Health and Safety.
Although computers and information systems are generally regarded as agents of "progress," they can adversely affect individuals' health and safety. To illustrate this point, we consider two issues associated with IT: job stress and long-term use of the keyboard.

An increase in an employee's workload and/or responsibilities can trigger *job stress*. Although computerization has benefited organizations by increasing productivity, it also has created an ever-expanding workload for some employees. Some workers feel overwhelmed and have become increasingly anxious about their job performance. These feelings of stress and anxiety can actually diminish rather than improve workers' productivity while jeopardizing their physical and mental health. Management can help alleviate these problems by providing training, redistributing the workload among workers, and hiring more workers.

On a more specific level, the long-term use of keyboards can lead to *repetitive strain injuries* such as backaches and muscle tension in the wrists and fingers. *Carpal tunnel syndrome* is a particularly painful form of repetitive strain injury that affects the wrists and hands.

Designers are aware of the potential problems associated with the prolonged use of computers. To address these problems, they continually attempt to design a better computing environment. The science of designing machines and work settings that minimize injury and illness is called **ergonomics**. The goal of ergonomics is to create an environment that is safe, well lit, and comfortable. Examples of ergonomically designed products are antiglare screens that alleviate problems of fatigued or damaged eyesight and chairs that contour the human body to decrease backaches. FIGURE 1.6 displays some sample ergonomic products.

IT Provides Opportunities for People with Disabilities.
Computers can create new employment opportunities for people with disabilities by integrating speech-recognition and vision-recognition capabilities. For example, individuals who cannot type can use a voice-operated keyboard, and individuals who cannot travel can work at home.

Going further, adaptive equipment for computers enables people with disabilities to perform tasks they normally would not be able to do. For example, the Web and graphical user interfaces (GUIs; e.g., Windows) can be difficult for people with impaired vision to use. To address this problem, manufacturers have added audible screen tips and voice interfaces, which essentially restore the functionality of computers to the way it was before GUIs become standard.

Other devices help improve the quality of life in more mundane, but useful, ways for people with disabilities. Examples are a two-way writing telephone, a robotic page turner, a hair brusher, and a hospital-bedside video trip to the zoo or the museum. Several organizations specialize in IT designed for people with disabilities.

— BEFORE *YOU GO ON....* —

1. Why should employees in all functional areas become knowledgeable about IT?

2. Describe how IT might change the manager's job.

3. Discuss several ways in which IT impacts employees at work.

Media Bakery
(a)

Media Bakery
(b)

Media Bakery
(c)

Media Bakery
(d)

Figure 1.6 Ergonomic products protect computer users.

Apply The Concept 1.3

LEARNING OBJECTIVE 1.3 Discuss ways in which information technology can affect managers and nonmanagerial workers.

STEP 1 – Background

Section 1.3 demonstrated that the essential reason businesses use information systems is to add value to their daily activities. In fact, IS have radically transformed the nature of both managerial and nonmanagerial work. Managers employ IS to instantly track information that previously was available only in monthly reports. Support staff can view calendars and schedules for all employees and can schedule meetings more easily. Sales managers can view current product availability while visiting with clients. This list does not even scratch the surface of the countless ways technology has changed the nature of work in modern businesses.

STEP 2 – Activity

Think of an industry in which you are interested in pursuing a career. Photography? Dentistry? Banking? Fashion? Real estate? Transportation? After you have selected an area (or two or three), search the Web for "how information systems have changed [insert your chosen area here]." For example, a search for "how information systems have changed dentistry" generates lots of interesting information.

STEP 3 – Assignment

Based on your findings, write a few paragraphs to discuss at least three ways in which information technology can affect managers and nonmanagerial workers. Submit this essay to your professor. Make certain to include the links that you used to find your information.

1.4 Importance of Information Systems to Society

This section explains in greater detail why IT is important to society as a whole. Other examples of the impact of IT on society appear throughout the text.

IT Affects Our Quality of Life

IT has significant implications for our quality of life. The workplace can be expanded from the traditional 9-to-5 job at a central location to 24 hours a day at any location. IT can provide employees with flexibility that can significantly improve the quality of leisure time, even if it doesn't increase the total amount of leisure time.

From the opposite perspective, however, IT also can place employees on "constant call," which means they are never truly away from the office, even when they are on vacation. In fact, surveys reveal that the majority of respondents take their laptops and smartphones on their vacations, and 100 percent took their cell phones. Going further, the majority of respondents did some work while vacationing, and almost all of them checked their e-mail regularly.

The Robot Revolution Is Here Now

Once restricted largely to science fiction movies, robots that can perform practical tasks are becoming more common. In fact, "cyberpooches," "nursebots," and other mechanical beings may be our companions before we know it. Around the world, quasi-autonomous devices have become increasingly common on factory floors, in hospital corridors, and in farm fields. For home use, iRobot (www.irobot.com) produces the Roomba to vacuum our floors, the Scooba to wash our floors, the Dirt Dog to sweep our garages, the Verro to clean our pools, and the Looj to clean our gutters. Chapter closing case 2 takes a look at Baxter, a new, more human-like robot.

Robots are increasingly being utilized in a variety of areas. IT's About Business 1.2 discusses three additional types of robots: telepresence robots, autonomous cars, and drones.

IT'S ABOUT BUSINESS 1.2

Different Types of Robots

Telepresence robots. Telepresence robots allow people to move virtually through a distant building by remotely controlling a wheeled robot equipped with a camera, microphone, loudspeaker, and screen displaying live video of the face of the person controlling the robot. Advocates of these robots claim that by placing a remotely controlled embodiment of yourself in another location you can enhance your contacts, increase your influence, and assert your authority. The robots enable an individual to maintain a consistent connection with coworkers, customers, and clients. Interestingly, the robots actually break down barriers of awkwardness that people sometimes feel in person-to-person meetings.

Telepresence robots are designed to help companies save money on travel and expensive teleconferencing technology. They enable people in remote offices or locations to have a rich communications experience without using a complicated videoconference system.

In addition to conducting business, telepresence robots are being employed in a variety of fields. For example, they enable homebuyers to virtually tour distant properties, they provide an inexpensive method to patrol workplaces at night, they allow managers to supervise factory floors, and they allow parents who are out to dinner to stay in touch with their children at home.

In a particularly valuable practice known as *telemedicine*, telepresence robots enable doctors to conduct bedside consultations from a distance. In one specific example, Brazil's Olympic Organizing Committee will place telepresence robots in operating rooms for the 2016 Olympic Games in Rio de Janeiro. The committee's chief medical officer explains that doctors who are unable to accompany their athletes to the games will be able to advise Brazilian surgeons during operations.

Autonomous Cars. *Autonomy* is commonly defined as the ability of a machine to make decisions without human intervention. The best-known example of an autonomous, or self-driving, car is the Google driverless car. Google has announced that its autonomous cars had completed some half-million accident-free, self-driving miles. As of mid-2014, four states had passed laws permitting autonomous cars on roads: Nevada, Florida, California, and Michigan. Nevertheless, Google had not announced any plans to commercially develop the system. An attorney for the California Department of Motor Vehicles raised concerns that Google's technology is "ahead of the law in many areas," citing state laws that "all presume to have a human being operating the vehicle."

Audi, Toyota, Cadillac, and Ford, among other car brands, are developing autonomous cars as well. It is worth noting that each of Google's driverless test cars contains about $150,000 in equipment. With so many automobile manufacturers developing autonomous cars, the price will undoubtedly drop quickly.

Drones. An unmanned aerial vehicle (UAV), commonly known as a *drone*, is an aircraft that does not have a human pilot on board. Its flight is controlled either autonomously by computers contained in the vehicle or via remote control by a pilot located either on the ground or in another vehicle. UAVs are deployed predominately for military applications, but they are also utilized in a growing number of civil applications including police work, firefighting, and nonmilitary security work such as border control and surveillance of pipelines. One interesting application of drones is in the retail sector. In 2014, Jeff Bezos, the CEO of Amazon, announced that his company was evaluating the use of drones to deliver packages under 5 pounds in weight to its customers.

The ultimate goal in the development of autonomous technology in UAVs is to replace the human pilot. To this end, artificial intelligence has advanced to the point where UAVs are capable of taking off, landing, and flying by themselves. It remains to be seen, however, whether the perception of autonomous technology, and, most importantly, the political climate surrounding the use of such technology, will limit the development and utility of autonomous UAVs.

There is a great deal of controversy concerning the use of UAVs inside the United States. (The U.S. military is currently deploying them in foreign countries such as Pakistan and Yemen.) Drones are powerful surveillance tools, capable of carrying facial recognition systems, license plate scanners, thermal imaging cameras, open Wi-Fi scanners, and many other types of sensors. On January 10, 2012, the Electronic Frontier Foundation (EFF), an advocacy group for free speech and privacy rights in technology-related areas, filed a Freedom of Information Act lawsuit against the Federal Aviation Administration. In response, the FAA, for the first time, released a list of the names of all public and private entities that have applied for authorization to fly drones domesti-

cally. Among these organizations are the U.S. Customs and Border Protection Agency (CBP), located within the Department of Homeland Security (DHS). The CBP has used UAVs to patrol U.S. borders since 2005. Other organizations on the list include the FBI, the Department of Defense, and local law enforcement agencies.

Significantly, U.S. citizens currently have few legal privacy protections from aerial surveillance conducted with UAVs. In one case, the U.S. Supreme Court held that individuals do not have the right to privacy from police observation from public airspace, even on their private property. The weakness of legal protections from UAV surveillance has led civil liberties advocacy groups to pressure the U.S. government to issue laws and regulations that establish both privacy protections and greater transparency regarding the use of UAVs to gather information about individuals.

Sources: Compiled from T. Simonite, "A Telepresence Machine to Watch the Kids or Visit Grandma," *MIT Technology Review*, January 15, 2014; R. Nakashima, "Carmakers: Driverless Cars Need Legal Framework," *ABC News*, January 10, 2014; H. Kelly, "Driverless Car Tech Gets Serious at CES," *CNN*, January 9, 2014; "Balancing Safety, Privacy in Use of Drones," *Star Tribune*, January 7, 2014; "Ford Joins Driverless Car Stampede," *Automotive News*, December 12, 2013; T. Jackovics, "Florida Aims to Lead Driverless Car Revolution," *The Tampa Tribune*, November 10, 2013; A. Vance, "Google Self-Driving Robot Cars Are Ruining My Commute," *Bloomberg BusinessWeek*, March 28, 2013; J. Horgen, "Unmanned Flight," *National Geographic*, March 2013; W. Knight, "The Perfect Parking Garage: No Drivers Required," *MIT Technology Review*, March 27, 2013; "Your Alter Ego on Wheels," *The Economist*, March 9, 2013; M. Whittington, "Law Proposed in Texas to Require Licensed Driver in Self-Driving Vehicles," *Yahoo! News*, March 8, 2013; M. Stewart, "Drones Patrolling U.S. Borders Spark Controversy Over Privacy," *TheDenverChannel.com*, February 24, 2013; J. Lynch, "FAA Releases New Drone List – Is Your Town on the Map?" *Electronic Freedom Foundation*, February 7, 2013; T. Chea, "Telepresence Robots Let Employees 'Beam' into Work," *Associated Press*, January 1, 2013; J. Oram, "Governor Brown Signs California Driverless Car Law at Google HQ," *WebProNews*, September 27, 2012; M. Slosson, "Google Gets First Self-Driven Car License in Nevada," *Reuters*, May 8, 2012; www.xaxxon.com, www.roboticsvalley.com, accessed March 23, 2014.

Questions

1. Discuss some disadvantages of (a) telepresence robots, (b) autonomous cars, and (c) drones.

2. Would you be willing to ride in an autonomous car? Why or why not?

3. Which occupations are most at risk from a widespread adoption of autonomous cars? Support your answer.

4. Debate the privacy issues associated with domestic use of drones by law enforcement agencies.

It probably will be a long time before we see robots making decisions by themselves, handling unfamiliar situations, and interacting with people. Nevertheless, robots are extremely helpful in various environments, particularly those that are repetitive, harsh, or dangerous to humans.

Improvements in Healthcare

IT has brought about major improvements in healthcare delivery. Medical personnel use IT to make better and faster diagnoses and to monitor critically ill patients more accurately. IT also has streamlined the process of researching and developing new drugs. Expert systems now help doctors diagnose diseases, and machine vision is enhancing the work of radiologists. Surgeons use virtual reality to plan complex surgeries. They also employ surgical robots to perform long-distance surgery. Finally, doctors discuss complex medical cases via videoconferencing. New computer simulations recreate the sense of touch, allowing doctors-in-training to perform virtual procedures without risking harm to an actual patient.

Not all uses of information technology to improve health are expensive and sophisticated. IT's About Business 1.3 illustrates how Zamzee is using gamification to help young people lose weight.

IT'S ABOUT BUSINESS 1.3

Getting Kids in Shape

Jerry never paid much attention to how much physical activity he engaged in. However, one day he played basketball while wearing a small activity tracker called a Zamzee on his waist. Later, he plugged the device into his computer's USB port and uploaded the data captured by the device's *accelerometers*: devices that measure the speed and distance covered by the person wearing them. Unlike a FitBit (www.fitbit.com), a popular pedometer geared to adults, Jerry's Zamzee did not tell him how many steps he took or how many calories he burned. Instead, it awarded him points—758, in fact—for his movements. These points are the currency that he can spend in the virtual world of Zamzee.com, where he created an avatar representing himself. If Jerry continues to exercise, he can eventually collect enough "Zamz" to be able to purchase real items like an iPod Nano (16,000 Zamz) or a Wii console (18,000 Zamz).

 Jerry's experience illustrates the goals of Zamzee (www.zamzee.com), a company that is testing the idea that the addictiveness of games can be harnessed to solve a difficult social problem – in this case, childhood obesity. The concept is called *gamification*, which is the use of game thinking and game mechanics in a non-game context to engage users and solve problems.

Rather than focusing on weight loss or diet, Zamzee hopes to reward movement of any kind in children ages 11 to 14. Zamzee has targeted this demographic because research indicates that these are the ages when physical activity drops precipitously. Significantly, this is also the period when children adopt lifelong habits.

Zamzee is a for-profit venture started by HopeLab, the nonprofit foundation funded by eBay founder Pierre Omidyar and his wife, Pam. Zamzee launched in the fall of 2013. By mid-2013, however, pilot programs were already underway in schools and community centers in Atlanta, Chicago, Honolulu, and San Francisco.

© monkeybusinessimages/iStockphoto

Jerry is one of the middle-school boys who have been trying Zamzee at a Boys & Girls Club in Atlanta. Georgia ranks second among the states for childhood obesity, and more than half of its middle-school students fail to meet the Center for Disease Control's recommendations for daily activity. The situation is so serious that Children's Healthcare of Atlanta, a system of pediatric centers, recently launched an ad campaign aimed at overweight children.

Zamzee concentrates on carrots rather than sticks. Parents put money into an account to fund the rewards that their children can try to earn with their Zamz (although some donors, such as the Mayo Clinic, are providing funding during the pilot tests).

Neuroscientist Sandra Aamodt, the author of *Welcome to Your Child's Brain*, praises Zamzee's focus on physical activity instead of weight. She cautions, however, that research has revealed that intrinsic motivation outlasts extrinsic rewards. (Intrinsic motivation comes from inside an individual rather than from external rewards, such as money or grades.) With that in mind, Zamzee's developers have been testing multiple methods for motivating children. They have found that combining virtual (electronic) and monetary rewards can be successful.

And the bottom line? According to Zamzee, studies confirm that young people who use Zamzee move almost 60 percent more on average than their counterparts who do not.

Sources: Compiled from "New Zamzee for Groups Program Curriculum Helps Instructors Increase Youth Physical Activity," *Boston Globe*, November 21, 2013; "Zamzee Partners with Safe Routes to School Initiative in West Coast Communities," *San Jose Mercury News*, November 13, 2013; "Zamzee Improves Kids' Health Using Gamification Tools from Bunchball," *Yahoo! Finance*, March 8, 2013; N. Mott, "Zamzee Cracks Gamified Fitness....For the Children," *Pandodaily.com*, October 5, 2012; M. Frazier, "Virtual World Takes on Childhood Obesity," *MIT Technology Review*, May 16, 2012; J. Temple, "Jury Out on Zamzee, Other Forms of 'Gamification'," *San Francisco Chronicle*, February 26, 2012; H. Shaughnessy, "The Day I Knew Gamification Would be a Winner," *Forbes*, February 8, 2012; www.zamzee.com, accessed April 5, 2014.

 uestions

1. Why is Zamzee using games to help kids lose weight?

2. In your opinion, would Zamzee be as successful for adult weight loss? Why or why not?

Among the thousands of other healthcare applications, administrative systems are critically important. These systems perform functions ranging from detecting insurance fraud, to creating nursing schedules, to financial and marketing management.

The Internet contains vast amounts of useful medical information (see www.webmd.com, for example). In an interesting study, researchers at the Princess Alexandra Hospital in Brisbane, Australia, identified 26 difficult diagnostic cases published in the *New England Journal of Medicine*. They selected three to five search terms from each case and then conducted a Google search. Next, they recorded the three diagnoses that Google ranked most prominently and that appeared to fit the symptoms and signs. Finally, they compared these results with the correct diagnoses as published in the journal. The researchers discovered that their Google searches had found the correct diagnosis in 15 of the 26 cases, a success rate of 57 percent. Despite these results, the research team cautions against self-diagnosis. They maintain that people should use diagnostic information gained from Google and medical Web sites such as WebMD (www.webmd.com) only to ask questions of their physicians. In chapter closing case 1 of Chapter 2, you will see the medical applications of IBM's Watson system.

BEFORE YOU GO ON....

1. What are some of the quality-of-life improvements made possible by IT? Has IT had any negative effects on our quality of life? If so, explain, and provide examples.

2. Describe the robotic revolution, and consider its implications for humans.

3. Explain how IT has improved healthcare practices.

Apply The Concept 1.4

LEARNING OBJECTIVE 1.4 Identify positive and negative societal effects of the increased use of information technology.

STEP 1 – Background

As you have just read, the increased use of IS has had a significant impact on society. Section 1.4 focused on three areas—quality of life improvements, robotics, and healthcare—to spark your interest in the ways our lives are being touched. Unfortunately, the technologies that provide quality-of-life improvements can also create economic and political problems. For example, robots that make production more streamlined also eliminate jobs. Similarly, healthcare improvements raise concerns regarding shared data and privacy violations.

STEP 2 – Activity

Conduct a Web search for "technology and work/life balance." Look for programs, articles, research, suggestions, and other materials that help you understand the positive and negative effects of the increased use of information technologies.

Create a table that identifies the positive and negative effects for the following areas: quality of life, robotics, healthcare, and work/life balance. Set your table up as in the example below, and submit it to your instructor.

	Positive	Negative
Quality of life		
Robotics		
Healthcare		
Work/life balance		

What's in for ME?

In Section 1.2, we discussed how IT supports each of the functional areas of the organization. Here we examine the MIS function.

 FOR THE MIS MAJOR

The MIS function directly supports all other functional areas in an organization. That is, the MIS function is responsible for providing the information that each functional area needs in order to make decisions. The overall objective of MIS personnel is to help users improve performance and solve business problems using IT. To accomplish this objective, MIS personnel must understand both the information requirements and the technology associated with each functional area. Given their position, however, they must think "business needs" first and "technology" second.

SUMMARY

1. Identify the reasons why being an informed user of information systems is important in today's world.

    The benefits of being an informed user of IT include the following:

    > You will benefit more from your organization's IT applications because you will understand what is "behind" those applications.

    > You will be able to provide input into your organization's IT applications, thus improving the quality of those applications.

    > You will quickly be in a position to recommend, or participate in the selection of IT applications that your organization will use.

    > You will be able to keep up with rapid developments in existing information technologies, as well as the introduction of new technologies.

    > You will understand the potential impacts that "new and improved" technologies will have on your organization and therefore will be qualified to make recommendations concerning their adoption and use.

    > You will play a key role in managing the information systems in your organization.

    > You will be in a position to use IT if you decide to start your own business.

2. Describe the various types of computer-based information systems in an organization.

    > Transaction processing systems (TPS) support the monitoring, collection, storage, and processing of data from the organization's basic business transactions, each of which generates data.

> Functional area information systems (FAISs) support a particular functional area within the organization.

> Interorganizational information systems (IOSs) support many interorganizational operations, of which supply chain management is the best known.

> Enterprise resource planning (ERP) systems correct a lack of communication among the FAISs by tightly integrating the functional area ISs via a common database.

> Electronic commerce (e-commerce) systems enable organizations to conduct transactions with other organizations (called business-to-business (B2B) electronic commerce), and with customers (called business-to-consumer (B2C) electronic commerce).

> Office automation systems (OASs) typically support the clerical staff, lower and middle managers, and knowledge workers, by enabling them to develop documents (word processing and desktop publishing software), schedule resources (electronic calendars), and communicate (e-mail, voice mail, videoconferencing, and groupware).

> Business intelligence (BI) systems provide computer-based support for complex, nonroutine decisions, primarily for middle managers and knowledge workers.

> Expert systems (ESs) attempt to duplicate the work of human experts by applying reasoning capabilities, knowledge, and expertise within a specific domain.

3. Discuss ways in which information technology can affect managers and nonmanagerial workers.

Potential IT impacts on managers:

> IT may reduce the number of middle managers;

> IT will provide managers with real-time or near real-time information, meaning that managers will have less time to make decisions;

> IT will increase the likelihood that managers will have to supervise geographically dispersed employees and teams.

Potential IT impacts on nonmanagerial workers:

> IT may eliminate jobs;

> IT may cause employees to experience a loss of identity;

> IT can cause job stress and physical problems, such as repetitive stress injury.

4. List positive and negative societal effects of the increased use of information technology.

Positive societal effects:

> IT can provide opportunities for people with disabilities;

> IT can provide people with flexibility in their work (e.g., work from anywhere, anytime);

> Robots will take over mundane chores;

> IT will enable improvements in healthcare.

Negative societal effects:

> IT can cause health problems for individuals;

> IT can place employees on constant call;

> IT can potentially misinform patients about their health problems.

>>>CHAPTER GLOSSARY

application (or app) A computer program designed to support a specific task or business process.

business intelligence (BI) systems Provide computer-based support for complex, nonroutine decisions, primarily for middle managers and knowledge workers.

computer-based information system (CBIS) An information system that uses computer technology to perform some or all of its intended tasks.

dashboards A special form of IS that support all managers of the organization by providing rapid access to timely information and direct access to structured information in the form of reports.

data items An elementary description of things, events, activities, and transactions that are recorded, classified, and stored but are not organized to convey any specific meaning.

database A collection of related files or tables containing data.

electronic commerce (e-commerce) systems A type of interorganizational information system that enables organizations to conduct transactions, called business-to-business (B2B) electronic commerce, and customers to conduct transactions with businesses, called business-to-consumer (B2C) electronic commerce.

enterprise resource planning (ERP) systems Information systems that correct a lack of communication among the functional area ISs by tightly integrating the functional area ISs via a common database.

ergonomics The science of adapting machines and work environments to people; focuses on creating an environment that is safe, well lit, and comfortable.

expert systems (ES) Attempt to duplicate the work of human experts by applying reasoning capabilities, knowledge, and expertise within a specific domain.

functional area information systems (FAISs) ISs that support a particular functional area within the organization.

hardware A device such as a processor, monitor, keyboard, or printer. Together, these devices accept, process, and display data and information.

information Data that have been organized so that they have meaning and value to the recipient.

information system (IS) Collects, processes, stores, analyzes, and disseminates information for a specific purpose.

information technology (IT) Relates to any computer-based tool that people use to work with information and support the information and information-processing needs of an organization.

information technology components Hardware, software, databases, and networks.

information technology infrastructure IT components plus IT services.

information technology platform Formed by the IT components of hardware, software, networks (wireline and wireless), and databases.

information technology services IT personnel use IT components to perform these IT services: develop information systems, oversee security and risk, and manage data.

informed user A person knowledgeable about information systems and information technology.

interorganizational information systems (IOSs) Information systems that connect two or more organizations.

knowledge Data and/or information that have been organized and processed to convey understanding, experience, accumulated learning, and expertise as they apply to a current problem or activity.

knowledge workers Professional employees such as financial and marketing analysts, engineers, lawyers, and accountants, who are experts in a particular subject area and create information and knowledge, which they integrate into the business.

network A connecting system (wireline or wireless) that permits different computers to share resources.

procedures The set of instructions for combining hardware, software, database, and network components in order to process information and generate the desired output.

software A program or collection of programs that enable the hardware to process data.

supply chain The flow of materials, information, money, and services from suppliers of raw materials through factories and warehouses to the end customers.

transaction processing system (TPS) Supports the monitoring, collection, storage, and processing of data from the organization's basic business transactions, each of which generates data.

>>>DISCUSSION QUESTIONS

1. Describe a business that you would like to start. Discuss how information technology could: (a) help you find and research an idea for a business; (b) help you formulate your business plan; and (c) help you finance your business.

2. Your university wants to recruit high-quality high school students from your state. Provide examples of (1) the data that your recruiters would gather in this process, (2) the information that your recruiters would process from these data, and (3) the types of knowledge that your recruiters would infer from this information.

3. Can the terms data, information, and knowledge have different meanings for different people? Support your answer with examples.

4. Information technology makes it possible to "never be out of touch." Discuss the pros and cons of always being available to your employers and clients (regardless of where you are or what you are doing).

5. Robots have the positive impact of being able to relieve humans from working in dangerous conditions. What are some negative impacts of robots in the workplace?

6. Is it possible to endanger yourself by accessing too much medical information on the Web? Why or why not? Support your answer.

7. Describe other potential impacts of IT on societies as a whole.

8. What are the major reasons why it is important for employees in all functional areas to become familiar with IT?

9. Refer to the study at Princess Alexandra Hospital (in the "Improvements in Healthcare" section). How do you feel about Google searches finding the correct diagnosis in 57 percent of the cases? Are you impressed with these results? Why or why not? What are the implications of this study for self-diagnosis?

10. Is the vast amount of medical information on the Web a good thing? Answer from the standpoint of a patient and from the standpoint of a physician.

>>>PROBLEM-SOLVING ACTIVITIES

1. Visit some Web sites that offer employment opportunities in IT. Prominent examples are: www.dice.com, www.monster.com, www.collegerecruiter.com, www.careerbuilder.com, www.jobcentral.com, www.job.com, www.career.com, www.simplyhired.com, and www.truecareers.com. Compare the IT salaries to salaries offered to accountants, marketing personnel, financial personnel, operations personnel, and human resources personnel. For other information on IT salaries, check *Computerworld*'s annual salary survey.

2. Enter the Web site of UPS (www.ups.com).

   a. Find out what information is available to customers before they send a package.

   b. Find out about the "package tracking" system.

   c. Compute the cost of delivering a 10" × 20" × 15" box, weighing 40 pounds, from your hometown to Long Beach, California (or to Lansing, Michigan, if you live in or near Long Beach). Compare the fastest delivery against the least cost. How long did this process take? Look into the business services offered by UPS. How do they make this process easier when you are a business customer?

3. Surf the Internet for information about the Department of Homeland Security (DHS). Examine the available information, and comment on the role of information technologies in the department.

4. Access www.irobot.com, and investigate the company's Education and Research Robots. Surf the Web for other companies that manufacture robots, and compare their products with those of iRobot.

STEP 1 – Background

This chapter has discussed the many ways in which IS have transformed the modern business environment. As you will learn through this text, there are many jobs that have now been created as a result of the growth of IS; for example, software developers who write word processing programs. (Of course, other positions, such as typists, have been eliminated.) This exercise will expose you to a variety of real-world functional area systems and the positions they support.

STEP 2 – Activity

Divide a team of at least five members into the following functional areas: marketing, accounting, finance, human resources, and logistics. You will begin the project individually in your assigned area and then finish it collaboratively with your teammates.

Individually, research your assigned functional area to identify the types of systems an employee would need to become familiar with to obtain employment in that area (such as ADP for Human Resources). Also, research these systems to understand how they support the functional area.

After each member has completed his or her research, reconvene as a team, and have a conversation about the current job market and the technologies that are supporting each functional area.

STEP 3 – Deliverable

Compile the information you found in your individual efforts in a table as shown in the example below. Use Google Drive to share your work with everyone on your team. Then, write a summary of your team experience to inform your instructor about the most valuable information you found and how you will use this information moving forward.

Functional Area	Functional System	How the System Supports the Functional Area

CLOSING **CASE 1** > Information Technology Impacts a Wide Array of Industries

THE BUSINESS PROBLEM >>> As of mid-2014, the technology required to transform industries through software has been developed and integrated and can be delivered globally. Billions of people now access the Internet via broadband connections. Worldwide, more than 5 billion people use cell phones. Of those users, more than 1 billion have smartphones that provide them with instant access to the Internet at all times, from multiple locations.

In addition, software programming tools and Internet-based services enable companies in many industries to launch new software-powered startups without investing in new infrastructure or training new employees. For example, in 2000, operating a basic Internet application cost businesses approximately $150,000 per month. Today, operating that same application in Amazon's cloud (we discuss cloud computing in detail in Plug IT In 4) costs less than $1,000 per month.

In essence, software is impacting every industry, and every organization must prepare for these impacts. Numerous companies have attempted to meet this challenge: Some have succeeded, and some have failed.

SOFTWARE IMPACTS >>> Let's look at examples of software disruption across several industries. Many of these examples focus on two scenarios: (1) industries where software disrupted the previous market-leading companies and (2) industries where a new company (or companies) used software to achieve a competitive advantage.

- *The book industry:* A dramatic example of software disruption is the fate of Borders bookstore. In 2001, Borders agreed to hand over its online business to Amazon because the bookstore was convinced that online book sales were nonstrategic and unimportant. Ten years later, Borders filed for bankruptcy. That same year, the www.borders.com Web site was replaced with a redirect link to the Barnes & Noble Web site (www.bn.com). Then, in January 2012, Barnes & Noble warned analysts that it would lose twice as much money in 2012 as it had previously predicted. On April 30, 2012, the bookstore entered into a partnership with Microsoft that will spin off the Nook and college businesses into a subsidiary.

  Today, the world's largest bookseller, Amazon, is a software company. Its core capability is its software engine, which can sell virtually anything online without building or maintaining any retail stores. Amazon has even reorganized its Web site to promote its Kindle digital books over physical books. (In August 2012, Amazon announced that it sold more electronic books than hardback books and paperback books combined.) Now, even the books themselves are software products. (We note here that, in mid-2014, electronic books are gaining in popularity, but approximately 80 percent of book sales are for print books.)

- *The music industry:* Today's dominant music companies are software companies: Apple's iTunes (www.apple.com/itunes), Spotify (www.spotify.com), and Pandora (www.pandora.com). Traditional record labels now exist largely to provide those software companies with content. In mid-2014, the Recording Industry Association of America (RIAA) continues to fight battles over copyright infringement and the illegal download and sharing of digital music files. For example, in April 2014, the RIAA sued Megaupload (www.megaupload.com) for copyright infringement. Interestingly, the United States Department of Justice closed the Megaupload Web site in 2012.

- *The video industry:* Blockbuster—which rented and sold videos and ancillary products through its chain of stores—was the industry leader until it was disrupted by a software company, Netflix (www.netflix.com). In mid-2014, Netflix has the largest subscriber base of any video service with some 40 million subscribers. Meanwhile, Blockbuster declared bankruptcy in February 2011 and was acquired by satellite television provider Dish Networks a month later.

- *The software industry:* Incumbent software companies such as Oracle and Microsoft are increasingly threatened by software-as-a-service (SAAS) products (e.g., Salesforce.com) and Android, an open-source operating system developed by the Open Handset Alliance (www.openhandsetalliance.com). (We discuss operating systems in Plug IT In 2 and SAAS in Plug IT In 4.)

  MIS

- *The videogame industry:* Today, the fastest-growing entertainment companies are videogame makers—again, software. Examples are:

  ○ Zynga (www.zynga.com), the creator of FarmVille, delivers its games entirely online.

  ○ Rovio (www.rovio.com), the maker of Angry Birds, recorded almost $200 million in sales in 2012. The company was nearly bankrupt when it launched Angry Birds on the iPhone in late 2009.

  ○ Minecraft (www.minecraft.net), another video game delivered exclusively over the Internet, was first released in 2009. By September 2013, more than 33 million people had downloaded it. Interestingly, the creator of Minecraft, Markus Persson, has never spent any money to market his game. Instead, sales resulted entirely from word of mouth.

- *The photography industry:* This industry was disrupted by software years ago. Today it is virtually impossible to buy a mobile phone that does not include a software-powered camera. In addition, people can upload photos automatically to the Internet for permanent archiving and global sharing. The leading photography companies include Shutterfly (www.shutterfly.com), Snapfish (www.snapfish.com), Flickr (www.flickr.com), and Instagram (www.instagram.com). Meanwhile, the long-time market leader, Kodak—whose name was almost synonymous with cameras—declared bankruptcy in January 2012.

  ○ Each day people upload more than 350 million digital photos just to Facebook. Snapchat (www.snapchat.com) is a smartphone app that enables users to send a photo (or video) to someone and have it "self-destruct" within seconds. Snapchat users are now sharing more than 100 million "snaps" daily.

- *The marketing industry:* Today's largest direct marketing companies include, for example, Facebook (www.facebook.com), Google (www.google.com), and Foursquare (www.foursquare.com). All of these companies are using software to disrupt the retail marketing industry.

  MKT

- *The recruiting industry:* LinkedIn (www.linkedin.com) is a fast-growing company that is disrupting the traditional job recruiting industry. For the first time on a publicly accessible Web site, employees and job searchers can maintain their resumes on LinkedIn for recruiters to search in real time.

- *The financial services industry:* Software has transformed the financial services industry. Practically every financial transaction is now performed by software. Also, many of the leading innovators in financial services are software companies. For example, Square (https://squareup.com) allows anyone to accept credit card payments with a mobile phone.

  FIN

- *Fundraising*: In early 2013, Joel Silver and Rob Thomas, the producers of *Veronica Mars*, a feature film, used Kickstarter (www.kickstarter.com) to raise money to produce the film. They achieved their goal of $2 million in just 10 hours. Kickstarter takes a 5 percent cut of every transaction.

- *Genomics*: Illumina (www.illumina.com) reduced the cost of sequencing a human genome from more $1 million in 2007 to under $1,000 in 2014. Illumina's technology has helped medical researchers develop anticancer drugs that target specific genetic mutations that can cause cancer.

- *The motion picture industry*: The process of making feature-length computer-generated films has become incredibly IT intensive. Studios require state-of-the-art information technologies, including massive numbers of servers (described in Plug IT In 2), sophisticated software (described in Plug IT In 2), and an enormous amount of storage (described in Plug IT In 2).

Consider DreamWorks Animation (www.dreamworksanimation.com), a motion picture studio that creates animated feature films, television programs, and online virtual worlds. The studio has released 26 feature films, including the franchises of *Shrek*, *Madagascar*, *Kung Fu Panda*, and *How to Train Your Dragon*. By late 2013, its feature films had grossed more than $10 billion globally.

For a single motion picture such as *The Croods*, the studio manages more than 500,000 files and 300 terabytes (a terabyte is 1 trillion bytes) of data, and it uses about 80 million central processing unit (CPU; described in Plug IT In 2) hours. As DreamWorks executives state, "In reality, our product is data that looks like a movie. We are a digital manufacturing company."

Software is also disrupting industries that operate primarily in the physical world. Consider these examples:

- *The automobile industry:* In modern cars, software is responsible for running the engines, controlling safety features, entertaining passengers, guiding drivers to their destinations, and connecting the car to mobile, satellite, and GPS networks. Other software functions in modern cars include Wi-Fi receivers, which turn your car into a mobile hot spot; software, which helps maximize fuel efficiency; and ultrasonic sensors, which enable some models to parallel-park automatically.

  POM

  The next step is to network all vehicles together, a necessary step toward driverless cars. The creation of software-powered driverless cars is already being undertaken at Google as well as several major car companies (see IT's About Business 1.2).

- *The logistics industry*: Today's leading real-world retailer, Walmart, uses software to power its logistics and distribution capabilities. This technology has enabled Walmart to become dominant in its industry.

- *The postal industry*: FedEx, which early in its history adopted the view that "the information about the package is as important as the package itself," now employs hundreds

of developers who build and deploy software products for 350,000 customer sites to help customers with their mailing and shipping needs.

- *The oil and gas industry:* Companies in this industry were early innovators in supercomputing and data visualization and analysis, which are critical to oil and gas exploration efforts.

- *The agriculture industry:* Agriculture is increasingly powered by software, including satellite analysis of soils linked to per-acre seed selection software algorithms. In addition, precision agriculture makes use of automated, driverless tractors controlled by global positioning systems and software.

- *National defense:* Even national defense is increasingly software based. The modern combat soldier is embedded in a web of software that provides intelligence, communications, logistics, and weapons guidance. Software-powered drone aircraft launch airstrikes without placing human pilots at risk. (Recall that we discussed drone technology in IT's About Business 1.2.) Intelligence agencies perform large-scale data mining with software to uncover and track potential terrorist plots.

- *The retail industry*: Women have long "borrowed" special-occasion dresses from department stores, buying them and then returning them after wearing them for one evening. Now, Rent the Runway (www.renttherunway.com) has redefined the fashion business, making expensive clothing available to more women than ever before. The firm is also disrupting traditional physical retailers. After all, why buy a dress when you can rent one for a very low price? Some department stores feel so threatened by Rent the Runway that they have reportedly told vendors that they will pull floor merchandise if it ever shows up on that company's Web site.

  Rent the Runway employs 200 people, including one of the nation's largest dry-cleaning operations. Their Web site has more than 3 million members, and it features 35,000 dresses and 7,000 accessories created by 170 designers.

- *The television industry*: Aereo (www.aereo.com) has developed a new distribution model. The firm captures free over-the-air broadcasts on tiny antennas in a datacenter (one antenna for each subscriber) and then sends the shows over the Internet to the subscribers' mobile devices or other connection. The service began in February 2012. Immediately following the company's launch, a consortium of major broadcasters (including CBS, Comcast's NBC, Disney's ABC, and 21st Century Fox) sued Aereo for copyright infringement.

  On April 1, 2013, a federal appeals court upheld a lower court's finding that Aereo's video streams to subscribers were not "public performances" and thus did not constitute copyright infringement. The issue may ultimately be decided by the U.S. Supreme Court.

- *Education*: College graduates owe approximately $1 trillion in student debt, a crippling burden for many recent graduates. UniversityNow (www.unow.com) was founded to make college more accessible to working adults by offering online, self-paced degrees. Two key characteristics distinguish UniversityNow from an increasing number of rivals: (1) very low fees (as little as $2,600, which includes tuition and books for as many courses as students can complete in one year) and (2) fully accredited degrees, from an associate's degree to an M.B.A.

- *The legal profession*: Today, electronic discovery (e-discovery) software applications can analyze documents in a fraction of the time that human lawyers would take, at a fraction of the cost. For example, Blackstone Discovery (www.blackstone discovery.com) helped one company analyze 1.5 million documents for less than $100,000. That company estimated that the process would have cost $1.5 million had it been performed by lawyers.

  E-discovery applications go beyond simply finding documents rapidly using relevant terms. They can also extract relevant concepts, even in the absence of specific terms, from millions of documents. These applications can also analyze documents for information pertaining to the activities and interactions of people—who did what and when, and who talked to whom.

- *The medical profession*: Several startup companies are providing devices and accompanying software that can perform some of the duties of a physician. For example, EyeNetra (www.eyenetra.com) has produced a device called the Netra-G that measures the refractive error of the eye—i.e., whether you are farsighted or nearsighted—using a smartphone screen and an inexpensive pair of plastic binoculars.

  Two other startups are AliveCor and Cellscope. AliveCor (www.alivecor.com) sells a heart monitor that attaches to an iPhone, and Cellscope (www.cellscope .com) is developing a smartphone camera that could let parents diagnose a child's ear infection.

THE RESULTS >>> Clearly, then, an increasing number of major businesses and industries are being run on software and delivered as online services—from motion pictures to agriculture to national defense. Regardless of the industry, companies face constant competitive threats from both established rivals and entrepreneurial technology companies that are developing disruptive software. These threats will force companies to become more agile and to respond to competitive threats more quickly, efficiently, and effectively.

Sources: Compiled from S. Young, "Computer-Controlled Anesthesia Could be Safer for Patients," *MIT Technology Review*, October 31, 2013; "How to Use an iPhone to Diagnose Eye Disease," *KurzweilAI.net*, September 26, 2013; A. Regalado, "When Smartphones Do a Doctor's Job," *MIT Technology Review*, September 13, 2013; D. Talbot, "Aereo's on a Roll," *MIT Technology Review*, May 15, 2013; C. Howard, M. Noer, and T. Post, "Disruptors," *Forbes*, April 15, 2013; S. Mendelson, "Can Fox and DreamWorks Combined Challenge Disney's Animation Empire?" *Forbes*, April 10, 2013; S. Greengard, "DreamWorks Takes a Picture-Perfect Approach to IT," *Baseline Magazine*, April 1, 2013; M. K. Rodriguez, "Traditional vs. Disruptive Tech: What's Best for Your Business?" *Amadeus Consulting White Paper*, February 28, 2013; S. Noonoo, "How Disruptive Technologies Are Leading the Next Great Education Revolution," *T.H.E. Journal*, January 16, 2013; J. Leber, "Parents Could Skip the Doctor's Office with This Device," *MIT Technology Review*, June 14, 2012; De La Merced, "Eastman Kodak Files for Bankruptcy," *The Wall Street Journal*, January 19, 2012; J. Trachtenberg and M. Peers, "Barnes & Noble Seeks Next Chapter," *The Wall Street Journal*, January 6, 2012; "Driverless Car: Google Awarded U.S. Patent for Technology," *BBC News*, December 15, 2011; J. McKendrick, "Five Non-IT Companies That Are Now Indistinguishable from Software Companies," *ZDNet*, December 7, 2011; A. Bleicher, "Five Reasons Every Company Should Act Like a Software Startup," *Forbes*, November 14, 2011; B. Austen, "The End of Borders and the Future of Books," *Bloomberg BusinessWeek*, November 10, 2011; A. Regalado, "Your Heartbeat on an iPhone," *MIT Technology Review*, September 14, 2011; M. Andreessen, "Why Software Is Eating the World," *The Wall Street Journal*, August 20, 2011; J. Knee, "Why Content Isn't King," *The Atlantic*, July/August, 2011; J. Checkler and J. Trachtenberg, "Bookseller Borders Begins a New Chapter . . . 11," *The Wall Street Journal*, February 17, 2011.

Questions

1. Given that information technology is impacting every industry, what does this mean for a company's employees? Provide specific examples to support your answer.

2. Given that information technology is impacting every industry, what does this mean for students attending a college of business? Provide specific examples to support your answer.

CLOSING **CASE 2 >** Baxter:
Coming to Work Right Next to You

THE PROBLEM >>> Manufacturing constitutes a $2 trillion sector of the U.S. economy. For the past 60 years, worker productivity in the manufacturing sector has increased by about 3.7 percent per year.

POM

In the past, the United States has retained higher-value-added manufacturing jobs while allowing lower-value-added jobs to go elsewhere. Interestingly, the definition of "elsewhere" has changed over time. For example, the manufacture of simple goods such as toys is constantly moving to the location with the lowest wages. After the end of World War II, there was an abundance of low-cost labor in Japan, so manufacturing moved there. As the Japanese economy recovered, the standard of living rose, and with it the costs of producing goods. As a result, low-cost manufacturing moved to South Korea, where a scenario similar to Japan took place. Manufacturing simple goods then moved to Taiwan, to mainland China, and, most recently, to Vietnam.

From the perspective of a manufacturing company, a more highly educated and skilled workforce typically has less interest in low-skilled jobs designed to manufacture simple goods. As a result, the world will eventually run out of places where low-cost labor is available. Therefore, the question is "What will it take to break out of the cycle of making inexpensive goods by hand with unskilled, inexpensive labor?" Perhaps robots are the answer.

THE INITIAL SOLUTION: INDUSTRIAL ROBOTS >>>
The first industrial robot developed in the United States was put to work in 1961 in a General Motors factory located in Ewing, New Jersey. The robot, called the Unimate, placed hot, forged car parts into a liquid bath to cool them. At that time, companies could not place a computer on an industrial robot, because computers cost millions of dollars and were room-sized. Sensors were also extremely expensive. As a result, early industrial robots were effectively blind and very dumb, and they performed repeated actions only by following a closely defined physical path dictated by a computer program.

Today's industrial robots still perform well on very narrowly defined, repeatable tasks. However, they are not adaptable, flexible, or easy to use, and they are very expensive. In addition, most industrial robots are not safe for people to be around. Moreover, it typically takes 18 months to integrate an industrial robot into a factory operation.

As of mid-2014, about 70 percent of all industrial robots in the United States were being utilized in automobile factories. These machines are often thought of as money savers for companies. However, the cost to integrate one of today's industrial robots into a factory operation is often 3 to 5 times the cost of the robot itself. Such integration requires the services of computer programmers and machine specialists. In addition, companies must place safety cages around the robots so that they do not strike people while they are operating. Further, most industrial robots have no sensors or means to detect what is happening in their environment.

There are some 300,000 small manufacturing companies in the United States that have fewer than 500 employees. Almost none of these firms has an industrial robot, for the reasons we have just discussed. In addition, almost all of these firms have relatively small production runs, meaning that they are constantly changing the design and manufacturing procedures for what they produce. Some of these companies, called "job shops," produce a wide variety of goods for other companies. They specialize in manufacturing a type of product that can be highly customized to an individual client's needs. In a typical factory that uses an industrial robot, a production run is rarely less than four months long. For a job shop, a production run can be as short as one hour. Clearly, then, small manufacturing firms need a different kind of robot.

A NEXT-GENERATION SOLUTION: BAXTER
>>> Rapid improvements in computer vision, processing power and storage, and low-cost sensors, coupled with new software algorithms that enable robots to plan and move in cluttered environments, are changing the nature of robotics. Rethink Robotics (www.rethinkrobotics.com) is putting these technological developments to work with Baxter, a new kind of industrial robot that sells for $22,000. Baxter is very different from existing industrial robots. It does not need an expensive or elaborate safety cage, and factory operators do not need to segregate it from human workers. In fact, humans actually share a workspace with Baxter.

Unlike other industrial robots, Baxter works right out of the box. It can be integrated into a factory's work flow in about an hour. Baxter also requires no special programming.

Interacting with Baxter is more like working with a person than operating a traditional industrial robot. If Baxter picks up something it shouldn't on the assembly line, for instance, workers can take its arm and move the robot to put the object down.

Baxter also contains a variety of sensors, including depth sensors as well as cameras in its wrists, so it "sees" with its hands. It is constantly building and adjusting a mathematical model of the world in front of it, enabling it to recognize different objects.

Another benefit of Baxter is that other factory workers can train it. In fact, a factory worker who has never seen a robot before can learn to train Baxter to perform simple tasks in five minutes. For example, a worker can show Baxter a part of the task she is asking the robot to perform, and Baxter can infer the rest of the task. Also, if a human is interacting with Baxter or doing part of the task, the robot can figure out how to perform the rest of the task.

THE RESULTS >>>
Rethink Robotics launched Baxter on September 18, 2012. Since that time Baxter has been "hired" by several companies. For example, Baxter is working at a K'Nex (www.knex.com) plant outside Philadelphia, helping to stack Super Mario toys and ship them to China. Baxter is also working at three plastics companies: Rodon (www.rodongroup.com), Nypro (www.nypro.com), and Vanguard Plastics Corporation (www.vanguardplastics.com).

Let's take a closer look at Vanguard Plastics, a small company with $6 million in annual revenue. Vanguard operates state-of-the-art automated electric presses that crush plastic pellets into different shapes under 1,000 atmospheres of pressure. Custom-built industrial robots—running on overhead tracks—swing down to collect the finished parts and place them on a conveyor.

Vanguard's key statistic is sales divided by man-hours. Vanguard executives claim that for the company to stay in business, this statistic must improve by 1 percent or more every year. The only way to accomplish this goal is to increase productivity.

One routine job that is still performed by hand is packing parts. For example, coming off one of the presses are small, textured, plastic cups, which Vanguard sells for 2 cents each to a medical company that uses them to package liquid medicines. A worker from a temporary agency, earning $9 per hour, stacks the cups and then flicks a plastic bag over the stacks. This is the job for which Vanguard is using Baxter. Vanguard maintains that for Baxter to be cost-effective, the robot must replace one temporary worker—a move that would earn back the company's investment in a single year.

Rethink Robotics asserts that Baxter empowers factory workers by providing them with user-friendly machines they can manage themselves. In fact, Rethink claims it is on a mission to rescue American manufacturing through technological innovation. That is, Baxter can help American manufacturers lower costs sufficiently to compete with manufacturers overseas who employ low-cost labor.

However, Baxter raises the question of the future of low-skilled labor in the United States: How fast will Baxter replace these workers, and what will they do after they are replaced?

Sources: Compiled from J. Morton, "Baxter the Robot Rolls On In," *The New Zealand Herald*, January 21, 2014; B. Trebilcock, "Is There a Robot in Your Distribution Future?" *Modern Materials Handling*, December 1, 2013; S. Castellanos, "Rethink Robotics to Distribute Baxter in Japan," *Boston Business Journal*, November 6, 2013; M. Naitove, "'Collaborative' Robot Works Safely, Comfortably Alongside Human Workers," *Plastics Technology*, November 2013; J. Markoff, "Making Robots More Like Us," *The New York Times*, October 28, 2013; K. Alspach, "New Brain for Baxter: Rethink Robotics Releases Baxter 2.0 Software," *Boston Business Journal*, September 23, 2013; B. Jackson, "Baxter the Friendly Robot," *Yale Daily News Magazine*, September 8, 2013; R. Brooks, "Robots at Work: Toward a Smarter Factory," *The Futurist*, May-June, 2013; G. Anderson, "Help Wanted: Robots to Fill Service Jobs," *Retail Wire*, April 10, 2013;

J. Young, "The New Industrial Revolution," *The Chronicle of Higher Education*, March 25, 2013; L. Kratochwill, "Rethink's Baxter Robot Got a Job Packaging Toys and Sending Them to China," *Fast Company*, February 26, 2013; A. Regalado, "Small Factories Give Baxter the Robot a Cautious Once-Over," *MIT Technology Review*, January 16, 2013; T. Geron, "The Robots Are Coming," *Forbes*, November 12, 2012; W. Knight, "This Robot Could Transform Manufacturing," *MIT Technology Review*, September 18, 2012; F. Harrop, "Buckle Up for the Robot Revolution," *Rasmussen Reports*, September 18, 2012; K. Alspach, "Rethink Robotics Unveils 'Human-Like' Robot," *Boston Business Journal*, September 18, 2012; J. Markoff, "Skilled Work, Without the Worker," *The New York Times*, August 19, 2012; J. Leber, "The Next Wave of Factory Robots," *MIT Technology Review*, July 23, 2012; www.rethinkrobotics.com, accessed April 4, 2013.

Questions

1. Rethink Robotics claims that Baxter will not necessarily replace workers; rather, it will enable workers to transition into higher-paying jobs (e.g., programming Baxter robots and supervising Baxter robots). Will Baxter replace workers in small manufacturing companies? Why or why not? Support your answer.

2. Discuss the possible reactions of labor unions to Baxter.

3. Discuss additional potential applications for Baxter.

INTERNSHIP ACTIVITY> ● first noble bank

Information systems impact every facet of an organization. This is especially true in the banking industry, where IS have revolutionized the ways customers interact with banks, pay bills, manage their accounts, and generally conduct most of their banking activities. From the banks' perspective, IS make it easier to communicate with customers via e-statements, make loan decisions, monitor account status, and much, much more.

For this Internship Activity, you will work for Jeremy Farr, Associate Vice President and IT Officer of First Noble Bank. Jeremy is working hard to bring First Noble "into the 21st Century" in regards to mobile offerings for his customers. Below is your e-mail from Jeremy that provides instructions for this assignment.

To:	IT Intern
From:	Jeremy Farr
Subject:	Help Reviewing Banking Customer Information Systems

Hello!

I have a very important project for you to help me with. I am looking for a mobile platform to offer our customers. As you know, most banks do not build their own platforms. Instead, they find a software provider that meets both their business needs and their customers' needs. I would like you to search the Web for examples of how other banks have implemented a mobile platform to their advantage. Specifically, complete the following steps.

First, examine the Web sites of at least three local financial institutions, such as banks and credit unions. What mobile banking tools do they offer their customers? Do they provide different tools for business and personal customers? Which tools seem to be standard, and which ones are offered as part of a fee-based account? Take some notes to use as a comparison.

Next, visit YouTube, and search for "ACI Provides Universal Online Banking in a Single Platform." I ran across this video the other day, but I did not have time to watch it or to review the company's mobile product offerings. You can probably find the company's Web address through the video or by searching Google. If you don't have any luck finding the video, then search the Web for ACI Worldwide, and look for their Mobile Channel Manager.

Finally, put together a short report for me that answers the following questions:

1. Based on your review of local banks, what tools do you think we need to make available in a mobile format?
2. Will ACI's mobile solution work for our business customers and our consumer customers?
3. Will the ACI products allow us to set up different offerings for different types/levels of customers?
4. Will we need other systems, or will this system satisfy all of our needs?
5. What is your overall impression of the company after exploring their Web site? Do they seem credible?

Thanks in advance for your assistance.
Jeremy Farr

Note: All links mentioned in this e-mail are available at http://www.wiley.com/go/rainer/MIS3e/internship.

SPREADSHEET ACTIVITY > INTRODUCTION TO SPREADSHEETS

STEP 1 – Background

A spreadsheet is a powerful tool for organizing and analyzing data. A single spreadsheet is made up of numerous columns and rows of cells that contain data. These data can be manipulated using formulas that range from basic mathematical calculations to highly complex statistical models. The results can be presented in numeric format or in charts and graphs.

A collection of spreadsheets is called a *workbook*. Workbooks are more powerful than individual spreadsheets because they allow users to integrate data stored on separate sheets into a single calculation. The most popular spreadsheet program is Microsoft Excel. Google's free cloud-based program Sheets is gaining popularity as Google adds more features to the service.

STEP 2 – Activity

Imagine that you have been asked to total the individual items for LaQuita's travel expense report. There are the following six expenses:

Hotel	$453.48	Airport	311.26
Meals	$84.35	Personal car mileage	$44.31
Rental car	$112.94	Miscellaneous	$25.00

Your task is to calculate the total. One obvious method is to simply use a calculator. When you add these numbers, LaQuita's expense report comes to $1031.34.

However, you can also perform this operation using a spreadsheet.

Create a spreadsheet that calculates the total of the numb ers listed above. Use the "Sum" formula. If you need assistance with this formula, access the Help feature in the spreadsheet program you have chosen. Although this is an easy activity, it will demonstrate the power of using a spreadsheet.

STEP 3 – Deliverable

Visit http://www.wiley.com/go/rainer/MIS3e/spreadsheet, and download the file linked for Spreadsheet Activity 1. This is an .XLS file that will open in any spreadsheet tool. The file contains three sheets:

- A list of the miles that three rental cars were driven for each day of the year
- The number of patients seen in an emergency room (ER)
- Sales per region

(Navigate between the sheets using the tabs at the bottom of the page.) Use your newly acquired knowledge of the Sum formula to quickly calculate the totals for each of the three sheets.

Follow the instructions in the spreadsheet and submit your final work to your instructor.

Additional help with this spreadsheet skill is available in WileyPLUS. Open the "Microsoft Office 2013 Lab Manual Spreadsheet Module: Excel 2013," and review Lesson 1: Launching Excel and Lesson 2: Entering Data and Issuing Commands.

DATABASE ACTIVITY > INTRODUCTION TO DATABASES

STEP 1 – Background

A database is a group of logically related files that stores data and the associations among them. It is best illustrated by highlighting the difference in a single file and multiple files. Imagine the following data represent a customer information file.

Name	Address	Order	Items	Sales Rep	Payment	Balance

Now imagine multiple customers with multiple orders on this same table. There will be a great deal of data duplication (name and address on every row), which will increase the risk that inconsistent or inaccurate data will appear in the table.

A database would split, or normalize, the data into multiple tables and would then create a single data item, known as the primary key, to tie everything together. These tables are reproduced below. Note that the customer information has to be entered only one time; it is then tied to a customer ID. The major benefit of this system is that the user can update this information in a single location—Customer ID—and the updated information automatically appears every time the customer is referenced.

The beauty of this design is that it allows very complex data structures and analysis. This example is very simple. Imagine, however, a database that touches every function within an organization. These databases, which are referred to as enterprise resource planning (ERP), contain more than 75,000 tables!

STEP 2 – Activity

In this activity you will download an Access database and familiarize yourself with its functions. In particular, you need to learn about the ribbons, commands, menus, help options, and views that are available to you. The objective of this first activity is to learn how to navigate an Access database.

STEP 3 – Deliverable

Visit http://www.wiley.com/go/rainer/MIS3e/database, and download the file linked for Database Activity 1. There will also be an instructional PDF that will provide more detailed instructions on the deliverable, which is a series of questions that guide you through the database.

Additional help with this database skill is available in WileyPLUS. Open the "Microsoft Office 2013 Lab Manual Database Module: Access 2013," and review Lesson 1: Launching Access.

CHAPTER 2

Organizational Strategy, Competitive Advantage, and Information Systems

LEARNING OBJECTIVES >>>

2.1 Identify effective IT responses to different kinds of business pressures.

2.2 Describe the strategies that organizations typically adopt to counter Porter's five competitive forces.

OPENING **CASE** > GrubHub Seamless

In August 2013, two formerly separate companies—Seamless (www.seamless.com) and GrubHub (www.grubhub.com)—merged to form a combined organization, called GrubHub Seamless (GS). The new organization, which has retained both brands, is the leading company in food delivery. The two brands offer similar products.

- GrubHub's diner products include the GrubHub.com Web site and the mobile app Track Your Grub, which is GrubHub's system for providing diners with real-time notifications and order tracking. GrubHub's restaurant products include OrderHub, an in-restaurant tablet that helps streamline the order confirmation process, and DeliveryHub, an app that helps delivery drivers plan their routes more efficiently. These two products collaborate to provide real-time updates to GrubHub diners through Track Your Grub.
- Seamless's diner products include the Seamless.com Web site and the mobile app Food Tracker, which is Seamless's system for providing diners with real-time order tracking. Seamless's restaurant product is Boost, an in-restaurant tablet that helps streamline the order confirmation process. Seamless allows businesses

to consolidate all food ordering and subsequent billing into a single account. It provides three ordering options: individual meals, group ordering, and corporate catering.

© Tijana87/iStockphoto

Visitors to GS begin by entering their physical address. The service then returns a list of restaurants that deliver to that address, as well as takeout restaurants situated within a predetermined radius. Users are also able to browse restaurants in their city or search by cuisine, restaurant name, or specific item. Once users decide what they want, they can place their order either through the GS Web site or over the phone. GS also provides its users with access to reviews, coupons, special deals, and a 24/7 customer service team that tracks and monitors each order.

GS's expertise is concentrated primarily on the technical side of the industry. Though the company employs many former servers, it has not focused on recruiting people with high-level restaurant expertise. Therefore, since late 2013, GS has been sending employees from its headquarters to work in kitchens and to accompany drivers on deliveries.

GS provides restaurants with tablets to manage orders. The company also employs account managers to advise restaurants based on industry sales data. For example, sports bars know they will sell more hot wings during National Football League games than at other times. GS claims, however, that it can accurately predict how much chicken the restaurants in a particular neighborhood will need. In fact, GS claims that, when restaurants run out of an item on the menu, employees can instantly adjust their online menus using the tablets. Half of all GS orders are now processed on the tablets.

GS's strategy is to integrate itself into restaurants' operations to justify its commissions, which range from 10 to more than 20 percent of the food order. Small businesses in particular are typically skeptical of companies offering data services, especially when their commissions are as high as GS's. Convenient tablets may not be enough to offset a 10 to 20 percent revenue cut. Industry analysts note that the primary value of OrderHub is to GS, not the restaurants. In fact, these analysts claim it is in the restaurants' best interests to play GS against competing services such as Delivery (www.delivery.com) and Eat24 (www.eat24.com).

Despite these problems and a competitive marketplace, by mid-2014 GS was filling an average of 150,000 online orders per day from 26,500 restaurants in more than 600 U.S. cities as well as London. The company served more than 3 million unique diners in 2013.

Sources: Compiled from J. Brustein, "GrubHub Puts Data on Its Menu," *Bloomberg BusinessWeek*, December 23, 2013–January 5, 2014; L. Lazare, "GrubHub and Seamless Complete Merger," *Chicago Business Journal*, August 9, 2013; A. Moscaritolo, "GrubHub 'Track Your Grub' Lets You Keep Tabs on Your Order," *PC Magazine*, November 13, 2012; A. Shontell, "The Digital 100: The World's Most Valuable Private Tech Companies," *Business Insider*, November 7, 2012; www.grubhub.com, www.seamless.com, accessed February 14, 2014.

Questions

1. Look ahead in this chapter. Which one of Porter's strategies for competitive advantage is GrubHub Seamless pursuing? Explain your answer.
2. Propose additional applications that GS could develop to gain a competitive advantage in the marketplace.

Introduction

Organizations operate in the incredible complexity of the modern high-tech world. As a result, they are subject to a myriad of business pressures. Information systems are critically important in helping organizations respond to business pressures and in supporting organizations' global strategies. As you study this chapter, you will see that any information system can be *strategic*, meaning that it can provide a competitive advantage if it is used properly.

Competitive advantage refers to any assets that provide an organization with an edge against its competitors in some measure such as cost, quality, or speed. A competitive advantage helps an organization to control a market and to accrue larger-than-average profits. Significantly, both strategy and competitive advantage take many forms.

Although there are many companies that use technology in more expensive ways, GrubHub Seamless, which is discussed in the chapter opening case, demonstrates that an entrepreneurial spirit coupled with a solid understanding of what IT can do for you will provide competitive advantages to entrepreneurs just as it does for Wall Street CIOs. As you study this chapter, think of the small businesses in your area that are utilizing popular technologies in interesting and novel ways. Have any of them found an innovative use for Twitter? Facebook? Amazon? PayPal? If not, then can you think of any businesses that would benefit from employing these technologies?

This chapter is important for you for several reasons. First, the business pressures we address in the chapter will affect your organization. Just as important, however, they also will affect *you*. Therefore, you must understand how information systems can help you—and eventually your organization—respond to these pressures.

In addition, acquiring competitive advantage is essential for your organization's survival. Many organizations achieve competitive advantage through the efforts of their employees. Therefore, becoming knowledgeable about strategy and how information systems affect strategy and competitive position will help you throughout your career.

This chapter encourages you to become familiar with your organization's strategy, mission, and goals and to understand its business problems and how it makes (or loses) money. It will help you understand how information technology contributes to organizational strategy. Further, you likely will become a member of business/IT committees that decide (among many other things) how to use existing technologies more effectively and whether to adopt new ones. After studying this chapter, you will be able to make immediate contributions in these committees when you join your organizations.

Information systems can be just as strategic to a small or medium-sized company as they are to a large firm. The chapter opening case about GrubHub Seamless illustrates how information systems are strategically important to GrubHub, an online food ordering service.

In this chapter, you will see how information systems enable organizations to respond to business pressures. Next, you will learn how information systems help organizations gain competitive advantages in the marketplace.

2.1 Business Pressures, Organizational Responses, and Information Technology Support

Modern organizations compete in a challenging environment. To remain competitive they must react rapidly to problems and opportunities that arise from extremely dynamic conditions. In this section, you examine some of the major pressures confronting modern organizations and the strategies that organizations employ to respond to these pressures.

Business Pressures

The **business environment** is the combination of social, legal, economic, physical, and political factors in which businesses conduct their operations. Significant changes in any of these factors are likely to create business pressures on organizations. Organizations typically respond to these pressures with activities supported by IT. FIGURE 2.1 illustrates the

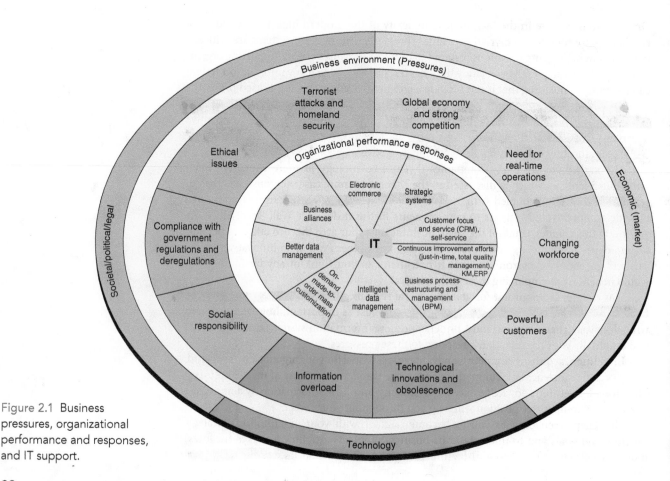

Figure 2.1 Business pressures, organizational performance and responses, and IT support.

relationships among business pressures, organizational performance and responses, and IT support. You will learn about three major types of business pressures: market, technology, and societal pressures.

Market Pressures. Market pressures are generated by the global economy, intense competition, the changing nature of the workforce, and powerful customers. Let's look more closely at each of these factors.

Globalization. **Globalization** is the integration and interdependence of economic, social, cultural, and ecological facets of life, made possible by rapid advances in information technology. In his book *The World Is Flat*, Pulitzer Prize-winning author Thomas Friedman argues that technology is leveling the global competitive playing field, thereby making it "flat."

Friedman identifies three eras of globalization. The first era, Globalization 1.0, lasted from 1492 to 1800. During this era, the force behind globalization was how much muscle, horsepower, wind power, or steam power a country could deploy.

The second era, Globalization 2.0, lasted from 1800 to 2000. In this era, the force behind globalization was the emergence of multinational companies, that is, companies that had their headquarters in one country but operated in several countries. In the first half of this era, globalization was driven by falling transportation costs, generated by the development of the steam engine and the railroads. In the second half, the driving force was falling telecommunications costs resulting from the telegraph, telephones, computers, satellites, fiber-optic cable, and the Internet and World Wide Web. The modern global economy began to evolve during this era.

Around the year 2000, the world entered Globalization 3.0. In this era, globalization has been driven by the convergence of 10 forces that Friedman calls "flatteners." Table 2.1 identifies these forces.

According to Friedman, each era has been characterized by a distinctive focus. The focus of Globalization 1.0 was on countries, the focus of Globalization 2.0 was on companies, and the focus of Globalization 3.0 is on groups and individuals.

As you look at Table 2.1, note that 9 of Friedman's 10 flatteners directly relate to information technology (all except the fall of the Berlin Wall). These flatteners enable individuals to connect, compute, communicate, collaborate, and compete everywhere and anywhere, anytime and all the time; to access limitless amounts of information, services, and entertainment; to exchange knowledge; and to produce and sell goods and services. People and organizations can now operate without regard to geography, time, distance, or even language barriers. The bottom line? Globalization is markedly increasing competition.

These observations highlight the importance of market pressures for you. Simply put, you and the organizations you join will be competing with people and organizations from all over a flat world.

Let's consider some examples of globalization. Regional agreements such as the North American Free Trade Agreement (NAFTA), which includes the United States, Canada, and Mexico, have contributed to increased world trade and increased competition. Further, the rise of India and China as economic powerhouses has increased global competition.

One important pressure that businesses in a global market must contend with is the cost of labor, which varies widely among countries. In general, labor costs are higher in developed countries such as the United States and Japan than in developing countries such as China and El Salvador. Also, developed countries usually offer greater benefits, such as healthcare, to employees, driving the cost of doing business even higher. Therefore, many labor-intensive industries have moved their operations to countries with low labor costs. IT has made such moves much easier to implement.

However, manufacturing overseas is no longer the bargain it once was, and manufacturing in the United States is no longer as expensive. For example, manufacturing wages in China have more than doubled between 2002 and 2013, and they continue to rise. Meanwhile, the value of China's currency has steadily risen.

The Changing Nature of the Workforce. The workforce, particularly in developed countries, is becoming more diversified. Increasing numbers of women, single parents, minorities, and persons with disabilities are now employed in all types of positions.

TABLE 2.1 Friedman's 10 Flatteners

- **Fall of the Berlin Wall on November 9, 1989**
  - Shifted the world toward free-market economies and away from centrally planned economies.
  - Led to the emergence of the European Union and early thinking about the world as a single, global market.

- **Netscape goes public on August 9, 1995**
  - Popularized the Internet and the World Wide Web.

- **Development of workflow software**
  - Enabled computer applications to work with one another without human intervention.
  - Enabled faster, closer collaboration and coordination among employees, regardless of their location.

- **Uploading**
  - Empowered all Internet users to create content and put it on the Web.
  - Led the transition from a passive approach to content to an active, participatory, collaborative approach.

- **Outsourcing**
  - Contracting with an outside company to perform a specific function that your company was doing itself and then integrating their work back into your operation; for example, moving customer call centers to India.

- **Offshoring**
  - Relocating an entire operation, or certain tasks, to another country; for example, moving an entire manufacturing operation to China.

- **Supply chaining**
  - Technological revolution led to the creation of networks composed of companies, their suppliers, and their customers, all of which could collaborate and share information for increased efficiency.

- **Insourcing**
  - Delegating operations or jobs within a business to another company that specializes in those operations; for example, Dell hires FedEx to "take over" Dell's logistics process.

- **Informing**
  - The ability to search for information, best illustrated by search engines.

- **The Steroids** (computing, instant messaging and file sharing, wireless technologies, Voice over Internet Protocol, videoconferencing, and computer graphics)
  - Technologies that amplify the other flatteners.
  - Enable all forms of computing and collaboration to be digital, mobile, and personal.

IT is easing the integration of these employees into the traditional workforce. IT is also enabling people to work from home, which can be a major benefit for parents with young children and for people confronted with mobility and/or transportation issues.

Powerful Customers. Consumer sophistication and expectations increase as customers become more knowledgeable about the products and services they acquire. Customers can use the Internet to find detailed information about products and services, to compare prices, and to purchase items at electronic auctions.

Organizations recognize the importance of customers and they have increased their efforts to acquire and retain them. Modern firms strive to learn as much as possible about their customers to better anticipate and address their needs. This process, called *customer intimacy,* is an important component of *customer relationship management* (CRM), an organization-wide effort toward maximizing the customer experience. You will learn about CRM in Chapter 12.

Technology Pressures. The second category of business pressures consists of those pressures related to technology. Two major technology-related pressures are technological innovation and information overload.

Technological Innovation and Obsolescence. Few and improved technologies rapidly create or support substitutes for products, alternative service options, and superb quality. As a result, today's state-of-the-art products may be obsolete tomorrow. For example, how fast are new versions of your smartphone being released? How quickly are electronic versions of books, magazines, and newspapers replacing traditional hard copy versions? These changes force businesses to keep up with consumer demands.

Consider the rapid technological innovation of the Apple iPad (www.apple.com/ipad).

- Apple released the first iPad in April 2010 and sold 3 million devices in just 80 days.
- Apple released the iPad 2 on March 11, 2011, only 11 months later.
- Apple released the iPad 3 on March 7, 2012.
- Apple released its fourth-generation iPad on November 2, 2012, along with the iPad mini.
- On November 1, 2013, Apple released the fifth generation of its iPad, called the iPad Air.
- On November 12, 2013, Apple released its new iPad mini with Retina Display.

One manifestation of technological innovation is "bring your own device (BYOD)." BYOD refers to the policy of permitting employees to bring personally owned mobile devices (laptops, tablet computers, and smartphones) to the workplace and to use those devices to connect to the corporate network as well as for personal use as well. The academic version of BYOD involves students' utilizing personally owned devices in educational settings to connect to their school's network.

The rapid increase in BYOD represents a huge challenge for IT departments. Not only has IT lost the ability to fully control and manage these devices, but employees are now demanding that they be able to conduct company business from multiple personal devices.

The good news is that BYOD has increased worker productivity and satisfaction. In fact, some employees with BYOD privileges actually work longer hours with no additional pay.

The bad news is security concerns. Many companies with BYOD policies have experienced an increase in malware (malicious software, discussed in Chapter 7). Further, there is an increased risk of losing sensitive, proprietary information. Such information might not be securely stored on a personal, mobile device, which can be lost or stolen.

BYOD is causing concern to organizational IT departments, as you see in IT's About Business 2.1.

IT'S ABOUT BUSINESS 2.1

"Bring Your Own Device" Can Cause Problems

Hamilton Fraser (HF; www.hamiltonfraser.co.uk), located in North London, is an insurance company that specializes in home insurance. The firm is one of Great Britain's major contractors for its deposit protection system, which assigns an independent arbitrator to both tenants and landlords to resolve any disputes when a tenant moves from a rented property.

Information security is the IT group's highest priority because credibility is critical to the company's success. HF began to focus specifically on security threats from "bring your own device (BYOD)" when younger employees began using their mobile devices to play games and contact their friends on social networks. However, these employees also used their devices to access corporate applications, store corporate data, and access corporate e-mail. In addition, senior executives began to access their e-mail on mobile devices when they were out of the office.

HF had already embraced mobile computing by allowing its employees to use their iPhones and iPads to access the company network. However, employees were using other devices—particularly Android devices—on the company network. HF turned to

MobileIron (www.mobileiron.com), a firm that provides mobile device management and security to large enterprises.

MobileIron enabled HF to decide which mobile devices the company would support. HF utilized the MobileIron software to keep track of how many employees were accessing the firm's network for business purposes (as opposed to, for example, playing games or shopping) and whether these employees were using an approved device. The company's human resources department developed an acceptable use policy, and it began to conduct short training sessions to raise employee awareness of this policy. The policy dictates that employees who use mobile devices must download an application to their smartphone or tablet that will enable the IT department to erase any corporate data from the device if it is lost or stolen, or to erase all of the data if the employee so wishes.

HRM

Sources: Compiled from "BYOD & the Implications for IT," *NEC White Paper*, 2013; J. Gold, "Has BYOD Peaked?" *Computerworld*, March 21, 2013; J. Scott, "Case Study: Hamilton Fraser Embraces BYOD with MobileIron," *Computer Weekly*, March 20, 2013; G. Marks, "Do You Really Need a BYOD Policy?" *Forbes*, February 25, 2013; M. Endler, "4 Big BYOD Trends for 2013," *InformationWeek*, February 21, 2013; T. Kaneshige, "BYOD to Change the Face of IT in 2013," *CIO*, February 7, 2013; T. Kemp, "Beyond BYOD: The Shift to People-Centric IT," *Forbes*, January 14, 2013; L. Mearian, "Nearly Half of IT Shops Ignore BYOD," *Computerworld*, November 29, 2012; E. Lai, "Infographic: The Ten Things We Fear (and Love) About BYOD," *Forbes*, July 16, 2012; www.hamiltonfraser.co.uk, www.mobileiron.com, accessed April 14, 2014.

Questions

1. What are the advantages of allowing employees to use any mobile device to connect to the corporate network? The disadvantages?

2. Why is it necessary to be able to erase corporate data when a mobile device is lost or stolen?

Information Overload. The amount of information available on the Internet doubles approximately every year, and much of it is free. The Internet and other telecommunications networks are bringing a flood of information to managers. To make decisions effectively and efficiently, managers must be able to access, navigate, and utilize these vast stores of data, information, and knowledge. Information technologies, such as search engines (discussed in Chapter 4) and data mining (Chapter 5), provide valuable support in these efforts.

Societal/Political/Legal Pressures. The third category of business pressures includes social responsibility, government regulation/deregulation, spending for social programs, spending to protect against terrorism, and ethics. This section will explain how all of these elements affect modern businesses. We start with social responsibility.

Social Responsibility. Social issues that affect businesses and individuals range from the state of the physical environment, to company and individual philanthropy, to education. Some corporations and individuals are willing to spend time and/or money to address various social problems. These efforts are known as **organizational social responsibility** or **individual social responsibility**.

Studio Frank/Image Source

One critical social problem is the state of the physical environment. A growing IT initiative, called *green IT*, is addressing some of the most pressing environmental concerns. IT is instrumental in organizational efforts to "go green" in three areas.

- *Facilities design and management.* Organizations are creating more environmentally sustainable work environments. Many organizations are pursuing Leadership in Energy and Environmental Design (LEED) certification from the U.S. Green Building Council, a nonprofit group that promotes the construction of environmentally friendly buildings. One impact of this development is that IT professionals are expected to help create green facilities. IT personnel must understand the system's complex monitors and sensors involved with green facilities. Further, utilities are offering incentives to commercial customers who take certain energy conservation steps, such as enabling computer power management across their networks and designing energy-efficient data centers. Finally, utilities are also offering variable rate incentives depending on when companies use electricity and how much they use. To address these issues, organizations must utilize IT systems that can regulate electricity usage.

- *Carbon management.* As companies try to reduce their carbon footprints, they are turning to IT executives to develop the systems needed to monitor carbon throughout the organization and its supply chain, which can be global in scope. Therefore, IT employees need to become knowledgeable about embedded carbon and how to measure it in the company's products and processes. Consider, for example, application development. IT managers will have to ask whether an application will require new hardware to test and run, or how much additional server space (and thus energy) it will require—and how these issues translate into carbon output.

- *International and U.S. environmental laws.* IT executives must deal with federal and state laws and international regulations that impact everything from the IT products they buy, to how they dispose of them, to their company's carbon footprint. IT managers must understand environmental compliance issues so that they can ask their vendors the right questions regarding specific state, national, and international environmental standards before they purchase, deploy, and dispose of equipment.

Continuing our discussion of social responsibility, social problems all over the world may be addressed through corporate and individual philanthropy. In some cases, questions arise as to what percentage of contributions actually goes to the intended causes and recipients and what percentage goes to the charity's overhead. Another problem that concerns contributors is that they often exert little influence over the selection of projects their contributions will support. The Internet can help address these concerns and facilitate generosity and connection. Consider the following examples:

- *PatientsLikeMe* (www.patientslikeme.com), or any of the thousands of message boards dedicated to infertility, cancer, and various other ailments. People use these sites and message boards to obtain information about life-and-death decisions based on volunteered information, while also receiving much-needed emotional support from strangers.

- *GiftFlow* (www.giftflow.org): GiftFlow is a virtual community where you can obtain things you need for free and find people who need the "stuff" you have to give away. GiftFlow connects community organizations, businesses, governments, and neighbors in a network of reciprocity.

- *Sparked* (www.sparked.com): Sparked is an online "microvolunteering" Web site where large and small organizations list opportunities for people looking to volunteer.

- *Collaborative Consumption* (www.collaborativeconsumption.com): This Web site is an online hub for discussions about the growing business of sharing, resale, reuse, and barter (with many links to Web sites engaged in these practices).

- *Kiva* (www.kiva.org): Kiva is a nonprofit enterprise that provides a link between lenders in developed countries and entrepreneurs in developing countries. Users pledge interest-free loans rather than tax-deductible donations. Kiva directs 100 percent of the loans to borrowers.

- *DonorsChoose* (www.donorschoose.org): DonorsChoose is an education-oriented Web site that functions entirely within the United States. Users make donations rather than loans. The Web site addresses the huge problem of underfunded public schools.

Still another social problem that affects modern business is the digital divide. The **digital divide** refers to the wide gap between those individuals who have access to information and communications technology and those who do not. This gap exists both within and among countries.

Many government and international organizations are trying to close the digital divide. As technologies develop and become less expensive, the speed at which the gap can be closed will accelerate. On the other hand, the rapid pace of technological development can make it more difficult for groups with few resources to keep up with more affluent groups.

One well-known project to narrow the divide is the One Laptop per Child (OLPC) project (http://one.laptop.org). OLPC is a nonprofit association dedicated to developing a very inexpensive laptop—a technology that aims to revolutionize how the world can educate its children.

The first generation of inexpensive laptops appeared in 2007 with a price of $188, which was too high for individuals and groups with limited resources. The second generation was scrapped because the price remained too high. The next generation, a touchscreen tablet computer for schoolchildren in the developing world, uses less power than a light bulb and is unbreakable, waterproof, and half as thick as an iPhone. IT's About Business 2.2 discusses an interesting experiment by the OLPC in the East African nation of Ethiopia.

IT'S ABOUT BUSINESS 2.2

Solar-Powered Tablets in Ethiopia

Nearly 100 million children in the world never make it to first grade, not only because there are no schools, but also because there are very few literate adults to educate them. To address this problem, the OLPC designed an experiment.

The experiment took place in two Ethiopian villages: Wonchi and Wolonchete. The literacy rate in these two villages was very close to zero. In fact, the children—as well as most of the adults—had never even seen a written word. They had no books, no newspapers, no street signs, and no labels on packaged foods or goods.

The OLPC set out to determine whether children with no previous exposure to written words could learn to read all by themselves, without intervention by teachers or other adults. In early 2013, the organization delivered approximately 1,000 solar-powered tablet computers (Motorola Xoom) to the children in the two villages. Each tablet was preloaded with alphabet-training games, electronic books, movies, cartoons, paintings, and many other applications—a total of 500 for each tablet. Each tablet also contained a memory card with tracking software to record how it was being used. Significantly, the OLPC team left the boxes containing the tablets in each village closed and taped shut. The team offered no instructions to either the adults or the children.

The results were amazing. Within four minutes, one child not only opened the box containing the tablets, but also found the on/off switch and turned the tablet on. This feat was very impressive, considering that he had never before seen an on/off switch. Within five days, the children were using an average of 47 apps each per day. Within two weeks, they were singing ABC songs in English. Within five months, the children had accessed the Android operating system. The OLPC had disabled the cameras in the tablets, and the children turned them back on and began taking pictures of themselves. The OLPC had also frozen the tablets' desktop settings. So, the children disabled the OLPC's settings, and each child customized his or her desktop.

Although the early results were promising, in early 2014 the children still were not really literate. That is, they were

© karelnoppe/iStockphoto

not able, yet, to read on their own. The OLPC concluded that the children needed more time, and so the experiment continues.

Despite this limitation, however, the OLPC also observed an unforeseen yet highly positive result. The children were teaching their parents what they had learned, and the adults were moving toward literacy along with their children.

Sources: Compiled from J. Brakel, "Tablets Without Teachers Improving Literacy in Ethiopia," *Gulf Times*, September 28, 2013; "Tablet as Teacher: Poor Ethiopian Kids Learn ABCs," *Associated Press*, December 24, 2012; E. Ackerman, "Ethiopian Kids, Hack OLPCs in 5 Months with Zero Instruction," *DVICE*, October 30, 2012; D. Talbot, "Given Tablets but No Teachers, Ethiopian Children Teach Themselves," *MIT Technology Review*, October 29, 2012.

Questions

1. What advantages could result from increasing the literacy of 100 million children around the world? Be specific.

2. In this experiment, the tablets were not connected to the Internet. Discuss the advantages and disadvantages to the children if the tablets were connected.

Compliance with Government Regulations. Another major source of business pressures is government regulations regarding health, safety, environmental protection, and equal opportunity. Businesses tend to view government regulations as expensive constraints on their activities. In general, government deregulation intensifies competition.

In the wake of 9/11 and numerous corporate scandals, the U.S. government passed many new laws, including the Sarbanes–Oxley Act, the USA PATRIOT Act, the Gramm–Leach–Bliley Act, and the Health Insurance Portability and Accountability Act (HIPAA). Organizations must be in compliance with the regulations contained in these statutes. The process of becoming and remaining compliant is expensive and time consuming. In almost all cases, organizations rely on IT support to provide the necessary controls and information for compliance.

Protection Against Terrorist Attacks. Since September 11, 2001, organizations have been under increased pressure to protect themselves against terrorist attacks. In addition, employees who are in the military reserves have been called up for active duty, creating personnel problems. Information technology can help protect businesses by providing security systems and possibly identifying patterns of behavior associated with terrorist activities, including cyberattacks (discussed in Chapter 7).

An example of protection against terrorism is the Department of Homeland Security's (DHS) Office of Biometric Identity Management (OBIM) program. (We discuss biometrics in Chapter 7.) OBIM is a network of biometric screening systems, such as fingerprint and iris and retina scanners, that ties into government databases and watch lists to check the identities of millions of people entering the United States. The system is now operational in more than 300 locations, including major international ports of entry by air, sea, and land. As another example, refer to chapter closing case 2 on the Palantir system.

Ethical Issues. Ethics relates to general standards of right and wrong. Information ethics relates specifically to standards of right and wrong in information processing practices. Ethical issues are very important because, if handled poorly, they can damage an organization's image and destroy its employees' morale. The use of IT raises many ethical issues, ranging from monitoring e-mail to invading the privacy of millions of customers whose data are stored in private and public databases. Chapter 6 covers ethical issues in detail.

Clearly, then, the pressures on organizations are increasing, and organizations must be prepared to take responsive actions if they are to succeed. You will learn about these organizational responses in the next section.

Organizational Responses

Organizations are responding to the various pressures just discussed by implementing IT such as strategic systems, customer focus, make-to-order and mass customization, and e-business. This section explores each of these responses.

Strategic Systems. Strategic systems provide organizations with advantages that enable them to increase their market share and/or profits, to better negotiate with suppliers, and to prevent competitors from entering their markets. IT's About Business 2.3 provides another example of how strategically important information systems can be by examining The Weather Channel.

'S ABOUT BUSINESS 2.3

The Weather Channel

The Weather Channel (TWC; www.weather.com) is a cable and satellite television channel that is owned as a joint venture by NBC Universal and two investment firms: The Blackstone Group and Bain Capital. The channel broadcasts weather forecasts along with weather-related news, documentaries, and entertainment. In addition to its programming on the cable channel, TWC provides forecasts for terrestrial and satellite radio stations, newspapers, and Web sites. TWC maintains its online presence at www.weather.com as well as via a set of mobile smartphone and table applications.

Despite its powerful and well-known brand, TWC is losing viewers. According to Nielsen, TWC averaged a five-year low of 211,000 daily viewers in 2013, down nearly 23 percent from 273,000 the previous year.

One reason for this decline was the unusual absence of catastrophic weather events in the United States in 2013, which typically translate into higher television ratings. (Recall that 2012 was the year of Hurricane Sandy, which decimated parts of the East Coast, including New York City.) In addition, TWC viewers are increasingly using mobile devices instead of television as their primary source of weather information. In 2013, according to analytics firm Distimo (www.distimo.com), the total number of weather apps for the iPhone and android devices doubled to nearly 10,000.

TWC also has to contend with changing user expectations about what a weather forecast should be. "Nowcasting"—highly accurate short-term weather predictions for a specific location—is finding favor among weather watchers who dislike semi-reliable five-day forecasts. TWC has typically relied on methods that can actually delay forecasts, such as having meteorologists interpret data for longer-term predictions over a broader geographical area.

Regardless of these competitive pressures, thanks largely to its brand recognition, TWC's mobile app is the category's most popular, with approximately 100 million users. However, a group of startup companies, including Dark Sky (www.darkskyapp.com), Sky Motion (www.skymotion.com), and WeatherSphere (www.weathersphere.com), are beginning to cut into TWC's lead.

Whereas TWC's app can present conditions in 15-minute intervals, Dark Sky, for example, predicts to the minute—often with startling precision—when it is going to start raining or snowing within the next hour. Sky Motion does the same for the upcoming two hours. WeatherSphere's product, Radar Cast, can navigate drivers around oncoming storms.

These startups can predict the weather with such accuracy because they integrate and analyze data from National Weather Service radar, satellites, and personal weather stations to improve short-term forecasting. Interestingly, Dark Sky's $3.99 app has been downloaded about 400,000 times since 2012.

Another competitor, IBM (www.ibm.com), has been in the weather forecasting arena since it initiated its Deep Thunder project in 1996. Deep Thunder provides local, high-resolution weather predictions, customized to weather-sensitive specific business operations. For example, the system could predict up to 84 hours in advance the wind velocity at an Olympic diving platform or which locations are at risk for flooding or damaged power lines.

To combat viewer migration, TWC revamped its TV channel in November 2013, implementing major changes to both its appearance and its coverage. The channel now supports a graphic display on the bottom third of the television screen that shows local hourly weather conditions 24/7,

even during commercials. The channel is also deploying technology that allows it to televise location-specific information to a defined geographical area, called "hyperlocal" forecasting. This technology involves having TWC's 220 meteorologists divide the country into 4000 different zones. Viewers can now watch weather pertinent to their geographical location.

TWC is also developing mobile projects to compete with the startups. For example, it created an app called Radius that lets weather watchers share user-generated photos with other people in their areas.

Another new technology, called Forecast on Demand, could be transformative. This technology incorporates elements of nowcasting but can also create a detailed forecast, at the request of a user, for more than 2 billion points around the globe. The application runs on a Web site that features a world map. As the user clicks on a location, Forecast on Demand instantly generates real-time forecasts for that specific geographical point, using the most current information available from its more than 75,000 data sources. This technology disrupts traditional forecasting, which relies on pre-generated predictions.

Not surprisingly, the competition is not standing still. In 2013, Dark Sky created a service that makes short-term and long-term forecasts available to other up-and-coming companies, encroaching even further into TWC's territory. In addition, the company is negotiating with auto companies to install its technology in their vehicles, which could dramatically expand its user base.

Sources: Compiled from J. McCorvey, "A Storm Brews Over Weather," *Fast Company*, February, 2014; K. Bell, "Hyperlocal Weather App Dark Sky Gets 24-Hour and 7-Day Forecasts," *Mashable*, January 27, 2014; D. Lu, "13 Best Weather Apps to Take Your Day by Storm," *Mashable*, August 12, 2013; S. Gallagher, "How IBM's Deep Thunder Delivers 'Hyper-Local' Forecasts 3½ Days Out," *Arstechnica*, March 14, 2012; "Dark Sky Reinvents Weather Apps with Hyper-Local Forecasts," *Fast Company*, November 8, 2011; H. Czerski, "150 Years Since the First UK Weather 'Forecast'," *BBC*, August 1, 2011; www.twc.com, www.darksky.com, www.ibm.com, accessed February 6, 2014.

Questions

1. Identify several reasons (not discussed in the case) why accurate weather predictions are so important. Can an accurate weather prediction be considered a competitive advantage for an organization that receives this information? Why or why not? Support your answer with specific examples.

2. Will Dark Sky, Sky Motion, and WeatherSphere have a lasting competitive advantage over The Weather Channel? Why or why not? Support your answer.

Customer Focus. Organizational attempts to provide superb customer service can make the difference between attracting and retaining customers versus losing them to competitors. Numerous IT tools and business processes have been designed to keep customers happy. (As you see in Plug IT In 1, a *business process* is a collection of related activities that produce a product or a service of value to the organization, its business partners, and/or its customers.) Consider Amazon, for example. When you visit Amazon's Web site anytime after your first visit, the site welcomes you back by name and it presents you with information about items that you might like, based on your previous purchases. In another example, Dell guides you through the process of purchasing a computer by providing information and choices that help you make an informed buying decision.

Make-to-Order and Mass Customization. **Make-to-order** is a strategy of producing customized (made to individual specifications) products and services. The business problem is how to manufacture customized goods efficiently and at a reasonably low cost. Part of the solution is to change manufacturing processes from mass production to mass customization. In mass production, a company produces a large quantity of identical items. An early example of mass production was Henry Ford's Model T, where buyers could pick any color—as long as it was black.

Ford's policy of offering a single product for all of its customers eventually gave way to *consumer segmentation*, in which companies provided standard specifications for different consumer groups, or segments. Clothes manufacturers, for example, designed their products in different sizes and colors to appeal to different customers. The next step was *configured mass customization*, in which companies offer features that allow each shopper to customize his or her product or service with a range of components. Examples are ordering a car, a computer, or a smartphone, where the customer can specify which features he or she wants.

In the current strategy, known as **mass customization**, a company produces a large quantity of items, but it customizes them to match the needs and preferences of individual customers. Mass customization is essentially an attempt to perform make-to-order on a large scale. Bodymetrics (www.bodymetrics.com) is an excellent example of mass customization that involves men's and women's jeans and swimsuits. Bodymetrics provides a "body scanner" that customers can access either at home or in a store. This technology scans the customer's body, captures more than 150 measurements, and produces a digital replica of the customer's size and shape. This scan is then used to provide made-to-measure jeans and swimsuits.

E-Business and E-Commerce. Conducting business electronically is an essential strategy for companies that are competing in today's business environment. *Electronic commerce* (EC or e-commerce) describes the process of buying, selling, transferring, or exchanging products, services, or information via computer networks, including the Internet. *E-business* is a somewhat broader concept. In addition to the buying and selling of goods and services, e-business also refers to servicing customers, collaborating with business partners, and performing electronic transactions within an organization. Chapter 9 focuses extensively on this topic. In addition, e-commerce applications appear throughout the text.

┌─ **BEFORE** *YOU GO ON....* ─
1. What are the characteristics of the modern business environment?
2. Discuss some of the pressures that characterize the modern global business environment.
3. Identify some of the organizational responses to these pressures. Are any of these responses specific to a particular pressure? If so, which ones?

You now have a general overview of the pressures that affect companies in today's business environment and the responses that they choose to manage these pressures. To plan for the most effective responses, companies formulate strategies. In the new digital economy, these strategies rely heavily on information technology, especially strategic information systems. You examine these topics in the next section.

Apply The Concept 2.1

LEARNING OBJECTIVE 2.1 Identify effective IT responses to different kinds of business pressures.

STEP 1 – Background (Here is what you are learning.)

Businesses face immense pressures today from every angle imaginable. The market is constantly shifting, technology becomes obsolete almost as quickly as it is implemented, society expects businesses to take more responsibility for the communities their work impacts, and legal compliance is required. Businesses increasingly employ cutting-edge technologies to navigate these difficult waters.

STEP 2 – Activity (Here is what you do.)

Pick one business pressure from each of the three broad categories presented in the chapter: market, technology, and societal/political/legal. Now search for a real-world business story related to each of the pressures you have chosen.

STEP 3 – Deliverable (Here is what you turn in.)

After you have selected your three examples, identify an effective IT response to each one. Feel free to use the responses listed in the chapter. Explain why you feel this is an appropriate response to the business pressure you have identified.

Perhaps there is a response outlined in the story you have found. If so, determine whether the response was truly effective in dealing with the business pressure. Your submission should follow the outline below.

- Broad Category: _____
- Business Pressure: _____
- IT Response: _____
- Description: _____

2.2 Competitive Advantage and Strategic Information Systems

A *competitive strategy* is a statement that identifies a business's approach to compete, its goals, and the plans and policies that will be required to carry out those goals (Porter, 1985).[1] A strategy, in general, can apply to a desired outcome, such as gaining market share. A competitive strategy focuses on achieving a desired outcome when competitors want to prevent you from reaching your goal. Therefore, when you create a competitive strategy, you must plan your own moves, but you must also anticipate and counter your competitors' moves.

Through its competitive strategy, an organization seeks a competitive advantage in an industry. That is, it seeks to outperform its competitors in a critical measure such as cost, quality, and time-to-market. Competitive advantage helps a company function profitably with a market and generate larger-than-average profits.

Competitive advantage is increasingly important in today's business environment, as you will note throughout the text. In general, the *core business* of companies has remained the same. That is, information technologies simply offer tools that can enhance an organization's success through its traditional sources of competitive advantage, such as low cost, excellent customer service, and superior supply chain management. **Strategic information systems (SISs)** provide a competitive advantage by helping an organization implement its strategic goals and improve its performance and productivity. Any information system that helps an organization either achieve a competitive advantage or reduce a competitive disadvantage qualifies as a strategic information system.

[1] Porter, M.E. (1985) *Competitive Advantage*, Free Press, New York.

Porter's Competitive Forces Model

The best-known framework for analyzing competitiveness is Michael Porter's **competitive forces model** (Porter, 1985). Companies use Porter's model to develop strategies to increase their competitive edge. Porter's model also demonstrates how IT can make a company more competitive.

Porter's model identifies five major forces that can endanger or enhance a company's position in a given industry. FIGURE 2.2 highlights these forces. Although the Web has changed the nature of competition, it has not changed Porter's five fundamental forces. In fact, what makes these forces so valuable as analytical tools is that they have not changed for centuries. Every competitive organization, no matter how large or small, or what business it is in, is driven by these forces. This observation applies even to organizations that you might not consider competitive, such as local governments. Although local governments are not for-profit enterprises, they compete for businesses to locate in their districts, for funding from higher levels of government, for employees, and for many other things.

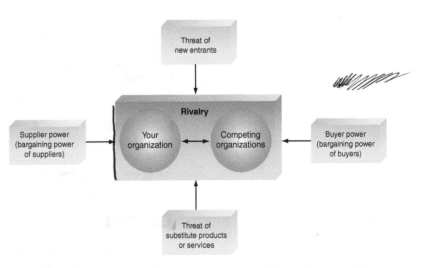

Figure 2.2 Porter's competitive forces model.

Significantly, Porter (2001)[2] concludes that the *overall* impact of the Web is to increase competition, which generally diminishes a firm's profitability. Let's examine Porter's five forces and the ways that the Web influences them.

1. *The threat of entry of new competitors.* The threat that new competitors will enter your market is high when entry is easy and low when there are significant barriers to entry. An **entry barrier** is a product or service feature that customers have learned to expect from organizations in a certain industry. A competing organization must offer this feature in order to survive in the marketplace. There are many types of entry barriers. Consider, for example, legal requirements such as admission to the bar to practice law or a license to serve liquor, where only a certain number of licenses are available.

   Suppose you want to open a gasoline station. In order to compete in that industry, you would have to offer pay-at-the-pump service to your customers. Pay-at-the-pump is an IT-based barrier to entering this market because you must offer it for free. The first gas station that offered this service gained first-mover advantage and established barriers to entry. This advantage did not last, however, because competitors quickly offered the same service and thus overcame the entry barrier.

   For most firms, the Web *increases* the threat that new competitors will enter the market because it sharply reduces traditional barriers to entry, such as the need for a sales force or a physical storefront. Today, competitors frequently need only to set up a Web site. This threat of increased competition is particularly acute in industries that perform an *intermediation role*, which is a link between buyers and sellers (e.g., stock brokers and travel agents), as well as in industries where the primary product or service is digital (e.g., the music industry). In addition, the geographical reach of the Web enables distant competitors to compete more directly with an existing firm.

   In some cases, the Web increases barriers to entry. This scenario occurs primarily when customers have come to expect a nontrivial capability from their suppliers. For example, the first company to offer Web-based package tracking gained a competitive advantage from that service. Competitors were forced to follow.

2. *The bargaining power of suppliers.* Supplier power is high when buyers have few choices from whom to buy and low when buyers have many choices. Therefore, organizations

---

[2] Porter, M.E. (2001) "Strategy and the Internet," *Harvard Business Review*, March.

would rather have more potential suppliers so that they will be in a stronger position to negotiate price, quality, and delivery terms.

The Internet's impact on suppliers is mixed. On the one hand, it enables buyers to find alternative suppliers and to compare prices more easily, thereby reducing the supplier's bargaining power. On the other hand, as companies use the Internet to integrate their supply chains, participating suppliers prosper by locking in customers.

3. *The bargaining power of customers (buyers).* Buyer power is high when buyers have many choices from whom to buy and low when buyers have few choices. For example, in the past, there were few locations where students could purchase textbooks (typically, one or two campus bookstores). In this situation, students had low buyer power. Today, the Web provides students with access to a multitude of potential suppliers as well as detailed information about textbooks. As a result, student buyer power has increased dramatically.

In contrast, *loyalty programs* reduce buyer power. As their name suggests, loyalty programs reward customers based on the amount of business they conduct with a particular organization (e.g., airlines, hotels, and rental car companies). Information technology enables companies to track the activities and accounts of millions of customers, thereby reducing buyer power. That is, customers who receive "perks" from loyalty programs are less likely to do business with competitors. (Loyalty programs are associated with customer relationship management, which you will study in Chapter 12.)

4. *The threat of substitute products or services.* If there are many alternatives to an organization's products or services, then the threat of substitutes is high. If there are few alternatives, then the threat is low. Today, new technologies create substitute products very rapidly. For example, customers today can purchase wireless telephones instead of landline telephones, Internet music services instead of traditional CDs, and ethanol instead of gasoline in cars.

Information-based industries experience the greatest threat from substitutes. Any industry in which digitized information can replace material goods (e.g., music, books, and software) must view the Internet as a threat because the Internet can convey this information efficiently and at low cost and high quality.

Even when there are many substitutes for their products, however, companies can create a competitive advantage by increasing switching costs. *Switching costs* are the costs, in money and time, imposed by a decision to buy elsewhere. For example, contracts with smartphone providers typically include a substantial penalty for switching to another provider until the term of the contract expires (quite often, two years). This switching cost is monetary.

As another example, when you buy products from Amazon, the company develops a profile of your shopping habits and recommends products targeted to your preferences. If you switch to another online vendor, that company will need time to develop a profile of your wants and needs. In this case, the switching cost involves time rather than money.

5. *The rivalry among existing firms in the industry.* The threat from rivalry is high when there is intense competition among many firms in an industry. The threat is low when the competition is among fewer firms and is not as intense.

In the past, proprietary information systems—systems that belong exclusively to a single organization—have provided strategic advantage to firms in highly competitive industries. Today, however, the visibility of Internet applications on the Web makes proprietary systems more difficult to keep secret. In simple terms, when I see my competitor's new system online, I will rapidly match its features to remain competitive. The result is fewer differences among competitors, which leads to more intense competition in an industry.

To understand this concept, consider the highly competitive grocery industry, where Walmart, Kroger, Safeway, and other companies compete essentially on price. Some of these companies have IT-enabled loyalty programs in which customers receive discounts and the store gains valuable business intelligence on customers' buying preferences.

Stores use this business intelligence in their marketing and promotional campaigns. (You will learn about business intelligence in Chapter 5.)

Grocery stores are also experimenting with wireless technologies such as *radio-frequency identification* (RFID, discussed in Chapter 10) to speed up the checkout process, track customers through the store, and notify customers of discounts as they pass by certain products. Grocery companies also use IT to tightly integrate their supply chains for maximum efficiency and thus reduce prices for shoppers.

Competition also is being affected by the extremely low variable cost of digital products. That is, once a digital product has been developed, the cost of producing additional "units" approaches zero. Consider the music industry as an example. When artists record music, their songs are captured in digital format. Physical products, such as CDs or DVDs of the songs for sale in music stores, involve costs. The costs of a physical distribution channel are much higher than those involved in delivering the songs digitally over the Internet.

In fact, in the future companies might give away some products for free. For example, some analysts predict that commissions for online stock trading will approach zero because investors can search the Internet for information to make their own decisions regarding buying and selling stocks. At that point, consumers will no longer need brokers to give them information that they can obtain themselves, virtually for free.

Porter's Value Chain Model

Organizations use Porter's competitive forces model to design general strategies. To identify specific activities where they can use competitive strategies for greatest impact, they use his value chain model (1985). A **value chain** is a sequence of activities through which the organization's inputs, whatever they are, are transformed into more valuable outputs, whatever they are. The **value chain model** identifies points where an organization can use information technology to achieve competitive advantage (see FIGURE 2.3).

According to Porter's value chain model, the activities conducted in any organization can be divided into two categories: primary activities and support activities. **Primary activities** relate to the production and distribution of the firm's products and services. These

Administration and management	Legal, accounting, finance management	Electronic scheduling and message systems; collaborative workflow intranet
Human resource management	Personnel, recruiting, training, career development	Workforce planning systems; employee benefits intranet
Product and technology development	Product and process design, production engineering, research and development	Computer-aided design systems; product development extranet with partners
Procurement	Supplier management, funding, subcontracting, specification	E-commerce Web portal for suppliers

SUPPORT ACTIVITIES

PRIMARY ACTIVITIES

FIRM ADDS VALUE

Inbound logistics	Operations	Outbound logistics	Marketing and sales	Customer service
Quality control; receiving; raw materials control; supply schedules	Manufacturing; packaging; production control; quality control; maintenance	Finishing goods; order handling; dispatch; delivery; invoicing	Customer management; order taking; promotion; sales analysis; market research	Warranty; maintenance; education and training; upgrades
Automated warehousing systems	Computer-controlled machining systems; computer-aided flexible manufacturing	Automated shipment scheduling systems; online point of sale and order processing	Computerized ordering systems; targeted marketing	Customer relationship management systems

Figure 2.3 Porter's value chain model.

activities create value for which customers are willing to pay. The primary activities are buttressed by **support activities**. Unlike primary activities, support activities do not add value directly to the firm's products or services. Rather, as their name suggests, they contribute to the firm's competitive advantage by supporting the primary activities.

Next, you will see examples of primary and support activities in the value chain of a manufacturing company. Keep in mind that other types of firms, such as transportation, healthcare, education, retail, and others, have different value chains. The key point is that *every* organization has a value chain.

In a manufacturing company, primary activities involve purchasing materials, processing the materials into products, and delivering the products to customers. Manufacturing companies typically perform five primary activities in the following sequence:

1. Inbound logistics (inputs)
2. Operations (manufacturing and testing)
3. Outbound logistics (storage and distribution)
4. Marketing and sales
5. Services

As work progresses in this sequence, value is added to the product in each activity. Specifically, the following steps occur:

1. The incoming materials are processed (in receiving, storage, and so on) in activities called *inbound logistics*.
2. The materials are used in operations, where value is added by turning raw materials into products.
3. These products are prepared for delivery (packaging, storing, and shipping) in the outbound logistics activities.
4. Marketing and sales sell the products to customers, increasing product value by creating demand for the company's products.
5. Finally, the company performs after-sales service for the customer, such as warranty service or upgrade notification, adding further value.

As noted above, the primary activities are buttressed by support activities. Support activities consist of the following:

1. The firm's infrastructure (accounting, finance, management)
2. Human resources management
3. Product and technology development (R&D)
4. Procurement

Each support activity can be applied to any or all of the primary activities. In addition, the support activities can also support one another.

A firm's value chain is part of a larger stream of activities, which Porter calls a **value system**. A value system, or an *industry value chain*, includes the suppliers that provide the inputs necessary to the firm along with their value chains. After the firm creates products, these products pass through the value chains of distributors (which also have their own value chains), all the way to the customers. All parts of these chains are included in the value system. To achieve and sustain a competitive advantage, and to support that advantage with information technologies, a firm must understand every component of this value system.

Strategies for Competitive Advantage

Organizations continually try to develop strategies to counter the five competitive forces identified by Porter. You will learn about five of those strategies here. Before we go into specifics, however, it is important to note that an organization's choice of strategy involves trade-offs. For example, a firm that concentrates only on cost leadership might not have the resources available for research and development, leaving the firm unable to innovate. As another example, a company that invests in customer happiness (customer orientation strategy) will experience increased costs.

Companies must select a strategy and then stay with it, because a confused strategy cannot succeed. This selection, in turn, decides how a company will utilize its information systems. A new information system that can improve customer service but will increase costs slightly will be welcomed at a high-end retailer such as Nordstrom's, but not at a discount store such as Walmart. The following list presents the most commonly used strategies. FIGURE 2.4 provides an overview of these strategies.

Figure 2.4 Strategies for competitive advantage.

1. *Cost leadership strategy.* Produce products and/or services at the lowest cost in the industry. An example is Walmart's automatic inventory replenishment system, which enables Walmart to reduce inventory storage requirements. As a result, Walmart stores use floor space only to sell products, and not to store them, thereby reducing inventory costs.

2. *Differentiation strategy.* Offer different products, services, or product features than your competitors. Southwest Airlines, for example, has differentiated itself as a low-cost, short-haul, express airline. This has proved to be a winning strategy for competing in the highly competitive airline industry. Also, Dell has differentiated itself in the personal computer market through its mass customization strategy.

3. *Innovation strategy.* Introduce new products and services, add new features to existing products and services, or develop new ways to produce them. A classic example is the introduction of automated teller machines (ATMs) by Citibank. The convenience and cost-cutting features of this innovation gave Citibank a huge advantage over its competitors. Like many innovative products, the ATM changed the nature of competition in the banking industry. Today, an ATM is a competitive *necessity* for any bank.

4. *Operational effectiveness strategy.* Improve the manner in which a firm executes its internal business processes so that it performs these activities more effectively than its rivals. Such improvements increase quality, productivity, and employee and customer satisfaction while decreasing time to market.

5. *Customer orientation strategy.* Concentrate on making customers happy. Web-based systems are particularly effective in this area because they can create a personalized, one-to-one relationship with each customer.

Business–Information Technology Alignment

The best way for organizations to maximize the strategic value of IT is to achieve business–information technology alignment. In fact, the "holy grail" of organizations is business–information technology alignment, or strategic alignment (which we will call simply *alignment*). **Business–information technology alignment** is the tight integration of the IT function with the organization's strategy, mission, and goals. That is, the IT function directly supports the business objectives of the organization. There are six characteristics of excellent alignment:

- Organizations view IT as an engine of innovation that continually transforms the business, often creating new revenue streams.

- Organizations view their internal and external customers and their customer service function as supremely important.

- Organizations rotate business and IT professionals across departments and job functions.

- Organizations provide overarching goals that are completely clear to each IT and business employee.

- Organizations ensure that IT employees understand how the company makes (or loses) money.

- Organizations create a vibrant and inclusive company culture.

Unfortunately, many organizations fail to achieve this type of close alignment. In fact, according to a McKinsey & Company survey on IT strategy and spending, only 16 percent of the IT and business executives who participated agreed that their organization had adequate alignment between IT and the business. Given the importance of business–IT alignment, why do so many organizations fail to implement this policy? The major reasons are the following:

- Business managers and IT managers have different objectives.
- The business and IT departments are ignorant of the other group's expertise.
- A lack of communication.

Put simply, business executives often know little about information technology, and IT executives understand the technology but may not understand the real needs of the business. One solution to this problem is to foster a collaborative environment in organizations so that business and IT executives can communicate freely and learn from each other.

Businesses can also utilize enterprise architecture to foster alignment. Originally developed as a tool to organize a company's IT initiatives, the enterprise architecture concept has evolved to encompass both a technical specification (the information and communication technologies and the information systems used in an organization) and a business specification (a collection of core business processes and management activities). IT's About Business 2.4 illustrates effective business–IT alignment at the University of Pittsburgh Medical Center.

IT'S ABOUT BUSINESS 2.4

The University of Pittsburgh Medical Center Makes Effective Use of IT

The University of Pittsburgh Medical Center (UPMC; www.upmc.com) is one of the country's largest nonprofit healthcare organizations. Its revenues for fiscal year 2013 totaled more than $10 billion. UPMC operates more than 20 hospitals and 400 physician offices and outpatient sites in Pennsylvania. It is also one of the state's largest health insurance plans. In its dual role of provider and payer, UPMC services more than 2 million customers. The center takes an aggressive approach to implementing and developing information technology to make healthcare more effective and efficient.

UPMC's IT organization performs several major roles. For example, it must improve the operations of the company's hospitals and health insurance plan, enhance patient care, and drive down the company's costs. In addition, it should be profitable for UPMC rather than function as a cost center. Finally, it has the mandate to develop unique technologies that the company can sell to other healthcare providers and insurers.

UPMC's IT initiatives are developed at its Technology Development Center (TDC), a business incubator and lab located in Pittsburgh. The TDC's mission is to develop new healthcare technologies and then to provide resources for startup companies to develop these technologies. (A business incubator is an organization that speeds up the growth and success of startup and early-stage companies. Just a few of the services provided by incubators include help with business basics; marketing assistance; high-speed Internet

© Squaredpixels/iStockphoto

access; help with accounting and financial management; and help with bank loans.)

The TDC initially attempts to use off-the-shelf technology to meet the needs of its clinicians, insurance teams, and other business groups. For example, it uses electronic health record (EHR) systems from Cerner (www.cerner.com) and Epic (www.epic.com). If it cannot find the technology it needs, then it will look to develop that technology, often in a joint venture with a large vendor. Another strategy is to purchase a stake in a startup, in which case it can influence the development process.

One example of a technology that TDC is developing is a telemedicine system called Virtual Care Collaboration (VCC). VCC combines videoconferencing with medical records. The greatest obstacle to telemedicine is not the technology, but the business model. For example, health insurance plans often will not pay for telemedicine consultations, and licensing rules can prevent doctors from treating patients across state lines. To combat these problems and provide impetus for the practice of telemedicine, the UPMC health plan and some other insurers are starting to cover telemedicine appointments.

UPMC's IT group is also utilizing cloud computing, a system in which tasks are performed by networked computers in remote locations ("the cloud"). (We discuss cloud computing in Plug IT In 4.) Cloud computing presents problems for the healthcare industry because it typically requires patient data to leave the healthcare providers' data centers. In mid-2014, UPMC had about 5 petabytes of data, with that volume doubling every 18 months. These data include medical images, genomic data, and remote patient monitoring data. UPMC could not afford to spend tens of millions of dollars to build data centers with the capacity to store all of that data. Therefore, the center turned to the cloud. Specifically, it rents storage infrastructure from cloud computing vendors such as Amazon and IBM.

UPMC's IT group is also creating a data warehouse that combines clinical, genomic, insurance, financial, and other information from more than 200 data sources. (We discuss data warehouses in detail in Chapter 3.) This initiative ties into the aspect of the U.S. healthcare reform that intends to change how healthcare is delivered and paid for. Providers will be paid to keep a group of people—for example, all the employees at a company—healthy rather than treat them after they become ill. This arrangement creates a financial incentive for providers to increase their preventive care efforts and to minimize mishaps that lead to hospital readmissions.

UPMC cannot accomplish its goals without analytics. Consider a recent UPMC study of the use of a particular catheter. The study found that the catheter was not used consistently, although on average it led to better outcomes. However, the catheter was also more expensive. These findings led to the next analysis, which examined which patients

benefited from the catheter and under which circumstances. The findings will be presented to doctors to help them make decisions about the use of the catheter. Ongoing projects include analyzing patients' individual genomes so that health providers can personalize their treatments.

UPMC has experienced some IT problems. For example, problems occurred in the implementation of electronic health records needed to comply with government mandates and financial incentives. As one example, new technologies allow physicians to cut and paste electronic records. As a result, an in-hospital progress note that used to present the patient's daily status in less than 1 page can now total 19 pages.

Sources: Compiled from N. Versel, "The Evolution of Health IT Continues," *U.S. News & World Report*, February 6, 2014; "Information Technology Is Changing the Healthcare System," *The Washington Post*, January 12, 2014; D. Gardner, "Healthcare Turns to Big Data Analytics for Improved Patient Outcomes," *ZDNet*, December 12, 2013; C. Murphy, "UPMC Plays to Win in the Tech Game," *InformationWeek*, September 9, 2013; E. McCann, "Clinical Data Analytics Next Big Thing," *Healthcare IT News*, August 27, 2013; V. Ramachandran, "How Is Information Technology Changing Healthcare?" *Mashable*, August 15, 2013; S. Tibkin, "Numbers, Numbers, and More Numbers," *The Wall Street Journal*, February 14, 2013; E. Topol, "The Future of Healthcare: Information Technology," *Modern Healthcare*, July 25, 2011; www.upmc.com, accessed February 20, 2014.

Questions

1. Describe the strategic advantages that IT provides to UPMC.

2. Which of Porter's competitive strategies is UPMC employing? Support your answer.

3. Describe how UPMC illustrates effective business–IT alignment.

Apply The Concept 2.2

LEARNING OBJECTIVE 2.2 Describe the strategies that organizations typically adopt to counter Porter's five competitive forces.

STEP 1 – Background

This section has exposed you to Porter's five forces model, which explains how various forces can affect an organization. The threat of entry of new competitors, bargaining power of suppliers, bargaining power of customers, threat of substitute products or services, and rivalry among existing firms in the industry all have an impact on the organization's success. Based on this model, the chapter presents five strategies for competitive advantage: cost leadership, differentiation, innovation, operational effectiveness, and customer orientation.

Walmart is a worldwide company that focuses on a cost leadership strategy. Review the ways Walmart uses the five

BEFORE *YOU GO ON....*

1. What are strategic information systems?

2. According to Porter, what are the five forces that could endanger a firm's position in its industry or marketplaces?

3. Describe Porter's value chain model. Differentiate between Porter's competitive forces model and his value chain model.

4. What strategies can companies use to gain competitive advantage?

5. What is business–IT alignment?

6. Give examples of business–IT alignment at your university, regarding student systems. (*Hint:* What are the "business" goals of your university with regard to student registration, fee payment, grade posting, etc.?)

forces (or controls them) to maintain their position as a global cost leader. Although it may be somewhat easy to perform this exercise with a global giant such as Walmart, it is very difficult to apply these concepts to small businesses.

STEP 2 – Activity

Visit your favorite restaurant, and ask to speak to the manager. Asking only a few questions, evaluate whether the manager has a grasp of the five forces model. Do *not* ask anything specifically about Porter. Rather, inquire about rivals, substitutes, customers' bargaining power, suppliers' power, and so on. A good manager should be familiar with these concepts regardless of whether he or she uses the term "Porter's five forces." Finally, ask the manager what strategy he or she uses. Then, try to classify that strategy as a cost leadership, differentiation, innovation, operational effectiveness, and customer orientation strategy.

STEP 3 – Deliverable

Identify which of the five forces are at work based on the manager's feedback. Then, describe the strategies that COULD help deal with these particular forces, and explain IF this is what the restaurant is currently attempting to do. If it is not, then explain what they should do differently. Your submission will have two parts: a definition of the forces, and a description of the strategies at play in response to those forces.

What's in for ME?

MIS FOR ALL MAJORS

All functional areas in any organization must work together in an integrated fashion in order for the firm to respond adequately to business pressures. These responses typically require each functional area to utilize a variety of information systems to support, document, and manage cross-functional business processes. In today's competitive global marketplace, the timeliness and accuracy of these responses are even more critical.

Closely following this discussion, all functional areas must work together for the organization to gain competitive advantage in its marketplace. Again, the functional areas use a variety of strategic information systems to achieve this goal. BPR and BPI process change efforts contribute to the goal as well.

You have seen why companies must be concerned with strategic advantage. But why is this chapter so important for you? There are several reasons. First, the business pressures you have learned about have an impact on your organization, but they also affect you as an individual. So, it is critical that you understand how information systems can help you, and eventually your organization, respond to these pressures.

In addition, achieving competitive advantage is essential for your organization's survival. In many cases, you, your team, and all your colleagues will be responsible for creating a competitive advantage. Therefore, having general knowledge about strategy and about how information systems affect the organization's strategy and competitive position will help you in your career.

You also need a basic knowledge of your organization's strategy, mission, and goals, as well as its business problems and how it makes (or loses) money. You now know how to analyze your organization's strategy and value chain, as well as the strategies and value chains of your competitors. You also have acquired a general knowledge of how information technology contributes to organizational strategy. This knowledge will help you to do your job better, to be promoted more quickly, and to contribute significantly to the success of your organization.

SUMMARY

1. Identify effective IT responses to different kinds of business pressures.

   > *Market pressures*: An example of a market pressure is powerful customers. Customer relationship management is an effective IT response that helps companies achieve customer intimacy.

   > *Technology pressures*: An example of a technology pressure is information overload. Search engines and business intelligence applications enable managers to access, navigate, and utilize vast amounts of information.

   > *Societal/political/legal pressures*: An example of a societal/political/legal pressure is social responsibility, such as the state of the physical environment. Green IT is one response that is intended to improve the environment.

2. Describe the strategies that organizations typically adopt to counter Porter's five competitive forces.

   Porter's five competitive forces:

   > *The threat of entry of new competitors*: For most firms, the Web increases the threat that new competitors will enter the market by reducing traditional barriers to entry. Frequently, competitors need only to set up a Web site to enter a market. The Web can also increase barriers to entry, as when customers come to expect a nontrivial capability from their suppliers.

   > *The bargaining power of suppliers*: The Web enables buyers to find alternative suppliers and to compare prices more easily, thereby reducing suppliers' bargaining power. From a different perspective, as companies use the Web to integrate their supply chains, participating suppliers can lock in customers, thereby increasing suppliers' bargaining power.

   > *The bargaining power of customers (buyers)*: The Web provides customers with incredible amounts of choices for products, as well as information about those choices. As a result, the Web increases buyer power. However, companies can implement loyalty programs in which they use the Web to monitor the activities of millions of customers. Such programs reduce buyer power.

   > *The threat of substitute products or services*: New technologies create substitute products very rapidly, and the Web makes information about these products available almost instantly. As a result, industries (particularly information-based industries) are in great danger from substitutes (e.g., music, books, newspapers, magazines, software). However, the Web also can enable a company to build in switching costs, so that it will cost customers time and/or money to switch from your company to a competitor.

   > *The rivalry among existing firms in the industry*: In the past, proprietary information systems provided strategic advantage for firms in highly competitive industries. The visibility of Internet applications on the Web makes proprietary systems more difficult to keep secret. Therefore, the Web makes strategic advantage more short-lived.

   The five strategies are as follows:

   > *Cost leadership strategy*—produce products and/or services at the lowest cost in the industry.

   > *Differentiation strategy*—offer different products, services, or product features.

   > *Innovation strategy*—introduce new products and services, put new features in existing products and services, or develop new ways to produce them.

   > *Operational effectiveness strategy*—improve the manner in which internal business processes are executed so that a firm performs similar activities better than its rivals.

   > *Customer orientation strategy*—concentrate on making customers happy.

>>>CHAPTER GLOSSARY

business environment The combination of social, legal, economic, physical, and political factors in which businesses conduct their operations.

business–information technology alignment The tight integration of the IT function with the strategy, mission, and goals of the organization.

competitive advantage An advantage over competitors in some measure such as cost, quality, or speed; leads to control of a market and to larger-than-average profits.

competitive forces model A business framework devised by Michael Porter that analyzes competitiveness by recognizing five major forces that could endanger a company's position.

digital divide The gap between those who have access to information and communications technology and those who do not.

entry barrier Product or service feature that customers expect from organizations in a certain industry; an organization trying to enter this market must provide this product or service at a minimum to be able to compete.

globalization The integration and interdependence of economic, social, cultural, and ecological facets of life, enabled by rapid advances in information technology.

individual social responsibility See **organizational social responsibility**.

make-to-order The strategy of producing customized products and services.

mass customization A production process in which items are produced in large quantities but are customized to fit the desires of each customer.

organizational social responsibility (also **individual social responsibility**) Efforts by organizations to solve various social problems.

primary activities Those business activities related to the production and distribution of the firm's products and services, thus creating value.

strategic information systems (SISs) Systems that help an organization gain a competitive advantage by supporting its strategic goals and/or increasing performance and productivity.

support activities Business activities that do not add value directly to a firm's product or service under consideration but support the primary activities that do add value.

value chain A sequence of activities through which the organization's inputs, whatever they are, are transformed into more valuable outputs, whatever they are.

value chain model Model that shows the primary activities that sequentially add value to the profit margin; also shows the support activities.

value system Includes the producers, suppliers, distributors, and buyers, all with their value chains.

>>>DISCUSSION QUESTIONS

1. Explain why IT is both a business pressure and an enabler of response activities that counter business pressures.

2. What does a flat world mean to you in your choice of a major? In your choice of a career? Will you have to be a "lifelong learner"? Why or why not?

3. What might the impact of a flat world be on your standard of living?

4. Is IT a strategic weapon or a survival tool? Discuss.

5. Why might it be difficult to justify a strategic information system?

6. Describe the five forces in Porter's competitive forces model, and explain how increased access to high-speed Internet has affected each one.

7. Describe Porter's value chain model. What is the relationship between the competitive forces model and the value chain model?

8. Describe how IT can be used to support different value chains for different companies.

9. Discuss the idea that an information system by itself can rarely provide a sustainable competitive advantage.

>>>PROBLEM-SOLVING ACTIVITIES

1. Surf the Internet for information about the Department of Homeland Security. Examine the available information, and comment on the role of information technologies in the department.

2. Experience mass customization by designing your own shoes at www.nike.com, your car at www.jaguar.com, your CD at www.easternrecording.com, your business card at www.iprint.com, and your diamond ring at www.bluenile.com. Summarize your experiences.

3. Access www.go4customer.com. What does this company do and where is it located? Who are its customers? Which of Friedman's flatteners does this company fit? Provide examples of how a U.S. company would use its services.

4. Enter Walmart China (www.wal-martchina.com/english/index.htm). How does Walmart China differ from your local Walmart (consider products, prices, services, etc.)? Describe these differences.

5. Apply Porter's value chain model to Costco (www.costco.com). What is Costco's competitive strategy? Who are Costco's major competitors? Describe Costco's business model. Describe the tasks that Costco must accomplish for each primary value chain activity. How would Costco's information systems contribute to Costco's competitive strategy, given the nature of its business?

6. Apply Porter's value chain model to Dell (www.dell.com). What is Dell's competitive strategy? Who are Dell's major

competitors? Describe Dell's business model. Describe the tasks that Dell must accomplish for each primary value chain activity. How would Dell's information systems contribute to Dell's competitive strategy, given the nature of its business?

7. The market for optical copiers is shrinking rapidly. It is estimated that 90 percent of all duplicated documents are generated by computer printers. Can a company such as Xerox Corporation survive?

   a. Read about the problems and solutions of Xerox from 2000 to 2010 at www.fortune.com, www.findarticles.com, and www.google.com.

   b. Identify all the business pressures on Xerox.

   c. Find some of Xerox's response strategies (see www.xerox.com, www.yahoo.com, and www.google.com).

   d. Identify the role of IT as a contributor to the business technology pressures (e.g., obsolescence).

   e. Identify the role of IT as a facilitator of Xerox's critical response activities.

>>> COLLABORATION EXERCISE

STEP 1 – Background

Imagine you work for a company based in Atlanta, Georgia. Recent significant growth on the West Coast has made it necessary to open an office there. Because of the time lost in traveling across the country, the company has decided that it can conduct 95 percent of its meetings over the Web.

You and a few colleagues from other departments are assigned the job of determining which platform would best support your company's upcoming Web meetings. Many companies—Adobe Connect, Webex, and Fuze Meeting, among others—offer webcasting-type technologies, each of which has certain distinctive features. Obviously, these companies offer different price packages, but the one with the lowest cost may not be the best option.

STEP 2 – Activity

Form a team with your classmates (preferably some who are majoring in other areas) to determine which online tool will best serve your company's needs. First, decide what activities the system has to support in a Web meeting. Will Marketing need the ability to present product videos? Will Accounting need to share spreadsheets? Is it necessary to have a streaming video of the participants? (These are arbitrary questions, but your answer will make a difference. There is not a right or wrong choice.) Based on your decisions, list the tools that will be required of the system. Finally, review the online systems that are mentioned above along with any others you find. Use your list of requirements to guide your decision.

STEP 3 – Deliverable

To accomplish your group task, create a new Google document (this will require a Gmail account), and share it with your team members. Make certain that everyone is online at the same time and is working together to determine which webcasting solution is the best to meeting the needs of your company. Be creative in your document, using tables, colors, or other enhancements to help your readers understand how the solution you have chosen fits the criteria identified by your company.

You now need to submit your work. At the bottom of your report, compose a short paragraph that explains how this particular online meeting program will support your company. Export the Google document you created to a pdf, and submit it according to the instructions your professor has specified. Make certain to include the names of all group members and the role that each one played, particularly which department each one represented.

CLOSING **CASE 1** > IBM's Watson

THE PROBLEM >>> Computer scientists have long sought to design computer-based information systems (CBISs) that interact in natural human terms across a range of applications and processes, comprehending the questions that humans ask and providing answers that humans can understand. A major step toward achieving this goal is the development of the IBM Watson system.

AN INTERESTING IT SOLUTION >>> IBM (www.ibm.com) has developed an artificial intelligence (we discuss artificial intelligence in Plug IT In 5) CBIS capable of answering questions posed in natural language. IBM named the system "Watson," after the company's founder, Thomas J. Watson, Sr. IBM describes Watson as an application of advanced natural language processing, information retrieval, knowledge representation and reasoning, and machine learning technologies to the field of open-domain (general) question answering.

IBM developed Watson specifically to answer questions on the quiz show *Jeopardy!*. In 2011, Watson competed on *Jeopardy!* against former winners Brad Rutter and Ken Jennings. Watson won the game series and received the first prize of $1 million. (In *Jeopardy!*, the host reads the answer, and the contestants must then provide the correct question.)

For *Jeopardy!*, Watson had access to 200 million pages of structured and unstructured content consuming 4 terabytes of disk storage, including the full text of *Wikipedia* (see www.wikipedia.org). Significantly, however, Watson was *not* connected to the Internet during the game. For each clue, Watson's three most probable responses were displayed on the television screen. The probabilities represented Watson's level of confidence in any given answer.

Following the television performance, IBM executives immediately turned their attention to commercializing Watson. They decided to focus on a field in which Watson could have a distinctive social impact while also proving its ability to master a complex body of knowledge. The team chose medicine.

Medicine was a logical choice. Although some health information is structured—for example, blood pressure readings and cholesterol counts—the vast majority is unstructured. This information includes textbooks, medical journals, patient records, and nurse and physician notes. In fact, modern medicine entails so much unstructured information that its rapid growth has surpassed the ability of healthcare practitioners to keep up. It is important to note here that IBM has made it clear that Watson is *not* intended to replace doctors. Rather, its purpose is to assist them in avoiding medical errors and sharpening their medical diagnoses.

Enter Watson. Watson can ingest more data in one day than any human could in a lifetime. It can read all of the world's medical journals in seconds. Simultaneously, it can read patient histories, monitor the latest drug trials, examine the potency of new therapies, and closely follow state-of-the-art guidelines that help doctors choose the best treatments. Watson can also analyze images such as MRIs and EKGs. "Healthcare Watson" (to distinguish the system from "*Jeopardy!* Watson") is now connected to the Internet.

THE RESULTS: INITIAL USES OF WATSON >>>

- **Watson at WellPoint.** IBM partnered with WellPoint (www.wellpoint.com), the largest managed for-profit healthcare company in the Blue Cross and Blue Shield Association, to increase the efficiency of health insurance decisions and claims by utilizing Watson's analytic capabilities. At WellPoint, Watson was trained with more than 25,000 test case scenarios and 1,500 real-life cases. It acquired the ability to analyze queries in the context of complex medical data and human natural language, including doctor's notes, patient records, and medical annotations and clinical feedback. In addition, nurses spent more than 14,700 hours of hands-on training with Watson.

  As of mid-2014, WellPoint was using two Watson-based products: Interactive Care Guide and Interactive Care Reviewer. These products help employees review clinicians' suggested treatments against their patients' insurance plans. Watson continues to learn on the job, while working with the WellPoint nurses who originally conducted its training.

- **Watson at Memorial Sloan-Kettering.** The Memorial Sloan-Kettering Cancer Center (MSK; www.mskcc.org) in Manhattan utilizes Watson to help physicians diagnose and treat lung cancer. Watson's role is to analyze a patient's specific symptoms, medical history, and hereditary history, and then synthesize those data with available unstructured and structured medical information, including published medical books and articles. MSK has immersed Watson in the complexities of cancer as well as the explosion of genetic research that has set the stage for changing treatment practices for many cancer patients by basing their treatments on their personal genetic profiles.

- **Watson at the Cleveland Clinic.** The Cleveland Clinic Lerner College of Medicine of Case Western Reserve University is continuing Watson's medical training by increasing its health expertise. As with other installations of Watson, the goal is for Watson to assist medical professionals in diagnosing and treating patients.

  The Cleveland Clinic has helped IBM develop two new Watson-based products that are designed to help physicians make more informed and accurate decisions more quickly and to obtain new insights from electronic medical records. With the first product, WatsonPaths, the system interacts naturally with physicians and nurses, enabling them to more easily understand the structured and unstructured data sources that Watson consulted and the decision path Watson adopted in offering treatment options. The second product, Watson EMR Assistant, enables physicians to uncover key information from patients' medical records to help improve the quality and efficiency of medical care.

- **Watson at Citigroup.** IBM intends to use Watson in other information-intensive fields, such as telecommunications, financial services, and government. At Citigroup (www.citigroup.com), for example, Watson analyzes financial, regulatory, economic, and social data across financial exchanges, currencies, and funds to help simplify and improve the bank's digital interactions with its customers.

- **The Watson Engagement Advisor.** The Watson Engagement Advisor is designed to help customer-facing personnel assist consumers with deeper insights more quickly than was previously possible. Engagement Advisor's "Ask Watson" feature can quickly address customers' questions, offer feedback to guide their purchase decisions, and troubleshoot their problems. Companies using the Engagement Advisor include the Australian bank ANZ, the Royal Bank of Canada, Nielsen, the publishing and research company IHS, and the grocery chain Kroger.

- **Other Interesting Uses of Watson.** Macy's uses Watson to better target millennials by interpreting their social signals on social media. BNSF Railway is using Watson to help detect faulty sections in the company's 32,500 miles of track before they break.

In November 2013, IBM announced that it will make Watson available to developers in the cloud so that they can build apps using the technology. (We discuss cloud computing in Plug IT In 4.) In February 2014, IBM announced that it was deploying Watson to Africa to encourage business opportunities across the world's

 fastest-growing continent. Watson eventually will be available for use in key areas such as education, water and sanitation, and agriculture.

One last point: In mid-2014, IBM executives noted that Watson was 240 percent faster than, and less than 10 percent the size of, the system that won *Jeopardy!*.

Sources: Compiled from "IBM's $100M 'Project Lucy' Brings Watson to Africa," *KurzweilAI.net*, February 7, 2014; D. Henschen, "With Watson, Is IBM Riding the Right Wave?" *InformationWeek*, January 10, 2014; A. Regalado, "Facing Doubters, IBM Expands Plans for Watson," *MIT Technology Review*, January 9, 2014; L. Dignan, "IBM Form Watson Business Group: Will Commercialization Follow?" *ZDNet*, January 9, 2014; "IBM to Announce Low-Cost, More Powerful Cloud-Based Watson," *KurzweilAI .net*, November 14, 2013; "IBM to Take Watson to the Cloud, Opens to App Developers," *KurzweilAI.net*, November 14, 2013; J. Best, "IBM Watson: How

the Jeopardy-Winning Supercomputer Was Born and What It Wants to Do Next," *TechRepublic*, November 4, 2013; "MD Anderson Cancer Center Taps IBM Watson to Power Its Mission to Eradicate Cancer," *KurzweilAI.net*, October 20, 2013; "IBM Research Unveils Two New Watson-Related Projects from Cleveland Clinic Collaboration," *KurzweilAI.net*, October 20, 2013; J. Hempel, "IBM's Massive Bet on Watson," *Fortune*, October 7, 2013; D. Talbot, "New Answer from IBM's Watson: A Recipe for Swiss–Thai Fusion Quiche," *MIT Technology Review*, October 3, 2013; T. Simonite, "Trained on Jeopardy, Watson Is Headed for Your Pocket," *MIT Technology Review*, May 28, 2013; "IBM Watson Engagement Advisor Hopes to Improve Customer Service," *KurzweilAI.net*, May 22, 2013; D. Taft, "IBM Watson Masters Customer Service as Engagement Advisor," *eWeek*, May 21, 2013; E. Kolawole, "Watson Goes to Washington: IBM Shows Off Latest Health-Care Work to Lawmakers," *The Washington Post*, May 17, 2013; "Watson Provides Cancer Treatment Options to Doctors in Seconds," *KurzweilAI .net*, February 11, 2013; N. Leske, "Doctors Seek Help on Cancer Treatment from IBM Supercomputer," *Reuters*, February 8, 2013; B. Upbin, "IBM's Watson Gets Its First Piece of Business in Healthcare," *Forbes*, February 8, 2013; J. Fitzgerald, "Watson Supercomputer Offers Medical Expertise," *USA Today*, February 8, 2013; M. Lev-Ram, "The Supercomputer Will See You Now," *Fortune*, December 3, 2012; "IBM's Watson Goes to Medical School," *KurzeilAI.net*, November 2, 2012; J. Gertner, "Calling Dr. Watson," *Fast Company*, November, 2012; B. Keim, "Paging Dr. Watson: Artificial Intelligence as a Prescription for Health Care," *Wired*, October 16, 2012; J. Gertner, "IBM's Watson Is Learning Its Way to Saving Lives," *Fast Company*, October 15, 2012; D. Zax, "Will Watson Be the New Siri?" *MIT Technology Review*, August 28, 2012; http://www-03.ibm.com/innovation/us/ watson/, accessed April 14, 2014.

Questions

1. What applications can you think of for Watson in a university setting?

2. What are potential disadvantages of using Watson in healthcare settings?

3. Would you consider being diagnosed only by Watson? Why or why not?

4. Would you consider being diagnosed by your personal physician, if he or she consulted Watson? Why or why not?

CLOSING **CASE 2** > A Tool to Combat Terrorism and Fight Crime

THE PROBLEM >>> In the months leading up to the terrorist attacks of September 11, 2001, the U.S. government had all the necessary clues to stop the al Qaeda perpetrators. The attackers were from countries known to harbor terrorists, they entered the United States on temporary visas, they had trained to fly civilian airliners, and they purchased one-way airplane tickets on September 11.

Unfortunately, those clues were located in different databases scattered across many government agencies. Organizations such as the CIA and the FBI maintain thousands of databases, each with its own data: financial records, DNA samples, voice and other sound samples, video clips, maps, floor plans, human intelligence reports from all over the world, and many other types of data. Integrating all of those data into a coherent whole is potentially overwhelming. In 2001, there was no tool available that would have enabled government analysts to integrate all of these different types of data that were dispersed across so many locations.

A POTENTIAL IT SOLUTION >>> Today, more than a decade after the terrorist attacks, the government has an important new tool at its disposal, known as Palantir (www.palantir.com). Palantir has become the "go to" company for mining massive datasets for intelligence and law enforcement applications. The company examines, tags, and integrates a company's data and then can analyze problems as different as terrorism, disaster response, and human trafficking.

The origins of Palantir go back to PayPal. Because PayPal was so successful, it attracted criminals who used it to carry out money laundering and fraud. By 2000, PayPal was in financial trouble because the existing antifraud software tools could not keep up with the criminal activity. Each time PayPal analysts caught onto one ploy, the perpetrators simply changed tactics.

To deal with these issues, PayPal's analysts created software that could view each transaction as a part of a pattern, rather than as just a single database entry. This process enabled analysts to spot networks of suspicious accounts and to discover patterns that PayPal's computers had missed. PayPal utilized this software to freeze suspicious payments before they were processed. The software saved the company hundreds of millions of dollars.

Several PayPal engineers who had worked on the software collaborated with computer scientists from Stanford University to form a startup company to develop PayPal's fraud-detection tool into a data analysis system. This system would have the capacity to integrate pattern recognition, artificial intelligence software, and human cognitive skills. They named the tool Palantir for the "Seeing Stones" in the *Lord of the Rings*.

Palantir technology essentially solves the types of intelligence problems that allowed September 11 to occur. That is, it helps organizations spot patterns in the vast amounts of data they analyze every day. Palantir software combs through all of the available databases, identifies related pieces of information, and integrates everything into a unified picture.

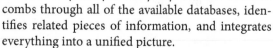

THE RESULTS >>> Palantir's customer list currently includes the U.S. Department of Defense, the CIA, the FBI, the Army, the Marines, the Air Force, the police departments of New York and Los Angeles, and an increasing number of financial institutions that have an interest in detecting bank fraud. Most of Palantir's government work remains classified, but information on some cases has leaked out.

In April 2010, for example, security researchers in Canada used Palantir software to crack a spy operation called the Shadow Network that, among other things, had broken into the Indian Defense Ministry and infiltrated the Dalai Lama's e-mail account. Palantir has also been used to unravel child abuse and abduction cases, to locate suspects in the murder of a U.S. Immigration and Customs Enforcement special agent, and to uncover bombing networks in Syria, Afghanistan, and Pakistan.

U.S. Marines used to spend years gathering fingerprint and DNA evidence from IEDs and trying to match those data against a database of similar information collected from villagers. Usually, by the time they obtained any results, the bombers had disappeared. In contrast, field operatives can now upload fingerprint/DNA evidence from villagers, along with location data, anonymous tips, and social media posts into Palantir and instantly find matches from past attacks.

Wall Street banks are also utilizing Palantir to search their transaction databases for criminal fraud, trading insights, and even new ways to price mortgages. One of the world's largest banks employs Palantir software to break up a popular scam called BustOut. In this scam, criminals steal or purchase access to thousands of people's online identities and then break into their bank and credit card accounts. Rather than act immediately, however, they spend weeks biding their time until someone on their radar purchases a plane ticket or leaves on a holiday. They then siphon money out of the accounts as quickly as they can while the victim is in transit. The criminals hide their trails by anonymizing their computing activity and disabling alert systems in the bank and credit card accounts. When the bank identifies a small number of compromised accounts, it uses Palantir to discern the characteristics of those accounts. Palantir then helps the bank discover thousands of other accounts with those characteristics that have not yet been hacked.

In the area of law enforcement, the FBI utilizes Palantir technology to compile thorough dossiers on U.S. citizens. For example, agents can integrate surveillance videos with credit card transactions, cell phone records, e-mails, air itineraries, and Web search information. Privacy advocates worry that Palantir will make the FBI and other government agencies even more intrusive consumers of personal data. One specific event that raised concerns among privacy advocates concerned a Palantir engineer who was exposed by the hacker collective Anonymous for participating in a plot to break into the personal computers of WikiLeaks supporters. The engineer was placed on leave but later was quietly rehired.

Palantir responds to these concerns by asserting that it has developed very sophisticated privacy protection technology. Its software creates audit trails that detail who is privy to certain pieces of information and what they have done with the information. Palantir also has a permission system that ensures that agency workers who employ their software can access only the data allowed by their clearance level.

Sources: Compiled from S. Doshi, "Data as a Company's Secret Weapon," *TechCrunch*, January 25, 2014; A. Greenberg and R. Mac, "Big Brother's Brain," *Forbes*, September 2, 2013; N. Ungerleider, "Google, Palantir, Salesforce Fight Human Traffickers," *Fast Company*, April 9, 2013; J. Gould, "Army May Work with Palantir on Intel Software," *The Army Times*, January 3, 2013; M. Hoffman, "Army Considers Palantir to Boost Intelligence Architecture," *Defense.org*, December 20, 2012; J. Lonsdale, "How Did Palantir Build Such a Strong Brand?" *Forbes*, December 12, 2012; R. Scarborough, "Army's Own Data Mining System Fails Test," *The Washington Times*, December 2, 2012; R. Scarborough, "Military Leaders Urgently Push for New Counterterrorism Software," *The Washington Times*, August 27, 2012; A. Good, "Who Actually

Uses Palantir Finance?" *Forbes*, August 15, 2012; W. Hickey, "This Peter Thiel Company Is Ripping the Army Intelligence Community Apart," *Business Insider*, August 3, 2012; A. Vance and B. Stone, "Palantir, the War on Terror's Secret Weapon," *Bloomberg BusinessWeek*, November 22, 2011; "Husky Names Palantir as Software and Consulting Partner," *Oil & Gas Financial Journal*, November 4, 2011; P. Gobry, "Secretive Spy Tech Company Palantir Technologies Raises Another $50 Million," *Business Insider*, May 11, 2011; D. Primack, "Analyze This: Palantir Worth More than $2 Billion," *CNN Money*, May 6, 2011; A. Greenberg, "Palantir Apologizes for WikiLeaks Attack Proposal, Cuts Ties with HBGary," *Forbes*, February 11, 2011; www.palantir.com, accessed February 16, 2014.

Questions

1. Is the Palantir system a strategic information system to the organization using it? Why or why not? Support your answer.

2. What are potential problems that could arise with this high-level, massive amount of data integration?

INTERNSHIP ACTIVITY> OXFORD ORTHOPAEDICS

Information systems have drastically altered the ways we conduct business in healthcare. Every day there seems to be another breakthrough in research, product development, or treatments that is made possible by technology. One critical innovation—electronic health records—has moved to the forefront in the last few years because of the strong positives and potentially serious negatives they bring to the table. For professionals in the business of running a healthcare business, however, the practice management side of technology has made more of a difference.

For this Internship Activity, you will work for Chad Prince, Practice Administrator for Oxford Orthopaedics Associates in

Oxford, AL. Chad has recently taken on the role of Practice Administrator, and he is learning the ins and outs of managing a healthcare organization. His first task is to familiarize himself with the market offerings for practice management. A quick Web search for "Healthcare Practice Management Software" will reveal plenty of information on the relationship between practice management and electronic health records.

Below is a letter from Chad outlining his expectations for your project.

To:	IT Intern
From:	Chad Prince
Subject:	Help Creating Marketing Programs

Hello!

I have recently become the Administrator for Oxford Orthopaedics, and I need to learn more about the management of a healthcare business and the software that supports day-to-day operations. I have compiled a list of questions that will help me understand the relationships between the people and processes both inside and outside a healthcare organization. The profession refers to this set of relationships as practice management (PM). I have been advised to research a product called PrimeSuite by Greenway. Try to find a demo of their software on the Web to review. As you do so, consider the following questions.

1. *Internal People:* The front office deals with most of the initial customer interaction. How will the PM software help our personnel who are primarily responsible for scheduling, coordinating, and planning our business activities? How will it help me (the Administrator) manage the business of the medical practice?

2. *Internal Processes:* A medical practice involves myriad processes, including employee scheduling, record keeping, accounting, and records. How many of these processes does the PM software manage?

3. *External People:* Clients engage with the practice to schedule their visits, register for care, submit insurance claims, and pay bills. Insurance companies interact with us regarding claims.

4. *External Processes:* Insurance companies have many considerations when it comes to processing payment for healthcare. How can healthcare information systems help manage these processes?

I want to thank you in advance for your work. I am looking forward to reading what you find on these topics!
Chad

Note: Any links referenced in this letter can be found at http://www.wiley.com/go/rainer/MIS3e/internship.

SPREADSHEET ACTIVITY > BASIC FUNCTIONS: SUM, SUMIF, COUNT, COUNTIF

STEP 1 – Background

Part of the power of a spreadsheet comes from built-in formulas that provide a great deal of functionality. Some of the most basic functions perform simple activities such as calculate a sum (Sum) (as we saw in Spreadsheet Activity 1), calculate a conditional sum (Sumif), provide a count of items (Count), and provide a conditional count (Countif).

It is important at this stage to understand the basics of how a formula is constructed. There are four parts to a formula: the function, the reference cell, the constant, and the operator. Constants and operators are optional; we use them only if we need them. Functions and references, in contrast, are required for the spreadsheet to calculate anything.

The function describes the calculation(s) you are trying to perform. In this activity, the functions are Sum, Sumif, Count, and Countif. The reference cells are the cells on the spreadsheet that are involved in the function. A group of reference cells is called a *range*. A range is denoted by the column letter and the row number of the upper left-hand cell and the column letter and row number of the bottom right-hand cell. (Sometimes a range exists within a single column.)

As previously explained, some formulas involve constants. For example, if you want to divide every number in a column by 2, then the number 2 would be the constant. Finally, the operator is the sign that will tell the spreadsheet what to do. To divide by 2, for example, you would use a forward slash "/" as your operator with the constant "2" after the operator.

This may seem like a lot of information to digest, but after you perform a few calculations it will begin to make sense.

STEP 2 – Activity

Imagine you are the manager of a Sales Department for a regional grocery distribution company and you have two sales representatives, Huang and Sally. You are interested in keeping track of the number of sales they close and the total revenue they generate. Below are their data from the past month.

	Sales Amount
Huang	$3,132
Sally	$8,245
Sally	$6,365
Huang	$7,282
Huang	$6,245

Of course, you can add up these numbers with a calculator and see that Huang has three sales with a total of $16,659 while Sally has two sales with a total of $14,610. If you are looking at data for an entire year, however, then these calculations will involve much more work. This is exactly where the Sum, Sumif, Count, and Countif formulas come in.

STEP 3 – Deliverable

Visit http://www.wiley.com/go/rainer/MIS3e/spreadsheet, and download the file linked for Spreadsheet Activity 2. This is an XLS file that will open in any spreadsheet tool. You will find a list of sales from the past year and instructions written into the spreadsheet indicating what you should calculate.

Follow the instructions in the spreadsheet and submit your final work to your intstructor.

Additional help with this spreadsheet skill is available in WileyPLUS. Open the "Microsoft Office 2013 Lab Manual Spreadsheet Module: Excel 2013," and review Lesson 5: Using Formulas and Built-In Functions and Lesson 10: The IF Function.

DATABASE ACTIVITY > TABLES

STEP 1 – Background

In this activity, you will learn how to create Access tables from an existing design. The construction of any database begins with creating its data tables. If you cannot create tables, then you cannot create a database. Even if you use an existing database, knowing where the tables come from will help you understand how you can utilize the database and why it sometimes behaves in ways that you otherwise might not expect.

STEP 2 – Activity

Imagine that you are building a database for your university. The following diagram is called an entity–relationship diagram (ERD), as you will learn in Plug IT

In 3. It describes some of your university's data. Specifically, this part of the database stores data related to four entities: Department, Course, Student, and Grade.

The lines, or relationships, in the ERD tell us that

- Each department can have several courses, or it might not have any.
- Each course belongs to only one department.
- Each course can have several students, but it might not have any. (This would be a temporary situation when registration starts.)
- Each student in the course receives one grade.

- Each student can take several courses, but he or she might not be registered for any (yet).
- Each course gives that student one grade.

Based on this information, it is possible to begin building tables and establishing the relationships—that is, primary key to foreign key—between the tables.

STEP 3 – Deliverable

Submit your database file with at least the Department and Course tables. Include Department and Course information from your university in the database.

Additional help with this database skill is available in WileyPLUS. Open the "Microsoft Office 2013 Lab Manual Database Module: Access 2013," and review Lesson 2: Creating a Table Structure.

CHAPTER 3

Data and Knowledge Management

LEARNING OBJECTIVES >>>

3.1 Discuss ways that common challenges in managing data can be addressed using data governance.

3.2 Discuss the advantages and disadvantages of relational databases.

3.3 Define *Big Data*, and discuss its basic characteristics.

3.4 Recognize the necessary environment to successfully implement and maintain data warehouses.

3.5 Describe the benefits and challenges of implementing knowledge management systems in organizations.

OPENING CASE > Flurry Gathers Data from Smartphone Users

A woman waits in an airline lounge. She scrolls through her iPhone and launches a free mobile game. An instant before the app loads, there is an auction targeted specifically for her that is run by a company you have probably never heard of, called Flurry (www.flurry.com). Flurry presents the woman to dozens of advertisers in multiple capacities: a new mother, a business traveler, a fashion follower, a woman in her late 20's, and someone located near the Atlanta airport. In a fraction of a second, the Flurry auction picks the highest bidder, an advertiser who is also most likely to be offering goods or services that the woman might want. The woman then views an ad for designer sunglasses. Significantly, she is completely unaware that any of this background activity has occurred.

Flurry is in the business of mobile, *real-time bidding* (RTB). RTB refers to the process whereby advertising inventory is bought and sold on a per-impression basis, via instantaneous auction. With real-time bidding, advertising buyers bid on an impression, and the winner's ad is instantly displayed. (An impression is a measure of the number of times an ad is seen. Each time an ad displays is counted as one impression.) A typical transaction begins with a user visiting a mobile website. This visit triggers a bid request that can include various pieces of data such as the user's demographic information, browsing history, location, and the page being loaded. The request is

forwarded to an ad exchange, which submits it and the accompanying data to multiple advertisers.

© AndreyPopov/iStockphoto

In turn these advertisers submit bids in real time to place their ads. The impression goes to the highest bidder, and their ad is served on the mobile page. In essence, Flurry provides a high-speed auction system for targeting ads to individuals.

Mobile RTB permits advertisers to bid for each impression. This system is in sharp contrast to a static auction, in which the advertisers typically bundle impressions in groups of 1,000.

Flurry recently launched a pair of real-time mobile ad exchanges that uniquely handle both demand and supply in the ad marketplace. Flurry maintains it has sufficient data to link the two exchanges together.

Flurry's other major selling point is the massive amount of data that it collects on mobile app users. The reason that you have never heard of Flurry is that *you never put it on your smartphone.* App makers did. In fact, in a typical device the software is contained in 7–10 apps. Why? The answer is that Flurry gives away an analytics tool that informs app makers as to how people are using their apps. More than 400,000 apps now use the Flurry tool. In return, they send much of that user data back to Flurry. Flurry, therefore, has a pipeline to more than 1.2 billion devices globally. The company collects, on average, 3 terabytes of data *every day.*

Flurry solves a huge problem for apps that are designed to sell ads. On a desktop computer, advertisers can target consumers by using cookies, which are tiny data files attached your browser. (We discuss cookies in Chapter 7.) In contrast, mobile phones do not have cookies in their browser, so advertisers don't know who you are. Flurry's software assists advertisers by encrypting and combining identifying bits of data about each user to create an anonymous ID for each device. Specifically, it classifies each user into one of roughly 100 "personas"; that is, psychographic profiles such as "business travel" and "sports fanatic." Note that each persona has multiple characteristics. Advertisers use the characteristics of these personas to target ads.

While providing a major benefit to advertisers, Flurry's policy of encrypting personal information into an anonymous ID has raised serious concerns among privacy advocates. For example, one legal researcher in Europe charges that Flurry is already in breach of the European Union's (EU) E-Privacy Directive, which applies to mobile devices. The directive states that end users should be notified of cookies or tracking programs above and beyond the opt-out option that Flurry offers. The researcher maintains that to satisfy these requirements Flurry should be required to obtain consent from each user. Specifically, each time an EU resident opens an app that uses Flurry, a pop-up must inform this individual that the tool is tracking him or her. Flurry counters by reassuring users that the company does not collect personally identifiable information.

Sources: Compiled from K. Andrew, "Is Christmas Losing Its Sparkle? Flurry Points to Drop Off in Yuletide Download Growth," *PocketGamer.biz*, February 13, 2014; J. Aquino, "Why App Re-Engagement Ads Are the Next Big Thing in Mobile Advertising," *AdExchanger*, January 7, 2014; P. Olson, "We Know Everything," *Forbes*, November 18, 2013; C. Gibbs, "Real-Time Bidding for Mobile Ads: Promising in the Short Term, Questionable in the Long Term," *GigaOM*, May 8, 2013; P. Elmer-Dewitt, "Report: Americans Spend 2:38 Hours a Day Glued to Their Tablets and Smartphones," *CNN Money*, April 3, 2013; www.flurry.com, accessed February 22, 2014.

Questions

1. Do you feel that Flurry should be installed on your smartphone by various app makers without your consent? Why or why not? Support your answer.

2. What problems would Flurry encounter if someone other than the smartphone's owner uses the device? (*Hint:* Note how Flurry gathers data.)

3. Can Flurry survive the privacy concerns that are being raised about its business model?

Introduction

Information technologies and systems support organizations in managing—that is, acquiring, organizing, storing, accessing, analyzing, and interpreting—data. As you noted in Chapter 1, when these data are managed properly, they become *information* and then *knowledge.* (Recall our discussion of data, information, and knowledge in Section 1.2). Information and knowledge are invaluable organizational resources that can provide any organization with a competitive advantage.

So, just how important are data and data management to organizations? From confidential customer information, to intellectual property, to financial transactions, to social media posts, organizations possess massive amounts of data that are critical to their success. Of course, to benefit from these data, they need to manage them effectively. This type of management, however, comes at a huge cost. According to Symantec's (www.symantec.com) State of Information Survey, digital information costs organizations worldwide $1.1 trillion annually, and it makes up roughly half of an organization's total value. The survey found that large organizations spend an average of some $40 million annually to maintain and utilize data, and small-to-medium-sized businesses spend almost $350,000.

This chapter will examine the processes whereby data are transformed first into information and then into knowledge. Managing data is critically important in all organizations. Few business professionals are comfortable making or justifying business decisions that are not based on solid information. This is especially true today, when modern information systems make access to that information quick and easy. For example, we have technology that formats data in a way that managers and analysts can easily understand. Consequently, these professionals can access these data themselves and then analyze them according to their needs. The result is useful *information.* Executives can then apply their experience to use this information to address a business problem, thereby producing *knowledge.* Knowledge management, enabled by information technology, captures and stores knowledge in forms that all organizational employees can access and apply, thereby creating the flexible, powerful "learning organization."

Organizations store data in databases. Recall from Chapter 1 that a *database* is a collection of related data files or tables containing data. We discuss databases in Section 3.3.

Clearly, data and knowledge management are vital to modern organizations. But, why should *you* learn about them? The reason is that you will play an important role in the development of database applications. The structure and content of your organization's database depend on how users (you) define your business activities. For example, when database developers in the firm's MIS group build a database, they use a tool called entity-relationship (ER) modeling. This tool creates a model of how users view a business activity. When you understand how to create and interpret an ER model, then you can evaluate whether the developers have captured your business activities correctly.

Keep in mind that decisions about data last longer, and have a broader impact, than decisions about hardware or software. If decisions concerning hardware are wrong, then the equipment can be replaced relatively easily. If software decisions turn out to be incorrect, they can be modified, though not always painlessly or inexpensively. Database decisions, in contrast, are much harder to undo. Database design constrains what the organization can do with its data for a long time. Remember that business users will be stuck with a bad database design, while the programmers who created the database will quickly move on to their next projects. This is why it is so important to get database designs right the first time—and you will play a key role in these designs.

In addition, you might want to create a small, personal database using a software product such as Microsoft Access. In that case, you will need to be familiar with at least the basics of the product.

After the data are stored in your organization's databases, they must be accessible to users in a form that helps them make decisions. Organizations accomplish this objective by developing *data warehouses*. You should become familiar with data warehouses because they are invaluable decision-making tools. We discuss data warehouses in Section 3.4.

You will also make extensive use of your organization's knowledge base to perform your job. For example, when you are assigned a new project, you will likely research your firm's knowledge base to identify factors that contributed to the success (or failure) of previous, similar projects. We discuss knowledge management in Section 3.5.

You begin this chapter by examining the multiple problems involved in managing data. You then study the database approach that organizations use to help solve these problems. You turn your attention to Big Data, which organizations must manage in today's business environment. Next, you study data warehouses and data marts, and you learn how to utilize them for decision making. You finish the chapter by examining knowledge management.

3.1 Managing Data

All IT applications require data. These data should be of high quality, meaning that they should be accurate, complete, timely, consistent, accessible, relevant, and concise. Unfortunately, the process of acquiring, keeping, and managing data is becoming increasingly difficult.

The Difficulties of Managing Data

Because data are processed in several stages and often in multiple locations, they are frequently subject to problems and difficulties. Managing data in organizations is difficult for many reasons.

First, the amount of data increases exponentially with time. Much historical data must be kept for a long time, and new data are added rapidly. For example, to support millions of customers, large retailers such as Walmart have to manage petabytes of data. (A petabyte is approximately 1,000 terabytes, or trillions of bytes; see Plug IT In 2.)

In addition, data are also scattered throughout organizations, and they are collected by many individuals using various methods and devices. These data are frequently stored in numerous servers and locations and in different computing systems, databases, formats, and human and computer languages. IT's About Business 3.1 demonstrates how New York City is benefiting from the system it utilizes to manage its data management problems.

IT'S ABOUT BUSINESS 3.1

New York City Opens Its Data to All

Obtaining and using government data has never been easy. In most cases, these data are stored in proprietary formats. Historically it has been impossible to obtain these data and then to reconfigure them into accessible and open formats. To address this problem, New York City passed Local Law 11 of 1998, which mandated that city agencies systematically categorize data and make them available to the public.

To accommodate this initiative, the city had to redefine its data practices. So, in September 2012, it created an "Open Data Policy and Technical Standards Manual," which outlines how city agencies can gather, structure, and automate data flows to meet the requirements of Local Law 11. To ensure that the process was collaborative and that it met the needs of city residents, the city's Department of Information Technology and Telecommunications (DoITT) enlisted the help of the civic technology community and city agencies to create the document. The agency also launched a wiki (http://nycopendata.pediacities.com/wiki/index.php/NYC_Open_Data) that let citizens amend or comment on the document as it was being created.

This initiative has changed the way that the New York City government functions. As of mid-2014, the city had made some 2,000 unique representations of more than 1,000 raw datasets available at no charge via NYC Open-Data. These datasets include more than 60 city agencies, commissions, and business improvement districts. They span the breadth of city operations, including cultural affairs, education, health, housing, property, public safety, social services, and transportation. Most of the data can be viewed through a standard Web browser and downloaded in multiple file formats. The data include:

- Ten years of city performance data; building information, including building complaints, permits, and building jobs;
- Emergency information encompassing evacuation zones and evacuation centers;
- Crime data spanning the previous 12 years;
- A list of licensed taxi drivers that is updated on a daily basis;
- Data from the Department of Finance's Automated City Register Information System

© mura/iStockphoto

(ACRIS) that allows users to search property records for Manhattan, Queens, the Bronx, and Brooklyn;

- Data from the Environmental Control Board related to violations from 13 of NYC's ticket-issuing agencies;
- Daily updated data from the Department of Education on the status of school bus routes, bus delays, and daily school-wide attendance;
- Monthly data from the Department of Environmental Protection on wastewater treatment plant performance and weekly data on water quality;
- Annual data from the New York Police Department showing precinct-based comparisons of various crimes.

New York City is now using data and analysis in unprecedented ways to develop policies, drive operations, and improve services for its citizens. The goal is to enable developers, entrepreneurs, and academics to put data to work in new and innovative ways. Literally anyone can employ his or her skills and creativity to utilize these data to improve the city's quality of life.

One of the initiative's fundamental objectives is to encourage creative projects aimed at defining and illuminating public policy questions—for example, overlays of data pertaining to gang activity and the availability of youth programs, in-depth analysis of traffic crashes, school performance, noise problems, affordable housing, and homelessness. These are all age-old urban problems that can be examined in new ways as the data become available online and people use them in innovative ways.

FIN

This effort is ongoing. In mid-2014, the DoITT had published an open-data compliance plan that (1) categorizes all public datasets held by the city and (2) outlines plans to make these datasets available by the end of 2018. As New York City Council Member Gale Brewer noted, "We are putting an end to the days of city agencies posting information in confusing formats that cannot be searched or manipulated."

Sources: Compiled from A. Wiederspahn, "Manhattan's Borough President Logs In," *The New York World*, January 23, 2014; T. Cashman, "NYC Uses Open Data for Public Good," *Socrata.com*, October 16, 2013; M. Neubauer, "New York City's Latest Open Data Release," *TechPresident*, September 23, 2013; J. Naidoo, "Open Data Platforms: A Tool to Revolutionise Governance," *The Guardian*, April 16, 2013; S. Greengard, "New York City Takes an Open Approach to Data," *Baseline Magazine*, March 20, 2013; S. Goodyear, "Why New York City's Open Data Law Is Worth Caring About," *The Atlantic Cities*, March 8, 2013; B. Morrissey, "New York's Data Deluge Begins," *The New York World*, March 7, 2013; J. Pollicino, "Bloomberg Signs NYC 'Open Data Policy' into Law, Plans Web Portal for 2018," *Engadget.com*, March 12, 2012; "New York City to Mandate Open Data," *Government Technology*, March 2, 2012; www.nyc.gov, accessed April 15, 2014.

Questions

1. What are some other creative applications addressing city problems that could be developed using NYC's open data policy?

2. List some disadvantages of providing all city data in an open, accessible format.

Another problem is that data are generated from multiple sources: internal sources (for example, corporate databases and company documents); personal sources (for example, personal thoughts, opinions, and experiences); and external sources (for example, commercial databases, government reports, and corporate Web sites). Data also come from the Web, in the form of clickstream data. **Clickstream data** are those data that visitors and customers produce when they visit a Web site and click on hyperlinks (described in Chapter 4). Clickstream data provide a trail of the users' activities in the Web site, including user behavior and browsing patterns.

Adding to these problems is the fact that new sources of data, such as blogs, podcasts, videocasts, and RFID tags and other wireless sensors, are constantly being developed and the data these technologies generate must be managed. In addition, data degrade over time. For example, customers move to new addresses or change their names, companies go out of business or are bought, new products are developed, employees are hired or fired, and companies expand into new countries.

Data are also subject to *data rot*. Data rot refers primarily to problems with the media on which the data are stored. Over time, temperature, humidity, and exposure to light can cause physical problems with storage media and thus make it difficult to access the data. The second aspect of data rot is that finding the machines needed to access the data can be difficult. For example, it is almost impossible today to find 8-track players. Consequently, a library of 8-track tapes has become relatively worthless, unless you have a functioning 8-track player or you convert the tapes to a modern medium such as CDs.

Data security, quality, and integrity are critical, yet they are easily jeopardized. In addition, legal requirements relating to data differ among countries as well as among industries, and they change frequently.

Another problem arises from the fact that, over time, organizations have developed information systems for specific business processes, such as transaction processing, supply chain management, and customer relationship management. Information systems that specifically support these processes impose unique requirements on data, which results in repetition and conflicts across the organization. For example, the marketing function might maintain information on customers, sales territories, and markets. These data might be duplicated within the billing or customer service functions. This situation can produce inconsistent data within the enterprise. Inconsistent data prevent a company from developing a unified view of core business information—data concerning customers, products, finances, and so on—across the organization and its information systems.

Two other factors complicate data management. First, federal regulations—for example, the Sarbanes–Oxley Act of 2002—have made it a top priority for companies to better account for how they are managing information. Sarbanes–Oxley requires that (1) public companies evaluate and disclose the effectiveness of their internal financial controls and (2) independent auditors for these companies agree to this disclosure. The law also holds CEOs and CFOs personally responsible for such disclosures. If their companies lack satisfactory data management policies and fraud or a security breach occurs, the company officers could be held liable and face prosecution.

Second, companies are drowning in data, much of which is unstructured. As you have seen, the amount of data is increasing exponentially. To be profitable, companies must develop a strategy for managing these data effectively.

There are two additional problems with data management: Big Data and data hoarding. Big Data, which we discuss in chapter-closing case 1, is so important that we devote the entire Section 3.3 to this topic. We examine data hoarding in chapter-closing case 2.

Data Governance

To address the numerous problems associated with managing data, organizations are turning to data governance. **Data governance** is an approach to managing information across an entire organization. It involves a formal set of business processes and policies that are designed to ensure that data are handled in a certain, well-defined fashion. That is, the organization follows unambiguous rules for creating, collecting, handling, and protecting its information. The objective is to make information available, transparent, and useful for the people who are authorized to access it, from the moment it enters an organization until it is outdated and deleted.

One strategy for implementing data governance is master data management. **Master data management** is a process that spans all organizational business processes and applications. It provides companies with the ability to store, maintain, exchange, and synchronize a consistent, accurate, and timely "single version of the truth" for the company's master data.

Master data are a set of core data, such as customer, product, employee, vendor, geographic location, and so on, that span the enterprise information systems. It is important to distinguish between master data and transaction data. *Transaction data*, which are generated and captured by operational systems, describe the business's activities, or transactions. In contrast, master data are applied to multiple transactions and are used to categorize, aggregate, and evaluate the transaction data.

Let's look at an example of a transaction: You (Mary Jones) purchase one Samsung 42-inch plasma television, part number 1234, from Bill Roberts at Best Buy, for $2,000, on April 20, 2014. In this example, the master data are "product sold," "vendor," "salesperson," "store," "part number," "purchase price," and "date." When specific values are applied to the master data, then a transaction is represented. Therefore, transaction data would be, respectively, "42-inch plasma television," "Samsung," "Best Buy," "Bill Roberts," "1234," "$2,000," and "April 20, 2014."

An example of master data management is Dallas, Texas, which implemented a plan for digitizing the city's public and private records, such as paper documents, images, drawings, and video and audio content. The master database can be utilized by any of the 38 government departments that have appropriate access. The city is also integrating its financial and billing processes with its customer relationship management program. (You will learn about customer relationship management in Chapter 12.)

How will Dallas utilize this system? Imagine that the city experiences a water-main break. Before it implemented the system, repair crews had to search City Hall for records that were filed haphazardly. Once the workers found the hard-copy blueprints, they would take them to the site and, after examining them manually, would decide on a plan of action. In contrast, the new system delivers the blueprints wirelessly to the laptops of crews in the field, who can magnify or highlight areas of concern to generate a rapid response. This process reduces the time it takes to respond to an emergency by several hours.

Along with data governance, organizations use the database approach to efficiently and effectively manage their data. We discuss the database approach in the Section 3.2.

Apply The Concept 3.1

LEARNING OBJECTIVE 3.1 Discuss ways that common challenges in managing data can be addressed using data governance.

STEP 1 – Background (Here is what you are learning.)

The amount of data we create today is absolutely mind-boggling. EMC is a global company that focuses on helping organizations manage their data. Recently, the company sponsored a study to determine exactly how big the "digital universe" actually is and to envision its projected growth. There are some amazing findings in this study that point to a dramatic growth in data and an increase in virtual data centers. In the future (as it is now) it will be possible to run your information systems in data centers that do not operate on your premises.

STEP 2 – Activity (Here is what you do.)

Visit YouTube, and search for a video titled "IDC Study: Digital Universe: Sponsored by EMC." Although it is somewhat dated (2011), the concepts it presents are still valid. Watch this 5-minute video, and consider how the trends it presents relate to the challenges discussed in this section. Now, imagine that your parents own their own business. It is successful, but it is also struggling under pressure to upgrade IT services for its employees and customers. How could you help them look ahead to the future rather than keeping the status quo?

STEP 3 – Deliverable (Here is what you turn in.)

Write an e-mail to your parents to explain how data and data management are likely to evolve over the next 10 years. Describe the common challenges they face, and discuss how data governance can help address these issues. Also, based on the video, highlight the qualities they should look for in new employees. Finally, identify the types of training they should provide for their current employees.

Submit your e-mail to your instructor.

3.2 The Database Approach

From the mid-1950s, when businesses first adopted computer applications, until the early 1970s, organizations managed their data in a *file management environment*. This environment evolved because organizations typically automated their functions one application at a time. Therefore, the various automated systems developed independently from one another, without any overall planning. Each application required its own data, which were organized in a data file.

A **data file** is a collection of logically related records. In a file management environment, each application has a specific data file related to it. This file contains all of the data records the application requires. Over time, organizations developed numerous applications, each with an associated, application-specific data file.

For example, imagine that most of your information is stored in your university's central database, but a club to which you belong maintains its own files, the athletics department has separate files for student athletes, and your instructors maintain grade data on their personal computers. It is easy for your name to be misspelled in one of these databases or files but not in others. Similarly, if you move, then your address might be updated correctly in one database or file but not in others.

Using databases eliminates many problems that arose from previous methods of storing and accessing data, such as file management systems. Databases are arranged so that one set of software programs—the database management system—provides all users with

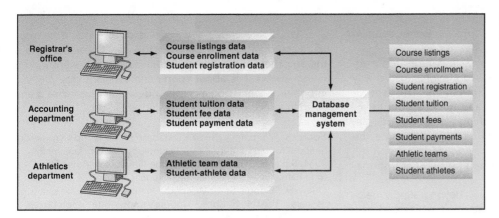

Figure 3.1 Database management system.

access to all of the data. (You will study database management systems later in this chapter.) Database systems minimize the following problems:

- *Data redundancy:* The same data are stored in multiple locations.
- *Data isolation:* Applications cannot access data associated with other applications.
- *Data inconsistency:* Various copies of the data do not agree.

In addition, database systems maximize the following:

- *Data security:* Because data are "put in one place" in databases, there is a risk of losing a lot of data at one time. Therefore, databases must have extremely high security measures in place to minimize mistakes and deter attacks.
- *Data integrity:* Data meet certain constraints; for example, there are no alphabetic characters in a Social Security number field.
- *Data independence:* Applications and data are independent of one another; that is, applications and data are not linked to each other, so all applications are able to access the same data.

FIGURE 3.1 illustrates a university database. Note that university applications from the registrar's office, the accounting department, and the athletics department access data through the database management system. Google's Knowledge Graph is an interesting example of a database, as you see in IT's About Business 3.2.

IT'S ABOUT BUSINESS 3.2

Google's Knowledge Graph

When a person conducts a Google search, the conventional results are based on algorithms that look for matches with the search terms, rather than the actual meaning of the information entered into the search box. Google's algorithms first refer to data from past searches to determine which words in the query are most likely to be important, based on how often they have been used by previous searchers. Next, software accesses a list of Web pages known to contain information related to these search terms. Finally, another calculation ranks the results displayed to the searcher.

Google's Knowledge Graph can be considered as a vast database that allows Google software to connect facts on people, places, and things to one another. The purpose of the Knowledge Graph is to enable Google's future products to truly understand the people who use them and the things they care about. The Knowledge Graph will enable searchers to use information to resolve their queries without having to navigate to other sites and assemble information themselves.

Google began the Knowledge Graph project when it bought a startup called Metaweb in 2010. At that time, Metaweb contained only 12 million entries. Today, the

Knowledge Graph has more than 600 million entries containing more than 18 billion links.

Google designed the Knowledge Graph to interpret a searcher's query in a much more sophisticated way and directly retrieve relevant information. The Knowledge Graph adds useful context and detail to the list of links that Google provides. Searching for certain people, places, or things produces a box of facts alongside the regular search results. However, the Knowledge Graph still uses data from past searches to determine what information is most relevant.

The Knowledge Graph has uses beyond simply helping people who are searching for facts online. For example, Google has integrated Knowledge Graph into YouTube, where it is being used to organize videos by topic and to suggest new videos to users, based on the videos they just watched. The Knowledge Graph can also be used to connect and recommend news articles based on specific facts mentioned in stories.

The Knowledge Graph is a database that represents what Google knows about the world. A good analogy for the Knowledge Graph is maps. For a maps product, you have to build a database of the real world and know that, in the physical world, there are entities called streets, rivers, and countries, among many others. Therefore, a map is a structure for the physical world.

The Knowledge Graph provides such a structure for the world of ideas and common sense. For example, Google has entities in the Knowledge Graph for foods, recipes, products, ideas in philosophy and history, famous people, and a myriad of others. The relationships among entities enable the Knowledge Graph to determine, for example, that these two people are married, that this place is located in this country, or that this person appears in this movie.

As Google crawls and indexes documents, it can now understand what each document is about. For example, if the document is about famous tennis players, the Knowledge Graph knows it is about sports and tennis. Every piece of information that Google crawls, indexes, or researches is analyzed in the context of the Knowledge Graph.

Sources: T. Simonite, "How a Database of the World's Knowledge Shapes Google's Future," *MIT Technology Review*, January 27, 2014; S. Perez, "Google's Knowledge Graph Now Being Used to Enhance Search Results," *TechCrunch*, January 22, 2014; A. Orlowski, "Google Stabs Wikipedia in the Front," *The Register*, January 13, 2014; G. Kohs, "Google's Knowledge Graph Boxes: Killing Wikipedia?" *Wikipediocracy*, January 6, 2014; J. Lee, "OK Google: 'The End of Search as We Know It'," *Search Engine Watch*, May 16, 2013; A. Isidoro, "Google's Knowledge Graph: One Step Closer to the Semantic Web?" *eConsultancy*, February 28, 2013; C. Newton, "How Google Is Taking the Knowledge Graph Global," *CNET*, December 14, 2012; T. Simonite, "Google's New Brain Could Have a Big Impact," *MIT Technology Review*, June 14, 2012.

Questions

1. Refer to the definition of a relational database. In what way can the Knowledge Graph be considered a database? Provide specific examples to support your answer.

2. Refer to the definition of an expert system in Plug IT In 5. Could the Knowledge Graph be considered an expert system? If so, provide a specific example to support your answer.

3. What are the advantages of the Knowledge Graph over traditional Google searches?

A database can contain vast amounts of data. To make these data more understandable and useful, they are arranged in a hierarchy.

The Data Hierarchy

Data are organized in a hierarchy that begins with bits and proceeds all the way to databases (see FIGURE 3.2). A **bit** (*binary digit*) represents the smallest unit of data a computer can process. The term *binary* means that a bit can consist only of a 0 or a 1. A group of eight bits, called a **byte**, represents a single character. A byte can be a letter, a number, or a symbol. A logical grouping of characters into a word, a small group of words, or an identification number is called a **field**. For example, a student's name in a university's computer files would appear in the "name" field, and her or his Social Security number would appear in the "Social Security number" field. Fields can also contain data other than text and numbers. They can contain an image, or any other type of multimedia. Examples are a motor vehicle department's licensing database that contains a driver's photograph and a field that contains a voice sample to authorize access to a secure facility.

A logical grouping of related fields, such as the student's name, the courses taken, the date, and the grade, comprises a **record**. In the Apple iTunes Store, a song is a field in a record,

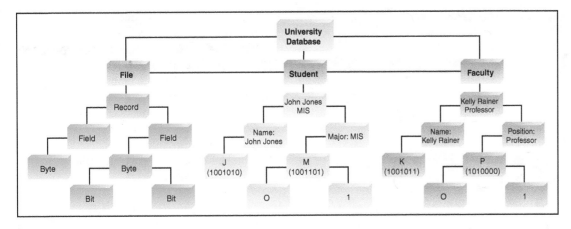

Figure 3.2 Hierarchy of data for a computer-based file.

with other fields containing the song's title, its price, and the album on which it appears. A logical grouping of related records is called a **data file** or a **table**. For example, a grouping of the records from a particular course, consisting of course number, professor, and students' grades, would constitute a data file for that course. Continuing up the hierarchy, a logical grouping of related files constitutes a *database*. Using the same example, the student course file could be grouped with files on students' personal histories and financial backgrounds to create a student database. In the next section, you will learn about relational database model.

The Relational Database Model

A **database management system (DBMS)** is a set of programs that provide users with tools to create and manage a database. Managing a database refers to the processes of adding, deleting, accessing, modifying, and analyzing data stored in a database. An organization can access the data by using query and reporting tools that are part of the DBMS or by using application programs specifically written to perform this function. DBMSs also provide the mechanisms for maintaining the integrity of stored data, managing security and user access, and recovering information if the system fails. Because databases and DBMSs are essential to all areas of business, they must be carefully managed.

There are a number of different database architectures, but we focus on the relational database model because it is popular and easy to use. Other database models (for example, the hierarchical and network models) are the responsibility of the MIS function and are not used by organizational employees. Popular examples of relational databases are Microsoft Access and Oracle.

Most business data—especially accounting and financial data—traditionally were organized into simple tables consisting of columns and rows. Tables allow people to compare information quickly by row or column. In addition, users can retrieve items rather easily by locating the point of intersection of a particular row and column.

The **relational database model** is based on the concept of two-dimensional tables. A relational database generally is not one big table—usually called a *flat file*—that contains all of the records and attributes. Such a design would entail far too much data redundancy. Instead, a relational database is usually designed with a number of related tables. Each of these tables contains records (listed in rows) and attributes (listed in columns).

To be valuable, a relational database must be organized so that users can retrieve, analyze, and understand the data they need. A key to designing an effective database is the data model. A **data model** is a diagram that represents entities in the database and their relationships. An **entity** is a person, place, thing, or event—such as a customer, an employee, or a product—about which information is maintained. Entities can typically be identified in the user's work environment. A record generally describes an entity. An **instance** of an entity refers to each row in a relational table, which is a specific, unique representation of the entity. For example, your university's student database contains an entity called STUDENT. An instance of the STUDENT entity would be a particular student. For

Figure 3.3 Student database example.

instance, you are an instance of the STUDENT entity in your university's student database.

Each characteristic or quality of a particular entity is called an **attribute**. For example, if our entities were a customer, an employee, and a product, entity attributes would include customer name, employee number, and product color.

Consider the relational database example about students diagrammed in FIGURE 3.3. The table contains data about the entity called students. As you can see, each row of the table corresponds to one student record. (You have your own row in your university's student database.) Attributes of the entity are student name, undergraduate major, grade point average, and graduation date. The rows are the records on Sally Adams, John Jones, Jane Lee, Kevin Durham, Juan Rodriguez, Stella Zubnicki, and Ben Jones. Of course, your university keeps much more data on you than our example shows. In fact, your university's student database probably keeps hundreds of attributes on each student.

Every record in the database must contain at least one field that uniquely identifies that record so that it can be retrieved, updated, and sorted. This identifier field (or attribute) is called the **primary key**. For example, a student record in a U.S. university would use a unique student number as its primary key. (*Note*: In the past, your Social Security number served as the primary key for your student record. However, for security reasons, this practice has been discontinued.) You see that Sally Adams is uniquely identified by her student ID of 012345.

In some cases, locating a particular record requires the use of secondary keys. A **secondary key** is another field that has some identifying information, but typically does not identify the record with complete accuracy. For example, the student's major might be a secondary key if a user wanted to identify all of the students majoring in a particular field of study. It should not be the primary key, however, because many students can have the same major. Therefore, it cannot uniquely identify an individual student.

A **foreign key** is a field (or group of fields) in one table that uniquely identifies a row of another table. A foreign key is used to establish and enforce a link between two tables. We discuss foreign keys in more detail in Plug IT In 3.

Organizations implement databases to efficiently and effectively manage their data. There are a variety of operations that can be performed on databases. We look at three of these operations in detail in Plug IT In 3: query languages, normalization, and joins.

As we noted earlier in this chapter, organizations must manage huge quantities of data. Such data consist of structured and unstructured data and are called Big Data (discussed in Section 3.3). To manage Big Data, many organizations are using special types of databases, which we also discuss in Section 3.3.

Because databases typically process data in real time (or near real time), it is not practical to allow users access to the databases. After all, the data will change while the user is looking at them! As a result, data warehouses have been developed to allow users to access data for decision making. You will learn about data warehouses in Section 3.4.

Apply The Concept 3.2

LEARNING OBJECTIVE 3.2 Discuss the advantages and disadvantages of relational databases.

STEP 1 – Background

This section has exposed you to the advantages and disadvantages of using a relational database. This is one of those concepts that cannot really be appreciated until you work through the process of designing a database. Even though very few people go on to become database administrators, it is still valuable to have some understanding of how a database is built and administered. In this activity you will be presented with a scenario, and you will then apply the concepts you have just read about. In the process you will develop a solid foundation to discuss the advantages and disadvantages of relational databases.

— BEFORE *YOU GO ON*.... —

1. What is a data model?
2. What is a primary key? A secondary key?
3. What is an entity? An attribute? An instance?
4. What are the advantages and disadvantages of relational databases?

STEP 2 – Activity

You are employed as the coordinator of multiple ongoing projects within a company. Your responsibilities include keeping track of the company's commercial projects, its employees, and the employees' participation in each project. Usually, a project will have multiple team members, but some projects have not been assigned to any team members. For each project, the company must keep track of the project's title, description, location, estimated budget, and due date.

Each employee can be assigned to one or more projects. Some employees can also be on leave and therefore will not be working on any assignments. Project leaders usually need to know the following information about their team members: name, address, phone number, Social Security number, highest degree attained, and his or her expertise (for example, IS, accounting, marketing, and finance).

Your manager has instructed you to present an overview of the advantages and disadvantages of a database that would support the company's efforts to manage the data described in this scenario. At a minimum, you should define the tables and the relationships among the key variables to provide structure to the information that would be included in the database.

STEP 3 – Deliverable

Using the relational database design you created in Step 2, prepare a discussion of the advantages and disadvantages of this database. How will it benefit the company? What additional challenges might it create?

Submit your design and your discussion to your instructor.

3.3 Big Data

We are accumulating data and information at an increasingly rapid pace from many diverse sources. In fact, organizations are capturing data about almost all events—including events that, in the past, firms never used to think of as data at all, such as a person's location, the vibrations and temperature of an engine, and the stress at numerous points on a bridge—and then analyzing those data.

Organizations and individuals must process a vast amount of data that continues to rapidly increase. According to IDC (a technology research firm), the world generates exabytes of data each year (an exabyte is 1 trillion terabytes). Furthermore, the amount of data produced worldwide is increasing by 50 percent each year. As we discussed at the beginning of the chapter, we refer to the superabundance of data available today as Big Data. That is, **Big Data** is a collection of data so large and complex that it is difficult to manage using traditional database management systems. (We capitalize *Big Data* to distinguish the term from large amounts of traditional data.)

We are awash in data that we have to make sense of and manage. To deal with the growth and the diverse nature of digital data, organizations must employ sophisticated techniques for data management.

At its core, Big Data is about predictions. Predictions do not come from "teaching" computers to "think" like humans. Instead, predictions come from applying mathematics to huge quantities of data to infer probabilities. Consider these examples:

- The likelihood that an e-mail message is spam;
- The likelihood that the typed letters "teh" are supposed to be "the";

- The likelihood that the trajectory and velocity of a person jaywalking indicates that he will make it across the street in time, meaning that a self-driving car need only slow down slightly.

Big Data systems perform well because they contain huge amounts of data on which to base their predictions. Moreover, these systems are configured to improve themselves over time by searching for the most valuable signals and patterns as more data are input.

Defining Big Data

It is difficult to define Big Data. Here we present two descriptions of the phenomenon. First, the technology research firm Gartner (www.gartner.com) defines Big Data as diverse, high-volume, high-velocity information assets that require new forms of processing to enable enhanced decision making, insight discovery, and process optimization. Second, the Big Data Institute (TBDI; www.the-bigdatainstitute.com) defines Big Data as vast datasets that:

- Exhibit variety;
- Include structured, unstructured, and semi-structured data;
- Are generated at high velocity with an uncertain pattern;
- Do not fit neatly into traditional, structured, relational databases; and
- Can be captured, processed, transformed, and analyzed in a reasonable amount of time only by sophisticated information systems.

Big Data generally consists of the following:

- Traditional enterprise data—examples are customer information from customer relationship management systems, transactional enterprise resource planning data, Web store transactions, operations data, and general ledger data.
- Machine-generated/sensor data—examples are smart meters; manufacturing sensors; sensors integrated into smartphones, automobiles, airplane engines, and industrial machines; equipment logs; and trading systems data.
- Social data—examples are customer feedback comments; microblogging sites such as Twitter; and social media sites such as Facebook, YouTube, and LinkedIn.
- Images captured by billions of devices located throughout the world, from digital cameras and camera phones to medical scanners and security cameras.

Let's take a look at a few specific examples of Big Data:

- In 2014 Google was processing more than 27 petabytes of data every day.
- Facebook members upload more than 10 million new photos every hour. In addition, they click a "like" button or leave a comment nearly 3 billion times every day.
- The 800 million monthly users of Google's YouTube service upload more than an hour of video every second.
- The number of messages on Twitter is growing at 200 percent every year. By mid-2014, the volume exceeded 550 million tweets per day.
- As recently as the year 2000, only 25 percent of the stored information in the world was digital. The other 75 percent was analog; that is, it was stored on paper, film, vinyl records, and the like. By 2014, the amount of stored information in the world was over 98 percent digital and less than 2 percent non-digital.

Characteristics of Big Data

Big Data has three distinct characteristics: volume, velocity, and variety. These characteristics distinguish Big Data from traditional data.

- *Volume*: We have noted the incredible volume of Big Data in this chapter. Consider machine-generated data, which are generated in much larger quantities than nontraditional data. For instance, sensors in a single jet engine can generate 10 terabytes of data in 30 minutes. With more than 25,000 airline flights per day, the daily volume of data from just this single source is incredible. Smart electrical meters, sensors in heavy industrial equipment, and telemetry from automobiles compound the volume problem.

- *Velocity:* The rate at which data flow into an organization is rapidly increasing. Velocity is critical because it increases the speed of the feedback loop between a company and its customers. For example, the Internet and mobile technology enable online retailers to compile histories not only on final sales, but on their customers' every click and interaction. Companies that can quickly utilize that information—for example, by recommending additional purchases—gain competitive advantage.

- *Variety:* Traditional data formats tend to be structured and relatively well described, and they change slowly. Traditional data include financial market data, point-of-sale transactions, and much more. In contrast, Big Data formats change rapidly. They include satellite imagery, broadcast audio streams, digital music files, Web page content, scans of government documents, and comments posted on social networks.

Irrespective of their source, structure, format, and frequency, Big Data are valuable. If certain types of data appear to have no value today, it is because we have not yet been able to analyze them effectively. For example, several years ago when Google began harnessing satellite imagery, capturing street views, and then sharing these geographical data for free, few people understood its value. Today, we recognize that such data are incredibly valuable because analyses of Big Data yield deep insights. We discuss analytics in detail in Chapter 5.

Issues with Big Data

Despite its extreme value, Big Data does have issues. In this section, we take a look at data integrity, data quality, and the nuances of analysis that are worth noting.

- *Big Data can come from untrusted sources:* As we discussed above, one of the characteristics of Big Data is variety, meaning that Big Data can come from numerous, widely varied sources. These sources may be internal or external to the organization. For instance, a company might want to integrate data from unstructured sources such as e-mails, call center notes, and social media posts with structured data about its customers from its data warehouse. The question is, How trustworthy are those external sources of data? For example, how trustworthy is a tweet? The data may come from an unverified source. Further, the data itself, reported by the source, can be false or misleading.

- *Big Data is dirty:* Dirty data refers to inaccurate, incomplete, incorrect, duplicate, or erroneous data. Examples of such problems are misspelling of words and duplicate data such as retweets or company press releases that appear numerous times in social media.

  Suppose a company is interested in performing a competitive analysis using social media data. The company wants to see how often a competitor's product appears in social media outlets as well as the sentiments associated with those posts. The company notices that the number of positive posts about the competitor is twice as large the number of positive posts about itself. This finding could simply be a case where the competitor is pushing out its press releases to multiple sources, in essence "blowing its own horn." Alternatively, the competitor could be getting many people to retweet an announcement.

- *Big Data changes, especially in data streams:* Organizations must be aware that data quality in an analysis can change, or the data itself can change, because the conditions under which the data are captured can change. For instance, imagine a utility company that analyzes weather data and smart-meter data to predict customer power usage. What happens when the utility is analyzing this data in real time and it discovers data missing from some of its smart meters?

Managing Big Data

Big Data makes it possible to do many things that were previously impossible; for example, to spot business trends more rapidly and accurately, prevent disease, track crime, and so on. When properly analyzed, Big Data can reveal valuable patterns and information that were previously hidden because of the amount of work required to discover them. Leading corporations, such as Walmart and Google, have been able to process Big Data for years, but only at great expense. Today's hardware, cloud computing (see Plug IT In 4), and open-source software make processing Big Data affordable for most organizations.

The first step for many organizations toward managing Big Data was to integrate information silos into a database environment and then to develop data warehouses for decision making. (An information silo is an information system that does not communicate with other, related information systems in an organization.) After completing this step, many organizations turned their attention to the business of information management—making sense of their proliferating data. In recent years, Oracle, IBM, Microsoft, and SAP have spent billions of dollars purchasing software firms that specialize in data management and business intelligence. (You will learn about business intelligence in Chapter 5.)

In addition, many organizations are turning to NoSQL databases (think of them as "not only SQL" (structured query language) databases) to process Big Data. (We discuss SQL in Plug IT In #3). These databases provide an alternative for firms that have more and different kinds of data (Big Data) in addition to the traditional, structured data that fit neatly into the rows and columns of relational databases.

As you have seen in this chapter, traditional relational databases such as Oracle and MySQL store data in tables organized into rows and columns. Recall that each row is associated with a unique record and each column is associated with a field that defines an attribute of that account.

In contrast, NoSQL databases can manipulate structured as well as unstructured data and inconsistent or missing data. For this reason, NoSQL databases are particularly useful when working with Big Data. Many products utilize NoSQL databases, including Cassandra (http://cassandra.apache.org), CouchDB (http://couchdb.apache.org), MongoDB (www.mongodb.org), and Hadoop (http://hadoop.apache.org). IT's About Business 3.3 focuses on MongoDB, a leading NoSQL database vendor.

IT'S ABOUT BUSINESS 3.3

The MetLife Wall

Founded in 1868, the Metropolitan Life Insurance Company (MetLife; www.metlife.com) is among the largest global providers of insurance, annuities, and employee benefit programs, with 90 million customers in more than 60 countries. As a result of acquisitions, new products, and various software deployments over the years, MetLife had grown into a $68 billion company with 70 software systems that could not communicate with one another. To make matters worse, each system had its own database. These problems made it difficult for MetLife to communicate with its policyholders. For example, customer service representatives could not always tell if a client with an automobile insurance policy also had a disability plan with the company.

FIN

MetLife had to rely heavily on humans to integrate its separate systems and databases. Customer service representatives and claims researchers had to access multiple applications and utilize as many as 40 screens just to gather all the data and documents required to answer customer questions. That process decreased both worker productivity and customer satisfaction. Because MetLife offers multiple lines of insurance as well as annuities and other lines of business, it was critical that the company develop a unified, consolidated view of its customers.

To accomplish this task, in 2013, MetLife turned to MongoDB, a document-oriented NoSQL database, to integrate all relevant customer data on a single screen. MetLife called the project, which was inspired by the Facebook Wall, the MetLife Wall. With the deployment of the Wall, MetLife representatives no longer view policyholders merely as ID numbers scattered among different insurance products. The MetLife Wall integrates different sources of customer data to let representatives review customers' histories, their conversations with the company, any claims filed and paid, and their various policies—all on a simple timeline. Representatives can access these data with one click, and they can settle issues more efficiently and quickly assess how a customer feels about the company. The MetLife Wall has significantly increased customer satisfaction. Since the company implemented a limited launch in April 2013, more than 1000 customer service representatives and claims researchers in the United States and Europe have been using MetLife's Wall successfully.

In addition to the MetLife Wall, MetLife is using MongoDB for two other applications. The first is a recruiting site to store résumés, which makes the résumés easier to analyze than would be the case if the résumés were stored in Word files or PDFs. Next, MetLife deployed a customer-facing mobile app that allows its customers to upload documents, videos, photos, and other content that they can schedule to be shared only with selected individuals at some future

date. For example, access to a life insurance policy can be made available to the beneficiaries after the policy holder has passed away.

Sources: Compiled from "5 Lessons Learned from the MetLife Wall," *inetpost.mobi*, May 1, 2014; J. Alserver, "Technology Is the Best Policy," *Fortune*, November 18, 2013; J. Alsever, "At MetLife, Technology Is the Best Policy," *CNN Money*, October 31, 2013; K. Nicole, "MetLife's Big Data Revolution," *Forbes*, October 11, 2013; D. Henschen, "When NoSQL Makes Sense," *InformationWeek*, October 7, 2013; D. Harris, "The Promise of Better Data Has MetLife Investing $300 M in New Tech," *GigaOM*, May 7, 2013; www.metlife.com, accessed February 27, 2014.

Questions

1. Describe the problems that MetLife was experiencing with customer data before it implemented the MetLife Wall.

2. Describe how these problems originated.

Putting Big Data to Use

Organizations must manage Big Data and gain value from it. There are several ways to do this.

Making Big Data Available. Making Big Data available for relevant stakeholders can help organizations gain value. For example, consider open data in the public sector. Open data is accessible public data that individuals and organizations can use to create new businesses and solve complex problems. In particular, government agencies gather very large amounts of data, some of which is Big Data. Making that data available can provide economic benefits. The Open Data 500 study at the GovLab at New York University found some 500 examples of U.S.-based companies whose business models depend on analyzing open government data.

Enabling Organizations to Conduct Experiments. Big Data allows organizations to improve performance by conducting controlled experiments. For example, Amazon (and many other companies such as Google and LinkedIn) constantly experiments by offering slight different "looks" on its Web site. These experiments are called A/B experiments, because each experiment has only two possible outcomes. Here is how an experiment works: Hundreds of thousands of people who click on Amazon.com will see one version of the Web site, and hundreds of thousands of others will see the other version. One experiment might change the location of the "Buy" button on the Web page. Another might change the size of a particular font on the Web page. (Amazon conducts literally hundreds of A/B experiments when evaluating its Web page.) Amazon captures data on an assortment of variables from all of the clicks, including which pages users visited, the time they spent on each page, and whether the click led to a purchase. Amazon then analyzes all of these data to "tweak" its Web site to provide the optimal user experience.

Micro-Segmentation of Customers. Segmentation of a company's customers means dividing them up into groups that share one or more characteristics. Micro-segmentation simply means dividing customers up into very small groups, or even down to the individual level.

For example, Paytronix Systems (www.paytronix.com) provides loyalty and rewards program software for thousands of different restaurants. Paytronix gathers restaurant guest data from a variety of sources beyond loyalty and gift programs, including social media.

Paytronix analyzes this Big Data to help its restaurant clients micro-segment their guests. Restaurant managers are now able to more precisely customize their loyalty and gift programs. In doing so, the managers are noting improved performance in their restaurants in terms of profitability and customer satisfaction.

Creating New Business Models. Companies are able to use Big Data to create new business models. For example, a commercial transportation company operated a large fleet of large, long-haul trucks. The company recently placed sensors on all its trucks. These sensors wirelessly communicate large amounts of information to the company, a process called telematics. The sensors collect data on vehicle usage (including acceleration, braking, cornering, etc.), driver performance, and vehicle maintenance.

By analyzing this Big Data, the transportation company was able to improve the condition of its trucks through near-real-time analysis that proactively suggested preventive maintenance. In addition, the company was able to improve the driving skills of its operators by analyzing their driving styles.

The transportation company then made its Big Data available to its insurance carrier. Using this data, the insurance carrier performed risk analysis on driver behavior and the condition of the trucks, resulting in a more precise assessment. The insurance carrier offered the transportation company a new pricing model that lowered the transportation company's premiums by 10 percent.

Organizations Can Analyze Far More Data. In some cases, organizations can even process all the data relating to a particular phenomenon, meaning that they do not have to rely as much on sampling. Random sampling works well, but it is not as effective as analyzing an entire dataset. In addition, random sampling has some basic weaknesses. To begin with, its accuracy depends on ensuring randomness when collecting the sample data. However, achieving such randomness is problematic. Systematic biases in the process of data collection can cause the results to be highly inaccurate. For example, consider political polling using landline phones. This sample tends to exclude people who use only cell phones. This bias can seriously skew the results, because cell phone users are typically younger and more liberal than people who rely primarily on landline phones.

BEFORE *YOU GO ON....*

1. Define Big Data.
2. Describe the characteristics of Big Data.
3. Describe how companies can use Big Data to gain competitive advantage.

Apply The Concept 3.3

LEARNING OBJECTIVE 3.3 Define Big Data, and discuss its basic characteristics.

STEP 1 – Background

This section describes Big Data as an ongoing phenomenon that is providing businesses with access to vast amounts of information. The key "ingredients" that make the Big Data phenomenon a reality are volume, velocity, and variety. These elements are described in Section 3.2.

STEP 2 – Activity

TIBCO is a company that provides a real-time event-processing software platform that brings customers and vendors together in a very interactive and engaging way. It uses vast amounts of data (volume), in real time (velocity), from multiple sources (variety) to bring this solution to its customers. Visit YouTube, and search for two videos—"Deliver Personalized Retail Experiences Using Big Data" and "Harnessing Big Data and Social Media to Engage Customers"—both by user "TIBCOSoftware."

As you view these videos, watch carefully for the three "ingredients" mentioned above.

STEP 3 – Deliverable

Choose one of the videos mentioned in Step 2, and write a review. In your review, define Big Data, and discuss its basic characteristics relative to the video.

Submit your review to your instructor.

3.4 Data Warehouses and Data Marts

Today, the most successful companies are those that can respond quickly and flexibly to market changes and opportunities. A key to this response is the effective and efficient use of data and information by analysts and managers. The challenge is providing users with access to corporate data so that they can analyze the data to make better decisions. Let's look at an example. If the manager of a local bookstore wanted to know the profit margin on used books at her store, she could obtain that information from her database, using SQL or QBE. However, if she needed to know the trend in the profit margins on used books over the past 10 years, she would have to construct a very complicated SQL or QBE query.

This example illustrates several reasons why organizations are building data warehouses and/or data marts. First, the bookstore's databases contain the necessary information to answer the manager's query, but this information is not organized in a way that makes it easy for her to find what she needs. Second, the organization's databases are designed to process millions of transactions every day. Therefore, complicated queries might take a long time to answer, and they also might degrade the performance of the databases. Third, transactional databases are designed to be updated. This update process requires extra processing. Data warehouses and data marts are read-only, and the extra processing is eliminated because data already contained in the data warehouse are not updated. Fourth, transactional databases are designed to access a single record at a time. Data warehouses are designed to access large groups of related records.

As a result of these problems, companies are using a variety of tools with data warehouses and data marts to make it easier and faster for users to access, analyze, and query data. You will learn about these tools in Chapter 5 on Business Analytics.

Describing Data Warehouses and Data Marts

In general, data warehouses and data marts support business intelligence (BI) applications. As you will see in Chapter 5, business intelligence encompasses a broad category of applications, technologies, and processes for gathering, storing, accessing, and analyzing data to help business users make better decisions. A **data warehouse** is a repository of historical data that are organized by subject to support decision makers in the organization.

Because data warehouses are so expensive, they are used primarily by large companies. A **data mart** is a low-cost, scaled-down version of a data warehouse that is designed for the end-user needs in a strategic business unit (SBU) or an individual department. Data marts can be implemented more quickly than data warehouses, often in less than 90 days. Further, they support local rather than central control by conferring power on the user group. Typically, groups that need a single or a few BI applications require only a data mart, rather than a data warehouse.

The basic characteristics of data warehouses and data marts include the following:

- *Organized by business dimension or subject.* Data are organized by subject—for example, by customer, vendor, product, price level, and region. This arrangement differs from transactional systems, where data are organized by business process, such as order entry, inventory control, and accounts receivable.
- *Use online analytical processing.* Typically, organizational databases are oriented toward handling transactions. That is, databases use *online transaction processing* (OLTP), where business transactions are processed online as soon as they occur. The objectives are speed and efficiency, which are critical to a successful Internet-based business operation. Data warehouses and data marts, which are designed to support decision makers but not OLTP, use online analytical processing. *Online analytical processing* (OLAP) involves the analysis of accumulated data by end users. We consider OLAP in greater detail in Chapter 5.
- *Integrated.* Data are collected from multiple systems and then integrated around subjects. For example, customer data may be extracted from internal (and external) systems and then integrated around a customer identifier, thereby creating a comprehensive view of the customer.

- *Time variant.* Data warehouses and data marts maintain historical data (i.e., data that include time as a variable). Unlike transactional systems, which maintain only recent data (such as for the last day, week, or month), a warehouse or mart may store years of data. Organizations utilize historical data to detect deviations, trends, and long-term relationships.

- *Nonvolatile.* Data warehouses and data marts are nonvolatile—that is, users cannot change or update the data. Therefore, the warehouse or mart reflects history, which, as we just saw, is critical for identifying and analyzing trends. Warehouses and marts are updated, but through IT-controlled load processes rather than by users.

- *Multidimensional.* Typically the data warehouse or mart uses a multidimensional data structure. Recall that relational databases store data in two-dimensional tables. In contrast, data warehouses and marts store data in more than two dimensions. For this reason, the data are said to be stored in a **multidimensional structure**. A common representation for this multidimensional structure is the *data cube*.

The data in data warehouses and marts are organized by *business dimensions*, which are subjects such as product, geographic area, and time period that represent the edges of the data cube. If you look ahead briefly to FIGURE 3.6 for an example of a data cube, you see that the product dimension is comprised of nuts, screws, bolts, and washers; the geographic area dimension is comprised of East, West, and Central; and the time period dimension is comprised of 2012, 2013, and 2014. Users can view and analyze data from the perspective of these business dimensions. This analysis is intuitive because the dimensions are presented in business terms that users can easily understand.

A Generic Data Warehouse Environment

The environment for data warehouses and marts includes the following:

- Source systems that provide data to the warehouse or mart
- Data-integration technology and processes that prepare the data for use
- Different architectures for storing data in an organization's data warehouse or data marts
- Different tools and applications for the variety of users. (You will learn about these tools and applications in Chapter 5.)
- Metadata, data-quality, and governance processes that ensure that the warehouse or mart meets its purposes

FIGURE 3.4 depicts a generic data warehouse/data mart environment. Let's drill-down into the component parts.

Figure 3.4 Data warehouse framework.

(a) 2012

Product	Region	Sales
Nuts	East	50
Nuts	West	60
Nuts	Central	100
Screws	East	40
Screws	West	70
Screws	Central	80
Bolts	East	90
Bolts	West	120
Bolts	Central	140
Washers	East	20
Washers	West	10
Washers	Central	30

(b) 2013

Product	Region	Sales
Nuts	East	60
Nuts	West	70
Nuts	Central	110
Screws	East	50
Screws	West	80
Screws	Central	90
Bolts	East	100
Bolts	West	130
Bolts	Central	150
Washers	East	30
Washers	West	20
Washers	Central	40

(c) 2014

Product	Region	Sales
Nuts	East	70
Nuts	West	80
Nuts	Central	120
Screws	East	60
Screws	West	90
Screws	Central	100
Bolts	East	110
Bolts	West	140
Bolts	Central	160
Washers	East	40
Washers	West	30
Washers	Central	50

Figure 3.5 Relational databases.

Source Systems. There is typically some "organizational pain" (i.e., business need) that motivates a firm to develop its BI capabilities. Working backward, this pain leads to information requirements, BI applications, and source system data requirements. The data requirements can range from a single source system, as in the case of a data mart, to hundreds of source systems, as in the case of an enterprisewide data warehouse.

Modern organizations can select from a variety of source systems: operational/transactional systems, enterprise resource planning (ERP) systems, Web site data, third-party data (e.g., customer demographic data), and more. The trend is to include more types of data (e.g., sensing data from RFID tags). These source systems often use different software packages (e.g., IBM, Oracle) and store data in different formats (e.g., relational, hierarchical).

A common source for the data in data warehouses is the company's operational databases, which can be relational databases. To differentiate between relational databases and multidimensional data warehouses and marts, imagine your company manufactures four products—nuts, screws, bolts, and washers—and has sold them in three territories—East, West, and Central—for the previous three years—2012, 2013, and 2014. In a relational database, these sales data would resemble FIGURE 3.5(a)–(c). In a multidimensional database, in contrast, these data would be represented by a three-dimensional matrix (or data cube), as depicted in FIGURE 3.6. This matrix represents sales *dimensioned by* products and regions and year. Notice that FIGURE 3.5(a) presents only sales for 2012. Sales for 2013 and 2014 are presented in FIGURE 3.5(b) and (c), respectively. FIGURE 3.7(a)–(c) illustrates the equivalence between these relational and multidimensional databases.

Unfortunately, many source systems that have been in use for years contain "bad data" (e.g., missing or incorrect data) and are poorly documented. As a result, data-profiling software should be used at the beginning of a warehousing project to better understand the data. For example, this software can provide statistics on missing data, identify possible primary and foreign keys, and reveal how derived values (e.g., column 3 = column 1 + column 2) are calculated. Subject area database specialists (e.g., marketing, human resources) can also assist in understanding and accessing the data in source systems.

Organizations need to address other source systems issues as well. Often there are multiple systems that contain some of the same data and the best system must be selected as the source system. Organizations must also decide how granular (i.e., detailed) the data should be. For example, does the organization need daily sales figures or data at the individual transaction level? The conventional wisdom is that it is best to store data at a highly granular level because someone will likely request the data at some point.

Figure 3.6 Data cube.

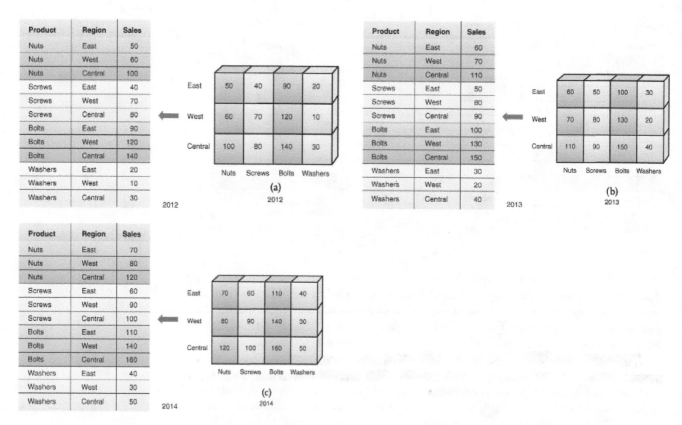

Figure 3.7 Equivalence between relational and multidimensional databases.

Data Integration. In addition to storing data in their source systems, organizations need to extract the data, transform them, and then load them into a data mart or warehouse. This process is often called ETL, although the term *data integration* is increasingly being used to reflect the growing number of ways that source system data can be handled. For example, in some cases, data are extracted, loaded into a mart or warehouse, and then transformed (i.e., ELT rather than ETL).

Data extraction can be performed either by handwritten code (e.g., SQL queries) or by commercial data-integration software. Most companies employ commercial software. This software makes it relatively easy to specify the tables and attributes in the source systems that are to be used, map and schedule the movement of the data to the target (e.g., a data mart or warehouse), make the required transformations, and ultimately load the data.

After the data are extracted they are transformed to make them more useful. For example, data from different systems may be integrated around a common key, such as a customer identification number. Organizations adopt this approach to create a 360-degree view of all of their interactions with their customers. As an example of this process, consider a bank. Customers can engage in a variety of interactions: visiting a branch, banking online, using an ATM, obtaining a car loan, and more. The systems for these touch points—defined as the numerous ways that organizations interact with customers, such as e-mail, the Web, direct contact, and the telephone—are typically independent of one another. To obtain a holistic picture of how customers are using the bank, the bank must integrate the data from the various source systems into a data mart or warehouse.

Other kinds of transformations also take place. For example, format changes to the data may be required, such as using *male* and *female* to denote gender, as opposed to 0 and 1 or M and F. Aggregations may be performed, say on sales figures, so that queries can use the summaries rather than recalculating them each time. Data-cleansing software may be used to "clean up" the data; for example, eliminating duplicate records for the same customer.

Finally, data are loaded into the warehouse or mart during a specific period known as the "load window." This window is becoming smaller as companies seek to store ever-fresher data in their warehouses. For this reason, many companies have moved to real-time data warehousing where data are moved (using data-integration processes) from source systems to the data warehouse or mart almost instantly. For example, within 15 minutes of a purchase at Walmart, the details of the sale have been loaded into a warehouse and are available for analysis.

Storing the Data. A variety of architectures can be used to store decision-support data. The most common architecture is *one central enterprise data warehouse*, without data marts. Most organizations use this approach, because the data stored in the warehouse are accessed by all users and represent the *single version of the truth*.

Another architecture is *independent data marts*. This architecture stores data for a single application or a few applications, such as marketing and finance. Limited thought is given to how the data might be used for other applications or by other functional areas in the organization. This is a very application-centric approach to storing data.

The independent data mart architecture is not particularly effective. Although it may meet a specific organizational need, it does not reflect an enterprise-wide approach to data management. Instead, the various organizational units create independent data marts. Not only are these marts expensive to build and maintain, but they often contain inconsistent data. For example, they may have inconsistent data definitions such as: What is a customer? Is a particular individual a potential or current customer? They might also use different source systems (which may have different data for the same item, such as a customer address). Although independent data marts are an organizational reality, larger companies have increasingly moved to data warehouses.

Still another data warehouse architecture is the *hub and spoke*. This architecture contains a central data warehouse that stores the data plus multiple dependent data marts that source their data from the central repository. Because the marts obtain their data from the central repository, the data in these marts still comprise the *single version of the truth* for decision-support purposes.

The dependent data marts store the data in a format that is appropriate for how the data will be used and for providing faster response times to queries and applications. As you have learned, users can view and analyze data from the perspective of business dimensions and measures. This analysis is intuitive because the dimensions are in business terms, easily understood by users.

Metadata. It is important to maintain data about the data, known as *metadata*, in the data warehouse. Both the IT personnel who operate and manage the data warehouse and the users who access the data need metadata. IT personnel need information about data sources; database, table, and column names; refresh schedules; and data-usage measures. Users' needs include data definitions, report/query tools, report distribution information, and contact information for the help desk.

Data Quality. The quality of the data in the warehouse must meet users' needs. If it does not, users will not trust the data and ultimately will not use it. Most organizations find that the quality of the data in source systems is poor and must be improved before the data can be used in the data warehouse. Some of the data can be improved with data-cleansing software, but the better, long-term solution is to improve the quality at the source system level. This approach requires the business owners of the data to assume responsibility for making any necessary changes to implement this solution.

To illustrate this point, consider the case of a large hotel chain that wanted to conduct targeted marketing promotions using zip code data it collected from its guests when they checked in. When the company analyzed the zip code data, they discovered that many of the zip codes were 99999. How did this error occur? The answer is that the clerks were not asking customers for their zip codes, but they needed to enter something to complete the registration process. A short-term solution to this problem was to conduct the marketing campaign using city and state data instead of zip codes. The long-term solution was to make certain the clerks entered the actual zip codes. The latter solution required the hotel managers to take the responsibility for making certain their clerks enter the correct data.

Governance. To ensure that BI is meeting their needs, organizations must implement *governance* to plan and control their BI activities. Governance requires that people, committees, and processes be in place. Companies that are effective in BI governance often create a senior-level committee comprised of vice presidents and directors who (1) ensure that the business strategies and BI strategies are in alignment, (2) prioritize projects, and (3) allocate resources. These companies also establish a middle management–level committee that oversees the various projects in the BI portfolio to ensure that these projects are being completed in accordance with the company's objectives. Finally, lower-level operational committees perform tasks such as creating data definitions and identifying and solving data problems. All of these committees rely on the collaboration and contributions of business users and IT personnel.

Users. Once the data are loaded in a data mart or warehouse, they can be accessed. At this point the organization begins to obtain business value from BI; all of the prior stages constitute creating BI infrastructure.

There are many potential BI users, including IT developers; frontline workers; analysts; information workers; managers and executives; and suppliers, customers, and regulators. Some of these users are *information producers* whose primary role is to create information for other users. IT developers and analysts typically fall into this category. Other users—including managers and executives—are *information consumers*, because they utilize information created by others.

Companies have reported hundreds of successful data-warehousing applications. You can read client success stories and case studies at the Web sites of vendors such as NCR Corp. (www.ncr.com) and Oracle (www.oracle.com). For a more detailed discussion, visit the Data Warehouse Institute (http://tdwi.org). The benefits of data warehousing include the following:

- End users can access needed data quickly and easily via Web browsers because these data are located in one place.
- End users can conduct extensive analysis with data in ways that were not previously possible.
- End users can obtain a consolidated view of organizational data.

These benefits can improve business knowledge, provide competitive advantage, enhance customer service and satisfaction, facilitate decision making, and streamline business processes. IT's About Business 3.4 demonstrates the benefits of data warehousing to the Nordea Bank in Scandinavia.

Despite their many benefits, data warehouses have some limitations. First, they can be very expensive to build and to maintain. Second, incorporating data from obsolete mainframe systems can be difficult and expensive. Finally, people in one department might be reluctant to share data with other departments.

IT'S ABOUT BUSINESS 3.4

Data Warehouse Gives Nordea Bank a Single Version of the Truth

Financial institutions across Europe must improve their data-management practices if they are to comply with the demanding legislation that arose from the global financial crisis of 2008. Banks must comply with numerous regulations developed by various authorities around the globe. These regulations require banks to report how much capital they hold and to document how they report risk.

FIN

In Europe, these regulations include Basel III affecting capital ratios, the European Central Bank demanding faster and more detailed reporting with MFI 3, and the European Banking Authority developing new financial reporting with Finrep. Meanwhile, in 2010 the United States passed the Foreign Account Tax Compliance Act (FACTA), which also places greater reporting requirements on banks operating in the country.

© halbergman/iStockphoto

The new regulations, together with ongoing business challenges, had pushed data to the top of the agenda at Nordea Bank AB (www.nordea.com). As a result, the bank developed a data warehouse.

Nordea, which is headquartered in Stockholm, Sweden, advertises itself as "the largest financial services group in

Northern Europe." Although the institution has a long history, the modern organization was formed in 2001 when major banks in Norway, Sweden, Denmark, and Finland merged their resources and operations. Today Nordea has more than 1,400 branches that conduct business in 19 countries. Its clientele includes 10 million private customers and 600,000 corporate clients. The group also operates an Internet bank, which services 6 million online customers.

Nordea's finance group agreed to lead a data warehouse project with a budget of €100 million. The project was managed by the finance group because that group "owned" the data and the data-management processes. The project had two overriding objectives: to improve customer service and to comply with all of the relevant regulations.

As noted, Nordea was created from the merger of four separate financial institutions, each with its own legacy information systems. (A legacy system refers to outdated information systems or application software that is used instead of available upgraded versions.) Data at Nordea were governed by manual processes, stored on spreadsheets, and managed locally. This arrangement was inadequate to meet the demands of a modern global banking system.

As a result of these data management problems, the most important principle for the data warehouse was to create a single version of the truth. The finance team was able to build common data definitions and master data necessary to compare variables across geographies and business functions. Based in Stockholm, the data warehouse stores 11 terabytes of data, including more than 7 billion records.

Nordea deployed the data warehouse, with impressive results. Reporting lead times decreased from eight to four days. This process enabled the bank to conduct analyses more quickly and accurately at lower costs. All managers and financial controllers now receive the branch results in the same format, at the same time. They can drill down to the customer, account, and product data, all from the same coherent, consistent source.

The data warehouse enabled Nordea to introduce a customer profitability application for relationship managers. Once these managers meet with customers, they can then prepare easily, instead of spending time obtaining the data from different databases.

The current financial climate requires banks to focus more carefully on compliance. At the same time, however, these institutions must pursue opportunities to improve business performance. If banks can share data across the business uniformly and consistently, they will reduce the costs of compliance, which in turn will enable them to reallocate capital to address needs in other areas of the business.

Sources: Compiled from "Nordea Builds on a Financial Data Warehouse," *TechandFinance.com*, October 27, 2013; R. Nielsen, "Nordea's 'One Platform:' Business Value with a Financial Data Warehouse," *Teradata Conference and Expo*, October, 2013; L. Clark, "European Banks Pull Data Together for Business and Legal Compliance," *Computer Weekly Europe*, September, 2013; L. Clark, "European Banks Raise Data Management Game in Response to New Regulations," *Computer Weekly Europe*, September, 2013; P. Swabey, "Nordea Prepares for Wave of Regulation with New Data Warehouse," *Information Age*, April 15, 2013; www.nordea.com, accessed February 27, 2014.

Questions

1. What are other advantages (not mentioned in the case) that Nordea Bank might realize from its data warehouse?

2. What recommendations would you give to Nordea Bank about incorporating Big Data into their bank's data management? Provide specific examples of what types of Big Data you think Nordea should consider.

Apply The Concept 3.4

LEARNING OBJECTIVE 3.4 Recognize the necessary environment to successfully implement and maintain data warehouses.

STEP 1 – Background

Section 3.2 presented a general set of "ingredients" that characterize Big Data. A similar set of general ingredients is required for organizations to effectively utilize the power of data marts and data warehouses. FIGURE 3.4 presents this information. Healthcare as an industry has not been centralized for many business, legal, and ethical reasons. However, the overall health implications of a centralized data warehouse are unimaginable.

STEP 2 – Activity

Visit http://www.wiley.com/go/rainer/MIS3e/applytheconcept, and read the article in *WIRED* magazine from March 6, 2014, titled "Gadgets like Fitbit Are Remaking How Doctors Treat You." As you read this article, you will see that several key ingredients exist, though no one has built a medical data warehouse as described in the article. (The term "warehouse" is not used, but the concept is applicable.) Also, although the article seems to

> ┌─ **BEFORE** *YOU GO ON....* ─┐
> 1. Differentiate between data warehouses and data marts.
> 2. Describe the characteristics of a data warehouse.
> 3. What are three possible architectures for data warehouses and data marts in an organization?

focus on real-time data usage, imagine the possibilities of compiling years of this type of data in a data warehouse.

To demonstrate that you recognize the environmental factors necessary to implement and maintain a data warehouse, imagine that the date is exactly five years in the future. Write a newspaper article titled "Data from Gadgets like Fitbit Remade How Doctors Treated Us." In your article imagine that all of the ingredients necessary in the environment have come together. Discuss what the environment was like five years ago (today) and how things have evolved to create the right mix of environmental factors.

Be aware that there is no right/wrong answer to this exercise. The objective is for you to recognize the necessary environment for a successful data warehouse implementation. The healthcare-related example simply provides a platform to accomplish this task.

3.5 Knowledge Management

As we have noted throughout this text, data and information are critically important organizational assets. Knowledge is a vital asset as well. Successful managers have always valued and utilized intellectual assets. These efforts were not systematic, however, and they did not ensure that knowledge was shared and dispersed in a way that benefited the overall organization. Moreover, industry analysts estimate that most of a company's knowledge assets are not housed in relational databases. Instead, they are dispersed in e-mail, word processing documents, spreadsheets, presentations on individual computers, and in people's heads. This arrangement makes it extremely difficult for companies to access and integrate this knowledge. The result frequently is less-effective decision making.

Concepts and Definitions

Knowledge management (KM) is a process that helps organizations manipulate important knowledge that comprises part of the organization's memory, usually in an unstructured format. For an organization to be successful, knowledge, as a form of capital, must exist in a format that can be exchanged among persons. In addition, it must be able to grow.

Knowledge. In the information technology context, knowledge is distinct from data and information. As you learned in Chapter 1, data are a collection of facts, measurements, and statistics; information is organized or processed data that are timely and accurate. Knowledge is information that is *contextual*, *relevant*, and *useful*. Simply put, knowledge is information in action. **Intellectual capital** (or **intellectual assets**) is another term for knowledge.

To illustrate, a bulletin listing all of the courses offered by your university during one semester would be considered data. When you register, you process the data from the bulletin to create your schedule for the semester. Your schedule would be considered information. Awareness of your work schedule, your major, your desired social schedule, and characteristics of different faculty members could be construed as knowledge, because it can affect the way you build your schedule. You see that this awareness is contextual and relevant (to developing an optimal schedule of classes) as well as useful (it can lead to changes in your schedule). The implication is that knowledge has strong experiential and reflective elements that distinguish it from information in a given context. Unlike information, knowledge can be utilized to solve a problem.

Numerous theories and models classify different types of knowledge. Here you will focus on the distinction between explicit knowledge and tacit knowledge.

Explicit and Tacit Knowledge. **Explicit knowledge** deals with more objective, rational, and technical knowledge. In an organization, explicit knowledge consists of the policies, procedural guides, reports, products, strategies, goals, core competencies, and IT infrastructure of the enterprise. In other words, explicit knowledge is the knowledge that has been codified (documented) in a form that can be distributed to others or transformed into a process or a strategy. A description of how to process a job application that is documented in a firm's human resources policy manual is an example of explicit knowledge.

In contrast, **tacit knowledge** is the cumulative store of subjective or experiential learning. In an organization, tacit knowledge consists of an organization's experiences, insights, expertise, know-how, trade secrets, skill sets, understanding, and learning. It also includes the organizational culture, which reflects the past and present experiences of the organization's people and processes, as well as the organization's prevailing values. Tacit knowledge is generally imprecise and costly to transfer. It is also highly personal. Finally, because it is unstructured, it is difficult to formalize or codify, in contrast to explicit knowledge. A salesperson who has worked with particular customers over time and has come to know their needs quite well would possess extensive tacit knowledge. This knowledge is typically not recorded. In fact, it might be difficult for the salesperson to put into writing, even if he or she were willing to share it.

Knowledge Management Systems

The goal of knowledge management is to help an organization make the most productive use of the knowledge it has accumulated. Historically, management information systems have focused on capturing, storing, managing, and reporting explicit knowledge. Organizations now realize they need to integrate explicit and tacit knowledge into formal information systems. **Knowledge management systems (KMSs)** refer to the use of modern information technologies—the Internet, intranets, extranets, databases—to systematize, enhance, and expedite intrafirm and interfirm knowledge management. KMSs are intended to help an organization cope with turnover, rapid change, and downsizing by making the expertise of the organization's human capital widely accessible.

Organizations can realize many benefits with KMSs. Most importantly, they make **best practices**—the most effective and efficient ways of doing things—readily available to a wide range of employees. Enhanced access to best-practice knowledge improves overall organizational performance. For example, account managers can now make available their tacit knowledge about how best to manage large accounts. The organization can then utilize this knowledge when it trains new account managers. Other benefits include improved customer service, more efficient product development, and improved employee morale and retention.

At the same time, however, implementing effective KMSs presents several challenges. First, employees must be willing to share their personal tacit knowledge. To encourage this behavior, organizations must create a knowledge management culture that rewards employees who add their expertise to the knowledge base. Second, the organization must continually maintain and upgrade its knowledge base. Specifically, it must incorporate new knowledge and delete old, outdated knowledge. Finally, companies must be willing to invest in the resources needed to carry out these operations.

The KMS Cycle

A functioning KMS follows a cycle that consists of six steps (see FIGURE 3.8). The reason the system is cyclical is that knowledge is dynamically refined over time. The knowledge in an effective KMS is never finalized because the environment changes over time and knowledge must be updated to reflect these changes. The cycle works as follows:

1. *Create knowledge.* Knowledge is created as people determine new ways of doing things or develop know-how. Sometimes external knowledge is brought in.

2. *Capture knowledge.* New knowledge must be identified as valuable and be represented in a reasonable way.

3. *Refine knowledge.* New knowledge must be placed in context so that it is actionable. This is where tacit qualities (human insights) must be captured along with explicit facts.

4. *Store knowledge.* Useful knowledge must then be stored in a reasonable format in a knowledge repository so that other people in the organization can access it.

Figure 3.8 The knowledge management system cycle.

5. *Manage knowledge.* Like a library, the knowledge must be kept current. It must be reviewed regularly to verify that it is relevant and accurate.

6. *Disseminate knowledge.* Knowledge must be made available in a useful format to anyone in the organization who needs it, anywhere and anytime.

BEFORE *YOU GO ON....*

1. What is knowledge management?
2. What is the difference between tacit knowledge and explicit knowledge?
3. Describe the knowledge management system cycle.

Apply The Concept 3.5

LEARNING OBJECTIVE 3.5 Describe the benefits and challenges of implementing knowledge management systems in organizations.

STEP 1 – Background

As you have learned in this text, data are captured, stored, analyzed, and shared to create knowledge within organizations. This knowledge is exposed in meetings when colleagues are interpreting the information they received from the latest report, in employee presentations, in e-mail among coworkers, and in numerous other scenarios. The problem many organizations face is that there are massive amounts of knowledge that are created and shared, but this information is not stored in a centralized, searchable format.

STEP 2 – Activity

Visit http://www.wiley.com/go/rainer/MIS3e/applytheconcept, and click on the links provided for Apply the Concept 3.5. They will take you to two YouTube videos: "Discover What You Know" by user "Ken Porter" and "Lee Bryant—Knowledge Management" by user "usnowfilm." Both videos illustrate the importance of capturing knowledge within an organization so it can be shared with the right person at the right time to support effective decision making.

STEP 3 – Deliverable

Write a short paragraph or two to discuss the benefits and challenges faced by companies when they attempt to implement a knowledge management system. How many of these elements are technical, and how many are social? Also, discuss the ways that companies can use Web 2.0 technologies to help capture and share knowledge.

Submit this essay to your instructor.

What's in for ME?

FOR THE
ACCOUNTING MAJOR

The accounting function is intimately concerned with keeping track of the transactions and internal controls of an organization. Modern databases enable accountants to perform these functions more effectively. Databases help accountants manage the flood of data in today's organizations so that they can keep their firms in compliance with the standards imposed by Sarbanes–Oxley.

Accountants also play a role in cost justifying the creation of a knowledge base and then auditing its cost-effectiveness. In addition, if you work for a large CPA company that provides management services or sells knowledge, you will most likely use some of your company's best practices that are stored in a knowledge base.

FOR THE FINANCE MAJOR

Financial managers make extensive use of computerized databases that are external to the organization, such as CompuStat or Dow Jones, to obtain financial data on organizations in their industry. They can use these data to determine if their organization meets industry benchmarks in return on investment, cash management, and other financial ratios.

Financial managers, who produce the organization's financial status reports, are also closely involved with Sarbanes–Oxley. Databases help these managers comply with the law's standards.

 FOR THE MARKETING MAJOR

Databases help marketing managers access data from the organization's marketing transactions, such as customer purchases, to plan targeted marketing campaigns and to evaluate the success of previous campaigns. Knowledge about customers can make the difference between success and failure. In many databases and knowledge bases, the vast majority of information and knowledge concerns customers, products, sales, and marketing. Marketing managers regularly use an organization's knowledge base, and they often participate in its creation.

 FOR THE PRODUCTION/ OPERATIONS MANAGEMENT MAJOR

Production/operations personnel access organizational data to determine optimum inventory levels for parts in a production process. Past production data enable production/operations management (POM) personnel to determine the optimum configuration for assembly lines. Firms also collect quality data that inform them not only about the quality of finished products but also about quality issues with incoming raw materials, production irregularities, shipping and logistics, and after-sale use and maintenance of the product.

Knowledge management is extremely important for running complex operations. The accumulated knowledge regarding scheduling, logistics, maintenance, and other functions is very valuable. Innovative ideas are necessary for improving operations and can be supported by knowledge management.

 FOR THE HUMAN RESOURCE MANAGEMENT MAJOR

Organizations keep extensive data on employees, including gender, age, race, current and past job descriptions, and performance evaluations. HR personnel access these data to provide reports to government agencies regarding compliance with federal equal opportunity guidelines. HR managers also use these data to evaluate hiring practices, evaluate salary structures, and manage any discrimination grievances or lawsuits brought against the firm.

Databases help HR managers provide assistance to all employees as companies turn over more and more decisions about healthcare and retirement planning to the employees themselves. The employees can use the databases for help in selecting the optimal mix among these critical choices.

HR managers also need to use a knowledge base frequently to find out how past cases were handled. Consistency in how employees are treated not only is important, but it also protects the company against legal actions. In addition, training for building, maintaining, and using the knowledge system sometimes is the responsibility of the HR department. Finally, the HR department might be responsible for compensating employees who contribute their knowledge to the knowledge base.

 FOR THE MIS MAJOR

The MIS function manages the organization's data as well as the databases. MIS database administrators standardize data names by using the data dictionary. This process ensures that all users understand which data are in the database. Database personnel also help users access needed data and generate reports with query tools.

SUMMARY

1. Discuss ways that common challenges in managing data can be addressed using data governance.

The following are three common challenges in managing data:

> Data are scattered throughout organizations and are collected by many individuals using various methods and devices. These data are frequently stored in numerous servers and locations and in different computing systems, databases, formats, and human and computer languages.

> Data come from multiple sources.

> Information systems that support particular business processes impose unique requirements on data, which results in repetition and conflicts across an organization.

One strategy for implementing data governance is master data management. Master data management provides companies with the ability to store, maintain, exchange, and synchronize a consistent, accurate, and timely "single version of the truth" for the company's core master data. Master data management manages data gathered from across an organization, manages data from multiple sources, and manages data across business processes in an organization.

2. Discuss the advantages and disadvantages of relational databases.

Relational databases allow people to compare information quickly by row or column. In addition, items are easy to retrieve by finding the point of intersection of a particular row and column. On the other hand, large-scale relational databases can be composed of many interrelated tables, making the overall design complex with slow search and access times.

3. Define Big Data, and discuss its basic characteristics.

Big Data is composed of high volume, high velocity, and high variety information assets that require new forms of processing to enable enhanced decision making, insight discovery, and process optimization. Big Data has three distinct characteristics, which are volume, velocity, and variety. These characteristics distinguish Big Data from traditional data.

> *Volume:* Big Data consists of vast quantities of data.
> *Velocity:* Big Data flows into an organization at incredible speeds.
> *Variety:* Big Data includes a huge variety of different data in differing data formats.

4. Explain the elements necessary to successfully implement and maintain data warehouses.

To successfully implement and maintain a data warehouse, an organization must:

> Link source systems that provide data to the warehouse or mart.

> Prepare the necessary data for the data warehouse using data integration technology and processes.

> Decide on an appropriate architecture for storing data in the data warehouse or data mart.

> Select the tools and applications for the variety of organizational users.

> Ensure that metadata, data quality, and governance processes are in place to ensure that the data warehouse or mart meets its purposes.

5. Describe the benefits and challenges of implementing knowledge management systems in organizations.

Organizations can realize many benefits with KMSs.

> Best practices are readily available to a wide range of employees.
> Improved customer service;
> More efficient product development;
> Improved employee morale and retention.

Challenges to implementing KMSs include:

> Employees must be willing to share their personal tacit knowledge;
> Organizations must create a knowledge management culture that rewards employees who add their expertise to the knowledge base
> The knowledge base must be continually maintained and updated.
> Companies must be willing to invest in the resources needed to carry out these operations.

>>>**CHAPTER GLOSSARY**

attribute Each characteristic or quality of a particular entity.

best practices The most effective and efficient ways to do things.

Big Data A collection of data so large and complex that it is difficult to manage using traditional database management systems.

bit A binary digit—that is, a 0 or a 1.

byte A group of eight bits that represents a single character.

clickstream data Data collected about user behavior and browsing patterns by monitoring users' activities when they visit a Web site.

data file (also table) A collection of logically related records.

data governance An approach to managing information across an entire organization.

data mart A low-cost, scaled-down version of a data warehouse that is designed for the end-user needs in a strategic business unit (SBU) or a department.

data model A diagram that represents entities in the database and their relationships.

data warehouse A repository of historical data that are organized by subject to support decision makers in the organization.

database management system (DBMS) The software program (or group of programs) that provides access to a database.

entity Any person, place, thing, or event of interest to a user.

explicit knowledge The more objective, rational, and technical types of knowledge.

field A characteristic of interest that describes an entity.

foreign key A field (or group of fields) in one table that uniquely identifies a row (or record) of another table.

instance Each row in a relational table, which is a specific, unique representation of the entity.

intellectual capital (or intellectual assets) Other terms for knowledge.

knowledge management (KM) A process that helps organizations identify, select, organize, disseminate, transfer, and apply information and expertise that are part of the organization's memory and that typically reside within the organization in an unstructured manner.

knowledge management systems (KMSs) Information technologies used to systematize, enhance, and expedite intra- and interfirm knowledge management.

master data A set of core data, such as customer, product, employee, vendor, geographic location, and so on, that spans an enterprise's information systems.

master data management A process that provides companies with the ability to store, maintain, exchange, and synchronize a consistent, accurate, and timely "single version of the truth" for the company's core master data.

multidimensional structure Storage of data in more than two dimensions; a common representation is the *data cube*.

primary key An field (or attribute) of a record that uniquely identifies that record so that it can be retrieved, updated, and sorted.

record A grouping of logically related fields.

relational database model Data model based on the simple concept of tables in order to capitalize on characteristics of rows and columns of data.

secondary key A field that has some identifying information, but typically does not uniquely identify a record with complete accuracy.

table A grouping of logically related records.

tacit knowledge The cumulative store of subjective or experiential learning, which is highly personal and hard to formalize.

>>>DISCUSSION QUESTIONS

1. Is Big Data really a problem on its own, or are the use, control, and security of the data the true problems? Provide specific examples to support your answer.

2. What are the implications of having incorrect data points in your Big Data? What are the implications of incorrect or duplicated customer data? How valuable are decisions that are based on faulty information derived from incorrect data?

3. Explain the difficulties involved in managing data.

4. What are the problems associated with poor-quality data?

5. What is master data management? What does it have to do with high-quality data?

6. Explain why master data management is so important in companies that have multiple data sources.

7. Describe the advantages and disadvantages of relational databases.

8. Explain why it is important to capture and manage knowledge.

9. Compare and contrast tacit knowledge and explicit knowledge.

>>>PROBLEM-SOLVING ACTIVITIES

1 Access various employment Web sites (e.g., www .monster.com and www.dice.com) and find several job descriptions for a database administrator. Are the job descriptions similar? What are the salaries offered in these positions?

2. Access the Web sites of several real estate companies. Find the sites that take you through a step-by-step process for buying a home, that provide virtual reality tours of homes in your price range (say, $200,000 to $250,000) and location, that provide mortgage and interest rate calculators, and that offer financing for your home. Do the sites require that you register to access their services? Can you request that an e-mail be sent to you when properties in which you might be interested become available? How does the process outlined influence your likelihood of selecting this company for your real estate purchase?

3. It is possible to find many Web sites that provide demographic information. Access several of these sites and

see what they offer. Do the sites differ in the types of demographic information they offer? If so, how? Do the sites require a fee for the information they offer? Would demographic information be useful to you if you wanted to start a new business? If so, how and why?

4. Search the Web for uses of Big Data in homeland security. Specifically, read about the spying by the U.S. National Security Agency (NSA). What role did technology and Big Data play in this questionable practice?

5. Visit the website for HowStuffWorks (www.howstuffworks .com), and search for "Big Data: Friend or Foe?" What points does this article present concerning the delicate balance between shared data and customer privacy?

6. Access the Web sites of IBM (www.ibm.com), Sybase (www.sybase.com), and Oracle (www.oracle.com), and trace the capabilities of their latest data management products, including Web connections.

7. Enter the Web site of the Gartner Group (www.gartner.com). Examine the company's research studies pertaining to data management. Prepare a report on the state of the art.

8. Calculate your personal digital footprint at http://www.emc.com/digital_universe/downloads/web/personal-ticker.htm.

9. Diagram a knowledge management system cycle for a fictional company that sells customized T-shirts to students.

>>> **COLLABORATION EXERCISE**

STEP 1 – Background

Data can come from multiple sources. This in itself does not pose a problem. Problems arise, however, when there is no consistent process for capturing and storing those data. For example, if one sales representative keeps her data in a spreadsheet and another keeps his data in individual Word files, then combining the two datasets will be extremely difficult. This example highlights issues involving different storage methods. Multiple problems can also arise in situations that involve different pieces of data, duplicate data, or inconsistent data.

STEP 2 – Activity

Your team is a group of sales representatives from five different sales regions: New England, East, South, Midwest, and West. You work for a company that sells food and food-preparation products to restaurants. Each of you collects data in a unique format because your organization has not created a centralized method for storing data. Visit http://www.wiley.com/go/rainer/MIS3e/collaboration and download the individual data files that you have created through your experience.

Each team member should download one file. The team should then collaborate (using Google Drive) to create a single Google spreadsheet of your data. Make notes of any issues that arise as you try to combine your data.

STEP 3 – Deliverable

"Clean" and prepare the data for a database, and submit the single combined file to your professor. Along with your single file, submit a list of notes/best practices for future data collection so that future representatives will not experience the problems you have just overcome. Congratulations! You have just worked through a major process in managing a database!

CLOSING **CASE 1** > Tapping the Power of Big Data

Analysts have coined the term *Big Data* to refer to the vast and ever-increasing amounts of data that modern organizations need to capture, store, process, and analyze. Managing Big Data represents a fundamental challenge for every business. The following examples illustrate how companies are utilizing Big Data in creative and profitable ways. The fundamental concept that underlies all of these examples is that Big Data will continue to get "bigger," so organizations will have to devise evermore innovative solutions to manage these data.

- **Human Resources.** Employee benefits, particularly healthcare, represent a major business expense. Consequently, some companies have turned to Big Data to better manage these benefits. Caesars Entertainment (www.caesars.com), for example, analyzes health-insurance claim data for its 65,000 employees and their covered family members. Managers can track thousands of variables that indicate how employees use medical services, such as the number of emergency room visits and whether employees choose a generic or brand name drug.

  Consider the following scenario: Data revealed that too many employees with medical emergencies were being treated at hospital emergency rooms rather than at less-expensive urgent-care facilities. The company launched a campaign to remind employees of the high cost of emergency room visits, and they provided a list of alternative facilities. Subsequently, 10,000 emergencies shifted to less-expensive alternatives, for a total savings of $4.5 million.

  Big Data is also having an impact on *hiring*. An example is Catalyst IT Services (www.catalystitservices.com), a technology outsourcing company that hires teams for programming jobs. In 2013, the company planned to screen more than 10,000 candidates. Not only is traditional recruiting too slow, but too often the hiring managers subjectively choose candidates who are not the best fit for the job. Catalyst addresses this problem by requiring candidates to fill out an online assessment. It then uses the assessment to collect thousands of data points about each candidate. In fact, the company collects more data based on *how* candidates answer than on *what* they answer.

For example, the assessment might give a problem requiring calculus to an applicant who is not expected to know the subject. How the candidate responds—laboring over an answer, answering quickly and then returning later, or skipping the problem entirely—provides insight into how that candidate might deal with challenges that he or she will encounter on the job. That is, someone who labors over a difficult question might be effective in an assignment that requires a methodical approach to problem solving, whereas an applicant who takes a more aggressive approach might perform better in a different job setting.

The benefit of this big-data approach is that it recognizes that people bring different skills to the table and that there is no one-size-fits-all person for any job. Analyzing millions of data points can reveal which attributes candidates bring to specific situations.

As one measure of success, employee turnover at Catalyst averages about 15 percent per year, compared with more than 30 percent for its U.S. competitors and more than 20 percent for similar companies overseas.

- **Product Development.** Big Data can help capture customer preferences and put that information to work in designing new products. In this area, both online companies and traditional companies are using Big Data to achieve competitive advantage.

Physical manufacturers are using Big Data to measure customer interest. For example, as Ford Motor Company (www.ford.com) was designing the first subcompact model on its new global platform—a common set of components that Ford would incorporate into its cars and trucks around the world—the company had to decide which features that were common in one region should be made available in all regions. One feature the company considered was a "three blink" turn indicator that had been available on its European cars for years. Unlike the turn signals on its U.S. vehicles, this indicator flashes three times at the driver's touch and then automatically shuts off.

Ford decided that conducting a full-scale market research test on this blinker would be too costly and time consuming. Instead, it examined auto-enthusiast Web sites and owner forums to discover what drivers were saying about turn indicators. Using text-mining algorithms, researchers culled more than 10,000 mentions and then summarized the most relevant comments.

The results? Ford introduced the three-blink indicator on the new Ford Fiesta in 2010, and by 2013 it was available on most Ford products. Although some Ford owners complained online that they have had trouble getting used to the new turn indicator, many others defended it. Ford managers note that the use of text-mining algorithms was critical in this effort because they provided the company with a complete picture that would not have been available using traditional market research.

- **Operations.** For years, companies have been using information technology to make their operations more efficient. They can now use Big Data to capture much more information from a wealth of new sources.

Consider United Parcel Service (UPS). The company has long relied on data to improve its operations. Specifically, it uses sensors in its delivery vehicles that can, among other things, capture the truck's speed and location, the number of times it is placed in reverse, and whether the driver's seat belt is buckled. These data are uploaded at the end of each day to a UPS data center, where they are analyzed overnight. By combining GPS information and data from sensors installed on more than 46,000 vehicles, UPS reduced fuel consumption by 8.4 million gallons, and it cut 85 million miles off its routes.

- **Marketing.** Marketing managers have long used data to better understand their customers and to target their marketing efforts more directly. Today, Big Data enables marketers to craft much more personalized messages.

Like many hoteliers, United Kingdom's InterContinental Hotels Group (IHG; www.ihg.com) has gathered details about the 71 million members of its Priority Club rewards program, such as income levels and whether members prefer family-style or business-traveler accommodations. The company then consolidated all of this information into a single data warehouse that extracts information from social media Web sites and processes queries very quickly. Using its data warehouse and analytics software, the hotelier launched a new marketing campaign in January 2013. Where previous marketing campaigns generated, on average, between 7 and 15 customized marketing messages, the new campaign generated more than 1,500. IHG rolled out these messages in stages to an initial core of 12 customer groups, each of which is defined by 4,000 attributes. One group, for instance, tends to stay on weekends, redeem reward points for gift cards, and register through IHG marketing partners. Utilizing this information, IHG sent these customers a marketing message that alerted them to local weekend events.

The campaign proved to be highly successful. It generated a 35 percent higher rate of customer conversions, or acceptances, than previous, similar campaigns.

- **Government Operations.** With 55 percent of the population of the Netherlands living under the threat of flooding, water management is critically important to the Dutch government. The government operates a sophisticated water management system, managing a network of dykes or levees, canals, locks, harbors, dams, rivers, storm-surge barriers, sluices, and pumping stations.

In its water management efforts, the government makes use of a vast number of sensors embedded in every physical structure used for water control. The sensors generate at least 2 petabytes of data annually. As the sensors are becoming cheaper, the government is deploying more of them, increasing the amount of data generated.

In just one example of the use of sensor data, sensors in dykes can provide information on the structure of the dyke, how well it is able to handle the stress of the water it controls, and whether it is likely to fail. Further, the sensor data are providing valuable insights for new designs for Dutch dykes. The result is that Dutch authorities have reduced the costs of managing water by 15 percent.

Sources: Compiled from "Big Data Management," The Data Warehousing Institute, January, 2014; "Big Data: An Overview," ZDNet, October 1, 2013; T. Wolpe, "Big Data Deluge: How Dutch Water Is Trying to Turn the Tide," *ZDNet*, October 1, 2013; S. Sikular, "Gartner's Big Data Definition Consists of Three Parts, Not to Be Confused with Three 'V's," *Forbes*, March 27, 2013; G. Fowler, "Data, Data Everywhere," *The Wall Street Journal*, March 13, 2013; G. Press, "What's To Be Done About Big Data?" *Forbes*, March 11, 2013; S. Rosenbush and M. Totty, "How Big Data Is Changing the Whole Equation for Business," *The Wall Street Journal*, March 11, 2013; D. Clark, "How Big Data Is Transforming the Hunt for Talent," *Forbes*, March 8, 2013; G. Satell, "The Limits of Big Data Marketing," *Forbes*, March 6, 2013; V. Mayer-Schonberger and K. Cukier, "Big Data: A Revolution That Will Transform How We Live, Work, and Think," Eamon Dolan/Houghton Mifflin Harcourt, March 5, 2013; "Big Data: What's Your Plan?" *McKinsey & Company Insights*, March, 2013; D. Henshen, "Big Data Revolution Will Be Led by Revolutionaries," *InformationWeek*, December 12, 2012; "Integrate for Insight," *Oracle White Paper*, October 27, 2012; "Big Data Now," *O'Reilly Media*, October, 2012; S. Greengard, "Big Data Challenges Organizations," *Baseline Magazine*, June 13, 2012; S. Lohr, "The Age of Big Data," *The New York Times*, February 11, 2012; "Big Data: Lessons From the Leaders," *The Economist (Economist Intelligence Unit)*, 2012; www.the-bigdatainstitute.com, accessed April 17, 2014.

Questions

1. Select two examples from the case, and summarize how Big Data is adding value over traditional data.

2. Select one area and describe the future value anticipated from Big Data, given the current trends.

3. How does Big Data improve customer stratification and profiling? What concerns should managers address about these processes?

CLOSING **CASE 2 >** Can Organizations Have Too Much Data?

THE PROBLEM >>> Organizations are hoarding (over-retaining) data they no longer need. This massive accumulation of unnecessary data results from several technological and organizational factors. From a technology standpoint, the growth of high-bandwidth Internet connections (discussed in Chapter 4) and the decrease in the price of hard drive storage (discussed in Plug IT In 2) have made it relatively easy and inexpensive to move and store vast amounts of documents and files.

From an organizational perspective, few managers are concerned about what is being stored when it seems on the surface to be so inexpensive simply to keep everything. In fact, in most organizations, no one is responsible for limiting the amount of data that is being stored. Business unit managers typically do not see a budget line item for all of the costs associated with unused or unneeded data, so they do not make it a management priority—at least, not until huge amounts of corporate data are involved in a legal matter or a government investigation.

Although storing vast amounts of hoarded data seems to have little or no cost, this is not really the case. Hoarding data actually involves significant costs. These costs fall into three broad categories: infrastructure costs; hidden costs; and legal, compliance, and regulatory costs.

- **Infrastructure Costs.** When companies closely analyze their data, they typically find that 80 percent of their ostensibly "active" files and folders have not been accessed for three to five years. This situation results in unnecessary IT expenditures for electronic data storage, disaster recovery, and data migration as old servers and systems are retired. Some organizations also have tens of thousands of backup tapes in storage, many of which are essentially useless. Nevertheless, they are generating storage fees and excess costs if they are included in the discovery process for litigation (discussed below).

- **Hidden Costs.** Other costs associated with unnecessary data hoarding are hidden—out of sight, and out of mind. One all-too common example of hidden costs is lost productivity when employees have to search through volumes of unused and unwanted materials to find the information they need.

- **Legal, Compliance, and Regulatory Costs.** The largest costs of over-retained data frequently arise when a company becomes entangled in legal actions. In these scenarios, the court issues a legal hold for all data pertaining to the matter. A *legal hold* requires an organization to preserve all relevant information when litigation is reasonably anticipated. A company cannot dispose of *any* relevant data after the hold is issued. In essence, the legal hold supersedes the company's right to dispose of information that is not required for any specific operational or regulatory requirements. The process of examining a company's data to find if they are pertinent to a legal case is called *discovery*.

The discovery process can be extraordinarily expensive. In many cases, companies must hire attorneys to examine data files to determine whether they are pertinent to discovery requests or subpoenas. Even if companies use electronic discovery software, the costs are still substantial. For example, although an e-discovery company, Blackstone Discovery (www.blackstonediscovery.com), helped one company analyze 1.5 million documents for less than $100,000, that firm still incurred those costs. The key point here is that if the company had disposed of the data before the legal matter arose, these costs would have been substantially lower. As this example illustrates, companies should proactively and appropriately dispose of unnecessarily hoarded data.

In addition, companies increasingly must adhere to state privacy legislation that requires them to notify state officials and implicated state citizens if private information such as Social Security numbers or credit card numbers is breached or disclosed. For example, Belmont Bank in Massachusetts discovered that a backup tape had been left on a table and disposed of by the cleaning crew. It appeared that the tape had been incinerated and therefore was not actually disclosed to any third parties. Nevertheless, the bank had to pay a $7,500 civil penalty.

Companies also incur costs when legal problem arise from incidents involving the actual loss of credit card information. Security experts estimated the cost of the Target breach to exceed $1 billion. (See chapter-closing case 1 in Chapter 7). Obviously, hackers and thieves cannot take what organizations no longer possess. One excellent protection against a breach is to dispose of data as soon as they are no longer needed for business purposes or legal matters.

THE SOLUTION >>> So, how can a company reduce the risks and costs associated with data hoarding? First, companies must understand that the key to avoiding legal difficulties is to take all reasonable steps to meet record-keeping obligations and to document those steps. Legal obligations do not require perfection; good-faith efforts generally suffice. Furthermore, companies normally are obligated to keep only "a" copy of relevant information, not "all" copies. That is, there is little or no need to keep all backups. Companies that recognize this simple fact can sometimes dispose of tens of thousands of unneeded backup files, generating enormous savings in the process.

Second, companies should hire a properly insured external consultant or expert who will go on record as authorizing the final disposition of data files. Organizational employees are not typically comfortable saying "throw out those data," and many employees are too busy to devote the time that an electronic data housecleaning (e-housecleaning) project requires. Going further, employees may not be familiar with the legal standards governing the disposition of information. As a result, organizations are more comfortable delegating the responsibility for directing data disposal to external experts. In fact, these experts are frequently the persons whose deposition is ultimately taken if anyone questions the company's disposition decisions.

Third, companies should launch an e-housecleaning project. The first step is to review company policies regulating records retention and legal holds to confirm that the company is operating in a reasonable and defensible manner. The basic inquiry here is whether the company appears to be placing the proper documents and information on hold when litigation arises.

The next step is to inventory physical data containers, such as hard drives, servers, tapes, and other media, and to make reasonable efforts to determine their source. If the data are required for business, regulatory or legal hold purposes, then companies should place them on retention schedules. If not, then companies should dispose of them.

Finally, for maximum protection, the external expert should draft an opinion letter explaining the process and directing the final disposition of unneeded data. This step ensures that if the data disposition is ever challenged, the company can point to this process and its associated documentation as evidence of their good-faith effort to comply with their record-keeping obligations.

THE RESULTS >>> Properly performed e-housecleaning efforts offer a large return on investment. Some companies have been able to remove thousands of backup files that have been determined to be irrelevant to legal hold. Others have freed up significant amounts of storage space, in addition to avoiding discovery and data breach costs.

In some firms, an executive or business unit insists on holding onto unused data, claiming they may someday need to access those data. The most effective strategy for dealing with "just-in-case hoarders" is to allow them keep their data, but with the understanding that they are now the "owner" of the data, meaning they must accept all of the responsibilities that ownership entails. Therefore, they will assume all ownership costs, including data storage, backup, and data breaches, as well as all legal costs associated with reviewing and producing the data if the data are ever swept into litigation discovery or governmental investigations. Once these individuals understand the full costs associated with ownership, they usually opt to dispose of the data instead.

Sources: Compiled from B. Greenberg, "Seven Questions Every CIO Should Be Able to Answer about eDiscovery and Legal Holds," *General System Dynamics*, February 25, 2014; S. Mathieson, "Civil Servants Are Not to Blame for Government Data Hoarding," *The Guardian*, April 10, 2013; J. Clark, "Big Data or Big Data Hoarding?" *The Datacenter Journal*, March 14, 2013; "Security Implications of Improper Data Disposal?" *InfoShield Security*, March 11, 2013; A. Kidman, "Data Disposal 101: Don't Use Rubbish Bins," *lifehacker.com.au*, February 21, 2013; J. Jaeger, "Changing Your Data-Hoarding Ways," *Compliance Week*, February 5, 2013; A. Samuel, "E-Discovery Trends for 2013," *CMS Wire*, January 17, 2013; J. Dvorak, "Stop Your Data Hoarding!" *PC Magazine*, December 11, 2012; L. Luellig, "A Modern Governance Strategy for Data Disposal," *CIO Insight*, December 5, 2012; A. Kershaw, "Hoarding Data Wastes Money," *Baseline Magazine*, April 16, 2012; T. Claburn, "Google Apps Vault Promises Easy E-Discovery," *InformationWeek*, March 29, 2012; T. Harbert, "E-Discovery in the Cloud? Not So Easy," *Computerworld*, March 6, 2012; B. Kerschberg, "E-Discovery and the Rise of Predictive Coding," Forbes, March 23, 2011; M. Miller, "Data Theft: Top 5 Most Expensive Data Breaches," *The Christian Science Monitor*, May 4, 2011; E. Savitz, "The Problem with Packrats: The High Cost of Digital Hoarding," *Forbes*, March 25, 2011; J. Markoff, "Armies of Expensive Lawyers, Replaced by Cheaper Software," *The New York Times*, March 4, 2011.

Questions

1. Compare and contrast this case with the material in this chapter on Big Data. That is, given the disadvantages of over-retained data, how should an organization manage Big Data?

2. Are there any advantages to over-retaining data? Support your answer.

3. Storage media are becoming much cheaper, with increasing capacity. Would it be easier and cheaper to over-retain data than it would be to pay employees to dispose of data properly and to hire an outside expert to oversee this process?

INTERNSHIP ACTIVITY> ● first noble bank

Industry; Banking

Data are "huge" when it comes to understanding customer patterns. The more data you have, and the more analysis you are able to do, the better you will understand what makes customers tick. In fact, data have become such a "big" part of understanding customers that we have a unique name for them—BIG DATA.

Today, using Big Data means that we have not only vast *amounts* of data, but also many *types* of data. Most databases are designed to use structured data. However, Big Data makes use of unstructured data from multiple sources and computes with the data it has. Traditional databases need all of the variables to create a model, and they do not work well when data are missing.

Below is an e-mail message from Jeremy Farr. You worked with Jeremy in the Internship Activity for Chapter 1. This e-mail will explain the task he has chosen for you today.

To:	IT Intern
From:	Jeremy Farr
Subject:	Big Data and Banking

Hello again!

Recently, I watched a video on YouTube by IBM Big Data and Analytics about the use of Big Data in the banking industry. It is so interesting to consider what can happen when we create a full picture—some people call it a 360° view—of our customer. The video demonstrates real-time marketing based on data such as social media. This type of marketing seems impossible to me because I am so unfamiliar with these technologies.

I have not encountered any companies at our banking trade shows that perform this type of analysis. I conducted a quick Web search, however, and I found MarkLogic, who seem to come close. They offer the 360° view of the customer, analysis of unstructured data, real-time diagnostics, and other valuable features.

Unfortunately, MarkLogic does not offer a public demo of their product. I believe, however, that you can provide me with a quality review of their solutions by watching the YouTube video mentioned above for the concepts and then reading about the MarkLogic solution for banking and other industries. After you watch the videos and review the company's Web site, answer these questions about Big Data and banking.

1. How effective can Big Data be without the use of mobile banking?
2. How will I know if my customers want me to have a 360° view of them?
3. Will Big Data be seen as Big Brother?
4. What legal issues could arise from creating this 360° view of our customers?

Thanks for your help!
Jeremy

Note: All links mentioned in this letter are available at http://www.wiley.com/go/rainer/MIS3e/internship.

SPREADSHEET ACTIVITY > BASIC FUNCTIONS: AVERAGE, MIN, MAX, AVERAGEIF

STEP 1 – Background

In addition to Sum, Sumif, Count, and Countif from Spreadsheet Activities 1 and 2, it is often useful to be able to calculate averages and to find the minimum and maximum values within a given range. For example, whereas a sales manager might want to know the total number of sales, a quality control manager would likely find averages and range (minimum to maximum) numbers more useful.

Additionally, you can calculate conditional averages with the Averageif function. This function enables you to compare individual averages against the overall average.

STEP 2 – Activity

Calculating averages (total and conditional) and min and max is fairly simple when the list of numbers you are averaging is small. For example, Achilles teaches and likes to show his students the total average and the high and low scores on their exams so that they know where their score fell relative to the class. On the last exam, his 20 students scored 54, 95, 83, 75, 85, 77, 88, 79, 94, 65, 83, 77, 89, 84, 94, 88, 74, 93, 82, and 99. If you put these scores in a spreadsheet or a calculator, you will quickly see that the average is 82.9 with a low score of 54 and a high score of 99. However, when you are measuring quality data on an industrial scale, calculating averages by hand is far too cumbersome.

STEP 3 – Deliverable

Aaisa works as the Quality Control Manager in a Michelin tire-manufacturing plant that produces 3,000 tires per day. She is responsible for ensuring that all Michelin tires are of outstanding quality. This means that tire specs must measure within an acceptable range for each of the following metrics: uniformity, weight, balance, and X-ray inspection. Calculating averages for 3,000 tires each day is nearly impossible to do by hand, much less handling the averages for a year or more of data.

Visit http://www.wiley.com/go/rainer/MIS3e/spreadsheet, and download the file linked for Spreadsheet Activity 3. This is an XLS file that will open in any spreadsheet tool. You will find data and instructions written into the spreadsheet indicating what you should calculate.

Follow the instructions in the spreadsheet and submit your final work to your instructor.

Additional help with this spreadsheet skill is available in WileyPLUS. Open the "Microsoft Office 2013 Lab Manual Spreadsheet Module: Excel 2013," and review Lesson 5: Using Formulas and Built-In Functions and Lesson 10: The IF Function.

DATABASE ACTIVITY > ENTITY–RELATIONSHIP DIAGRAM

STEP 1 – Background

Just as every house begins with an architectural drawing, every database begins with a data model. In this activity, you will develop the most common type of data model: an entity–relationship diagram (ERD). Plug IT In 3 introduces you to data modeling—specifically, entity–relationship diagramming—as a key element of database management. This activity applies those concepts.

Understanding the structure of a database is critical to developing and using one. This knowledge reduces the chances of errors, which typically are very difficult to correct after the database has been developed. In addition, professional database developers communicate with ERDs when they design a database for business needs. The ERD defines what the database will be. Knowing their language will improve your chances of acquiring a database that meets your needs.

STEP 2 – Activity

Imagine that your university has requested your assistance in designing a database. They give you the following facts:

- The database will store information on departments, courses, sections, and students.
- Each department can teach many courses.
- Each course is taught by one department.
- Each course can have many sections.
- Each section belongs to one course.
- Each section has many students.
- Each student enrolls in many sections.

STEP 3 – Deliverable

Draw an ERD for a database that will convey the information listed above. You can use the graphics program of your choice or, if you prefer, paper and pencil. Regardless of how you create the ERD, it must convey the following information:

- All of the relationships among the entities.
- The primary key of each entity, displayed in a separate area at the top of the entity box.
- At least three attributes of each entity, based on your understanding of the situation. If you cannot think of three attributes, then show whichever ones you have.

Submit your ERD for your instructor to review.

Additional help with this database skill is available in Plug IT In 3.

CHAPTER 4

Telecommunications and Networking

LEARNING OBJECTIVES >>>

4.1 Compare and contrast the major types of networks.

4.2 Describe the wireline communications media and transmission technologies.

4.3 Describe the most common methods for accessing the Internet.

4.4 Explain the impact that networks have had on business and everyday life for each of the six major categories of network applications.

OPENING **CASE** > Get Rid of E-Mail? Seriously?

© beaucroft/iStockphoto

The first e-mail message was sent in 1971. Since then, e-mail has become the dominant means of communication and collaboration in business. (In fact, e-mail is probably the dominant means of communication between faculty and students at your university.)

Over time, however, organizations have begun to associate e-mail with information overload and stress. Time-pressed managers are finding it more difficult to get work done than they did five years ago as their workloads increase and organizational resources become scarcer.

Adding to their workloads, managers are spending much of their time sifting through a seemingly endless barrage of e-mail messages. By compulsively checking e-mail, managers become distracted and are unable to devote sufficient time to other, more productive work. In addition, managers frequently assert that many of the e-mails they have to read and respond to add little or no value to their organization.

Even managers who are disciplined enough to check their e-mails only at certain times can become frustrated. At the end of a day, they may have an inbox full of messages that need to be addressed before the next morning. This process can be exhausting, particularly if e-mail is the only means of communication between managers and their teams.

How are organizations responding to these problems? One organization, Atos SE (http://atos.net), took a rather drastic step: They banned e-mail.

Atos SE is a French multinational information technology (IT) services corporation headquartered in Bezons, France. The firm provides IT consulting, systems integration, and managed IT services. Atos also receives contracts for outsourced public IT services from some governments, such as the United Kingdom.

In 2011, Atos introduced a Zero Email initiative that banned e-mail as a form of internal communications, except for use with customers and prospects. One reason for the ban was an internal research study at Atos that found that a sample of 300 employees collectively sent or received some 85,000 e-mails in one week.

As part of its Zero Email initiative, Atos acquired the French software company blueKiwi (www.bluekiwi-software.com) in 2012 and deployed its ZEN enterprise social networking software across the organization. This software allows employees to selectively subscribe to relevant subject and networking groups composed of employees with common business interests and activities. Atos discovered that its 76,000 employees are able to reduce or even eliminate e-mails by participating (or posting as on Facebook) in relevant groups.

Group communities are the central information and communication hub for different work topics (e.g., a project). Employees use blogs, wikis, instant messaging, and social media tools in place of e-mail.

And the results? By mid-2014, Zero Email had made great strides in reducing (but not eliminating) internal electronic mail at Atos. Additionally, Atos's initiative has attracted interest from other businesses. Although not as drastic as the Atos approach, Volkswagen, for example, now prevents its BlackBerry servers from sending e-mail messages to employees outside work hours. Other companies are encouraging their employees to take e-mail breaks. That is, for them to devote a defined time period for e-mails is much like a coffee break.

Sources: Compiled from P. Karcher, "What You Can Learn from Atos's Zero Email Initiative," *Forrester*, December 11, 2013; P. Karcher, "Enterprise Social Does Not Stem Email Overload," *Forrester*, October 31, 2013; B. Profitt, "30 Days with Inbox Zero: Cleaning Out Messages – And Stress," *ReadWrite*, April 15, 2013; L. Timmins, "Why Atos Is Eliminating Email," *Computer Weekly*, March 22, 2013; P. Taylor, "Atos' 'Zero Email Initiative' Succeeding," *Financial Times*, March 7, 2013; D. du Preez, "Atos Drives for Zero Email with blueKiwi Roll Out," *ComputerWorldUK*, November 7, 2012; L. Magid, "Zero Email Has Zero Chance, But How About an Email Diet," *Forbes*, December 2, 2011; M. Colchester and G. Amiel, "The IT Boss Who Shuns Email," *The Wall Street Journal*, November 28, 2011; http://atos.net, accessed March 4, 2014.

Questions

1. Is it feasible for your university to eliminate e-mail? Why or why not? Would you support such a policy at your school? Why or why not?

2. Describe the advantages and disadvantages of eliminating e-mail from an organization. Provide specific examples to support your answers.

Introduction

There are three fundamental points about network computing you need to know. First, in modern organizations computers do not work in isolation. Rather, they constantly exchange data with one another. Second, this exchange of data—facilitated by telecommunications technologies—provides companies with a number of very significant advantages. Third, this exchange can take place over any distance and over networks of any size.

Without networks, the computer on your desk would be merely another productivity-enhancement tool, just as the typewriter once was. The power of networks, however, turns your computer into an amazingly effective tool for accessing information from thousands of sources, thereby making both you and your organization more productive. Regardless of the type of organization (profit/not-for-profit, large/small, global/local) or industry (manufacturing, financial services, healthcare), networks in general, and the Internet in particular, have transformed—and will continue to transform—the way we do business.

Networks support new and innovative ways of doing business, from marketing to supply chain management to customer service to human resources management. In particular, the Internet and private intranets—networks located within a single organization—have an enormous impact on our lives, both professionally and personally.

For all organizations regardless of their size, having a telecommunications and networking system is no longer just a source of competitive advantage. Rather, it is necessary for survival.

Computer networks are essential to modern organizations, for many reasons. First, networked computer systems enable organizations to become more flexible so that they can adapt to rapidly changing business conditions. Second, networks allow companies to share hardware, computer applications, and data across the organization and among different organizations. Third, networks make it possible for geographically dispersed employees and workgroups to share documents, ideas, and creative insights. This sharing encourages teamwork, innovation, and more efficient and effective interactions. In addition, networks are a critical link between businesses, their business partners, and their customers.

Clearly, networks are essential tools for modern businesses. But, why do *you* need to be familiar with networks? The simple fact is that if you operate your own business or work in a business, you cannot function without networks. You will need to communicate rapidly with your customers, business partners, suppliers, employees, and colleagues. Until about 1990, you would have used the postal service or the telephone system with voice or fax capabilities for business communication. Today, however, the pace of business is much faster—almost real time. To keep up with this incredibly fast pace, you will need to use computers, e-mail, the Internet, cell phones, and mobile devices. Furthermore, all of these technologies will be connected via networks to enable you to communicate, collaborate, and compete on a global scale.

Networking and the Internet are the foundations for commerce in the twenty-first century. Recall that one important objective of this book is to help you become an informed user of information systems. A knowledge of networking is an essential component of modern business literacy.

You begin this chapter by learning what a computer network is and identifying the various types of networks. You then study network fundamentals and follow by turning your attention to the basics of the Internet and the World Wide Web. You conclude the chapter by seeing the many network applications available to individuals and organizations—that is, what networks help you do.

4.1 What Is a Computer Network?

A **computer network** is a system that connects computers and other devices (e.g., printers) via communications media so that data and information can be transmitted among them. Voice and data communication networks are continually becoming faster—that is, their bandwidth is increasing—and cheaper. **Bandwidth** refers to the transmission capacity of a network; it is stated in bits per second. Bandwidth ranges from narrowband (relatively low transmission capacity) to broadband (relatively high network capacity).

The telecommunications industry itself has difficulty defining the term **broadband**. In 2010, the Federal Communications Commission (FCC) defined broadband as the transmission capacity of a communications medium (discussed later in this chapter) faster than 4 megabits per second (Mbps). In mid-2014, the FCC is soliciting public comments on whether a new minimum for broadband service should be established as 10 Mbps or as high as 25 Mbps. For the purposes of this book, we will use the 2010 FCC criteria of 4 Mbps. The definition of broadband remains fluid, however, and it will undoubtedly continue to change to reflect greater transmission capacities in the future.

You are likely familiar with certain types of broadband connections, such as **digital subscriber line (DSL)** and cable to your homes and dorms. DSL and cable fall within the range of transmission capacity mentioned here and are thus defined as broadband connections.

The various types of computer networks range from small to worldwide. They include (from smallest to largest) personal area networks (PANs), local area networks (LANs), metropolitan area networks (MANs), wide area networks (WANs), and the ultimate WAN, the Internet. PANs are short-range networks—typically a few meters—that are used for communication among devices close to one person. They can be wired or wireless. (You will learn about wireless PANs in Chapter 8.) MANs are relatively large computer networks that cover a metropolitan area. MANs fall between LANs and WANs in size. WANs typically cover large geographical areas; in some cases they can span the entire planet.

Local Area Networks

Regardless of their size, networks represent a compromise among three objectives: speed, distance, and cost. Organizations typically must select two of the three. To cover long distances, organizations can have fast communication if they are willing to pay for it, or cheap communication if they are willing to accept slower speeds. A third possible combination of the three trade-offs is fast, cheap communication with distance limitations. This is the idea behind local area networks.

A **local area network (LAN)** connects two or more devices in a limited geographical region, usually within the same building, so that every device on the network can communicate with every other device. Most LANs today use Ethernet (discussed later in this chapter). FIGURE 4.1 illustrates an Ethernet LAN that consists of four computers, a server, and a printer, all of which connect via a shared cable. Every device in the LAN has a *network interface card* (NIC) that allows the device to physically connect to the LAN's communications medium. This medium is typically unshielded twisted-pair wire (UTP).

Although it is not required, many LANs have a **file server** or **network server**. The server typically contains various software and data for the network. It also houses the LAN's network operating system, which manages the server and routes and manages communications on the network.

Wide Area Networks

When businesses have to transmit and receive data beyond the confines of the LAN, they use wide area networks. Interestingly, the term *wide area network* did not even exist until local area networks appeared. Before that time, what we call a wide area network today was simply called a "network."

A **wide area network (WAN)** is a network that covers a large geographical area. WANs typically connect multiple LANs. They are generally provided by common carriers such as telephone companies and the international networks of global communications services providers. WANs have large capacity, and they typically combine multiple channels (e.g., fiber-optic cables, microwave, and satellite). The Internet is an example of a WAN.

WANs also contain routers. A **router** is a communications processor that routes messages from a LAN to the Internet, across several connected LANs, or across a wide area network such as the Internet.

Enterprise Networks

Organizations today have multiple LANs and may have multiple WANs. All of these networks are interconnected to form an **enterprise network.** FIGURE 4.2 displays a model of enterprise computing. Note that the enterprise network in the figure has a **backbone network.** Corporate backbone networks are

Figure 4.1 Ethernet local area network.

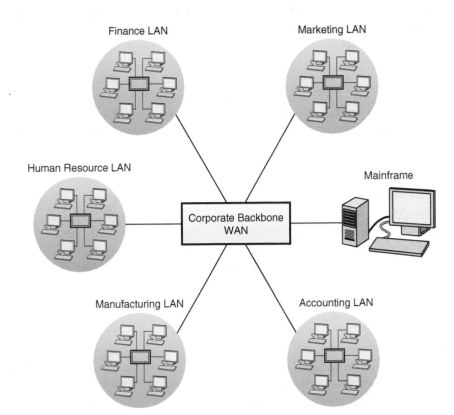

Figure 4.2 Enterprise network.

1. What are the primary business reasons for using networks?

2. What is the difference between LANs and WANs?

3. Describe an enterprise network.

high-speed central networks to which multiple smaller networks (such as LANs and smaller WANs) connect. The LANs are called *embedded LANs* because they connect to the backbone WAN.

Apply The Concept 4.1

LEARNING OBJECTIVE 4.1 Compare and contrast the major types of networks.

STEP 1 – Background (Here is what you are learning.)

Section 4.1 has introduced you to the different types of networks that connect businesses around the world. These networking capabilities enable modern organizations to spread out over many geographical locations. Frequently, a company's headquarters are located in one city with various branches in other countries. In addition, employees frequently work from home rather than commute to a physical office. The computer network is the technology that allows all of this to happen. For a network to function, a few components are required. In this activity, you will place these components in the appropriate places to create a computer network.

STEP 2 – Activity (Here is what you do.)

Consider the following company, called JLB TechWizards, and these potential network components.

1. Headquarters: JLB TechWizards manufactures, sells, and services computer equipment. The company's headquarters, which are located in Chicago, house several key functions, including marketing, accounting, HR, and manufacturing. Each office has a number of PCs that connect to the main server. All offices share data and printers.

2. Sales force: The company has about 15 technicians who service equipment sold within the United States. Each technician has a laptop that needs to connect to the database (at headquarters) about three hours each day to check inventory, enter repairs, and place orders. Technicians are constantly on the road, and they need to be able to check inventory whether they are in a hotel or at a customer site. In addition, each evening the technicians must log on to check for updates and to post their daily activities.

3. Employees from home: JLB TechWizards has a number of employees who work from home part time on flextime. These employees need a fast, secure connection because some of them are dealing with financial data stored in the main computer and its databases at headquarters. They all live within 20 miles of their workplace.

STEP 3 – Deliverable (Here is what you turn in.)

Use the description presented above to compare and contrast the types of networks discussed in this section. Explain how these networks will or will not meet the needs of each situation. A table may be useful to present this information, but it is not required. Create a Word document with your description and explanations and submit it to your instructor.

4.2 Network Fundamentals

In this section you will learn the basics of how networks actually operate. You will then distinguish between analog and digital signals and understand how modems enable computer networks to "translate" among them. You follow by studying wireline communications media, which enable computers in a network to transmit and receive data. You conclude this section by looking at network protocols and types of network processing.

Analog and Digital Signals

Networks transmit information with two basic types of signals, analog and digital. **Analog signals** are continuous waves that transmit information by altering the characteristics of the waves. Analog signals have two parameters, *amplitude* and *frequency*. All sounds—including the human voice—are analog, traveling to human ears in the form of waves. The higher the waves (or amplitude), the louder the sound; the more closely packed the waves, the higher the frequency or pitch. In contrast, **digital signals** are discrete pulses that are either on or off, representing a series of *bits* (0s and 1s). This quality allows digital signals to convey information in a binary form that can be interpreted by computers. FIGURE 4.3 illustrates both analog and digital signals.

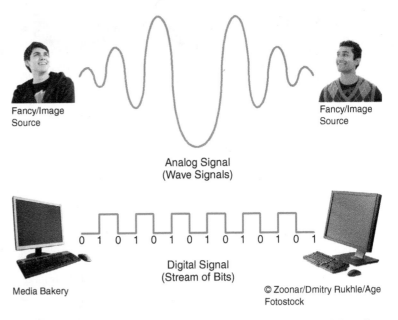

Figure 4.3 Analog and digital signals.

The function of a **modem** is to convert digital signals to analog signals—a process called *modulation*—and analog signals to digital signals—a process called *demodulation*. (The name *modem* is a contraction of *modulator–demodulator*.) Modems are used in pairs. The modem at the sending end converts a computer's digital information into analog signals for transmission over analog lines, such as telephone lines. At the receiving end, another modem converts the analog signal back into digital signals for the receiving computer. There are three types of modems: dial-up modems, cable modems, and DSL modems.

The U.S. public telephone system was originally designed as an analog network to carry voice signals or sounds in an analog wave format. In order for this type of circuit to carry digital information, that information must be converted into an analog wave pattern by a *dial-up modem*. Dial-up modems have transmission speeds of up to 56 kilobytes per second (Kbps). They are almost extinct in most parts of the developed world.

Cable modems are modems that operate over coaxial cable—for example, cable TV. They offer broadband access to the Internet or corporate intranets. Cable modem speeds vary widely. Most providers offer bandwidth between 1 and 6 million bits per second (Mbps) for downloads (from the Internet to a computer) and between 128 and 768 thousand bits per second (Kbps) for uploads. Cable modem services share bandwidth among subscribers in a locality. That is, the same cable line connects to many households. Therefore, when large numbers of neighbors access the Internet at the same time, cable speeds can decrease significantly.

DSL (discussed later in this chapter) *modems* operate on the same lines as voice telephones and dial-up modems. DSL modems always maintain a connection, so an Internet connection is immediately available.

Communications Media and Channels

Communicating data from one location to another requires some form of pathway or medium. A **communications channel** is such a pathway. It is comprised of two types of media: cable (twisted-pair wire, cable, or fiber-optic cable) and broadcast (microwave, satellite, radio, or infrared).

Wireline media or **cable media** use physical wires or cables to transmit data and information. Twisted-pair wire and coaxial cables are made of copper, and fiber-optic cable is made of glass. The alternative is communication over **broadcast media** or **wireless media**. The key to mobile communications in today's rapidly moving society is data transmissions over electromagnetic media—the "airwaves." In this section you will study the three wireline channels. Table 4.1 summarizes the advantages and disadvantages of each of these channels. You will become familiar with wireless media in Chapter 8.

Twisted-Pair Wire. **Twisted-pair wire** is the most prevalent form of communications wiring; it is used for almost all business telephone wiring. As the name suggests, it consists

TABLE 4.1 Advantages and Disadvantages of Wireline Communications Channels

Channel	Advantages	Disadvantages
Twisted-pair wire	Inexpensive	Slow (low bandwidth)
	Widely available	Subject to interference
	Easy to work with	Easily tapped (low security)
Coaxial cable	Higher bandwidth than twisted-pair	Relatively expensive and inflexible
		Easily tapped (low to medium security)
	Less susceptible to electromagnetic interference	Somewhat difficult to work with
Fiber-optic cable	Very high bandwidth	Difficult to work with (difficult to splice)
	Relatively inexpensive	
	Difficult to tap (good security)	

Figure 4.4 Twisted-pair wire.

of strands of copper wire twisted in pairs (see FIGURE 4.4). Twisted-pair wire is relatively inexpensive to purchase, widely available, and easy to work with. However, it also has some significant disadvantages. Specifically, it is relatively slow for transmitting data, it is subject to interference from other electrical sources, and it can be easily tapped by unintended receivers to gain unauthorized access to data.

Coaxial Cable. Coaxial cable (FIGURE 4.5) consists of insulated copper wire. Compared with twisted-pair wire, it is much less susceptible to electrical interference, and it can carry much more data. For these reasons, it is commonly used to carry high-speed data traffic as well as television signals (thus the term *cable TV*). However, coaxial cable is more expensive and more difficult to work with than twisted-pair wire. It is also somewhat inflexible.

Fiber Optics. Fiber-optic cable (FIGURE 4.6) consists of thousands of very thin filaments of glass fibers that transmit information via light pulses generated by lasers. The fiber-optic cable is surrounded by cladding, a coating that prevents the light from leaking out of the fiber.

Fiber-optic cables are significantly smaller and lighter than traditional cable media. They also can transmit far more data, and they provide greater security from interference and tapping. As of mid-2014, optical fiber had reached data transmission rates of more than 50 trillion bits (terabits) per second in laboratory experiments. Fiber-optic cable is typically

Cross-section view

How coaxial cable looks to us

Figure 4.5 Two views of coaxial cable.

Phillip Hayson/Science Source
Cross-section view

Chris Knapton/Science Source
How fiber-optic cable looks to us

Figure 4.6 Two views of fiber-optic cable.

used as the backbone for a network, whereas twisted-pair wire and coaxial cable connect the backbone to individual devices on the network.

Network Protocols

Computing devices that are connected to the network must access and share the network to transmit and receive data. These devices are often referred to as *nodes* of the network. They work together by adhering to a common set of rules and procedures—known as a **protocol**— that enable them to communicate with one another. The two major protocols are the Ethernet and Transmission Control Protocol/Internet Protocol.

Ethernet. A common LAN protocol is Ethernet. Many organizations use 100-gigabit Ethernet, where the network provides data transmission speeds of 100 gigabits (100 billion bits) per second.

Transmission Control Protocol/Internet Protocol. The **Transmission Control Protocol/Internet Protocol (TCP/IP)** is the protocol of the Internet. TCP/IP uses a suite of protocols, the main ones being the Transmission Control Protocol (TCP) and the Internet Protocol (IP). The TCP performs three basic functions: (1) It manages the movement of data packets (see below) between computers by establishing a connection between the computers, (2) it sequences the transfer of packets, and (3) it acknowledges the packets that have been transmitted. The **Internet Protocol (IP)** is responsible for disassembling, delivering, and reassembling the data during transmission.

Before data are transmitted over the Internet, they are divided into small, fixed bundles called *packets*. The transmission technology that breaks up blocks of text into packets is called *packet switching*. Each packet carries the information that will help it reach its destination— the sender's IP address, the intended receiver's IP address, the number of packets in the message, and the number of the particular packet within the message. Each packet travels independently across the network and can be routed through different paths in the network. When the packets reach their destination, they are reassembled into the original message.

It is important to note that packet-switching networks are reliable and fault tolerant. For example, if a path in the network is very busy or is broken, packets can be dynamically ("on the fly") rerouted around that path. Also, if one or more packets do not get to the receiving computer, then only those packets need to be resent.

Why do organizations use packet switching? The main reason is to achieve reliable end-to-end message transmission over sometimes unreliable networks that may have transient (short-acting) or persistent (long-acting) faults.

The packets use the TCP/IP protocol to carry their data. TCP/IP functions in four layers (see FIGURE 4.7). The *application layer* enables client application programs to access the other layers, and it defines the protocols that applications use to exchange data.

Figure 4.7 The four layers of the TCP/IP reference model.

Sending Email

Receiving Email

Email: Sending a Message via SMPT (Simple Mail Transfer Protocol)	Application	Email: Message received
Break Message into packets and determine order	Transport	Packets reordered and replaced (if lost)
Assign sending and receiving IP addresses and apply to each packet	Internet	Packets routed through internal network to desired IP address
Determine path across network/ Internet to intended destination	Network Interface	Receipt of packets

One of these application protocols is the **Hypertext Transfer Protocol (HTTP)**, which defines how messages are formulated and how they are interpreted by their receivers. (We discuss hypertext in Section 4.3.) The *transport layer* provides the application layer with communication and packet services. This layer includes TCP and other protocols. The *Internet layer* is responsible for addressing, routing, and packaging data packets. The IP is one of the protocols in this layer. Finally, the *network interface layer* places packets on, and receives them from, the network medium, which can be any networking technology.

Two computers using TCP/IP can communicate even if they use different hardware and software. Data sent from one computer to another proceed downward through all four layers, beginning with the sending computer's application layer and going through its network interface layer. After the data reach the receiving computer, they travel up the layers.

TCP/IP enables users to send data across sometimes unreliable networks with the assurance that the data will arrive in uncorrupted form. TCP/IP is very popular with business organizations because of its reliability and the ease with which it can support intranets and related functions.

Let's look at an example of packet switching across the Internet. FIGURE 4.8 illustrates a message being sent from New York City to Los Angeles over a packet-switching network. Note that the different colored packets travel by different routes to reach their destination in Los Angeles, where they are reassembled into the complete message.

Types of Network Processing

Organizations typically use multiple computer systems across the firm. **Distributed processing** divides processing work among two or more computers. This process enables

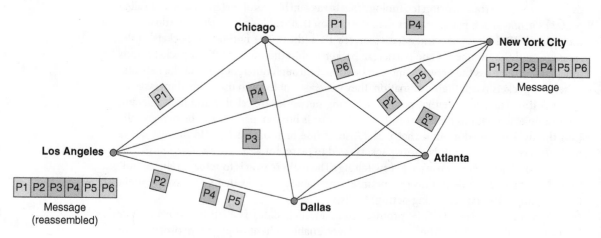

Figure 4.8 Packet switching.

computers in different locations to communicate with one another via telecommunications links. A common type of distributed processing is client/server processing. A special type of client/server processing is peer-to-peer processing.

Client/Server Computing.

Client/server computing links two or more computers in an arrangement in which some machines, called *servers*, provide computing services for user PCs, called *clients*. Usually, an organization performs the bulk of its processing or application/data storage on suitably powerful servers that can be accessed by less powerful client machines. The client requests applications, data, or processing from the server, which acts on these requests by "serving" the desired commodity.

Client/server computing leads to the ideas of "fat" clients and "thin" clients. As discussed in Plug IT In 2, *fat clients* have large storage and processing power and therefore can run local programs (such as Microsoft Office) if the network goes down. In contrast, *thin clients* may have no local storage and only limited processing power. Thus, they must depend on the network to run applications. For this reason, they are of little value when the network is not functioning.

Peer-to-Peer Processing.

Peer-to-peer (P2P) processing is a type of client/server distributed processing where each computer acts as *both* a client and a server. Each computer can access (as assigned for security or integrity purposes) all files on all other computers.

There are three basic types of peer-to-peer processing. The first type accesses unused CPU power among networked computers. An application of this type is **SETI@home** (http://setiathome.ssl.berkeley.edu). These applications are from open-source projects, and they can be downloaded at no cost.

The second form of peer-to-peer is real-time, person-to-person collaboration, such as Microsoft SharePoint Workspace (http://office.microsoft.com/en-us/sharepoint-workspace). This product provides P2P collaborative applications that use buddy lists to establish a connection and allow real-time collaboration within the application.

The third peer-to-peer category is advanced search and file sharing. This category is characterized by natural language searches of millions of peer systems. It enables users to discover other users, not just data and Web pages. One example of this category is BitTorrent.

BitTorrent (www.bittorrent.com) is an open-source, free, peer-to-peer file-sharing application that simplifies the problem of sharing large files by dividing them into tiny pieces, or "torrents." BitTorrent addresses two of the biggest problems of file sharing: (1) downloading bogs down when many people access a file at once, and (2) some people leech, meaning they download content but refuse to share it. BitTorrent eliminates the bottleneck by enabling all users to share little pieces of a file at the same time—a process called *swarming*. The program prevents leeching because users must upload a file while they download it. Thus, the more popular the content, the more efficiently it zips over a network.

BEFORE *YOU GO ON....*

1. Compare and contrast the three wireline communications channels.
2. Describe the various technologies that enable users to send high-volume data over any network.
3. Describe the Ethernet and TCP/IP protocols.
4. Differentiate between client/server computing and peer-to-peer processing.

Apply The Concept 4.2

LEARNING OBJECTIVE 4.2

Describe the wireline communications media and transmission technologies.

STEP 1 – Background

Section 4.2 covers network channels, protocols, and other network fundamentals. These computer networks enable businesses to receive and share information with customers, suppliers, and employees. Made up of several possible cable types and protocols, they are quite literally the backbone of modern businesses.

STEP 2 – Activity

Imagine that you work in the billing department of a midsized hospital. Recently, your supervisor stated that hospital growth had created a need for office space to be repurposed, and your work would now be done from home. You would be reimbursed for any expenses involved in preparing your home office, and your home Internet (required connection speed of 1.5 MB/second minimum) would also be reimbursed quarterly. The only requirement is that you finalize the same number of bills each day from home as you did in the office. You can schedule your own time, as long as the work gets done.

Visit http://www.wiley.com/go/rainer/MIS3e/applytheconcept to watch a few videos about telecommuting.

STEP 3 – Deliverable

Describe the wireline communication media and the transmission technologies (protocols) that would be used to support telecommuting. Your description should (at a minimum) include the home Internet connection, use of the Web, and connections within the office. It should also describe the protocols that operate to support these connections. Submit your description to your instructor.

4.3 The Internet and the World Wide Web

The **Internet ("the Net")** is a global WAN that connects approximately 1 million organizational computer networks in more than 200 countries on all continents, including Antarctica. It has become so widespread that it features in the daily routine of nearly 2.5 billion people. Participating computer systems include smartphones, PCs, LANs, databases, and mainframes.

The computers and organizational nodes on the Internet can be of different types and makes. They are connected to one another by data communications lines of different speeds. The primary network connections and telecommunications lines that link the nodes are referred to as the **Internet backbone**. For the Internet, the backbone is a fiber-optic network that is operated primarily by large telecommunications companies.

As a network of networks, the Internet enables people to access data in other organizations and to communicate, collaborate, and exchange information seamlessly around the world, quickly and inexpensively. Thus, the Internet has become a necessity for modern businesses.

The Internet grew out of an experimental project of the Advanced Research Project Agency (ARPA) of the U.S. Department of Defense. The project began in 1969 as the *ARPAnet*. Its purpose was to test the feasibility of a WAN over which researchers, educators, military personnel, and government agencies could share data, exchange messages, and transfer files.

Today, Internet technologies are being used both within and among organizations. An **intranet** is a network that uses Internet protocols so that users can take advantage of familiar applications and work habits. Intranets support discovery (easy and inexpensive browsing and search), communication, and collaboration inside an organization.

In contrast, an **extranet** connects parts of the intranets of different organizations. In addition, it enables business partners to communicate securely over the Internet using virtual private networks (VPNs) (explained in Chapter 7). Extranets offer limited accessibility to the intranets of participating companies, as well as necessary interorganizational communications. They are widely used in the areas of business-to-business (B2B) electronic commerce (see Chapter 9) and supply chain management (SCM) (see Chapter 13).

No central agency manages the Internet. Instead, the costs of its operation are shared among hundreds of thousands of nodes. Thus, the cost for any one organization is small. Organizations must pay a small fee if they wish to register their names, and they need to install their own hardware and software to operate their internal networks. The organizations are obliged to move any data or information that enter their organizational network, regardless of the source, to their destination, at no charge to the senders. The senders, of course, pay the telephone bills for using either the backbone or regular telephone lines.

Companies from every country conduct business on the Internet. China has the largest number of people accessing the Internet—some 618 million people. Let's take a look at its leading Internet firms.

- *Qihoo 360* (http://corp.360.cn) is best known for its online security software, which has more than 400 million users. In addition, in 2012 it launched a search engine that now claims almost 25 percent of the Chinese market.

- *JD.com* (www.jd.com) is an online retailer with 140 million users that operates in a similar way to Amazon.com. JD.com has an English-language Web site that offers free global shipping for purchases over $49, with a delivery time of at least one week.

- *Jiayuan.com* (www.jiayuan.com) is one of China's oldest and best-known dating sites, with 100 million users. China's one child policy has created a gender gap in the population that is skewed toward males. At the same time, the media refer to women in their late 20s as "leftover women." Jiaynan, which means "beautiful destiny," is tailored to users looking to get married.

- *Netease* (www.netease.com) is a major news portal for China, with more than 590 million users. The site offers an e-mail service, search, online video, social networking, and online games.

- *58.com* (www.58.com), China's version of Craigslist, covers 380 cities and 130 million monthly users who post jobs, special offers, and personal ads.

Accessing the Internet

You can access the Internet in several ways. From your place of work or your university, you can utilize your organization's LAN. A campus or company backbone connects all of the various LANs and servers in the organization to the Internet. You can also log onto the Internet from your home or on the road, using either wireline or wireless connections.

Connecting via an Online Service. You can also access the Internet by opening an account with an Internet service provider. An **Internet service provider (ISP)** is a company that provides Internet connections for a fee. Large ISPs include America Online (www.aol.com), Juno (www.juno.com), Earthlink (www.earthlink.com), and NetZero (www.netzero.net). In addition, many telephone providers and cable companies such as Verizon and Time Warner sell Internet access, as do computer companies such as Microsoft. To use this service, you need a modem and standard communication software.

ISPs connect to one another through **network access points (NAPs)**. NAPs are exchange points for Internet traffic. They determine how traffic is routed. NAPs are key components of the Internet backbone. FIGURE 4.9 displays a schematic of the Internet. The white links at the top of the figure represent the Internet backbone; the brown dots where the white links meet are the NAPs.

Connecting via Other Means. There have been several attempts to make access to the Internet cheaper, faster, and easier. For example, terminals known as Internet kiosks have been located in such public places as libraries and airports (and even in convenience stores in some countries) for use by people who do not have their own computers. Accessing the Internet from smartphones and iPads is common, and fiber-to-the-home (FTTH) is growing rapidly. FTTH involves connecting fiber-optic cable directly to individual homes. This system initially was restricted to new residential developments, but it is rapidly spreading. Table 4.2 summarizes the various means of connecting to the Internet.

Other countries use cybercafes, which are places that provide Internet access to the public, usually for a time-based fee. These businesses often provide snacks and drinks, hence the café in the name. IT's About Business 4.1 illustrates how Cuba approaches Internet access.

© mstay/iStockphoto

Figure 4.9 Internet (backbone in white).

TABLE 4.2 Internet Connection Methods

Service	Description
Dial-up	Still used in the United States where broadband is not available
DSL	Broadband access via telephone companies
Cable modem	Access over your cable TV coaxial cable. Can have degraded performance if many of your neighbors are accessing the Internet at once
Satellite	Access where cable and DSL are not available
Wireless	Very convenient, and WiMAX will increase the use of broadband wireless
Fiber-to-the-home (FTTH)	Expensive and usually placed only in new housing developments

IT'S ABOUT BUSINESS 4.1

Internet Access in Cuba

The Internet in Cuba is among the most tightly controlled in the world. It is characterized by a low number of connections, limited bandwidth, extensive censorship, and high costs. Beginning in 2007, the situation seemed to show signs of improving. In 2013, analysts estimated that slightly more than 25 percent of the Cuban population had some type of Internet access. Although this statistic indicated some progress, Cuba still has the lowest Internet penetration rate in the western hemisphere.

Cuban citizens do have access, however, to a national intranet. The Cuban intranet provides a government-operated e-mail service and "government-friendly" Web sites hosted in the .cu domain. All of these services are subject to review by Cuba's Department of Revolutionary Orientation.

In spring 2013, Cuba linked up with two undersea fiber-optic Internet cables, and the country's state telecommunications company, ETECSA, opened 118 cybercafes with access to the wider Internet. However, Cubans are not allowed to access the new Internet service at home. Cuba's focus is on "collective points of access," as Cuba's deputy communications minister stated in the Communist Party daily newspaper, *Granma*.

In addition, at the cybercafes, connecting to the closed Cuban intranet costs only 70 cents per hour. In contrast, connecting to the Internet costs $5 per hour. Making matters worse, Cubans must show their national ID when signing up for Internet time. Some users have even been required to sign agreements not to do "anything online that might jeopardize 'public security.'"

Cuba demonstrates that when the government controls online communications, it is possible to allow "expanded" Internet access without providing much, if any, digital freedom. Interestingly, many Cubans have been able to circumvent government restrictions using satellite smartphones, many of which are paid for by friends and relatives abroad.

© LanceB/iStockphoto

Sources: Compiled from S. Willis, "Cuba's Internet: It's Bad But It Might Get Better," *Fusion.net*, October 25, 2013; "A Cyber Café in Cuba? No Chance," *Translating Cuba*, October 20, 2013; "Cuba Plans Internet in Homes by Late 2014," *Fox News Latino*, June 22, 2013; D. Talbot, "Cuba's New Internet Service Is Also No Bed of Roses," *MIT Technology Review*, July 16, 2013; F. Revsberg, "Cuba's New Cybercafes: A Piecemeal Strategy," *Havana Times*, May 30, 2013; R. Schoon, "Cuba to Offer Public Internet at Cyber Cafes, But Access Comes with Hefty Price Tag," *Latinos Post*, May 28, 2013; M. Frank, "Cuba's Mystery Fiber-Optic Internet Cable Stirs to Life," *Reuters*, January 22, 2013; www.cuba.cu, accessed March 1, 2014.

Questions

1. Describe the advantages and disadvantages of the global Internet to Cuban citizens.

2. Describe the advantages and disadvantages of the global Internet to the Cuban government.

Addresses on the Internet. Each computer on the Internet has an assigned address, called the **Internet Protocol (IP) address**, that distinguishes it from all other computers. The IP address consists of sets of numbers, in four parts, separated by dots. For example, the IP address of one computer might be 135.62.128.91. You can access a Web site by typing this number in the address bar of your browser.

Currently, there are two IP addressing schemes. The first scheme, IPv4, is the most widely used. IP addresses using IPv4 consist of 32 bits, meaning that there are 2^{32} possibilities for IP addresses, or 4,294,967,295 distinct addresses. Note that the IP address in the preceding paragraph (135.62.128.91) is an IPv4 address. At the time that IPv4 was developed, there were not as many computers that need addresses as there are today. Therefore, a new IP addressing scheme has been developed, IPv6.

IP addresses using IPv6 consist of 128 bits, meaning that there are 2^{128} possibilities for distinct IP addresses, which is an unimaginably large number. IPv6, which is replacing IPv4, will accommodate the rapidly increasing number of devices that need IP addresses, such as smartphones. (IP addresses using IPv4 consisted of 32 bits. Note that 2^{32} is a vastly smaller number than 2^{128}.)

IP addresses must be unique so that computers on the Internet know where to find one another. The Internet Corporation for Assigned Names (ICANN) (www.icann.org) coordinates these unique addresses throughout the world. Without that coordination, we would not have one global Internet.

Because the numeric IP addresses are difficult to remember, most computers have names as well. ICANN accredits certain companies called *registrars* to register these names, which are derived from a system called the domain name system (DNS). Domain names consist of multiple parts, separated by dots, that are read from right to left. For example, consider the domain name *business.auburn.edu*. The rightmost part (or zone) of an Internet name is its top-level domain (TLD). The letters *edu* in business.auburn.edu indicate that this is an educational site. The following are popular U.S. TLDs:

com	commercial sites
edu	educational sites
mil	military government sites
gov	civilian government sites
org	organizations

To conclude our domain name example, *auburn* is the name of the organization (Auburn University), and *business* is the name of the particular machine (server) within the organization to which the message is being sent.

A top-level domain (TLD) is the domain at the highest level in the hierarchical Domain Name System of the Internet. The top-level domain names are located in the root zone (rightmost zone) of the name. Management of most TLDs is delegated to responsible organizations by ICANN. ICANN operates the Internet Assigned Numbers Authority (IANA), which is in charge of maintaining the DNS root zone. Today, IANA distinguishes the following groups of TLDs:

- Country-code top-level domains (ccTLD): Two letter domains established for countries or territories. For example, *de* stands for Germany, *it* for Italy, and *ru* for Russia.

- Internationalized country code top-level domains (IDN ccTLD): These are ccTLDs in non-Latin character sets (e.g., Arabic or Chinese).

- Generic top-level domains (gTLD): Top-level domains with three or more characters. gTLDs initially consisted of .gov, .edu, .com, .mil, .org, and .net. In late 2000, ICANN introduced .aero, .biz, .coop, .info, .museum, .name, and .pro. In June 2012, ICANN revealed nearly 2,000 applications for new top-level domains.

The Future of the Internet

Consumer demand for content delivered over the Internet is increasing rapidly. Telecommunications industry analysts estimate that Internet traffic has reached some 64 exabytes per month in 2014. (1 exabyte is 1 million terabytes.) Many experts are now concerned that Internet users will experience brownouts from three factors: (1) the increasing number of people who work online, (2) the soaring popularity of Web sites such as YouTube that require large amounts of bandwidth, and (3) the tremendous demand for high-definition television delivered over the Internet. These brownouts will cause computers to go offline for several minutes at a time. Researchers assert that if Internet bandwidth is not improved rapidly, then within a few years the Internet will be able to function only at a much reduced speed.

Even today, the Internet sometimes is too slow for data-intensive applications such as full-motion video files (movies) and large medical files (X-rays). In addition, the Internet is unreliable and is not secure. As a result, Internet2 has been developed by more than 200 U.S. universities collaborating with industry and government. **Internet2** develops and deploys advanced network applications such as remote medical diagnosis, digital libraries, distance education, online simulation, and virtual laboratories. It is designed to be fast, always on, everywhere, natural, intelligent, easy, and trusted. Note that Internet2 is not a separate physical network from the Internet. At the end of 2013, Internet2 had over 500 members, including 251 institutions of higher education and 76 members from industry. For more details, see www.internet2.edu.

The World Wide Web

Many people equate the Internet with the World Wide Web. However, they are not the same thing. The Internet functions as a transport mechanism, whereas the World Wide Web is an application that uses those transport functions. Other applications, such as e-mail, also run on the Internet.

The **World Wide Web (The Web, WWW, or W3)** is a system of universally accepted standards for storing, retrieving, formatting, and displaying information via a client/server architecture. The Web handles all types of digital information, including text, hypermedia, graphics, and sound. It uses graphical user interfaces (GUIs) (explained in Plug IT In 2), so it is very easy to navigate.

Hypertext is the underlying concept defining the structure of the World Wide Web. Hypertext is the text displayed on a computer display or other electronic device with references, called hyperlinks, to other text that the reader can immediately access, or where text can be revealed progressively at additional levels of details. A **hyperlink** is a connection from a hypertext file or document to another location or file, typically activated by clicking on a highlighted word or image on the screen, or by touching the screen.

Organizations that wish to offer information through the Web must establish a *home page*, which is a text and graphical screen display that usually welcomes the user and provides basic information on the organization that has established the page. In most cases, the home page will lead users to other pages. All the pages of a particular company or individual are collectively known as a **Web site**. Most Web pages provide a way to contact the organization or the individual. The person in charge of an organization's Web site is its *Webmaster*. (*Note: Webmaster* is a gender-neutral title.)

To access a Web site, the user must specify a **uniform resource locator (URL)**, which points to the address of a specific resource on the Web. For instance, the URL for Microsoft is http://www.microsoft.com. Recall that HTTP stands for hypertext transport protocol. The remaining letters in this URL—www.microsoft.com—indicate the domain name that identifies the Web server that stores the Web site.

Users access the Web primarily through software applications called **browsers**. Browsers provide a graphical front end that enables users to point-and-click their way across the Web, a process called *surfing*. Web browsers became a means of universal access because they deliver the same interface on any operating system on which they run.

BEFORE *YOU GO ON....*

1. Describe the various ways that you can connect to the Internet.
2. Identify each part of an Internet address.
3. Describe the difference between the Internet and the World Wide Web.
4. What are the functions of browsers?

Apply The Concept 4.3

LEARNING OBJECTIVE 4.3 Describe the most common methods for accessing the Internet.

STEP 1 – Background

Section 4.3 has explained the difference between the Internet and the World Wide Web. Although many people use these terms interchangeably, they are very different. Most computers today are continuously connected to the Internet, although they are not always accessing the Web. Offices and other places of employment typically set up an Internet connection via a local area network (LAN). However, at home you have several options to consider.

STEP 2 – Activity

Visit http://www.wiley.com/go/rainer/MIS3e/applytheconcept, and watch the YouTube videos listed there. These videos go into a little more detail about the types of connections mentioned in Table 4.2. You will learn about advantages, disadvantages, and things to consider for the different methods of connecting to the Internet.

STEP 3 – Deliverable

Imagine that your parents are "technologically challenged" (some of you may not have to imagine). They have just bought a house at the beach, and they are getting ready to set up an Internet connection. At home, there is only one provider, so DSL vs. cable vs. cellular vs. satellite is not an issue. However, there are several options at the beach, and your parents don't know where to begin.

Compose an e-mail to your parents that describes the most common methods for accessing the Internet to help them develop criteria for making their choice.

4.4 Network Applications

Now that you have a working knowledge of what networks are and how you can access them, the key question is, How do businesses use networks to improve their operations? This section addresses that question. Stated in general terms, networks support businesses and other organizations in all types of functions.

This section will explore numerous network applications, including discovery, communication, collaboration, e-learning and distance learning, virtual universities, and telecommuting. These applications, however, are merely a sampling of the many network applications currently available to users. Even if these applications formed an exhaustive list today, they would not do so tomorrow when something new will be developed. Furthermore, placing network applications in categories is difficult because there will always be borderline cases. For example, the difference between chat rooms (in the communications category) and teleconference (in the collaboration category) is only one of degree.

Discovery

The Internet enables users to access or discover information located in databases all over the world. By browsing and searching data sources on the Web, users can apply the Internet's discovery capability to areas ranging from education to government services to entertainment to commerce. Although having access to all this information is a great benefit, it is critically important to realize that there is no quality assurance for information on the Web. The Web is truly democratic in that *anyone* can post information to it. Therefore, the fundamental rule about information on the Web is "User beware!"

In addition, the Web's major strength—the vast stores of information it contains—also presents a major challenge. The amount of information on the Web can be overwhelming, and it doubles approximately each year. As a result, navigating through the Web and gaining access to necessary information are becoming more and more difficult. To accomplish these tasks, people increasingly are using search engines, directories, and portals.

Search Engines and Metasearch Engines. A **search engine** is a computer program that searches for specific information by keywords and then reports the results. A search engine maintains an index of billions of Web pages. It uses that index to find pages that match a set of user-specified keywords. Such indexes are created and updated by *webcrawlers*, which are computer programs that browse the Web and create a copy of all visited pages. Search engines then index these pages to provide fast searches.

In mid-2014, four search engines accounted for almost all searches in the United States. They are, in order, Google (www.google.com), Bing (www.bing.com), Yahoo! (www.yahoo.com), and Ask (www.ask.com). In addition, there are an incredible number of other search engines that are quite useful, many of which perform very specific searches. (See an article on "The Top 100 Alternative Search Engines" that appeared on www.readwriteweb.com.) The leading search engine in China is Baidu, which claimed 78 percent of the Chinese market in April 2014.

For an even more thorough search, you can use a metasearch engine. Metasearch engines search several engines at once and then integrate the findings to answer users' queries. Examples are Surf-wax (www.surfwax.com), Metacrawler (www.metacrawler.com), Mamma (www.mamma.com), KartOO (www.kartoo.com), and Dogpile (www.dogpile.com).

One interesting Q&A Web site is Quora. IT's About Business 4.2 explains how Quora works.

 'S ABOUT BUSINESS 4.2

Just Exactly What Is Quora?

The Merriam-Webster online dictionary (www.merriam-webster.com) has amazing breadth and scope. However, there is only so much that any encyclopedia, limited to verifiable facts about discrete nouns, can capture about the entirety of human knowledge. On the other end of the "knowledge" spectrum, Web sites such as Facebook and Twitter allow people to describe their lives and make personal observations. On such networks, however, it is difficult to separate informed opinions from pure speculation.

The large gap between the two approaches—the objective (Merriam-Webster) and the subjective (social networks)—is that area that Quora (www.quora.com) occupies. For years, blogs have occupied this space, but their idiosyncratic style has made their insights difficult to search.

Quora fills an existing need with Web sites devoted to answering questions. Many Internet searches are framed as searches. For example, Yahoo! Answers, a Q&A Web site, attracts millions of users in the United States per month. However, this site cannot satisfy most searches because the questions are often silly, and the replies tend to be guesswork offered by people with no knowledge of the subject.

On Quora's Web site, you can begin with the page—framed as a question—about getting started on Quora. Or, you can begin by looking through random questions that are displayed in the center of the screen. At the top of the page is a search bar. Using keywords, you can find questions that other visitors have already posed, or you can choose topics to follow so that the Web site can begin serving up queries more suited to your interests. You can also start following people. That way, the questions they ask, answer, and follow will show up in your feed. You can also vote "up" answers you think are helpful and vote "down" those you think are not.

Permitting users to vote an answer up or down helps to push high-quality responses to the top and to push down (if not off the page entirely) frivolous and poorly conceived posts. The Quora site has a button that allows users to deem an answer "not helpful"—a signal to the Quora team or to one of the site's volunteers that perhaps they should consider deleting it.

Real names are mandatory, so there is a heavy social cost to acting the fool. Quora does allow anonymous posts however, which helps when asking about a personal health issue, for example, or responding about your experience as a fellow sufferer.

Quora encourages answers that are thorough and in-depth. In Quora's community, the most valued responses reflect your honest intelligence and wisdom.

In contrast to Facebook, everything you write in Quora can be edited by one of the site's volunteers. Volunteers often send answers back to their authors marked up with suggested edits. Questions, too, can be extensively reworded.

By creating an environment in which members can post and answer questions as well as rate the quality of other users' answers, Quora is building a searchable repository of information and knowledge. The Quora community hopes to attract so many users that their subjective, experiential, inherent knowledge will construct a comprehensive picture of the world.

Questions persist about poor content on Quora. Some people pose silly questions. Worse, some people push up other users' answers that are off the point and not helpful. Quora responds that it can predict which content is useful and show its users only that content.

The site uses machine learning to identify its user's interests, based on signals such as which topics they read or follow on the site and answers they have voted on. (Machine learning concerns the construction and study of systems that can learn from data.) Many users give Quora access to their accounts on other services (e.g., social media), so the site can see what they do there. Quora also maintains a "map" of experts in different areas, so the site can direct questions to the people who should be able to provide the best answers.

When someone writes a new answer on Quora, the site must decide very quickly if it is good. Quora already knows something about the person who wrote it, his or her previous answers, who liked those answers, and who did not. Quora quickly shows new answers to other users. The site can learn within minutes whether a new answer (a) is likely to be a blockbuster and (b) meets a certain quality threshold. If the answer meets these criteria, then Quora surfaces it on the site and notifies the people who are following that topic or question. The most notable topics on Quora include start-ups, psychology, social media, medicine and health, software development, parenting, and U.S. politics.

Quora encourages people to write down their personal experiences, expertise, and advice. Since the site was founded in 2010, it has compiled high-quality content. Examples range from an astronaut trainer explaining pre-launch procedures to an inside account of Apple's (www .apple.com) culture of secrecy. If Quora can fulfill its vision—convincing experts to engage in conversation and thus generate searchable and authoritative answers to thousands of questions—then it may someday collect more page views than Wikipedia by filling in the gaps that no encyclopedia can address.

Sources: Compiled from Q. Hardy, "Quora and the Search for Truth," *The New York Times*, February 9, 2014; K. Yeung, "Quora Reveals the Secret to How It Organizes Content and the Most Popular Topics on Its Q&A Service," *TheNextWeb*, February 7, 2014; M. Nisen, "Is Quora the Future of the Press Release?" *Quartz*, February 5, 2014; L. Gannes, "Quora Gives Its Writers a Stats Dashboard," *AllThingsD*, November 12, 2013; T. Simonite, "Quora's Search for What the Internet Doesn't Know," *MIT Technology Review*, September 25, 2013; K. Fratti, "BBC.com and Quora Partner Up for New Column," *Mediabistro*, September 24, 2013; J. Novet, "Quora Looks to the Crowd to Solve Machine Learning Problems," *GigaOM*, July 10, 2013; G. Rivlin, "Does Quora Really Have all the Answers?" *Wired*, April 26, 2011; M. Lowman, "The Mystery Behind Quora," *BostInnovation*, February 1, 2011; www.quora.com, accessed March 1, 2014.

Questions

1. Is Quora a search engine, a knowledge-management system, or both? Provide specific examples to support your answer.

2. Is there an inherent problem with Quora itself selecting experts to whom the site sends questions? Support your answer.

Publication of Material in Foreign Languages. Not only is there a huge amount of information on the Internet, but it is also written in many different languages. How, then, do you access this information? The answer is that you use an *automatic translation* of Web pages. Such translation is available to and from all major languages, and its quality is improving with time. Some major translation products are Microsoft's Bing translator (http://www.microsofttranslator.com) and Google (www.google.com/language_tools) (see FIGURE 4.10), as well as products and services available at Trados (www.trados.com).

Should companies invest their time and resources to make their Web sites accessible in multiple languages? The answer is, absolutely. In fact, multilingual Web sites are now a competitive necessity because of the global nature of the business environment. Companies increasingly are looking outside their home markets to grow revenues and attract new

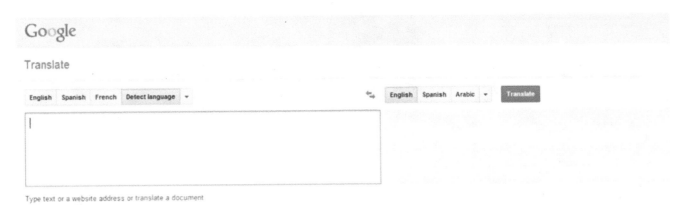

Figure 4.10 Google Translate. (Google and the Google logo are registered trademarks of Google Inc., used with permission)

customers. When companies are disseminating information around the world, getting that information correct is essential. It is not enough for companies to translate Web content. They must also localize that content and be sensitive to the needs of the people in local markets.

To reach 80 percent of the world's Internet users, a Web site needs to support a minimum of 10 languages: English, Chinese, Spanish, Japanese, German, Korean, French, Italian, Russian, and Portuguese. At 20 cents and more per word, translation services are expensive. Companies supporting 10 languages can spend $200,000 annually to localize information and another $50,000 to maintain the Web sites. Translation budgets for major multinational companies can run in millions of dollars. Many large companies use Systran S.A. (www.systransoft.com) for high-quality machine translation services.

Portals. Most organizations and their managers encounter information overload. Information is scattered across numerous documents, e-mail messages, and databases at different locations and systems. Finding relevant and accurate information is often time-consuming and may require users to access multiple systems.

One solution to this problem is to use portals. A **portal** is a Web-based, personalized gateway to information and knowledge that provides relevant information from different IT systems and the Internet using advanced search and indexing techniques. After reading the next section, you will be able to distinguish among four types of portals: commercial, affinity, corporate, and industrywide. The four types of portals are differentiated by the audiences they serve.

A **commercial (public) portal** is the most popular type of portal on the Internet. It is intended for broad and diverse audiences, and it offers routine content, some of it in real time (e.g., a stock ticker). Examples are Lycos (www.lycos.com) and Microsoft Network (www.msn.com).

In contrast, an **affinity portal** offers a single point of entry to an entire community of affiliated interests, such as a hobby group or a political party. Your university most likely has an affinity portal for its alumni. FIGURE 4.11 displays the affinity portal for the University of West Georgia. Other examples of affinity portals are www.techweb.com and www.zdnet.com.

As the name suggests, a **corporate portal** offers a personalized, single point of access through a Web browser to critical business information located inside and outside an

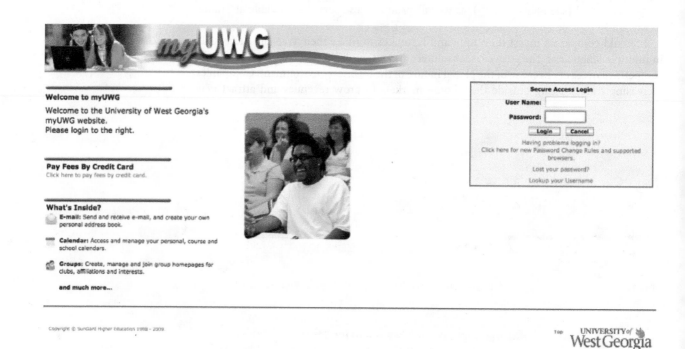

Figure 4.11 University of West Georgia affinity portal. (Courtesy of the University of West Georgia)

organization. These portals are also known as *enterprise portals*, *information portals*, and *enterprise information portals*. In addition to making it easier to find needed information, corporate portals offer customers and employees self-service opportunities.

Whereas corporate portals are associated with a single company, an **industrywide** portal serves entire industries. An example is TruckNet (www.truck.net), a portal for the trucking industry and the trucking community, including professional drivers, owner/operators, and trucking companies. TruckNet provides drivers with personalized Web-based e-mail, access to applications to leading trucking companies in the United States and Canada, and access to the Drivers Round Table, a forum where drivers can discuss issues of interest. The portal also provides a large database of trucking jobs as well as general information related to the trucking industry.

Communication

The second major category of network applications is communication. There are many types of communication technologies, including e-mail, call centers, chat rooms, and voice. You learn about each one in this section. You will read about another type of communication, blogging, in Chapter 8.

Electronic Mail. Electronic mail (e-mail) is the largest-volume application running over the Internet. Studies have found that almost all companies conduct business transactions via e-mail, and the vast majority confirm that e-mail is tied to their means of generating revenue. In fact, for many users, e-mail has all but replaced the telephone.

Web-Based Call Centers. Effective personalized customer contact is becoming an important aspect of Web-based customer support. Such service is provided through *Web-based call centers*, also known as *customer care centers*. For example, if you need to contact a software vendor for technical support, you will usually be communicating with the vendor's Web-based call center, using e-mail, a telephone conversation, or a simultaneous voice/Web session. Web-based call centers are sometimes located in foreign countries such as India. Such *offshoring* is an important issue for the U.S. companies. (We will discuss offshoring in detail in Chapter 14.)

Significantly, some of the U.S. companies are moving their call center operations back to the United States, for several reasons. First, they believe they have less control of their operations when the centers are located overseas. They must depend on the vendor company to uphold their standards, such as quality of service. A second difficulty is language differences, which can create serious communication problems. Third, companies that manage sensitive information risk breaching customer confidentiality and security. Finally, the call center representatives typically work with many companies. As a result, they may not deliver the same level of customer services that each company requires.

Electronic Chat Rooms. *Electronic chat* refers to an arrangement whereby participants exchange conversational messages in real time. A chat room is a virtual meeting place where many people (in fact, anyone) come to chat. Chat programs allow you to send messages to people who are connected to the same channel of communication at the same time. Anyone can join in the conversation. Messages are displayed on your screen as they arrive, even if you are in the middle of typing a message.

There are two major types of chat programs. The first type is Web based, which allows you to send messages to Internet users by using a Web browser and visiting a Web chat site (e.g., http://messenger.yahoo.com). The second type is e-mail based (text only); it is called *Internet Relay Chat* (IRC). A business can use IRC to interact with customers, provide online experts for answers to questions, and so on.

Voice Communication. When people need to communicate with one another from a distance, they use the telephone more frequently than any other communication device. With the plain old telephone service (POTS), every call opened up a dedicated circuit for the duration of the call. A dedicated circuit connects you to the person with whom you are talking and is devoted only to your call. In contrast, as you saw earlier in this chapter, the Internet divides data into packets, which traverse the Internet in random order and are reassembled at their destination.

With **Internet telephony**, also known as **Voice-over-Internet Protocol** or **VoIP**, phone calls are treated as just another kind of data. That is, your analog voice signals are digitized, sectioned into packets, and then sent over the Internet. In the past, to utilize VoIP you needed a computer with a sound card and a microphone. Today, however, you do not need special phones or headsets for your computer.

VoIP can reduce your monthly phone bills. However, packet switching can cause garbled communications. For example, if the packets of a message arrive out of order, that is not a problem when you are sending an e-mail or transmitting a photo. Incorrect reassembly of the packets of a voice message, however, will garble the message. Fortunately, this is less of a problem than in the past, because VoIP software continues to improve, and typical communications links have become much faster. So, although VoIP is not perfect, it is ready for prime time.

Skype (www.skype.com) provides several VoIP services for free: voice and video calls to users who also have Skype, instant messaging, short message service, voice mail, one-to-one and group chats, and conference calls with up to nine people. As of mid-2014, the most current version of Skype offered full-screen, high-definition video calling, Skype Access (to access WiFi hotspots), call transfer to a Skype contact on either a mobile or a landline phone, improved quality of calls, and ease of use. It also provided additional functions for which users pay. For example, SkypeOut allows you to make calls to landline phones and mobile phones. SkypeIn provides a number that your friends can call from any phone, and you pick up the call in Skype.

Vonage (www.vonage.com) also provides VoIP services, but for a fee (approximately $25 per month). With Vonage you make and receive calls with your existing home phone through your broadband Internet connection. Your phone actually connects to Vonage instead of an actual phone company. The person whom you are calling does not need to have Vonage or even an Internet connection.

Unified Communications. In the past, organizational networks for wired and wireless data, voice communications, and videoconferencing operated independently, and the IT department managed each network separately. This arrangement increased costs and reduced productivity.

Unified communications (UC) simplifies and integrates all forms of communications—voice, voice mail, fax, chat, e-mail, instant messaging, short message service, presence (location) services, and videoconferencing—on a common hardware and software platform. *Presence services* enable users to know where their intended recipients are and if they are available, in real time.

UC unifies all forms of human and computer communications into a common user experience. For example, UC allows an individual to receive a voice mail message and then read it in his or her e-mail inbox. In another example, UC enables users to seamlessly collaborate with another person on a project, regardless of where the users are located. One user could quickly locate the other user by accessing an interactive directory, determining whether that user is available, engaging in a text messaging session, and then escalating the session to a voice call or even a video call, all in real time.

Collaboration

The third major category of network applications is collaboration. An important feature of modern organizations is that people collaborate to perform work. **Collaboration** refers to efforts by two or more entities—that is, individuals, teams, groups, or organizations—who work together to accomplish certain tasks. The term **workgroup** refers specifically to two or more individuals who act together to perform some task.

Workflow is the movement of information as it progresses through the sequence of steps that make up an organization's work procedures. Workflow management makes it possible to pass documents, information, and tasks from one participant to another in a way that is governed by the organization's rules or procedures. Workflow systems are tools for automating business processes.

If group members are working in different locations, they constitute a **virtual group (team)**. Virtual groups conduct *virtual meetings*—that is, they "meet" electronically. **Virtual**

collaboration (or *e-collaboration*) refers to the use of digital technologies that enable organizations or individuals who are geographically dispersed to collaboratively plan, design, develop, manage, and research products, services, and innovative applications. Organizational employees frequently collaborate virtually with one another. In addition, organizations collaborate virtually with customers, suppliers, and other business partners to become more productive and competitive.

One type of collaboration is **crowdsourcing**, in which an organization outsources a task to an undefined, generally large group of people in the form of an open call. Crowdsourcing provides many potential benefits to organizations. First, crowds can explore problems—and often resolve them—at relatively low cost, and often very quickly. Second, the organization can tap a wider range of talent than might be present among its employees. Third, by listening to the crowd, organizations gain firsthand insight into their customers' desires. Finally, crowdsourcing taps into the global world of ideas, helping companies work through a rapid design process. Let's look at some examples of crowdsourcing.

- *Crowdsourcing help desks:* IT help desks are a necessary service on college campuses because students depend on their computers and Internet access to complete their schoolwork and attend class online. At Indiana University at Bloomington, new IT help desks use crowdsourcing to alleviate the cost and pressure of having to answer so many calls. Students and professors post their IT problems on an online forum, where other students and amateur IT experts answer them.

- *Recruitment:* Champlain College in Vermont developed a Champlain For Reel program, inviting students to share via YouTube videos recounting their experiences at the school and the ways they benefited from their time there. The YouTube channel serves to recruit prospective students and even updates alumni on campus and community events.

- *Scitable* (www.nature.com/scitable) combines social networking and academic collaboration. Through crowdsourcing, students, professors, and scientists discuss problems, find solutions, and swap resources and journals. Scitable is a free site that lets each individual user turn to crowdsourcing for answers even while helping others.

- Procter & Gamble (P&G) uses InnoCentive (www.innocentive.com), where company researchers post their problems. P&G offers cash rewards to problem solvers.

- SAP launched the Idea Place with the purpose of generating ideas for not-yet-developed software improvements and innovation. Any person can view the content in the Idea Place. The Idea Place is organized into numerous sessions, or categories, under which the ideas are organized. Once you have posted your idea, other users can vote on it and add comments. Status updates on your idea allow you to follow it as it progresses through the Idea Place. Every idea is reviewed by a team of experts made up of engineers, product managers, and community managers who evaluate the potential for implementation. The ideas with the most votes will receive a higher level of attention from SAP.

Although crowdsourcing has numerous success stories, there are many questions and concerns about this system, including the following:

- Should the crowd be limited to experts? If so, then how would a company go about implementing this policy?

- How accurate is the content created by the nonexperts in the crowd? How is accuracy maintained?

- How is crowd-created content being updated? How can companies be certain the content is relevant?

- The crowd may submit too many ideas, with most of them being worthless. In this scenario, evaluating all of these ideas can be prohibitively expensive. For example, during the BP oil spill in 2010, crowds submitted more than 20,000 suggestions on how to stem the flow of oil. The problem was very technical, so there were many poor suggestions. Nevertheless, despite the fact that BP was under severe time constraints, the company had to evaluate all of the ideas.

- Content contributors may violate copyrights, either intentionally or unintentionally.

- The quality of content (and therefore subsequent decisions) depends on the composition of the crowd. The best decisions may come if the crowd is made up of people with diverse opinions and ideas. In many cases, however, companies do not know the makeup of the crowd in advance.

Collaboration can be *synchronous*, meaning that all team members meet at the same time. Teams may also collaborate *asynchronously* when team members cannot meet at the same time. Virtual teams, whose members are located throughout the world, typically must collaborate asynchronously.

A variety of software products are available to support all types of collaboration. Among the most prominent are Microsoft SharePoint Workspace, Google Drive, IBM Lotus Quickr, and Jive. In general, these products provide online collaboration capabilities, workgroup e-mail, distributed databases, bulletin whiteboards, electronic text editing, document management, workflow capabilities, instant virtual meetings, application sharing, instant messaging, consensus building, voting, ranking, and various application development tools.

These products also provide varying degrees of content control. Wikis, Google Drive, Microsoft SharePoint Workspace, and Jive provide for shared content with *version management*, whereas Microsoft SharePoint Workspace and IBM Lotus Quickr offer *version control*. Products that provide version management track changes to documents and provide features to accommodate multiple people working on the same document at the same time. In contrast, version-control systems provide each team member with an account that includes a set of permissions. Shared documents are located in shared directories. Document directories are often set up so that users must check out documents before they can edit them. When one team member checks out a document, no other member can access it. Once the document has been checked in, it becomes available to other members.

In this section, we review the major collaboration software products. We then shift our attention to two tools that support collaboration—electronic teleconferencing and videoconferencing.

Microsoft SharePoint. Microsoft's SharePoint product (www.microsoft.com/Sharepoint/default.mspx) provides shared content with version control. SharePoint supports document directories and has features that enable users to create and manage surveys, discussion forums, wikis, member blogs, member Web sites, and workflow. It also has a rigorous permissions structure, which allows organizations to control users' access based on their organizational role, team membership, interest, security level, or other criteria.

One company that has used SharePoint effectively is Continental Airlines. When new federal regulations regarding long runway delays went into effect, Continental responded by implementing a SharePoint system that puts various aspects of flight operations—aircraft status, pilots, crews, and customer care—on the same page. Under this system, the 135 general managers at the airline's domestic airports fill out a 16-page form online. The form includes the names and numbers of airport workers, from the airport authority to the person who drives the stairs to planes waiting on the runway. The general managers have to specify how they would manage delays of an hour, two hours, and two-and-one-half hours. The Sharepoint system includes a dashboard for Continental's centralized system operations center. People in the center can use the dashboard to quickly find information about delays and to communicate with pilots, crews, and dispatchers to decide what to do to mitigate any delays.

Google Drive. Google Drive (http://drive.google.com) is a free Web-based word processor, spreadsheet, and presentation application. It enables users to create and edit documents online while collaborating with other users. In contrast to Microsoft SharePoint Workspace, Google Docs allows multiple users to open, share, and edit documents at the same time.

IBM Lotus Quickr. IBM's Lotus Quickr (www.ibm.com/lotus/quickr) product provides shared content with version control in the form of document directories with check-in and check-out features based on user privileges. Quickr provides online team spaces where members can share and collaborate by utilizing team calendars, discussion forums, blogs, wikis, and other collaboration tools for managing projects and other content.

Jive. Jive's (www.jivesoftware.com) newest product, Clearspace, uses Web collaboration and communication tools such as forums, wikis, and blogs to allow people to share content with version management via discussion rooms and calendars. For example, Nike originally used Clearspace Community to run a technical support forum on Nike Plus (http://nikerunning.nike.com), a Web site where runners track their miles and calories burned using a sensor in their shoes. The company soon noticed that runners were also using the forum to meet other athletes. In response, Nike expanded its forum to include a section where runners could meet and challenge one another to races. Since that time, 40 percent of visitors to the site who did not own the Nike Plus sensor ended up buying the product.

Electronic Teleconferencing. **Teleconferencing** is the use of electronic communication technology that enables two or more people at different locations to hold a conference. There are several types of teleconferencing. The oldest and simplest is a telephone conference call, where several people talk to one another from multiple locations. The biggest disadvantage of conference calls is that they do not allow the participants to communicate face to face. In addition, participants in one location cannot see graphs, charts, and pictures at other locations.

To overcome these shortcomings, organizations are increasingly turning to video teleconferencing or videoconferencing. In a **videoconference**, participants in one location can view participants, documents, and presentations at other locations. The latest version of videoconferencing, called *telepresence*, enables participants to seamlessly share data, voice, pictures, graphics, and animation by electronic means. Conferees can also transmit data along with voice and video, which allows them to work together on documents and to exchange computer files.

Several companies are offering high-end telepresence systems. For example, Hewlett-Packard's Halo system (www.hp.com), Cisco's TelePresence 3000 (www.cisco.com), and Polycom's HDX (www.polycom.com) use massive high-definition screens up to eight feet wide to show people sitting around conference tables (see FIGURE 4.12). Telepresence systems also have advanced audio capabilities that let everyone talk at once without canceling out any voices. For example, financial firms such as the Blackstone Group (www.blackstone.com), a private equity firm, and consulting firms like Deloitte & Touche (www.deloitte.com) are using telepresence systems.

Let's look at an example of how a law firm uses these various collaboration technologies. Burr & Forman (www.burr.com), a full-service law firm based in Atlanta, Georgia, uses Microsoft SharePoint as a content and document repository. SharePoint allows users to find and share the documents they need faster and with less effort. Furthermore, Burr can quickly, easily, and securely provide its clients with access to whatever documents they need. The firm is also able to consolidate nine different document libraries into a single library that all of its employees can access.

Burr also uses AdobeConnect (www.adobe.com) to provide online training. This feature enables the firm to train multiple people in different offices at one time. Burr also uses the tool for continuing education training, which requires input to prove that the person watches the entire video session.

In addition, Burr employs Cisco System's (www.cisco.com) Tandberg video conferencing system for internal meetings, depositions, interviews, and other events. The firm has realized decreased travel costs as a result of using videoconferencing.

E-Learning and Distance Learning

E-learning and distance learning are not the same thing, but they do overlap. E-learning refers to learning supported by the Web. It can take place inside classrooms as a support to conventional teaching, such as when students work on the Web during class. It also can take place in virtual classrooms, in which all coursework is completed

HO Marketwire Photos/Newscom

Figure 4.12 Telepresence system.

online and classes do not meet face-to-face. In these cases, e-learning is a part of distance learning. **Distance learning (DL)** refers to any learning situation in which teachers and students do not meet face-to-face.

Today, the Web provides a multimedia interactive environment for self-study. Web-enabled systems make knowledge accessible to those who need it, when they need it, anytime, anywhere. For this reason, e-learning and DL can be useful for both formal education and corporate training.

There are many benefits of e-learning. For example, online materials can deliver very current content that is of high quality (created by content experts) and consistent (presented the same way every time). It also gives students the flexibility to learn at any place, at any time, and at their own pace. In corporate training centers that use e-learning, learning time generally is shorter, which means that more people can be trained within a given time frame. This system reduces training costs and eliminates the expense of renting facility space.

Despite these benefits, e-learning has some drawbacks. For one, students must be computer literate. Also, they may miss the face-to-face interaction with instructors and fellow students. In addition, accurately assessing students' work can be problematic because instructors really do not know who completed the assignments.

E-learning does not usually replace the classroom setting. Rather, it enhances it by taking advantage of new content and delivery technologies. Advanced e-learning support environments, such as Blackboard (www.blackboard.com), add value to traditional learning in higher education.

A new form of distance learning has recently appeared, called *massive open online courses* or *MOOCs*. MOOCs are a tool for democratizing higher education. Hundreds of thousands of students around the world who lack access to universities are using MOOCs to acquire sophisticated skills and high-paying jobs without having to pay tuition or obtain a college degree.

MOOCs are highly automated, with computer-graded assignments and exams. Nonetheless, they provide many opportunities for social interaction, as you see in Stanford University's MOOC.

In fall 2011, 160,000 students in 190 countries enrolled in a single Machine Learning (a type of artificial intelligence) course offered at Stanford. The course gave rise to its own online community, including a Facebook group, online discussions among participants, and volunteer translators who made the course available in 44 languages. The 23,000 students who completed the course received a PDF file by e-mail that indicated their percentile score. However, the file did not contain the name "Stanford University." A total of 248 students, none of them from Stanford, earned grades of 100 percent.

In February 2012, the Massachusetts Institute of Technology (MIT), which had been posting materials online for 10 years, opened registration for its first MOOC. In addition to universities, two for-profit startups, Udacity (www.udacity.com) and Udemy (www.udemy.com), offer a variety of MOOCs. Both companies plan to help their students find jobs. To accomplish this task, they obtain students' permission to sell leads to recruiters.

Virtual Universities

Virtual universities are online universities in which students take classes via the Internet either at home or in an off-site location. A large number of existing universities offer online education of some form. Some universities, such as the University of Phoenix (www.phoenix.edu), California Virtual Campus (www.cvc.edu), and the University of Maryland (www.umuc.edu), offer thousands of courses and dozens of degrees to students worldwide, all of them online. Other universities offer limited online courses and degrees, but they employ innovative teaching methods and multimedia support in the traditional classroom.

Telecommuting

Knowledge workers are being called the distributed workforce, or "digital nomads." This group of highly prized workers is now able to work anywhere and anytime, a process called **telecommuting**. Distributed workers are those who have no permanent office at their companies, preferring to work at home offices, in airport lounges, or client conference rooms, or on a high school stadium bleacher. The growth of the distributed workforce is driven by globalization, extremely long commutes to work, rising gasoline prices, ubiquitous broadband communications links (wireline and wireless), and powerful laptop computers and computing devices.

Telecommuting offers a number of potential advantages for employees, employers, and society. For employees, the benefits include reduced stress and improved family life. In addition, telecommuting offers employment opportunities for housebound people such as single parents and persons with disabilities. Benefits for employers include increased productivity, the ability to retain skilled employees, and the ability to attract employees who do not live within commuting distance.

However, telecommuting also has some potential disadvantages. For employees, the major disadvantages are increased feelings of isolation, possible loss of fringe benefits, lower pay (in some cases), no workplace visibility, the potential for slower promotions, and lack of socialization. In a 2013 study, researchers at Stanford University found that telecommuting employees are 50 percent less likely to receive a promotion than onsite workers. The researchers concluded that a lack of "face time" with bosses caused careers to stall.

In addition, telecommuting employees often have difficulties "training" their families to understand that they are at work even though they are physically at home. Families have to understand that they should not disturb the telecommuter for anything that they would not have disturbed him or her about in a "real" office. The major disadvantages to employers are difficulties in supervising work and potential data security problems. IT's About Business 4.3 underscores the intense debate about telecommuting in today's workplace.

IT'S ABOUT BUSINESS 4.3

Yahoo! CEO Marissa Mayer Bans Telecommuting

According to the U.S. Census Bureau, approximately 9 percent of American workers work from home at least one day per week, and that percentage is increasing rapidly. However, Yahoo! (www.yahoo.com) seems to be reversing this trend.

In February 2013, Yahoo! CEO Marissa Mayer controversially terminated the company's policy of allowing its employees to work offsite. According to an anonymous source, Mayer checked the logins on Yahoo!'s virtual private network and discovered that her remote employees did not log into the company network often enough. In addition, Mayer was frustrated because the Yahoo! parking lot was slow to fill up in the morning and quick to empty by 5:00 PM, a situation not typical of the company's rivals in Silicon Valley.

In an internal memo republished in multiple media outlets, Mayer announced: "To become the absolute best place to work, communication and collaboration will be important, so we need to be working side-by-side. That is why it is critical that we are all present in our offices. Some of the best decisions and insights come from hallway and cafeteria discussions, meeting new people, and impromptu team meetings. Speed and quality are often sacrificed when we work from home." Some observers speculated that Mayer was trying to trim unproductive workers without incurring the costs associated with layoffs. Unfortunately, in the process, she may have received more negative publicity than she had anticipated. Hundreds of Yahoo! employees—including those who

work from home only one or two days per week—will have to decide whether to come to the office every day or lose their jobs.

For her part, Mayer is a well-known workaholic. She created a controversy

© LajosRepasi/iStockphoto

when she took the top job at Yahoo! when she was five months pregnant and then took only two weeks of maternity leave. When she returned to work, she built a nursery next to her office at Yahoo! at her own expense so that she could be closer to her infant son and yet work even longer hours.

A backlash to Mayer's announcement threatened to overshadow any progress that she had made in reversing Yahoo!'s long decline. For example, working mothers are protesting because they believe that Mayer is setting them back by taking away their flexible working arrangements. Many people view telecommuting as the only way time-stressed women who do not enjoy the pay, privilege, and perks that come with being the chief executive of a Fortune 500 company can care for young children and advance their careers at the same time.

Mayer's decision to ban telecommuting intensified the debate about the subject. In contrast to Mayer's claims that working outside the office makes employees less productive and creative, several studies have concluded that telecommuting brings positive outcomes to organizations. For example, one broad, inclusive study by the consulting firm Workshifting (www.workshifting.com) discovered that, on average, productivity among telecommuting employees increased 27 percent. Overall, nearly 70 percent of the employers surveyed, including British Telecom (www.bt.com), Dow Chemical (www.dow.com), and American Express (www.americanexpress.com), reported higher productivity among telecommuting employees than those working in-house. One of the most impressive examples of telecommuting advantages involves Cisco (www.cisco.com), which, in contrast to Mayer's assertion, found that its telecommuters communicated and collaborated effectively. Cisco has also benefited from improved employee retention by allowing its employees to telecommute. Similarly, a 2011 study by WorldatWork (www.worldatwork.org) concluded that companies that embrace flexibility exhibited lower turnover rates and greater employee satisfaction, motivation, and engagement.

In addition to increased productivity, a study by Global Workplace Analytics (www.teleworkresearchnetwork.com) revealed that telecommuting generates significant environmental savings. Specifically, allowing employees to telecommute half-time could reduce carbon emissions by more than 51 million metric tons per year—the equivalent of taking all of greater New York's commuters off the road.

Mayer's ban on telecommuting is widely viewed as a risky step that could further damage Yahoo! employee morale and performance and undermine recruiting efforts in a very competitive job market. As of March 2014, the impact of Yahoo!'s ban on telecommuting remained to be seen. That is, is Marissa Mayer right or wrong?

About a month after Mayer's announcement, electronics retailer Best Buy (www.bestbuy.com) followed suit by banning telecommuting for the roughly 4,000 employees at its headquarters. This move eliminated an innovative program called Results Only Work Environment, which had allowed workers to complete projects out of the office. Employees essentially had free rein as long as they met their superiors' expectations.

In October 2013, Hewlett-Packard (HP) also banned telecommuting during a critical turnaround period. As with Yahoo!, the impact of Best Buy's and HP's bans on telecommuting remains to be seen.

Despite being prohibited at Yahoo!, Best Buy, and HP, telecommuting continues to grow. One national survey of full-time employed adults found that 31 percent perform most of their work away from their employers' location. Their "worksites" include their home, a business center, shared office space, or a coffee shop. These studies support the value of telecommuting, and an increasing number of employers are allowing or even requiring employees to work remotely at least part of the time. Fueling this increase is not just savings in real estate costs, but the fact that telecommuting enables employers to hire the best (and least expensive) candidates, regardless of where they live.

Sources: Compiled from J. Ludden, "Telework: Not Just for Moms and Millenials," *NPR.org*, February 27, 2014; M. Biro, "Telecommuting Is the Future of Work," *Forbes*, January 12, 2014; J. Parris, "Hewlett-Packard Bans Telecommuting? Not Quite," *Flexjobs*, October 17, 2013; A. Lee, "First Yahoo! Now HP Cracks Down on Telecommuting," *Cruxial CIO*, October 9, 2013; J. Kotkin, "Marissa Mayer's Misstep and the Unstoppable Rise of Telecommuting," *Forbes*, March 26, 2013; M. Patrick, "Yahoo! Ban on Telecommuting Causes Debate," *U.S. News and World Report*, March 22, 2013; T. Hsu, "After Yahoo!, Best Buy Also Rethinks Telecommuting," *Los Angeles Times*, March 6, 2013; B. Belton, "Best Buy Copies Yahoo!, Reins in Telecommuting," *USA Today*, March 6, 2013; R. Silverman and Q. Fottrell, "The Home Office in the Spotlight," *The Wall Street Journal*, February 27, 2013; J. Guynn, "Yahoo! CEO Marissa Mayer Causes Uproar with Telecommuting Ban," *Los Angeles Times*, February 26, 2013; www.yahoo.com, accessed March 27, 2013.

Questions

1. Do you feel that Yahoo! is making the correct decision of banning telecommuting?
   a. Present the pro side of this issue (i.e., Mayer's side).
   b. Present the con side of this issue.

2. This IT's About Business was written in March 2014. Take a look at www.yahoo.com to see how the company is doing. Also, check on news articles about the ongoing fallout from Mayer's decision.

3. Discuss Mayer's internal memo quoted above. Do you agree or disagree with it? Support your answer.

Apply The Concept 4.4

LEARNING OBJECTIVE 4.4

Explain the impact that networks have had on business and everyday life for each of the six major categories of network applications.

STEP 1 – Background

This section identified the six major categories of network applications. *Discovery* occurs when you find information in other places that is useful to you. *Communication* takes place when you send information to other people that is helpful to them, and *collaboration* exists when two or more people work on information at the same time. Corporate networks (intranets) are designed to enable communication and collaboration within an organization by making data accessible to employees in different departments. Employees who access these data off-site are often telecommuting. *E-learning* (and distance learning) and *virtual universities* are sister applications of networks because they allow instruction to take place outside the boundaries of a traditional campus.

STEP 2 – Activity

All of the categories discussed above have pros and cons. For this activity, search the Web for advantages and disadvantages of each category. Then consider how these advantages and disadvantages apply to businesses and everyday life.

STEP 3 – Deliverable

Build a table that explains the impact (positive and negative) that networks have on business and on everyday life for each of the six categories listed above. The table should be formatted like the following example:

┌─ **BEFORE** *YOU GO ON....* ─────────────

1. Discuss the network applications that you studied in this section and the tools and technologies that support each one.

2. Identify the business conditions that have made videoconferencing more important.

3. Differentiate between e-learning and distance learning.

4. Describe virtual universities.

5. What is telecommuting? Would you like to telecommute? Why or why not?

Network Application	Business Impact	Everyday Life Impact
Discovery	Positive: Negative	Positive: Negative
Communication	Positive: Negative	Positive: Negative
Collaboration	Positive: Negative	Positive: Negative
E-Learning and Distance Learning	Positive: Negative	Positive: Negative
Virtual Universities	Positive: Negative	Positive: Negative
Telecommuting	Positive: Negative	Positive: Negative

What's in for ME?

FOR THE ACCOUNTING MAJOR

Accounting personnel use corporate intranets and portals to consolidate transaction data from legacy systems to provide an overall view of internal projects. This view contains the current costs charged to each project, the number of hours spent on each project by individual employees, and an analysis of how actual costs compare with projected costs. Finally, accounting personnel use Internet access to government and professional Web sites to stay informed on legal and other changes affecting their profession.

FOR THE FINANCE MAJOR

Corporate intranets and portals can provide a model to evaluate the risks of a project or an investment. Financial analysts use two types of data in the model: historical transaction data from corporate databases via the intranet and industry data obtained via the Internet. In addition, financial services firms can use the Web for marketing and to provide services.

FOR THE MARKETING MAJOR

Marketing managers use corporate intranets and portals to coordinate the activities of the sales force. Sales personnel access corporate portals via the intranet to discover updates on pricing, promotion, rebates, customer information, and information about competitors. Sales staff can also download and customize presentations for their customers. The Internet, particularly the Web, opens a completely new marketing channel for many industries. Just how advertising, purchasing, and information dispensation should occur appears to vary from industry to industry, product to product, and service to service.

POM **FOR THE** PRODUCTION/ OPERATIONS MANAGEMENT MAJOR

Companies are using intranets and portals to speed product development by providing the development team with three-dimensional models and animation. All team members can access the models for faster exploration of ideas and enhanced feedback. Corporate portals, accessed via intranets, enable managers to carefully supervise their inventories as well as real-time production on assembly lines. Extranets are also proving valuable as communication formats for joint research and design efforts among companies. The Internet is also a great source of cutting-edge information for POM managers.

 FOR THE HUMAN RESOURCES MANAGEMENT MAJOR

Human resources personnel use portals and intranets to publish corporate policy manuals, job postings, company telephone directories, and training classes. Many companies deliver online training obtained from the Internet to employees through their intranets. Human resources departments use intranets to offer employees healthcare, savings, and benefit plans, as well as the opportunity to take competency tests online. The Internet supports worldwide recruiting efforts; it can also be the communications platform for supporting geographically dispersed work teams.

MIS **FOR THE** MIS MAJOR

As important as the networking technology infras-tructure is, it is invisible to users (unless something goes wrong). The MIS function is responsible for keeping all organizational networks up and running all the time. MIS personnel, therefore, provide all users with an "eye to the world" and the ability to compute, communicate, and collaborate anytime, anywhere. For example, organizations have access to experts at remote locations without having to duplicate that expertise in multiple areas of the firm. Virtual teaming allows experts physically located in different cities to work on projects as though they were in the same office.

SUMMARY

1. Compare and contrast the two major types of networks.

   The two major types of networks are local area networks (LANs) and wide area networks (WANs). LANs encompass a limited geographical area and are usually composed of one communications medium. In contrast, WANs encompass a broad geographical area and are usually composed of multiple communications media.

2. Describe the wireline communications media and channels.

   Twisted-pair wire, the most prevalent form of communications wiring, consists of strands of copper wire twisted in pairs. It is relatively inexpensive to purchase, widely available, and easy to work with. However, it is relatively slow for transmitting data, it is subject to interference from other electrical sources, and it can be easily tapped by unintended receivers.

   Coaxial cable consists of insulated copper wire. It is much less susceptible to electrical interference than is twisted-pair wire and it can carry much more data. However, coaxial cable is more expensive and more difficult to work with than twisted-pair wire. It is also somewhat inflexible.

   Fiber-optic cables consist of thousands of very thin filaments of glass fibers that transmit information via light pulses generated by lasers. Fiber-optic cables are sig-

nificantly smaller and lighter than traditional cable media. They can also transmit far more data, and they provide greater security from interference and tapping. Fiber-optic cable is often used as the backbone for a network, whereas twisted-pair wire and coaxial cable connect the backbone to individual devices on the network.

3. Describe the most common methods for accessing the Internet.

   Common methods for connecting to the Internet include dial-up, DSL, cable modem, satellite, wireless, and fiber to the home.

4. Explain the impact that networks have had on business and everyday life for each of the six major categories of network applications.

   > *Discovery* involves browsing and information retrieval, and provides users the ability to view information in databases, download it, and/or process it. Discovery tools include search engines, directories, and portals. Discovery tools enable business users to efficiently find needed information.

   > Networks provide fast, inexpensive *communications*, via e-mail, call centers, chat rooms, voice communications,

and blogs. Communications tools provide business users with a seamless interface among team members, colleagues, business partners, and customers.

> *Collaboration* refers to mutual efforts by two or more entities (individuals, groups, or companies) who work together to accomplish tasks. Collaboration is enabled by workflow systems. Collaboration tools enable business users to collaborate with colleagues, business partners, and customers.

> *E-learning* refers to learning supported by the Web. Distance learning refers to any learning situation in which teachers and students do not meet face-to-face.

E-learning provides tools for business users to enable their lifelong learning.

> *Virtual universities* are online universities in which students take classes via the Internet at home or an off-site location. Virtual universities make it possible for students to obtain degrees while working full time, thus increasing their value to their firms.

> *Telecommuting* is the process whereby knowledge workers are able to work anywhere and anytime. Telecommuting provides flexibility for employees, with many benefits and some drawbacks.

CHAPTER GLOSSARY

affinity portal A Web site that offers a single point of entry to an entire community of affiliated interests.

analog signals Continuous waves that transmit information by altering the amplitude and frequency of the waves.

backbone networks High-speed central networks to which multiple smaller networks (e.g., LANs and smaller WANs) connect.

bandwidth The transmission capacity of a network, stated in bits per second.

broadband The transmission capacity of a communications medium faster than 4 Mbps.

broadcast media (also called **wireless media**) Communications channels that use electromagnetic media (the "airwaves") to transmit data.

browsers Software applications through which users primarily access the Web.

cable media (also called **wireline media**) Communications channels that use physical wires or cables to transmit data and information.

chat room A virtual meeting place where groups of regulars come to "gab" electronically.

client/server computing Form of distributed processing in which some machines (servers) perform computing functions for end-user PCs (clients).

clients Computers, such as users' personal computers, that use any of the services provided by servers.

coaxial cable Insulated copper wire; used to carry high-speed data traffic and television signals.

collaboration Mutual efforts by two or more individuals who perform activities in order to accomplish certain tasks.

commercial (public) portal A Web site that offers fairly routine content for diverse audiences; offers customization only at the user interface.

communications channel Pathway for communicating data from one location to another.

computer network A system that connects computers and other devices via communications media so that data and information can be transmitted among them.

corporate portal A Web site that provides a single point of access to critical business information located inside and outside of an organization.

crowdsourcing A process in which an organization outsources a task to an undefined, generally large group of people in the form of an open call.

digital signals A discrete pulse, either on or off, that conveys information in a binary form.

digital subscriber line (DSL) A high-speed, digital data-transmission technology using existing analog telephone lines.

distance learning (DL) Learning situations in which teachers and students do not meet face-to-face.

distributed processing Network architecture that divides processing work between two or more computers, linked together in a network.

domain name system (DNS) The system administered by the Internet Corporation for Assigned Names (ICANN) that assigns names to each site on the Internet.

domain names The name assigned to an Internet site, consisting of multiple parts, separated by dots, which are translated from right to left.

e-learning Learning supported by the Web; can be done inside traditional classrooms or in virtual classrooms.

enterprise network An organization's network composed of interconnected multiple LANs and WANs.

Ethernet A common local area network protocol.

extranet A network that connects parts of the intranets of different organizations.

fiber-optic cable A communications medium consisting of thousands of very thin filaments of glass fibers, surrounded by cladding, that transmit information via light pulses generated by lasers.

file server (also called **network server**) A computer that contains various software and data files for a local area network and contains the network operating system.

hyperlink A connection from a hypertext file or document to another location or file, typically activated by clicking on a highlighted word or image on the screen, or by touching the screen.

hypertext Text displayed on a computer display with references, called hyperlinks, to other text that the reader can immediately access.

Hypertext Transport Protocol (HTTP) The communications standard used to transfer pages across the WWW portion of the Internet; defines how messages are formulated and transmitted.

industrywide portal A Web-based gateway to information and knowledge for an entire industry.

Internet (the Net) A massive global WAN that connects approximately 1 million organizational computer networks in more than 200 countries on all continents, including Antarctica, and features in the daily routine of almost 2 billion people. Participating computer systems include smartphones, PCs, LANs, databases, and mainframes.

Internet backbone The primary network connections and telecommunications lines that link the computers and organizational nodes of the Internet.

Internet Protocol (IP) A set of rules responsible for disassembling, delivering, and reassembling packets over the Internet.

Internet Protocol (IP) address An assigned address that uniquely identifies a computer on the Internet.

Internet service provider (ISP) A company that provides Internet connections for a fee.

Internet telephony (Voice-over-Internet Protocol or VoIP) The use of the Internet as the transmission medium for telephone calls.

Internet2 A new, faster telecommunications network that deploys advanced network applications such as remote medical diagnosis, digital libraries, distance education, online simulation, and virtual laboratories.

intranet A private network that uses Internet software and TCP/IP protocols.

local area network (LAN) A network that connects communications devices in a limited geographic region, such as a building, so that every user device on the network can communicate with every other device.

metasearch engine A computer program that searches several engines at once and integrates the findings of the various search engines to answer queries posted by users.

modem Device that converts signals from analog to digital and vice versa.

network access points (NAPs) Computers that act as exchange points for Internet traffic and determine how traffic is routed.

network server See file server.

packet switching The transmission technology that divides blocks of text into packets.

peer-to-peer (P2P) processing A type of client/server distributed processing that allows two or more computers to pool their resources, making each computer both a client and a server.

portal A Web-based personalized gateway to information and knowledge that provides information from disparate information systems and the Internet, using advanced search and indexing techniques.

protocol The set of rules and procedures governing transmission across a network.

router A communications processor that routes messages from a LAN to the Internet, across several connected LANs, or across a wide area network such as the Internet.

search engine A computer program that searches for specific information by keywords and reports the results.

servers Computers that provide access to various network services, such as printing, data, and communications.

synchronous optical network (SONET) An interface standard for transporting digital signals over fiber-optic lines; allows the integration of transmissions from multiple vendors.

telecommuting A work arrangement whereby employees work at home, at the customer's premises, in special workplaces, or while traveling, usually using a computer linked to their place of employment.

teleconferencing The use of electronic communication that allows two or more people at different locations to have a simultaneous conference.

Transmission Control Protocol/Internet Protocol (TCP/IP) A file transfer protocol that can send large files of information across sometimes unreliable networks with assurance that the data will arrive uncorrupted.

twisted-pair wire A communications medium consisting of strands of copper wire twisted together in pairs.

unified communications Common hardware and software platform that simplifies and integrates all forms of communications—voice, e-mail, instant messaging, location, and videoconferencing—across an organization.

uniform resource locator (URL) The set of letters that identifies the address of a specific resource on the Web.

videoconference A virtual meeting in which participants in one location can see and hear participants at other locations and can share data and graphics by electronic means.

virtual collaboration The use of digital technologies that enable organizations or individuals to collaboratively plan, design, develop, manage, and research products, services, and innovative information systems and electronic commerce applications.

virtual group (team) A workgroup whose members are in different locations and who meet electronically.

virtual universities Online universities in which students take classes via the Internet at home or at an off-site location.

Voice-over-Internet Protocol (VoIP) See **Internet telephony**.

Web site Collectively, all of the Web pages of a particular company or individual.

wide area network (WAN) A network, generally provided by common carriers, that covers a wide geographical area.

wireless media See **broadcast media**.

wireline media See **cable media**.

workgroup Two or more individuals who act together to perform some task, on either a permanent or on a temporary basis.

workflow The movement of information as it flows through the sequence of steps that make up an organization's work procedures.

World Wide Web (the Web, WWW, or W3) A system of universally accepted standards for storing, retrieving, formatting, and displaying information via a client/server architecture; it uses the transport functions of the Internet.

DISCUSSION QUESTIONS

1. What are the implications of having fiber-optic cable to everyone's home?

2. What are the implications of BitTorrent for the music industry? For the motion picture industry?

3. Discuss the pros and cons of P2P networks.

4. Should the Internet be regulated? If so, by whom?

5. Discuss the pros and cons of delivering this book over the Internet.

6. Explain how the Internet works. Assume you are talking with someone who has no knowledge of information technology (in other words, keep it very simple).

7. How are the network applications of communication and collaboration related? Do communication tools also support collaboration? Give examples.

8. Search online for the article from *The Atlantic:* "Is Google Making Us Stupid?" *Is* Google making us stupid? Support your answer.

9. Refer to the chapter opening case:

   a. How do you feel about the net neutrality issue?

   b. Do you believe heavier bandwidth users should pay for more bandwidth?

   c. Do you believe wireless carriers should operate under different rules than wireline carriers?

   d. Evaluate your own bandwidth usage. (For example: Do you upload and download large files, such as movies?) If network neutrality were to be eliminated, what would the impact be for you?

   e. Should businesses monitor network usage? Do see a problem with employees using company-purchased bandwidth for personal use? Please explain your answer.

PROBLEM-SOLVING ACTIVITIES

1. Calculate how much bandwidth you consume when using the Internet every day. How many e-mails do you send daily and what is the size of each? (Your e-mail program may have e-mail file size information.) How many music and video clips do you download (or upload) daily and what is the size of each? If you view YouTube often, surf the Web to find out the size of a typical YouTube file. Add up the number of e-mail, audio, and video files you transmit or receive on a typical day. When you have calculated your daily Internet usage, determine if you are a "normal" Internet user or a "power" Internet user. What impact does network neutrality have on you as a "normal" user? As a "power" user?

2. Access several P2P applications, such as SETI@home. Describe the purpose of each application, and indicate which ones you would like to join.

3. Access http://ipv6.com and www.ipv6news.info and learn about more advantages of IPv6.

4. Access www.icann.org and learn more about this important organization.

5. Set up your own Web site using your name for the domain name (e.g., KellyRainer).

   a. Explain the process for registering a domain.

   b. Which top-level domain will you use and why?

6. Access www.icann.org and obtain the name of an agency or company that can register a domain for the TLD that you selected. What is the name of that agency or company?

7. Access the Web site for that agency or company (in question 6) to learn the process that you must use. How much will it initially cost to register your domain name? How much will it cost to maintain that name in the future?

8. You plan to take a two-week vacation in Australia this year. Using the Internet, find information that will help you plan the trip. Such information includes, *but is not limited to*, the following:

   a. Geographical location and weather conditions at the time of your trip

   b. Major tourist attractions and recreational facilities

   c. Travel arrangements (airlines, approximate fares)

   d. Car rental; local tours

   e. Alternatives for accommodation (within a moderate budget) and food

   f. Estimated cost of the vacation (travel, lodging, food, recreation, shopping, etc.)

   g. Country regulations regarding the entrance of your dog

   h. Shopping

   i. Passport information (either to obtain one or to renew one)

   j. Information on the country's language and culture

   k. What else do you think you should research before going to Australia?

9. From your own experience or from the vendor's information, list the major capabilities of Lotus Notes/Domino. Do the same for Microsoft Exchange. Compare and contrast the products. Explain how the products can be used to support knowledge workers and managers.

10. Visit Web sites of companies that manufacture telepresence products for the Internet. Prepare a report. Differentiate between telepresence products and videoconferencing products.

11. Access Google (or YouTube) videos and search for "Cisco Magic." This video shows Cisco's next-generation telepresence system. Compare and contrast it with current telepresence systems.

12. Access the Web site of your university. Does the Web site provide high-quality information (right amount, clear, accurate, etc.)? Do you think a high-school student who is thinking of attending your university would feel the same way?

13. Compare and contrast Google Sites (www.google.com/sites) and Microsoft Office Live (www.liveoffice.com). Which site would you use to create your own Web site? Explain your choice.

14. Access the Web site of the Recording Industry Association of America (www.riaa.com). Discuss what you find there regarding copyright infringement (i.e., downloading music files). How do you feel about the RIAA's efforts to stop music downloads? Debate this issue from your point of view and from the RIAA's point of view.

15. Research the companies involved in Internet telephony (Voice-over IP). Compare their offerings as to price, necessary technologies, ease of installation, and so on. Which company is the most attractive to you? Which company might be the most attractive for a large company?

16. Access various search engines other than Google. Search for the same terms on several of the alternative search engines and on Google. Compare the results on breadth (number of results found) and precision (results are what you were looking for).

17. Second Life (www.secondlife.com) is a three-dimensional, online world built and owned by its residents. Residents of Second Life are avatars who have been created by real people. Access Second Life, learn about it, and create your own avatar to explore this world. Learn about the thousands of people who are making "real-world" money from operations in Second Life.

18. Access Microsoft's Bing translator (http://www.microsofttranslator.com) or Google (www.google.com/language_tools) translation pages. Type in a paragraph in English and select, for example, English-to-French. When you see the translated paragraph in French, copy it into the text box, and select French-to-English. Is the paragraph that you first entered the same as the one you are looking at now? Why or why not? Support your answer.

>>> COLLABORATION EXERCISE

STEP 1 – Background

Napster was one of the first online services that allowed users to share files, primarily music files. The site was based on a peer-to-peer (P2P) network. In response to a lawsuit initiated by the recording industry, Napster was convicted of copyright violations and forced to close its doors. However, Napster opened the door for many subsequent ventures. Visit http://www.wiley.com/go/rainer/MIS3e/collaboration to watch a YouTube video about the rise and fall of Napster.

Today there are numerous sites that allow users to share files, often in the cloud. In contrast to Napster, these sites are both legal and highly useful. At the same link listed above, also watch the video titled "Cloud File Storage."

STEP 2 – Activity

Work with a group to imagine the type of data sharing you may experience on your job. Divide your group into functional areas. What kinds of files would benefit from a centralized file-sharing site? This site would not be a database.

Rather, it would involve large files that are more easily managed through file-sharing services; for example, handbooks, catalogs, manuals, policies, maps, and reference books. Files such as these are often too large to e-mail. In addition, they are regularly updated, so they need to be stored in a central location where users can access the latest version.

For the functional area to which you are assigned, search the Web for different types of files that are too large for e-mail. Download at least three of these files. Once everyone in your group has his or her files (make sure they are all public files), create a shared folder on Google Drive, and let everyone upload the files they have found. Create a new document in that folder titled "Contents" to list and describe the files contained in the folder.

STEP 3 – Deliverable

Share your folder and the "Contents" document with your instructor. Include an explanation of your experience as a group of using the Web for discovery, communication, and collaboration.

CLOSING **CASE 1** > Network Neutrality Wars

THE PROBLEM >>> The explosive growth of streaming video and mobile technologies is beginning to create bandwidth problems over the Internet. The Internet was designed to transmit content such as e-mails and Web pages. However, media items being transmitted through the Web today, such as high-definition movies, are vastly larger in size than the types of information the Internet was originally designed to handle. To compound this problem, there are now nearly 150 million smartphone users in the United States, many of whom use the Internet to stream video content to their phones.

Put simply, the number of users uploading and downloading huge files such as videos has skyrocketed within the past few years and will likely continue to increase. Internet traffic has reached some 64 exabytes per month in mid-2014, and more than 90 percent of that traffic consists of video uploads, downloads, and streaming.

The Internet bandwidth issue is as much about economics as it is about technology. Currently, consumers can send 1-kilobyte e-mails or watch the latest 30-gigabyte movie on their large-screen televisions for the same monthly broadband fee. Unlike the system used for power and water bills where higher usage results in higher fees, monthly broadband fees are not tied to consumer usage.

A study from Juniper Networks (www.juniper.net) highlights this "revenue-per-bit" problem. The report predicts that Internet revenue for carriers such as AT&T (www.att .com) and Comcast (www.comcast.com) will grow by 5 percent per year through 2020. At the same time, Internet traffic will increase by 27 percent annually, meaning that carriers will have to increase their bandwidth investment by 20 percent per year just to keep up with demand. Under this model, the carriers' business models will face pressures, because their total necessary investment will come to exceed revenue growth.

Few industry analysts expect carriers to stop investing in new capacity, but analysts agree that a financial crunch is coming. As Internet traffic soars, analysts expect revenue per megabit to decrease. These figures translate into a far lower return on investment (ROI). Although carriers can find ways to increase their capacity, it will be difficult for them to reap any revenue benefits from doing so.

The heart of the problem is that, even if the technology is equal to the task of transmitting huge amounts of data, no one is sure how to pay for these technologies. One proposed solution is to eliminate network neutrality.

A POSSIBLE SOLUTION >>> *Network neutrality* is an operating model under which Internet service providers (ISPs) must allow customers equal access to content and applications, regardless of the source or nature of the content. That is, Internet backbone carriers must treat all Web traffic equally, not charging different rates by user, content, site, platform, or application.

Telecommunications and cable companies want to replace network neutrality with an arrangement in which they can charge differentiated prices based on the amount of bandwidth consumed by the content that is being delivered over the Internet. These companies believe that differentiated pricing is the most equitable method by which they can finance the necessary investments in their network infrastructures.

To bolster their argument, ISPs point to the enormous amount of bandwidth required to transmit pirated versions of copyrighted materials over the Internet. In fact, Comcast reported in 2010 that illegal file sharing of copyrighted material was consuming 50 percent of its network capacity. In 2008, the company slowed down the transmission of BitTorrent (www.bittorrent.com) files, a form of peer-to-peer transmission that is frequently used for piracy and illegal sharing of copyrighted materials. In response, the Federal Communications Commission (FCC) ordered Comcast to restore its previous service. Comcast then filed a lawsuit challenging the FCC's authority to enforce network neutrality. In April 2010, the Washington D.C. Circuit Court of Appeals ruled in favor of Comcast, declaring that the FCC did not have the authority to regulate how an ISP manages its network. By endorsing differentiated pricing, the court struck a major blow against network neutrality.

ISPs further contend that net neutrality hinders U.S. international competitiveness by decreasing innovation and discouraging capital investments in new network technologies. Without such investments and innovations, ISPs will be unable to handle the exploding demand for Internet and wireless data transmission.

From the opposite perspective, proponents of network neutrality are petitioning Congress to regulate the industry to prevent network providers from adopting strategies similar to Comcast. They argue that the risk of censorship increases when network providers can selectively block or slow access to certain content, such as access to competing low-cost services such as Skype and Vonage. They also assert that a neutral Internet encourages innovation. Finally, they contend that the neutral Internet has helped to create many new businesses.

Most analysts expect that those users who consume the most data eventually will have to pay more, most likely in the form of tiered pricing plans. Americans, however, have never had to contend with limits on the amount of data they upload and download, so there may be pushback from users.

Despite the 2010 court ruling against network neutrality, on December 21, 2010, the FCC approved network neutrality rules that prohibited wireline-based broadband providers —but not mobile broadband providers—from engaging in "unreasonable discrimination" against Web traffic. These rules are known as the Open Internet Order.

THE RESULTS >>> In 2012, Verizon initiated a legal action against the FCC, claiming that the agency had overstepped its authority and that its network neutrality rules are unconstitutional. Verizon may have a valid point. The FCC can regulate the physical infrastructure over which packets travel on the network. It is less clear, however, whether it can also regulate the actual service or content those packets deliver.

In January 2014 Verizon won a partial victory in its appeal of the FCC's Open Internet Order. The U.S. Court of Appeals for the Washington D.C. circuit rejected Verizon's claim that the FCC lacks jurisdiction over broadband providers. However, it also ruled that the FCC cannot regulate broadband service providers the same way it regulates telephone companies. This ruling suggests that network neutrality cannot be enforced without further legislative intervention.

On February 23, 2014, Netflix agreed to a deal with Comcast to ensure that its movies and TV shows stream more quickly. This agreement demonstrates a shift in the balance of power in favor of ISPs and the likelihood of rising prices for consumers. Meanwhile the battle over network neutrality continued.

On May 15, 2014, the FCC decided to consider two options regarding the network neutrality issue: (1) permit fast and slow broadband lanes, which would compromise network neutrality; or (2) reclassify broadband as a telecommunications service, which would preserve network neutrality.

As of June 2014, the FCC has not announced its decision.

Sources: "Searching for Fairness on the Internet," *The New York Times*, May 15, 2014; Carr, D. "Warnings Along F.C.C.'s Fast Lane," *The New York Times*, May 11, 2014; R. Yu, "Netflix Deal Has Its Catches," *USA Today*, February, 24, 2014; D. Talbot, "Is Netflix Slowing Down? Good Luck Finding Out Why," *MIT Technology Review*, February 21, 2014; E. Malykhina, "FCC: We're Not Done with Net Neutrality," *Information Week*, February 20, 2014; J. Feldman, "Why Carriers Won't Win War on Netflix," *Information Week*, February 6, 2014; B. Butler, "Verizon Denies Throttling Amazon's Cloud, Netflix Services," *Network World*, February 5, 2014; D. Talbot, "Around the World, Net Neutrality Is Not a Reality," *MIT Technology Review*, January 20, 2014; J. Feldman, "Net Neutrality: Regulation Makes Evil Empire Giggle," *Information Week*, January 17, 2014; J. Feldman, "Net Neutrality Court Ruling Won't Ruin the Internet,"

Information Week, January 15, 2014; G. Gross, "Appeals Court Strikes Down FCC Net Neutrality Rule," *Network World*, January 14, 2014; T. Claburn, "FCC Net Neutrality Rules Rejected," *Information Week*, January 14, 2014; S. Higginbotham, "Analyst: Verizon's Network Neutrality Challenge May Have to Wait Until Fall," *GigaOM*, March 25, 2013; J. Brodkin, "Time Warner, Net Neutrality Foes Cry Foul over Netflix Super HD Demands," *Ars Technica*, January 17, 2013; M. Reardon, "Verizon to FCC: Free Speech Trumps Net Neutrality Rules," *CNET News*, July 3, 2012; J. Hamilton, "AT&T Must Give Shareholders Net Neutrality Vote," *Bloomberg*, February 14, 2012; W. Plank, "Confessions of an iPhone Data Hog," *The Wall Street Journal*, January 27, 2012; J. Engebretson, "Verizon Confirms It Will Appeal Newly Published Net Neutrality Rules Soon," *Connected Planet*, September 27, 2011; E. Wyatt, "House Votes Against 'Net Neutrality,'" *The New York Times*, April 8, 2011; L. Segall, "Verizon Challenges FCC Net Neutrality Rules," *CNN Money*, January 21, 2011; K. Corbin, "Net Neutrality 2011: What Storms May Come," *Internet News*, December 30, 2010; C. Albanesius, "What Do the FCC's Net Neutrality Rules Mean for You?" *PC Magazine*, December 22, 2010; G. Gross, "FCC Approves Compromise Net Neutrality Rules," *Network World*, December 21, 2010; P. Burrows, "Will Video Kill the Internet, Too?" *Bloomberg BusinessWeek*, December 6–12, 2010; A. Schatz and S. Ante, "FCC Web Rules Create Pushback," *Wall Street Journal*, May 6, 2010; www.comcast.com, www.att.com, www.verizon.com, accessed March 13, 2014.

Questions

1. Are the ISPs correct in claiming that network neutrality will limit their development of new technologies? Support your answer.

2. Are the content providers (e.g., Netflix) correct in claiming that eliminating network neutrality will encourage censorship by the ISPs? Support your answer.

3. Are the content providers correct in claiming that eliminating network neutrality will result in consumers paying higher prices for the content they watch over the Internet? Support your answer.

CLOSING **CASE 2** > Fiber to All of Us?

THE PROBLEM >>> Cable distribution giants such as Verizon (www.verizon.com), Time Warner Cable (www.timewarnercable.com), and Comcast (www.comcast.com) are enjoying healthy profit margins on their Internet services. Verizon's (www.verizon.com) fiber-optic network, called FiOS, serves the largest number of home subscribers in the nation. Verizon has made FiOS available to some 11 million U.S. households at a cost to Verizon of $23 billion. FiOS offers basic service starting at 15 megabits per second (Mbps), which can be upgraded in some areas to as much as 300 Mbps. Comcast's Xfinity Platinum service also offers 300 Mbps download cable service in some locations for about $300 per month.

None of these companies, however, appear to have plans to extend these services to additional geographical areas.

Rather, their business goal is to sign up more people in their existing service areas. Why have they adopted this strategy? The answer is that this approach adds the most revenue without increasing the companies' capital costs. Essentially, there are no compelling business incentives for the established cable companies to expand their service offerings. This policy is unfortunate because most Americans have no choice but to do business with their local cable company. To compound this problem, few outside companies have the money to compete with the existing, cash-heavy telecommunications companies who control existing cable networks. Given these realities, what would it take to implement ultrafast fiber service throughout the United States?

POSSIBLE SOLUTIONS >>> One possible solution involves Google (www.google.com), which is installing and operating ultrafast fiber-optic cable service, known as Google Fiber, in several U.S. cities. Google has invited 34 cities in 9 metropolitan areas to collaborate with Google to explore strategies to bring gigabit-speed Google Fiber to their cities.

Google Fiber was first deployed to homes in Kansas City (Kansas and Missouri). Google secured guarantees from the Kansas City government that the company would receive rapid responses on matters such as city inspections, access to rights-of-way, and permission to place fiber in sewers.

Google's fiber and connections are off-the-shelf technologies, and Google's fiber service is priced at just $70 per month, or $120 with bundled television. For the television service, Google made content deals that include some sports channels, although HBO is not yet part of Google's service content. Google Fiber comes with 2 terabytes of DVR storage, 1 additional terabyte of cloud storage, and a Nexus 7 Android tablet for use as a remote control.

How can Google offer this level of service for such a low price? The answer is that Google appears to be willing to accept lower operating margins and profits for compelling business reasons. The company's long-term corporate fortunes are closely linked to heavy Web usage. Therefore, more Web traffic, and more people watching that traffic, translate to more ad revenue for Google.

MKT

There are many cities where it may not be feasible to deploy fiber; for example, cities that have areas that are not densely populated or where construction costs are too high. Furthermore, in California, the provisions for securing environmental permits make such a project cost-prohibitive.

Google is not the only organization that is bringing ultrafast fiber services to underserved areas. Some cities are taking matters into their own hands. For example, in 2010 the local power utility in Chattanooga Tennessee, received $111 million in federal stimulus money to accelerate the build-out of a 1-gigabit per second (Gbps) network for a smart electric grid. In 2013, the utility began offering 1-Gbps Internet access for about $300 per month, depending on the television service the customer chooses.

THE RESULTS >>> Kansas City families are delighted with Google Fiber. For instance, in late 2012, an installer wired one home, making the Internet access speed 50 times faster while substantially improving the television service. This entire package cost $125 per month, which was just a few dollars more than the family had been paying Time Warner Cable for their previous, slower service. The family was able to simultaneously stream four high-definition television shows, recording three of them on the included 2-terabyte DVR. That was two more shows than they could previously watch at once, with plenty of capacity to spare.

At one level, this project reflects Google's policy of developing new businesses by providing customers with ultrafast speeds and then offering them experimental services such as Google TV. However, if Google's business model for deploying fiber services works, then it may create a new era for privately built broadband.

On another level, ultrafast Internet access may encourage local entrepreneurship. For example, Kansas City has implemented a policy of attracting information technology startups. An effort called Homes for Hackers is trying to

convince Kansas City homeowners with Google Fiber to give free rooms to developers for three months in hopes that these developers will form startup companies. Consider RareWire (www.rarewire.com), a Kansas City startup that develops apps for mobile devices. Google Fiber gave RareWire a chance to compete on a much larger scale, and hopefully a better chance to be successful. Similarly, Google Fiber enables Sports Photos (www.sportsphotos.com) to upload thousands of high-resolution photos in a matter of hours. Previously such a project would have taken days or weeks to accomplish.

Despite these successes, however, there are problems associated with expanding ultrafast fiber in the United States. One of the major impediments is industry lobbying. For example, in 2011, after the city of Wilson, North Carolina, built its own fast network—which competed with the existing carriers—the North Carolina legislature, under pressure from industry lobbyists, passed a law that made it more difficult for local governments to develop their own networks. In addition, the law prevented Wilson from expanding its network beyond the county line.

The FCC has called for broadband providers and state and city officials to build out at least one "gigabit community" in all 50 states by 2015. In fact, Google is expanding its Google Fiber service to three additional cities: Olathe, Kansas; Austin, Texas; and Provo, Utah. And the bottom line? Efforts such as Google's are an encouraging start. Nevertheless, the United States has a long way to go to achieve widespread 1-Gbps service.

In mid-2014, Google has its fiber service operating in Kansas City, Austin, Texas, and Provo, Utah. The company is considering expanding its fiber service to nine new markets: Atlanta, Georgia; Charlotte, North Carolina; Nashville, Tennessee; Phoenix, Arizona; Portland, Oregon; Raleigh-Durham, North Carolina; San Antonio, Texas; Salt Lake City, Utah; and San Jose, California.

Sources: Compiled from "Gigabit Internet May Be Coming to 35 U.S. Cities," *KurzweilAI.net*, February 20, 2014; J. Sartain, "Google's Gigabit Internet: Not Coming to a Neighborhood Near You," *Network World*, November 19, 2013; D. Talbot, "Not So Fast: A Google Fiber One-Gigabit Mystery," *MIT Technology Review*, September 20, 2013; P. Olson, "The Google Effect," *Forbes*, May 27, 2013; D. Talbot, "Google Fiber's Ripple Effect," *MIT Technology Review*, April 26, 2013; J. Calacanis, "Google's Fiber Takeover Plan Expands, Will Kill Cable and Carriers," *Pandodaily.com*, April 19, 2013; M. Gottfried, "Google Prepares for Fiber Warfare," *The Wall Street Journal*, April 9, 2013; P. Olson, "Google Turns Up the Heat on Cable Companies, Expanding Fiber to Austin, Texas," *Forbes*, April 9, 2013; D. Talbot, "A Tale of Two Genachowsis," *MIT Technology Review*, March 22, 2013; S. Gustin, "Google Fiber Expanding Superfast Internet Service to Olathe, Kansas," *Time*, March 20, 2013; B. Paynter, "Google: For Adding Fiber to Our Internet Diet", *Fast Company*, March, 2013; D. Talbot, "When Will the Rest of Us Get Google Fiber?" *MIT Technology Review*, February 4, 2013; P. Kafka, "A Peak at TV's Future, Via Google Fiber," *All Things Digital*, November 21, 2012; D. Talbot, "Google's Internet Service Might Actually Bring the U.S. Up to Speed," *MIT Technology Review*, November 19, 2012; "Google Fiber Installations Kick Off Today," *Google Fiber Blog*, November 13, 2012; A. Knapp, "The Google Highway," *Forbes*, October 22, 2012; S. Gustin, "Google Fiber Issues Public Challenge: Get Up to Speed!" *Time*, September 14, 2012; "Super-Fast Google Fiber for Kansas City," *KurzweilAI.net*, July 27, 2012; R. Metz, "Google Launches a Superfast Internet and TV Business," *MIT Technology Review*, July 26, 2012; D. Talbot, "City with Superfast Internet Invites Innovators to Play," *MIT Technology Review*, February 28, 2012; http://fiber.google.com/about/, accessed March 25, 2014.

Questions

1. Why would a "search company" such as Google decided to enter the fiber services business?

Describe the benefits that Google expects to obtain from this new business venture.

2. Describe the various outcomes that might occur in an area that receives ultrafast fiber, regardless of the provider.

INTERNSHIP ACTIVITY>   OXFORD ORTHOPAEDICS

Industry: Healthcare

Networks create the connections that allow organizations to share data with the right people at the right time. User needs change (data, devices, access, etc.), so networks must also change to address those needs.

When Chad Prince took on the role of Practice Administrator at Oxford Orthopaedics, he was faced with the task of updating their entire network because they were implementing a new practice management/electronic health records (PM/EHR) system that required new hardware and network components. Less than three years later, the PM/EHR software vendor is pushing their clients to move into the cloud rather than constantly updating their networks. Chad is concerned about the latency of receiving information when it is housed 50–600 miles away rather than on a server around the corner.

Below is a letter from Chad with the specifics of how you can help him on this project.

To:	IT Intern
From:	Chad Prince
Subject:	Big Data and Banking

Hello!

Recently I helped my organization, Oxford Orthopaedics, navigate the implementation of a practice management/electronic health records (PM/EHR) solution. Now, less than three years later, my software vendor is pushing their clients to move into the cloud rather than constantly updating their networks. I am concerned about the latency of receiving information when it is housed 50–600 miles away rather than on a server around the corner.

I would like you to conduct a Web search for information concerning latency in the cloud environment. This issue is not exclusive to healthcare. Anyone who intends to use the cloud to provide a thin client environment (everything is hosted in the cloud) as opposed to a thick client (everything running locally on the client computer) will run into this problem. Each situation is unique depending on the complexity of the program being hosted, the number of users online simultaneously, and the need for immediate access to information.

What I am looking for is a benchmarking tool that will enable me to compare our current network performance with a cloud-based performance. Check out http://cloudharmony.com/services for information on cloud-based benchmarking. I believe you can even run some sample benchmark comparisons under the "Benchmark" tab. After perusing this site, answer the following questions.

- What are the major network latency concerns I should have regarding moving to the cloud?
- How can I compare my cloud performance with my current network?
- Do I need to purchase some type of cloud-based performance tool, or should I pay a vendor like CloudHarmony to do this for me?

Thank you in advance for your research and recommendations on this project.
Chad

SPREADSHEET ACTIVITY > BASIC FUNCTIONALITY: TEXT EDITING

STEP 1 – Background

As you may have learned in a Marketing or Business Communications course, presentation is very important. As powerful as spreadsheets are, they are not very elegant. They do, however, offer a broad array of formatting choices to make your data a bit more user-friendly and easier to the eyes. You do not want the "clunkiness" of the spreadsheet to detract from your data. In this activity, we will focus on text justification (left, right, center, full), border color, fill color, text alignment, text wrapping, and other formatting options.

STEP 2 – Activity

Johanna is a Sales Representative for BJ's Office Supply store, a family-owned business with annual sales of approximately $900,000. BJ's offers several product categories. Imagine that Johanna is preparing a presentation of last year's sales data for the business owners, as displayed in the accompanying table. As you can see, the format of the presentation is not particularly pleasing. Some of the words are hidden, sales data are not listed as currency, and the various categories are difficult to pick out.

STEP 3 – Deliverable

Visit http://www.wiley.com/go/rainer/MIS3e/spreadsheet, and download Johanna's spreadsheet. The sheet will contain instructions to help you use some of the basic tools listed above to create a better format for sharing these data with the owners.

Follow the instructions in the spreadsheet and submit your final work to your instructor.

Additional help with this spreadsheet skill is available in WileyPLUS. Open the "Microsoft Office 2013 Lab Manual Spreadsheet Module: Excel 2013," and review Lesson 6: Changing Cell Appearance and Lesson 13: Enhancing Worksheet Appearance.

DATABASE ACTIVITY > REPORTS: GROUPING AND SUMMARIES

STEP 1 – Background

In this activity, you will learn how to create an Access report, with groupings and summaries. A database is not useful if it doesn't provide the information you need. Users frequently obtain information by creating reports. Reports can connect data from several tables, organize the data, sort them, group them, summarize them, and much more. After you have designed a database you can run it as needed to access real-time data.

STEP 2 – Activity

In this activity you will select a database and use it to create multilevel reports. You will then add summary fields to this report and reformat it to improve its appearance.

Visit http://www.wiley.com/go/rainer/MIS3e/database, and download and open the Chapter 04 NeTrouble database. You should recognize this database if you have completed the Chapter 1 activity. This version does not include the report, query, or form you used there. Here, you will create two reports from the same underlying data.

Your first report should display trouble tickets by user. Include the following information: Department Name, Ticket Submitted, Ticket Resolved, and Ticket Status. Set Department Name as the main grouping, and sort the data by the order of when the tickets were submitted.

The second report will add summaries to this one. Use the "Group and Totals" options to create a report that will display a count of the tickets that each Department submits. Because the "Ticket Submitted" field always contains a value, use this field as the means of counting. "Count Record" options have been built into the database that will create this for you.

This report needs a formatting upgrade. Modify the column headings to make sense to a reader who isn't familiar with them. Finally, create a copy of your work to this point to make certain your professor can see it.

STEP 3 – Deliverable

Print your two reports to PDF, and submit them to your instructor.

Additional help with this database skill is available in WileyPLUS. Open the "Microsoft Office 2013 Lab Manual Database Module: Access 2013," and review Lesson 11: Creating a Report Template.

CHAPTER 5

Business Intelligence

LEARNING OBJECTIVES >>>

5.1 Identify the phases in the decision-making process, and use a decision support framework to demonstrate how technology supports managerial decision making.

5.2 Describe and provide examples of different ways that organizations use business intelligence (BI).

5.3 Specify the BI application available to users for data analysis, and provide examples of how each application can be used to solve a business problem at your university.

5.4 Describe three BI applications that present the results of data analyses to users, and offer examples of how businesses and government agencies can use each of these applications.

OPENING CASE > How Much Rent Can You Charge?

Renting out single-family homes was largely a mom-and-pop business until the U.S. housing bust (roughly from 2006 until 2012). In the aftermath of the bust, large investment firms began investing substantial sums of money in this market. For example, Blackstone Group (www.blackstone.com), the largest investor, has spent $4 billion on 24,000 homes. The big investors initially focused on the most depressed markets, including Phoenix, Arizona, and Atlanta, Georgia.

FIN As competition from other bargain hunters grew and prices in those areas rose, Blackstone started looking across the country for other opportunities.

Enter RentRange (www.rentrange.com). RentRange provides analyses about purchasing foreclosed and low-priced single-family homes and then renting them out. Using data from 12 million properties around the United States, RentRange can estimate how much monthly rent a property is likely to generate. Such predictive analyses provide critical input into the financial models that investors use to determine where to buy homes to convert to rentals, as well as how much rent they can charge.

Wally Charnoff, who founded RentRange in 2008, used his own money to purchase data from property managers, rental listing Web sites, and landlords. RentRange's predictive algorithms integrate those raw data with additional data, such as whether dogs or smoking have been, and are, allowed

© xeni4ka / iStockphoto

and whether the local area is already saturated with rental homes, to predict a likely rent.

Customers pay $50,000 for five years of RentRange data at regional, county, city, and zip code levels to help identify potentially profitable markets. Once investors pick a market, they pay $2 to $12 for rental estimates for specific properties.

How accurate are RentRange's rent predictions? One large investment firm manager claims that RentRange's estimates have generally been within 1 to 3 percent of what the firm ultimately charged.

RentRange, which has a staff of 22, has seen its revenue increase 1,900 percent between 2011 and 2014. The company became profitable in 2012. Company officials claim that almost 19,000 users, including 50 institutional clients, buy data directly from RentRange.

Renters now occupy 35 percent of all single-family homes in the United States, up from 30 percent in 2005, according to the Goldman Sachs Group (www.goldmansachs.com). As a result, it is not clear how long the buy-to-rent boom will last, as rising home prices make the process less profitable. In 2014, Clear Capital, a provider of real estate data and analysis, noted that home prices increased about 10 percent over 2013.

If the buy-to-rent market does lose momentum, then RentRange has other customers to fall back on. For example, some credit card companies have begun using RentRange's predictions to evaluate applicants' creditworthiness.

Sources: Compiled from "Looking to Buy to Rent?" *The Melton Times*, March 8, 2014; J. Gittelsohn and H. Perlberg, "Goldman Sachs Said to Lead American Homes 4 Rent Bond Deal," *Bloomberg Business Week*, January 29, 2014; "PRAXIS Launches Fourth Single Family Home 'Buy to Rent' Fund," *PR Web*, January 23, 2014; D. Bloomquist, "Foreclosure Auction Discounts Shrinking Under Buy-to-Rent Spotlight," *Forbes*, December 20, 2013; "Blackstone Establishes Single-Family Buy-to-Rent Lending Platform," *Blackstone Group*, November 15, 2013; "Single Family Homes as Rentals Remains a Viable Investment," *National Mortgage Professional*, September 9, 2013; K. Weise and H. Perlberg, "The Data King of the Rental Market," *Bloomberg Business Week*, May 6–12, 2013; T. Durden, "Is the 'Buy to Rent' Party Over?" *Zerohedge*, March 18, 2013; www.rentrange.com, accessed March 8, 2014.

Questions

1. What additional sources of data could RentRange collect to enhance its predictive accuracy? Provide examples to support your answer.

2. What other companies or institutions could utilize RentRange's predictions?

Introduction

The chapter opening case illustrates the importance and far-reaching nature of business intelligence applications. **Business intelligence (BI)** is a broad category of applications, technologies, and processes for gathering, storing, accessing, and analyzing data to help business users make better decisions. BI applications enable decision makers to quickly ascertain the status of a business enterprise by examining key information. Large firms that want to invest in single-family homes to rent need current, timely, and accurate information to predict the rents they can charge to maximize their return on investment (ROI). RentRange's BI applications provided the information that the investing firms needed.

Before we proceed, we need to distinguish between the terms "business intelligence" and "business analytics." In his book *Analytics at Work: Smarter Decisions, Better Results*, Thomas Davenport argued that business intelligence should be divided into querying, reporting, online analytical processing, and business analytics. He defined business analytics as a subset of BI based on statistics, prediction, and optimization. Essentially, BI can answer questions such as: What happened, how many, how often, where the problem is, and what actions are needed? In contrast, business analytics can answer questions such as: Why is this happening, what will happen if these trends continue, what will happen next, and what is the best (or worst) that can happen?

Despite this distinction, however, both BI and business analytics rely on data (particularly Big Data) and statistical methods. In fact, many experts argue that the terms should be used interchangeably. In this chapter, we adopt this approach.

This chapter describes information systems that support *decision making*. It begins by reviewing the manager's job and the nature of modern managerial decisions. This discussion will help you to understand why managers need computerized support. It then considers how business intelligence can support individuals, groups, and entire organizations.

It is impossible to overstate the importance of business intelligence within modern organizations. Recall from Chapter 1 that the essential goal of information systems is to provide the right information to the right person, in the right amount, at the right time, in the right format. In essence, BI achieves this goal. BI systems provide business intelligence that you can act on in a timely fashion.

It is also impossible to overstate the importance of your input into the BI process within an organization, for several reasons. First, you (the user community) will decide what data should be stored in your organization's data warehouse. You will then work closely with the MIS department to obtain these data.

Further, you will use your organization's BI applications, probably from your first day on the job. With some BI applications such as data mining and decision support systems, you will decide how you want to analyze the data (user-driven analysis). With other BI applications such as dashboards, you will decide which data you need and in which format. Again, you will work closely with your MIS department to ensure that these applications meet your needs.

Much of this chapter is concerned with large-scale BI applications. You should keep in mind, however, that smaller organizations, and even individual users, can implement small-scale BI applications as well. For example, Excel spreadsheets provide some BI functions, as do SQL queries of a database. The chapter opening case illustrates how a small company uses analytics to predict how much rent investors can charge in the single-family-home market.

The most popular BI tool by far is Excel. For years, BI vendors "fought" against the use of Excel. Eventually, however, they decided to "join it" by designing their software so that it interfaces with Excel. How does this process work? Essentially, users download plug-ins that add functionality (e.g., the ability to list the top 10 percent of customers, based on purchases) to Excel. This process can be thought of as creating "Excel on steroids." Excel then connects to the vendor's application server—which provides additional data analysis capabilities—which in turn connects to a backend database, such as a data mart or warehouse. This arrangement gives Excel users the functionality and access to data typical of sophisticated BI products, while allowing them to work with a familiar client—Excel.

Microsoft has made similar changes to its product line. Specifically, Excel now can be used with MS SQL Server (a database product), and it can be utilized in advanced BI applications, such as dashboards and data mining/predictive analysis.

After you finish this chapter, you will have a basic understanding of decision making, the business intelligence process, and the incredibly broad range of BI applications employed in modern organizations. This knowledge will enable you to immediately and confidently provide input into your organization's BI processes and applications. Further, the hands-on exercises in this chapter will familiarize you with the actual use of BI software. These exercises will enable you to use your organization's BI applications to effectively analyze data and thus make better decisions. Enjoy!

5.1 Managers and Decision Making

Management is a process by which an organization achieves its goals through the use of resources (people, money, materials, and information). These resources are considered to be *inputs*. Achieving the organization's goals is the *output* of the process. Managers oversee this process in an attempt to optimize it. A manager's success often is measured by the ratio between the inputs and outputs for which he or she is responsible. This ratio is an indication of the organization's **productivity**.

The Manager's Job and Decision Making

To appreciate how information systems support managers, you first must understand the manager's job. Managers do many things, depending on their position in the organization, the type and size of the organization, the organization's policies and culture, and the personalities of the managers themselves. Despite these variations, however, all managers perform three basic roles (Mintzberg, 1973):[1]

1. *Interpersonal roles*: figurehead, leader, liaison
2. *Informational roles*: monitor, disseminator, spokesperson, analyzer
3. *Decisional roles*: entrepreneur, disturbance handler, resource allocator, negotiator

[1]Mintzberg, H. (1973) *The Nature of Managerial Work*, Harper & Row, New York.

Early information systems primarily supported the informational roles. In recent years, however, information systems have been developed that support all three roles. In this chapter, you will focus on the support that IT can provide for decisional roles.

A **decision** refers to a choice among two or more alternatives that individuals and groups make. Decisions are diverse and are made continuously. Decision making is a systematic process. Economist Herbert Simon (1977)[2] described decision making as composed of three major phases: intelligence, design, and choice. Once the choice is made, the decision is implemented. FIGURE 5.1 illustrates this process, highlighting the tasks that are in each phase. Note that there is a continuous flow of information from intelligence, to design, to choice (bold lines). At any phase, however, there may be a return to a previous phase (broken lines).

This model of decision making is quite general. Undoubtedly, you have made decisions where you did not construct a model of the situation, validate your model with test data, or conduct a sensitivity analysis. The model we present here is intended to encompass *all* of the conditions that might occur when making a decision. For some decisions, some steps or phrases may be minimal, implicit (understood), or completely absent.

Media Bakery; © Sigrid Olsson/Photo Alto/Age Fotostock; Image Source; © nyul/iStockphoto

The decision-making process starts with the *intelligence phase*, in which managers examine a situation and then identify and define the problem or opportunity. In the *design phase*, decision makers construct a model for addressing the situation. They perform this task by making assumptions that simplify reality and by expressing the relationships among all of the relevant variables. Managers then validate the model by using test data. Finally, decision makers set criteria for evaluating all of the potential solutions that are proposed. The *choice phase* involves selecting a solution or course of action that seems best suited to resolve the problem. This solution (the decision) is then implemented. Implementation is successful if the proposed solution solves the problem or seizes the opportunity. If the solution fails, then the process returns to the previous phases. Computer-based decision support assists managers in the decision-making process.

Why Managers Need IT Support?

Making good decisions is very difficult without solid information. Information is vital for each phase and activity in the decision-making process. Even when information is available, however, decision making is difficult due to the following trends:

- The *number of alternatives* is constantly *increasing*, due to innovations in technology, improved communications, the development of global markets, and the use of the Internet and e-business. A key to good decision making is to explore and compare many relevant alternatives. The greater the number of alternatives, the more a decision maker needs computer-assisted searches and comparisons.

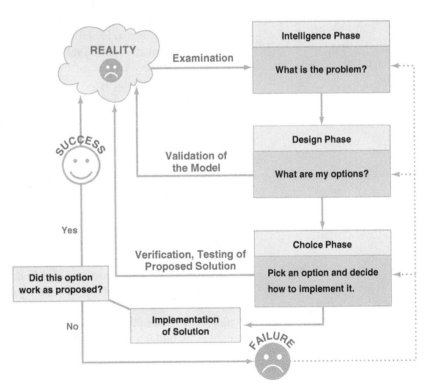

Figure 5.1 The process and phases in decision making.

[2]Simon, H.A. (1997) *The New Science of Management Decision*, Prentice-Hall, Englewood Cliffs, NJ.

- Most decisions must be made *under time pressure*. It often is not possible to manually process information fast enough to be effective.

- Due to increased uncertainty in the decision environment, decisions are becoming more complex. It is usually necessary to *conduct a sophisticated analysis* in order to make a good decision.

- It often is necessary to rapidly access remote information, consult with experts, or conduct a group decision-making session, all without incurring major expenses. Decision makers, as well as the information they need to access, can be situated in different locations. Bringing everything together quickly and inexpensively represents a serious challenge.

These trends create major difficulties for decision makers. Fortunately, as you will see throughout this chapter, a computerized analysis can be of enormous help.

What Information Technologies Are Available to Support Managers?

In addition to discovery, communication, and collaboration tools (Chapter 4) that indirectly support decision making, several other information technologies have been successfully used to support managers. As you saw earlier, these technologies are collectively referred to as *business intelligence*. BI is closely linked to data warehousing, which provides the data needed for BI. You will now learn about additional aspects of decision making that place our discussion of BI in context. First, you will look at the different types of decisions that managers face.

A Framework for Computerized Decision Analysis

To better understand BI, note that various types of decisions can be placed along two major dimensions: problem structure and the nature of the decision (Gorry and Scott Morton, 1971).[3] FIGURE 5.2 provides an overview of decision making along these two dimensions.

Problem Structure. The first dimension is *problem structure*, where decision-making processes fall along a continuum ranging from highly structured to highly unstructured (see the left column in FIGURE 5.2). *Structured decisions* deal with routine and repetitive problems for which standard solutions exist, such as inventory control. In a structured decision, the first three phases of the decision process—intelligence, design, and choice—are laid out in a particular sequence, and the procedures for obtaining the best (or at least a good enough) solution are known. Two basic criteria used to evaluate proposed solutions are minimizing costs and maximizing profits. These types of decisions are candidates for decision automation.

At the other extreme of complexity are *unstructured decisions*. These decisions are intended to deal with "fuzzy," complex problems for which there are no cut-and-dried solutions. An unstructured decision is one in which there is no standardized procedure for carrying out any of the three phases. In making such a decision, human intuition and judgment often play an important role. Typical unstructured decisions include planning new service offerings, hiring an executive, and choosing a set of research and development (R&D) projects for the coming year. Although BI cannot make unstructured decisions, it can provide information that assists decision makers.

Located between structured and unstructured decisions are *semistructured* decisions, in which only some of the decision process phases are structured. Semistructured decisions require a combination of standard solution procedures and individual judgment. Examples of semistructured decisions are evaluating employees, setting marketing budgets for consumer products, performing capital acquisition analysis, and trading bonds.

The Nature of Decisions. The second dimension of decision support deals with the *nature of decisions*. All managerial decisions fall into one of three broad categories:

[3]Gorry, G.A. and Scott Morton, M. (1971) "A Framework for Management Information Systems," *Sloan Management Review*, Fall, 21–36.

	Operational Control	Management Control	Strategic Planning	IS Support
Structured	Accounts receivable, order entry . **1**	Budget analysis, short-term forecasting, personnel reports, make-or-buy analysis **2**	 **3**	MIS, statistical models (management science, financial, etc.)
Semistructured	Production scheduling, inventory control **4**	Credit evaluation, budget preparation, plant layout, project scheduling, reward systems design **5**	Building a new plant, mergers and acquisitions, planning (product, quality assurance, compensation, etc.) **6**	Decision support systems, business intelligence
Unstructured	 **7**	Negotiating, recruiting an executive, buying hardware, lobbying **8**	New technology development, product R&D, social responsibility planning **9**	Decision support systems, expert systems, enterprise resource planning, neural networks, business intelligence, big data

Figure 5.2 Decision support framework. Technology is used to support the decisions shown in the column at the far right and in the bottom row.

1. *Operational control*—executing specific tasks efficiently and effectively.
2. *Management control*—acquiring and using resources efficiently in accomplishing organizational goals.
3. *Strategic planning*—the long-range goals and policies for growth and resource allocation.

These categories are displayed along the top row of FIGURE 5.2.

Note that strategic decisions define the context in which management control decisions are made. In turn, management control decisions define the context in which operational control decisions are made.

The Decision Matrix. The three primary classes of problem structure and the three broad categories of the nature of decisions can be combined in a decision support matrix that consists of nine cells, as diagrammed in FIGURE 5.2. Lower-level managers usually perform the tasks in cells 1, 2, and 4. The tasks in cell 5 are usually the responsibility of middle managers and professional staff. Finally, the tasks in cells 6, 8, and 9 are generally carried out by senior executives.

Computer Support for Structured Decisions. Examples of computer support that might be used for the nine cells in the matrix are displayed in the right-hand column and the bottom row of FIGURE 5.2. Structured and some semistructured decisions, especially of the operational and management control type, have been supported by computers since the 1950s. Decisions of this type are made in all functional areas, but particularly in finance and operations management.

Problems that lower-level managers encounter on a regular basis typically have a high level of structure. Examples are capital budgeting (e.g., replacing equipment), allocating resources, distributing merchandise, and controlling inventory. For each type of structured decision, prescribed solutions have been developed, which often include mathematical formulas. This approach is called *management science* or *operations research*, and it also is executed with the aid of computers.

BEFORE YOU GO ON....

1. Describe the decision-making process proposed by Simon.

2. You are registering for classes next semester. Apply the decision-making process to your decision about how many and which courses to take. Is your decision structured, semistructured, or unstructured?

3. Consider your decision-making process when registering for classes next semester. Explain how information technology supports (or does not support) each phase of this process.

Apply The Concept 5.1

LEARNING OBJECTIVE 5.1 Identify the phases in the decision-making process, and use a decision support framework to demonstrate how technology supports managerial decision making.

STEP 1 – Background (Here is what you are learning.)

If you look back through this section you will see that Henry Mintzberg's 1973 book, *The Nature of Managerial Work*, was referenced when the three basic roles of a manager were presented. This text focuses on the decisional role because that is the one that is most supported by information systems. However, Mintzberg's work goes much farther than just the decisional role.

STEP 2 – Activity (Here is what you do.)

Visit http://www.wiley.com/go/rainer/MIS3e/applytheconcept, and click on the link provided for Apply the Concept 5.1. The link will take you to a YouTube video titled "Data-Driven Decision Making" by user "Minnetonka Schools." This video mentions a strategic plan, operational control, and decisional control. As you view the video, make certain to watch for these key points, and pay special attention to how they are supported by data.

STEP 3 – Deliverable (Here is what you turn in.)

Write a short paper (a couple of paragraphs is plenty) for your professor that will identify the phases in the decision-making process for Minnetonka Schools. Be sure to demonstrate how technology supports their decision making in each phase.

5.2 What Is Business Intelligence?

To provide users with access to corporate data, many organizations are implementing data warehouses and data marts, which you learned about in Chapter 3. Users analyze the data in warehouses and marts using a wide variety of BI tools. Many vendors offer integrated packages of these tools under the overall label of *business intelligence software*. Major BI software vendors include SAS (www.sas.com), Hyperion (www.hyperion.com, now owned by Oracle), Business Objects (www.businessobjects.com, now owned by SAP), Information Builders (www.informationbuilders.com), SPSS (www.spss.com, now owned by IBM), and Cognos (www.ibm.com/cognos).

As you have seen, BI is vital to modern decision making and organizational performance. Let's consider in greater detail the technical foundation for BI and the variety of ways that BI can be used. (Recall our earlier discussion contrasting BI and business analytics, and that we are using the terms interchangeably throughout this chapter.)

The phrase *business intelligence* is relatively new. Business and IT analyst Howard Dresner coined the term in 1989 while he was an analyst at Gartner, a market research firm. The expression is especially popular in industry, where it is used as an umbrella term that encompasses all decision support applications.

BI encompasses not only applications, but also technologies and processes. It includes both "getting data in" (to a data mart or warehouse) and "getting data out" (through BI applications).

In addition, a significant change is taking place within the BI environment. In the past, organizations used BI only to support management. Today, however, BI applications are increasingly available to front-line personnel (e.g., call center operators), suppliers, customers, and even regulators. These groups rely on BI to provide them with the most current information.

The Scope of Business Intelligence

The use of BI in organizations varies considerably. In smaller organizations, BI may be limited to Excel spreadsheets. In larger ones, BI often is enterprisewide, and it includes applications such as data mining/predictive analytics, dashboards, and data visualization. It is important to recognize that the importance of BI to organizations continues to grow. In fact, it is not an exaggeration to assert that for many firms, BI is now a requirement for competing in the marketplace, as is illustrated in IT's About Business 5.1.

IT'S ABOUT BUSINESS 5.1

Predicting Airplane Arrivals More Accurately

Travelers are accustomed to long flight delays and cancellations for any number of reasons. Few customers realize that airlines themselves are not particularly accurate at predicting when a flight will arrive at its destination even when it is ready to leave the gate. Making a pinpoint-accurate prediction on gate arrival times is notoriously tricky, because many factors alter flight times. Weather and wind are the most common, but there are also ground issues, such as the passenger who neglects to board his flight on time, causing his bags to have to be offloaded. As a result, airline predictions are off by an average of seven minutes across the industry.

Flights normally operate according to a flight plan put together a few hours in advance of a flight's scheduled departure. After the flight takes off it is tracked by a dispatcher, who may be monitoring 15 flights simultaneously. So, for example, if headwinds increase, then the pilot must talk to a dispatcher, who may decide to reprogram the "cost index" of the flight, revise the flight plan, and give permission to the pilot to pick up speed (and therefore use more fuel) to arrive on time.

Airlines have been looking to automate these kinds of processes to save costs and also to provide travelers with a better flying experience. Gary Beck, vice president of flight operations for Alaska Airlines, maintains that airlines need to eliminate the human part of these communications in favor of automation.

MIS

To encourage this process, Alaska Airlines (www.alaskaair.com) and General Electric (GE; www.ge.com) sponsored a Flight Quest contest aimed at developing an algorithm that could help airlines better predict flight arrival times and reduce passenger delays. The contest, which was set up on the contest Web site Kaggle (www.kaggle.com), provided contestants with two months of flight data, such as arrivals, departures, weather, and latitudes and longitudes along the routes. Such data are typically not available to the public because they are owned by the airlines and manufacturers.

A team from Singapore won the contest and the $100,000 prize. The winning algorithm produced flight arrival estimates that were nearly 40 percent more accurate than existing estimates. The algorithm could help airlines reduce gate congestion, manage crews more efficiently, and save travelers up to five minutes at the gate. Each minute saved in a flight saves $1.2 million in annual crew costs and $5 million in annual fuel savings for a midsized airline.

A second Flight Quest contest, with a $250,000 prize, challenged data scientists to determine the most efficient flight routes, speeds, and altitudes at any moment, taking into account variables such as weather, wind, and airspace constraints. The winning model proved to be up to 12 percent more efficient when compared with data from past actual flights.

GE plans to develop software and services that incorporate the results of the two Flight Quest contests. It is important to note that GE's goal is not to replace pilot decisions, but to create smart assistants for pilots.

It may take some time, however, before software can be used to fundamentally change how commercial flights operate. For example, Alaska Airlines, which frequently lands planes under difficult weather conditions, has pioneered the use of satellite navigation, as opposed to relying on ground-based instruments for navigation. The use of satellite navigation lowers the standard minimum elevations for a plane's approach upon landing. The airline is working with the U.S. Federal Aviation Administration to spread the technique, which also saves fuel, to the lower 48 states. Beck claims that the greatest challenge has been to alter the practices and official handbooks of air traffic controllers, who would no longer need to tell planes where and when to turn. He maintains that satellite navigation systems essentially transform air traffic controllers into air traffic monitors.

Sources: Compiled from "Alaska Airlines Could Be Set to Soar," *Nasdaq.com*, January 27, 2014; "How Data Geeks Could Save the Airlines Millions – And Get You Home Quicker," *Bloomberg BusinessWeek*, May 7, 2013; R. Boyle, "Invented: A Much Better Way to Predict Airline Delays," *Popular Science*, April 4, 2013; "GE Flight Quest: Winners Use Algorithms on Flight Data to Help Reduce Delays," *FlightStats*, April 4, 2013; J. Novet, "On Kaggle, GE Finds Data Science Solutions for Patients and Pilots," *GigaOM*, April 3, 2013; J. Leber, "A Data-Crunching Prize to Cut Flight Delays," *MIT Technology Review*, April 3, 2013; J. Bruner, "New Data Competition Tackles Airline Delays," *O'Reilly Radar*, November 29, 2012; www.ge.com, www.alaskaair.com, www.kaggle.com, accessed March 8, 2014.

1. Do you think that satellite-based navigation will meet resistance among air traffic controllers? Why or why not?

2. Do you think that pilots will object to having "smart assistants" help them make decisions? Why or why not?

3. Do you think the overall response of the airlines to satellite-based navigation and smart assistants for pilots will be positive or negative? Support your answer.

4. What is the relationship between analytics and smart assistants for pilots?

Not all organizations use BI in the same way. For example, some organizations employ only one or a few applications, whereas others utilize enterprisewide BI. In this section, you will examine three specific BI targets that represent different levels of change:

- The development of one or a few related BI applications
- The development of infrastructure to support enterprisewide BI
- Support for organizational transformation

These targets differ in terms of their focus; scope; level of sponsorship, commitment, and required resources; technical architecture; impact on personnel and business processes; and benefits.

The Development of One or a Few Related BI Applications.
This BI target often is a point solution for a departmental need, such as campaign management in marketing. Sponsorship, approval, funding, impacts, and benefits typically occur at the departmental level. For this target, organizations usually create a data mart to store the necessary data. Organizations must be careful that the data mart—an "independent" application—does not become a "data silo" that stores data that are inconsistent with, and cannot be integrated with, data used elsewhere in the organization.

The Development of Infrastructure to Support Enterprisewide BI.
This BI target supports both current and future BI needs. A crucial component of BI at this level is an enterprise data warehouse. Because it is an enterprisewide initiative, senior management often provides sponsorship, approval, and funding. In addition, the impacts and benefits are felt throughout the organization.

An example of this target is the 3M Corporation. Traditionally, 3M's various divisions had operated independently, using separate decision support platforms. Not only was this arrangement costly, but it prevented 3M from integrating the data and presenting a "single face" to its customers. For example, sales representatives did not know whether or how business customers were interacting with other 3M divisions. The solution was to develop an enterprise data warehouse that enabled 3M to operate as an integrated company. As an added benefit, the costs of implementing this system were offset by savings resulting from the consolidation of the various platforms.

Support for Organizational Transformation.
With this target, a company uses BI to fundamentally transform the ways it competes in the marketplace. BI supports a new business model, and it enables the business strategy. Because of the scope and importance of these changes, critical elements such as sponsorship, approval, and funding originate at the highest organizational levels. The impact on personnel and processes can be significant, and the benefits accrue across the organization.

This BI target is closely aligned with corporate performance management. **Corporate performance management (CPM)** is involved with monitoring and managing an organization's performance according to *key performance indicators* (KPIs) such as revenue, return on investment, overhead, and operational costs. For online businesses,

CPM includes additional factors such as the number of page views, server load, network traffic, and transactions per second. BI applications allow managers and analysts to analyze data to obtain valuable information and insights concerning the organization's KPIs. Chapter closing case 2 demonstrates how social sentiment analysis is impacting the performance of two entire industries: the motion picture industry and the television industry. (*Sentiment analysis* refers to the use of natural language processing, text analysis, machine learning, and statistics to identify and extract subjective information in source materials.)

Harrah's Entertainment (a brand of Caesars Entertainment; www.caesars.com) provides another good example of this BI target. Harrah's developed a customer loyalty program known as *Total Rewards*. To implement the program, Harrah's created a BI infrastructure (a data warehouse) that collected data from casino, hotel, and special event systems (e.g., wine-tasting weekends) across all the various customer touchpoints (e.g., slot machines, table games, and Internet). Harrah's utilized these data to reward loyal customers and to reach out to them in personal and appealing ways, such as through promotional offers. These efforts helped the company to become a leader in the gaming industry. IT's About Business 5.2 illustrates how Cardlytics uses analytics to predict customer behavior so that merchants can present targeted offers to them through the banks that issue their credit and debit cards.

In Chapter 3, you studied the basics of data warehouses and data marts. In this section, you have seen how important data warehouses and marts are to the different ways that organizations use BI. In the next section, you will learn how the user community can analyze the data in warehouses and marts, how the results of these analyses are presented to users, and how organizations can use the results of these analyses.

'S ABOUT BUSINESS 5.2

Cardlytics Analyzes Customer Buying Behaviors

Card swipe data used to be an untapped source of data for banks. Banks wanted to use that data to increase their revenues and to attract loyalty by targeting deals to their customers. The banks, however, needed a "middleman" to analyze the data and actually deliver the offers.

Many banks have selected Cardlytics (http://cardlytics .com) to perform this role. Cardlytics has helped pioneer a data-driven advertising niche called merchant-funded rewards. The company collects data from 70 percent of U.S. bank customers. Its systems read some 11 billion U.S. transactions in 2013, amounting to $500 billion in spending. The company's algorithms present 1 billion ads per month to more than 35 million customers on the Web sites and mobile apps of 400 banks, including Bank of America, PNC, Regents, and Lloyd's of London.

ACCT

Cardlytics tracks and understands consumer buying behaviors. That is, the company targets people based on what they buy, not on who they are. Cardlytics works on the principle that if you know where and how people are spending money, then you know many things about them even if you can't access their personally identifying information. For example, if a woman is going to McDonald's and then to Target and finally to Babies "R" Us, then she would probably be young mother. Likewise, if a man makes his purchases at bars and Taco Bell, he is probably single.

© Juanmonino / iStockphoto

Merchants can utilize Cardlytics data analyses based on actual customer buying behaviors to present precisely targeted, relevant advertisements to clients of financial institutions. These ads also include offers to participate in merchant rewards programs. Offers are distributed via secure bank channels including online banking, mobile banking, secure text, e-mail, and/or ATM machines.

Consider this example. The Sports Authority wants to connect with customers who spend more than $100 per month on sporting goods at its competitors' stores. Cardlytics serves up a Sports Authority offer to those shoppers, and Cardlytics and the banks share a commission from the merchant, typically about 10 percent of any resulting purchases.

Many critics raise privacy concerns about merchant-funded rewards. To address these concerns, the banks prohibit Cardlytics and its competitors from moving data off banks' servers. In fact, banks do not ever share individual customer information with Cardlytics or the merchants. Further, there are limits to what Cardlytics can know or wants to know. The company sees only store-level data, so if customers use their bank cards at a CVS pharmacy, Cardlytics does not know whether they purchased Xanax or chewing gum. Another concern is that the success of merchant-funded rewards could prompt banks and brands to move into sensitive categories such as healthcare and gambling.

Other organizations want to access Cardlytics's analytics. For example, hedge funds want to use the firm's insights to better predict earnings. Further, Cardlytics accumulates enough data to predict whether any retailer's sales will increase or decrease for a particular quarter.

FIN

Sources: Compiled from A. Tanner, "Reading Your Financial Footprints," *Forbes*, December 16, 2013; D. Gardner, "Cardlytics on HP Vertica Powers Millions of Swiftly Tailored Marketing Offers to Bank Card Customers," *BriefingsDirect*, November 13, 2013; "Merchant-Funded Rewards Have a Bright Future with U.S. Consumers, Says Auriemma Consulting Group," *Globe News Wire*, November 12, 2013; P. Britt, "Merchant-Funded Loyalty Programs Poised for Growth," *Loyalty360.org*, September 6, 2012; S. Zhen, "US Bank Offers Merchant-Funded Rewards via FreeMonee," mybanktracker.com, April 13, 2012; http://cardlytics.com, accessed March 4, 2014.

Questions

1. Discuss the advantages and disadvantages of Cardlytics's data analyses for the customer. Use specific examples in your answers.

2. Discuss the advantages and disadvantages of Cardlytics's data analyses for the merchants. Use specific examples in your answers.

BEFORE YOU GO ON....

1. Define BI.

2. Discuss the breadth of support provided by BI applications to organizational employees.

3. Identify and discuss the three basic targets of BI.

Apply The Concept 5.2

LEARNING OBJECTIVE 5.2 Describe and provide examples of different ways that organizations use business intelligence.

STEP 1 – Background

In this section, you have learned that BI is a concept that encompasses everything from the collection, analysis, and dissemination of data to the technology tools that enable this process to take place. In particular, organizations use BI to support

- Specific departmental needs
- Organizational change

STEP 2 – Activity

There are several companies that provide data management and BI tools to help make decisions. Two of these companies are Avitas and Intricity. Visit http://www.wiley.com/go/rainer/MIS3e/applytheconcept to watch a short YouTube video about BI by each of these companies. While you watch, look for examples of how their tools support departments, enterprises, and/or organizational change.

STEP 3 – Deliverable

Describe the different BI tools available to modern organizations, and provide examples from the videos of how these tools are supported by technology providers.

5.3 Business Intelligence Applications for Data Analysis

A good strategy to study the ways in which organizations use business intelligence applications is to consider how the users analyze data, how they present the results of their analyses, and how managers and executives (who can also be users) implement these results.

Recall from Chapter 3 that the data are stored in a data warehouse or data mart. The user community analyzes these data employing a variety of BI applications. The results of these analyses can be presented to users via other BI applications. Finally, managers and executives put the overall results to good use. You will become familiar with data analysis, data presentation, and data use in the next three sections.

A variety of BI applications for analyzing data are available. They include multidimensional analysis (also called *online analytical processing*, or *OLAP*), data mining, and decision support systems.

Multidimensional Analysis or Online Analytical Processing

Some BI applications include **online analytical processing**, also referred to as **multidimensional analysis** capabilities. OLAP involves "slicing and dicing" data stored in a dimensional format, drilling down in the data to greater detail, and aggregating the data.

Consider our example from Chapter 3. Recall FIGURE 3.6 illustrating the data cube. The product is on the *x*-axis, geography is on the *y*-axis, and time is on the *z*-axis. Now, suppose you want to know how many nuts the company sold in the West region in 2012. You would slice and dice the cube, using *nuts* as the specific measure for product, *West* as the measure for geography, and 2012 as the measure for time. The value or values that remain in the cell(s) after our slicing and dicing is (are) the answer to our question. As an example of drilling down, you also might want to know how many nuts were sold in January 2012. Alternatively, you might want to know how many nuts were sold during 2011–2013, which is an example of aggregation, also called "rollup."

Data Mining

Data mining refers to the process of searching for valuable business information in a large database, data warehouse, or data mart. Data mining can perform two basic operations: (1) predicting trends and behaviors, and (2) identifying previously unknown patterns. BI applications typically provide users with a view of what has happened; data mining helps to explain *why* it is happening, and it predicts what will happen in the future.

Regarding the first operation, data mining automates the process of finding predictive information in large databases. Questions that traditionally required extensive hands-on analysis now can be answered directly and quickly from the data. For example, *targeted marketing* relies on predictive information. Data mining can use data from past promotional mailings to identify those prospects who are most likely to respond favorably to future mailings. Another business problem that uses predictive information is the forecasting of bankruptcy and other forms of default.

Data mining can also identify previously hidden patterns in a single step. For example, it can analyze retail sales data to discover seemingly unrelated products that people often purchase together. The classic example is beer and diapers. Data mining found that young men tend to buy beer and diapers at the same time when shopping at convenience stores.

One significant pattern discovery operation is detecting fraudulent credit card transactions. Over time a pattern emerges of the typical ways you use your credit card and your typical shopping behaviors—the places in which you use your card, the amounts you spend, and so on. If your card is stolen and used fraudulently, then the usage often varies noticeably from your established pattern. Data mining tools can discern this difference and bring the issue to your attention.

Numerous data mining applications are used in business and in other fields. According to a Gartner report (www.gartner.com), most Fortune 1000 companies worldwide currently use data mining, as the following representative examples illustrate. Note that in most cases the purpose of data mining is to identify a business opportunity in order to create a sustainable competitive advantage.

- *Retailing and sales.* Predicting sales, preventing theft and fraud, and determining correct inventory levels and distribution schedules among outlets. For example, retailers such as AAFES (stores on military bases) use Fraud Watch from SAP (www.sap.com) to combat fraud by employees in their 1,400 stores.

- *Banking.* Forecasting levels of bad loans and fraudulent credit card use, predicting credit card spending by new customers, and determining which kinds of customers will best respond to (and qualify for) new loan offers.

- *Manufacturing and production.* Predicting machinery failures, and finding key factors that help optimize manufacturing capacity.

- *Insurance.* Forecasting claim amounts and medical coverage costs, classifying the most important elements that affect medical coverage, and predicting which customers will buy new insurance policies.

- *Policework.* Tracking crime patterns, locations, and criminal behavior; identifying attributes to assist in solving criminal cases. Several cities have teamed up with IBM to analyze crime history and to strategically deploy police officers. Memphis, which reduced its crime rate by 14 percent in 2013, employed this system. Chicago adopted the "predictive policing" system in 2013 in hopes of reducing the city's 500 homicides in 2012. Chicago reported 415 homicides in 2013, but there is disagreement about the causes of the decrease.

- *Healthcare.* Correlating demographics of patients with critical illnesses, and developing better insights on how to identify and treat symptoms and their causes. In March 2013, Microsoft and Stanford University announced that they had mined the search data of millions of users to successfully identify unreported side effects of certain medications.

- *Marketing.* Classifying customer demographics that can be used to predict which customers will respond to a mailing or buy a particular product.

- *Politics.* In his FiveThirtyEight blog, Nate Silver famously analyzed polling and economic data to predict the results of the 2008 presidential election, calling 49 out of 50 states correctly. He then correctly predicted all 50 states in the 2012 presidential election.

- *Weather.* The National Weather Service is predicting weather with increasing accuracy and precision.

- *Higher education.* Desire2Learn (www.desire2learn.com) provides an application called Degree Compass that recommends courses based on students' majors, transcripts, and past course success rates. In March 2013, Degree Compass reported a 92 percent accuracy rate across four universities in predicting the grade that a student would receive in a course.

- *Social good.* Datakind (www.datakind.org) is an organization that serves as a bridge between social and "mission-driven" organizations that require assistance in interpreting their data and data scientists who provide their talents, usually for free, for noncommercial purposes. For example, Datakind has collaborated with the Sunlight Foundation (www.sunlightfoundation.com) in the United States to explore the influence of lobbyists on legislators. This type of research has been conducted before. Nevertheless, by gathering enormous amounts of data—congressional votes, fundraisers, parties, donations, and all of the House of Representatives transcripts going back to the early 1800s—analysts have far more potential to explore and expose relevant issues.

Decision Support Systems

Decision support systems (DSSs) combine models and data to analyze semistructured problems and some unstructured problems that involve extensive user involvement. **Models** are simplified representations, or abstractions, of reality. DSSs enable business managers and analysts to access data interactively, to manipulate these data, and to conduct appropriate analyses.

Decision support systems can enhance learning and contribute to all levels of decision making. DSSs also employ mathematical models. Finally, they have the related capabilities of sensitivity analysis, what–if analysis, and goal-seeking analysis, which you will learn about next. You should keep in mind that these three types of analysis are useful for any type of decision support application. Excel, for example, supports all three.

Sensitivity Analysis. *Sensitivity analysis* is the study of the impact that changes in one or more parts of a decision-making model have on other parts. Most sensitivity analyses examine the impact that changes in input variables have on output variables.

Most models include two types of input variables: decision variables and environmental variables. "What is our reorder point for these raw materials?" is a decision variable (internal to the organization). "What will the rate of inflation be?" is an environmental variable (external to the organization). The output in this example is the total cost of raw materials. Companies generally perform a sensitivity analysis to determine the impact of environmental variables on the result of the analysis.

Sensitivity analysis is extremely valuable because it enables the system to adapt to changing conditions and to the varying requirements of different decision-making situations. It provides a better understanding of the model as well as of the problem that the model purports to describe.

What–If Analysis. A model builder must make predictions and assumptions regarding the input data, many of which are based on the assessment of uncertain futures. The results depend on the accuracy of these assumptions, which can be highly subjective. *What–if analysis* attempts to predict the impact of a change in the assumptions (input data) on the proposed solution. For example, what will happen to the total inventory cost *if* the originally assumed cost of carrying inventories is 12 percent rather than 10 percent? In a well-designed BI system, managers themselves can interactively ask the computer these types of questions as often as they need to.

Goal-Seeking Analysis. *Goal-seeking analysis* represents a "backward" solution approach. It attempts to calculate the value of the inputs necessary to achieve a desired level of output. For example, let's say that an initial BI analysis predicted a profit of $2 million. Management might want to know what sales volume would be necessary to generate a profit of $3 million. To find out, they would perform a goal-seeking analysis.

The managers, however, cannot simply press a button labeled "increase sales." Instead, the company will need to take certain actions to bring about the sales increase. Options include lowering prices, increasing funding for research and development, paying the sales force a higher commission rate, enhancing the advertising program, and, of course, implementing some combination of these actions. Whatever actions the company chooses, they will cost money, and the goal-seeking analysis must take this fact into account.

FIN

> ### BEFORE *YOU GO ON....*
>
> 1. Describe multidimensional analysis.
> 2. What are the two basic operations of data mining?
> 3. What is the purpose of decision support systems?

Apply The Concept 5.3

LEARNING OBJECTIVE 5.3 Specify the BI application available to users for data analysis, and provide examples of how each one might be used to solve a business problem at your university.

STEP 1 – Background

This section has explained that data are more abundant today than ever before. One thing we are learning is that there is much we *can* know that we *do not* know. In fact, there are many questions we are not even aware we should be asking! For such questions, we use multidimensional analysis and data mining tools to extract valuable insights from the data. When we know the questions, we frequently employ decision support systems to run sensitivity, what–if, or goal-seeking analysis.

STEP 2 – Activity

Consider your university. Various departments focus on teaching, student academic support, financial aid, admissions, recruitment, administration, and much more. Each of these departments has its special purpose, but overall the enterprise exists to support student learning.

Visit your university's Web site, and look for these various functions. What can you learn about their purpose? Based on this knowledge, what can you imply about the types of BI applications they might use?

STEP 3 – Deliverable

Provide examples of how each of the BI applications mentioned in this section might be used to solve a business problem at your university.

TABLE 5.1 The Capabilities of
Dashboards

Capability	Description
Drill down	The ability to go to details, at several levels; it can be done by a series of menus or by clicking on a drillable portion of the screen.
Critical success factors (CSFs)	The factors most critical for the success of business. These can be organizational, industry, departmental, or for individual workers.
Key performance indicators	The specific measures of CSFs.
Status access	The latest data available on KPI or some other metric, often in real time.
Trend analysis	Short-, medium-, and long-term trend of KPIs or metrics, which are projected using forecasting methods.
Exception reporting	Reports that highlight deviations larger than certain thresholds. Reports may include only deviations.

5.4 Business Intelligence Applications for Presenting Results

The results of the types of data analyses you just learned about can be presented with dashboards and data visualization technologies. Today, users are increasingly relying on data that are real time or almost real time. Therefore, you also study real-time BI in this section.

Dashboards

Dashboards evolved from executive information systems, which were information systems designed specifically for the information needs of top executives. Today, however, many employees, business partners, and customers can use digital dashboards.

A dashboard provides easy access to timely information and direct access to management reports. It is user friendly, it is supported by graphics, and, most importantly, it enables managers to examine exception reports and drill down into detailed data. Table 5.1 summarizes the various capabilities common to many dashboards. Moreover, some of the capabilities discussed in this section have been incorporated into many BI products, as illustrated in FIGURE 5.3.

Figure 5.3 Sample performance dashboard. *Source:* Image Courtesy of Dundas Data Visualization, Inc., 2014 (www.dundas.com)

One outstanding example of a dashboard is the Bloomberg Terminal. Bloomberg LP (www.bloomberg.com), a privately held company, provides a subscription service that sells financial data, software to analyze these data, trading tools, and news (electronic, print, TV, and radio). All of this information is accessible through a color-coded Bloomberg keyboard that displays the desired information on a computer screen, either the user's screen or one that Bloomberg provides. Users can also set up their own computers to access the service without a Bloomberg keyboard. The subscription service plus the keyboard is called the Bloomberg Terminal. It literally represents a do-it-yourself dashboard, because users can customize their information feeds as well as the look and feel of those feeds (see FIGURE 5.4).

In another example, a human resources dashboard/scorecard developed by iDashboards, one of the leading BI software vendors. At a glance, users can see employee productivity, hours, team, department, and division performance in graphical, tabular, summary, and detailed form. The selector box to the left enables the user to easily change between specific analyses to compare their performance.

© Carlos Osorio/Toronto Star/ZUMAPRESS.com

Figure 5.4 Bloomberg Terminal. (*Source:* Carlos Osario/Zuma Press)

A unique and interesting application of dashboards to support the informational needs of executives is the Management Cockpit. Essentially, a Management Cockpit is a strategic management room containing an elaborate set of dashboards that enable top-level decision makers to pilot their businesses better. The goal is to create an environment that encourages more efficient management meetings and boosts team performance via effective communication. To help achieve this goal, the dashboard graphically displays KPIs and information relating to critical success factors on the walls of a meeting room called the *Management Cockpit Room* (see FIGURE 5.5). The cockpit-like arrangement of instrument panels and displays helps managers visualize how all of the different factors in the business interrelate.

HRM

Within the room, the four walls are designated by color: Black, Red, Blue, and White. The Black Wall displays the principal success factors and financial indicators. The Red Wall measures market performance. The Blue Wall projects the performance of internal processes and employees. Finally, the White Wall indicates the status of strategic projects. The Flight Deck, a six-screen, high-end PC, enables executives to drill down to detailed information. External information needed for competitive analyses can easily be imported into the room.

Board members and other executives hold meetings in the Management Cockpit Room. Managers also meet there with the comptroller to discuss current business issues. The Management Cockpit can implement various what–if scenarios for this purpose. It also provides a common basis for information and communication. Finally, it supports efforts to translate a corporate strategy into concrete activities by identifying performance indicators.

Data Visualization Technologies

After data have been processed, they can be presented to users in visual formats such as text, graphics, and tables. This process, known as *data visualization*, makes IT applications more attractive and understandable to users. Data visualization is becoming increasingly popular

The Management Cockpit is a registered trademark of SAP, created by Professor M. Georges.

Figure 5.5 Management Cockpit. (*Source:* The Management Cockpit is a registered trademark of SAP, created by Professor Patrick M. Georges)

on the Web for decision support. A variety of visualization methods and software packages that support decision making are available. Two particularly valuable applications are geographic information systems and reality mining.

Geographic Information Systems. A **geographic information system (GIS)** is a computer-based system for capturing, integrating, manipulating, and displaying data using digitized maps. Its most distinguishing characteristic is that every record or digital object has an identified geographical location. This process, called *geocoding*, enables users to generate information for planning, problem solving, and decision making. In addition, the graphical format makes it easy for managers to visualize the data.

Today, relatively inexpensive, fully functional PC-based GIS packages are readily available. Representative GIS software vendors are ESRI (www.esri.com), Intergraph (www.intergraph.com), and Pitney Bowes MapInfo (now Pitney Bowes Business Insight; www.pbinsight.com/welcome/mapinfo). In addition, both government sources and private vendors provide diversified commercial GIS data. Some of these GIS packages are free, for example, downloadable material from the Environmental Systems Research Institute (ESRI; www.esri.com) and http://data.geocomm.com.

There are countless applications of GISs to improve decision making in both the public and private sectors. IT's About Business 5.3 focuses on ESRI and illustrates the many uses of GIS. The following example shows how ESRI impacts a huge number of organizations.

IT'S ABOUT BUSINESS 5.3

Geographical Information Systems Have Many Uses

Founded as the Environmental Systems Research Institute in 1969, ESRI (www.esri.com) is an international supplier of geographic information system software and geodatabase management applications. Industry analysts estimate that about 70 percent of GIS users employ ESRI products, particularly an ESRI product called ArcGIS. ArcGIS is used for creating and using maps, compiling geographic data, analyzing mapped information, sharing and discovering geographic information, using maps and geographic information across a wide range of applications, and managing geographic information in a database.

MIS

Essentially, ESRI makes GIS available to be used by people to solve real problems. Let's consider some of the applications where ESRI products are being used.

- Consider this scenario, in which a park ranger uses ESRI's ArcGIS software tool. A hiker is missing on one of the trails in a national park. As the head park ranger, your job is to lead a search-and-rescue mission to find him. Sunset is approaching, and in some parts of the park the temperature will be below freezing in a few hours. What do you do?

  Many experienced hikers know that the recommended course of action when you are lost is to follow a stream downhill, which should eventually lead to civilization. However, you cannot assume that the missing hiker is aware of this. He might stay put, or, if he has a phone,

© AdrianHillman / iStockphoto

he might move *uphill* to find a signal. You also do not know if he is injured.

You open ArcGIS on your computer, and a computer map of the park appears on the screen. You also have access to a database of records from 30,000 lost hiker search-and-rescue missions. You query the database and learn that 66 percent of lost hikers are found within two miles of the spot where they were last seen. You draw a ring on your map reflecting this two-mile perimeter. You then learn that 52 percent of lost hikers are found downhill. You impose an elevation limit on the area with all land above the last point seen shaded in one color and the land beneath it shaded in another color.

Again querying the database, you discover that lost hikers usually quit walking after about three hours. You can now create a predictive model, which describes a priority list of places to look for the lost hiker. When you run the model through ArcGIS, the software provides three concentric circles depicting the hiker's most likely location. The inner circle is the hiker's most likely location, etc.

Next, you share this map with the public, targeting people who mentioned on Twitter and Facebook that they would be hiking in the park that day. You enable these people to place points on the map where they saw something that might be a clue, such as an article of clothing. You take anything they mention and add it to your predictive model. ArcGIS then produces a new map with new concentric circles, which gives you a reasonable chance to find the hiker before the sun sets.

- A typical utility company serving millions of customers uses GIS to manage its complex infrastructure. The utility uses GIS for customer service, emergency response, electricity or water distribution, infrastructure maintenance, automated mapping, network tracing, flow or power analysis, and other aspects of engineering, operations, administration, and finance.

- An irrigation district serves thousands of farmers and maintains hundreds of miles of waterways. It uses GIS for engineering and operations.

- The attendance boundaries for public schools are drawn using GIS. For example, a city has to build a new elementary school due to an increase in the number of elementary-school-aged children. School boards use GIS at public meetings to demonstrate the new boundaries to parents.

- Cities use GIS to manage their transportation infrastructures. GIS supports planning, inventory, design, construction, operations, and maintenance.

- More than 80 percent of the information used to manage road, rail, and port facilities has a spatial component. Facility managers use GIS in designing and operating the facilities.

- The telecommunications industry is deploying new broadband networks. The industry uses GIS to support the design, implementation, and management of the new network infrastructure.

- GIS is used for the management of coastal resources, including shoreline, aquatic, and terrestrial habitats and biological resources. With GIS and the appropriate scientific database, coastal erosion can be better understood and managed.

- Restaurant companies use GIS to help select optimal locations for new outlets.

- The vast majority of information used in law enforcement is map-based. Agencies need to display the location of incidents and be able to view incidents by categories, time, or date. Advanced GIS capabilities can generate maps that are used to predict the probability of crimes occurring.

- State legislatures make extensive use of GIS to redraw congressional districts after each national census.

Sources: Compiled from G. Baldwin, "Geospatial Efforts Often Rely on a Single Go-Getter," *Health Data Management*, March 13, 2014; J. Stromberg, "Do You Live Within 50 Miles of a Nuclear Power Plant?" *Smithsonian Magazine*, March 13, 2014; J. Marks, "How Maps Drive Decisions at EPA," *NextGov*, March 12, 2014; "ESRI Maps Offer Geographic Perspective on Third Anniversary of Fukushima Disaster," *The American Surveyor*, March 11, 2014; B. McCann, "GIS Expands into Law Enforcement, Healthcare: ESRI Opens Up," *CivSource*, March 10, 2014; A. Wills, "Crisis in Crimea: A Story Map of the Place Everyone's Watching," *Mashable*, March 6, 2014; J. Tierney, "Mapping the Anxiety About College Admissions," *The Atlantic*, March 6, 2014; S. Postema, "The Future of Journalism: Real-Time Story Maps," *Dutch News Design*, February 27, 2014; P. Tucker, "Mapping the Future with Big Data," *The Futurist*, July/August 2013; www.esri.com, accessed March 9, 2014.

Questions

1. Describe how your university might use GIS. Provide specific examples in your answer.

2. What are potential disadvantages of GIS? Provide specific examples in your answer.

Reality Mining. One important emerging trend is the integration of GISs and global positioning systems (GPSs, discussed in Chapter 10). Using GISs and GPSs together can produce an interesting new type of technology called *reality mining*. **Reality mining** allows analysts to extract information from the usage patterns of mobile phones and other wireless devices. If you want to catch a cab in New York City, the next example will show you how.

EXAMPLE

New York City. Is there some kind of secret formula for finding a cab in New York City? The answer is, yes. The most popular corners to catch a yellow cab in Manhattan now can be pinpointed at any hour of any day of the week, thanks to a record 90 million actual taxi trips that have been tracked by the city.

Using the city's GPS data, Sense Networks (www.sensenetworks.com) examined the pickup point of every New York City cab ride taken over a six-month period. The result was a free mobile application called CabSense (www.cabsense.com). This app lets would-be taxi riders view a map of nearby street corners, ranked by the number of taxi hails they attract at that hour on that day of the week. The company uses an algorithm that takes into account parades, street construction, and other factors that could skew the results.

Here are two results from CabSense. The Upper East Side is more dependent on cabs than are its neighbors across Central Park. In one particular month, more than 2 million trips started on the Upper East Side, nearly twice as many as on the Upper West Side. Also, a neighborhood-by-neighborhood breakdown confirms what most New Yorkers already know: It is easier to get a cab below 96th Street in Manhattan, and much harder above 96th Street.

Singapore. The idea of making it easier to find a cab has traveled to Singapore. Commuters who cannot find a cab use an app that points them to places where they are more likely to find one. The Agency for Science, Technology, and Research gathered sensor data from taxis on the road, including time, place, speed, and whether the taxis were occupied. Researchers developed a predictive mobile application that informs passengers where they are most likely to find empty cabs and cabbies where they are most likely to find fares. The app even tells train commuters where to get off the train so that they will have the best chance of finding a taxi.

Interestingly, taxi companies in Singapore are not pleased with the app. They do not want the app to bypass their own dispatch systems.

Other Major Cities. Taxibeat (https://taxibeat.com) and Easy Taxi (www.easytaxi .com) help users find taxis in major cities, including Paris, São Paulo, Rio de Janeiro, Bucharest, and Oslo. The apps locate your position and contact a cab near you. They indicate the taxi's location and the speed at which it is arriving. Significantly, they identify both taxis and customers, which enhances both security and quality assurance. Quality assurance comes from the fact that customers and cab drivers can rate each other. In fact, one of Taxibeat's developers noted that when the app became popular in Athens, the city's taxi drivers became much more courteous. They actually got out of their cars to open doors for passengers, in hopes of receiving a higher rating.

Sources: Compiled from J. Racoma, "Rocket Internet's Easy Taxi: Having Competition Drives Business Up," *e27.com*, August 22, 2013; S. O'Hear, "Taxibeat Raises $2M and Rides into Mexico to Start the Meter on Rocket Internet's Easy Taxi," *Tech Crunch*, July 15, 2013; C. Tan, "Can't Find a Cab? New App Can Help," *The Straits Times*, March 12, 2013; J. Haha, "10 Apps Every New Yorker Needs," *Complex Tech*, February 4, 2013; "Taxibeat: A Greek Startup Makes Finding a Cab Easier and More Reliable," *Capgemini.com*, December 26, 2012; L. Dignan, "Meet CabSense: Now Your Apple iPhone and Android Device Will Hail a Cab for You," *ZDNet*, March 31, 2010; M. Grynbaum, "Need a Cab? New Analysis Shows Where to Find One," *The New York Times*, April 2, 2010; www.sensenetworks.com, www.cabsense.com, https://taxibeat .com, www.easytaxi.com, accessed April 7, 2014.

Real-Time BI

Until recently, BI focused on the use of historical data. This focus has changed with the emergence of technology for capturing, storing, and using real-time data. Real-time BI enables users to employ multidimensional analysis, data mining, and decision support systems to analyze data in real time. In addition, it helps organizations to make decisions and to interact with customers in new ways.

FIGURE 5.6 presents a typical support center operations dashboard. The dashboard enables the manager to see, in greater detail, a performance overview of the support center regions as well as specific support centers within those regions. The top visualization is called a microchart, which allows the manager to see numerous KPIs at once for all four support regions. The manager can see that all support regions have exceeded their target for cases that were closed in under one week. By selecting a specific support region, the manager can see the historical trend for the past 12 months for the KPIs through the bar chart on the bottom left. In addition, the manager can see certain performance statistics for individual support centers through the bubble chart on the bottom right.

With this dashboard, the manager can quickly understand that the New York support center has generated the most revenue in the North America region. In addition, it appears that the steps that have been taken to address customer satisfaction have been successful, as customer satisfaction has improved in the past few months. Lastly, without leaving her screen, the manager can move on to an analysis of the product's performance by clicking the "Product Performance" tab in the upper right hand corner, making for a more efficient and comprehensive performance analysis.

MicroStrategy, Inc.

Figure 5.6 Support Center Operations Dashboard.

BEFORE YOU GO ON....

1. What is a dashboard? Why are dashboards so valuable to employees?

2. Explain the difference between geographic information systems and reality mining, and provide examples of how each of these technologies can be used by businesses and government agencies.

3. What is real-time BI, and why is this technology valuable to an organization's managers and executives?

Apply The Concept 5.4

LEARNING OBJECTIVE 5.4 Describe three BI applications that present the results of data analyses to users, and offer examples of how businesses and government agencies can use each of these technologies.

STEP 1 – Background

Section 5.4 discusses visualization tools that help users understand the information contained in a dataset. These tools are valuable because it is much easier and quicker to glance at a graph than it is to look at a page full of numbers. Data analysis was one of the keys to President Obama's reelection in 2012. The president's campaign staff were able to communicate with the right people in the swing states to win 332 electoral votes to Mitt Romney's 206 even though the popular vote was much closer (62,611,250 to 59,134,475).

STEP 2 – Activity

Visit http://www.wiley.com/go/rainer/MIS3e/applytheconcept, and click on the link provided for Apply the Concept 5.4. This link will take you to a video that describes how the Obama campaign used data to convey the appropriate messages to the right people to help win the election. There is also a link to a results page that displays a geographic map of the results.

STEP 3 – Deliverable

Based on the video and any of your own Web research, describe and give examples of how the three BI applications that present the results of data analyses to users helped drive the Obama campaign to victory in the 2012 presidential election.

What's in for ME?

 ### FOR THE
ACCOUNTING MAJOR

BI is used extensively in auditing to uncover irregularities. It also is used to uncover and prevent fraud. CPAs use BI for many of their duties, ranging from risk analysis to cost control.

 ### FOR THE FINANCE MAJOR

People have been using computers for decades to solve financial problems. Innovative BI applications have been created for activities such as making stock market decisions, refinancing bonds, assessing debt risks, analyzing financial conditions, predicting business failures, forecasting financial trends, and investing in global markets.

 ### FOR THE MARKETING MAJOR

Marketing personnel utilize BI in many applications, from planning and executing marketing campaigns, to allocating advertising budgets, to evaluating alternative routings of salespeople. New marketing approaches such as targeted marketing and database marketing depend heavily on IT in general, and on data warehouses and business intelligence applications in particular.

 ### FOR THE PRODUCTION/
OPERATIONS MANAGEMENT
MAJOR

BI supports complex operations and production decisions from inventory control, to production planning, to supply chain integration.

 ### FOR THE HUMAN RESOURCES
MANAGEMENT MAJOR

Human resources personnel use BI for many of their activities. For example, BI applications can find resumes of applicants posted on the Web and sort them to match needed skills and to support management succession planning.

 ### FOR THE MIS MAJOR

MIS provides the data infrastructure used in BI. MIS personnel are also involved in building, deploying, and supporting BI applications.

SUMMARY

1. Identify the phases in the decision-making process, and use a decision support framework to demonstrate how technology supports managerial decision making.

When making a decision, either organizational or personal, the decision maker goes through a three-step process: intelligence, design, and choice. When the choice is made, the decision is implemented.

Several information technologies have been successfully used to directly support managers. Collectively, they are referred to as *business intelligence information systems*. FIGURE 5.2 provides a matrix that shows how technology supports the various types of decisions that managers must make.

2. Describe and provide examples of the three different ways in which organizations use business intelligence.

There are three major ways that organizations use BI:

> The development of one or a few related BI applications. This BI target often is a point solution for a departmental need, such as campaign management in marketing. A data mart usually is created to store necessary data.

> The development of infrastructure to support enterprisewide BI. This target supports current and future BI needs. A critical component is an enterprise data warehouse.

> Support for organizational transformation. With this target, BI is used to fundamentally change how a company competes in the marketplace. BI supports a new business model and enables the business strategy.

3. Specify the BI applications available to users for data analysis, and provide examples of how each one might be used to solve a business problem at your university.

Users have a variety of BI applications available to help them analyze data. These applications include multidimensional analysis, data mining, and decision support systems.

Multidimensional data analysis, also called *online analytical processing*, involves "slicing and dicing" data stored in a dimensional format, drilling down to greater data detail, and aggregating data. Data mining refers to the process of searching for valuable business information in a large database, data warehouse, or data mart. Decision support systems combine models and data in an attempt to analyze semistructured and some unstructured problems with extensive user involvement. (We leave it to you to provide examples of using each application at your university.)

4. Describe three BI applications that present the results of data analyses to users, and offer examples of how businesses and government agencies can use each of these technologies.

A dashboard provides easy access to timely information and direct access to management reports. A geographic information system is a computer-based system for capturing, integrating, manipulating, and displaying data using digitized maps. Reality mining analyzes information extracted from the usage patterns of mobile phones and other wireless devices. (Examples of how these technologies might be used by businesses and government agencies, we leave to you.)

>>>CHAPTER GLOSSARY

business intelligence (BI) A broad category of applications, technologies, and processes for gathering, storing, accessing, and analyzing data to help business users make better decisions.

corporate performance management (CPM) The area of business intelligence involved with monitoring and managing an organization's performance, according to key performance indicators such as revenue, return on investment, overhead, and operational costs.

dashboard A BI application that provides rapid access to timely information and direct access to management reports.

data mining The process of searching for valuable business information in a large database, data warehouse, or data mart.

decision A choice that individuals and groups make among two or more alternatives.

decision support systems (DSSs) Business intelligence systems that combine models and data in an attempt to solve semistructured and some unstructured problems with extensive user involvement.

geographic information system (GIS) A computer-based system for capturing, integrating, manipulating, and displaying data using digitized maps.

management A process by which organizational goals are achieved through the use of resources.

model (in decision making) A simplified representation, or abstraction, of reality.

multidimensional data analysis See **online analytical processing (OLAP)**.

online analytical processing (OLAP) (or **multidimensional data analysis**) A set of capabilities for "slicing and dicing" data using dimensions and measures associated with the data.

productivity The ratio between the inputs to a process and the outputs from that process.

reality mining Allows analysts to extract information from the usage patterns of mobile phones and other wireless devices.

1. Your company is considering opening a new factory in China. List several typical activities involved in each phase of the decision (intelligence, design, and choice).

2. Recall that data mining found that young men tend to buy beer and diapers at the same time when they shop at convenience stores. Now that you know this relationship exists, can you provide a rationale for it?

3. American Can Company announced that it was interested in acquiring a company in the health maintenance organization (HMO) field. Two decisions were involved in this act: (1) the decision to acquire an HMO, and (2) the decision of which HMO to acquire. How can the use of BI assist the company in this endeavor?

4. Discuss the strategic benefits of BI systems.

5. Will BI replace business analysts? (*Hint*: See W. McKnight, "Business Intelligence: Will Business Intelligence Replace the Business Analyst?" *DMReview*, February 2005.)

>>> **COLLABORATION EXERCISE**

STEP 1 – Background

In this chapter, a company named MicroStrategy has been mentioned several times. MicroStrategy provides multiple products that are intended to help businesses manage and interpret their data. One of these products is a free tool called "MicroStrategy Personal Cloud," which enables you to upload your data and then let MicroStrategy software create reports for you. Go to http://www.wiley.com/go/rainer/MIS3e/collaboration, and click on the link provided. The link will take you to MicroStrategy's Web site where you can find information on several "cloud" tools for personal data analysis.

STEP 2 – Activity

Organize teams of five members. Each member will open up a Google spreadsheet, and create data that reflects the money you spend on food for a week. Each team member should create 10 rows of data in the shared spreadsheet. (You will first have to agree on the type of data you will create and the column titles so that everyone's data will be uniform. In fact, you may find it easier to use a Google Form to create your spreadsheet and keep everything in the same format.) After you have created the data, export them to an Excel spreadsheet. Finally, upload your data into the MicroStrategy Personal Cloud.

STEP 3 – Deliverable

Review your new intelligence as a team. Consider the charts, diagrams, reports, and any information you can find on the Web site. Then, compile a report for your professor based on the data your team put together. Include images of your visuals, and discuss your findings. Also, highlight anything in this analysis that surprises you.

CLOSING **CASE 1 >** Conoco Phillips Uses Business Intelligence to Produce More Oil and Gas

THE BUSINESS PROBLEM >>> ConocoPhillips (CP; www.conocophillips.com) is a $9 billion U.S. multinational energy corporation. It is the world's largest independent energy exploration and production company. The company explores for, produces, transports, and markets crude oil and natural gas on a worldwide basis.

POM

Finding oil and gas is a first step for CP. The next step is to invest millions of dollars to drill each well to extract those resources. The company must then spend additional money to manage the natural decline in production at each well. With returns and profitability directly linked to production, CP must try to collect every barrel of oil or cubit foot of gas it can from its wells.

THE IT SOLUTION >>> There is nothing new about energy companies using analytics to find and produce more oil and gas. An excellent example of analytics at work in the energy industry is the custom-developed plunger lift surveillance and optimization software tool (PLOT) from CP. PLOT allows the company to optimize a well to its true capacity. The tool gathers data specifically related to CP's use of plunger lifts, which are installed inside a well to lift accumulated fluids that are stopping the flow of gas. PLOT enables the energy giant to maximize the lift's capabilities as well as to recognize sooner when the plunger lift will need maintenance.

Plunger lift technology has been around for decades. Wells dating to the 1950s using this technology offer only basic gas pressure and flow rate data. CP stored and compiled data from these wells in spreadsheets, and any analyses performed on the data were manual and labor intensive.

In the PLOT initiative, CP installed additional sensors to capture pressure and temperature readings, and it is sampling those readings every 30 to 60 seconds, as opposed to once per hour or per day. PLOT gathers approximately 4.5 million daily data points from monitoring CP's wells.

PLOT calculates pressure and temperature at different parts of the well, enabling well operators to identify which wells are producing efficiently and which ones are not. Company managers claim that PLOT enables them to see so much more because they have higher-frequency data. One manager stated that with CP's old technology, analyzing data was similar to looking at snapshots at certain points in time. In contrast, with PLOT, analyzing data resembles looking at a movie because managers are analyzing nearly real-time data.

PLOT provides 43 performance dashboards for individual wells and gas fields. Simple threshold alerts let well operators know when plunger lift operating cycles must be adjusted to eliminate fluid buildup restricting the flow of gas. The dashboards remotely monitor wells and notify well operators when problems are likely to occur, so that the operators can quickly recognize problems.

To continuously connect more of its far-flung wells, the company is building its own radio and Wi-Fi towers to cover remote energy fields in South Texas, where commercial carriers do not offer mobile coverage. This private communications network will transmit data from wells to company data centers in Houston and Bartlesville, Oklahoma, where the information is stored and analyzed.

ConocoPhillips did face an interesting challenge when implementing PLOT, specifically, change management. Many well operators adopted the new dashboards quickly, adjusted plunger lift cycles, and tweaked well operations every day to increase output. Others were trained, but either they did not understand what to change or they just did not follow through on recommended actions from PLOT. To resolve this problem, CP is moving to a centralized approach, where a dozen people in an operation center monitor all the wells in a geographic area and direct optimization efforts rather than count on the hundreds of well operators—the people who travel from well to well to make adjustments and maintain equipment—to interpret the dashboards and determine which actions to take. The operations center staff will be able to identify which wells are operating within expected parameters and which ones are not. They will also be able to instruct the operators as to which wells to visit and what to do when they arrive on site.

THE RESULTS >>> Interestingly, CP did not spend large amounts of money on PLOT. Nevertheless, the system has generated significant benefits for the company. PLOT has increased production from more than 4,500

natural gas wells by an average of 5 percent. As a result, PLOT has improved the company's revenue from its wells, reduced greenhouse gas emissions tied to inefficient wells, and eliminated unnecessary operator trips to each well by using remote monitoring. The project is also reducing U.S. dependence on imported oil by making the most of domestic energy sources.

CP has realized another advantage from PLOT—improved data quality. Data quality has been a major challenge with the company. The company has deployed different generations of computers and sensors stationed in and at the wells themselves, as well as different communications methods (over cellular, radio, and Wi-Fi), which have contributed to data complexity and variability.

These benefits are just a start. ConocoPhillips is now using PLOT in thousands of additional plunger-lift-style gas wells in the United States and Canada. In addition, the company is applying the techniques and lessons learned from PLOT to other types of gas wells. For example, CP is expanding PLOT to its gas fields in Canada and the North Slope of Alaska.

Sources: Compiled from G. Allouche, "Mining for Oil with Big Data," *Toad World*, February 10, 2014; "A PLOT to Increase Production," *ConocoPhillips Onshore*, 2014; "The Big Deal About Big Data in Upstream Oil and Gas," *Hitachi Data Systems White Paper*, 2014; C. Murphy, "ConocoPhillips CIO Talks Live on Big Data Analytics," *InformationWeek*, December 16, 2013; M. DiLallo, "How ConocoPhillips Plots to Use Technology to Improve Production," *The Motley Fool*, October 1, 2013; "Data Analysis Tool Helps ConocoPhillips Boost Natural Gas Production," *SmartBrief*, September 11, 2013; D. Henschen, "Drilling Down into Big Data," *InformationWeek*, September 9, 2013; D. Henschen, "ConocoPhillips Taps Big Data for Gas Well Gains, *InformationWeek*, September 5, 2013; D. McDonald, "Even Oil Companies Are Using the New Oil, Big Data Analytics," *Teradata*, December 11, 2012; "How Big Data Is Changing the Oil & Gas Industry," *Analytics Magazine*, November/December 2012; R. Thomas, "The Looming Global Analytics Talent Mismatch in Oil and Gas," *Accenture White Paper*, October 2012; www.conocophillips.com, accessed March 7, 2014.

Questions

1. Describe the impact of the PLOT system on the quantity and quality of the data collected from ConocoPhillips's wells. Now, describe the impact of these data on the quality of the analyses from the PLOT system. What is the relationship that you can infer between the quality and quantity of data and the quality of the analysis performed on that data?

2. If plunger lift technology had been in place for some 50 years, why is ConocoPhillips just now developing its PLOT system?

3. Speculate how well operators will react to PLOT. Positively or negatively? Support your answer.

CLOSING **CASE 2** > Social

Sentiment Analysis

THE BUSINESS PROBLEM >>> Sentiment analysis refers to the use of natural language processing, text analysis, machine learning, and statistics to identify and extract subjective information in source materials. A basic task in sentiment analysis is classifying whether the expressed opinion in a document, sentence, Web page, online news, Internet discussion group, blog, Facebook post, or tweet is positive, negative, or neutral. Advanced sentiment analysis examines emotional states such as angry, sad, and happy.

The rise of social media in particular has increased interest in sentiment analysis. (We discuss social computing in detail in Chapter 8.) With the proliferation of reviews, ratings, and recommendations, online opinion has become a critical information resource for businesses that want to market their products, identify new opportunities, and manage their reputations. Businesses must understand the conversations, identify relevant content, and take appropriate actions based on these findings.

THE IT SOLUTION >>> At the University of Southern California's (USC; www.usc.edu) Annenberg Innovation Lab, researchers are using sentiment analysis to analyze, in real time, the sentiment of conversations on a range of topics that thrive on social media. The research analyzes the positive and negative sentiments of 40 million tweets to gain insights on a variety of topics. The researchers hope to help businesses, nonprofit organizations, and government agencies gain new insights from millions of online conversations.

The problem is that most sentiment analysis algorithms use simple terms to express sentiment about a product or a service. However, cultural factors, linguistic nuances, and differing contexts make it very difficult to classify online content as positive, negative, or neutral. Additionally, the fact that humans often disagree on the sentiment expressed in a message demonstrates how difficult it is for algorithms to correctly classify sentiment. In fact, the shorter a piece of text, the harder the classification task becomes.

In every subject area—politics, entertainment, technology, etc.—people often use jargon, and sometimes sarcasm, to convey their ideas and opinions. To help improve the accuracy of sentiment analytics, researchers must train the software to learn these nuances of language. Researchers found that almost 70 percent of tweets on politics are sarcastic.

As an example, consider the difference between sarcasm and enthusiasm, a distinction that is difficult for sentiment analysis software to discern. The Annenberg Lab brought in many people both physically and virtually—the latter via Amazon's Mechanical Turk—to address the challenge of distinguishing if a tweet is sarcastic. The participants examined tweets and determined whether each one was sarcastic. Their findings were used to fine-tune the sentiment analysis software. The research team learned a great deal about sarcasm. For example, they found that if someone puts a word in quotes, then it probably means just the opposite.

THE RESULTS >>> Let's consider some examples of sentiment analysis at work. First, the Annenberg Lab analyzed social media posts related to new motion picture releases. They looked at this question: "Could you determine how movies would open based on the social buzz?" That is, how much money would a movie make in its opening days? The research found that the ability to understand public sentiment in real time was an excellent predictor of how a movie would open and what types of advertising were effective.

For instance, the researchers found that just before its release, the film *Twilight: Breaking Dawn* received a 90 percent positive sentiment on Twitter. However, soon after its release, the positive sentiment dropped to 75 percent. Though it appeared that viewers had been disappointed after the initial excitement, a closer analysis revealed that the negative sentiment was not directed against the movie. Rather, *Twilight* fans were "sad" that the series was ending.

In another example, the researchers tracked the DreamWorks' movie *Puss in Boots*, and they found that the Twitter conversations surrounding the film were negative. Responding to this feedback, the movie's marketers created a large television advertising campaign for the film. Within two days, the researchers noticed that *Puss in Boots* not only became the most talked-about movie on social media, but the mentions were overwhelmingly positive. To the marketers, this sentiment shift constituted evidence that the ad campaign had been successful.

These examples indicate that film producers and movie marketers can utilize sentiment analysis to assess popular opinions building up around a film as its release time nears. They can then create a custom message and marketing campaign based on this information. After the film is released, they can predict how well it will do over time.

In television, these insights could change the system by which networks develop shows. Television today is measured the same way as it was measured in the 1950s, with the Nielsen ratings (www.nielsen.com). The current ratings system reveals only which channel is turned on in 2,500 homes in America. It describes nothing about whether the viewers are engaged and how they feel about the programs.

Today, however, it is possible to examine a million tweets around a piece of television programming. For example, researchers examined the *Oscars* television show to see in real time what people thought about every segment of the show's programming and advertising. The show's producers could actually see where the sentiment became negative in the program (say, at minute 36), and then look at the tweets to understand what viewers did not like.

The business opportunities that sentiment analysis offers for the media, entertainment, and advertising industries are significant. Sentiment analysis can provide marketing managers with near-real-time insight into what consumers are thinking, so they can adjust their strategies and offers while it is still possible to influence the outcomes. Even more compelling, however, are the social implications of sentiment analytics. It could influence everything from election strategies to public policies to emergency responses.

For example, the Annenberg Lab analyzed tweets during a political debate, where each candidate had a sentiment meter. The debate was literally a real-time, 800,000-person focus group. The researchers observed that when members of the audience perceived that a candidate had made a mistake, the sentiment changed negatively on the dashboard in seconds.

Social sentiment analysis will be valuable to governments as well. People in developing nations use Twitter and Facebook extensively. If government officials in developing nations could monitor a malaria epidemic or a civil conflict by analyzing huge volumes of Twitter data, they could identify areas where problems are developing and then act proactively to resolve them.

Sources: Compiled from M. Sponder, "The Dollars and Sense of Sentiment," *CMS Wire*, March 7, 2014; I. Lunden, "Thomson Reuters Taps into Twitter for Big Data Sentiment Analysis," *TechCrunch*, February 3, 2014; E. Washington, "Human Sentiment Analysis," *Growing Social Media*, November 6, 2013; R. Munro, "Why Is Sentiment Analysis Hard?" *idibon*, September 6, 2013; "Sentiment Analysis: The New Game Changer for Entertainment Industry," *Shout Analytics*, July 12, 2013; J. Burn-Murdoch, "Social Media Analytics: Are We Nearly There Yet?" The Guardian, June 10, 2013; G. Parker, "Tool Developed by USC Annenberg Innovation Lab Explores True Sentiment of Social Media," *USC Annenberg School for Communication and Journalism*, January 30, 2013; "Case Study: Advanced Sentiment Analysis," *Paragon Poll*, 2013; "Case Study: University of Southern California Annenberg Innovation Lab," *IBM Software Information Management*, 2013; J. Taplin, "Social Sentiment Analysis Changes the Game for Hollywood," *Building a Smarter Planet*, November 30, 2012; "USC Annenberg, IBM, and Los Angeles Times Conduct Academy Awards Social Sentiment Analysis," *USC Annenberg School for Communication and Journalism*, February 8, 2012; M. Ogneva, "How Companies Can Use Sentiment Analysis to Improve Their Business," *Mashable*, April 19, 2010; http://annenberg.usc.edu, www.ibm.com, accessed March 8, 2014.

Questions

1. Describe areas in which social sentiment analysis would be beneficial for your university. Provide specific examples to support your answer.

2. Describe potential disadvantages that organizations might experience when using social sentiment analysis.

3. What impacts could social sentiment analysis have on television reality shows? Provide specific examples in your answer.

INTERNSHIP ACTIVITY> OXFORD ORTHOPAEDICS

Industry: Healthcare

Dashboards are a popular tool for viewing business data. Many companies have developed "off-the-shelf" dashboards that enable them to quickly and easily assess their organizational health based on a few key indicators. Of course, no two companies are exactly alike. Ultimately, a dashboard is helpful only if it is showing you what you need to see.

Oxford Orthopaedics recently migrated to a new practice management/electronic health records (PM/HER) system. The company can now collect data in ways they previously were unable to. However, Chad Prince, the Practice Administrator, is having a difficult time determining which measures are helpful. Although many types of information may be interesting to look at, if they are not a good measure of the organization's health, then they are not serving any useful purpose.

Below you will find a letter from Chad requesting your assistance with his Business Intelligence (BI) Dashboard.

To:	IT Intern
From:	Chad Prince
Subject:	Help reviewing PM/HER Dashboards

Hello!

As you know from previous projects, Oxford Orthopaedics has recently implemented Greenway Medical's Electronic Health Records/Practice Management PrimeSuite software package. Although we are enjoying many of the benefits offered by this software, we are also struggling under a bit of information overload. I have watched their demo online and have learned a lot about how to use the package. However, I want an outside perspective. Look up NextGen (another PM/EHR solution), and find their Practice Management Dashboard Demonstration. You may have to register to gain access. If this is the case, then select "student" as your role if you are given the option. Watch this demo, and take notes on the key features that you think will make their BI Dashboard tool helpful.

Finally, search the Web for "BI Dashboard Best Practices," and learn as much as you can. Then, send me a summary of what you have found. Include the Web links so that I can visit the sites myself.

Thanks for your efforts in this endeavor. It's funny . . . I never thought I would have a problem with too much information!
Chad

SPREADSHEET ACTIVITY > BASIC FUNCTIONALITY: PROTECTING A SPREADSHEET

STEP 1 – Background

Any time you store data, you should take steps to secure those data. Spreadsheets frequently contain private or personal data that employees and/or customers do not want to be lost or released.

To prevent data loss, it is a good idea to understand spreadsheet protection at three levels: workbook protection, worksheet protection, and range protection (including a single cell). *Workbook protection* requires the user to enter a password to access the entire workbook. This is an effective strategy to prevent unauthorized parties from accessing the data. *Worksheet* protection within a protected workbook maintains the consistency of all of the data in the worksheet. Perhaps there are a few pages of data that do NOT need to be altered. Protecting those worksheets while allowing others to be modified will ensure that those data will not been changed. Finally, *range protection* allows users to modify data in some cells on a worksheet without affecting the data in other cells.

It is important to note that protecting a workbook does not encrypt the workbook. Rather, the data are stored in traditional spreadsheet files. The underlying idea in protecting a workbook is either to lock out unauthorized people completely or to keep authorized users from modifying something they should not.

STEP 2 – Activity

Recently, Juanita signed up for a Debt Management course, but she didn't want her family, friends, and coworkers to know that she had problems with debt. However, the course manager's computer was hacked, and the spreadsheet—which was not protected—was posted on the Internet. Research the three methods of protecting spreadsheets, and be prepared to give advice on which method would have been the most appropriate for the course manager: workbook, worksheet, or range.

STEP 3 – Deliverable

Charles is the teacher whose computer was hacked in the example in Step 2. Visit http://www.wiley.com/go/rainer/MIS3e/spreadsheet, and download Charles's spreadsheet. The workbook will include instructions to guide you in helping Charles to protect his data so that even if his computer is hacked, at least the spreadsheet will be inaccessible. Submit your protected workbook to your professor with another document of notes that contains your passwords so that your professor will be able to access your work.

Follow the instructions in the spreadsheet and submit your final work to your instructor.

DATABASE ACTIVITY > SORTING AND FILTERING

STEP 1 – Background

All organizations keep critical information in databases. Security and privacy policies govern who can access each database and which data they are authorized to view. Simply put, users can access some parts of a database but not others. Hence, the way users select which parts of a database to view is closely connected to privacy and security considerations.

In this activity, you will learn how to select only the useful rows of a table, hiding the others, and how to sort a table on any column in it. A database has no value if you cannot use it to obtain the information you need. Access offers many options to help you accomplish this task. Some of these options are simple, but limited. Others are more comprehensive, but they require more work. Filtering and sorting a table are at the low end, but they are still often useful. We will start with these functions and then proceed to more complex (but more capable) methods in later activities.

STEP 2 – Activity

Visit http://www.wiley.com/go/rainer/MIS3e/database, and download the database linked for Chapter 5. This database has one table that contains the same information as NeTrouble, which you worked with in

Chapter 4, minus some columns (such as employee date of birth and date of hire) to save screen space.

This is usually a poor way to organize a database. It violates the normalization rules you read about in Plug IT In 3. However, this "flat file" data structure is common. When you have this type of file, this is where filtering works best.

Suppose you want to see the trouble tickets for various devices. Open TroubleTbl in NetSimple. Make certain it is in Datasheet view (it should open that way). The second column of the table, DeviceName, identifies the type of device. Imagine that the Marketing Department has recently updated their equipment and you are no longer interested in the tickets contained on their old equipment. Filter the data so that all other department tickets are listed in the order of newest to oldest for the "Bridge" device.

STEP 3 – Deliverable

Use the same set of filters to show each of the devices as described above for the "Bridge." (Print a PDF of each one as well.) Then, write a summary of what you learned about the devices and the problems that are showing up in each department.

Additional help with this database skill is available in WileyPLUS. Open the "Microsoft Office 2013 Lab Manual Database Module: Access 2013," and review Lesson 9: Sorting Records.

CHAPTER 6

Ethics and Privacy

LEARNING OBJECTIVES >>>

6.1 Define ethics, list and describe the three fundamental tenets of ethics, and describe the four categories of ethical issues related to information technology.

6.2 Identify three places that store personal data, and for each one, discuss at least one potential threat to the privacy of the data stored there.

OPENING CASE > Tapad Can Track You Across Devices

© tiridifilm / iStockphoto

Targeting potential customers is simple on a desktop. Just add cookies—bits of code that tag visitors—to a Web site, and advertisers can follow prospects with ads as they surf the Web. Visit a Web site for your university's football team, for instance, and you might see ads for team paraphernalia. Because these ads appear only to people who have visited a brand's Web site, they have a click-through rate of up to three times that of banner ads notes AdRoll, a San Francisco digital advertising company.

Cookies, however, can track on only one device. The trail goes cold when you leave your desktop and use your phone. Today, it is not unusual for users to switch devices many times within just one hour, leaving marketers in the dark. Tapad (www.tapad.com), a rapidly growing digital advertising startup, claims that it can track and target the same consumer across multiple devices—desktop computers, smartphones, and tablets—using software algorithms.

Tapad analyzes 150 billion data points—from cookies, smartphone IDs (which link individual phones to app downloads and Web browsing), Wi-Fi connections, Web site registrations, browsing history, and other inputs that it will not reveal. In essence, Tapad is searching for commonalities that link one device with another.

For instance, if a tablet and a laptop share the same Wi-Fi network, that is a positive sign. In a similar fashion, browsing patterns are also important—say, two devices that share a history of visiting sports Web sites. Each correlation increases the likelihood that the same person owns both devices. Based on these probabilities, Tapad clients serve ads to potential customers across devices. Thus, the same customer might see one ad on a work computer, another ad on the mobile Web on the commute home, and a third ad while sitting with a tablet on the couch.

Significantly, Tapad encountered a major problem right from the start. Agencies and marketing departments are often divided into mobile, desktop, and television advertising divisions. Tapad had to sell its product to all three groups.

In August 2011, Tapad secured its first client, a U.S. wireless network. The startup ran a month-long campaign that increased the network's click-through rates by 300 percent. That higher rate enabled the network to fine-tune its marketing budget, because it knew which devices, when used at key times, correlated with a specific transaction.

By mid-2014, Tapad had acquired 160 clients, including Audi, American Airlines, and TurboTax, serving 2 billion ads each month. However, the company's success is running the risk of irritating Congress, regulators, and privacy advocates.

Success breeds scrutiny, and not just from competitors such as Drawbridge (http://drawbrid.ge). The U.S. Senate

Commerce Committee may force advertisers to adopt "Do Not Track" technology, which requires Web browsers to offer an easy opt-out. (We discuss opt-out and opt-in later in the chapter.) Tapad protests that it does not collect data that can be used to pinpoint users by name. Furthermore, the company includes opt-out buttons in all of its ads. Tapad employs a privacy lawyer in Washington to ensure that the company is functioning within the law while it continues to expand rapidly.

Sources: Compiled from T. Peterson, "Google Tests Desktop-to-Mobile Retargeting with Brand Data," *Advertising Age*, March 12, 2014; "Introducing AdRoll Retargeting for Mobile: A New Way to Retarget Across Devices," *PR Newswire*, February 20, 2014; J. Colao, "The Stalker," *Forbes*, June 10, 2013; N. Dujnic, "Tapad & the Multiscreen World," *Live Intent*,

June 5, 2013; J. McDermott, "Can Mobile Targeting Ever Be as Accurate as Cookies on the Desktop?" *Advertising Age*, March 21, 2013; "Tapad and TRUSTe Forge Partnership," *TRUSTe.com*, March 12, 2013; J. Del Rey, "Tapad Brings Retargeting to Phones, Tablets, But Marketers Aren't Talking," *Advertising Age*, March 7, 2012; www.tapad.com, accessed March 29, 2014.

Questions

1. Is Tapad's business model ethical? Why or why not?
2. What is the relationship between Tapad's business model and your privacy? Provide specific examples to support your answer.

Introduction

The chapter opening case about Tapad and chapter closing case 1 concerning surveillance programs at the National Security Agency (NSA) address the two major issues you will study in this chapter: ethics and privacy. The two issues are closely related to each other and also to IT, and both raise significant questions involving access to information in the digital age. For example: Are the actions of the two organizations ethical? Does either organization violate the privacy of governments, organizations, and individuals? The answers to these questions are not straightforward. In fact, IT has made finding answers to these questions even more difficult.

You will encounter numerous ethical and privacy issues in your career, many of which will involve IT in some manner. This chapter will provide insights into how to respond to these issues. Furthermore, it will help you to make immediate contributions to your company's code of ethics and its privacy policies. You will also be able to provide meaningful input concerning the potential ethical and privacy impacts of your organization's information systems on people within and outside the organization.

For example, suppose your organization decides to adopt social computing technologies (which you will study in Chapter 8) to include business partners and customers in new product development. You will be able to analyze the potential privacy and ethical implications of implementing these technologies.

All organizations, large and small, must be concerned with ethics. In particular, small business (or startup) owners face a very difficult situation when their employees have access to sensitive customer information. There is a delicate balance between access to information and the appropriate use of that information. This balance is best maintained by hiring honest and trustworthy employees who abide by the organization's code of ethics. Ultimately this issue leads to another question: Does the small business, or a startup, even have a code of ethics to fall back on in this type of situation?

6.1 Ethical Issues

Ethics refers to the principles of right and wrong that individuals use to make choices that guide their behavior. Deciding what is right or wrong is not always easy or clear-cut. Fortunately, there are many frameworks that can help us make ethical decisions.

Ethical Frameworks

There are many sources for ethical standards. Here we consider four widely used standards: the utilitarian approach, the rights approach, the fairness approach, and the common good approach. There are many other sources, but these four are representative.

© AlexMax/iStockphoto

The *utilitarian approach* states that an ethical action is the one that provides the most good or does the least harm. The ethical corporate action would be the one that produces the greatest good and does the least harm for all affected parties—customers, employees, shareholders, the community, and the physical environment.

The *rights approach* maintains that an ethical action is the one that best protects and respects the moral rights of the affected parties. Moral rights can include the rights to make one's own choices about what kind of life to lead, to be told the truth, not to be injured, and to enjoy a degree of privacy. Which of these rights people are actually entitled to—and under what circumstances—is widely debated. Nevertheless, most people acknowledge that individuals are entitled to some moral rights. An ethical organizational action would be one that protects and respects the moral rights of customers, employees, shareholders, business partners, and even competitors.

The *fairness approach* posits that ethical actions treat all human beings equally, or, if unequally, then fairly, based on some defensible standard. For example, most people might believe it is fair to pay people higher salaries if they work harder or if they contribute a greater amount to the firm. However, there is less certainty regarding CEO salaries that are hundreds or thousands of times larger than those of other employees. Many people question whether this huge disparity is based on a defensible standard or whether it is the result of an imbalance of power and hence is unfair.

Finally, the *common good approach* highlights the interlocking relationships that underlie all societies. This approach argues that respect and compassion for all others is the basis for ethical actions. It emphasizes the common conditions that are important to the welfare of everyone. These conditions can include a system of laws, effective police and fire departments, healthcare, a public educational system, and even public recreation areas.

If we combine these four standards, we can develop a general framework for ethics (or ethical decision making). This framework consists of five steps:

- Recognize an ethical issue:

  - Could this decision or situation damage someone or some group?

  - Does this decision involve a choice between a good and a bad alternative?

  - Does this issue involve more than simply legal considerations? If so, then in what way?

- Get the facts:

  - What are the relevant facts of the situation?

  - Do I have sufficient information to make a decision?

  - Which individuals and/or groups have an important stake in the outcome?

  - Have I consulted all relevant persons and groups?

- Evaluate alternative actions:

  - Which option will produce the most good and do the least harm? (the utilitarian approach)

  - Which option best respects the rights of all stakeholders? (the rights approach)

  - Which option treats people equally or proportionately? (the fairness approach)

  - Which option best serves the community as a whole, and not just some members? (the common good approach)

- Make a decision and test it:

  - Considering all the approaches, which option best addresses the situation?

- Act and reflect on the outcome of your decision:

  - How can I implement my decision with the greatest care and attention to the concerns of all stakeholders?

  - How did my decision turn out, and what did I learn from this specific situation?

Now that we have created a general ethical framework, we will focus specifically on ethics in the corporate environment.

Ethics in the Corporate Environment

Many companies and professional organizations develop their own codes of ethics. A **code of ethics** is a collection of principles intended to guide decision making by members of the organization. For example, the Association for Computing Machinery (www.acm.org), an organization of computing professionals, has a thoughtful code of ethics for its members (see www.acm.org/constitution/code.html).

© Marcopolo9442 / iStockphoto

Keep in mind that different codes of ethics are not always consistent with one another. Therefore, an individual might be expected to conform to multiple codes. For example, a person who is a member of two large professional computing-related organizations may be simultaneously required by one organization to comply with all applicable laws and by the other organization to refuse to obey unjust laws.

Fundamental tenets of ethics include responsibility, accountability, and liability.

Responsibility means that you accept the consequences of your decisions and actions.

Accountability refers to determining who is responsible for actions that were taken.

Liability is a legal concept that gives individuals the right to recover the damages done to them by other individuals, organizations, or systems.

Before you go any further, it is critical that you realize that what is *unethical* is not necessarily *illegal*. For example, a bank's decision to foreclose on a home can be technically legal, but it can raise many ethical questions. In many instances, then, an individual or organization faced with an ethical decision is not considering whether to break the law. As the foreclosure example illustrates, however, ethical decisions can have serious consequences for individuals, organizations, and society at large.

We have witnessed a large number of extremely poor ethical decisions, not to mention outright criminal behavior, at many organizations. During 2001 and 2002, three highly publicized fiascos occurred at Enron, WorldCom, and Tyco. At each company, executives were convicted of various types of fraud for using illegal accounting practices. These actions led to the passage of the Sarbanes-Oxley Act in 2002. Sarbanes-Oxley requires publicly held companies to implement financial controls and company executives to personally certify financial reports.

Then, the subprime mortgage crisis exposed unethical lending practices throughout the mortgage industry. The crisis also highlighted pervasive weaknesses in the regulation of the U.S. financial industry as well as the global financial system. It ultimately contributed to a deep recession in the global economy. Along these same lines, financier Bernie Madoff was convicted in 2009 of operating a Ponzi scheme and sentenced to 150 years in federal prison. In addition, several of Madoff's employees were convicted in 2014.

Advancements in information technologies have generated a new set of ethical problems. Computing processing power doubles roughly every 18 months, meaning that organizations are more dependent than ever on their information systems. Organizations can store increasing amounts of data at decreasing costs. As a result, they can maintain more data on individuals for longer periods of time. Going further, computer networks, particularly the Internet, enable organizations to collect, integrate, and distribute enormous amounts of information on individuals, groups, and institutions. These developments have created numerous ethical problems concerning the appropriate collection and use of customer information, personal privacy, and the protection of intellectual property, as chapter closing case 2 illustrates.

These developments affect the academic world as well. For example, vast amounts of information on the Internet make it easier for students to plagiarize papers and essays. IT's About Business 6.1 addresses the plagiarism problem.

Cheating Is Risky for Business Students

For $29.99, an MBA applicant can access the Web site Wordprom (http://wordprom.com) and purchase an admissions essay that got someone else accepted to another university. If that person is daring, he or she might even try to pass parts of that essay off as his or her own.

Unfortunately, cheating has become more common at business schools. Between 2002 and 2004, Rutgers Business School professor Don McCabe surveyed 5,000 graduate students and found that MBA students confessed to cheating more than their nonbusiness peers. In fact, the managing director of the MBA program at Pennsylvania State University's Smeal College of Business claims that recycled essays are the school's biggest problem.

However, it is becoming much more difficult to fool admissions staff and instructors, because a growing number of schools use plagiarism-detection software such as Turnitin (www.turnitin.com). For years, classroom instructors have employed Turnitin to uncover plagiarized material on term papers. Essays submitted through online admission portals at business schools are now passed through Turnitin, which crawls the Web to identify plagiarized passages. The software has matched material to *Wikipedia* and *Bloomberg BusinessWeek*, among many other sites. Turnitin's database also includes academic research papers and a growing repository of college papers. The software issues an alert when substantial parts of an essay match an entry by a different author stored in the system.

Smeal College provides an excellent illustration of this process. Since the school began to use Turnitin in 2010, it has rejected 85 applicants for plagiarizing their admissions essays, including 40 in 2013 alone. Overall, the number of MBA admissions offices using Turnitin more than doubled in 2013 to 15, and it is likely to increase even faster now that the tool is being marketed as an add-on to a widely used software suite (see www.iparadigms.com) for processing applications. Significantly, Turnitin keeps its client roster private, and most business schools do not disclose whether they are using the service. Among those that do, Smeal College is the only one that has notified suspected plagiarizers. All other schools have rejected applicants without offering any explanation. Wordprom's CEO maintains that its Web site is intended to give applicants samples of effective work so that they can

get a feel for structure and style when drafting their own original essays. The site does warn users that it has an agreement to provide Turnitin with access to its database.

© Dmitriy Shironosov/iStockphoto

Some experts contend that tools like Turnitin are a deterrent but not a cure, because applicants can still hire someone to write their essays for them. Moreover, even cheaters are turning to content-tracking services such as Turnitin. They want to make certain that the authors they hire to write their essays are not plagiarizing themselves or selling the essays to multiple customers.

A Ukraine-based competitor of Turnitin, Plagtracker (www.plagtracker.com), reports that its client base is growing rapidly. The site claims that 60 percent of its customers are either students or prospective students.

Sources: Compiled from C. Straumsheim, "Turnitin Put to the Test," *Inside Higher Ed*, February 6, 2014; J. Bailey, "New Turnitin Study on the Impact of Plagiarism Detection in Higher Education," *Plagiarism Today*, February 5, 2014; M. Saltzman, "Turnitin: Plagiarizing Students Beware New App for iPad," *USA Today*, September 17, 2013; E. Zlomek, "Master's in Plagiarism," *Bloomberg BusinessWeek*, April 22–28, 2013; N. Heckler, M. Rice, and C. Bryan, "Turnitin Systems: A Deterrent to Plagiarism in College Classrooms," *Journal of Research on Technology in Education*, March 6, 2013; "Why Students Cheat, and What To Do About It," *Hult Labs*, February 9, 2013; D. McCabe, "MBAs Cheat. But Why?" *Harvard Business Review blog*, April 13, 2009; www.turnitin.com, www.iparadigms.com, www.plagtracker.com, accessed March 30, 2014.

Questions

1. As the Turnitin database expands rapidly by incorporating a growing number of papers and essays, what will be the impact on subsequent papers submitted to it?

2. Discuss the ethical implications of writing a paper yourself that you know contains some plagiarized material and then using Turnitin's service yourself.

Ethics and Information Technology

All employees have a responsibility to encourage ethical uses of information and information technology. Many of the business decisions you will face at work will have an ethical dimension. Consider the following decisions that you might have to make:

- Should organizations monitor employees' Web surfing and e-mail?
- Should organizations sell customer information to other companies?

- Should organizations audit employees' computers for unauthorized software or illegally downloaded music or video files?

The diversity and ever-expanding use of IT applications have created a variety of ethical issues. These issues fall into four general categories: privacy, accuracy, property, and accessibility.

1. *Privacy issues* involve collecting, storing, and disseminating information about individuals.
2. *Accuracy issues* involve the authenticity, fidelity, and correctness of information that is collected and processed.
3. *Property issues* involve the ownership and value of information.
4. *Accessibility issues* revolve around who should have access to information and whether they should pay a fee for this access.

Table 6.1 lists representative questions and issues for each of these categories. In addition, Online Ethics Cases presents 14 scenarios that raise ethical issues. These scenarios will provide a context for you to consider situations that involve ethical or unethical behavior.

Many of the issues and scenarios discussed in this chapter involve privacy as well as ethics. In the next section, you will learn about privacy issues in more detail.

┌─ BEFORE *YOU GO ON....* ─┐

1. What does a code of ethics contain?
2. Describe the fundamental tenets of ethics.

TABLE 6.1 A Framework for Ethical Issues

Privacy issues

What information about oneself should an individual be required to reveal to others?

What kinds of surveillance can an employer use on its employees?

What types of personal information can people keep to themselves and not be forced to reveal to others?

What information about individuals should be kept in databases, and how secure is the information there?

Accuracy issues

Who is responsible for the authenticity, fidelity, and accuracy of the information collected?

How can we ensure that the information will be processed properly and presented accurately to users?

How can we ensure that errors in databases, data transmissions, and data processing are accidental and not intentional?

Who is to be held accountable for errors in information, and how should the injured parties be compensated?

Property issues

Who owns the information?

What are the just and fair prices for its exchange?

How should we handle software piracy (illegally copying copyrighted software)?

Under what circumstances can one use proprietary databases?

Can corporate computers be used for private purposes?

How should experts who contribute their knowledge to create expert systems be compensated?

How should access to information channels be allocated?

Accessibility issues

Who is allowed to access information?

How much should companies charge for permitting access to information?

How can access to computers be provided for employees with disabilities?

Who will be provided with the equipment needed for accessing information?

What information does a person or an organization have a right to obtain, under what conditions, and with what safeguards?

Apply The Concept 6.1

LEARNING OBJECTIVE 6.1 Define ethics, list and describe the three fundamental tenets of ethics, and describe the four categories of ethical issues related to information technology.

STEP 1 – Background (Here is what you are learning)

As you begin your career, you need to be aware of the current trends affecting the four areas of concern presented in Section 6.1. Privacy (what people know about you), property (who owns the data about you), accuracy (are the data about you accurate), and accessibility (who can access your data) are major topics in the today's high-tech world. They are especially important in the migration to electronic health records, mobile wallets, social media, and government-run databases, to name a few.

STEP 2 – Activity (Here is what you are doing)

Visit http://www.wiley.com/go/rainer/MIS3e/applytheconcept, and read the article posted on the *Huffington Post* Web site from November 2013. The article describes an unusual (or not-so-unusual) action on the part of Goldman Sachs. It seems they have decided that their junior bankers should have weekends off!

Understand that it isn't illegal to require your employees to work weekends, nor is it illegal to give them time off. It also isn't illegal to work people 75 hours a week. Many of the talking points in this article focus expressly on ethics. An employer is trying to do the "right" thing, and they have used a new standard to define "right."

STEP 3 – Deliverable (Here is what you turn in)

Summarize the article for your professor. In your summary, make certain to define ethics and to describe how the three fundamental tenets of ethics (responsibility, liability, and accountability) played a role in Goldman Sach's decision. Finally, (not from the article) discuss how these same bankers deal with the four areas of ethical concern with regards to your financial information.

6.2 Privacy

In general, **privacy** is the right to be left alone and to be free of unreasonable personal intrusions. **Information privacy** is the right to determine when, and to what extent, information about you can be gathered and/or communicated to others. Privacy rights apply to individuals, groups, and institutions. The right to privacy is recognized today in all the U.S. states and by the federal government, either by statute or in common law.

Privacy can be interpreted quite broadly. However, court decisions in many countries have followed two rules fairly closely:

1. The right of privacy is not absolute. Privacy must be balanced against the needs of society.

2. The public's right to know supersedes the individual's right of privacy.

These two rules illustrate why determining and enforcing privacy regulations can be difficult.

As we discussed earlier, rapid advances in information technologies have made it much easier to collect, store, and integrate vast amounts of data on individuals in large databases. On an average day, data about you are generated in many ways: surveillance cameras located on toll roads, on other roadways, in busy intersections, in public places, and at work; credit card transactions; telephone calls (landline and cellular); banking transactions; queries to search engines; and government records (including police records). These data can be integrated to produce a **digital dossier**, which is an electronic profile of you and your habits. The process of forming a digital dossier is called **profiling**.

Data aggregators, such as LexisNexis (www.lexisnexis.com), ChoicePoint (www.choicepoint.com), and Acxiom (www.acxiom.com), are prominent examples of profilers.

These companies collect public data such as real estate records and published telephone numbers, in addition to nonpublic information such as Social Security numbers; financial data; and police, criminal, and motor vehicle records. They then integrate these data to form digital dossiers on most adults in the United States. They ultimately sell these dossiers to law enforcement agencies and companies that conduct background checks on potential employees. They also sell them to companies that want to know their customers better, a process called *customer intimacy*.

Data on individuals can also be used in more controversial manners. For example, a controversial map in California identifies the addresses of donors who supported Proposition 8, the referendum approved by California voters in the 2008 election that outlawed same-sex marriage in that state (see www.eightmaps.com). Gay activists created the map by combining Google's satellite mapping technology with publicly available campaign records that listed Proposition 8 donors who contributed $100 or more. These donors were outraged, claiming that the map invaded their privacy.

Electronic Surveillance

According to the American Civil Liberties Union (ACLU), tracking people's activities with the aid of information technology has become a major privacy-related problem. The ACLU notes that this monitoring, or **electronic surveillance**, is rapidly increasing, particularly with the emergence of new technologies. Electronic surveillance is conducted by employers, the government, and other institutions.

Americans today live with a degree of surveillance that would have been unimaginable just a few years ago. For example, surveillance cameras track you at airports, subways, banks, and other public venues. In addition, inexpensive digital sensors are now everywhere. They are incorporated into laptop webcams, video-game motion sensors, smartphone cameras, utility meters, passports, and employee ID cards. Step out your front door and you could be captured in a high-resolution photograph taken from the air or from the street by Google or Microsoft, as they update their mapping services. Drive down a city street, cross a toll bridge, or park at a shopping mall, and your license plate will be recorded and time-stamped.

Emerging technologies such as low-cost digital cameras, motion sensors, and biometric readers are helping to increase the monitoring of human activity. In addition, the costs of storing and using digital data are rapidly decreasing. The result is an explosion of sensor data collection and storage.

In fact, your smartphone has become a sensor. The average price of a smartphone has increased 17 percent since 2000. However, the phone's processing capability has increased by 13,000 percent during that time, according to technology market research firm ABI Research (www.abiresearch.com). As you will study in Chapter 10, smartphones can now record video, take pictures, send and receive e-mail, search for information, access the Internet, and locate you on a map, among many other things. Your phone also stores large amounts of information about you that can be collected and analyzed. A special problem arises with smartphones that are equipped with global positioning system (GPS) sensors. These sensors routinely *geotag* photos and videos, embedding images with the longitude and latitude of the location shown in the image. Thus, you could be inadvertently supplying criminals with useful intelligence by posting personal images on social networks or photo-sharing Web sites. These actions would show the criminals exactly where you live.

Another example of how new devices can contribute to electronic surveillance is facial recognition technology. Just a few years ago, this software worked only in very controlled settings such as passport checkpoints. However, this technology can now match faces even in regular snapshots and online images. For example, Intel and Microsoft have introduced in-store digital billboards that can recognize your face. These billboards can keep track of the products you are interested in based on your purchases or browsing behavior. One marketing analyst has predicted that your experience in every store will soon be customized.

Google and Facebook are using facial-recognition software—Google Picasa and Facebook Photo Albums—in their popular online photo-editing and sharing services. Both companies encourage users to assign names to people in photos, a practice referred to as *photo tagging*. Facial-recognition software then indexes facial features. Once an individual in a photo is tagged, the software searches for similar facial features in untagged photos. This process allows the user to quickly group photos in which the tagged person appears. Significantly, the individual is not aware of this process.

Why is tagging important? The reason is that once you are tagged in a photo, that photo can be used to search for matches across the entire Internet or in private databases, including databases fed by surveillance cameras. How could this type of surveillance affect you? As one example, a car dealer can take a picture of you when you step onto the car lot. He or she could then quickly profile you (find out information about where you live, your employment, etc.) on the Web to achieve a competitive edge in making a sale. Even worse, a stranger in a restaurant could photograph you with a smartphone and then go online to profile you for reasons of his or her own. One privacy attorney has asserted that losing your right to anonymity would have a chilling effect on where you go, whom you meet, and how you live your life. IT's About Business 6.2 illustrates another type of surveillance technology employed by retailers.

IT'S ABOUT BUSINESS 6.2

Those Mannequins Are Watching You

Store mannequin maker Almax (www.almax-italy.com) is deploying the EyeSee, a mannequin equipped with technology that is typically used to identify criminals at airports. The mannequins allow retailers to gather demographic data and shopping patterns from customers as they move through stores. Although retailers are reluctant to discuss the mannequins' use, Almax says that several companies are using them in three European countries and the United States.

The EyeSee looks like an ordinary mannequin from the outside. Internally, however, a camera in one eye feeds data into demographic-profiling software to determine each customer's age, gender, and race. To give the EyeSee ears as well as eyes, Almax is developing technology that recognizes words. This feature will allow retailers to eavesdrop on shoppers' comments regarding the mannequins' attire.

The EyeSee is designed for merchants who increasingly use technology to help personalize their product offerings. Merchants are enthusiastic over technology that can help profile customers while keeping their customers' identities anonymous.

Whereas some stores deploy similar technology to watch shoppers from overhead security cameras, Almax contends that the EyeSee provides better data because it stands at eye level and thus invites customer attention. The mannequin led one store to change its window displays after it revealed that men who shopped in the first two days of a sale spent more money than women did. Another store discovered that one-third of visitors who accessed one of its doors after 4 PM were Asian, prompting the store to place Chinese-speaking staff by that entrance.

Regulations imposed by the United States and Europe permit the use of cameras for security purposes, but they also require retailers to place signs in their stores warning customers that they may be filmed. However, watching people solely for commercial gain could be construed as gathering personal data without consent. One legal expert notes that when you access Facebook, before you start the registration process, you can see exactly what information the site will collect and what the site will do with that information. In contrast, with the EyeSee, what can customers do? Almax counters that because the EyeSee does not store any images, retailers can use it as long as they have a closed-circuit television license.

© parema / iStockphoto

Sources: Compiled from "Retailers Are Watching: The EyeSee Mannequin," *The Barcoding Blog*, January 2, 2014; "Retailers Go High-Tech to Track Shoppers," *CBS News*, December 11, 2013; "EyeSee Mannequins Monitor Footfall Traffic," *Fashion United*, December 9, 2013; A. Roberts, "In Some Stores, All Eyes Are on You," *Bloomberg BusinessWeek*, December 10–16, 2012; K. Hill, "Why Do Mannequins That Spy On Us Creep Us Out?" *Forbes*, November 28, 2012; J. Stern, "Department Store Mannequins Are Watching You. No, Really." *ABC News*, November 26, 2012; L. Clark, "Mannequins Are Spying on Shoppers for Market Analysis," *Wired*, November 23, 2012; www.almax-italy.com, accessed March 30, 2014.

Questions

1. Is using EyeSee mannequins in stores an ethical practice? Why or why not? Support your answer.

2. If stores notify people that they may be filmed, do the stores have to indicate how they might be filmed (i.e., by mannequins)? What are the ethical implications of how stores make these notifications?

3. Would knowing that the mannequins may be watching you change your shopping behavior? Why or why not? Explain your answer.

4. What are the privacy implications of the EyeSee mannequins, given that stores already have security cameras placed in strategic locations?

The scenarios we just considered deal primarily with your personal life. However, electronic surveillance has become a reality in the workplace as well. In general, employees have very limited legal protection against surveillance by employers. The law supports the right of employers to read their employees' e-mail and other electronic documents and to monitor their employees' Internet use. Today, more than three-fourths of organizations routinely monitor their employees' Internet usage. In addition, two-thirds use software to block connections to inappropriate Web sites, a practice called *URL filtering*. Furthermore, organizations are installing monitoring and filtering software to enhance security by blocking malicious software and to increase productivity by discouraging employees from wasting time.

In one organization, the chief information officer (CIO) monitored roughly 13,000 employees for three months to determine the type of traffic they engaged in on the network. He then forwarded the data to the chief executive officer (CEO) and the heads of the human resources and legal departments. These executives were shocked at the questionable Web sites the employees were visiting, as well as the amount of time they were spending on those sites. The executives quickly decided to implement a URL filtering product.

In general, surveillance is a concern for private individuals regardless of whether it is conducted by corporations, government bodies, or criminals. As a nation, the United States is still struggling to define the appropriate balance between personal privacy and electronic surveillance, especially in situations that involve threats to national security.

Personal Information in Databases

Modern institutions store information about individuals in many databases. Perhaps the most visible locations of such records are credit-reporting agencies. Other institutions that store personal information include banks and financial institutions; cable TV, telephone, and utilities companies; employers; mortgage companies; hospitals; schools and universities; retail establishments; government agencies (Internal Revenue Service, your state, your municipality); and many others.

© Pamela Moore/iStockphoto

There are several concerns about the information you provide to these record keepers. Some of the major concerns are as follows:

- Do you know where the records are?
- Are the records accurate?
- Can you change inaccurate data?
- How long will it take to make a change?
- Under what circumstances will the personal data be released?
- How are the data used?
- To whom are the data given or sold?
- How secure are the data against access by unauthorized people?

Information on Internet Bulletin Boards, Newsgroups, and Social Networking Sites

Every day we see more and more *electronic bulletin boards, newsgroups, electronic discussions* such as chat rooms, and *social networking sites* (discussed in Chapter 8). These sites appear on the Internet, within corporate intranets, and on blogs. A *blog*, short for "Weblog," is an informal, personal journal that is frequently updated and is intended for general public reading. How does society keep owners of bulletin boards from disseminating information that may be offensive to readers or simply untrue? This is a difficult problem because it involves the conflict between freedom of speech on the one hand and privacy on the other. This conflict is a fundamental and continuing ethical issue in the United States and throughout the world.

There is no better illustration of the conflict between free speech and privacy than the Internet. Many Web sites contain anonymous, derogatory information on individuals, who typically have little recourse in the matter. The vast majority of the U.S. firms use the Internet in examining job applications, including searching on Google and on social networking sites (see closing case 1 in Chapter 8). Consequently, derogatory information contained on the Internet can harm a person's chances of being hired.

New information technologies can also present serious privacy concerns. IT's About Business 6.3 examines Google Glass and its potential for invading your privacy.

IT'S ABOUT BUSINESS 6.3

Google Glass: Big Brother Really Is Watching You

We live in a world where the boundaries between what is private and what is public are blurring. New information technologies are largely responsible for this reality. Social media such as Twitter, as well as the widespread use of smartphones with image and video cameras that can upload their content immediately, have caused us to become more comfortable with these technologies. In fact, we are already used to being filmed; for example, closed-circuit television (CCTV) has become a normal part of our lives. (Think of all the CCTV security cameras located on city streets and in your university buildings.) Despite our increasing acceptance of electronic surveillance, however, a new technology known as Google Glass (www.google.com/glass/start) is causing privacy concerns.

Google Glass is an augmented reality, wearable computer with a head-mounted display. The glasses display information in a hands-free, smartphone-type format, and they can interact with the Internet via natural language voice commands. The device receives data through Wi-Fi, and it contains a GPS chip (global positioning system). (We discuss Wi-Fi and GPS in Chapter 10.) Users issue voice commands by first saying "OK glass" followed by the command. Alternatively, they can use their finger to scroll through the options located along the side of the device. Google Glass can record video, take pictures, start Google1 hangout, perform search, translate, perform facial recognition, provide directions, answer queries, use Google Now, and send a message. Essentially, these glasses can instantly capture and store every movement of every individual around the person wearing them.

Consider these questions relating to the privacy implications of Google Glass. What if someone around you who is wearing Google Glass records you on video or takes your picture and you don't even know he or she is doing it? Or, suppose you are being recorded during a business meeting at lunch? Can a child properly consent to being recorded? Is an adult who happens to be visible in the camera's peripheral vision in a bar consenting? Would you like a stranger to be able to automatically identify you with the glasses' facial recognition feature? These are only a few of the questions regarding the privacy concerns associated with Google Glass.

Perhaps the most fundamental questions are as follows: Who owns the data generated by Google Glass? Who receives these data? What happens to the data after they are captured? Presumably the data flow to Google, where they are analyzed to provide more personalized search results as well as more targeted advertising. After all, advertising is a significant source of revenue for Google. Imagine that you are wearing Google Glasses and, whenever you look at something—a shirt, for example—a special offer for that shirt pops up on your glasses. For many people, that process would be simply too intrusive.

Some analysts contend that we are too worried over the privacy implications of Google Glass. They note that our courts have outlined a definition of "reasonable expectation of privacy." If we reach a point where our surveillance technology is intrusive to a degree that everyone finds exploitative, then concerned parties will initiate legal challenges to these practices. In response, the government will create new laws or reinterpret exiting ones to address excessive cases.

As of mid-2014, Google Glass was in its initial stages of introduction. It remains to be seen if the functionality offered by this technology will outweigh the privacy concerns it raises. Some individuals and institutions, however, are already addressing these concerns. For example, a Seattle bar known as the 5 Point Café has banned Google Glass. The Café's managers are concerned about their customers' privacy. The bar's policy already prohibits customers from videotaping or photographing inside the bar without the permission of the managers as well as the people being videoed or photographed. The managers contend that banning Google Glass is simply an extension of this policy. Another bar, The Willows, in San Francisco, has also banned Google Glass.

Caesars Palace in Las Vegas will not allow Google Glass in its casino. Gaming regulations prohibit the use of computers or recording devices by persons who are gambling. If individuals did attempt to gamble while wearing Google Glass, they would be subject to arrest under the State of Nevada's gaming regulations. Theater owners are also banning Google Glass in case the glasses are used to illegally record a motion picture.

In San Francisco, a woman reported that she was attacked for wearing Google Glass at a bar. She said she was showing someone at the bar how the glasses work, when two women confronted her. Then, a man ripped the Google Glass off her face. She said she later recovered her Google Glass along with the video on the device that shows the man who ripped the glasses off her face. Witnesses said that she was very friendly, but that some people inside the bar got upset about the possibility of being recorded by the glasses.

Responding to these problems, Google launched a public relations campaign. The company is holding nationwide forums for people to try the product. Also, in February 2014, it released an etiquette guide for its beta testers, so they do not become "glassholes."

Sources: Compiled from E. Weise, "San Francisco Bar Bans 'Glassholes'," *USA Today*, March 5, 2014; K. Alexander, "Google Glass Attack Offers a New Lens on Privacy Concerns," *SFGate*, February 26, 2014; J. Vazquez, "Woman Wearing Google Glass Says She Was Attacked in San Francisco Bar, *CBS*, February 25, 2014; C. Castaneda, "Google Glass Guidelines Tell Users Don't Be 'Creepy or Rude' or a 'Glasshole'," CBS, February 19, 2014; S. Gaudin, "Caesars Palace Deals Google Glass Out of Its Game," *Computerworld*, May 7, 2013; L. Moran, "Google Glasses Prompt Ban from Seattle Bar," *New York Daily News*, March 11, 2013; B. Woods, "Google Glass: You'll Kiss Your Privacy Goodbye, and You Won't Mind a Bit," *ZDNet*, March 7, 2013; C. Arthur, "Google Glass: Is It a Threat to Our Privacy?" *The Guardian*, March 6, 2013; S. Bradner, "Privacy as Product Differentiation: Is It Time?" *Computerworld*, March 5, 2013; D. Zax, "Privacy Fears with Google Glass Are Overblown," *MIT Technology Review*, March 4, 2013; G. Marshall, "Google Glass: Say Goodbye to Your Privacy," *TechRadar*, March 1, 2013; A. Keen, "Why Life Through Google Glass Should Be for Our Eyes Only," *CNN News*, February 26, 2013; www.google.com/glass/start, accessed March 6, 2014.

Questions

1. Apply the general framework for ethical decision making to Google Glass.

2. Do you feel that the functionality offered by Google Glass outweighs the potential loss of privacy that the technology could create? Why or why not? Support your answer.

3. Would you use Google Glasses? Why or why not? Support your answer.

4. If you were at a party or at a bar, would you be comfortable speaking to someone who was wearing Google Glasses? Would you be comfortable just being in the room with someone wearing Google Glasses? Why or why not? Support your answer.

Privacy Codes and Policies

Privacy policies or **privacy codes** are an organization's guidelines for protecting the privacy of its customers, clients, and employees. In many corporations, senior management has begun to understand that when they collect vast amounts of personal information, they must protect it. In addition, many organizations give their customers some voice in how their information is used by providing them with opt-out choices. The **opt-out model** of informed consent permits the company to collect personal information until the customer specifically requests that the data not be collected. Privacy advocates prefer the **opt-in model** of informed consent, which prohibits an organization from collecting any personal information unless the customer specifically authorizes it.

One privacy tool available to consumers is the *Platform for Privacy Preferences* (P3P), a protocol that automatically communicates privacy policies between an electronic commerce Web site and visitors to that site. P3P enables visitors to determine the types of personal data that can be extracted by the sites they visit. It also allows visitors to compare a site's privacy policy to the visitors' preferences or to other standards, such as the Federal Trade Commission's (FTC) Fair Information Practices Standard or the European Directive on Data Protection.

Table 6.2 provides a sampling of privacy policy guidelines. The last section, "Data Confidentiality," refers to security, which we consider in Chapter 7. All of the good privacy intentions in the world are useless unless they are supported and enforced by effective security measures.

Despite privacy codes and policies, and despite opt-out and opt-in models, guarding whatever is left of your privacy is becoming increasingly difficult. However, several companies are providing help in maintaining your privacy, as you see in chapter closing case 2.

International Aspects of Privacy

As the number of online users has increased globally, governments throughout the world have enacted a large number of inconsistent privacy and security laws. This highly complex global legal framework is creating regulatory problems for companies. Approximately 50 countries have some form of data protection laws. Many of these laws conflict with those of other countries, or they require specific security measures. Other countries have no privacy laws at all.

TABLE 6.2 Privacy Policy Guidelines: A Sampler

Data collection

Data should be collected on individuals only for the purpose of accomplishing a legitimate business objective.

Data should be adequate, relevant, and not excessive in relation to the business objective.

Individuals must give their consent before data pertaining to them can be gathered. Such consent may be implied from the individual's actions (e.g., applications for credit, insurance, or employment).

Data accuracy

Sensitive data gathered on individuals should be verified before they are entered into the database.

Data should be kept current, where and when necessary.

The file should be made available so that the individual can ensure that the data are correct.

In any disagreement about the accuracy of the data, the individual's version should be noted and included with any disclosure of the file.

Data confidentiality

Computer security procedures should be implemented to ensure against unauthorized disclosure of data. These procedures should include physical, technical, and administrative security measures.

Third parties should not be given access to data without the individual's knowledge or permission, except as required by law.

Disclosures of data, other than the most routine, should be noted and maintained for as long as the data are maintained.

Data should not be disclosed for reasons incompatible with the business objective for which they are collected.

The absence of consistent or uniform standards for privacy and security obstructs the flow of information among countries (*transborder data flows*). The European Union (EU), for one, has taken steps to overcome this problem. In 1998 the European Community Commission (ECC) issued guidelines to all of its member countries regarding the rights of individuals to access information about themselves. The EU data protection laws are stricter than the U.S. laws and therefore could create problems for the U.S.-based multinational corporations, which could face lawsuits for privacy violations.

The transfer of data into and out of a nation without the knowledge of either the authorities or the individuals involved raises a number of privacy issues. Whose laws have jurisdiction when records are stored in a different country for reprocessing or retransmission purposes? For example, if data are transmitted by a Polish company through a U.S. satellite to a British corporation, which country's privacy laws control the data, and at what points in the transmission? Questions like these will become more complicated and frequent as time goes on. Governments must make an effort to develop laws and standards to cope with rapidly changing information technologies to solve some of these privacy issues.

The United States and the European Union share the goal of privacy protection for their citizens, but the United States takes a different approach. To bridge the different privacy approaches, the U.S. Department of Commerce, in consultation with the European Union, developed a "safe harbor" framework to regulate the way that the U.S. companies export and handle the personal data (e.g., names and addresses) of European citizens. See www.export.gov/safeharbor and http://ec.europa.eu/justice_home/fsj/privacy/index_en.htm.

BEFORE YOU GO ON....

1. Describe the issue of privacy as it is affected by IT.

2. Discuss how privacy issues can impact transborder data flows.

Apply The Concept 6.2

LEARNING OBJECTIVE 6.2 Identify three places that store personal data, and for each one, discuss at least one potential threat to the privacy of the data stored there.

STEP 1 – Background

Section 6.2 has defined privacy as the right to be left alone and to be free of unreasonable personal intrusions. Information privacy is the right to determine when, and to what extent, information about you can be gathered and/or communicated to others. And, where our data are concerned, we are in control, right? If so, then why do people always seem to fear that "Big Brother" is spying on us and violating our privacy? Going further, the law generally assigns a higher priority to society's right to access information than to an individual's right to privacy.

The 2002 movie *Minority Report* presented a future where a special police unit could predict when and where crimes were going to occur before they actually did. This unit could arrest "criminals" before they committed the crime. Along these same lines, a 2008 movie titled *Eagle Eye* focused on a highly intelligent computer system that chose to abide by the Constitution even if it meant having the president of the United States assassinated.

STEP 2 – Activity

Movie night! If you have not seen these two films, then schedule a movie night, and watch them from the perspective of privacy and information security. Discuss the movies with your friends, and obtain their thoughts on these issues. If you don't have time to watch the movies, then visit http://www.wiley.com/go/rainer/MIS3e/applytheconcept to read a synopsis of both films on IMDB.com.

STEP 3 – Deliverable

After considering the plots in these movies, prepare a paper identifying three places where you store personal data. For each location, discuss at least one potential threat to your personal privacy that arises from storing your information there. Make them major threats—on the scale of the movies. Consider just how far your seemingly innocent decisions can take you! Present your paper to the class and submit it to your instructor.

What's in for ME?

FOR THE ACCOUNTING MAJOR

Public companies, their accountants, and their auditors have significant ethical responsibilities. Accountants now are being held professionally and personally responsible for increasing the transparency of transactions and assuring compliance with Generally Accepted Accounting Principles (GAAP). In fact, regulatory agencies such as the SEC and the Public Company Accounting Oversight Board (PCAOB) require accounting departments to adhere to strict ethical principles.

FOR THE FINANCE MAJOR

As a result of global regulatory requirements and the passage of Sarbanes-Oxley, financial managers must follow strict ethical guidelines. They are responsible for full, fair, accurate, timely, and understandable disclosure in all financial reports and documents that their companies submit to the Securities and Exchange Commission (SEC) and in all other public financial reports. Furthermore, financial managers are responsible for compliance with all applicable governmental laws, rules, and regulations.

FOR THE MARKETING MAJOR

Marketing professionals have new opportunities to collect data on their customers, for example, through business-to-consumer electronic commerce (discussed in Chapter 9). Business ethics clearly mandate that these data should be used only within the company and should not be sold to anyone else. Marketers do not want to be sued for invasion of privacy over data collected for the marketing database.

Customers expect their data to be properly secured. However, profit-motivated criminals want that data. Therefore, marketing managers must analyze the risks of their operations. Failure to protect corporate and customer data will cause significant public relations problems and outrage customers. Customer relationship management (discussed in Chapter 12) operations and tracking customers' online buying habits can expose unencrypted data to misuse or result in privacy violations.

FOR THE PRODUCTION/OPERATIONS MANAGEMENT MAJOR

POM professionals decide whether to outsource (or offshore) manufacturing operations. In some cases, these operations are sent overseas to countries that do not have strict labor laws. This situation raises serious ethical questions. For example: Is it ethical to hire employees in countries with poor working conditions in order to reduce labor costs?

FOR THE HUMAN RESOURCE MANAGEMENT MAJOR

Ethics is critically important to HR managers. HR policies explain the appropriate use of information technologies in the workplace. Questions such as the following can arise: Can employees use the Internet, e-mail, or chat systems for personal purposes while at work? Is it ethical to monitor employees? If so, how? How much? How often? HR managers must formulate and enforce such policies while at the same time maintaining trusting relationships between employees and management.

FOR THE MIS MAJOR

Ethics might be more important for MIS personnel than for anyone else in the organization, because these individuals have control of the information assets. They also have control over a huge amount of the employees' personal information. As a result, the MIS function must be held to the highest ethical standards.

SUMMARY

1. Define ethics, list and describe the three fundamental tenets of ethics, and describe the four categories of ethical issues related to information technology.

   Ethics refers to the principles of right and wrong that individuals use to make choices that guide their behavior.

   Fundamental tenets of ethics include responsibility, accountability, and liability. Responsibility means that you accept the consequences of your decisions and actions. Accountability refers to determining who is responsible for actions that were taken. Liability is a legal concept that gives individuals the right to recover the damages done to them by other individuals, organizations, or systems.

   The major ethical issues related to IT are privacy, accuracy, property (including intellectual property), and access to information. Privacy may be violated when data are held in databases or transmitted over networks.

   Privacy policies that address issues of data collection, data accuracy, and data confidentiality can help organizations avoid legal problems.

2. Identify three places that store personal data, and for each one, discuss at least one personal threat to the privacy of the data stored there.

   Privacy is the right to be left alone and to be free of unreasonable personal intrusions. Threats to privacy include advances in information technologies, electronic surveillance, personal information in databases, Internet bulletin boards, newsgroups, and social networking sites. The privacy threat in Internet bulletin boards, newsgroups, and social networking sites is that you might post too much personal information that many unknown people can see.

>>>CHAPTER GLOSSARY

accountability A tenet of ethics that refers to determining who is responsible for actions that were taken.

code of ethics A collection of principles intended to guide decision making by members of an organization.

digital dossier An electronic description of an individual and his or her habits.

electronic surveillance Tracking people's activities with the aid of computers.

ethics The principles of right and wrong that individuals use to make choices to guide their behaviors.

information privacy The right to determine when, and to what extent, personal information can be gathered by and/or communicated to others.

liability A legal concept that gives individuals the right to recover the damages done to them by other individuals, organizations, or systems.

opt-in model A model of informed consent in which a business is prohibited from collecting any personal information unless the customer specifically authorizes it.

opt-out model A model of informed consent that permits a company to collect personal information until the customer specifically requests that the data not be collected.

privacy The right to be left alone and to be free of unreasonable personal intrusions.

privacy codes See privacy policies.

privacy policies (also known as **privacy codes**) An organization's guidelines for protecting the privacy of customers, clients, and employees.

profiling The process of forming a digital dossier.

responsibility A tenet of ethics in which you accept the consequences of your decisions and actions.

>>>DISCUSSION QUESTIONS

1. In 2008, the Massachusetts Bay Transportation Authority (MBTA) obtained a temporary restraining order barring three Massachusetts Institute of Technology (MIT) students from publicly displaying what they claimed to be a way to get "free subway rides for life." Specifically, the 10-day injunction prohibited the students from revealing vulnerabilities of the MBTA's fare card. The students were scheduled to present their findings in Las Vegas at the DEFCON computer hacking conference. Were the students' actions legal? Were their actions ethical? Discuss your answer from the students' perspective and then from the perspective of the MBTA.

2. Frank Abagnale, the criminal played by Leonardo DiCaprio in the motion picture *Catch Me If You Can*, ended up in prison. After he left prison, however, he worked as a consultant to many companies on matters of fraud.

   a. Why do these companies hire the perpetrators (if caught) as consultants? Is this a good idea?

   b. You are the CEO of a company. Discuss the ethical implications of hiring Frank Abagnale as a consultant.

3. Access various search engines to find information relating to the use of drones (unmanned aerial vehicles (UAVs)) for electronic surveillance purposes in the United States.

   a. Take the position favoring the use of drones for electronic surveillance.

   b. Take the position against the use of drones for electronic surveillance.

>>>PROBLEM-SOLVING ACTIVITIES

1. An information security manager routinely monitored Web surfing among her company's employees. She discovered that many employees were visiting the "sinful six" Web sites. (*Note:* The "sinful six" are Web sites with material related to pornography, gambling, hate, illegal activities, tastelessness, and violence.) She then prepared a list of the employees and their surfing histories and gave the list to management. Some managers punished their employees. Some employees, in turn, objected to the monitoring, claiming that they should have a right to privacy.

   a. Is monitoring of Web surfing by managers ethical? (It is legal.) Support your answer.

   b. Is employee Web surfing on the "sinful six" ethical? Support your answer.

   c. Is the security manager's submission of the list of abusers to management ethical? Why or why not?

   d. Is punishing the abusers ethical? Why or why not? If yes, then what types of punishment are acceptable?

   e. What should the company do in this situation? (*Note:* There are a variety of possibilities here.)

2. Access the Computer Ethics Institute's Web site at www.cpsr.org/issues/ethics/cei. The site offers the "Ten Commandments of Computer Ethics." Study these rules and decide whether any others should be added.

3. Access the Association for Computing Machinery's code of ethics for its members (see www.acm.org/constitution/code.html). Discuss the major points of this code. Is this code complete? Why or why not? Support your answer.

4. Access www.eightmaps.com. Is the use of data on this Web site illegal? Unethical? Support your answer.

5. The Electronic Frontier Foundation (www.eff.org) has a mission of protecting rights and promoting freedom in the "electronic frontier." Review the organization's suggestions about how to protect your online privacy, and summarize what you can do to protect yourself.

6. Access your university's guidelines for ethical computer and Internet use. Are there limitations as to the types of Web sites that you can visit and the types of material you can view? Are you allowed to change the programs on the lab computers? Are you allowed to download software

from the lab computers for your personal use? Are there rules governing the personal use of computers and e-mail?

7. Access http://www.albion.com/netiquette/corerules .html. What do you think of this code of ethics? Should it be expanded? Is it too general?

8. Access www.cookiecentral.com and www.epubliceye .com. Do these sites provide information that helps you protect your privacy? If so, then explain how.

9. Do you believe that a university should be allowed to monitor e-mail sent and received on university computers? Why or why not? Support your answer.

>>> COLLABORATION EXERCISE

STEP 1 – Background

We all receive multiple privacy statements in the mail each month. But, how many of us actually read them? Do you take the time to read every statement you agree to when you click the "I Agree" button? Periodically it is a good idea to skim over these statements to know exactly what you are agreeing to when you check the box. It is even more important to study the revisions when the company sends out an updated version to see what has changed.

STEP 2 – Activity

Work with your team to research various privacy statements. Use popular sites like Facebook, Google, Twitter, LinkedIn, and Pinterest as your primary information sources.

For example, in 2012 Google updated its privacy and information-sharing policy and would not allow anyone

to opt out of it. You either agreed to Google's policy or you stopped using Google. What about Facebook and its privacy statements? Have each team member analyze a company and report back to the team. In most cases, you will be able to find Web sites that have already analyzed and put together histories of privacy issues.

STEP 3 – Deliverable

Create and share a Google Presentation. Have each team member contribute two to three slides on the company he or she has researched. Include discussion points on whether the company's privacy policies are ethical. Remember, the fact that a policy is not illegal does not mean it is ethical.

Share your presentation with your professor.

CLOSING **CASE 1** > The National Security Agency's Surveillance Programs

THE HUGE PROBLEM >>> The surveillance efforts of the U.S. National Security Agency (NSA) (www.nsa .gov) expanded dramatically under laws passed following the September 11, 2001 terrorist attacks. In 2006, the U.S. Congress approved changes to the Patriot Act that made it easier for the government to collect phone subscriber data under the Foreign Intelligence Surveillance Act (FISA). These changes helped the NSA collection programs become institutionalized, rather than being conducted only under the authority of the president. At the same time, advances in information technology have enabled the agency to accumulate and analyze far larger volumes of phone, Internet, social, and financial data to search for potential terrorist activities.

In 2007, the NSA launched another data collection effort, called PRISM, that obtains stored Internet communications from companies such as Google and Apple. These companies are legally required to turn over any data that match search terms approved by the U.S. Foreign Intelligence Surveillance Court (FISC). In addition, the nation's leading Internet firms were providing the NSA and the FBI with "direct access" to their servers and thus to the e-mails, photos, and other private information of hundreds of millions of users both in the

United States and around the world. The NSA developed similar relationships with credit card companies.

The NSA's data collection programs had attracted very limited public scrutiny until June 2013 when a computer expert named Edward Snowden, who had previously worked for Booz Allen Hamilton, a major NSA contractor, leaked numerous classified NSA documents. Snowden maintained that he disclosed details of the programs in the hopes of creating a debate over the U.S. surveillance policies. On June 6, 2013, *The Washington Post* (www.washingtonpost.com) and the British newspaper *The Guardian* (www.theguardian.com) published Snowden's disclosures.

The public release of these documents forced the Obama administration to acknowledge that it had been collecting many billions of U.S. phone records and monitoring the Internet communications of foreign individuals and organizations that are conducted through Microsoft, Google, Facebook, Apple, and other U.S. technology companies. These revelations immediately generated a storm of controversy.

In fact, the NSA possesses only limited legal authority to spy on the U.S. citizens. Nevertheless, the agency has created a surveillance network that covers the Internet communications of more Americans than officials had publicly disclosed. The system has the capacity to reach roughly 75 percent of all the U.S. Internet traffic in the search for foreign intelligence, including a wide array of communications by foreigners and Americans. In some cases, the NSA retains the written content of e-mails sent between citizens within the United States. It also filters domestic phone calls made with Internet technology.

The NSA's filtering process, carried out with the cooperation of the telecommunications companies, is designed to search for communications that either originate or end abroad, or are entirely foreign but happen to be passing through the United States. In its first analysis of the data, the NSA requires telecommunications companies to submit various streams of Internet traffic it believes most likely to contain foreign intelligence. The telecommunications companies must hand over any data the NSA requests under orders from the secret FISC. This initial step does not involve all Internet traffic. Rather, it focuses on certain areas of interest. In its second analysis, the NSA briefly copies the traffic and decides which communications to retain based on what the agency has identified as "strong selectors." A strong selector could be an e-mail address or a large block of computer addresses that correspond to an organization that the NSA is monitoring. The NSA examines the content of the communications as well as the ancillary information concerning who is sending and receiving the communications.

According to the documents released by Snowden, the NSA logs almost 5 billion mobile phone location records around the world every day, via its CO-TRAVELER system. The agency obtains these data by tapping into the cables that connect mobile networks globally. These cables serve both the U.S. and foreign mobile phones.

The NSA's monitoring of Americans includes customer records from the three major phone networks (Verizon, AT&T, and Sprint Nextel) as well as e-mails and Web searches. In addition, the agency also cataloged credit card transactions. The arrangement with the country's three largest phone companies means that every time the majority of Americans make a call, NSA obtains a record of the location, the number called, the time of the call, and the length of the conversation. This practice, which evolved from warrantless wiretapping programs implemented after 2001, was approved by all three branches of the U.S. government. Telephone and Internet companies find themselves in the uncomfortable position of balancing extensive government demands for information against the need to maintain their customers' trust.

The NSA surveillance programs are not limited to private citizens. Rather, the agency collects data from foreign governments and other targets by accessing thousands of classified documents. Significantly, the NSA routinely spies on allies as well as on foes. The agency's official mission list includes using its surveillance powers to achieve "diplomatic advantage" over such allies as France and Germany and "economic advantage" over Japan and Brazil, among other countries. In just one instance, in September 2013, President Obama was standing uncomfortably beside Brazilian President Dilma Rousseff, who was furious when she learned she was a target of NSA eavesdropping. In addition, there have been protests from Mexico, France, Germany, Spain, and the European Union.

Encryption methods are essential to securing personal and corporate information around the world. This technology is considered the backbone of modern digital security, and it is used to protect e-mail systems, personal data, Internet searching, and banking information. However, Snowden also revealed that the U.S. and British intelligence agencies have cracked encryption designed to provide online privacy and security. In a secret effort to defeat encryption, the NSA, along with its British counterpart, the Government Communications Headquarters (GCHQ), have used supercomputers to crack encryption codes and have inserted secret "back doors" into software with the help of technology companies.

The NSA went even further. According to a report by Reuters, the NSA paid $10 million to vendor RSA in a secret deal to incorporate a deliberately flawed encryption algorithm into widely used security software. The contract was a part of a NSA campaign to weaken encryption standards in order to aid the agency's surveillance programs.

THE REACTION >>> Critics contend that neither the FISC nor the Congress has made a serious effort to restrict the NSA's data-gathering efforts. They emphasize, for example, that from 1979 through 2012, the FISC has rejected only 11 of the more than 33,900 surveillance applications by the U.S. government, according to annual Justice Department reports to Congress.

From its perspective, the NSA defends its practices as legal and respectful of Americans' privacy. In an attempt to ensure Americans' privacy, NSA programs employ complex software algorithms that, in effect, operate like filters placed over a stream with holes designed to allow certain pieces of information flow through. After 9/11, the NSA widened the holes to capture more information when the government broadened its definition of what constitutes "reasonable" data collection.

The U.S. intelligence officials and the White House argue that the NSA's surveillance programs provide early warnings of terror threats that do not respect geographical boundaries. In August 2013, President Obama announced plans to overhaul key parts of the NSA's surveillance programs. The most significant proposal would restructure the FISC by adding an advocate for privacy concerns.

THE RESULTS >>> The fallout from Snowden's revelations continues. Technology companies that pass data to the NSA under the PRISM program could face legal action in the European Union. That is, companies that operate in the European Union and serve citizens of the bloc are subject to its relatively strict data protection laws. These laws limit the actions of companies that collect data, and they require these companies to be transparent about how this information will be used and to whom it could be disclosed.

In addition, in March 2014, President Obama unveiled a legislative proposal to drastically overhaul the NSA's once-secret phone data collection program. The president asserted he wanted to get the NSA out of the business of collecting call records in bulk, while preserving the program's capabilities.

And Edward Snowden? As of mid-2014, he had been granted asylum in Russia.

Sources: Compiled from C. Savage, "Obama Is Set to Curb NSA on Call Data," *New York Times*, March 25, 2014; M. Ferranti, "Report on NSA 'Secret' Payments to RSA Fuels Encryption Controversy," *Network World*, December 22, 2013; B. Gellman and A. Soltani, "NSA Tracking Cellphone Locations Worldwide, Snowden Documents Show," *The Washington Post*, December 4, 2013; S. Shane, "No Morsel Too Minuscule for All-Consuming NSA," *New York Times*, November 2, 2013; November 6–8, 2013; M. Winter, "NSA Cracks Internet Privacy," *USA Today*, September[Thomson1]; S. Gorman and J. Valentino-DeVries, "NSA's Reach into U.S. Net Is Deep, Wide," *The Wall Street Journal*, August 21, 2013; S. Gorman, C. Lee, and J. Hook, "Obama Vows Spying Overhaul," *The Wall Street Journal*, August 10–11, 2013; B. Stone and J. Brustein, "This Prism Isn't Reflecting Much Light," *Bloomberg BusinessWeek*, June 24–30, 2013; G. Greenwald and J. Ball, "The Top Secret Rules That Allow NSA to Use US Data Without a Warrant," *The Guardian*, June 20, 2013; G. Greenwald and E. MacAskill, "Boundless Informant: The NSA's Secret Tool to Track Global Surveillance Data," *The Guardian*, June 11, 2013; S. Gorman, A. Entous, and A. Dowell, "Technology Emboldened NSA," *The Wall Street Journal*, June 10, 2013; D. Barrett and D. Yadron, "Contractor Says He Is Source of NSA Leak," *The Wall Street Journal*, June 10, 2013; G. Greenwald, E. MacAskill, and L. Poitras, "Edward Snowden: The Whistleblower Behind the NSA Surveillance Revelations," *The Guardian*, June 9, 2013; S. Gorman, E. Perez, and J. Hook, "U.S. Collects Vast Data Trove," *The Wall Street Journal*, June 7, 2013; N. Hopkins, "UK Gathering Secret Intelligence Via Covert NSA Operation," *The Guardian*, June 7, 2013; G. Greenwald and E. MacAskill, "NSA Prism Program Taps in to User Data of Apple, Google, and Others," *The Guardian*, June 6, 2013; G. Greenwald, "NSA Collecting Phone Records of Millions of Verizon Customers Daily," *The Guardian*, June 5, 2013; www.nsa.gov, accessed March 29, 2014.

Questions

1. Present the pros and cons of the NSA's actions.
2. Present the pros and cons of Edward Snowden's actions.
3. Are the NSA's actions legal? Support your answer with specific examples.
4. Are the NSA's actions ethical? Support your answer with specific examples.
5. Were Edward Snowden's actions legal? Support your answer with specific examples.
6. Were Edward Snowden's actions ethical? Support your answer with specific examples.

CLOSING **CASE 2 >** Protecting Your Privacy

THE PROBLEM >>> Competition is intense for the control of personal data, which some observers call the "new oil" of the 21st century. Facebook's market value illustrates the value of maintaining detailed data about more than 1 billion people. Companies constantly seek to obtain increasing amounts of data on all of us so that they can more precisely target advertising messages to each of us. For example, the ubiquitous "Like" and "Share" buttons deployed by Web sites to make it easier to promote their content enable Facebook (via Facebook Connect) to track people online.

However, the National Security Agency (NSA) spying scandal has generated new fears on the part of Web surfers of being tracked and traced by countless ad networks, data miners, and data brokers. The Federal Trade Commission (FTC) is pressuring browser companies, consumer advocates, and advertisers to establish a "Do Not Track" option for Internet users. Negotiations have broken down, however, because advertisers and privacy advocates cannot agree on how much protection consumers are entitled to.

A VARIETY OF SOLUTIONS >>> As a result of the privacy problem, a number of companies have launched in recent years around privacy and software tools to support it. Let's take a closer look at some of them.

- Snapchat (www.snapchat.com): This smartphone app is a picture and video viewer, marketed to teenagers, that offers the illusion of security because "snaps" automatically self-destruct. The app also contains a notification feature that lets you know if someone performs a "screen grab" of any photos that you send.

- Wickr (https://www.mywickr.com): This smartphone app allows you to send military-grade encrypted texts, photos, and videos to other Wickr users. (We discuss encryption in Chapter 7.) In addition, it deletes information such as location and type of device from files before sending them. Nothing is stored on Wickr's servers that could be used to track (or subpoena) the sender.

- Burn Note (https://burnnote.com): This smartphone app sends encrypted notes that self-destruct after a set amount of time. The notes are deleted from the recipient's computer, and they are not stored on Burn Note servers. Burn Note also displays only a specific spotlit area of a note as the recipient mouses over it. As a result, it is difficult for a screenshot to capture an entire note.

- TigerText (www.tigertext.com): This app is marketed to businesses—particularly healthcare—that require a secure messaging system. For example, your physician can use TigerText to securely text X-rays of your knee to a colleague. TigerText also allows senders to retrieve messages that they have already sent.

- Reputation (www.reputation.com): This company manages your online reputation, which is the process of making individuals and businesses look their best on the Internet. Reputation will search for damaging content online and destroy it. In addition, it helps its clients prevent private information from being made public.

- Silent Circle (https://silentcircle.com): This company produces a smartphone app that allows people to easily make secure, encrypted phone calls and send secure, encrypted texts. In addition, the sender can specify a time period after which the file will automatically be deleted from both devices (sending and receiving). Silent Circle makes life easier and safer for journalists, political dissidents, diplomats, and companies that are trying to evade state surveillance or corporate espionage.

According to the company, in early 2013, a reporter in South Sudan used the app to record a video of brutality that occurred at a vehicle checkpoint. He then encrypted the video and sent it to Europe. Within a few minutes, the video was automatically deleted from the sender's device. Even if authorities had arrested and searched the sender, they would not have found the footage on his phone. Meanwhile, the film, which included location data showing exactly where it was taken, was already in safe hands, where it can eventually be used to build a case documenting human rights abuses.

Law enforcement agencies have concerns that criminals will use the Silent Circle app. The FBI, for instance, wants all communications providers to build in backdoors (discussed in Chapter 7) so that the agency can secretly spy on suspects. Silent Circle, however, has an explicit policy that it will not comply with eavesdropping requests from law enforcement entities.

- Personal (www.personal.com) provides users with personal data lockers in which they store a single account with information about themselves. Businesses would pay for these data because the data enable them to offer personalized products and advertising. Furthermore, because people retain control over the data in their lockers, they can demand something of value in return, such as discounts on products or cash.

- iPredator (https://www.ipredator.se) is a virtual private networking service (discussed in Chapter 7) with the stated goal of providing Internet privacy.

- Disconnect (https://disconnect.me) is a shareware tool that places a green D next to the search bar and displays the number of requests and the requesting companies for your personal data being made on that Web site. Disconnect then blocks those requests, speeding up surfing

dramatically. (Shareware is software that is available free of charge and is often distributed for consumer evaluation, after which a fee may be requested for continued use.) The most current version of Disconnect blocks more than 2,000 parties from collecting your data.

- Burner (http://burnerapp.com) is an iPhone app that provides temporary phone numbers, so you can send and receive calls and texts from disposable digits. After you have finished your business, you "nuke" the number so that it cannot be easily traced back to you. Unlike Silent Circle, Burner complies with law enforcement requests.

THE RESULTS >>> Ultimately, the results for each of us will be different, depending on our Web presence (or our digital footprint), how much information we share on social media, and many other factors. Therefore, as you try any or all of these privacy products, you will be able to determine the impact(s) on your privacy.

Sources: Compiled from "How to Protect Your Privacy Online," *The Wall Street Journal,* October 21, 2013; M. Carney, "TigerText Takes Its Secure Messaging Platform Freemium, Targeting Both Enterprises and Consumers," *Pando Daily,* October 3, 2013; K. Hill, "Track Me If You Can," *Forbes,* August 12, 2013; B. Tekspert, "How Can I Protect My Privacy Online?" *Senior Planet,* August 6, 2013; M. Lee, "Encryption Works: How to Protect Your Privacy in the Age of NSA Surveillance," *Freedom of the Press Foundation,* July 2, 2013; R. Gallagher, "The Threat of Silence," *Slate,* February 4, 2013; J. Brustein, "Start-Ups Seek to Help Users Put a Price on Their Personal Data," *New York Times,* February 12, 2012; www.snapchat.com, https://www.mywickr.com, https://burnnote.com, www.tigertext.com, www.reputation.com, https://silentcircle.com, www.personal.com, www.ipredator.se, https://disconnect.me, http://burnerapp.com, accessed March 29, 2014.

Questions

1. Describe how each of the companies discussed above can protect your privacy in some way.

2. Describe the disadvantages to you from using any of the services described in this case.

INTERNSHIP ACTIVITY> FIRST NOBLE BANK

Banking

At the end of the day, banks have to make money to survive. They make their money by charging interest on loans and by selling certificates of deposit (CDs). In both cases, the strategy is to make money off your money! Before a bank enters into a legal contract with you as their customer, they want to learn as much as they can about you, your financial history, your current situation, and your financial future so that they can

make a wise choice. In collecting this information, banks walk very fine lines of ethics and privacy.

For this activity, you again will be working with Jeremy Farr of First Noble Bank (you met Jeremy in the Internship Activity for Chapter 1). Jeremy wants to put together some information to make certain the bank's employees understand that violating ethical standards and privacy codes is a serious offense.

Below is a letter from Jeremy that details his expectations for this project.

Hello again!

I recently heard about a group of loan officers who met to work through their pending loan applications. As the group considered a particular loan, they looked at all of the information on the application and concluded that everything seemed positive. Then, one officer spoke up and shared information that was "off the record" concerning one applicant's personal life, family life, work habits, and general health. Sharing this information was both unethical and a violation of the individual's privacy. Nevertheless, this information was now on the table and in everyone's mind.

Fortunately, no such incident has occurred at Noble Bank. To make certain we avoid such incidents, I put together some information to make certain our employees understand that this type of behavior would seriously violate ethical standards and privacy codes.

Your specific project is to research the privacy policies of 10 banks and then provide written guidelines for a new written policy for Noble Bank.

Based on your research, please provide the following information in your report.

1. Outline the sections that an effective Privacy Policy will include.

2. Describe the internal actions I should take to make certain the bank's employees are aware of the need to comply with the policy.

I am very much looking forward to your findings and recommendations.

Thanks!
Jeremy

SPREADSHEET ACTIVITY > BASIC FUNCTIONALITY: COPYING FORMULAS WITH ABSOLUTE AND RELATIVE REFERENCES

STEP 1 – Background

If you have worked through the previous activities, then you are beginning to appreciate the power of a spreadsheet. This next skill will be a great addition to your spreadsheet tool belt.

Writing a formula can be time consuming because all of the cell references must be correct and all of the data must be calculated properly. After you have successfully applied a formula once, however, you can copy that formula to other cells to calculate the data contained in that column or row. For example, imagine that you have numbers in cells a1 and b1 and you want to use the Sum formula in cell c1 to add these numbers together. (You learned about the Sum formula in Activities 1 and 2.) If you copy your formula from cell c1 to c2, it will then sum the data in cells a2 and b2. This is called a *relative reference*. Formulas are always, by default, relative to the location.

Sometimes you need to keep part of a reference pointing to a single row, column, or cell. To do this you insert a dollar sign ($) before the column letter, the row number, or both if you want your calculation to remain in a single cell. To continue the above example, if you want to add the number in cell a1 to the numbers in column b, then you would insert a dollar sign before both the column letter and the row number in the formula. Your formula would read "=a11b2." It would then allow you to copy your formula while remaining fixed on cell a1.

STEP 2 – Activity

Lisa owns a small business where she purchases plastic cups and bowls and then custom-decorates them with paint and vinyl stickers. Creating these products involves multiple combinations of options and time. Lisa's objective is to make a 25% profit per item and then add a $20/hour charge for the amount of time it takes to create each item. For a cup item that initially costs $2.50 and takes 30 minutes to decorate, the final cost would be $2.50 1 25% 1 $10 (half an hour at

$20/hour). The total comes out to $13.13. This type of calculation would become rather cumbersome given the numerous product combinations available to Lisa.

STEP 3 – Deliverable

Visit http://www.wiley.com/go/rainer/MIS3e/spreadsheet, and download a spreadsheet that contains Lisa's product information. The workbook will contain instructions to guide you in helping Lisa determine the final prices for her products.

Follow the instructions in the spreadsheet and submit your final work to your instructor.

Additional help with this spreadsheet skill is available in WileyPLUS. Open the "Microsoft Office 2013 Lab Manual Spreadsheet Module: Excel 2013," and review Lesson 11: Freezing Titles and Absolute Addressing.

DATABASE ACTIVITY > TABLES: DEFAULT VALUES, RANGE CHECKS, AND VALUE CHECKS

STEP 1 – Background

Information systems must be able to catch errors in the entry and analysis of data before those data lead to bad decisions. Incorrect data can cause a company to produce the wrong products, to order too many or too few supplies, to send messages to one group that were meant for a different group, and so on. If you develop a database for yourself or your team, you should create a system that checks for as many errors as possible. The Design View mode of your Access database allows you to embed and enforce edits and checks when you are entering data in the Datasheet View.

Not all errors can be caught, of course. If a street address is entered as 63 Elm instead of 36 Elm, a database cannot tell it is wrong. Many errors can be caught, however. In this activity you will apply default values, range checks, and value checks against a list.

STEP 2 – Activity

Visit http://www.wiley.com/go/rainer/MIS3e/database, and download the database linked for the Chapter 6 Activity. This database has tables for customers, orders, line items, and products. Its structure resembles the example in Section of the book. The Ordered Parts table there corresponds to the line item table here. Complete the following steps.

- Open the Line Item table in Design View, and specify a default value of 1 for line item quantity.

- Open the Customer table in Design View, and enter a default value of 0 for customer discount. Also, for the same field, add a rule to limit the discount to a range of 0–25. (If this column was formatted as a percentage, you would have to enter the upper limit as 0.25, not 25. Access can display fractions as percentages, but that is just for display. The program treats them as fractions internally and validates them that way. Here, however, because the column is not formatted as a percentage, use 25.) Enter an error message to display if a user tries to enter a value outside this range. (*Hint:* Use validation text.)

- In the Order table, add a validation rule to the order date: The date cannot be later than today. (The limiting value, today, is allowable.)

- Create a table CountryList with one column: countries from which you expect orders. Enter 10 countries into it, including your home country, the other countries in the sample data, and enough others of your choice to make 10. (*Hint:* Use the Lookup Tab under Design View.) Link the table to the Country field in the Customer table. The user should be allowed to enter a new country in the Customer table if a customer's country does not appear in the list. (Because the table contains data, you will have to re-enter the country names when you are finished. If you cannot identify them from the city names, then write them down first.)

STEP 3 – Deliverable

Submit your completed database with your built-in checks to your professor.

Additional help with this database skill is available in WileyPLUS. Open the "Microsoft Office 2013 Lab Manual Database Module: Access 2013," and review Lesson 6: Viewing Table Data.

Information Security

LEARNING OBJECTIVES >>>

7.1 Identify the five factors that contribute to the increasing vulnerability of information resources, and provide a specific example of each one.

7.2 Compare and contrast human mistakes and social engineering, and provide a specific example of each one.

7.3 Discuss the 10 types of deliberate attacks.

7.4 Define the three risk mitigation strategies, and provide an example of each one in the context of owning a home.

7.5 Identify the three major types of controls that organizations can use to protect their information resources, and provide an example of each one.

OPENING **CASE** > Shodan: Good Tool or Bad Tool?

Jim Smith got a terrible surprise from a stranger on his birthday. After the celebration, he heard an unfamiliar voice coming from his daughter's room. The person was telling his sleeping 2-year-old, "Wake up." When Smith rushed into her bedroom, he discovered that the voice was coming from his baby monitor and that whoever had taken control of the monitor was also able to manipulate the camera. Significantly, the monitor enables users to monitor audio and video over the Internet from anywhere in the world. Smith immediately unplugged the monitor, which is made by Foscam (www.foscam.us) of Shenzhen, China.

Months before Smith's experience, security researchers had discovered software flaws in the monitor that enabled attackers to take control of the monitor remotely if they entered the username "admin." Foscam had already developed a fix, but it had not aggressively informed users about it. When Smith checked his Foscam account, he discovered that the hacker had added his own username so that he could sign in whenever he wanted to. Smith is now considering initiating a class action against Foscam.

© blyjak/iStockphoto

He could find other plaintiffs by using a search engine called Shodan (www.shodanhq.com). In fact, Shodan is probably the tool that the attacker used to find Smith!

Shodan crawls the Internet searching for devices, many of which are programmed to answer. It has discovered a broad array of systems including cars, fetal heart monitors, office building heating control systems, water treatment facilities, power plant controls, traffic lights, and glucose meters. A search for the type of baby monitor used by the Smiths reveals that more than 40,000 other people are using the monitor—and all of them may be vulnerable to hackers!

Shodan has become a critical tool for security researchers, law enforcement officials, and hackers searching for devices that should not be on the Internet or that are vulnerable to being hacked. An industry report from the Swedish technology company Ericsson estimated that by 2020 some 50 billion devices will be networked into an "Internet of Things." (We discuss the Internet of Things in Chapter 10.)

Hackers have used Shodan to find Webcams whose security is so poor that the hackers only needed to type an Internet Protocol (IP) address into their browser to look into people's homes, security offices, hospital operating rooms, childcare centers, and drug dealer operations. Shodan has also found banks, apartment buildings, convention centers, and even Google's headquarters in Australia, in which the security, lights, and heating and cooling systems operated online and therefore could be controlled by a hacker. In late 2013, one security analyst noted that there were 2,000 facilities on the Internet that hackers could take control of if they could determine the IP address. That same year, the Department of Homeland Security (DHS) revealed that hackers had used Shodan to virtually break into the energy management systems of a "state government facility" and a "New Jersey manufacturing company."

Shodan's freemium model allows users to obtain 10 search results for free. Approximately 10,000 users pay a nominal one-time fee of up to $20 to obtain 10,000 results per search. A dozen institutional users, all of them cybersecurity firms, pay five figures annually for access to Shodan's entire database of 1.5 billion connected devices.

Shodan is extremely valuable for calling attention to the mistakes that gadget companies make when they configure their products as well as consumer's inattention to the security of the products they buy. Every device that connects to the Internet should be password-protected, yet many are not. Nor should these devices ship with a default username and password, yet many do. How vulnerable are these devices to attacks? Consider that in 2013 an anonymous user took control of more than 400,000 Internet-connected devices using just four default passwords.

Sources: Compiled from A. Stern, "Getting Rid of Shady Toolbars," Kaspersky Labs Daily, March 27, 2014; A. Grau, "Shutting the Door on Shodan," Manufacturing.net, December 16, 2013; K. Hill, "A Google for Hackers," Forbes, September 23, 2013; A. Couts, "Shodan, the Search Engine That Points Hackers Directly to Your Webcam," Digital Trends, September 5, 2013; R. McMillan, "The Internet of Things: Shodan," Wired, July 8, 2013; D. Goldman, "Shodan: The Scariest Search Engine on the Internet," CNN Money, April 8, 2013; www.shodanhq.com, accessed March 27, 2014.

Questions

1. Is Shodan more useful for hackers or for security defenders? Provide specific examples to support your choice.

2. What impact should Shodan have on the manufacturers of devices that connect to the Internet?

3. As an increasingly large number of devices are connected to the Internet, what will Shodan's impact be? Provide examples to support your answer.

Introduction

The lessons that you can learn from the opening case address a major problem with information security: software tools (i.e., Shodan) that are valuable to defenders are just as valuable to attackers. The most important question raised by the opening case, however, is whether it is possible to secure the Internet. The answer to this question impacts each and every one of us.

The answers to these questions and others are not clear. As you learn about information security in the context of information technology, you will acquire a better understanding of these issues, their importance, their relationships, and their trade-offs. Keep in mind that the issues involved in information security impact individuals and small organizations as well as large companies.

Information security is especially important to small businesses. Large organizations that experience an information security problem have greater resources to bring to both resolve and survive the problem. In contrast, small businesses have fewer resources and therefore can be destroyed by a data breach.

When properly used, information technologies can have enormous benefits for individuals, organizations, and entire societies. In Chapters 1 and 2, you read about diverse ways in which IT has made businesses more productive, efficient, and responsive to consumers. You also explored fields such as medicine and philanthropy in which IT has improved people's health and well-being. Unfortunately, information technologies can also be misused, often with devastating consequences. Consider the following scenarios:

- Individuals can have their identities stolen.

- Organizations can have customer information stolen, leading to financial losses, erosion of customer confidence, and legal action.

- Countries face the threat of *cyberterrorism* and *cyberwarfare*, terms for Internet-based attacks. Cyberwarfare is a critical problem for the U.S. government. In fact, President Obama signed a cyberwarfare directive in October 2012. In that directive, the White House, for the first time, laid out specific ground rules for how and when the U.S. military can carry out offensive and defensive cyber operations against foreign threats. The directive emphasizes the Obama administration's focus on cybersecurity as a top priority.

Clearly, the misuse of information technologies has come to the forefront of any discussion of IT. Studies have revealed that each security breach costs an organization millions of dollars. For example, consider the Target breach described in chapter closing case 1. The direct costs of a data breach include hiring forensic experts, notifying customers, setting up telephone hotlines to field queries from concerned or affected customers, offering free credit monitoring, and providing discounts for future products and services. The more intangible costs of a breach include the loss of business from increased customer turnover—called *customer churn*—and decreases in customer trust.

Unfortunately, employee negligence caused many of the data breaches, meaning that organizational employees are a weak link in information security. It is therefore very important for you to learn about information security so that you will be better prepared when you enter the workforce.

7.1 Introduction to Information Security

Security can be defined as the degree of protection against criminal activity, danger, damage, and/or loss. Following this broad definition, **information security** refers to all of the processes and policies designed to protect an organization's information and information systems (IS) from unauthorized access, use, disclosure, disruption, modification, or destruction. You have seen that information and information systems can be compromised by deliberate criminal actions and by anything that can impair the proper functioning of an organization's information systems.

Before continuing, let's consider these key concepts. Organizations collect huge amounts of information and employ numerous information systems that are subject to myriad threats. A **threat** to an information resource is any danger to which a system may be exposed. The **exposure** of an information resource is the harm, loss, or damage that can result if a threat compromises that resource. An information resource's **vulnerability** is the possibility that the system will be harmed by a threat.

Today, five key factors are contributing to the increasing vulnerability of organizational information resources, making it much more difficult to secure them:

© pressureUA/iStockphoto

Human mistakes such as unattended equipment often leave resources vulnerable to theft.

- Today's interconnected, interdependent, wirelessly networked business environment

- Smaller, faster, cheaper computers and storage devices

- Decreasing skills necessary to be a computer hacker

- International organized crime taking over cybercrime

- Lack of management support

The first factor is the evolution of the IT resource from mainframe-only to today's highly complex, interconnected, interdependent, wirelessly networked business environment. The Internet now enables millions of computers and computer networks to communicate freely and seamlessly with one another. Organizations and individuals are exposed to a world of untrusted networks and potential attackers. A *trusted network*, in general, is any network within your organization. An *untrusted network*, in general, is any network external to your organization. In addition, wireless technologies enable employees to compute, communicate, and access the Internet anywhere and anytime. Significantly, wireless is an inherently nonsecure broadcast communications medium.

The second factor reflects the fact that modern computers and storage devices (e.g., thumb drives or flash drives) continue to become smaller, faster, cheaper, and more portable, with greater storage capacity. These characteristics make it much easier to steal or lose a computer or storage device that contains huge amounts of sensitive information. Also, far more people are able to afford powerful computers and connect inexpensively to the Internet, thus raising the potential of an attack on information assets.

The third factor is that the computing skills necessary to be a hacker are *decreasing*. The reason is that the Internet contains information and computer programs called *scripts* that users with few skills can download and use to attack any information system connected to the Internet. (Security experts can also use these scripts for legitimate purposes, such as testing the security of various systems.)

The fourth factor is that international organized crime is taking over cybercrime. **Cybercrime** refers to illegal activities conducted over computer networks, particularly the Internet. iDefense (http://labs.idefense.com), a company that specializes in providing security information to governments and Fortune 500 companies, maintains that groups of well-organized criminal organizations have taken control of a global billion-dollar crime network. The network, powered by skillful hackers, targets known software security weaknesses. These crimes are typically nonviolent, but quite lucrative. Consider, for example, that losses from armed robberies average hundreds of dollars, and those from white-collar crimes average tens of thousands of dollars. In contrast, losses from computer crimes average hundreds of thousands of dollars. Also, computer crimes can be committed from anywhere in the world, at any time, effectively providing an international safe haven for cybercriminals. Computer-based crimes cause billions of dollars in damages to businesses each year, including the costs of repairing information systems and of lost business.

The fifth, and final, factor is lack of management support. For the entire organization to take security policies and procedures seriously, senior managers must set the tone. Unfortunately, senior managers often do not do so. Ultimately, however, lower-level managers may be even more important. These managers are in close contact with employees every day and thus are in a better position to determine whether employees are following security procedures.

BEFORE YOU GO ON....

1. Define information security.
2. Differentiate among a threat, an exposure, and a vulnerability.
3. Why are the skills needed to be a hacker decreasing?

Apply The Concept 7.1

LEARNING OBJECTIVE 7.1 Identify the five factors that contribute to the increasing vulnerability of information resources, and provide a specific example of each one.

STEP 1 – Background (Here is what you are learning.)

Section 7.1 has taught you about the importance of information security, particularly when you are conducting business over the Web. It is important to note that a chain is only as strong as its weakest link. Therefore, although you may have been careful to maintain security across your network, if your business partners have not done so as well, then as your information passes over their networks it will be at risk.

Visit http://www.wiley.com/go/rainer/MIS3e/applytheconcept, and click on the link to VeriSign's Web site. As you read over this page, keep in mind that VeriSign is in the business of protecting Web sites and Web users, which is something we all appreciate. In fact, it is likely that you feel some level of comfort when you see the VeriSign symbol on an e-commerce site.

STEP 3 – Deliverable (Here is what you turn in.)

After reading the article, compose a brief memo from VeriSign to a potential client. Identify the five factors that contribute to the increasing vulnerability of information resources, and provide examples of how VeriSign can help protect the client's digital assets against these threats. Submit your memo to your instructor.

7.2 Unintentional Threats to Information Systems

Information systems are vulnerable to many potential hazards and threats, as you can see in FIGURE 7.1. The two major categories of threats are unintentional threats and deliberate threats. This section discusses unintentional threats, and the next section addresses deliberate threats.

Unintentional threats are acts performed without malicious intent that nevertheless represent a serious threat to information security. A major category of unintentional threats is human error.

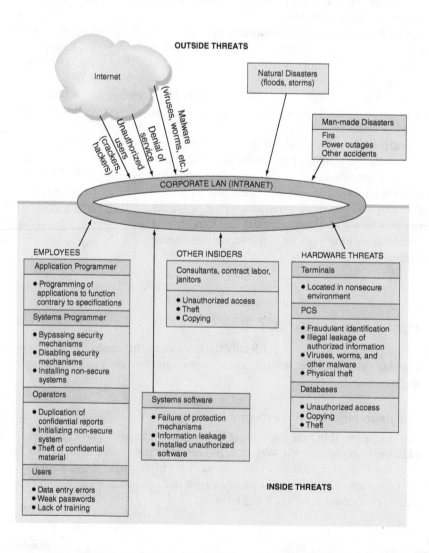

Figure 7.1 Security threats.

Human Errors

Organizational employees span the breadth and depth of the organization, from mail clerks to the CEO, and across all functional areas. There are two important points to be made about employees. First, the higher the level of employee, the greater the threat he or she poses to information security. This is true because higher-level employees typically have greater access to corporate data, and they enjoy greater privileges on organizational information systems. Second, employees in two areas of the organization pose especially significant threats to information security: human resources and information systems. Human resources employees generally have access to sensitive personal information about all employees. Likewise, IS employees not only have access to sensitive organizational data, but also often control the means to create, store, transmit, and modify those data.

Other employees include contract labor, consultants, and janitors and guards. Contract labor, such as temporary hires, may be overlooked in information security arrangements. However, these employees often have access to the company's network, information systems, and information assets. Consultants, although technically not employees, perform work for the company. Depending on the nature of their work, they may also have access to the company's network, information systems, and information assets.

Finally, janitors and guards are the most frequently ignored people in information security systems. Companies frequently outsource their security and janitorial services. As with contractors, then, these individuals work for the company although they technically are not employees. Moreover, they are usually present when most—if not all—other employees have gone home. They typically have keys to every office, and nobody questions their presence in even the most sensitive parts of the building. In fact, an article from *2600: The Hacker Quarterly* described how to get a job as a janitor for the purpose of gaining physical access to an organization.

Human errors or mistakes by employees pose a serious problem. These errors are typically the result of laziness, carelessness, or a lack of awareness concerning information security. This lack of awareness arises from poor education and training efforts by the organization. Human mistakes manifest themselves in many different ways, as illustrated in Table 7.1.

TABLE 7.1 Human Mistakes

Human Mistake	Description and Examples
Carelessness with laptops	Losing or misplacing laptops, leaving them in taxis, and so on.
Carelessness with computing devices	Losing or misplacing these devices, or using them carelessly so that **malware** is introduced into an organization's network.
Opening questionable e-mails	Opening e-mails from someone unknown, or clicking on links embedded in e-mails (see *phishing attack* in Table 7.2).
Careless Internet surfing	Accessing questionable Web sites; can result in malware and/or alien software being introduced into the organization's network.
Poor password selection and use	Choosing and using weak passwords (see *strong passwords* in the "Authentication" section later in this chapter).
Carelessness with one's office	Leaving desks and filing cabinets unlocked when employees go home at night; not logging off the company network when leaving the office for any extended period of time.
Carelessness using unmanaged devices	Unmanaged devices are those outside the control of an organization's IT department and company security procedures. These devices include computers belonging to customers and business partners, computers in the business centers of hotels, and so on.
Carelessness with discarded equipment	Discarding old computer hardware and devices without completely wiping the memory; includes computers, smartphones, BlackBerry® units, and digital copiers and printers.
Careless monitoring of environmental hazards	These hazards, which include dirt, dust, humidity, and static electricity, are harmful to the operation of computing equipment.

The human errors you have just studied, although unintentional, are committed entirely by employees. However, employees also can make unintentional mistakes in response to actions by an attacker. Attackers often employ social engineering to induce individuals to make unintentional mistakes and disclose sensitive information.

Social Engineering

Social engineering is an attack in which the perpetrator uses social skills to trick or manipulate legitimate employees into providing confidential company information such

Blend/Image Source

Who is real and who is engaged in social engineering? Can you tell?

as passwords. The most common example of social engineering occurs when the attacker impersonates someone else on the telephone, such as a company manager or an information systems employee. The attacker claims he forgot his password and asks the legitimate employee to give him a password to use. Other common ploys include posing as an exterminator, an air-conditioning technician, or a fire marshal. Examples of social engineering abound.

In one company, a perpetrator entered a company building wearing a company ID card that looked legitimate. He walked around and put up signs on bulletin boards reading "The help desk telephone number has been changed. The new number is 555-1234." He then exited the building and began receiving calls from legitimate employees thinking they were calling the company help desk. Naturally, the first thing the perpetrator asked for was username and password. He now had the information necessary to access the company's information systems.

Two other social engineering techniques are tailgating and shoulder surfing. *Tailgating* is a technique designed to allow the perpetrator to enter restricted areas that are controlled with locks or card entry. The perpetrator follows closely behind a legitimate employee and, when the employee gains entry, the attacker asks him or her to "hold the door." *Shoulder surfing* occurs when a perpetrator watches an employee's computer screen over the employee's shoulder. This technique is particularly successful in public areas such as in airports and on commuter trains and airplanes.

BEFORE *YOU GO ON....*

1. What is an unintentional threat to an information system?

2. Provide examples of social engineering attacks other than the ones just discussed.

Apply The Concept 7.2

LEARNING OBJECTIVE 7.2 Compare and contrast human mistakes and social engineering, and provide a specific example of each one.

STEP 1 – Background

Sensitive information is generally stored in a safe location, both physically and digitally. However, as you have just read, this information is often vulnerable to unintentional threats that result from careless mistakes. As one example, employees frequently use USB (flash) drives to take information home. Although these actions are perfectly legal, the USB drive makes it easy to lose the information or to copy it onto unauthorized machines. In fact, any device that stores information can become a threat to information security—backup drives, CDs, DVDs, and even printers!

Printers?! Because people can "copy" information? Not quite. Continue the activity to find out more.

STEP 2 – Activity

Go to http://www.wiley.com/go/rainer/MIS3e/applytheconcept, and click on the link provided for Apply the Concept 7.2. You will find an article about how the hard drive in a printer sometimes stores images of all of the documents that have been copied. In the past when these printers were discarded their hard drives were not erased, leaving medical records, police reports, and other private information in a vulnerable state.

STEP 3 – Deliverable

Compare and contrast human mistakes and social engineering using the example above. How might someone make a mistake with a printer? How might someone use social engineering to access or create copies of personal information? Put your thoughts into a report and submit it to your instructor.

7.3 Deliberate Threats to Information Systems

There are many types of deliberate threats to information systems. We provide a list of 10 common types for your convenience.

- Espionage or trespass
- Information extortion
- Sabotage or vandalism
- Theft of equipment or information
- Identity theft
- Compromises to intellectual property
- Software attacks
- Alien software
- Supervisory control and data acquisition (SCADA) attacks
- Cyberterrorism and cyberwarfare

Espionage or Trespass

Espionage or trespass occurs when an unauthorized individual attempts to gain illegal access to organizational information. It is important to distinguish between competitive intelligence and industrial espionage. Competitive intelligence consists of legal information-gathering techniques, such as studying a company's Web site and press releases, attending trade shows, and similar actions. In contrast, industrial espionage crosses the legal boundary.

Information Extortion

Information extortion occurs when an attacker either threatens to steal, or actually steals, information from a company. The perpetrator demands payment for not stealing the information, for returning stolen information, or for agreeing not to disclose the information.

Sabotage or Vandalism

Sabotage and vandalism are deliberate acts that involve defacing an organization's Web site, potentially damaging the organization's image and causing its customers to lose faith. One form of online vandalism is a hacktivist or cyberactivist operation. These are cases of high-tech civil disobedience to protest the operations, policies, or actions of an organization or government agency. For example, the English Twitter account for the Arabic news network Al Jazeera was subject to hacktivism. The Associated Press reported that supporters of Syrian President Bashar Assad used the account to tweet pro-Assad links and messages.

Theft of Equipment or Information

Computing devices and storage devices are becoming smaller yet more powerful with vastly increased storage (e.g., laptops, personal digital assistants, smartphones, digital cameras, thumb drives, and iPods). As a result, these devices are becoming easier to steal and easier for attackers to use to steal information.

Table 7.1 points out that one type of human mistake is carelessness with laptops. In fact, many laptops have been stolen due to such carelessness. The cost of a stolen laptop includes the loss of data, the loss of intellectual property, laptop replacement, legal and regulatory costs, investigation fees, and lost productivity.

One form of theft, known as *dumpster diving*, involves rummaging through commercial or residential trash to find discarded information. Paper files, letters, memos, photographs, IDs, passwords, credit cards, and other forms of information can be found in dumpsters. Unfortunately, many people never consider that the sensitive items they throw in the trash might be recovered. When this information is recovered, it can be used for fraudulent purposes.

Dumpster diving is not necessarily theft, because the legality of this act varies. Because dumpsters are usually located on private premises, dumpster diving is illegal in some parts of the United States. Even in these cases, however, these laws are enforced with varying degrees of rigor.

Identity Theft

Identity theft is the deliberate assumption of another person's identity, usually to gain access to his or her financial information or to frame him or her for a crime. Techniques for illegally obtaining personal information include the following:

- Stealing mail or dumpster diving
- Stealing personal information in computer databases
- Infiltrating organizations that store large amounts of personal information (e.g., data aggregators such as Acxiom) (www.acxiom.com)
- Impersonating a trusted organization in an electronic communication (phishing)

Recovering from identity theft is costly, time consuming, and burdensome. Victims also report problems in obtaining credit and obtaining or holding a job, as well as adverse effects on insurance or credit rates. In addition, victims state that it is often difficult to remove negative information from their records, such as their credit reports.

Your personal information can be compromised in other ways. For example, your identity can be uncovered just by examining your searches in a search engine. The ability to analyze all searches by a single user can enable a criminal to identify who the user is and what he or she is doing. To demonstrate this fact, *The New York Times* tracked down a particular individual based solely on her AOL searches.

Compromises to Intellectual Property

Protecting intellectual property is a vital issue for people who make their livelihood in knowledge fields. **Intellectual property** is the property created by individuals or corporations that is protected under *trade secret*, *patent*, and *copyright* laws.

A **trade secret** is an intellectual work, such as a business plan, that is a company secret and is not based on public information. An example is the formula for Coca-Cola. A **patent** is an official document that grants the holder exclusive rights on an invention or a process for a specified period of time. **Copyright** is a statutory grant that provides the creators or owners of intellectual property with ownership of the property, also for a designated period. Current U.S. laws award patents for 20 years and copyright protection for the life of the creator plus 70 years. Owners are entitled to collect fees from anyone who wants to copy their creations. It is important to note that these are definitions under U.S. law. There is some international standardization of copyrights and patents, but it is far from total. Therefore, there can be discrepancies between U.S. law and other countries' laws.

The most common intellectual property related to IT deals with software. In 1980, the U.S. Congress amended the Copyright Act to include software. The amendment provides protection for the *source code* and *object code* of computer software, but it does not clearly identify what is eligible for protection. For example, copyright law does not protect fundamental concepts, functions, and general features such as pull-down menus, colors, and icons. However, copying a software program without making payment to the owner—including giving a disc to a friend to install on his or her computer—is a copyright violation. Not surprisingly, this practice, called **piracy**, is a major problem for software vendors. The BSA (www.bsa.org) Global Software Piracy Study found that the commercial value of software theft totals billions of dollars per year.

Software Attacks

Software attacks have evolved from the early years of the computer era, when attackers used malicious software to infect as many computers worldwide as possible, to the profit-driven, Web-based attacks of today. Modern cybercriminals use sophisticated, blended malware attacks, typically via the Web, to make money. Table 7.2 displays a variety of software attacks. These attacks are grouped into three categories: remote attacks requiring user action; remote attacks requiring no user action; and software attacks initiated by programmers during the development of a system. IT's About Business 7.1 provides an example of a software attack.

TABLE 7.2 Types of Software Attacks

Type	Description
(1) Remote Attacks Requiring User Action	
Virus	Segment of computer code that performs malicious actions by attaching to another computer program.
Worm	Segment of computer code that performs malicious actions and will replicate, or spread, by itself (without requiring another computer program).
Phishing attack	Phishing attacks use deception to acquire sensitive personal information by masquerading as official-looking e-mails or instant messages.
Spear phishing	Phishing attacks target large groups of people. In spear phishing attacks, attack the perpetrators find out as much information about an individual as possible to improve their chances that phishing techniques will obtain sensitive, personal information.
(2) Remote Attacks Needing No User Action	
Denial-of-service attack	An attacker sends so many information requests to a target computer system that the target cannot handle them successfully and typically crashes (ceases to function).
Distributed denial-of-service attack	An attacker first takes over many computers, typically by using malicious software. These computers are called **zombies** or **bots**. The attacker uses these bots—which form a **botnet**—to deliver a coordinated stream of information requests to a target computer, causing it to crash.
(3) Attacks by a Programmer Developing a System	
Trojan horse	Software programs that hide in other computer programs and reveal their designed behavior only when they are activated.
Back door	Typically a password, known only to the attacker, that allows him or her to access a computer system at will, without having to go through any security procedures (also called a **trap door**).
Logic bomb	A segment of computer code that is embedded within an organization's existing computer programs and is designed to activate and perform a destructive action at a certain time or date.

IT'S ABOUT BUSINESS 7.1

Stealing Cash from ATMs with Text Messages

Security firm Symantec (www.symantec.com)—which manufactures Norton Internet security software—is warning the banking industry that it is facing a serious risk of cyberattacks aimed at their ATMs. A group of cybercriminals has developed a method to obtain cash from an ATM–by text message. The malware, called "Ploutus," is engineered to compromise a certain type of standalone ATM. Ploutus is not easy to install, because the cybercriminals must physically access the ATM itself. That is probably the reason they target standalone ATMs.

Here is how the ATM hack works: The criminals first connect a mobile phone to the ATM through a USB port. (They have to physically break open the ATM to do this.) The attackers then infect the ATM with Ploutus malware. Because the phone is connected to the ATM through the USB port, the phone also draws power from the connection, which charges the phone's battery indefinitely.

Ploutus monitors network traffic going in and out of the ATM. When the compromised ATM receives a valid code from the phone, it is ready to receive commands from the criminals. The criminals can now send specific short message service commands to the phone attached to the ATM. When the phone detects a new message from the criminals, it forwards the message to the ATM through the USB cable.

The criminal boss employs "money mules" to perform the actual ATM hacks. A mule is someone hired to do the risky job of stopping by the ATM to pick up the cash. In previous manual versions of Ploutus, the boss had to share a code (16-digit number) with the mule. The mule would enter this code on the ATM keyboard and then withdraw cash from the machine. However, the boss would not know how much cash the mule withdrew, meaning that the mule could skim money from the boss.

In the latest version of Ploutus, the boss sends a text message to the phone attached to the ATM. The phone then informs the boss of the amount of cash in the ATM, denomination by denomination. The boss instructs the ATM as to how much cash to dispense, and in what denominations. The mule stands in front of the compromised ATM, looking as if he or she were making a legitimate withdrawal. The ATM dispenses the cash. Significantly, the mule never sees the code. This system provides the boss with additional security while enabling him to centrally control the cash withdrawals.

Using SMS messages to remotely control the ATM is a much more convenient method for all parties involved in this theft. The boss knows exactly how much money the mule will collect from the ATM, and the mule does not need to linger around the ATM for extended periods waiting for it to issue the cash. The boss and the mule can synchronize their actions so that the money is issued just as the mule pretends to withdraw cash or is walking past the ATM.

To prevent this type of attack, modern ATMs have incorporated enhanced security features, such as encrypted hard drives. For older ATMs that still run on Windows XP, however, protecting against this type of attack is more challenging, especially when ATMs are placed in remote locations. To make this process much more difficult for criminals, banks can upgrade to Windows 7 or 8. They can also provide adequate physical protection and consider closed-circuit television monitoring for the ATM.

MIS

Sources: Compiled from F. D'Sa, "Windows XP ATMs Being Hacked by a Simple SMS," *Deccan Chronicle*, March 26, 2014; L. Seltzer, "Robbing ATMs by SMS: Not in the Real World," *ZDNet*, March 25, 2014; J. Kirk, "ATM Malware, Controlled by a Text Message, Spews Cash," *Financial IT*, March 25, 2014; D. Regalado, "Texting ATMs for Cash Shows Cybercriminals' Increasing Sophistication," *Symantec.com*, March 24, 2014; K. Higgins, "Criminals Control, Cash Out Bank's ATM Machines," *Dark Reading*, February 13, 2014; C. Smith, "The Latest Malware Innovation: Infect ATMs and Have Them Pump Out Cash," *BGR*, January 1, 2014; T. Kitten, "ATM Malware: Sign of New Trend?" *Bank Info Security*, October 14, 2013; www.symantec.com, accessed March 27, 2014.

Questions

1. Other than the ones mentioned in this case, what countermeasures could banks take to defend against ATM hacks such as these?

2. Why are some banks still using Windows XP on their ATMs, when newer, more secure operating systems are available?

Not all cybercriminals are sophisticated, however. For example, a student at a U.S. university was sentenced to one year in prison for using keylogging software (discussed later in this chapter) to steal 750 fellow students' passwords and vote himself and four of his fraternity brothers into the student government's president and four vice president positions. The five positions would have combined to bring the students a combined $36,000 in stipends.

The student was caught when university security personnel noticed strange activity on the campus network. Authorities identified the computer used in the activity from its IP address. On this computer, which belonged to the student in question, authorities found a PowerPoint presentation detailing the scheme. Authorities also found research on his computer, with queries such as "how to rig an election" and "jail time for keylogger."

Once the university caught onto the scheme, the student reportedly turned back to hacking to try to get himself out of trouble. He created new Facebook accounts in the names of actual classmates, going as far as conducting fake conversations between the accounts to try to deflect the blame. Those actions contributed to the one-year prison sentence, which the judge imposed even after the student pleaded guilty and requested probation.

Alien Software

Many personal computers have alien software, or *pestware*, running on them that the owners are unaware of. **Alien software** is clandestine software that is installed on your computer through duplicitous methods. It typically is not as malicious as viruses, worms, or Trojan horses, but it does use up valuable system resources. In addition, it can enable other parties to track your Web surfing habits and other personal behaviors.

The vast majority of pestware is **adware**—software that causes pop-up advertisements to appear on your screen. Adware is common because it works. According to advertising agencies, for every 100 people who close a pop-up ad, 3 click on it. This "hit rate" is extremely high for Internet advertising.

Spyware is software that collects personal information about users without their consent. Two common types of spyware are keystroke loggers and screen scrapers.

Keystroke loggers, also called *keyloggers*, record both your individual keystrokes and your Internet Web browsing history. The purposes range from criminal—for example, theft of passwords and sensitive personal information such as credit card numbers—to annoying—for example, recording your Internet search history for targeted advertising.

Companies have attempted to counter keyloggers by switching to other forms of identifying users. For example, at some point all of us have been forced to look at wavy, distorted letters and type them correctly into a box. That string of letters is called a *CAPTCHA*, and it is a test. The point of CAPTCHA is that computers cannot (yet) accurately read those distorted letters. Therefore, the fact that you can transcribe them means that you are probably not a software program run by an unauthorized person, such as a spammer. As a result, attackers have turned to *screen scrapers*, or *screen grabbers*. This software records a continuous "movie" of a screen's contents rather than simply recording keystrokes.

Spamware is pestware that uses your computer as a launch pad for spammers. **Spam** is unsolicited e-mail, usually advertising for products and services. When your computer is infected with spamware, e-mails from spammers are sent to everyone in your e-mail address book, but they appear to come from you.

Not only is spam a nuisance, but it wastes time and money. Spam costs U.S. companies billions of dollars every year. These costs arise from productivity losses, clogged e-mail systems, additional storage, user support, and antispam software. Spam can also carry viruses and worms, making it even more dangerous.

Cookies are small amounts of information that Web sites store on your computer, temporarily or more or less permanently. In many cases, cookies are useful and innocuous. For example, some cookies are passwords and user IDs that you do not want to retype every time you access the Web site that issued the cookie. Cookies are also necessary for online shopping because merchants use them for your shopping carts.

Tracking cookies, however, can be used to track your path through a Web site, the time you spend there, what links you click on, and other details that the company wants to record, usually for marketing purposes. Tracking cookies can also combine this information with your name, purchases, credit card information, and other personal data to develop an intrusive profile of your spending habits.

Most cookies can be read only by the party that created them. However, some companies that manage online banner advertising are, in essence, cookie-sharing rings.

These companies can track information such as which pages you load and which ads you click on. They then share this information with their client Web sites, which may number in the thousands.

Supervisory Control and Data Acquisition Attacks

SCADA refers to a large-scale, distributed measurement and control system. SCADA systems are used to monitor or to control chemical, physical, and transport processes such as those used in oil refineries, water and sewage treatment plants, electrical generators, and nuclear power plants. Essentially, SCADA systems provide a link between the physical world and the electronic world.

SCADA systems consist of multiple sensors, a master computer, and communications infrastructure. The sensors connect to physical equipment. They read status data such as the open/closed status of a switch or a valve, as well as measurements such as pressure, flow, voltage, and current. They control the equipment by sending signals to it, such as opening or closing a switch or a valve or setting the speed of a pump.

The sensors are connected in a network, and each sensor typically has an Internet address (Internet Protocol, or IP, address, discussed in Chapter 4). If attackers gain access to the network, they can cause serious damage, such as disrupting the power grid over a large area or upsetting the operations of a large chemical or nuclear plant. Such actions could have catastrophic results.

Cyberterrorism and Cyberwarfare

Cyberterrorism and **cyberwarfare** refer to malicious acts in which attackers use a target's computer systems, particularly via the Internet, to cause physical, real-world harm or severe disruption, often to carry out a political agenda (see IT's About Business 7.2). These actions range from gathering data to attacking critical infrastructure (e.g., via SCADA systems). We treat the two types of attacks as synonymous here, even though cyberterrorism typically is carried out by individuals or groups, whereas cyberwarfare is carried out by nation states. The following example examines cyberattacks perpetrated against Estonia and the Republic of Georgia, formerly parts of the Soviet Union.

IT'S ABOUT BUSINESS 7.2

The Mask

A report from Kaspersky Labs (www.kaspersky.com), a global information security firm, revealed what could be the most sophisticated malware yet discovered in the wild (on the Internet). The software, called Careto (which means "The Mask" in Spanish), is a sophisticated suite of software tools for compromising computers and collecting information from them. In fact, the software is so sophisticated that it remained undiscovered for more than five years. That is, the software had been downloaded on victims' computers but they were unaware of it.

Whoever is behind Careto sends out spear phishing e-mails, with addresses designed to be mistaken for the Web sites of mainstream newspapers such as *The Washington Post* and *The Guardian*. If users click on a link, it takes them to a Web site that scans their systems for vulnerabilities and attempts to infect them. There are multiple versions of the software, designed to attack Windows, Mac OS X, Linux, iOS, and Android.

After Careto has compromised a system, it collects sensitive information from it. The software can intercept network traffic, collect keystrokes, monitor Skype conversations, analyze Wi-Fi traffic, collect all of the information communicated via wireless devices, perform screen captures, and monitor all of the computer's operations. It can also capture any encryption keys found on the compromised computer, which the perpetrators can utilize to launch attacks against other computer systems.

© aetb/iStockphoto

Careto is highly targeted. Most of the attacks have been directed against government institutions, embassies, oil and gas companies, research organizations, private equity firms, and activists. Kaspersky found that more than 380 victims in 31 countries had been targeted.

The question is: Who is behind the malware? It is likely that only national intelligence agencies have the resources to build software of this complexity and sophistication. (Recall the Stuxnet malware of several years ago.) Fragments of Spanish embedded in the malware's code suggest that the culprit is a native Spanish speaker. However, it is not clear which Spanish-speaking nation would build such a sophisticated intelligence-gathering operation, or why. Further, the researchers note that the fragments of Spanish may be a "false flag" operation. That is, the authors may have deliberately inserted Spanish slang into the software's source code to divert attention from them.

Regardless of who is responsible for Careto, the emergence of the malware underscores the fact that software-based espionage is an important new source of power. In 2013, documents leaked by Edward Snowden revealed that the National Security Agency (NSA; see closing case 1 in Chapter 6) has established a large "Tailored Access Operations" department dedicated to building offensive hacking capabilities. If the NSA did not build Careto, then it is a good bet that the agency possesses similar software. In addition, intelligence agencies in China, Russia, and other international powers are also likely working on this type of software.

Sources: Compiled from "Careto Detection: The Most Dangerous Malicious Code Security in History!" *Bubblews*, March 9, 2014; J. Plafke, "Sophisticated Malware Poses as Your Favorite News Site, Steals Your Data," *Extreme Tech*, February 13, 2014; S. Bansal, "The Mask, A Malware Campaign That Remained Undetected for 7 Years," *The Hacker News*, February 11, 2014; "Kaspersky Lab Uncovers 'The Mask': One of the Most Advanced Global Cyber-Espionage Operations to Date Due to the Complexity of the Toolset Used by the Attackers," *Kaspersky Labs Press Release*, February 11, 2014; L. Constantin, "Cyberespionage Operation 'The Mask' Compromised Organizations in 30-Plus Countries," *Network World*, February 10, 2014; K. Higgins, "Researchers Uncover 'The Mask' Global Cyberspying Operation," *Dark Reading*, February 10, 2014; T. Lee, "This Malware Is Frighteningly Sophisticated, and We Don't Know Who Created It," *The Washington Post*, February 10, 2014; www.kaspersky.com, accessed March 27, 2014.

Questions

1. Discuss the implications of the targeted nature of the Careto malware.

2. Analyze the statement: "Nations use malware such as Careto when their only alternative is to go to war."

3. Discuss the impacts that such sophisticated malware could have on all of us.

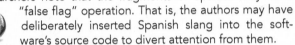

Apply The Concept 7.3

LEARNING OBJECTIVE 7.3 Discuss the 10 types of deliberate attacks.

┌─ BEFORE *YOU GO ON....* ─┐

1. Why has the theft of computing devices become more serious over time?

2. What are the three types of software attacks?

3. Define alien software, and explain why it is a serious problem.

4. What is a SCADA system? Why can attacks against SCADA system have catastrophic consequences

STEP 1 – Background

Unfortunately, there are many people who take advantage of others. Fraud, espionage, information extortion, identity theft, cyberterrorism, spamming, phishing, and many other deliberate acts have created a world where we must always confirm the identity of the people we share information with.

STEP 2 – Activity

Go to http://www.wiley.com/go/rainer/MIS3e/applytheconcept, and click on the links provided for Apply the Concept 7.3. The link will take you to a video about foreign lotteries and a Web site the U.S. Postal Service provides to help people realize when they are being scammed. This type of scam has taken advantage of many people who are not aware that such scams exist. After watching the video, search the Web for other fraudulent activities that involve Craigslist, eBay, and any other sites you find.

STEP 3 – Deliverable

Imagine you are the owner of a site such as Craigslist. Draft a memo to your users—both buyers and sellers—explaining your intention to run a "clean" site where all parties are safe. In your memo, discuss the 10 types of deliberate attacks that you want your users to be aware of as they conduct business on your site. Submit your memo to your instructor.

7.4 What Organizations Are Doing to Protect Information Resources

Why is stopping cybercriminals such a challenge? Table 7.3 illustrates the many major difficulties involved in protecting information. Because organizing an appropriate defense system is so important to the entire enterprise, it is one of the major responsibilities of any prudent CIO as well as of the functional managers who control information resources. In fact, IT security is the business of *everyone* in an organization.

In addition to the problems listed in Table 7.3, another reason why information resources are difficult to protect is that the online commerce industry is not particularly willing to install safeguards that would make completing transactions more difficult or complicated. As one example, merchants could demand passwords or personal identification numbers for all credit card transactions. However, these requirements might discourage people from shopping online. For credit card companies, it is cheaper to block a stolen credit card and move on than to invest time and money prosecuting cybercriminals.

Despite these difficulties, the information security industry is battling back against cybercrime. Companies are developing software and services that deliver early warnings of trouble on the Internet. Unlike traditional antivirus software, which is reactive, early-warning systems are *proactive*, scanning the Web for new viruses and alerting companies to the danger.

Organizations spend a great deal of time and money protecting their information resources. Before doing so, they perform risk management.

A **risk** is the probability that a threat will impact an information resource. The goal of **risk management** is to identify, control, and minimize the impact of threats. In other words, risk management seeks to reduce risk to acceptable levels. Risk management consists of three processes: risk analysis, risk mitigation, and controls evaluation.

Organizations perform risk analyses to ensure that their IS security programs are cost effective. **Risk analysis** involves three steps: (1) assessing the value of each asset being protected, (2) estimating the probability that each asset will be compromised, and (3) comparing the probable costs of the asset's being compromised with the costs of protecting that asset. The organization then considers how to mitigate the risk.

In **risk mitigation**, the organization takes concrete actions against risks. Risk mitigation has two functions: (1) implementing controls to prevent identified threats from occurring, and (2) developing a means of recovery if the threat becomes a reality. There are several risk mitigation strategies that organizations can adopt. The three most common are risk acceptance, risk limitation, and risk transference.·

TABLE 7.3 The Difficulties in Protecting Information Resources

Hundreds of potential threats exist.
Computing resources may be situated in many locations.
Many individuals control or have access to information assets.
Computer networks can be located outside the organization, making them difficult to protect.
Rapid technological changes make some controls obsolete as soon as they are installed.
Many computer crimes are undetected for a long period of time, so it is difficult to learn from experience.
People tend to violate security procedures because the procedures are inconvenient.
The amount of computer knowledge necessary to commit computer crimes is usually minimal. As a matter of fact, a potential criminal can learn hacking, for free, on the Internet.
The costs of preventing hazards can be very high. Therefore, most organizations simply cannot afford to protect themselves against all possible hazards.
It is difficult to conduct a cost–benefit justification for controls before an attack occurs because it is difficult to assess the impact of a hypothetical attack.

- **Risk acceptance**: Accept the potential risk, continue operating with no controls, and absorb any damages that occur.
- **Risk limitation**: Limit the risk by implementing controls that minimize the impact of the threat.
- **Risk transference**: Transfer the risk by using other means to compensate for the loss, such as by purchasing insurance.

Finally, in controls evaluation, the organization examines the costs of implementing adequate control measures against the value of those control measures. If the costs of implementing a control are greater than the value of the asset being protected, the control is not cost effective. In the next section, you will study the various controls that organizations use to protect their information resources.

┌─ BEFORE *YOU GO ON....* ─┐

1. Describe several reasons why it is difficult to protect information resources.
2. Compare and contrast risk management and risk analysis.

Apply The Concept 7.4

LEARNING OBJECTIVE 7.4 Define the three risk mitigation strategies, and provide an example of each one in the context of owning a home.

STEP 1 – Background

Section 7.4 has discussed at length the ways businesses deal with risk. Risk management is so important that companies frequently assign an entire department to oversee risk analysis and mitigation. When companies address risk, they have three basic methods to choose from: risk acceptance, risk limitation, and risk transference. Significantly, we do the same thing when it comes to our personal assets.

Like businesses, homeowners face intentional and unintentional threats. To mitigate against these threats, almost all homeowners take certain actions. These actions reflect, among other things, where your home is located. For example, a home on the beach is much more susceptible to hurricanes than is a home in Arkansas. However, the home in Arkansas is (perhaps) more susceptible to tornadoes than is the home on the beach.

STEP 2 – Activity

Imagine that you own your home. What risks do you need to manage? What property do you need to assess? What is the probability that any asset will be compromised? (*Note*: You will need to assess the risk to each asset.) What are the costs associated with each asset being compromised?

STEP 3 – Deliverable

In a document, define the three risk management strategies, and provide an example of each one in the context of owning a home. Submit your document to your instructor.

7.5 Information Security Controls

To protect their information assets, organizations implement **controls**, or defense mechanisms (also called *countermeasures*). These controls are designed to protect all of the components of an information system, including data, software, hardware, and networks. Because there are so many diverse threats, organizations utilize layers of controls, or *defense-in-depth*.

Controls are intended to prevent accidental hazards, deter intentional acts, detect problems as early as possible, enhance damage recovery, and correct problems. Before you study controls in more detail, it is important to emphasize that the single most valuable control is user education and training. Effective and ongoing education makes every member of the organization aware of the vital importance of information security.

Figure 7.2 Where defense mechanisms are located. (*Sources:* © sergeytitov1977/iStockphoto; © fatihoca/iStockphoto)

In this section, you will learn about three major types of controls: physical controls, access controls, and communications controls. FIGURE 7.2 illustrates these controls. In addition to applying controls, organizations plan for business continuity in case of a disaster, and they periodically audit their information resources to detect possible threats. You will study these topics in this section as well.

Physical Controls

Physical controls prevent unauthorized individuals from gaining access to a company's facilities. Common physical controls include walls, doors, fencing, gates, locks, badges, guards, and alarm systems. More sophisticated physical controls include pressure sensors, temperature sensors, and motion detectors. One shortcoming of physical controls is that they can be inconvenient to employees.

Guards deserve special mention because they have very difficult jobs, for at least two reasons. First, their jobs are boring and repetitive and generally do not pay well. Second, if guards perform their jobs thoroughly, the other employees harass them, particularly if they slow up the process of entering the facility.

Organizations also implement physical security measures that limit computer users to acceptable login times and locations. These controls also limit the number of unsuccessful login attempts, and they require all employees to log off their computers when they leave for the day. In addition, they set the employees' computers to automatically log off the user after a certain period of disuse.

Access Controls

Access controls restrict unauthorized individuals from using information resources. These controls involve two major functions: authentication and authorization. **Authentication** confirms the identity of the person requiring access. After the person is authenticated (identified), the next step is authorization. **Authorization** determines which actions, rights, or privileges the person has, based on his or her verified identity. Let's examine these functions more closely.

Authentication. To authenticate (identify) authorized personnel, an organization can use one or more of the following methods: something the user is, something the user has, something the user does, and/or something the user knows.

Something the user is, also known as **biometrics**, is an authentication method that examines a person's innate physical characteristics. Common biometric applications are fingerprint scans, palm scans, retina scans, iris recognition, and facial recognition. Of these applications, fingerprints, retina scans, and iris recognition provide the most definitive identification. The following example shows how powerful biometrics can be for identification purposes.

EXAMPLE   The Biometric Identification Project of India

India has vast numbers of anonymous poor citizens. To address this problem, the nation instituted its Unique Identification Project, also known as Aadhaar, which means "the foundation" in several Indian languages. The goal of the project is to issue identification numbers linked to the fingerprints and iris scans of every individual in India. This process will ultimately encompass some 1.2 billion people who speak more than 300 languages and dialects. The biometrics and the Aadhaar identification number will serve as a verifiable, portable, and unique national ID. The Aadhaar project should enable millions of poor Indian citizens to access government services that previously were out of reach to them.

Aadhaar seeks to remedy a critical problem that afflicts poor people. The Indian government does not officially acknowledge the existence of many impoverished citizens because these individuals do not possess birth certificates and other official documentation. Therefore, they cannot access government services to which they are entitled, nor can they open bank accounts. When the project started, many Indian households were "unbanked," meaning they had to stash their savings in cash around their homes.

Aadhaar went into operation in September 2010, when officials armed with iris scanners, fingerprint scanners, digital cameras, and laptops began to register the first few villagers as well as slum dwellers in the country's capital city, Delhi. One of the most daunting challenges confronting the project is to ensure that each individual's record in the database is matched to one and only one person. For this process, Aadhaar must check all 10 fingerprints and both irises of each person against those of everyone else in the country. Using 10 prints and both irises boosts the accuracy rate to 99 percent. However, in a country the size of India, 99 percent accuracy means that 12 million people could end up with faulty records.

Additionally, Aadhaar faces enormous physical and technical challenges: reaching millions of illiterate Indians who have never seen a computer, persuading them to have their irises scanned, ensuring that their scanned information is accurate, and safeguarding the resulting massive amounts of data. In addition, civil libertarians object to the project on privacy grounds.

In September 2013, an Indian court ruled that people cannot be required to have the controversial Aadhaar ID to collect state subsidies. The court stated that "no person should suffer for not getting the Aadhaar card." The project was created via an executive order rather than by legislation enacted by India's parliament. As a result, its legality can be challenged.

Further, a number of people have complained that the Aadhaar cards they have received contain errors in their names, addresses, and other personal information. One newspaper reported that an Aadhaar recipient received a card that had the face of a dog in place of his photograph.

As of mid-2014, Aadhaar had enrolled some 850 million people (8.5 billion fingerprints, 1.7 billion iris images, 850 million facial photos), comprising 10 petabytes of data. At the current rate of enrollment, Aadhaar planners hope to reach the entire population of India by mid-2016.

Sources: Compiled from B. Rohith, "Aadhaar Drive Loses Its Pace," *The Times of India*, March 15, 2014; J. Ribeiro, "Indian Biometric ID Project Faces Court Hurdle," *PC World*, September 24, 2013; S. Rai, "Why India's Identity Scheme Is Groundbreaking," *BBC News*, June 5, 2012; E. Hannon, "For India's Undocumented Citizens, an ID at Last," *NPR.org*, March 1, 2012; "World's Biggest Biometric ID Scheme Forges Ahead," *BBC News India*, February 12, 2012; M. Magnier, "India's Biometric ID Number Plan Divided by Bureaucracy," *Los Angeles Times*, January 28, 2012; B. Turbeville, "Cashless Society: India Implements First Biometric ID Program for All of Its 1.2 Billion Residents," *Infowars.com*, January 12, 2012; V. Beiser, "Identified," *Wired*, September 2011; www.iaadhaar.com, accessed April 25, 2014.

Questions

1. Describe the problems that India is facing in implementing this biometric identification system.
2. Describe the benefits that India hopes to gain in implementing the biometric identification system.
3. Describe the benefits that the biometric identification system should provide to India's impoverished citizens.

Something the user has is an authentication mechanism that includes regular identification (ID) cards, smart ID cards, and tokens (see chapter closing case 2). *Regular ID cards*, or *dumb cards*, typically have the person's picture and often his or her signature. *Smart ID cards* have an embedded chip that stores pertinent information about the user. (Smart ID cards used for identification differ from smart cards used in electronic commerce, which you learn about in Chapter 9. Both types of card have embedded chips, but they are used for different purposes.) *Tokens* have embedded chips and a digital display that presents a login number that the employees use to access the organization's network. The number changes with each login.

Something the user does is an authentication mechanism that includes voice and signature recognition. In *voice recognition*, the user speaks a phrase (e.g., his or her name and department) that has been previously recorded under controlled conditions. The voice recognition system matches the two voice signals. In *signature recognition*, the user signs his or her name, and the system matches this signature with one previously recorded under controlled, monitored conditions. Signature recognition systems also match the speed and the pressure of the signature.

Something the user knows is an authentication mechanism that includes passwords and passphrases. **Passwords** present a huge information security problem in all organizations. Most of us have to remember numerous passwords for different online services, and we typically must choose complicated strings of characters to make them harder to guess. Security experts examined the frequency and usage of passwords belonging to 500,000 computer users. They found that each person had an average of 6.5 passwords that he or she used for 25 different online accounts. Unfortunately, as you see in chapter closing case 2, passwords (even strong passwords) are terribly vulnerable to attack.

All users should use *strong passwords*, which are difficult for hackers to discover. The basic guidelines for creating strong passwords are the following:

- They should be difficult to guess.
- They should be long rather than short.
- They should have uppercase letters, lowercase letters, numbers, and special characters.
- They should not be recognizable words.
- They should not be the name of anything or anyone familiar, such as family names or names of pets.
- They should not be a recognizable string of numbers, such as a Social Security number or a birthday.

Unfortunately, strong passwords are more difficult to remember than weak ones. Consequently, employees frequently write them down, which defeats their purpose. The ideal solution to this dilemma is to create a strong password that is also easy to remember. To achieve this objective, many people use passphrases.

A *passphrase* is a series of characters that is longer than a password but is still easy to memorize. Examples of passphrases are "maytheforcebewithyoualways" and "goaheadmakemyday." A passphrase can serve as a password itself, or it can help you create a strong password. You can turn a passphrase into a strong password in this manner. Starting with the last passphrase above, take the first letter of each word. You will have "gammd." Then, capitalize every other letter to create "GaMmD". Finally, add special characters and numbers to create "9GaMmD//*." You now have a strong password that you can remember.

To identify authorized users more efficiently and effectively, organizations frequently implement more than one type of authentication, a strategy known as *multifactor authentication*. This system is particularly important when users log in from remote locations.

Single-factor authentication, which is notoriously weak, commonly consists simply of a password. Two-factor authentication consists of a password plus one type of biometric identification (e.g., a fingerprint). Three-factor authentication is any combination of three authentication methods. In most cases, the more factors the system utilizes, the more reliable it is. However, stronger authentication is also more expensive, and, as with strong passwords, it can be irritating to users.

Authorization. After users have been properly authenticated, the rights and privileges to which they are entitled on the organization's systems are established in a process called *authorization*. A **privilege** is a collection of related computer system operations that a user is authorized to perform. Companies typically base authorization policies on the principle of **least privilege**, which posits that users be granted the privilege for an activity only if there is a justifiable need for them to perform that activity.

Communications Controls

Communications controls (also called **network controls**) secure the movement of data across networks. Communications controls consist of firewalls, anti-malware systems, whitelisting and blacklisting, encryption, virtual private networks (VPNs), secure socket layer (SSL), and employee monitoring systems.

Firewalls. A **firewall** is a system that prevents a specific type of information from moving between untrusted networks, such as the Internet, and private networks, such as your company's network. Put simply, firewalls prevent unauthorized Internet users from accessing private networks. All messages entering or leaving your company's network pass through a firewall. The firewall examines each message and blocks those that do not meet specified security rules.

Firewalls range from simple, for home use, to very complex for organizational use. FIGURE 7.3(a) illustrates a basic firewall for a home computer. In this case, the firewall is implemented as software on the home computer. FIGURE 7.3(b) shows an organization that has implemented an external firewall, which faces the Internet, and an internal firewall, which faces the company network. Corporate firewalls typically consist of software running on a computer dedicated to the task. A **demilitarized zone (DMZ)** is located between the two firewalls. Messages from the Internet must first pass through the external firewall. If they conform to the defined security rules, they are then sent to company servers located in the DMZ. These servers typically handle Web page requests and e-mail. Any messages designated for the company's internal network (e.g., its intranet) must pass through the internal firewall, again with its own defined security rules, to gain access to the company's private network.

Figure 7.3 (a) Basic firewall for home computer. (b) Organization with two firewalls and demilitarized zone. (*Source:* © f9photos/iStockphoto)

The danger from viruses and worms is so severe that many organizations are placing firewalls at strategic points *inside* their private networks. In this way, if a virus or worm does get through both the external and internal firewalls, then the internal damage may be contained.

Anti-malware Systems. **Anti-malware systems**, also called *antivirus*, or *AV*, software, are software packages that attempt to identify and eliminate viruses and worms, and other malicious software. AV software is implemented at the organizational level by the IS department. Hundreds of AV software packages are currently available. Among the best known are Norton AntiVirus (www.symantec.com), McAfee VirusScan (www.mcafee.com), and Trend Micro PC-cillin (www.trendmicro.com). IT's About Business 7.3 provides an example of how a software program known as FireEye helps protect organizations from malware.

IT'S ABOUT BUSINESS 7.3

A Tale of Two Cybersecurity Firms

FireEye (www.fireeye.com) and Mandiant (www.mandiant.com) are two of the world's most effective private cybercrime fighters. The companies defend corporations and governments against targeted malicious software. Their clients include Fortune 500 companies and members of the U.S. intelligence community.

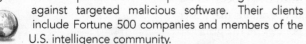

The companies' software examines the entire life cycle of malicious software, when the malware penetrated the network, how the malware operates within a network, what the malware is searching for, which servers delivered the malware, and from which control servers the malware receives its orders. Let's look at an example of each company in action.

FireEye vs. the Rustock Botnet.
Consider FireEye's confrontation with the Rustock botnet, the most advanced botnet ever released onto the Web. Rustock reeled people in by putting out spam that advertised fake drugs, online pharmacies, and Russian stocks. Then, from 2007 to 2011, it quietly and illegally took control of more than 1 million computers around the world. In the process, it generated profits estimated to be in the millions of dollars.

FireEye collaborated with Microsoft and Pfizer to plot a counterattack. Microsoft and Pfizer became involved because Rustock was selling fake Viagra, a Pfizer product, as well as sham lotteries using the Microsoft logo. Working from FireEye's intelligence, in March 2011 U.S. marshals stormed seven Internet data centers across the United States where Rustock had hidden its 96 command servers. Microsoft lawyers and technicians and computer forensics experts also participated in the raids. A team deployed to the Netherlands confiscated two additional Rustock command servers.

Although the operation was executed flawlessly, Rustock was able to fight back. From an unknown location, the *botmaster* (the person or persons controlling the bots, or zombie computers) remotely sneaked back into its network, locked out Microsoft's technicians, and began to erase files. After some difficulty, the Microsoft technicians were able to regain control of the servers. However, the data that were erased in the 30 minutes that the Microsoft technicians required to regain control of their servers may be lost forever.

Microsoft also offered (and was still offering as of mid-2014) $250,000 for information about the identity of the person or persons operating the botnet. Unfortunately, the Rustock perpetrators still have

© PN_Photo/iStockphoto

not been caught, and security experts believe that more than 600,000 computers around the world are still infected with Rustock malware.

Mandiant and Chinese Hacking.
In a wave of cyberattacks beginning in 2009, sophisticated hackers based in China breached the corporate networks of Google, Yahoo!, Juniper Networks, Adobe Systems, and dozens of other prominent technology companies and tried to access their source code. Experts believed the cyberattacks were intended to steal intellectual property and narrow the marketplace advantages enjoyed by U.S. companies over Chinese competitors such as Huawei Technology and ZTE, neither of which has been implicated in the attacks.

Then in 2013, a series of news stories reported that the computer systems of major news organizations including the *New York Times*, *Wall Street Journal*, and *Washington Post* had been breached by hackers with connections to the Chinese government. China's censors were apparently trying to stifle dissent by exposing the anonymous sources of Western journalists who have written negative stories about the country or its government.

For instance, Mandiant believes that the *New York Times* was targeted by APT 12, a group known primarily for attacking defense contractors. According to Mandiant, the attackers had obtained complete access to the newspaper's internal network. However, they had only searched the files of two reporters who had authored a series of stories about the personal wealth of China's Communist Party leadership.

Today, China's targets appear to be much broader. Wiley Rein (www.wileyrein.com), a Washington law firm working on a trade case against China, was attacked in 2011. Even more ominous, the White House itself was attacked in 2012.

Hacking groups with ties to the Chinese government have also aggressively targeted Western oil and gas companies (and often their law firms and investment banks) to obtain proprietary financial information, sometimes in advance of an acquisition by a Chinese company. For instance, when Chesapeake Energy put natural gas holdings worth billions of dollars on the market, its investment bank, Jefferies, was targeted around the time a Chinese government official visited Chesapeake's Oklahoma headquarters.

To prevent such hacks, Mandiant uses unconventional methods. Teams of three to five specialists are assigned to track each victim company's computer system, a painstaking process that can take months. After the specialists have identified every security vulnerability and every piece of malware in the company's network, Mandiant removes the malware, in some cases by replacing every infected computer within 48 hours. For companies that fear their secrets might be lost before the malware is removed, the process can be suspenseful.

And the latest news from the two companies? On January 2, 2014, FireEye (www.fireeye.com) purchased Mandiant for more than $1 billion in cash and stock, creating a new giant in the cybersecurity marketplace.

Here is how the new company will work:

- Clients will pay a monthly fee for a license for FireEye (the name of the combined company).

- FireEye will make recommendations concerning best security practices.

- The client's security operations team will operate the security environment, keep it up to date, and analyze attacks as they occur. They will send data from any attacks to FireEye's operations center for further analysis.

- Another monthly fee will cover automated advanced analysis of the company's security data and incident response. When the client's security team cannot identify a problem, security professionals from Mandiant will come in and fix it.

Sources: Compiled from J. Xavier, "FireEye's Kevin Mandia on the $1B Mandiant Acquisition," *Silicon Valley Business Journal,* February 28, 2014; D. Woods, "The Product Management Logic of the FireEye–Mandiant Deal," *New York Times*, January 3, 2014; "Report: Chinese Hackers Attacked Crucial Government Election Website," *CNN*, December 17, 2013; J. Vijayan, "China-Based Hacking Group Behind Hundreds of Attacks on U.S. Companies," *Computerworld*, September 17, 2013; "New York Times: Chinese Hackers Attacked Our Computers for Months," *CBS News*, August 7, 2013; C. Joye, "Anatomy of a Cyberattack on Business," *Financial Review*, June 4, 2013; D. Sanger and N. Perlroth, "Hackers From China Resume Attacks on U.S. Targets," *New York Times*, May 19, 2013; B. Stone and M. Riley, "Hacked? Who Ya Gonna Call?" *Bloomberg BusinessWeek*, February 11–17, 2013; "FireEye Testimonials," *FireEye Information Center* (www.fireeye.com), January 8, 2013; S. Ragan, "Dutch Police Takedown C&Cs Used by Grum Botnet," *Security Week*, July 17, 2012; P. Cohan, "FireEye: Silicon Valley's Hottest Security Start-up," *Forbes*, May 24, 2012; K. Higgins, "Microsoft Offers $250,000 for Rustock Botnet Operator Identity," *InformationWeek*, July 19, 2011; C. Stewart, "Botnet Busters," *Bloomberg BusinessWeek*, June 20–26, 2011; "Spammers Sought After Botnet Takedown," *BBC News*, March 25, 2011; M. Schwartz, "Microsoft, Feds Knock Rustock Botnet Offline," *InformationWeek*, March 18, 2011; www.fireeye.com, www.mandiant.com, accessed March 28, 2014.

Questions

1. Describe why it was so important for law enforcement officials to capture all 96 Rustock command servers at one time.

2. If the perpetrators of Rustock are ever caught, will it be possible to prove that they were responsible for the malware? Why or why not? Support your answer.

3. Mandiant has stated that it has no definitive proof that Chinese hackers are behind the numerous attacks on U.S. companies and government agencies. Is such proof even possible to obtain? Why or why not? Support your answer. If such proof were possible to obtain, would it matter? Why or why not? Support your answer.

4. Discuss the advantages for FireEye of purchasing Mandiant. Then, discuss the benefits that Mandiant obtained from the sale.

Anti-malware systems are generally reactive. Whereas firewalls filter network traffic according to categories of activities that are likely to cause problems, anti-malware systems filter traffic according to a database of specific problems. These systems create definitions, or signatures, of various types of malware and then update these signatures in their products. The anti-malware software then examines suspicious computer code to determine whether it matches a known signature. If the software identifies a match, then it removes the code. For this reason, organizations regularly update their malware definitions.

Because malware is such a serious problem, the leading vendors are rapidly developing anti-malware systems that function proactively as well as reactively. These systems evaluate behavior rather than relying entirely on signature matching. In theory, therefore, it is possible to catch malware before it can infect systems.

Whitelisting and Blacklisting. A report by the Yankee Group (www.yankeegroup .com), a technology research and consulting firm, stated that 99 percent of organizations had installed anti-malware systems, but 62 percent still suffered malware attacks. As we have seen, anti-malware systems are usually reactive, and malware continues to infect companies.

One solution to this problem is **whitelisting**. Whitelisting is a process in which a company identifies the software that it will allow to run on its computers. Whitelisting permits acceptable software to run, and it either prevents any other software from running or lets new software run only in a quarantine environment until the company can verify its validity.

Whereas whitelisting allows nothing to run unless it is on the whitelist, **blacklisting** allows everything to run unless it is on the blacklist. A blacklist, then, includes certain types of software that are not allowed to run in the company environment. For example, a company might blacklist peer-to-peer file sharing on its systems. In addition to software, people, devices, and Web sites can also be whitelisted and blacklisted.

Encryption. Organizations that do not have a secure channel for sending information use encryption to stop unauthorized eavesdroppers. **Encryption** is the process of converting an original message into a form that cannot be read by anyone except the intended receiver.

All encryption systems use a key, which is the code that scrambles and then decodes the messages. The majority of encryption systems use public-key encryption. **Public-key encryption**—also known as *asymmetric encryption*—uses two different keys: a public key and a private key (see FIGURE 7.4). The public key (locking key) and the private key (the unlocking key) are created simultaneously using the same mathematical formula or algorithm. Because the two keys are mathematically related, the data encrypted with one key can be decrypted by using the other key. The public key is publicly available in a directory that all parties can access. The private key is kept secret, never shared with anyone, and never sent across the Internet. In this system, if Hannah wants to send a message to Harrison, she first obtains Harrison's public key (locking key), which she uses to encrypt her message (put the message in the "two-lock box"). When Harrison receives Hannah's message, he uses his private key to decrypt it (open the box).

Although this arrangement is adequate for personal information, organizations that conduct business over the Internet require a more complex system. In these cases, a third party, called a **certificate authority**, acts as a trusted intermediary between the companies. The certificate authority issues digital certificates and verifies the integrity of the certificates. A **digital certificate** is an electronic document attached to a file that certifies that the file is from the organization it claims to be from and has not been modified from its original format. As you can see in FIGURE 7.5, Sony requests a digital certificate from VeriSign, a certificate authority, and it uses this certificate when it conducts business with Dell. Note that the digital certificate contains an identification number, the issuer, validity dates, and the requester's public key. For examples of certificate authorities, see www.entrust.com, www.verisign.com, www.cybertrust.com, www.secude.com, and www.thawte.com.

Virtual Private Networking. A **virtual private network** is a private network that uses a public network (usually the Internet) to connect users. VPNs essentially integrate the global connectivity of the Internet with the security of a private network and thereby extend the reach of the organization's networks. VPNs are called *virtual* because they have no separate physical existence. They use the public Internet as their infrastructure. They are created by using logins, encryption, and other techniques to enhance the user's **privacy**, which we defined in Chapter 6 as the right to be left alone and to be free of unreasonable personal intrusion.

VPNs have several advantages. First, they allow remote users to access the company network. Second, they provide flexibility. That is, mobile users can access the organization's network from properly configured remote

Courtesy of Brad Prince.

Figure 7.4 How public-key encryption works. (*Source:* Omnisec AG)

Figure 7.5 How digital certificates work. Sony and Dell, business partners, use a digital certificate from VeriSign for authentication.

devices. Third, organizations can impose their security policies through VPNs. For example, an organization may dictate that only corporate e-mail applications are available to users when they connect from unmanaged devices.

To provide secure transmissions, VPNs use a process called tunneling. **Tunneling** encrypts each data packet to be sent and places each encrypted packet inside another packet. In this manner, the packet can travel across the Internet with confidentiality, authentication, and integrity. FIGURE 7.6 illustrates a VPN and tunneling.

Transport Layer Security (TLS). **Transport layer security**, formerly called *secure socket layer*, is an encryption standard used for secure transactions such as credit card purchases and online banking. TLS encrypts and decrypts data between a Web server and a browser end to end.

TLS is indicated by a URL that begins with "https" rather than "http," and it often displays a small padlock icon in the browser's status bar. Using a padlock icon to indicate a secure connection and placing this icon in a browser's status bar are artifacts of specific browsers. Other browsers use different icons (e.g., a key that is either broken or whole). The important thing to remember is that browsers usually provide visual confirmation of a secure connection.

Employee Monitoring Systems. Many companies are taking a proactive approach to protecting their networks against what they view as one of their major security threats, namely, employee mistakes. These companies are implementing **employee monitoring systems**, which scrutinize their employees' computers, e-mail activities, and Internet surfing activities. These products are useful to identify employees who spend too much time surfing on the Internet for personal reasons, who visit questionable Web sites, or who download music illegally. Vendors that provide monitoring software include SpectorSoft (www.spectorsoft.com) and Websense (www.websense.com).

Business Continuity Planning

A basic security strategy for organizations is to be prepared for any eventuality. A critical element in any security system is a *business continuity plan*, also known as a *disaster recovery plan*.

Business continuity is the chain of events linking planning to protection and to recovery. The purpose of the business continuity plan is to provide guidance to people who keep the business operating after a disaster occurs. Employees use this plan to prepare for, react to, and recover from events that

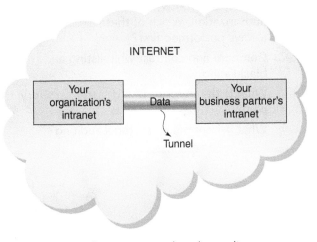

Figure 7.6 Virtual private network and tunneling.

affect the security of information assets. The objective is to restore the business to normal operations as quickly as possible following an attack. The plan is intended to ensure that critical business functions continue.

In the event of a major disaster, organizations can employ several strategies for business continuity. These strategies include hot sites, warm sites, and cold sites. A *hot site* is a fully configured computer facility with all of the company's services, communications links, and physical plant operations. A hot site duplicates computing resources, peripherals, telephone systems, applications, and workstations. A *warm site* provides many of the same services and options as the hot site. However, it typically does not include the actual applications the company needs. A warm site includes computing equipment such as servers, but it often does not include user workstations. A *cold site* provides only rudimentary services and facilities, such as a building or a room with heating, air conditioning, and humidity control. This type of site provides no computer hardware or user workstations.

Hot sites reduce risk to the greatest extent, but they are the most expensive option. Conversely, cold sites reduce risk the least, but they are the least expensive option.

Information Systems Auditing

Companies implement security controls to ensure that information systems function properly. These controls can be installed in the original system, or they can be added after a system is in operation. Installing controls is necessary but not sufficient to provide adequate security. In addition, people responsible for security need to answer questions such as: Are all controls installed as intended? Are they effective? Has any breach of security occurred? If so, what actions are required to prevent future breaches?

These questions must be answered by independent and unbiased observers. Such observers perform the task of *information systems auditing*. In an IS environment, an **audit** is an examination of information systems, their inputs, outputs, and processing.

Types of Auditors and Audits.

There are two types of auditors and audits: internal and external. IS auditing is usually a part of accounting *internal auditing*, and it is frequently performed by corporate internal auditors. An *external auditor* reviews the findings of the internal audit as well as the inputs, processing, and outputs of information systems. The external audit of information systems is frequently a part of the overall external auditing performed by a certified public accounting (CPA) firm.

IS auditing considers all of the potential hazards and controls in information systems. It focuses on issues such as operations, data integrity, software applications, security and privacy, budgets and expenditures, cost control, and productivity. Guidelines are available to assist auditors in their jobs, such as those from the Information Systems Audit and Control Association (www.isaca.org).

How Is Auditing Executed?

IS auditing procedures fall into three categories: (1) auditing around the computer, (2) auditing through the computer, and (3) auditing with the computer.

Auditing around the computer means verifying processing by checking for known outputs using specific inputs. This approach is most effective for systems with limited outputs. In *auditing through the computer*, auditors check inputs, outputs, and processing. They review program logic, and they test the data contained within the system. *Auditing with the computer* means using a combination of client data, auditor software, and client and auditor hardware. This approach enables the auditor to perform tasks such as simulating payroll program logic using live data.

BEFORE *YOU GO ON....*

1. What is the single most important information security control for organizations?

2. Differentiate between authentication and authorization. Which of these processes is always performed first?

3. Compare and contrast whitelisting and blacklisting.

4. What is the purpose of a disaster recovery plan?

5. What is information systems auditing?

Apply The Concept 7.5

LEARNING OBJECTIVE 7.5 Identify the three major types of controls that organizations can use to protect their information resources, and provide an example of each one.

STEP 1 – Background

Security controls are designed to protect all components of an information system, including data, software, hardware, and networks. Because there are so many diverse threats, organizations utilize layers of controls. One security feature discussed in this chapter is public-key encryption. This feature requires a public key and a private key. The public key is shared and is used to encrypt a message that only the individual's private key can decrypt.

STEP 2 – Activity

Visit http://www.wiley.com/go/rainer/MIS3e/applytheconcept, and click on the link provided for Apply the Concept 7.5. The link will take you to an article about the 2004 movie *National Treasure*. Watching the actual film is preferable, but you may not have access to it. For this activity, reading about it will suffice.

In this movie, Ben Gates (played by Nicholas Cage) steals one of our nation's most sacred documents—the Declaration of Independence. In the process, you see how the thief breaches all three of the major types of controls.

STEP 3 – Deliverable

Identify the three major types of controls that the National Archives employs—and that Gates ultimately penetrates—and provide examples of them from the movie. Prepare a document with the three types of controls and examples from the movie, and submit it to your instructor.

What's in for ME?

FOR THE ACCOUNTING MAJOR

Public companies, their accountants, and their auditors have significant information security responsibilities. Accountants are now being held professionally responsible for reducing risk, assuring compliance, eliminating fraud, and increasing the transparency of transactions according to Generally Accepted Accounting Principles (GAAP). The SEC and the Public Company Accounting Oversight Board (PCAOB), among other regulatory agencies, require information security, fraud prevention and detection, and internal controls over financial reporting. Forensic accounting, a combination of accounting and information security, is one of the most rapidly growing areas in accounting today.

FOR THE FINANCE MAJOR

Because information security is essential to the success of organizations today, it is no longer just the concern of the CIO. As a result of global regulatory requirements and the passage of Sarbanes–Oxley Act, responsibility for information security lies with the CEO and CFO. Consequently, all aspects of the security audit, including the security of information and information systems, are a key concern for financial managers.

In addition, CFOs and treasurers are increasingly involved with investments in information technology. They know that a security breach of any kind can have devastating financial effects on a company. Banking and financial institutions are prime targets for computer criminals. A related problem is fraud involving stocks and bonds that are sold over the Internet. Finance personnel must be aware of both the hazards and the available controls associated with these activities.

FOR THE MARKETING MAJOR

Marketing professionals have new opportunities to collect data on their customers, for example, through business-to-consumer electronic commerce. Customers expect their data to be properly secured. However, profit-motivated criminals want those data. Therefore, marketing managers must analyze the risk of their operations. Failure to protect corporate and customer data will cause significant public relations problems, make customers very angry, may lead to lawsuits, and may result in losing customers to competitors. CRM operations and tracking customers' online buying habits can expose data to misuse (if they are not encrypted) or result in privacy violations.

FOR THE PRODUCTION/ OPERATIONS MANAGEMENT MAJOR

Every process in a company's operations—inventory purchasing, receiving, quality control, production, and shipping—can be disrupted by an information technology security breach or an IT security breach at a business partner. Any weak link in supply chain management or enterprise resource management systems puts the entire chain at risk. Companies may be held liable for IT security failures that impact other companies.

FOR THE HUMAN RESOURCE MANAGEMENT MAJOR

HR managers have responsibilities to secure confidential employee data. In addition, they must ensure that all employees explicitly verify that they understand the company's information security policies and procedures.

FOR THE MIS MAJOR

The MIS function provides the security infrastructure that protects the organization's information assets. This function is critical to the success of the organization, even though it is almost invisible until an attack succeeds. All application development, network deployment, and introduction of new information technologies have to be guided by IT security considerations. MIS personnel must customize the risk exposure security model to help the company identify security risks and prepare responses to security incidents and disasters.

Senior executives of publicly held companies look to the MIS function for help in meeting Sarbanes–Oxley Act requirements, particularly in detecting "significant deficiencies" or "material weaknesses" in internal controls and remediating them. Other functional areas also look to the MIS function to help them meet their security responsibilities.

SUMMARY

1. Identify the five factors that contribute to the increasing vulnerability of information resources, and provide a specific example of each one.

   The five factors are the following:

   > Today's interconnected, interdependent, wirelessly networked business environment.

   >> *Example*: The Internet.

   > Smaller, faster, cheaper computers and storage devices.

   >> *Examples*: Netbooks, thumb drives, iPads.

   > Decreasing skills necessary to be a computer hacker.

   >> *Example*: Information system hacking programs circulating on the Internet.

   > International organized crime taking over cybercrime.

   >> *Example*: Organized crime has formed transnational cybercrime cartels. Because it is difficult to know exactly where cyberattacks originate, these cartels are extremely hard to bring to justice.

   > Lack of management support.

   >> *Example*: Suppose that your company spent $10 million on information security countermeasures last year, and they did not experience any successful attacks on their information resources. Short-sighted management might conclude that the company could spend less during the next year and obtain the same results. Bad idea.

2. Compare and contrast human mistakes and social engineering, and provide a specific example of each one.

   Human mistakes are unintentional errors. However, employees can also make unintentional mistakes as a result of actions by an attacker, such as social engineering. *Social engineering* is an attack where the perpetrator uses social skills to trick or manipulate a legitimate employee into providing confidential company information.

   An example of a human mistake is tailgating. An example of social engineering is when an attacker calls an employee on the phone and impersonates a superior in the company.

3. Discuss the 10 types of deliberate attacks.

   The 10 types of deliberate attacks are the following:

   Espionage or trespass occurs when an unauthorized individual attempts to gain illegal access to organizational information.

   Information extortion occurs when an attacker either threatens to steal, or actually steals, information from a company. The perpetrator demands payment for not stealing the information, for returning stolen information, or for agreeing not to disclose the information.

   Sabotage and vandalism are deliberate acts that involve defacing an organization's Web site, possibly causing the organization to lose its image and experience a loss of confidence by its customers.

   Theft of equipment and information is becoming a larger problem because computing devices and storage devices are becoming smaller yet more powerful with vastly increased storage, making these devices easier and more valuable to steal.

Identity theft is the deliberate assumption of another person's identity, usually to gain access to his or her financial information or to frame him or her for a crime.

Preventing *compromises to intellectual property* is a vital issue for people who make their livelihood in knowledge fields. Protecting intellectual property is particularly difficult when that property is in digital form.

Software attacks occur when malicious software penetrates an organization's computer system. Today, these attacks are typically profit-driven and Web-based.

Alien software is clandestine software that is installed on your computer through duplicitous methods. It typically is not as malicious as viruses, worms, or Trojan horses, but it does use up valuable system resources.

Supervisory control and data acquisition refers to a large-scale, distributed measurement and control system. SCADA systems are used to monitor or control chemical, physical, and transport processes. A *SCADA attack* attempts to compromise such a system in order to cause damage to the real-world processes that the system controls.

With both *cyberterrorism* and *cyberwarfare*, attackers use a target's computer systems, particularly via the Internet, to cause physical, real-world harm or severe disruption, usually to carry out a political agenda.

4. Define the three risk mitigation strategies, and provide an example of each one in the context of owning a home.

The three risk mitigation strategies are the following:

Risk acceptance, where the organization accepts the potential risk, continues operating with no controls, and absorbs any damages that occur. If you own a home, you may decide not to insure it. Thus, you are practicing risk acceptance. Clearly, this is a bad idea.

Risk limitation, where the organization limits the risk by implementing controls that minimize the impact of threats. As a homeowner, you practice risk limitation by putting in an alarm system or cutting down weak trees near your house.

Risk transference, where the organization transfers the risk by using other means to compensate for the loss, such as by purchasing insurance. The vast majority of homeowners practice risk transference by purchasing insurance on their houses and other possessions.

5. Identify the three major types of controls that organizations can use to protect their information resources, and provide an example of each one.

Physical controls prevent unauthorized individuals from gaining access to a company's facilities. Common physical controls include walls, doors, fencing, gates, locks, badges, guards, and alarm systems. More sophisticated physical controls include pressure sensors, temperature sensors, and motion detectors.

Access controls restrict unauthorized individuals from using information resources. These controls involve two major functions: authentication and authorization. Authentication confirms the identity of the person requiring access. An example is biometrics. After the person is authenticated (identified), the next step is authorization. Authorization determines which actions, rights, or privileges the person has, based on his or her verified identity. Authorization is generally based on least privilege.

Communications (network) controls secure the movement of data across networks. Communications controls consist of firewalls, anti-malware systems, whitelisting and blacklisting, encryption, virtual private networking, secure socket layer, and vulnerability management systems.

>>>CHAPTER GLOSSARY

access controls Controls that restrict unauthorized individuals from using information resources and are concerned with user identification.

adware Alien software designed to help pop-up advertisements appear on your screen.

alien software Clandestine software that is installed on your computer through duplicitous methods.

anti-malware systems (antivirus software) Software packages that attempt to identify and eliminate viruses, worms, and other malicious software.

audit An examination of information systems, their inputs, outputs, and processing.

authentication A process that determines the identity of the person requiring access.

authorization A process that determines which actions, rights, or privileges the person has, based on verified identity.

back door Typically a password, known only to the attacker, that allows the attacker to access the system without having to go through any security procedures.

biometrics The science and technology of authentication (i.e., establishing the identity of an individual) by measuring the subject's physiological or behavioral characteristics.

blacklisting A process in which a company identifies certain types of software that are not allowed to run in the company environment.

bot A computer that has been compromised by, and under the control of, a hacker.

botnet A network of computers that have been compromised by, and under control of, a hacker, who is called the botmaster.

business continuity The chain of events linking planning to protection and to recovery.

certificate authority A third party that acts as a trusted intermediary between computers (and companies) by issuing digital certificates and verifying the worth and integrity of the certificates.

communications controls (also **network controls**) Controls that deal with the movement of data across networks.

controls Defense mechanisms (also called *countermeasures*).

cookie Small amounts of information that Web sites store on your computer, temporarily or more or less permanently.

copyright A grant that provides the creator of intellectual property with ownership of it for a specified period of time, currently the life of the creator plus 70 years.

cybercrime Illegal activities executed on the Internet.

cyberterrorism Can be defined as a premeditated, politically motivated attack against information, computer systems, computer programs, and data that results in violence against noncombatant targets by subnational groups or clandestine agents.

cyberwarfare War in which a country's information systems could be paralyzed from a massive attack by destructive software.

demilitarized zone (DMZ) A separate organizational local area network that is located between an organization's internal network and an external network, usually the Internet.

denial-of-service attack A cyberattack in which an attacker sends a flood of data packets to the target computer, with the aim of overloading its resources.

digital certificate An electronic document attached to a file certifying that this file is from the organization it claims to be from and has not been modified from its original format or content.

distributed denial-of-service (DdoS) attack A denial-of-service attack that sends a flood of data packets from many compromised computers simultaneously.

employee monitoring systems Systems that monitor employees' computers, e-mail activities, and Internet surfing activities.

encryption The process of converting an original message into a form that cannot be read by anyone except the intended receiver.

exposure The harm, loss, or damage that can result if a threat compromises an information resource.

firewall A system (either hardware, software, or a combination of both) that prevents a specific type of information from moving between untrusted networks, such as the Internet, and private networks, such as your company's network.

identity theft Crime in which someone uses the personal information of others to create a false identity and then uses it for some fraud.

information security Protecting an organization's information and information systems from unauthorized access, use, disclosure, disruption, modification, or destruction.

intellectual property The intangible property created by individuals or corporations, which is protected under trade secret, patent, and copyright laws.

least privilege A principle that users be granted the privilege for some activity only if there is a justifiable need to grant this authorization.

logic bombs Segments of computer code embedded within an organization's existing computer programs.

malware Malicious software such as viruses and worms.

network controls See communications controls.

password A private combination of characters that only the user should know.

patent A document that grants the holder exclusive rights on an invention or process for a specified period of time, currently 20 years.

phishing attack An attack that uses deception to fraudulently acquire sensitive personal information by masquerading as an official-looking e-mail.

physical controls Controls that restrict unauthorized individuals from gaining access to a company's computer facilities.

piracy Copying a software program (other than freeware, demo software, etc.) without making payment to the owner.

privacy The right to be left alone and to be free of unreasonable personal intrusion.

privilege A collection of related computer system operations that can be performed by users of the system.

public-key encryption (also called *asymmetric encryption*) A type of encryption that uses two different keys, a public key and a private key.

risk The likelihood that a threat will occur.

risk acceptance A strategy in which the organization accepts the potential risk, continues to operate with no controls, and absorbs any damages that occur.

risk analysis The process by which an organization assesses the value of each asset being protected, estimates the probability that each asset might be compromised, and compares the probable costs of each being compromised with the costs of protecting it.

risk limitation A strategy in which the organization limits its risk by implementing controls that minimize the impact of a threat.

risk management A process that identifies, controls, and minimizes the impact of threats, in an effort to reduce risk to manageable levels.

risk mitigation A process whereby the organization takes concrete actions against risks, such as implementing controls and developing a disaster recovery plan.

risk transference A process in which the organization transfers the risk by using other means to compensate for a loss, such as by purchasing insurance.

secure socket layer (SSL) (also known as **transport layer security**) An encryption standard used for secure transactions such as credit card purchases and online banking.

security The degree of protection against criminal activity, danger, damage, and/or loss.

social engineering Getting around security systems by tricking computer users inside a company into revealing sensitive information or gaining unauthorized access privileges.

spam Unsolicited e-mail.

spamware Alien software that uses your computer as a launch platform for spammers.

spyware Alien software that can record your keystrokes and/or capture your passwords.

threat Any danger to which an information resource may be exposed.

trade secret Intellectual work, such as a business plan, that is a company secret and is not based on public information.

transport layer security (TLS) See **secure socket layer**.

trap doors See **back door**.

Trojan horse A software program containing a hidden function that presents a security risk.

tunneling A process that encrypts each data packet to be sent and places each encrypted packet inside another packet.

virtual private network (VPN) A private network that uses a public network (usually the Internet) to securely connect users by using encryption.

viruses Malicious software that can attach itself to (or "infect") other computer programs without the owner of the program being aware of the infection.

vulnerability The possibility that an information resource will be harmed by a threat.

whitelisting A process in which a company identifies acceptable software and permits it to run, and either prevents anything else from running or lets new software run in a quarantined environment until the company can verify its validity.

worms Destructive programs that replicate themselves without requiring another program to provide a safe environment for replication.

zombie computer See **bot**.

>>>DISCUSSION QUESTIONS

1. Why are computer systems so vulnerable?

2. Why should information security be a prime concern to management?

3. Is security a technical issue? A business issue? Both? Support your answer. (*Hint*: Read Kim Nash, "Why Technology Isn't the Answer to Better Security," *CIO* (www.cio.com), October 15, 2008.)

4. Compare information security in an organization with insuring a house.

5. Why are authentication and authorization important to e-commerce?

6. Why is cross-border cybercrime expanding rapidly? Discuss possible solutions.

7. Discuss why the Sarbanes–Oxley Act is having an impact on information security.

8. What types of user authentication are used at your university and/or place of work? Do these measures seem to be effective? What if a higher level of authentication were implemented? Would it be worth it, or would it decrease productivity?

9. Why are federal authorities so worried about SCADA attacks?

>>>PROBLEM-SOLVING ACTIVITIES

1. A critical problem is assessing how far a company is legally obligated to go in order to secure personal data. Because there is no such thing as perfect security (i.e., there is always more that you can do), resolving this question can significantly affect cost.

   a. When are security measures that a company implements sufficient to comply with its obligations?

   b. Is there any way for a company to know if its security measures are sufficient? Can you devise a method for any organization to determine if its security measures are sufficient?

2. Assume that the daily probability of a major earthquake in Los Angeles is 0.07 percent. The chance that your computer center will be damaged during such a quake is 5 percent. If the center is damaged, the estimated damage to the computer center will be $4.0 million.

   a. Calculate the expected loss in dollars.

   b. An insurance agent is willing to insure your facility for an annual fee of $25,000. Analyze the offer, and discuss whether to accept it.

3. Enter www.scambusters.org. Find out what the organization does. Learn about e-mail scams and Web site scams. Report your findings.

4. Visit www.dhs.gov/dhspublic (Department of Homeland Security). Search the site for "National Strategy to Secure Cyberspace" and write a report on their agenda and accomplishments to date.

5. Enter www.alltrustnetworks.com and other vendors of biometrics. Find the devices they make that can be used to control access into information systems. Prepare a list of products and major capabilities of each vendor.

6. Software piracy is a global problem. Access the following Web sites: www.bsa.org and www.microsoft.com/piracy/. What can organizations do to mitigate this problem? Are some organizations dealing with the problem better than others?

7. Investigate the Sony PlayStation Network hack that occurred in April 2011.

   a. What type of attack was it?

   b. Was the success of the attack due to technology problems at Sony, management problems at Sony, or a combination of both? Provide specific examples to support your answer.

   c. Which Sony controls failed?

   d. Could the hack have been prevented? If so, how?

   e. Discuss Sony's response to the hack.

   f. Describe the damages that Sony incurred from the hack.

STEP 1 – Background

This chapter has highlighted the importance of information security. The "What's in IT for Me?" section explained how each functional area must contribute to security maintenance.

STEP 2 – Activity

Divide your team into functional areas. Assign one person to each of the following areas: vice president of accounting, vice president of finance, vice president of human resources, and vice president of production. Imagine that your chief executive officer (CEO) is having a hard time understanding why you need to invest in a chief information officer (CIO) to oversee your information systems. Right now each department is doing its own thing and managing its own systems.

Everyone needs help and direction from an expert, and the vice presidents have agreed that you need a CIO.

STEP 3 – Deliverable

Create and share a Google document with your team. Write an executive summary that accompanies an "imaginary" (meaning you don't have to write this part) full report. The imaginary report should include a full description of how the CIO would help each functional area. Therefore, the executive summary will include the highlights of what this position would mean to each team member. Have each team member research from his or her perspective why you need a CIO to help maintain information security. Finally, submit your executive summary to your professor. For help formatting your executive summary, search Google for "Executive Summary Template." You will find many examples there to help you.

CLOSING **CASE 1** > Lessons

Learned from the Data Breach at Target

THE BUSINESS PROBLEM >>> Target Corporation (Target; www.target.com), a U.S. retailing company, is the nation's second-largest discount retailer, after Walmart. In late 2013, Target disclosed that it had been the victim of a massive data breach. The breach has been compared with the 2009 non-retail Heartland Payment Systems breach, which affected 130 million card holders, and with the 2007 retail TJX Companies breach, which affected 90 million card holders.

Let's take a closer look at the attack. Just prior to Thanksgiving 2013, an unknown individual or group installed malware (malicious software) in Target's security and payments system. The malware was designed to steal every credit card used at the company's nearly 1,800 U.S. stores.

Amazingly, Target was prepared for the attack. Six months prior to Thanksgiving, the company had installed a malware detection tool manufactured by the computer security firm FireEye (www.fireeye.com; see IT's About Business 7.3). In addition, Target had assembled a team of security specialists in Bangalore to monitor its computers around the clock. If Bangalore noticed anything suspicious, they would notify Target's security operations center in Minneapolis, Minnesota.

Around Thanksgiving, Target's antivirus system, Symantec Endpoint Protection (www.symantec.com), identified suspicious behavior over several days. Target ignored the system's warnings.

On November 30, 2013, the attackers loaded malware to transfer stolen credit card numbers—first to staging points (computers) around the United States to cover their tracks, then into their computers in Russia. FireEye spotted the attackers and alerted Bangalore. In turn, Bangalore alerted the Target security team in Minneapolis. And … nothing happened. For some reason, Minneapolis did not respond to the alert. Even worse, the FireEye system includes an option to automatically delete malware as it is detected. Target's security team had turned off the option.

On December 18, 2013, security expert Brian Krebs (see IT's About Business 8.1 in Chapter 8) broke the news that Target was investigating a major data breach. His report quickly spread across news channels. On December 19, Target confirmed the incident via a press release, revealing that the attack took place between November 27 and December 15. Target warned that up to 40 million consumer credit and debit cards may have been compromised. The attackers gained access to customer names, card numbers, expiration dates, and card security codes (also called card verification codes) of the cards issued by financial institutions.

On December 27, Target disclosed that debit card PIN data had also been stolen in encrypted form, reversing a previous assertion that PIN data were not included in the breach. On January 10, 2014, Target further announced that the names, mailing addresses, phone numbers, and/or e-mail addresses of up to 70 million additional people had also been stolen, raising the possible number of customers affected to 110 million.

The attackers sent 11 gigabytes of data to a Moscow-based hosting service called vpsville.ru. A Target spokesman defended the company by arguing it has too many clients to monitor all of them effectively.

Investigators from the U.S. Secret Service, the agency leading the government's investigation into the Target breach, visited the offices of Fazio Mechanical Services (www.faziomechanical.com), a refrigeration and HVAC (heating, ventilation, and air conditioning) systems provider. The investigators believe that Target's attackers first accessed the retailer's network on November 15, 2013, using access credentials they had stolen from Fazio in a phishing attack. The attackers then used those credentials to access Target's payment processing and point-of-sale (POS) systems. (It is important to note that as of mid-2014, none of these points have been proved, as the investigation is ongoing.)

Significantly, Fazio purportedly used a free version of an antivirus software product called Malwarebytes (www.malwarebytes.com) for protection. Significantly, the free version is intended for consumer use only. Therefore, if Fazio had used this version, then the company would be in violation of Malwarebytes' license. Further, the free version of Malwarebytes does not provide real-time scanning of files for malware, meaning that free antivirus software is not an industry best practice. Fazio responded that "our IT system and security measures are in full compliance with industry practices."

Fazio had access to Target's network because Target relies on HVAC systems with IP addresses that can be remotely monitored and adjusted by Fazio to manage store environments. (*Note:* This practice is standard for retailers, supermarkets, and similar businesses.)

Target's system, like any standard corporate network, is segmented so that the most sensitive areas—including customer payments and personal data—are walled off from other parts of the network, particularly the Internet. Clearly, Target's internal walls had holes. As a result, the attackers could proceed from the part of the network that its vendors could access to more sensitive parts of the network where customer data were located.

Questions involving the Target breach focused on the security processes in place at Fazio, as well as the controls in place at Target. Target is liable, per Payment Card Industry Data Security Standards (PCI-DSS), for any of its third-party contractors' security faults. Notably, PCI-DSS requires that merchants "incorporate two-factor authentication for remote access to the network by employees, administrators, and third parties."

However, one challenge when granting remote access to a third party (e.g., a contractor) is that multiple employees of that contractor may have access to those credentials. For example, a contractor may have many technicians who require access on a revolving basis.

Among the most pertinent questions regarding the Target attack are the following:

- Did Target secure Fazio's access to its network using two-factor authentication?
- What level of network access did Target grant to Fazio?
- Was Target actively monitoring Fazio's access?
- Were Target's HVAC appliances located on an isolated network segment that should have prevented attackers from accessing other network systems?

TARGET'S RESPONSE >>>

Target encouraged customers who shopped at its U.S. stores (online orders were not affected) during the specified time frame to closely monitor their credit and debit cards for irregular activity. The retailer is also cooperating with law enforcement, including the Secret Service, to bring the responsible parties to justice.

Gregg Steinhafel, Target's CEO, apologized to the retailer's customers in a press release. As a further apology to the public, all Target stores in the United States awarded retail shoppers a 10 percent storewide discount for the weekend of December 21–22, 2013. Finally, Target offered free credit monitoring via Experian to affected customers.

THE RESULTS FROM THE BREACH >>>

Security analysts at the technology research firm Gartner (www.gartner.com) estimated that the cost of the breach will eventually exceed $1 billion. These costs include paying card networks to cover losses and expenses in reissuing cards, lawsuits, government investigations, and enforcement proceedings. As of mid-2014, more than 90 lawsuits had been filed against Target by customers and banks that issued the credit cards for negligence and compensatory damages. Target's net income for the fourth quarter of 2013 fell 46 percent.

Target also announced that it was implementing encrypted "chip and PIN" credit card technology, to be completed by the first quarter of 2015. The retailer will reissue its store credit cards with this technology, and it plans to deploy new card readers in all of its U.S. stores.

On March 6, 2014, Target announced the resignation of its chief information officer and an overhaul of the company's information security practices. In a further step to restore customer faith, the retailer announced it would search outside the company for a new CIO. Target also announced an external search for a newly created position, chief compliance officer.

On May 5, 2014, Target announced the resignation of its CEO, Gregg Steinhafel. He was with the company for 35 years.

Ultimately, the really unfortunate finding from the Target breach is that if the company's security team had responded appropriately when it was supposed to, the theft never would have occurred.

Sources: Compiled from M. Schwartz, "Target Ignored Data Breach Alarms," *InformationWeek*, March 14, 2014; M. Riley, B. Elgin, D. Lawrence, and C. Matlack, "The Epic Hack," *Bloomberg BusinessWeek*, March 13, 2014; A. Shrivastava and M. Thomas, "Target Announces Technology Overhaul, CIO Departure," *Reuters*, March 5, 2014; B. Horovitz, "Breach Takes Toll on Target," *USA Today*, February 27, 2014; E. Harris, "Data Breach Hurts Profit at Target," *The New York Times*, February 27, 2014; J. Pagliery, "Why Retailers Aren't Protecting You from Hackers," *CNN Money*, February 18, 2014; A. Gonsalves, "Experts Question Security Used in Target Breach," *CSO Online*, February 13, 2014; M. Schwartz, "Target Breach: Phishing Attack Implicated," *InformationWeek*, February 13, 2014; L. MacVittie, "Target Breach Takeaway: Secure Your Remote Access," *InformationWeek*, February 10, 2014; M. Schwartz, "Target Breach: HVAC Contractor Systems Investigated," *InformationWeek*, February 6, 2014; D. Leger, "Target to Rush Card Chip Security," *USA Today*, February 5, 2014; H. Stout, "Target Vows to Speed Anti-Fraud Technology," *The New York Times*, February 5, 2014; E. Harris, N. Periroth, and N. Popper, "Neiman Marcus Data Breach Worse than First Said," *The New York Times*, January 24, 2014; M. Feibus, "A Tale of Two Cyberheists," *InformationWeek*, January 22, 2014; "Why the Target Data Hack Is Just the Beginning," *Bloomberg BusinessWeek*, January 16, 2014; M. Schwartz, "Target Breach: 8 Facts on Memory-Scraping Malware," *InformationWeek*, January 14, 2014; A. d'Innocenzio and M. Chapman, "Target: Breach Affected Millions More Customers," *Associated Press*, January 10, 2014; P. McNamara, "Target Confesses: Breach Victim Total

Soars to 70 Million," *Network World*, January 10, 2014; D. Goldman, "Target Confirms PIN Data Was Stolen in Breach," *CNN Money*, December 27, 2013; C. Woodyard, "Target Offers 10% Off as Credit Fraud Apology," *USA Today*, December 22, 2013; J. Ribeiro, "Target Says 40 Million Cards Likely Skimmed in Security Breach," *Network World*, December 19, 2013; "Target Confirms Unauthorized Access to Payment Card Data in U.S. Stores," *Target Pressroom*, December 19, 2013; B. Krebs, "Sources: Target Investigating Data Breach," *Krebs on Security*, December 18, 2013; www.target.com, www.krebsonsecurity.com, accessed March 10, 2014.

Questions

1. Describe the flaws in Target's security system that enabled the breach.

2. Was Target's response to the breach appropriate? Why or why not?

3. What should you do as a consumer to protect yourself against losing your personal data from establishments where you shop?

CLOSING **CASE 2** > A Startup Develops a New Process for Multifactor Authentication

THE PROBLEM >>> We bank online, track our finances online, fill out our tax returns online, and store our photos, our documents, and our data online. As a result, the amount of personal information being stored online has exploded. Further, we typically link our various online accounts, using our e-mail addresses as universal usernames, a problem that becomes worse as the number of our online accounts increases. The combination of our e-mail address as username with a password creates a single point of failure that can be exploited with devastating results.

How did this problem start? Companies that conduct business over the Internet had to devise a method to make people feel secure about conducting online transactions and storing personal information on merchants' Web sites. To function in the real world, the security systems provided by online merchants must effectively manage the trade-off between convenience and security. The most secure system is useless if it is too difficult for users to access. For example, if the merchant requires customer passwords to be 50 characters in length and to include special symbols, these passwords might keep their customers' accounts safe, but they would be impossible to remember.

We have all bought into the idea that a password is sufficient to protect all of our data, as long as it is sufficiently elaborate. In reality, however, passwords by themselves can no longer protect us, regardless of how unique or complex we make them.

Attackers can employ a number of strategies to obtain our passwords, no matter how strong they are. Among the most common methods are the following:

- Attackers can steal them. User carelessness is the greatest security risk of all. Therefore, the most basic hacking method is simply to guess correctly. Despite years of being told not to, people still use weak, predictable passwords such as birthdays.

- They can crack them. With modern computers, cracking passwords utilizing brute-force computation takes just a few seconds. The software simply tries every possible combination of letters, numbers, and special characters until it

discovers the password.

- They can obtain them online. Since 2011, hackers have dumped more than 280 million "hashes"—that is, encrypted but readily crackable passwords—online for everyone to see.

- They can discover them through phishing and spear phishing attacks.

- They can employ hidden malware that secretly sends your data to other people. For example, keylogger software captures every keystroke you type.

The ultimate problem with passwords is that they are a single point of failure, subject to many types of attacks. It is impossible for any password-based security system to be memorable enough to allow mobile logins, flexible enough to vary from Web site to Web site, convenient enough to be easily reset, and yet also secure against brute-force hacking. So, what are users and businesses supposed to do?

A VARIETY OF POTENTIAL SOLUTIONS >>> Several initiatives are underway to improve the authentication process. For instance, security startup Nok Nok Labs (www.noknok.com) has designed a new protocol to help clients make certain that end users are who they say they are. Although this solution is not perfectly secure, it is considerably more secure than usernames and alphanumeric passwords.

Nok Nok's objective is to revolutionize online authentication with tools that already exist on user devices, such as a camera, a touchscreen, and a microphone. The company's software allows customers to store both their login data and their biometric data—voice, facial features, and fingerprints—on their personal computers, smartphones, and tablets.

Companies can sign up for the Nok Nok protocol, which offers individual users the option of using these authentication methods on their devices instead of a password. When the user provides a valid match, his or her device connects securely to the desired Web site. This process provides strong multifactor authentication. Hackers looking to compromise such a system would need to steal a user's device, as well as his or her finger and eye.

The Nok Nok protocol offers many security advantages. For example, the strong authentication process will be effective as more companies allow employees to access data on public clouds from their mobile devices. In addition, if an employee accidentally leaves a tablet on an airplane, it would be nearly impossible for the person who finds to replicate the owner's voice or fingerprints. This enhanced protection could prevent a security breach.

Additional initiatives are being developed under the auspices of the Fast Identity Online (FIDO) Alliance to "kill the password." The concept underlying all of these products is that identifiers such as a person's fingerprint, iris scan, and the unique identifier of any USB device or contactless ring will not be sent over the Internet. Rather, they will be checked locally. The only data that will be transferred over the Internet are cryptographic keys that cannot be reverse-engineered to steal a person's identify. Let's consider a few examples:

- Synaptics (www.synaptics.com) manufactures fingerprint readers that are embedded in some business laptops and the HTC One Max smartphone. The company also makes compact sensors that capture a fingerprint with a tap. These sensors can also be integrated into a button, such as the button in Apple's 5S iPhone.
- Bionym (www.bionym.com) manufactures a wristband called the Nymi that verifies phone users' identity by the unique signals generated by their heartbeat.
- Eyelock (www.eyelock.com) manufactures the Myris, a device that scans your eyes to allow you to access your computer and online accounts. To use this device, you stare into the small mirror on its underside for 15 seconds, during which time an infrared video camera captures 240 identification points in each iris. On the basis of the individual signature that it detects, the software can enter passwords into Web sites or unlock a computer.
- Yubico (www.yubico.com) manufactures the YubiKey Neo, an authentication device similar to flash drive. The Neo works when you insert it into a USB port or you tap it against a mobile device when you need to log into an app or a Web service.
- The NFC Ring (http://nfcring.com) and the Google ring are rings that you wear. They contain contactless RFID technology that can automatically unlock an NFC-capable phone when a person picks it up. In addition, they can operate other RFID devices such as door locks.

THE RESULTS >>> In the future, online identity verification will no longer be a password-based system. Instead, the password, if used at all, will be a less significant component of a multifactor process. Each online account will have to integrate many pieces of information: who we are and what we do; where we go and when; what we have with us; and how

we act when we are there—true multifactor authentication. Biometrics will undoubtedly play an important role in future authentication systems.

Of course, as measures such as these are implemented, future security systems will require significant sacrifices to our privacy. These systems will need to draw upon our location and habits, and perhaps even our speech patterns or our DNA. The only path to improved security is to allow our movements to be tracked in all sorts of ways and to have those movements and metrics tied to our actual identity. This shift will involve significant investments and inconvenience. Also, it will likely raise concerns among privacy advocates.

Sources: Compiled from M. Dickey, "This Startup Lets You Use Your Heartbeat as a Password, and It's Awesome," *Business Insider*, January 9, 2014; T. Simonite, "CES 2014: A Technological Assault on the Password," *MIT Technology Review*, January 8, 2014; M. Flores, "Eyelock's Myris: You'll Never Have to Enter Another Password Again," *Tech Radar*, January 7, 2014; "FPC and Nok Nok Labs Deliver Infrastructure for Fingerprint-Based Strong Authentication," *PR Newswire*, November 26, 2013; M. Flacy, "NFC Ring Can Unlock Your Smartphone or Front Door," *Digital Trends*, August 8, 2013; M. Kelly, "Nok Nok Labs Improving Two-Factor Authentication with $4 M in Debt Financing," *VentureBeat*, June 18, 2013; O. Kharif, "An End to the Traditional Password," *Bloomberg BusinessWeek*, April 1–7, 2013; K. Hill, "Google Ordered to Teach America How to Put Passwords on Wi-Fi Networks," *Forbes*, March 13, 2013; R. Metz, "A Password You Wear on Your Wrist," *MIT Technology Review*, February 27, 2013; T. Simonite, "PayPal, Lenovo Launch New Campaign to Kill the Password," *MIT Technology Review*, February 12, 2013; J. Daly, "Passwords, Security, and the Future of Authentication," *EdTech Magazine*, February 11, 2013; C. Albanesius, "Sony Fined 250,000 British Pounds Over Playstation Hack," *PC Magazine*, January 24, 2013; R. Greenfield, "What the Future Without Passwords Will Look Like," *Yahoo! News*, January 22, 2013; M. Honan, "Kill the Password," *Wired*, December 2012; R. Metz, "Instead of a Password, Security Software Just Checks Your Eyes," *MIT Technology Review*, December 3, 2012; www.noknok.com, accessed March 27, 2014.

Questions

1. What are the advantages, if any, of the Nok Nok process over strong passwords?

2. Examine the strength of the passwords that you use. How vulnerable are your passwords to guessing? To brute-force hacking?

3. Does the security burden fall primarily on the user? On the company that the user is doing business with? On both? Support your answer.

4. Is it possible to ever have complete security in your online transactions? Why or why not? Explain your answer.

INTERNSHIP ACTIVITY> 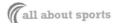 all about sports

Industry: Retail

Customer relationship management (CRM) tools are vital for successful businesses. You will learn more about these tools in Chapter 12. For now, you simply need to know that they maintain massive amounts of data on customers, purchases, preferences, and products. All of these data need to be kept secure.

For this activity you will be working for Hannah Shaw, Marketing Director for All About Sports, a regional sporting goods retailer. Having chosen salesforce.com as their CRM tool, All About Sports has set out to create a unique experience for customers. The company can now maintain a complete customer profile that includes the ages and gender of their children (based on the sizes of athletic wear purchased), the sports the children are engaged in (based on product purchases), spontaneous purchases (do they buy candy when they come in for baseballs?), outside team affiliations (do they wear and buy Atlanta Braves' memorabilia?), and more. All of this information is rather private, especially when it concerns children. Parents might be a bit unnerved if they realized how much All About Sports knew about their family habits!

Below is a letter from Hannah with the details of what she needs from this project.

To:	IT Intern
From:	Hannah Shaw
Subject:	Help reviewing Security Policies

Hi!

We at All About Sports have recently chosen salesforce.com as our CRM tool. Our goal is to create a unique experience for our customers. I am very concerned, however, about maintaining the privacy of our customers' information, especially information about their children.

To help me out, I would like you to review a fairly recent framework published by the U.S. government. It is called the *Framework for Improving Critical Infrastructure Cybersecurity*, and it can be found by searching for that title. I believe Section 3.0 of this document describes "How to Use the Framework." This section provides specific suggestions concerning the actions I would need to take both electronically and physically to secure my customers' information.

Read over this document, and prepare a summary for me. Don't copy and paste it—I can read the entire document myself if I want to. Let me know how I should proceed to ensure that my relationship with salesforce.com will be secure and well designed for my customers.

Thanks so much!
Hannah

Note: All links mentioned in this letter are available at http://www.wiley.com/go/rainer/MIS3e/internship.

SPREADSHEET ACTIVITY > LOGICAL FUNCTIONS

STEP 1 – Background

Logical functions allow users to build arguments into their spreadsheets so that the formula will evaluate information and provide a logical response. Excel offers seven logical functions in particular that you should be aware of. Four of them are defined below.

1. IF: Performs a prescribed action based on the outcome of a logical test.
2. IFERROR: Returns an ERROR if the outcome of a logical test is outside the specified margins. Otherwise, it leaves the outcome.
3. AND: Checks multiple criteria and returns TRUE if all prescribed arguments are true, or FALSE if any of the criteria are not true.
4. OR: Checks multiple criteria and returns TRUE if any of the criteria are true.

STEP 2 – Activity

Several business scenarios use logical functions. Banks, for example, employ many logical considerations when they consider whether to loan money to a customer.

Tommy is a loan officer at his bank. He becomes very frustrated when the committee meets to discuss weekly loan applications and they do not have all of the necessary paperwork. There are also a few items that need to be predetermined based on their numbers. For example, even though no application can be reviewed until it is complete, no one checks the application prior to the meeting. Additionally, if someone has filed for bankruptcy within the past six months or has been denied a loan within the past two weeks, then the bank will not consider the application. Finally, if an applicant has satisfied these requirements, then the committee pre-approves the loan for final consideration. Although you could check all of these factors by hand, having a computer program perform most of this analysis before the meeting would save everyone on the committee time.

The AND function can help determine whether the application is complete, and the OR function can determine whether someone either has filed for bankruptcy or has been denied a loan. The IF function can determine whether the average credit score is a reliable descriptive measure by assessing whether any of the other requirements disqualify the applicant. Finally, the AND statement can also be used to determine an applicant's status.

STEP 3 – Deliverable

Visit http://www.wiley.com/go/rainer/MIS3e/spreadsheet, and download a spreadsheet that summarizes all of the loan applications that Tommy dealt with the previous week. The workbook contains instructions to guide you in helping Tommy write the appropriate formulas to provide his committee with all of the information they need.

Follow the instructions in the spreadsheet and submit your final work to your instructor.

Additional help with this spreadsheet skill is available in WileyPLUS. Open the "Microsoft Office 2013 Lab Manual Spreadsheet Module: Excel 2013," and review Lesson 10: the IF Function. The AND and OR functions use a similar logic to the IF function.

DATABASE ACTIVITY > FORMS

STEP 1 – Background

In this activity, you will learn how to view and enter new data using forms that select columns of interest from one or more related tables. So far we have entered all of our data directly into our tables, and we have looked at most of the data in tables (except for reports). We opened tables in Datasheet view, selected a row, and either keyed in the data or examined them. However, working with one table at a time is not ideal, for two major reasons:

1. To understand information in a meaningful way, you frequently need to examine more than one table.
2. A table may contain hundreds of columns, and most likely you will not need to examine all of them at the same time.

Using forms solves both of these problems, as this activity will demonstrate.

STEP 2 – Activity

Visit http://www.wiley.com/go/rainer/MIS3e/database, and download the database linked for the Chapter 7 activity. This database contains three tables: members, photos, and comments. Each comment was created by a member, and it concerns a photo posted by a member. (The members may be the same—that is, a member may comment on his or her own photo.) Open the relationship map, found under the Database Tools ribbon tab, to see how they are related.

1. From the Member Table, create a form that will allow you to input new member information.

(*Hint*: Use Form Wizard under the Create ribbon.) Save this form as "newmemberform," and then open it. Enter yourself as a new member with the current date as the date of joining the club.

2. Using the Photo Table and the Member Table, create a form that displays all of an individual member's photos. Save this form as "photosbymember." Test your form by submitting a new photo for one user. Then, view that user's information to see whether your new photo is displayed. (Database Activity 7 does not contain actual photos, just photo metadata, so you will see a photo only after you submit one with the form.)

3. Use the Photo Table, Member Table, and Comments Table to create a form that shows comments along with member photos. To accomplish this task, you need to create a subform that displays both photos and comments. You then embed this subform into the primary form to display members, photos, and comments in a single form. Save this form as "photocommentsbymember."

STEP 3 – Deliverable

Submit your completed database with all of the forms to your professor.

Additional help with this database skill is available in WileyPLUS. Open the "Microsoft Office 2013 Lab Manual Database Module: Access 2013," and review Lesson 5: Editing Records.

CHAPTER 8

Social Computing

LEARNING OBJECTIVES >>>

8.1 Describe six Web 2.0 tools and two major types of Web 2.0 sites.

8.2 Describe the benefits and risks of social commerce to companies.

8.3 Identify the methods used for shopping socially.

8.4 Discuss innovative ways to use social networking sites for advertising and market research.

8.5 Describe how social computing improves customer service.

8.6 Discuss different ways in which human resource managers make use of social computing.

OPENING CASE > Disappearing Images

A generation of young people are beginning to recognize the potential dangers associated with social media. The Web is a scary place, where every mistake becomes permanent. For instance, college administrators review prospective students' social media profiles before admitting them. Similarly, potential employers view the tangible evidence of youthful indiscretions committed by recent graduates.

Disappearing photo-sending service Snapchat (www.snapchat.com) wants to tap into these fears. Snapchat's signature feature allows users to take photos, record videos, add text and drawings, and then send these files to a controlled list of recipients. These photos and videos are known as "Snaps." Users set a time limit for how long recipients can view their Snaps (as of mid-2014, the range was 1–10 seconds). After the time limit expires, the Snaps are hidden from the recipient's device and deleted from Snapchat's servers. Just as e-mail revolutionized the way people "talk" to one another at work and Twitter is transforming the way people broadcast information, Snapchat has become the "language" of a younger generation.

© Antonio_Diaz/iStockphoto

Snapchat began to catch on in 2011. The first users were Orange County (Los Angeles area) high school students who had learned about the app from one of the founder's cousins. From those humble beginnings, Snapchat has mushroomed into a giant service with tens of millions of users, who send as many as 400 million Snaps per day. And, it continues to grow.

Early on, Snapchat caught the attention of Mark Zuckerberg, CEO of Facebook. Facebook initially responded by experimenting with a copycat feature called "Poke," but the effort failed. Subsequently, in the fall of 2013, Zuckerberg tried to purchase Snapchat for $3 billion. Snapchat's founders, however, refused to sell. Shortly thereafter, Google offered $4 billion. Again, the founders declined the offer.

In October 2013, Snapchat introduced a new feature called "Snapchat Stories" in which photos do not immediately disappear. Users and their friends can use Stories to build "chains" of photos, which are basically a digital photo album that is available to all of their contacts for 24 hours. Stories represent an evolution for Snapchat, offering users slightly less privacy and urgency, while moving toward the kind of product that marketers would find appealing. As of mid-2014, the response to Stories had been tepid.

Thus far only a few marketers are running tests on Snapchat. Taco Bell (www.tacobell.com), for instance, used Snapchat in May 2013 to distribute photos of its new Beefy Crunch Burrito, and it publicized its photo campaign on Twitter. Other companies that are trying Snapchat include Web retailer Kamaloop (www.kamaloop.com) and 16 Handles (http://16handles.com), a New York frozen yogurt chain.

The "disappearing" nature of transactions on Snapchat, which is the essence of its service, is a huge negative to marketers, who want to monitor and track customers' every move. To survive, Snapchat must persuade **MKT** marketers that the benefits of reaching its coveted youth audience outweigh the relative anonymity of that audience. One chief marketing officer put it this way: How does Snapchat, which collects no data on its users, sell itself to marketers?

Of course, there are other ways for Snapchat to make money. Game publishers have used messaging platforms in Asia, including Chinese online giant Tencente's WeChat (www.wechat.com), to publicize their games and to allow users to share their experiences. Snapchat could perform a similar function. After building a larger user base, Snapchat could also experiment with premium services, such as storing photos.

Snapchat suffered a setback of sorts when it was hacked on December 31, 2013. The breach revealed parts of approximately 4.6 million user names and phone numbers. In January 2014, Snapchat responded by releasing an updated version of its application that would let users opt out of the "Find Friends" feature, which required users to store their phone numbers so that other users could easily locate them.

Sources: Compiled from R. Bushey, "Snapchat Finally Apologizes after 4.6 Million User Phone Numbers Leak – Here's How to Make Sure It Doesn't Happen Again," *Business Insider*, January 9, 2014; R. Lawler, "Snapchat Acknowledges Hack, Updated App Coming That Lets Users Opt-Out of Find Friends," *Engadget*, January 2, 2014; M. Peckham, "How to Survive the Snapchat Hack (and Others)," *Time*, January 2, 2014; J. Leyden, "Snapchat: In 'Theory' You Could Hack. . . . Oh CRAP Is That 4.6 MILLION Users' Details?" *The Register*, January 2, 2014; J. Hempel and A. Lashinsky, "Countdown to the Snapchat Revolution," *Fortune*, December 18, 2013; J. Kleinman, "Snapchat Allegedly Rejected $4B Buyout Offer from Google," *TechnoBuffalo*, November 15, 2013; E. Rusli and D. MacMillan, "Snapchat Spurned $3B Acquisition Offer from Facebook," *The Wall Street Journal*, November 13, 2013; A. Holpuch, "Snapchat Admits to Handing Unopened 'Snaps' to U.S. Law Enforcement, *The Guardian*, October 15, 2013; D. Etherington, "Snapchat Gets Its Own Timeline with Snapchat Stories, 24-Hour Photo & Video Tales," *TechCrunch*, October 3, 2013; N. Kemp, "What Marketers Should Know About Snapchat," *Brand Republic*, June 13, 2013; www.snapchat.com, accessed March 23, 2014.

Questions

1. Describe the advantages and disadvantages of Snapchat to its users. Provide specific examples of both to support your answer.

2. Do you think that Snapchat can become profitable (i.e., survive) in the marketplace? Why or why not? Support your answer with specific examples.

3. How will the Snapchat breach affect marketers who are considering using the app in their campaigns?

4. Should Snapchat's founders have sold the service to Facebook or Google? Why or why not? If you were the founder of Snapchat, would you have accepted one of these offers? Why or why not?

Introduction

Humans are social individuals. Therefore, human behavior is innately social. Humans typically orient their behavior around other members of their community. As a result, people are sensitive to the behavior of people around them, and their decisions are generally influenced by their social context.

Traditional information systems support organizational activities and business processes, and they concentrate on cost reductions and productivity increases. A variation of this traditional model, **social computing,** is a type of IT that combines social behavior and information systems to create value. Social computing is focused on improving collaboration and interaction among people and on encouraging user-generated content. Significantly, in social computing, social information is not anonymous. Rather, it is important precisely because it is linked to particular individuals, who in turn are linked to their own networks of individuals.

Social computing makes socially produced information available to everyone. This information may be provided directly, as when users rate a movie (e.g., at Rotten Tomatoes), or indirectly, as with Google's PageRank algorithm, which sequences search results.

In social computing, users, rather than organizations, produce, control, use, and manage content via interactive communications and collaboration. As a result, social computing is transforming power relationships within organizations. Employees and customers are empowered by their ability to use social computing to organize themselves. Thus, social computing can influence people in positions of power to listen to the concerns and issues of "ordinary people." Organizational customers and employees are joining this social computing phenomenon, with serious consequences for most organizations.

Significantly, most governments and companies in modern developed societies are not prepared for the new social power of ordinary people. Today, managers, executives, and government officials can no longer control the conversation around policies, products, and other issues.

In the new world of business and government, organizational leaders will have to demonstrate authenticity, even-handedness, transparency, good faith, and humility. If they do not, then customers and employees may distrust them, to potentially disastrous effects. For example, customers who do not like a product or service can quickly broadcast their disapproval. Another example is that prospective employees do not have to take their employers at their word for what life is like at their companies—they can find out from people who already work there. A final example is that employees now have many more options to start their own companies, which could compete with their former employers.

As you see from these examples, the world is becoming more democratic and reflective of the will of ordinary people, enabled by the power of social computing. On the one hand, social power can help keep a company vital and can enable customers and employee activists to become a source of creativity, innovation, and new ideas that will move a company forward. On the other hand, companies that show insensitivity toward customers or employees quickly find themselves on a downward slide.

For instance, Kenneth Cole came under fire for suggesting on Twitter that news of its spring collection led to riots in Egypt, and American Apparel was blasted online for offering a Hurricane Sandy sale. Lesson to be learned: If companies want to win the favor and loyalty of customers, they should refrain from making comments that may suggest that they were trying to profit from other people's misery.

Another example is CVS Pharmacy. CVS asked its customers to sign up for the company's Twitter account, become followers, and offer feedback. However, CVS's account was locked, so customers could not follow it or view tweets without asking for permission. Lesson to be learned: Make certain you understand the mechanics of how a social media platform works before you try to use it.

Social computing is exploding worldwide, with China having the world's most active social media population. In one McKinsey survey, 91 percent of Chinese respondents reported that they had visited a social media site in the previous six months, compared with 70 percent in South Korea, 67 percent in the United States, and 30 percent in Japan. Interestingly, the survey found that social media has a greater influence on purchasing decisions for Chinese consumers than for consumers anywhere else in the world.

Social computing is also increasing dramatically in Africa. Facebook in particular is growing rapidly in African countries, and it is the dominant social network in most of them. However, Facebook does have rivals in Africa, including the following:

- In South Africa, Mxit (www.mxit.com) has 10 million active users, more than double Facebook's number.
- In Ghana, a mobile social network called Saya.im (www.saya.im) gained more than 50,000 members in six weeks after the site launched.
- In Kenya, a mobile social network called iCow (www.icow.co.ke) provides farmers and other members with livestock management and other agricultural information.

Businesses today are using social computing in a variety of innovative ways, including marketing, customer relationship management, and human resource management. In fact, so many organizations are competing to use social computing in as many new ways as possible that an inclusive term for the use of social computing in business has emerged: *social commerce*. Because social computing is facilitated by Web 2.0 tools and sites, you begin this chapter by examining these technologies. You then turn your attention to a diverse number of social commerce activities, including shopping, advertising, market research, customer relationship management, and human resource management. You conclude by studying the risks and concerns associated with social computing.

When you complete this chapter, you will have a thorough understanding of social computing and the ways in which modern organizations use this technology. You will be familiar with the advantages and disadvantages of social computing as well as the risks and rewards it can bring to your organization. For example, most of you already have pages on social networking sites, so you are familiar with the positive and negative features of these sites. This chapter will enable you to apply this knowledge to your organization's efforts in the social computing arena. You will be in a position to contribute to your organization's policies on social computing. You will also be able to help your organization create a strategy to utilize social computing. Finally, social computing offers incredible opportunities for entrepreneurs who want to start their own businesses.

8.1 Web 2.0

The World Wide Web, which you learned about in Chapter 4, first appeared in 1990. Web 1.0 was the first generation of the Web. We did not use this term in Chapter 4 because there was no need to say "Web 1.0" until Web 2.0 emerged.

The key developments of Web 1.0 were the creation of Web sites and the commercialization of the Web. Users typically had minimal interaction with Web 1.0 sites. Rather, they passively received information from those sites.

Web 2.0 is a popular term that has proved difficult to define. According to Tim O'Reilly, a noted blogger, **Web 2.0** is a loose collection of information technologies and applications, plus the Web sites that use them. These Web sites enrich the user experience by encouraging user participation, social interaction, and collaboration. Unlike Web 1.0 sites, Web 2.0 sites are not so much online places to visit as Web locations that facilitate information sharing, user-centered design, and collaboration. Web 2.0 sites often harness collective intelligence (e.g., wikis); deliver functionality as services, rather than packaged software (e.g., Web services); and feature remixable applications and data (e.g., mashups).

In the following sections, we discuss six Web 2.0 information technology tools: AJAX, tagging, Really Simple Syndication (RSS), blogs, microblogs, and wikis. We then turn our attention to the two major types of Web 2.0 sites: social networking sites and mashups.

AJAX

Most Web 2.0 applications have rich, user-friendly interfaces based on AJAX. **AJAX** is a Web development technique that enables users to reload portions of Web pages with fresh data instead of having to reload the entire Web page. This process speeds up response time and increases user satisfaction.

Tagging

A **tag** is a keyword or term that describes a piece of information—for example, a blog, a picture, an article, or a video clip. Users typically choose tags that are meaningful to them. Tagging allows users to place information in multiple, overlapping associations rather than in rigid categories. For example, a photo of a car might be tagged with "Corvette," "sports car," and "Chevrolet." Tagging is the basis of *folksonomies*, which are user-generated classifications that use tags to categorize and retrieve Web pages, photos, videos, and other Web content.

One specific form of tagging, known as *geotagging*, refers to tagging information on maps. For example, Google Maps allows users to add pictures and information, such as restaurant or hotel ratings, to maps. Therefore, when users access Google Maps, their experience is enriched because they can see pictures of attractions, reviews, and things to do, posted by everyone, and all related to the map location they are viewing.

Really Simple Syndication

Really Simple Syndication is a Web 2.0 feature that allows you to receive the information you want (customized information), when you want it, without having to surf thousands of Web sites. RSS allows anyone to syndicate (publish) his or her blog, or any other content, to anyone who has an interest in subscribing to it. When changes to the content are made, subscribers receive a notification of the changes and an idea of what the new content contains. Subscribers can then click on a link that will take them to the full text of the new content.

For example, CNN.com provides RSS feeds for each of its main topic areas, such as world news, sports news, technology news, and entertainment news. NBC uses RSS feeds to allow viewers to download the most current version of shows such as *Meet the Press* and *NBC Nightly News.*

You can find thousands of Web sites that offer RSS feeds at Syndic8 (www.syndic8.com) and NewsIsFree (www.newsisfree.com). FIGURE 8.1 illustrates how to search an RSS and locate RSS feeds.

To use RSS, you can utilize a special newsreader that displays RSS content feeds from the Web sites you select. Many such readers are available, several of them for free. Examples are AmphetaDesk (www.disobey.com/amphetadesk) and Pluck (www.pluck.com). In addition, most browsers have built-in RSS readers. For an excellent RSS tutorial, visit www.mnot.net/rss/tutorial.

Blogs

A **weblog** (**blog** for short) is a personal Web site, open to the public, in which the site creator expresses his or her feelings or opinions via a series of chronological entries.

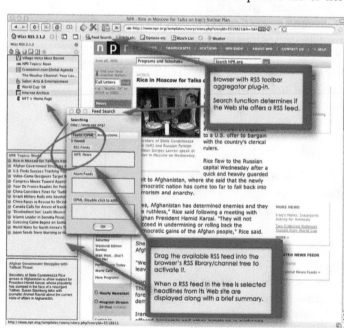

Figure 8.1 The Web site of National Public Radio (NPR) with RSS toolbar aggregator and search function. (Courtesy of NPR. Used with permission.)

Bloggers—people who create and maintain blogs—write stories, convey news, and provide links to other articles and Web sites that are of interest to them. The simplest method of creating a blog is to sign up with a blogging service provider, such as www.blogger.com (now owned by Google), www.xanga.com, and www.sixapart.com. The **blogosphere** is the term for the millions of blogs on the Web.

Many companies listen to consumers in the blogosphere who express their views on the companies' products. Marketers refer to these views as *consumer-generated media*. For example, Nielsen (www.nielsen-online.com) "mines" the blogosphere to provide information for its clients in several areas. Nielsen helps clients find ways to serve potential markets, ranging from broad-based to niche markets. The company also helps clients detect false rumors before these rumors appear in the mainstream media, and it gauges the potency of a marketing push or the popularity of a new product.

Blogs often provide incredibly useful information, often before the information becomes available in traditional media outlets (e.g., television, newspapers). IT's About Business 8.1 describes Brian Krebs's blog on information security.

Brian Krebs Blogs on Information Security

Brian Krebs has built a business exposing security breaches. He has an outstanding record of security scoops, exposing organizational weaknesses in online security in his blog (http://krebsonsecurity.com). Krebs typically posts step-by-step details, without revealing his sources, of how he has uncovered which hackers breached whose corporate defenses. Krebs's blog covers profit-seeking cybercriminals, many of them based in Eastern Europe, who make billions of dollars off fraudulent pharmaceutical sales, malware, spam, frauds, and heists like the recent ones at Adobe, Target, and Neiman Marcus that Krebs was the first to uncover.

Krebs's blog performs a valuable service for consumers. Unlike physical crime—for example, a bank robbery—that quickly becomes public knowledge, online thefts are frequently hushed up by companies that worry that the disclosure will inflict more damage than the theft by frightening away customers. For this reason, hackers can raid multiple companies before consumers hear about it. Therefore, when Krebs uncovers a data breach and quickly publicizes it, the public gains valuable information even though the company might try to keep it quiet.

In 2005, Krebs started the *Washington Post's* Security Fix blog, and he began to infiltrate the online forums and chat rooms where criminals often operate. He learned hacker slang, listened to hundreds of hours of Russian language lessons, and persuaded industry sources to share their security knowledge and techniques.

Krebs was the first person to report the existence of the Stuxnet virus, which we discussed in Chapter 7. He also broke the news of a hack at Adobe Systems, and he uncovered how the credit bureau Experian was tricked into selling consumer data to identity thieves.

In mid-December 2013, Krebs began to hear of a major data breach. A source at a large bank directed him to Web sites that were selling stolen information from credit cards it had issued, all of which had recently been used at various Target stores. Krebs checked with a source at a second bank that also had witnessed a spike in fraud. Together, they visited one Web site and bought a number of stolen cards. Again, the cards appeared to have one thing in common: They had been used at Target from late November to mid-December 2013.

Krebs had corroborated the information he had received in mid-December. Then, on December 18, 2013, he posted that hackers had stolen the financial data of tens of millions of Target customers (see Chapter 7 closing case 1). Krebs then identified a Ukrainian man he had concluded was selling the stolen data. In an online chat that Krebs later posted, the man offered him $10,000 to back off. Krebs declined, and he ran the story. In the following weeks, Krebs discovered breaches at Neiman Marcus and White Lodging, which manages franchises for major hotel chains like Hilton, Marriott, and Starwood hotels. The total number of victims from the breaches at these stores exceeds one-third of the U.S. population.

Krebs maintains he now makes more money than he did at the *Washington Post*. Security businesses such as Authentify and IBM's Trusteer division advertise on his Web site, which attracted about 800,000 unique visitors in December 2013 alone. Krebs also gives a dozen paid speeches per year, and he takes on the occasional data-mining project, usually for financial companies.

Krebs also has become well known internationally. Many security industry experts request his assistance in understanding how the Eastern European criminals operate, how they work with one another, and who is doing what to whom. Krebs is so entrenched in the digital underground that he is on a first-name basis with some of Russia's major cybercriminals. Many of them call him regularly, leak him documents about their rivals, and try to bribe and threaten him to keep their names and dealings off his blog. For example, when two Russian spammers who processed payments for fraudulent online pharmacies hacked each other, each one sent the other's accounting files to Krebs. Krebs is turning that story into a book due out in 2014 from the independent publisher Sourcebooks.

Krebs's readership is expanding. However, there are risks involved in functioning as a one-man operation. Cybercriminals have exhibited their loathing of him in various ways. In the summer of 2013, for example, Krebs received 13 packets of heroin at his home. Even worse, in March 2013, a SWAT team arrived at his home, lured by a fake report of a hostage situation. At precisely the same time, Krebs's computer system was experiencing a distributed denial-of-service attack.

Sources: Compiled from N. Perlroth, "Reporting from the Web's Underbelly," *The New York Times*, February 17, 2014; K. Weise, "The Blogger Hackers Love to Hate," *Bloomberg BusinessWeek*, January 20–26, 2014; M. Stencel, "Tech Reporter Brian Krebs Hacks It on His Own, One Scoop at a Time," *Poynter*, January 16, 2014; N. Perlroth, "Who Is Selling Target's Data?" *The New York Times*, December 24, 2013; J. Bort, "Security Blogger Brian Krebs Is Trying to Track Down the Target Hacker by Talking to Suspected Credit Card Thieves," *SFGate*, December 24, 2013; C. Franzen, "Security Blogger Brian Krebs Suffers Simultaneous Cyber Attack, Police Raid," *The Verge*, March 15, 2013; J. Waters, "What to Do If You Fear Your Credit Card's Hacked," *MarketWatch*, March 30, 2012; M. Gross, "A Declaration of Cyber-War," *Vanity Fair*, April, 2011; krebsonsecurity.com, accessed January 21, 2014.

Questions

1. List various ways in which Krebs can make money from his blog.

2. You are the Chief Security Officer for a company. How would you incorporate Krebs's blog into your security efforts?

Although blogs can be very useful, they also have shortcomings. Perhaps the primary value of blogs is their ability to bring current, breaking news to the public in the fastest time possible. Unfortunately, in doing so, bloggers sometimes cut corners, and their blogs can be inaccurate. Regardless of their various problems, however, blogs have transformed the ways in which people gather and consume information.

Microblogging

Microblogging is a form of blogging that allows users to write short messages (or capture an image or embedded video) and publish them. These messages can be submitted via text messaging from mobile phones, instant messaging, e-mail, or simply over the Web. The content of a microblog differs from that of a blog because of the limited space per message (usually up to 140 characters). A popular microblogging service is Twitter.

Twitter is a free microblogging service that allows its users to send messages and read other users' messages and updates, known as **tweets**. Tweets are displayed on the user's profile page and delivered to other users who have signed up to receive them.

Twitter is becoming a very useful business tool. It allows companies to quickly share information with people interested in their products, thereby creating deeper relationships with their customers. Businesses also use Twitter to gather real-time market intelligence and customer feedback. As an individual user, you can use Twitter to inform companies about your experiences with their business, offer product ideas, and learn about great offers.

Sina Weibo (http://english.sina.com/weibo/) is the most popular microblogging service in China. Closing case 2 discusses how many multinational companies are using this service in their marketing efforts in China.

Wikis

A **wiki** is a Web site made up entirely of content posted by users. Wikis have an "edit" link on each page that allows any user to add, change, or delete material, thus fostering easy collaboration.

Wikis take advantage of the combined input of many individuals. Consider Wikipedia (www.wikipedia.org), an online encyclopedia that is the largest existing wiki. Wikipedia contains more than 4.5 million articles in English (as of mid-2014), which attract some 500 million views every day. Wikipedia relies on volunteer administrators who enforce a neutral point of view, and it encourages users to delete copy that displays a clear bias. Nevertheless, there are still major debates over the reliability of Wikipedia articles. Many educators will not allow students to cite references from Wikipedia because Wikipedia content is of uncertain origin. Moreover, Wikipedia does not provide any quality assessment or fact checking by experts. Therefore, academics and other professionals have major concerns about the accuracy of user-provided content.

Organizations use wikis in several ways. In project management, for example, wikis provide a central repository for capturing constantly updated product features and specifications, tracking issues, resolving problems, and maintaining project histories. In addition, wikis enable companies to collaborate with customers, suppliers, and other business partners on projects. Wikis are also valuable in knowledge management. For example, companies use wikis to keep enterprisewide documents, such as guidelines and frequently asked questions, accurate and current.

Social Networking Web Sites

A **social network** is a social structure composed of individuals, groups, or organizations linked by values, visions, ideas, financial exchange, friendship, kinship, conflict, or trade. **Social networking** refers to activities performed using social software tools (e.g., blogging) or social networking features (e.g., media sharing).

A social network can be described as a map of all relevant links or connections among the network's members. For each individual member that map is his or her **social graph**. Mark Zuckerberg of Facebook originally coined this term to refer to the social network of relationships among Facebook users. The idea was that Facebook would take advantage of relationships among individuals to offer a richer online experience.

Social networks can also be used to determine the social capital of individual participants. **Social capital** refers to the number of connections a person has within and between social networks.

Participants congregate on *social networking Web sites* where they can create their own profile page for free and on which they can write blogs and wikis; post pictures, videos, or music; share ideas; and link to other Web locations they find interesting. Social networkers chat using instant messaging and Twitter, and they tag posted content with their own key words, making content searchable and facilitating interactions and transactions. Social networkers converse, collaborate, and share opinions, experiences, knowledge, insights, and perceptions with one another. They also use these Web sites to find like-minded people online, either to pursue an interest or a goal or just to establish a sense of community among people who may never meet in the real world.

© Logorilla/iStockphoto

Social networking allows convenient connections to those of similar interest.

Participants who post on social networking sites tend to reveal a great deal of personal information. As a result, if they are not careful, bad things can happen. IT's About Business 8.2 illustrates a negative outcome that resulted from a Facebook post.

IT'S ABOUT BUSINESS 8.2

Trip to Europe: Cancelled

Patrick Snay was the headmaster at Gulliver Preparatory School in Miami for several years. In 2010, the school did not renew his contract. Snay sued his former employer for age discrimination and for retaliation that involved his daughter, a student at the school.

Gulliver settled the case in November 2011, agreeing to pay Snay $10,000 in back wages and an $80,000 settlement, as well as $60,000 to Snay's attorneys. The settlement depended on a confidentiality agreement that required Snay and his wife to keep the "terms and existence" of the agreement private. Snay immediately informed his daughter, Dana, that he had settled with Gulliver and was happy with the results.

Rather than keeping this news private, Dana bragged about the case on Facebook. Her post read: "Mama and Papa Snay won the case against Gulliver. Gulliver is now officially paying for my vacation to Europe this summer. SUCK IT."

Dana had 1,200 Facebook friends, many of whom were current and former Gulliver students. News of the post made its way back to the school's lawyers, who appealed the verdict in the Snay case to a circuit court.

©zimmytws/iStockphoto

Snay won this round when the court upheld the settlement. The school then appealed to the Third District Court of Appeals, which threw out the settlement. This court ruled that Snay and his daughter had breached the terms of a confidentiality agreement when she posted about it on Facebook.

Snay is now headmaster at Riviera Preparatory Academy in Coral Gables, Florida. He is allowed to file a motion for rehearing and also to appeal to the Florida Supreme Court. However, attorneys maintain that the odds of his winning an appeal are slim. They note that Facebook is a public forum and that is where the mistake was made.

And the irony of it all? It seems that Dana was just kidding about the European vacation.

Sources: Compiled from J. Allen, "Dana Snay's Facebook Post Costs Father $80K," *WebProNews*, March 6, 2014; P. Caufield, "Daughter's Facebook Post Botches Dad's $80,000 Settlement," *New York Daily News*, March 3, 2014; T. Greene, "Who Is Dana Snay? College Student's Facebook Bragging Costs Father $80,000 Lawsuit Settlement," *International Business Times*, February 28, 2014; E. Sole, "Daughter's Facebook Brag Costs Her Family $80,000," *Yahoo! Shine*, February 28, 2014; K. Waldman, "Teen's Facebook Post Costs Her Dad $80,000. Oops," *Slate*, February 28, 2014; "80,000 Mistake: Who Is to Blame?" *Babysitter Community*, February 28, 2014; D. Smiley, "Daughter's Facebook Boast Costs Former Gulliver Prep Headmaster $80,000 Discrimination Settlement," *Miami Herald*, February 26, 2014.

Questions

1. Should you be careful of what you post on Facebook? Support your answer in relation to this case.

2. What mistake did the parents make when they informed Dana about the settlement? Telling her at all? Not telling her about the dangers of posting details on social media?

Table 8.1 displays the variety of online social networking platforms. Social networking Web sites allow users to upload their content to the Web in the form of text, voice, images, and videos.

TABLE 8.1 Categories of Social Networking Web Sites

Socially oriented: Socially focused public sites, open to anyone

- Facebook (www.facebook.com)
- Google Orkut (www.orkut.com)
- Google+ (https://plus.google.com)
- Hi5 (www.hi5.com)

Professional networking: Focused on networking for business professionals

- LinkedIn (www.linkedin.com)

Media sharing

- *Netcasting* includes podcasting (audio) and videocasting (audio and video). For example, educational institutions use netcasts to provide students with access to lectures, lab demonstrations, and sports events. In 2007, Apple launched iTunes U, which offers free content provided by major U.S. universities such as Stanford and MIT.
- *Web 2.0 media* sites allow people to come together and share user-generated digital media, such as pictures, audio, and video.
  - Video (Amazon Video on Demand, YouTube, Hulu, Facebook)
  - Music (Amazon MP3, Last.fm, Rhapsody, Pandora, Facebook, iTunes)
  - Photographs (Photobucket, Flickr, Shutterfly, Picasa, Facebook)

Communication

- *Blogs*: Blogger, LiveJournal, Open Diary, TypePad, WordPress, Vox, Expression Engine, Xanga
- *Microblogging/Presence applications*: Twitter, Plurk, Tumblr, Yammer, Qaiku

Collaboration: Wikis (Wikimedia, PBworks, Wetpaint)

Social bookmarking (or *social tagging*): Focused on helping users store, organize, search, and manage bookmarks of Web pages on the Internet

- Delicious (www.delicious.com)
- StumbleUpon (www.stumbleupon.com)
- Google Reader (http://reader.google.com)
- CiteULike (www.citeulike.com)

Social news: Focused on user-posted news stories that are ranked by popularity based on user voting

- Digg (www.digg.com)
- Chime.in (http://chime.in)
- Reddit (www.reddit.com)

Events: Focused on alerts for relevant events, people you know nearby, etc.

- Eventful (www.eventful.com)
- Meetup (www.meetup.com)
- Foursquare (www.foursquare.com)

Virtual meeting place: Sites that are essentially three-dimensional worlds, built and owned by the residents (the users)

- Second Life (www.secondlife.com)

Interesting new social networks

- Empire Avenue (www.empireavenue.com) is a social exchange network where members invest virtual currency in people and brands that interest them.
- Color (www.color.com) is a free mobile app that creates an instant social network based on users' locations and proximity to others. Users can instantly share images, videos, and text conversations with other nearby users.
- Foursquare (http://foursquare.com) is a location-based mobile service that enables participants to share their location with friends by checking in via a smartphone app.
- Hunch (www.hunch.com) maps people's interests by asking them a series of questions. The site creates a "taste graph," which tracks everything that a user likes and dislikes.

Online marketplaces for microjobs

- For example, TaskRabbit (www.taskrabbit.com) and Zaarly (www.zaarly.com) enable people to farm out chores to a growing number of temporary personal assistants. Thousands of unemployed and underemployed workers use these sites. The part-time or full-time tasks are especially popular with stay-at-home moms, retirees, and students. Workers choose their jobs and negotiate their rates.

Enterprise Social Networks

Business-oriented social networks can be public, such as LinkedIn.com. As such, they are owned and managed by an independent company.

However, an increasing number of companies have created in-house, private social networks for their employees, former employees, business partners, and/or customers. Such networks are "behind the firewall" and are often referred to as *corporate social networks*. Employees utilize these networks to create connections that allow them to establish virtual teams, bring new employees up to speed, improve collaboration, and increase employee retention by creating a sense of community. Employees are able to interact with their coworkers on a level that is typically absent in large organizations or in situations where people work remotely.

Corporate social networks are used for many processes, including

- Networking and community building, both inside and outside an organization

- *Social collaboration:* collaborative work and problem solving using wikis, blogs, instant messaging, collaborative office, and other special-purpose Web-based collaboration platforms; for example, see Laboranova (www.laboranova.com)

- *Social publishing:* employees and others creating, either individually or collaboratively, and posting contents—photos, videos, presentation slides, and documents—into a member's or a community's accessible-content repository such as YouTube, Flickr, SlideShare, and DocStoc

- Social views and feedback

- *Social intelligence and social analytics:* monitoring, analyzing, and interpreting conversations, interactions, and associations among people, topics, and ideas to gain insights. Social intelligence is useful for examining relationships and work patterns of individuals and groups and for discovering people and expertise. IT's About Business 8.3 illustrates how the Chicago Police Department uses social analytics to gather social intelligence about gang members.

Social Network Analysis Applied to Gangs

Gang violence typically is not random. Rather, it involves territorial disputes or personal disagreements. That is, gang violence is related to geographic, cultural, and social connections. Some police departments have enjoyed some success monitoring social networks such as Facebook for clues about where violence might occur next. However, a new kind of software being implemented in Chicago can turn an entire database of arrest records into visual portrayals of real-life social networks. This technology might enable police officers to quickly identify a person's friends and enemies, and hopefully identify locations where violence might erupt.

Major Paulo Shakarian, an assistant professor at the U.S. Military Academy at West Point, had been developing software to better understand networks of insurgents abroad. The software had been tested in Afghanistan, but was not widely deployed. In 2012, Chicago police officer John Bertetto came across one of Shakarian's papers and asked him a question: "Could social network analysis help Chicago?"

Shakarian and Bertetto created the Organizational, Relationship, and Contact Analyzer (ORCA), a software program that in seconds generates networks that would take people with whiteboards and unstructured databases hours or days to produce. In summer 2013 they put ORCA to the test. The software analyzed three years of anonymized arrests (5,418 total) from one district, turning the arrests into social connection visualizations and reports on individuals. (Anonymized arrests are those where personally identifiable information has been removed.)

ORCA begins by linking people who had been arrested together, which is the most objective way a record indicates that, at the very least, people have been at the same place at the same time. From there, ORCA categorizes individuals who had admitted a gang affiliation. Then, based on social links, the software assigns other persons a numerical probability of having a particular affiliation. ORCA further analyzes clusters of people within the network to identify groups and subgroups. A subgroup occupying a street corner, for example, could be one of a gang's "crews." By zeroing in on people who are connected across many groups and subgroups, ORCA singles out the most influential individuals.

The analysis revealed more than 11,000 relationships among the arrested individuals. From this analysis, ORCA created a social network consisting of 1,468 individuals who are members of 18 gangs. ORCA identified "seed sets," which are small groups within a gang who are highly connected and therefore highly influential. ORCA also found individuals known as "connectors" who link one gang with another. Such individuals, for instance, may sell drugs from one gang to another. Interestingly, ORCA performed all of these analyses on a standard laptop in 34 seconds.

ORCA remains under development. Future iterations may integrate geolocation data, time-based data, and intelligence from informants. The time element is particularly important because gang members switch allegiances and regularly start new gangs.

Sources: Compiled from M. Mruk, "Building a Social Network of Crime," *Popular Science*, January 14, 2014; C. Wood, "Counter-Insurgency Software Goes Stateside," *Government Technology*, July 24, 2013; P. Ball, "Unmasking Organised Crime Networks with Data," *BBC News*, July 9, 2013; "How Military Counterinsurgency Software Is Being Adapted to Tackle Gang Violence in Mainland USA," *Small Wars Journal*, July 9, 2013; D. Coldewey, "Gangs' Pecking Order Revealed by Army Software," *NBC News*, July 8, 2013; K. Campbell-Dollaghan, "The Army's Insurgent Tracking Software Is Now Being Used to Track Gangs," *Gizmodo*, July 7, 2013; "How Military Counterinsurgency Software Is Being Adapted to Tackle Gang Violence in Mainland USA," *MIT Technology Review*, July 4, 2013.

Questions

1. What other data could the Chicago Police Department add to ORCA?

2. What are the potential disadvantages of ORCA? Provide specific examples to support your answer.

Mashups

A **mashup** is a Web site that takes different content from a number of other Web sites and mixes them together to create a new kind of content. The launch of Google Maps is credited with providing the start for mashups. A user can take a map from Google, add his or her data, and then display a map mashup on his or her Web site that plots crime scenes, cars for sale, or anything else (see FIGURE 8.2).

There are many examples of mashups (for a complete list of mashups, see www.programmableweb.com):

- Craigslist developed a dynamic map of all available apartments in the United States that are listed on their Web site (www.housingmaps.com).

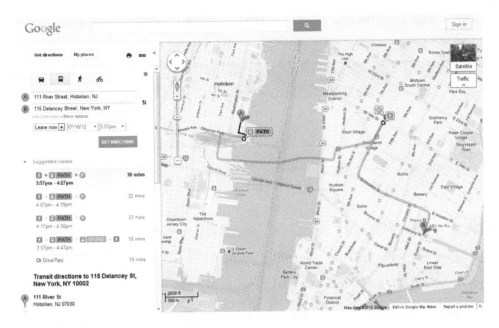

Figure 8.2 GoogleMaps (www.googlemaps.com) is a classic example of a mashup. In this case, GoogleMaps is pulling in information from public transportation Web sites to provide the customer with transit directions.

- **Everyblock.com** is a mashup of Web services that integrates content from newspapers, blogs, and government databases to inform citizens of cities such as Chicago, New York, and Seattle about what is happening in their neighborhoods. This information includes criminal activities, restaurant inspections, and local photos posted on Flickr.

> — **BEFORE** *YOU GO ON....* —
> 1. Differentiate between blogs and wikis.
> 2. Differentiate between social networking Web sites and corporate social networks.

Apply The Concept 8.1

LEARNING OBJECTIVE 8.1 Describe six Web 2.0 tools and the two major types of Web 2.0 sites.

STEP 1 – Background (Here is what you are learning)

This section differentiates Web 1.0, which consists of places to visit, from Web 2.0, where users interact and share information. Whether or not you have thought of these media in these terms, you are familiar with these differences. No doubt you are much more accustomed to Web 2.0, and businesses have begun to integrate information sharing into their public sites.

STEP 2 – Activity (Here is what you are doing)

Visit http://www.wiley.com/go/rainer/MIS3e/applytheconcept, and click on the link for Apply the Concept 8.1. This video provides a valuable overview of Web 2.0 technologies. Take notes of the various features that Web 2.0 makes available, and then click on the second link. This link will take you to a CNN Money Web page that provides a rank-order list of the Fortune 500 companies. Visit the Web sites of the top 10 firms, and identify the Web 2.0 technologies they employ on their sites.

STEP 3 – Deliverable (Here is what you turn in)

Create a table similar to the one shown below that displays the following information about 5 of the top 10 companies on the CNN Money rankings.

- The company's name
- The company's rank
- The industry (e.g., retail, consulting services, and communications)

- A description of the Web 2.0 technologies/applications that each company uses
- A description of the Web 2.0 tools the company does not use

Name	Rank	Industry	Web 2.0 Used	Web 2.0 Not Used

Submit your table to your professor.

8.2 Fundamentals of Social Computing in Business

Social computing in business, or **social commerce,** refers to the delivery of electronic commerce activities and transactions through social computing. Social commerce also supports social interactions and user contributions, allowing customers to participate actively in the marketing and selling of products and services in online marketplaces and communities. With social commerce, individuals can collaborate online, obtain advice from trusted individuals, and find and purchase goods and services. Below we list a few examples of social commerce:

- Disney allows people to book tickets on Facebook without leaving the social network.
- PepsiCo provides a live notification when its customers are close to physical stores (grocery, restaurants, and gas stations) that sell Pepsi products. The company then uses Foursquare to send them coupons and discount information.
- Mountain Dew attracts video game lovers and sports enthusiasts via Dewmocracy contests. The company also encourages the most dedicated community members to contribute ideas on company products.
- Levi's advertises on Facebook by enabling consumers to populate a "shopping cart" based on what their friends think they would like.
- Wendy's uses Facebook and Twitter to award $50 gift cards to people who submit the funniest and quirkiest responses to various challenges.

Social commerce offers numerous benefits to both customers and vendors, as described in Table 8.2.

Despite all of its benefits, social computing does involve risks. It is problematic, for example, to advertise a product, brand, or company on social computing Web sites where content is user generated and is not edited or filtered. Companies that employ this strategy must be willing to accept negative reviews and feedback. Of course, negative feedback can be some of the most valuable information that a company receives, if it utilizes this information properly.

Companies that engage in social computing are always concerned with negative posts. For example, when a company creates a Facebook business page, by default the site allows other members of the Web site—potentially including disgruntled customers or unethical competitors—to post notes on the firm's Facebook Wall and to comment on what the firm has posted.

Going further, if the company turns off the feature that lets other users write on its Wall, people may wonder what the company is afraid of. The company will also be eliminating its opportunity to engage in great customer conversations, particularly conversations that could market the firm's products and services better than the company could do itself. Similarly, the company could delete posts. However, that policy only encourages the post author to scream even louder about being censored.

Another risk is the 20–80 rule of thumb, which posits that a minority of individuals (20 percent) contribute most of the content (80 percent) to blogs, wikis, social computing

TABLE 8.2 Potential Benefits of Social Commerce

Benefits to customers

- Better and faster vendor responses to complaints, because customers can air their complaints in public (on Twitter, Facebook, and YouTube)
- Customers can assist other customers (e.g., in online forums)
- Customers' expectations can be met more fully and quickly
- Customers can easily search, link, chat, and buy while staying on a social network's page

Benefits to businesses

- Can test new products and ideas quickly and inexpensively
- Learn a lot about their customers
- Identify problems quickly and alleviate customer anger
- Learn about customers' experiences via rapid feedback
- Increase sales when customers discuss products positively on social networking site
- Create more effective marketing campaigns and brand awareness
- Use low-cost user-generated content, for example, in marketing campaigns
- Obtain free advertising through viral marketing
- Identify and reward influential brand advocates

Web sites, etc. For example, in an analysis of thousands of submissions to the news voting site Digg over a three-week time frame, the *Wall Street Journal* reported that roughly 33 percent of the stories that made it to Digg's homepage were submitted by 30 contributors (out of 900,000 registered members).

Other risks of social computing include the following:

- Information security concerns
- Invasion of privacy
- Violation of intellectual property and copyright
- Employees' reluctance to participate
- Data leakage of personal information or corporate strategic information
- Poor or biased quality of users' generated content
- Cyberbullying/cyberstalking and employee harassment

Consider Rosetta Stone (www.rosettastone.com), which produces software for language translation. To obtain the maximum possible mileage out of social computing and limit the firm's risks on social media, Rosetta Stone implemented a strategy to control its customer interaction on Facebook. The strategy involves both human intervention and software to help monitor the firm's Facebook presence. Specifically, the software helps to monitor Wall posts and respond to them constructively.

Fans of facebook.com/RosettaStone who post questions on its Wall are likely to receive a prompt answer because the Facebook page is integrated with customer service software from Parature (www.parature.com). The software scans Wall posts and flags those posts that require a company response, as opposed to those in which fans of the company are talking among themselves. Rosetta Stone customer service representatives are also able to post responses to the Wall that are logged in the Parature issue tracking database.

Companies are engaged in many types of social commerce activities, including shopping, advertising, market research, customer relationship management, and human resource management. In the next sections of this chapter, you will learn about each social commerce activity.

BEFORE YOU GO ON....

1. Briefly describe the benefits of social commerce to customers.
2. Briefly describe the risks of social commerce to businesses.

Apply The Concept 8.2

LEARNING OBJECTIVE 8.2 Describe the benefits and risks of social commerce to companies.

STEP 1 – Background

Section 8.2 has described many concerns about social computing, including privacy, security, copyright (and other intellectual property right issues), and poor quality content. Despite these problems, however, social computing is too valuable to ignore! It is truly a double-edged sword.

Of course, social commerce did not create negative customer opinions. Rather, it provided customers with a platform on which to share such comments. Social computing is creating a world in which customer experiences, company products, and company practices are more transparent. Companies must truly "put the customer first," or else they will be "outed" on social media very quickly.

STEP 2 – Activity

Visit http://www.wiley.com/go/rainer/MIS3e/applytheconcept, and click on the link for Apply the Concept 8.2. This link will take you to a blog article that focuses on a negative YouTube video about Nestlé. When the video went viral, the company's legal team demanded that it be removed. The article then discusses various strategies for dealing with such negative publicity on social networks.

Next, click on the second link for Apply the Concept 8.2. Here you will view a story about a FedEx driver who threw a fragile package over a fence. This video also went viral, but FedEx did not ask for it to be removed. FedEx responded that they had identified the driver and that he was subject to internal disciplinary measures.

Consider the two approaches to handling the risks involved in social computing. Which approach do you think is better?

STEP 3 – Deliverable

Based on the videos and the material in the section, write and submit a paragraph summarizing what you have learned about the benefits and risks of social commerce to companies.

8.3 Social Computing in Business: Shopping

Social shopping is a method of electronic commerce that takes all of the key aspects of social networks—friends, groups, voting, comments, discussions, reviews, etc.—and focuses them on shopping. Social shopping helps shoppers connect with one another based on tastes, location, age, gender, and other selected attributes.

The nature of shopping is changing, especially shopping for brand-name clothes and related items. For example, popular brands such as Gap, Shopbop, InStyle, and Lisa Klein are joining communities on Stylehive (www.stylehive.com) to help promote the season's latest fashion collections. Shoppers are using sites like ThisNext (www.thisnext.com) to create profiles and blogs about their favorite products in social communities. Shoppers can tag each item, so that all items become searchable. Moreover, searching within these Web sites can yield results targeted specifically to individual customers.

There are several methods to shop socially. You will learn about each of them in the next section.

Ratings, Reviews, and Recommendations

Prior to making a purchase, customers typically collect information such as what brand to buy, from which vendor, and at what price. Online customers obtain this information via shopping aids such as comparison agents and Web sites such as Epinions (www.epinions.com). Today, customers also use social networking to guide their purchase decisions. They are increasingly utilizing ratings, reviews, and recommendations from friends, fans, followers, and experienced customers.

Ratings, *reviews*, and *recommendations* are usually available in social shopping. In addition to seeing what is already posted, shoppers have an opportunity to contribute their own ratings and reviews and to discuss ratings and reviews posted by other shoppers (see FIGURE 8.3). The ratings and reviews come from the following sources:

- *Customer ratings and reviews*: integrated into the vendor's Web page, a social network page, a customer review site, or in customer feeds (e.g., Amazon, iTunes, Buzzillions, Epinions).
- *Expert ratings and reviews*: views from an independent authority (e.g., Metacritic).
- *Sponsored reviews*: paid-for reviews (e.g., SponsoredReviews, PayPerPost).
- *Conversational marketing*: individuals converse via e-mail, blog, live chat, discussion groups, and tweets. Monitoring these conversations yields rich data for market research and customer service.

As one example, Maui Jim (www.mauijim.com), the sunglass company, employed favorable word-of-mouth marketing as a key sales driver. The company uses Bazaarvoice's Ratings & Reviews to allow customers to contribute 5-point ratings and authentic product reviews on the company's entire line of sunglasses and accessories. In effect, Maui Jim extended customers' word-of-mouth reviews across the Web.

Maui Jim encourages its customers to share their candid opinions on the style, fit, and performance of all of its sunglass models. To accomplish this goal, the company integrates customer reviews into its Web site search function to ensure that shoppers who are interested in a particular product will see that product's rating in the search results. Customer response to this rating system has been overwhelmingly positive.

Social recommendation Web sites such as ShopSocially (www.shopsocially.com), Blippy (www.blippy.com), and Swipely (www.swipely.com) encourage conversations about purchases. The product recommendations are submitted by users' friends and acquaintances and arguably are more trustworthy than reviews posted by strangers.

ThisNext (www.thisnext.com) is a Web site where people recommend their favorite products to others. The site blends two powerful elements of real-world shopping: word-of-mouth recommendations from trusted sources and the ability to browse products in a way that naturally leads to discovery.

Figure 8.3 Epinions (www.epinions.com) is a Web site that allows customers to rate anything from cars to music. In this screenshot, customers review a popular children's film.

Group Shopping

Group shopping Web sites such as Groupon (www.groupon.com) and LivingSocial (www.livingsocial.com, see FIGURE 8.4) offer major discounts or special deals during a short time frame. Group buying is closely associated with special deals (flash sales).

People who sign up with LivingSocial receive e-mails that offer deals at, for example, a restaurant, a spa, or an event in a given city. They can click on either "Today's Deal" or "Past Deal" (some past deals can still be active). They can also click on an icon and receive the deal the next day. Customers who purchase a deal receive a unique link to share with their friends. If a customer convinces three or more people to buy that specific deal using his or her link, then the customer's deal is free.

Vinobest is a French wine merchant that uses Facebook for group buying and flash deals. The company offers opinions by oenologists (wine experts) and selections by sommeliers (wine stewards) for group-buying deals. Vinobest offers active pricing—the more people who buy, the cheaper the wine.

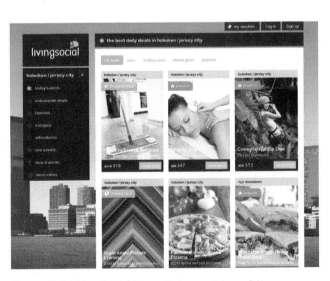

Figure 8.4 LivingSocial (www.livingsocial.com) is a popular example of a group shopping web site.

Individuals can also shop together virtually in real time. In this process, shoppers log on to a Web site and then contact their friends and family. Everyone then shops online at the same time. Some real-time shopping providers, such as DoTogether (www.dotogether.com) and Wet Seal (www.wetseal.com), have integrated their shopping service directly into Facebook. Customers log in to Facebook, install the firm's app, and then invite their friends to join them on a virtual retail shopping experience.

Shopping Communities and Clubs

Shopping clubs host sales for their members that last just a few days and usually feature luxury brands at heavily discounted prices. Club organizers host three to seven sales per day, usually via e-mail messages that entice club members to shop at more than 70 percent off retail—but quickly, before supplies run out.

Luxury brands effectively partner with online shopping clubs to dispose of special-run, sample, overstock, or liquidation goods. These clubs are rather exclusive, which prevents the brands' images from being diminished. Examples are Beyond the Rack (www.beyondtherack.com), Gilt Groupe (www.gilt.com), Rue La La (www.ruelala.com), and One King's Lane (www.onekingslane.com).

Kaboodle (www.kaboodle.com) is another example of a shopping community. Kaboodle is a free service that lets users collect information from the Web and store it on a Kaboodle list that they can share with other shoppers. Kaboodle simplifies shopping by making it easier for people to find items they want in a catalog and by allowing users to share recommendations with one another using Kaboodle lists and groups. People can also use Kaboodle lists for planning vacations, sharing research for work and school, sharing favorite bands with friends, and basically everything else they might want to collect and share information about.

Social Marketplaces and Direct Sales

Social marketplaces act as online intermediaries that harness the power of social networks for introducing, buying, and selling products and services. A social marketplace helps members market their own creations (see Etsy in FIGURE 8.5). Other examples are as follows:

- Craigslist (www.craigslist.com) provides online classifieds in addition to supporting social activities such as meetings and events.

- Fotolia (www.fotolia.com) is a social marketplace for the community of creative people who enjoy sharing, learning, and expressing themselves through images, forums, and blogs; members provide royalty-free stock images that other individuals and professionals can legally buy and share.

- Flipsy (www.flipsy.com) can be used by anyone to list, buy, and sell books, music, movies, and games.

Peer-to-Peer Shopping Models

Peer-to-peer shopping models are the high-tech version of old-fashioned bazaars and bartering systems. Individuals use these models to sell, buy, rent, or barter online with other individuals. For example, many Web sites have emerged to facilitate online sharing. SnapGoods created a community of people who rent goods to people in need, usually for the short term. SnapGoods helps these people connect over the Internet.

All of these peer-to-peer sites encourage **collaborative consumption**—that is, peer-to-peer sharing or renting. This trend accelerated as the result of the recession, because people had less money to spend and turned to sharing and renting. However, collaborative consumption has an environmentally "green" aspect as well. Producing a product has significant environmental impacts when the natural resources

Figure 8.5 Etsy (www.etsy.com) is a social marketplace for all handmade or vintage items.

(e.g., water, lumber, minerals, and electricity) needed to product it are taken into account. Sharing goods among people is much more resource efficient than everyone buying those same goods.

One of the most surprising benefits of collaborative consumption, however, turns out to be social. In an era when we may hardly know our neighbors, sharing things—even with strangers we have just met online—allows us to make meaningful connections. Some people share cars, and others invite travelers to stay in their homes for free. The following example illustrates the benefits of collaborative consumption.

EXAMPLE Collaborative Consumption

An entirely new generation of businesses is emerging, created by the intersection of the economic crisis, environmental concerns, and the maturation of social computing. These firms help interested parties share cars, clothing, couches, apartments, tools, meals, and even skills. The basic characteristic of these sharing marketplaces is that they extract value out of the "stuff" we already possess.

The premise of collaborative consumption is simple: Having access to goods and skills is more important than owning them. There are three types of collaborative consumption:

- Product-service systems that enable people to share or rent a product (e.g., car sharing)
- Redistribution markets, through which a product can be renowned (e.g., Craigslist)
- Collaborative lifestyles in which participants can share assets and skills (e.g., coworking spaces)

Consider our second-most expensive asset, our cars. (Our homes are the most expensive.) Across the United States, Canada, and Western Europe, the average person uses his or her car only 8 percent of the time. In fact, cars are the ultimate expensive, underutilized commodity. In 2000, Zipcar started convincing city dwellers that they could enjoy the perks of access without the expense of actually owning a car.

Zipcar is a U.S. membership-based car-sharing company that provides automobile reservations to its members, billable by both the hour and the day. Members can reserve Zipcars online or by phone at any time. To access a car, members use an access card that works with the car's technology to unlock the door. (The keys are already located inside.) Zipcar also offers an iPhone and Android application that allows members to honk the horn to locate a Zipcar and to unlock the doors. Zipcar charges a one-time application fee, an annual fee, and a reservation charge. Gas, parking, insurance, and maintenance are included in the price.

Competitors are emerging for Zipcar. Companies like RelayRides (http://relayrides.com), Zimride (www.zimride.com), Spride (www.spride.com), and Getaround (www.getaround.com) do not own any cars—they simply enable individuals to share them. For example, the average person who allows his or her car to be rented at RelayRides makes $250 per month. In fact, some users are making enough money on RelayRides to cover their entire car payment. Moreover, because RelayRides includes a $1 million insurance policy that covers both owners and renters during each reservation, renting from RelayRides is a low-risk arrangement.

In addition to its financial benefits, car sharing offers environmental benefits as well. When people's mobility costs shift from being fixed (ownership) to variable (renting), they make more efficient decisions about when and how frequently they actually need to drive. Research has demonstrated that the average car sharer drives 40 percent less than the average owner.

The German car manufacturer Daimler is taking car sharing seriously. Its Car2Go (www.car2go.com) service is similar to Zipcar's, except that it does not require a reservation or a two-way trip. Car2Go's mobile app allows a person walking down a city street to locate a car on that block, access it immediately via a windshield card reader and PIN number, drive it anywhere locally, and leave it there for someone else to use. The fuel-efficient Smart car has a 100-watt solar roof, which powers the car's telematics (discussed in Chapter 10) and its battery.

Daimler is also developing an app called Car2Gether (www.car2gether.com), which matches local drivers with people who are looking for a ride. Riders submit a request to a driver of any type of car, and both profiles are linked to their Facebook pages and Twitter feeds. After the ride, both the driver and the rider rate each other.

Perhaps the greatest concern associated with car sharing is trust. Sharing works well only when the participants' reputations are involved. Most sharing platforms try to address this issue by creating a self-policing community. Almost all platforms require profiles of both parties, and they feature community rating systems.

Startups like TrustCloud (http://trustcloud.com) are endeavoring to become the portable reputation system for the Web. The company has built an algorithm that collects (if you choose to opt in) your online "data exhaust"—the trail you leave as you engage with others on Facebook, LinkedIn, Twitter, commentary-filled sites like TripAdvisor, and others. It then calculates your reliability, consistency, and responsiveness. The result is a contextual badge that you carry to any Web site, a trust rating similar to the credit rating you have in the "offline" world.

Of course, Facebook is already collecting a huge amount of your data exhaust on its own site. Thus, Facebook could become the arbiter of online trust.

Collaborative consumption has the potential to become extremely disruptive to existing organizations. For example, if the people formerly known as "consumers" began consuming 10 percent less and sharing 10 percent more, traditional corporations would inevitably see their profits decline.

Sources: Compiled from D. Brodwin, "The Rise of the Collaborative Consumption Economy," *U.S. News and World Report*, August 9, 2012; D. Sacks, "The Sharing Economy," *Fast Company*, May, 2011; www.collaborativeconsumption.com, www.car2go.com, http://trustcloud.com, accessed March 30, 2013.

 uestions

1. What are some potential disadvantages of car sharing?
2. Describe how collaborative consumption can be disruptive to traditional organizations. How might the organizations respond to this challenge?

BEFORE *YOU GO ON....*

1. Why are ratings, reviews, and recommendations so important to potential customers?
2. Define collaborative consumption, and describe how collaborative consumption is a "green" phenomenon.

Apply The Concept 8.3

LEARNING OBJECTIVE 8.3 Identify the methods used for shopping socially.

STEP 1 – Background

Section 8.3 defines shopping socially as taking the key aspects of social networks—e.g., groups, reviews, and discussions—and applying them to shopping. This phenomenon is not new. People have shopped socially for years, through general conversation.

Today, most consumers conduct a lot of research before they make a purchase by reading reviews posted by other customers. Recently, however, the validity of these reviews has been questioned. As you learn about social shopping, you should also become aware of the potential fraud that takes place online.

STEP 2 – Activity

Go to http://www.wiley.com/go/rainer/MIS3e/applytheconcept, and click on the link for Apply the Concept 8.3. This link will take you to an article from the *New York Times* and one from the *Denver Post*. Both articles deal with the issue of falsified recommendations and ratings.

Talk to some of your classmates about this topic, and record their feedback. How did they respond to the fact that product ratings may not be legitimate? Ask them the following questions:

- What star rating do you rely on when you are considering a product?
- Do you read reviews or simply notice the number of stars?
- If you read reviews, do you read only the good ones, only the bad ones, or a mixture of both?
- Do you rely on reviews more than a third-party company such as *Consumer Reports*?

STEP 3 – Deliverable

Considering the material you have read and your conversations with your classmates, identify various methods of shopping socially, and discuss the role that trust plays in each method. Prepare a paper or presentation for your professor documenting what you have learned.

8.4 Social Computing in Business: Marketing

Marketing can be defined as the process of building profitable customer relationships by creating value for customers and capturing value in return. There are many components to a marketing campaign, including (1) define your target audience; (2) develop your message (i.e., how you will solve their problem); (3) decide on how you will deliver your message (e.g., e-mail, snail mail, Web advertising, and/or social networks); and (4) follow up. Social computing is particularly useful for two marketing processes: advertising and market research.

Advertising

Social advertising refers to advertising formats that make use of the social context of the user viewing the ad. Social advertising is the first form of advertising to leverage forms of social influence such as peer pressure and friend recommendations and likes.

Many experts believe advertising is the solution to the challenge of making money from social networking sites and social commerce sites. Advertisers have long noted the large number of visitors on social networks and the amount of time they spend there. As a result, they are willing to pay to place ads and run promotions on social networks. Advertisers now post ads on all major social networking Web sites.

Most ads in social commerce consist of branded content paid for by advertisers. These ads belong to two major categories: *social advertisements* (or *social ads*) and *social apps*. Social advertisements are ads placed in paid-for media space on social media networks. Social apps are branded online applications that support social interactions and user contributions (e.g., Nike+).

Viral marketing—that is, word-of-mouth advertising—lends itself especially well to social networking. For example, Stormhoek Vineyards (www.stormhoek.com) initiated a marketing campaign by offering bloggers a free bottle of wine. Within six months, roughly 100 of these bloggers had posted voluntary comments—the majority of them positive—about the winery on their blogs. In turn these comments were read by other bloggers.

There are other innovative methods to advertise in social media. Consider the following:

- Use a company Facebook page, including a store that attracts fans and lets them "meet" other customers. Then, advertise in your Facebook store.
- Tweet business success stories to your customers.
- Integrate ads into YouTube videos.
- Mercedes-Benz launched a "Tweet Race," which challenged four teams to drive across the country in Mercedes automobiles to Dallas, Texas, where the 2011 Super Bowl was being played. Each team collected Twitter followers with the help of a celebrity coach. Each tweet or retweet earned the team points, as did other activities, such as photographing other Mercedes cars during the road trip. The team that accumulated the most points by the end of the trip was declared the winner.
- Facebook has introduced a feature called the "sponsored story." When a member chats with friends and one of them indicates that he or she "checked into" a place or "liked it," say at Starbucks, a boxed "sponsored story" (an advertisement) will appear with the Starbucks logo (fee paid to Facebook). Furthermore, the name "Starbucks" will also appear in the user's news feed (another fee paid to Facebook). The users have the option to delete the boxed advertisement.

For an interesting example of social advertising, you need look no further than YouTube. IT's About Business 8.4 illustrates how YouTube is battling traditional television to provide online content and in the process is increasing its ad revenue.

IT'S ABOUT BUSINESS 8.4

YouTube versus Television

YouTube (www.youtube.com) is growing rapidly. Viewership increased by about 50 percent in 2013, an astonishing growth rate for a Web site that already attracts 1 billion users each month from around the world. Its viewers consume 6 billion hours of YouTube videos per month, and many devoted fans enjoy their favorite shows day after day. With traditional television audiences stagnating, YouTube has emerged as a leading platform for professional artists and producers who want to connect directly to audiences.

YouTube and its content partners are transforming the site from a chaotic collection of cat videos and viral hits like "Gangnam Style" into a legitimate destination for a new generation of professional videos. The viral hits and zany clips are still there, of course, and they continue to draw the largest and most global entertainment audience anywhere.

YouTube is not going to kill television, but it is definitely starting to disrupt mainstream entertainment. Americans have their TV sets on for 34 hours per week, according to Nielsen. In contrast, they watch only 1 hour of video on the Internet per week. However, viewing habits among young people point to a dramatic shift: 18- to 24-year-olds watch just 23 hours of TV and 2.5 hours of online video.

If the first era of video entertainment was network television with a few channels and the second era was cable with hundreds of channels, then the third era is the Web with tens of thousands of channels increasingly tailored to niche audiences. In this third era, YouTube is not only the largest distribution platform but also the era's organizing force. Essentially, YouTube is an open platform where anyone can upload content. In turn, YouTube collects nearly half of the revenue from all of the ads that run on the site.

© Aigars Reinholds/Shutterstock

More searches are conducted on YouTube than on any other search engine other than Google. The video-sharing site helps Google deliver the right audiences for advertisers, particularly on mobile devices, where the consumption of video is growing most rapidly.

YouTube also provides a wealth of data about consumer behavior that helps Google fine-tune its services. Going further, YouTube has fortified the advertising industry by empowering brands to become content creators and publishers that increasingly plan to create their own viral hits.

Other technology companies are developing Web video platforms. Amazon, Hulu, Yahoo!, and Microsoft are all competing in the online entertainment marketplace. Furthermore, Netflix has commissioned high-quality original programming such as *House of Cards*. However, none of these companies rivals YouTube for producing made-for-Web content that is quickly becoming a mainstay for a new generation of viewers.

YouTube executives describe traditional television as a wholesale business, with producers selling their programs to a broadcast or cable network that acts as a content gatekeeper. YouTube, in contrast, is all about retailing. Creators develop shows designed to appeal to their audiences rather than the middlemen who have traditionally purchased distribution rights to the content. YouTube performers and producers receive instant feedback from their viewers, and they make programming decisions based on this feedback. The YouTube medium is truly interactive, with the audience responding to content with comments, shares, and sometimes their own videos. In fact, Google executives note that traditional television is one-way, whereas YouTube "talks back."

Consider AwesomenessTV, an American sketch-comedy reality series targeted to young teens that launched as a YouTube channel in July 2013. Awesomeness's marketing team hoped to attract 100,000 subscribers in its first year. In fact, the channel reached that mark in *one month*. In mid-2014, DreamWorks Animation purchased Awesomeness for $33 million.

Google now collects $3.6 billion in annual revenue on YouTube, almost all of it from advertising. Industry experts predict that YouTube revenue will increase by 20 percent in 2014. Keep in mind, however, that traditional network television remains a cash cow, thanks to continued strong advertising fees for sporting events as well as the high fees paid by cable operators and telecommunications companies.

Sources: Compiled from A. Taube, "If YouTube Were a TV Channel, Its Revenues Would Terrify Its Broadcast Network Rivals," *Business Insider*, December 13, 2013; M. Helft, "How YouTube Changes Everything," *Fortune*, August 12, 2013; A. Penny, "Why the Battle between YouTube and TV Matters to Brands," *The Guardian*, June 28, 2013; "YouTube: Battle with TV Is Already Over," Associated Press, May 2, 2013; A. Knapp, "Indie Hip-Hop Star Destorm Power on YouTube and the Future of Music," *Forbes*, March 1, 2012; H. Shaughnessy, "YouTube Creators and the Rise of Social Entertainment," *Forbes*, February 21, 2012; A. Knapp, "Meredith Valiando Is Bringing YouTube to Concert Halls," *Forbes*, February 18, 2012; H. Shaughnessy, "Where Is the Big Time Headed? RockStar, Comic, Actor, and the Story of the Social Brand," *Forbes*, February 1, 2012; J. Perez, "YouTube to Boost Original, Professional Programming," *CIO*, October 29, 2011; www.youtube.com, accessed March 22, 2014.

Questions

1. Describe the differences in how traditional television and YouTube provide online content to audiences.

2. If you were the CEO of a traditional television network, how would you combat YouTube?

Market Research

Traditionally, marketing professionals used demographics compiled by market research firms as one of their primary tools to identify and target potential customers. Obtaining this information was time-consuming and costly, because marketing professionals had to ask potential customers to provide it. Today, however, members of social networks provide this information voluntarily on their pages! (Think about all the information that you provide on your favorite social networking Web sites.) Because of the open nature of social networking, merchants can easily find their customers, see what they do online, and learn who their friends are.

This information provides a new opportunity to assess markets in near real time. Word of mouth has always been one of the most powerful marketing methods—more often than not, people use products that their friends like and recommend. Social media sites can provide this type of data for numerous products and services.

Companies are utilizing social computing tools to obtain feedback from customers. This trend is referred to as *conversational marketing*. These tools enable customers to supply feedback via blogs, wikis, online forums, and social networking sites. Again, customers are providing much of this feedback to companies voluntarily and for free.

Social computing not only generates faster and cheaper results than traditional focus groups but also fosters closer customer relationships. For example, Dell Computer operates a feedback Web site called IdeaStorm that allows customers to suggest and vote on improvements in its offerings (see FIGURE 8.6).

Retailers are aware that customers, especially younger ones, not only want to be heard but also want to know whether other customers agree with them. Consequently, retailers are increasingly opening up their Web sites to customers, allowing them to post product reviews, ratings, and, in some cases, photos and videos.

As a result of this strategy, customer reviews are emerging as prime locations for online shoppers to visit. Approximately one-half of consumers consult reviews before making an

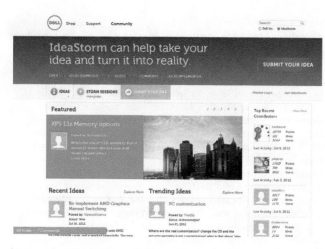

Figure 8.6 Customers share their ideas and feedback with Dell via IdeaStorm (www.ideastorm.com).

online purchase, and almost two-thirds are more likely to purchase from a site that offers ratings and reviews.

Using social computing for market research is not restricted to businesses. Customers also enjoy the capabilities that social computing offers when they are shopping.

Conducting Market Research Using Social Networks

Customer sentiment expressed on Twitter, Facebook, and similar sites represents an incredibly valuable source of information for companies. Customer activities on social networking sites generate huge amounts of data that must be analyzed, so that management can conduct better marketing campaigns and improve their product design and their service offerings. The monitoring, collection, and analysis of socially generated data, and the resultant strategic decisions are combined in a process known as **social intelligence**.

An example of social intelligence is Wendy's International (www.wendys.com), which uses software to sift through the more than 500,000 customer messages the fast-food chain collects each year. Using Clarabridge (www.clarabridge.com) text analytics software, Wendy's analyzes comments from its online notes, e-mails, receipt-based surveys, and social media. Prior to adopting this software, the company used a combination of spreadsheets and keyword searches to review comments in what it describes as a slow and expensive manual approach. In contrast, the new software enables Wendy's to track customer experiences at the store level within minutes.

Social networks provide excellent sources of valuable information for market research. In this section you will see illustrative examples of how to use Facebook, Twitter, and LinkedIn for market research.

Using Facebook for Market Research. There are several ways to use Facebook for market research. Consider the following examples:

- Obtain feedback from your Facebook fans (and their friends if possible) on advertising campaigns, market research, etc. It is the equivalent of holding a free focus group.

- Test-market your messages. Provide two or three options, and ask fans which one they prefer and why.

- Use Facebook for survey invitations (i.e., to recruit participants). Essentially, turn Facebook into a giant panel, and ask users to participate in a survey. Facebook offers a self-service model for displaying ads, which can function as invitations to take a survey. Facebook also allows you to target your audience very specifically based on traditional demographic criteria such as age and gender.

Using Twitter for Market Research. Your customers, your prospects, and industry thought leaders all use Twitter, making it a rich source of instantly updated information. Consider the following examples:

- Visit Twitter Search (www.twitter.com/search). Enter a company's Twitter name. Not only can you follow what the company is saying, you can also follow what everyone is saying to them. Monitoring replies to your competitors and their employees will help you develop your own Twitter strategy by enabling you to observe (a) what your competitors are doing and, more importantly, (b) what people think about them. You can also follow the company's response to this feedback.

- Take advantage of the tools that enable you to find people in the industries in which they operate. Use search.twitter.com to monitor industry-specific keywords. Check out Twellow (www.twellow.com). This site automatically categorizes a Twitter user into one to three industries based on that person's bio and tweets.

- Do you want to know what topic is on most people's minds today? If so, then review the chart on TweetStats (www.tweetstats.com). It will show you the most frequently used words in all of Tweetdom, so you can be a part of those conversations.

- An increasing number of companies are utilizing Twitter to solicit information from customers and to interact with them. Examples are Dell (connecting with customers), JetBlue (learning about customers), Teusner Wines (gathering feedback, sharing information), and Pepsi (rapid response time in dealing with complaints).

Using LinkedIn for Market Research. Post a question (e.g., solicit advice) regarding the topic or issue you are interested in. You may obtain a better result if you go to a specific LinkedIn group.

BEFORE *YOU GO ON....*

1. Is social advertising more effective than advertising without a social component? Why or why not?

2. Describe how marketing professionals use social networks to perform marketing research.

Apply The Concept 8.4

LEARNING OBJECTIVE 8.4 Discuss innovative ways to use social networking sites for advertising and market research.

STEP 1 – Background

Section 8.4 focused on how some businesses employ social advertising to create a competitive advantage. These enterprises allow customers to share product information and make purchases right in the social network. You have probably received a note from a social network that asked you to share it with five of your friends. This type of social commerce is here to stay. The question is: How many people can you actually reach with this type of virtual word-of-mouth marketing?

For example, imagine you want to know how many users could be reached at the third level of friends away from the initial group, when the initial group consists of 100 people and each person shares the message with 3 people. For this example, assume that each person shares with three unique individuals.

The table below is completed for you based on the assumption that each person shares with only two people. (We leave the table for you when each person shares with three people.) This process will help you understand how to find the total reach when each person shares with three people.

Level 1 is the initial 100 people. Level 2 is the initial 100 multiplied by 2 because each individual shares with 2 people. This equals a reach of 200 people at this level. This group then shares with 2 more people, for a reach of 400 people at level 3. After one more share, level 4 will reach 800 people. The total—1,500 people—is the sum of everyone who has been reached at each level.

Level	100 Share with 2	100 Share with 3	200 Share with 2
1	100	100	200
2	200 (100 × 2 = 200)		
3	400 (200 × 2 = 400)		
4	800 (400 × 2 = 800)		
Total	1500 (800 + 400 + 200 + 100)		

STEP 2 – Activity

Expand this table to level 5 to see how quickly social commerce can reach potential customers. Label your columns as indicated in the table.

STEP 3 – Deliverable

After seeing how quickly social networking can reach customers through viral communication, write a paragraph to discuss innovative ways to utilize the power of social commerce. Specifically, focus on how this tool can be used for advertising and market research. Submit your paragraph to your instructor.

8.5 Social Computing in Business: Customer Relationship Management

The customer service profession has undergone a significant transformation, both in the ways that customer service professionals conduct business and in the ways that customers adapt to interacting with companies in a newly connected environment. Social computing has vastly altered both the expectations of customers and the capabilities of corporations in the area of customer relationship management. (We discuss customer relationship management in detail in Chapter 12.)

How Social Computing Improves Customer Service

Customers are now incredibly empowered. Companies are closely monitoring social computing not only because they are mindful of the negative comments posted by social network members but also because they perceive an opportunity to involve customers proactively to reduce problems through improved customer service.

Empowered customers know how to use the wisdom and power of crowds and communities to their benefit. These customers choose how they interact with companies and brands, and they have elevated expectations concerning their experiences with a company. They are actively involved with businesses, not just as purchasers but also as advocates and influencers. As a result, businesses must respond to customers quickly and appropriately. Fortunately, social computing provides many opportunities for businesses to do just that, thereby offering businesses the opportunity to turn disgruntled customers into champions for the firm.

Consider this example: Papa John's Pizza fired a cashier at one of its New York restaurants and apologized to an Asian-American customer for a receipt that identified her as "lady chinky eyes." Minhee Cho, a communications manager at the nonprofit investigative journalism group ProPublica, posted a photo of the receipt on her Twitter account, and it was viewed almost 200,000 times in a single day. John Schnatter, chairman and CEO of Papa John's, immediately posted an apology on Facebook. In his apology, he asserted that he had apologized personally to Ms. Cho as well.

— BEFORE YOU GO ON.... —

1. Discuss why social computing is so important in customer relationship management.
2. Describe how social computing improves customer service.

Apply The Concept 8.5

LEARNING OBJECTIVE 8.5 Describe how social computing improves customer service.

STEP 1 – Background

Social customer relationship management involves using social networks to maintain customer loyalty. One company that employs this strategy quite skillfully is ZAGG (Zealous

About Great Gadgets). ZAGG makes and sells accessories for mobile devices such as smartphones and tablets. To help sell its products, the company has developed one of the best social customer relationship management plans around.

When ZAGG develops a new product, it not only posts notes about the product on its social networking page but also involves customers in the process. For example, when ZAGG was releasing its ZAGGFolio for the iPad, the company allowed fans to vote on the colors of the new product.

ZAGG is also proficient at monitoring the social network for product-related issues. It is not uncommon for a customer to complain and then receive feedback from a ZAGG employee. Not only does the company retain that individual customer, but it also develops a sense of trust with all of its customers who are confident they would receive the same treatment.

STEP 2 – Activity

Go to http://www.wiley.com/go/rainer/MIS3e/applytheconcept and click on the link to ZAGG's Web site. At the bottom of the page you will find a link to all of the company's social networks. Visit their Facebook page, and review their timeline. Search for customer complaints and for how the company deals with them. Did you find a customer representative present on the social networking site? Does the site offer any competitions? Polls? Giveaways? Can you reverse-engineer the company's social customer relationship management methodology?

STEP 3 – Deliverable

Imagine that you are a marketing manager, and you have been selected to present a report to the president on how social computing improves customer service. Create the outline that you would use to make your points and present it to the class and to your instructor.

8.6 Social Computing in Business: Human Resource Management

Human resource (HR) departments in many organizations use social computing applications outside their organizations (recruiting) and inside their organizations (employee development). For example, Deloite Touche Tohmatsu created a social network to assist its HR managers in downsizing and regrouping teams.

Recruiting

Both recruiters and job seekers are moving to online social networks as recruiting platforms. Enterprise recruiters are scanning online social networks, blogs, and other social resources to identify and find information about potential employees. If job seekers are online and active, there is a good chance that they will be seen by recruiters. In addition, on social networks there are many passive job seekers—people who are employed but would take a better job if one appeared. So, it is important that both active and passive job seekers maintain online profiles that accurately reflect their background and skills. Closing case 1 takes a look at the rewards and the difficulties inherent in the online recruiting process. It also provides some tips to assist you in a job search.

In another example, one HR director uses the HR social media management software Bullhorn Reach (www.bullhornreach.com), which allows her to post jobs to eight different social networks simultaneously. Bullhorn Reach also enables her to analyze metrics that measure the effectiveness of her social recruiting efforts.

Employee Development

Human resource managers know that the best strategy to enable, encourage, and promote employee development is to build relationships with employees. To this end, a number of

HR professionals are using enterprise social tools such as Chatter (www.salesforce.com/chatter), Yammer (www.yammer.com), and Tibbr (www.tibbr.com) to tap into the wisdom of every employee. These tools help connect employees to work efficiently across organizations and to collaborate on sales opportunities, campaigns, and projects. They help companies simplify workflows and capture new ideas. They enable HR managers to find subject matter experts within the organization, recommending relevant people for every project team, sales team, and other functions.

As HR managers learn more about employees' skills, expertise, and passions through such tools, they can better motivate them, thereby helping them become more engaged and excited about their work. Employees can then be better rewarded for their expertise.

Another area of employee development is training. A large percentage of the time and expense of employee education and learning management can be minimized by utilizing e-learning and interactive social learning tools. These tools help create connections among learners, instructors, and information. Companies find that these tools facilitate knowledge transfer within departments and across teams. Examples of these tools are Moodle (http://moodle.com), Joomia (www.joomia.org), and Bloomfire (www.bloomfire.com).

BEFORE *YOU GO ON....*

1. Explain why LinkedIn has become so important in the recruiting process.

2. If you are looking for a job, what is the major problem with restricting your search to social networks?

Apply The Concept 8.6

LEARNING OBJECTIVE 8.6 Discuss different ways in which human resource managers make use of social computing.

STEP 1 – Background

Social human resource management is redefining the ways we search and apply for jobs and make hiring decisions. Going digital was a natural step, but it was also an awkward one. When position announcements went from the bulletin board and local newspaper to Monster.com, the number of positions and applicants exploded. We are so connected today that it is impossible to go back. After you graduate you will no doubt use social networks to find and apply for jobs.

STEP 2 – Activity

Visit http://www.wiley.com/go/rainer/MIS3e/applytheconcept and click on the first link for Apply the Concept 8.6. This link will take you to LinkedIn, a professional social network. Create a profile that includes the college you currently attend. Connect to your classmates as they also complete this activity. You never know when you will need to call on one of these individuals.

Next, search the Web for "Job Search Websites," and see which ones will allow you to connect with your LinkedIn profile. As you connect with these professional sites, consider the differences between a professional and a personal social network.

STEP 3 – Deliverable

In a paper, discuss the various ways in which human resource managers will make use of social computing and how you can best present yourself online. Present your paper to your instructor.

What's in for ME?

 FOR THE
ACCOUNTING MAJOR

Audit teams use social networking technologies internally to stay in touch with team members who are working on multiple projects. These technologies serve as a common channel of communications. For example, an audit team manager can create a group, include his or her team members as subscribers, and then push information regarding projects to all members at once. Externally, these technologies are useful in interfacing with clients and other third parties for whom the firm and its staff provide services.

 FOR THE FINANCE MAJOR

Many of the popular social networking sites have users who subscribe to finance-oriented subgroups. Among these groups are finance professionals who collaborate and share knowledge as well as nonfinancial professionals who are potential clients.

 FOR THE MARKETING MAJOR

Social computing tools and applications enable marketing professionals to become closer to their customers in a variety of ways, including blogs, wikis, ratings, and recommendations. Marketing professionals now receive almost real-time feedback on products.

 FOR THE PRODUCTION/ OPERATIONS MANAGEMENT MAJOR

Social computing tools and applications allow production personnel to "enlist" business partners and customers in product development activities.

 FOR THE HUMAN RESOURCE MANAGEMENT MAJOR

Social networks offer tremendous benefits to human resource professionals. HR personnel can perform a great deal of their recruiting activities by accessing such sites as LinkedIn. They can also check out potential new hires by accessing a large number of social networking sites. Internally, HR personnel can utilize private, internal social networks for employee expertise and experience in order to find the best person for a position or project team.

FOR THE MIS MAJOR

The MIS department is responsible for two aspects of social computing usage: (1) monitoring employee usage of social computing applications while at work, both time and content, and (2) developing private, internal social networks for company employees and then monitoring the content of these networks.

SUMMARY

1. Describe six Web 2.0 tools and two major types of Web 2.0 sites.

AJAX is a Web development technique that enables portions of Web pages to reload with fresh data instead of requiring the entire Web page to reload.

A *tag* is a keyword or term that describes a piece of information (e.g., a blog, a picture, an article, or a video clip).

Really Simple Syndication allows you to receive the information you want (customized information), when you want it, without having to surf thousands of Web sites.

A *weblog* (*blog* for short) is a personal Web site, open to the public, in which the site creator expresses his or her feelings or opinions with a series of chronological entries.

Microblogging is a form of blogging that allows users to write short messages (or capture an image or embedded video) and publish them.

A *wiki* is a Web site on which anyone can post material and make changes to already posted material. Wikis foster easy collaboration and they harness the collective intelligence of Internet users.

Social networking Web sites allow users to upload their content to the Web in the form of text (e.g., blogs), voice (e.g., podcasts), images, and videos (e.g., videocasts).

A *mashup* is a Web site that takes different content from a number of other Web sites and mixes them together to create a new kind of content.

2. Describe the benefits and risks of social commerce to companies.

Social commerce refers to the delivery of electronic commerce activities and transactions through social computing.

Benefits of social commerce to customers include the following: better and faster vendors' response to complaints; customers can assist other customers; customers' expectations can be met more fully and quickly; customers can easily search, link, chat, and buy while staying in the social network's page.

Benefits of social commerce to vendors include the following: can test new products and ideas quickly and inexpensively; learn much about their customers; identify problems quickly and alleviate anger; learn from customers' experiences with rapid feedback; increase sales when customers discuss products positively on social networking site; create better marketing campaigns and brand awareness; use low-cost user-generated content, for example, in marketing campaigns; get free advertising through viral marketing; identify influential brand advocates and reward them.

Risks of social computing include information security concerns; invasion of privacy; violation of intellectual property and copyright; employees' reluctance to participate; data leakage of personal information or corporate strategic information; poor or biased quality of users' generated content; cyberbullying/cyberstalking and employee harassment.

3. Identify the methods used for shopping socially.

Social shopping is a method of electronic commerce that takes all of the key aspects of social networks—friends, groups, voting, comments, discussions, reviews, etc.—and focuses them on shopping.

Methods for shopping socially include what other shoppers say; group shopping; shopping communities and clubs; social marketplaces and direct sales; and peer-to-peer shopping.

4. Discuss innovative ways to use social networking sites for advertising and market research.

Social advertising represents advertising formats that employ the social context of the user viewing the ad.

Innovative ways to advertise in social media include the following: create a company Facebook page; tweet business success stories to your customers; integrate ads into YouTube videos; add a Facebook "Like" button with its sponsored story to your product; use sponsored stories.

> *Using Facebook for market research*: get feedback from your Facebook fans (and their friends if possible) on advertising campaigns, market research, etc.; test-market your messages; use Facebook for survey invitations.

> *Using Twitter for market research*: use Twitter Search; use Twellow; look at the chart on TweetStats.

> *Using LinkedIn for market research*: post a question (e.g., solicit advice) regarding the topic or issue you are interested in.

5. Describe how social computing improves customer service.

Customers are now incredibly empowered. Companies are closely monitoring social computing not only because they are mindful of the negative comments posted by social network members but also because they see an opportunity to involve customers proactively to reduce problems by improved customer service.

Empowered customers know how to use the wisdom and power of crowds and communities to their benefit. These customers choose how they interact with companies and brands, and they have elevated expectations. They are actively involved with businesses, not just as purchasers but also as advocates and influencers. As a result, businesses must respond to customers quickly and accurately. Fortunately, social computing provides many opportunities for businesses to do just that, thereby giving businesses the opportunity to turn disgruntled customers into champions for the firm.

6. Discuss different ways in which human resource managers make use of social computing.

> *Recruiting*: Both recruiters and job seekers are moving to online social networks as new recruiting platforms. Enterprise recruiters are scanning online social networks, blogs, and other social resources to identify and find information about potential employees. If job seekers are online and active, there is a good chance that they will be seen by recruiters. In addition, on social networks there are many passive job seekers—people who are employed but would take a better job if it appeared. So, it is important that both active and passive job seekers maintain profiles online that truly reflect them.

> *Employee development*: HR managers are using social tools to build relationships with employees. As HR managers learn more about employees, they can help them become more engaged and excited about their work.

>>>CHAPTER GLOSSARY

AJAX A Web development technique that allows portions of Web pages to reload with fresh data rather than requiring the entire Web page to reload

blog (weblog) A personal Web site, open to the public, in which the site creator expresses his or her feelings or opinions with a series of chronological entries

blogosphere The term for the millions of blogs on the Web

collaborative consumption Peer-to-peer sharing or renting

mashup Web site that takes different content from a number of other Web sites and mixes them together to create a new kind of content

microblogging A form of blogging that allows users to write short messages (or capture an image or embedded video) and publish them

Really Simple Syndication A technology that allows users to receive the information they want, when they want it, without having to surf thousands of Web sites

social advertising Advertising formats that make use of the social context of the user viewing the ad

social capital The number of connections a person has within and between social networks

social commerce The delivery of electronic commerce activities and transactions through social computing

social computing A type of information technology that combines social behavior and information systems to create value

social graph A map of all relevant links or connections for one member of a social network

social intelligence The monitoring, collection, and analysis of socially generated data and the resultant strategic decisions

social marketplaces These act as online intermediaries that harness the power of social networks for introducing, buying, and selling products and services

social network A social structure composed of individuals, groups, or organizations linked by values, visions, ideas, financial exchange, friendship, kinship, conflict, or trade

social networking Activities performed using social software tools (e.g., blogging) or social networking features (e.g., media sharing)

social shopping A method of electronic commerce that takes all of the key aspects of social networks—friends, groups, voting, comments, discussions, reviews, etc.—and focuses them on shopping

tag A keyword or term that describes a piece of information

tweet Messages and updates posted by users on Twitter

Twitter A free microblogging service that allows its users to send messages and read other users' messages and updates

Web 2.0 A loose collection of information technologies and applications, plus the Web sites that use them

Web 2.0 media Any Web site that provides user-generated media content and promotes tagging, rating, commenting, and other interactions among users and their media contributions

weblog (see blog)

wiki A Web site on which anyone can post material and make changes to other material

>>>DISCUSSION QUESTIONS

1. How would you describe Web 2.0 to someone who has not taken a course in information systems?

2. If you were the CEO of a company, would you pay attention to blogs about your company? Why or why not? If yes, would you consider some blogs to be more important or more reliable than others? If so, which ones? How would you find blogs relating to your company?

3. Do you have a page on a social networking Web site? If yes, why? If no, what is keeping you from creating one? Is there any content that you definitely would *not* post on such a page?

4. How can an organization best employ social computing technologies and applications to benefit its business processes?

5. What factors might cause an individual, an employee, or a company to be cautious in the use of social networks?

6. Why are advertisers so interested in social networks?

7. What sorts of restrictions or guidelines should firms place on the use of social networks by employees? Are social computing sites a threat to security? Can they tarnish a firm's reputation? If so, how? Can they enhance a firm's reputation? If so, how?

8. Why are marketers so interested in social networks?

9. Why are human resource managers so interested in social networks?

>>>PROBLEM-SOLVING ACTIVITIES

1. Enter www.programmableweb.com and study the various services that the Web site offers. Learn how to create mashups and then propose a mashup of your own. Present your mashup to the class.

2. Go to Amazon's Mechanical Turk Web site (www.mturk.com). View the available Human Intelligence Tasks (HITs). Are there any HITs that you would be interested in to make some extra money? Why or why not?

3. Access Pandora (www.pandora.com). Why is Pandora a social networking site?

4. Access ChatRoulette (www.chatroulette.com). What is interesting about this social networking site?

5. Using a search engine, look up the following:
   - *Most popular or most visited blogs.* Pick two and follow some of the posts. Why do you think these blogs are popular?

   - *Best blogs* (try www.bloggerschoiceawards.com). Pick two and consider why they might be the "best blogs."

6. Research how to be a successful blogger. What does it take to be a successful blogger? What time commitment might be needed? How frequently do successful bloggers post?

>>> COLLABORATION EXERCISE

STEP 1 – Background

This chapter has illustrated many positive and many negative features associated with social computing. However, in spite of the negatives, social computing is a reality that you will have to deal with as a job applicant, an employee, and perhaps as a business manager.

In some cases, you will need to develop your own social tools. To provide you with some experience in this area, this collaboration exercise will have you create a social network for a small business venture.

STEP 2 – Activity

You are the cofounder of a local bicycle shop, and you need some publicity. To help address this need, you have decided to sponsor an annual bike race in your neighborhood. There is already a local runner's club from which you hope to attract some participants.

Even though you are a very small enterprise, assume that you have a support team (classmates) comprised of representatives from marketing, logistics, finance, and legal services. If your team does not include members who are majoring in these (or similar) areas, then each team member should select a role and research the activity from that perspective.

Visit http://www.wiley.com/go/rainer/MIS3e/collaboration, and click on the link. It will take you to the Web site for Ning, a company that allows you to create your own social network. The site offers training videos and plenty of helpful information. Explore this site with your teammates, and determine how creating your personal social network might be superior to utilizing an existing network.

STEP 3 – Deliverable

As a team, Use Google Drive to create a shared Google Sheet (Google Doc) and write a proposal for or against using Ning. If you feel it is better to utilize existing social networks rather than creating your own with Ning, then make certain to explain why that is superior to having your own social network. Present your proposal to your instructor.

CLOSING **CASE 1** > So You Want to Find a Job

Let's say you want to find a job. Like the majority of job hunters, you will probably conduct at least part of your search online, typically on job sites such as www.monster.com, www.careerbuilder.com, and www.simplyhired.com. After all, the vast majority of entry-level positions in the United States are now listed only online.

Job sites are the fastest, least expensive, and most efficient method to connect employers with potential employees. Unfortunately, these sites can be overwhelmed with résumés, making it impossible for them to process these résumés efficiently and effectively.

Luckily for you, job sites now have access to vast amounts of computing power (see cloud computing in Plug IT In 3), and they use new, more efficient search algorithms to help manage millions of résumés. In addition, you have access to many companies whose job is to assist you in your search.

In perhaps the most dramatic shift in the online employment business, job searchers are turning away from traditional job sites and toward social networks such as LinkedIn. Applicants like you have helped LinkedIn raise its market share in job searches from 4.7 percent in 2010 to more than 12 percent by mid-2014. This shift explains why Simply Hired incorporated social networking into its search process, a move that enabled job seekers to integrate their networks with Simply Hired's job listings, thereby facilitating contacts and referrals to target companies.

To find a job, your best bet is to begin with LinkedIn (www.linkedin.com), which has roughly 165 million members. You should definitely have a profile on LinkedIn, which, by the way, is free. (See the end of this case for mistakes to avoid on your LinkedIn profile.)

LinkedIn has focused on selling the company's Recruiter product to corporate talent scouts. Thousands of human resource departments use the tool.

Perhaps the fundamental reason for LinkedIn's success has been its ability to accurately identify its market segment. The company's automated approach does not lend itself well to the upper tier of the job market—for example, CEO searches—where traditional face-to-face searches continue to be the preferred strategy. At the other end of the spectrum—that is, low-paying, low-skill jobs such as cashiers and truck drivers—job boards provide faster results. LinkedIn targets the vast sweet spot between these two extremes, helping to fill high-skill jobs that pay anywhere from $50,000 to $250,000 or more per year. This is the spot you will likely occupy when you graduate.

LinkedIn is also invaluable in finding hidden candidates whom traditional searches would overlook. Consider the hiring manager for Wireless Vision, a mobile phone retailer. She was asked to find an accounting manager with an entrepreneurial spirit. Regular job ads produced only 100 candidates, all of them unsuitable. So, she crafted a search on LinkedIn. Her target: accountants who had worked in similar retail companies and whose profiles included keywords such as "launched," "created," and "built." Within days she had found an Avis veteran who had developed billing systems on his own. The two individuals talked, and Wireless Vision had its new accounting manager.

A number of job-search companies are competing with LinkedIn. These companies are trying to create better-targeted matching systems that leverage social networking functionality. Here are two examples:

- Jobvite (http://recruiting.jobvite.com) helps client companies by integrating social networking with the personal referrals that employers prefer. Clients' employees are allowed to send their online "friends" a "jobvite" to apply for an opening.

- Dice Open Web (www.dice.com/openweb) searches across online sites, identifies active and passive information technology candidates, and assembles public information about them from more than 50 social media sites, including GitHub, Stack Overflow, Gravatar, Quora, Blogger, MS Inquire, Google Plus, Twitter, Facebook, and Flickr. Open Web finds professionals who match predetermined criteria by integrating pieces of information residing at these sites. The result is a profile that includes a candidate's professional experience, contributions, history, and capabilities, as well as his or her passions and interests.

The bottom line for all job sites is that they do not want to produce 2,000 satisfactory candidates, but rather 20 great candidates. The most important secret to making online job search sites work for you is to use them carefully. When you are looking for a job, it is too easy to spend all day on your keyboard, combing through listings and experimenting with endless search filters. Job coaches advise you to spend 80 percent of your day networking and directly contacting the people in charge of jobs you want. Devote another 10 percent to headhunters. Spend only the remaining 10 percent of your time online.

Here is how to make your time online count. To start with, as you saw above, you should have a profile on LinkedIn.

Next, access the Google-like job aggregators, such as Indeed (www.indeed.com) and SimplyHired. Both of these sites list millions of jobs, and they make it easy to narrow your search using filters. These filters include title, company name, location, and many others. Indeed allows you to search within a specific salary range. SimplyHired lets you sort for friendly, socially responsible, and even dog-friendly workplaces.

Both sites have advanced search options. Try plugging in the name of a company you might want to work for or an advanced degree that qualifies you for specialized work. For example, you could enter "CFA" if you are a certified financial analyst or "LEED" if you are a building engineer with expertise in environmental efficiency.

SimplyHired has a useful tool called "Who do I know." If you have a LinkedIn profile, then this tool will instantly display your LinkedIn contacts with connections to various job listings. "Who do I know" also syncs with Facebook.

One more trick to using the aggregators: Configure them to deliver listings to your inbox. Set up an e-mail alert that delivers new job postings to you every day.

You should also search for niche sites that are specific to your field. For technology-related jobs, for instance, Dice (www.dice.com) has a strong reputation. For nonprofit jobs, try Idealist (www.idealist.org). For government jobs, the U.S. government's site is an excellent resource: www.usajobs.gov.

One more great online resource is Craigslist (www.craigslist.com). It is one site the aggregators do not tap. Craigslist focuses on local listings, and it is especially useful for entry-level jobs and internships.

Beyond locating listings for specific jobs, career coaches contend that job sites can be a resource for keywords and phrases that you can pull from job descriptions and include in your résumé, cover letters, and e-mails. Use the language from a job description in your cover letter.

Web sites like Vault (www.vault.com), Monster, and CareerBuilder provide some helpful career tips. Vault, in particular, offers very useful career guides.

The bottom line: It is critical to extend most of your efforts *beyond* an online search. There is just too much competition online.

MISTAKES NOT TO MAKE ON YOUR LINKEDIN PROFILE

- Do have a current, professional picture. (No dogs, no spouses, no babies, etc.)

- Do make certain your LinkedIn Status is correct and current.

- Do join groups related to your field of study or even to your personal interests.

- Do list an accurate skill set. Do not embellish.

- Do not use the standard connection request. Do some research on that person, and tailor your connection request to that person.

- Do not neglect LinkedIn's privacy settings. When you have a job and are looking for another one, you will want to be discreet. You can set your privacy settings so that your boss does not see that you are looking for opportunities.

- Do not skip the Summary. The Summary is a concise way of selling yourself. Write it in the first person.

- Do not eliminate past jobs or volunteer work.

- Do not say you have worked with someone when you have not.

Sources: Compiled from S. Greengard, "Online Recruiter Adopts a New Web-Based Tool," *Baseline Magazine*, April 26, 2013; J. Leber, "A Startup That Scores Job Seekers, Whether They Know It or Not," *MIT Technology Review*, March 7, 2013; LearnVest, "8 Mistakes You Should Never Make on LinkedIn," *Forbes*, March 4, 2013; G. Anders, "LinkedIn's Fast-Lane Ambition: Watch These 5 Moves in 2013," *Forbes*, February 7, 2013; C. Ceniza-Levine, "What Recruiters Want from Job Seekers Today," *Forbes*, February 1, 2013; G. Anders, "The Other Social Network," *Forbes*, July 16, 2012; R. Sylvestre-Williams, "How Recruiters Use LinkedIn," *Forbes*, May 31, 2012; T. Team, "LinkedIn Looks to Hitch Ride from Mobile Ads," *Forbes*, February 14, 2012; R. Silverman, "No More Resumes, Say Some Firms," *The Wall Street Journal*, January 24, 2012; L. Weber, "Your Resume vs. Oblivion," *The Wall Street Journal*, January 24, 2012; S. Adams, "Secrets of Making the Most of Job Search Websites," *Forbes*, January 18, 2012; G. Anders, "The Rare Find," *Bloomberg BusinessWeek*, October 17–23, 2011; www.monster.com, www.linkedin.com, www.careerbuilder.com, www.jobvite.com, www.simplyhired.com, www.indeed.com, www.dice.com, www.idealist.org, www.usajobs.gov, www.craigslist.com, www.vault.com, www.gild.com, accessed March 5, 2014.

Questions

1. What are the advantages of using online job sites when you look for your first job?

2. What are the disadvantages of using online job sites when you look for your first job?

CLOSING **CASE 2** > Establishing a Presence in China via Microblogging

THE BUSINESS PROBLEM >>> Multinational companies are looking for cost-effective methods to market their products to the vast, rapidly growing market of China. Many of these companies believe they have found such a solution to establish, consolidate, or increase their market presence in China: microblogging. They are using microblogging to enhance communications with consumers, launch business campaigns, deliver positive information about their products, and build their brands.

THE IT SOLUTION >>> Mercedes-Benz, Starbucks, and Nokia have widely different lines of business. Nevertheless, in China they share the same marketing platform: They are participants in the "virtual town square." In China, the virtual town square is a microblog, a platform that is now an integral component of global companies' strategies to expand their operations in China.

The leading microblogging Web site in China is Sina Weibo (called Weibo; http://english.sina.com/weibo/). In 2013 this site attracted an estimated 500 million users, according to the China Internet Network Information Center. The Center further reported that there were more than 260,000 active company accounts on microblogs in 2013, with more than 1,000 of these accounts belonging to multinational companies. These companies span 22 different industries.

Since their Chinese debut in August 2009, microblogs have developed into a huge online society where people from all walks of life share personal experiences, participate in social activities, and voice opinions on diverse topics. From a commercial perspective, the power to influence opinion and ultimately increase purchases makes microblogs appealing to multinational companies. In addition, microblogs have become an effective means for companies to reduce spending on conventional advertising. For example, it is difficult and expensive for companies to establish a marketing presence throughout such a vast country because television marketing is so expensive.

Chinese microblogs differ from their Western counterparts such as Twitter in terms of the added features they offer. The fundamental difference between Chinese and Western microblogs lies in Twitter's relatively low penetration rate in the U.S. market. Of the 74 percent of U.S. adults who use the Internet, only 8 percent use Twitter, according to a recent study by Pew Research Center (www.pewresearch.org). In contrast, by the end of 2012, the proportion of microbloggers among Chinese adults who use the Internet reached 55 percent.

Another key difference is that Weibo allows users to watch videos and view pictures seamlessly. In contrast, Twitter typically presents video and pictures in the form of a hyperlink that users have to click to access the content. Going further, Twitter limits users to 140 characters for each post. Weibo, by contrast, allows 140 characters in addition to various other features such as pictures, videos, and hyperlinks. These additional features enable companies to create more vivid marketing campaigns.

THE RESULTS >>> Let's review some examples of how several multinational companies have fared using microblogs in China.

- **Mercedes-Benz** (www.mercedes-benz.com). The German luxury brand Mercedes-Benz knows the power of microblogging in China. In January 2013, the company initiated a campaign to sell a limited edition of its Smart cars in China, and it decided to conduct this campaign via a microblog. The result? Mercedes-Benz sold all 666 units of the Smart 2013 New Year Edition offered via Weibo in *eight hours*!

- **Starbucks** (www.starbucks.com). Starbucks opened its Weibo account in May 2012. Today the coffee giant has more than 700,000 followers in China. The company's initiative started with routine marketing campaigns. Starbucks quickly discovered, however, that targeted marketing campaigns can be converted into real-time store purchases.

  In 2013, Starbucks introduced a campaign to increase Frappuccino sales on its microblog. During the two-month warm-up campaign, Starbucks put up more than 60 posts on its microblog, which generated 234,541 reposts and comments, according to JWT Shanghai, the advertising company that conducted the campaign.

  In terms of quantifiable returns, the company's 500,000 yuan ($80,600) microblog campaign resulted in more than 95 million friend-to-friend recommendations and helped generate a 14 percent growth in Frappuccino sales in China.

- **Ikea** (www.ikea.com). The Swedish furniture retailer set up its account on Weibo in October 2010. Its microblog performs a dual role: listening to consumer feedback and suggestions, and providing positive, timely feedback on their concerns and needs. Ikea's daily schedule includes answering consumers' questions, forwarding complaints to relevant after-sales departments, supervising keywords, and overseeing comments relating to sensitive topics on other microblogs that could affect the company.

- **McDonald's** (www.mcdonalds.com). In March 2012, China Central Television reported that McDonald's was selling expired food at its branch in the upmarket Sanlitun area in eastern Beijing. Within one hour of that report, the U.S. fast food giant announced the suspension of business at that branch. It also apologized on its microblog, triggering nearly 389,000 posts. This strategy enabled the company to quickly and successfully resolve the crisis.

All of these examples convey good news. Now, what is the bad news? Approximately 28 million people abandoned Weibo in 2013, according to a Chinese government report. Why? The answer is that the Chinese government has blocked Twitter since 2009, so many Chinese were using Weibo as a source of unfiltered information. Weibo attracted the attention of Chinese authorities, who moved to silence dissenting voices online. The government passed a law that empowered the authorities to jail microbloggers, and dozens were arrested.

These developments have put a damper on multinational companies' marketing efforts. However, citizens have turned to instant mobile messaging services, such as WeChat (www.wechat.com), whose user base has expanded dramatically. Therefore, multinationals might turn to WeChat for future marketing efforts.

Sources: Compiled from C. Bailey, "Weibo Wants You to Ride China's Micro-Blogging Explosion," *The Street*, March 20, 2014; "Chinese Microblogging Site Weibo Files $500M IPO," *Reuters*, March 14, 2014; "A Record of Over 800K Weibo Posts Published in the First Minute of Year of the Horse," *China Internet Watch*, February 19, 2014; "China Microblogging Site Weibo Sees Decline in Users," *BBC News Asia*, January 17, 2014; "9 Facts About Microblog Marketing in China," *Advangent*, October 29, 2013; K. Tang, "Why Starbucks Is Suddenly Becoming Rebel Chic in China," *BuzzFeed*, October 22, 2013; H. Shao, "Updated: Critizue of Starbucks by China's State Broadcaster Backfires," *Forbes*, October 22, 2013; "China Employs Two Million Microblog Monitors State Media Say," *BBC News China*, October 4, 2013; G. Hamblin, "Social Media Marketing: Microblogging," *TruCounsel Marketing*, August 14, 2013; V. Chu, A. Girdhar, and R. Sood, "Couching Tiger Tames the Dragon," *Business Today*, July 21, 2013; L. Jing and C. Yingqun, "Talking It Up Online," *China Daily*, April 22, 2013; "Mercedes-Benz Becomes First Brand to Sell Cars Via Weibo," *Tech & Science*, January 24, 2013; "Mercedes-Benz Experiments with Selling Smart Cars on China's Sina Weibo Microblog," *TheNextWeb*, January 21, 2013; N. Madden, "Marketers Like Starbucks Are Learning to Use Microblog Sina Weibo in China," *Advertising Age*, September 28, 2011; http://english.sina.com/weibo/, accessed March 22, 2014.

Questions

1. Describe the various advantages and benefits that multinational companies hope to attain from their marketing efforts on Weibo.

2. Describe the disadvantages that multinational companies might encounter from their marketing efforts on Weibo.

INTERNSHIP ACTIVITY> 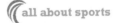 all about sports

Retail/Entertainment Industry

Social computing has become a powerful tool used by retailers around the world. Group shopping sites such as Groupon and LivingSocial offer discounts when a certain number of people purchase a given product. This arrangement creates a bit of peer pressure when friends tell friends about a great deal they really want, but will get only if enough people purchase the product. This peer pressure can be very powerful in compelling people to open their wallets when they really don't want to.

For this Internship Activity, you will be working for All About Sports and, specifically, for Hannah Shaw, the Marketing Director. Below is an e-mail from Hannah that conveys her ideas for using the power of social media to drive sales.

To:	IT Intern
From:	Hannah Shaw
Subject:	Help Creating Marketing Programs

Hello!

I have a very interesting project for you. The sporting goods store I work for, All About Sports, has lost sales to several large online retailers. These companies are able to sell much more merchandise than I am and therefore can sell items at a lower cost. I have tried running ads and specials in the newspaper, but I just haven't made any headway in improving our sales.

I would like to use social computing to help boost sales by offering group discounts. My hope is that I can put together product discounts for group purchases, such as a single team. These discounts don't have to be restricted to a single team, however. I could offer group purchases that would benefit anyone playing a team sport, but at the same time make a recommendation that an entire team match. Here are a few things I need help with to get started.

First, I would like you to research some of the companies that offer these group discounts. Start with companies like Groupon and LivingSocial. Find out all you can about how these discounts would work if I were their customer. I need to know how much money these companies get from these deals and the parameters I have to work within. Also, I think it is possible for me just to run the special by myself and not even go through them. What do you recommend?

Also, try to locate videos on the Web that deal with this type of marketing. I am certain there are some consulting groups that provide information on YouTube on how to use group purchases to fuel sales.

After you have learned as much as you can from these Web sites and videos, draw up a recommendation for me on whom I should target, when and why I should target them, and how I should design a deal that will benefit them as well as us.

I am very excited about this project, and I look forward to receiving your proposal.
Hannah

Note: All links mentioned in this letter are available at http://www.wiley.com/go/rainer/MIS3e/internship.

SPREADSHEET ACTIVITY > VALIDATION

STEP 1 – Background

The automation of data entry benefits modern organizations because it reduces the risk that inaccurate data will be presented. In a spreadsheet, ensuring that data are presented appropriately is often referred to as validation. Essentially, you validate data by creating rules to which the data must conform.

STEP 2 – Activity

You work as a receptionist, and you frequently take calls for your fellow employees. Sometimes you forget to ask important questions. So, you decide to create a spreadsheet to make certain you obtain the necessary information from each caller. The following are few of the items you want to capture:

Caller's Name
Called Name
Caller's Number
Reason for Call
E-mail Address
Urgency Rating
Best Time to Return Call

Of course, you could try to remember this information, or you could transfer the caller to voicemail. However, callers often fail to leave some key information. Ultimately, to make certain you don't leave anything out, you decide to create a spreadsheet that will validate each data point.

Validation means that the data in your spreadsheet have to conform to certain preset standards. For example, you can set your data to fall between certain dates. Then, if someone tries to enter a date that falls before or after your prescribed range, the spreadsheet will return an error.

STEP 3 – Deliverable

Visit http://www.wiley.com/go/rainer/MIS3e/spreadsheet, and download a spreadsheet that you can use to start your call log. Instructions for validation are included on the sheet. Complete the activity as directed in the spreadsheet and submit your call log to your instructor.

Follow the instructions in the spreadsheet and submit your final work to your instructor.

DATABASE ACTIVITY > FORMS

STEP 1 – Background

In this activity, you will create a three-table form directly, using the Form Wizard, and you will improve the appearance of your forms. You were introduced to forms in the Chapter 7 activity. There, you created three forms: one based on a single table, one based on two tables, and one based on three tables where you had to create a subform to manage complex table relationships. Here, you will extend your knowledge to more complex form design issues.

In this activity you will use a database similar to one a store might use. The database contains data on items the store sells, the manufacturers of these items, and the distributors who supply them to the store. A distributor may supply items from several manufacturers. The relationship map, accessed via the Database Tools ribbon, displays the complicated relationships among these tables.

STEP 2 – Activity

Visit http://www.wiley.com/go/rainer/MIS3e/database, and download the database linked for the Chapter 8 Activity. This activity will instruct you to create a form similar to the one you designed for the Chapter 7 Activity. For this activity, however, you will generate this form using the Form Wizard. (Database 8 has four tables: customer, order, line item, and product.)

To begin, use the Form Wizard to select the Distributors Table, the Manufacturers Table, and the Product Table. Create a form that displays Distributor Information and contains data from two subforms: a Manufacturer Subform and a Product Subform. Organize your form by "DistTable," and specify using "forms with subforms." Save your Distributor Form as "DistForm," and close your work. Reopen it, and you can see that the Form Wizard may put together the information you have requested, but it doesn't do much for you in the way of formatting.

Next, create an identical form using the Form Wizard. This time, name it "DistForm2." Rename your form to a common name (not database titles), and resize any text that is not easily legible. There is quite a bit to change, so be prepared to spend some time creating and reformatting this form.

STEP 3 – Deliverable

Submit your database with both forms included. You have now learned how to create complex forms from scratch and clean up the formatting to make your forms more presentable.

Additional help with this database skill is available in WileyPLUS. Open the "Microsoft Office 2013 Lab Manual Database Module: Access 2013," and review Lesson 5: Editing Records. Help is also available from the Microsoft Support Web site at the link shown above.

Business and E-Commerce

LEARNING OBJECTIVES >>>

9.1 Describe the six common types of electronic commerce.

9.2 Describe the various online services of business-to-consumer (B2C) commerce, providing specific examples of each.

9.3 Describe the three business models for business-to-business electronic commerce.

9.4 Identify the ethical and legal issues related to electronic commerce, providing examples.

OPENING CASE > Swipely

Founded in 2009, Swipely (www.swipely.com) is a service that processes credit card transactions for merchants. The online software works with point-of-sale systems and terminals used by independent businesses, including restaurants, salons, boutiques, grocers, and other retailers without requiring these businesses to implement additional hardware. Merchants in the Swipely network use the product to integrate customer spending, social media, and other data to obtain valuable insights into customer behavior.

Swipely's competitive advantage lies in helping merchants to better understand their customers. Its cloud servers (we describe cloud computing in detail in Plug IT In 4) analyze the data left by card swipes, delete personally identifying factors for security, and then present the data to merchants in the form of customer dashboards that reveal what each card number purchased and when. The dashboards are capable of very finely tuned analyses, such as how a rainy Tuesday affects profits. Swipely integrates with a merchant's social accounts so that owners can see how campaigns on Facebook or reviews on Yelp affect business in their restaurants or stores.

MKT

Swipely becomes even more effective if customers provide merchants with their name and e-mail address, which 20 percent are willing to do. These additional data enable the dashboards to incorporate marketing histories

such as responses to e-mail or coupon offers. This type of customer management software can cost hundreds of dollars per month, but Swipely adds it free.

EdBockStock/Shutterstock

Swipely competes with numerous payment processing services, including Square (www.squareup.com), Heartland Payment Systems (www.heartlandpaymentsystems.com), and Chase Paymentech (www.chasepaymentech.com). Many companies are competing in this arena because information about customers' spending habits is extremely valuable. Square (www.squareup.com), for example, is competing for the same customers as Swipely. One of these customers—the Blue Bottle Coffee Company (www.bluebottlecoffee.com), which has more than a dozen locations in Oakland, San Francisco, and New York —recently switched its registers to Square. It would be a small step for Square to offer its clients analytics on customer behaviors.

Swipely's competitive advantage over Square, for now, is price. Swipely takes an average of 2.65 percent of its merchants' customer transactions. Swipely's average charge is 10 basis points less per swipe than Square. (A basis point is 1/100 of 1 percent.) Furthermore, because Swipely is a cloud-based service that can communicate with more than 50 register systems, merchants do not have to purchase equipment to train on and then discard.

So, how is Swipely doing? At the end of 2013, the enterprise was processing more than $1 billion of customer transactions with its participating merchants.

Sources: Compiled from E. Ducoff, "Swipely Reveals How Menu and Server Performance Impact Sales," *Swipely Press Release,* February 11, 2014; "Swipely Release Helps Operators Track Behavior," *QSR Magazine,* January 24, 2014; A. Wilhelm, "Now Processing $1B Annually, Swipely Announces a Partner Network to Support Growth," *TechCrunch,* September 24. 2013; E. Carlyle, "Plastic Insights," *Forbes,* May 27, 2013; O. Thomas, "When Hurricane Sandy Struck, This Company Changed Its Entire Sales Plan – In Minutes," *Business Insider,* January 19, 2013;

L. Baverman, "Swipely Brings Big Data to Small Biz," *Upstart Business Journal,* November 8, 2012; T. Geron, "Swipely Expands Credit Card-Based Loyalty Service," *Forbes,* December 15, 2011; L. Gannes, "Swipely Aims to (Politely) Turn Purchases into Conversations," *GigaOM,* May 10, 2010; www.swipely.com, accessed February 4, 2014.

Questions

1. Describe the advantages that Swipely offers merchants that help it maintain a competitive advantage in the marketplace.

2. Refer back to Chapter 2. Does Swipely function as a strategic information system for a merchant? Why or why not?

Introduction

One of the most profound changes in the modern world of business is the emergence of electronic commerce. **Electronic commerce (EC or e-commerce)** describes the process of buying, selling, transferring, or exchanging products, services, or information via computer networks, including the Internet. E-commerce is transforming all of the business functional areas we discussed in Chapter 1 as well as their fundamental tasks, from advertising to paying bills. Its impact is so pervasive that it is affecting almost every modern organization. Regardless of where you land a job, your organization likely will be practicing electronic commerce.

Electronic commerce influences organizations in many significant ways. First, it increases an organization's *reach,* defined as the number of potential customers to whom the company can market its products. In fact, e-commerce provides unparalleled opportunities for companies to expand worldwide at a small cost, to increase market share, and to reduce costs. By utilizing electronic commerce, many small businesses can now operate and compete in market spaces that formerly were dominated by larger companies.

Another major impact of electronic commerce has been to remove many of the barriers that previously impeded entrepreneurs seeking to start their own businesses. E-commerce offers amazing opportunities for you to open your own business by developing an e-commerce Web site.

Electronic commerce is also fundamentally transforming the nature of competition through the development of new online companies, new business models, and the diversity of EC-related products and services. Recall your study of competitive strategies in Chapter 2, particularly the impact of the Internet on Porter's five forces. You learned that the Internet can both endanger and enhance a company's position in a given industry.

This chapter's opening case illustrates how Swipely is using an e-commerce application to add value to the e-commerce operations of merchants. Furthermore, Swipely is helping merchants achieve competitive advantage in their highly competitive marketplaces.

It is important for you to have a working knowledge of electronic commerce because your organization almost certainly will be employing e-commerce applications that will affect its strategy and business model. This knowledge will make you more valuable to your organization, and it will enable you to quickly contribute to the e-commerce applications employed in your functional area. As you read What's in IT for Me? at the end of the chapter, envision yourself performing the activities discussed in your functional area.

Going further, you may decide to become an entrepreneur and start your own business, as illustrated in the chapter opening case and IT's About Business 9.1. It is interesting that the two founders of FlightCar were 17 years old. If you start your own business, it is even more essential for you to understand electronic commerce, because e-commerce, with its broad reach, will probably be critical for your business to survive and thrive.

In this chapter, you will discover the major applications of e-business, and you will be able to identify the services necessary for its support. You will then study the major types of electronic commerce: business-to-consumer (B2C), business-to-business (B2B), consumer-to-consumer (C2C), business-to employee (B2E), and government-to-citizen (G2C). You conclude by examining several legal and ethical issues that have arisen as a result of the rapid growth of e-commerce.

IT'S ABOUT BUSINESS 9.1

FlightCar

Airport parking in most major cities represents a major challenge. Parking places can be difficult to locate and expensive as well. In addition, your car just sits there until you return. Now, FlightCar (www.flightcar.com) wants to transform your car into a revenue generator while you are away.

FlightCar lets its customers park their cars for free in the FlightCar parking lot at the airport. Then, FlightCar rents the cars out while its customers are traveling. Airports are fighting the startup, but FlightCar is moving ahead.

FlightCar insures all rentals up to $1 million, and it pre-screens all renters to root out poor drivers. If you put your car up for rent, then you park for free at the FlightCar location. After the team checks you in on an iPad, they drive you to the airport and drop you off. If your car is rented while you are gone, they pay you 20 cents per mile.

When you return, you either call 1-866-FLIGHTCAR for a pickup or use FlightCar's Web app. The company then sends a town car to pick you up from curbside. If you do not want to wait for a town car, then you can take a cab to the FlightCar lot, and the company will reimburse you for your cab fare. When you arrive at FlightCar's parking lot, your car will have been washed and vacuumed. You later receive a check in the mail if your car was rented.

Thus far FlightCar has not experienced any major accidents. If a car is involved in an accident, then FlightCar will contact the owner's insurance provider and, if the owner approves, will attempt to have the car fixed by the time the owner returns. If the company is not able to have the car fixed by the owner's return, then they provide loaner cars.

As of mid-2014, FlightCar had facilitated about 6,000 rentals in Boston, Los Angeles, and San Francisco, to 13,000 customers. One user has used the company about 10 times over the course of one year to rent out his 2011 Hyundai Accent. His car was rented half of those times, and he has made about $100 on those rentals. He has also saved more than that amount in airport parking fees. He identifies FlightCar's value as a combination of convenience and customer service.

MKT

FlightCar does have problems. The city of San Francisco, for example, refuses to acknowledge a difference between peer-to-peer car sharing and car rentals. As a result, it is suing FlightCar over lost fees and taxes. (The city collects fees and taxes from car rental companies.)

Another problem is the competition. RelayRides (https://relayrides.com) and Hubber (www.drivehubber.com) provide similar services at airports. It remains to be seen what the results of this fierce competition will be.

Sources: Compiled from R. Lawler, "Peer-to-Peer Car Rental Startup FlightCar Lands Some Senior Execs," *TechCrunch*, March 19, 2014; C. Forrest, "How Two 17-Year-Olds Disrupted the Transportation Industry, Got Sued, Got Funded," *TechRepublic*, February 21, 2014; J. Leo, "For Inexpensive Car Rental, Consider FlightCar.com," *The Los Angeles Times*, February 16, 2014; "FlightCar Launches New Service for Frequent Business Travelers to Participate in Peer-to-Peer Car Sharing," *PR Web*, February 4, 2014; "Travelport Teams Up with FlightCar," *Auto Rental News*, December 18, 2013; R. Lawler, "Airport Car Rental Startup FlightCar Launches at LAX, Unveils Mobile Web App," *TechCrunch*, November 13, 2013; C. Deamicis, "Let the Fight to the Car Sharing Death Begin: FlightCar Moves into Hubber's Territory," *Pando Daily*, November 13, 2013; J. Melvin, "Flightcar: San Francisco Sues Unruly SFO Car Rental Startup from Santa Clara," *San Jose Mercury News*, June 4, 2013; www.flightcar.com, www.drivehubber.com, https://relayrides.com, accessed March 20, 2014.

Questions

1. What are possible disadvantages of FlightCar's business model for its customers? Provide specific examples to support your answer.

2. Can FlightCar survive in its marketplace? Why or why not? Support your answer.

3. Would you allow FlightCar to rent your car while you were traveling? Why or why not? Support your answer. Does your answer to this question have any bearing on your answer to Question 2?

9.1 Overview of E-Business and E-Commerce

Any entrepreneur or company that decides to practice electronic commerce must develop a strategy to do so effectively. The first step is to determine exactly *why* you want to do business over the Internet using a Web site. There are several reasons for employing Web sites:

- To sell goods and services
- To induce people to visit a physical location
- To reduce operational and transaction costs
- To enhance your reputation

A Web site can accomplish any of these goals. Unless a company (or you) has substantial resources, it is difficult to accomplish all of them at the same time. The appropriate Web site for achieving each goal will be somewhat different. As you set up your Web site, you must consider how the site will generate and retain traffic, as well as a host of other issues. The point here is that when you are studying the various aspects of electronic commerce, you should keep in mind the strategy of the organization or entrepreneur. This will help you determine the type of Web site to use.

This section examines the basics of e-business and e-commerce. First, we define these two concepts. You then become familiar with pure and partial electronic commerce. You then examine the various types of electronic commerce. Next, you focus on e-commerce mechanisms, which are the ways that businesses and people buy and sell over the Internet. You conclude this section by considering the benefits and limitations of e-commerce.

Definitions and Concepts

Recall that electronic commerce describes the process of buying, selling, transferring, or exchanging products, services, or information via computer networks, including the Internet. **Electronic business** (e-business) is a somewhat broader concept. In addition to the buying and selling of goods and services, **e-business** refers to servicing customers, collaborating with business partners, and performing electronic transactions within an organization.

Electronic commerce can take several forms depending on the degree of digitization involved. The *degree of digitization* is the extent to which the commerce has been transformed from physical to digital. This concept can relate to both the product or service being sold and the delivery agent or intermediary. In other words, the product can be either physical or digital, and the delivery agent can also be either physical or digital.

In traditional commerce, both dimensions are physical. Purely physical organizations are referred to as **brick-and-mortar organizations.** (You may also see the term *bricks-and-mortar.*) In contrast, in *pure EC* all dimensions are digital. Companies engaged only in EC are considered **virtual** (or **pure-play**) **organizations**. All other combinations that include a mix of digital and physical dimensions are considered *partial* EC (but not pure EC). **Clicks-and-mortar organizations** conduct some e-commerce activities, yet their primary business is carried out in the physical world. A common alternative to the term *clicks-and-mortar* is *clicks-and-bricks.* You will encounter both terms. Therefore, clicks-and-mortar organizations are examples of partial EC. E-commerce is now so well established that people generally expect companies to offer this service in some form.

Purchasing a shirt at Walmart Online or a book from Amazon.com is an example of partial EC because the merchandise, although bought and paid for digitally, is physically delivered by FedEx or UPS. In contrast, buying an e-book from Amazon.com or a software product from Buy.com constitutes pure EC because the product itself as well as its delivery, payment, and transfer are entirely digital. To avoid confusion, we use the term *electronic commerce* to denote both pure and partial EC.

Types of E-Commerce

E-commerce can be conducted between and among various parties. In this section, you will identify the six common types of e-commerce, and you will learn about three of them—C2C, B2E, and e-government—in detail. You then consider B2C and B2B in separate sections because they are very complex. We discuss mobile commerce in detail in Chapter 10.

- *Business-to-consumer electronic commerce (B2C):* In B2C, the sellers are organizations, and the buyers are individuals. You learn about B2C electronic commerce in Section 9.2.

- *Business-to-business electronic commerce (B2B):* In B2B transactions, both the sellers and the buyers are business organizations. B2B comprises the vast majority of EC volume. You will learn more about B2B electronic commerce in Section 9.3. FIGURE 1.5 also illustrates B2B electronic commerce.

- *Consumer-to-consumer electronic commerce (C2C):* In C2C (also called customer-to-customer), an individual sells products or services to other individuals. The major strategies for conducting C2C on the Internet are auctions and classified ads.

In dozens of countries, the volume of C2C selling and buying on auction sites is exploding. Most auctions are conducted by intermediaries such as eBay (www.ebay.com). Consumers can also select general sites such as www.auctionanything.com, a company that sells software and services that help individuals and organizations conduct their own auctions. In addition, many individuals are conducting their own auctions.

The major categories of online classified ads are similar to those found in print ads: vehicles, real estate, employment, pets, tickets, and travel. Classified ads are available through most Internet service providers (AOL, MSN, etc.), at some portals (Yahoo!, etc.), and from Internet directories and online newspapers. Many of these sites contain search engines that help shoppers narrow their searches. Craigslist (www.craigslist.org) is the largest online classified ad provider.

Internet-based classified ads have one major advantage over traditional types of classified ads: They provide access to an international, rather than a local, audience. This wider audience greatly increases both the supply of goods and services and the number of potential buyers. It is important to note that the value of expanded geographical reach depends greatly on what is being bought or sold. For example, you might buy software from a company located 1,000 miles from you, but you would not buy firewood from someone at such a distance.

- *Business-to-employee (B2E):* In B2E, an organization uses EC internally to provide information and services to its employees. For example, companies allow employees to manage their benefits and to take training classes electronically. In addition, employees can buy discounted insurance, travel packages, and tickets to events on the corporate intranet. They can also order supplies and materials electronically. Finally, many companies have electronic corporate stores that sell the company's products to its employees, usually at a discount.

- *E-government:* E-government is the use of Internet technology in general and e-commerce in particular to deliver information and public services to citizens (called government-to-citizen or G2C EC) and to business partners and suppliers (called government-to-business or G2B EC). G2B EC is much like B2B EC, usually with an overlay of government procurement regulations. That is, G2B EC and B2B EC are similar conceptually. However, the functions of G2C EC are conceptually different from anything that exists in the private sector (e.g., B2C EC).

- E-government is also an efficient way of conducting business transactions with citizens and businesses and within the governments themselves. E-government makes government more efficient and effective, especially in the delivery of public services. An example of G2C electronic commerce is electronic benefits transfer, in which governments transfer benefits, such as Social Security and pension payments, directly to recipients' bank accounts.

- *Mobile commerce (m-commerce):* The term *m-commerce* refers to e-commerce that is conducted entirely in a wireless environment. An example is using cell phones to shop over the Internet. You will learn about m-commerce in Chapter 10.

Each type of EC is executed in one or more business models. A **business model** is the method by which a company generates revenue to sustain itself. Table 9.1 summarizes the major EC business models.

TABLE 9.1 E-Commerce
Business Models

Online direct marketing	Manufacturers or retailers sell directly to customers. Very efficient for digital products and services. Can allow for product or service customization (www.dell.com)
Electronic tendering system	Businesses request quotes from suppliers. Uses B2B with a reverse auction mechanism
Name-your-own-price	Customers decide how much they are willing to pay. An intermediary tries to match a provider (www.priceline.com)
Find-the-best-price	Customers specify a need; an intermediary compares providers and shows the lowest price. Customers must accept the offer in a short time, or they may lose the deal (www.hotwire.com)
Affiliate marketing	Vendors ask partners to place logos (or banners) on partner's site. If customers click on logo, go to vendor's site, and make a purchase, then the vendor pays commissions to the partners
Viral marketing	Recipients of your marketing notices send information about your product to their friends
Group purchasing (e-coops)	Small buyers aggregate demand to create a large volume; the group then conducts tendering or negotiates a low price
Online auctions	Companies run auctions of various types on the Internet. Very popular in C2C, but gaining ground in other types of EC as well (www.ebay.com)
Product customization	Customers use the Internet to self-configure products or services. Sellers then price them and fulfill them quickly (*build-to-order*) (www.jaguar.com)
Electronic marketplaces and exchanges	Transactions are conducted efficiently (more information to buyers and sellers, lower transaction costs) in electronic marketplaces (private or public)
Bartering online	Intermediary administers online exchange of surplus products and/or company receives "points" for its contribution, which it can use to purchase other needed items (www.bbu.com)
Deep discounters	Company offers deep price discounts. Appeals to customers who consider only price in their purchasing decisions (www.half.com)
Membership	Only members can use the services provided, including access to certain information, conducting trades, etc. (www.egreetings.com)

Major E-Commerce Mechanisms

Businesses and customers can buy and sell on the Internet through a number of mechanisms. The most widely used mechanisms are as follows:

- Electronic catalogs
- Electronic auctions
- E-storefronts
- E-malls
- E-marketplaces

Let's look at each one more closely.

Catalogs have been printed on paper for generations. Today, however, they are available over the Internet. Electronic catalogs consist of a product database, a directory and search capabilities, and a presentation function. They are the backbone of most e-commerce sites.

An **auction** is a competitive buying and selling process in which prices are determined dynamically by competitive bidding. Electronic auctions (e-auctions) generally increase revenues for sellers by broadening the customer base and shortening the cycle time of the auction. Buyers generally benefit from e-auctions because they can bargain for lower prices. In addition, they do not have to travel to an auction at a physical location.

The Internet provides an efficient infrastructure for conducting auctions at lower administrative costs and with a greater number of involved sellers and buyers. Both individual consumers and corporations can participate in auctions.

There are two major types of auctions: forward and reverse. In **forward auctions**, sellers solicit bids from many potential buyers. Usually, sellers place items at sites for auction, and buyers bid continuously for them. The highest bidder wins the items. Both sellers and buyers can be either individuals or businesses. The popular auction site eBay. com is a forward auction.

In **reverse auctions**, one buyer, usually an organization, wants to purchase a product or a service. The buyer posts a request for quotation (RFQ) on its Web site or on a third-party site. The RFQ provides detailed information on the desired purchase. Interested suppliers study the RFQ and then submit bids electronically. Everything else being equal, the lowest-price bidder wins the auction. The reverse auction is the most common auction model for large purchases (in terms of either quantities or price). Governments and large corporations frequently use this approach, which may provide considerable savings for the buyer.

Auctions can be conducted from the seller's site, the buyer's site, or a third party's site. For example, eBay, the best-known third-party site, offers hundreds of thousands of different items in several types of auctions. Overall, more than 300 major companies, including Amazon.com and Dellauction.com, sponsor online auctions.

An *electronic storefront* is a Web site that represents a single store. An *electronic mall*, also known as a *cybermall* or an *e-mall*, is a collection of individual shops consolidated under one Internet address. Electronic storefronts and electronic malls are closely associated with B2C electronic commerce. You will study each one in more detail in Section 9.2.

An *electronic marketplace* (*e-marketplace*) is a central, virtual market space on the Web where many buyers and many sellers can conduct e-commerce and e-business activities. Electronic marketplaces are associated with B2B electronic commerce. You will learn about electronic marketplaces in Section 9.3.

Electronic Payment Mechanisms

Implementing EC typically requires electronic payments. **Electronic payment mechanisms** enable buyers to pay for goods and services electronically, rather than writing a check or using cash. Payments are an integral part of doing business, whether in the traditional manner or online. Traditional payment systems have typically involved cash and/or checks.

In most cases, traditional payment systems are not effective for EC, especially for B2B. Cash cannot be used because there is no face-to-face contact between buyer and seller. Not everyone accepts credit cards or checks, and some buyers do not have credit cards or checking accounts. Finally, contrary to what many people believe, it may be *less* secure for the buyer to use the telephone or mail to arrange or send payments, especially from another country, than to complete a secured transaction on a computer. For all of these reasons, a better method is needed to pay for goods and services in cyberspace. This method is electronic payment systems. Let's take a closer look at four types of electronic payment: electronic checks, electronic cards, purchasing cards, and electronic cash.

Electronic Checks. *Electronic checks* (*e-checks*), which are used primarily in B2B, are similar to regular paper checks. A customer who wishes to use e-checks must first establish a checking account with a bank. Then, when the customer buys a product or a service, he or she e-mails an encrypted electronic check to the seller. The seller deposits the check in a bank account, and the funds are transferred from the buyer's account into the seller's account.

Like regular checks, e-checks carry a signature (in digital form) that can be verified (see www.authorize.net). Properly signed and endorsed e-checks are exchanged between financial institutions through electronic clearinghouses. (See www.eccho.org and www .troygroup.com for details.)

Electronic Cards. There are a variety of electronic cards, and they are used for different purposes. The most common types are electronic credit cards, virtual credit cards, purchasing cards, stored-value money cards, and smart cards.

Electronic credit cards allow customers to charge online payments to their credit card account. These cards are used primarily in B2C and in shopping by small-to-medium enterprises (SMEs). Here is how e-credit cards work (see FIGURE 9.1).

- Step 1: When you purchase a book from Amazon, for example, your credit card information and purchase amount are encrypted in your browser. This procedure ensures the information is safe while it is "traveling" on the Internet to Amazon.

- Step 2: When your information arrives at Amazon, it is not opened. Rather, it is transferred automatically (in encrypted form) to a *clearinghouse*, where it is decrypted for verification and authorization.

- Step 3: The clearinghouse asks the bank that issued you your credit card (the card issuer bank) to verify your credit card information.

- Step 4: Your card issuer bank verifies your credit card information and reports this to the clearinghouse.

- Step 5: The clearinghouse reports the result of the verification of your credit card to Amazon.

- Step 6: Amazon reports a successful purchase and amount to you.

- Step 7: Your card issuer bank sends funds in the amount of the purchase to Amazon's bank.

- Step 8: Your card issuer bank notifies you (either electronically or in your monthly statement) of the debit on your credit card.

- Step 9: Amazon's bank notifies Amazon of the funds credited to its account.

Virtual credit cards allow customers to shop online (see FIGURE 9.2). These cards can be used only once. The reason for this limitation is to thwart criminals by using a different, random card number every time you shop online. Going further, a virtual number is good only on the Web site where you make your purchase. An online purchase made with a virtual card number shows up on your bill just like any other purchase.

Purchasing cards are the B2B equivalent of electronic credit cards (see FIGURE 9.3). In some countries, purchasing cards are the primary form of payment between companies. Unlike credit cards, where credit is provided for 30–60 days (for free) before payment is made to the merchant, payments made with purchasing cards are settled within a week.

Stored-value money cards allow you to store a fixed amount of prepaid money and then spend it as necessary. These cards are used to pay for photocopies in your library, for transportation, and for telephone calls. Each time you use the card, the amount is reduced by the amount you spent. FIGURE 9.4 illustrates a New York City Metro (subway and bus) card.

Finally, **smart cards** contain a chip that can store a considerable amount of information—more than 100 times the amount contained on a stored-value money card (see FIGURE 9.5). Smart cards are frequently multipurpose—that is, you can use them as a credit card, a debit card, a stored-value money card, or a loyalty card. Smart cards are ideal for *micropayments*, which are small payments of a few dollars or less.

Person-to-Person Payments. **Person-to-person payments** enable two individuals, or an individual and a business, to transfer funds without using a credit card. One of the first companies to offer this service was PayPal (an eBay company). An attractive security feature of PayPal is that you have to put only enough money in your PayPal account to cover any upcoming transactions. Therefore, if anyone should gain access to your account, that person will not have access to all of your money.

Figure 9.1 How e-credit cards work. (The numbers 1–9 indicate the sequence of activities.)

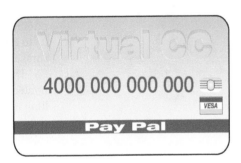

Figure 9.2 Example of virtual credit card.

Mike Clarke/AFP/Getty Images/NewsCom

Figure 9.3 Example of purchasing card.

© Clarence Holmes Photography/Alamy

Figure 9.4 The New York City Metro Card.

© MARKA/Alamy

Figure 9.5 Smart cards are frequently multipurpose.

Person-to-person payment services work this way. First, you select a service and open up an account. Basically, this process entails creating a user name, selecting a password, and providing the service with a credit card or bank account number. Next, you transfer funds from your credit card or bank account to your new account. Now you are ready to send money to someone over the Internet. You access the service—for example, PayPal—with your user name and password, and you specify the e-mail address of the person to receive the money, along with the dollar amount that you want to send. The service then sends an e-mail to the payee's e-mail address. The e-mail contains a link back to the service's Web site. When the recipient clicks on the link, he or she is taken to the service. There, the recipient is asked to set up an account to which the money that you sent will be credited. The recipient can then credit the money from this account to either a credit card or a bank account. The service charges the payer a small amount, roughly $1 per transaction.

Benefits and Limitations of E-Commerce

Few innovations in human history have provided as many benefits to organizations, individuals, and society as e-commerce has. E-commerce benefits organizations by making national and international markets more accessible and by lowering the costs of processing, distributing, and retrieving information. Customers benefit by being able to access a vast number of products and services, around the clock. The major benefit to society is the ability to easily and conveniently deliver information, services, and products to people in cities, rural areas, and developing countries.

 Despite all these benefits, EC has some limitations, both technological and nontechnological, that have restricted its growth and acceptance. One major technological limitation is the lack of universally accepted security standards. Also, in less-developed countries, telecommunications bandwidth often is insufficient, and accessing the Web is expensive. Nontechnological limitations include the perceptions that EC is insecure, has unresolved legal issues, and lacks a critical mass of sellers and buyers. As time passes, these limitations, especially the technological ones, will diminish or be overcome. In fact, IT's About Business 9.2 describes two instances of how these limitations are being overcome in the developing world.

IT'S ABOUT BUSINESS 9.2

Overcoming the Limitations of Electronic Commerce in the Developing World

China. A series of food safety scandals has created a demand in China's big cities for natural or traditionally grown food. Two beneficiaries of this new market are Li Chengcai (83 years old) and Cheng Youfang (76 years old), who grow radishes on their tiny farm. Although the couple are both illiterate and speak only their local dialect, they sell their produce via electronic commerce to urban customers who are willing to pay extra for flavorful, safe food. Here is how they became engaged in e-commerce.

Zhang Yu, a 26-year-old "young village official"—that is her actual title—and other young village officials launched an account on Sina Weibo (http://english.sina.com/weibo), a Chinese microblogging Web site, to post items about the fresh, traditionally grown produce of their region. Soon afterward, they opened an online store through Alibaba Group's Taobao (www.engtaobao.com) Web site to connect local

farmers with urban buyers. The online grocery, officially known as the Young Village Officials' Farm, has customers in Beijing, Shanghai, and elsewhere, and about 10,000 followers on Weibo. Customers place orders online, and Zhang visits farmers to verbally inform them of the order. Zhang handles the logistics, shipping, and quality control of the produce.

Zhang maintains the reason for the success of the grocery is a renewed interest in local farming traditions—which she documents in photographs on social media—and strict quality control. In an area where the average monthly household income is only about 600 yuan ($99), farmers selling produce through the online grocery store can increase their income by one-third.

Nigeria. There is an old saying in Nigeria that "You can outfit your entire home in a single drive across Lagos." Today, you can buy everything from cutlery and furniture to food and décor from the thousands of hawkers who aggressively sell their goods along, and in the middle of, the congested city's potholed streets. Unfortunately, shopping locally historically has meant higher prices, less selection, and often sitting in traffic for hours to get to stores, which rely on generators to cope with almost daily power outages.

Today, however, Nigerians have another option for comprehensive shopping: online marketplace Jumia (www.jumia .com.ng). For example, when Gbemiga Omotoso bought a Samsung tablet last year, he handed over his cash to a man in a van. The transaction was part of online retailer Jumia's attempt to adapt its operation to the unique challenges of selling in Nigeria. With many of the country's 160 million residents suspicious of paying online, the Lagos-based retailer wins over skeptical shoppers by accepting payment on delivery and offering free returns.

Jumia and local rival Konga (www.konga.com) are delivering electronics, clothes, and even refrigerators to the front doors of Nigerians. To combat fears of online fraud and to educate Nigerians about shopping online securely, the company has a direct sales team of about 200 who travel around major cities such as Lagos and Port Harcourt carrying tablet computers. They wear outfits with Jumia's logo and hold impromptu shopping sessions in businesses, churches, and homes, showing consumers how to order and answering questions.

Jumia is building its own fleet of about 200 vehicles. Almost two-thirds are motorbikes that are easier to navigate through the country's traffic jams. To keep robberies at a minimum, the last deliveries take place at 7 PM. The company promises to deliver any item in its 90,000 square foot central warehouse in Lagos to any location in the city within a single day, and anywhere in the entire country within five days.

Jumia has 600 employees. The company also sells in Kenya, Morocco, Ivory Coast, Egypt, Uganda, and South Africa. Although not yet profitable, Jumia claims monthly revenues of "a couple of million" dollars as well as rapidly increasing sales.

Sources: Compiled from "'Taobao Village' Phenomenon Boosts E-Commerce in Rural China," *Fashionbi 247*, March 5, 2014; C. Larson, "In Rural China, You Don't Have to Read to Buy and Sell Online," *Bloomberg BusinessWeek*, February 17–23, 2014; "Ecommerce Transforms Rural Chinese Villages," *Financial Times*, February 16, 2014; B. Marino, "Alibaba Opens Ecommerce Door for Chinese Villagers," *Financial Times*, February 16, 2014; J. Erickson, "Viral Villages: E-Commerce Is Spreading in China's Agrarian Hinterlands," *Alizila*, February 11, 2014; K. Mbote, "Uganda: Jumia Extends Services to Uganda," *CIO East Africa*, February 8, 2014; P. Adepoju, "Jumia Nigeria Wins Best Online Retail Brand of the Year Award," *Biz Community*, January 31, 2014; B. Tan, "The Social Side of E-Commerce: Lessons from Rural China," *The Conversation*, January 6, 2014; "E-Commerce Booming in Africa," *IT Web Retail Technology*, December 10, 2013; C. Kay, C. Spillane, and J. Kew, "Trying to Build the Next Amazon – In Nigeria," *Bloomberg BusinessWeek*, November 25–December 1, 2013; C. Sheets, "Nigeria's Jumia: The Company Behind the 'Amazonification' of Africa," *International Business Times*, September 18, 2013; http://english.sina.com/weibo, www.jumia.com.ng, accessed March 21, 2014.

Questions

1. Describe how the Young Village Officials Farm and Jumia are trying to overcome the limitations of electronic commerce. Provide specific examples to support your answer.

2. What are the advantages of electronic commerce to rural farmers in China (above and beyond increased income)?

3. What are the advantages of electronic commerce to the people of Nigeria?

Apply The Concept 9.1

LEARNING OBJECTIVE 9.1 Describe the six common types of electronic commerce.

STEP 1 – Background (Here is what you are learning.)

Today there are many companies that specialize in making e-commerce a reality for small businesses. Amazon, Yahoo!, PayPal, and other entities offer services that provide everything a small business needs to sell products and accept payment over the Internet. In fact, many consumers prefer for their transactions to go through these larger global companies because they trust these companies' security.

STEP 2 – Activity (Here is what you are doing.)

Visit http://www.wiley.com/go/rainer/MIS3e/applytheconcept, and click on the link provided for Apply the Concept 9.1. This link will take you to PayPal's Web site. Click on the business link at the top of the page. You will find that PayPal offers easy solutions for both businesses and customers.

Create and submit a table that lists and describes the six common types of e-commerce. Which ones are supported by PayPal, and which are not? For the second group, can you explain why they are not supported? Should PayPal move into these areas of e-commerce as well?

9.2 Business-to-Consumer (B2C) Electronic Commerce

B2B EC is much larger than B2C EC by volume, but B2C EC is more complex. The reason is that B2C involves a large number of buyers making millions of diverse transactions per day from a relatively small number of sellers. As an illustration, consider Amazon, an online retailer that offers thousands of products to its customers. Each customer purchase is relatively small, but Amazon must manage every transaction as if that customer were its most important one. The company needs to process each order quickly and efficiently, and ship the products to the customer in a timely manner. In addition, it has to manage returns. Multiply this simple example by millions, and you get an idea of how complex B2C EC can be. Overall, B2B complexities tend to be more business related, whereas B2C complexities tend to be more technical and volume related.

This section addresses the primary issues in B2C EC. We begin by studying the two basic mechanisms that customers utilize to access companies on the Web: electronic storefronts and electronic malls. In addition to purchasing products over the Web, customers also access online services. Therefore, the next section covers several online services, such as banking, securities trading, job searching, and travel. The complexity of B2C EC creates two major challenges for sellers: channel conflict and order fulfillment. We examine these two topics in detail. Finally, companies engaged in B2C EC must "get the word out" to prospective customers. Therefore, this section concludes with a look at online advertising.

Electronic Storefronts and Malls

For several generations, home shopping from catalogs, and later from television shopping channels, has attracted millions of customers. Today, shopping online offers an alternative to catalog and television shopping. **Electronic retailing (e-tailing)** is the direct sale of products and services through electronic storefronts or electronic malls, usually designed around an electronic catalog format and/or auctions.

Like any mail-order shopping experience, e-commerce enables you to buy from home and to do so 24 hours a day, 7 days a week. Compared with mail order, however, EC offers a wider variety of products and services, including the most unique items, often at lower prices. Furthermore, within seconds, shoppers can access very detailed supplementary product information. In addition, they can easily locate and compare competitors' products and prices. Finally, buyers can find hundreds of thousands of sellers. Two popular online shopping mechanisms are electronic storefronts and electronic malls.

Electronic Storefronts.
As we saw earlier in the chapter, an **electronic storefront** is a Web site that represents a single store. Today, Internet shoppers can access hundreds of thousands of electronic storefronts. Each storefront has a unique uniform resource locator (URL), or Internet address, at which buyers can place orders. Some electronic storefronts are extensions of physical stores such as Hermes, The Sharper Image, and Walmart. Others are new businesses started by entrepreneurs who discovered a niche on the Web (e.g., Restaurant.com and Alloy.com). Manufacturers (e.g., www.dell.com) and retailers (e.g., www.officedepot.com) also use storefronts.

Electronic Malls

Whereas an electronic storefront represents a single store, an **electronic mall**, also known as a *cybermall* or an *e-mall*, is a collection of individual shops grouped under a single Internet address. The basic idea of an electronic mall is the same as that of a regular shopping mall: to provide a one-stop shopping place that offers a wide range of products and services. A cybermall may include thousands of vendors. For example, Microsoft Shopping (now Bing shopping, www.bing.com/shopping) includes tens of thousands of products from thousands of vendors.

There are two types of cybermalls. In the first type, known as *referral malls* (e.g., www.hawaii.com), you cannot buy anything. Instead, you are transferred from the mall to a participating storefront. In the second type of mall (e.g., http://shopping .google.com), you can actually make a purchase. At this type of mall, you might shop from several stores, but you make only one purchase transaction at the end. You use an *electronic shopping cart* to gather items from various vendors and then pay for all of them in a single transaction. The mall organizer, such as Google, takes a commission from the sellers for this service.

Online Service Industries

In addition to purchasing products, customers can also access needed services via the Web. Selling books, toys, computers, and most other products on the Internet can reduce vendors' selling costs by 20–40 percent. Further reduction is difficult to achieve because the products must be delivered physically. Only a few products, such as software and music, can be digitized and then delivered online for additional savings. In contrast, services, such as buying an airline ticket and purchasing stocks or insurance, can be delivered entirely through e-commerce, often with considerable cost reduction. Not surprisingly, then, online delivery of services is growing very rapidly, with millions of new customers being added each year.

One of the most pressing EC issues relating to online services (as well as in marketing tangible products) is **disintermediation**. Intermediaries, also known as middlemen, have two functions: (1) they provide information, and (2) they perform value-added services such as consulting. The first function can be fully automated and most likely will be assumed by e-marketplaces and portals that provide information for free. When this development occurs, the intermediaries who perform only (or primarily) this function are likely to be eliminated. The process whereby intermediaries are eliminated is called disintermediation. IT's About Business 9.3 provides an example of disintermediation.

T'S ABOUT BUSINESS 9.3

Penske Used Trucks

Throughout 2009 and 2010, used trucks grew more appealing to businesses because the economy was in poor shape. Penske Truck Leasing (www.pensketruckleasing.com), which has a steady supply of used trucks coming off leases, realized that it was missing out on revenue by selling those trucks at reduced prices to wholesalers rather than directly to would-be buyers.

To sell its used trucks, Penske had relied on a bare-bones Web site used primarily by wholesale buyers, as well as by local Penske used-truck coordinators who visited the site for reference material when assisting wholesalers. Penske needed a high-quality Web site that would generate sales to wholesalers as well as directly to the end customers, such as the owner of a flower store or hardware store who needed a cargo van or box truck.

The result, PenskeUsedTrucks (www.penskeusedtrucks .com), illustrates how various business units must work

together to implement a major electronic commerce project. Penske's vehicle remarketing group first recognized the value of used trucks, and it realized that the company was losing money with its current business model. This

© Hasenonkel/iStockphoto

group brought in the company's marketing staff to evaluate how Penske could employ a new Web site to attract more buyers. The two groups then collaborated with the information technology group to build the Web site.

Penske face several challenges in creating the site. To begin with, the site had to incorporate the correct terminology and keywords to attract the attention of shoppers and search engines. To address this challenge, IT and marketing interviewed customers to obtain feedback concerning effective keywords. For example, Penske calls one type of truck a "cargo van," but some potential customers refer to it as a "high cube" or a "box truck." Ultimately, the additional keywords and cross-referencing expanded Penske's keyword base from roughly 100 vehicle names to more than 2,000.

MIS

Another problem was collecting and organizing photos. In most cases obtaining images for a Web site is a fairly straightforward process. Unfortunately, in Penske's case this task was more complicated because the company does not have a centralized truck lot. Rather, its fleet operates out of 2,500 locations nationwide. The solution required reengineering Penske's fleet management system and requiring that whenever the company lists a new vehicle for sale on its Web site, five images must come with the vehicle.

POM

The resulting Web site resembles CarMax (www.carmax.com) more than it does Penske's previous site: a Web-based catalog. Every type of Penske vehicle, from a standard cargo van to a refrigerated 18-wheel trailer truck, is searchable on the site, and Penske updates the inventory every day. The number of vehicles for sale can vary from 3,500 to 5,000 units. A vehicle comparison tool enables a buyer to compare up to five trucks side-by-side in terms of price, mileage, weight, horsepower, and other specifications. Maintenance reports display a vehicle's repair and maintenance history of the previous three years. Buyers can close the sale on a single truck or a fleet of trucks by phone via Penske's call center.

Offering a good product and building a useful Web site are basic strategic necessities in the digital era. Successful companies must do better than this. Attracting customers requires an aggressive search engine optimization (SEO) and social media strategy as well. (*Search engine optimization* is the process of maximizing the number of visitors to a particular Web site by ensuring that the site appears high on the list of results returned by a search engine.)

The Penske marketing team followed Google's SEO advice to incorporate keywords that customers use when searching across the Web site. For Web site traffic analytics, Penske uses Adobe Analytics (www.adobe.com) software for information such as which keywords drive visitors to the Web site, where buyers are coming from, how long they stay on the site, and which pages they visit.

Google search results also include rich details such as the price and availability of a vehicle. The SEO helped increase Google search traffic by 37 percent for the Penske site.

For social media and blogging, Penske's marketing team uses a company blog called Move Ahead (blog.gopenske.com) as a content hub where the team posts daily truck specials and directs traffic to the PenskeUsedTrucks.com Web site. The team also tweets about daily truck specials in the morning and evening. Furthermore, Penske has active company pages on Facebook, YouTube, Pinterest, and Google+. In October 2013, Penske added a mobile version of PenskeUsedTrucks.com.

Sources: Compiled from M. Hernandez, "Dominate SEO with Long Tail Keywords," *Huffington Post*, March 17, 2014; J. Martin, "20 SEO Tips, Trends and Predictions for 2014," *CIO*, January 16, 2014; "Penske Ranked Fourth on InformationWeek 500 List for Used Truck Website," *PR Newswire*, September 10, 2013; S. O'Neill, "Website Drives Used Truck Sales," *InformationWeek*, September 9, 2013; S. O'Neill, "What Penske Learned from Rebuilding Its E-Commerce Site," *Information Week*, September 5, 2013; www.pensketruckleasing.com, www.penskeusedtrucks.com, accessed January 29, 2014.

Questions

1. Describe how disintermediation works in this case. Provide an example to support your answer.

2. Why is it so important for different functional areas in an organization to work together in designing an organizational Web site?

3. Referencing question 2, discuss the implications of this statement: "Regardless of your major, an understanding of information technology will be of value to you."

In contrast to simply providing information, performing value-added services requires expertise. Unlike the information function, then, this function can be only partially automated. Thus, intermediaries who provide value-added services not only are likely to survive but they may also actually prosper. The Web helps these employees in two situations: (1) when the number of participants is enormous, as with job searches, and (2) when the information that must be exchanged is complex.

In this section, you will examine some leading online service industries: banking, trading of securities (stocks, bonds), job matching, travel services, and advertising.

Cyberbanking. *Electronic banking*, also known as **cyberbanking**, involves conducting various banking activities from home, at a place of business, or on the road instead of at a physical bank location. Electronic banking has capabilities ranging from paying bills to applying for a loan. For customers, it saves time, and it is convenient. For banks, it offers an inexpensive alternative to branch banking—for example, about 2 cents cost per transaction versus $1.07 at a physical branch. Cyberbanking also enables banks to attract remote customers. In addition to regular banks with added online services, **Internet-only banks**, which are dedicated solely to Internet transactions, are emerging, as you see in IT's About Business 9.4. Another example of an Internet-only bank is First Internet Bank of Indiana (www.firstib.com).

IT'S ABOUT BUSINESS 9.4

Can Simple Disrupt Traditional Banking?

Consumer banking is an industry that is ready to be disrupted. Banks are known for hidden fees, confusing language, and customer frustration. Online-only banks may provide the business model that can help solve these problems and increase customer satisfaction.

One such bank, Simple (www.simple.com), was founded in 2009 and launched commercially in July 2012. Instead of seeking a new bank charter, Simple chose to partner with Bancorp to sponsor them in the payment networks and to ensure that all of their banking services are FDIC insured. Simple was founded on the idea that traditional banks do not provide adequate online and mobile tools to properly service their customers.

Think of Simple as an online-only bank with a heavy focus on customer service that incorporates financial tracking and budgeting tools similar to those offered by Mint (www.mint.com). Mint is a free, Web-based personal financial management service for the United States and Canada. Mint's primary service allows users to track bank, credit card, investment, and loan transactions and balances, as well as make budgets. Intuit (www.intuit.com) acquired Mint in 2009.

Simple's plan is to provide easy-to-use, cloud-based apps and great customer service. The Web site and apps are attractive and uncluttered, with a minimalist design that is easy to navigate. They focus on Simple's financial management tools like Goals, which allows customers to establish financial goals to save toward, for example, a vacation or a down payment on a car. Goals then regularly updates customers as to how much progress they are making toward that goal. Another innovative tool is Safe to Spend, which displays the amount in the checking account that will be available after customers pay their scheduled bills and set aside money toward their goals.

Simple also offers a unique feature called "push notification" that it sends to customers' smartphones after they make a purchase. With push notification, customers can take a picture of a purchase, which is automatically geotagged (location data are added to the image) and then add notes about the purchase for their records. (See Chapter 6 for a discussion of geotagging.) This information can help customers to better understand their spending habits and to track specific types of purchases they have made in the past.

Simple makes money from interest margins and interchange revenue from payment networks, which is the fee that companies pay to be able to accept card-based transactions. Simple has no IT infrastructure to support and no physical branches, so they are able to operate on a lower profit margin than traditional banks.

Simple's market is paradoxical, in that banking customers desire the convenience of Internet banking, but they remain wary of the Internet itself. (For example, see the

© Anatoliy Babiy/iStockphoto

case about the Target breach in Chapter 7.) Despite these concerns, however, Pew research (www.pewresearch.org) reported in 2013 that 51 percent of all the U.S. adults conduct some banking online.

Simple experienced rapid growth, attracting roughly 100,000 customers across the United States by the end of 2013. That year the bank completed $1.6 billion in transactions. Then, in February 2014, Simple was purchased by BBVA Compass Bank (www.bbvacompass.com) for $117 million. Simple promised that it would continue to operate as it always had and that nothing would change for its existing customers. **FIN**

Despite these assurances, however, the purchase raised several serious questions:

- How can Simple, which built a loyal following by criticizing annoying banking practices, keep its business model intact as a subsidiary of a huge traditional bank?
- Can Simple retain its current customer base?
- What does BBVA intend to do with Simple? Will it allow Simple to maintain its traditional business practices? How much independence will it allow the bank?
- Given that Internet-only banks are typically small start-ups, what does this purchase mean for the future of such banks?
- What are the implications of this purchase for the disruption of the banking industry as a whole?

At the time of this writing, it remains to be seen how this purchase will impact both Simple and the overall online banking industry.

Sources: Compiled from D. Wolman, "The Bank and the Anti-Bank," *The New Yorker*, February 26, 2014; D. Etherington, "Banking Startup Simple Acquired for $117M, Will Continue to Operate," *TechCrunch*, February 20, 2014; "BBVA Acquires Digital Banking Service Pioneer Simple," *BBVA Press Release*, February 20, 2014; C. Forrest, "Appetite for Disruption: Can Simple and the Web Reinvent Banking?" *TechRepublic*, January 17, 2014; A. Jeffries, "Simple's Online-Only Banking App Launches on Android," *The Verge*, January 15, 2013; A. Robertson, "Banking Substitute Simple Releases iPhone App," *The Verge*, May 9, 2012; www.simple.com, accessed March 20, 2014.

Questions

1. Would you be willing to bank with an Internet bank? Why or why not?

2. What are the disadvantages of Simple's banking model? Provide examples to support your answer.

International banking and the ability to handle trading in multiple currencies are critical for international trade. Transfers of electronic funds and electronic letters of credit are vital services in international banking. An example of support for EC global trade is provided by TradeCard, in conjunction with MasterCard. TradeCard is an international company that provides a secure method for buyers and sellers to make digital payments anywhere on the globe (see the demo at www.tradecard.com). In another example, banks and companies such as Oanda (www.oanda.com) provide conversions of more than 160 currencies.

Online Securities Trading. Millions of Americans use computers to trade stocks, bonds, and other financial instruments. In fact, several well-known securities companies, including E*Trade, Ameritrade, and Charles Schwab, offer only online trading. In Korea, more than half of stock traders are already using the Internet for that purpose. Why? Because it is cheaper than a full-service or discount broker. On the Web, investors can find a considerable amount of information regarding specific companies or mutual funds in which to invest (e.g., http://money.cnn.com and www.bloomberg.com).

Let's say, for example, that you have an account with Scottrade. You access Scottrade's Web site (www.scottrade.com) from your personal computer or your Internet-enabled mobile device, enter your account number and password to access your personalized Web page, and then click on "stock trading." Using a menu, you enter the details of your order—buy or sell, margin or cash, price limit, market order, and so on. The computer informs you of the current "ask" and "bid" prices, much as a broker would do over the telephone. You can then approve or reject the transaction.

The Online Job Market. The Internet offers a promising new environment for job seekers and for companies searching for hard-to-find employees. Thousands of companies and government agencies advertise available positions, accept resumes, and take applications via the Internet.

Job seekers use the online job market to reply online to employment ads, to place resumes on various sites, and to use recruiting firms (e.g., www.monster.com, www.simplyhired.com, www.linkedin.com, and www.truecareers.com). Companies that have jobs to offer advertise these openings on their Web sites, and they search the bulletin boards of recruiting firms. In many countries (including the United States), governments must advertise job openings on the Internet.

Travel Services. The Internet is an ideal place to plan, explore, and arrange almost any trip economically. Online travel services allow you to purchase airline tickets, reserve hotel rooms, and rent cars. Most sites also offer a fare-tracker feature that sends you e-mail messages about low-cost flights. Examples of comprehensive online travel services are Expedia.com, Travelocity.com, and Orbitz.com. Online services are also provided by all major airline vacation services, large conventional travel agencies, car rental agencies, hotels (e.g., www.hotels.com), and tour companies. In a variation of this process, Priceline.com allows you to set a price you are willing to pay for an airline ticket or hotel accommodations. It then attempts to find a vendor that will match your price.

One costly problem that e-commerce can cause is "mistake fares" in the airline industry. For example, on August 6, 2012, El Al (www.elal.com), Israel's national airline, offered flights to Israel worth up to $1,600 for as little as some $300. This price was incorrect; the actual price was higher. By the time El Al noticed the mistake and pulled the fare, however, several tickets had been sold, thanks in part to online travel discussion groups.

Online Advertising. *Advertising* is the practice of disseminating information in an attempt to influence a buyer–seller transaction. Traditional advertising on TV or in newspapers involves impersonal, one-way mass communication. In contrast, direct response marketing, or telemarketing, contacts individuals by direct mail or telephone and requires them to respond in order to make a purchase. The direct response approach personalizes advertising and marketing. At the same time, however, it can be expensive, slow, and ineffective. It can also be extremely annoying to the consumer.

Internet advertising redefines the advertising process, making it media rich, dynamic, and interactive. It improves on traditional forms of advertising in a number of ways. First, Internet ads can be updated any time at minimal cost and therefore can be kept current. In addition, these ads can reach very large numbers of potential buyers all over the world. Furthermore, they are generally cheaper than radio, television, and print ads. Finally, Internet ads can be interactive and targeted to specific interest groups and/or individuals.

Advertising Methods. The most common online advertising methods are banners, pop-ups, and e-mail. **Banners** are simply electronic billboards. Typically, a banner contains a short text or a graphical message to promote a product or a vendor. It may even contain video clips and sound. When customers click on a banner, they are transferred to the advertiser's home page. Banner advertising is the most commonly used form of advertising on the Internet.

A major advantage of banners is that they can be customized to the target audience. If the computer system knows who you are or what your profile is, it might send you a banner that is specifically intended to match your interests. A major disadvantage of banners is that they can convey only limited information because of their small size. Another drawback is that many viewers simply ignore them.

Pop-up and pop-under ads are contained in a new browser window that is automatically launched when you enter or exit a Web site. A **pop-up ad** appears in front of the current browser window. A **pop-under ad** appears underneath the active window; when users close the active window, they see the ad. Many users strongly object to these ads, which they consider intrusive. Modern browsers let users block pop-up ads, but this feature must be used with caution because some Web sites depend on pop-up capabilities to present content other than advertising. For example, when you log on to your Verizon e-mail page, you also see a brief (one line each) summary of recent news stories. If you hover your mouse over one of them, you get a pop-up window with an extended summary (a few paragraphs) of that story. Another example is the WebCT Vista software for online instruction, where discussion group posts appear in pop-up windows. In the first example, blocking pop-ups would make the feature less useful. In the second example it would eliminate important functionality.

E-mail is emerging as an Internet advertising and marketing channel. It is generally cost-effective to implement, and it provides a better and quicker response rate than other advertising channels. Marketers develop or purchase a list of e-mail addresses, place them in a customer database, and then send advertisements via e-mail. A list of e-mail addresses can be a very powerful tool because the marketer can target a group of people or even individuals.

As you have probably concluded by now, there is a potential for misuse of e-mail advertising. In fact, some consumers receive a flood of unsolicited e-mail, or *spam*. **Spamming** is the indiscriminate distribution of electronic ads without the permission of the receiver. Unfortunately, spamming is becoming worse over time.

Two important responses to spamming are permission marketing and viral marketing. **Permission marketing** asks consumers to give their permission to voluntarily accept online advertising and e-mail. Typically, consumers are asked to complete an electronic form that asks what they are interested in and requests permission to send related marketing information. Sometimes, consumers are offered incentives to receive advertising.

Permission marketing is the basis of many Internet marketing strategies. For example, millions of users periodically receive e-mails from airlines such as American and Southwest.

Users of this marketing service can ask to be notified of low fares from their hometown or to their favorite destinations. Significantly, they can easily unsubscribe at any time. Permission marketing is also extremely important for market research (e.g., search for "Media Metrix" at www.comscore.com).

In one particularly interesting form of permission marketing, companies such as Clickdough.com, ExpressPaidSurveys.com, and CashSurfers.com have built customer lists of millions of people who are happy to receive advertising messages whenever they are on the Web. These customers are paid $0.25–0.50 an hour to view messages while they do their normal surfing.

Viral marketing refers to online word-of-mouth marketing. The strategy behind viral marketing is to have people forward messages to friends, family members, and other acquaintances suggesting they "check this out." For example, a marketer can distribute a small game program embedded with a sponsor's e-mail that is easy to forward. The marketer releases only a few thousand copies, with the expectation that the recipients in turn will forward the program to many more thousands of potential customers. In this way, viral marketing enables companies to build brand awareness at a minimal cost without having to spam millions of uninterested users.

Issues in E-Tailing

Despite e-tailing's increasing popularity, many e-tailers continue to face serious issues that can restrict their growth. Perhaps the two most significant issues are channel conflict and order fulfillment.

Clicks-and-mortar companies may face a conflict with their regular distributors when they sell directly to customers online. This situation, known as **channel conflict**, can alienate the distributors. Channel conflict has forced some companies to avoid direct online sales. For example, Walmart, Lowe's, and Home Depot would rather have customers come to their stores. Therefore, although all three companies maintain e-commerce Web sites, their sites place more emphasis on providing information—products, prices, specials, and store locations—than on online sales.

Channel conflict can arise in areas such as pricing and resource allocation—for example, how much money to spend on advertising. Another potential source of conflict involves the logistics services provided by the offline activities to the online activities. For example, how should a company handle returns of items purchased online? Some companies have completely separated the "clicks" (the online portion of the organization) from the "mortar" or "bricks" (the traditional bricks-and-mortar part of the organization). However, this approach can increase expenses, reduce the synergy between the two organizational channels, and alienate customers. As a result, many companies are integrating their online and offline channels, a process known as **multichanneling**. In fact, many companies are calling this process omni-channeling, as you see in closing case 2.

Multichanneling has created the opportunity for showrooming. *Showrooming* occurs when shoppers visit a brick-and-mortar store to examine a product in person. They then conduct research about the product on their smartphones. Often, they purchase the product from the Web site of a competitor of the store they are visiting. Showrooming is causing problems for brick-and-mortar retailers, such as Target, Best Buy, and others. At the same time, showrooming benefits Amazon, eBay, and other online retailers.

The second major issue confronting e-commerce is order fulfillment, which can create problems for e-tailers as well. Any time a company sells directly to customers, it is involved in various order-fulfillment activities. It must perform the following activities: quickly find the products to be shipped; pack them; arrange for the packages to be delivered speedily to the customer's door; collect the money from every customer, either in advance, by COD, or by individual bill; and handle the return of unwanted or defective products.

It is very difficult to accomplish these activities both effectively and efficiently in B2C, because a company has to ship small packages to many customers and do it quickly. For this reason, companies involved in B2C activities often experience difficulties in their supply chains.

In addition to providing customers with the products they ordered and doing it on time, order fulfillment provides all related customer services. For example, the customer must receive assembly and operation instructions for a new appliance. In addition, if the customer is unhappy with a product, the company must arrange an exchange or a return.

In the late 1990s, e-tailers faced continuous problems in order fulfillment, especially during the holiday season. These problems included late deliveries, delivering wrong items, high delivery costs, and compensation to unsatisfied customers. For e-tailers, taking orders over the Internet is the easy part of B2C e-commerce. Delivering orders to customers' doors is the hard part. In contrast, order fulfillment is less complicated in B2B. These transactions are much larger, but they are fewer in number. In addition, these companies have had order fulfillment mechanisms in place for many years.

BEFORE *YOU GO ON....*

1. Describe electronic storefronts and malls.
2. Discuss various types of online services, such as cyberbanking, securities trading, job searches, travel services, and so on.
3. Discuss online advertising, its methods, and its benefits.
4. Identify the major issues related to e-tailing.
5. What are spamming, permission marketing, and viral marketing?

Apply The Concept 9.2

LEARNING OBJECTIVE 9.2 Describe the various online services of business-to-consumer (B2C) commerce, providing specific examples of each.

STEP 1 – Background

At this point in your "buying" career, you have probably purchased something online, visited an auction site (and possibly won a bid), and engaged in some form of online banking. Your generation is very comfortable with the retail side of e-commerce. While you were engaging in B2C e-commerce, you probably created an account with a few vendors and received some e-mail advertisements. No doubt you have also received some pop-up ads promoting products during your Internet searches.

Another aspect of modern business that has changed is that companies now want you to do their advertising for them. The text refers to this development as viral marketing.

STEP 2 – Activity

Imagine that you and some friends decide to start a new online thrift store. To become a member, an individual has to donate to the thrift. For every 10 items a person donates, he or she is awarded a two-month membership. However, you have no IT platform for e-commerce. After some research, you determine that Shopify is your best provider. Shopify is an e-commerce platform that enables individuals and businesses to create online stores.

Visit http://www.wiley.com/go/rainer/MIS3e/applytheconcept, and click on the link provided for Apply the Concept 9.2. This link will take you to Shopify's Web site. Near the top of the page you will see a link to "Examples" of other providers. Look through the examples to identify ideas you would like to incorporate into your store.

STEP 3 – Deliverable

After reviewing the Shopify site, prepare a presentation or a document that describes the various online services of B2C commerce provided by Shopify. Provide specific examples of services that attracted your attention, and discuss how you would apply these services to your store.

9.3 Business-to-Business (B2B) Electronic Commerce

In *business to business* (*B2B*) e-commerce, the buyers and sellers are business organizations. B2B comprises about 85 percent of EC volume. It covers a broad spectrum of applications that enable an enterprise to form electronic relationships with its distributors, resellers, suppliers, customers, and other partners. Organizations can use B2B to restructure their supply chains and their partner relationships.

B2B applications utilize any of several business models. The major models are sell-side marketplaces, buy-side marketplaces, and electronic exchanges.

Sell-Side Marketplaces

In the **sell-side marketplace** model, organizations attempt to sell their products or services to other organizations electronically from their own private e-marketplace Web site and/or from a third-party Web site. This model is similar to the B2C model in which the buyer is expected to come to the seller's site, view catalogs, and place an order. In the B2B sell-side marketplace, however, the buyer is an organization.

The key mechanisms in the sell-side model are forward auctions and electronic catalogs that can be customized for each large buyer. Sellers such as Dell Computer (www.dellauction.com) use auctions extensively. In addition to conducting auctions from their own Web sites, organizations can use third-party auction sites, such as eBay, to liquidate items. Companies such as Ariba (www.ariba.com) are helping organizations to auction old assets and inventories.

The sell-side model is used by hundreds of thousands of companies. It is especially powerful for companies with superb reputations. The seller can be either a manufacturer (e.g., Dell or IBM), a distributor (e.g., www.avnet.com), or a retailer (e.g., www.bigboxx .com). The seller uses EC to increase sales, reduce selling and advertising expenditures, increase delivery speed, and lower administrative costs. The sell-side model is especially suitable to customization. Many companies allow their customers to configure their orders online. For example, at Dell (www.dell.com), you can determine the exact type of computer that you want. You can choose the type of chip, the size of the hard drive, the type of monitor, and so on. Similarly, the Jaguar Web site (www.jaguar.com) allows you to customize the Jaguar you want. Self-customization greatly reduces any misunderstandings concerning what customers want, and it encourages businesses to fill orders more quickly.

Buy-Side Marketplaces

Procurement is the overarching function that describes the activities and processes to acquire goods and services. Distinct from purchasing, procurement involves the activities necessary to establish requirements, sourcing activities such as market research and vendor evaluation, and negotiation of contracts. *Purchasing* refers to the process of ordering and receiving goods and services. It is a subset of the procurement process.

The **buy-side** marketplace is a model in which organizations attempt to procure needed products or services from other organizations electronically. A major method of procuring goods and services in the buy-side model is the reverse auction.

The buy-side model uses EC technology to streamline the procurement process. The goal is to reduce both the costs of items procured and the administrative expenses involved in procuring them. In addition, EC technology can shorten the procurement cycle time.

Procurement by using electronic support is referred to as e-procurement. **E-procurement** uses reverse auctions, particularly group purchasing. In **group purchasing**, multiple buyers combine their orders so that they constitute a large volume and therefore attract more seller attention. In addition, when buyers place their combined orders on a reverse auction, they can negotiate a volume discount. Typically, the orders of small buyers are aggregated by a third-party vendor, such as the United Sourcing Alliance (www.usa-llc.com).

Electronic Exchanges

Private exchanges have one buyer and many sellers. Electronic marketplaces (e-marketplaces), called **public exchanges** or just **exchanges**, are independently owned by a third party, and they connect many sellers with many buyers. Public exchanges are open to all business organizations. They are frequently owned and operated by a third party. Public exchange managers provide all of the necessary information systems to the participants. Thus, buyers and sellers merely have to "plug in" in order to trade. B2B public exchanges are often the initial point of contacts between business partners. Once the partners make contact, they may move to a private exchange or to private trading rooms provided by many public exchanges to conduct their subsequent trading activities.

Electronic exchanges deal in both direct and indirect materials. *Direct materials* are inputs to the manufacturing process, such as safety glass used in automobile windshields and windows. *Indirect materials* are those items, such as office supplies, that are needed for maintenance, operations, and repairs (MRO).

There are three basic types of public exchanges: vertical, horizontal, and functional. All three types offer diversified support services, ranging from payments to logistics.

Vertical exchanges connect buyers and sellers in a given industry. Examples of vertical exchanges are www.plasticsnet.com in the plastics industry and www.papersite.com in the paper industry. The vertical e-marketplaces offer services that are particularly suited to the community they serve. Vertical exchanges are frequently owned and managed by a *consortium*, a term for a group of major players in an industry. For example, Marriott and Hyatt own a procurement consortium for the hotel industry, and Chevron owns an energy e-marketplace.

Horizontal exchanges connect buyers and sellers across many industries. They are used primarily for MRO materials. Examples of horizontal exchanges are TradersCity (www.traderscity .com), Globalsources (www.globalsources.com), and Alibaba (www.alibaba.com).

Finally, in *functional exchanges*, needed services such as temporary help or extra office space are traded on an "as-needed" basis. For example, Employease (www.employease .com) can find temporary labor by searching employers in its Employease Network.

┌─ **BEFORE** *YOU GO ON....* ─────────
│
│ 1. Briefly differentiate between the sell-side
│   marketplace and the buy-side marketplace.
│
│ 2. Briefly differentiate among vertical
│   exchanges, horizontal exchanges, and
│   functional exchanges.
│
└────────────────────────────────────

Apply The Concept 9.3

LEARNING OBJECTIVE 9.3 Describe the three business models for business-to-business electronic commerce.

STEP 1 – Background

Section 9.3 describes forward auctions, reverse auctions, and exchanges. Forward auctions are used when a seller is trying to reach several buyers, and reverse auctions are used when a buyer is soliciting from several sellers. In an exchange, both buyers and sellers come to a central Web site to quickly and easily establish a B2B relationship. Some of these Web sites or exchanges are for materials involved in manufacturing a product; others involve materials that help run the business.

STEP 2 – Activity

Visit http://www.wiley.com/go/rainer/MIS3e/applytheconcept, and click on the link provided for Apply the Concept 9.3. This link will take you to one of the horizontal exchanges (an exchange for many buyers and sellers across industries) listed in the section. As you examine the available products, you should get a better understanding of the breadth of a horizontal exchange.

STEP 3 – Deliverable

Describe the three business models for B2B e-commerce by comparing and contrasting them with Globalsource. Submit your description to your professor.

9.4 Ethical and Legal Issues in E-Business

Technological innovation often forces a society to reexamine and modify its ethical standards. In many cases, the new standards are incorporated into law. In this section, you will learn about two important ethical considerations—privacy and job loss—as well as various legal issues arising from the practice of e-business.

Ethical Issues

Many of the ethical and global issues related to IT also apply to e-business. Here you will learn about two basic issues: privacy and job loss.

By making it easier to store and transfer personal information, e-business presents some threats to privacy. To begin with, most electronic payment systems know who the buyers are. It may be necessary, then, to protect the buyers' identities. Businesses frequently use encryption to provide this protection.

Another major privacy issue is tracking. For example, individuals' activities on the Internet can be tracked by cookies (discussed in Chapter 7). Cookies store your tracking history on your personal computer's hard drive, and any time you revisit a certain Web site, the server recognizes the cookie. In response, antivirus software packages routinely search for potentially harmful cookies.

In addition to compromising individual privacy, the use of EC may eliminate the need for some of a company's employees, as well as brokers and agents. The manner in which these unneeded workers, especially employees, are treated can raise ethical issues: How should the company handle the layoffs? Should companies be required to retrain employees for new positions? If not, how should the company compensate or otherwise assist the displaced workers?

Legal and Ethical Issues Specific to E-Commerce

Many legal issues are related specifically to e-commerce. A business environment in which buyers and sellers do not know one another and cannot even see one another creates opportunities for dishonest people to commit fraud and other crimes. During the first few years of EC, the public witnessed many such crimes. These illegal actions ranged from creating a virtual bank that disappeared along with the investors' deposits to manipulating stock prices on the Internet. Unfortunately, fraudulent activities on the Internet are increasing. In the following section, you explore some of the major legal issues that are specific to e-commerce.

Fraud on the Internet. Internet fraud has grown even faster than Internet use itself. In one case, stock promoters falsely spread positive rumors about the prospects of the companies they touted in order to boost the stock price. In other cases, the information provided might have been true, but the promoters did not disclose that they were paid to talk up the companies. Stock promoters specifically target small investors who are lured by the promise of fast profits.

Stocks are only one of many areas where swindlers are active. Auctions are especially conducive to fraud, by both sellers and buyers. Other types of fraud include selling bogus investments and setting up phantom business opportunities. Because of the growing use of e-mail, financial criminals now have access to many more potential victims. The U.S. Federal Trade Commission (FTC) (www.ftc.gov) regularly publishes examples of scams that are most likely to be spread via e-mail or to be found on the Web. Later in this section, you will see some ways in which consumers and sellers can protect themselves from online fraud.

Domain Names. Another legal issue is competition over domain names. Domain names are assigned by central nonprofit organizations that check for conflicts and possible infringement of trademarks. Obviously, companies that sell goods and services over the Internet want customers to be able to find them easily. In general, the closer the domain name matches the company's name, the easier the company is to locate.

A domain name is considered legal when the person or business who owns the name has operated a legitimate business under that name for some time. Companies such as Christian Dior, Nike, Deutsche Bank, and even Microsoft have had to fight or pay to acquire the domain name that corresponds to their company's name. Consider the case of Delta Air Lines. Delta originally could not obtain the Internet domain name delta.com because Delta Faucet had already purchased it. Delta Faucet had been in business under that name since 1954, so it had a legitimate business interest in using the domain name. Delta Air Lines had to settle for delta-airlines.com until it bought the domain name from Delta Faucet. Delta Faucet is now at deltafaucet.com. Several cases of disputed domain names are currently in court.

Cybersquatting. **Cybersquatting** refers to the practice of registering or using domain names for the purpose of profiting from the goodwill or the trademark that belongs to someone else. The Anti-Cybersquatting Consumer Protection Act (1999) permits trademark owners in the United States to sue for damages in such cases.

However, some practices that could be considered cybersquatting are not illegal, although they may well be unethical. Perhaps the more common of these practices is "domain tasting." Domain tasting lets registrars profit from the complex money trail of pay-per-click advertising. The practice can be traced back to the policies of the organization responsible for regulating Web names, the Internet Corporation for Assigned Names and Numbers (ICANN) (www.icann.org). In 2000, ICANN established the "create grace period," a five-day period during which a company or person can claim a domain name and then return it for a full refund of the $6 registry fee. ICANN implemented this policy to allow someone who mistyped a domain to return it without cost. In some cases, companies engage in cybersquatting by registering domain names that are very similar to their competitors' domain names in order to generate traffic from people who misspell Web addresses.

Domain tasters exploit this policy by claiming Internet domains for five days at no cost. These domain names frequently resemble those of prominent companies and organizations. The tasters then jam these domains full of advertisements that come from Yahoo! and Google. Because this process involves zero risk and 100 percent profit margins, domain tasters register millions of domain names every day—some of them over and over again. Experts estimate that registrants ultimately purchase less than 2 percent of the sites they sample. In the vast majority of cases, they use the domain names for only a few days to generate quick profits.

Taxes and Other Fees. In offline sales, most states and localities tax business transactions that are conducted within their jurisdiction. The most obvious example is sales taxes. Federal, state, and local authorities are now scrambling to create some type of taxation policy for e-business. This problem is particularly complex for interstate and international e-commerce. For example, some people claim that the state in which the *seller* is located deserves the entire sales tax (in some countries, it is a value-added tax (VAT)). Others contend that the state in which the *server* is located should also receive some of the tax revenues.

In addition to the sales tax, there is a question about where—and in some cases, whether—electronic sellers should pay business license taxes, franchise fees, gross receipts taxes, excise taxes, privilege taxes, and utility taxes. Furthermore, how should tax collection be controlled? Legislative efforts to impose taxes on e-commerce are opposed by an organization named the Internet Freedom Fighters.

In December 2013, the U.S. Supreme Court declined to get involved in state efforts to force Web retailers such as Amazon to collect sales tax from customers even in places where the companies do not have a physical presence. The court's decision to stay out of the issue may put pressure on Congress to come up with a national solution, as both online and traditional retailers complain about a patchwork of state laws and conflicting lower court decisions. As of mid-2014, all but five states impose sales taxes on online purchases, and an increasing number have passed legislation to force online retailers to begin collecting those taxes from customers.

Even before electronic commerce over the Internet emerged, the basic law was that as long as a retailer did not have a physical presence in the state where the consumer was shopping, that retailer did not have to collect a sales tax. Shoppers are supposed to track such purchases and then pay the taxes owed in their annual tax filings. Few people, however, do this or are even aware of it.

The result is that online retailers have been able to undercut the prices of their non-Internet (e.g., brick-and-mortar stores) competitors for years. As state and local governments have increasingly experienced large cash shortcomings since the recession, they have fought back. As of mid-2014, some 19 states required Amazon to collect sales taxes.

Copyright. Recall from Chapter 6 that intellectual property is protected by copyright laws and cannot be used freely. This point is significant because many people mistakenly believe that once they purchase a piece of software, they have the right to share it with others. In fact, what they have bought is the right to *use* the software, not the right to *distribute* it. That right remains with the copyright holder. Similarly, copying material from Web sites without permission is a violation of copyright laws. Protecting intellectual property rights in e-commerce is extremely difficult, however,

> BEFORE *YOU GO ON*....
>
> 1. List and explain some ethical issues in EC.
> 2. Discuss the major legal issues associated with EC.
> 3. Describe buyer protection and seller protection in EC.

because it involves hundreds of millions of people in 200 countries with differing copyright laws who have access to billions of Web pages.

Apply The Concept 9.4

LEARNING OBJECTIVE 9.4 Identify the ethical and legal issues related to electronic commerce, providing examples.

STEP 1 – Background

Amazon.com is the world's largest online retailer. In fact, it is one of a kind in many ways. It competes with Apple, Google, Microsoft, and Walmart, some of the biggest names in the tech and retail universe (online and in-store).

Did you know, however, that there is a huge controversy surrounding Amazon? Specifically, the retailer does not collect sales tax in all states. No big deal, right? Not exactly. A quick Web search for "Amazon Sales Tax" will quickly bring you up to speed on this issue. Of course, Amazon considers their tax-free status to be their competitive advantage. Not surprisingly, the retailer has used its considerable power to discourage state governments from revising their tax policies to alter this status.

From the opposite perspective, if you purchase something online and do not pay sales tax, you are supposed to include this purchase on your income tax statement and pay the taxes at that time. But, do you? Do you think anybody does?

STEP 2 – Activity

Search the Web to find out if Amazon collects sales tax in your state. If it doesn't, then it is likely that the issue has been raised. Imagine that Amazon has fulfillment centers in your state, meaning it operates in your state and therefore should collect sales tax. How would you feel if the retailer charges you tax but doesn't charge consumers in other states? Next, suppose a business in your state uses Amazon's fulfillment services and does not collect sales tax. Should Amazon's partnership with that company require it to collect tax on every purchase in your state?

STEP 3 – Deliverable

Take a little time to consider this controversy. Then, create a list of arguments for and against requiring Amazon.com to collect sales tax in *all* states. Make certain your argument identifies both the ethical and legal aspects of this issue.

What's in for ME?

FOR THE
ACCOUNTING MAJOR

Accounting personnel are involved in several EC activities. Designing the ordering system and its relationship with inventory management requires accounting attention. Billing and payments are also accounting activities, as are determining cost and profit allocation. Replacing paper documents with electronic means will affect many of the accountant's tasks, especially the auditing of EC activities and systems. Finally, building a cost-benefit and cost-justification system to determine which products/services to take online and creating a chargeback system are critical to the success of EC.

FOR THE FINANCE MAJOR

The worlds of banking, securities and commodities markets, and other financial services are being reengineered because of EC. Online securities trading and its supporting infrastructure are growing more rapidly than any other EC activity. Many innovations already in place are changing the rules of economic and financial incentives for financial analysts and managers. Online banking, for example, does not recognize state boundaries, and it may create a new framework for financing global trades. Public financial information is now accessible in seconds. These innovations will dramatically change the manner in which finance personnel operate.

FOR THE MARKETING MAJOR

A major revolution in marketing and sales is taking place because of EC. Perhaps its most obvious feature is the transition from a physical to a virtual marketplace. Equally important, however, is the radical transformation to one-on-one advertising and sales and to customized and interactive marketing. Marketing channels are being combined, eliminated, or recreated. The EC revolution is creating new products and markets and significantly altering existing ones. Digitization of products and services also has implications for marketing and sales. The direct producer-to-consumer channel is expanding rapidly and is fundamentally changing the nature of customer service. As the battle for customers intensifies, marketing and sales personnel are becoming the most critical success factor in many organizations. Online marketing can be a blessing to one company and a curse to another.

FOR THE PRODUCTION/ OPERATIONS MANAGEMENT MAJOR

EC is changing the manufacturing system from product-push mass production to order-pull mass customization. This change requires a robust supply chain, information support, and reengineering of processes that involve suppliers and other business partners. Suppliers can use extranets to monitor and replenish inventories without the need for constant reorders. In addition, the Internet and intranets help reduce cycle times. Many production/operations problems that have persisted for years, such as complex scheduling and excess inventories, are being solved rapidly with the use of Web technologies. Companies can now use external and internal networks to find and manage manufacturing operations in other countries much more easily. Also, the Web is reengineering procurement by helping companies conduct electronic bids for parts and subassemblies, thus reducing cost. All in all, the job of the progressive production/operations manager is closely tied in with e-commerce.

FOR THE HUMAN RESOURCE MANAGEMENT MAJOR

HR majors need to understand the new labor markets and the impacts of EC on old labor markets. Also, the HR department may use EC tools for such functions as procuring office supplies. Moreover, becoming knowledgeable about new government online initiatives and online training is critical. In addition, HR personnel must be familiar with the major legal issues related to EC and employment.

FOR THE MIS MAJOR

The MIS function is responsible for providing the information technology infrastructure necessary for electronic commerce to function. In particular, this infrastructure includes the company's networks, intranets, and extranets. The MIS function is also responsible for ensuring that electronic commerce transactions are secure.

SUMMARY

1. Describe the six common types of electronic commerce.

    In *business-to-consumer* (B2C) electronic commerce, the sellers are organizations and the buyers are individuals. In *business-to-business* (B2B) electronic commerce, the sellers and the buyers are businesses. In *consumer-to-consumer* (C2C) electronic commerce, an individual sells products or services to other individuals. In *business-to-employee* (B2E) electronic commerce, an organization uses EC internally to provide information and services to its employees. *E-government* is the use of Internet technology in general and e-commerce in particular to deliver information and public services to citizens (called government-to-citizen or G2C EC) and business partners and suppliers (called government-to-business or G2B EC). *Mobile commerce* refers to e-commerce that is conducted entirely in a wireless environment. We leave the examples of each type to you.

2. Describe the various online services of business-to-consumer (B2C) commerce, providing specific examples of each.

    Electronic banking, also known as cyberbanking, involves conducting various banking activities from home, at a place of business, or on the road instead of at a physical bank location.

    Online securities trading involves buying and selling securities over the Web.

    Online job matching over the Web offers a promising environment for job seekers and for companies searching for hard-to-find employees. Thousands of companies and government agencies advertise available positions, accept resumes, and take applications via the Internet.

    Online travel services allow you to purchase airline tickets, reserve hotel rooms, and rent cars. Most sites also offer a fare-tracker feature that sends you e-mail messages about low-cost flights. The Internet is an ideal place to plan, explore, and arrange almost any trip economically.

Online advertising over the Web makes the advertising process media-rich, dynamic, and interactive.

We leave the examples to you.

3. Describe the three·business models for business-to-business electronic commerce.

In the *sell-side marketplace* model, organizations attempt to sell their products or services to other organizations electronically from their own private e-marketplace Web site and/or from a third-party Web site. Sellers such as Dell Computer (www.dellauction.com) use sell-side auctions extensively. In addition to auctions from their own Web sites, organizations can use third-party auction sites, such as eBay, to liquidate items.

The *buy-side marketplace* is a model in which organizations attempt to buy needed products or services from other organizations electronically.

E-marketplaces, in which there are many sellers and many buyers, are called *public exchanges*, or just exchanges. Public exchanges are open to all business organizations. They are frequently owned and operated by a third party.

There are three basic types of public exchanges: vertical, horizontal, and functional. *Vertical exchanges* connect buyers and sellers in a given industry. *Horizontal exchanges* connect buyers and sellers across many industries. In *functional exchanges*, needed services such as temporary help or extra office space are traded on an "as-needed" basis.

4. Identify the ethical and legal issues related to electronic commerce, providing examples.

E-business presents some threats to privacy. First, most electronic payment systems know who the buyers are. It may be necessary, then, to protect the buyers' identities with encryption. Another major privacy issue is tracking, where individuals' activities on the Internet can be tracked by cookies.

The use of EC may eliminate the need for some of a company's employees, as well as brokers and agents. The manner in which these unneeded workers, especially employees, are treated can raise ethical issues: How should the company handle the layoffs? Should companies be required to retrain employees for new positions? If not, how should the company compensate or otherwise assist the displaced workers?

We leave the examples to you.

>>>CHAPTER GLOSSARY

auction A competitive process in which either a seller solicits consecutive bids from buyers or a buyer solicits bids from sellers, and prices are determined dynamically by competitive bidding.

banner Electronic billboards, which typically contain a short text or graphical message to promote a product or a vendor.

brick-and-mortar organizations Organizations in which the product, the process, and the delivery agent are all physical.

business model The method by which a company generates revenue to sustain itself.

business-to-business electronic commerce (B2B) Electronic commerce in which both the sellers and the buyers are business organizations.

business-to-consumer electronic commerce (B2C) Electronic commerce in which the sellers are organizations and the buyers are individuals; also known as e-tailing.

business-to-employee electronic commerce (B2E) An organization using electronic commerce internally to provide information and services to its employees.

buy-side marketplace B2B model in which organizations buy needed products or services from other organizations electronically, often through a reverse auction.

channel conflict The alienation of existing distributors when a company decides to sell to customers directly online.

clicks-and-mortar organizations Organizations that do business in both the physical and digital dimensions.

consumer-to-consumer electronic commerce (C2C) Electronic commerce in which both the buyer and the seller are individuals (not businesses).

cyberbanking Various banking activities conducted electronically from home, a business, or on the road instead of at a physical bank location; also known as *electronic banking*.

cybersquatting Registering domain names in the hope of selling them later at a higher price.

disintermediation Elimination of intermediaries in electronic commerce.

e-government The use of electronic commerce to deliver information and public services to citizens, business partners, and suppliers of government entities, and those working in the public sector.

electronic business (e-business) A broader definition of electronic commerce, including buying and selling of goods and services, and servicing customers, collaborating with business partners, conducting e-learning, and conducting electronic transactions within an organization.

electronic commerce (EC or e-commerce) The process of buying, selling, transferring, or exchanging products, services, or information via computer networks, including the Internet.

electronic mall A collection of individual shops under one Internet address; also known as a *cybermall* or an *e-mall*.

electronic marketplace A virtual market space on the Web where many buyers and many sellers conduct electronic business activities.

electronic payment mechanisms Computer-based systems that allow customers to pay for goods and services electronically, rather than writing a check or using cash.

electronic retailing (e-tailing) The direct sale of products and services through storefronts or electronic malls, usually designed around an electronic catalog format and/or auctions.

electronic storefront The Web site of a single company, with its own Internet address, at which orders can be placed.

e-procurement Purchasing by using electronic support.

exchanges (see **public exchanges**)

forward auctions Auctions that sellers use as a selling channel to many potential buyers; the highest bidder wins the items.

group purchasing The aggregation of purchasing orders from many buyers so that a volume discount can be obtained.

mobile commerce (m-commerce) Electronic commerce conducted in a wireless environment.

multichanneling A process in which a company integrates its online and offline channels.

permission marketing Method of marketing that asks consumers to give their permission to voluntarily accept online advertising and e-mail.

person-to-person payments A form of electronic cash that enables the transfer of funds between two individuals, or between an individual and a business, without the use of a credit card.

pop-under ad An advertisement that is automatically launched by some trigger and appears underneath the active window.

pop-up ad An advertisement that is automatically launched by some trigger and appears in front of the active window.

public exchanges (or exchanges) Electronic marketplaces in which there are many sellers and many buyers, and entry is open to all; frequently owned and operated by a third party.

reverse auctions Auctions in which one buyer, usually an organization, seeks to buy a product or a service, and suppliers submit bids; the lowest bidder wins.

sell-side marketplace B2B model in which organizations sell to other organizations from their own private e-marketplace and/or from a third-party site.

smart cards Cards that contain a microprocessor (chip) that enables the card to store a considerable amount of information (including stored funds) and to conduct processing.

spamming Indiscriminate distribution of e-mail without the receiver's permission.

stored-value money cards A form of electronic cash on which a fixed amount of prepaid money is stored; the amount is reduced each time the card is used.

viral marketing Online word-of-mouth marketing.

virtual banks Banking institutions dedicated solely to Internet transactions.

virtual (or pure play) organizations Organizations in which the product, the process, and the delivery agent are all digital.

>>>DISCUSSION QUESTIONS

1. Discuss the major limitations of e-commerce. Which of these limitations are likely to disappear? Why?

2. Discuss the reasons for having multiple EC business models.

3. Distinguish between business-to-business forward auctions and buyers' bids for RFQs.

4. Discuss the benefits to sellers and buyers of a B2B exchange.

5. What are the major benefits of G2C electronic commerce?

6. Discuss the various ways to pay online in B2C. Which method(s) would you prefer and why?

7. Why is order fulfillment in B2C considered difficult?

8. Discuss the reasons for EC failures.

9. Should Mr. Coffee sell coffeemakers online? *Hint:* Take a look at the discussion of channel conflict in this chapter.

10. In some cases, individuals engage in cybersquatting so that they can sell the domain names to companies expensively. In other cases, companies engage in cybersquatting by registering domain names that are very similar to their competitors' domain names in order to generate traffic from people who misspell Web addresses. Discuss each practice in terms of its ethical nature and legality. Is there a difference between the two practices? Support your answer.

11. Do you think information technology has made it easier to do business? Or has *it* only raised the bar on what is required to be able to do business in the 21st century? Support your answer with specific examples.

12. With the rise of electronic commerce, what do you think will happen to those without computer skills, Internet access, computers, smartphones, and so on? Will they be able to survive and advance by hard work?

>>>PROBLEM-SOLVING ACTIVITIES

1. Assume you are interested in buying a car. You can find information about cars at numerous Web sites. Access five Web sites for information about new and used cars, financing, and insurance. Decide which car you want to buy. Configure your car by going to the car manufacturer's Web site. Finally, try to find the car from www.autobytel.com. What information is most supportive of your decision-making process? Write a report about your experience.

2. Compare the various electronic payment methods. Specifically, collect information from the vendors cited in this chapter and find additional vendors using Google.com. Pay attention to security level, speed, cost, and convenience.

3. Conduct a study on selling diamonds and gems online. Access such sites as www.bluenile.com, www.diamond.com, www.thaigem.com, www.tiffany.com, and www.jewelryexchange.com.

   a. What features do these sites use to educate buyers about gemstones?

   b. How do these sites attract buyers?

   c. How do these sites increase customers' trust in online purchasing?

   d. What customer service features do these sites provide?

4. Access www.nacha.org. What is NACHA? What is its role? What is the ACH? Who are the key participants in an ACH e-payment? Describe the "pilot" projects currently underway at ACH.

5. Access www.espn.com. Identify at least five different ways the site generates revenue.

6. Access www.queendom.com. Examine its offerings and try some of them. What type of electronic commerce is this? How does this Web site generate revenue?

7. Access www.ediets.com. Prepare a list of all the services the company provides. Identify its revenue model.

8. Access www.theknot.com. Identify the site's revenue sources.

9. Access www.mint.com. Identify the site's revenue model. What are the risks of giving this Web site your credit and debit card numbers, as well as your bank account number?

10. Research the case of www.nissan.com. Is Uzi Nissan cybersquatting? Why or why not? Support your answer. How is Nissan (the car company) reacting to the www.nissan.com Web site?

11. Enter www.alibaba.com. Identify the site's capabilities. Look at the site's private trading room. Write a report. How can such a site help a person who is making a purchase?

12. Enter www.grubhub.com. Explore the site. Why is the site so successful? Could you start a competing site? Why or why not?

13. Enter www.dell.com, go to "Desktops," and configure a system. Register to "My Cart" (no obligation). What calculators are used there? What are the advantages of this process as compared with buying a computer in a physical store? What are the disadvantages?

14. Enter www.checkfree.com and www.lmlpayment.com to identify their services. Prepare a report.

15. Access various travel sites such as www.travelocity.com, www.orbitz.com, www.expedia.com, www.kayak.com, and www.pinpoint.com. Compare these Web sites for ease of use and usefulness. Note differences among the sites. If you ask each site for the itinerary, which one gives you the best information and the best deals?

16. Access www.outofservice.com, and answer the musical taste and personality survey. When you have finished, click on "Results" and see what your musical tastes say about your personality. How accurate are the findings about you?

17. Tips for Safe Electronic Shopping

   • Look for reliable brand names at sites such as Walmart Online, Disney Online, and Amazon. Before purchasing, make sure that the site is authentic by entering the site directly and not from an unverified link.

   • Search any unfamiliar selling site for the company's address and phone and fax numbers. Call up and quiz the employees about the seller.

   • Check out the vendor with the local Chamber of Commerce or Better Business Bureau (www.bbbonline.org). Look for seals of authenticity such as TRUSTe.

   • Investigate how secure the seller's site is by examining the security procedures and by reading the posted privacy policy.

   • Examine the money-back guarantees, warranties, and service agreements.

   • Compare prices with those in regular stores. Too low prices are too good to be true and some catch is probably involved.

   • Ask friends what they know. Find testimonials and endorsements on community Web sites and well-known bulletin boards.

   • Find out what your rights are in case of a dispute. Consult consumer protection agencies and the National Consumer League's Fraud Center (www.fraud.org).

   • Check Consumerworld (www.consumerworld.org) for a collection of useful resources.

   • For many types of products, www.resellerratings.com is a useful resource.

STEP 1 – Background

Converting a business from bricks-and-mortar to e-business is a rather complicated task. At the turn of the 20th century (the early 1900s), Sears & Roebuck was the dominant retailer. This company's business model—mailing out a catalog, receiving payment and orders, processing, and fulfillment—was years ahead of the local "general store." To better understand the mail-order catalog model, search Wikipedia and other sources for more information on the history of Sears.

STEP 2 – Activity

Divide your team into the following activities: consumer, order processing, accounts receivable, product fulfillment, shipping, inventory, and sales. For each activity, work through a catalog order that includes five different items. To facilitate this process, assume that full payment is received.

Beginning with the consumer, have each person create a Google Doc with all of the necessary information to forward to the next person in the process. For example, the consumer will create two documents to pass to the order processing person: the order and the payment. Next, the order processing person will create documents that include new information needed as the order moves through the purchase process. This person will also keep a copy for himself or herself. As this order progresses through the "company," you will see how many documents are created and how much information is generated by traditional business processes.

STEP 3 – Deliverable

As a team, visit http://www.wiley.com/go/rainer/MIS3e/collaboration, and watch the YouTube video about Amazon.com. Then, write a summary as a team of your experience that compares Amazon.com's e-commerce model with the traditional commerce that you modeled in your experiment. Did anyone make a mistake when transferring the information? How could computer information systems (and therefore e-commerce) have helped to make the process flow better?

Submit your paper to your instructor.

CLOSING **CASE 1** > Uber:

Disrupting the Taxi Industry

THE BUSINESS PROBLEM >>> The problem is universal. As a passenger, what is the best way to find a cab when you need one?

The taxi industry has problems. Take San Francisco, for example. The city, like other major urban centers, has a longstanding policy of limiting the number of operating licenses for taxis, despite that its population has increased. In addition, dispatchers at the major cab companies do not seem to care about prompt customer service because they make their money primarily by leasing their cars to drivers. As one Massachusetts Institute of Technology professor stated, "The taxi industry is characterized by high prices, poor service, and no accountability."

Another problem is that taxis tend to be scarce when passengers need them. A Princeton University economist found that New York City taxi drivers tend to go home after they reach their target income for the day. Common sense would dictate that on days when demand is high—such as when it is raining—drivers would keep driving to maximize their income. However, it turns out that cabbies prefer to stabilize their income from day to day. Therefore, when the weather is bad and the demand for taxis is greater than normal, taxis are actually more difficult to find. The reason is not simply that more people are hailing cabs. Rather, the supply is constricted, by cabbies who have made their daily quota more rapidly and have turned on the off-duty sign. In short, the taxi industry has long been ripe for disruption. Today, information technology is enabling that disruption.

A POSSIBLE SOLUTION >>> Uber (www.uber.com), founded in 2010, allows passengers to directly book the nearest cab or limousine by smartphone and then track the vehicle on a map as it approaches their location. After the ride, Uber automatically compensates the driver from the customer's credit card—no tipping required. It is a simple experience and a much more pleasant way to get a ride than stepping onto a busy street and waving vigorously at oncoming traffic.

How Uber Works. The company recruits partners—either limousine companies or individual drivers, all of whom own their own cars and assume responsibility for the licensing, vehicle maintenance, gas, and auto insurance—and trains them on using the software. Uber also performs background checks on its drivers. Drivers normally keep 80% of the fare. Uber does not always provide the best deal for its drivers—they can sometimes make more money with other services—but the drivers like the flexibility and assignment flexibility that Uber offers.

A newer option, UberX, offers lower-priced rides from drivers who pilot their personal vehicles. Uber restricts this program to certain late-model cars, and drivers undergo the same background screening as others in the service.

Uber drivers can choose when they work. Some drivers have credited Uber for increasing their potential earnings by 30 percent. Their cars are held to high standards and are rigorously inspected. Drivers and riders rate each other after each trip. This arrangement improves the experience for both the driver and the rider.

The one complaint by Uber drivers involves the company's tipping policies. Uber informs potential customers that the ride might cost slightly more than a cab ride, but they do not have to tip. Uber's pricing is similar to metered taxis, although all hiring and payment are handled exclusively through Uber and not with the driver personally.

To fulfill its promise of a ride within five minutes of the touch of a smartphone button, Uber must constantly optimize the algorithms that govern, among other things, how many of its cars are on the road, where they go, and how much a ride costs. In the company's San Francisco headquarters, a software tool called God View displays all of the vehicles on the Uber system moving at once. Tiny eyeballs on the same map indicate the location of every customer who is currently accessing the Uber app on his or her smartphone. Uber's job is to bring those cars and those eyeballs together as seamlessly as possible.

Uber offers standard local rates for its various options. It increases these rates, however, at times of peak demand. Uber refers to this policy as "surge pricing." Some critics (and customers) call it "price gouging." Uber denies these accusations. The company maintains that to meet increased demand, drivers need an extra incentive to get out on the road. Uber also notes that many goods are dynamically priced; for example, airline tickets and happy hour cocktails.

Battles with the Establishment. Uber has a significant problem with the "establishment," including the taxi industry and local authorities. Regulators and politicians claim that Uber cars are breaking the law by not following the same regulatory rules as taxi and limousine companies. Uber contends that because it is a software provider and not a taxi or limousine operator, it should not be subject to the same regulatory oversight. Rather, the responsibility to observe the rules falls on its drivers.

Local governments in several of Uber's markets have taken legal action to shut down Uber. The $6 billion taxi industry has declared an unofficial war on the company. Numerous professional limo services have attacked it over its business tactics.

For example, San Francisco's transportation agency issued Uber a cease-and-desist letter, calling the company an unlicensed taxi service. Again, Uber argued that it merely provided the software that connected drivers and riders. The company continued to offer rides, building its stature among its customers, a constituency that city politicians are reluctant to alienate.

Uber has also encountered government and industry hostility in other cities, notably New York, Chicago, Boston, and Washington, DC. The Washington city council ultimately passed a legal framework in favor of Uber that the company called "an innovative model for city transportation legislation across the country." The city law includes the following:

- It explicitly defines a separate class of for-hire vehicles that operate through digital dispatch and charge by time and distance.

- It creates a single operator license for taxis, sedans, and limousines and requires the Washington, DC Taxi Commission to actually issue licenses.

- It sets standards for price transparency that will benefit consumers.

- It brings regulatory certainty to the vehicle-for-hire marketplace, making it clear that Uber and its partners, the licensed/regulated sedan companies and drivers, cannot be regulated out of existence.

Uber drivers can also get caught between local government regulations and Uber's rules. Several drivers were ticketed for dropping off passengers at San Francisco International Airport after the airport began enforcing a policy that requires them to be regulated as a taxi service. The drivers had to choose whether to continue their airport service and run the risk of being ticketed. Significantly, most drivers, who had grown accustomed to the flexible schedule and decent income, decided it was worth the risk.

Uber has won enough of these fights to threaten the market share of the entrenched players. The company not only offers a more efficient way to hail a ride but also provides drivers with an entirely new method to identify the areas where the demand is the greatest. In the process, Uber is opening up sections of cities that taxis and car services previously had ignored.

In addition to its battles with the establishment, Uber faces competition from lower cost real-time ridesharing startups such as Lyft (www.lyft.me) and SideCar (https://www.side.cr). To compete at lower price levels, Uber has introduced UberTaxi (partnerships with local taxi commissions). This strategy has led to dissatisfaction among existing Uber limo drivers who have seen their earnings decrease.

RESULTS >>> On Valentine's Day 2013, Uber offered customers flowers in 15 cities. On that day, customers could select the "Rose button" on the Uber app, and an Uber driver would deliver a dozen long-stemmed red roses to a sweetheart. A few months later, Uber launched another one-day special, offering to send an ice cream truck to any customer who hit a special button. These specials represent more than simple brand-building efforts. They are tests to see whether Uber can become not just a car service but also a delivery service; that is, an on-the-ground logistics network with the capability to move many types of products and experiences on the fly.

With its efficient algorithms and on-the-ground reach—all those vehicles roaming around picking up and dropping off people on any given day—Uber may become a local logistics network that can transport anything anywhere on a moment's notice, challenging firms such as FedEx and UPS.

If Uber were to expand into delivery, its competition—for now other ridesharing startups such as Lyft and Sidecar—could grow to include Amazon, eBay, and Walmart as well. One strategy for Uber to navigate its rivalry with such giants is to offer itself as the backend technology that can power same-day online retail. Consider the following scenario. In the fall of 2013, Google launched its shopping express service in San Francisco. The program allows customers to shop online at local stores through a Google-powered app. Google then delivers their purchases via courier the same day. That courier could be a Uber driver.

By mid-2014, Uber had expanded to 60 cities on six continents and has more than 400 employees. In addition, company revenues increased at a rate of nearly 18 percent every month during 2013. Uber will not disclose the figures, but it is rumored to be on track for $125 million in sales in 2014.

Sources: Compiled from B. Stone, "Invasion of the Taxi Snatchers: Uber Leads an Industry's Disruption," *Bloomberg BusinessWeek*, February 20, 2014; R. Dillet, "Protesting Taxi Drivers Attack Uber Car Near Paris," *Tech Crunch*, January 13, 2014; M. Wohlsen, "Uber in Overdrive," *Wired*, January, 2014; J. Hempel, "Why the Surge-Pricing Fiasco Is Great for Uber," *Fortune*, December 30, 2013; B. Fung, "How Uber Could Reinforce Car Culture," *The Washington Post*, December 24, 2013; J. Roberts, "Uber CEO Taunts Price Critics, Points to Airline 'Surge Pricing,'" *GigaOM*, December 24, 2013; M. Wolff, "Wolff: The Tech Company of the Year Is Uber," *USA Today*, December 22, 2013; N. Bolton, "Customers Out in the Cold Balk at Uber's Surge Pricing," *The New York Times*, December 16, 2013; J. Hempel, "Hey Taxi Company, You Talkin' to Me?" *Fortune*, October 7, 2013; K. Yeung, "California Becomes First State to Regulate Ridesharing Services Benefiting Uber, Lyft, Sidecar, and InstantCab," *TheNextWeb*, September 19, 2013; T. Knowlton, "Uber Toronto Activates Surge Pricing During Storm, Triggering a Bad PR Storm of Its Own," *Techvibes.com*, July 9, 2013; R. Lawler, "Look Out, Lyft: Uber CEO Travis Kalanick Says It Will Do Ride Sharing, Too," *TechCrunch*, September 12, 2012; C. Albanesius, "Uber Rolling Out On-Demand Ice Cream Trucks," *PC Magazine*, July 12, 2012; N. Jackson, "Hailing a Cab with Your Phone," *The Atlantic*, November 16, 2010; www.uber.com, www.lyft.me, www.side.cr, accessed January 21, 2014.

Questions

1. Discuss how taxi companies could combat Uber, Lyft, and SideCar. *Hint:* Why couldn't taxi companies deploy similar types of information technology?

2. Describe the disadvantages of Uber's business model. Provide specific examples to support your answer.

CLOSING **CASE 2** > The Omni-Channel Strategy to Compete with Amazon

THE BUSINESS PROBLEM >>> In recent years, the traditional bricks-and-mortar strategy for large retailers, with its accompanying high overhead costs, has become a liability rather than an asset for retailers. Amazon (www.amazon.com), which has no stores, has achieved major market share—and expanded into the world's largest Internet retailer—through a combination of lower prices and huge selection. The third battleground is location, and retailers are not conceding that to Amazon.

Regarding location, Amazon poses additional problems to traditional retailers. For same-day delivery, Amazon customer pay an extra $8.99 or more at checkout. For $99 per year, the company's Prime service, which includes free two-day shipping for most items, offers same-day service starting at $3.99.

Going further, Amazon's same-day delivery system works only if (a) Amazon has the item in stock at a nearby warehouse or (b) a third-party seller can immediately ship the order. To improve its delivery times, Amazon is adding robots, storage space, and refrigerators at more than 90 of its warehouses.

Amazon routes deliveries via carriers such as FedEx and UPS, and now on Sundays using the U.S. Postal Service. To reach more U.S. customers faster, Amazon has spent about $14 billion since 2011 on new warehouses. The company is adding some 5,000 full-time warehouse jobs.

As of mid-2014, Amazon can reach about 15 percent of Americans with same-day delivery. The company is building another five warehouses, and it hopes to be able to reach 50 percent of Americans if it can secure storage space near the top 20 metropolitan areas.

THE SOLUTION >>> To compete with Amazon, some of the world's largest retailers are adopting an omni-channel strategy. In this strategy, customers seamlessly combine their experience of online shopping on any device with in-store shopping. This strategy is becoming increasingly important as Amazon builds its own fulfillment centers closer to customers. In California, for instance, the company is constructing several giant warehouses one to two hours' drive from San Francisco and Los Angeles.

To implement the omni-channel strategy, the retailers are turning their stores into mini-distribution hubs to help them compete more effectively online against Amazon. Instead of fulfilling Web orders from warehouses located hundreds of miles from shoppers' homes, retailers such as Walmart (www.walmart.com), Best Buy (www.bestbuy.com), Target (www.target.com), Nordstrom (www.nordstrom.com), Macy's (www.macys.com), Lowe's (www.lowes.com), and Gap (www.gap.com) are routing orders to nearby stores. Store employees pick products from shelves, pack them into boxes, and drop them into FedEx and UPS trucks that take the items to customers.

This trend, known as *ship-from-store*, saves money through shorter delivery routes. More importantly, it speeds deliveries, avoids expensive markdowns on unsold products, and recoups sales that have been lost to Amazon. Let's take a closer look at Gap's omni-channel strategy.

As the largest specialty apparel chain in the United States, Gap (www.gap.com) must keep its shelves well stocked at its more than 2,500 U.S. stores and 3,000 worldwide stores. This process requires Gap to maintain an extensive in-store inventory. At the same time, Gap needs sufficient inventory in its e-commerce fulfillment channel to meet the growing demand for its products. One element of Gap's mission is to make shopping seamless to its customers through its digital strategy.

To integrate its in-store inventory and its e-commerce inventory, Gap developed an algorithm, known as Ship From Store, which it implemented in its Web site e-commerce system. Ship From Store allows online shoppers to buy directly from store inventory. The system is integrated seamlessly into Gap's e-commerce system, so that customers are not aware of it.

Ship From Store is not available from all stores, a factor that is critical to making the new feature profitable. The challenge was that the e-commerce system would bog down if it had to check the inventory of every store, which changes hour by hour. So, knowing which stores to include in the system is "the secret sauce," according to Gap's senior vice president of information technology. Claiming that the information is proprietary, Gap will not reveal how many stores the system taps, or what percentage of online shoppers receive items from warehouses compared with the situation before Ship From Store was implemented.

Another reason why not all Gap locations are included: The staff in participating stores must be trained and equipped to receive an order and ship the goods, just as they would in a fulfillment and distribution center. When the Web site informs a customer that a purchase will be delivered the next day, then it is up to Gap staffers to make that happen.

The blurring lines between the physical channel (stores) and the online channel help explain why Gap's IT and product management teams are located next to each other in the retailer's headquarters. They also explain why both groups are located within the company's growth, innovation, and digital business unit.

Most customers engage in preshopping, meaning they go to the company's Web site and browse the merchandise. For customers who want to see an item, feel its fabric, or try it on, Gap added a Find In Store function, which advises shoppers where to find the nearest store that stocks that item. Find In Store led to Reserve In Store, where a shopper can place a hold on an item for 24 hours.

The progression demonstrates that Ship From Store was not a single project that the IT group launched into production and then moved on to the next project. With the added functionalities, IT must constantly review how the system as a whole is functioning and make any necessary revisions. The algorithm is not static.

RESULTS >>> Let's take a closer look at three retailers: Walmart, Best Buy, and Gap. In mid-2014, Walmart was shipping online orders from 35 stores. This ship-from-store strategy has exceeded expectations, and Walmart is planning to expand the service to hundreds of its stores.

Two-thirds of the U.S. population live within five miles of a Walmart, so the company is using store locations as nodes in a broader distribution network that includes storage warehouses and specific fulfillment centers for online orders. In mid-2014, 10 percent of the items ordered on Walmart.com were shipped from stores, and the majority of those packages were delivered in two days or less. Walmart charges a $10 fee for same-day delivery service. In some cases, the company uses third-party carriers to ship items from its stores. In addition, Walmart employees sometimes deliver products by car.

Best Buy, the largest U.S. consumer electronics retailer, was labeled a "Big Box Zombie" on the cover of *Bloomberg BusinessWeek* magazine in October 2012. However, the company is experiencing a rebound. A crucial part of this turnaround is the ship-from-store process, which Best Buy has deployed in about 50 stores.

Best Buy receives about 1 billion online visits per year. In 2–4 percent of those cases, shoppers cannot buy products because they are out of stock in the company's e-commerce warehouses. However, in 80 percent of those cases, Best Buy has the products in one of its physical stores. Best Buy predicts that ship-from-store could generate an extra $6 billion in sales and $168 million in profits in 2014.

Ship From Store was first implemented at Gap stores, and the retailer has added this service to the e-commerce systems of two Gap-owned chains, Banana Republic and Athleta. Not coincidentally, Gap's annual revenue increased by $500 million in 2013.

Sources: Compiled from R. Borison, "Gap Expands Omnichannel Inventory Program for Added Convenience," *Mobile Commerce Daily*, November 22, 2013; "Gap and Banana Republic Make Shopping Easier for Customers This Holiday Season," *MarketWatch*, November 20, 2013; "Get Online Orders in a Matter of Hours," *Bloomberg BusinessWeek*, November 14, 2013; A. Barr, "'Ship From Store' Strategy Saves Money Through Shorter Delivery Routes," *USA Today*, October 6, 2013; T. Stapleton, "Retail Innovation Shout Out: Gap Blurs Channel Lines with 'Ship From Store' Service," *Kalypso Viewpoints*, September 17, 2013; C. Babcock, "Gap Connects Store and Web,"

InformationWeek, September 9, 2013; C. Babcock, "How Gap Connects Store and Online Channels," *InformationWeek*, September 5, 2013; A. Blair, "Gap Pilots Reserve-In-Store Capability for Online Shoppers," *Retail Information System News*, June 3, 2013; A. Barr, "E-Tailers Embrace Same-Day Delivery, but U.S. Shoppers Shrug: Survey," *Reuters*, March 5, 2013; www.gap .com, accessed January 29, 2014.

2. Describe the problems retailers face in implementing a ship-from-store strategy.

3. Identify some strategies that Amazon could employ to counter the ship-from-store strategy from traditional bricks-and-mortar retailers.

Questions

1. Why is an "omni-channel" strategy such an important part of retailers' missions today?

INTERNSHIP ACTIVITY>

Industry: Retail

One difficulty in moving a small business from a traditional retail store to an online store is channel complications. In many cases, the store needs to reconsider all of its business activities. For example, how will you communicate with your customers? How will your customers find product information? How will you accept orders? Manage payments? Shipping?

These questions and many more have kept Harrison Kirby from making the e-commerce plunge. Harrison runs a regional sporting goods store, All About Sports (the same one as in Internship Activities 1, 7, and 8), which carries roughly 250 consistent items and 400 seasonal items. He would love to have a Web site that would help his store expand its reach.

Below you will find a letter from Harrison explaining what he would like you to do.

To:	IT Intern
From:	Harrison Kirby
Subject:	Help Moving to E-commerce

Hi!

I have an interesting project for you. I am interested in developing an online and mobile presence for my sporting goods store. Specifically, I want to offer online shopping with local pickup. Have you ever been in a hurry to get to a practice or a game and you needed that one special piece of equipment? What if you could order and pay online and have your item waiting for you when you got to the store?

I don't mind shipping, but I would prefer to use a single shipping partner (UPS, FedEx, or USPS). In general, however, I really want to encourage my customers to order online and then pick up the items in the store. Plus, when they come into the store, I could encourage a compulsory purchase by offering a 25 percent discount or $25 off (whichever is the lesser amount) on any item in the store

Keep in mind that my shop is a small business, and I do not possess the resources to manage a complicated system. I need something that is fairly easy to implement, use, and manage. I have heard of online, cloud, as-a-service platforms that do not require local hardware. I think this type of setup would be most useful to me, but I have no idea what type of software I should use to support my business. One of my friends suggested Volusion. Perhaps you can find information about them on the Web.

After you complete your research, please send me a report with an overview of solutions you explored. Indicate whether you think I can handle something like this myself or I need to hire someone to run the e-commerce part of the business.

I am very excited to see your work!
Harrison

Note: Any links or Web sites referenced in this letter can be found at http://www.wiley.com/go/rainer/MIS3e/ internship.

SPREADSHEET ACTIVITY > SORTING, FILTERING, AND TABLES

STEP 1 – Background

It is frequently quite useful to be able to sort our data into a different order, whether alphabetically, numerically, or based on some other criteria. Spreadsheets have built-in sorting tools that allow this functionality. You can sort an entire dataset, or just a selection of the data. In addition, filters allow you to remove certain parts of a dataset. For example, if you have data that include four different regions, you can filter those data to see only one, two, or three of them. This functionality makes it much easier to digest large datasets.

Tables have this functionality built in, so you can sort and filter your data without having to use the sort and filter tools.

STEP 2 – Activity

In the "dark ages" of education, teachers kept a paper grade book in which they recorded everything. The only option for sorting was the alphabetical order in which the students' names were written. However, sometimes it is helpful to sort according to activity grades to see how students compare.

First name	Last name	Act 1	Act 2	Act 3	Act 4	Act 5	Act 6
Bobby	Caldwell	85	74	95	94	45	62
Ian	Jacqueness	65	96	87	94	89	79
Warren	Yelch	63	84	91	85	75	81

As you can see, when you have only three students, rearranging these data in the order of highest to lowest grade on Activity 5 would not be difficult. But, imagine that you have 50 students, or 150! The task becomes much more difficult without spreadsheet tools.

STEP 3 – Deliverable

Visit http://www.wiley.com/go/rainer/MIS3e/spreadsheet, and download a sales spreadsheet that includes sales data by region and sales representative. The spreadsheet will provide instructions that will guide you through the process of sorting, filtering, and using tables.

Follow the instructions in the spreadsheet and submit your final work to your instructor.

Additional help with this spreadsheet skill is available in WileyPLUS. Open the "Microsoft Office 2013 Lab Manual Spreadsheet Module: Excel 2013," and review Lesson 14: Filters and Pivot Tables. Help is also available from the Microsoft Support Web site at the link shown above.

DATABASE ACTIVITY > QUERIES

STEP 1 – Background

In this activity you will learn how to create a query based on more than one table, with multiple criteria. Business questions frequently involve data from multiple tables, so a query that can combine these data is more useful than one that cannot.

In the Chapter 5 activity, you selected records from a table by filtering. Sometimes the selection criteria are too complex for that approach, especially if more than one table is involved. Or, perhaps you would like to set up a database so that a user who is not familiar with Access can accomplish the same thing. Queries let you do that.

STEP 2 – Activity

Visit http://www.wiley.com/go/rainer/MIS3e/database, and download the database linked for Database Activity 9. This database belongs to a chain of donut shops. Much of the company's business comes from people who are driving or walking by its stores. The company has a smartphone application that (1) determines the customer's location from the phone's GPS data, (2) lets the customer order online and pay by credit card, (3) sends a bar code to the phone as a graphic, and then (4) lets the customer pick up the order by holding the bar code up to a reader located at the counter or drive-in window.

The database you will work with supports that application. It has five tables: stores, customers, products, orders, and line items. You can see their relationships in the relationship map of the database.

In this activity, you will create three queries to answer the following questions:

1. How often does a customer use the mobile order feature?
2. How many customers shop in a given store?
3. Which customers order expensive products?

To accomplish this task you need to be familiar with the relationship layout of the database, and you have to carefully select the tables and data that will be searched as part of the query.

STEP 3 – Deliverable

Save your database, and submit it to your professor with the three queries as described above.

Additional help with this database skill is available in WileyPLUS. Open the "Microsoft Office 2013 Lab Manual Database Module: Access 2013," and review Lesson 7: The Query Command.

CHAPTER **10**

Wireless, Mobile Computing, and Mobile Commerce

CHAPTER OUTLINE

10.1 Wireless Technologies

10.2 Wireless Computer Networks and Internet Access

10.3 Mobile Computing and Mobile Commerce

10.4 Pervasive Computing

10.5 Wireless Security

LEARNING OBJECTIVES >>>

10.1 Identify advantages and disadvantages of each of the four main types of wireless transmission media.

10.2 Explain how businesses can use short-range, medium-range, and long-range wireless networks, respectively.

10.3 Provide a specific example of how each of the five major m-commerce applications can benefit a business.

10.4 Describe technologies that underlie pervasive computing, providing examples of how businesses can utilize each one.

10.5 Explain how the four major threats to wireless networks can damage a business.

OPENING **CASE** > Mobile Commerce via Telemedicine at the Miami Children's Hospital

The Miami Children's Hospital (MCH; www.mch.com) deployed its telehealth command center to expand the reach of pediatric care while creating new sources of revenue for the hospital. The $2 million command center provides high-definition cameras and large monitors to enable physician-to-patient and physician-to-physician communications as well as remote reading of diagnostic tests. MCH used the command center to develop three telemedicine models—mobile, semistatic, and extremely static—through which patients from as far away as Ecuador and Ukraine can connect with MCH specialists.

Mobile Model

In the mobile model, MCH IT developers created an iPad app that acts as a virtual examination room. Families download the app, log in from home, and request an appointment with a general physician ($30 out-of-pocket

per consultation) or a specialist ($50). MCH views this app as a cash business that sidesteps the usual billing process that inevitably involves an insurance company. The

© Blend_Images/iStockphoto

cloud-based app provides an interface for clinical care and patient billing. (We discuss cloud computing in Plug IT In 4).

A separate physician app allows doctors to log in from the MCH command center or from their own devices and choose patients who are online in the virtual waiting room. They then select a patient and engage in an encrypted video consult. This app is most appropriate for consultative services because the physician is limited to a visual examination. It is intended for patients with nonemergency symptoms such as a cold or sinus infection.

MCH is also integrating at-home diagnostic medical tools into the mobile app. These tools include Bluetooth-enabled medical devices—such as blood pressure cuffs and stethoscopes—that families use to provide data to physicians. MCH plans to broaden the geographic reach of the mobile app, with physicians staffed at the command center around the clock.

The app also integrates with MCH's electronic health record (EHR) by Cerner (www.cerner.com). MCH executives are confident that patients and family members will find the experience similar to consumer services such as Apple's FaceTime.

In addition to using the iPad for telehealth, the tablet platform has been integrated into MCH's administrative infrastructure. Patients register using an app that allows them to input initial medical, billing, and demographic information through the tablet. MCH collects payment when patients swipe a credit card through a device attached to the iPad. Patients can also read and sign consent forms on the iPad.

MCH has focused its technology strategy on reducing the time it takes to get patients through registration. The iPad-enabled registration process is part of the improvement, as is a transition from a paper system to an electronic system that uses Bluetooth-enabled medical devices to transmit patient data directly into the EHR. Previously, a nurse would take a patient's vital signs, write down the data on paper, and then manually input those data into the EHR. Now, the data are transmitted from the blood pressure cuff or stethoscope directly to the EHR. These technology-enabled process changes will help healthcare providers make more effective use of IT.

Semistatic Model

In the semistatic model, MCH has deployed a number of medical carts equipped with videoconferencing technology and clinical tools (such as a stethoscope, blood pressure cuff, and examination camera) to hospitals in the United States and abroad. For $100 per hour, patients can receive a live consultation with an MCH specialist working out of the Miami command center. A local hospital physician is present with the patient to operate the clinical tools and conduct a physician-to-physician conversation with the patient in the room. Clinicians can move the cart around the hospital as needed. MCH has placed carts in hospitals in Ecuador, the Cayman Islands, the Vatican, Ukraine, and other international locations.

MCH leases the carts to hospitals for about $1000 per year. The carts are leased rather than sold so that MCH can ensure that the technology stays up to date.

Extremely Static Model

In the extremely static model, MCH is partnering with HealthSpot (www.healthspot.net), a medical kiosk producer, to bring medical care to retail environments such as malls and shopping centers. The kiosk has videoconferencing equipment and clinical tools such as thermometer, stethoscope, blood pressure cuff, and otoscope (for checking ears), but a physician is not physically present. Instead, a nurse or other practitioner assists with the consult as an MCH physician conducts a virtual examination via videoconference. All the consultations are recorded and can be referenced by both the physician and the patient.

The kiosks create new market opportunities for MCH. For example, there is a shortage of pediatric subspecialists. With the kiosks, these providers can be present in rural counties and areas where the demand is greatest. The kiosks are intended for non-urgent care patients. Beyond shopping malls, MCH envisions kiosks at places such as airports, and even cruise ship ports.

Sources: Compiled from B. Guarino, "Telemedicine Shows Satisfaction and Safety, but Obstacles Remain," *Pharmacy Practice News*, February 28, 2014; D. Alexander, "Kiosk Company Wants to Bring the Doctor's Office to Workplaces, Pharmacies, and Impoverished Villages," *Forbes*, February 17, 2014; A. Rudansky, "Telemedicine Creates Opportunity," *Information Week*, September 9, 2013; D. Brazell, "Telemedicine to Help Save More Lives," *Medical University of South Carolina*, August 2, 2013; S. Wunker, "A New Age for Healthcare Kiosks – Five Ways Next Generation Kiosks Disrupt Medicine and Healthcare Marketing," *Forbes*, July 16, 2013; E. Huizenga, "Pediatric Care Benefiting from the Advantages of Telemedicine," *SearchHealthIT*, May 3, 2013; "HealthSpot and Miami Children's Hospital Pursue a Superior Healthcare Experience," *EMRandEHRNews*, January 8, 2013; www.mch.com, accessed March 1, 2014.

Questions

1. Describe the advantages and the disadvantages of the iPad mobile app for patients. Do the same thing for medical carts and medical kiosks.

2. Describe the advantages and the disadvantages of the iPad mobile app for Miami Children's Hospital. Do the same thing for medical carts and medical kiosks.

Introduction

The traditional working environment that required users to come to a wired computer is ineffective and inefficient. The solution was to build computers that are small enough to carry or wear and that can communicate via wireless networks. The ability to communicate anytime and anywhere provides organizations with a strategic advantage by increasing productivity and speed and improving customer service. The term **wireless** is used to describe telecommunications in which electromagnetic waves, rather than some form of wire or cable, carry the signal between communicating devices such as computers, smartphones, and iPads.

Before you continue, it is important to distinguish between the terms *wireless* and *mobile*, because they can mean different things. The term *wireless* means exactly what it says: without wires. In contrast, *mobile* refers to something that changes its location over time. Some wireless networks, such as MiFi (discussed later in this chapter), are also mobile. Others, however, are fixed. For example, microwave towers form fixed wireless networks.

Wireless technologies enable individuals and organizations to conduct mobile computing, mobile commerce, and pervasive computing. We define these terms here, and then we discuss each one in detail later in the chapter.

Mobile computing refers to a real-time, wireless connection between a mobile device and other computing environments, such as the Internet or an intranet. *Mobile commerce*—also known as *m-commerce*—refers to e-commerce (EC) transactions (see Chapter 9) conducted with a mobile device. *Pervasive computing*, also called *ubiquitous computing*, means that virtually every object has processing power with either wireless or wired connections to a global network.

Wireless technologies and mobile commerce are spreading rapidly, replacing or supplementing wired computing. In fact, Cisco (www.cisco.com) predicts that the volume of mobile Web traffic will continue to increase rapidly over the next decade.

Almost all (if not all) organizations utilize wireless computing. Therefore, when you begin your career, you likely will be assigned a company smartphone and a wirelessly enabled computer. Clearly, then, it is important for you to learn about wireless computing not only because you will be using wireless applications but also because wireless computing will be so important to your organization. In your job, you will be involved with customers who conduct wireless transactions, with analyzing and developing mobile commerce applications, and with wireless security. And the list goes on.

Simply put, an understanding of wireless technology and mobile commerce applications will make you more valuable to your organization. When you look at "What's in IT for Me?" at the end of the chapter, envision yourself performing the activities discussed in your functional area. In addition, for those of you who are so inclined, an understanding of wireless technology can help you start and grow your own business.

The wireless infrastructure upon which mobile computing is built may reshape the entire IT field. The technologies, applications, and limitations of mobile computing and mobile commerce are the focus of this chapter. You begin the chapter by learning about wireless devices and wireless transmission media. You continue by examining wireless computer networks and wireless Internet access. You then look at mobile computing and mobile commerce, which are made possible by wireless technologies. Next, you turn your attention to pervasive computing. You conclude by familiarizing yourself with a critical component of the wireless environment—namely, wireless security.

10.1 Wireless Technologies

Wireless technologies include both wireless devices, such as smartphones, and wireless transmission media, such as microwave, satellite, and radio. These technologies are fundamentally changing the ways organizations operate.

Individuals are finding wireless devices convenient and productive to use, for several reasons. First, people can make productive use of time that was formerly wasted—for example, while commuting to work on public transportation. Second, because people can take these devices with them, their work locations are becoming much more flexible. Third, wireless technology enables them to schedule their working time around personal and professional obligations.

Wireless Devices

Wireless devices provide three major advantages to users:

- They are small enough to easily carry or wear.
- They have sufficient computing power to perform productive tasks.
- They can communicate wirelessly with the Internet and other devices.

Modern smartphones exhibit a process called *dematerialization*. Essentially, dematerialization occurs when the functions of many physical devices are included in one other physical device. Consider that your smartphone includes the functions of digital cameras for images and video, radios, televisions, Internet access via Web browsers, recording studios, editing suites, movie theaters, GPS navigators, word processors, spreadsheets, stereos, flashlights, board games, card games, video games, an entire range of medical devices, maps, atlases, encyclopedias, dictionaries, translators, textbooks, watches, alarm clocks, books, calculators, address books, credit card swipers, magnifying glasses, money and credit cards, car keys, hotel keys, cellular telephony, Wi-Fi, e-mail access, text messaging, a full QWERTY keyboard, and many, many others. FIGURE 10.1 illustrates the process of dematerialization with smartphones.

One downside of smartphones is that people can use them to copy and pass on confidential information. For example, if you were an executive at Intel, would you want workers snapping pictures of their colleagues with your secret new technology in the background? After all, one of the functions of a smartphone is that of a digital camera that can transmit wirelessly. New jamming devices are being developed to counter the threat. Some companies, such as Samsung (www.samsung.com), have recognized the danger and have banned these devices from their premises altogether. Regardless of any disadvantages, however, cell phones, and particularly smartphones, have had a far greater impact on human society than most of us realize.

Consider Africa, for example. One in six of Africa's 1 billion inhabitants now use a cell phone. These phones are transforming healthcare across the continent in many ways:

- For the first time, medical personnel are obtaining high-quality data that can inform them of who is dying and from what causes, who is sick, and where clusters of disease are occurring.

Figure 10.1 Dematerialization with smartphones.

TABLE 10.1 Advantages and Disadvantages of Wireless Media

Channel	Advantages	Disadvantages
Microwave	High bandwidth Relatively inexpensive	Must have unobstructed line of sight Susceptible to environmental interference
Satellite	High bandwidth Large coverage area	Expensive Must have unobstructed line of sight Signals experience propagation delay Must use encryption for security
Radio	High bandwidth Signals pass through walls Inexpensive and easy to install	Creates electrical interference problems Susceptible to snooping unless encrypted
Infrared	Low to medium bandwidth	Must have unobstructed line of sight Used only for short distances

- Cell phones are now making it possible for parents to register the birth of a child very easily and for governments to more accurately plan healthcare interventions, such as vaccination schedules.

- Cell phones are improving vaccine supply chains, preventing unnecessary stockouts, and ensuring that vaccines are available when children are brought into clinics to be immunized.

- Healthcare workers in the field can access health records and schedule appointments with patients.

Wireless Transmission Media

Wireless media, or broadcast media, transmit signals without wires. The major types of wireless media are microwave, satellite, radio, and infrared. Table 10.1 lists the advantages and disadvantages of each type.

Microwave. **Microwave transmission** systems transmit data via electromagnetic waves. These systems are used for high-volume, long-distance, line-of-sight communication. *Line-of-sight* means that the transmitter and receiver are in view of each other. This requirement creates problems because the Earth's surface is curved rather than flat. For this reason, microwave towers usually cannot be spaced more than 30 miles apart.

Clearly, then, microwave transmissions offer only a limited solution to data communications needs, especially over very long distances. In addition, microwave transmissions are susceptible to environmental interference during severe weather such as heavy rain and snowstorms. Although long-distance microwave data communications systems are still widely used, they are being replaced by satellite communications systems.

Satellite. **Satellite transmission** systems make use of communication satellites. Currently, there are three types of satellites circling Earth: geostationary-earth-orbit (GEO), medium-earth-orbit (MEO), and low-earth-orbit (LEO). Each type has a different orbit, with the GEO being farthest from Earth and the LEO the closest. In this section, you examine the three types of satellites and then discuss two major satellite applications: global positioning systems and Internet transmission via satellites. Table 10.2 compares and contrasts the three types of satellites.

As with microwave transmission, satellites must receive and transmit data via line-of-sight. However, the enormous *footprint*—the area of Earth's surface reached by a satellite's transmission—overcomes the limitations of microwave data relay stations. The most basic rule governing footprint size is simple: The higher a satellite orbits, the larger its footprint. Thus, medium-earth-orbit satellites have a smaller footprint than geostationary satellites, and low-earth-orbit satellites have the smallest footprint of all. FIGURE 10.2 compares the footprints of the three types of satellites.

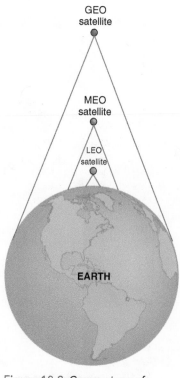

Figure 10.2 Comparison of satellite footprints.

Type	Characteristics	Orbit	Number	Use
GEO	• Satellites stationary relative to point on Earth • Few satellites needed for global coverage • Transmission delay (approximately 0.25 second) • Most expensive to build and launch • Longest orbital life (many years)	22,300 miles	8	TV signal
MEO	• Satellites move relative to point on Earth • Moderate number needed for global coverage • Requires medium-powered transmitters • Negligible transmission delay • Less expensive to build and launch • Moderate orbital life (6–12 years)	6,434 miles	10–12	GPS
LEO	• Satellites move rapidly relative to point on Earth • Large number needed for global coverage • Requires only low-power transmitters • Negligible transmission delay • Least expensive to build and launch • Shortest orbital life (as low as 5 years)	400–700 miles	Many	Telephone

TABLE 10.2 Three Basic Types of Telecommunications Satellites

There are an incredible number of applications of satellites, one of which is commercial images from orbit. IT's About Business 10.1 illustrates how Skybox is providing users with high-quality images.

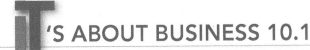

'S ABOUT BUSINESS 10.1

Skybox Imaging Provides Commercial Images from Earth's Orbit

Of the 1,000 or more satellites orbiting the Earth at any given time, only about 100 transmit visual data. Of those 100, only 12 send back high-resolution pictures, which are defined as an image in which each pixel represents a square meter or less of ground. Further, only 9 of these 12 sell to the commercial space-based imaging market and 80 percent of that market is controlled by the U.S. government, which has priority over all other buyers. Basically, if government agencies decide that they want satellite time for themselves, they can simply demand it.

In January 2013, after the government reduced its imaging budget, the market's two largest companies—

DigitalGlobe (www.digitalglobe.com) and GeoEye, which between them operated five of the nine commercial geo-imaging satellites—were forced to merge under the name DigitalGlobe. Due to only nine satellites and the government's claim on satellite operations, ordering and obtaining an image of a specific place on Earth can take days, weeks, or even months.

With the image resolutions—*resolution* means sharpness or clarity—allowed by the government for commercial purposes, an orbiting satellite can clearly show individual cars and other objects that are just a few feet across. As a result, an almost entirely untapped source of data—information that companies and governments sometimes try to keep secret—is orbiting in space right above us.

A startup called Skybox Imaging (Skybox; www .skyboximaging.com) has designed and built something unprecedented. Using inexpensive consumer hardware, the company plans to ring the Earth with constellations of imaging satellites that are dramatically less expensive to build and maintain than existing satellites. By blanketing the Earth's orbit with its cameras, Skybox will quickly disrupt the commercial space-imaging industry. Even with only six small satellites orbiting Earth, Skybox can provide practically real-time images of the same spot twice a day at a fraction of the current cost.

Over the long term, Skybox's real payoff will not be in the images that the company sells. Instead, the payoff will derive from the massive collection of unsold images its satellites capture every day—images that, when analyzed either by computer vision or by humans, can be translated into extremely useful, desirable, and valuable data. Let's consider some examples of these kinds of data:

- The number of cars in the parking lot of every Walmart in America.
- The number of fuel tankers on the roads of the three fastest-growing economic zones in China.
- The size of the pits and slag heaps outside the largest gold mines in southern Africa. These images would allow analysts to estimate a mine's productivity.
- The rate at which the electrical wattage along key stretches of the Ganges River in India is growing brighter as a result of population growth and industrialization.

These images contain clues about the economic health of countries, industries, and individual businesses. Skybox has already brainstormed entirely practical ways to estimate major economic indicators for any country, based entirely on satellite images. The same analysis process will yield even more direct insight into the revenues of a retail chain, a mining company, or an electronics company, once the analyst determines which of the trucks leaving their factories are shipping out goods or key components.

Many people want real-time access to these data—investors, environmentalists, activists, journalists—and no one currently has it, with the exception of certain government agencies. Skybox can dramatically alter this situation by putting enough satellites into orbit, transmitting the image streams back to Earth, and then analyzing them. This is exactly what the company has done.

Significantly, Skybox has made only incremental changes to existing inexpensive off-the-shelf technologies, which anyone can purchase. The company started with CubeSat (www.cubesat.org), a type of low-cost satellite built entirely from inexpensive components or prepackaged kits. The result was a cube, 4 inches on each side, containing a basic sensor and communications payload, solar panels, and a battery, that could be built and launched for less than $60,000.

Skybox launched the first CubeSats in 2003. Since that time there have been astounding advances in computer processing power and speed, and similar advances in telecommunications technologies. Consequently, Skybox engineers were able to build a 220-pound satellite about 3 feet tall, with a payload of optics equipment designed to capture commercial-grade images. Also, Skybox uses a 6-foot antenna to communicate with a dish the size of a dinner plate instead of

the much more expensive 30-foot antenna that commercial satellite-imaging companies typically require.

Rather than hardware, Skybox focused on software. Consider the cameras that Skybox uses. Compared with most satellites, they are cheap, low resolution, and unsophisticated. But, by writing custom-built software algorithms to integrate dozens of images, Skybox creates one super-high-quality image that enables users to distinguish things they cannot see in any one of the individual images. This focus on *off-board processing* (i.e., processing handled by computers on the ground, not on the satellite itself) means that less processing has to be performed on the satellite, allowing it to be lighter and less expensive.

As an analogy to what Skybox has accomplished, consider your smartphone. There was a time when you had a phone, a pocket organizer (such as the Palm), a personal computer, and also a camera. Now, information and communications technologies have improved to such an extent that all of these functions are integrated into a much smaller physical package (today's smartphones) at a much lower cost.

Skybox launched its first satellite, SkySat-1, on November 21, 2013, from Yasny, Russia, aboard a Dnepr rocket. The satellite began capturing its first images just hours after the payload door opened. The image quality exceeded Skybox's expectations. Even in the photos' uncalibrated state, it is possible to make out details such as car windshields, varying car colors, and road markings. Given the cost-effectiveness of these satellites, Skybox intends to launch 24 of them to provide comprehensive coverage of Earth, beaming back images in near real time.

Skybox does face problems. The disruptive threat that the company poses to the space-based commercial imaging market could present a threat to U.S. national security. As a result, the government could deny the company licenses, seize its technology or bandwidth, and place restrictions on the frequency and users of its service. In the end, the government will likely commandeer some of Skybox's imaging capabilities under similar terms to those imposed on other vendors. However, Skybox feels confident that its network will be so wide and so nimble that there will be plenty of images and data left over for everyone else.

At least two other startups are also building a business around satellite imagery. One, Urthecast (www.urthecast.com), has the rights to images collected by a powerful telescope attached to the International Space Station. The other, Planet Labs (www.planet-labs.com), plans to launch a network of ultra-low-cost (though also less powerful) satellites.

Sources: Compiled from M. Kelley, "HD Video from Space Is Going to Change the World," *Business Insider*, March 7, 2014; B. Mason, "Incredible HD Video of Earth from Space Brings Maps to Life," *Wired*, March 4, 2014; R. Sharma, "All Set for Take-Off: Silicon Valley Startups Redefine Space Imaging Market," *Forbes*, February 26, 2014; "Satellite Images of the Protests in Kiev," *The New York Times*, February 18, 2014; "Emirates Space Imaging Ties Up with Skybox Imaging for Meena," *Skybox Imaging Press Release*, February 13, 2014; D. Werner, "Planet Labs CubeSats Deployed from ISS with Many More to Follow," *Space News*, February 11, 2014; D. Butler, "Many Eyes on Earth," *Nature*, January 8, 2014; R. Meyer, "Silicon Valley's New Spy Satellites," *The Atlantic*,

January 7, 2014; R. Meyer, "For the First Time Ever, You Can Buy HD Video of Earth from Space," *The Atlantic*, December 27, 2013; "Exelis to Help Advance Near Real-Time Global Observation," *The Wall Street Journal*, December 17, 2013; A. Truong, "Proof That Cheaper Satellites Can Take Incredibly Detailed Photos of Earth," *Fast Company*, December 11, 2013; "Skybox Unveils First Images from Newly Launched Earth-Observation Satellite," *Space News*, December 11, 2013; "Skybox Launch Successful," *Directions Magazine*, November 22, 2014; D. Samuels, "The Watchers," *Wired*, July 2013; J. Dorrier, "Tiny CubeSat Satellites Spur Revolution in Space," *Singularity Hub*, June 23, 2013; www .skyboximaging.com, www.urthecast.com, www.planet-labs.com, accessed March 13, 2014.

Questions

1. Describe other applications of Skybox Imaging (not mentioned in the case).

2. Why might the U.S. government object to Skybox Imaging's business? Provide specific examples in your answer.

3. Might other nations object to Skybox Imaging's business? If so, which ones, and why?

In contrast to line-of-sight transmission with microwave, satellites use *broadcast* transmission, which sends signals to many receivers at one time. So, even though satellites are line-of-sight like microwave, they are high enough for broadcast transmission, thus overcoming the limitations of microwave.

Types of Orbits. *Geostationary-earth-orbit satellites* orbit 22,300 miles directly above the Equator. These satellites maintain a fixed position above Earth's surface because, at their altitude, their orbital period matches the 24-hour rotational period of Earth. For this reason, receivers on Earth do not have to track GEO satellites. GEO satellites are excellent for sending television programs to cable operators and for broadcasting directly to homes.

One major limitation of GEO satellites is that their transmissions take a quarter of a second to send and return. This brief pause, one kind of **propagation delay**, makes two-way telephone conversations difficult. Also, GEO satellites are large and expensive, and they require substantial amounts of power to launch.

Medium-earth-orbit satellites are located about 6,000 miles above Earth's surface. MEO orbits require more satellites to cover Earth than GEO orbits because MEO footprints are smaller. MEO satellites have two advantages over GEO satellites: They are less expensive, and they do not have an appreciable propagation delay. However, because MEO satellites move with respect to a point on Earth's surface, receivers must track these satellites. (Think of a satellite dish slowly turning to remain oriented to a MEO satellite.)

Low-earth-orbit satellites are located 400 to 700 miles above Earth's surface. Because LEO satellites are much closer to Earth, they have little, if any, propagation delay. Like MEO satellites, however, LEO satellites move with respect to a point on Earth's surface and therefore must be tracked by receivers. Tracking LEO satellites is more difficult than tracking MEO satellites because LEO satellites move much more quickly relative to a point on Earth.

Unlike GEO and MEO satellites, LEO satellites can pick up signals from weak transmitters. This feature makes it possible for satellite telephones to operate via LEO satellites, because they can operate with less power using smaller batteries. Another advantage of LEO satellites is that they consume less power and cost less to launch.

At the same time, however, the footprints of LEO satellites are small, which means that many satellites are needed to cover the planet. For this reason, a single organization often produces multiple LEO satellites, known as *LEO constellations*. Two examples are Iridium and Globalstar.

Iridium (www.iridium.com) has placed a LEO constellation in orbit that consists of 66 satellites and 12 in-orbit spare satellites. The company claims it provides complete satellite communications coverage of Earth's surface, including the polar regions. Globalstar (www .globalstar.com) also has a LEO constellation in orbit.

Jeff Chiu/AP Images

Figure 10.3 Obtaining GPS information in an automobile. (*Source:* Image Source)

Global Positioning Systems. The **global positioning system (GPS)** is a wireless system that utilizes satellites to enable users to determine their position anywhere on Earth. GPS is supported by 24 MEO satellites that are shared worldwide. The exact position of each satellite is always known because the satellite continuously broadcasts its position along with a time signal. By using the known speed of the signals and the distance from three satellites (for two-dimensional location) or four satellites (for three-dimensional location), it is possible to find the location of any receiving station or user within a range of 10 feet. GPS software can also convert the user's latitude and longitude to an electronic map.

Most of you are probably familiar with GPS in automobiles, which "talks" to drivers when giving directions. FIGURE 10.3 illustrates two ways for drivers to obtain GPS information in a car: a dashboard navigation system and a GPS app (in this case, TomTom; www.tomtom.com) on an iPhone.

Commercial use of GPS for activities such as navigating, mapping, and surveying has become widespread, particularly in remote areas. Cell phones in the United States now must have a GPS embedded in them so that the location of a person making an emergency call—for example, 911, known as **wireless 911**—can be detected immediately.

Three other global positioning systems are either planned or operational. The Russian GPS, *GLONASS*, was completed in 1995. However, the system fell into disrepair with the collapse of the Russian economy. In 2010, however, GLONASS achieved 100 percent coverage of Russian territory. The European Union GPS is called *Galileo*. The first determination of a position relying on Galileo satellites occurred in March 2013. The entire Galileo system is expected to be completed by 2019. China expects to complete its GPS, *Beidou*, by 2020.

Internet over Satellite. In many regions of the world, Internet over Satellite (IoS) is the only option available for Internet connections because installing cables is either too expensive or physically impossible. IoS enables users to access the Internet via GEO satellites from a dish mounted on the side of their homes. Although IoS makes the Internet available to many people who otherwise could not access it, it has its drawbacks. Not only do GEO satellite transmissions involve a propagation delay, but they also can be disrupted by environmental influences such as thunderstorms.

Radio. **Radio transmission** uses radio-wave frequencies to send data directly between transmitters and receivers. Radio transmission has several advantages. First, radio waves travel easily through normal office walls. Second, radio devices are fairly inexpensive and easy to install. Third, radio waves can transmit data at high speeds. For these reasons, radio increasingly is being used to connect computers to both peripheral equipment and local area networks (LANs; discussed in Chapter 4).

As with other technologies, however, radio transmission has its drawbacks. First, radio media can create electrical interference problems. Also, radio transmissions are susceptible to snooping by anyone who has similar equipment that operates on the same frequency.

Another problem with radio transmission is that when you travel too far away from the source station, the signal breaks up and fades into static. Most radio signals can travel only 30 to 40 miles from their source. However, satellite radio overcomes this problem. **Satellite radio** (or *digital radio*) offers uninterrupted, near CD-quality transmission that is beamed to your radio, either at home or in your car, from space. In addition, satellite radio offers a broad spectrum of stations, including many types of music, news, and talk.

XM Satellite Radio and Sirius Satellite Radio were competitors that launched satellite radio services. XM broadcast its signals from GEO satellites, while Sirius used MEO satellites. In July 2008, the two companies merged to form Sirius XM (www.siriusxm.com). Listeners subscribe to the service for a monthly fee.

Infrared. The final type of wireless transmission is infrared transmission. **Infrared** light is red light that is not commonly visible to human eyes. Common applications of infrared light are found in remote control units for televisions and DVD and CD players. In addition, like radio transmission, infrared transceivers are used for short-distance connections between computers and peripheral equipment and local area networks. A *transceiver* is a device that can both transmit and receive signals.

┌─ BEFORE *YOU GO ON....* ─┐

1. Describe the most common types of wireless devices.

2. Describe the various types of transmission media.

Apply The Concept 10.1

LEARNING OBJECTIVE 10.1 Identify advantages and disadvantages of each of the four main types of wireless transmission media.

STEP 1 – Background (Here is what you are learning.)

As stated in this section, mobile communication has changed our world more rapidly and dramatically than any other technology. Although several wireless transmission media are available, rarely will one technology meet all of a business's needs by itself. Vislink is a global technology firm that collects and delivers high-quality video broadcasts. These broadcasts are utilized in sports, news, law enforcement, and other areas. Although Vislink specializes in video, they rely on multiple mobile transmission media to obtain live feeds from multiple locations. Rajant is one of the providers that Vislink has utilized for their wireless media.

STEP 2 – Activity (Here is what you are doing.)

Visit http://www.wiley.com/go/rainer/MIS3e/applytheconcept, and click on the link provided for Apply the Concept 10.1. There are three links. One will take you to Vislink's Web site, another to Rajant's Web site, and the last to a YouTube video in which Vislink demonstrates how they can provide live video feed to law enforcement agencies using Rajant's wireless mesh network.

STEP 3 – Deliverable (Here is what you turn in.)

As you watch the video, listen for the wireless transmission media they mention, and pay attention to how many of them are discussed in this section of the book. Write and submit a summary of your findings that highlights the advantages and disadvantages of the transmission media types and explains why they were or were not used in the product that Vislink/Rajant demonstrated.

10.2 Wireless Computer Networks and Internet Access

You have learned about various wireless devices and how these devices transmit wireless signals. These devices typically form wireless computer networks, and they provide wireless Internet access. In this section, you will study wireless networks, which we organize by their effective distance: short range, medium range, and wide area.

Short-Range Wireless Networks

Short-range wireless networks simplify the task of connecting one device to another. In addition, they eliminate wires, and they enable users to move around while they use the devices. In general, short-range wireless networks have a range of 100 feet or less. In this section, you consider three basic short-range networks: Bluetooth, ultra-wideband (UWB), and near-field communications (NFC).

Bluetooth. **Bluetooth** (www.bluetooth.com) is an industry specification used to create small personal area networks. A **personal area network** is a computer network used for communication among computer devices—for example, telephones, personal digital assistants, and smartphones—located close to one person. Bluetooth 1.0 can link up to eight devices within a 10-meter area (about 30 feet) with a bandwidth of 700 kilobits per second (Kbps) using low-power, radio-based communication. Bluetooth 4.0 can transmit up to approximately 25 megabits per second (Mbps) up to 100 meters (roughly 300 feet). Ericsson, the Scandinavian mobile handset company that developed this standard, called it Bluetooth after the tenth-century Danish King Harald Blatan (*Blatan* means "Bluetooth"). Ericsson selected this name because Blatan unified previously separate islands into the nation of Denmark.

Common applications for Bluetooth are wireless handsets for cell phones and portable music players. Advantages of Bluetooth include low power consumption and the fact that it uses omnidirectional radio waves—that is, waves that are emitted in all directions from a transmitter. For this reason, you do not have to point one Bluetooth device at another to create a connection.

Bluetooth low energy, marketed as Bluetooth Smart, enables applications in the healthcare, fitness, security, and home entertainment industries. Compared to "classic" Bluetooth, Bluetooth Smart is less expensive and consumes less power, although it has a similar communication range.

Ultra-Wideband.

Ultra-wideband is a high-bandwidth wireless technology with transmission speeds in excess of 100 Mbps. This very high speed makes UWB a good choice for applications such as streaming multimedia from, say, a personal computer to a television.

Time Domain (www.timedomain.com), a pioneer in UWB technology, has developed many UWB applications. One interesting application is the PLUS Real-Time Location System (RTLS). An organization can utilize PLUS to locate multiple people and assets simultaneously. Employees, customers, and/or visitors wear the PLUS Badge Tag. PLUS Asset Tags are placed on equipment and products. PLUS is extremely valuable for healthcare environments, where knowing the real-time location of caregivers (e.g., doctors, nurses, technicians) and mobile equipment (e.g., laptops, monitors) is critical.

Near-Field Communications.

Near-field communications has the smallest range of any short-range wireless networks. It is designed to be embedded in mobile devices such as cell phones and credit cards. For example, using NFC, you can swipe your device or card within a few centimeters of POS terminals to pay for items.

Medium-Range Wireless Networks

Medium-range wireless networks are the familiar **wireless local area networks** (WLANs). The most common type of medium-range wireless network is Wireless Fidelity, or Wi-Fi. WLANs are useful in a variety of settings, some of which may be challenging.

Wireless Fidelity.

Wireless Fidelity is a medium-range WLAN, which is a wired LAN but without the cables. In a typical configuration, a transmitter with an antenna, called a **wireless access point** (see FIGURE 10.4), connects to a wired LAN or to satellite dishes that provide an Internet connection. A wireless access point provides service to a number of users within a small geographical perimeter (up to approximately 300 feet), known as a **hotspot**. Multiple wireless access points are needed to support a larger number of users across a larger geographical area. To communicate wirelessly, mobile devices, such as laptop PCs, typically have a built-in wireless network interface capability.

© Roman Samokhin/Shutterstock

Figure 10.4 Wireless access point.

Wi-Fi provides fast and easy Internet or intranet broadband access from public hotspots located at airports, hotels, Internet cafés, universities, conference centers, offices, and homes. Users can access the Internet while walking across a campus, to their office, or through their homes. In addition, users can access Wi-Fi with their laptops, desktops, or PDAs by adding a wireless network card. Most PC and laptop manufacturers incorporate these cards in their products.

The Institute of Electrical and Electronics Engineers (IEEE) has established a set of standards for wireless computer networks. The IEEE standard for Wi-Fi is the 802.11 family. As of mid-2014, there were several standards in this family:

- 802.11a: supports wireless bandwidth up to 54 Mbps; high cost; short range; difficulty penetrating walls.

- 802.11b: supports wireless bandwidth up to 11 Mbps; low cost; longer range.
- 802.11g: supports wireless bandwidth up to 54 Mbps; high cost; longer range.
- 802.11n: supports wireless bandwidth exceeding 600 Mbps; higher cost than 802.11g; longer range than 802.11g.
- 802.11ac: will support wireless bandwidth of 1.3 Gbps (1.3 billion bits per second); will provide the ability to fully support a "multimedia home" in which high-definition video can be streamed simultaneously to multiple devices. Essentially, you will be able to wirelessly network your TV, DVR, smartphone, and sound system for complete on-demand access through any Internet-enabled device.
- 802.11 ad: supports wireless bandwidth up to 7 Gbps; targeted to the "wireless office" as opposed to the "wireless home."

The major benefits of Wi-Fi are its low cost and its ability to provide simple Internet access. It is the greatest facilitator of the wireless Internet—that is, the ability to connect to the Internet wirelessly.

Corporations are integrating Wi-Fi into their strategies. For example, Starbucks, McDonald's, Panera, and Barnes & Noble offer customers Wi-Fi in many of their stores, primarily for Internet access. The Winter Olympic Games in Sochi, Russia utilized Wi-Fi extensively, as you see in IT's About Business 10.2.

IT'S ABOUT BUSINESS 10.2

A Wi-Fi Network Provides Communications at the 2014 Winter Olympic Games

Sochi, Russia, a city of some 350,000 people located on the Black Sea, hosted the 2014 Winter Olympic Games. There were two Olympic venues—the Olympic village in Sochi and a group of Alpine venues in the nearby Krasnaya Polyana Mountains. In addition to investing in a telecommunications infrastructure, Russia spent billions of dollars to upgrade Sochi's electric power grid, its transportation system, and its sewage treatment facilities. Unfortunately, Russia had to start from zero to build the information technology (IT) infrastructure for the games.

One essential component of this infrastructure was communications. To meet this need, Avaya (www.avaya.com), a California-based business solutions company, built a Wi-Fi network for the Winter Games. The network was designed to handle 54 terabits (trillions of bits or Tbps) per second when the games opened on February 7, 2014.

One of the reasons that the International Olympic Committee (IOC) chose Avaya was that the company had built the Wi-Fi network for the 2010 Winter Olympic Games in Vancouver, Canada. However, the Sochi games were a stark contrast from the 2010 Games, where the wireless network was capable of handling only 4 Tbps. In Vancouver, Avaya installed an Internet Protocol (IP) voice, data, and video network. This project gave the company invaluable experience, which enabled it to deploy the same type of IP

network at Sochi. Interestingly, in Vancouver, Avaya allowed only one mobile device per user. At that time in Vancouver, wired traffic at the Games outnumbered wireless traffic by 4:1. In Sochi, wireless traffic outnumbered wired **MIS** traffic by the same margin.

Building the Wi-Fi network in Sochi presented numerous challenges for Avaya. Let's consider some of them.

- The network had to serve 40,000 athletes and their families, administrators and staff, media, IOC officials, and volunteers with data, voice, video, and full Internet access across 11 competition venues, 3 Olympic villages, multiple media centers, celebration centers, and data centers.
- Avaya knew that the athletes, journalists, and roughly 75,000 daily visitors at the Games would have an unprecedented number of smartphones, tablets, and other mobile devices. To meet this challenge, Avaya actually installed the capacity to support up to 120,000 devices on the Sochi Wi-Fi network, without issues or interruptions. To maintain this system, the company also installed 2,500 wireless access points.
- Avaya had to deliver 30 Internet Protocol high-definition Olympic television channels, all of which had to be available to Olympic family users over the network. Internet Protocol Television (IPTV) support eliminated the need for a separate cable television (CATV) network.
- Still another challenge was moving goods into Russia, a process that can be time consuming in the best of situations. To expedite this process, Avaya placed employees

in Sochi 18 months before the opening ceremony, coordinating the logistics and ensuring that supplies arrived where and when they were needed. This was a nervous experience for Avaya. Consider, for example, that one of its equipment trucks lost radio contact for days while traveling through rural Kazakhstan. Another truck arrived in Sochi with unprotected/uncushioned computer hardware after driving over hundreds of miles of bumpy roads. Fortunately, in both cases the equipment arrived in usable shape.

- Another challenge was training. In line with their agreement with Avaya's Russian partners, the company trained 170 Russian technicians to provide network support during the Games.

- Avaya had to design its network equipment to operate in extreme weather, in case such weather occurred.

Despite these many challenges, Avaya successfully deployed its Wi-Fi network in Sochi, in time for the opening ceremonies. The network consisted of five subnetworks: one for the athletes, two for media (one free, one paid), one for the Olympics staff, and one for dignitaries. Avaya provided each group with its own access password, and it added extra layers of password protection where needed. The company distributed the Wi-Fi traffic with approximately 2,500 802.11n wireless access points across the Olympics Games sites, including, for the first time, inside the stands. It also provided voice services and more than 6,500 voicemail inboxes at the Games.

The Avaya network was headquartered in a primary Technical Operations Center (TOC) in the coastal city of Adler. The secondary TOC was located at the Sochi Olympic Park, 10 miles northeast of Adler at the Games site. While one TOC was in use, the other was kept in standby mode by a skeleton crew. Each TOC was connected to the outside world by 10 gigabit-per-second wireline cables provided by Rostelecom (www.rostelecom.ru), Russia's national telecommunications operator. The TOCs were placed in separate locations to ensure redundancy in the case of a natural disaster or man-made incident.

What type of traffic did Avaya's Wi-Fi network have to handle? According to the company's network analytics, during *just a four-hour period* within the first week of the Games, the network managed 5,130 megabytes of data from Twitter, 2,222 megabytes from Facebook, 1,475 megabytes from Skype, and 746 megabytes from Instagram.

After the Games concluded on February 23, much of Avaya's infrastructure was removed. However, the telecommunications facilities it built for the Games—including the telephone and IP networking for the Olympics skiing venue in the Caucasus, where a new resort town is being built—will remain.

Sources: Compiled from N. Cochrane, "The Most Data-Intensive Games Ever, Sochi Takes Mobile Gold," *The Sydney Morning Herald*, February 24, 2014; K. Bent, "Game Time: How Avaya's Technology Fueled the 2014 Winter Olympics," *CRN*, February 21, 2014; N. Shchelko, "Forget Its Hotels, Sochi's Tech Has Been Up for the Olympic Challenge," *Ars Technica*, February 20, 2014; L. Leavitt, "Sochi Is the First Truly Connected Olympics," *Forbes*, February 18, 2014; "Avaya Technology Firsts Keep the Sochi 2014 Olympic Winter Games Connected," *Evoke Telecom*, February 13, 2014; S. Leaks, "How Avaya Will Keep Sochi Connected for the 2014 Winter Olympics," *Sport Techie*, February 7, 2014; D. Poeter, "Mid Olympic Hacking Fears, Avaya Offers Safer Surfing in Sochi," *PC Magazine*, February 6, 2014; J. Careless, "Avaya Builds Massive Wi-Fi Net for 2014 Winter Olympics," *Network World*, December 16, 2013; E. Lai, "Going for Gold," *Avaya Innovations Magazine*, Quarter 3, 2013; www.avaya.com, accessed January 28, 2014.

Questions

1. Describe why wireless communications were critical to the success of the 2014 Winter Olympic Games. Provide specific examples to support your answer.

2. What other potential problems did Avaya have to consider that were not mentioned in this case? Provide specific examples to support your answer.

Although Wi-Fi has become extremely popular, it is not without problems. Three factors are preventing the commercial Wi-Fi market from expanding even further: roaming, security, and cost.

- At this time, users cannot roam from hotspot to hotspot if the hotspots use different Wi-Fi network services. Unless the service is free, users have to log on to separate accounts and, where required, pay a separate fee for each service. (Some Wi-Fi hotspots offer free service, while others charge a fee.)

- Security is the second barrier to greater acceptance of Wi-Fi. Because Wi-Fi uses radio waves, it is difficult to shield from intruders.

- The final limitation to greater Wi-Fi expansion is cost. Even though Wi-Fi services are relatively inexpensive, many experts question whether commercial Wi-Fi services can survive when so many free hotspots are available to users.

Wi-Fi Direct. Until late 2010, Wi-Fi could operate only if the hotspot contained a wireless antenna. Because of this limitation, organizations have typically used Wi-Fi for communications of up to about 800 feet. For shorter, peer-to-peer connections they have used Bluetooth.

This situation changed following the introduction of a new iteration of Wi-Fi known as Wi-Fi Direct. Wi-Fi Direct enables peer-to-peer communications, so devices can connect directly. It allows users to transfer content among devices without having to rely on a wireless antenna. It can connect pairs or groups of devices at Wi-Fi speeds of up to 250 Mbps and at distances of up to 800 feet. Further, devices with Wi-Fi Direct can broadcast their availability to other devices just as Bluetooth devices can. Finally, Wi-Fi Direct is compatible with the more than 1 billion Wi-Fi devices currently in use.

Wi-Fi Direct will probably challenge the dominance of Bluetooth in the area of device-to-device networking. It offers a similar type of connectivity but with greater range and much faster data transfer.

MiFi. MiFi is a small, portable wireless device that provides users with a permanent Wi-Fi hotspot wherever they go. Thus, users are always connected to the Internet. The range of the MiFi device is about 10 meters (roughly 30 feet). Developed by Novatel, the MiFi device is also called an intelligent mobile hotspot. Accessing Wi-Fi through the MiFi device allows up to five persons to be connected at the same time, sharing the same connection. MiFi also allows users to use voice-over-IP technology (discussed in Chapter 4) to make free (or cheap) calls, both locally and internationally.

MiFi provides broadband Internet connectivity at any location that offers 3G cellular network coverage. One drawback is that MiFi is expensive both to acquire and to use.

Super Wi-Fi. The term *Super Wi-Fi* was coined by the U.S. Federal Communications Commission (FCC) to describe a wireless network proposal that creates long-distance wireless Internet connections. (Despite the name, Super Wi-Fi is *not* based on Wi-Fi technology.) Super Wi-Fi uses the lower-frequency "white spaces" between broadcast TV channels. These frequencies enable the signal to travel further and penetrate walls better than normal Wi-Fi frequencies.

Super Wi-Fi is already in use in Houston, Texas, Wilmington, North Carolina, and the University of West Virginia. The technology threatens cell phone carriers' 3G technology, and it could eventually bring broadband wireless Internet access to rural areas.

Wireless Mesh Networks. **Mesh networks** use multiple Wi-Fi access points to create a wide area network that can be quite large. Mesh networks could have been included in the long-range wireless section, but you see them here because they are essentially a series of interconnected local area networks.

Around the United States, public wireless mesh programs have stalled and failed (e.g., in Philadelphia, in Boston, and on Long Island, New York). Service providers that partnered with cities to maintain the systems are dropping out, largely because the projects' costs are escalating and the revenue models are unclear.

Despite these problems, there are many examples of successful mesh network applications. Consider the following:

- U.S. military forces are using wireless mesh networks to connect their laptops in field operations.

- Electric meters are now being placed on residences to transfer their readings to the central office for billing, without the need to employ human readers or to connect the meters with cables.

- The LEO Iridium constellation operates as a mesh network, with wireless links among adjacent satellites. Calls between two satellite phones are routed through the mesh, from one satellite to another across the constellation, without having to pass through an Earth-based station. As a result, the signal travels a shorter distance, reducing any transmission lag. In addition, the constellation can operate with fewer Earth stations.

Wide-Area Wireless Networks

Wide-area wireless networks connect users to the Internet over a geographically dispersed territory. These networks typically operate over the licensed spectrum—that is, they use por-

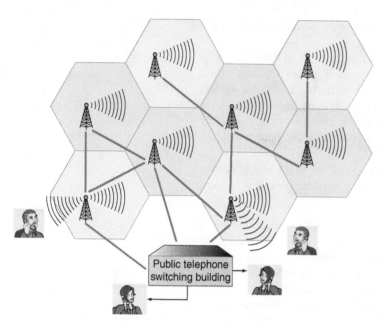

Figure 10.5 Smartphone and GPS system. (*Sources:* Image Source; © Engine Images-Fotolia.com; © AP/Wide World Photos)

tions of the wireless spectrum that are regulated by the government. In contrast, Bluetooth, Wi-Fi, and Super Wi-Fi operate over the unlicensed spectrum and are therefore more prone to interference and security problems. In general, wide-area wireless network technologies fall into two categories: cellular radio and wireless broadband.

Cellular Radio. **Cellular telephones (cell phones)** provide two-way radio communications over a cellular network of base stations with seamless handoffs. Cellular telephones differ from cordless telephones, which offer telephone service only within a limited range through a single base station attached to a fixed landline—for example, within a home or an office.

The cell phone communicates with radio antennas, or towers, placed within adjacent geographic areas called *cells* (see FIGURE 10.5). A telephone message is transmitted to the local cell—that is, the antenna—by the cell phone and then is passed from cell to cell until it reaches the cell of its destination. At this final cell, the message either is transmitted to the receiving cell phone or it is transferred to the public switched telephone system to be transmitted to a wireline telephone. This is why you can use a cell phone to call other cell phones as well as standard wireline phones.

Although we typically think of cellular networks as spanning huge distances, it is possible for them to be very small. IT's About Business 10.3 provides an example of a tiny cellular network in a remote area of Indonesia.

IT'S ABOUT BUSINESS 10.3

A Tiny Cellular Network for a Remote Tribe in Indonesia

Around the world, hundreds of millions of people, primarily in remote rural areas, lack even basic cellular coverage. Major wireless carriers—such as Indonesia's Telkomsel (www.telkomsel.com)—are often unable to make a business case for serving such areas. In these situations, communities have to provide the coverage themselves.

The indigenous people in the remote highlands of Papua, Indonesia, avoided contact with the outside world until scientists stumbled upon them in 1938. It is in this area, a four-hour drive from the nearest cellular coverage, that a tiny cellular network has been established. The network uses an inexpensive base station roped into a treetop. A base station is a multichannel, two-way radio that provides the connection between mobile phones and a larger network such as a telecommunications company's network, or even the Internet.

A team from the University of California, Berkeley, set up the tiny network. The project leader noted that the network "is a telecommunications company in a box that is placed in

a tree." The "box in the tree" is the base station, which performs the function of a cell tower.

The team built the network partly with existing infrastructure. It used a small hydropower generator and a satellite dish that provided Internet connectivity to a local school. The team added a wireless access point for local cellular connectivity, a battery for nighttime usage, a Wi-Fi router for a local Internet hot spot, and a billing system.

The network operates in a low-power "sleep mode" at night, and users can switch it on. All they have to do to make a call or send a message during the night is visit one of three devices placed in central locations in the village and press a red button to "wake up" the wireless access point. Incoming calls or text messages also "wake up" the system, but the call or message is delayed 20 seconds while the power amplifier starts. This delay enables the signal to become available. This process provides 24-hour availability while saving about half the power that the system would use if it were fully on all night.

The villagers are delighted that they can make calls and send short messages (via SMS) to communicate with family members in other parts of Indonesia or just to send messages across their valley. A trip to the next village across the valley takes hours of hiking up and down steep, slippery hillsides.

The network is now operated by a stand-alone telecommunications company managed by a local nongovernmental organization (NGO), with a laptop for local billing and a satellite connection to the rest of the world via the Internet. The network relies on Swedish phone numbers because no local telecommunications company would provide them.

The network started operating in 2013 with an initial $10,000 investment. As of mid-2014, it has 187 cellular subscribers and average monthly revenues of $830, including $368 in profits. The company provides several jobs, including three for people who sell airtime credits to villagers. The team notes that it received tacit approval for the network from high-level figures in the Indonesian government, but it has no formal license.

This technology could provide a new model for self-managed "last mile" mobile coverage in the world's hardest-to-reach areas, where traditional top-down telecommunications business models do not work. The network in Papua is a demonstration that remote areas and populations can profitably and sustainably manage their own networks. They do not need existing telecommunications companies. They can do it themselves.

Sources: Compiled from K. Heimerl, "Cellular Repeaters for Rural Coverage," *Technology and Infrastructure for Emerging Regions*, January 8, 2014; K. Heimerl, S. Hassan, K. Ali, E. Brewer, and T. Parikh, "Local, Sustainable, Small-Scale Cellular Networks," *Proceedings of the International Conference on Information and Communication Technologies and Development*, Cape Town, South Africa, 2013; D. Talbot, "How Remote Places Can Get Cellular Coverage by Doing It Themselves," *MIT Technology Review*, December 11, 2013; K. Heimerl, "The Village Base Station Goes Live in Rural Papua," *Technology and Infrastructure for Emerging Regions*, February 14, 2013; "Deploying the Village Base Station in Papua," *Technology and Infrastructure for Emerging Regions*, November 10, 2012.

uestions

1. Describe several advantages of the network for the villagers.

2. Describe several advantages of the network for the Indonesian government.

Cellular technology is quickly evolving, moving toward higher transmission speeds and richer features. The technology has progressed through several stages:

- *First generation* (*1G*) cellular networks used analog signals and had low bandwidth (capacity).

- *Second generation* (*2G*) uses digital signals primarily for voice communication; it provides data communication up to 10 Kbps.

- *2.5G* uses digital signals and provides voice and data communication up to 144 Kbps.

- *Third generation* (*3G*) uses digital signals and can transmit voice and data up to 384 Kbps when the device is moving at a walking pace, 128 Kbps when it is moving in a car, and up to 2 Mbps when it is in a fixed location. 3G supports video, Web browsing, and instant messaging.

3G does have disadvantages. Perhaps the most fundamental problem is that cellular companies in North America use two separate technologies: Verizon and Sprint use Code Division Multiple Access (CDMA), while AT&T and T-Mobile use Global System for Mobile Communications (GSM). CDMA companies are currently using *Evolution-Data Optimized* (*EV-DO*) technology, which is a wireless broadband cellular radio standard.

In addition, 3G is relatively expensive. In fact, most carriers limit how much information you can download and what you can use the service for. For instance, some carriers prohibit you from downloading or streaming audio or video. If you exceed the carriers' limits, they reserve the right to cut off your service.

- *Fourth generation* (*4G*) is not one defined technology or standard. The International Telecommunications Union (ITU) has specified speed requirements for 4G: 100 Mbps (million bits per second) for high-mobility communications such as cars and trains, and 1 Gbps (billion bits per second) for low-mobility communications such as pedestrians. A 4G system is expected to provide a secure all-IP-based mobile broadband system to all types of mobile devices. Many of the current "4G" offerings do not meet the ITU specified speeds, but they call their service 4G nonetheless. See "IT's Personal" for more information.

- *Fifth generation* (5G) is expected to be deployed by 2020. 5G networks are predicted to be faster and more intelligent than previous generations of cellular networks. With 5G, wearable computers (e.g., Fitbit), smartphones, tablets, and other devices with sensors that are location- and context-aware will work together with apps and services that you use.

Wireless Broadband or WiMAX. Worldwide Interoperability for Microwave Access, popularly known as WiMAX, is the name for IEEE Standard 802.16. WiMAX has a wireless access range of up to 31 miles, compared to 300 feet for Wi-Fi. WiMAX also has a data transfer rate of up to 75 Mbps. It is a secure system, and it offers features such as voice and video. WiMAX antennas can transmit broadband Internet connections to antennas on homes and businesses located miles away. For this reason, WiMAX can provide long-distance broadband wireless access to rural areas and other locations that are not currently being served.

IT'S PERSONAL: WIRELESS AND MOBILE

What the GSM3GHSDPA+4GLTE???

This chapter explains the many mobile platforms that are available to you as a consumer. Specifically, it discusses cellular, Bluetooth, Wi-Fi, satellite, and other wireless options. Within the cellular area, however, things get confusing because the telecommunications companies use so many acronyms these days. Have you ever wondered if Verizon 3G was equivalent to AT&T 3G? What about 4G and 4G LTE? Of course, most people assume that 4G is faster than 3G, but by how much?

To appreciate this confusion, consider that when Apple released an update to its mobile operating system (iOS), AT&T suddenly began to display 4G rather than 3G on the iPhone. And, that was with no phone upgrade! Pretty nice, right? Wrong. In this instance, the "upgrade" was simply a change in terminology rather than a change in technology. The speed of the 3G/4G network had not changed. (*Note:* AT&T "4G LTE" is a different technology that does offer significantly higher speeds than AT&T 3G or 4G.)

Actual connection speeds are described in bit rates, meaning how many bits (1s or 0s) a device can transmit in one second. For example, a speed listed as 1.5 Mbps translates to 1.5 million bits per second. That sounds like a tremendous rate. Knowing the bits per second, however, is only part of understanding the actual speed. In reality, connection speed is not the same as throughput. (Throughput is the amount of bandwidth actually available to you to use.) Actual throughput will always be less than the connection speed.

To understand this point, consider how your car operates. Your car is probably capable of driving more than 100 mph. However, you are "throttled down" by various speed limits, so you never reach your potential speed. Your actual speed varies depending on the route you take, the speed limits imposed along that route, the weather, the amount of traffic, and many other factors. In the same way, even though AT&T, Verizon, Sprint, and other companies boast incredible wireless speeds ("Up to 20 Mbps!"), they will always say "up to" because they know that you will never actually download a file at that rate.

The best method for determining the actual speeds of the various networks is to go to your local wireless store and run a speed test using the demo model they have on display. This will give you first-hand experience of the actual throughput speed you can expect from their network. This number is much more realistic than terms such as 3G, 4G, and 4G LTE.

Here is how to perform the test: First, make certain the unit is connected only to a cellular network (not Wi-Fi). Then go to http://speedtest.net, and click "Begin Test." I just ran this test from my iPhone 4S on AT&T's 4G (not 4G LTE) network. My download speed was 3.80 Mbps, and my upload speed was 1.71 Mbps. These numbers are more informative than any name they are given (3G, 4G, etc.) because they indicate exactly what you can expect from your wireless connection. Run this test at competing stores (AT&T, Verizon, Sprint, T-Mobile, etc.), and you will have real data to compare. As names change, you can always run a test to find the facts.

BEFORE *YOU GO ON....*
1. What is Bluetooth? What is a WLAN?
2. Describe Wi-Fi, cellular service, and WiMAX.

Apply The Concept 10.2

LEARNING OBJECTIVE 10.2 Explain how businesses can use technology employed by short-range, medium-range, and long-range networks, respectively.

STEP 1 – Background

Many cellular phones today contain multiple radios. Both the iPhone 5s and the Galaxy S4 contain three radio transceivers and one radio receiver. The radio transceivers are Cellular (4G

LTE, 4G, or 3G depending on your carrier), Bluetooth, and Wi-Fi. GPS is the radio receiver. The Samsung S4 also includes infrared and an NFC chip. With all of these radios embedded in a small mobile device, the possibilities of connectivity are nearly endless because one device can utilize short-range, mid-range, and wide-range connectivity.

STEP 2 – Activity

Visit http://www.wiley.com/go/rainer/MIS3e/applytheconcept, and view the video demonstration by Serial IO. There is also a link to their Web site, where you will find several examples of wireless products intended for business use. Although most of these products are short-range devices, you must assume they will be connected to some mid-range and/or wide-range wireless network. In fact, these devices support Windows, Mac, Android, iOS, BlackBerry, and other platforms.

STEP 3 – Deliverable

Based on the video and the Serial IO Web site, create and submit a table to explain how businesses can use the technologies employed by short-range, medium-range, and long-range networks to achieve their business purposes.

10.3 Mobile Computing and Mobile Commerce

In the traditional computing environment, users come to a computer, which is connected with wires to other computers and to networks. Because these networks need to be linked by wires, it is difficult or even impossible for people on the move to use them. In particular, salespeople, repair people, service employees, law enforcement agents, and utility workers can be more effective if they can use IT while in the field or in transit. Mobile computing was designed for workers who travel outside the boundaries of their organizations as well as for anyone traveling outside his or her home.

Mobile computing refers to a real-time connection between a mobile device and other computing environments, such as the Internet or an intranet. This innovation is revolutionizing how people use computers. It is spreading at work and at home; in education, healthcare, and entertainment; and in many other areas.

Mobile computing has two major characteristics that differentiate it from other forms of computing: mobility and broad reach. *Mobility* means that users carry a device with them and can initiate a real-time contact with other systems from wherever they happen to be. *Broad reach* refers to the fact that when users carry an open mobile device, they can be reached instantly, even across great distances.

Mobility and broad reach create five value-added attributes that break the barriers of geography and time: ubiquity, convenience, instant connectivity, personalization, and localization of products and services. A mobile device can provide information and communication regardless of the user's location (*ubiquity*). With an Internet-enabled mobile device, users can access the Web, intranets, and other mobile devices quickly and easily, without booting up a PC or placing a call via a modem (*convenience* and *instant connectivity*). A company can customize information and send it to individual consumers as a short message service (SMS) (*customization*). And, knowing a user's physical location helps a company advertise its products and services (*localization*). Mobile computing provides the foundation for mobile commerce (m-commerce).

Mobile Commerce

In addition to affecting our everyday lives, mobile computing is also transforming the way organizations conduct business by allowing businesses and individuals to engage in mobile commerce. As you saw at the beginning of this chapter, **mobile commerce** (or *m-commerce*) refers to electronic commerce (EC) transactions that are conducted in a wireless environment, especially via the Internet. Like regular EC applications, m-commerce can be transacted via the Internet, private communication lines, smart cards, and other infrastructures. M-commerce creates opportunities for businesses to deliver new services to existing customers and to attract new customers. To see how m-commerce applications are classified by industry, visit www.wirelessresearch.eu.

The development of m-commerce is driven by the following factors:

- *Widespread availability of mobile devices.* By mid-2014, some 6 billion cell phones were in use throughout the world. Cell phones are spreading more quickly in the developing world than the developed world. Experts estimate that within a few years about 70 percent of cell phones in developed countries will have Internet access. Mobile Internet access in developing countries will increase rapidly as well. Thus, a mass market has developed for mobile computing and m-commerce.

- *Declining prices.* The price of wireless devices is declining and will continue to decline.

- *Bandwidth improvement.* To properly conduct m-commerce, you need sufficient bandwidth for transmitting text, voice, video, and multimedia. Wi-Fi, 4G cellular technology, and WiMAX all provide the necessary bandwidth.

Mobile computing and m-commerce include many applications, which result from the capabilities of various technologies. You will examine these applications and their impact on business activities in the next section.

Mobile Commerce Applications

Mobile commerce applications are many and varied. The most popular applications include location-based applications, financial services, intrabusiness applications, accessing information, and telemetry. The rest of this section examines these various applications and their effects on the ways people live and do business.

Location-Based Applications and Services. M-commerce B2C applications include location-based services and location-based applications. Location-based mobile commerce is called **location-based commerce** (or **L-commerce**).

Location-based services provide information that is specific to a given location. For example, a mobile user can (1) request the nearest business or service, such as an ATM or a restaurant; (2) receive alerts, such as a warning of a traffic jam or an accident; and (3) find a friend. Wireless carriers can provide location-based services such as locating taxis, service personnel, doctors, and rental equipment; scheduling fleets; tracking objects such as packages and train boxcars; finding information such as navigation, weather, traffic, and room schedules; targeting advertising; and automating airport check-ins.

Consider, for example, how location-based advertising can make the marketing process more productive. Marketers can use this technology to integrate the current locations and preferences of mobile users. They can then send user-specific advertising messages concerning nearby shops, malls, and restaurants to consumers' wireless devices. Apple's iBeacon app is an interesting location-based service, which is illustrated in IT's About Business 10.4.

 'S ABOUT BUSINESS 10.4

Apple's iBeacons

Apple's (www.apple.com) iBeacon, a new feature found in iOS 7, is a location-based iPhone app that provides location-aware, contextual information to users. iBeacon uses a collection of beacons, which are Bluetooth low energy (also called Bluetooth Smart; see Section 10.2) transmitters. The beacons, which can be placed anywhere that contextual information would be valuable, are tiny discs a little wider and thicker than a quarter. They locate a smartphone's location by broadcasting Bluetooth signals.

The purpose of iBeacon is to allow advertisers and business partners to deliver information, coupons, and other media relevant to a person's location.

© gpointstudio/iStockphoto

Reported uses for iBeacon span a wide range of interactive applications for museums, city tours, and shopping experiences. Users can view location-relevant information on exhibits, be guided around on a city tour, and receive notifications for deals while walking past or into stores, without relying on GPS technology. iBeacons also enable shoppers to make purchases at point-of-sale terminals without having to remove their wallet or credit card.

As an example of the use of iBeacons, let's look at Major League Baseball (MLB; www.mlb.com). At Citi Field, home of the New York Mets, iBeacons provide messages such as a simple greeting or a discount at the stadium store. For example, as a fan nears the threshold of the gates from the walkway to the ballpark, a message appears on his iPhone 5S, "Welcome to Citi Field." When he is within a few feet of the stadium turnstiles, the app opens on his smartphone. A prompt asks him if he would like to view his ticket for that day's game. (With this app, fans would not create logjams at the turnstiles looking for their tickets on their e-mail.) When he encounters the Mets Home Run Apple in front of the stadium, he holds his iPhone near a sign by the landmark, and a video appears on his smartphone detailing the landmark's history.

When he enters the stadium, another message pops up, this time greeting him as a first-time visitor to Citi Field. The stadium "knows" how many times he has been there. It can utilize this knowledge to send special coupons and discounts to fans who, for instance, are attending their 10th game.

Major League Baseball is also collaborating with Apple to integrate the iBeacon app with MLB's At the Ballpark app. MLB prefers Bluetooth Smart over other technologies because it is more flexible. The iBeacon app can be tuned for a wide variety of distances, all depending on the application. Only fans who walk through the door of the Mets store, for instance, will be sent a coupon. Other fans who walk past the store will not be sent anything.

The iBeacon app became commercially available in ballparks in 2014, with individual stadiums offering different features depending on the preferences of the ball club. MLB is also investigating mobile payments powered by iBeacon and Bluetooth Smart at the ballparks.

Location-based services such as iBeacon are challenging to implement. Although retailers love the idea of targeting customers who walk by their stores, there is an inherent unease associated with knowing too much about individuals. Some customers may appreciate offers, whereas others might be nervous or irritated by the idea that stores are tracking their movements. To avoid alienating potential customers, most retailers use an "opt in" feature. For instance, MLB purposely designed its app so that only users who are running the At the Ballpark app (even in the background) will receive offers. MLB maintains that it does not want to surprise any fans

Privacy concerns have not stopped other businesses from employing technologies that can track a person's location. Significantly, each of these technologies has its own drawbacks. GPS is not particularly accurate indoors, and its use quickly drains a device's battery. Quick response (QR) codes require users to open a specific app and take a clear photo of the code. NFC requires users to tap a specific spot on their devices. Even then, it does not always function correctly.

Consider a shoe store, for example. When a customer visits the store, an iBeacon mounted under a shelf will alert her smartphone that she (Jane, loyalty card number 12345) is in a particular physical location in front of the Nike shoe section. The store owner can monitor her behavior: How long is she looking at Nike shoes? As a result, the store can send her a discount coupon for Nike shoes.

Other interesting applications of iBeacon:

- An indoor location app for a museum that (1) provides a map for you to use in navigating the museum, (2) knows which gallery you are visiting, and (3) offers information about the exhibits in that gallery as you move around.

- A conference management system that tracks which sessions you attend as you enter each session and automatically downloads the session videos to your smartphone after they are published.

- Imagine approaching your front door and having it automatically unlock as you are a step away. When you enter your living room, the television automatically turns on—to your favorite channel.

- For gas stations, customers become more valuable when they do more than buy gas. Thanks to an iBeacon, the station could know when a customer is pumping gas. That is the perfect chance to offer a discount on a sandwich or a drink.

Sources: Compiled from A. Bohna, "iBeacons: An Overview," *YMC*, February 6, 2014; M. McFarland, "How iBeacons Could Change the World Forever," *The Washington Post*, January 7, 2014; M. Panzarino, "inMarket Rolls Out iBeacons to 200 Safeway, Giant Eagle Grocery Stores to Reach Shoppers When It Matters," *Tech Crunch*, January 6, 2014; K. Vanhemert, "4 Reasons Why Apple's iBeacon Is About to Disrupt Interaction Design," *Wired*, December 11, 2013; "iBeacon – The Game Changer in InStore Navigation," *Technopark Living*, December 8, 2013; L. Tung, "Apple Launches iBeacon in 254 Stores to Streamline Shopping Experience," *ZD Net*, December 6, 2013; E. Anderson, "Shelfbucks Shares Use Cases for Apple's iBeacon for Retailers," *Bestfit Mobile*, November 20, 2013; "Apple iBeacons Explained – Smart Home Occupancy Sensing Explained?" *Automated Home*, October 3, 2013; J. O'Grady, "iBeacons: Coming Soon to a Baseball Stadium Near You," *ZD Net*, October 1, 2013; R. Cheng, "Baseball's Beacon Trials Hint at Apple's Location Revolution," *CNET*, September 28, 2013; www.apple.com, accessed March 18, 2014.

Questions

1. What other uses for iBeacon can you think of?

2. Other than privacy concerns, what are other possible disadvantages of the iBeacon app? Provide specific examples to support your answer.

Financial Services. Mobile financial applications include banking, wireless payments and micropayments, money transfers, wireless wallets, and bill payment services. The bottom line for mobile financial applications is to make it more convenient for customers to transact business regardless of where they are or what time it is. Harried customers are demanding such convenience.

In many countries, banks increasingly offer mobile access to financial and account information. For example, Citibank (www.citibank.com) alerts customers on their digital cell phones about changes to their account information.

If you took a taxi ride in Frankfurt, Germany, you could use your cell phone to pay the taxi driver. Such very small purchase amounts (generally less than $10) are called *micropayments*.

Web shoppers historically have preferred to pay with credit cards. Because credit card companies sometimes charge fees on transactions, however, credit cards are an inefficient way to make very small purchases. The growth of relatively inexpensive digital content, such as music (e.g., iTunes), ring tones, and downloadable games, is driving the growth of micropayments, as merchants seek to avoid paying credit card fees on small transactions.

Ultimately, however, the success of micropayment applications will depend on the costs of the transactions. Transaction costs will be small only when the volume of transactions is large. One technology that can increase the volume of transactions is wireless **mobile wallets** (m-wallets). Various companies offer m-wallet technologies that enable cardholders to make purchases with a single click from their mobile devices.

In China, SmartPay allows people to use their mobile phones to pay their phone bills and utility bills, buy lottery tickets and airline tickets, and make other purchases. SmartPay launched 172.com (see www.172.com), a portal that centralizes the company's mobile, telephone, and Internet-based payment services for consumers. The company designed the portal to provide a convenient, centralized source of information for all of these transactions.

Intrabusiness Applications. Although business-to-consumer (B2C) m-commerce receives considerable publicity, most of today's m-commerce applications actually are used *within* organizations. In this section, you will see how companies use mobile computing to support their employees.

Mobile devices increasingly are becoming an integral part of workflow applications. For example, companies can use non-voice mobile services to assist in dispatch functions—that is, to assign jobs to mobile employees, along with detailed information about the job. Target areas for mobile delivery and dispatch services include transportation (delivery of food, oil, newspapers, cargo; courier services; tow trucks; taxis), utilities (gas, electricity, phone, water); field service (computers, office equipment, home repair); healthcare (visiting nurses, doctors, social services); and security (patrols, alarm installation).

Accessing Information. Another vital function of mobile technology is to help users obtain and utilize information. Two types of technologies—mobile portals and voice portals—are designed to aggregate and deliver content in a form that will work within the limited space available on mobile devices. These portals provide information to users anywhere and at any time.

A **mobile portal** aggregates and provides content and services for mobile users. These services include news, sports, and e-mail; entertainment, travel, and restaurant information; community services; and stock trading. The world's best-known mobile portal—i-mode from NTT DoCoMo (www.nttdocomo.com)—has more than 40 million subscribers, primarily in Japan. Major players in Europe are Vodafone, O2, and T-Mobile. Some traditional portals—for example, Yahoo!, AOL, and MSN—have mobile portals as well.

A **voice portal** is a Web site with an audio interface. Voice portals are not Web sites in the normal sense because they can also be accessed through a standard phone or a cell phone. A certain phone number connects you to a Web site, where you can request information verbally. The system finds the information, translates it into a computer-generated voice reply, and tells you what you want to know. Most airlines utilize voice portals to provide real-time information on flight status.

Another example of a voice portal is the voice-activated 511 travel-information line developed by Tellme.com. This technology enables callers to inquire about weather, local restaurants, current traffic, and other valuable information. In addition to retrieving information, some sites provide true interaction. For example, iPing (www.iping.com) is a reminder and notification service that allows users to enter information via the Web and receive reminder calls. This service can even call a group of people to notify them of a meeting or conference call.

Telemetry Applications. **Telemetry** is the wireless transmission and receipt of data gathered from remote sensors. Telemetry has numerous mobile computing applications. For example, technicians can use telemetry to identify maintenance problems in equipment. As another example, doctors can monitor patients and control medical equipment from a distance.

Car manufacturers use telemetry applications for remote vehicle diagnosis and preventive maintenance. For instance, drivers of many General Motors cars use its OnStar system (www.onstar.com) in numerous ways.

An interesting telemetry application for individuals is an iPhone app called Find My iPhone. Find My iPhone is a part of the Apple iCloud (www.apple.com/icloud). This app provides several very helpful telemetry functions. If you lose your iPhone, for example, it offers two ways to find its approximate location on a map. First, you can sign into the Apple iCloud from any computer. Second, you can use the Find My iPhone app on another iPhone, iPad, or iPod touch.

If you remember where you left your iPhone, you can write a message and display it on your iPhone's screen. The message might say, "Left my iPhone. Please call me at 301-555-1211." Your message appears on your iPhone, even if the screen is locked. And, if the map indicates that your iPhone is nearby—perhaps in your office under a pile of papers—you can tell Find My iPhone to play a sound that overrides the volume or silent setting.

If you left your iPhone in a public place, you may want to protect its contents. You can remotely set a four-digit passcode lock to prevent people from using your iPhone, accessing your personal information, or tampering with your settings. Going further, you can initiate a remote wipe (erase all contents) to restore your iPhone to its factory settings. If you eventually find your phone, then you can connect it to your computer and use iTunes to restore the data from your most recent backup.

If you have lost your iPhone and you do not have access to a computer, you can download the Find My iPhone app to a friend's iPhone, iPad, or iPod touch and then sign in to access all the Find My iPhone features.

┌─ BEFORE *YOU GO ON....* ─┐

1. What are the major drivers of mobile computing?
2. Describe mobile portals and voice portals.
3. Describe wireless financial services.
4. Discuss some of the major intrabusiness wireless applications.

Apply The Concept 10.3

LEARNING OBJECTIVE 10.3 Provide a specific example of how each of the five major m-commerce applications can benefit a business.

STEP 1 – Background

Mobile connectivity has not only changed the lives of consumers, but also drastically reformulated the rules for what is possible for a business. Of course, possible and legal are not always the same, so what is possible may not be plausible. Nonetheless, thanks to location-aware devices interconnected by short-range, medium-range, and wide-range networks, the possibilities truly are endless!

STEP 2 – Activity

Visit http://www.wiley.com/go/rainer/MIS3e/applytheconcept, and watch the YouTube video about Apple's iBeacon and its use in Citi Field for the New York Mets. Also, reread (assuming you have already read) IT's About Business 10.4. This box describes Apple's iBeacon technology, and it illustrates all of the applications mentioned in this section, even though it does not specifically name them. Those applications of mobile technology are (meaning uses of mobile ... not necessarily mobile apps) location, financial, intrabusiness, accessing information, and telemetry.

STEP 3 – Deliverable

Provide specific examples of how each of the five major m-commerce applications can benefit the New York Mets, Major League Baseball, and their customers. Submit your examples to your instructor.

10.4 Pervasive Computing

Media Bakery

A world in which virtually every object has processing power and is connected to a global network either via a wireline or wirelessly is the world of **pervasive computing** (or **ubiquitous computing**). Pervasive computing is invisible "everywhere computing" that is embedded in the objects around us—the floor, the lights, our cars, the washing machine, our cell phones, our clothes, and so on.

For example, in a *smart home*, your home computer, television, lighting and heating controls, home security system, and many appliances can communicate with one another via a home network. You can control these linked systems through various devices, including your pager, cell phone, television, home computer, and even your automobile. One of the key elements of a smart home is the *smart appliance*, an Internet-ready appliance that can be controlled by a small handheld device or a desktop computer via a home network, either wireline or wireless. Two technologies provide the infrastructure for pervasive computing: radio-frequency identification and wireless sensor networks.

Radio-Frequency Identification

Radio-frequency identification (RFID) technology allows manufacturers to attach tags with antennas and computer chips on goods and then track their movement through radio signals. RFID was developed to replace bar codes.

A typical bar code, known as the *Universal Product Code* (*UPC*), is made up of 12 digits that are batched in various groups. The first digit identifies the item type, the next five digits identify the manufacturer, and the next five identify the product. The last digit is a check digit for error detection. Bar codes have worked well, but they have limitations. First, they require a line of sight to the scanning device. This system works well in a store, but it can pose substantial problems in a manufacturing plant or a warehouse or on a shipping/receiving dock. Second, because bar codes are printed on paper, they can be ripped, soiled, or lost. Third, the bar code identifies the manufacturer and product but not the actual item.

© Ecken, Dominique/Keystone Pressedienst/ZUMA Press

Figure 10.6 Small RFID reader and RFID tag. (*Source:* © Ecken, Dominique/Keystone Pressedienst/Zuma Press)

RFID systems use tags with embedded microchips, which contain data, and antennas to transmit radio signals over a short distance to RFID readers. The readers pass the data over a network to a computer for processing. The chip in the RFID tag is programmed with information that uniquely identifies an item. It also contains information about the item such as its location and where and when it was made. FIGURE 10.6 shows a small RFID reader and RFID tag.

There are two basic types of RFID tags: active and passive. *Active RFID tags* use internal batteries for power, and they broadcast radio waves to a reader. Because active tags contain batteries, they are more expensive than passive RFID tags, and they can be read over greater distances. Therefore, they are used primarily for more expensive items. In contrast, *passive RFID tags* rely entirely on readers for their power. They are less expensive than active tags, but they can be read only up to 20 feet. For these reasons, they are generally applied to less expensive merchandise. Problems with RFID include expense and the comparatively large size of the tags. There are many uses for RFID technology, as you see in IT's About Business 10.5.

Marks & Spencer Embraces RFID

Marks & Spencer (M&S; www.marksandspencer.com) is one of the United Kingdom's leading retailers, with 766 UK stores. More than 21 million people visit its stores each week to shop for high-quality clothing, home products, and innovative food items. Traditionally, M&S relied on optical scanners and bar codes to track its inventory. However, the process was too slow and error prone. As a result, M&S decided to implement RFID technology. The company has since become a pioneer in RFID use.

M&S intends to transform itself from a traditional British retailer into a leading international, multichannel retailer. The firm, which operates 418 international stores across Europe, the Middle East, and Asia, announced in 2013 that it will enter four new European markets with the launch of localized customer Web sites in Austria, Belgium, Germany, and Spain. The company's CEO notes that the strategy to become a global retailer is not directly linked to RFID. However, tracking items with RFID improves inventory accuracy, which will help significantly in fulfilling customer orders.

In 2001, M&S began attaching reusable RFID tags to food trays to track deliveries of fresh food between its suppliers and distribution centers and to determine how well the RFID technology functioned. M&S suppliers place information on the tags regarding the content and expiration dates of the items on the trays. The tags are read upon entry to the receiving depots, and they are then used to ensure that fresh merchandise is shipped rapidly to M&S stores. Empty trays are returned to suppliers to be washed, after which they are refilled and recoded. The RFID deployment worked so well that M&S now tracks approximately 10 million RFID-tagged food trays, as well as trays containing fresh flowers and plants, as they move along its supply chain.

Based on the success of its initial efforts, in 2004 M&S deployed RFID to tag and track 10,000 items of men's suits, shirts, and ties. This effort increased inventory accuracy so impressively that M&S expanded the deployment to additional types of clothing, such as men's formal and casual trousers, jackets, and shirts, as well as ladies' knitwear, coats, formal and casual trousers, and suits, in 550 UK stores.

When M&S began RFID-tagging clothing, the concept of using the technology to track items was new in the industry. M&S chose to initially tag men's suits, shirts, and ties because these items represent different methods by which clothing is delivered from the company's distribution centers to its stores. Suits are shipped on hangers and shirts are moved flat in reusable carriers, then transferred to hangers prior to being shipped to stores.

The clothing items are identified using RFID tags from Avery Dennison Corporation, which had supplied M&S with nearly 1 billion tags as of mid-2014. Avery Dennison is a global manufacturer of pressure-sensitive adhesive materials, apparel labels and tags, and RFID tags.

© albln/iStockphoto

Initially, M&S used fixed RFID readers that were built into carts equipped with lead acid batteries as a power source. In 2006 and 2007, the company replaced these readers with two-piece readers that consisted of a reader linked to a handheld scanner via Bluetooth. The readers are stored in the back office and are deployed on the sales floor either in the early morning or in the evening.

Sales assistants select a store department from a drop-down menu on the handheld device and then read each item located on the sales floor and within the store's stockroom. The RFID system enables M&S to accurately read merchandise at a rate of up to 15,000 items per hour. It also removes duplicate reads. After the scanning is completed, the mobile device transmits the data to a central RFID database via the store's wireless network. The company then uses this information to automatically update the store's database.

The item-level tagging of clothing provided M&S with a number of benefits. Perhaps most importantly, the retailer knows the exact amount of each particular item at each of its stores. Thanks to the new technology, M&S can ensure that the correct products are shipped to the right stores at the proper time. Inventory turnover has been improved by 50 percent, and out-of-stock products have been reduced by 40 percent.

Essentially, RFID creates a "single version of the truth" for the inventory levels in a particular store. These inventory levels are then used by all other M&S systems to calculate the correct allocation of stock for each store. Missing items in each store are replenished by the distribution system as part of the normal daily store deliveries. Also, the company's ability to keep the right sizes of garments in stores has improved customer satisfaction.

Another benefit of the RFID system is the time savings generated by the reduced number of calls that individual stores make to the head office or distribution center to order missing stock. The stores are confident that if stock is available, it will be sent to them. This process has enabled store teams to focus on customer service rather than on stock inventories and adjustments.

In 2012, M&S began deploying Generation 2 RFID technology on home goods such as bedding, accessories, and kitchenware. Generation 2 RFID technology enables users to manage multiple RFID readers and multiple RFID applications in close proximity. That is, it can manage interference between RFID readers. It is also faster and more accurate than Generation 1 technology.

M&S deployed between 8 and 10 types of Generation 2 RFID tags, all of which were supplied by Avery Dennison. The company will use some tags for various apparel goods, others for beauty products, and still others for items containing metal. M&S is also working with Avery Dennison to develop a tag for liquid products. (Metal and thick liquids can interfere with RFID signals and typically require more powerful RFID tags.)

At the same time, M&S is deploying handheld readers capable of reading older RFID tags as well as Generation 2 RFID tags. The company is also developing proprietary software to manage its RFID system. It intends to use its existing database, also developed in-house, to store RFID data.

M&S executives feel confident that RFID generates a more accurate picture of where and when products are manufactured and where they need to go. RFID also enables more complete product descriptions, including size, color, style, and many other features.

Finally, RFID provides M&S with greater visibility into its supply chain in addition to more accurate item-level inventory. The retailer has reduced the costs associated with taking inventory annually, with excessive markdowns, and with theft and fraud. RFID also offers the M&S the opportunity to implement an entire range of customer information services that help seamlessly integrate the multiple channels through which customers interact with the retailer.

In 2014, M&S achieved a landmark when it became the first retailer to have 100 percent of its merchandise tagged with RFID technology.

Sources: Compiled from "Marks & Spencer Expands RFID Rollout," *RFID24-7*, February 27, 2014; "Marks & Spencer Introduce RFID Enabled Footwear Inspiration Station," *Retail Innovation*,

February 23, 2014; "Accurate Inventory Tracking Benefits M&S," *Retail Technology*, February 18, 2014; "RFID Leader Marks & Spencer Drives Apparel Sales with Accurate Inventory Tracking," *Avery Dennison Press Release*, 2013; B. Violino, "Marks & Spencer Rolls Out RFID to All Its Stores," *RFID Journal*, March 25, 2013; "M&S Extends RFID Across Departments," *Logistics Manager*, January 17, 2013; T. Sharma, "Marks & Spencer Extends Its Use of RFID Technology," *RFID Ready*, January 17, 2013; L. Barrie, "Marks & Spencer Expands RFID to All Clothing," *Just-Style*, January 15, 2013; L. Bateman, "M&S Sets Its Sights on Becoming Closed Loop," *Greenwise Business*, June 19, 2012; C. Swedberg, "Marks & Spencer to Tag Items at 120 Stores," *RFID Journal*, November 16, 2006; J. Collins, "Marks & Spencer to Extend Trial to 53 Stores," *RFID Journal*, February 18, 2005; B. Violino, "EPC in Fashion at Marks & Spencer," *RFID Journal*, April 10, 2003; www.marksandspencer.com, accessed March 12, 2014.

Questions

1. Describe how RFID technology can generate increased customer satisfaction.

2. What are potential disadvantages to implementing RFID technology in a retailer such as Marks & Spencer?

3. Why did Marks & Spencer initially deploy RFID technology on a limited basis? In your opinion, was this the correct strategy? Why or why not? Be specific.

QR code

RFID tag

Barcode

© Oehoeboeroe/iStockphoto;
© ra-photos/iStockphoto;
Media Bakery

Figure 10.7 Bar codes, RFID tags, and QR codes.

QR codes are also being developed to replace bar codes. FIGURE 10.7 illustrates bar codes, QR codes, and an RFID tag.

A QR code is a two-dimensional code, readable by dedicated QR readers and camera phones. QR codes have several advantages over bar codes:

- QR codes can store much more information.

- Data types stored in QR codes include numbers, text, URLs, and even Japanese characters.

- QR codes are smaller because they store information both horizontally and vertically.

- QR codes can be read from any direction or angle, so they are less likely to be misread.

- QR codes are more resistant to damage.

Wireless Sensor Networks

Wireless sensor networks (WSNs) are networks of interconnected, battery-powered, wireless sensors called *motes* that are placed into the physical environment. The motes collect data from many points over an extended space. A mote contains processing, storage, and radio-frequency sensors and antennas. Each mote "wakes up" or activates for a fraction of a second when it has data to transmit. It then relays those data to its nearest neighbor. So, instead of every mote transmitting its data to a remote computer at a base station, the data are moved mote by mote until they reach a central computer where they are stored and analyzed. An advantage of a wireless sensor network is that if one mote fails, then another one can pick up the data. This process makes WSNs very efficient and reliable. Also, if the network requires more bandwidth, it is easy to boost performance by placing new motes when and where they are required.

The motes provide information that enables a central computer to integrate reports of the same activity from different angles within the network. Therefore, the network can determine with much greater accuracy information such as the direction in which a person is moving, the weight of a vehicle, and the amount of rainfall over a field of crops.

There are many applications of wireless sensors. Nest Labs (www.nest.com; now owned by Google) produces a "digital thermostat" that combines sensors and Web technology. The thermostat senses not only air temperature, but also the movements of people in a house. It then adjusts room temperatures accordingly to save energy.

Placing sensors in all kind of products makes the products "smart." Smart equipment includes sensors in bridges and oil rigs that alert their human minders when they need repairs, before equipment failure occurs. Sensors in jet engines produce data on the operating performance of the engines in real time. Sensors in fruit and vegetable cartons can track location and "sniff" the produce, warning in advance of spoilage, so shipments can be rerouted or rescheduled.

In Dubuque, Iowa, IBM has initiated a long-term project with the local government to use sensors, software, and the Internet to improve the city's use of water, electricity, and transportation. In a pilot project introduced in 2011, digital water meters were installed in 151 homes. These meters contain software that monitors water use and patterns. It then informs residents about ways to consume less, and it alerts them to likely leaks. The pilot program decreased water use by 65 million gallons per year in the city.

Another valuable application of sensors is to use them in smart electrical meters, thereby forming a smart grid. Smart meters monitor electricity usage, and they transmit that data to the utility company.

The Internet of Things

Wireless sensors are an underlying technology of the Internet of Things. The **Internet of Things (IoT)** is a scenario in which objects, animals, and people are provided with unique identifiers and the ability to automatically transfer data over a network without requiring human-to-human or human-to-computer interaction. The first Internet appliance was a Coke machine at Carnegie Mellon University in the early 1980s. Programmers at the university could connect to the machine over the Internet, monitor the machine's status, and determine whether a cold drink would be awaiting them if they decided to make the trip to the machine.

In the IoT, a *thing* can be a person with a heart monitor implant, a farm animal with a biochip transmitter, an automobile with sensors to alert the driver when tire pressure is low, or any other natural or man-made object that can be assigned an IP address and provided with the ability to transfer data over a network. Using IPv6, we can assign an IP address to every "thing" on the planet. (We discuss IPv6 in detail in Chapter 4.)

As of mid-2014, the IoT had been most closely associated with *machine-to-machine* (M2M) communication in manufacturing and in the power, oil, and gas utilities. Products build with M2M communication capabilities are often referred to as *smart products.*

For example, the IoT will enable us to track and count everything and greatly reduce waste, loss, and cost. We would know when things need to be repaired, replaced, or recalled. We would also know if perishable products were fresh or past their "best." From a different perspective, the IoT raises new concerns about individual data privacy, data sovereignty (who owns what data), and data security.

> **BEFORE** *YOU GO ON....*
>
> 1. Define pervasive computing, RFID, and wireless sensor networks.
> 2. Provide two specific business uses of RFID technology.
> 3. What is the Internet of Things?

Apply The Concept 10.4

LEARNING OBJECTIVE 10.4 Describe technologies that underlie pervasive computing, providing examples of how businesses can utilize each one.

Pervasive computing is something to be both thankful for and concerned about. The fact that devices around us could be collecting data on our movements, purchases, vital signs, decisions, and so on frightens many people. At the same time, however, these devices could help us make better decisions by providing access to real-time data or by including factors in our decision-making process that we have not considered.

STEP 2 – Activity

RFID and WSNs are the underlying technologies that make pervasive computing possible. Here we focus on their positive uses, though a simple YouTube search for "RFID" brings up more videos that are against its use than are for it. Visit http://www.wiley.com/go/rainer/MIS3e/applytheconcept to watch two videos. The first is about RFID inventory management, and the second is about WSNs used in agriculture.

STEP 3 – Deliverable

Write and submit a paragraph that describes the technologies that allow pervasive computing to exist, and explain how the businesses depicted in the videos are using them. Also in your paragraph, provide one additional business example beyond those in the videos.

10.5 Wireless Security

Clearly, wireless networks provide numerous benefits for businesses. However, they also present a huge challenge to management—namely, their inherent lack of security. Wireless is a broadcast medium, and transmissions can be intercepted by anyone who is close enough and has access to the appropriate equipment. There are four major threats to wireless networks: rogue access points, war driving, eavesdropping, and radio-frequency jamming.

A *rogue access point* is an unauthorized access point to a wireless network. The rogue could be someone in your organization who sets up an access point meaning no harm but fails to inform the IT department. In more serious cases, the rogue is an "evil twin"—someone who wishes to access a wireless network for malicious purposes.

In an evil twin attack, the attacker is in the vicinity with a Wi-Fi-enabled computer and a separate connection to the Internet. Using a *hotspotter*—a device that detects wireless networks and provides information on them (see www.canarywireless.com)—the attacker simulates a wireless access point with the same wireless network name, or SSID, as the one that authorized users expect. If the signal is strong enough, users will connect to the attacker's system instead of the real access point. The attacker can then serve them a Web page asking for them to provide confidential information such as usernames, passwords, and account numbers. In other cases, the attacker simply captures wireless transmissions. These attacks are more effective with public hotspots (e.g., McDonald's and Starbucks) than with corporate networks.

War driving is the act of locating WLANs while driving (or walking) around a city or elsewhere. To war drive or walk, you simply need a Wi-Fi detector and a wirelessly enabled computer. If a WLAN has a range that extends beyond the building in which it is located, then an unauthorized user might be able to intrude into the network. The intruder can then obtain a free Internet connection and possibly gain access to important data and other resources.

Eavesdropping refers to efforts by unauthorized users to access data that are traveling over wireless networks. Finally, in *radio-frequency* (*RF*) *jamming*, a person or a device intentionally or unintentionally interferes with your wireless network transmissions.

As you see, wireless systems can be difficult to secure. Plug IT In 7 discusses a variety of techniques and technologies that you should implement to help you avoid these threats.

BEFORE *YOU GO ON....*

1. Describe the four major threats to the security of wireless networks.

2. Which of the four threats is the most dangerous for a business? Which is the most dangerous for an individual? Support your answers.

Apply The Concept 10.5

LEARNING OBJECTIVE 10.5 Explain how the four major threats to wireless networks can damage a business.

STEP 1 – Background

Generally, innovation is intended to accomplish some good purpose. In time, however, most innovations exhibit weaknesses that are exploited by people with negative intentions. This section has discussed four security issues that must be addressed: rogue access points, war driving, eavesdropping, and radio-frequency jamming.

One of the most frightening aspects of technology is that it has become so easy to share information. Although that is also one of technology's most popular and useful features, it makes it very easy for people with bad intentions to share the tools needed to perform illegal activities. For example, YouTube provides several videos on how to create a rogue access point. Simply displaying these videos is not illegal. What people do with that rogue access point, however, can be highly illegal.

STEP 2 – Activity

Visit Wikipedia (the link can be found at http://www.wiley.com/go/rainer/MIS3e/applytheconcept), and search for each of the four wireless network threats. Also, look through the examples and external links. Take notes on the types of damage that can be inflicted on network owners by these actions.

STEP 3 – Deliverable

Create a table that explains the damages that businesses can incur from each of the four major threats presented in Steps 1 and 2. Submit your table to your professor.

What's in for ME?

FOR THE ACCOUNTING MAJOR

Wireless applications help accountants to count and audit inventory. They also expedite the flow of information for cost control. Price management, inventory control, and other accounting-related activities can be improved with the use of wireless technologies.

FOR THE FINANCE MAJOR

Wireless services can provide banks and other financial institutions with a competitive advantage. For example, wireless electronic payments, including micropayments, are more convenient (anywhere, anytime) than traditional means of payment, and they are less expensive. Electronic bill payment from mobile devices is becoming more popular, increasing security and accuracy, expediting cycle time, and reducing processing costs.

FOR THE MARKETING MAJOR

Imagine a whole new world of marketing, advertising, and selling, with the potential to increase sales dramatically. Such is the promise of mobile computing. Of special interest for marketing are location-based advertising as well as the new opportunities resulting from pervasive computing and RFID. Finally, wireless technology also provides new opportunities in sales force automation (SFA), enabling faster and better communications with both customers (CRM) and corporate services.

FOR THE PRODUCTION/ OPERATIONS MANAGEMENT MAJOR

Wireless technologies offer many opportunities to support mobile employees of all kinds. Wearable computers enable off-site employees and repair personnel working in the field to service customers faster, better, and less expensively. Wireless devices can also increase productivity within factories by enhancing communication and collaboration as well as managerial planning and control. In addition, mobile computing technologies can improve safety by providing quicker warning signs and instant messaging to isolated employees.

 FOR THE HUMAN RESOURCE MANAGEMENT MAJOR

Mobile computing can improve HR training and extend it to any place at any time. Payroll notices can be delivered as SMSs. In addition, wireless devices can make it even more convenient for employees to select their own benefits and update their personal data.

MIS **FOR THE** MIS MAJOR

MIS personnel provide the wireless infrastructure that enables all organizational employees to compute and communicate anytime, anywhere. This convenience provides exciting, creative, new applications for organizations to reduce expenses and improve the efficiency and effectiveness of operations (e.g., to achieve transparency in supply chains). Unfortunately, as you saw earlier, wireless applications are inherently insecure. This lack of security is a serious problem with which MIS personnel must contend.

SUMMARY

1. Identify advantages and disadvantages of each of the four main types of wireless transmission media.

   Microwave transmission systems are used for high-volume, long-distance, line-of-sight communication. One advantage is the high volume. A disadvantage is that microwave transmissions are susceptible to environmental interference during severe weather such as heavy rain and snowstorms.

   Satellite transmission systems make use of communication satellites, and they receive and transmit data via line-of-sight. One advantage is that the enormous footprint—the area of Earth's surface reached by a satellite's transmission—overcomes the limitations of microwave data relay stations. Like microwaves, satellite transmissions are susceptible to environmental interference during severe weather.

   Radio transmission systems use radio-wave frequencies to send data directly between transmitters and receivers. An advantage is that radio waves travel easily through normal office walls. A disadvantage is that radio transmissions are susceptible to snooping by anyone who has similar equipment that operates on the same frequency.

   Infrared light is red light that is not commonly visible to human eyes. Common applications of infrared light are in remote control units for televisions and DVD and CD players. An advantage of infrared is that it does not penetrate walls and so does not interfere with other devices in adjoining rooms. A disadvantage is that infrared signals can be easily blocked by furniture.

2. Explain how businesses can use short-range, medium-range, and long-range wireless networks, respectively.

   Short-range wireless networks simplify the task of connecting one device to another, eliminating wires, and enabling people to move around while they use the devices. In general, short-range wireless networks have a range of 100 feet or less. Short-range wireless networks include Bluetooth, ultra-wideband, and near-field communications. A business application of ultra-wideband is the

PLUS Real-Time Location System from Time Domain. Using PLUS, an organization can locate multiple people and assets simultaneously.

   Medium-range wireless networks include Wi-Fi and mesh networks. *Wi-Fi* provides fast and easy Internet or intranet broadband access from public hotspots located at airports, hotels, Internet cafés, universities, conference centers, offices, and homes. *Mesh networks* use multiple Wi-Fi access points to create a wide area network that can be quite large.

   Wide-area wireless networks connect users to the Internet over geographically dispersed territory. They include cellular telephones and wireless broadband. *Cellular telephones* provide two-way radio communications over a cellular network of base stations with seamless handoffs. *Wireless broadband* has a wireless access range of up to 31 miles and a data transfer rate of up to 75 Mbps. WiMAX can provide long-distance broadband wireless access to rural areas and remote business locations.

3. Provide a specific example of how each of the five major m-commerce applications can benefit a business.

   Location-based services provide information specific to a location. For example, a mobile user can (1) request the nearest business or service, such as an ATM or restaurant; (2) receive alerts, such as a warning of a traffic jam or an accident; and (3) find a friend. With *location-based advertising*, marketers can integrate the current locations and preferences of mobile users. They can then send user-specific advertising messages about nearby shops, malls, and restaurants to wireless devices.

   Mobile financial applications include banking, wireless payments and micropayments, money transfers, wireless wallets, and bill payment services. The bottom line for mobile financial applications is to make it more convenient for customers to transact business regardless of where they are or what time it is.

Intrabusiness applications consist of m-commerce applications that are used *within* organizations. Companies can use non-voice mobile services to assist in dispatch functions—that is, to assign jobs to mobile employees, along with detailed information about the job.

When it comes to *accessing information*, mobile portals and voice portals are designed to aggregate and deliver content in a form that will work within the limited space available on mobile devices. These portals provide information anywhere and anytime to users.

Telemetry is the wireless transmission and receipt of data gathered from remote sensors. Company technicians can use telemetry to identify maintenance problems in equipment. Car manufacturers use telemetry applications for remote vehicle diagnosis and preventive maintenance.

4. Describe technologies that underlie pervasive computing, providing examples of how businesses can utilize each one.

Pervasive computing is invisible and everywhere computing that is embedded in the objects around us. Two technologies provide the infrastructure for pervasive computing: *radio-frequency identification* and *wireless sensor networks*.

RFID is the term for technologies that use radio waves to automatically identify the location of individual items equipped with tags that contain embedded microchips. *WSNs* are networks of interconnected, battery-powered, wireless devices placed in the physical environment to collect data from many points over an extended space.

5. Explain how the four major threats to wireless networks can damage a business.

The four major threats to wireless networks are rogue access points, war driving, eavesdropping, and radio-frequency jamming. A *rogue access point* is an unauthorized access point to a wireless network. *War driving* is the act of locating WLANs while driving around a city or elsewhere. *Eavesdropping* refers to efforts by unauthorized users to access data that are traveling over wireless networks. *Radio-frequency jamming* occurs when a person or a device intentionally or unintentionally interferes with wireless network transmissions.

>>>CHAPTER GLOSSARY

Bluetooth Chip technology that enables short-range connection (data and voice) between wireless devices.

cellular telephones (cell phones) Phones that provide two-way radio communications over a cellular network of base stations with seamless handoffs.

global positioning system (GPS) A wireless system that uses satellites to enable users to determine their position anywhere on Earth.

hotspot A small geographical perimeter within which a wireless access point provides service to a number of users.

infrared A type of wireless transmission that uses red light not commonly visible to human eyes.

Internet of Things (IoT) A scenario in which objects, animals, and people are provided with unique identifiers and the ability to automatically transfer data over a network without requiring human-to-human or human-to-computer interaction.

location-based commerce (L-commerce) Mobile commerce transactions targeted to individuals in specific locations, at specific times.

mesh networks Networks composed of multiple Wi-Fi access points that create a wide area network that can be quite large.

microwave transmission A wireless system that uses microwaves for high-volume, long-distance, point-to-point communication.

mobile commerce (or m-commerce) Electronic commerce transactions that are conducted with a mobile device.

mobile computing A real-time connection between a mobile device and other computing environments, such as the Internet or an intranet.

mobile portal A portal that aggregates and provides content and services for mobile users.

mobile wallet (m-wallet) A technology that allows users to make purchases with a single click from their mobile devices.

near-field communications (NFC) The smallest of the short-range wireless networks that is designed to be embedded in mobile devices such as cell phones and credit cards.

personal area network A computer network used for communication among computer devices close to one person.

pervasive computing (or ubiquitous computing) A computer environment where virtually every object has processing power with wireless or wired connections to a global network.

propagation delay Any delay in communications from signal transmission time through a physical medium.

radio-frequency identification (RFID) technology A wireless technology that allows manufacturers to attach tags with antennas and computer chips on goods and then track their movement through radio signals.

radio transmission Uses radio-wave frequencies to send data directly between transmitters and receivers.

satellite radio (or digital radio) A wireless system that offers uninterrupted, near CD-quality music that is beamed to your radio from satellites.

satellite transmission A wireless transmission system that uses satellites for broadcast communications.

telemetry The wireless transmission and receipt of data gathered from remote sensors.

ubiquitous computing See pervasive computing.

ultra-wideband (UWB) A high-bandwidth wireless technology with transmission speeds in excess of 100 Mbps that can be used for applications such as streaming multimedia from, say, a personal computer to a television.

voice portal A Web site with an audio interface.

wireless Telecommunications in which electromagnetic waves carry the signal between communicating devices.

wireless 911 911 emergency calls made with wireless devices.

wireless access point An antenna connecting a mobile device to a wired local area network.

Wireless Fidelity (Wi-Fi) A set of standards for wireless local area networks based on the IEEE 802.11 standard.

wireless local area network (WLAN) A computer network in a limited geographical area that uses wireless transmission for communication.

wireless sensor networks (WSNs) Networks of interconnected, battery-powered, wireless sensors placed in the physical environment.

>>>DISCUSSION QUESTIONS

1. Given that you can lose a cell phone as easily as a wallet, which do you feel is a more secure way of carrying your personal data? Support your answer.

2. If mobile computing is the next wave of technology, would you ever feel comfortable with handing a waiter or waitress your cell phone to make a payment at a restaurant the way you currently hand over your credit or debit card? Why or why not?

3. What happens if you lose your NFC-enabled smartphone or it is stolen? How do you protect your personal information?

4. In your opinion, is the mobile (or digital) wallet a good idea? Why or why not?

5. Discuss how m-commerce can expand the reach of e-business.

6. Discuss how mobile computing can solve some of the problems of the digital divide.

7. List three to four major advantages of wireless commerce to consumers and explain what benefits they provide to consumers.

8. Discuss the ways in which Wi-Fi is being used to support mobile computing and m-commerce. Describe the ways in which Wi-Fi is affecting the use of cellular phones for m-commerce.

9. You can use location-based tools to help you find your car or the closest gas station. However, some people see location-based tools as an invasion of privacy. Discuss the pros and cons of location-based tools.

10. Discuss the benefits of telemetry in healthcare for the elderly.

11. Discuss how wireless devices can help people with disabilities.

12. Some experts say that Wi-Fi is winning the battle with 3G cellular service. Others disagree. Discuss both sides of the argument and support each one.

13. Which of the applications of pervasive computing do you think are likely to gain the greatest market acceptance over the next few years? Why?

>>>PROBLEM-SOLVING ACTIVITIES

1. Investigate commercial applications of voice portals. Visit several vendors, for example, Microsoft and Nuance (links to both Web sites are available via http://www.wiley.com/go/rainer/MIS3e/problemsolving). What capabilities and applications do these vendors offer?

2. Using a search engine, try to determine whether there are any commercial Wi-Fi hotspots in your area. (*Hint*: Access http://www.wiley.com/go/rainer/MIS3e/problemsolving.)

3. Examine how new data-capture devices such as RFID tags help organizations accurately identify and segment their customers for activities such as targeted marketing. Browse the Web, and develop five potential new applications not listed in this chapter for RFID technology. What issues would arise if a country's laws mandated that such devices be embedded in everyone's body as a national identification system?

4. Investigate commercial uses of GPS. Start with www.neigps.com. Can some of the consumer-oriented products be used in industry? Prepare a report on your findings.

5. Access www.bluetooth.com. Examine the types of products being enhanced with Bluetooth technology. Present two of these products to the class and explain how they are enhanced by Bluetooth technology.

6. Explore www.nokia.com. Prepare a summary of the types of mobile services and applications Nokia currently supports and plans to support in the future.

7. Enter www.ibm.com. Search for "wireless e-business." Research the resulting stories to determine the types of wireless capabilities and applications IBM's software and hardware support. Describe some of the ways these applications have helped specific businesses and industries.

8. Research the status of 3G and 4G cellular service by visiting the links available via http://www.wiley.com/go/rainer/MIS3e/problemsolving. Prepare a report on the status of 3G and 4G based on your findings.

9. Enter Pitney Bowes Business Insight (www.pbinsight.com). Click on "MapInfo Professional," then click on the "Resources" tab, then on the "Demos" tab. Look for the location-based services demos. Try all the demos. Summarize your findings.

10. Enter www.packetvideo.com. Examine the demos and products and list their capabilities.

11. Enter www.onstar.com. What types of *fleet* services does OnStar provide? Are these any different from the services OnStar provides to individual car owners? (Play the movie.)

12. Access various search engines to find articles about the "Internet of Things." What is the "Internet of Things"? What types of technologies are necessary to support it? Why is it important?

>>> COLLABORATION EXERCISE

STEP 1 – Background

Greenway Medical Technologies sells electronic health record (EHR) and practice management (PM) software. Some of the company's products enable physicians to access patient records from their mobile devices. Many doctors enjoy the flexibility of being able to share information quickly and easily with colleagues for a second opinion. They also appreciate the ability to catch up on charts from home, the road, the train, and other remote locations. Patients, however, have legitimate security concerns about how their information is being shared across cellular networks and mobile devices.

STEP 2 – Activity

Divide your team into the following perspectives: patient, doctor, nurse, business administrator, and IT director. Use the Web to locate information on how each party would use mobile devices in their professional activities. In addition, search for the security/privacy concerns regarding mobile access to such private information. Record your concerns to share with the group.

Create a Google Form that will capture the following information: position (by a dropdown box), positive perspective (paragraph textbox), and negative perspective (paragraph textbox). Finally, include a place for team members to vote for or against the use of mobile devices. Remember, you are voting from your *assigned* perspective, not from your *personal* opinion.

STEP 3 – Deliverable

Meet as a team, and review the results of your work. Did a consensus emerge either in favor of or against the use of mobile devices? Are there any arguments that seem consistent across all perspectives? Export your team's voting results and comments from the Google spreadsheet to a PDF.

CLOSING **CASE 1** > Republic Wireless and FreedomPop Might Disrupt the Wireless Industry

THE BUSINESS PROBLEM >>> In 2012, according to Cisco Systems (www.cisco.com), more than 30 percent of all data traffic from smartphones passed through a Wi-Fi router. Cisco expects that figure to rise to almost 50 percent by 2017. This trend is even more pronounced with tablets, nearly 70 percent of which connect to the Internet exclusively through Wi-Fi. That is, this trend represents a problem for large U.S. carriers, who have purchased land on which to place their transmitter towers as well as exclusive rights to a part of the electromagnetic spectrum. Their strategy is to sell faster, more expensive data plans as their revenue from voice plans decreases.

In contrast, Wi-Fi networks were substantially less expensive to build. The transmitter is the router in the corner of your living room. You do not pay for the spectrum, because Wi-Fi does not require a license from the Federal Communications Commission, and you are already paying for access to the Internet with your home Internet service.

After a decade in which the big four U.S. wireless carriers—AT&T, www.att.com; Verizon, www.verizon.com; T-Mobile, www.t-mobile.com; and Sprint, www.sprint.com—spent tens of billions of dollars to upgrade their networks, arguably the fastest and largest network is the one we have all been building together, namely, Wireless Fidelity.

Cisco's report indicated that traffic over cellular networks did not grow as much as expected in 2012, partly because mobile device users adjusted their settings to automatically jump to their home and office Wi-Fi networks whenever possible. This strategy enabled the users to avoid the fees for exceeding carriers' new limits on data.

Industry analysts note that the rule of thumb in the wireless industry is that a smartphone uses four gigabytes of data per month. One gigabyte travels over a cellular network, and the remaining three gigabytes travel through Wi-Fi, usually at home. The question for the carrier is: "How can I make money from the three gigabytes?" The question for the consumer is: "How can I minimize the cost of the one gigabyte?"

Large carriers typically are too focused on their 4G cellular networks to pay attention to Wi-Fi. In the United States, AT&T

is the only major carrier that currently offers what the industry calls "seamless offloading." Seamless offloading works like this. AT&T has agreements with about 32,000 Wi-Fi hotspots at businesses and other public places. A customer walks into range, the hotspot recognizes his or her smartphone, and it immediately logs him or her onto the Wi-Fi network. Once on Wi-Fi, the customer no longer pays for data. China Mobile (www.chinamobileltd.com), TIM Participacoes (www.tim.com.br) in Brazil, and O$_2$ (www.o2.co.uk) in the United Kingdom provide seamless offloading as well.

MIS With its hotspots, AT&T has recognized that in some places Wi-Fi is more economical not just for the smartphone user but for the carrier as well. An efficient method to improve a wireless network is to densely pack the transmitters that send and receive data. For a crowded area such as a mall, the carrier receives greater benefits from working with the property owner to build a number of shorter-range Wi-Fi cells than from building a massive tower somewhere nearby. For big carriers, this process could mean billions in savings over time. Elsewhere in the world, the shift to Wi-Fi has prompted wireline Internet service providers such as British Telecom (http://home.bt.com) in the United Kingdom, France's Free Mobile (http://mobile.free.fr), and Japan's KDDI (www.kddi.com) to realize that they actually own an extra wireless network because they power the Wi-Fi of every customer.

With only one major carrier in the U.S. offering seamless offloading, and with Wi-Fi networks so prevalent and essentially free to use, the wireless industry appears to be ripe for disruption. A potential disruption is called "inverting" the network. A network is "inverted" when Wi-Fi is a carrier's primary service and cellular network functions as its backup service. Both Republic Wireless and FreedomPop invert the network.

TWO DISRUPTIVE SOLUTIONS >>> Republic Wireless (https://republicwireless.com) is a wireless communications service provider that offers unlimited calls and texts for $5 per month and unlimited data for an additional $40 per month. Republic can offer such low prices because it has not built a cellular network. Instead, for its customers who travel, the company rents network capacity from Sprint. All other Republic calls, texts, and data use Wi-Fi. Wi-Fi constitutes 50 percent of its calls and texts and 90 percent of its data.

Republic launched its wireless service in November 2013. The carrier requires the upfront purchase of an Android smartphone that is modified to use a customer's home or business Wi-Fi network to make phone calls.

Republic relies on a proprietary Voice-over-Internet Protocol (VoIP) for the Android operating system, which can seamlessly switch between Sprint's mobile network and Wi-Fi (assuming Wi-Fi service is available). Republic users can switch between service plans directly from their devices so that they can take advantage of Wi-Fi, 3G, and 4G cellular signals based on their individual needs. Further, members can change their plans up to twice per month.

FreedomPop (www.freedompop.com) sells refurbished Android phones for $99 to $199, with no contract. In addition, it gives away 500 megabytes of 4G data per month, plus unlimited texting and 200 anytime call minutes, as well as unlimited calls to other FreedomPop phones. FreedomPop sells 2 or more gigabytes of data starting at $18 per month. Compare these figures with a "Share Everything" plan from Verizon iPhone plan, which costs $40 per month for unlimited voice and text plus $60 for 2 gigabytes of data. Therefore, FreedomPop charges $18 for what Verizon offers for $100.

FreedomPop uses VoIP to transmit voice and data, which it transmits over bandwidth purchased from Sprint. The startup entices new customers with its free plan, but it then offers them many $3.99 services such as faster download speeds, monthly rollover of unused data, and device insurance. Over half of its customers now pay something, either via monthly plans (25 percent of customers) or added features (28 percent of customers). These add-on services have gross margins of 90 percent.

FreedomPop uses proven social marketing tactics. Anyone with a FreedomPop device can share minutes with another user, which increases customer loyalty and boosts usage. Customers also receive free data rewards when they sign up friends. How attractive is this feature? Consider that the company generates 17 invites on its site from each subscriber.

THE RESULTS >>> As of mid-2014, both Republic Wireless and FreedomPop were essentially startups. As such, it is unclear as to whether either company will find success. It is also unclear how they will impact the major carriers. It does appear, though, that the ultimate winners will be the consumers.

Sources: Compiled from R. Broida, "The One Real Problem with Republic Wireless," *CNET*, March 10, 2014; B. Greeley, "The Biggest, Cheapest Network of All," *Bloomberg BusinessWeek*, January 6–12, 2014; M. Reardon, "Is Republic Wireless Too Good to Be True?" *CNET*, January 4, 2014; D. McNay, "Republic Wireless: Game Changer in Revolution Against AT&T, Verizon," *The Huffington Post*, November 26, 2013; "W. Mossberg, "Smartphone with Wi-Fi Smarts," *The Wall Street Journal*, November 26, 2013; A. Atkins, "Wi-Fi vs. Cellular Networks: Why Wi-Fi Wins Every Time," Scratch Wireless, November 25, 2013; M. Miller, "Republic Wireless Moto X Review: Top Consumer Smartphone and Low Cost Service Are a Killer Combo," *ZD Net*, November 25, 2013; "Republic Wireless Offers Moto X for $299 and Four New Plans Starting at $5 Per Month," *Republic Wireless Press Release*, November 13, 2013; T. Geron, "Data for Nothing, Calls for Free," Forbes, June 24, 2013; S. Vaughan-Nichols, "The Merger of Cellular and Wi-Fi: The Wireless Network's Future," *ZD Net*, January 9, 2013; S. Segan, "Republic Wireless: It's All About Wi-Fi," *PC Magazine*, November 8, 2011; https://republicwireless.com, www.freedompop.com, accessed March 11, 2014.

Questions

1. Describe how Republic Wireless and FreedomPop can be disruptive to the major U.S. cellular service providers.

2. What actions should the major cellular service providers take to combat Republic and FreedomPop's business models?

CLOSING **CASE 2** > Has Facebook Solved the Mobile Ad Problem?

THE BUSINESS PROBLEM >>> In 2012, Facebook (www.facebook.com) was unsuccessfully managing the shift of online activities from computers to smartphones and tablets. Immediately before its initial public offering (IPO) in May 2012, the company revealed that it was not earning "any significant revenue" from either its mobile Web site or its mobile app, despite the fact that more than half of its members used its service on their mobile devices.

Facebook had to deal with the two most common problems associated with mobile devices: small screens and gaps in marketers' ability to measure the impact of mobile ads. These factors made ads look far less effective on mobile devices. Consequently, marketers were less willing to pay for them.

Facebook's advertising team was also too preoccupied with pushing a new kind of desktop Web ad, called Sponsored Stories, to pay much attention to mobile. These ads are actions by a Facebook member, such as "liking" a page or checking in at a store, that marketers can then promote, for a fee, to the member's friends. CEO Mark Zuckerberg viewed these ads as the future of Facebook advertising because users were less likely to ignore real posts from friends.

By August 2013, the widening gap between mobile usage and revenue caused Facebook shares to drop by 50 percent of their offering price. Zuckerberg admitted in September 2013 that the company had made a "bunch of missteps" in mobile.

THE IT SOLUTION >>> Facebook discovered that integrating ads directly into a user's flow of natural activities—in Facebook's case, the main feed where people view updates from friends—works far better than banners and pop-up ads. Although these "native ads" might be controversial, they appear to be advertising's most successful adaptation yet to mobile computing.

Facebook began running its ads not just in the right-hand section reserved for ads but also on its prime real estate: the news feed, where people spend most of their time on the social network. Facebook executives knew that this was a risky step—particularly when they extended the same type of ads to mobile as well. What if the ads in the news feed really annoyed people?

That fear did not materialize. Sponsored Stories got more clicks. However, the mobile ads got twice as many clicks and commanded nearly three times as much revenue from advertisers as ads on the desktop, according to a study by advertising agency TBG Digital. Within a short period of time, the mobile ads were grossing $500,000 per day.

Facebook then launched other mobile ads, including one that allowed makers of mobile apps to encourage users to install their games or programs. This step was an even bigger leap. It was the first ad in the mobile news feed that did not require advertisers to wait for a "like" or some other social action to create it. Advertisers instead could use Facebook's huge quantity of biographical data from user profiles to target likely prospects, as they already did with traditional ads.

This process worked as well. For instance, Cie Games used app installation ads to draw players for its first iPhone game, Car Town Streets. The cost of acquiring the ads was 40 percent lower using Facebook's ads than using those from other mobile ad networks. In addition, Walmart purchases 50 million mobile ads from Facebook annually.

THE RESULTS >>> From near zero in May 2012, revenue from mobile ads had increased to $305 million for the last three months of that year. That figure amounted to 23 percent of overall Facebook ad sales, and it helped to restore the value of Facebook shares to more than $30 by January 2013. For the fourth quarter of 2013, Facebook reported that mobile ads accounted for 53 percent of the company's total ad revenue, for a total of $1.24 billion.

Facebook's success has exploded several myths concerning mobile marketing. Advertisers often complain that they cannot run big, flashy ads on tiny screens. However, Facebook's mobile ads take up a larger part of the screen than desktop ads do, which is one reason why they attract so many clicks. In fact, an increasing number of mobile ads now contain photographs, and Facebook is actively looking to incorporate video into mobile ads.

Industry analysts worried that users might balk at ads mixed with posts from friends. So far, that has not happened. Research revealed that the ads reduced comments, likes, and other interaction with posts by only 2 percent, a decline that Facebook considers acceptable. However, Facebook will have to be careful not to overdo mobile ads to the point of overloading its users' feeds.

Despite this demonstrated success, Facebook is still far behind the mobile-ad revenue leader, Google. In 2013, Google earned $39 billion of the $118 billion—a total of 33 percent—spent globally on mobile ads.

Sources: Compiled from A. Campos, "Why Facebook Is Releasing News Feed Video Ads," *The Motley Fool*, March 17, 2014; Z. Terrelonge, "Facebook Officially Launches 15-Second 'Premium Video Ads,'" *Mobile Entertainment*, March 14, 2014; S. Parkerson, "New Premium Video Ads Are Facebook's Latest Move to Dominate Ad Dollars," *App Developer Magazine*, March 14, 2014; E. Price, "Prepare Yourself: Facebook Video Ads Are Headed Your Way Soon," *Engadget*, March 13, 2014; J. Edwards, "Facebook Is Powering Millions of App Downloads a Year," *Slate*, March 13, 2014; H. Weber, "Facebook Finally Launches Autoplaying Video Ads on Desktop and Mobile," *VentureBeat*, March 13, 2014; R. Tate, "Facebook Lures Developers with Mobile Ads and a Promise of Riches," *Wired*, March 12, 2014; D. Serfaty, "Why CMOs Must Change Their Plans for Facebook," *Forbes*, March 11, 2014; L. White, "Digital Ad Spend Quickly Shifting to Mobile: Are You Ready?" *Marketing Land*, February 27, 2014; M. Mawad, "Facebook Mobile Strength Breeds Apps in Hunt for Ad Dollars," *Bloomberg*, February 24, 2014; M. Charski, "Facebook, Twitter Retargeting Tools Appeal to Creators of Mobile Ads," *Data Informed*, February 18, 2014; R. Hof, "How Facebook Slew the Mobile Monster," *MIT Technology Review*, May 6, 2013; www.facebook.com, accessed March 18, 2014.

uestions

1. Explain why mobile ads are so effective on Facebook. Provide specific examples to support your answer.

2. You are accessing Facebook on your smartphone or tablet. Would ads placed directly into your news feed bother you? Why or why not?

3. You are accessing Facebook from your desktop computer. Would ads placed directly into your news feed bother you? Why or why not?

4. If there is a difference in your answers to questions 2 and 3 above, explain why.

INTERNSHIP ACTIVITY> ⊙ FIRST NOBLE BANK

Banking Industry

Mobile communications have changed our lives dramatically over the past 15 years. We have progressed from being connected to households by landline telephones to being connected to individuals by wireless devices. Wireless devices are much more than just phones. Often referred to as "smartphones," they enable us to stay connected via social media, text messages, video calls, photo sharing, e-mail, and yes, even phone calls. It is no surprise, then, that businesses are utilizing these powerful devices to reach out to customers.

For this Internship Activity, you will work for Jeremy Farr, Associate Vice President and IT Officer of First Noble Bank. Jeremy is particularly interested in learning about some of the new mobile developments his bank could use to allow their customers to access account information on the mobile Web or through mobile apps.

Below you will find a letter from Jeremy regarding this project.

To:	IT Intern
From:	Jeremy Farr
Subject:	Help with Mobile Banking Apps

Hello!

I want to begin by thanking you for the good work you have done for me during your internship. Now, I want to turn your attention to a topic that is of great interest to me.

I am very interested in learning how my bank can use mobile technologies to allow our customers to access their account information on their smartphones or tablets. Your job will be to research potential mobile app providers and offer feedback on the strengths and limitations of different partners (an example is D3 Banking). I would also like you to explore the mobile offerings of the banks in your local area, as well as those "big banks"—Chase, Nationwide, and so on—that serve customers on a national basis.

After you have developed a working knowledge of the mobile app functionality offered by the competition AND the mobile functionality offered by mobile app providers, identify the partners you feel would best position our bank to compete in the marketplace based on mobile app functionality.

Thanks in advance,
Jeremy

Note: All Web sites recommended in the letter from Jeremy are available at http://www.wiley.com/go/rainer/MIS3e/internship.

SPREADSHEET ACTIVITY > PIVOT TABLES

STEP 1 – Background

As you saw in the last exercise, sorting, filtering, and tables are very useful tools in a spreadsheet. Pivot tables are even more powerful than standard tables, in part because they enable users to "slice and dice" data in ways they otherwise could not.

A pivot table is comprised of data that are in tabular format with column headers. It allows you to move columns to rows and to choose how your data will be displayed: as sums, averages, counts, or other functions. There are four parts to a pivot table that are built out of the data headers.

Pivot tables are very complex, and the only way you can understand them is to see one. For a basic introduction to pivot tables, visit http://www.wiley.com/go/rainer/MIS3e/spreadsheet.

STEP 2 – Activity

Recall the sales data from the Chapter 9 activity where you learned to sort and filter the data. Now, imagine that you have been given the information requests as listed below. You will need to do more than sort and filter to find this information. A pivot table will be required to complete the following instructions.

1. First, find the sum of total sales for each product (saddle 1, saddle 2, and saddle 3) by region.
2. Second, help identify the overall top-performing sales representative. In Spreadsheet Activity 9,

Scylance and Krystyna achieved the highest total sales. Which one of them is the top seller by product?
3. Finally, determine the top two saddles in each market.

STEP 3 – Deliverable

Visit http://www.wiley.com/go/rainer/MIS3e/spreadsheet, and download the spreadsheet to complete the work listed in Step 2. After you have completed your work in the spreadsheet and answered the above questions, find one additional fact you find interesting. Create one last pivot table to support the final question you have decided to answer. Submit your spreadsheet with all four pivot tables.

Follow the instructions in the spreadsheet and submit your final work to your instructor.

Additional help with this spreadsheet skill is available in WileyPLUS. Open the "Microsoft Office 2013 Lab Manual Spreadsheet Module: Excel 2013," and review Lesson 14: Filters and Pivot Tables. Help is also available from the Microsoft Support Web site at the link shown above.

DATABASE ACTIVITY > ADVANCED REPORTS

STEP 1 – Background

The Chapter 9 activity taught you how to combine data from more than one table and to select the rows of combined data that you want. In this activity, you will learn how to create a report that uses a query, rather than tables, as its data source.

For this assignment, you will combine the selection and table-joining capabilities of queries with the layout and summary capabilities of reports. This combination creates a powerful tool for presenting data to businesspeople who need it.

STEP 2 – Activity

Visit http://www.wiley.com/go/rainer/MIS3e/database, and download the database linked for the Chapter 10 activity. This work will be an extension of the Chapter 9 activity. Open the Store Order Query, and add a column that will query for discarded orders. You do not want to see orders that were not complete on your report. Although this task is fairly simple, you will need to modify the formatting so that the report makes sense. When you remove all of the discarded orders,

you are left with a column that reports unneeded information. You can hide a column and still have it complete its query in the background.

You will need to use a combination of Design and Layout views to accomplish the above task. Create a new report that includes Customer Name, Order Date, and Order Total that is based on the updated Store Order Query. The report should summarize Order Total by customer. Name the report "CustomerInCity."

If you recall, the StoreOrderQry is Boston data. Recreate this report with Chicago data, and name it "ChicagoCityReport."

STEP 3 – Deliverable

Submit your report with both the enhanced Boston report and the Chicago report.

Additional help with this database skill is available in WileyPLUS. Open the "Microsoft Office 2013 Lab Manual Database Module: Access 2013," and review Lesson 11: Creating a Report Template, Lesson 12: Printing a Report, and Lesson 13: Modifying a Report Template. Help is also available from the Microsoft Support Web site linked at the URL listed in Step 2.

Information Systems within the Organization

CHAPTER OUTLINE

11.1 Transaction Processing Systems

11.2 Functional Area Information Systems

11.3 Enterprise Resource Planning (ERP) Systems

11.4 ERP Support for Business Processes

LEARNING OBJECTIVES >>>

11.1. Explain the purpose of transaction processing systems.

11.2. Explain the types of support that information systems can provide for each functional area of the organization.

11.3. Identify advantages and drawbacks to businesses implementing an enterprise resource planning system.

11.4. Describe the three main business processes supported by ERP systems.

OPENING CASE > The Lion King Roars Back

© Apples Eyes Studio / Shutterstock

The Lion King opened on Broadway in 1997 to critical acclaim. The play went on to win six Tony Awards, including best musical. Like many Broadway hit shows, *The Lion King* enjoyed increasing ticket sales early on, often grossing $1 million per week. Earnings eventually leveled off, however, as newer musicals such as *The Producers* (2001) became hot attractions. To reverse this trend, Disney actually discounted tickets to *The Lion King* for a period of time.

In 2006, Disney moved *The Lion King* from the New Amsterdam Theater to the slightly smaller Minskoff Theater to make way for its *Mary Poppins* musical. At this time, Disney executives were occupied with opening new musicals such as *The Little Mermaid*. The entertainment giant made the mistake of bundling those shows with *The Lion King* in their ads, even though the target audiences for the two shows were different. Ticket sales for *The Lion King* remained uneven, both before and after the 2008 recession. By March 2009 weekly gross revenues had declined to $813,000.

To reinvigorate ticket sales, in 2011 the show's producers, Disney Theatrical Productions, implemented a proprietary yield management system (YMS) (also known as dynamic pricing) to recommend the highest ticket prices that audiences would likely to pay for each of the 1,700 seats at every performance at the Minskoff. Although other shows employ YMSs to increase seat prices during tourist-heavy holiday weeks, only Disney has reached the level of yield management sophistication achieved by the airline and hotel industries. Disney uses its system to analyze and set prices based on demand and ticket purchasing patterns.

FIN

Yield management systems enable businesses to implement a variable pricing strategy, based on understanding, anticipating, and influencing consumer behavior to maximize revenue from a fixed, perishable resource (e.g., airline seats, hotel rooms, and theater seats). YMSs are designed to sell inventory to the right customer at the right time for the right price.

In the case of *The Lion King*, Disney's YMS analyzes historical data for 11.5 million audience members. It then recommends prices for different types of performances—for example, peak dates such as Christmas, off-peak dates such as a weeknight in February, and periods in between. Historical ticket demand for a particular week, for instance, will influence price recommendations for that week in subsequent years.

To help keep audience demand strong, Disney has made a highly unusual choice among Broadway hit shows. The company has factored in an upper ticket price limit of $227 in its YMS. This price is well below the top prices for blockbuster shows such as *The Book of Mormon* ($477), *Kinky Boots* ($349), and *Wicked* ($300). This pricing strategy provides at least three benefits: (1) It makes *The Lion King* relatively affordable for large groups and families. (2) It reduces the chance of buyer's remorse, which can generate negative word-of-mouth feedback. (3) It offers Disney the flexibility to raise prices over the long term.

Based on the results Disney obtained from its YMS, the company abandoned the traditional strategy of charging one price for entire sections of seats. Instead, the producers raise prices for busy weeks by making predictions based on the show's historical data. An interactive seating map accompanies the YMS, thus allowing customers to visually pick their seats. Disney has discovered that customers often choose better, pricier seats when they examine the seating chart.

How successful was Disney's yield management system? In 2013 *The Lion King* stunned Broadway by replacing *Wicked* as the Number 1 earner, a position it had not enjoyed for 10 years. By March 2014 the play was grossing $1.5 million per week. Additionally, consumer demand has grown. In 2013 the show attracted 700,000 theater goers, which was 50,000 more than in 2008.

Sources: Compiled from A. Phadnis, "SpiceJet Revenue Management GM Quits Two Days After Discount Sale," *Business Standard*, April 3, 2014; J. Gereben, "Dynamic Ticket Pricing," *San Francisco Classical Voice*, March 18, 2014; S. Sluis, "Dynamic Pricing Finds a Seat on Broadway," *Destination CRM*, March 17, 2014; P. Healy, "Ticket Pricing Puts 'Lion King' Atop Broadway's Circle of Life," *New York Times*, March 17, 2014; L. Homer, "3 Rules for Pricing Right," *TRG Arts*, October 16, 2013; C. Jones, "How Theater Ticket Prices Are Changing Like Airline Fares," *Chicago Tribune*, October 22, 2012; "Marriott Takes Revenue Management to the Next Level," *Marriott Press Release*, June 4, 2012; P. Healy, "Broadway Hits Make Most of Premium Pricing," *New York Times*, November 24, 2011; www.lionking.com, accessed April 8, 2014.

Questions

1. Why are yield management systems so important to the producers of Broadway shows? *Hint:* What is the value of an unsold seat once the curtain goes up?

2. Describe potential disadvantages of Disney's yield management system.

Introduction

The opening case illustrates the integral part that information systems (IS) play in an organization's success. Indeed, it is arguable that *The Lion King* might have finished its run on Broadway had Disney not implemented its yield management system. IS are everywhere, and they affect organizations in countless ways. Although IS are frequently discussed within the context of large organizational settings, they also play a critical role in small organizations.

It is important to note that "systems within organizations" do not have to be owned by the organization itself. Instead, organizations can deploy very productive IS that are owned by an external vendor. The key point here is that "systems within an organization" are intended to support internal processes, regardless of who actually owns the systems.

It is important for you to have a working knowledge of IS within your organization, for a variety of reasons. First, your job will require you to access corporate data that are supplied primarily by your firm's transaction processing systems and enterprise resource planning systems. Second, you will have a great deal of input into the format and content of the reports that you receive from these systems. Third, you will utilize the information contained in these reports to perform your job more productively.

This chapter will teach you about the various information systems that modern organizations utilize. You begin by considering transaction processing systems, the most fundamental organizational information systems. You continue with the functional area management information systems, and you conclude with enterprise resource planning systems.

11.1 Transaction Processing Systems

Millions (sometimes billions) of transactions occur in large organizations every day. A **transaction** is any business event that generates data worthy of being captured and stored in a database. Examples of transactions are a product manufactured, a service sold, a person hired, and a payroll check generated. In another example, when you are checking out of Walmart, each time the cashier swipes an item across the bar code reader is one transaction.

A **transaction processing system (TPS)** supports the monitoring, collection, storage, and processing of data from the organization's basic business transactions, each of which generates data. The TPS collects data continuously, typically in *real time*—that is, as soon as the data are generated—and it provides the input data for the corporate databases. The TPSs are critical to the success of any enterprise because they support core operations.

In the modern business world, TPSs are inputs for the functional area information systems and business intelligence systems, as well as business operations such as customer relationship management, knowledge management, and e-commerce. TPSs have to efficiently handle both high volumes of data and large variations in those volumes (e.g., during periods of peak processing). In addition, they must avoid errors and downtime, record results accurately and securely, and maintain privacy and security. FIGURE 11.1 illustrates how TPSs manage data. Consider these examples of how TPSs handle the complexities of transactional data:

- When more than one person or application program can access the database at the same time, the database has to be protected from errors resulting from overlapping updates. The most common error is losing the results of one of the updates.

- When processing a transaction involves more than one computer, the database and all users must be protected against inconsistencies arising from a failure of any component at any time. For example, an error that occurs at some point in an ATM withdrawal can enable a customer to receive cash, although the bank's computer indicates that he or she did not. (Conversely, a customer might not receive cash, although the bank's computer indicates that he or she did.)

- It must be possible to reverse a transaction in its entirety if it turns out to have been entered in error. It is also necessary to reverse a transaction when a customer returns a purchased item. For example, if you return a sweater that you have purchased, then the store must credit your credit card for the amount of the purchase, refund your cash, or offer you an in-store credit to purchase another item. In addition, the store must update its inventory.

- It is frequently important to preserve an audit trail. In fact, for certain transactions an audit trail may be legally required.

These and similar issues explain why organizations spend millions of dollars on expensive mainframe computers. In today's business environment, firms must have the dependability, reliability, and processing capacity of these computers to handle their transaction processing loads.

Regardless of the specific data processed by a TPS, the actual process tends to be standard, whether it occurs in a manufacturing firm, a service firm, or a government organization. As the first step in this procedure, people or sensors collect data, which are entered into the computer via any input device. Generally speaking, organizations try to automate the TPS data entry as much as possible because of the large volume involved, a process called *source data automation* (discussed in Plug IT In 2).

Next, the system processes data in one of two basic ways: batch processing and online

Figure 11.1 How transaction processing systems manage data.

processing. In **batch processing**, the firm collects data from transactions as they occur, placing them in groups or *batches*. The system then prepares and processes the batches periodically (say, every night).

In **online transaction processing (OLTP)**, business transactions are processed online as soon as they occur. For example, when you pay for an item at a store, the system records the sale by reducing the inventory on hand by one unit, increasing sales figures for the item by one unit, and increasing the store's cash position by the amount you paid. The system performs these tasks in real time by means of online technologies.

> **BEFORE** *YOU GO ON....*
>
> 1. Define TPS.
> 2. List the key functions of a TPS.

Apply The Concept 11.1

LEARNING OBJECTIVE 11.1 Explain the purpose of transaction processing systems.

STEP 1 – Background (This is what you are learning.)

Section 11.1 has explained that transaction processing systems (TPS) capture data and then automatically transmit those data to the various functional area systems. Most TPS are designed based on an organization's existing processes. To better understand how a TPS operates, you should consider the flow of data through the student application process.

STEP 2 – Activity (This is what you are doing.)

Visit http://www.wiley.com/go/rainer/MIS3e/applytheconcept, and click on the link provided for Apply the Concept 11.1. This link will take you to a Web page that describes the process of creating data flow diagrams (DFDs). The page uses the example of a college student application to demonstrate the flow of data through the organization. Review this description, and identify the transactions that take place in this process.

STEP 3 – Deliverable (This is what you turn in.)

Prepare a memo explaining the purpose of a TPS, incorporating the student application DFD. Submit your memo to your instructor.

11.2 Functional Area Information Systems

Each department or functional area within an organization has its own collection of application programs, or information systems. Each of these **functional area information systems** (FAISs) supports a particular functional area in the organization by increasing each area's internal efficiency and effectiveness. FAISs often convey information in a variety of reports, which you will see later in this chapter. Examples of FAISs are accounting IS, finance IS, production/operations management (POM) IS, marketing IS, and human resources IS.

As illustrated in FIGURE 11.1, the FAIS access data from the corporate databases. The following sections discuss the support that FAISs provide for these functional areas.

Information Systems for Accounting and Finance

A primary mission of the accounting and finance functional areas is to manage money flows into, within, and out of organizations. This mission is very broad because money is involved in all organizational functions. Therefore, accounting and finance information systems are very diverse and comprehensive. In this section, you focus on certain selected activities of the accounting/finance functional area.

Financial Planning and Budgeting. Appropriate management of financial assets is a major task in financial planning and budgeting. Managers must plan for both acquiring and utilizing resources.

- *Financial and economic forecasting.* Knowledge about the availability and cost of money is a key ingredient for successful financial planning. Cash flow projections are particularly important because they inform organizations what funds they need, when they need them, and how they will acquire them.

  Funds for operating organizations come from multiple sources, including stockholders' investments, bond sales, bank loans, sales of products and services, and income from investments. Decisions concerning funding for ongoing operations and for capital investment can be supported by decision support systems and business intelligence applications (discussed in Chapter 5), as well as expert systems (discussed in Plug IT In 5). In addition, numerous software packages for conducting economic and financial forecasting are available. Many of these packages can be downloaded from the Internet, some of them for free.

- *Budgeting.* An essential component of the accounting/finance function is the annual budget, which allocates the organization's financial resources among participants and activities. The budget allows management to distribute resources in the way that best supports the organization's mission and goals.

  Several software packages are available to support budget preparation and control and to facilitate communication among participants in the budget process. These packages can reduce the time involved in the budget process. Furthermore, they can automatically monitor exceptions for patterns and trends.

Managing Financial Transactions. Many accounting/finance software packages are integrated with other functional areas. For example, Peachtree by Sage (www.peachtree.com) offers a sales ledger, a purchase ledger, a cash book, sales order processing, invoicing, stock control, a fixed assets register, and more.

Companies involved in electronic commerce need to access customers' financial data (e.g., credit line), inventory levels, and manufacturing databases (to determine available capacity and place orders). For example, Microsoft Dynamics GP (formerly Great Plains Software) offers 50 modules that meet the most common financial, project, distribution, manufacturing, and e-business needs.

Organizations, business processes, and business activities operate with, and manage, financial transactions. Consider these examples:

- *Global stock exchanges.* Financial markets operate in global, 24/7/365, distributed electronic stock exchanges that use the Internet both to buy and sell stocks and to broadcast real-time stock prices.

- *Managing multiple currencies.* Global trade involves financial transactions that are carried out in different currencies. The conversion ratios of these currencies are constantly in flux. Financial and accounting systems utilize financial data from different countries, and they convert the currencies from and to any other currency in seconds. Reports based on these data, which formerly required several days to generate, can now be produced in only seconds. In addition to currency conversions, these systems manage multiple languages as well.

- *Virtual close.* Companies traditionally closed their books (accounting records) quarterly, usually to meet regulatory requirements. Today, many companies want to be able to close their books at any time, on very short notice. Information systems make it possible to close the books quickly in what is called a *virtual close.* This process provides almost real-time information on the organization's financial health.

- *Expense management* automation. *Expense management automation* (EMA) refers to systems that automate the data entry and processing of travel and entertainment expenses. EMA systems are Web-based applications that enable companies to quickly and consistently collect expense information, enforce company policies and contracts, and reduce unplanned purchases as well as airline and hotel expenses. They also allow companies to reimburse their employees more quickly because expense approvals are not delayed by poor documentation.

Investment Management. Organizations invest large amounts of money in stocks, bonds, real estate, and other assets. Managing these investments is a complex task, for several reasons. First, organizations have literally thousands of investment alternatives dispersed throughout the world to choose from. In addition, these investments are subject to complex regulations and tax laws, which vary from one location to another.

Investment decisions require managers to evaluate financial and economic reports provided by diverse institutions, including federal and state agencies, universities, research institutions, and financial services firms. In addition, thousands of Web sites provide financial data, many of them for free.

To monitor, interpret, and analyze the huge amounts of online financial data, financial analysts employ two major types of IT tools: (1) Internet search engines and (2) business intelligence and decision support software.

Control and Auditing. One major reason why organizations go out of business is their inability to forecast and/or secure a sufficient cash flow. Underestimating expenses, overspending, engaging in fraud, and mismanaging financial statements can lead to disaster. Consequently, it is essential that organizations effectively control their finances and financial statements. Let us examine some of the most common forms of financial control.

- *Budgetary control.* After an organization has finalized its annual budget, it divides those monies into monthly allocations. Managers at various levels monitor departmental expenditures and compare them against the budget and the operational progress of corporate plans.

- *Auditing.* Auditing has two basic purposes: (1) to monitor how the organization's monies are being spent and (2) to assess the organization's financial health. Internal auditing is performed by the organization's accounting/finance personnel. These employees also prepare for periodic external audits by outside CPA firms.

- *Financial ratio analysis.* Another major accounting/finance function is to monitor the company's financial health by assessing a set of financial ratios. Included here are liquidity ratios (the availability of cash to pay debt), activity ratios (how quickly a firm converts noncash assets to cash assets), debt ratios (measure the firm's ability to repay long-term debt), and profitability ratios (measure the firm's use of its assets and control of its expenses to generate an acceptable rate of return).

Information Systems for Marketing

It is impossible to overestimate the importance of customers to any organization. Therefore, any successful organization must understand its customers' needs and wants and then develop its marketing and advertising strategies around them. Information systems provide numerous types of support to the marketing function. In fact, customer-centric organizations are so important that we devote Chapter 12 to this topic.

Information Systems for Production/Operations Management

The POM function in an organization is responsible for the processes that transform inputs into useful outputs as well as for the overall operation of the business. Because of the breadth and variety of POM functions, you see only four here: in-house logistics and materials management, planning production and operation, computer-integrated manufacturing (CIM), and product lifecycle management (PLM).

The POM function is also responsible for managing the organization's supply chain. Because supply chain management is vital to the success of modern organizations, we address this topic in detail in Chapter 13.

In-House Logistics and Materials Management. Logistics management deals with ordering, purchasing, inbound logistics (receiving), and outbound logistics (shipping) activities. Related activities include inventory management and quality control.

Inventory Management. As the name suggests, inventory management determines how much inventory an organization should maintain. Both excessive inventory and insufficient inventory create problems. Overstocking can be expensive, because of

© paci77/iStockphoto

A "Quality Guarantee" requires data collection and analysis throughout production to maintain standards.

storage costs and the costs of spoilage and obsolescence. However, keeping insufficient inventory is also expensive, because of last-minute orders and lost sales.

Operations personnel make two basic decisions: when to order and how much to order. Inventory models, such as the economic order quantity (EOQ) model, support these decisions. A large number of commercial inventory software packages are available that automate the application of these models.

Many large companies allow their suppliers to monitor their inventory levels and ship products as they are needed. This strategy, called *vendor-managed inventory* (VMI), eliminates the need for the company to submit purchasing orders. We discuss VMI in Chapter 13.

Quality Control. Quality control systems used by manufacturing units provide information about the quality of incoming material and parts, as well as the quality of in-process semifinished and finished products. These systems record the results of all inspections and then compare these results with established metrics. They also generate periodic reports that contain information about quality—for example, the percentage of products that contain defects or that need to be reworked. Quality control data, collected by Web-based sensors, can be interpreted in real time. Alternatively, they can be stored in a database for future analysis.

Planning Production and Operations. In many firms, POM planning is supported by IT. POM planning has evolved from material requirements planning (MRP) to manufacturing resource planning (MRP II), to enterprise resource planning (ERP). We briefly discuss MRP and MRP II here, and we examine ERP in detail later in this chapter.

Inventory systems that use an EOQ approach are designed for items for which demand is completely independent—for example, the number of identical personal computers a computer manufacturer will sell. In manufacturing operations, however, the demand for some items is interdependent. Consider, for example, a company that makes three types of chairs, all of which use the same screws and bolts. In this case, the demand for screws and bolts depends on the total demand for all three types of chairs and their shipment schedules. The planning process that integrates production, purchasing, and inventory management of interdependent items is called *material requirements planning* (MRP).

MRP deals only with production scheduling and inventories. More complex planning also involves allocating related resources, such as money and labor. For these cases, more complex, integrated software, called *manufacturing resource planning* (MRP II), is available. MRP II integrates a firm's production, inventory management, purchasing, financing, and labor activities. Thus, MRP II adds functions to a regular MRP system. In fact, MRP II has evolved into enterprise resource planning.

Computer-Integrated Manufacturing. Computer-integrated manufacturing (CIM) (also called *digital manufacturing*) is an approach that integrates various automated factory systems. CIM has three basic goals: (1) to simplify all manufacturing technologies and techniques, (2) to automate as many of the manufacturing processes as possible, and (3) to integrate and coordinate all aspects of design, manufacturing, and related functions via computer systems.

Product Lifecycle Management. Even within a single organization, designing and developing new products can be expensive and time consuming. When multiple organizations are involved, the process can become very complex. *Product lifecycle management* (PLM) is a business strategy that enables manufacturers to share product-related data that support product design and development and supply chain operations. PLM applies Web-based collaborative technologies to product development. By integrating formerly disparate functions, such as a manufacturing process and the logistics that support it, PLM enables these functions to collaborate, essentially forming a single team that manages the product from its inception through its completion.

Information Systems for Human Resource Management

Initial human resource information system (HRIS) applications dealt primarily with transaction processing systems, such as managing benefits and keeping records of vacation days. As organizational systems have moved to intranets and the Web, so have HRIS applications.

Product Life Cycle.

Many HRIS applications are delivered via an HR portal. (See our discussion of LinkedIn in Chapter 8.) For example, numerous organizations use their Web portals to advertise job openings and to conduct online hiring and training. In this section, you consider how organizations are using IT to perform some key HR functions: recruitment, HR maintenance and development, and HR planning and management.

Recruitment. Recruitment involves finding potential employees, evaluating them, and deciding which ones to hire. Some companies are flooded with viable applicants; others have difficulty finding the right people. IT can be helpful in both cases. In addition, IT can assist in related activities such as testing and screening job applicants.

With millions of resumes available online (in particular, LinkedIn), it is not surprising that companies are trying to find appropriate candidates on the Web, usually with the help of specialized search engines. Companies also advertise hundreds of thousands of jobs on the Web. Online recruiting can reach more candidates, which may bring in better applicants. In addition, the costs of online recruitment are usually lower than traditional recruiting methods such as advertising in newspapers or in trade journals.

Human Resources Development. After employees are recruited, they become part of the corporate human resources pool, which means they must be evaluated and developed. IT provides support for these activities.

Most employees are periodically evaluated by their immediate supervisors. In addition, in some organizations, peers or subordinates also evaluate other employees. Evaluations are typically digitized, and they are used to support many decisions, ranging from rewards to transfers to layoffs.

IT also plays an important role in training and retraining. Some of the most innovative developments are taking place in the areas of intelligent computer-aided instruction and the application of multimedia support for instructional activities. For example, companies conduct much of their corporate training over their intranet or via the Web.

Human Resources Planning and Management. Managing human resources in large organizations requires extensive planning and detailed strategy. IT support is particularly valuable in the following three areas:

- *Payroll and employees' records.* The HR department is responsible for payroll preparation. This process is typically automated, meaning that paychecks are printed or money is transferred electronically into employees' bank accounts.

- *Benefits administration.* In return for their work contributions to their organizations, employees receive wages, bonuses, and various benefits. These benefits include healthcare and dental care, pension contributions (in a decreasing number of organizations), 401K contributions, wellness centers, and child care centers.

  Managing benefits is a complex task because multiple options are available and organizations typically allow employees to choose and trade off their benefits. In many organizations, employees can access the company portal to self-register for specific benefits.

- *Employee relationship management.* In their efforts to better manage employees, companies are developing *employee relationship management* (ERM) applications. A typical ERM application is a call center for employees' problems.

Table 11.1 provides an overview of the activities that the FAIS support. FIGURE 11.2 shows many of the information systems that support these five functional areas.

Reports

All information systems produce reports: transaction processing systems, functional area information systems, ERP systems, customer relationship management systems, business intelligence systems, and so on. We discuss reports here because they are so closely associated with FAIS and ERP systems. These reports generally fall into three categories: routine, ad hoc (on-demand), and exception.

Monthly sales report.

TABLE 11.1 Activities
Supported by Functional Area
Information Systems

Accounting and Finance

Financial planning—and cost of money
Budgeting—allocates financial resources among participants and activities
Capital budgeting—financing of asset acquisitions
Managing financial transactions
Handling multiple currencies
Virtual close—the ability to close the books at any time on short notice
Investment management—managing organizational investments in stocks, bonds, real estate, and other investment vehicles
Budgetary control—monitoring expenditures and comparing them against the budget
Auditing—ensuring the accuracy of the organization's financial transactions and assessing the condition of the organization's financial health
Payroll

Marketing and Sales

Customer relations—know who customers are and treat them like royalty
Customer profiles and preferences
Sales force automation—using software to automate the business tasks of sales, thereby improving the productivity of salespeople

Production/Operations and Logistics

Inventory management—when to order new inventory, how much inventory to order, and how much inventory to keep in stock
Quality control—controlling for defects in incoming material and defects in goods produced
Materials requirements planning—planning process that integrates production, purchasing, and inventory management of interdependent items (MRP)
Manufacturing resource planning—planning process that integrates an enterprise's production, inventory management, purchasing, financing, and labor activities (MRP II)
Just-in-time systems—a principle of production and inventory control in which materials and parts arrive precisely when and where needed for production (JIT)
Computer-integrated manufacturing—a manufacturing approach that integrates several computerized systems, such as computer-assisted design (CAD), computer-assisted manufacturing (CAM), MRP, and JIT
Product lifecycle management—business strategy that enables manufacturers to collaborate on product design and development efforts, using the Web

Human Resource Management

Recruitment—finding employees, testing them, and deciding which ones to hire
Performance evaluation—periodic evaluation by superiors
Training
Employee records
Benefits administration—retirement, disability, unemployment, and so on

Routine reports are produced at scheduled intervals. They range from hourly quality control reports to daily reports on absenteeism rates. Although routine reports are extremely valuable to an organization, managers frequently need special information that is not included in these reports. At other times, they need the information that is normally included in routine reports, but at different times ("I need the report today, for the last three days, not for one week").

Such out-of-the routine reports are called **ad hoc (on-demand) reports**. Ad hoc reports can also include requests for the following types of information:

- **Drill-down reports** display a greater level of detail. For example, a manager might examine sales by region and decide to "drill down" by focusing specifically on sales by store and then by salesperson.

- **Key indicator reports** summarize the performance of critical activities. For example, a chief financial officer might want to monitor cash flow and cash on hand.

- **Comparative reports** compare, for example, the performances of different business units or of a single unit during different times.

				Sales Forecasting, Advertising Planning	**STRATEGIC**
Profitability Planning	Financial Planning	Employment Planning, Outsourcing	Product Life Cycle Management	Sales Forecasting, Advertising Planning	**STRATEGIC**
Auditing, Budgeting	Investment Management	Benefits Administration, Performance Evaluation	Quality Control, Inventory Management	Customer Relations, Sales Force Automation	**TACTICAL**
Payroll, Accounts Payable, Accounts Receivable	Manage Cash, Manage Financial Transactions	Maintain Employee Records	Order Fulfillment, Order Processing	Set Pricing, Profile Customers	**OPERATIONAL**
ACCOUNTING	**FINANCE**	**HUMAN RESOURCES**	**PRODUCTION/ OPERATIONS**	**MARKETING**	

Figure 11.2 Examples of information systems supporting the functional areas.

Some managers prefer exception reports. **Exception reports** include only information that falls outside certain threshold standards. To implement *management by exception,* management first establishes performance standards. The company then creates systems to monitor performance (via the incoming data about business transactions such as expenditures), to compare actual performance to the standards, and to identify exceptions to the standards. The system alerts managers to the exceptions via exception reports.

Let us use sales as an example. First, management establishes sales quotas. The company then implements an FAIS that collects and analyzes all of the sales data. An exception report would identify only those cases where sales fell outside an established threshold—for example, more than 20 percent short of the quota. It would *not* report expenditures that fell *within* the accepted range of standards. By leaving out all "acceptable" performances, exception reports save managers time, thus helping them focus on problem areas.

BEFORE *YOU GO ON....*

1. Define a functional area information system and list its major characteristics.

2. How do information systems benefit the finance and accounting functional area?

3. Explain how POM personnel use information systems to perform their jobs more effectively and efficiently.

4. What are the most important HRIS applications?

5. Compare and contrast the three basic types of reports.

Apply The Concept 11.2

LEARNING OBJECTIVE 11.2 Explain the types of support that information systems can provide for each functional area of the organization.

STEP 1 – Background

Section 11.2 introduced you to the concept of functional area information systems (FAIS). As you can see, every area of business has processes in place that define how data are stored, analyzed, applied, and distributed across the area. For example, inventory management is easy to manage with a computer system because it involves simply keeping track of your materials and products. However, when you integrate inventory management with production and operations management (POM), you have a very effective functional system that supports the internal production line.

Visit http://www.wiley.com/go/rainer/MIS3e/applytheconcept, and click on the link provided for Apply the Concept 11.2. You will be directed to four Web sites that present real-world examples of the information systems discussed in this section. Read over them, and look for any specific material that you can tie back into the concepts covered in the chapter.

STEP 3 – Deliverable

Prepare a report that explains the types of support the IS reviewed in Step 2 can provide for each functional area within an organization. Submit your report to your instructor.

11.3 Enterprise Resource Planning Systems

Historically, the functional area information systems were developed independent of one another, resulting in *information silos*. These silos did not communicate well with one another, and this lack of communication and integration made organizations less efficient. This inefficiency was particularly evident in business processes that involve more than one functional area, such as procurement and fulfillment.

Enterprise resource planning (ERP) systems are designed to correct a lack of communication among the functional area IS. ERP systems resolve this problem by tightly integrating the functional area IS via a common database. For this reason, experts credit ERP systems with greatly increasing organizational productivity. **ERP systems** adopt a business process view of the overall organization to integrate the planning, management, and use of all of an organization's resources, employing a common software platform and database.

The major objectives of ERP systems are to tightly integrate the functional areas of the organization and to enable information to flow seamlessly across them. Tight integration means that changes in one functional area are immediately reflected in all other pertinent functional areas. In essence, ERP systems provide the information necessary to control the business processes of the organization.

It is important to understand here that ERP systems are an evolution of FAIS. That is, ERP systems have much the same functionality as FAIS, and they produce the same reports. ERP systems simply integrate the functions of the individual FAIS.

Although some companies have developed their own ERP systems, most organizations use commercially available ERP software. The leading ERP software vendor is SAP (www.sap.com). Other major vendors include Oracle (www.oracle.com) and PeopleSoft (www.peoplesoft.com), now an Oracle company. (With more than 700 customers, PeopleSoft is the market leader in higher education). For up-to-date information on ERP software, visit http://erp.ittoolbox.com.

Although implementing ERP systems can be difficult because they are large and complicated, many companies have done so successfully. IT's About Business 11.1 recounts a successful ERP deployment at a large German engineering company.

IT'S ABOUT BUSINESS 11.1

GEA Group Uses SAP for Financial Reporting

With 25,000 employees worldwide, GEA Group (GEA) (www.gea.com) develops, produces, and sells innovative and energy-efficient systems in the food and energy industries. The company's goals are to help its customers process food using highly efficient methods and to conserve scarce energy resources. Sales in these two industries account for 70 percent of the company's revenue, which totaled approximately $8 billion in 2013.

As a public corporation whose stock is listed on the MDAX index (a stock index that lists German companies), GEA is required to publish its quarterly, midyear, and year-end financial statements by specific deadlines. GEA

© lukas_zb/iStockphoto

provides the consolidated balance sheet, profit and loss (P&L) statement, cash flow statement, statement of stockholders' equity, notes concerning these statements, as well as management reporting, the firm's business outlook, and other stock-related information.

Creating these financial statements was a time-consuming process. At GEA, the responsibility for this task lies with a relatively small team within the accounting department, which is based in the company's headquarters located in Dusseldorf, Germany. The team begins by gathering the required financial data from the business divisions, which it then consolidates to create a draft report. As new and more current data and financial figures are added on an ongoing basis, the team constantly has to modify and update the content and the graphics of its reports.

This process was extremely time consuming, because most of the processes for creating the reports were manual and were not standardized. Furthermore, manual data manipulation carries with it a high risk of introducing errors and of circulating different versions of the same report. In short, GEA did not have a satisfactory solution for the inherent weaknesses in the processes it used to generate its financial statements.

To resolve these problems, GEA implemented the SAP (www.sap.com) Disclosure Management application, one of the SAP solutions for enterprise performance management. This software delivers all of the financial data and information necessary for preparing financial statements. It provides GEA with a consistent data repository, which enables the firm to set up end-to-end workflows (business processes) in accounting. In addition, it enables multiple users to process a single report simultaneously, in parallel.

In collaboration with SAP partner cundus AG, the accounting department at GEA successfully implemented the new solution in only eight weeks. The approximately 20 users required only minimal training because the application is user-friendly and straightforward. Many of the functions are self-explanatory. The implementation took place in parallel with the generation of the firm's quarterly financial statements.

GEA now gathers all of the data and information necessary for creating financial statements and manages it in the accounting department. For the team members, many processes have become simpler. All of the data required to produce the financial reports—the balance sheet figures, notes, text, graphics, and tables from the business divisions—now flow seamlessly into the SAP solution.

At the same time, all of the steps of the process are documented in an audit-compliant manner, while built-in authorization requirements precisely govern access rights. Therefore, both the company's management and external auditors can use the audit trail created by the solution to track the source of the financial figures and to determine who changed them and when.

Furthermore, GEA can now produce reports in all of the desired and required formats—including Microsoft Word, Microsoft Excel, Microsoft PowerPoint, and Adobe PDF files. The simplification of the process extends to the external graphic design agency, which can now create the print version of the financial statements more quickly.

The GEA accounting department now has a clear view of the current status of a report at any time. The result has been a tangible improvement in the flow of information to GEA's management. The new solution also offers integrated version control, a feature that prevents multiple versions of the same report from being circulated.

Thanks to the SAP solution, GEA can create their financial reports 20 percent faster than previously. As a result, the company is better able to meet the increasingly tough legal requirements within Germany and abroad regarding timely external reporting.

Sources: Compiled from "GEA Revenue and Profit Hit New Record High in 2013," *GEA Press Release*, 2014; "Innovating for Sustainable Business Practices," *SAP Customer Success Story*, 2014; www.gea.com, accessed April 9, 2014.

Questions

1. Discuss the reasons why financial reports must be timely.

2. Explain how SAP enabled the GEA Group to produce their financial reports in an efficient, timely manner.

3. What are the advantages of the SAP solution to the GEA Group?

ERP II Systems

ERP systems were originally deployed to facilitate business processes associated with manufacturing, such as raw materials management, inventory control, order entry, and distribution. However, these early ERP systems did not extend to other functional areas, such as sales and marketing. They also did not include any customer relationship management (CRM) capabilities that enable organizations to capture customer-specific information. Finally, they did not provide Web-enabled customer service or order fulfillment.

Over time, ERP systems evolved to include administrative, sales, marketing, and human resources processes. Companies now employ an enterprisewide approach to ERP that utilizes the Web and connects all facets of the value chain. (You might want to review our discussion of value chains in Chapter 2.) These systems are called ERP II.

ERP II systems are interorganizational ERP systems that provide Web-enabled links among a company's key business systems—such as inventory and production—and its customers, suppliers, distributors, and other relevant parties. These links integrate internal-facing ERP

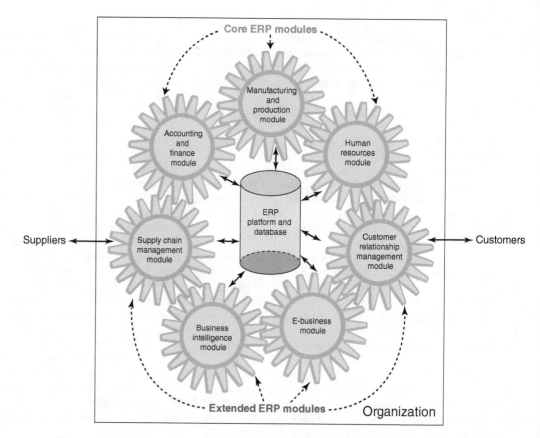

Figure 11.3 ERP II system.

applications with the external-focused applications of supply chain management and customer relationship management. FIGURE 11.3 illustrates the organization and functions of an ERP II system.

The various functions of ERP II systems are now delivered as e-business suites. The major ERP vendors have developed modular, Web-enabled software suites that integrate ERP, customer relationship management, supply chain management, procurement, decision support, enterprise portals, and other business applications and functions. Examples are Oracle's e-Business Suite and SAP's mySAP. The goal of these systems is to enable companies to execute most of their business processes using a single Web-enabled system of integrated software rather than a variety of separate e-business applications.

ERP II systems include a variety of modules that are divided into core ERP modules—financial management, operations management, and human resource management—and extended ERP modules—customer relationship management, supply chain management, business intelligence, and e-business. If a system does not have the core ERP modules, then it is not a legitimate ERP system. The extended ERP modules, in contrast, are optional. Table 11.2 describes each of these modules.

Benefits and Limitation of ERP Systems

ERP systems can generate significant business benefits for an organization. The major benefits fall into the following categories:

- *Organizational flexibility and agility.* As you have seen, ERP systems break down many former departmental and functional silos of business processes, information systems, and information resources. In this way, they make organizations more flexible, agile, and adaptive. The organizations can therefore respond quickly to changing business conditions and capitalize on new business opportunities.

- *Decision support.* ERP systems provide essential information on business performance across functional areas. This information significantly improves managers' ability to make better, more timely decisions.

TABLE 11.2 ERP Modules

CORE ERP MODULES

Financial Management. These modules support accounting, financial reporting, performance management, and corporate governance. They manage accounting data and financial processes such as general ledger, accounts payable, accounts receivable, fixed assets, cash management and forecasting, product-cost accounting, cost-center accounting, asset accounting, tax accounting, credit management, budgeting, and asset management.

Operations Management. These modules manage the various aspects of production planning and execution such as demand forecasting, procurement, inventory management, materials purchasing, shipping, production planning, production scheduling, materials requirements planning, quality control, distribution, transportation, and plant and equipment maintenance.

Human Resource Management. These modules support personnel administration (including workforce planning, employee recruitment, assignment tracking, personnel planning and development, and performance management and reviews), time accounting, payroll, compensation, benefits accounting, and regulatory requirements.

EXTENDED ERP MODULES

Customer Relationship Management. (Discussed in detail in Chapter 12.) These modules support all aspects of a customer's relationship with the organization. They help the organization to increase customer loyalty and retention, and thus improve its profitability. They also provide an integrated view of customer data and interactions, helping organizations to be more responsive to customer needs.

Supply Chain Management. (Discussed in detail in Chapter 13.) These modules manage the information flows between and among stages in a supply chain to maximize supply chain efficiency and effectiveness. They help organizations plan, schedule, control, and optimize the supply chain from the acquisition of raw materials to the receipt of finished goods by customers.

Business Intelligence. (Discussed in detail in Chapter 5.) These modules collect information used throughout the organization, organize it, and apply analytical tools to assist managers with decision making.

E-Business. (Discussed in detail in Chapter 9.) Customers and suppliers demand access to ERP information including order status, inventory levels, and invoice reconciliation. Furthermore, they want this information in a simplified format that can be accessed via the Web. As a result, these modules provide two channels of access into ERP system information—one channel for customers (B2C) and one for suppliers and partners (B2B).

- *Quality and efficiency.* ERP systems integrate and improve an organization's business processes, generating significant improvements in the quality of production, distribution, and customer service.

Despite all of their benefits, however, ERP systems do have drawbacks. The major limitations of ERP implementations include the following:

The business processes in ERP software are often predefined by the best practices that the ERP vendor has developed. *Best practices* are the most successful solutions or problem-solving methods for achieving a business objective. As a result, companies may need to change their existing business processes to fit the predefined business processes incorporated into the ERP software. For companies with well-established procedures, this requirement can create serious problems, especially if employees do not want to abandon their old ways of working and therefore resist the changes.

At the same time, however, an ERP implementation can provide an opportunity to improve and in some cases completely redesign inefficient, ineffective, or outdated procedures. In fact, many companies benefit from implementing best practices for their accounting, finance, and human resource processes, as well as other support activities that companies do not consider a source of competitive advantage.

Recall from Chapter 2, however, that different companies organize their value chains in different configurations to transform inputs into valuable outputs and achieve competitive advantage. Therefore, although the vendor's best practices, by definition, are appropriate for most organizations, they might not be the "best" one for your company if they change those processes that give you competitive advantage.

ERP systems can be extremely complex, expensive, and time consuming to implement. (We discuss the implementation of ERP systems in detail in the next section.) In fact, the costs and risks of failure in implementing a new ERP system are substantial. Quite a few companies have experienced costly ERP implementation failures. Specifically, they have suffered losses in revenue, profits, and market share when core business processes and information systems failed or did not work properly. In many cases, orders and shipments were lost, inventory changes were not recorded correctly, and unreliable inventory levels caused major stock outs. Companies such as Hershey Foods, Nike, A-DEC, and Connecticut General sustained losses in amounts up to hundreds of millions of dollars. In the case of FoxMeyer Drugs, a $5 billion pharmaceutical wholesaler, the ERP implementation was so poorly executed that the company had to file for bankruptcy protection.

In almost every ERP implementation failure, the company's business managers and IT professionals underestimated the complexity of the planning, development, and training that were required to prepare for a new ERP system that would fundamentally transform their business processes and information systems. The following are the major causes of ERP implementation failure:

- Failure to involve affected employees in the planning and development phases and in change management processes
- Trying to accomplish too much too fast in the conversion process
- Insufficient training in the new work tasks required by the ERP system
- The failure to perform proper data conversion and testing for the new system

Implementing ERP Systems

Companies can implement ERP systems by using either on-premise software or software-as-a-service (SaaS). We differentiate between these two methods in detail in Plug IT In 4.

On-Premise ERP Implementation. Depending on the types of value chain processes managed by the ERP system and a company's specific value chain, there are three strategic approaches to implementing an on-premise ERP system:

The vanilla approach: In this approach, a company implements a standard ERP package, using the package's built-in configuration options. When the system is implemented in this way, it will deviate only minimally from the package's standardized settings. The vanilla approach can enable the company to perform the implementation more quickly. However, the extent to which the software is adapted to the organization's specific processes is limited. Fortunately, a vanilla implementation provides general functions that can support the firm's common business processes with relative ease, even if they are not a perfect fit for those processes.

The custom approach: In this approach, a company implements a more customized ERP system by developing new ERP functions designed specifically for that firm. Decisions concerning the ERP's degree of customization are specific to each organization. To utilize the custom approach, the organization must carefully analyze its existing business processes to develop a system that conforms to the organization's particular characteristics and processes. In addition, customization is expensive and risky because computer code must be written and updated every time a new version of the ERP software is released. Going further, if the customization does not perfectly match the organization's needs, then the system can be very difficult to use.

The best of breed approach: This approach combines the benefits of the vanilla and customized systems while avoiding the extensive costs and risks associated with complete customization. Companies that adopt this approach mix and match core ERP modules as well as other extended ERP modules from different software providers to best fit their unique internal processes and value chains. Thus, a company may choose several core ERP modules from an established vendor to take advantage of industry best practices—for example, for financial management and human resource management. At the same time, it may also choose specialized software to support its unique business processes—for example, for manufacturing, warehousing, and distribution. Sometimes companies arrive at the best of breed approach the hard way. For example, Dell wasted millions of dollars trying to customize an integrated ERP system from a major vendor to match its unique processes before it realized that a smaller, more flexible system that integrated well with other corporate applications was the answer.

Software-as-a-Service ERP Implementation. Companies can acquire ERP systems without having to buy a complete software solution (i.e., on-premise ERP implementation). Many organizations are utilizing software-as-a-service (SaaS) (discussed in Chapter 14 and Plug IT In 4) to acquire cloud-based ERP systems. (We discuss cloud computing in Plug IT In 4.)

In this business model, the company rents the software from an ERP vendor who offers its products over the Internet using the SaaS model. The ERP cloud vendor manages software updates and is responsible for the system's security and availability.

Cloud-based ERP systems can be a perfect fit for some companies. For instance, companies that cannot afford to make large investments in IT, yet already have relatively structured business processes that need to be tightly integrated, might benefit from cloud computing.

The relationship between the company and the cloud vendor is regulated by contracts and by service level agreements (SLAs). (We discuss SLAs in Chapter 14.) The SLAs define the characteristics and quality of service; for instance, a guaranteed uptime, or the percentage of time that the system is available. Cloud vendors that fail to meet these conditions can face penalties.

The decision about whether to use on-premise ERP or SaaS ERP is specific to each organization, and it depends on how the organization evaluates a series of advantages and disadvantages. The following are the three major advantages of using a cloud-based ERP system:

- The system can be used from any location that provides Internet access. Consequently, users can work from any location using online shared and centralized resources (data and databases). Users access the ERP system via a secure virtual private network (VPN) connection (discussed in Chapter 4) with the provider.

- Companies using cloud-based ERP avoid the initial hardware and software expenses that are typical of on-premise implementations. For instance, to run SAP on-premise, a company must purchase SAP software as well as a license to use SAP. The magnitude of this investment can hinder small- to medium-sized enterprises (SMEs) from adopting ERP.

- Cloud-based ERP solutions are scalable, meaning it is possible to extend ERP support to new business processes and new business partners (e.g., suppliers) by purchasing new ERP modules.

There are also disadvantages of adopting cloud-based ERP systems that a company must carefully evaluate. The following are the three major disadvantages of using a cloud-based ERP system:

- It is not clear whether cloud-based ERP systems are more secure than on-premise systems. In fact, a 2012 survey conducted by North Bridge Venture Partners indicated that security was the primary reason why organizations did not adopt cloud-based ERP.

- Companies that adopt cloud-based ERP systems sacrifice their control over a strategic IT resource. For this reason, some companies prefer to implement an on-premise ERP system, utilizing a strong in-house IT department that can directly manage the system.

- A third disadvantage is a direct consequence of the lack of control over IT resources. This disadvantage occurs when the ERP system experiences problems; for example, some ERP functions are temporarily slow or are not available. In such cases, having an internal IT department that can solve problems immediately rather than dealing with the cloud vendor's system support can speed up the system recovery process.

This situation is particularly important for technology-intensive companies. In such companies, IT is crucial to conduct any kind of business with customers.

Examples are e-commerce companies, banks, and government organizations that manage emergencies or situations that might involve individual and national security (e.g., healthcare organizations, police, homeland security department, antiterrorism units, and others).

Finally, slow or unavailable software from a cloud-based ERP vendor creates business continuity problems for the client. (We discuss business continuity in Chapter 7.) That is, a sudden system problem or failure makes it impossible for the firm to operate. Companies lose money when they lose business continuity because customers cannot be serviced and employees cannot do their jobs. A loss of business continuity also damages the company's reputation because customers lose trust in the firm.

Enterprise Application Integration

For some organizations, integrated ERP systems are not appropriate. This situation is particularly true for companies that find the process of converting from their existing system too difficult or time consuming.

Such companies, however, may still have isolated information systems that need to be connected with one another. To accomplish this task, these companies can use enterprise application integration. An **enterprise application integration (EAI) system** integrates existing systems by providing software, called *middleware*, that connects multiple applications. In essence, the EAI system allows existing applications to communicate and share data, thereby enabling organizations to utilize existing applications while eliminating many of the problems caused by isolated information systems. EAI systems also support implementation of "best of breed" ERP solutions by connecting software modules from different vendors.

BEFORE *YOU GO ON....*

1. Define ERP, and describe its functions.
2. What are ERP II systems?
3. Differentiate between core ERP modules and extended ERP modules.
4. List some drawbacks of ERP software.
5. Highlight the differences between ERP configuration, customization, and best of breed implementation strategies.

Apply The Concept 11.3

LEARNING OBJECTIVE 11.3 Identify advantages and drawbacks to businesses implementing an enterprise resource planning system.

STEP 1 – Background

Section 11.3 explained that enterprise resource planning (ERP) works toward removing information silos within an organization by implementing a single system to support all of the functional areas. One example of an ERP system is SAP Business One. SAP is an industry-leading ERP company. In this activity you will consider the advantages and drawbacks of using an ERP such as SAP.

STEP 2 – Activity

Visit http://www.wiley.com/go/rainer/MIS3e/applytheconcept, and click on the link provided for Apply the Concept 11.3. This link will take you to a YouTube video titled "SAP-Business-One.wmv" by user "angeltechdotit."

As you watch the video, consider how many departments the representative would have to contact to find the information that SAP Business One can present in just a few moments. If this organization operated out of silos, the representative would have to take extensive notes, visit multiple departments, and call the customer back at a later time with the answers.

STEP 3 – Deliverable

After considering how complicated it would be for OEC to handle the customer's requests without an ERP, identify the advantages and drawbacks to OEC of using the SAP Business One ERP. Submit your thoughts to your professor.

11.4 ERP Support for Business Processes

ERP systems effectively support a number of standard business processes. In particular, ERP systems manage end-to-end, cross-departmental processes. A **cross-departmental process** is one that (1) originates in one department and ends in a different department or (2) originates and ends in the same department but involves other departments.

The Procurement, Fulfillment, and Production Processes

The following are the three prominent examples of cross-departmental processes:

- The *procurement process*, which originates in the warehouse department (need to buy) and ends in the accounting department (send payment)
- The *fulfillment process*, which originates in the sales department (customer request to buy) and ends in the accounting department (receive payment)
- The *production process*, which originates and ends in the warehouse department (need to produce and reception of finished goods) but involves the production department as well

These three processes are examined in more detail in the following sections, focusing on the steps that are specific to each one.

The Procurement Process.

The **procurement process** originates when a company needs to acquire goods or services from external sources, and it concludes when the company receives and pays for them. Let's consider a procurement process where the company needs to acquire physical goods. This process involves three main departments—Warehouse, Purchasing, and Accounting—and it consists of the following steps:

- The process originates in the Warehouse department, which generates a purchase requisition to buy the needed products.
- The Warehouse forwards the requisition to the Purchasing department, which creates a purchase order (PO) and forwards it to a vendor. Generally, companies can choose from a number of vendors, and they select the one that best meets their requirements in terms of convenience, speed, reliability, and/or other characteristics.
- After the company places the order, it receives the goods in its Warehouse department, where someone physically checks the delivery to make certain that it corresponds to what the company ordered. He or she performs this task by comparing a packing list attached to the shipment against the PO.
- If the shipment matches the order, then the Warehouse issues a goods receipt document.
- At the same time or shortly thereafter, the Accounting department receives an invoice from the vendor. Accounting then checks that the PO, the goods receipt document, and the invoice match. This process is called the *three-way-match*.
- After Accounting verifies the match, it processes the payment and sends it to the vendor.

FIGURE 11.4 illustrates the procurement process.

The Order Fulfillment Process.

In contrast to procurement, in which the company purchases goods from a vendor, in the **order fulfillment process**, also known as the order-to-cash process, the company sells goods to a customer. Fulfillment originates when the company receives a customer order, and it concludes when the company receives a payment from the customer.

Figure 11.4 Departments and documents flow in the procurement process.

The fulfillment process can follow two basic strategies: sell-from-stock and configure-to-order. *Sell-from-stock* involves fulfilling customer orders directly using goods that are in the warehouse (stock). These goods are standard, meaning that the company does not customize them for buyers. In contrast, in *configure-to-order*, the company customizes the product in response to a customer request.

A fulfillment process involves three main departments: Sales, Warehouse, and Accounting. This process includes the following steps:

- The Sales department receives a customer inquiry, which essentially is a request for information concerning the availability and price of a specific good. (We restrict our discussion here to fulfilling a customer order for physical goods rather than services.)
- After Sales receives the inquiry, it issues a quotation that indicates availability and price.
- If the customer agrees to the price and terms, then Sales creates a customer purchase order (PO) and a sales order.
- Sales forwards the sales order to the Warehouse. The sales order is an interdepartmental document that helps the company keep track of the internal processes that are involved in fulfilling a specific customer order. In addition, it provides details of the quantity, price, and other characteristics of the product.
- The Warehouse prepares the shipment and produces two other internal documents: the picking document, which it uses to remove goods from the Warehouse, and the packing list, which accompanies the shipment and provides details about the delivery.
- At the same time, Accounting issues an invoice for the customer.
- The process concludes when Accounting receives a payment that is consistent with the invoice.

FIGURE 11.5 shows the fulfillment process. Note that it applies to both sell-from-stock and configure-to-order, because the basic steps are the same for both strategies.

The Production Process. The **production process** does not occur in all companies because not all companies produce physical goods. In fact, many businesses limit their activities to buying (procurement) and selling products (e.g., retailers).

The production process can follow two different strategies: make-to-stock and make-to-order. (See the discussion of the pull model and the push model in Chapter 13.) *Make-to-stock* occurs when the company produces goods to create or increase an *inventory*; that is, finished products that are stored in the warehouse and are available for sales. In contrast, *make-to-order* occurs when production is generated by a specific customer order.

Manufacturing companies that produce their own goods manage their interdepartmental production process across the Production and Warehouse departments. The production process involves the following steps:

- The Warehouse department issues a planned order when the company needs to produce a finished product, either because the Warehouse has insufficient inventory or because the customer placed a specific order for goods that are not currently in stock.
- Once the planned order reaches Production, the production controller authorizes the order and issues a production order, which is a written authorization to start the production of a certain amount of a specific product.

Figure 11.5 Departments and documents flow in the fulfillment process.

Figure 11.6 Departments and documents flow in the production process.

- To assemble a finished product, Production requires a number of materials (or parts). To acquire these materials, Production generates a material withdrawal slip, which lists all of the needed parts, and forwards it to the Warehouse.

- If the parts are available in the Warehouse, then the Warehouse delivers them to Production. If the parts are not available, then the company must purchase them via the procurement process.

- After Production has created the products, it updates the production order specifying that, as planned, a specific number of units of product can now be shipped to the Warehouse.

- As soon as the Warehouse receives the finished goods, it issues a goods receipt document that certifies how many units of a product it received that are available for sales.

This overview of the Production process is a highly simplified one. In reality, the process is very complex, and it frequently involves additional steps. In addition, ERP systems collect a number of other documents and pieces of information such as the bill of materials (a list of all materials needed to assemble a finished product), the list of work centers (locations where the production takes place), and the product routing (production steps). All of these topics require an in-depth analysis of the production process and are therefore beyond the scope of our discussion here. FIGURE 11.6 illustrates the production process.

A number of events can occur that create exceptions or deviations in the procurement, fulfillment, and production processes. Deviations may include the following:

- A delay in the receipt of products
- Issues related to an unsuccessful three-way-match regarding a shipment and its associated invoice (procurement)
- Rejection of a quotation
- A delay in a shipment
- A mistake in preparing the shipment or in invoicing the customer (fulfillment)
- Overproduction of a product
- Reception of parts that cannot be used in the production process
- Nonavailability of certain parts from a supplier

Companies use ERP systems to manage procurement, fulfillment, and production because these systems track all of the events that occur within each process. Furthermore, the system stores all of the documents created in each step of each process in a centralized database, where they are available as needed in real time. Therefore, any exceptions or mistakes made during one or more interdepartmental processes are handled right away by simply querying the ERP system and retrieving a specific document or piece of information that needs to be revised or examined more carefully. Therefore, it is important to follow each step in each process and to register the corresponding document into the ERP system.

FIGURE 11.7 portrays the three cross-functional business processes we just discussed. It specifically highlights the integration of the three processes, which is made possible by ERP systems.

Figure 11.7 Integrated processes with ERP systems.

Interorganizational Processes: ERP with SCM and CRM

Although the procurement and the fulfillment processes involve suppliers and customers, they are considered (together with the production process) intraorganizational processes because they originate and conclude within the company. However, ERP systems can also manage processes that originate in one company and conclude in another company. These processes are called *interorganizational processes*, and they typically involve supply chain management (SCM) and customer relationship management (CRM) systems. You can find a more detailed description of CRM in Chapter 12 and SCM in Chapter 13. Here, we focus on the integration of these processes within a firm's industry value chain.

SCM and CRM processes help multiple firms in an industry coordinate activities such as the production-to-sale of goods and services. Let's consider a chain of grocery stores whose supply chain must properly manage perishable goods. On the one hand, store managers need to stock only the amount of perishable products that they are reasonably sure they will sell before the products' expiration dates. On the other hand, they do not want to run out of stock of any products that customers need.

ERP SCM systems have the capability to place automatic requests to buy fresh perishable products from suppliers in real time. That is, as each perishable product is purchased, the system captures data on that purchase, adjusts store inventory levels, and transmits these data to the grocery chain's warehouse as well as the products' vendors. The system executes this process by connecting the point-of-sale barcode scanning system with the Warehouse and Accounting departments, as well as with the vendors' systems. In addition, SCM systems utilize historical data to predict when fresh products need to be ordered before the store's supply becomes too low.

ERP CRM systems also benefit businesses by generating forecasting analyses of product consumption based on critical variables such as geographical area, season, day of the week, and type of customer. These analyses help grocery stores coordinate their supply chains to meet customer needs for perishable products. Going further, CRM systems identify particular customer needs and then utilize this information to suggest specific product campaigns. These campaigns can transform a potential demand into sales opportunities, and convert sales opportunities into sales quotations and sales orders. This process is called the *demand-to-order* process.

BEFORE YOU GO ON....

1. What are the three main intraorganizational processes that are typically supported by ERP systems?

2. Why is it important that all steps in each process generate a document that is stored in the ERP system?

3. What is the difference between intraorganizational and interorganizational processes?

4. What are the two main ES systems that support interorganizational processes?

Apply The Concept 11.4

LEARNING OBJECTIVE 11.4 Describe the three main business processes supported by ERP systems.

STEP 1 – Background

We have discussed reports that you can receive from TPS, FAIS, and ERP systems earlier in this chapter. In particular, these reports truly are the power of an ERP. Getting the right information to the right person at the right time to make the right decision is the underlying purpose for installing and utilizing an ERP. Recall from earlier in the text that managers need IT decision-support tools because decisions are becoming more complex, there is less time to make decisions, there are more options, and the costs of making incorrect decisions are increasing.

STEP 2 – Activity

Visit http://www.wiley.com/go/rainer/MIS3e/applytheconcept, and click on the link provided for Apply the Concept 11.4. This link will take you to a YouTube video titled "Phoebus ERP—Customized Dashboard" by user "kinhvan69." This video will introduce you to the dashboard tool provided by Phoebus, which individual users can customize to provide the specific information they need. This type of dashboard pulls together the many reports you have learned about in this chapter.

As you watch the video, look for examples of the three major types of processes (procurement, fulfillment, and production) that are supported by ERP systems as discussed in this section.

STEP 3 – Deliverable

Discuss the three major types of processes and the ways that an ERP can support them. Use what you learned in the dashboard video to discuss the types of information that could be presented in a dashboard to support these processes.

What's in for ME?

 FOR THE ACCOUNTING MAJOR

Understanding the functions and outputs of TPSs effectively is a major concern of any accountant. It is also necessary to understand the various activities of all functional areas and how they are interconnected. Accounting information systems are a central component in any ERP package. In fact, all large CPA firms actively consult with clients on ERP implementations, using thousands of specially trained accounting majors.

FOR THE FINANCE MAJOR

IT helps financial analysts and managers perform their tasks better. Of particular importance is analyzing cash flows and securing the financing required for smooth operations. In addition, financial applications can support such activities as risk analysis, investment management, and global transactions involving different currencies and fiscal regulations.

Finance activities and modeling are key components of ERP systems. Flows of funds (payments), at the core of most supply chains, must be executed efficiently and effectively. Financial arrangements are especially important along global supply chains, where currency conventions and financial regulations must be considered.

FOR THE MARKETING MAJOR

Marketing and sales expenses are usually targets in a cost-reduction program. Also, sales force automation improves not only salespeoples' productivity (and thus reduces costs) but also customer service.

FOR THE PRODUCTION/ OPERATIONS MANAGEMENT MAJOR

Managing production tasks, materials handling, and inventories in short time intervals, at a low cost, and with high quality is critical for competitiveness. These activities can be achieved only if they are properly supported by IT. In addition, IT can greatly enhance interaction with other functional areas, especially sales. Collaboration in design, manufacturing, and logistics requires knowledge of how modern information systems can be connected.

FOR THE HUMAN RESOURCE MANAGEMENT MAJOR

Human resources managers can increase their efficiency and effectiveness by using IT for some of their routine functions.

Human resources personnel need to understand how information flows between the HR department and the other functional areas. Finally, the integration of functional areas via ERP systems has a major impact on skill requirements and scarcity of employees, which are related to the tasks performed by the HRM department.

MIS FOR THE MIS MAJOR

The MIS function is responsible for the most fundamental information systems in organizations: the transaction processing systems. The TPSs provide the data for the databases. In turn, all other information systems use these data. MIS personnel develop applications that support all levels of the organization (from clerical to executive) and all functional areas. The applications also enable the firm to do business with its partners.

SUMMARY

1. Explain the purpose of transaction processing systems.

   TPSs monitor, store, collect, and process data generated from all business transactions. These data provide the inputs into the organization's database.

2. Explain the types of support that information systems can provide for each functional area of the organization.

   The major business functional areas are production/operations management, marketing, accounting/finance, and human resources management. Table 11.1 provides an overview of the many activities in each functional area supported by FAIS.

3. Identify advantages and drawbacks to businesses of implementing an ERP system.

   Enterprise resource planning (ERP) systems integrate the planning, management, and use of all of the organization's resources. The major objective of ERP systems is to tightly integrate the functional areas of the organization. This integration enables information to flow seamlessly across the various functional areas.

   The following are the major benefits of ERP systems:

   > Because ERP systems integrate organizational resources, they make organizations more flexible, agile, and adaptive. The organizations can therefore react quickly to changing business conditions and capitalize on new business opportunities.

   > ERP systems provide essential information on business performance across functional areas. This information significantly improves managers' ability to make better, more timely decisions.

   > ERP systems integrate organizational resources, resulting in significant improvements in the quality of customer service, production, and distribution.

   The following are the major drawbacks of ERP systems:

   > The business processes in ERP software are often predefined by the best practices that the ERP vendor has developed. As a result, companies may need to change existing business processes to fit the predefined business processes of the software. For companies with well-established procedures, this requirement can be a huge problem.

   > ERP systems can be extremely complex, expensive, and time consuming to implement. In fact, the costs and risks of failure in implementing a new ERP system are substantial.

4. Describe the three main business processes supported by ERP systems.

   The *procurement process*, which originates in the warehouse department (need to buy) and ends in the accounting department (send payment).

   The *fulfillment process* that originates in the sales department (customer request to buy) and ends in the accounting department (receive payment).

   The *production process* that originates and ends in the warehouse department (need to produce and reception of finished goods), but involves the production department as well.

   We leave the details of the steps in each of these processes to you.

>>>CHAPTER GLOSSARY

ad hoc (on-demand) reports Nonroutine reports that often contain special information that is not included in routine reports.

batch processing Transaction processing system (TPS) that processes data in batches at fixed periodic intervals.

comparative reports Reports that compare performances of different business units or times.

computer-integrated manufacturing (CIM) An information system that integrates various automated factory systems; also called *digital manufacturing*.

cross-departmental process A business process that originates in one department and ends in another department, and/or originates and ends in the same department while involving other departments.

drill-down reports Reports that show a greater level of details than is included in routine reports.

enterprise application integration (EAI) system A system that integrates existing systems by providing layers of software that connect applications together.

enterprise resource planning (ERP) systems Information systems that take a business process view of the overall organization to integrate the planning, management, and use of all of an organization's resources, employing a common software platform and database.

ERP II systems Interorganizational ERP systems that provide Web-enabled links among key business systems (e.g., inventory and production) of a company and its customers, suppliers, distributors, and others.

exception reports Reports that include only information that exceeds certain threshold standards.

functional area information systems (FAIS) Systems that provide information to managers (usually midlevel) in the functional areas, in order to support managerial tasks of planning, organizing, and controlling operations.

key indicator reports Reports that summarize the performance of critical activities.

online transaction processing (OLTP) Transaction processing system (TPS) that processes data after transactions occur, frequently in real time.

order fulfillment process A cross-functional business process that originates when the company receives a customer order, and it concludes when it receives a payment from the customer.

procurement process A cross-functional business process that originates when a company needs to acquire goods or services from external sources, and it concludes when the company receives and pays for them.

production process A cross-functional business process in which a company produces physical goods.

routine reports Reports produced at scheduled intervals.

transaction Any business event that generates data worth capturing and storing in a database.

transaction processing system (TPS) Information system that supports the monitoring, collection, storage, and processing of data from the organization's basic business transactions, each of which generates data.

>>>DISCUSSION QUESTIONS

1. Why is it logical to organize IT applications by functional areas?

2. Describe the role of a TPS in a service organization.

3. Describe the relationship between TPS and FAIS.

4. Discuss how IT facilitates the budgeting process.

5. How can the Internet support investment decisions?

6. Describe the benefits of integrated accounting software packages.

7. Discuss the role that IT plays in support of auditing.

8. Investigate the role of the Web in human resources management.

9. What is the relationship between information silos and enterprise resource planning?

>>>PROBLEM-SOLVING ACTIVITIES

1. Finding a job on the Internet is challenging as there are almost too many places to look. Visit the following sites: www.careerbuilder.com, www.craigslist.org, www.linkedin.com, www.jobcentral.com, and www.monster.com. What does each of these sites provide you as a job seeker?

2. Enter www.sas.com and access *revenue optimization* there. Explain how the software helps in optimizing prices.

3. Enter www.eleapsoftware.com and review the product that helps with online training (training systems). What are the most attractive features of this product?

4. Check out Microsoft Dynamics demos at http://www.wiley.com/go/rainer/MIS3e/problemsolving. View three of the demos in different functional areas of your choice. Prepare a report on each product's capabilities.

5. Examine the capabilities of the following (and similar) financial software packages: Financial Analyzer (from

Oracle) and CFO Vision (from SAS Institute). Prepare a report comparing the capabilities of the software packages.

6. Surf the Net and find free accounting software. (Try CNet's software at http://www.wiley.com/go/rainer/MIS3e/problemsolving, www.rkom.com, www.tucows.com, www.passtheshareware.com, and www.freeware-guide.com.) Download the software and try it. Compare the ease of use and usefulness of each software package.

7. Examine the capabilities of the following financial software packages: TekPortal (from www.tekknowledge.com), Financial Analyzer (from www.oracle.com), and Financial Management (from www.sas.com). Prepare a report comparing the capabilities of the software packages.

8. Find Simply Accounting Basic from Sage Software (http://us.simplyaccounting.com). Why is this product recommended for small businesses?

9. Enter www.halogensoftware.com and www.successfactors.com. Examine their software products and compare them.

10. Enter www.iemployee.com and find the support it provides to human resources management activities. View the demos and prepare a report on the capabilities of the products.

>>> COLLABORATION EXERCISE

STEP 1 – Background

Transaction processing systems, functional area systems, and enterprise resource planning systems provide extensive decision support within an organization. Frequently, all of the data reside in a few databases or data warehouses and are then accessed by the various systems that provide support for decision makers.

STEP 2 – Activity

Divide your team into the following positions, based as much as possible on members' majors (if you do not have enough majors to divide, then choose by preference): inventory, sales, production, human resources, and accounting. Imagine that you are a manufacturing company that sells widgets and that your top salesperson just closed a deal for 10,000 units.

For each of the systems mentioned in this chapter (transaction, function, and enterprise), describe the information your area would need to capture, store, analyze, and distribute for this transaction.

After all members have completed their list of data needs, meet as a team to create and share a Google Form that will capture all of the information needed for this transaction, and incorporate it into a spreadsheet. Next, create new sheets that pull area-specific data (inventory, sales, production, labor, etc.) from the transaction sheet.

STEP 3 – Deliverable

Even though this is a very rudimentary exercise, it will give you some appreciation for the complexity of designing a system that captures and shares data across an organization. As a team, write a summary of your experience using Google Forms to build a TPS. Submit your summary and a link to your Google Form and your Google Spreadsheet.

CLOSING **CASE 1 >** General Motors Transforms Its Information Technology Strategy

THE PROBLEM >>> General Motors (GM; www.gm.com) is in the middle of transforming information technology (IT) operations and strategy away from outsourcing and toward hiring thousands of U.S. technology professionals. This process is called *insourcing*.

Currently, however, GM's most pressing issue arises from allegations that the carmaker was far too slow to recall Chevy Cobalt and other vehicles with faulty ignition switches. These failures are linked to 13 deaths, and they have sparked a series of lawsuits as well as a congressional investigation. The recall covers 1.6 million vehicles built between 2003 and 2007. This crisis makes improving the company's IT infrastructure all the more critical.

Discovering vehicle quality problems early on has been complicated by the fact that GM did not consolidate its manufacturing data for analysis. Instead, the data were divided by brands and then subdivided by vehicle models inside those brands. Reporters asked, "Would the current enterprise data warehouse (EDW) have helped GM identify a problem like the faulty ignition switches and deal with it sooner?" GM's CIO, Randy Mott, responded, "Had we had an easy-to-use, broad way to analyze data, would we have come to different conclusions in the past? I'm sure we would." (We discussed enterprise data warehouses in detail in Chapter 5.)

THE IT SOLUTION >>> Creating a single EDW for quality analysis and other purposes was always part of the IT transformation plan at GM. By mid-2014, GM had moved 1.1 petabytes of data relating to product development, procurement, logistics, quality, manufacturing, customer care, sales, marketing, finance, and other functions into its new warehouse, and it plans to incorporate more data. The EDW's primary function is to help GM plan for the future. In fact, GM has started using the data to improve vehicle quality. With the EDW, GM is able to segment and analyze the data down to the vehicle identification number (VIN), to improve safety and quality, and to assess profitability.

GM has collapsed 55 of the 200 data marts scattered across its operations and regions worldwide into its EDW. The company is inputting both structured and unstructured data from its 170 factories worldwide. GM is also incorporating data from new applications that its IT team is building, such as an app that helps GM dealers manage their service operations. The company estimates that by the end of 2015, it will have transferred 100 percent of IT operations data, 90 percent of quality data, and 50 percent of logistics and procurement data into the EDW.

Beyond its EDW efforts, GM is moving forward with other elements of its IT transformation. Mott believes that employees are more cost-effective, drive more innovation, and obtain results faster than outsourced IT teams. Accordingly, the carmaker is moving from performing 10 percent of its IT work in-house (as of January 2013) to 90 percent by the end of 2015. As a result of this transformation, GM expects to have about 12,000 in-house IT professionals by 2018, with 2,000 of them performing "run the business" IT functions and the rest focusing on new application development.

Mott is skeptical of classical IT outsourcing, such as for application development and data center operations. He is examining GM's logistics contracts, and is requesting that their IT component perhaps be moved in-house. Why does Mott believe that GM could perform logistics-related IT better than a company that specializes in this field? He notes that at GM's scale, the carmaker can usually deliver technology that is cheaper and better aligned to its unique needs. He further contends that GM is already "moving" $142 billion worth of components around the world. So why shouldn't the firm provide the IT to support its logistics function?

GM transitioned more than 340 mainframe applications from the data centers of outsourcing vendors to GM's new data center over two weekends in October 2013. Mott points to that successful process as proof that his in-house IT team is a professional operation.

The real test will be whether GM's IT team delivers innovation that is better than its competitors. Let's look at several examples. One innovation is a tablet app that GM will give its dealers free of charge. The app will enable salespeople to look up the inventory, products in the supply chain, and incentives for a vehicle on a mobile device without having to go back to their desktops. GM is also deploying a new service lane automation application aimed at helping dealers better manage their vehicle service operations, in hopes of providing a better customer experience.

GM is also focused on simplifying engineers' systems so that they spend less time moving and managing data and more time on developing vehicles. GM is also increasing its high-performance computing initiatives to provide more accurate simulations for crash tests and to speed up new vehicle development. In manufacturing, the automaker is applying monitoring and analytics to processes such as understanding the quality of a plant's paint jobs in real time, so that problems are spotted before vehicles reach final inspection or even the dealer's lot.

THE RESULTS >>> Mary Barra, GM's CEO since January 2014, has apologized for how GM mismanaged the recall. She also initiated an investigation into what went wrong. In addition, she created the new position of vice president for global vehicle safety, whose mandate is to use data to prevent safety problems. This individual will scan the entire organization, identify and analyze safety data, and provide GM with an accurate, real-time safety performance picture of all of its vehicles around the globe.

It is too early to report on the results of the numerous initiatives discussed above. However, GM reported revenue of $155 billion in calendar year 2013, a 2 percent increase over the previous year.

Sources: Compiled from P. Lebeau, "Many GM Cars Unlikely to Get Faults Fixed, Despite Major Recall," *NBC News*, April 8, 2014; S. Glinton, "Just How New Is the 'New' GM?" *NPR*, April 8, 2014; G. Wallace, "General Motors Owners Still Waiting for Recall Repairs," *CNN Money*, April 7, 2014; J. Nocera, "GM's Cobalt Crisis," *New York Times*, April 7, 2014; C. Murphy, "GM's Data Strategy Pushed to Center Stage," *InformationWeek*, March 27, 2014; S. Frizell, "General Motors Hit with Class Action Lawsuit Over Recall," *Time*, March 15, 2014; S. Gallagher, "General Motors Is Literally Tearing Its Competition to Bits," *Ars Technica*, September 26, 2013; A. Luft, "Why Did GM Choose Arizona, Texas, Georgia, and Michigan for Its 4 IT Innovation Centers?" *GM Authority*, March 12, 2013; M. Wayland, "GM Announces $21 Million Innovation Center, Final in 'IT Transformation,'" *MLive*, March 6, 2013; "GM Hiring 1,000 Information Technology Workers in Arizona," *Automotive News*, March 6, 2013; P. Lucas, "GM: Information Technology Center in Roswell, Ga., Will Create 1,000 Jobs," *The Augusta Chronicle*, January 10, 2013; "GM Now Hiring – 10,000 Information Technology Workers," *NBC News*, October 8, 2012; www.gm.com, accessed April 8, 2014.

Questions

1. Take the "pros" side and discuss GM's insourcing strategy.
2. Take the "cons" side and discuss GM's insourcing strategy.
3. Discuss the ways in which information technology at GM can help to prevent safety problems such as the 2014 recall.

CLOSING CASE 2 > Airlines Use Information Technology to Combat Flight Cancellations

THE PROBLEM >>> A very difficult winter in 2013–2014 led to the cancellation of tens of thousands of airline flights, leaving airlines scrambling to find alternative ways to enable travelers reach their destinations. Once a flight is cancelled, it takes an estimated 18 hours for travelers to reach their destinations, according to masFlight (www.masflight.com), a data and software company that specializes in air travel. On February 14, 2014, masFlight reported that the airline industry had already experienced 76,400 cancellations that year, affecting 5.7 million passengers and making the winter of 2014 the worst for flight operations since 2010.

However, the weather is not the only problem in cancelled flights. Federal regulations that require pilots to get more rest time and threaten airlines with fines if they keep passengers on a plane that is sitting on the tarmac for longer than three hours are also increasing the number of flight cancellations.

THE IT SOLUTION >>>

Although the cancellation rate increased during the winters of 2013–2014, the ability of the airlines to utilize information technology to efficiently get passengers to their destinations has increased as well. Airlines are now taking proactive steps before a storm breaks out, and they have implemented software that automatically rebooks fliers when their flights are cancelled. Furthermore, passengers can use the airlines' Web sites and mobile applications to reroute their trips.

For instance, when Delta receives advance notice about a weather event, it starts waiving ticket change fees 24–36 hours before the weather strikes. This policy affords passengers the opportunity to travel before, as well as after the storm. Passengers who elect to cancel rather than reschedule their flights will receive a refund.

The major airlines have multiple hubs, which makes reworking an itinerary somewhat easier. For example, if Atlanta (a Delta hub) is experiencing bad weather, passengers can be rerouted through Detroit, Minneapolis, or Salt Lake City. Improved booking software has smoothed out the process of rebooking passengers. Previously, this process was manual and time intensive. The newer rebooking systems have automated this process, enabling the airlines to find accommodations on other flights much more quickly.

THE RESULTS >>>

So, how are the airlines' systems working? To answer this question, let's consider the case of Fred Jones. In the middle of February's (2014) winter storm, which bombarded the South and Northeast with snow and ice, Jones was scheduled to fly from Atlanta to Houston. However, thanks to a call from his airline, he was able to get around the storm. The airline alerted him to potential cancellations arising from the storm, and he was rerouted successfully, enabling him to attend an important business meeting. Unfortunately, Fred is only a single, successful example. In fact, during that winter storm in February 2014, many people had to sleep in various airports around the country while the airlines were working to get them to their destinations.

Sources: Compiled from M. Schlangenstein, "American Airlines Says Winter Storms Cut $115 Million in Revenue," *Bloomberg BusinessWeek*, April 8, 2014; A. Langfield, "Pent-Up Winter Demand to Boost Business Travel Spending," *CNBC*, April 7, 2014; C. Jones, "Airlines, Airports Improve Technology for Passengers," *USA Today*, April 7, 2014; C. Jones, "Airlines Better at Getting Stuck Fliers Up in Air," *USA Today*, February 27, 2014; J. Mouawad, "Airlines Work to Catch Up to the Digital Age," *New York Times*, June 4, 2010; www.masflight.com, accessed April 8, 2014.

Questions

1. Describe how the airlines' new information systems benefit travelers.

2. What are possible problems with these information systems?

3. Refer to Chapter 2. Would you categorize the airlines' new information systems as strategic information systems? Why or why not?

INTERNSHIP ACTIVITY> southwest wire A PRODUCTION COMPANY

Manufacturing Industry

Implementing an enterprise resource planning (ERP) system is a lofty goal for any organization, especially an organization with existing systems. Migrating to a new system involves much more than simply updating software. It also requires the organization to modify its business processes and behaviors, train its employees, and convince both management and users to buy into the new system.

For this activity, you will work for Halle Smith, CIO of Southwest Wire, a wire manufacturing company. Halle has been charged with finding and implementing an ERP to help clean up the flow of data and operations within the organization. She knows this will be an uphill battle. Your task will be to research unsuccessful ERP implementations to help Halle understand why these endeavors often fail.

Below is a letter from Halle.

To:	IT Intern
From:	Halle Smith
Subject:	ERP Implementation

Hello!

I am very excited to have an Intern available to help me on this project. Honestly, when they asked me to begin the research process to implement an ERP, I was very nervous because there are so many options and I have heard about so many failures. My understanding is that most ERP systems can be implemented in modules. The idea is to identify the modules you can successfully implement upfront to gain support and traction throughout the organization.

OpenERP is an open-source solution that I have heard about at some conferences. It is a cloud-based software suite that should be easy to implement on the technology side. I would like you to review the OpenERP system and provide some feedback on an implementation plan. Specifically, I am interested in implementing the Project Management, MRP, Warehouse Management, and Purchase Management modules in our initial phase. How well will these products work together?

It also might be helpful to review some unsuccessful projects (Hershey's is a good example) so that you can advise me on how NOT to implement an ERP. Ultimately, I would appreciate your feedback on the combination of ERP applications I have listed above from OpenERP and a list of considerations you learned from Hershey's ERP failure.

I very much appreciate your work on this project.
Halle

Note: All Web sites referenced in this document are available at http://www.wiley.com/go/rainer/MIS3e/internship.

SPREADSHEET ACTIVITY > BASIC CHARTS: PIE CHARTS, LINE CHARTS, AND SCATTER PLOTS

STEP 1 – Background
Visual displays of data are extremely helpful. Most spreadsheets offer some automatic charting features for this purpose. These charts can be built and formatted for viewing with minimal setup.

Three standard charting formats are pie charts, line charts (or line graphs), and scatter plots. Pie charts display data in a circle in which different "slices" represent different parts of a whole. Stock portfolios are often visualized with a pie chart to illustrate how different funds are distributed. Line charts display data trends over a period of time. Stock prices are often displayed on a line chart to indicate

their rise and fall. Although line charts do not have any predictive ability, they do convey trends. Finally, scatter plots show where data fall within two categories. In some cases they help you identify how items group together.

STEP 2 – Activity
This activity will require you to work in three different worksheets, all of which are contained within the same workbook. One sheet is a list of closing values from the S&P 500 Stock Index for every open day in 2013. This will be the easiest of the charts to build. A line graph will display these data in a format

that will enable you to view the 252 data points at a glance.

The second sheet is a stock portfolio. Your first task is to calculate percentage breakdowns for the different stocks/funds held in the portfolio. You will then build both a pie chart and a bar chart to present these data.

The final sheet displays data for all cars that were built with a four-cylinder engine in 2013. It indicates miles per gallon (MPG) for both city and highway driving, along with combined MPG. You will use these data to create a scatter plot to determine whether there are obvious "groups" of four-cylinder cars. You may have to use the sorting and filtering

skills you acquired in previous activities to define the groups.

STEP 3 – Deliverable

Visit http://www.wiley.com/go/rainer/MIS3e/spreadsheet, and download the workbook mentioned above. You will find the three sheets described in Step 2 along with additional instructions on how to complete this activity.

Follow the instructions in the spreadsheet and submit your final work to your instructor.

Additional help with this spreadsheet skill is available in WileyPLUS. Open the "Microsoft Office 2013 Lab Manual Spreadsheet Module: Excel 2013," and review Lesson 12: Creating Charts.

DATABASE ACTIVITY > ADVANCED QUERIES

STEP 1 – Background

In this activity you will learn how to use parameters to simplify the process of entering query selection criteria. Until now, if you needed to query for information, you used something like a design grid. This approach is not ideal for casual users. This activity will show you how to use query parameters to avoid this step.

People who work with customer information frequently must specify whose information they need to review. Queries can perform this task. However, a customer service agent should not have to modify the query design for each question. A parameter in Access is a user-entered value that determines what data a query returns. Each time the query is run, Access will prompt the user to enter a value. No fixed value is built into the query.

STEP 2 – Activity

Before starting this activity, you should visit http://www.wiley.com/go/rainer/MIS3e/database to download a fresh copy of the database you worked with in the Chapter 10 activity.

For this activity you will provide a simple interface to enter data for a query. Create a new Query

Design with Customer, Order, and Store tables. Enter CustName, StoreCity, OrderDate, and OrderTotal in the grid. Rather than entering a value in a query, use a prompt string to require the user to choose which value (customer, city, product, etc.) he or she wants to query, rather than having to create a new query.

1. In the query you created above, add a parameter that will ask the user to enter a Customer Name before the query runs. Run the query to ensure it displays the correct prompt. Save this query as CustOrderParamQry.
2. Using Product Price, Product Name, and Customer Name, create a query that uses a parameter to require the user to state a dollar amount that you want to use as the cutoff value. Next, find customers who spend more than that amount. Run the query twice: once with $1.50 and again with $5.00 as the cutoff values. Save this query as ExpensiveProdParamQry.
3. Queries can calculate a column based on other data in the same row. These can be data you choose not to show, as long as they come from a table in the query. Create a query to help the staff price out orders involving multiple units

of a particular item. (In a real store, this function would be performed electronically, but the query is still a good example.) Using Product Table, select ProdName and ProdPrice to create your expressions. Build expressions that state the amount that two of the same item cost. Create additional items for customers who want—three, four, and five. Save this query as ProdPriceQry.

STEP 3 – Deliverable

Submit your database with the three queries listed above. If you need additional help, visit the Microsoft Support Web site at the link identified in Step 2.

Customer Relationship Management

LEARNING OBJECTIVES >>>

1. Identify the primary functions of both customer relationship management (CRM) and collaborative CRM strategies.

2. Describe how businesses might utilize applications of each of the two major components of operational CRM systems.

3. Discuss the benefits of analytical CRM systems to businesses.

4. Explain the advantages and disadvantages of mobile CRM systems, on-demand CRM systems, and open-source CRM systems.

OPENING **CASE** > Rating Online Customer Service

© JuSun/iStockphoto

In the past year, how many times have you interacted online with a retailer? Of those times, how often did you provide feedback? Chances are that you have done so very few times, if at all. In fact, consumers typically provide feedback only when their experience is either incredibly good or incredibly bad. Unfortunately for retailers, these instances fail to capture roughly 95 percent of customer interactions. However, these experiences are the sweet spot for StellaService.

StellaService (www.stellaservice.com) wants to rate online customer service just as J.D. Power & Associates (www.jdpower.com) rates new car quality and long-term dependability and Nielsen (www.nielsen.com) rates television viewers, radio listeners, and newspaper readers. That is, the enterprise measures and rates the customer service performance of online retailers via a process audited by the global accounting and auditing firm KPMG (www.kpmg.com). Their mission is to enhance transparency in online customer care.

To implement this policy, StellaService employees act as real-life customers at Sears and thousands of other retailers, ordering and returning $10 shirts, $1,000 bicycle parts, and almost every conceivable product in between. These anonymous shoppers stress-test and track 300 or so metrics in 20,000 Internet transactions each month. StellaService then sells these data back to companies such as Sears—and their competitors. In the case of Sears, for example, their "package fit and quality" and Twitter response time to shopper queries receive high marks, but their speed at refunding returns could use some improvement.

In mid-2014, retailers who had signed up to receive StellaService's service included Amazon and its shoe subsidiary Zappos, Diapers.com, 1-800-Flowers.com, and

MKT

boutique sites such as GiltGroupe. Retailers who provide consistently high-quality customer service are awarded StellaService's seal of approval, a logo they can then display on their Web site and their advertising materials.

Companies can spend more than $100,000 per year for feedback on their online services. Only 50 percent of the businesses that pay StellaService for evaluations win a seal of approval. These businesses can also peruse their competitors' data to discover what they are doing wrong.

StellaService has also entered into a partnership with Google's Trusted Stores initiative. How does this arrangement work? As an example, a Google search for a pair of earrings will display StellaService data alongside Goggle's check mark of approval. These approvals will make shoppers more confident that they are buying from online merchants that consistently provide a superior experience.

Let's look at an example of StellaService in action. According to data provided by the company, wait times to contact Target after its massive data breach spiked. (See closing case 1 in Chapter 7.) Following news of the breach, callers employed by StellaService were disconnected from the line during three separate calls they made on each of two days. In two other instances, the caller waited on hold for 20 minutes before terminating the call. StellaService also noted that Target experienced spikes in e-mail communications to its customer support center, particularly from December 18–25, with the longest response time being 2 days and 18 hours on December 23. By comparison, the retailer's average response time over the three months prior to the breach had been less than eight hours.

Sources: Compiled from K. Gustafson, "Target Shoppers Faced Long Waits Post-Security Breach," *CNBC*, January 8, 2014; G. Marvin, "Google Trusted Stores Now Integrates with AdWords, Shows StellaService Ratings in US," *Search Engine Land*, November 25, 2013; C. O'Connor, "Thinking Inside the Box," *Forbes*, September 23, 2013; L. Stangel, "Google Rolling Out E-Commerce Customer Service Ratings," *Silicon Valley Business Journal*, May 30, 2013; A. Barr, "Google to License Retailer Ratings from StellaService," *Reuters*, May 29, 2013; M. Creamer, "StellaService Strives to Give E-Tailers Credibility They Desire," *Advertising Age*, March 29, 2011; www.stellaservice.com, accessed April 1, 2014.

Questions

1. Why is it so valuable for an online retailer to be able to post StellaService's seal of approval on its Web site and advertising materials?
2. Why doesn't StellaService provide the same service for bricks-and-mortar retailers?

Introduction

The chapter opening case provides examples of the evolving nature of the business–customer relationship, particularly in today's social media arena. As personal technology usage changes, so too must the methods that businesses use to interface with their customers. As you see with StellaService, it is important to rate online customer service for two reasons. First, customers can see how well companies are performing in a variety of areas. Second, companies can see how well they and their competitors are performing. The StellaService rating is particularly important given the increase in online shopping, which is typically more impersonal than in-store shopping.

Organizations increasingly are emphasizing a customer-centric approach to their business practices because they realize that long-term customer relationships provide sustainable value that extends beyond an individual business transaction. Significantly, **customer relationship management** (CRM) is not important solely for large enterprises. Rather, it is essential for small organizations as well.

At this point, you might be asking yourself: Why should *I* learn about CRM? The answer, as you will see in this chapter, is that customers are supremely important to *all* organizations. Regardless of your job, you will have an impact, whether direct or indirect, on managing your firm's customers. When you read the What's in IT for Me? section at the end of the chapter, you will learn about opportunities to make immediate contributions on your first job. Therefore, it is essential that you acquire a working knowledge of CRM and CRM systems.

In Chapter 11, you learned about information systems that supported organizational activities within the organization. In this chapter, you study information systems that support organizational activities that extend outside the organization to customers, appropriately titled customer relationship management systems. CRM and CRM systems are critical to the success of modern businesses.

12.1 Defining Customer Relationship Management

Before the supermarket, the mall, and the automobile, people purchased goods at their neighborhood store. The owners and employees recognized customers by name and knew their preferences and wants. For their part, customers remained loyal to the store and made repeated purchases. Over time, however, this personal customer relationship became impersonal as people moved from farms and small towns to cities, consumers became mobile, and supermarkets and department stores achieved economies of scale through mass marketing. Although prices were lower and products were more uniform in quality, the relationship with customers became nameless and impersonal.

The customer relationship has become even more impersonal with the rapid growth of the Internet and the World Wide Web. In today's hypercompetitive marketplace, customers are increasingly powerful; if they are dissatisfied with a product and/or a service from one organization, a competitor is often just one mouse click away. Furthermore, as more and more customers shop on the Web, an enterprise does not even have the opportunity to make a good first impression *in person*.

Customer relationship management returns to personal marketing. That is, rather than market to a mass of people or companies, businesses market to each customer individually. By employing this approach, businesses can use information about each customer—for example, previous purchases, needs, and wants—to create highly individualized offers that customers are more likely to accept. That is, the CRM approach is designed to achieve *customer intimacy*.

Customer relationship management is a customer-focused and customer-driven organizational strategy. That is, organizations concentrate on assessing customers' requirements for products and services and then providing a high-quality, responsive customer experience. CRM is not a process or a technology per se; rather, it is a customer-centric way of thinking and acting. The focus of modern organizations has shifted from conducting business transactions to managing customer relationships. In general, organizations recognize that customers are the core of a successful enterprise, and the success of the enterprise depends on effectively managing relationships with them.

The CRM approach is enabled by information technology in the form of various systems and applications. However, CRM is not only about the software. Sometimes the problem with managing relationships is simply time and information. Old systems may contain the needed information, but this information may take too long to access and may not be usable across a variety of applications. The result is that companies have less time to spend with their customers.

In contrast, modern CRM strategies and systems build sustainable long-term customer relationships that create value for the company as well as for the customer. That is, CRM helps companies acquire new customers and to retain and expand their relationships with profitable existing customers. Retaining customers is particularly important because repeat customers are the largest generator of revenue for an enterprise. Also, organizations have long understood that winning back a customer who has switched to a competitor is vastly more expensive than keeping that customer satisfied in the first place. One company that has become successful and famous for its customer-centric policies is Amazon, as you see in IT's About Business 12.1.

IT'S ABOUT BUSINESS 12.1

Amazon: Truly Superb Customer Service

Customer experience is a top priority for 86 percent of executives, according to Gartner's "Amplifying the Enterprise: The CIO Agenda." Amazon (www.amazon.com) is amazingly effective at managing customer relationships. The company has achieved its phenomenal success by combining data efficiency and customer service in ways that no previous business has ever managed to do.

Amazon's basic customer relationship management (CRM) strategy has always focused on anticipation and prevention. Amazon realizes that after a customer orders a product, his or her next question is, "When will I receive it?" Therefore, the retailer proactively informs customers (either by e-mail or on the purchase page), "You will receive your order on Tuesday." This process eliminates phone calls and impresses customers with Amazon's level of service.

Consider Amazon's optimized product information pages, which include the following:

- Product details, including specifications, special features, and competitive advantages
- Real-time inventory and availability
- Price comparisons
- Shipping and payment options, special offers, and product promotions
- Cross-sold products frequently purchased along with the current product
- Predictable product delivery timing

By presenting such information in a single, user-friendly view, Amazon helps shoppers make informed and efficient buying decisions. When customers return to the site, Amazon analyzes their transaction histories, including products previously browsed, to present a personalized, sales-optimized page that encourages additional purchases. All of this information is accurate, real-time, and integrated, including product details, user reviews, product availability, fulfillment information, and payment options.

MKT

Essentially, Amazon has radically disrupted the business model of retailing: how customers interact with businesses, what customers expect of businesses, how products are handled, and how shipping and delivery are managed. Amazon has restored the customer experience into something that is highly personalized. The company provides a vast but manageable set of services to customers on a platform that allows them to choose which products they want, when they want them.

To better understand Amazon's CRM philosophy, let's consider two innovative services: Amazon Prime and Mayday. Amazon Prime began as a service to provide customers with less expensive two-day shipping. Today, it offers not only free shipping but also thousands of free videos that customers can watch and download. Amazon has found that its Prime customers spend 40 percent more than they did before joining the service.

Mayday is another popular customer service. Amazon's tablet—the Amazon Kindle HDX series—contains a Mayday button. Click on that button, and within 15 seconds a live customer service representative appears in a small video window on the screen. The representative has the ability to take over your tablet (with your permission) to handle your customer service questions. Mayday is available 24/7/365.

In addition to these services, Amazon is planning a future innovation: Amazon Prime Air. In late 2013, Amazon founder Jeff Bezos announced that the company was exploring the use of unmanned, autonomous, flying drones to deliver packages. The packages will be lifted off the shipping lines by "octocopters" and then flown to the delivery address via GPS coordinates. Amazon acknowledges that there are

© 4774344sean/iStockphoto

many obstacles to implementing such a delivery system (think about the Federal Aviation Administration's regulations, for example). Nevertheless, the company is, once again, relentlessly focused on providing superb customer services.

And the results of this focus? In March 2014, the office supplies company Staples (www.staples.com) announced that it will close 225 brick-and-mortar stores in the United States and Canada. This decision suggests that online sales will determine the future of retail. In 2013 Staples sales had declined to about $6 billion. Moreover, nearly half of those sales were generated by its online channel. Staples joins other retailers that have struggled to keep pace with Amazon. For example, RadioShack (www.radioshack.com) similarly announced that it would close 1,100 stores after a huge decline in profits. BestBuy (www.bestbuy.com) is also continuing to suffer decreases in revenues. This trend has been called the "Amazon Effect."

Sources: Compiled from M. Wulfraat, "Logistics Comment: How the 'Amazon Effect' Is Changing the American Manufacturing Industry," *Supply Chain Digest*, March 26, 2014; I. Lunden, "The Amazon Effect: Staples to Close 225 Stores, Says It's Now Making Half of All Sales Online," *TechCrunch*, March 6, 2014; "How Technology Contributes to Customer Experience," *Baseline Magazine*, March 6, 2014; J. Bort, "Larry Ellison: Amazon, Salesforce.com Are Now Oracle's Biggest Competitors," *Business Insider*, January 2014; P. Greenberg, "Why Customer-Obsessed Amazon Is Our Most Important Business Force," *ZDNet*, January 22, 2014; S. Raisch, "Retailers Need to Adapt to the Amazon Effect," *Today's Garden Center*, January 6, 2014; D. Gross, "Amazon's Drone Delivery: How Would It Work?" *CNN Technology News*, December 2, 2013; J. Talton, "Digging into the 'Amazon Effect'," *The Seattle Times*, July 30, 2013; S. Duplessie, "IT Is About to Meet the Amazon Effect," *Computerworld*, June 5, 2013; K. Liyakasa, "Uncovering the 'Amazon Effect'," *Destination CRM*, August 16, 2012; www.amazon.com, accessed April 7, 2014.

Questions

1. Describe the advantages that Amazon has over bricks-and-mortar retailers.

2. Describe the many facets of Amazon's relentless focus on customer relationship management.

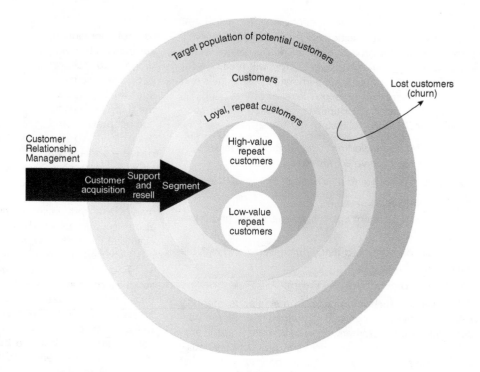

Figure 12.1 The customer relationship management process.

FIGURE 12.1 depicts the CRM process. The process begins with marketing efforts, where the organization solicits prospects from a target population of potential customers. A certain number of these prospects will make a purchase and thus become customers. A certain number of these customers will become repeat customers. The organization then segments its repeat customers into low- and high-value repeat customers. An organization's overall goal is to maximize the *lifetime value* of a customer, which is that customer's potential revenue stream over a number of years.

Over time all organizations inevitably lose a certain percentage of customers, a process called *customer churn*. The optimal result of the organization's CRM efforts is to maximize the number of high-value repeat customers while minimizing customer churn.

CRM is a fundamentally simple concept: Treat different customers differently, because their needs differ, and their value to the company may also differ. A successful CRM strategy not only improves customer satisfaction but also makes the company's sales and service employees more productive, which in turn generates increased profits. In fact, researchers at the National Quality Research Center at the University of Michigan discovered that a 1 percent increase in customer satisfaction can lead to as much as a 300 percent increase in a company's *market capitalization*, defined as the number of shares of the company's stock outstanding multiplied by the price per share of the stock. Put simply, a minor increase in customer satisfaction can generate a major increase in a company's overall value.

Up to this point, you have been looking at an organization's CRM strategy. It is important to distinguish between a CRM *strategy* and CRM *systems*. Basically, CRM systems are information systems designed to support an organization's CRM strategy. For organizations to pursue excellent relationships with their customers, they need to employ CRM systems that provide the infrastructure needed to support those relationships. Because customer service and support are essential to a successful business, organizations must place a great deal of emphasis on both their CRM strategy and their CRM systems.

Broadly speaking, CRM systems lie along a continuum, from *low-end CRM systems*—designed for enterprises with many small customers—to *high-end CRM systems*—for enterprises with a few large customers. An example of a low-end system

© Spencer Grant/PhotoEdit

is Amazon, which uses its CRM system to recommend books to returning customers. An example of a high-end system is Boeing, which uses its CRM system to coordinate staff activities in a campaign to sell its new 787 aircraft to Delta Airlines. As you study the cases and examples in this chapter, consider where on the continuum a particular CRM system would fall.

Although CRM varies according to circumstances, all successful CRM policies share two basic elements. First, the company must identify the many types of customer touch points. Second, it needs to consolidate data about each customer. Let's examine these two elements in more detail.

Customer Touch Points

Organizations must recognize the numerous and diverse interactions they have with their customers. These interactions are referred to as **customer touch points**. Traditional customer touch points include telephone contact, direct mailings, and actual physical interactions with customers during their visits to a store. Organizational CRM systems, however, must manage many additional customer touch points that occur through the use of popular personal technologies. These touch points include e-mail, Web sites, and communications via smartphones (see FIGURE 12.2).

Data Consolidation

Data consolidation is also critical to an organization's CRM efforts. The organization's CRM systems must manage customer data effectively. In the past, customer data were stored in isolated systems (or silos) located in different functional areas across the business—for example, in separate databases in the finance, sales, logistics, and marketing departments. Consequently, data for individual customers were difficult to share across the various functional areas.

As you saw in Chapter 3, modern interconnected systems built around a data warehouse now make all customer-related data available to every unit of the business. This complete data set on each customer is called a *360° view* of that customer. By accessing this view, a company can enhance its relationship with its customers and ultimately make more productive and profitable decisions.

Figure 12.2 Customer touch points. (*Sources:* "Oleksiy Mark/Shutterstock" for the smartphone and "Media Bakery" for the service center and "Media Bakery" for the physical store)

Data consolidation and the 360° view of the customer enable the organization's functional areas to readily share information about customers. This information sharing leads to collaborative CRM. **Collaborative CRM systems** provide effective and efficient interactive communication with the customer throughout the entire organization. That is, they integrate communications between the organization and its customers in all aspects of marketing, sales, and customer support. Collaborative CRM systems also enable customers to provide direct feedback to the organization. As you read in Chapter 8, Web 2.0 applications such as blogs and Wikis are very important to companies that value customer input into their product and service offerings, as well as into new product development.

An organization's CRM system contains two major components: operational CRM systems and analytical CRM systems. You will learn about these components in the next two sections.

BEFORE *YOU GO ON....*

1. What is the definition of customer relationship management?
2. Why is CRM so important to any organization?
3. Define and provide examples of customer touch points.

Apply The Concept 12.1

LEARNING OBJECTIVE 12.1 Identify the primary functions of both customer relationship management (CRM) and collaborative CRM strategies.

STEP 1 – Background (Here is what you are learning.)

Section 12.1 has introduced the concept of a CRM system, and it has suggested that it is better to focus on relationships than on transactions. The idea is that relationships create transactions, so if you grow the relationship, you keep the customers (and the transactions)!

STEP 2 – Activity (Here is what you are doing.)

Visit http://www.wiley.com/go/rainer/MIS3e/applytheconcept, and click on the link provided for Apply the Concept 12.1. This link will take you to a YouTube video that illustrates how Recreational Equipment Incorporated (REI) uses CRM to service their customers.

STEP 3 – Deliverable (Here is what you submit.)

In a report, identify the primary functions of both customer relationship management (CRM) and collaborative CRM strategies. What are REI's approaches to CRM? Can you make any suggestions to help them improve? Submit your report to your professor.

12.2 Operational Customer Relationship Management Systems

Operational CRM systems support front-office business processes. **Front-office processes** are those that directly interact with customers; that is, sales, marketing, and service. The two major components of operational CRM systems are customer-facing applications and customer-touching applications (discussed below).

Operational CRM systems provide the following benefits:

- Efficient, personalized marketing, sales, and service
- A 360° view of each customer
- The ability of sales and service employees to access a complete history of customer interaction with the organization, regardless of the touch point

An example of an operational CRM system involves Caterpillar, Inc. (www.cat.com), an international manufacturer of industrial equipment. Caterpillar uses its CRM tools to accomplish the following objectives:

- Improve sales and account management by optimizing the information shared by multiple employees and by streamlining existing processes (e.g., taking orders using mobile devices)

- Form individualized relationships with customers, with the aim of improving customer satisfaction and maximizing profits
- Identify the most profitable customers, and provide them with the highest level of service
- Provide employees with the information and processes necessary to know their customers
- Understand and identify customer needs, and effectively build relationships among the company, its customer base, and its distribution partners

Customer-Facing Applications

In **customer-facing CRM applications,** an organization's sales, field service, and customer interaction center representatives interact directly with customers. These applications include customer service and support, sales force automation, marketing, and campaign management.

Customer Service and Support. Customer service and support refers to systems that automate service requests, complaints, product returns, and requests for information. Today, organizations have implemented **customer interaction centers (CIC)**, where organizational representatives use multiple channels such as the Web, telephone, fax, and face-to-face interactions to communicate with customers. The CIC manages several different types of customer interaction.

One of the most well-known customer interaction centers is the *call center*, a centralized office set up to receive and transmit a large volume of requests by telephone. Call centers enable companies to respond to a large variety of questions, including product support and complaints.

Organizations also use the CIC to create a call list for the sales team, whose members contact sales prospects. This type of interaction is called *outbound telesales*. In these interactions, the customer and the sales team collaborate in discussing products and services that can satisfy customers' needs and generate sales.

Customers can communicate directly with the CIC to initiate a sales order, inquire about products and services before placing an order, and obtain information about a transaction they have already made. These interactions are referred to as *inbound teleservice*. Teleservice representatives respond to requests either by utilizing service instructions stored in an organizational knowledge base or by noting incidents that can be addressed only by field service technicians.

The CIC also provides the Information Help Desk. The Help Desk assists customers with their questions concerning products or services, and it also processes customer complaints. Complaints generate follow-up activities such as quality control checks, delivery of replacement parts or products, service calls, generation of credit memos, and product returns.

New technologies are extending the traditional CIC's functionality to include e-mail and Web interaction. For example, Epicor (www.epicor.com) provides software solutions that combine Web channels, such as automated e-mail reply, with Web knowledge bases. The information the software provides is available to CIC representatives and field service personnel. Another new technology, live chat, allows customers to connect to a company representative and conduct an instant messaging session. The advantage of live chat over a telephone conversation is that live chat enables the participants to share documents and photos (see www.livechatinc.com and www.websitealive.com). Some companies conduct the chat with a computer using natural language processing rather than with a real person.

Sales Force Automation. **Sales force automation (SFA)** is the component of an operational CRM system that automatically records all of the components in a sales transaction process. SFA systems include a *contact management system*, which tracks all communications between the company and the customer, the purpose of each communication, and any necessary follow-up. This system eliminates duplicated contacts and redundancy, which in turn reduces the risk of irritating customers. SFA also includes a *sales lead tracking system*, which lists potential customers or customers who have purchased related products; that is, products similar to those that the salesperson is trying to sell to the customer.

Other elements of an SFA system can include a *sales forecasting system*, which is a mathematical technique for estimating future sales, and a *product knowledge system*, which is a comprehensive source of information regarding products and services. More-developed SFA systems also have online product-building features, called *configurators*, that enable customers to model the product to meet their specific needs. For example, you can customize your own running shoe at NikeID (http://nikeid.nike.com). Finally, many of the current SFA systems enable the salesperson in the field to connect remotely with customers and the home office via Web-based interfaces that can be displayed on smartphones.

Marketing. Thus far, you have focused primarily on how sales and customer service personnel can benefit from CRM systems. However, CRM systems have many important applications for an organization's marketing department as well. For example, they enable marketers to identify and target their best customers, to manage marketing campaigns, and to generate quality leads for the sales teams. Additionally, CRM marketing applications can sift through volumes of customer data—a process known as data mining (discussed in Chapter 5)—to develop a *purchasing profile*; that is, a snapshot of a consumer's buying habits that may lead to additional sales through cross-selling, upselling, and bundling.

Cross-selling is the marketing of additional related products to customers based on a previous purchase. This sales approach has been used very successfully by banks. For example, if you have a checking and savings account at your bank, then a bank officer will recommend other products for you, such as certificates of deposit (CDs) or other types of investments.

Upselling is a strategy in which the salesperson provides customers with the opportunity to purchase related products or services of greater value in place of, or along with, the consumer's initial product or service selection. For example, if a customer goes into an electronics store to buy a new television, a salesperson may show him a pricey 1080i HD LED television placed next to a less expensive LCD television in the hope of selling the more expensive set (assuming that the customer is willing to pay more for a sharper picture). Other common examples of upselling are warranties on electronics merchandise and the purchase of a carwash after buying gas at the gas station.

Finally, **bundling** is a form of cross-selling in which a business sells a group of products or services together at a lower price than their combined individual prices. For example, your cable company might bundle cable TV, broadband Internet access, and telephone service at a lower price than you would paid for each service separately.

Campaign Management. **Campaign management applications** help organizations plan campaigns that send the right messages to the right people through the right channels. Organizations manage their campaigns very carefully to avoid targeting people who have opted out of receiving marketing communications. Furthermore, companies use these applications to personalize individual messages for each particular customer.

Customer-Touching Applications

Corporations have used manual CRM systems for many years. In the mid-1990s, for example, organizations began to utilize the Internet, the Web, and other electronic touch points (e.g., e-mail, point-of-sale terminals) to manage customer relationships. In contrast with customer-facing applications, where customers deal with a company representative, customers who utilize these technologies interact directly with the applications themselves. For this reason, these applications are called **customer-touching CRM applications** or **electronic CRM (e-CRM) applications**. Customers typically can use these applications to help themselves. There are many types of e-CRM applications. Let's examine some of the major ones.

Search and Comparison Capabilities. It is often difficult for customers to find what they want from the vast array of products and services available on the Web. To assist customers, many online stores and malls offer search and comparison capabilities, as do independent comparison Web sites (see www.mysimon.com).

Technical and Other Information and Services. Many organizations offer personalized experiences to induce customers to make purchases or to remain loyal. For example, Web sites often allow customers to download product manuals. One example is General Electric's Web site (www.ge.com), which provides detailed technical and maintenance information and sells replacement parts to customers who need to repair outdated home appliances. Another example is Goodyear's Web site (www.goodyear.com), which provides information about tires and their use.

Customized Products and Services. Another customer-touching service that many online vendors use is mass customization, a process in which customers can configure their own products. For example, Dell (www.dell.com) allows customers to configure their own computer systems. The Gap (www.gap.com) enables customers to "mix and match" an entire wardrobe. Web sites such as Hitsquad (www.hitsquad.com), MusicalGreeting (www.musicalgreeting.com), Apple iTunes (www.apple.com/itunes), and Surprise (www.surprise.com) allow customers to pick individual music titles from a library and customize a CD, a feature that traditional music stores do not offer.

In addition, customers can now view account balances or check the shipping status of orders at any time from their computers or smartphones. If you order books from Amazon, for example, you can look up the anticipated arrival date. Many other companies, including FedEx and UPS, provide similar services (see www.fedex.com and www.ups.com).

© Amy Eira/PhotoEdit

Personalized Web Pages. Many organizations permit their customers to create personalized Web pages. Customers use these pages to record purchases and preferences, as well as problems and requests. For example, American Airlines generates personalized Web pages for each of its registered travel-planning customers.

FAQs. Frequently asked questions (FAQs) are a simple tool for answering repetitive customer queries. Customers may find the information they need by using this tool, thereby eliminating the need to communicate with an actual person.

E-mail and Automated Response. The most popular tool for customer service is e-mail. Inexpensive and fast, companies use e-mail not only to answer customer inquiries but also to disseminate information, send alerts and product information, and conduct correspondence on any topic.

Loyalty Programs. Loyalty programs recognize customers who repeatedly use a vendor's products or services. Loyalty programs are appropriate when two conditions are met: a high frequency of repeat purchases, and limited product customization for each customer.

Although loyalty programs are frequently referred to as "rewards programs," their actual purpose is not to reward *past* behavior, but, rather, to influence *future* behavior. Significantly, the most profitable customers are not necessarily those whose behavior can be most easily influenced. As one example, most major U.S. airlines provide some "elite" benefits to anyone who flies 25,000 miles with them and their partners over the course of a year. Customers who fly first class pay much more for a given flight than those who fly in discount economy. Nevertheless, they reach elite status only 1.5–2 times faster than economy-class passengers. Why is this true? The reason is that, although first-class passengers are far more profitable than discount seekers, they also are less influenced by loyalty programs. Discount flyers respond much more enthusiastically to the benefits of frequent flyer programs. Therefore, airlines award more benefits to discount flyers than to first-class flyers (relative to their spending).

The airlines' frequent flyer programs are probably the best-known loyalty programs. Other popular loyalty programs are casino players' clubs, which reward frequent players, and supermarkets, which reward frequent shoppers. Loyalty programs use a database or data warehouse to maintain a record of the points (or miles) a customer has accrued and the rewards to which he or she is entitled. The programs then use analytical tools to mine the data and learn about customer behavior.

BEFORE *YOU GO ON....*

1. Differentiate between customer-facing applications and customer-touching applications.

2. Provide examples of cross-selling, upselling, and bundling (other than the examples presented in the text).

Apply The Concept 12.2

LEARNING OBJECTIVE 12.2 Describe how businesses might utilize applications of each of the two major components of operational CRM systems.

STEP 1 – Background

Section 12.2 has introduced you to the concept of customer-facing and customer-touching CRM applications, the two major components of operational CRM systems. Many organizations use a combination of both types of systems to establish, develop, and maintain relationships with consumers. This activity will help you to see these systems in action when you do business on a Web site or in a brick-and-mortar business.

STEP 2 – Activity

Visit a physical store where you like to shop (or recall a recent visit and discuss it with some friends), and visit the store's Web site. Make certain to select a company that has both an Internet site and a physical store so that you can compare the two channels.

As you walked through the store, did you notice any cues that could tie a customer to a CRM? Did the business have a customer loyalty programs? Are there any significant advantages to joining the program? Is the in-store membership tied to anything online? If so, how? Or, does the store seem to have separate in-store and online memberships?

STEP 3 – Deliverable

After considering the points mentioned in Step 2, describe how businesses might utilize both the customer-facing and customer-touching applications of a CRM to integrate the online and traditional shopping experiences. Prepare a report and submit it to your instructor.

12.3 Analytical Customer Relationship Management Systems

Whereas operational CRM systems support front-office business processes, **analytical CRM systems** provide business intelligence by analyzing customer behavior and perceptions. For example, analytical CRM systems typically provide information concerning customer requests and transactions, as well as customer responses to the organization's marketing, sales, and service initiatives. These systems also create statistical models of customer behavior and the value of customer relationships over time, as well as forecasts about acquiring, retaining, and losing customers. FIGURE 12.3 illustrates the relationship between operational CRM systems and analytical CRM systems.

Important technologies in analytical CRM systems include data warehouses, data mining, decision support, and other business intelligence technologies. After these systems have completed their various analyses, they supply information to the organization in the form of reports and digital dashboards. We discuss all of these topics in Chapter 5.

Analytical CRM systems analyze customer data for a variety of purposes:

- Designing and executing targeted marketing campaigns
- Increasing customer acquisition, cross-selling, and upselling
- Providing input into decisions relating to products and services (e.g., pricing and product development)
- Providing financial forecasting and customer profitability analysis

---

BEFORE YOU GO ON....

1. What is the relationship between operational CRM systems and analytical CRM systems?
2. What are some of the functions of analytical CRM systems?

Operational CRM

Customer-facing applications
Sales
Marketing
Customer service and support
Campaign management

Image Source

Customer-touching applications
Search and comparison
Customized products
Technical information
Personalized Web pages
FAQ
E-mail/auto response
Loyalty programs

J-C & D.PRATT/PhotoNonStop/Glow Images

Analytical CRM

Customer data warehouse

Data mining
Decision support
Business intelligence
OLAP

Figure 12.3 The relationship between operational CRM and analytical CRM.

Apply The Concept 12.3

LEARNING OBJECTIVE 12.3 Discuss the benefits of analytical CRM systems to businesses.

STEP 1 – Background

Section 12.3 defined analytical CRM as systems that create statistical models of customer behavior and the value of customer relationships over time, as well as forecasts about acquiring, retaining, and losing customers. Put simply, the more frequently you shop at a Web site, the more that site will learn about you. Google is a prime example.

STEP 2 – Activity

Visit http://www.wiley.com/go/rainer/MIS3e/applytheconcept, and click on the link provided for Apply the Concept 12.3. This link will take you to an Oracle Web site dedicated to PeopleSoft CRM Analytics. As you read this article, consider CRM from a business perspective, focusing on how businesses can benefit from an analytical CRM system.

STEP 3 – Deliverable

Imagine today is your first day on your new job and you had an opportunity to use your company's CRM system. At lunch a coworker was complaining about having to use this system as part of her sales program. Write down how you would explain to her the benefits of analytical CRM systems to businesses. Submit your thoughts to your instructor.

12.4 Other Types of Customer Relationship Management Systems

Now that you have examined operational and analytical CRM systems, let's shift our focus to other types of CRM systems. Four exciting developments in this area are on-demand CRM systems, mobile CRM systems, open-source CRM systems, and social CRM.

On-Demand CRM Systems

Customer relationship management systems may be implemented as either *on-premise* or *on-demand*. Traditionally, organizations utilized on-premise CRM systems, meaning that they purchased the systems from a vendor and then installed them on site. This arrangement was expensive, time consuming, and inflexible. Some organizations, particularly smaller ones, could not justify the costs of these systems.

On-demand CRM systems became a solution for the drawbacks of on-premise CRM systems. An **on-demand CRM system** is one that is hosted by an external vendor in the vendor's data center. This arrangement spares the organization the costs associated with purchasing the system. In addition, because the vendor creates and maintains the system, the organization's employees need to know only how to access and utilize it. The concept of on-demand is also known as *utility computing* or *software-as-a-service* (SaaS) (see Plug IT In 4).

Salesforce (www.salesforce.com) is the best-known on-demand CRM vendor. The company's goal is to provide a new business model that allows companies to rent the CRM software instead of buying it. The secret to their success appears to be that CRM has common requirements across many customers. Consequently, Salesforce's product meets the demands of its customers without a great deal of customization.

One Salesforce customer is Babson College (www.babson.edu) in Wellesley, Massachusetts. Babson's goal is to deliver the best applicant experience possible. To accomplish this mission, the school decided to use Salesforce to bring together all of the information on prospective students in a single location. All personnel who are involved with admissions have immediate access to candidate contact information, applications, and reports that indicate the status of each applicant within the enrollment process. This system makes it easy for administrators to deliver valuable information to applicants at the right time.

Using the Salesforce platform, Babson built an admissions portal with a fully personalized user experience for prospective students. The portal consolidates all of the information that potential students need. Furthermore, it displays different information to students at different points in the application process.

Despite their benefits, on-demand CRM systems have potential problems. First, the vendor could prove to be unreliable, in which case the client company would have no CRM functionality at all. Second, hosted software is difficult or impossible to modify, and only the vendor can upgrade it. Third, vendor-hosted CRM software may be difficult to integrate with the organization's existing software. Finally, giving strategic customer data to vendors always carries security and privacy risks.

Mobile CRM Systems

A **mobile CRM** system is an interactive system that enables an organization to conduct communications related to sales, marketing, and customer service activities through a mobile medium for the purpose of building and maintaining relationships with its customers. Simply put, mobile CRM systems involve interacting directly with consumers through portable devices such as smartphones. Many forward-thinking companies believe that mobile CRM systems have tremendous potential to create personalized customer relationships that may be accessed anywhere and at any time. In fact, the opportunities offered by mobile marketing appear so rich that many companies have already identified mobile CRM systems as a cornerstone of their future marketing activities. Chapter closing case 1 discusses a mobile CRM application at Disney World.

Open-Source CRM Systems

As explained in Plug IT In 2, the source code for open-source software is available at no cost. **Open-source CRM systems**, therefore, are CRM systems whose source code is available to developers and users.

Open-source CRM systems provide the same features or functions as other CRM software, and they may be implemented either on-premise or on-demand. Leading open-source CRM vendors include SugarCRM (www.sugarcrm.com), Concursive (www.concursive.com), and Vtiger (www.vtiger.com).

The benefits of open-source CRM systems include favorable pricing and a wide variety of applications. In addition, these systems are easy to customize. This is an attractive feature for organizations that need CRM software that is designed for their specific needs. Finally, updates and bug (software error) fixes for open-source CRM systems are rapidly distributed, and extensive support information is available free of charge. IT's About Business 12.2 explains how uShip obtained many benefits from implementing SugarCRM.

IT'S ABOUT BUSINESS 12.2

uShip Benefits from SugarCRM

uShip (www.uship.com) is a global online marketplace for shipping services. Individuals and businesses post items they need shipped in a variety of categories, including automobile transport, boat shipping, home and office moving and removal services, and the transport of heavy industrial equipment.

POM

Transportation service providers on uShip place competing bids for the right to haul a customer's shipment. For some categories, including boats, automobiles, and less-than-truckload (LTL) freight, customers can (1) select an upfront quote for transport services or (2) enter an acceptable price to be matched with a transporter. Customers can either book a shipment immediately from these quotes or opt to wait for auction bids, similar to eBay's "buy it now" feature. The site's reverse auction format reduces the cost of shipping by enabling service providers to find shipments along their routes and to fill empty cargo space.

uShip uses a feedback rating system for both service providers and customers. Transport companies maintain company profiles that feature past customer feedback in several service categories, equipment photos, videos, cargo insurance data, and information about the U.S. Department of Transportation licensing, operating authority, and licensing verification.

Fans of A&E's reality TV show *Shipping Wars* are familiar with uShip. It is the shipping marketplace used by the show, where six independent shippers bid to transport items that traditional carriers will not transport.

At first, uShip focused primarily on the consumer market, building a partnership with eBay. Then, in late 2013, the company began to develop two segments of its commercial business: full truckload (FTL) and less-than-truckload (LTL). However, uShip did not have infrastructure to support its rapid growth. The company needed a centralized point of access for customer contact information, such as notes and call data. Complicating the customer management issues, commercial accounts require longer-term management than retail customers, so uShip required a system that accommodated both. In addition, uShip's LTL sales team is field based, whereas the retail and FTL sales teams are located in-house. uShip wanted all of its sales teams to utilize the same CRM platform.

uShip selected SugarCRM (www.sugarcrm.com) as its CRM platform. SugarCRM had the capability to integrate with uShip's telephony system, its databases, the uship.com Web site, and its help desk application. To help implement the SugarCRM solution, uShip chose the systems integration firm Epicom (www.epicom.com). Epicom employed a phased approach in the system's implementation. Phase 1 developed a solution for uShip's commercial accounts, Phase 2 developed a solution for its retail accounts, and Phase 3 developed a solution for its telephony system.

SugarCRM enables uShip to efficiently in-process new customers, manage hundreds of disparate accounts utilizing a single interface, provide a superior customer experience, and support the company's rapid growth. The new system has also enabled every area of uShip's business to enhance their speed and productivity. In fact, it has increased uShip's overall efficiency by 20 percent.

As one example, if a problem arises that needs to be handled by customer service, in the past it had taken uShip just a minute or two to find the account. With SugarCRM, the account is displayed to the uShip customer representative instantly. Company reporting is also more efficient and effective, saving six to eight hours per week per employee. In addition, the workload of the analytics group has been substantially reduced. Without the SugarCRM package, uShip would have had to hire additional staff to manage this workload.

Sources: Compiled from "uShip, eBay Deal Puts Spotlight on Larger-Than-Parcel Shipping," *Business Wire*, March 10, 2014; "New Service for LTL Spot Rate Marketplace from uShip," *Fleet News Daily*, March, 2014; J. Berman, "uShip Introduces Online LTL Spot Rate Marketplace," Logistics Management, January 23, 2014; A. Heim, "Online Shipping Marketplace uShip Plans on Leveraging Brazil's Logistics Woes to Bolster Its Business," *TheNextWeb*, January 23, 2013; "uShip," *SugarCRM Case Study*, 2012; www.uship.com, www.sugarcrm.com, www.epicom.com, accessed April 2, 2014.

Questions

1. Describe the advantages provided to uShip by the SugarCRM system.

2. Describe the business needs of uShip that led to the company's decision to implement a CRM system.

Like all software, however, open-source CRM systems have certain risks. The most serious risk involves quality control. Because open-source CRM systems are created by a large community of unpaid developers, there sometimes is no central authority responsible for overseeing the quality of the product. (We discuss open-source software in Plug IT In 2). Furthermore, for best results, companies must have the same IT platform in place as the one on which the open-source CRM system was developed.

Social CRM

Social CRM is the use of social media technology and services to enable organizations to engage their customers in a collaborative conversation in order to provide mutually beneficial value in a trusted and transparent manner. In fact, social CRM is the company's response to the customers' ownership of this two-way conversation. In social CRM, organizations monitor services such as Facebook, Twitter, and LinkedIn (among many others) for relevant mentions of their products, services, and brand, and they respond accordingly.

Social media are also providing methods that customers are using to obtain faster, better customer service. IT's About Business 12.3 recounts how one customer was pleasantly surprised when Morton's Steakhouse responded to his tweet.

IT'S ABOUT BUSINESS 12.3

Morton's Steakhouse Surprises a Customer

© peshkov/iStockphoto

Peter Shankman was tied up in meetings all day, and he had to take a later flight home that caused him to miss his dinner. So, he jokingly tweeted Morton's Steakhouse (www.mortons.com) and requested that the restaurant meet him at the airport with a porterhouse steak when he landed.

Morton's saw the Tweet, discovered that the tweeter was a frequent customer (and frequent tweeter—Shankman has 100,000 Twitter followers), pulled data on what he typically ordered, identified the flight he was on, and then sent a delivery person to Newark Airport (New Jersey) to serve him his dinner. When Shankman got to the reception lobby at the airport, he noticed a man in a tuxedo holding a card with Shankman's name. The man was also carrying a bag that contained a 24-ounce Porterhouse steak, an order of Colossal shrimp, a side order of potatoes, bread, two napkins, and silverware.

The closest Morton's restaurant was 24 miles from the airport, and Shankman's flight took only two hours. This scenario says a lot about both Morton's customer service and the speed of social media. Admittedly, the entire scenario was a publicity stunt that went explosively viral over the Internet. This is not the point, however. The question businesses should be asking themselves is: Would your company even consider doing something like this?

Sources: C. Chan, "Morton's Steakhouse Met a Man at the Airport with a Steak After He Asked for One on Twitter," *Gizmodo*, August 19, 2011; M. Flacy, "After a Single Tweet, Air Traveler Gets a Morton's Surprise at Newark Airport," *Digital Trends*, August 18, 2011; "Peter Shankman Tweet Joke Leads to Morton's Surprise Steak Dinner at Newark Airport," *The Huffington Post*, August 11, 2013; www.mortons.com, accessed March 31, 2014.

Questions

1. Explain how Morton's monitoring of social media illustrates how CRM is reviving personal marketing.

2. Do you see any disadvantages in such close monitoring of social media? Provide specific examples to support your answer.

BEFORE *YOU GO ON....*

1. Define on-demand CRM.
2. Define mobile CRM.
3. Define open-source CRM.

Apply The Concept 12.4

LEARNING OBJECTIVE 12.4 Explain the advantages and disadvantages of mobile CRM systems, on-demand CRM systems, and open-source CRM systems.

STEP 1 – Background

Section 12.4 has outlined different CRM systems—not operational or analytical—but, instead, the different ways you can actually implement a CRM system. For example, you can run mobile CRM, open-source CRM, on-demand CRM (cloud), and more. You will have most—if not all—of these options with any system you plan to implement!

STEP 2 – Activity

Visit http://www.wiley.com/go/rainer/MIS3e/applytheconcept, and click on the links provided for Apply the Concept 12.4. One link will take you to a YouTube video that describes an on-demand CRM system (Salesforce). Another will take you to a video that highlights an open-source CRM (SugarCRM). The final link will illustrate a hybrid approach, Sales Cloud (mobile-cloud CRM). Watch these videos, paying special attention to the advantages and disadvantages of each approach. The advantages will be easy to spot (these are promotional videos). The disadvantages of each one will become obvious as you compare the advantages of the others because you may notice particular functions that system one cannot perform but the others can.

STEP 3 – Deliverable

Build a table that highlights the advantages and disadvantages of each approach. Do the differences reside in the capabilities of the software or in the user experience? Submit your table to your instructor.

What's in **T** for ME?

 FOR
ACCOUNTING MAJORS

CRM systems can help companies establish controls for financial reporting related to interactions with customers in order to support compliance with legislation. For example, Sarbanes-Oxley requires companies to establish and maintain an adequate set of controls for accurate financial reporting that can be audited by a third party. Other sections [302 and 401(b)] have implications for customer activities, including the requirements that sales figures reported for the prior year be correct. Section 409 requires companies to report material changes to financial conditions, such as the loss of a strategic customer or significant customer claims about product quality.

CRM systems can track document flow from a sales opportunity to a sales order, to an invoice, to an accounting document, thus enabling finance and accounting managers to monitor the entire flow. CRM systems that track sales quotes and orders can be used to incorporate process controls that identify questionable sales transactions. CRM systems can provide exception-alert capabilities to identify instances outside defined parameters that put companies at risk.

FIN ### FOR THE FINANCE MAJOR

CRM systems allow companies to track marketing expenses, collecting appropriate costs for each individual marketing campaign. These costs then can be matched to corporate initiatives and financial objectives, demonstrating the financial impact of the marketing campaign.

Pricing is another key area that impacts financial reporting. For example, what discounts are available? When can a price be overridden? Who approves discounts? CRM systems can put controls into place for these issues.

MKT ### FOR THE MARKETING MAJOR

CRM systems are an integral part of every marketing professional's work activities. CRM systems contain the consolidated customer data that provides the foundation for making informed marketing decisions. Using these data, marketers develop well-timed and targeted sales campaigns with customized product mixes and established price points that enhance potential sales opportunities and therefore increase revenue. CRM systems also support the development of forecasting models for future sales to existing clients through the use of historical data captured from previous transactions.

 ### FOR THE PRODUCTION/ OPERATIONS MANAGEMENT MAJOR

Production is heavily involved in the acquisition of raw materials, conversion, and distribution of finished goods. However, all of these activities are driven by sales. Increases or decreases in the demand for goods result in a corresponding increase or decrease in a company's need for raw materials. Integral to a company's demand is forecasting future sales, an important part of CRM systems. Sales forecasts are created from the historical data stored in CRM systems.

This information is critically important to a production manager who is placing orders for manufacturing processes. Without an accurate future sales forecast, production managers may face inventory problems (discussed in detail in this chapter). The use of CRM systems for production and operational support is critical to efficiently managing the resources of the company.

 ### FOR THE HUMAN RESOURCES MAJOR

Companies trying to enhance their customer relationships must recognize that employees who interact with customers are critical to the success of CRM strategies. Essentially, the success of CRM is based on the employees' desire and ability to promote the company and its CRM initiatives. In fact, research analysts have found that customer loyalty is based largely on employees' capabilities and their commitment to the company.

As a result, human resource managers know that a company that desires valued customer relationships needs valued relationships with its employees. Therefore, HR managers are implementing programs to increase employee satisfaction and are training employees to execute CRM strategies

FOR THE MIS MAJOR

The IT function in the enterprise is responsible for the corporate databases and data warehouse, as well as the correctness and completeness of the data in them. That is, the IT department provides the data used in a 360° view of the customer. Furthermore, IT personnel provide the technologies underlying the customer interaction center.

SUMMARY

1. Identify the primary functions of both customer relationship management (CRM) and collaborative CRM.

   Customer relationship management (CRM) is an organizational strategy that is customer focused and customer driven. That is, organizations concentrate on assessing customers' requirements for products and services and then on providing high-quality, responsive services. CRM functions include acquiring new customers, retaining existing customers, and growing relationships with existing customers.

   Collaborative CRM is an organizational CRM strategy where data consolidation and the 360° view of the customer enable the organization's functional areas to readily share information about customers. The functions of collaborative CRM include integrating communications between the organization and its customers in all aspects of marketing, sales, and customer support processes, and enabling customers to provide direct feedback to the organization.

2. Describe how businesses might use applications of each of the two major components of operational CRM systems.

   Operational CRM systems support the front-office business processes that interact directly with customers (i.e., sales, marketing, and service). The two major components of operational CRM systems are customer-facing applications and customer-touching applications.

   Customer-facing CRM applications include customer service and support, sales force automation, marketing, and campaign management. *Customer-touching applications* include search and comparison capabilities, technical and other information and services, customized products and services, personalized Web pages, FAQs, e-mail and automated response, and loyalty programs.

3. Discuss the benefits of analytical CRM systems to businesses.

   Analytical CRM systems analyze customer behavior and perceptions in order to provide business intelligence.

   Organizations use analytical systems for many purposes, including designing and executing targeted marketing campaigns; increasing customer acquisition, cross-selling, and upselling; providing input into decisions relating to products and services (e.g., pricing, and product development); and providing financial forecasting and customer profitability analysis.

4. Explain the advantages and disadvantages of mobile CRM systems, on-demand CRM systems, and open-source CRM systems.

   On-demand CRM systems are those hosted by an external vendor in the vendor's data center. Advantages of on-demand CRM systems include lower costs and a need for employees to know only how to access and utilize the software. Drawbacks include possibly unreliable vendors, difficulty in modifying the software, and difficulty in integrating vendor-hosted CRM software with the organization's existing software.

   Mobile CRM systems are interactive systems where communications related to sales, marketing, and customer service activities are conducted through a mobile medium for the purpose of building and maintaining customer relationships between an organization and its customers. Advantages of mobile CRM systems include convenience for customers and the chance to build a truly personal relationship with customers. A drawback could be difficulty in maintaining customer expectations; that is, the company must be extremely responsive to customer needs in a mobile, near-real-time environment.

   Open-source CRM systems are those whose source code is available to developers and users. The benefits of open-source CRM systems include favorable pricing, a wide variety of applications, easy customization, rapid updates and bug (software error) fixes, and extensive free support information. The major drawback of open-source CRM systems is quality control.

>>>CHAPTER GLOSSARY

analytical CRM system CRM system that analyzes customer behavior and perceptions in order to provide actionable business intelligence.

bundling A form of cross-selling where an enterprise sells a group of products or services together at a lower price than the combined individual price of the products.

campaign management applications CRM applications that help organizations plan marketing campaigns that send the right messages to the right people through the right channels.

collaborative CRM system A CRM system where communications between the organization and its customers are integrated across all aspects of marketing, sales, and customer support processes.

cross-selling The practice of marketing additional related products to customers based on a previous purchase.

customer-facing CRM applications Areas where customers directly interact with the organization, including customer service and support, sales force automation, marketing, and campaign management.

customer interaction center (CIC) A CRM operation where organizational representatives use multiple communication channels to interact with customers in functions such as inbound teleservice and outbound telesales.

customer relationship management (CRM) A customer-focused and customer-driven organizational strategy that concentrates on addressing customers' requirements for products and services, and then providing high-quality, responsive services.

customer-touching CRM applications (also called **electronic CRM** or **e-CRM**) Applications and technologies with which customers interact and typically help themselves.

customer touch point Any interaction between a customer and an organization.

electronic CRM (e-CRM) See **customer-touching CRM applications**.

front-office processes Those processes that directly interact with customers; that is, sales, marketing, and service.

loyalty program Programs that offer rewards to customers to influence future behavior.

mobile CRM system An interactive CRM system where communications related to sales, marketing, and customer service activities are conducted through a mobile medium for the purpose of building and maintaining customer relationships between an organization and its customers.

on-demand CRM system A CRM system that is hosted by an external vendor in the vendor's data center.

open-source CRM system CRM software whose source code is available to developers and users.

operational CRM system The component of CRM that supports the front-office business processes that directly interact with customers (i.e., sales, marketing, and service).

sales force automation (SFA) The component of an operational CRM system that automatically records all the aspects in a sales transaction process.

social CRM The use of social media technology and services to enable organizations to engage their customers in a collaborative conversation in order to provide mutually beneficial value in a trusted and transparent manner.

upselling A sales strategy where the organizational representative provides to customers the opportunity to purchase higher-value related products or services in place of, or along with, the consumer's initial product or service selection.

>>>DISCUSSION QUESTIONS

1. How do customer relationship management systems help organizations achieve customer intimacy?

2. What is the relationship between data consolidation and CRM systems?

3. Discuss the relationship between CRM and customer privacy.

4. Distinguish between operational CRM systems and analytical CRM systems.

5. Differentiate between customer-facing CRM applications and customer-touching CRM applications.

6. Explain why Web-based customer interaction centers are critical for successful CRM systems.

7. Why are companies so interested in e-CRM applications?

8. Discuss why it is difficult to justify CRM applications.

9. You are the CIO of a small company with a rapidly growing customer base. Which CRM system would you use: an on-premise CRM system, an on-demand CRM system, or an open-source CRM system? Remember that open-source CRM systems may be implemented either on-premise or on-demand. Discuss the pros and cons of each type of CRM system for your business.

10. Refer to the example concerning the CRM efforts of Caterpillar. Where on the CRM continuum (low-end to high-end) does the company's CRM strategy fit? Explain your answer.

>>>PROBLEM-SOLVING ACTIVITIES

1. Access www.ups.com and www.fedex.com. Examine some of the IT-supported customer services and tools provided by the two companies. Compare and contrast the customer support provided on the two companies' Web sites.

2. Enter www.anntaylor.com, www.hermes.com, and www.tiffany.com. Compare and contrast the customer service activities offered by these companies on their Web sites. Do you see marked similarities? Differences?

3. Access your university's Web site. Investigate how your university provides for customer relationship management. (*Hint:* First decide who your university's customers are.)

4. Access www.sugarcrm.com, and take the interactive tour. Prepare a report on SugarCRM's functionality to the class.

STEP 1 – Background

Customer relationship management (CRM) tools typically provide information to the marketing department. As you have read in other chapters, the information in one department will affect the activities in other departments. For example, when a company establishes its production targets for the next quarter, required labor is updated, suppliers are updated, and information from that decision is shared with other decision makers within the organization so that they can make appropriate plans.

STEP 2 – Activity

Imagine that you are the owner of an automobile manufacturer. Your supply chain has both B2B relationships (manufacturers and their suppliers) and B2C relationships (dealerships and their customers). Therefore, the marketing department encompasses both B2B and B2C channels. This situation creates an interesting mix of customer relationships. Is it possible that a single CRM solution can provide support to both B2B and B2C relationships?

Divide your team into two groups. One group should represent employees of the manufacturing company. The second group should represent the dealerships. The manufacturing group will visit http://www.wiley.com/go/rainer/

MIS3e/collaboration, and watch the video that demonstrates how Hyundai builds cars in its Montgomery, Alabama, plant. Watch for clues about data that are being collected and shared, and take notes on where those data may have been generated. The dealerships group will visit the Web site of the closest Hyundai dealership, and look for clues about data they are collecting and sharing. Both groups should try to reverse-engineer their respective marketing strategies and messages and identify their target market.

Each group should then search the Web for a CRM solution that will help them manage their customer relationships. Remember, the manufacturing company is dealing with other businesses (B2B) and the dealers are dealing with individual customers (B2C). Are you generally looking for operational or analytical CRM systems? Do you think a cloud, mobile, open-source, or some combination of these systems is the best alternative? Support your answer.

STEP 3 – Deliverable

Using Google Drive, create and share a Google Document. Each group (manufacturing and dealerships) should comment on their findings. Draft a memo for your company that recommends how you can utilize CRM to support both their manufacturing initiatives and those of their dealerships.

CLOSING **CASE 1** > Mobile

CRM at Disney World

THE BUSINESS PROBLEM >>> In the past, guests at Disney World (https://disneyworld.disney.go.com) passed through entrance turnstiles, redeemed paper tickets, decided which rides to take, and bought food and merchandise with cash or credit cards. They could also use Disney hotel key cards to charge items. People would race to Fast-Pass kiosks, which dispensed a limited number of free line-skipping tickets. However, gridlock quickly set in and people waited and waited.

THE SOLUTION >>> Disney has introduced a mobile CRM system called MyMagic+ that has drastically changed the way Disney World guests—some 30 million people per year—do just about everything. The intent of MyMagic+ is to make the experience of visiting Disney parks less difficult and more reflective of modern customer behavior. Disney is betting that MyMagic+ will make guests happier and less stressed, so they will spend more money at the company's parks.

MyMagic+ allows users of a new Web site and app—called My Disney Experience—to preselect three FastPasses before they leave home. Customers can use these passes for rides or V.I.P. seating for parades, fireworks displays, and character meet-and-greets. Orlando-bound guests can also preregister

for RFID bracelets, called MagicBands. These bands function as room key, park ticket, FastPass, and credit card.

With MyMagic+, Disney World has no entry turnstiles, and guests do not need cash. To enter the park, guests tap their MagicBands on a post, eliminating the need for turnstiles. Guests' MagicBands are encoded with credit card information, so they can buy corn dogs and Mickey Mouse ears with a tap of the wrist. Smartphone alerts signal when it is time to ride Space Mountain without standing in line.

MagicBands are also encoded with personal details, which allow customers to interact with Disney employees in a more personalized manner. Previously, the employee playing Cinderella could say hello only in a general way. Now—if parents opt in—hidden sensors will read MagicBand data, providing information needed for a personalized greeting: "Hi, Susan," the character might say without prompting. "I understand today is your birthday!"

Disney World also uses these data to make waiting areas for rides less boring. A new Magic Kingdom ride called Under the Sea, for instance, features a robotic version of Scuttle the seagull from "The Little Mermaid" that is able to chitchat with MagicBand wearers. Disney wants to take experiences that historically have been passive and make them as interactive as possible.

To alleviate privacy concerns, Disney will not require guests to use the MagicBand system. Moreover, customers who use it will decide how much information they want to share. An online options menu, for example, offers various controls: Do you want park employees to know your name? Do you want Disney to send you special offers when you get home? What about during your stay? However, even if a guest chooses the most restrictive settings, the MagicBand will still gather general information about how he or she uses the park.

The logistical challenges involved in deploying MyMagic+ and MagicBand were considerable. Disney World has 60,000 employees, many of whom had to be retrained to use the new technology. Disney World had already installed Wi-Fi, so smartphone users can access the My Disney experience app more readily. In addition, all of the new technology and procedures must be communicated to Super Bowl-sized crowds every day.

What happens if your MagicBand is lost or stolen? You have two options. First, park employees are trained to deactivate them. Alternatively, you can use the My Disney Experience app in place of your band. As a safety precaution, Disney requires guests to enter a PIN when using the wristbands to make purchases of $50 or more. Disney notes that the bands themselves contain no personally identifiable information.

THE RESULTS >>> *The Good News.* MyMagic+ helps Disney track its guests as they move about its parks, enabling the company to manage and allocate its workforce more efficiently. MyMagic+ allows guests to plan in advance how they will tour the parks. Hopefully, this capability will discourage them from, for example, making impromptu visits to Universal's Wizarding World of Harry Potter. This process will cut down on long lines and wait times.

The Potentially Bad News. The new CRM system places Disney in the middle of the debate on privacy and personal data collection. Like most major companies, Disney wants

MKT to collect as much information about its customers' preferences as it can, so that it can market to them more efficiently.

Disney is aware of potential privacy concerns, especially regarding children. However, Disney has decided that

MyMagic+ is essential to its marketing and CRM strategies. The company argues that it must aggressively integrate new technology into the customer experience at its parks—without damaging the sense of nostalgia on which the experience depends—or risk becoming irrelevant to future generations of guests.

When asked about privacy issues, one Disney guest replied: "As far as 'Big Brother' watching us as we wander the parks, anyone worried about 'real' privacy would not be wandering around a theme park already full of security cameras."

Sources: Compiled from B. Barnes, "Billion-Dollar Bracelet Is Key to Magical Kingdom," *New York Times*, April 2, 2014; D. Peterson, "Walt Disney World Offers MyMagic+, FastPass+, and MagicBands to Day Guests," *Examiner*, March 31, 2014; D. Bevil, "Disney World: MyMagic+, MagicBands Ready for Day Guests," *Orlando Sentinel*, March 31, 2014; K. Gambacorta, "Putting Disney MagicBands to the Test," *Fox News*, March 21, 2014; R. Brigante, "Walt Disney World Readies Full Rollout of MyMagic+ as MagicBands Become Available for Annual Passholders," *Inside the Magic*, March 7, 2014; W. Pramik, "New Disney MagicBands Make Touring – and Spending – Easy," *Cleveland Plain Dealer*, March 5, 2014; D. Lansky, "What Disney Got Wrong with Its Magic Bands," *The Huffington Post*, March 4, 2014; S. Sekula, "Disney Gets Personal with New MyMagic+ System," *USA Today*, February 25, 2014; E. Dockterman, "Now Disney Can Track Your Every Move with NSA-Style Wristbands," *Time*, January 2, 2014; L. Jenkins, "MyMagic+ Debuts at Disney," *Fodor's Travel*, December 13, 2013; J. Burstein, "Disney's Latest Experiment with Technology: MagicBands," *Miami Herald*, November 27, 2013; B. Barnes, "At Disney Parks, a Bracelet Meant to Build Loyalty (and Sales)," *New York Times*, January 7, 2013; https://disneyworld.disney.go.com, accessed April 1, 2014.

Questions

1. How do MyMagic+ and MagicBands contribute positively to the customer experience at Disney parks? Provide specific examples to support your answer.

2. Other than privacy, what are other disadvantages of MyMagic+ and MagicBands to guests? To Disney? To Disney employees? Provide specific examples to support your answer.

CLOSING **CASE 2 >** Organic and Beyond Corporation Manages Its New B2C Channel

Food safety has drawn increasing attention from the Chinese government and the Chinese populace, and this interest opened an opportunity for the organic agriculture market in China. In 2013, total organic food sales in China approached US$2 billion, with an expected annual growth rate of more than 30 percent.

Founded in 2007, Organic and Beyond Corporation (OABC) (www.oabc.cc/en/) cultivates, produces, distributes, and delivers organic food. Headquartered in Beijing,

the company has six branches in China. The company has established farms to grow organic vegetables, fruits, grains, Chinese lake crabs, and many other products.

As late as 2013, OABC operated a primarily business-to-business (B2B) model, selling produce to retail establishments such as restaurants. In contrast, the company's business-to-consumer (B2C) channel was relatively small. However, OABC wanted to expand this channel to increase its revenues. To accomplish this task, the enterprise had to reconfigure its information systems—which were designed to manage bulk sales and deliveries—so that they could also handle potentially millions of small orders. To make this transition possible, OABC had to reinvent itself to find new ways to service the B2C marketplace.

OABC engaged IBM Global Business Services to implement customer-centric business processes and systems that would encompass the entire customer fulfillment business process. OABC and IBM selected Oracle's Siebel Customer Relationship Management (CRM) system to provide a foundation for OABC's B2C operations.

OABC was able to transform customer management, thereby enhancing sales management, optimizing distribution, decreasing order fulfillment time, and personalizing service. The company also implemented systems that enable managers to visualize the order process, the delivery process, and overall company performance.

The near-real-time information systems allow OABC to understand its new B2C market, adjust its production and delivery processes to match demand, and operate at very low costs with minimal waste. In addition, the company can now closely track sales performance and identify opportunities for improvement.

Today OABC is able to service 30,000 consumers and to operate profitably, seizing a significant share of the B2C organic foods marketplace. The company's B2C channel provides home delivery services to more than 200,000 families in six metropolitan areas. The company reported an annual revenue of US$30 million in 2013.

Sources: Compiled from "EnfoDesk: China B2C Market Hit 763.71 Billion Yuan in 2013," *China Internet Watch*, March 19, 2014; "China Online Shopping Maintains High Growth in Q3 2013," *iResearch China*, December 3, 2013; "China B2C Online Shopping Industry Report, 2013–2016," *PRNewswire*, October 17, 2013; "OABC Grows Organically to Reach More than 400,000 Consumers," *IBM Sales and Distribution Success Story*, September, 18, 2013; S. Millward, "China's E-Commerce to Hit $71 Billion in Q2: These Are the Top 10 E-Stores," *Tech in Asia*, August 28, 2013; "Top 10 China B2C E-Commerce Websites," *Advangent*, August 20, 2013; M. Klein, "What B2B Can Learn from B2C," *Direct Marketing News*, August 2, 2013; www.oabc.cc/en/, accessed April 6, 2014.

Questions

1. Why is B2C electronic commerce so important in China?

2. Why is customer relationship management so important to B2C electronic commerce?

INTERNSHIP ACTIVITY> southwest wire A PRODUCTION COMPANY

Manufacturing Industry

Customer relationship management (CRM) and supply chain management (SCM) tools help organizations manage external relationships. In fact, CRM tools provide information that is useful to SCM systems even though the external entities they interact with are on opposite sides of the supply chain model.

This activity will focus on CRM, and the activity for the next chapter will focus on SCM. Imagine that, in addition to the work you completed on Chapter 11 (ERP) on the OpenERP implementation, you now are going to add CRM to the list of installed applications.

Below is another e-mail from Halle Smith, CIO of Southwest Wire.

To:	IT Intern
From:	Halle Smith
Subject:	CRM Implementation

Hello!

Thank you so much for your help on the OpenERP project. We have successfully implemented the Project Management, MRP, Warehouse Management, and Purchase Management modules. Now I want to add the CRM application.

OpenERP offers a CRM tool, but there are others available. SugarCRM is a popular tool that you can demo online. I think you will have to input your name and e-mail address, but I am interesting in seeing what they offer. Compare SugarCRM with the OpenERP tool, and let me know which one you feel is better suited to our needs. SugarCRM. Of course, one key consideration is the ease of implementation and integration. However, I do not want to acquire a subpar CRM just because it will integrate easily. Feel free to search the Web for any other CRM tools and review them as well. Basically, I want your feedback on the CRM tool that you feel is the most powerful, flexible, and useable.

I very much appreciate your work on this project.
Halle

Note: Any links or Web sites mentioned in this e-mail are available at http://www.wiley.com/go/rainer/MIS3e/internship.

SPREADSHEET ACTIVITY > BASIC CHARTS: CHART FORMATTING

STEP 1 – Background

Although individual charts are helpful, creating a series of charts is even more beneficial. An integrated collection of charts is called a *dashboard* because it allows you to quickly and easily view data and identify the key trends and activities within an organization.

It is also useful to be able to link to data located in separate worksheets. This capability allows you to update data in a single location rather than updating multiple copies. A database accomplishes this function through the use of relationships, but that is illustrated in another set of exercises.

STEP 2 – Activity

Imagine you are trying to manage your investment portfolio and you have multiple mutual funds and stocks to keep track of. Your entire portfolio is difficult to capture at a glance. You can review each individual stock, but it is difficult to see how all of your holdings translate into your "big picture."

Recall from the previous activity that you created pie charts, bar charts, scatter plots, and line graphs to display financial information. In this activity, you will perform the same tasks. However, the data will be stored on separate worksheets, and you will do more formatting to create something similar to a dashboard that enables you to view several charts at once.

Imagine how helpful it would be to see how slight changes in one fund price would impact the overall value of the portfolio!

STEP 3 – Deliverable

Visit http://www.wiley.com/go/rainer/MIS3e/spreadsheet, and download the required workbook. Additional instructions are provided to guide you through building four separate charts to create your personal investment portfolio dashboard. Complete your spreadsheet and submit it to your instructor.

Follow the instructions in the spreadsheet and submit your final work to your instructor.

Additional help with this spreadsheet skill is available in WileyPLUS. Open the "Microsoft Office 2013 Lab Manual Spreadsheet Module: Excel 2013," and review Lesson 12: Creating Charts and Lesson 13: Enhancing Worksheet Appearance. Help is also available from the Microsoft Support Web site at the link shown above. This page will also provide assistance with formatting charts and graphs.

DATABASE ACTIVITY > QUERY BY FORM

STEP 1 – Background

Forms and queries have a reciprocal relationship. Forms can be a relatively easy method to provide the input to a query. In turn, query results can be used in place of tables to drive forms. In this activity you will see how a form drives a query. Hopefully, this exercise will enhance your understanding of both functions. It also lets you replace a series of parameter entry dialogue boxes with a single form while allowing you to create a more attractive user interface. To use it, you must create both the query and the form.

STEP 2 – Activity

Visit http://www.wiley.com/go/rainer/MIS3e/database, and download the database linked for the Chapter 12 Activity. This database includes sales data for a chain of computer stores.

We want this query to identify which customers ordered products in a chosen category from a chosen store, and which products they ordered. To begin, display all five database tables in the upper pane of the query design window. Then, double-click on four fields to enter them into the query design: StoreCity from StoreTbl, ProdCategory from ProductTbl, CustName from CustomerTbl, and ProdDescrip from ProductTbl. Run the query to test it. You should see an unsorted list of all 312 purchases. If you do not, then review the previous steps to find the error. Finally, close the query, saving it as CS_Qry when prompted.

The next step is to create the form that will activate this query. Your final form should allow you to enter the store about which you want information as well as the product categories you are interested in. When you run this "query by form" without entering information in the boxes, your response will resemble the entire datasheet. Everything will show up. However, if you type in a store city and/or a product category, you should see only the data you requested.

STEP 3 – Deliverable

Once your form is working, query the database for different combinations of Store City and Product Category. Write down the answers, and comment on any differences among the combinations that you find.

CHAPTER **13**

Supply Chain Management

CHAPTER OUTLINE

13.1 Supply Chains

13.2 Supply Chain Management

13.3 Information Technology Support for Supply Chain Management

LEARNING OBJECTIVES >>>

13.1. Describe the three components and the three flows of a supply chain.

13.2. Identify popular strategies to solving different challenges of supply chains.

13.3. Explain the utility of each of the three major technologies that support supply chain management.

OPENING **CASE** > Coca-Cola Enterprises

Coca-Cola is one of the world's most recognizable and powerful brands. The beverage maker has dominated the global soft drink market for more than a century. Coca-Cola Enterprises (CCE) (www.cokecce.com) is a marketer, producer, and distributor of Coca-Cola products in Europe. CCE is the exclusive bottler for all of Belgium, continental France, Great Britain, Luxembourg, Monaco, The Netherlands, Norway, and Sweden. The enterprise purchases Coca-Cola concentrate from the Coca-Cola Company and combines it with other ingredients to create some of the most popular beverages in the countries in which it operates.

CCE produces and stores 11 billion bottles and cans at its 17 plants, 96 production lines, and 21 warehouses. The company delivers its products to more than 1 million retail outlets such as restaurants and food stores. In turn, these outlets provide 30 billion servings to more than 170 million consumers every year.

In its pursuit of long-term, sustainable growth, CCE faces similar challenges to other manufacturing and logistics businesses. Its top priority is replacing outdated information systems (IS) with a modernized information technology (IT) platform across its various markets to create a holistic, integrated view of its business metrics and to streamline its business processes.

 CCE executives recognized that establishing this IT platform was essential for the firm to expand its European operations. The platform would enable

CCE to implement a consistent set of standards and processes, which it could efficiently incorporate when it acquired and integrated new territories into its business.

CCE is a customer services enterprise with an elaborate supply chain. Therefore, it is critical that the company integrates its manufacturing plants all the way through the supply chain to the replenishment of shelves in its retail outlets. The company's objective was to integrate the manufacturing side of its business, which drives the *supply* of its products, with the shelf-replenishment side of its business, which drives the *demand* for its products.

© withGod/Shutterstock

CCE ultimately implemented a new supply chain management (SCM) solution at all of its European plants. The new system replaced and automated many of the company's existing supply chain processes. Significantly, deploying this system quickly and effectively required its employees to develop new skill sets. CCE selected CSC (www.csc.com) as a partner to help deliver the new system and to train users on the new business processes.

The new system is an integrated SAP (www.sap.com) enterprise resource planning (ERP) solution that replaces CCE's legacy systems in the business processes of "order to cash," "requisition to payment," and "record to report."

The system allows CCE to shorten cycle time in these processes while increasing the company's productivity. The new platform also brings more visibility into the company's supply chain operations, and it improves its decision-making processes.

Sources: Compiled from J. Stewart, "For Coke, Challenge Is Staying Relevant," *New York Times*, February 28, 2014; "Coca-Cola Supply Chain Management Success Story," *Scoop.it*, March 12, 2013; "Coca-Cola Enterprises," *CSC Success Story*, 2013; "Coca-Cola Supply Chain Improving," *i-Procure*, 2013; B. Hochfelder, "Things Go Better with Coke's Supply Chain," *Supply and Demand Chain Executive*, September 2, 2011; www.cokecce.com, accessed April 10, 2014.

Questions

1. Describe why new supply chain management technology is so important to CCE.
2. Describe the advantages of the new system to CCE.
3. Refer to Chapter 2. Is the new supply chain management system at CCE a strategic information system? Why or why not?

13.1 Supply Chains

Modern organizations are increasingly concentrating on their core competencies and on becoming more flexible and agile. To accomplish these objectives, they rely on other companies, rather than on companies they themselves own, to supply the goods and services they need. Organizations recognize that these suppliers can perform these activities more efficiently and effectively than they themselves can. This trend toward relying on an increasing number of suppliers has led to the concept of supply chains. A **supply chain** is the flow of materials, information, money, and services from raw material suppliers, through factories and warehouses, to the end customers. A supply chain also includes the *organizations* and *processes* that create and deliver products, information, and services to the end customers.

Supply chains enhance trust and collaboration among supply chain partners, thus improving supply chain visibility and inventory velocity. **Supply chain visibility** refers to the ability of all organizations within a supply chain to access or view relevant data on purchased materials as these materials move through their suppliers' production processes and transportation networks to their receiving docks. In addition, organizations can access or view relevant data on outbound goods as they are manufactured, assembled, or stored in inventory and then shipped through their transportation networks to their customers' receiving docks. The more quickly a company can deliver products and services after receiving the materials required to make them—that is, the higher the **inventory velocity**—the more satisfied the company's customers will be.

Supply chains are a vital component of the overall strategies of many modern organizations. To utilize supply chains efficiently, a business must be tightly integrated with its suppliers, business partners, distributors, and customers. A critical component of this integration is the use of information systems to facilitate the exchange of information among the participants in the supply chain.

You might ask, "Why do I need to study supply chain management?" The answer is that supply chains are critical to modern organizations. Therefore, regardless of your position within an organization, you will be involved with some aspect of your company's supply

Figure 13.1 Generic supply chain.

chain. You might think that supply chain management is only for large organizations. In fact, they have become essential to small and mid-sized organizations as well.

The Structure and Components of Supply Chains

The term *supply chain* comes from a picture of how the partnering organizations are linked together. FIGURE 13.1 illustrates a typical supply chain. (Recall that FIGURE 1.5 also illustrated a supply chain, in a slightly different way.) Note that the supply chain involves three segments:

1. *Upstream*, where sourcing or procurement from external suppliers occurs.

   In this segment, supply chain managers select suppliers to deliver the goods and services the company needs to produce its product or service. Furthermore, SC managers develop the pricing, delivery, and payment processes between a company and its suppliers. Included here are processes for managing inventory, receiving and verifying shipments, transferring goods to manufacturing facilities, and authorizing payments to suppliers.

2. *Internal*, where packaging, assembly, or manufacturing takes place.

   SC managers schedule the activities necessary for production, testing, packaging, and preparing goods for delivery. In addition, they monitor quality levels, production output, and worker productivity.

3. *Downstream*, where distribution takes place, frequently by external distributors.

   In this segment, SC managers coordinate the receipt of orders from customers, develop a network of warehouses, select carriers to deliver products to customers, and implement invoicing systems to receive payments from customers.

The flow of information and goods can be bidirectional. For example, damaged or unwanted products can be returned, a process known as *reverse flows* or *reverse logistics*. In the retail clothing industry, for example, reverse logistics involves clothing that customers return, either because the item had defects or because the customer did not like the item.

Tiers of Suppliers. FIGURE 13.1 shows several tiers of suppliers. As the diagram indicates, a supplier may have one or more subsuppliers, a subsupplier may have its own subsupplier(s), and so on. For an automobile manufacturer, for example, Tier 3 suppliers produce basic products such as glass, plastic, and rubber; Tier 2 suppliers use these inputs to make windshields, tires, and plastic moldings; and Tier 1 suppliers produce integrated components such as dashboards and seat assemblies.

The Flows in the Supply Chain. There are typically three flows in the supply chain: material, information, and financial. *Material flows* are the physical products, raw materials, supplies, and so forth that flow along the chain. Material flows also include the reverse flows discussed above. A supply chain thus involves a *product life cycle* approach, from "dirt to dust."

Information flows consist of data related to demand, shipments, orders, returns, and schedules, as well as changes in any of these data. Finally, *financial flows* involve money transfers, payments, credit card information and authorization, payment schedules, e-payments, and credit-related data.

Significantly, different supply chains have different numbers and types of flows. For instance, in service industries there may be no physical flow of materials, but frequently there is a flow of information, often in the form of documents (physical or electronic copies). For example, the digitization of software, music, and other content can create a supply chain without any physical flow. Notice, however, that in such a case there are two types of information flows: one that replaces materials flow (digitized software), and another that provides the supporting information (orders, billing, and so on). To manage the supply chain, an organization must coordinate all three flows among all of the parties involved in the chain, a topic we turn to next.

BEFORE *YOU GO ON....*

1. What is a supply chain?
2. Describe the three segments of a supply chain.
3. Describe the flows in a supply chain.

Apply The Concept 13.1

LEARNING OBJECTIVE 13.1 Describe the three components and the three flows of a supply chain.

STEP 1 – Background (Here is what you are learning.)

Section 13.1 has focused on supply chain flows, materials, and "positions" (upstream, internal, and downstream). It is important to understand how products move in the supply chain because data move along with them every step of the way. In fact, the data that travel with materials and products are more important to the efficiency of the operation than the products themselves!

STEP 2 – Activity (Here is what you are doing.)

Visit http://www.wiley.com/go/rainer/MIS3e/applytheconcept, and click on the link provided for Apply the Concept 13.1. This link will take you to a YouTube video titled "Module 1: What is Supply Chain Management? (ASU-WPC-SCM)" by user "wpcareyschool."

As you watch the video, consider the data that would be transferred with each product movement within the bottled water supply chain. Certain types of data, such as inventory updates, shipment information, quality checks, and supplier information, would deal just with the bottled water itself. In addition, there will be HR information, employee data, and machine data from the internal organization as well as from all of the suppliers!

STEP 3 – Deliverable (Here is what you turn in.)

Using the example you learned about in Step 2, describe the three components and the three flows of a water bottle supply chain in a report. Submit your report to your instructor.

13.2 Supply Chain Management

The function of **supply chain management (SCM)** is to improve the processes a company uses to acquire the raw materials it needs to produce a product or service and then deliver that product or service to its customers. That is, supply chain management is the process of planning, organizing, and optimizing the various activities performed along the supply chain. There are five basic components of SCM:

1. *Plan*: Planning is the strategic component of SCM. Organizations must have a strategy for managing all the resources that are involved in meeting customer demand for their product or service. Planning involves developing a set of metrics (measurable deliverables) to monitor the organization's supply chain to ensure that it is efficient and it delivers high quality and value to customers for the lowest cost.

2. *Source*: In the sourcing component, organizations choose suppliers to deliver the goods and services they need to create their product or service. Supply chain managers develop pricing, delivery, and payment processes with suppliers, and they create metrics to monitor and improve their relationships with their suppliers. They also develop processes for managing their goods and services inventory, including receiving and verifying shipments, transferring the shipped materials to manufacturing facilities, and authorizing supplier payments.

3. *Make*: This is the manufacturing component. Supply chain managers schedule the activities necessary for production, testing, packaging, and preparation for delivery. This component is the most metric-intensive part of the supply chain, where organizations measure quality levels, production output, and worker productivity.

4. *Deliver*: This component, often referred to as logistics, is where organizations coordinate the receipt of customer orders, develop a network of warehouses, select carriers to transport their products to their customers, and create an invoicing system to receive payments.

5. *Return*: Supply chain managers must create a responsive and flexible network for receiving defective, returned, or excess products back from their customers, as well as for supporting customers who have problems with delivered products.

Like other functional areas, SCM utilizes information systems. The goal of SCM systems is to reduce the problems, or friction, along the supply chain. Friction can increase time, costs, and inventories and decrease customer satisfaction. SCM systems, therefore, reduce uncertainty and risks by decreasing inventory levels and cycle time while improving business processes and customer service. These benefits make the organization more profitable and competitive.

Significantly, SCM systems are a type of interorganizational information system. In an **interorganizational information system (IOS)**, information flows among two or more organizations. By connecting the IS of business partners, IOSs enable the partners to perform a number of tasks:

- Reduce the costs of routine business transactions
- Improve the quality of the information flow by reducing or eliminating errors
- Compress the cycle time involved in fulfilling business transactions
- Eliminate paper processing and its associated inefficiencies and costs
- Make the transfer and processing of information easier for users

One of the most important goals of SCM systems is to give an organization visibility into its supply chain. *Supply chain visibility* is the ability of an organization to track products in transit from the manufacturer to their final destination. The goal of SCV is to improve the supply chain by making data readily available to all parties in the supply chain. Supply chain visibility promotes quick responses to problems or changes along the supply chain by enabling companies to shift products to where they are needed. IT's About Business 13.1 illustrates how Crate & Barrel improved its supply chain visibility.

IT'S ABOUT BUSINESS 13.1

Crate & Barrel Increases Its Supply Chain Visibility

Crate & Barrel (CB) (www.crateandbarrel.com), a leading retailer in the area of home furniture and furnishings, is finding that globalization brings many opportunities, but it also increases challenges and risk. The company has used an import model for much of its merchandise, meaning that when it sources (procures) goods from overseas, it ships those goods to the United States and then distributes them back to overseas markets. The retailer wants to improve its supply chain transparency significantly, so, for example, it can source goods from overseas and ship them directly to nearby overseas markets without going through the United States, an arrangement known as *international transfers*. That is, Crate & Barrel is working to evolve what had been a U.S.-centric supply chain into a truly global supply chain. The retailer's ultimate goal is to put any CB product anywhere in the world, quickly and cost-effectively.

 As of mid-2014, CB sourced from about three dozen different countries, and it was expanding its international store locations. As a result, the challenges of importing and exporting continue to increase. Adding to the complexity of its supply chain are myriad new regulations relating to product quality, plant security, and other related areas. Furthermore, these regulations are increasing both within the United Sates and globally.

© Lightspring/Shutterstock

In addition to globalization, electronic commerce has also created a number of opportunities and challenges. The opportunity occurs because consumers across the globe can purchase CB products online. The challenges occur because e-commerce also increases customer expectations in terms of service and information. In fact, the price transparency that comes with e-commerce has made cost reduction a key supply chain imperative for CB.

To reduce both supply chain costs and risk, CB set out to increase its supply chain visibility. To accomplish this process, the company needed data about the products in its supply chain such as what the products are, where they are, and when will they get to where they are supposed to be. CB implemented a new supply chain visibility system from Amber Road (www.amberroad.com), a provider of software solutions for global trade management.

The new system provides detailed end-to-end views of orders, inventory, shipments, events, and **POM** many more variables across CB's entire global supply chain. The system includes inbound import visibility, outbound export visibility, and international transfers.

Supply chain visibility enhances supply chain flexibility. Supply chain flexibility is necessary because problems inevitably occur along the supply chain, forcing companies to make appropriate adjustments on the fly. Using Amber

Road's system, Crate & Barrel can now identify where inventory is "stuck" in a location, and it can move this inventory to areas where it is needed. CB hopes that this process will enable it to make smaller, more frequent shipments that may actually cost more per unit shipped but will pay off in higher sales and reduced inventory costs. In essence, the costs that accompany inventory that a company owns too long, or that is in the wrong place in the company's supply chain, are higher than the costs of shipping less cost-effectively.

Sources: Compiled from A. Gonzalez, "Where Will You Find Supply Chain Innovation," *LinkedIn Pulse*, April 10, 2014; "Supply Chain News: eFulfillmente Wars Continue On, with New Ordering Gizmo from Amazon, New Retail Partners for eBay Now," *Supply Chain Digest*, April 7, 2014; "Ultriva's New Strategic Insights Regarding End to End Supply Chain Visibility Featuring Research from Gartner," *PR.com*, April 6, 2014; S. Hickman, "Indonesian Teak Farmers Achieve Traceability to the Tree Stump," *The Guardian*, March 18, 2014; "Crate & Barrel's Vision for Global Supply Chain Visibility Is Crystal Clear," *Supply Chain Digest*, January 16, 2014; B. Heaney, "Supply Chain Visibility," *Aberdeen Group*, May, 2013; D. Kent, "Finding Profitable Proximity," *EBN*, December 24, 2012; www.crateandbarrel.com, www.amberroad.com, accessed April 11, 2014.

Questions

1. Discuss the advantages of supply chain visibility for any organization.

2. Explain how an increase in shipping costs can actually generate higher revenues for Crate & Barrel.

The Push Model Versus the Pull Model

Many SCM systems employ the **push model**. In this model, also known as *make-to-stock*, the production process begins with a forecast, which is simply an educated guess as to customer demand. The forecast must predict which products customers will want and in what quantities. The company then produces the amount of products in the forecast, typically by using mass production, and sells, or "pushes," those products to consumers.

Push
© Milan Zeremski/iStockphoto

Pull
© Milan Zeremski/iStockphoto

Unfortunately, these forecasts are often incorrect. Consider, for example, an automobile manufacturer that wants to produce a new car. Marketing managers conduct extensive research, including customer surveys and analyses of competitors' cars, and then provide the results to forecasters. If the forecasters' predictions are too high—that is, if they predict that customers will purchase a certain number of these new cars but actual demand falls below this amount—then the automaker has excess cars in inventory and will incur large carrying costs (the costs of storing unsold inventory). Furthermore, the company will probably have to sell the excess cars at a discount.

From the opposite perspective, if the forecasters' predictions are too low—that is, actual customer demand exceeds expectations—then the automaker probably will have to run extra shifts to meet the demand, thereby incurring substantial overtime costs. Furthermore, the company risks losing business to its competitors if the car that customers want is not available. Thus, using the push model in supply chain management can cause problems, as you will see in the next section.

To avoid the uncertainties associated with the push model, many companies now employ the pull model of supply chain management, using Web-enabled information flows. In the **pull model**, also known as *make-to-order*, the production process begins with a customer order. Therefore, companies make only what customers want, a process closely aligned with mass customization (discussed in Chapter 1).

A prominent example of a company that uses the pull model is Dell Computer. Dell's production process begins with a customer order. This order not only specifies the type of computer the customer wants but also alerts each Dell supplier as to the parts of the order for which that supplier is responsible. That way, Dell's suppliers ship only the parts that Dell needs to produce the computer.

Not all companies can use the pull model. Automobiles, for example, are far more complicated and more expensive to manufacture than computers, so automobile companies require longer lead times to produce new models. Automobile companies do use the pull model, but only for specific automobiles that some customers order (e.g., Rolls-Royce, Bentley, and other extremely expensive cars).

Problems Along the Supply Chain

As you saw earlier, friction can develop within a supply chain. One major consequence of friction is poor customer service. In some cases, supply chains do not deliver products or services when and where customers—either individuals or businesses—need them. In other cases, the supply chain provides poor-quality products. Other problems associated with supply chain friction are high inventory costs and revenue loss.

The problems along the supply chain arise primarily from two sources: (1) uncertainties, and (2) the need to coordinate multiple activities, internal units, and business partners. A major source of supply chain uncertainties is the *demand forecast*. Demand for a product can be influenced by numerous factors such as competition, price, weather conditions, technological developments, overall economic conditions, and customers' general confidence. Another uncertainty is delivery times, which can be affected by numerous factors ranging from production machine failures to road construction and traffic jams. In addition, quality problems in materials and parts can create production delays, which also generate supply chain problems.

One major challenge that managers face in setting accurate inventory levels throughout the supply chain is known as the bullwhip effect. The **bullwhip effect** refers to erratic shifts in orders up and down the supply chain (see FIGURE 13.2). Basically, the variables that affect customer demand can become magnified when they are viewed through the eyes of managers at each link in the supply chain. If each distinct entity that makes ordering and inventory decisions places its interests above those of the chain, then stockpiling can occur at as many as seven or eight locations along the chain. Research has shown that in some cases such hoarding has led to as much as a 100-day supply of inventory that is waiting "just in case," versus the 10- to 20-day supply manufacturers normally keep at hand. Chapter closing case 2 illustrates how 3M is solving its supply chain problems.

Figure 13.2 The bullwhip effect.

Solutions to Supply Chain Problems

Supply chain problems can be very costly. Therefore, organizations are motivated to find innovative solutions. During the oil crises of the 1970s, for example, Ryder Systems, a large trucking company, purchased a refinery to control the upstream part of the supply chain and to ensure it had sufficient gasoline for its trucks. Ryder's decision to purchase a refinery is an example of vertical integration. **Vertical integration** is a business strategy in which a company purchases its upstream suppliers to ensure that its essential supplies are available as soon as the company needs them. Ryder later sold the refinery because it could not manage a business it did not understand and because oil became more plentiful.

Ryder's decision to vertically integrate was not the best method for managing its supply chain. In the remainder of this section, you will look at some other possible solutions to supply chain problems, many of which are supported by IT.

Using Inventories to Solve Supply Chain Problems. Undoubtedly, the most common solution to supply chain problems is *building inventories* as insurance against supply chain uncertainties. As you have learned, holding either too much or too little inventory can be very costly. Thus, companies make major attempts to optimize and control inventories.

Supply chain information that was previously obtained manually is increasingly being generated by sensors, RFID tags, meters, GPS, and other devices and systems. How does this transformation affect supply chain managers? For one thing, they now have real-time information on all products moving through their supply chains. Supply chains will therefore rely less on labor-based tracking and monitoring, because the new technology will allow shipping containers, trucks, products, and parts to report on their own status.

To illustrate this process, consider the case of Airbus. Airbus is one of the world's largest commercial aircraft manufacturers, producing more than half of the world's new aircraft with more than 100 seats per plane. As its suppliers became more geographically dispersed, Airbus was finding it increasingly difficult to track parts, components, and other assets as they moved from the warehouses of various suppliers to the company's 18 manufacturing sites.

To make its supply chain more visible, Airbus created a smart sensing solution that can detect any deviations of inbound shipments from their intended path. Here is how the sensing solution works: As parts move from suppliers' warehouses to the Airbus assembly line, they travel in smart containers fitted with RFID tags that hold important information. (We discuss RFID in detail in Chapter 10.) At each stop along the supply chain, RFID readers communicate with each tag. If shipments end up at the wrong location or they do not contain the correct parts, the RFID readers alert employees so that they can fix the problem before it disrupts production.

Airbus's supply chain solution, the largest of its kind in the manufacturing sector, has significantly reduced the number and severity of incorrect shipments and deliveries as well as the costs associated with correcting these problems. In turn, alleviating these problems has allowed Airbus to (1) reduce the number of overall travel containers by 8 percent, (2) avoid significant inventory carrying costs, and (3) increase the overall efficiency of its parts flow.

One widely utilized strategy to minimize inventories is the **just-in-time (JIT) inventory system**. Essentially, JIT systems deliver the precise number of parts, called *work-in-process* inventory, to be assembled into a finished product at precisely the right time.

Although JIT offers many benefits, it has certain drawbacks as well. To begin with, suppliers are expected to respond instantaneously to requests. As a result, they have to carry more inventory than they otherwise would. In this sense, JIT does not *eliminate* excess inventory; rather, it simply *shifts* it from the customer to the supplier. This process can still reduce the overall inventory size if the supplier can spread the increased inventory over several customers. However, that is not always possible.

In addition, JIT replaces a few large supply shipments with a large number of smaller ones. In terms of transportation, then, the process is less efficient.

Information Sharing. Another common approach to solving supply chain problems, and especially to improving demand forecasts, is *sharing information* along the supply chain. Information sharing can be facilitated by electronic data interchange and extranets, topics you will learn about in the next section.

One notable example of information sharing occurs between large manufacturers and retailers. For example, Walmart provides Procter & Gamble with access to daily sales information from every store for every item that P&G makes for Walmart. This access enables P&G to manage the *inventory replenishment* for Walmart's stores. By monitoring inventory levels, P&G knows when inventories fall below the threshold for each product at any Walmart store. These data trigger an immediate shipment.

Information sharing between Walmart and P&G is executed automatically. It is part of a vendor-managed inventory strategy. **Vendor-managed inventory (VMI)** occurs when the supplier, rather than the retailer, manages the entire inventory process for a particular product or group of products. Significantly, P&G has similar agreements with other major retailers. The benefit for P&G is accurate and timely information on consumer demand for its products. Thus, P&G can plan production more accurately, minimizing the bullwhip effect.

┌─ **BEFORE** *YOU GO ON....* ─┐

1. Differentiate between the push model and the pull model.

2. Describe various problems that can occur along the supply chain.

3. Discuss possible solutions to problems along the supply chain.

Apply The Concept 13.2

LEARNING OBJECTIVE 13.2 Identify popular strategies to solving different challenges of supply chains.

STEP 1 – Background

Section 13.2 has explained that managing a supply chain is not a simple task because consumer demand is so uncertain. Although organizations can forecast demand with some accuracy, actual demand almost inevitably will differ from the organizations' predictions. To manage demand fluctuations, organizations are moving toward JIT (just-in-time) inventory models, the amount of data shared along the supply chain increases. These data must be shared in a timely fashion if organizations are to remain flexible and capable of adapting to consumer demand.

STEP 2 – Activity

Visit http://www.wiley.com/go/rainer/MIS3e/applytheconcept, and click on the links provided for Apply the Concept 13.2. The first link will take you to an article that examines how the bullwhip effect wreaks havoc on the supply chain, and the second will take you to an activity where you will manage a supply chain for beer. This latter task might not sound difficult until you consider that there are serious timing issues due to the perishable nature of the product. The simulation begins with your supply chain in equilibrium, but it then suddenly shifts. Your job is to put things back in order!

As you work through the simulation, pay attention to how much information needs to be shared across the supply chain to make the entire operation function smoothly.

STEP 3 – Deliverable

Based on your experience, discuss how the popular strategies for dealing with supply chain challenges (building inventory, JIT inventory, vendor-managed inventory) would or would not work for this product. Write a report and submit it to your instructor.

13.3 Information Technology Support for Supply Chain Management

Clearly, SCM systems are essential to the successful operation of many businesses. As you have seen, these systems—and IOSs in general—rely on various forms of IT to resolve problems. Three technologies, in particular, provide support for IOSs and SCM systems: electronic data interchange, extranets, and Web services. You will learn about Web services in Plug IT In 4. In this section, you examine the other two technologies.

Electronic Data Interchange (EDI)

Electronic data interchange (EDI) is a communication standard that enables business partners to exchange routine documents, such as purchasing orders, electronically. EDI formats these documents according to agreed-upon standards (e.g., data formats). It then transmits messages over the Internet using a converter, called *translator*.

EDI provides many benefits that are not available with a manual delivery system. To begin with, it minimizes data entry errors, because each entry is checked by the computer. In addition, the length of the message can be shorter, and the messages are secured. EDI also reduces cycle time, increases productivity, enhances customer service, and minimizes paper usage and storage. FIGURE 13.3 contrasts the process of fulfilling a purchase order with and without EDI.

EDI does have some disadvantages. Business processes sometimes must be restructured to fit EDI requirements. Also, there are many EDI standards in use today, so one company might have to use several standards in order to communicate with multiple business partners.

In today's world, where every business has a broadband connection to the Internet and where multimegabyte design files, product photographs, and PDF sales brochures are routinely e-mailed, the value of reducing a structured e-commerce message from a few thousand XML bytes to a few hundred EDI bytes is negligible. As a result, EDI is being replaced by XML-based Web services. (You will learn about XML in Plug IT In 4.)

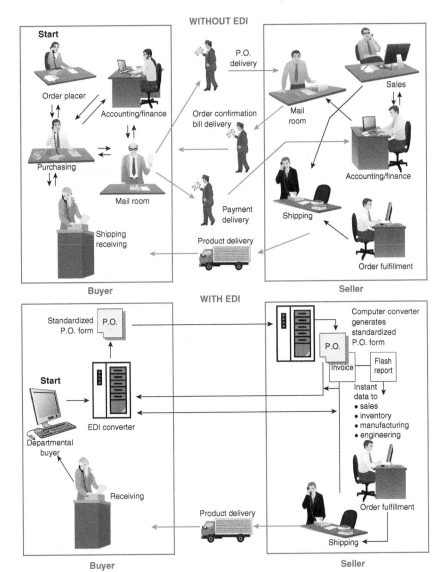

Figure 13.3 Comparing purchase order (PO) fulfillment with and without EDI. (*Source:* Drawn by E. Turban)

Extranets

To implement IOSs and SCM systems, a company must connect the intranets of its various business partners to create extranets. **Extranets** link business partners over the Internet by providing them access to certain areas of each other's corporate intranets (see FIGURE 13.4).

The primary goal of extranets is to foster collaboration between and among business partners. A business provides extranet access to selected B2B suppliers, customers, and other partners. These individuals access the extranet through the Internet. Extranets enable people located outside a company to collaborate with the company's internal employees. They also allow external business partners to enter the corporate intranet, via the Internet, to access data, place orders, check the status of those orders, communicate, and collaborate. Finally, they make it possible for partners to perform self-service activities such as checking inventory levels.

Extranets use virtual private network (VPN) technology to make communication over the Internet more secure. The major benefits of extranets are faster processes and information flow, improved order entry and customer service, lower costs (e.g., for communications, travel, and administrative overhead), and overall improved business effectiveness.

There are three major types of extranets. The type that a company chooses depends on the business partners involved and the purpose of the supply chain. We present each type below, along with its major business applications.

A Company and Its Dealers, Customers, or Suppliers.
This type of extranet centers on a single company. An example is the FedEx extranet, which allows customers to track the status of a delivery. Customers use the Internet to access a database on the FedEx intranet. Enabling customers to monitor deliveries saves FedEx the cost of hiring human operators to perform that task over the phone.

An Industry's Extranet.
Just as a single company can set up an extranet, the major players in an industry can team up to create an extranet that will benefit all of them. For example, ANXeBusiness (www.anx.com) enables companies to collaborate effectively through a network that provides a secure global medium for B2B information exchange. This network is used for mission-critical business transactions by leading international organizations in aerospace, automotive, chemical, electronics, financial services, healthcare, logistics, manufacturing, transportation, and related industries. It offers customers a reliable extranet as well as VPN services. IT's About Business 13.2 provides another example of an industry extranet.

Joint Ventures and Other Business Partnerships.
In this type of extranet, the partners in a joint venture use the extranet as a vehicle for communication and collaboration. An example is Bank of America's extranet for commercial loans. The partners involved in making these loans include a lender, a loan broker, an escrow company, and a title company. The extranet connects lenders, loan applicants, and the loan organizer, Bank of America. A similar case is Lending Tree (www.lendingtree.com), a company that provides mortgage quotes for homeowners and also sells mortgages online. Lending Tree uses an extranet for its business partners (e.g., the lenders).

Figure 13.4 The structure of an extranet.

IT'S ABOUT BUSINESS 13.2

India's New Automotive Supply Chain Extranet

© RicAguiar/iStockphoto

A major obstacle to implementing efficient and effective supply chain management is a lack of connectivity and integration among supply chain partners. Consider the automotive supply chain in India, for example. This supply chain includes more than 40 automotive original equipment manufacturers (OEMs) operating in India, as well as some 700 suppliers.

India's automotive supply chain relies primarily on manual communications in areas such as purchase orders, invoices, and forecasts. Furthermore, the methods by which the transactional data are shared in India among suppliers, manufacturers, suppliers, and customers have been highly inconsistent. As a result, the supply chain regularly experiences processing delays, inaccurate transactions, and other inefficiencies. For instance, a given supplier may be required to send data in dozens of different formats to meet the specific requirements of different manufacturers.

In mid-2014, in an attempt to address these issues, IBM (www.ibm.com) and two automotive industry associations in India launched a new SCM extranet that will electronically connect all of India's automobile manufacturers and suppliers. The two associations are the Society of Indian Automobile Manufacturers (SIAM) and the Automotive Components Manufacturers Association (ACMA).

In this extranet, suppliers will need to create data in only one standard format. They will then send those data to a cloud-based network, called Auto DX (www.autodx.org).

Manufacturers can work directly with those data. Alternatively, Auto DX will translate the message into a particular manufacturer's data format. The extranet supports many different electronic data interchange (EDI) transactions and document types. In addition, it provides Web-based software tools for suppliers that are not EDI-enabled.

POM

All participants in Auto DX, including the OEMs, will share in its cost of operations. India's manufacturers designed that cost structure from the beginning to avoid the impression that they were forcing a system on the suppliers and then requiring the suppliers to bear the entire cost.

The Indian automotive industry is anticipating that the extranet will improve efficiencies across the entire industry by standardizing the data definitions and data interchange formats and thereby expanding the possibilities for the automation of the supply chain. ACMA and SIAM expect a majority of their members to adopt Auto DX by the end of 2014.

Sources: Compiled from "IBM, Indian Auto Groups Launch Ambitious Connectivity Hub to Integrate OEMs, Parts Suppliers," *Supply Chain Digest*, April 2, 2014; J. Brandon, "Automotive CIOs Say Cloud Exchange Could Reduce Supply Chain Costs 80%," *Business Cloud News*, March 10, 2014; N. Roy, "IBM Cloud-Based AutoDX Exchange for Indian Automotive Industry," *Rush Lane*, March 6, 2014; "Auto DX to Improve Supply Chain in Automotive Sector," *Support Biz*, February 26, 2014; R. Mani, "Auto CIOs-Industry Get Into Turbo Mode: Launch AutoDX," *Dynamic CIO*, February 5, 2014; "SIAM, ACMA Launch AutoDX," *Gaadi.com*, February 4, 2014; www.autodx.org, accessed April 10, 2014.

Questions

1. Discuss the difficulties involved in implementing Auto DX.

2. Describe the advantages of Auto DX to the Indian automotive supply chain.

Portals and Exchanges

As you saw in Chapter 4, corporate portals offer a single point of access through a Web browser to critical business information in an organization. In the context of B2B supply chain management, these portals enable companies and their suppliers to collaborate very closely.

There are two basic types of corporate portals: procurement (sourcing) portals for a company's suppliers (upstream in the supply chain), and distribution portals for a company's customers (downstream in the supply chain). **Procurement portals** automate the business processes involved in purchasing or procuring products between a single buyer and multiple suppliers. For example, Boeing has deployed a procurement portal called the Boeing Supplier Portal through which it conducts business with its suppliers. **Distribution portals** automate the business processes involved in selling or distributing products from a single supplier to multiple buyers. For example, Dell services its business customers through its distribution portal at http://premier.dell.com.

Apply The Concept 13.3

LEARNING OBJECTIVE 13.3 Explain the utility of each of the three major technologies that support supply chain management.

STEP 1 – Background

Electronic data interchange (EDI) is defined in this section as a communication standard that enables business partners to exchange routine documents, such as purchasing orders, electronically. You should understand the need for electronic sharing of information if you have completed the activity in Apply the Concept 13.2. That activity required you to manage a supply chain on your own. Imagine the challenge of performing this function without being able to share data electronically!

STEP 2 – Activity

Visit http://www.wiley.com/go/rainer/MIS3e/applytheconcept, and click on the links provided for Apply the Concept 13.3. The link will take you to a YouTube video titled "What is EDI" by user "hitekequipment." You will also link to an article that defines EDI and discusses some of its standards.

As you watch the video, pay attention to the important components that are necessary to share information between two organizations. Then, consider the fact that suppliers rarely operate in only a single supply chain. In fact, suppliers typically have multiple customers, which means they are sharing information with many organizations via EDI.

STEP 3 – Deliverable

Based on the content of this section and the video you watched in Step 2, explain the utility of each of the three major technologies (EDI, extranets, and corporate portals) that support supply chain management. In other words, how might these technologies interact to enable the participating parties to exchange data? Put your explanation in a report and submit it to your instructor.

What's in for ME?

 FOR
ACCOUNTING MAJORS

The cost accountant will play an important role in developing and monitoring the financial accounting information associated with inventory and cost of goods sold. In a supply chain, much of the data for these accounting requirements will flow into the organization from various partners within the chain. It is up to the chief accountant, the comptroller or CFO, to prepare and review these data.

Going further, accounting rules and regulations and the cross-border transfer of data are critical for global trade. IOSs can facilitate such trade. Other issues that are important for accountants are taxation and government reports. In addition, creating information systems that rely on EDI requires the attention of accountants. Finally, fraud detection in global settings (e.g., transfers of funds) can be facilitated by appropriate controls and auditing.

FOR THE FINANCE MAJOR

In a supply chain, the finance major will be responsible for analyzing the data created and shared among supply chain partners. In many instances, the financial analyst will recommend actions to improve supply chain efficiencies and cash flow. This may benefit all the partners in the chain. These recommendations will be based on financial models that incorporate key assumptions such as supply chain partner agreements for pricing. Through the use of extensive financial modeling, the financial analyst helps to manage liquidity in the supply chain.

Many finance-related issues exist in implementing IOSs. For one thing, establishing EDI and extranet relationships involves structuring payment agreements. Global supply chains may involve complex financial arrangements, which may have legal implications.

FOR THE MARKETING MAJOR

A tremendous amount of useful sales information can be derived from supply chain partners through the supporting information systems. For example, many of the customer support activities take place in the downstream portion of the supply chain. For the marketing manager, an understanding of how the downstream activities of the supply chain relate to prior chain operations is critical.

Furthermore, a tremendous amount of data is fed from the supply chain supporting information systems into the CRM systems that are used by marketers. The information and a complete understanding of its genesis are vital for mixed-model marketing programs.

FOR THE PRODUCTION/ OPERATIONS MANAGEMENT MAJOR

The production/operations management major plays a major role in the supply chain development process. In many organizations, the production/operations management staff may even lead the supply chain integration process because of their extensive knowledge of the manufacturing components of the organization. Because they are in charge of procurement, production, materials control, and logistical handling, a comprehensive understanding of the techniques of SCM is vital for the production/operations staff.

The downstream segment of supply chains is where marketing, distribution channels, and customer service are conducted. An understanding of how downstream activities are related to the other segments is critical. Supply chain problems can reduce customer satisfaction and negate marketing efforts. It is essential, then, that marketing professionals understand the nature of such problems and their solutions. Also, learning about CRM, its options, and its implementation is important for designing effective customer services and advertising.

As competition intensifies globally, finding new global markets becomes critical. Use of IOSs provides an opportunity to improve marketing and sales. Understanding the capabilities of these technologies as well as their implementation issues will enable the marketing department to excel.

FOR THE HUMAN RESOURCES MAJOR

Supply chains require interactions among the employees of partners in the chain. These interactions are the responsibility of the Human Resources Manager. The HR Manager must be able to address supply chain issues that relate to staffing, job descriptions, job rotations, and accountability. All of these areas are complex within a supply chain and require the HR function to understand the relationship among partners as well as the movement of resources.

Preparing and training employees to work with business partners (frequently in foreign countries) requires knowledge about how IOSs operate. Sensitivity to cultural differences and extensive communication and collaboration can be facilitated with IT.

FOR THE MIS MAJOR

The MIS staff will be instrumental in the design and support of information systems—both internal organizational and interorganizational—that will underpin the business processes that are part of the supply chain. In this capacity, the MIS staff must have a concise knowledge of the business, the systems, and the points of intersection between the two.

SUMMARY

1. Describe the three components and the three flows of a supply chain.

A *supply chain* is the flow of materials, information, money, and services from raw material suppliers, through factories and warehouses, to the end customers. A supply chain involves three segments: upstream, where sourcing or procurement from external suppliers occurs; internal, where packaging, assembly, or manufacturing takes place; and downstream, where distribution takes place, frequently by external distributors.

There are three flows in the supply chain: *material flows*, which are the physical products, raw materials, supplies, and so forth; *information flows*, which consist of data related to demand, shipments, orders, returns, and schedules, as well as changes in any of these data; and *financial flows*, which involve money transfers, payments, credit card information and authorization, payment schedules, e-payments, and credit-related data.

2. Identify popular strategies to solving different challenges of supply chains.

Two major challenges in setting accurate inventory levels throughout a supply chain are the *demand forecast* and the bullwhip effect. Demand for a product can be influenced by numerous factors such as competition, prices, weather conditions, technological developments, economic conditions, and customers' general confidence. The *bullwhip effect* refers to erratic shifts in orders up and down the supply chain.

The most common solution to supply chain problems is *building inventories* as insurance against SC uncertainties. Another solution is the *just-in-time* (JIT) inventory system, which delivers the precise number of parts, called *work-in-process inventory*, to be assembled into a finished product at precisely the right time. The third possible solution is *vendor-managed inventory* (VMI), which occurs when the vendor, rather than the retailer, manages the entire inventory process for a particular product or group of products.

3. Explain the utility of each of the three major technologies that support supply chain management.

Electronic data interchange (EDI) is a communication standard that enables the electronic transfer of routine documents, such as purchasing orders, between business partners.

Extranets are networks that link business partners over the Internet by providing them access to certain areas of each other's corporate intranets. The main goal of extranets is to foster collaboration among business partners.

Corporate portals offer a single point of access through a Web browser to critical business information in an organization. In the context of business-to-business supply chain management, these portals enable companies and their suppliers to collaborate very closely

>>>CHAPTER GLOSSARY

bullwhip effect Erratic shifts in orders up and down the supply chain.

distribution portals Corporate portals that automate the business processes involved in selling or distributing products from a single supplier to multiple buyers.

electronic data interchange (EDI) A communication standard that enables the electronic transfer of routine documents between business partners.

extranets Networks that link business partners over the Internet by providing them access to certain areas of each other's corporate intranets.

interorganizational information system (IOS) An information system that supports information flow among two or more organizations.

inventory velocity The speed at which a company can deliver products and services after receiving the materials required to make them.

just-in-time (JIT) inventory system A system in which a supplier delivers the precise number of parts to be assembled into a finished product at precisely the right time.

procurement portals Corporate portals that automate the business processes involved in purchasing or procuring products between a single buyer and multiple suppliers.

pull model A business model in which the production process begins with a customer order and companies make only what customers want, a process closely aligned with mass customization.

push model A business model in which the production process begins with a forecast, which predicts the products that customers will want as well as the quantity of each product. The company then produces the amount of products in the forecast, typically by using mass production, and sells, or "pushes," those products to consumers.

supply chain The coordinated movement of *resources* from organizations through *conversion* to the end consumer.

supply chain management (SCM) An activity in which the leadership of an organization provides extensive oversight for the partnerships and processes that compose the supply chain and leverages these relationships to provide an operational advantage.

supply chain visibility The ability of all organizations in a supply chain to access or view relevant data on purchased materials as these materials move through their suppliers' production processes.

vendor-managed inventory (VMI) An inventory strategy where the supplier monitors a vendor's inventory for a product or group of products and replenishes products when needed.

vertical integration Strategy of integrating the upstream part of the supply chain with the internal part, typically by purchasing upstream suppliers, in order to ensure timely availability of supplies

>>>DISCUSSION QUESTIONS

1. List and explain the important components of a supply chain.

2. Explain how a supply chain approach may be part of a company's overall strategy.

3. Explain the important role that information systems play in supporting a supply chain strategy.

4. Would Rolls-Royce Motorcars (www.rolls-roycemotor-cars.com) use a push model or a pull model in its supply chain? Support your answer.

5. Why is planning so important in supply chain management?

1. Access www.ups.com and www.fedex.com. Examine some of the IT-supported customer services and tools provided by the two companies. Write a report on how the two companies contribute to supply chain improvements.

2. Enter www.supply-chain.org, www.cio.com, www.findarticles.com, and www.google.com, and search for recent information on supply chain management.

3. Surf the Web to find a procurement (sourcing) portal, a distribution portal, and an exchange (other than the examples presented in this chapter). List the features they have in common and those features that are unique.

STEP 1 – Background

Supply chain management is critical to organizations because it helps them manage inventory, which in turn is essential to reducing costs and increasing profits. SCM also deals with quality, legal contracts, deliveries, production schedules, forecasts, and other basic business issues.

STEP 2 – Activity

The class should divide into teams, and each team should research local businesses in different industries. For example, one group could research car dealerships (new and used); other teams can select gas stations, restaurants, auto parts, doctors' offices, or any other local businesses that employ a supply chain.

If possible, visit with the manager, and discuss the business's supply chain. If you are unable to visit with the managers, then research the industry online. What can you learn from this research? Also, what can you learn by investigating the types of product they sell?

STEP 3 – Deliverable

Using Google Drive, create a Google Drawing of a model of the supply chain for the industry your team investigated. Make certain to include upstream and downstream flows of material, information, and money. Share your model with your professor and your classmates to compare your supply chain with those of other teams. It will be interesting to find similarities and differences across multiple industries. One common element you should find is the need for information!

CLOSING **CASE 1** > Super Retail Group Consolidates Demand Forecasting and Replenishment

THE PROBLEM >>> Super Retail Group (Super) (www.superretailgroup.com.au) is one of the largest leisure retailers in Australia, with annual sales of more than AU$2 billion. Its seven retail brands focus on automotive products, cycling products, and sporting goods, which it sells through more than 600 stores in Australia and New Zealand.

Since 2005, Super has grown exponentially through a series of acquisitions. Although this growth has added sales volume and brand strength, it has also made the company's supply chain extremely complex. Historically, the company has operated each brand as a separate division. As a result, by 2011 it was managing seven distinct supply chains, which spanned from procurement in Asia to distribution in Australia and New Zealand. Adding to the complexity of managing Super's supply chains was the huge, yet sparsely populated geography of Australia.

Accordingly, Super's executives decided to invest more than AU$50 million in supply chain and inventory management improvements during 2012–2015. The initiative included centralizing a disparate set of distribution centers, consolidating procurement in Asia, developing online sales fulfillment for home delivery, and strengthening relationships with key trading partners.

In essence, the company's key strategic initiative was to consolidate demand forecasting and replenishment across its diverse brands. As the firm acquired other businesses and expanded its scale of private-label products, demand planning became increasingly important. The company needed to manage the lead times associated with procuring from Asia, as well as extreme seasonal and promotional volatility within its brands.

Super had also added more soft (digital) goods, which had different demand patterns than hard (physical) goods. In sum, the retailer needed a forecasting and replenishment model that could handle its geographical complexity, as well as the stock-keeping unit (SKU) complexity, and demand variation across its seven brands.

THE IT SOLUTION >>> To integrate demand planning and fulfillment and to increase its customer focus across brands, the retailer implemented software from JDA (www .jda.com) into its Leisure Retailing division. Within 10 months, the system was operational, thanks to a rapid deployment in JDA's cloud. (We discuss cloud computing in Plug IT In 4). The company elected to launch the software in a cloud environment not only to expedite the implementation but also to minimize expenses.

MIS Deploying the system in the cloud enabled Super Retail to contain its IT infrastructure costs. That is, the company was spared the expenses of purchasing hardware (servers and storage), software (the applications), and networking capabilities. The retailer understood that not all hardware and software expenses are obvious; rather, building an IT infrastructure frequently involves hidden costs. For example, Super estimated that hosting its own software solution would cost the firm AU$20,000 per month in electricity alone. Additionally, Super did not have the internal IT resources to implement the software, or the capacity to grow its IT team sufficiently to support the new software.

The pilot test in the Leisure Retailing division initially included 400,000 SKUs and was then expanded to accommodate 1.4 million SKUs. Because there was so much product complexity in Leisure Retailing, the division served as an effective pilot test for the new system. Consider one example. Because Australia is home to 68 targeted fishing species—more than anywhere else in the world—Super sells many different fishing lures, and it has to manage many regionally specific product ranges.

THE RESULTS >>> Not only has the cloud services model proved to be scalable across the division's enormous product diversity, but it has also proved to be very reliable. The system's availability has been nearly 100 percent—a critical factor given the enormous amounts of data the retailer needs to manage. After just six months of operation, Super realized tangible results from the pilot test. For instance, inventory had been reduced by 20 percent.

From a strategic perspective, Super's new system is helping to support the customer focus that the company needs to compete successfully in the marketplace. In fact, Super executives contend that the JDA software has made the firm's entire mindset more customer-centric.

Super completed its pilot test in the Leisure Retailing division and is now piloting the new system in its Auto Business division. The company's ultimate goal is to launch and manage all future JDA solutions in the cloud.

Sources: Compiled from S. Small, "Super Retail Group Posts Damp Profit Result after 'Internal' Issues," *Courier-Mail*, February 20, 2014; S. Davis, "Super Retail Group Ltd's 'Positive' Rating Reaffirmed at Deutsche Bank," *WKRB*, February 4, 2014; E. Knight, "Camping, Sporting Goods Company Super Retail Group Finds Life No Picnic of Late," *The Sydney Morning Herald*, January 18, 2014; M. King, "Why Super Retail Group Ltd Shares Sank," *The Motley Fool*, January 17, 2014; "Super Retail Group to Grow Store Footprint Following Solid Results," *Retail Biz*, October 24, 2013; L. Tay, "Super Retail Group Boosts IT Spend," *IT News*, February 20, 2013; "Catching Success Via the Cloud," *JDA Case Study*, 2012; www.superretailgroup.com.au, accessed April 10, 2014.

Questions

1. Describe the reasons why Super Retail Group decided to use JDA software along its supply chain.

2. Why did Super Retail Group pilot test in its Leisure Retailing division?

3. Why did Super Retail Group implement a cloud-based solution? Do you believe this was the correct decision? Why or why not?

CLOSING **CASE 2** > 3M Deals with Supply Chain Problems

3M (www.3m.com) manufactures 65,000 products, ranging from adhesive tape to film for solar energy panels to dental braces. It makes these products in 214 plants located in 41 countries. Over the years, 3M had developed extensive and highly complicated supply chains for many of its products.

One reason why the supply chains became so complicated was the company's risk-averse culture. Specifically, the culture at 3M is "make a little, sell a little." That is, the company does not purchase new machinery and/or construct plants until a product has proved itself in the market. Instead,

3M product developers utilized existing machines and expertise even if they were located hundreds of miles away. This strategy enabled 3M to keep its machinery running around the clock, thereby achieving efficiency. It also resulted in higher shipping costs and longer production cycles.

POM

Let's take a look at two 3M products with convoluted supply chains: Command picture-hanging hooks and Littmann stethoscopes.

3M's Command picture-hanging hooks are made of plastic and strips of sticky foam, and they do not look complicated. However, as recently as 2010, the Command production process literally stretched more than 1,300 miles through four factories in four U.S. states. The process began at a 3M plant in Springfield, Missouri, which made the adhesives. The plant then shipped those adhesives about 550 miles to a 3M plant in Hartford City, Indiana, where they were applied to polyethylene foam. Next, the foam was shipped 600 miles to a contractor's plant near Minneapolis, which imprinted the product with the 3M logo and sliced it into the standard sizes. Finally, the product was trucked about 200 miles to central Wisconsin, where another contractor bundled adhesive foam with plastic hooks and enclosed the product in blister packaging.

Littmann stethoscopes also had a convoluted supply chain. Until recently, the stethoscopes were produced in steps involving 14 outside contractors and three 3M plants.

When 3M became aware of these problems, it developed a strategic plan to simplify its supply chains, both to reduce costs and to increase flexibility in its manufacturing processes and along its supply chains. Long, convoluted supply chains increase inventory costs because each separate production stage maintains a buffer stock of unfinished items to cope with any disruptions in the flow from another plant or from suppliers. Holding that inventory is expensive in terms of space and cash spent for materials waiting to become merchandise. 3M set out to speed up production for in-demand products and to avoid convoluted supply chains.

3M has also developed 10 larger, more efficient plants, called *super hubs*, that are capable of making multiple products for a particular region of the world. Six of these hubs are located in the United States, and the remaining four are situated in Singapore, Japan, Germany, and Poland. By moving production closer to its customers, 3M can reduce shipping costs and currency risks while customizing its products to match regional tastes. Essentially, 3M wants to improve efficiency in the manufacturing of its major products. To accomplish this goal, the company plans to reduce *cycle times*—the period needed to complete the entire manufacturing process from ordering raw materials to delivering finished goods—by 25 percent.

3M Hefei, a branch of 3M, plans to become a super manufacturing hub for the U.S. company, with the capacity to make a variety of products. 3M currently relies on 10 single-product sites around China. The new plant is being built at a cost of 1 billion yuan ($16.3 million), and it will become 3M Hefei's largest site in China.

In 2010, 3M consolidated the steps involved in producing Command hooks at a super hub located in Hutchinson, Minnesota. This plant also produces adhesive tape, Nexcare bandages, furnace filters, and other items. In addition to creating finished Command products for the Americas, the Hutchinson plant exports giant rolls of unfinished sticky foam to Singapore and Poland, where they are tailored for Asian and European markets, respectively. The cycle time for making Command has dropped from 100 to 35 days.

And the Littman stethoscopes? All production is being centralized in a plant in Columbia, Missouri. The cycle time for this product has fallen from 165 to 50 days.

Sources: Compiled from B. Ferrari, "The Paradigm Shift Towards U.S. Manufacturing – More Evidence, Momentum, and Commitment," *Supply Chain Matters*, September 3, 2013; M. Chenguang and Z. Jun, "3M Eyes 1b Yuan Super Plant," *China Daily*, June 13, 2013; "Global Supply Chain Leaders to Discuss Reducing Cost and Improving Performance at 2013 LifeScience Alley Conference," *Medcity News*, October 31, 2013; S. Culp, "Supply Chain Disruption a Major Threat to Business," *Forbes*, February 15, 2013; A. Saltmarsh, "Creating a Super Hub," *Packaging Europe*, February 4, 2013; "3M to Establish Super Hub in Turkey," *Hurriyet Daily News*, October 10, 2012; "Industrial Giant 3M on Mission to Remove Its Supply Chain 'Hairballs'," *Supply Chain Digest*, June 6, 2012; J. Hagerty, "3M Begins Untangling Its 'Hairballs'," *The Wall Street Journal*, May 17, 2012; M. Mangelsdorf, "Understanding the 'Bullwhip' Effect in Supply Chains," *MIT Technology Review*, January 27, 2010; www.3m.com, accessed March 15, 2014.

Questions

1. Describe how large, complex organizations such as 3M can develop large, complex supply chains. Does this situation occur by accident? By design? Support your answer.

2. Describe the advantages of 3M using "super hubs."

3. Describe disadvantages of 3M using "super hubs."

4. Is 3M experiencing the bullwhip effect in this case? Why or why not? Support your answer.

INTERNSHIP ACTIVITY> southwest wire A PRODUCTION COMPANY

Manufacturing Industry

Customer relationship management (CRM) and supply chain management (SCM) tools help organizations manage external relationships. In fact, CRM tools provide information that is useful to SCM systems even though the external entities they interact with are on opposite sides of the supply chain model.

This activity will focus on SCM. It is similar to the review work you completed in the last chapter comparing CRM tools for Halle Smith, CIO of Southwest Wire.

Below is another e-mail from Halle.

Hello!

Thank you so much for your help on the CRM implementation project. We decided to go with the OpenERP CRM tool because the SugarCRM system was not sufficiently better to justify working through the integration issues. Now I want to add SCM application to our ERP system.

OpenERP does not offer an application specifically called SCM, but it has several applications that could be combined to perform this function. Recall from the last activity that we have already implemented the Project Management, MRP, Warehouse Management, and Purchase Management tools. My question involves any other OpenERP tools that would constitute a SCM "package" of apps. Obviously, it would be nice to have everything integrated in a single package. However, if another SCM tool is superior to OpenERP's offerings, then it would be hard to turn it down.

SAP is a huge ERP company. They operate worldwide, and they are wildly successful (though their ERP implementations often are not). Look up a demo of their SCM tool, and compare what you find there with the OpenERP tools. Identify which company will better address our needs, and explain the reasons for your choice.

I very much appreciate your work on this project.
Halle

Note: Any links or Web sites mentioned in this e-mail are available at http://www.wiley.com/go/rainer/MIS3e/internship.

SPREADSHEET ACTIVITY > BASIC CHARTS: CONDITIONAL FORMATTING

STEP 1 – Background

Although charts and graphs can be very helpful, sometimes you need to see specific numbers rather than a visual depiction of the summary. Also, sorting doesn't always give you the numbers you are looking for, because it will only order your quantitative data from largest to smallest or smallest to largest. Conditional formatting allows you to create a formula that searches for a value in a certain cell and then formats the entire row based on established criteria (perhaps a certain color) so that it highlights the data you have requested.

STEP 2 – Activity

Imagine that you are a teacher and you want to highlight the students who are struggling. If you have only five students, then it is fairly easy to review their data (see the attached table).

Shelly	85
Mileah	74
Lola Mae	98
Nicolas	78
Halle	80

In this example, you can see that Mileah and Nicolas scored the lowest on this exam. It is therefore possible that they need the most help. However, if you have 150 students in a large college lecture-style class, then it would be much more difficult to identify the students who are struggling.

STEP 3 – Deliverable

Visit http://www.wiley.com/go/rainer/MIS3e/spreadsheet, and download the workbook linked for this activity. The workbook contains a list of grades similar to the above example, except that there are 84 students rather than 5. It also provides specific instructions on how to format these grades. There are four activities and two exams that the instructor needs to format in different ways so that she can identify troubled students as well as those who are excelling.

The above Web page also contains links to Microsoft Support pages that will help you create conditional formatting in Excel. If you are using a different spreadsheet program, then you will likely find assistance in the "Help" section.

Follow the instructions in the spreadsheet and submit your final work to your instructor.

DATABASE ACTIVITY > ADVANCED FORMS

STEP 1 – Background

In this activity you will learn how to create a menu interface—a navigation form in Access terminology—that will allow users with no training to reach important elements of a system with relative ease. Consider what happens when you launch Access. An easy-to-navigate screen appears that asks questions such as "Do you want to open an existing database, start a blank one, or …?"

This method of navigation makes it easy for beginning users to make the right choices. With the complicated design out of the way, users of all levels can use the system based on prompts rather than code. We should design databases with the same ease of use. We can use navigation forms to accomplish this task.

STEP 2 – Activity

Visit http://www.wiley.com/go/rainer/MIS3e/database, and download the database linked for the Chapter 13 Activity. In this activity you will take an existing database with forms and reports, develop menus for using it, and set your database to launch with these menus.

When you examine this database, you will see that four reports already have been created. We want it to be simple for users to pick the reports. So, we need to create a navigation form. Creating a form requires you to work in stages. First, you need to create a navigation form that includes all four reports. Adjust the formatting to make the form more visually appealing (consider titles, column sizes, etc.). Save this form as "Report List."

Next, create a second form, using your new "Report List" as well as CustInfoForm with vertical tabs on the left. Check this new form to make certain it allows users to select from the reports listed in the previous paragraph. It is also helpful to include a back button for ease of navigation.

Finally, add an exit button to your form. Save your navigation form as "Customer Info," and then close it. Next, re-open and run it to confirm that it is pulling the information from the correct areas.

STEP 3 – Deliverable

Save your database with your two navigation forms, and submit it to your professor.

Additional help with this database skill is available from the Microsoft Support Web site which you can access at the URL provided in Step 2.

Acquiring Information Systems and Applications

LEARNING OBJECTIVES >>>

14.1 Discuss the different cost–benefit analyses that companies must take into account when formulating an IT strategic plan.

14.2 Discuss the four business decisions that companies must make when they acquire new applications.

14.3 Enumerate the primary tasks and the importance of each of the six processes involved in the systems development life cycle.

14.4 Describe alternative development methods and the tools that augment development methods.

14.5 Analyze the process of vendor and software selection.

OPENING CASE > LinkedIn's Fast Development Process Helps Save the Company

The May 2011 initial public offering (IPO) for the popular business networking site LinkedIn (www.linkedin.com) went very well. The stock's share price more than doubled in the first day of trading, giving the company a valuation of $9 billion. Behind the scenes though, the company's information systems were experiencing problems. In the ensuing months, hundreds of computer programmers struggled to hold the site together with the digital equivalent of duct tape.

By November 2011, LinkedIn was noticing that its systems were taxed as the site attracted an increasing number of users. Further, the programmers were burned out. To fix these problems, in February 2012 LinkedIn launched Operation InVersion. The company froze development on new features for two months so that programmers could overhaul the Web site's computing architecture. In the fast-moving world of social computing, such a freeze was sacrilege. It simply was not done.

As risky as the freeze was, it paid off. Today, LinkedIn provides extremely advanced coding tools for its programmers, enabling them to add new features on the fly such as a

© Erik Khalitov/iStockphoto

mobile version of the Web site. (Adding new features on the fly means that LinkedIn programmers code the new features and then insert them while the Web site is actually operating.) This coding agility was a key reason for LinkedIn's $18 billion valuation by mid-2013.

LinkedIn's programmers constantly run tests to identify which language and graphic choices keep users engaged and which tweaks enable mobile pages to load faster.

Changes—for example, a fresh look for a menu or a new service—are built into the live Web site almost immediately. LinkedIn updates its site three times a day, in contrast to rivals such as Facebook and Google, who typically update once a day or every few days.

When LinkedIn was founded in 2003, the company used Oracle software for its central database instead of the less expensive, more flexible open-source databases that now dominate Web computing. Immediately after its IPO, LinkedIn switched to NoSQL database software. (We discuss NoSQL database software in detail in Chapter 3.)

 The company has built its own data storage and messaging systems, both of which are being employed by other companies.

Among the keys to the success of the InVersion project are the artificial intelligence computer code checkers that examine software for any errors introduced by LinkedIn's programmers. Other technology companies have their own algorithmic software tools, but they also dispatch teams of people to oversee the process of adding new code to their company's live Web sites. At LinkedIn, the process is almost entirely automated.

Updating the Web site three times per day has caused at least one problem. Users have noticed that their LinkedIn homepages have become crowded with all types of services and feeds.

LinkedIn believes that its development work has primed the company for its next stage: mining users' economic and job data to spot trends early and to advise people on how to advance their careers. LinkedIn believes it will be able to identify trends such as, for example, which areas welders are migrating to and what skills the successful ones are learning. In short, LinkedIn plans to have information running in both directions: from its users, and back to its users.

Sources: Compiled from M. Nisen, "How LinkedIn Saved Its Engineers from Marathon Late-Night Coding Sessions," *Business Insider*, April 29, 2013; "How LinkedIn's Project Inversion Saved the Company," *Slashdot*, April 29, 2013; A. Vance, "LinkedIn's Hidden Horsepower," Bloomberg *Business Week*, April 15–21, 2013; A. Vance, "Inside Operation InVersion, the Code Freeze That Saved LinkedIn," *Bloomberg Business Week*, April 10, 2013; P. Houston, "Innovation Lesson: Disrupt Before You're Disrupted," *Information Week*, November 9, 2012; www.linkedin.com, accessed March 24, 2014.

Questions

1. Describe how freezing new feature development on its Web site "saved" LinkedIn.
2. Describe how rapid application development is enabling LinkedIn to add its next feature, mining users' economic and job data.

Introduction

As you learned from the chapter opening case, competitive organizations move as quickly as they can to acquire new information technologies or modify existing ones when they need to improve efficiencies and gain strategic advantage. Today, however, acquisition goes beyond building new systems in-house, and IT resources involve far more than software and hardware. The old model in which firms built their own systems is being replaced with a broader perspective of IT resource acquisition that provides companies with a number of options. Thus, companies now must decide which IT tasks will remain in-house, and even whether the entire IT resource should be provided and managed by outside organizations. Regardless of which approach an organization chooses, however, it must be able to manage IT projects adeptly.

In this chapter, you learn about the process of acquiring IT resources from a managerial perspective. This means from *your* perspective, because you will be closely involved in all aspects of acquiring information systems and applications in your organization. In fact, when we mention "users" in this chapter, we are talking about you. You will also study the available options for acquiring IT resources and how to evaluate those options. Finally, you will learn how organizations plan and justify the acquisition of new information systems.

14.1 Planning for and Justifying IT Applications

Organizations must analyze the need for applications and then justify each purchase in terms of costs and benefits. The need for information systems is usually related to organizational planning and to the analysis of its performance vis-à-vis its competitors. The cost–benefit justification must consider the wisdom of investing in a specific IT application versus spending the funds on alternative projects. This chapter focuses on the formal processes of large organizations. Smaller organizations employ less formal processes, or no processes

Figure 14.1 The information systems planning process.

at all. It is important to note, however, that even if a small organization does not have a formal process for planning and justifying IT applications, the steps of a formal process exist for a reason, and they have value. At the very least, decision makers in small organizations should consider each step when they are planning changes in their information systems.

When a company examines its needs and performance, it generates a prioritized list of both existing and potential IT applications, called the **application portfolio**. These are the applications that have to be added, or modified if they already exist.

IT Planning

The planning process for new IT applications begins with an analysis of the *organizational strategic plan*, which is illustrated in FIGURE 14.1. The organization's strategic plan identifies the firm's overall mission, the goals that follow from that mission, and the broad steps required to reach these goals. The strategic planning process modifies the organization's objectives and resources to match its changing markets and opportunities.

The organizational strategic plan and the existing IT architecture provide the inputs in developing the IT strategic plan. The *IT architecture* delineates the way an organization should utilize its information resources to accomplish its mission. It encompasses both the technical and the managerial aspects of information resources. The technical aspects include hardware and operating systems, networking, data management systems, and applications software. The managerial aspects specify how the IT department will be managed, how the functional area managers will be involved, and how IT decisions will be made.

The **IT strategic plan** is a set of long-range goals that describe the IT infrastructure and identify the major IT initiatives needed to achieve the organization's goals. The IT strategic plan must meet three objectives:

1. *It must be aligned with the organization's strategic plan.* This alignment is critical because the organization's information systems must support the organization's strategies. (Recall the discussion of organizational strategies and information systems in Chapter 2.)

    Consider the example of Nordstrom versus Walmart. An application that improves customer service at a small cost would be considered favorably at Nordstrom, but it would be rejected at Walmart. The reason is that the application would fit in favorably (i.e., align) with Nordstrom's service-at-any-cost strategy. However, it would not fit in well with Walmart's low-cost strategy. You see two department stores, same application, same cost and benefits—but different answers to the question "Should we develop the application?"

2. *It must provide for an IT architecture that seamlessly networks users, applications, and databases.*

3. *It must efficiently allocate IS development resources among competing projects so that the projects can be completed on time and within budget and still have the required functionality.*

The existing IT architecture is a necessary input into the IT strategic plan because it acts as a constraint on future development efforts. It is not an absolute constraint, however, because the organization can change to a new IT architecture. Companies prefer to avoid this strategy, however, because it is expensive and time consuming.

Consider this example. You have a Mac (Apple) system, and you need a new software application. You search and find several such packages for both Mac and MS Windows. Unfortunately, the best package runs only on Windows. How much better would this package have to be for you to justify switching from Mac to Windows?

POM

One critical component in developing and implementing the IT strategic plan is the **IT steering committee**. This committee, comprised of a group of managers and staff who represent the various organizational units, is created to establish IT priorities and to ensure that the MIS function is meeting the organization's needs. The committee's major tasks are to link corporate strategy with IT strategy, to approve the allocation of resources for the MIS function, and to establish performance measures for the MIS function and ensure they are met. The IT steering committee is important to you because it ensures that you get the information systems and applications that you need to do your job.

After a company has agreed on an IT strategic plan, it next develops the **IS operational plan**. This plan consists of a clear set of projects that the IS department and the functional area managers will execute in support of the IT strategic plan. A typical IS operational plan contains the following elements:

- *Mission:* The mission of the IS function (derived from the IT strategy).
- *IS environment:* A summary of the information needs of the individual functional areas and of the organization as a whole.
- *Objectives of the IS function:* The best current estimate of the goals of the IS function.
- *Constraints on the IS function:* Technological, financial, personnel, and other resource limitations on the IS function.
- *The application portfolio:* A prioritized inventory of present applications and a detailed plan of projects to be developed or continued during the current year.
- *Resource allocation and project management:* A listing of who is going to do what, how, and when.

Evaluating and Justifying IT Investment: Benefits, Costs, and Issues

Developing an IT plan is the first step in the acquisition process. Because all companies have limited resources, they must justify investing resources in some areas, including IT, rather than in others. Essentially, justifying IT investment involves calculating the costs, assessing the benefits (values), and comparing the two. This comparison is frequently referred to as cost–benefit analysis. Cost–benefit analysis is not a simple task.

FIN

Assessing the Costs. Calculating the dollar value of IT investments is not as simple as it may seem. One of the major challenges that companies face is to allocate fixed costs among different IT projects. *Fixed costs* are those costs that remain the same regardless of any change in the company's activity level. Fixed IT costs include infrastructure costs and the costs associated with IT services and IT management. For example, the salary of the IT director is fixed, and adding one more application will not change it.

Another complication is that the costs of a system do not end when the system is installed. Rather, costs for maintaining, debugging, and improving the system can accumulate over many years. This is a critical point because organizations sometimes fail to anticipate these costs when they make the investment.

A dramatic example of unanticipated expenses was the Year 2000 (Y2K) reprogramming projects, which cost organizations worldwide billions of dollars. In the 1960s, computer memory was very expensive. To save money, programmers coded the "year" in the date field 19_ _, instead of _ _ _ _. With the "1" and the "9" hard-coded in the computer program, only the last two digits varied, so computer programs needed less memory. However, this process meant that when the year 2000 rolled around, computers would display the year as 1900. This programming technique could have caused serious problems with financial applications, insurance applications, and countless other apps.

The Y2K example illustrates the point that database design choices tend to affect the organization for a long time. As the 21st century approached, no one still used hardware or software from the 1960s (other than a few legacy applications). Database design choices made in the 1960s, however, were often still in effect decades after the companies implemented them.

Assessing the Benefits. Evaluating the benefits of IT projects is typically even more complex than calculating their costs. Benefits may be more difficult to quantify, especially because many of them are intangible—for example, improved customer or partner relations and improved decision making. As an employee, you will probably be asked for input about the intangible benefits that an IS provides for you.

The fact that organizations use IT for multiple purposes further complicates benefit analysis. In addition, to obtain a return from an IT investment, the company must implement the technology successfully. In reality, many systems are not implemented on time, within budget, or with all of the features originally envisioned for them. Also, the proposed system may be "cutting edge." In these cases, there may be no precedent for identifying the types of financial payback the company can expect.

Conducting the Cost–Benefit Analysis. After a company has assessed the costs and benefits of IT investments, it must compare them. You have studied, or will study, cost–benefit analyses in more detail in your finance courses. The point is that real-world business problems do not come in neatly wrapped packages labeled "this is a finance problem" or "this is an IS problem." Rather, business problems span multiple functional areas.

There is no uniform strategy for conducting a cost–benefit analysis. Rather, an organization can perform this task in several ways. Here you see four common approaches: (1) net present value, (2) return on investment, (3) breakeven analysis, and (4) the business case approach.

- Analysts use the *net present value (NPV)* method to convert future values of benefits to their present-value equivalent by "discounting" them at the organization's cost of funds. They can then compare the present value of the future benefits with the cost required to achieve those benefits to determine whether the benefits exceed the costs.

- *Return on investment (ROI)* measures management's effectiveness in generating profits with its available assets. ROI is calculated by dividing the net income generated by a project by the average assets invested in the project. ROI is a percentage, and the higher the percentage return, the better.

- *Breakeven analysis* determines the point at which the cumulative dollar value of the benefits from a project equals the investment made in the project.

- In the *business case approach*, system developers write a business case to justify funding one or more specific applications or projects. IS professionals will be a major source of input when business cases are developed because these cases describe what you do, how you do it, and how a new system could better support you.

BEFORE *YOU GO ON....*

1. What are some problems associated with assessing the costs of IT?
2. Why are the intangible benefits from IT so difficult to evaluate?
3. Describe the NPV, ROI, breakeven analysis, and business case approaches.

Apply The Concept 14.1

LEARNING OBJECTIVE 14.1 Discuss the different cost–benefit analyses that companies must take into account when formulating an IT strategic plan.

You may not realize it, but you perform cost–benefit analyses all the time. Imagine that you want to go to the beach for the weekend, but you decide not to because you would have to drive eight hours each way and therefore would not get to spend much time there. In this case, the costs outweigh the benefits. However, if you could extend your stay another day, then the benefits might outweigh the costs. The difficulty in this example is that the benefits are difficult to measure. A cost–benefit analysis is designed to quantify all of the key elements, and sometimes there are subjective benefits for which there are no clear-cut numerical values.

STEP 2 – Activity (Here is what you are doing.)

Visit http://www.wiley.com/go/rainer/MIS3e/applytheconcept, and click on the links provided for Apply the Concept 14.1. You will watch three short videos that offer a financial explanation for net present value, return on investment, and breakeven analysis. The business case approach is not a financial approach, and it does not require further explanation.

STEP 3 – Deliverable (Here is what you turn in.)

Imagine you are creating a Web site to sell promotional items. You have no experience developing a site, so you will have to pay someone to do this for you. You research this service and discover that the site you have in mind will cost $3,500. (For this example, assume there are no monthly hosting fees.) This design will last five years, after which you will need to update it. You anticipate that you can make $500 in year 1, $750 in year 2, $750 in year 3, $1,000 in year 4, and $1,500 in year 5 from the site. Calculate the NPV, ROI, and breakeven analysis for this case, and discuss which metric is most helpful. Also, explain how a business case analysis would be helpful beyond what the numbers provide. Prepare a document with your figures and present it to your instructor.

14.2 Strategies for Acquiring IT Applications

After a company has justified an IT investment, it must then decide how to pursue it. As with cost–benefit analyses, there are several options for acquiring IT applications. To select the best option, companies must make a series of business decisions. The fundamental decisions are the following:

- *How much computer code does the company want to write?* A company can choose to use a totally prewritten application (write no computer code), to customize a prewritten application (write some computer code), or to custom-write an entire application (write all new computer code).

- *How will the company pay for the application?* Once the company has decided how much computer code to write, it must decide how to pay for it. With prewritten applications or customized prewritten applications, companies can buy them or lease them. With totally custom applications, companies use internal funding.

- *Where will the application run?* The next decision is whether to run the application on the company's platform or on someone else's platform. In other words, the company can employ either a software-as-a-service vendor or an application service provider. (You will examine these options later in this chapter.)

- *Where will the application originate?* Prewritten applications can be open-source software or they can come from a vendor. The company may choose to customize prewritten open-source applications or prewritten proprietary applications from vendors. Further, it may customize applications in-house, or it can outsource the customization. Finally, it can write totally custom applications in-house, or it can outsource this process.

In the following sections, you will find more details on the variety of options that companies looking to acquire applications can select from. A good rule of thumb is that an organization should consider all feasible acquisition methods in light of its business requirements. You will learn about the following acquisition methods:

- Purchase a prewritten application.
- Customize a prewritten application.
- Lease the application.
- Use application service providers and software-as-a-service vendors.
- Use open-source software.
- Use outsourcing.
- Employ custom development.

Purchase a Prewritten Application

Many commercial software packages contain the standard features required by IT applications. Therefore, purchasing an existing package can be a cost-effective and time-saving strategy compared with custom-developing the application in-house. Nevertheless, a company should carefully consider and plan the buy option to ensure that the selected package contains all of the features necessary to address the company's current and future needs. Otherwise, these packages can quickly become obsolete. Before a company can perform this process, it must decide which features a suitable package must include.

In reality, a single software package can rarely satisfy all of an organization's needs. For this reason, a company sometimes must purchase multiple packages to fulfill different needs. It then must integrate these packages with one another as well as with its existing software. TABLE 14.1 summarizes the advantages and limitations of the buy option.

Customize a Prewritten Application

Customizing existing software is an especially attractive option if the software vendor allows the company to modify the application to meet its needs. However, this option may not be attractive in cases where customization is the *only* method of providing the necessary flexibility to address the company's needs. It also is not the best strategy when the software is either very expensive or likely to become obsolete in a short time. Further, customizing a prewritten application can be extremely difficult, particularly for large, complex applications. IT's About Business 14.1 recounts a disastrous effort by Marin County, California, to implement a SAP system.

TABLE 14.1 Advantages and Limitations of the Buy Option

Advantages

Many different types of off-the-shelf software are available.

The company can try out the software before purchasing it.

The company can save much time by buying rather than building.

The company can know what it is getting before it invests in the product.

Purchased software may eliminate the need to hire personnel specifically dedicated to a project.

Disadvantages

Software may not exactly meet the company's needs.

Software may be difficult or impossible to modify, or it may require huge business process changes to implement.

The company will not have control over software improvements and new versions.

Purchased software can be difficult to integrate with existing systems.

Vendors may discontinue a product or go out of business.

Software is controlled by another company with its own priorities and business considerations.

The purchasing company lacks intimate knowledge about how and why the software functions as it does.

IT'S ABOUT BUSINESS 14.1

A Disastrous Development Project

In 2004, Marin County in California decided to replace its aging financial management, payroll, and human resources systems with a modern SAP enterprise resource planning (ERP) system. The county solicited proposals from various companies to act as software consultants on the implementation. Thirteen companies, including Oracle, PeopleSoft, and SAP, submitted proposals. In April 2005, the county selected Deloitte Consulting based on the firm's representations concerning its in-depth knowledge of SAP systems and the extensive experience of its consultants.

From 2005 to 2009, Marin County paid increasing consulting fees to Deloitte as the county grappled with serious fiscal problems. Essentially, the county's staff could not program the SAP system to perform even routine financial functions such as payroll and accounts receivable. A grand jury probe concluded that the system had cost taxpayers $28.6 million as of April 2009.

At that time, Marin County voted to stop the ongoing SAP project, implicitly acknowledging that it had wasted some $30 million on software and related implementation services from Deloitte. The Marin County Information Systems and Technology Group concluded that fixing the Deloitte-installed SAP system would cost nearly 25 percent more over a 10-year period than implementing a new system.

In 2010, Marin County filed a complaint alleging that Deloitte's representations were fraudulent. The complaint accused Deloitte of using the county's SAP project as a training ground to provide young consultants with public sector SAP experience, at the county's expense. The county further charged that Deloitte

1. intentionally failed to disclose its lack of SAP and public sector skills;
2. withheld information about critical project risks;
3. falsely represented to the county that the SAP system was ready to "go live" as originally planned;
4. conducted inadequate testing; and
5. concealed the fact that it had failed to perform necessary testing, thereby ensuring that system defects would remain hidden prior to the go-live date.
6. Finally, the county maintained that, although it had paid substantial consulting fees to Deloitte, the system continued to have crippling problems.

Deloitte filed a counterclaim over the county's failure to pay more than $550,000 in fees and interest. The company maintained that it had fulfilled all of its obligations under the contract, as evidenced by the fact that all of Deloitte's work was approved by the county officials who were responsible for overseeing the project.

In December 2010, Marin County sued Deloitte and two SAP subsidiaries, alleging that Deloitte had "engaged in a pattern of racketeering activity designed to defraud the county of more than $20 million." The county's lawsuit also named as a defendant Ernest Culver, a former county employee who

© AlexRaths/iStockphoto

served as director on the SAP project. The county alleged that Culver interviewed for jobs at Deloitte and SAP. It further claimed that during the SAP project, Culver "was approving Deloitte's deficient work on the project, approving payments, and causing Marin County to enter into new contracts with Deloitte and SAP Public Services, Inc."

In late December 2011, a judge ruled that Marin County failed to provide sufficient facts to bring a racketeering claim against SAP under the terms of the federal Racketeer Influenced and Corrupt Organizations Act (RICO). However, he also ruled that Marin County could file an amended complaint. The judge further found that Marin County had alleged sufficient facts to bring a "plausible" bribery claim against SAP with respect to Culver. Finally, the judge denied SAP's motion to dismiss claims against its SAP America division.

In mid-January 2012, Marin County filed an amended complaint in federal court related to its actions against SAP, Deloitte Consulting, and Ernest Culver. The president of the Marin County Board of Supervisors stated that the board is committed to ensuring accountability for its taxpayers.

In early 2013, Marin County settled its lawsuit with Deloitte Consulting. The settlement followed the court's dismissal of several of the county's claims as well as the county's conclusion, after a full investigation, that it should voluntarily dismiss its remaining fraud claims and its allegations of improper influence of a county employee (Culver) who managed the project. According to the *Marin Independent Journal*, the county received $3.9 million from Deloitte, which is less than it paid in legal fees.

It is important to note that neither Marin County nor Deloitte placed any blame on the SAP software. The dynamics between the customer and the system integrator caused this failure.

In November 2013, Marin County began searching for new ERP software to replace the existing SAP system. County officials approved a request for proposal (RFP) from vendors who wanted to bid on the job. Officials are focused on "Tier 2" vendors, which are generally smaller and more focused than their larger competitors. Responses to the RFP were expected in December, and officials hope that an approved contract will be signed by June 2014. Interestingly, officials claim that the county is open to using products from multiple vendors rather than implementing a single product to manage every functional area. The county has hired external consultants (for $600,000) to evaluate its business process needs and define the scope of the project.

County officials maintain they have learned many lessons from the failed SAP implementation, including the following:

- The need to consider "fit" between the software and the organization implementing it. Officials note that Tier 1 (the largest) ERP vendors have very complicated, expensive products that are not a particularly good fit with organizations the size and complexity of Marin County.

- The need to take employee input into account at all phases of the project, particularly in defining the business requirements for the software.
- The need for the county to create a formal business case document.
- The need for extensive user training and change management throughout the project.

Sources: Compiled from M. Krigsman, "Marin County Restarts ERP Project," *ZDNet*, November 8, 2013; C. Kanaracus, "Marin County Seeks New Software Vendor to Replace SAP System," *Government IT*, November 1, 2013; M. Krigsman, "Big Money: Marin County and Deloitte Settle ERP Lawsuit Under Gag Order," *ZDNet*, January 14, 2013; N. Johnson, "Marin County Cuts Its Losses, Settles Its Computer Lawsuit for $3.9 Million, " *Marin Independent Journal*, January 9, 2013; C. Kanaracus, "Judge Tosses Racketeering Claims in Marin County Lawsuit Against SAP," *PC World*, December 28, 2011; C. Kanaracus, "Marin County Alleges SAP, Deloitte Engaged in Racketeering," *Computerworld*, February 2, 2011; M. Krigsman, "Understanding Marin County's $30 Million ERP Failure," *ZDNet*, September 2, 2010; C. Kanaracus, "Marin County to Rip and Replace Ailing SAP System," *IDG News Service*, August 24, 2010; M. Krigsman, "Marin County Sues Deloitte: Alleges Fraud on SAP Project," *ZDNet*, June 3, 2010; J. Vijayan, "Deloitte Hit with $30M Lawsuit over ERP Project," *Computerworld*, June 3, 2010; T. Claburn, "Deloitte Sued Over Failed SAP Implementation," *InformationWeek*, June 1, 2010; www.co.marin.ca.us, www.deloitte.com, accessed March 14, 2013.

Questions

1. Debate the lawsuit from the point of view of Deloitte and SAP.
2. Debate the lawsuit from the point of view of Marin County.
3. Is it a good idea for Marin County to attempt another ERP implementation? Why or why not? Support your answer.
4. Are there other types of software that Marin County might use? (Hint: Consider cloud computing (see Plug IT In 4).)
5. Is it a good idea for Marin County to use software products from different vendors? Why or why not? Support your answer.

Lease the Application

Compared with the buy option and the option to develop applications in-house, the lease option can save a company both time and money. Of course, leased packages (like purchased packages) may not exactly fit the company's application requirements. However, as noted, vendor software generally includes the features that are most commonly needed by organizations in a given industry. Again, the company will decide which features are necessary.

Interested companies commonly apply the 80/20 rule when they evaluate vendor software. Put simply, if the software meets 80 percent of the company's needs, then the company should seriously consider modifying its business processes so that it can utilize the remaining 20 percent. Many times this is a better long-term solution than modifying the vendor software. Otherwise, the company will have to customize the software every time the vendor releases an updated version.

Leasing can be especially attractive to small and medium-sized enterprises (SMEs) that cannot afford major investments in IT software. Large companies may also prefer to lease packages to test potential IT solutions before committing to major investments. In addition, a company that does not employ sufficient IT personnel with the appropriate skills for developing custom IT applications may choose to lease instead of developing software in-house. Even those companies that employ in-house experts may not be able to afford the long wait for strategic applications to be developed in-house. Therefore, they lease (or buy) applications from external resources to establish a quicker presence in the market.

Leasing can be executed in one of three ways. The first way is to lease the application from a software developer, install it, and run it on the company's platform. The vendor can assist with the installation and frequently will offer to contract for the support and maintenance of the system. Many conventional applications are leased this way.

The other two options involve leasing an application and running it on the vendor's platform. Organizations can accomplish this process by using an application service provider or a software-as-a-service vendor.

Application Service Providers and Software-as-a-Service Vendors

An **application service provider (ASP)** is an agent or a vendor who assembles the software needed by enterprises and then packages it with services such as development, operations, and maintenance. The customer then accesses these applications via the Internet. FIGURE 14.2 illustrates the operation of an ASP. Note that the ASP hosts both an application and a database for each customer.

Software-as-a-service (SaaS) is a method of delivering software in which a vendor hosts the applications and provides them as a service to customers over a network, typically the Internet. Customers do not own the software; rather, they pay for using it. SaaS eliminates the need for customers to install and run the application on their own computers. Therefore, SaaS customers save the expense (money, time, IT staff) of buying, operating, and maintaining the software. For example, Salesforce (www.salesforce.com), a well-known SaaS provider for customer relationship management (CRM) software solutions, provides these advantages for its customers. FIGURE 14.3 displays the operation of a SaaS vendor. Note that the vendor hosts an application that multiple customers can use. The vendor also hosts a database that is partitioned for each customer to protect the privacy and security of each customer's data.

At this point, companies have made the first three decisions and must now decide where to obtain the application. Recall that in general, for prewritten applications, companies can use open-source software or obtain the software from a vendor. For customized prewritten applications, they can customize open-source software or customize vendor software. For totally custom applications, they can write the software in-house, or they can outsource the process.

Figure 14.2 Operation of an application service provider.

Use Open-Source Software

Organizations obtain a license to implement an open-source software product and either use it as is, customize it, or develop applications with it. Unless the company is one of the few that want to tinker with their source code, open-source applications are, basically, the same as a proprietary application except for licensing, payment, and support. Open-source software is really an alternative source of applications rather than a conceptually different development option. (We discuss open-source software in Plug IT In 2.)

Outsourcing

Acquiring IT applications from outside contractors or external organizations is called **outsourcing**. Companies can utilize outsourcing in many situations. For example, they might want to experiment with new IT technologies without making a substantial up-front investment. They also might use outsourcing to obtain access to outside experts. One disadvantage of outsourcing is that companies frequently must place their valuable corporate data under the control of the outsourcing vendor.

Several types of vendors offer services for creating and operating IT systems, including e-commerce applications. Many software companies, from IBM to Oracle, offer a range of outsourcing services for developing, operating, and maintaining IT applications. IT outsourcers, such as EDS, offer a variety of services. Also, the large CPA companies and management consultants—for example, Accenture—offer outsourcing services.

As the trend to outsource is on the rise, so is the trend to relocate these operations offshore, particularly in India and China. *Offshoring* can save money, but it includes risks as well. The risks depend on which services are being offshored. If a company is offshoring application development, then the major risk is poor communication between users and developers. In response to these risks, some companies are bringing outsourced jobs back in-house, a process called *reverse outsourcing*, or *insourcing*. IT's About Business 14.2 illustrates this process at General Motors.

Figure 14.3 Operation of a software-as-a-service vendor.

IT's ABOUT BUSINESS 14.2

General Motors Insources Its Information Technology Function

Software impacts every aspect of General Motors' business (www.gm.com), from how the company chooses manufacturing components to the ways that engineers and designers work together. Just as importantly, the automobiles themselves are becoming much more computerized. In fact, cars now have more software and computing power than the original Apollo mission in 1961. Modern autos contain a growing number of apps that interact with the dashboard. In addition, self-driving cars are coming soon. GM's Cadillac line is planning a partially self-driving car by 2015. Clearly, then, software is critical to the giant automaker.

When General Motors' new chief information officer, Randy Mott, assumed his position in February 2012, GM was outsourcing 90 percent of its IT work. This arrangement was creating several problems for the company, including long lead times for new application development and the vendors' lack of in-depth knowledge of the auto industry. Mott's response was to replace the existing system with an insourcing strategy. This strategy includes hiring up to 10,000 employees and opening four software innovation centers in the United States. GM is convinced that a much larger in-house IT staff, one that understands the automobile industry, could provide several advantages to the automaker, including the following:

- Reducing the number of software applications. Mott estimates that GM uses more than 4,000 applications throughout the world. Many of them are redundant and can be eliminated.

- Speeding up software application development to match the company's increased speed of new car and truck introductions.

- Replacing IT contractors who do not really understand the auto industry with in-house IT staff members who are familiar with the industry. GM is convinced these individuals will possess the knowledge to develop superior, innovative software applications.

General Motors is consolidating the company's 23 data centers into 2 much larger, more efficient centers. It is also building a global data warehouse that will enable executives to analyze detailed internal market and sales data and incorporate external information sources, including social media feedback, into their decision-making process. Finally, the company plans to hire additional IT professionals to staff the data centers and manage the data warehouse.

Sources: Compiled from B. Levishon, "General Motors Hits 52-Week High as Insourcing, Cutbacks, and Treasury Sale Boost Stock," *Barron's*, December 9, 2013; D. Burrus, "GM Is Insourcing Its Data Centers: What's Your Plan to Leverage High-Value Data?" *BigThink*, July 1, 2013; P. Ponticel, "GM Pushes IT Insourcing Strategy with Two New Data Centers," *SAE International*, May 14, 2013; S. Rosenbush and J. Bennett, "GM Opens New Data Center Modeled on Google, Facebook," *The Wall Street Journal*, May 13, 2013; J. Leber, "With Computerized Cars Ahead, GM Puts IT Outsourcing in the Rearview Mirror," *MIT Technology Review*, November 5, 2012; K. Flinders, "Could GM's Decision to Insource IT Start a Trend?" *Computer Weekly*, October 29, 2012; S. Overby, "GM Bets on Insourcing, Brings Back 10,000 IT Jobs," *CIO Magazine*, October 5, 2012; P. Thibodeau, "GM to Hire 10,000 IT Pros as It 'Insources' Work," *Computerworld*, September 7, 2012; C. Murphy, "General Motors Will Slash Outsourcing in IT Overhaul," *InformationWeek*, July 9, 2012; www.gm.com, accessed March 19, 2014.

Questions

1. What are potential disadvantages of Mott's insourcing strategy?

2. Why did GM's outsourcing strategy result in the company's using 4,000 software applications? In your opinion, will Mott's insourcing strategy resolve this problem? Why or why not?

Employ Custom Development

Another option is to custom-build an application. Companies can either perform this operation in-house or outsource the process. Although custom development is usually more time consuming and costly than buying or leasing, it often produces a better fit with the organization's specific requirements.

The development process starts when the IT steering committee (discussed previously in this chapter), having received suggestions for a new system, decides it is worth exploring. These suggestions come from users (who will be you in the near future). Understanding this process will help you obtain the systems that you need. Conversely, not understanding this process will reduce your chances, because other people who understand it better will make suggestions that use up available resources.

As the company goes through the development process, its mind-set changes. In systems investigation (the first stage of the traditional systems development life cycle), the organization is trying to decide whether to build something. Everyone knows it may or may not be built. In the later stages of the development process, the organization is committed to building the application. Although a project can be cancelled at any time, this change in attitude is still important.

The basic, backbone methodology for custom development is the systems development life cycle (SDLC), which you will read about in the next section. Section 14.4 examines the methodologies that complement the SDLC: prototyping, joint application development, integrated computer-assisted systems development tools, and rapid application development. You will also consider four other methodologies: agile development, end-user development, component-based development, and object-oriented development.

The SDLC is typically used for large-scale information systems development projects. However, entrepreneurs are also using custom development to deploy much smaller information systems such as mobile apps. IT's About Business 14.3 illustrates how entrepreneurs actually build apps themselves.

IT'S ABOUT BUSINESS 14.3

Build Your Apps Yourself

The rapid adoption of smartphones and tablets, coupled with the increased bandwidth of 4G wireless networks, has driven an explosion in mobile applications. The independent artist, the mom-and-pop store, and the local pizza parlor do not have the financial and technological resources to develop custom apps. However, entrepreneurs and small businesses can now develop their own mobile apps.

Many online tools, such as Appsme (www.appsme.com), AppMakr (www.appmakr.com), and Appsbar (www.appsbar.com), enable users to build simple apps by incorporating text, images, and other features into a ready-made template. However, these tools may be limited in scope, or they might require any additional features to be coded manually.

To fill in this knowledge gap, mobile developer boot camps now offer intensive do-it-yourself training. In a matter of weeks, programs such as the Pragmatic Studio claim that they can help turn a novice into a proficient coder, for fees of about $2,700 for four days of training.

Rather than go it alone, other entrepreneurs are using professional developers, who can charge more than $15,000 to produce sophisticated, polished apps. As we discussed earlier in the chapter, these costs can continue to rise after the app is developed. Each update to the operating system and every new device the company installs can affect the ways an app functions.

Let's examine a few examples of how this process functions.

Mike Vichich, a business consultant, had spent several years traveling almost continuously and accumulating many points on his credit cards. Cashing in those points gave him the idea for Glyph (www.paywithglyph.com), an iPhone app that tracks and maximizes credit-card rewards. Vichich faced one major obstacle, however: He did not know the first thing about developing a mobile app.

Vichich's case is not unusual. Many entrepreneurs can successfully manage a company in the fast-growing mobile apps market, but they do not possess the technical knowledge to build mobile apps on their own. Fortunately, they have several options to choose from, including (1) using online app-building tools, (2) taking crash courses in computer programming and coding languages, (3) hiring an expensive professional on contract, and (4) recruiting a full-time developer. Vichich combined options 1 and 3 and launched Glyph at the App Store in November 2013.

Michael Perry took 126 hours of training at CodeAcademy (www.codeacademy.com), a free online course that teaches a variety of programming languages. His business partner, an app developer who was working part time on their startup, had to devote more time to his other, full-time job. Perry, who had been in charge of business operations, realized he had to learn to code himself to launch the business—an app called GVING (https://gving.com) designed to help merchants to better track and reward their customers. The app is available at the App Store, and Perry now has a team of three developers who took over the programming side of the business.

Keith Brown, the owner of Austin Tree Experts from Austin, Texas, combined an online app builder with training to create an app that both employees and customers can use to identify and record details of trees. Austin Tree Experts' Web site and mobile app (www.austintreeexperts.com) are used by homeowners, local municipalities, apartment complexes, developers, engineers, architects, and contractors. The company offers many tree services, including trimming, pruning, removal, planting, fertilizing, consulting, construction site services, and more.

Codiqa (https://codiqa.com), an app builder, assisted with the basic code for the app's layout and general function.

Because Codiqa could not add a customized GPS feature to pin the location of the trees, or a photo-uploading capability to capture images of the trees, Brown turned to W3Schools.com (www.w3schools.com) and HTML5rocks.com (www.html5rocks.com) for online tutorials. He also submitted questions on StackOverflow.com, a developer forum, whenever he encountered problems. Brown admits that it took him 30 hours of hard work, but he successfully built the app.

Sources: Compiled from S. Hirsch, "The Democratization of App Building Has Created a New Paradigm," *Betanews*, March 12, 2014; S. Angeles, "14 Best App Makers of 2014," *Business News Daily*, February 20, 2014; P. Rubens, "DIY Apps and the Rise of 'Citizen Developers'," *BBC News*, February 6, 2014; E. Maltby and A. Loten, "App Building, the Do-It-Yourself Way," *The Wall Street Journal*, March 7, 2013; M. Carney, "New and Improved Glyph:

Hack Your Credit Card Utilization," *Pando Daily*, February 13, 2013; S. Perez, "Glyph's New iPhone App Tells You What Credit Cards to Use to Earn Better Rewards," *Tech Crunch*, November 13, 2012; C. Steele, "Do It Yourself: Create Your Own iOS or Android Apps," *PC Magazine*, March 16, 2012.

Questions

1. What are the advantages of learning to code so that you can build your own mobile apps? Provide specific examples to support your answer.

2. What are the disadvantages of learning to code so that you can build your own mobile apps? Provide specific examples to support your answer.

BEFORE *YOU GO ON....*

1. Describe the four fundamental business decisions that organizations must make when acquiring information systems.

2. Discuss each of the seven development methods in this section with regard to the four business decisions that organizations must make.

Apply The Concept 14.2

LEARNING OBJECTIVE 14.2 Discuss the four business decisions that companies must make when they acquire new applications.

STEP 1 – Background

Section 14.2 has discussed the many options available to acquire information systems. One of the more popular methods is software-as-a-service. SaaS is popular because it eliminates the need for the company purchasing the software to maintain the hardware that the software will run on. They simply need an Internet connection to access the software from the host company.

STEP 2 – Activity

Visit http://www.wiley.com/go/rainer/MIS3e/applytheconcept, and click on the links provided for Apply the Concept 14.2. There are two videos linked there that illustrate SaaS. As you watch these videos, consider the types of hardware that are required on both sides of the relationship. Also, give some thought to the legal nature of the relationship, given that the data will likely reside with the service provider.

STEP 3 – Deliverable

Imagine that a company has decided to use a SaaS model to acquire a new piece of software. Prepare a paper discussing the four business decisions they have made in light of this type of acquisition. Submit your paper to your instructor.

14.3 The Traditional Systems Development Life Cycle

The **systems development life cycle** is the traditional systems development method that organizations use for large-scale IT projects. The SDLC is a structured framework that consists of sequential processes by which information systems are developed. For our

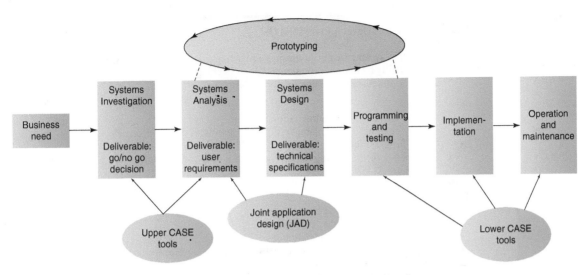

Figure 14.4 A six-stage systems development life cycle with supporting tools.

purposes (see FIGURE 14.4), we identify six processes, each of which consists of clearly defined tasks:

- Systems investigation
- Systems analysis
- Systems design
- Programming and testing
- Implementation
- Operation and maintenance

Alternative SDLC models contain more or fewer stages. The flow of tasks, however, remains largely the same. When problems occur in any phase of the SDLC, developers often must go back to previous phases.

Systems development projects produce desired results through team efforts. Development teams typically include users, systems analysts, programmers, and technical specialists. *Users* are employees from all functional areas and levels of the organization who interact with the system, either directly or indirectly. **Systems analysts** are IS professionals who specialize in analyzing and designing information systems. **Programmers** are IS professionals who either modify existing computer programs or write new programs to satisfy user requirements. **Technical specialists** are experts on a certain type of technology, such as databases or telecommunications. The **systems stakeholders** include everyone who is affected by changes in a company's information systems—for example, users and managers. All stakeholders are typically involved in systems development at various times and in varying degrees.

FIGURE 14.5 indicates that users have high involvement in the early stages of the SDLC, lower involvement in the programming and testing stage, and higher involvement in the later stages. TABLE 14.2 discusses the advantages and disadvantages of the SDLC.

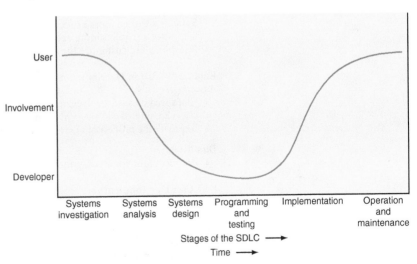

Figure 14.5 Comparison of user and developer involvement over the SDLC.

TABLE 14.2 Advantages and Disadvantages of System Acquisition Methods

Traditional Systems Development (SDLC)
Advantages
- Forces staff to systematically go through every step in a structured process.
- Enforces quality by maintaining standards.
- Has lower probability of missing important issues in collecting user requirements.

Disadvantages
- May produce excessive documentation.
- Users may be unwilling or unable to study the approved specifications.
- Takes too long to progress from the original ideas to a working system.
- Users have trouble describing requirements for a proposed system.

Prototyping
Advantages
- Helps clarify user requirements.
- Helps verify the feasibility of the design.
- Promotes genuine user participation.
- Promotes close working relationship between systems developers and users.
- Works well for ill-defined problems.
- May produce part of the final system.

Disadvantages
- May encourage inadequate problem analysis.
- Is not practical with large number of users.
- User may not want to give up the prototype when the system is completed.
- May generate confusion about whether the system is complete and maintainable.
- System may be built quickly, which can result in lower quality.

Joint Application Design
Advantages
- Involves many users in the development process.
- Saves time.
- Generates greater user support for the new system.
- Improves the quality of the new system.
- The new system is easier to implement.
- The new system has lower training costs.

Disadvantages
- It is difficult to get all users to attend the JAD meeting.
- The JAD approach is subject to all of the problems associated with any group meeting.

Integrated Computer-Assisted Software Engineering
Advantages
- Can produce systems with a longer effective operational life.
- Can produce systems that closely meet user requirements.
- Can speed up the development process.
- Can produce systems that are more flexible and adaptable to changing business conditions.
- Can produce excellent documentation.

Disadvantages
- Systems are often more expensive to build and maintain.
- The process requires more extensive and accurate definition of user requirements.
- It is difficult to customize the end product.

Rapid Application Development
Advantages
- Can speed up systems development.
- Users are intensively involved from the start.
- Improves the process of rewriting legacy applications.

Disadvantages
- Produces functional components of final systems, but not the final systems themselves.

End-User Development
Advantages
- Bypasses the IS department and avoids delays.
- User controls the application and can change it as needed.
- Directly meets user requirements.
- Promotes increased user acceptance of new system.
- Frees up IT resources.

Disadvantages
- May eventually require maintenance from IS department.
- Documentation may be inadequate.
- Leads to poor quality control.
- System may not have adequate interfaces to existing systems.
- May create lower-quality systems.

Object-Oriented Development
Advantages
- Objects model real-world entities.
- New systems may be able to reuse some computer code.

Disadvantages
- Works best with systems of more limited scope (i.e., with systems that do not have huge numbers of objects).

Systems Investigation

The initial stage in a traditional SDLC is systems investigation. Systems development professionals agree that the more time they invest in (1) understanding the business problem to be solved, (2) specifying the technical options for the systems, and (3) anticipating the problems they are likely to encounter during development, the greater the chances of success. For these reasons, **systems investigation** addresses *the business problem* (or business opportunity) by means of the feasibility study.

The primary task in the systems investigation stage is the **feasibility study**. Organizations have three basic solutions to any business problem relating to an information system: (1) do nothing and continue to use the existing system unchanged, (2) modify or enhance the existing system, and (3) develop a new system. The **feasibility study** analyzes which of these three solutions best fits the particular business problem. It also provides a rough assessment of the project's technical, economic, and behavioral feasibility, as explained below.

- *Technical feasibility* determines whether the company can develop and/or acquire the hardware, software, and communications components needed to solve the business problem. Technical feasibility also determines whether the organization can use its existing technology to achieve the project's performance objectives.

- *Economic feasibility* determines whether the project is an acceptable financial risk and, if so, whether the organization has the necessary time and money to successfully complete the project. You have already learned about the commonly used methods to determine economic feasibility: NPV, ROI, breakeven analysis, and the business case approach.

- *Behavioral feasibility* addresses the human issues of the systems development project. You will be heavily involved in this aspect of the feasibility study.

FIN

After the feasibility analysis is completed, a "go/no-go" decision is reached by the steering committee if there is one or by top management in the absence of a committee. The go/no-go decision does not depend solely on the feasibility analysis. Organizations often have more feasible projects than they can fund. Therefore, the firm must prioritize the feasible projects and pursue those with the highest priority. Unfunded feasible projects may not be presented to the IT department at all. These projects therefore contribute to the *hidden backlog*, which are projects that the IT department is not aware of.

If the decision is no-go, then the project either is put on the shelf until conditions are more favorable or is discarded. If the decision is go, then the project proceeds, and the systems analysis phase begins.

Systems Analysis

Once a development project has the necessary approvals from all participants, the systems analysis stage begins. **Systems analysis** is the process whereby systems analysts examine the business problem that the organization plans to solve with an information system.

The primary purpose of the systems analysis stage is to gather information about the existing system to determine the requirements for an enhanced system or a new system. The end product of this stage, known as the *deliverable*, is a set of *system requirements*.

Arguably, the most difficult task in systems analysis is to identify the specific requirements that the system must satisfy. These requirements are often called *user requirements*, because users (meaning you) provide them. When the systems developers have accumulated the user requirements for the new system, they proceed to the systems design stage.

Systems Design

Systems design describes how the system will resolve the business problem. The deliverable of the systems design phase is the set of *technical system specifications*, which specify the following:

- System outputs, inputs, and user interfaces
- Hardware, software, databases, telecommunications, personnel, and procedures
- A blueprint of how these components are integrated

When the system specifications are approved by all participants, they are "frozen." That is, they should not be changed. Adding functions after the project has been initiated causes **scope creep**, in which the time frame and expenses associated with the project expand beyond the agreed-upon limits. Scope creep endangers both the project's budget and its schedule. Because scope creep is expensive, successful project managers place controls on changes requested by users. These controls help to prevent runaway projects.

Programming and Testing

If the organization decides to construct the software in-house, then programming begins. **Programming** involves translating the design specifications into computer code. This process can be lengthy and time consuming, because writing computer code is as much an art as a science. Large-scale systems development projects can involve hundreds of computer programmers who are charged with creating hundreds of thousands of lines of computer code. These projects employ programming teams. The teams often include functional area users, who help the programmers focus on the business problem.

Thorough and continuous testing occurs throughout the programming stage. Testing is the process that assesses whether the computer code will produce the expected and desired results. It is also intended to detect errors, or bugs, in the computer code.

Implementation

Implementation (or *deployment*) is the process of converting from an old computer system to a new one. The conversion process involves organizational change. Only end users can manage organizational change, not the MIS department. The MIS department typically does not have enough credibility with the business users to manage the change process. Organizations use three major conversion strategies: direct, pilot, and phased.

In a **direct conversion**, the old system is cut off, and the new system is turned on at a certain point in time. This type of conversion is the least expensive. It is also the most risky because, if the new system does not work as planned, there is no support from the old system. Because of these risks, few systems are implemented using direct conversion.

A **pilot conversion** introduces the new system in one part of the organization, such as in one plant or one functional area. The new system runs for a period of time and is then assessed. If the assessment confirms that the system is working properly, then the system is implemented in other parts of the organization.

A **phased conversion** introduces components of the new system, such as individual modules, in stages. Each module is assessed. If it works properly, then other modules are introduced, until the entire new system is operational. Large organizations commonly combine the pilot and phased approaches. That is, they execute a phased conversion using a pilot group for each phase.

A fourth strategy is *parallel conversion*, in which the old and new systems operate simultaneously for a time. This strategy is seldom used today. One reason is that parallel conversion is totally impractical when both the old and new systems are online. Imagine that you are completing an order on Amazon, only to be told, "Before your order can be entered here, you must provide all the same information again, in a different form, and on a different set of screens." The results would be disastrous for Amazon.

Regardless of the type of implementation process that an organization uses, the new system may not work as advertised. In fact, the new system may cause more problems than the old system that it replaced. IT's About Business 14.4 illustrates how such an implementation caused serious problems at Avon Products.

IT'S ABOUT BUSINESS 14.4

Avon Writes Off $125 Million on Failed Software Implementation

Avon Products (Avon; www.avon.com) is a $10 billion American international manufacturer and distributor of beauty, household, and personal care products sold through representatives in more than 140 countries. Avon is the fifth-largest beauty company and the second-largest direct selling enterprise in the world, with 6.4 million independent salespeople or representatives. It is also a multilevel marketing company, in which the sales force is compensated not only for sales they personally generate, but also for the sales of the other salespeople that they recruit. Salespeople are expected to sell products directly to consumers by means of relationship referrals and word-of-mouth marketing.

In 2009, CEO and Chairperson Andrea Jung decided that "Avon ladies" (i.e., Avon sales representatives) should carry iPads so that they could "digitize the sales experience with the customer." Jung wanted Avon products ordered on the iPad so that the company's entire demand-driven supply chain would respond instantly. The Avon ladies would have access to product descriptions and inventories, and they would be able to place orders electronically.

To implement this program, Avon developed a SAP-based order management system. The system combined "back-end" (logistics and order fulfillment) software using SAP ERP modules with "front-end" (customer-facing) software using IBM electronic commerce software. Avon wanted to provide its reps with better insight into inventory as well as a better user experience. In May 2013, Avon launched a pilot system and its Web site in Canada.

When software development projects fail, the end users frequently suffer the most serious consequences. That is the case at Avon in Canada, where, in mid-2014, one independent salesperson was still struggling to cope with the hardships imposed by the failed order management system and Web site. She asserted that the system did not work properly when it was launched. Many sales representatives could not log into the new Web site. And, if they did gain access, the system did not accept orders, did not save orders properly, and did not reserve inventory properly. This rep further claimed that the Web site was too complex and required too many steps to place an order. She concluded that the new system "annihilated the business."

Ultimately, more than 100 of the 300 independent sales representatives who reported to her quit. The rep estimates that Avon lost as many as 16,000 representatives across

© pcatalin/iStockphoto

Canada. With all the trouble that sales reps encountered using the system, people who were making $50 or $100 per month decided that it simply was not worth their time and effort. The losses among the sales force are devastating to a multilevel marketing company such as Avon, which depends on its independent sale reps to generate revenues.

In late 2013, Avon halted the global deployment of the order management system because the pilot deployment in Canada caused "significant business disruption in that market and did not show a clear return on investment." However, Avon maintained that the new system actually worked, but it was so complicated to use that Avon salespeople left the company in large numbers. Therefore, the usability of the system was not consistent with the experiences that salespeople expect from consumer applications on tablets. Avon stated that it would continue to use the software in Canada despite the problems it caused. In fact, the company took a $125 million write down for associated software costs after it decided not to deploy the system globally.

In response to the problems Avon experienced with its pilot system, SAP maintained that it was involved only in the back-end applications of Avon's project, so it was not responsible for the front-end, sales-rep-facing application. The company also claimed that the order management system for Avon worked as designed.

The failure of the Avon system is a dramatic example of how usability has become a critical issue in the marketplace. People who are accustomed to using simple, well-designed applications in their personal lives (e.g., from Google, Amazon, and Apple) have no patience for disappointing and confusing applications at work. Essentially, consumer software has become so simple and intuitive to use that people expect business software to follow a similar model. If it does not, then users are much less patient than they were in the past.

As of mid-2014, Avon was still performing damage control in Canada. The company's goal is to stabilize its Canadian operations by intensifying recruitment and helping its sales force to utilize the new system.

Sources: Compiled from "With Friends Like These ... Uncovering Responsibility in Avon's Rollout Failure," *Enterprise Applications Consulting*, December 20, 2013; D. Henschen, "Inside Avon's Failed Order-Management Project," *InformationWeek*, December 16, 2013; N. Salerni, "Avon Cancels $125 Million Order Management System; Was the iPad App Too Hard to Use?" *iPhone in Canada*, December 15, 2013; "How NOT to Throw Out 125 Million Dollars," *Useful Usability*, December 12, 2013; D. Henschen,

"Avon Pulls Plug on $125 Million SAP Project," *InformationWeek*, December 12, 2013; D. Fitzgerald, "Avon to Halt Rollout of New Order Management System," *The Wall Street Journal*, December 11, 2013; S. Rosenbush, "Avon's Failed SAP Implementation Reflects Rise of Usability," *The Wall Street Journal*, December 11, 2013; www.avon.com, accessed March 10, 2014.

Questions

1. Is the Avon failure the fault of Avon? SAP? IBM? All three? Explain your answer.

2. Recall the discussion of strategic information systems in Chapter 2. Is Avon's new system a strategic information system? Why or why not? Explain your answer.

Operation and Maintenance

After the new system is implemented, it will operate for a period of time, until (like the old system it replaced) it no longer meets its objectives. Once the new system's operations are stabilized, the company performs audits to assess the system's capabilities and to determine if it is being utilized correctly.

Systems require several types of maintenance. The first type is *debugging* the program, a process that continues throughout the life of the system. The second type is *updating* the system to accommodate changes in business conditions. An example is adjusting to new governmental regulations, such as changes in tax rates. These corrections and upgrades usually do not add any new functions. Instead, they simply help the system to continue to achieve its objectives. In contrast, the third type of maintenance *adds new functions* to the existing system without disturbing its operation.

BEFORE *YOU GO ON....*

1. Describe the feasibility study.
2. What is the difference between systems analysis and systems design?
3. Describe structured programming.
4. What are the four conversion methods?

Apply The Concept 14.3

LEARNING OBJECTIVE 14.3 Enumerate the primary tasks and the importance of each of the six processes involved in the systems development life cycle.

STEP 1 – Background

The systems development life cycle uses a very systematic approach in which each stage builds on work completed at an earlier stage. It is an excellent model to follow, assuming that the right decisions are made at each stage of the SDLC and are appropriately communicated to the next stage of the SDLC.

STEP 2 – Activity

Visit http://www.wiley.com/go/rainer/MIS3e/applytheconcept, and watch the video titled "Software Development Life Cycle," which is linked to Apply the Concept 14.3. The video conveys a realistic (though perhaps a bit pessimistic) view of how poor communication can severely damage the software development process.

STEP 3 – Deliverable

After watching the video, build an outline that specifies the primary tasks and the importance of each of the six processes involved in the SDLC. Make certain to discuss the importance of communication from one step to the next.

14.4 Alternative Methods and Tools for Systems Development

Alternative methods for systems development include joint application design, rapid application development, agile development, and end-user development.

Joint Application Design

Joint application design (JAD) is a group-based tool for collecting user requirements and creating system designs. It is most often used within the systems analysis and systems design stages of the SDLC. JAD involves a group meeting attended by the analysts and all of the users that can be conducted either in person or via the computer. During this meeting, all users jointly define and agree on the systems requirements. This process saves a tremendous amount of time. TABLE 14.2 lists the advantages and disadvantages of the JAD process.

Rapid Application Development

Rapid application development (RAD) is a systems development method that can combine JAD, prototyping, and integrated computer-assisted software engineering (ICASE) tools (discussed later in this section) to rapidly produce a high-quality system. In the first RAD stage, developers use JAD sessions to collect system requirements. This strategy ensures that users are intensively involved early on. The development process in RAD is iterative; that is, requirements, designs, and the system itself are developed and then undergo a series, or sequence, of improvements. RAD uses ICASE tools to quickly structure requirements and develop prototypes. As the prototypes are developed and refined, users review them in additional JAD sessions. RAD produces the functional components of a final system, rather than prototypes. To understand how RAD functions and how it differs from SDLC, see FIGURE 14.6. TABLE 14.2 highlights the advantages and disadvantages of the RAD process.

Agile Development

Agile development is a software development methodology that delivers functionality in rapid iterations, which are usually measured in weeks. To be successful, this methodology requires frequent communication, development, testing, and delivery. Agile development focuses on rapid development and frequent user contact to create software that addresses the needs of business users. This software does not have to include every possible feature the user will require. Rather, it must meet only the user's more important and immediate needs. It can be updated later to introduce additional functions as they become necessary. The core tenet of agile development is to do only what you have to do to be successful right now.

One type of agile development uses the *scrum approach*. A key principle of scrum is that during a project users can change their minds about what they want and need. Scrum acknowledges that a development problem cannot be fully understood or defined from the start. Therefore, scrum focuses on maximizing the development team's ability to deliver iterations quickly and to respond effectively to additional user requirements as they emerge.

Figure 14.6 A rapid prototyping development process versus SDLC.
(Source: datawarehouse-training.com/Methodologies/rapidapplication-development)

Scrum contains sets of practices and predefined roles. The primary roles are the following:

- The *Scrum Master*: maintains the processes (typically replaces a project manager).
- The *Product Owner*: represents the business users and any other stakeholders in the project.
- The *Team*: a cross-functional group of about seven people who perform the actual analysis, design, coding, implementation, testing, and so on.

Scrum works this way: During each *sprint*—typically a 2- to 4-week period—the team creates a potentially shippable product increment, such as working and tested software. The set of features that goes into each sprint comes from the product backlog, which is a prioritized set of high-level work requirements to be completed.

The sprint planning meeting determines which backlog items will be addressed during a sprint. During this meeting, the Product Owner informs the team of the items in the product backlog that he or she wants to be completed. The team members then determine how many of these projects they can commit to during the next sprint, and they record this information in the sprint backlog.

During a sprint, no one is allowed to change the sprint backlog, which means that the requirements are frozen for the sprint. Each sprint must end on time. If the requirements are not completed for any reason, then they are left out and returned to the product backlog. After each sprint is completed, the team demonstrates how to use the software.

End-User Development

End-user development is an approach in which the organization's end users develop their own applications with little or no formal assistance from the IT department. TABLE 14.2 lists the advantages and disadvantages of end-user development.

Tools for Systems Development

Several tools can be used with various systems development methods. These tools include prototyping, integrated computer-assisted software engineering, component-based development, and object-oriented development.

Prototyping. The **prototyping** approach defines an initial list of user requirements, builds a model of the system, and then refines the system in several iterations based on users' feedback. Developers do not try to obtain a complete set of user specifications for the system at the outset, and they do not plan to develop the system all at once. Instead, they quickly develop a smaller version of the system known as a **prototype**. A prototype can take two forms. In some cases, it contains only the components of the new system that are of most interest to the users. In other cases, it is a small-scale working model of the entire system.

Users make suggestions for improving the prototype, based on their experiences with it. The developers then review the prototype with the users and utilize their suggestions to refine it. This process continues through several iterations until the users approve the system or it becomes apparent that the system cannot meet the users' needs. If the system is viable, then the developers can use the prototype to build the full system. One typical use of prototyping is to develop screens that a user will see and interact with. TABLE 14.2 describes the advantages and disadvantages of the prototyping approach.

A practical problem with prototyping is that a prototype usually looks more complete than it is. That is, it may not use the real database, it usually does not have the necessary error checking, and it almost never includes the necessary security features. Users who review a prototype that resembles the finished system may not recognize these problems. Consequently, they might have unrealistic expectations about how close the actual system is to completion.

Integrated Computer-Assisted Software Engineering Tools. **Computer-aided software engineering (CASE)** refers to a group of tools that automate many of the tasks in the SDLC. The tools that are used to automate the early stages of the SDLC (systems investigation, analysis, and design) are called **upper CASE tools**. The tools used to automate later stages in the SDLC (programming, testing, operation, and maintenance) are called **lower CASE tools**. CASE tools that provide links between upper CASE and lower CASE tools are called **integrated CASE (ICASE) tools**. TABLE 14.2 lists the advantages and disadvantages of ICASE tools.

Component-Based Development. **Component-based development** uses standard components to build applications. Components are reusable applications that generally have one specific function, such as a shopping cart, user authentication, or a catalog. Compared with other approaches, component-based development generally involves less programming and more assembly. Component-based development is closely linked with the idea of Web services and service-oriented architectures, which you will study in Plug IT In 4.

Many startup companies are pursuing the idea of component-based application development. One example is Ning (www.ning.com), which allows organizations to create, customize, and share their own social network.

Object-Oriented Development. **Object-oriented development** is based on a different view of computer systems than the perception that characterizes traditional development approaches. Traditional approaches can produce a system that performs the original task but may not be suited for handling other tasks. This limitation applies even when these other tasks involve the same real-world entities. For example, a billing system will handle billing, but it probably cannot be adapted to handle mailings for the marketing department or to generate leads for the sales force. This is true even though the billing, marketing, and sales functions all use similar data, including customer names, addresses, and purchases. In contrast, an *object-oriented (OO) system* begins not with the task to be performed, but with the aspects of the real world that must be modeled to perform that task. Therefore, in our example, if the firm has a good model of its customers and its interactions with them, then it can use this model equally well for billings, mailings, and sales leads.

The development process for an object-oriented system begins with a feasibility study and an analysis of the existing system. Systems developers identify the *objects* in the new system—the fundamental elements in OO analysis and design. Each object represents a tangible, real-world entity, such as a customer, bank account, student, or course. Objects have *properties*, or *data values*. For example, a customer has an identification number, a name, an address, an account number(s), and so on. Objects also contain the *operations* that can be performed on their properties. For example, operations that can be performed on the customer object may include obtain-account-balance, open-account, withdraw-funds, and so on. Operations are also referred to as *behaviors*.

This approach enables OO analysts to define all the relevant objects needed for the new system, including their properties and operations. The analysts then model how the objects interact to meet the objectives of the new system. In some cases, analysts can reuse existing objects from other applications (or from a library of objects) in the new system. This process saves the analysts the time they otherwise would spend coding these objects. In most cases, however, even with object reuse, some coding will be necessary to customize the objects and their interactions for the new system.

You have studied many methods that can be used to acquire new systems. TABLE 14.2 provides an overview of the advantages and disadvantages of each of these methods.

Apply The Concept 14.4

LEARNING OBJECTIVE 14.4 Describe alternative development methods and the tools that augment development methods.

STEP 1 – Background

The systems development life cycle is a very thorough method of development. However, it is also very time consuming and expensive. Section 14.4 discusses several alternative methods. Joint application design, rapid application development, and agile development are used in conjunction with several tools for systems development.

┌─ BEFORE YOU GO ON.... ─────

1. Describe the tools that augment the traditional SDLC.

2. Describe the alternate methods that can be used for systems development other than the SDLC.

Visit http://www.wiley.com/go/rainer/MIS3e/applytheconcept, and click on the link provided for Apply the Concept 14.4. This link will take you to a Vimeo video about prototyping.

Imagine that you are a developer of iPhone apps. At lunch the other day someone mentioned a very cool idea for a new camera app that would enable users to take pictures simply by opening the app and saying "click" rather than having to push a button.

What should this app look like? Draw up a sketch of at least two screens: the camera screen and the options screen. Discuss your prototype with a couple of your friends to see what they think. Also, try to find someone who has an iPhone to obtain his or her feedback.

STEP 3 – Deliverable

Based on your experience, describe the alternative development methods and how the tools discussed in this section might help you to develop your app. Put your descriptions in a document and submit it to your instructor.

14.5 Vendor and Software Selection

Few organizations, especially small and medium-sized enterprises, have the time, the financial resources, or the technical expertise required to develop today's complex IT or e-business systems. For this reason, business firms increasingly rely on outside vendors to provide software, hardware, and technical expertise. Consequently, selecting and managing these vendors and their software offerings has become a major aspect of developing an IT application. The following six steps in selecting a software vendor and an application package are useful.

Step 1: Identify Potential Vendors. Companies can identify potential software application vendors through various sources:

- Software catalogs
- Lists provided by hardware vendors
- Technical and trade journals
- Consultants and industry analysts experienced in the application area
- Peers in other companies
- Web searches

These sources often yield so many vendors and packages that the company must use some evaluation criteria to eliminate all but the most promising ones from further consideration. For example, it can eliminate vendors that are too small or that have a questionable reputation. It can also eliminate packages that do not have the required features or are not compatible with the company's existing hardware and/or software.

Step 2: Determine the Evaluation Criteria. The most difficult and crucial task in evaluating a vendor and a software package is to develop a detailed set of evaluation criteria. Some areas in which a customer should identify criteria are the following:

- Characteristics of the vendor
- Functional requirements of the system
- Technical requirements that the software must satisfy
- Amount and quality of documentation provided
- Vendor support of the package

These criteria should be set out in a **request for proposal**. An RFP is a document that is sent to potential vendors inviting them to submit a proposal that describes their software package and explains how it would meet the company's needs. The RFP provides the vendors with information about the system's objectives and requirements. Specifically, it describes the environment in which the system will be used, the general criteria that the company will use to evaluate the proposals, and the conditions for submitting proposals. The RFP may also request a list of current users of the package whom the company may

TABLE 14.3 Criteria for Selecting a Software Application Package

Functionality (Does the package do what the organization needs?)	Necessary hardware and networking resources
Cost and financial terms	Required training (check if provided by vendor)
Upgrade policy and cost	Security
Vendor's reputation and availability for help	Learning (speed of) for developers and users
Vendor's success stories (Visit the vendor's Web site, contact clients.)	Graphical presentation
System flexibility	Data handling
Ease of Internet interface	System-required hardware
Availability and quality of documentation	

contact. Finally, it can require the vendor to demonstrate the package at the company's facilities using specified inputs and data files.

Step 3: Evaluate Vendors and Packages. The responses to an RFP generate massive volumes of information that the company must evaluate. The goal of this evaluation is to determine the gaps between the company's needs (as specified by the requirements) and the capabilities of the vendors and their application packages. Often, the company gives the vendors and packages an overall score by (1) assigning an importance weight to each of the criteria, (2) ranking the vendors on each of the weighted criteria (say 1 to 10), and then (3) multiplying the ranks by the associated weights. The company can then shorten the list of potential suppliers to include only those vendors who achieved the highest overall scores. TABLE 14.3 lists the general criteria that companies use in this step.

Step 4: Choose the Vendor and Package. Once the company has shortened the list of potential suppliers, it can begin negotiations with these vendors to determine how their packages might be modified to remove any discrepancies with the company's IT needs. Thus, one of the most important factors in the decision is the additional development effort that may be required to tailor the system to the company's needs or to integrate it into the company's computing environment. The company must also consider the opinions of both the users and the IT personnel who will have to support the system.

Step 5: Negotiate a Contract. The contract with the software vendor is a vital element in the selection process. It specifies both the price of the software and the type and amount of support that the vendor agrees to provide. The contract will be the only recourse if either the system or the vendor does not perform as expected. It is essential, then, that the contract directly references the proposal, because this is the vehicle that the vendor used to document the functionality supported in its system. Furthermore, if the vendor is modifying the software to tailor it to the company's needs, then the contract must include detailed specifications (essentially the requirements) of the modifications. Finally, the contract should describe in detail the acceptance tests that the software package must pass.

Contracts are legal documents, and they can be quite tricky. For this reason, companies might need the services of experienced contract negotiators and lawyers. Many organizations employ software-purchasing specialists who assist in negotiations and write or approve the contract. These specialists should be involved in the selection process from the start.

Step 6: Establish a Service-Level Agreement. **Service-level agreements (SLAs)** are formal agreements that specify how work is to be divided between the company and its vendors. These specifications are based on a set of agreed-upon milestones, quality checks, and what–if situations. They describe how quality checks will be made and how disputes will be resolved. SLAs accomplish these goals by (1) defining the responsibilities of both partners, (2) providing a framework for designing support services, and (3) allowing the company to retain as much control as possible over its own systems. SLAs include such issues as performance, availability, backup and recovery, upgrades, and hardware and software ownership. For example, the SLA might specify that the application service provider make its system available to the customer 99.9 percent of the time.

┌─ **BEFORE** *YOU GO ON....* ─┐

1. List the major steps involved in selecting a vendor and a software package.
2. Describe a request for proposal.
3. Explain why SLAs play an important role in systems development.

Apply The Concept 14.5

LEARNING OBJECTIVE 14.5 Analyze the process of vendor and software selection.

STEP 1 – Background

A key element of acquiring information systems is determining exactly what you need. When a company decides to involve a third party (either in designing or in building the system), it typically posts a request for proposal, or RFP. This RFP explicitly communicates the company's expectations, its timeline, and sometimes its budgetary restrictions.

STEP 2 – Activity

Visit http://www.wiley.com/go/rainer/MIS3e/applytheconcept, and click on the link provided for Apply the Concept 14.5. This link will take you to a Web site that specializes in helping small and medium-sized enterprises with planning, documentation, examples, and other elements. In particular, it provides an example RFP. Download the sample, and review it.

STEP 3 – Deliverable

Considering that this is Step 2 of vendor and software selection, provide an analysis of how this RFP would fit into the rest of the process. What decisions did the company make to arrive at this RFP? How would this RFP lead the company through the rest of the process? Submit your analysis to your instructor.

What's in for ME?

ACCT

FOR THE ACCOUNTING MAJOR

Accounting personnel help perform the cost–benefit analyses on proposed projects. They may also monitor ongoing project costs to keep them within budget. Accounting personnel undoubtedly will find themselves involved with systems development at various points throughout their careers.

FIN

FOR THE FINANCE MAJOR

Finance personnel are frequently involved with the financial issues that accompany any large-scale systems development project (e.g., budgeting). They also are involved in cost–benefit and risk analyses. To perform these tasks, they need to stay abreast of the emerging techniques used to determine project costs and ROI. Finally, because they must manage vast amounts of information, finance departments are also common recipients of new systems.

MKT

FOR THE MARKETING MAJOR

In most organizations, marketing, like finance, involves massive amounts of data and information. Like finance, then, marketing is also a hotbed of systems development. Marketing personnel will increasingly find themselves participating in systems development teams. Such involvement increasingly means helping to develop systems, especially Web-based systems that reach out directly from the organization to its customers.

POM

FOR THE PRODUCTION/ OPERATIONS MANAGEMENT MAJOR

Participation in development teams is also a common role for production/operations people. Manufacturing is becoming increasingly computerized and integrated with other allied systems, from design to logistics to customer support. Production systems interface frequently with marketing, finance, and human resources. In addition, they may be part of a larger, enterprisewide system. Also, many end users in POM either develop their own systems or collaborate with IT personnel on specific applications.

HRM

FOR THE HUMAN RESOURCES MANAGEMENT MAJOR

The human resources department is closely involved with several aspects of the systems acquisitions process. Acquiring new systems may require hiring new employees, changing job descriptions, or terminating employees. Human resources staff performs all of these tasks. Further, if the organization hires consultants for the development project, or outsources it, the human resources department may handle the contracts with these suppliers.

 FOR THE MIS MAJOR

Regardless of the approach that the organization adopts for acquiring new systems, the MIS department spearheads it. If the organization chooses either to buy or to lease the application, the MIS department leads in examining the offerings of the various vendors and in negotiating with the vendors. If the organization chooses to develop the application in-house, then the process falls to the MIS department. MIS analysts work closely with users to develop their information requirements. MIS programmers then write the computer code, test it, and implement the new system.

SUMMARY

1. Discuss the different cost–benefit analyses that companies must take into account when formulating an IT strategic plan.

   The four common approaches to cost–benefit analysis are the following:

   > *The net present value* method converts future values of benefits to their present-value equivalent by "discounting" them at the organization's cost of funds. They can then compare the present value of the future benefits with the cost required to achieve those benefits to determine whether the benefits exceed the costs.

   > *Return on investment* measures management's effectiveness in generating profits with its available assets. ROI is calculated by dividing net income attributable to a project by the average assets invested in the project. ROI is a percentage, and the higher the percentage return, the better.

   > *Breakeven analysis* determines the point at which the cumulative dollar value of the benefits from a project equals the investment made in the project.

   > In the *business case approach*, system developers write a business case to justify funding one or more specific applications or projects.

2. Discuss the four business decisions that companies must make when they acquire new applications.

   > *How much computer code does the company want to write?* A company can choose to use a totally prewritten application (to write no computer code), to customize a prewritten application (to write some computer code), or to customize an entire application (write all new computer code).

   > *How will the company pay for the application?* Once the company has decided how much computer code to write, it must decide how to pay for it. With prewritten applications or customized prewritten applications, companies can buy them or lease them. With totally custom applications, companies use internal funding.

   > *Where will the application run?* Companies must now decide where to run the application. The company may run the application on its own platform or run the application on someone else's platform (use either a software-as-a-service vendor or an application service provider).

   > *Where will the application originate?* Prewritten applications can be open-source software or come from a vendor. Companies may choose to customize prewritten open-source applications or prewritten proprietary applications from vendors. Companies may customize applications in-house or outsource the customization. They also can write totally custom applications in-house or outsource this process.

3. Enumerate the primary tasks and importance of each of the six processes involved in the systems development life cycle.

   The six processes are the following:

   > *Systems investigation*: Addresses the business problem (or business opportunity) by means of the feasibility study; main task in the systems investigation stage is the feasibility study.

   > *Systems analysis*: Examines the business problem that the organization plans to solve with an information system; main purpose is to gather information about the existing system in order to determine the requirements for the new system; end product of this stage, known as the "deliverable," is a set of system requirements.

   > *Systems design*: Describes how the system will resolve the business problem; deliverable is the set of technical system specifications.

   > *Programming and testing*: Programming translates the design specifications into computer code; testing checks to see whether the computer code will produce the expected and desired results and detects errors, or bugs, in the computer code; deliverable is the new application.

   > *Implementation*: The process of converting from the old system to the new system via three major conversion strategies: direct, pilot, and phased; deliverable is properly working application.

   > *Operation and maintenance*: Types of maintenance include debugging, updating, and adding new functions when needed.

4. Describe alternative development methods and tools that augment development methods.

These are the *alternative methods*:

> *Joint application design* is a group-based tool for collecting user requirements and creating system designs.

> *Rapid application development* is a systems development method that can combine JAD, prototyping, and ICASE tools to rapidly produce a high-quality system.

> *Agile development* is a software development methodology that delivers functionality in rapid iterations, which are usually measured in weeks.

> *End-user development* refers to an organization's end users developing their own applications with little or no formal assistance from the IT department.

These are the *tools*:

> The *prototyping* approach defines an initial list of user requirements, builds a model of the system, and then improves the system in several iterations based on users' feedback.

> *Integrated computer-aided software engineering* combines upper CASE tools (automate systems investigation, analysis, and design) and lower CASE tools (programming, testing, operation, and maintenance).

> *Component-based development* uses standard components to build applications. Components are reusable applications that generally have one specific function, such as a shopping cart, user authentication, or a catalog.

> *Object-oriented development* begins with the aspects of the real world that must be modeled to perform that task. Systems developers identify the objects in the new system. Each object represents a tangible, real-world entity, such as a customer, bank account, student, or course. Objects have *properties*, or *data values*. Objects also contain the *operations* that can be performed on their properties.

TABLE 14.2 shows advantages and disadvantages of alternative methods and tools.

5. Analyze the process of vendor and software selection.

The process of vendor and software selection is composed of six steps:

> Identify potential vendors.

> Determine evaluation criteria.

> Evaluate vendors and packages.

> Choose the vendor and package.

> Negotiate a contract.

> Establish service-level agreements.

>>>CHAPTER GLOSSARY

agile development A software development methodology that delivers functionality in rapid iterations, measured in weeks, requiring frequent communication, development, testing, and delivery.

application portfolio The set of recommended applications resulting from the planning and justification process in application development.

application service provider (ASP) An agent or vendor who assembles the software needed by enterprises and packages them with outsourced development, operations, maintenance, and other services.

component-based development A software development methodology that uses standard components to build applications.

computer-aided software engineering (CASE) Development approach that uses specialized tools to automate many of the tasks in the SDLC; upper CASE tools automate the early stages of the SDLC and lower CASE tools automate the later stages.

direct conversion Implementation process in which the old system is cut off and the new system is turned on at a certain point in time.

end-user development Approach in which the organization's end users develop their own applications with little or no formal assistance from the IT department.

feasibility study Investigation that gauges the probability of success of a proposed project and provides a rough assessment of the project's feasibility.

implementation The process of converting from an old computer system to a new one.

integrated CASE (ICASE) tools CASE tools that provide links between upper CASE and lower CASE tools.

IS operational plan Consists of a clear set of projects that the IS department and the functional area managers will execute in support of the IT strategic plan.

IT steering committee A committee, comprised of a group of managers and staff representing various organizational units, set up to establish IT priorities and to ensure that the MIS function is meeting the needs of the enterprise.

IT strategic plan A set of long-range goals that describe the IT infrastructure and major IT initiatives needed to achieve the goals of the organization.

joint application design (JAD) A group-based tool for collecting user requirements and creating system designs.

lower CASE tools Tools used to automate later stages in the SDLC (programming, testing, operation, and maintenance)

object-oriented development A systems development methodology that begins with aspects of the real world that must be modeled to perform a task.

outsourcing Use of outside contractors or external organizations to acquire IT services.

phased conversion Implementation process that introduces components of the new system in stages, until the entire new system is operational.

pilot conversion Implementation process that introduces the new system in one part of the organization on a trial basis; when the new system is working properly, it is introduced in other parts of the organization.

programmers IS professionals who modify existing computer programs or write new computer programs to satisfy user requirements.

programming The translation of a system's design specifications into computer code.

prototype A small-scale working model of an entire system or a model that contains only the components of the new system that are of most interest to the users.

prototyping An approach that defines an initial list of user requirements, builds a prototype system, and then improves the system in several iterations based on users' feedback.

rapid application development (RAD) A development method that uses special tools and an iterative approach to rapidly produce a high-quality system.

request for proposal (RFP) Document that is sent to potential vendors inviting them to submit a proposal describing their software package and how it would meet the company's needs.

scope creep Adding functions to an information system after the project has begun.

service-level agreements (SLAs) Formal agreements regarding the division of work between a company and its vendors.

software-as-a-service (SaaS) A method of delivering software in which a vendor hosts the applications and provides them as a service to customers over a network, typically the Internet.

systems analysis The examination of the business problem that the organization plans to solve with an information system.

systems analysts IS professionals who specialize in analyzing and designing information systems.

systems design Describes how the new system will resolve the business problem.

systems development life cycle (SDLC) Traditional structured framework, used for large IT projects, that consists of sequential processes by which information systems are developed.

systems investigation The initial stage in the traditional SDLC that addresses the business problem (or business opportunity) by means of the feasibility study.

systems stakeholders All people who are affected by changes in information systems.

technical specialists Experts on a certain type of technology, such as databases or telecommunications.

upper CASE tools Tools that are used to automate the early stages of the SDLC (systems investigation, analysis, and design).

>>>DISCUSSION QUESTIONS

1. Discuss the advantages of a lease option over a buy option.

2. Why is it important for all business managers to understand the issues of IT resource acquisition?

3. Why is it important for everyone in business organizations to have a basic understanding of the systems development process?

4. Should prototyping be used on every systems development project? Why or why not?

5. Discuss the various types of feasibility studies. Why are they all needed?

6. Discuss the issue of assessing intangible benefits and the proposed solutions.

7. Discuss the reasons why end-user-developed information systems can be of poor quality. What can be done to improve this situation?

>>>PROBLEM-SOLVING ACTIVITIES

1. Access www.ecommerce-guide.com. Find the product review area. Read reviews of three software payment solutions. Assess them as possible components.

2. Use an Internet search engine to obtain information on CASE and ICASE tools. Select several vendors and compare and contrast their offerings.

3. Access www.ning.com. Observe how the site provides components for you to use to build applications. Build a small application at the site.

4. Enter www-01.ibm.com/software. Find its WebSphere product. Read recent customers' success stories. What makes this software so popular?

5. Enter the Web sites of the Gartner (www.gartner.com), the Yankee Group (www.yankeegroup.com), and CIO

(www.cio.com). Search for recent material about ASPs and outsourcing, and prepare a report on your findings.

6. StoreFront (www.storefront.net) is a vendor of e-business software. At its site, the company provides demonstrations illustrating the types of storefronts that it can create for shoppers. The site also provides demonstrations of how the company's software is used to create a store.

   a. Run the StoreFront demonstration to see how this is done.

   b. What features does StoreFront provide?

   c. Does StoreFront support smaller or larger stores?

   d. What other products does StoreFront offer for creating online stores? What types of stores do these products support?

STEP 1 – Background

Systems acquisition and implementation is fundamental to the life of an information system. A company can make the correct decision about what they need, but if the new system is not properly implemented, then the entire exercise is in vain. This chapter has covered many techniques for developing and implementing information systems.

STEP 2 – Activity

Your school has probably chosen a Learning Management System (LMS) that allows instructors to provide you with access to materials, grades, assignments, schedules, syllabi, and other materials. Perhaps your school uses Blackboard, WebCT, Desire2Learn, Moodle, or another type of LMS.

Assemble a group of classmates, and imagine that this system is just a demo to which you have been given access. Assume you are in one of the initial phases of rapid application development in which you get to provide feedback on the system's layout, functionality, and users' experiences.

STEP 3 – Deliverable

Create and share a Google Document in which each team member shares his or her personal review. Next, as a team, combine the comments into a single document that you will submit to your professor. Feel free to include screenshots with suggestions on how a modified layout could increase functionality.

CLOSING **CASE 1 >**

A Poor Start for Healthcare.gov

THE BUSINESS PROBLEM >>> Healthcare.gov (www.healthcare.gov) is a health insurance exchange Web site operated under the provisions of the 2010 Patient Protection and Affordable Care Act, commonly referred to as "Obamacare." The site was designed to serve the residents of the 36 U.S. states that opted not to create their own state exchanges. Healthcare.gov helps U.S. residents to purchase private health insurance plans, and it offers subsidies to people who earn less than four times the federal poverty line. In addition, it assists low-income people who are eligible for Medicaid, and it provides a separate marketplace for small businesses.

The front end, or customer-facing part of the Web site, presents the choices for the consumer and the necessary forms to fill out. The back end contains the databases and services. The Centers for Medicare and Medicaid Services oversaw the Web site design. A number of federal contractors, most prominently the CGI Group, built the actual site. CGI received a contract valued at nearly $300 million through 2013 for their work.

Unfortunately, Obama's team paid attention to crafting a healthcare reform policy but not to the details of actually implementing that policy. None of the participants in the White House meetings leading up to the launch of the Web site had any idea as to how well the site would function. Obama's team simply accepted the contractors' assurances that everything was ready to go for the launch. The White House's overriding concern was whether people would visit the exchanges. Unfortunately, they failed to consider what visitors would encounter when they accessed the site. The media concentrated on the marketing and enrollment hurdles as well. The

White House maintained this narrow focus despite numerous red flags indicating potential problems with Healthcare.gov that appeared for months prior to the rollout of the site. Federal auditors raised alarms as early as June 2013 when they warned of missed deadlines and unfinished work.

On October 1, 2013, Healthcare.gov was rolled out as planned. However, the launch was marred by serious technological problems, making it difficult (if not impossible) for the public to sign up for health insurance. In fact, the site was unusable to hundreds of thousands of Americans who wanted to enroll. Despite the pledges from Obama administration officials that the "glitches" would be quickly fixed, the list of bugs and problems continued to expand. Millward Brown Digital, a consulting firm, estimated that only 1 percent of the 3.7 million people who tried to register on the exchange in the first week were successful. Further, when people did log on, the site frequently shut down on them.

On October 4, 2013, President Obama publicly attributed the problems with Healthcare.gov to the overwhelming volume of attempted enrollments. The reality, however, was more serious. In fact, the architecture underlying the site was flawed in design, poorly tested, and ultimately nonfunctional. In addition, on the database side of the Web site (as opposed to the public-facing side), the data were garbled and, in some cases, unusable. The nightly reports on new enrollees that the insurance companies received from the federal government contained errors, including incorrect syntax and transposed or duplicate data. In other cases, insurers received multiple enrollments and cancellations from the same individual, but because the documents did not have time stamps, it was impossible to know which form was the most recent. Insurance companies resorted to contacting enrollees directly to obtain correct information, a solution that was possible only because so few people were able to sign up.

Even more alarming were the security flaws. An error message from the Web site relayed personal information over the Internet without encryption. In addition, the e-mail verification system could be bypassed without requiring access to the user's e-mail account.

To address these issues, administration officials put out a call for new contractors, as well as Silicon Valley talent, to fix the project. Unfortunately, these changes did not bring any new transparency to the site's myriad problems. In fact, Obama's aides refused to confirm the existence of any particular bugs or to describe what was wrong. Their primary concern was to maintain at least some public enthusiasm for the insurance marketplace.

On November 13, the government issued its first report on monthly enrollments, covering the disastrous October rollout. The report revealed that fewer than 27,000 people had enrolled through the federal exchange over the entire month. This number represented only 10 percent of the total the administration had been counting on.

THE SOLUTION >>> With Healthcare.gov in seeming disarray, President Obama and his chief of staff brought in an elite team of programmers from various IT organizations across the country to salvage the site. The team quickly found itself enmeshed in a situation in which multiple contractors were bickering with one another and no one would take ownership of any of the site's many deficiencies. Further, the contractors displayed a total lack of urgency, despite the fact that Healthcare.gov was becoming a national joke and was crippling Obama's healthcare legacy.

One of the team's most shocking discoveries was that the people operating Healthcare.gov had neglected to create a dashboard. As a result, programmers had no reliable method to measure what was actually occurring at the Web site, such as how many people were using it, what response times consumers encountered when they clicked on a feature, and where Web traffic was bottlenecked. The team immediately made implementing a dashboard a top priority.

By observing the dashboard, the team discovered a quick fix to an obvious mistake. Healthcare.gov had been constructed so that every time a user had to obtain information from the site's vast database, the site had to make a query into the database. Well-constructed, high-volume Web sites, particularly e-commerce sites, avoid this problem by storing the most frequently accessed information in a cache. (We discuss cache memory in Plug IT In 2). Queries to the cache are faster and do not tie up connections to the overall database. Not creating and using a cache created a huge, unnecessary bottleneck. The team immediately began to cache the data. As a result of these efforts, the Web site's overall response time—the time it took for a page to load—dropped from eight seconds to two. Although two seconds was still extremely slow, it still represented a significant improvement in the site's performance.

The day after the team successfully cached the data, they announced they could fix Healthcare.gov by the end of November, six weeks away, so that the "vast majority" of visitors could successfully access the site and enroll in a plan.

The team further discovered that the Healthcare.gov developers had made the most basic mistake that developers can make. E-commerce Web sites never open a service to everyone at once. Rather, they introduce it to smaller groups of customers and then expand it. In that way, they can monitor how the service functions, fix it if necessary, and then scale it (make it available to larger numbers of customers). The team concluded that Healthcare.gov should have been deployed via this method. Unfortunately, the government failed to adopt this approach.

Consider one particularly difficult problem that the team repaired. The unique identifier that the Web site had to issue to everyone who was trying to enroll was taking too long to generate. In fact, the ID generator had become so overloaded that the Web site was effectively nonfunctional. To resolve this problem, the team worked on a patch (new computer code). The patch was partially successful, but the team learned a few days later that the identifications it was generating did not have the correct number of digits to match the insurance companies' needs. As a result, the team had to remove the patch and restore the old ID generator. Then, in late November, the old generator effectively shut down the entire Web site. The team quickly developed a new patch, this time with the correct number of digits. They then executed a "hot fix," meaning that they inserted the patch into the site without testing it. Fortunately for the team, the patch worked.

While these experts were focusing on these immediate problems, other team members worked at a separate office to deal with longer-term issues that the site would face following the November 30 deadline. The most important issue was scale. Would the site be able to handle the volumes of traffic that a functional Healthcare.gov would generate?

THE RESULTS >>> On December 1, the team issued a public report card that documented Healthcare.gov's turnaround. A series of hardware upgrades had dramatically increased capacity; the system was now able to accommodate at least 50,000 simultaneous users. The team had performed more than 400 bug fixes. Web site availability had increased from an abysmal 43 percent at the beginning of November to 95 percent. Further, the average response time—originally a disastrous 8 seconds per page and then a slow 2 seconds per page—had decreased to an acceptable 0.343 seconds per page.

One of the key issues in preparing the site to scale was the error rate—the rate at which any click on the site generated a result that it was not supposed to. In October, the error rate had been an astoundingly high 6 percent. The report card indicated that the rate had declined significantly to 0.5 percent. (At the end of January 2014, the error rate was still decreasing.)

On December 23, the Web site handled 83,000 simultaneous users at one point. The result was 129,000 enrollments on that one day, almost five times as many as the site had handled in all of October. On Christmas Day, another 93,000 visitors enrolled.

In about one-tenth of the time that a group of Washington contractors had built a Web site that did not work at a cost of more than $300 million, this ad hoc team had rescued the site and, arguably, Obama's chance at a health reform legacy.

Government officials hoped to enroll 6 million people in Obamacare by March 31, 2014. If the system had attracted substantially fewer people, the costs could rise for other enrollees. At the end of May 2014, the White House stated that Healthcare.gov had processed some 8 million enrollments.

One final note: In April 2014, Kathleen Sebelius resigned as Secretary of Health and Human Services, in part as a result of the problems with the Healthcare.gov Web site.

Sources: Compiled from R. Abelson and K. Thomas, "A Final Push for Healthcare," *The New York Times*, March 25, 2014; L. Nichols, "Healthcare.gov Glitch Fixed Quickly Ahead of Open-Enrollment Deadline," *PR Week*, March 24, 2014; K. Kennedy, "4.2 Million Enrolled in Insurance Through February," *USA Today*, March 11, 2014; S. Brill, "Code Red," *Time*, March 10, 2014; A. Aigner-Treworgy and J. Acosta, "Obamacare Enrollment Hits 4 Million, Push Underway to Hit Revised Goal," *Political Ticker*, February 25, 2014; K. Diller, "How Developers Could Have Avoided HealthCare.gov Technical Problems," *SearchSoftwareQuality*, January 30, 2014; P. Wait, "Accenture Jumps into Healthcare.gov Hot Seat," *InformationWeek*, January 14, 2014; D. Talbot, "Diagnosis for Healthcare.gov: Unrealistic Technology Expectations," *MIT Technology Review*, December 2, 2013; M. Scherer, "More

Than a Glitch," *Time*, November 4, 2013; E. Scannell, "The IT Fundamentals That Healthcare.gov Ignored," *TechTarget*, November 1, 2013; P. Ford, "The Obamacare Website Didn't Have to Fail; How to Do Better Next Time," *Bloomberg BusinessWeek*, October 16, 2013; www.healthcare.gov, accessed February 15, 2014.

Questions

1. Were the problems with the Healthcare.gov Web site the result of management, technology, or both? Provide specific examples to support your answer.

2. What lessons can you draw from Healthcare.gov about successfully implementing very large information systems projects?

CLOSING **CASE 2 >**

The Federal Aviation Administration's Next Generation Air Transportation System

THE ORIGINAL PROBLEM >>> The U.S. air traffic system has achieved an impressive safety record. Nevertheless, many of the network's features are so antiquated that experts blame them for delays and other inefficiencies that cost billions of dollars each year. The Federal Aviation Administration (FAA; www.faa.gov) estimates that if the increasing congestion in the U.S. air transportation system is not addressed, it will cost the nation's economy some $22 billion annually in lost economic activity by 2022. Perhaps more seriously, it will also cause increasing safety issues, potentially endangering the flying public.

THE INTENDED SOLUTION >>> To resolve these problems, the FAA began to develop the Next Generation Air Transportation System (NextGen; www.faa.gov/nextgen) in 2004. (Development and deployment continue in mid-2014.) The purpose of NextGen is to transform America's air traffic control system from a ground-based system to a satellite-based system. NextGen uses global positioning system (GPS) technologies to shorten routes, save time and fuel, reduce traffic delays, increase the number of planes in the air traffic system, and permit controllers to monitor and manage aircraft with greater safety. Planes will be able to fly closer together, take more direct routes, and avoid delays caused when planes remain in holding patterns while they wait for an open runway. To implement NextGen, the FAA will have to transform the nation's entire air transportation system.

The FAA planned for a 20-year, $40 billion project, including upgraded information systems and radar, a new communications network to replace radios, and a satellite-based

surveillance system that indicates the locations of nearby planes without relying on air traffic controllers. The goal is to manage planes more precisely and automatically, thereby enabling them to fly closer and with greater safety. The FAA planned to deploy NextGen across the U.S. in stages between 2012 and 2025.

The FAA estimated that by 2018, NextGen will reduce aviation fuel consumption by 1.4 billion gallons, reduce carbon emissions by 14 million tons, and save billions of dollars in costs. Each mile in the air costs an airline about $0.10 to $0.15 per seat in operating expenses such as flight crew and fuel.

PROBLEMS WITH NEXTGEN'S IMPLEMENTATION >>> Uneven progress, budget overruns, and conflicts among regulators and airlines demonstrate how extremely challenging the task of modernizing the world's most complex air traffic management network really is. The slow pace of NextGen's implementation has drawn harsh criticism. An April 2013 report by the Government Accountability Office (GAO) found that, although the project exhibited some progress, the implementation has been hindered by bureaucracy, delays designing new navigation procedures, and fear of conflicts with airport neighbors and environmentalists. The report further stated that the FAA had failed to set realistic goals, budgets, or expectations for NextGen. The report raised concerns that NextGen's completion could slip to 2035, and its actual costs could be three times as great as its estimated costs.

FAA Administrator Michael Huerta responded that the agency had met 80 percent of its implementation goals since 2008. He asserted that the FAA will continue to develop NextGen despite government spending cuts.

There were early problems with NextGen. The FAA initially designed new flight paths without much industry input. Airlines, which are responsible for at least $7 billion of NextGen's total cost, have already invested in sophisticated computers and other cockpit equipment to enable pilots to fly more precise paths. Further, various interests have collided frequently. In just one example, simply reworking air routes to and from airports can take years, partly as a result of environmental assessments to address local noise concerns.

Difficulties in NextGen implementation have occurred nearly everywhere, from new landing procedures that were impossible for some planes to execute to aircraft tracking software that misidentified planes. Key initiatives are experiencing delays and are at risk of cost overruns. Further, the FAA lacks "an executable plan" for bringing NextGen fully online, according to the GAO.

Some airline officials, frustrated because they have not seen promised money-saving benefits, assert they want better results before they spend more money to equip planes to use NextGen, a vital step to the system's success. Lawmakers are also frustrated. NextGen has enjoyed broad bipartisan support in Congress, but with the government facing spending cuts, supporters fear the program will not receive the necessary funding to become fully operational. In September 2013, a government–industry advisory committee recommended that, given the likelihood of budget cuts, the FAA should concentrate on just 11 NextGen initiatives that are ready or nearly ready to come online. The committee concluded that the rest of NextGen's 150 initiatives can wait.

Even the use of GPS-based procedures has been slowed by unforeseen problems. Developing each procedure airport by airport takes several years. At large airports, new procedures are used only sporadically. During busy periods, controllers do not have time to switch back and forth between the new procedures, which most airliners can use, and older procedures that regional airliners and smaller planes still use. Consequently, all flights use the older procedure because all planes can fly them.

In mid-2014, an internal FAA report projected that NextGen will cost $120 billion to implement, three times more than the original estimate. Further, the FAA estimated that the system will not be fully operational until 2035.

THE RESULTS SO FAR (MID-2014) >>>

America's new information system to reduce airline delays—itself years behind schedule—is finally yielding results. Let's examine a few of them:

- According to the FAA, the implementation of a surface management (taxi) initiative in Boston saved more than 5,000 gallons of aviation fuel and reduced carbon dioxide emissions by 50 tons during one period of heavy congestion.

- A shared surface surveillance system combined with aircraft monitoring techniques reduced taxi-out time by 7,000 hours per year at New York's JFK airport and by 5,000 hours in Memphis, Tennessee.

- NextGen has also been tested in Memphis with Delta Air Lines and FedEx (www.fedex.com).

- The National Air Traffic Controllers Association conducted a demonstration at Dallas/Fort Worth International Airport of a new surveillance display called the Tower Flight Data Manager system that presented surveillance, flight data, weather, airport configuration, and other information critical to controllers.

- Specialized Optimized Profile Descents, also known as Initial Tailored Arrivals, are in operation at airports in San Francisco, Los Angeles, Miami, and Denver.

Let's take a closer look at one specific example, Alaska Air Group (www.alaskaair.com), where the future has arrived. Since spring 2013, pilots landing at its Seattle–Tacoma International Airport (Sea-Tac) hub no longer descend in steps that require frequent radio contact with air traffic controllers. Instead, they fly smoothly on autopilot, with their engines nearly idle.

One Alaska Air pilot recently demonstrated the new technology in a flight simulator, threading his GPS-guided Boeing 737 through a precise path that cut almost 20 miles from the old route. Significantly, this revised route included a tight turn that would have been impossible with the previous system. The new equipment enables pilots to descend smoothly and to guide planes through narrow bands of airspace. These procedures reduce the number of local residents who are affected by noise. The pilot needed only to monitor his plane's computers to ensure that the plane stayed on track.

Under the old system—which is still employed by planes that lack new equipment and for two arrival tracks that have not been modernized—planes approached Sea-Tac by following radio beacons. Controllers guided pilots in with multiple commands to change direction, altitude, and speed. Those steps frequently consumed extra fuel, and they increased mileage.

Alaska Air—not the FAA—initiated the efforts at Sea-Tac, in 2009. The airline had already been using radar-guided approaches to remote Alaskan airports that are famous for their bad weather. The FAA initially approved the plan and then took it over a year later. The agency eventually provided $4.8 million to update two of Sea-Tac's four arrival tracks with GPS guidance technologies.

More than 90 percent of Alaska Airlines pilots now use the two GPS approaches. Alaska Air executives claim that satellite-guided arrivals and departures at Seattle and a handful of other airports saved the carrier $17.6 million and 200,000 gallons of fuel in one year.

In sum, Alaska Air has successfully deployed some elements of NextGen. Nevertheless, as of mid-2014 the success of the entire project remained uncertain.

Sources: Compiled from C. Howard, "NextGen GA Fund Selects Banks to Help Finance General Aviation NextGen Installations, Accelerate FAA's NextGen Implementation," *Avionics Intelligence*, March 14, 2014; W. Bellamy, "NextGen Among Top US Transportation Issues for 2014," *Avionics Today*, December 17, 2013; J. Lowy, "The FAA's Next Big Issue Is Acting on Its NextGen Air Traffic Control Dreams," *Associated Press*, November 1, 2013; J. Lowy, "Air Traffic Control Modernization Hits Turbulence," *Associated Press*, October 31, 2013; S. Carey, "The FAA's $40 Billion Adventure," *The Wall Street Journal*, August 19, 2013; W. Jackson, "What's Keeping FAA's NextGen Air Traffic Control on the Runway?" *GCN.com*, July 22, 2013; S. Carey, "The FAA's $40 Billion Adventure," *The Wall Street Journal*, March 20, 2013; J. Mouawad, "Alaska Airlines, Flying Above an Industry's Troubles," *The New York Times*, March 2, 2013; J. Hoover, "Problems Plague FAA's NextGen Air Traffic Control Upgrade," *InformationWeek*, October 5, 2011; "Fact Sheet – Next Generation Air Transportation System," *FAA News*, May 27, 2010; www.faa.gov/nextgen, www.faa.gov, accessed January 30, 2014.

1. Describe the many problems that have caused problems with implementing NextGen.

2. In Plug IT In 2, you learned that hardware capabilities roughly double every 18 months or so (Moore's law). What impact will increases in hardware processing power, with accompanying decreases in size, have on the NextGen system? Support your answer.

3. Recall the discussion of cloud computing in Plug IT In 4. What impact might a cloud computing solution have on the future of the NextGen system? Support your answer.

INTERNSHIP ACTIVITY > southwest wire A PRODUCTION COMPANY

Manufacturing Industry

The last three Internship Activities have involved the manufacturing sector with Southwest Wire and its CIO, Halle Smith. Now that most of the initial ERP components have been implemented and both the SCM and CRM modules have been added, Halle wants to review the process to identify areas where the company could have made better decisions. Halle's decisions were based more on the opportunities afforded by the software packages than on the alignment within her organization, the needs of her users, or her organization's current processes.

In this activity, Halle is asking you to help her learn from her experiences so that she—and her organization—can make better implementation decisions in the future. Below is another e-mail from Halle.

To:	IT Intern
From:	Halle Smith
Subject:	General System Implementation Questions

Hello!

Thank you so much for your help on the ERP, SCM, and CRM implementation projects. They are all installed and running. Unfortunately, I have heard quite a few complaints that there are some things the old systems did better and some functions the new systems do not do at all. In general, we have been able to work around these problems, and the system is working. However, we need to learn from this experience to improve any future system implementations.

I have heard of a company in Australia called Holocentric that has a very high success rate in helping companies implement new systems. See if you can find anything on the Web that will clarify the differences between typical implementation methods and Holocentric's models. Perhaps you can even find a YouTube video that highlights this information.

Finally, I would like you to provide me with a descriptive comparison of the typical model to the Holocentric model. Moving forward I hope to use this information with future implementations.

I very much appreciate your work on this project.
Halle

Note: Any links or Web sites mentioned in this e-mail are available at http://www.wiley.com/go/rainer/MIS3e/internship.

SPREADSHEET ACTIVITY > VLOOKUP

STEP 1 – Background

You will frequently need to locate data in a table or chart and bring back a certain number based on another figure. VLOOKUP will accomplish this task for you. In fact, spreadsheets provide several "lookup" tools. However, once you understand the concept behind how one of them works, they all are fairly easy to pick up.

There are four components to a lookup function. The first is the *lookup value*. This component refers to the value you are searching for, which is contained in a particular cell. You typically don't specify this value; rather, you identify the cell in which it is found. This feature allows you to pick a different value to look up. The next component is the *table array*. This is simply the data where the match can be found. It should be in two columns arranged from least to greatest in the lookup column.

The third component is the *column index number*. This number specifies which of the two columns contains the data to return. Columns are numbered from left to right. Therefore, if the data you are returning are stored in the left-hand column, then you will place a 1 here. If the data are in the right-hand column, then you will place a 2 here. Finally, the spreadsheet needs to know if you require an exact match or the next highest value. If you require an exact match, then you will use the number 1; otherwise, use the number 2.

STEP 2 – Activity

Imagine that you work for a retail store that ships products to 50 zip codes within your state. Tax rates vary across the state depending on the county tax rate and whether the zip code falls within city limits. Combined tax rates are always different. You currently have to look up the correct tax rate on a table every time

a customer submits an order. Although this system is not ideal, it is manageable. However, you are concerned that as your business grows, this approach will become less reliable and accurate.

Using a spreadsheet to find the appropriate tax rates would be a better strategy. Specifically, the lookup tools mentioned in Step 1 would be ideal for this type of activity.

STEP 3 – Deliverable

Visit http://www.wiley.com/go/rainer/MIS3e/spreadsheet, and download the workbook linked for this activity. The workbook contains a list of 2,154 tax rates for the state of New York, including the county, city, and combined rates. For this activity, the combined rate is the one you want to return with VLOOKUP. The workbook provides specific instructions on how to complete this activity.

Follow the instructions in the spreadsheet and submit your final work to your instructor.

Additional help with this spreadsheet skill is available in WileyPLUS. Open the "Microsoft Office 2013 Lab Manual Advanced Spreadsheet Module: Excel 2013," and review Lesson 1: Enhanced Decision-Making—IF and LOOKUP, pages E104 and E105.

DATABASE ACTIVITY > CREATING A DATABASE FROM A TEMPLATE

STEP 1 – Background

In all of the database activities up to this point, you have been working with an existing database with existing data. You have learned how to write and modify queries and reports to analyze and present data in a meaningful way.

Suppose, however, that no database is available? What if you need to know something and no one has the data you need to answer your question? In this scenario, you might need to build your own database. Building a database completely from scratch is a very time-consuming activity. However, working with templates can save you a great deal of time.

STEP 2 – Activity

Imagine that your family has run a small building supply company for years. Fortunately, you haven't been hurt much by the "big box" stores because of your location. You are in a relatively rural area where it isn't profitable for Lowe's or Home Depot to move in and compete. Consequently, it is more convenient for your customers to shop with you.

After you completed an Operations Management class, you asked your grandfather how he manages his inventory. His answer was a bit vague. It seems that inventory is managed to a large degree by the employees who are instructed to inform management

when levels are beginning to run low. Apparently, no one knows how much product is lost, available, or on order.

You are convinced there has to be a better method of managing inventory. The store's computer already has Microsoft Access installed. So, rather than "reinventing the wheel," you decide to search for an inventory management template in Access.

Your assignment is to search the Web for "Microsoft Access Inventory Management Template," find a template, and download it to your computer. Then, open it and review the tables, relationships, queries, reports, navigation, and other features. How much would you have to customize this template to use it in your family's store?

STEP 3 – Deliverable

Work in the database layout to reformat the titles and labels, and make a list of other changes you would need to make. Then, submit your database and list of changes. Make a note in your list of whether you can work within the queries and reports to customize the template to meet your inventory management needs.

Additional help with this database skill is available in WileyPLUS. Open the "Microsoft Office 2013 Lab Manual Database Module: Access 2013," and review Lesson 2: Creating a Table Structure.

Business Processes and Business Process Management

LEARNING OBJECTIVES >>>

PI1.1 Discuss ways in which information systems enable cross-functional business processes and business processes for a single functional area.

PI1.2 Compare and contrast business process reengineering and business process management to determine the advantages and disadvantages of each.

PI1.1 Business Processes

A **business process** is an ongoing collection of related activities that create a product or a service of value to the organization, its business partners, and/or its customers. The process involves three fundamental elements:

- *Inputs:* Materials, services, and information that flow through and are transformed as a result of process activities
- *Resources:* People and equipment that perform process activities
- *Outputs:* The product or a service created by the process

If the process involves a customer, then that customer can be either internal or external to the organization. A manager who is the recipient of an internal reporting process is an example of an internal customer. In contrast, an individual or a business that purchases the organization's products is the external customer of the fulfillment process.

Successful organizations measure their process activities to evaluate how well they are executing these processes. Two fundamental metrics that organizations employ in assessing their processes are efficiency and effectiveness. *Efficiency* focuses on doing things well in the process; for example, progressing from one process activity to another without delay or without wasting money or resources. *Effectiveness* focuses on doing the things that matter; that is, creating outputs of value to the process customer—for example, high-quality products.

Many processes cross functional areas in an organization. For example, product development involves research, design, engineering, manufacturing, marketing, and distribution. Other processes involve only a single functional area. Table PI1.1 identifies the fundamental business processes performed in an organization's functional areas.

Cross-Functional Processes

All of the business processes in Table PI1.1 fall within a single functional area of the company. However, many other business processes, such as procurement and fulfillment, cut across multiple functional areas; that is, they are **cross-functional business processes**, meaning that no single functional area is responsible for their execution. Rather, multiple functional areas collaborate to perform the process. For a cross-functional process to be successfully completed, each functional area must execute its specific process steps in a coordinated, collaborative way. To clarify this point, let's take a look at the procurement and fulfillment cross-functional processes. We discuss these processes in greater detail in Chapter 11.

The *procurement process* includes all of the tasks involved in acquiring needed materials externally from a vendor. Procurement comprises five steps that are completed in three different functional areas of the firm: warehouse, purchasing, and accounting.

The process begins when the warehouse recognizes the need to procure materials, perhaps due to low inventory levels. The warehouse documents this need with a purchase requisition, which it sends to

POM

Accounting Business Processes
- Managing accounts payable
- Managing accounts receivable
- Reconciling bank accounts
- Managing cash receipts

- Managing invoice billings
- Managing petty cash
- Producing month-end close
- Producing virtual close

Finance Business Processes
- Managing account collection
- Managing bank loan applications
- Producing business forecasts
- Applying customer credit approval and credit terms

- Producing property tax assessments
- Managing stock transactions
- Generating financial cash flow reports

Marketing Business Processes
- Managing post-sale customer follow-up
- Collecting sales taxes
- Applying copyrights and trademarks
- Using customer satisfaction surveys
- Managing customer service

- Handling customer complaints
- Handling returned goods from customers
- Producing sales leads
- Entering sales orders
- Training sales personnel

Production/Operations Management Business Processes
- Processing bills of materials
- Processing manufacturing change orders
- Managing master parts list and files
- Managing packing, storage, and distribution
- Processing physical inventory
- Managing purchasing
- Managing quality control for finished goods

- Auditing for quality assurance
- Receiving, inspecting, and stocking parts and materials
- Handling shipping and freight claims
- Handling vendor selection, files, and inspections

Human Resources Business Processes
- Applying disability policies
- Managing employee hiring
- Handling employee orientation
- Managing files and records
- Applying healthcare benefits
- Managing pay and payroll

- Producing performance appraisals and salary adjustments
- Managing resignations and terminations
- Applying training/tuition reimbursement
- Managing travel and entertainment
- Managing workplace rules and guidelines
- Overseeing workplace safety

Management Information Systems Business Processes
- Antivirus control
- Computer security issues incident reporting
- Training computer users
- Computer user/staff training
- Applying disaster recovery procedures

- Applying electronic mail policy
- Generating Internet use policy
- Managing service agreements and emergency services
- Applying user workstation standards
- Managing the use of personal software

the purchasing department (Step 1). In turn, the purchasing department identifies a suitable vendor, creates a purchase order based on the purchase requisition, and sends the order to the vendor (Step 2). When the vendor receives the purchase order, it ships the materials, which are received in the warehouse (Step 3). The vendor then sends an invoice, which is received by the accounting department (Step 4). Accounting sends payment to the vendor, thereby completing the procurement process (Step 5).

The *fulfillment process* is concerned with processing customer orders. Fulfillment is triggered by a customer purchase order that is received by the sales department. Sales then validates the purchase order and creates a sales order. The sales order communicates data related to the order to other functional areas within the organization, and it tracks the progress

of the order. The warehouse prepares and sends the shipment to the customer. Once accounting is notified of the shipment, it creates an invoice and sends it to the customer. The customer then makes a payment, which accounting records.

An organization's business processes can create a competitive advantage if they enable the company to innovate or to execute more effectively and efficiently than its competitors. They can also be liabilities, however, if they make the company less responsive and productive. Consider the airline industry. It has become a competitive necessity for all of the airlines to offer electronic ticket purchases via their Web sites. To provide competitive advantage, however, these sites must be highly responsive and they must provide both current and accurate information on flights and prices. An up-to-date, user-friendly site that provides fast answers to user queries will attract customers and increase revenues. In contrast, a site that provides outdated or inaccurate information, or has a slow response time, will hurt rather than improve business.

Clearly, good business processes are vital to organizational success. But how can organizations determine if their business processes are well designed? The first step is to document the process by describing its steps, its inputs and outputs, and its resources. The organization can then analyze the process and, if necessary, modify it to improve its performance. We examine this procedure in Plug IT In 1.2.

To understand this point, let's consider the e-ticketing process. E-ticketing consists of four main process activities: searching for flights, reserving a seat, processing payment, and issuing an e-ticket. These activities can be broken down into more detailed process steps. The result may look like the process map in FIGURE PI1.1. Note that different symbols correspond to different types of process steps. For instance, rectangles (steps) are activities that are performed by process resources (reserve seats, issue e-ticket). Diamond-shaped boxes indicate decisions that need to be made (seats available?). Arrows are used as connectors between steps; they indicate the sequence of activities.

These symbols are important in the process flowchart (which is similar with a programming flowchart). Other symbols may be used to provide additional process details. For example, D-shaped boxes are used instead of rectangles when a waiting period is part of a process; ovals can show start and stop points; and process resources can be attached to activities with resource connector lines, or included as an annotation or property for each activity box.

The customers of the process are travelers planning a trip, and the process output is an e-ticket. Travelers provide inputs to the process: the desired travel parameters to begin the search, the frequent flyer miles number, and their credit card information. In addition, a computerized reservation system that stores information for many airlines also provides some of the process inputs—such as the seat availability and prices. The resources used in the process are the airline Web site, the computerized reservation system, and, if the customer calls the airline call center at any time during the process, the call center system and the human travel agents. The process creates customer value by efficiently generating an output that meets the customer search criteria—dates and prices. The performance of the process depends on efficiency metrics such as the time required to purchase an e-ticket, from the moment the customer initiates the ticket search until he or she receives the e-ticket. Effectiveness metrics include customer satisfaction with the airline Web site. Finally, the

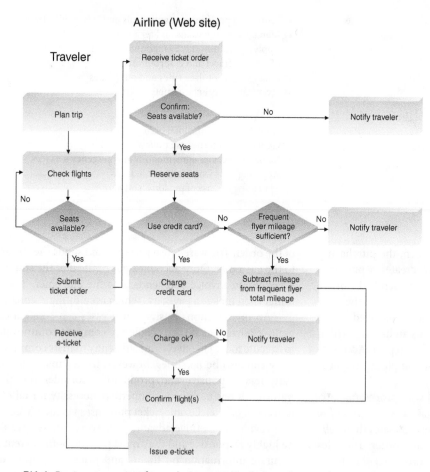

Figure PI1.1 Business process for ordering e-ticket from airline Web site.

performance of the process may be affected if the quality or the timeliness of the inputs is low—for example, if the customer enters the wrong dates—or if the process resources are not available—for example, if the Web site crashes before the purchase is finalized.

Information Systems and Business Processes

An information system (IS) is a critical enabler of an organization's business processes. Information systems facilitate communication and coordination among different functional areas, and allow easy exchange of, and access to, data across processes. Specifically, ISs play a vital role in three areas:

- Executing the process
- Capturing and storing process data
- Monitoring process performance

In this section, you will learn about each of these roles. In some cases the role is fully automated—that is, it is performed entirely by the IS. In other cases, the IS must rely on the manager's judgment, expertise, and intuition.

Executing the Process. An IS helps organizations execute processes efficiently and effectively. IS are typically embedded into the processes, and they play a critical role in executing the processes. In other words, an IS and processes are usually intertwined. If the IS does not work, the process cannot be executed. IS help execute processes by informing people when it is time to complete a task, by providing the necessary data to complete the task, and, in some cases, by providing the means to complete the task.

In the procurement process, for example, the IS generates the purchase requisitions and then informs the purchasing department that action on these requisitions is needed. The accountant will be able to view all shipments received to match an invoice that has been received from a supplier and verify that the invoice is accurate. Without the IS, these steps, and therefore the process, cannot be completed. For example, if the IS is not available, how will the warehouse know which orders are ready to pack and ship?

In the fulfillment process, the IS will inform people in the warehouse that orders are ready for shipment. It also provides them with a listing of what materials must be included in the order and where to find those materials in the warehouse.

Capturing and Storing Process Data. Processes create data such as dates, times, product numbers, quantities, prices, and addresses, as well as who did what, when, and where. IS capture and store these data, commonly referred to as *process data* or *transaction data*. Some of these data are generated and automatically captured by the IS. These are data related to who completes an activity, when, and where. Other data are generated outside the IS and must be entered into it. This data entry can occur in various ways, ranging from manual entry to automated methods involving data in forms such as bar codes and RFID tags that can be read by machines.

In the fulfillment process, for example, when a customer order is received by mail or over the phone, the person taking the order must enter data such as the customer's name, what the customer ordered, and how much he or she ordered. Significantly, when a customer order is received via the firm's Web site, then all customer details are captured by the IS. Data such as the name of the person entering the data (who), at which location the person is completing the task (where), and the date and time (when) are automatically included by the IS when it creates the order. The data are updated as the process steps are executed. When the order is shipped, the warehouse will provide data about which products were shipped and in what quantities, and the IS will automatically include data related to who, when, and where.

An important advantage of using an IS compared to a manual system or multiple functional area information systems is that the data need to be entered into the system only once. Further, once they are entered, other people in the process can easily access them, and there is no need to reenter them in subsequent steps.

The data captured by the IS can provide immediate feedback. For example, the IS can use the data to create a receipt or to make recommendations for additional or alternate products.

Monitoring Process Performance. A third contribution of IS is to help monitor the state of the various business processes. That is, the IS indicates how well a process is executing. The IS performs this role by evaluating information about a process. This information can be created either at the *instance level* (i.e., a specific task or activity) or the *process level* (i.e., the process as a whole).

For example, a company might be interested in the status of a particular customer order. Where is the order within the fulfillment process? Was the complete order shipped? If so, when? If not, then when can we expect it to be shipped? Or, for the procurement process, when was the purchase order sent to the supplier? What will be the cost of acquiring the material? At the process level, the IS can evaluate how well the procurement process is being executed by calculating the lead time, or the time between sending the purchase order to a vendor and receiving the goods, for each order and each vendor over time.

Not only can the IS help monitor a process, it can also detect problems with the process. The IS performs this role by comparing the information with a standard—that is, what the company expects or desires—to determine if the process is performing within expectations. Management establishes standards based on organizational goals.

If the information provided by the IS indicates that the process is not meeting the standards, then the company assumes that some type of problem exists. Some problems can be routinely and automatically detected by the IS, whereas others require a person to review the information and make judgments. For example, the IS can calculate the expected date that a specific order will be shipped and determine whether this date will meet the established standard. Or, the IS can calculate the average time taken to fill all orders over the last month and compare this information to the standard to determine if the process is working as expected.

Monitoring business processes, then, helps detect problems with these processes. Very often these problems are really symptoms of a more fundamental problem. In such cases, the IS can help diagnose the cause of the symptoms by providing managers with additional, detailed information. For example, if the average time to process a customer order appears to have increased over the previous month, this problem could be a symptom of a more basic problem.

A manager can then drill down into the information to diagnose the underlying problem. To accomplish this task, the manager can request a breakdown of the information by type of product, customer, location, employees, day of the week, time of day, and so on. After reviewing this detailed information, the manager might determine that the warehouse has experienced an exceptionally high employee turnover rate over the last month and that the delays are occurring because new employees are not sufficiently familiar with the process. The manager might conclude that this problem will work itself out over time, in which case there is nothing more to be done. Alternatively, the manager could conclude that the new employees are not being adequately trained and supervised. In this case, the company must take actions to correct the problem. Plug IT In 1.2 discusses several methodologies that managers can use to take corrective action when process problems are identified.

HRM

BEFORE *YOU GO ON....*

1. What is a business process?
2. Describe several business processes carried out at your university.
3. Define a cross-functional business process, and provide several examples of such processes.
4. Pick one of the processes described in Question 2 or 3 above, and identify its inputs, outputs, customer(s), and resources. How does the process create value for its customer(s)?

Apply The Concept PI1.1

LEARNING OBJECTIVE PI1.1 Discuss ways in which information systems enable cross-functional business processes and business processes for a single functional area.

STEP 1 – Background (This is what you are learning.)

This Plug IT In defines a business process as an ongoing collection of related activities that create a product or a service of value to the organization, its business partners, and/or its customers. Normally, we do not see everything that goes into a process; rather, we observe only the results of the process. For example, when you shop at a grocery store, you see stocked shelves. However, the inventory management processes that operate to keep the shelves stocked—as well as the information systems that support those processes—remain essentially invisible.

STEP 2 – Activity (This is what you are doing.)

Visit http://www.wiley.com/go/rainer/MIS3e/applytheconcept, and click on the link provided for Plug IT In 1.1. This link will take you to a YouTube video that focuses on workflow and business process management in a healthcare environment. As you watch the video, look for the ways that information systems enable cross-functional business processes and make the flow of data much easier and quicker for everyone involved.

STEP 3 – Deliverable (This is what you turn in.)

Based on the video from Step 2, write a brief description of how information systems enable both cross-functional business processes and business processes for a single functional area. Submit your description to your instructor.

PI1.2 Business Process Improvement, Business Process Reengineering, and Business Process Management

Excellence in executing business processes is widely recognized as the underlying basis for all significant measures of competitive performance in an organization. Consider these measures, for example:

- *Customer satisfaction:* The result of optimizing and aligning business processes to fulfill customers' needs, wants, and desires
- *Cost reduction:* The result of optimizing operations and supplier processes
- *Cycle and fulfillment time reduction:* The result of optimizing the manufacturing and logistics processes
- *Quality:* The result of optimizing the design, development, and production processes

- *Differentiation:* The result of optimizing the marketing and innovation processes
- *Productivity:* The result of optimizing each individual's work processes

The question is: How does an organization ensure business process excellence?

In their book *Reengineering the Corporation*, first published in 1993, Michael Hammer and James Champy argued that to become more competitive, American businesses needed to radically redesign their business processes to reduce costs and increase quality. The authors further asserted that information technology is the key enabler of such change. This radical redesign, called **business process reengineering (BPR)**, is a strategy for making an organization's business processes more productive and profitable. The key to BPR is for enterprises to examine their business processes from a "clean sheet" perspective and then determine how they can best reconstruct those processes to improve their business functions. BPR's popularity was propelled by the unique capabilities of information technology, such as automation and standardization of many process steps and error reduction due to improved communication among organizational information silos.

Although some enterprises have successfully implemented BPR, many organizations found this strategy too difficult, too radical, too lengthy, and too comprehensive. The impact on employees, on facilities, on existing investments in information systems, and even on organizational culture was overwhelming. Despite the many failures in BPR implementation, however, businesses increasingly began to organize work around business processes rather than individual tasks. The result was a less radical, less disruptive, and more incremental approach, called **business process improvement (BPI).**

BPI focuses on reducing variation in the process outputs by searching for root causes of the variation in the process itself (such as a broken machine on an assembly line) or among the process inputs (such as a decline in the quality of raw materials purchased from a certain supplier). BPI is usually performed by teams of employees that include a process expert—usually the process owner (the individual manager who oversees the process)—as well as other individuals who are involved in the process. These individuals can be involved directly; for example, the workers who actually perform process steps. Alternatively, these individuals can be involved indirectly; for example, customers who purchase the outputs from the process.

Six Sigma is a popular methodology for BPI initiatives. Its goal is to ensure that the process has no more than 3.4 defects per million outputs by using statistical methods to analyze the process. (A defect is defined as a faulty product or an unsatisfactory service.) Six Sigma was developed by Motorola in the 1980s, and it is now used by companies worldwide, thanks in part to promotional efforts by early adopters such as GE. Six Sigma is especially appropriate for manufacturing environments, where product defects can be easily defined and

measured. Over the years, the methodology has been modified so that it focuses less on defects and more on customer value. As a result, it can now be applied to services as well as products. Today, Six Sigma tools are widely used in financial services and healthcare institutions as components of process-improvement initiatives.

Regardless of the specific methodology you use, a successful BPI project generally follows five basic phases: define, measure, analyze, improve, and control, or DMAIC.

- In the *define phase*, the BPI team documents the existing "as is" process activities, process resources, and process inputs and outputs, usually as a graphical process map, or diagram. The team also documents the customer and the customer's requirements for the process output, together with a description of the problem that needs to be addressed.

- In the *measure phase*, the BPI team identifies relevant process metrics, such as time and cost to generate one output (product or service), and collects data to understand how the metrics evolve over time. Sometimes the data already exist, in which case they can be extracted from the IS that supports the process, as described in the previous section. Many times, however, the BPI team needs to combine operational process data already stored in the company's IS systems with other data sources, such as customer and employee observations, interviews, and surveys.

- In the *analysis phase*, the BPI team examines the "as is" process map and the collected data to identify problems with the process (e.g., decreasing efficiency or effectiveness) and their root causes. If possible, the team should also benchmark the process; that is, compare its performance with that of similar processes in other companies, or other areas of the organization. The team can employ IT applications such as statistical analysis software or simulation packages in this phase.

  It is often valuable to use process simulation software during the analysis phase. Utilizing this software provides two benefits. First, it enables a process manager to quickly simulate a real situation (e.g., with a certain number of people undertaking activities) for a specific amount of time (e.g., a working day, a week, or a month). The manager can then estimate the process performance over time without having to observe the process in practice. Second, it allows the manager to create multiple scenarios; for instance, using a different number of resources in the process and/or using a different configuration for the process steps. In addition, process simulation software can provide a number of outputs regarding a process including the time used by all resources to execute specific activities, the overall cycle time of a process, the identification of resources that are infrequently used, and the bottlenecks in the process. Simulating a process is extremely valuable for process managers because it is a risk-free and inexpensive test of an improvement solution that does not need to be conducted with real resources.

- In the *improve phase*, the BPI team identifies possible solutions for addressing the root causes, maps the resulting "to be" process alternatives, and selects and implements the most appropriate solution. Common ways to improve processes are eliminating process activities that do not add value to the output and rearranging activities in a way that reduces delays or improves resource utilization. The organization must be careful, however, not to eliminate internal *process controls*—those activities that safeguard company resources, guarantee the accuracy of its financial reporting, and ensure adherence to rules and regulations.

- In the *control phase*, the team establishes process metrics and monitors the improved process after the solution has been implemented to ensure the process performance remains stable. An IS system can be very useful for this purpose.

Although BPI initiatives do not deliver the huge performance gains promised by BPR, many organizations prefer them because they are less risky and less costly. BPI focuses on delivering quantifiable results—and if a business case cannot be made, the project is not continued. All employees can be trained to apply BPI techniques in their own work to identify opportunities for improvement. Thus, BPI projects tend to be performed more from the bottom-up, in contrast to BPR projects, which involve top-down change mandates. BPI projects take less time overall, and even if they are unsuccessful, they consume fewer organizational resources than BPR projects. However, if incremental improvements through BPI are no longer possible, or if significant changes occur in the firm's business environment, then the firm should consider BPR projects. One final consideration is that over time, employees can become overstretched or lose interest if the company undertakes too many BPI projects and does not have an effective system to manage and focus the improvement efforts.

To sustain BPI efforts over time, organizations can adopt **business process management (BPM)**, a management system that includes methods and tools to support the design, analysis, implementation, management, and continuous optimization of core business processes throughout the organization. BPM integrates disparate BPI initiatives to ensure consistent strategy execution.

Important components of BPM are process modeling, Web-enabled technologies, and business activity monitoring. BPM begins with *process modeling*, which is a graphical depiction of all of the steps in a process. Process modeling helps employees understand the interactions and dependencies among the people involved in the process, the information systems they rely on, and the information they require to optimally perform their tasks. Process modeling software can support this activity. IT's About Business PI1.1 shows how Chevron has employed BPR, BPI, and BPM.

Web-enabled technologies display and retrieve data via a Web browser. They enable an organization to integrate the necessary people and applications into each process, across functional areas and geographical locations.

Finally, *business activity monitoring* (BAM) is a real-time approach for measuring and managing business processes. Companies use BAM to monitor their business processes, identify failures or exceptions, and address these failures in real time. Further, because BAM tracks process operations and indicates whether they succeed or fail, it creates valuable records of process behaviors that organizations can use to improve their processes.

BPM activities are often supported by *business process management suites* (BPMS). A BPMS is an integrated set of applications that includes a repository of process information, such as process maps and business rules; tools for process modeling, simulation, execution, coordination across functions, and re-configuration in response to changing business needs; as well as process-monitoring capabilities.

BPM is growing in business value. In 2012, Capgemini (www.capgemini.com), an international consulting firm, surveyed more than 1,000 senior business executives. The majority of the respondents indicated that BPM would play a more prominent role in their organizations in 2013 and 2014.

Further, Gartner (www.gartner.com), a leading IT research and advisory firm, stated that companies need to focus on developing and mastering BPM skills throughout the organization. Gartner predicts that by 2016, high-performing companies will use BPM technologies such as real-time process monitoring, visualization, analytics, and intelligent automated decision making—all of them integrated in second-generation BPMS—to support intelligent business operations.

Another promising emerging trend is *social BPM*. This technology enables employees to collaborate, using social media tools on wired and mobile platforms, both internally across functions and externally with stakeholders (such as customers or experts), to exchange process knowledge and improve process execution.

BPM initially helps companies improve profitability by decreasing costs and increasing revenues. Over time, BPM can create a competitive advantage by improving organizational flexibility—making it easy to adapt to changing business conditions and to take advantage of new opportunities. For many companies, BPM can reduce costs, increase customer satisfaction, and ensure compliance with rules and regulations. In all cases, the company's strategy should drive the BPM effort. The following example illustrates these benefits.

— BEFORE *YOU GO ON....* —

1. What is business process reengineering?
2. What is business process improvement?
3. What is business process management?

Apply The Concept PI1.2

LEARNING OBJECTIVE PI1.2 Compare and contrast business process reengineering and business process management to determine the advantages and disadvantages of each.

STEP 1 – Background

One of the most difficult decisions related to business processes is whether they need to be reengineered or simply managed. Reengineering business processes is a "clean slate" approach where you build completely new processes to accomplish the current tasks. In contrast, managing these processes involves making the current processes more efficient. Put simply, reengineering is radical, whereas management is incremental.

STEP 2 – Activity

Consider the many processes involved in getting you (as a student) accepted, enrolled, registered, housed, fed, and, ultimately, educated. Do you recall the processes you went through to accomplish these tasks? Did any of these processes strike you as inefficient?

STEP 3 – Deliverable

Imagine that you are a student representative on a committee whose task is to consider reengineering or modifying (management) these business processes. Prepare a written statement for the committee that will compare and contrast BPR and BPM to determine the advantages and disadvantages of each strategy. Make a recommendation as to which one your university should follow and present your recommendation to your instructor.

EXAMPLE

The State of Alaska Streamlines Its Processes

The Alaska Department of Natural Resources (DNR) manages most state-owned land, water, and natural resources on behalf of Alaska residents. The group's primary mission is to responsibly develop and use Alaska's natural resources for the maximum benefit of the public.

One of the largest divisions of the DNR, the Division of Mining, Land, and Water (DMLW), is responsible for processing authorizations that allow individuals, corporations, or nonprofit organizations to use state resources. The authorization process begins when applicants submit a request. The DMLW then decides whether to allow the activity based on many criteria, such as how the activity will affect the adjoining properties, the neighbors, or current or future land development. It is advantageous for the state to process as many of these permit authorizations as possible because allowing such activity can generate significant revenue and an increase in jobs for the state and its residents. In fact, the state derives approximately 90 percent of its state budget from oil and gas revenue. In addition, these operations can create job opportunities that benefit the state economy.

However, for 20 years the DMLW has experienced a backlog of permit authorizations, resulting in missed revenue and business opportunities. Facing a mandate from the state legislature to fix the problem within three years, the Division needed to identify a solution that would enable it to streamline its processes and to eliminate the backlog (and prevent it from recurring).

In the past, the Division had used Microsoft Visio diagrams to map processes, and, on paper applications, to manage the permit authorization process. These manual, paper-based methods contributed to the backlog. Today, the Division uses IBM Business Process Manager Advanced software to handle the authorization process. Now, authorization requests are scanned and entered into a content management system. The act of entering the request triggers a new business process, which enables staff members to begin processing the application. Employees use the software to complete the adjudication process consistently and appropriately.

In the past, Division managers found it nearly impossible to easily assess the backlog. Managers had no way to effectively track the status of work in progress or work completed, resulting in processing delays. With the IBM software, managers use dashboards (you will learn about dashboards in Chapter 12) to quickly determine how much work is outstanding, the status of all work in process, and the target due dates of work in the queue.

The IBM software also helps the Division establish greater process consistency. Under the old system, where three regional offices employed manual and generally undocumented processes, enforcing consistency was a sometimes overwhelming challenge. An application that was approved by one office, for example, might be denied by another. Today, the new system guides employees through the application processes, and it coaches them on the next steps to take. By mid-2013, the backlog was decreasing, and all stakeholders were benefiting from the Division's improved authorization process management.

Sources: Compiled from "State of Alaska Streamlines Processes with Agile BPM Platform," *IBM Case Study*, March 4, 2013; S. Sweet, "Don't Even Start a BPM Project Without 5 Critical Pieces," *bpm.com*, December 5, 2012; J. vom Brocke and M. Rosemann, "Handbook on Business Process Management," *International Handbooks on Information Systems* (v. 1), Berlin: Springer, 2010; www.ibm.com, http://dnr.alaska.gov/mlw/, accessed April 12, 2014.

IT'S ABOUT BUSINESS PI1.1

BPR, BPI, and BPM at Chevron

Chevron, one of the world's largest oil and gas companies, and its subsidiaries are involved in exploration and production of oil and natural gas, as well as in manufacturing, transporting, and distributing petrochemical products, including gasoline and refined products. In 2013, Chevron employed more than 60,000 people worldwide, produced the equivalent of more than 2.6 million barrels of oil every day, and reported more than $230 billion in sales. Chevron has been involved in several process-reengineering and improvement efforts over the years, evolving from BPR to BPI and eventually to BPM, as described below.

In 1995, Chevron was less than half of its current size today, producing roughly 1 million barrels of oil per day across six plants. The company was divided into three major departments: Refining, Marketing, and Supply and Distribution (S&D). Management decided that they needed to improve their supply chain (see Chapter 11) to better integrate their multiple internal processes. A key figure in decision making concerning process management was Vice President Peter McCrea. McCrea was convinced that the best strategy to dramatically improve performance at Chevron was to re-engineer its end-to-end core processes, from the acquisition of crude oil crude through distribution of final products to Chevron customers.

POM

To accomplish this task, the Chevron team collaborated with a consultant company to create a model of the existing processes. The objective was to radically improve the existing processes to reflect Chevron's business goals. In other words, Chevron's strategy was not to analyze the existing processes to identify specific areas to improve. Rather, the project identified the desired outputs and then examined the supporting processes, utilizing BPR. As an added benefit, this holistic approach led the company to examine the interdependencies between processes executed in different business units. Adopting this holistic perspective ultimately improved the company's overall performance. In a 1996 report, Chevron claimed that the BPR project saved the company $50 million.

This complex BPR effort was initially followed by several smaller, employee-driven BPI initiatives. For example, in 1998, six Chevron employees initiated a project to improve water treatment processes at a company plant in California. Their efforts generated a 30 percent reduction in operating costs. Their success inspired other employees to initiate BPI projects in Indonesia, Angola, and other locations around the globe by employing Six Sigma improvement techniques. Although some managers were able to demonstrate benefits of BPI at the local level, BPI did not achieve company-wide recognition and corporate backing until 2006, when Lean Six Sigma, a methodology that combines statistical process analysis with techniques to eliminate waste and improve process flow, became the preferred improvement methodology at Chevron. Since then, hundreds of BPI projects have been executed worldwide, resulting in significant financial benefits. For example, from 2008 to 2010 Chevron reported more than $1 billion in BPI benefits. To support these internal improvement efforts, Chevron engaged its suppliers in BPI initiatives as well.

To coordinate these various BPI efforts, Chevron has adopted a unified BPM approach that involves standardizing processes across the entire company and consolidating process information within a central repository. Chevron estimates that only 20 percent of its processes can be fully automated—the rest involve a combination of manual and automated steps. Thus, process standardization involves not only supporting processes through integrated information systems, but also ensuring that relevant employees are familiar with the standards for manual activities. To facilitate this task, Chevron implemented Nimbus (nimbus.tibco.com), a BPMS that acts as an intelligent repository of standard, companywide business rules and procedures. In addition, Nimbus can provide employees with detailed work instructions.

Consider, for example, Chevron's shipping process, which experienced efficiency and risk problems due to its different execution in locations throughout Asia, Europe, and the United States. To establish uniform company standards, Chevron employed a BPI approach. The company analyzed "as is" operations across different geographical locations, identified best practices, and combined them into a common "to be" process. It then created documents that detailed these policies and procedures and distributed them to managers through the Web-based BPMS.

Chevron's BPM strategy is part of a larger companywide management system that focuses on operational excellence. The program requires all Chevron operating companies and business units to adopt a continuous improvement perspective, directed by guidelines, metrics, and targets that are reviewed and adapted every year. Apart from process efficiency, Chevron focuses on metrics related to safety, risk, and the environment. All employees participate in operational excellence activities, and managers receive specific operational excellence training to support the continuous improvement culture.

Sources: Compiled from "Operational Excellence," *chevron.com*, March 2012; "Chevron – using Nimbus Control software to manage processes," Finding FindingPetroleum.com, September 23, 2010; "Chevron Wins Boston Strategies International's 2010 Award for Lean Six Sigma Implementation in Oil and Gas Operations," www .bostonstrategies.com, September 22, 2010; "From the Bottom Up: Grassroots Effort Finds Footing at Chevron," *isixsigma.com*, March 1, 2010; "Business Process Improvement: A Talk With Chevron's Jim Boots," *Ebizq.net*, August 26, 2009; P. Harmon, *Business Process Management*, Elsevier, Burlington, MA, 2007; www.chevron.com, accessed May 14, 2014.

Questions

1. What was one of the main advantages of BPR at Chevron?
2. Why did Chevron adopt BPI?
3. How does Chevron apply BPM in its operations today?

What's in for ME?

FOR ALL BUSINESS MAJORS

All functional areas of any organization are literally composed of a variety of business processes, as we can see from the examples in this Plug IT In. Regardless of your major, you will be involved in a variety of business processes from your first day on the job. Some of these processes you will do by yourself, some will involve only your group, team, or department, while others will involve several (or all) functional areas of your organization.

It is important for you to be able to visualize processes, understand the inputs and outputs of each process, and know the "customer" of each process. If you can do these things, you will contribute to making processes more efficient and effective, which often means incorporating information technology in the process. It is also important for you to know how each process fits into your organization's strategy.

SUMMARY

1. Discuss ways in which information systems enable cross-functional business processes and processes for a single functional area.

A business process is an ongoing collection of related activities that produce a product or a service of value to the organization, its business partners, and/or its customers. Examples of business processes in the functional areas include managing accounts payable, managing accounts receivable, managing after-sale customer follow-up, managing bills of materials, managing manufacturing change orders, applying disability policies, employee hiring, computer user/staff training, and applying Internet use policy. The procurement and fulfillment processes are examples of cross-functional business processes.

2. Compare and contrast business process reengineering and business process management to determine the different advantages and disadvantages of each.

Business process reengineering (BPR) is a radical redesign of business processes that is intended to improve the efficiency and effectiveness of an organization's business processes. The key to BPR is for enterprises to examine their business processes from a "clean sheet" perspective and then determine how they can best reconstruct those processes to improve their business functions. Because BPR proved difficult to implement, organizations have turned to business process management. Business process management (BPM) is a management technique that includes methods and tools to support the design, analysis, implementation, management, and optimization of business processes.

business process A collection of related activities that create a product or a service of value to the organization, its business partners, and/or its customers.

business process management A management technique that includes methods and tools to support the design, analysis, implementation, management, and optimization of business processes.

business process reengineering A radical redesign of a business process that improves its efficiency and effectiveness, often by beginning with a "clean sheet" (i.e., from scratch).

cross-functional processes No single functional area is responsible for a process's execution.

>>>DISCUSSION QUESTIONS

1. Consider the student registration process at your university:

   - Describe the steps necessary for you to register for your classes each semester.

   - Describe how information technology is used (or is not used) in each step of the process.

2. Why is it so difficult for an organization to actually implement business process reengineering?

>>> COLLABORATION EXERCISE

STEP 1 – Background

BPM and BPR are fairly easy concepts to understand. You are taking existing processes and either modifying or recreating them. However, actually engaging in the process, making the decisions, and implementing the changes is an entirely different experience than simply reading about it.

STEP 2 – Activity

Recall the video you watched for the Apply the Concept PI1.1. Visit http://www.wiley.com/go/rainer/MIS3e/collaboration, and click on the link for Collaboration Exercise in Plug IT In 1. The link will take you to a video that explains the workflow of a doctor's office; specifically, receiving a patient, providing care, creating a claim for the insurance company, and receiving payment. Watch this part of the video closely, and divide your team into the following areas of responsibility: patient, front desk, physician, billing, and insurance company.

Using Google Drive, create and share a document for each stage of the process. For example, create something that is similar to a reception form, and then share it with the physician. Then, have the physician add an evaluation to that form and send it back to the front desk along with a billing form that is coded to indicate which services the doctor performed during the visit. Follow through the rest of the steps to experience what it might be like to engage in this process in real life.

After you are finished, visit http://www.wiley.com/go/rainer/MIS3e/collaboration, and click on the links to the Greenway videos to view a demo of Electronic Medical Records and Practice Management Software.

STEP 3 – Deliverable

Write a collective summary as a team that details the inefficiencies you experienced, as well as any ideas you have related to either managing or reengineering this process. How many of these ideas and suggestions can be implemented by using Electronic Medical Records and Practice Management Software? Submit your summary to your instructor.

INTERNSHIP ACTIVITY> `OXFORD ORTHOPAEDICS`

Healthcare

A key component of the alignment between corporate and IT strategy is a solid understanding of business workflow. If organizational personnel do not understand the current process models, then they cannot foresee, prepare for, or mitigate the impact that new information systems will have. At the same time, sometimes having this understanding does not simply help you foresee a problem. Rather, it may cause you to completely redesign your business processes! Business process management (BPM) is not about redesign. That is Business process redesign (BPR). BPM is about modifying and managing current processes with relatively minor increments to make profound improvements.

In this activity, you will work with Chad Prince of Oxford Orthopaedics to help him understand the typical business process of a doctor's office and the ways in which an information system can help things run more efficiently.

To:	IT Intern
From:	Chad Prince
Subject:	Business Process Management

Hello!

I am looking into a new practice management system for Oxford Orthopaedics. Before I delve too deeply into the research, however, I would like to learn about modeling business processes. I am quite certain that adding new technology will transform our existing practices, and I want to fully understand our current models to make certain we are improving our operations rather than causing setbacks.

First, I want you to search for relevant case studies. I understand that IBM has produced studies that highlight how the company has helped businesses improve their processes. Try to locate one, and learn from these experiences. Second, look for a YouTube video about the workflow of a typical doctor's office to understand at least some of the information that passes hands among patients, administration, doctors, insurance companies, banks, and other parties.

Finally, search for free business process modeling software, and use it to outline the workflow processes you saw in the YouTube video. This will be a huge help to me!

Thanks,

Chad Prince

Note: Any links or Web sites mentioned in this email are available at http://www.wiley.com/go/rainer/MIS3e/internship.

Hardware and Software

LEARNING OBJECTIVES >>>

PI2.1 Discuss strategic issues that link hardware design to business strategy.

PI2.2 Differentiate between the two major types of software.

Introduction

As you begin this Plug IT In, you might be wondering, why do I have to know anything about hardware and software? There are several reasons why you will benefit from understanding the basics of hardware and software. First, regardless of your major (and future functional area in an organization), you will be using different types of hardware and software throughout your career. Second, you will have input concerning the hardware and software that you will use. In this capacity, you will be required to answer many questions, such as "Is my hardware performing adequately for my needs? If not, what types of problems am I experiencing?" "Does my software help me do my job?" "Is this software easy to use?" "Do I need more functionality and, if so, what functionality would be most helpful to me?" Third, you will also have input into decisions when your functional area or organization upgrades or replaces its hardware and/or software. In addition, some organizations allocate the hardware and software budget to functional areas or departments. In such cases, you might be responsible for making hardware and software decisions (at least locally) yourself. MIS employees will act as advisors, but you will provide important input into such decisions.

This Plug IT In will help you better understand the hardware and software decisions your organization must make as well as better understand your personal computing decisions. Many of the design principles presented here apply to systems of all sizes, from an enterprisewide system to your home computer system. In addition, the dynamics of innovation and cost that you will read about can affect personal as well as corporate hardware and software decisions.

PI2.1 Introduction to Hardware

Recall from Chapter 1 that the term *hardware* refers to the physical equipment used for the input, processing, output, and storage activities of a computer system. Decisions about hardware focus on three interrelated factors: appropriateness for the task, speed, and cost. The incredibly rapid rate of innovation in the computer industry complicates hardware decisions because computer technologies become obsolete more quickly than other organizational technologies.

The overall trends in hardware are that it becomes smaller, faster, cheaper, and more powerful over time. In fact, these trends are so rapid that they make it difficult to know when to purchase (or upgrade) hardware. This difficulty lies in the fact that companies that delay hardware purchases will, more than likely, be able to buy more powerful hardware for the same amount of money in the future. It is important to note that buying more powerful hardware for the same amount of money in the future is a trade-off. An organization that delays purchasing computer hardware gives up the benefits of whatever it could buy today until the future purchase date arrives.

Hardware consists of the following:

- *Central processing unit (CPU).* Manipulates the data and controls the tasks performed by the other components.
- *Primary storage.* Temporarily stores data and program instructions during processing.
- *Secondary storage.* Stores data and programs for future use.
- *Input technologies.* Accept data and instructions and convert them to a form that the computer can understand.

- *Output technologies.* Present data and information in a form people can understand.
- *Communication technologies.* Provide for the flow of data from external computer networks (e.g., the Internet and intranets) to the CPU, and from the CPU to computer networks.

Strategic Hardware Issues

For most businesspeople, the most important issues are what the hardware enables, how it is advancing, and how rapidly it is advancing. In many industries, exploiting computer hardware is a key to achieving competitive advantage. Successful hardware exploitation comes from thoughtful consideration of the following questions:

- How do organizations keep up with the rapid price reductions and performance advancements in hardware? For example, how often should an organization upgrade its computers and storage systems? Will upgrades increase personal and organizational productivity? How can organizations measure such increases?
- How should organizations determine the need for the new hardware infrastructures, such as cloud computing? (We discuss cloud computing in Plug IT In 4.)
- Portable computers and advanced communications technologies have enabled employees to work from home or from anywhere. Will these new work styles benefit employees and the organization? How do organizations manage such new work styles?
- How do organizations manage employees who use their own portable devices (e.g., tablets and smartphones) for both personal and work purposes? That is, how do organizations handle the bring-your-own-device (BYOD) phenomenon?

Computer Hierarchy

The traditional standard for comparing classes of computers is their processing power. This section presents each class of computers, from the most powerful to the least powerful. It describes both the computers and their roles in modern organizations.

Supercomputers. The term **supercomputer** does not refer to a specific technology. Rather, it indicates the fastest computers available at any given time. At the time of this writing (mid-2014), the fastest supercomputers had speeds exceeding 10 petaflops (1 petaflop is 1,000 trillion floating point operations per second). A floating point operation is an arithmetic operation that involves decimals.

Because supercomputers are costly as well as very fast, they are generally used by large organizations to execute computationally demanding tasks involving very large datasets. In contrast to mainframes, which specialize in transaction processing and business applications, supercomputers typically run military and scientific applications. Although they cost millions of dollars, they are also being used for commercial applications where huge amounts of data must be analyzed. For example, large banks use supercomputers to calculate the risks and returns of various investment strategies, and healthcare organizations use them to analyze giant databases of patient data to determine optimal treatments for various diseases.

Mainframe Computers. Although mainframe computers are increasingly viewed as just another type of server, albeit at the high end of the performance and reliability scales, they remain a distinct class of systems differentiated by hardware and software features. **Mainframes** remain popular in large enterprises for extensive computing applications that are accessed by thousands of users at one time. Examples of mainframe applications are airline reservation systems, corporate payroll programs, Web site transaction processing systems (e.g., Amazon and eBay), and student grade calculation and reporting.

Today's mainframes perform at teraflop (trillions of floating point operations per second) speeds and can handle millions of transactions per day. In addition, mainframes provide a secure, robust environment in which to run strategic, mission-critical applications.

Midrange Computers. Larger midrange computers, called **minicomputers**, are relatively small, inexpensive, and compact computers that perform the same functions as mainframe computers, but to a more limited extent. In fact, the lines between minicomputers and mainframes have blurred in both price and performance. Minicomputers are a type of server—that is, a computer that supports computer networks and enables users to share files, software, peripheral devices, and other resources. Mainframes are a type of server as well because they provide support for entire enterprise networks.

Microcomputers. **Microcomputers**—also called *micros, personal computers,* or *PCs*—are the smallest and least expensive category of general-purpose computers. It is important to point out that people frequently define a PC as a computer that utilizes the Microsoft Windows operating system. In fact, a variety of PCs are available, and many of them do not use Windows. One well-known example is Apple Mac, which uses the Mac OS X operating system (discussed later in this Plug IT In). The major categories of microcomputers are desktops, thin clients, notebooks and laptops, netbooks, and tablets.

Desktop PCs. The *desktop personal computer* is the familiar microcomputer system that has become a standard tool for business and the home. A desktop generally includes a central processing unit—which you will learn about later—and a separate but connected monitor and keyboard. Modern desktop computers have gigabytes of primary storage, a rewriteable CD-ROM drive and a DVD drive, and up to several terabytes of secondary storage. Today, desktops are being replaced with portable devices such as laptops, netbooks, and tablets.

Thin-Client Systems. Before you address thin-client systems, recall that servers are computers that provide a variety of services for clients, including running networks, processing

Web sites, processing e-mail, and many other functions. *Clients* are typically computers on which users perform their tasks, such as word processing, spreadsheets, and others.

Thin-client systems are desktop computer systems that do not offer the full functionality of a PC. Compared to PCs, or **fat clients**, thin clients are less complex, particularly because they do not have locally installed software. When thin clients need to run an application, they access it from a server over a network instead of from a local disk drive.

For example, a thin client would not have Microsoft Office installed on it. Thus, thin clients are easier and less expensive to operate and support than PCs. The benefits of thin clients include fast application deployment, centralized management, lower cost of ownership, and easier installation, management, maintenance, and support. The main disadvantage of thin clients is that if the network fails, then users can do very little on their computers. In contrast, if users have fat clients and the network fails, they can still perform some functions because they have software, such as Microsoft Office, installed on their computers.

Laptop and Notebook Computers. **Laptop computers** (or **notebook computers**) are small, easily transportable, lightweight microcomputers that fit comfortably into a briefcase (FIGURE PI2.1). Notebooks and laptops are designed to be as convenient and easy to transport as possible. Just as important, they also provide users with access to processing power and data outside an office environment. However, they cost more than desktops for similar functionality.

Netbooks. A **netbook** is a very small, lightweight, low-cost, energy-efficient, portable computer. Netbooks are generally optimized for Internet-based services such as Web browsing and e-mail. In mid-2014, netbooks have been losing market share to tablet computers.

Tablet Computers. A **tablet computer** (or **tablet**) is a complete computer contained entirely in a flat touchscreen that users operate via a stylus, digital pen, or fingertip instead of a keyboard or mouse. Examples of tablets are the Apple iPad 3 (www.apple.com/ipad), the HP Slate 2 (www.hp.com), the Toshiba Thrive (www.toshiba.com), and the Motorola Xoom 2 (www.motorola.com).

Wearable Computers. Wearable computers are miniature computers that people wear under, with, or on top of their clothing. Key features of wearable computers are that there is constant interaction between the computer and the users and that the users can multitask, meaning they do not have to stop what they are doing to utilize the device. Examples of wearable computers are the Apple Watch (http://www.apple.com/watch/), the Sony SmartWatch (www.sony.com/SmartWatch), Samsung Gear S (http://www.samsung.com/global/microsite/gears/index.html), Google Glass (https://www.google.com/glass/start/), and Vuzix (http://www.vuzix.com) M100Smart Glasses (a Google Glass competitor).

Google Glass is an excellent example of a device that provides augmented reality. **Augmented reality** is a live, direct or indirect, view of a physical, real-world environment whose elements are augmented, or enhanced, by computer-generated sensory input such as sound, video, graphics, or GPS data. That is, augmented reality enhances the user's perception of reality. Note that, in contrast, virtual reality replaces the real world with a simulated world.

As an example of augmented reality with Google Glass, let's say that you are looking for a destination in an unfamiliar city. You ask Google Glass for directions, and the device will overlay your vision with a graphic display of a street map, with the route to your destination highlighted.

Laptop computer

© Dragonian/iStockphoto

Netbook

© yozks/iStockphoto

Motorola Xoom tablet

© PhotoEdit/Alamy

Apple iPad tablet

© Oleksiy Maksymenko/ Alamy Limited

Figure PI2.1 Laptop, notebook, and tablet computers.

IT'S PERSONAL: PURCHASING A COMPUTER

One day you will purchase a computer for yourself or your job. When that day comes, it will be important for you to know what to look for. Buying a computer can be very confusing if you just read the box. This Plug IT In has explained the major hardware components of a computer. There are more things you need to consider, however, when you purchase a computer: what you plan to do with it, where you plan to use it, and how long you need service from it? Let's look at each question more closely.

- What do you plan to do with your computer? Consider that when you buy a vehicle, your plans for using the vehicle determine the type of vehicle you will purchase. The same rules apply to purchasing a computer. You need to consider what you currently do with a computer and what you may do before you replace the one under consideration. Although many people simply buy as much as they can afford, they may overpay because they do not consider what they need the computer for.

- Where do you plan to use your computer? If you only plan to use it at home at your desk, then a desktop model will be fine. In general, you can get more computer for your money in a desktop model as opposed to a laptop (i.e., you pay extra for mobility). However, if you think you may want to take the computer with you, then you will need some type of a laptop or tablet computer. When portability is a requirement, you will want to reconsider what you plan to use the computer for because as computers become more portable (smaller), their functionality changes, and you want to make sure the computer will meet your needs.

- How long do you need service from this computer? Today, we anticipate that most of the devices we purchase will become outdated and need to be replaced in a few years. Therefore, the length of service is really more about warranty and the availability of repair services. In some cases, you should base your purchase decision on these issues rather than speed because they can extend the life of your computer.

Input and Output Technologies

Input technologies allow people and other technologies to enter data into a computer. The two main types of input devices are human data-entry devices and source-data automation devices. As their name implies, *human data-entry* devices require a certain amount of human effort to input data. Examples are keyboard, mouse, pointing stick, trackball, joystick, touchscreen, stylus, and voice recognition.

In contrast, *source-data automation* devices input data with minimal human intervention. These technologies speed up data collection, reduce errors, and gather data at the source of a transaction or other event. Barcode readers are an example of source-data automation. Table PI2.1 describes the various input devices.

The output generated by a computer can be transmitted to the user via several output devices and media. These devices

TABLE PI2.1 Input Devices

Input Device	Description
Human Data-Entry Devices	
Keyboards	Most common input device (for text and numerical data).
Mouse	Handheld device used to point the cursor at a point on screen, such as an icon; the user clicks a button on the mouse, instructing the computer to take some action.
Optical mouse	The mouse is not connected to computer by a cable; rather, it uses camera chip to take images of surface it passes over, comparing successive images to determine its position.
Trackball	User rotates a ball built into top of device to move the cursor (rather than moving an entire device such as a mouse).
Pointing stick	Small button-like device; the cursor moves in the direction of the pressure the user places on the stick. Located between the keys near the center of the keyboard.
Touchpad	User moves the cursor by sliding a finger across a sensitized pad and then can tap the pad when the cursor is in (also called a trackpad) the desired position to instruct the computer to take action (also called glide-and-tap pad).

Input Device	Description
Graphics tablet	A device that can be used in place of, or in conjunction with, a mouse or trackball; it has a flat surface for drawing and a pen or stylus that is programmed to work with the tablet.
Joystick	The joystick moves the cursor to the desired place on the screen; commonly used in video games and in workstations that display dynamic graphics.
Touchscreen	Users instruct computer to take some action by touching a particular part of the screen; commonly used in information kiosks such as ATM machines. Touchscreens now have gesture controls for browsing through photographs, moving objects around on a screen, flicking to turn the page of a book, and playing video games. For example, see the Apple iPhone.
Stylus	Pen-style device that allows user either to touch parts of a predetermined menu of options or to handwrite information into the computer (as with some PDAs); works with touch-sensitive screens.
Digital pen	Mobile device that digitally captures everything you write; built-in screen confirms that what you write has been saved; also captures sketches, figures, and so on with on-board flash memory
Web camera (Webcam)	A real-time video camera whose images can be accessed via the Web or instant messaging.
Voice recognition	Microphone converts analog voice sounds into digital input for a computer; critical technology for physically challenged people who cannot use other input devices.

Gesture-Based Input

Gesture recognition refers to technologies that enable computers to interpret human gestures. These technologies would be the first step in designing computers that can understand human body language. This process creates a richer interaction between machines and humans than has been possible via keyboards, graphical user interfaces, and the mouse. Gesture recognition enables humans to interact naturally with a computer without any intervening mechanical devices. With gesture-based technologies, the user can move the cursor by pointing a finger at a computer screen. These technologies could make conventional input devices (the mouse, keyboards, and touch-screens) redundant. Examples of gesture-based input devices are the Nintendo Wii (www.nintendo.com/wii), the Microsoft Kinect (www.xbox.com/kinect), and the Leap Motion Controller (www.leapmotion.com).

Wii	A video game console produced by Nintendo. A distinguishing feature of the Wii is its wireless controller, which can be used as a handheld pointing device and can detect movement in three dimensions.
Microsoft Kinect	A device that enables users to control and interact with the Xbox 360 through a natural interface using gestures and spoken commands. Kinect eliminates the need for a game controller.
Leap Motion Controller	A motion-sensing, matchbox-sized device placed on a physical desktop. Using two cameras, the device "observes" an area up to a distance of about three feet. It precisely tracks fingers or items such as a pen that cross into the observed area. The Leap can perform tasks such as navigating a Web site, using pinch-to-zoom gestures on maps, performing high-precision drawing, and manipulating complex three-dimensional visualizations. The smaller observation area and higher resolution of the device differentiates it from the Microsoft Kinect, which is more suitable for whole-body tracking in a space the size of a living room.

Source-Data Automation Input Devices

Automated teller machine (ATM)	A device that includes source-data automation input in the form of a magnetic stripe reader; human input via a keyboard; and output via a monitor, printer, and cash dispenser.
Magnetic stripe reader	A device that reads data from a magnetic stripe, usually on the back of a plastic card (e.g., credit and debit cards).
Point-of-sale terminals	Computerized cash registers that also may incorporate touchscreen technology and bar-code scanners to input data such as item sold and price.

Input Device	Description
Barcode scanners	Devices that scan black-and-white barcode lines printed on merchandise labels.
Optical mark reader	Scanner for detecting the presence of dark marks on a predetermined grid, such as multiple-choice test answer sheets.
Magnetic ink character reader	A device that reads magnetic ink printed on checks that identify the bank, checking account, and check number.
Optical character recognition	Software that converts text into digital form for input into computer.
Sensors	Devices that collect data directly from the environment and input data directly into computer; examples are vehicle airbag activation sensors and radio-frequency identification tags.
Cameras	Digital cameras capture images and convert them into digital files.
Radio–frequency identification (RFID)	Uses technology that uses active or passive tags (transmitters) to wirelessly transmit product information to electronic readers. (We discuss RFID in detail in Chapter 8.)

include monitors, printers, plotters, and voice. Table PI2.2 describes the various output devices.

Multimedia technology is the computer-based integration of text, sound, still images, animation, and digitized motion video. It usually consists of a collection of various input and output technologies. Multimedia merges the capabilities of computers with televisions, CD players, DVD players, video and audio recording equipment, and music and gaming technologies. High-quality multimedia processing requires powerful microprocessors and extensive memory capacity, including both primary and secondary storage.

TABLE PI2.2 Output Devices

Output Device	Description
Monitors	
Cathode ray tubes	Video screens on which an electron beam illuminates pixels on a display screen.
Liquid crystal displays (LCDs)	Flat displays that have liquid crystals between two polarizers to form characters and images on a backlit screen.
Flexible displays	Thin, plastic, bendable computer screens.
Organic light-emitting diodes (OLEDs)	Displays that are brighter, thinner, lighter, cheaper, faster, and take less power to run than LCDs.
Retinal scanning displays	Project image directly onto a viewer's retina; used in medicine, air traffic control, and controlling industrial machines.
Heads-up displays	Any transparent display that presents data without requiring the user to look away from his or her usual viewpoint; for example, see Microvision (www.microvision.com).
Printers	
Laser	Use laser beams to write information on photosensitive drums; produce high-resolution text and graphics.
Inkjet	Shoot fine streams of colored ink onto paper; usually less expensive to buy than laser printers but can be more expensive to operate; can offer resolution quality equal to laser printers.
Thermal	Produce a printed image by selectively heating coated thermal paper; when the paper passes over the thermal print head, the coating turns black in the areas where it is heated, producing an image.

Output Device	Description
Plotters	Use computer-directed pens for creating high-quality images, blueprints, schematics, drawing of new products, and so on.
Voice output	A speaker/headset that can output sounds of any type; voice output is a software function that uses this equipment.
Electronic book reader	A wireless, portable reading device with access to books, blogs, newspapers, and magazines. On-board storage holds hundreds of books (e.g., Amazon Kindle, Sony Reader, Barnes & Noble Nook).
Pocket projector	A projector in a handheld device that provides an alternative display method to alleviate the problem of tiny display screens in handheld devices. Pocket projectors will project digital images onto any viewing surface (e.g., see the Pico Projector).

The Central Processing Unit

The **central processing unit** performs the actual computation or "number crunching" inside any computer. The CPU is a **microprocessor** (e.g., Intel's Core i3, i5, and i7 chips with more to come) made up of millions of microscopic transistors embedded in a circuit on a silicon wafer or *chip*. For this reason, microprocessors are commonly referred to as chips.

As shown in FIGURE PI2.2, the microprocessor has different parts, which perform different functions. The **control unit** sequentially accesses program instructions, decodes them, and controls the flow of data to and from the arithmetic logic unit, the registers, the caches, primary storage, secondary storage, and various output devices. The **arithmetic logic unit (ALU)** performs the mathematical calculations and makes logical comparisons. The registers are high-speed storage areas that store very small amounts of data and instructions for short periods.

How the CPU Works. In the CPU, inputs enter and are stored until they are needed. At that point, they are retrieved and processed, and the output is stored and then delivered

Figure PI2.2 Parts of a microprocessor.

somewhere. FIGURE PI2.3 illustrates this process, which works as follows:

- The inputs consist of data and brief instructions about what to do with the data. These instructions come into the CPU from random access memory (RAM). Data

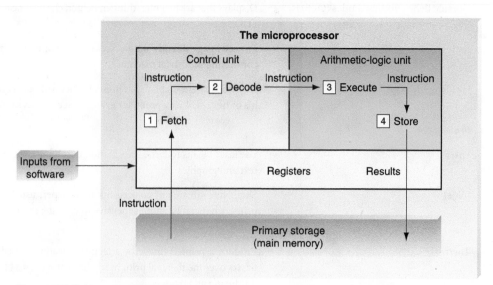

Figure PI2.3 How the CPU works.

might be entered by the user through the keyboard, for example, or read from a data file in another part of the computer. The inputs are stored in registers until they are sent to the next step in the processing.

- Data and instructions travel in the chip via electrical pathways called *buses*. The size of the bus—analogous to the width of a highway—determines how much information can flow at any time.

- The control unit directs the flow of data and instructions within the chip.

- The ALU receives the data and instructions from the registers and makes the desired computation. These data and instructions have been translated into **binary form**—that is, only 0s and 1s. A "0" or a "1" is called a **bit**. The CPU can process only binary data. All types of data, such as letters, decimal numbers, photographs, music, and so on, can be converted to a binary representation, which can then be processed by the CPU.

- The data in their original form and the instructions are sent to storage registers and then are sent back to a storage place outside the chip, such as the computer's hard drive. Meanwhile, the transformed data go to another register and then on to other parts of the computer (e.g., to the monitor for display or to storage).

Intel offers excellent demonstrations of how CPUs work: Search the web for "Intel" with "Explore the Curriculum" to find their demos. This cycle of processing, known as a *machine instruction cycle*, occurs billions of times per second.

Advances in Microprocessor Design. Innovations in chip designs are coming at a faster and faster rate, as described by **Moore's law.** In 1965, Gordon Moore, a cofounder of Intel Corporation, predicted that microprocessor complexity would double approximately every 18 months. His prediction has been amazingly accurate.

The advances predicted from Moore's law arise mainly from the following changes:

- Producing increasingly miniaturized transistors.
- Placing multiple processors on a single chip. Chips with more than one processor are called *multicore* chips. For example, the Cell chip, produced by a consortium of Sony, Toshiba, and IBM, contains nine processors. Computers using the Cell chip display very rich graphics. The chip is also used in TV sets and home theaters that can download and show large numbers of high-definition programs. Intel (www.intel.com) and AMD (www.amd.com) offer multicore chips.

- Intel's three-dimensional (3D) chips require less power than Intel's current chips while improving performance. These chips enhance the performance of all computers. However, they are particularly valuable in handheld devices, because they extend the device's battery life.

In addition to increased speeds and performance, Moore's law has had an impact on costs. For example, in 1997, a desktop computer with a Pentium II microprocessor, 64 megabytes of random access memory, a 4-gigabyte hard drive, and a 17-inch monitor cost $4,000. In mid-2014, a desktop computer with an Intel i7 quad-core processor, 8 gigabytes of random access memory, a 2-terabyte hard drive plus 32 gigabytes of solid-state storage, and a 27-inch touch-screen cost roughly $2,000.

Computer Memory

The amount and type of memory that a computer possesses has a great deal to do with its general utility. A computer's memory also determines the types of programs that the computer can run, the work it can perform, its speed, and its cost. There are two basic categories of computer memory. The first is *primary storage*. It is called "primary" because it stores small amounts of data and information that the CPU will use immediately. The second category is *secondary storage*, which stores much larger amounts of data and information (e.g., an entire software program) for extended periods.

Memory Capacity. As you have seen, CPUs process only binary units—0s and 1s—which are translated through computer languages into bits. A particular combination of bits represents a certain alphanumeric character or a simple mathematical operation. Eight bits are needed to represent any one of these characters. This 8-bit string is known as a **byte**. The storage capacity of a computer is measured in bytes. Bits typically are used as units of measure only for telecommunications capacity, as in how many million bits per second can be sent through a particular medium.

The hierarchy of terms used to describe memory capacity is as follows:

- *Kilobyte.* Kilo means "one thousand," so a kilobyte (KB) is approximately 1,000 bytes. Actually, a kilobyte is 1,024 bytes. Computer designers find it convenient to work with powers of 2: 1,024 is 2 to the 10th power, and 1,024 is close enough to 1,000 that for *kilobyte* people use the standard prefix *kilo*, which means exactly 1,000 in familiar units such as the kilogram or kilometer.

- *Megabyte.* Mega means "one million," so a megabyte (MB) is approximately 1 million bytes. Most personal computers have hundreds of megabytes of RAM memory.

- *Gigabyte.* Giga means "one billion," so a gigabyte (GB) is approximately 1 billion bytes.

- *Terabyte.* A terabyte is approximately 1 trillion bytes. The storage capacity of modern personal computers can be several terabytes.

- *Petabyte.* A petabyte is approximately 1,000 terabytes.

- *Exabyte.* An exabyte is approximately 1,000 petabytes.

- *Zettabyte.* A zettabyte is approximately 1,000 exabytes.

To get a feel for these amounts, consider the following example: If your computer has one terabyte of storage capacity on its hard drive (a type of secondary storage), it can store approximately 1 trillion bytes of data. If the average page of text contains about 2,000 bytes, then your hard drive could store approximately 10 percent of all the print collections of the Library of Congress. That same terabyte can store 70 hours of standard-definition compressed video.

Primary Storage.

Primary storage, or **main memory**, as it is sometimes called, stores three types of information for very brief periods of time: (1) data to be processed by the CPU, (2) instructions for the CPU as to how to process the data, and (3) operating system programs that manage various aspects of the computer's operation. Primary storage takes place in chips mounted on the computer's main circuit board, called the *motherboard*. These chips are located as close as physically possible to the CPU chip. As with the CPU, all the data and instructions in primary storage have been translated into binary code.

The four main types of primary storage are (1) register, (2) cache memory, (3) random access memory, and (4) read-only memory (ROM). You learn about each type of primary storage next.

Registers are part of the CPU. They have the least capacity, storing extremely limited amounts of instructions and data only immediately before and after processing.

Cache memory is a type of high-speed memory that enables the computer to temporarily store blocks of data that are used more often and that a processor can access more rapidly than main memory (RAM). Cache memory is physically located closer to the CPU than RAM. Blocks that are used less often remain in RAM until they are transferred to cache; blocks used infrequently remain in secondary storage. Cache memory is faster than RAM because the instructions travel a shorter distance to the CPU.

Random access memory is the part of primary storage that holds a software program and small amounts of data for processing. When you start most software programs (such as Microsoft Word) on your computer, the entire program is brought from secondary storage into RAM. As you use the program, small parts of the program's instructions and data are sent into the registers and then to the CPU. Compared with the registers, RAM stores more information and is located farther away from the CPU. However, compared with secondary storage, RAM stores less information and is much closer to the CPU.

RAM is temporary and, in most cases, *volatile*—that is, RAM chips lose their contents if the current is lost or turned off, as from a power surge, brownout, or electrical noise generated by lightning or nearby machines.

Most of us have lost data at one time or another due to a computer "crash" or a power failure. What is usually lost is whatever is in RAM, cache, or the registers at the time, because these types of memory are volatile. Therefore, you need greater security when you are storing certain types of critical data or instructions. Cautious computer users frequently save data to nonvolatile memory (secondary storage). In addition, most modern software applications have auto-save functions. Programs stored in secondary storage, even though they are temporarily copied into RAM when they are being used, remain intact because only the copy is lost, not the original.

Read-only memory is the place—actually, a type of chip—where certain critical instructions are safeguarded. ROM is nonvolatile, so it retains these instructions when the power to the computer is turned off. The read-only designation means that these instructions can only be read by the computer and cannot be changed by the user. An example of ROM is the instructions needed to start or "boot" the computer after it has been shut off.

Secondary Storage.

Secondary storage is designed to store very large amounts of data for extended periods. Secondary storage has the following characteristics:

- It is nonvolatile.
- It takes more time to retrieve data from it than from RAM.
- It is cheaper than primary storage (see FIGURE PI2.4).
- It can utilize a variety of media, each with its own technology, as you see next.

One secondary storage medium, magnetic tape, is kept on a large open reel or in a smaller cartridge or cassette. Although this is an old technology, it remains popular because it is the cheapest storage medium, and it can handle enormous amounts of data. As a result, many organizations (e.g., the U.S. Government Social Security Administration) use magnetic tape for archival storage. The downside is that it is the slowest method for retrieving data because all the data are placed on the tape sequentially. Sequential access means

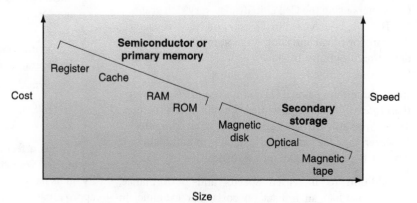

Figure PI2.4 Primary memory compared with secondary storage.

© Homiel/iStockphoto   © krzyscin/iStockphoto

Figure PI2.5 Traditional hard drives are less expensive, but solid-state drives are faster and are more reliable. (*Sources:* © АлексейБрагин/iStockphoto; © Krzysztof Krzyscin/iStockphoto)

that the system might have to run through the majority of the tape before it comes to the desired piece of data.

Magnetic disks (or **hard drives** or **fixed disk drives**) are the most commonly used mass storage devices because of their low cost, high speed, and large storage capacity. Hard disk drives read from, and write to, stacks of rotating (at up to 15,000 rpm) magnetic disk platters mounted in rigid enclosures and sealed against environmental and atmospheric contamination (see FIGURE PI2.5). These disks are permanently mounted in a unit that may be internal or external to the computer.

Solid-state drives (SSDs) are data storage devices that serve the same purpose as a hard drive and store data in memory chips. Whereas hard drives have moving parts, SSDs do not. SSDs use the same interface with the computer's CPU as hard drives and are therefore a seamless replacement for hard drives. SSDs offer many advantages over hard drives. They use less power, are silent and faster, and produce about one-third the heat of a hard drive. The major disadvantage of SSDs is that they cost more than hard drives.

Unlike magnetic media, **optical storage devices** do not store data via magnetism. Rather, a laser reads the surface of a reflective plastic platter. Optical disk drives are slower than magnetic hard drives, but they are less fragile and less susceptible to damage from contamination.

In addition, optical disks can store a great deal of information, both on a routine basis and when combined into storage systems. Types of optical disks include compact disk read-only memory and digital video disk.

Compact disk read-only memory (*CD-ROM*) storage devices feature high capacity, low cost, and high durability. However, because a CD-ROM is a read-only medium, it cannot be written on. *CD-R* can be written to, but once this is done, what was written on it cannot be changed later. That is, CD-R is writeable, which CD-ROM is not, but it is not rewriteable, which *CD-RW* (compact disk, rewritable) is. There are applications where not being rewriteable is a plus, because it prevents some types of accidental data destruction. CD-RW adds rewritability to the recordable compact disk market.

The digital video disk (*DVD*) is a 5-inch disk with the capacity to store about 135 minutes of digital video. DVDs can also perform as computer storage disks, providing storage capabilities of 17 gigabytes. DVD players can read current CD-ROMs, but current CD-ROM players cannot read DVDs. The access speed of a DVD drive is faster than that of a typical CD-ROM drive.

A dual-layer *Blu-ray disc* can store 50 gigabytes, almost three times the capacity of a dual-layer DVD. Development of Blu-ray technology is ongoing, with three-layered and four-layered Blu-ray discs available.

Flash memory devices (or *memory cards*) are nonvolatile electronic storage devices that contain no moving parts and use 30 times less battery power than hard drives. Flash devices are also smaller and more durable than hard drives. The trade-offs are that flash devices store less data than hard drives. Flash devices are used with digital cameras, handheld and laptop computers, telephones, music players, and video game consoles.

One popular flash memory device is the **thumb drive** (also called *memory stick, jump drive,* or *flash drive*). These devices fit into Universal Serial Bus (USB) ports on personal computers and other devices, and they can store many gigabytes. Thumb drives have replaced magnetic floppy disks for portable storage.

BEFORE *YOU GO ON....*

1. Decisions about hardware focus on what three factors?
2. What are the overall trends in hardware?
3. Define hardware and list the major hardware components.
4. Describe the computer hierarchy from the largest to the smallest computers.
5. Distinguish between human data-input devices and source-data automation.
6. Briefly describe how a microprocessor functions.
7. Distinguish between primary storage and secondary storage.

Apply The Concept PI2.1

STEP 1 – Background (Here is what you are learning.)

In the modern business environment, computer hardware components are inextricably linked to business strategy. Put simply, computers are tools that allow businesses to automate some transactions and make others more efficient. As technology evolves, businesses need to evolve the ways they use that technology to execute their business strategies. The generally accepted rule is that technology should NOT drive business strategy, but business strategy MUST consider how the organization can implement new types of hardware to achieve its goals.

STEP 2 – Activity (Here is what you are doing.)

Consider Lowe's (http://www.lowes.com). A large home improvement warehouse store might seem very distant from the use of technology. However, in 2011 Lowe's made significant improvements to its customer experience by implementing a type of hardware. What hardware is that? The answer is—smartphones.

Visit http://www.wiley.com/go/rainer/MIS3e/applytheconcept, and click on the link provided for Apply the Concept PI2.1. This link will take you to a *U.S. News and World Report* article that discusses how Lowe's implemented smartphone technology for their employees and their customers.

STEP 3 – Deliverable (Here is what you will turn in.)

Discuss strategic issues that link hardware design to business strategy, using the Lowe's case to illustrate these links.

PI2.2 Introduction to Software

Computer hardware is only as effective as the instructions you give it. Those instructions are contained in **software**. The importance of computer software cannot be overestimated. The first software applications for computers in business were developed in the early 1950s. At that time, software was less costly. Today, software comprises a much larger percentage of the cost of modern computer systems because the price of hardware has dramatically decreased, while both the complexity and the price of software have dramatically increased.

The ever-increasing complexity of software has also increased the potential for errors, or *bugs*. Large applications today may contain millions of lines of computer code, written by hundreds of people over the course of several years. Thus, the potential for errors is huge, and testing and debugging software is expensive and time consuming.

In spite of these overall trends—increasing complexity, cost, and numbers of defects—software has become an everyday feature of our business and personal lives. Your examination of software begins with definitions of some fundamental concepts. Software consists of computer programs, which are sequences of instructions for the computer. The process of writing or coding programs is called **programming**. Individuals who perform this task are called *programmers*.

Computer programs include documentation, which is a written description of the program's functions. Documentation helps the user operate the computer system, and it helps other programmers understand what the program does and how it accomplishes its purpose. Documentation is vital to the business organization. Without it, the departure of a key programmer or user could deprive the organization of the knowledge of how the program is designed and functions.

The computer can do nothing until it is instructed by software. Computer hardware, by design, is general purpose. Software enables the user to instruct the hardware to perform specific functions that provide business value. There are two major types of software: systems software and application software. FIGURE PI2.6 illustrates the relationship among hardware, systems software, and application software.

Systems software is a set of instructions that serves primarily as an intermediary between computer hardware and application programs. Systems software enables computer systems to perform self-regulatory functions by loading itself when the computer is first turned on and providing commonly used sets of instructions for all applications. Systems programming refers to both the creation and the maintenance of systems software.

Application software is a set of computer instructions that provides more specific functionality to a user. This functionality

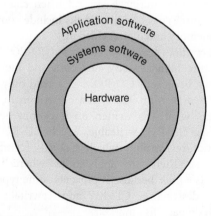

Figure PI2.6 Systems software services as intermediary between hardware and functional applications.

may be broad, such as general word processing, or narrow, such as an organization's payroll program. Essentially, an application program applies a computer to a certain need. *Application programming* refers to the creation, modification, and improvement of application software. Application software may be proprietary or off-the-shelf. As you will see, modern organizations use many different software applications.

Software Issues

The importance of software in computer systems has brought new issues to the forefront for organizational managers. These issues include software defects (bugs), licensing, open systems, and open-source software.

Software Defects. All too often, computer program code is inefficient, poorly designed, and riddled with errors. The Software Engineering Institute (SEI) at Carnegie Mellon University in Pittsburgh defines good software as usable, reliable, defect free, cost effective, and maintainable. As our dependence on computers and networks increases, the risks associated with software defects are becoming more serious.

The SEI maintains that, on average, professional programmers make between 100 and 150 errors in every 1,000 lines of code they write. Fortunately, the software industry recognizes this problem. Unfortunately, however, the problem is enormous, and the industry is taking only initial steps to resolve it. One critical step is better design and planning at the beginning of the development process (discussed in Chapter 13).

Software Licensing. Many people routinely copy proprietary software. However, making copies without the manufacturer's explicit permission—a practice known as *piracy*—is illegal. The Business Software Alliance (BSA; www.bsa.org), a nonprofit trade association dedicated to promoting a safe and legal digital world, collects, investigates, and acts on software piracy tips. The BSA has calculated

 that piracy costs software vendors around the world billions of dollars annually. Most of the tips the BSA receives come from current and past employees of offending companies.

To protect their investment, software vendors must prevent their products from being copied and distributed by individuals and other software companies. A company can copyright its software, which means that the U.S. Copyright Office grants the company the exclusive legal right to reproduce, publish, and sell that software.

The number of computing devices in organizations continues to grow, and businesses continue to decentralize, so IS managers are finding it increasingly difficult to supervise their software assets. In fact, the majority of chief information officers (CIOs) are not confident that their companies were in compliance with software licensing agreements. For example, one medium-size company was fined $10,000 for unknowingly using Microsoft Exchange mailbox licenses that had not been purchased. Worse, the company was also fined $100,000 for not having the necessary licenses for Autodesk, Inc.'s AutoCAD design software.

To help companies manage their software licenses, new firms have arisen that specialize in tracking software licenses for a fee. For example, Express Metrix (www.expressmetrix .com) will track and manage a company's software licenses to ensure they are in compliance with U.S. copyright laws.

Open Systems. The **open systems** concept refers to a group of computing products that work together. In an open system, the same operating system with compatible software is installed on all computers that interact within an organization. A complementary approach is to employ application software that will run across all computer platforms. Where hardware, operating systems, and application software are all designed as open systems, users can purchase the best software, called *best of breed*, for a job without worrying whether it will run on particular hardware.

Open-Source Software. Organizations today are increasingly selecting open-source software rather than proprietary software. **Proprietary software** is purchased software that has restrictions on its use, copying, and modification. Companies that develop proprietary software spend money and time developing their products, which they then sell in the marketplace. This software is labeled *proprietary* because the developer keeps the source code—the actual computer instructions—private (just as Coca-Cola does with its formula). Therefore, companies that purchase the software can utilize it in their operations, but they cannot change the source code themselves.

In contrast, the source code for **open-source software** is available at no cost to both developers and users. This software is distributed with license terms that ensure that its source code will always be available.

Open-source software is produced by worldwide "communities" of developers who write and maintain the code. Inside each community, however, only a small group of developers, called *core developers*, is allowed to modify the code directly. All the other developers must submit their suggested changes to the core developers.

There are advantages to implementing open-source software in an organization. According to OpenSource (www .opensource.org), open-source development produces high-quality, reliable, low-cost software. This software is also flexible, meaning that the code can be changed to meet users' needs. In many cases, open-source software can be more reliable than proprietary software. Because the code is available to many developers, more bugs are discovered early and quickly, and they are fixed immediately. Technical support for open-source software is also available from firms that offer products derived from the software. An example is Red Hat (www.redhat.com), a major Linux vendor that supplies solutions to problems associated with open-source technology. Specifically, Red Hat provides education, training, and technical support, for a fee.

Open-source software also has disadvantages, however. The major drawback is that companies that use open-source software depend on the continued goodwill of an army of volunteers for enhancements, bug fixes, and so on, even if they have signed a contract that includes support. Some companies will not accept this risk, although as a practical matter the support community for Linux, Apache, and Firefox is not likely to disappear. Further, organizations that do not have in-house technical experts will have to purchase maintenance–support contracts from a third party. In addition, open-source software poses questions concerning ease of use, the time and expense needed to train users, and compatibility with existing systems either within or outside the organization.

There are many examples of open-source software, including the GNU (GNU's Not UNIX) suite of software (www.gnu.org) developed by the Free Software Foundation (www.fsf.org); the Linux operating system (see www.linux-hq.com); Apache Web server (www.apache.org); sendmail SMTP (Send Mail Transport Protocol) e-mail server (www.sendmail.org); the Perl programming language (www.perl.org); the Firefox browser from Mozilla (www.mozilla.com); and Sun's StarOffice applications suite (www.sun.com/software/star/staroffice/index.jsp). In fact, more than 150,000 open-source projects are under way at SourceForge (www.sourceforge.net), the popular open-source hosting site.

Open-source software is moving to the mainstream, as you see by the many major companies that use this type of software. For example, Japan's Shinsei Bank (www.shinseibank.com) uses Linux on its servers; SugarCRM (www.sugarcrm.com) for certain customer relationship management tasks; and MySQL (www.mysql.com) open-source database management software. Further, the *Los Angeles Times* uses Alfresco (www.alfresco.com) to manage some of the images and video for its Web site.

Systems Software

As you saw earlier, the programs contained in systems software control and support the computer system and its information-processing activities. Systems software also helps users and IT personnel program, test, and debug their own computer programs. Systems software programs support application software by directing the computer's basic functions. For example, when the computer is turned on, the initialization program (a systems program) prepares and readies all devices for processing. The major type of systems software with which we are concerned is the operating system.

The **operating system (OS)** is the "director" of your computer system's operations. It supervises the overall operation of the computer by monitoring the computer's status, scheduling operations, and managing input and output processes. Well-known desktop operating systems include Microsoft Windows (www.microsoft.com), Apple Mac OS X (www.apple.com), Linux (www.linuxhq.com), and Google Chrome (www.google.com/chrome). When a new version with new features is released, the developers often give the new version a new designation. For example, in mid-2014, the latest version of Windows was Windows 8.1, and the latest version of OS X was Mavericks or OS X 10.9.

The operating system also provides an interface between the user and the hardware. This user interface hides the complexity of the hardware from the user. That is, you do not have to know how the hardware actually operates; you simply have to know what the hardware will do and what you need to do to obtain the desired results.

The ease or difficulty of the interaction between the user and the computer is determined to a large extent by the **graphical user interface (GUI)**. The **GUI** allows users to directly control the hardware by manipulating visible objects (such as icons) and actions that replace complex commands. Microsoft Windows provides a widely recognized GUI.

In mid-2014, GUI technology incorporates features such as virtual reality, head-mounted displays, speech input (user commands) and output, pen and gesture recognition, animation, multimedia, artificial intelligence, and cellular/wireless communication capabilities. These new interfaces, called *natural user interfaces* (NUIs), will combine social, haptic, and touch-enabled gesture-control interfaces. (A *haptic interface* provides tactile feedback through the sense of touch by applying forces, vibrations, or motions to the user.)

A **social interface** guides the user through computer applications by using cartoon-like characters, graphics, animation, and voice commands. The cartoon-like characters can be puppets, narrators, guides, inhabitants, or *avatars* (computer-generated human-like figures). Social interfaces are hard to create without being corny. For example, the assistant "Clippy" was so annoying to users of Microsoft Office 97 that it was eliminated from Office 2003 and all subsequent versions.

Motion control gaming consoles are another type of interface. Three major players currently offer this interface: the Xbox 360 Kinect, the PS3 PlayStation Move, and the Nintendo Wii.

- Kinect tracks your movements without a physical controller, has voice recognition, and accommodates multiple players.

  - The PlayStation Move uses a physical controller with motion-sensing electronics, making it the technological "cross" between Kinect and Wii. Move requires each player to use a wand.

- Wii uses a physical controller. Compared with Kinect and Move, Wii has been on the market longer, it has the biggest library of motion-sensing games, and it is the least expensive. On the negative side, Wii has the least accurate motion sensing of the three systems, and, unlike Kinect and Move, it is not available in high definition.

Touch-enabled gesture-control interfaces enable users to browse through photos, "toss" objects around a screen, "flick" to turn the pages of a book, play video games, and watch movies. Examples of this type of interface are Microsoft Surface and the Apple iPhone. Microsoft Surface is used in casinos such as Harrah's iBar in Las Vegas and in some AT&T stores. A very visible use of Surface was the touch wall used by the major television networks during their coverage of various elections.

Application Software

As you saw earlier, application software consists of instructions that direct a computer system to perform specific information-processing activities and also to provide functionality for users. Because there are so many different uses for computers, the number of application software programs is correspondingly large.

Application software may be developed in-house by the organization's information systems personnel, or it may be commissioned from a software vendor. Alternatively, the software can be purchased, leased, or rented from a vendor that develops applications and sells them to many organizations. This "off-the-shelf" software may be a standard package, or it may be customizable. Special-purpose programs or "packages" can be tailored for a specific purpose, such as inventory control and payroll. A **package, or software suite,** is a group of programs with integrated functions that has been developed by a vendor and is available for purchase in a prepackaged form. Microsoft Office is a well-known example of a package, or software suite.

General-purpose, off-the-shelf application programs designed to help individual users increase their productivity are referred to as **personal application software**. Table PI2.3 lists some of the major types of personal application software.

Speech-recognition software, also called *voice recognition*, is an input technology, rather than strictly an application, that enables users to provide input to systems software and application software. As the name suggests, this software recognizes and interprets human speech, either one word at a time (*discrete speech*) or in a conversational stream (*continuous speech*). Advances in processing power, new software algorithms, and better microphones have enabled developers to design extremely accurate speech-recognition software. Experts predict that, in the near future, voice recognition systems will be built into almost every device, appliance, and

TABLE PI2.3 Personal Application Software

Category of Personal Application Software	Major Functions	Examples
Spreadsheets	Use rows and columns to manipulate primarily numerical data; useful for analyzing financial information and for what–if and goal-seeking analyses	Microsoft Excel Corel Quattro Pro Apple iWork Numbers
Word processing	Allow users to manipulate primarily text with many writing and editing features	Microsoft Word Apple iWork Pages
Desktop publishing	Extend word processing software to allow production of finished, camera-ready documents, which may contain photographs, diagrams, and other images combined with text in different fonts	Microsoft Publisher QuarkXPress
Data management	Allow users to store, retrieve, and manipulate related data	Microsoft Access FileMaker Pro
Presentation	Allow users to create and edit graphically rich information to appear on electronic slides	Microsoft PowerPoint Apple iWork Keynote
Graphics	Allow users to create, store, and display or print charts, graphs, maps, and drawings	Adobe PhotoShop Corel DRAW
Personal information management	Allow users to create and maintain calendars, appointments, to-do lists, and business contacts	IBM Lotus Notes Microsoft Outlook
Personal finance	Allow users to maintain checkbooks, track investments, monitor credit cards, and bank and pay bills electronically	Quicken Microsoft Money
Web authoring	Allow users to design Web sites and publish them on the Web	Microsoft FrontPage Macromedia Dreamweaver
Communications	Allow users to communicate with other people over any distance	Novell Groupwise

machine that people use. Applications for voice recognition technology abound. Consider these examples:

- Call centers are using this technology. The average call costs $5 if it is handled by an employee, but only 50 cents with a self-service, speech-enabled system. The online brokerage firm E-Trade Financial uses Microsoft's Tellme (www.microsoft.com/en-us/tellme) to field about 50,000 calls per day, thereby saving at least $30 million annually.
  - Apple's Macintosh OS X and Microsoft's Windows 8 operating systems come with built-in voice technology.
  - Nuance's Dragon NaturallySpeaking (www.nuance.com) enables accurate voice-to-text and e-mail dictation.
  - Vocera Communications (www.vocera.com) has developed a communicator badge that combines voice recognition with wireless technologies. Among its first customers were medical workers, who used the badge to search hospital directories for the appropriate person to manage a patient problem or to find medical records.

- Vox-Tec's (www.voxtec.com) Phraselator, a handheld device about the size of a checkbook, listens to requests for a phrase and then translates it into any of 41 specified languages. U.S. troops in Iraq and Afghanistan are using it to provide translations in Arabic and Pashto, respectively.

BEFORE *YOU GO ON....*

1. What does the following statement mean? "Hardware is useless without software."
2. What are the differences between systems software and application software?
3. What is open-source software, and what are its advantages? Can you think of any disadvantages?
4. Describe the functions of the operating system.

Apply The Concept PI2.2

LEARNING OBJECTIVE PI2.2 Differentiate between the two major types of software.

STEP 1 – Background

There are two types of software (systems and application), two general ways of obtaining software licenses (proprietary vs. open-source), and two general types of uses (traditional vs. mobile). You should be sufficiently familiar with software to be able to categorize programs that you use.

STEP 2 – Activity

Visit http://www.wiley.com/go/rainer/MIS3e/applytheconcept, and click on the link for Apply the Concept PI2.2. This link will take you to CNET's Download.com. At this Web site, you should immediately notice one of the categories mentioned above. At the time of this writing, the site automatically recognized the type of computer operating system on the user's computer. For example, this author is writing on a Mac, and the system recognized the Mac OS and defaulted to the Mac software page.

Review the available software, and differentiate between the operating systems and the applications. Within applications, differentiate by method of obtaining a license—some you have to pay for, and some are available by open-source or freeware licensing.

STEP 3 – Deliverable

Build a table that differentiates between the two major types of software. To complete this task, list 10 applications you reviewed on the Web site mentioned in Step 2. Use the template provided below.

Application	Operating System	Licensing

What's in for ME?

HARDWARE

FOR ALL BUSINESS MAJORS

The design of computer hardware has profound impacts for businesspeople. Personal and organizational success can depend on an understanding of hardware design and a commitment to knowing where it is going and what opportunities and challenges hardware innovations will bring. Because these innovations are occurring so rapidly, hardware decisions both at the individual level and at the organizational level are difficult.

At the *individual level*, most people who have a home or office computer system and want to upgrade it, or people who are contemplating their first computer purchase, are faced with the decision of *when* to buy as much as *what* to buy and at what cost. At the *organizational level*, these same issues plague IS professionals. However, they are more complex and more costly. Most organizations have many different computer systems in place at the same time. Innovations may come to different classes of computers at different times or rates. Therefore, managers must decide when old hardware *legacy systems* still have a productive role in the organization and when they should be replaced. A legacy system is an old computer system or application that continues to be used, typically because it still functions for the users' needs, even though newer technology is available.

SOFTWARE

FOR THE
ACCOUNTING MAJOR

Accounting application software performs the organization's accounting functions, which are repetitive and performed in high volumes. Each business transaction (e.g., a person hired, a paycheck produced, an item sold) produces data that must be captured. Accounting applications capture these data and then manipulate them as necessary. Accounting applications adhere to relatively standardized procedures, handle detailed data, and have a historical focus (i.e., what happened in the past).

FOR THE
FINANCE MAJOR

Financial application software provides information about the firm's financial status to persons and groups inside and outside the firm. Financial applications include forecasting, funds management, and control applications. Forecasting applications predict and project the firm's future activity in the economic environment. Funds management applications use cash flow models to analyze expected cash flows. Control applications enable managers to monitor their financial performance, typically by providing information about the budgeting process and performance ratios.

FOR THE
MARKETING MAJOR

Marketing application software helps management solve problems that involve marketing the firm's products. Marketing software includes marketing research and marketing intelligence applications. Marketing applications provide information about the firm's products and competitors, its distribution system, its advertising and personal selling activities, and its pricing strategies. Overall, marketing applications help managers develop strategies that combine the four major elements of marketing: product, promotion, place, and price.

FOR THE

PRODUCTION/OPERATIONS MANAGEMENT MAJOR

Managers use production/operations management (POM) application software for production planning and as part of the physical production system. POM applications include production, inventory, quality, and cost software. These applications help management operate manufacturing facilities and logistics. Materials requirements planning (MRP) software also is widely used in manufacturing. This software identifies which materials will be needed, how much will be needed, and the dates on which they will be needed. This information enables managers to be proactive.

FOR THE

HUMAN RESOURCES MANAGEMENT MAJOR

Human resources management application software provides information concerning recruiting and hiring, education and training, maintaining the employee database, termination, and administering benefits. HRM applications include workforce planning, recruiting, workforce management, compensation, benefits, and environmental reporting subsystems (e.g., equal employment opportunity records and analysis, union enrollment, toxic substances, and grievances).

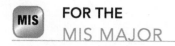

FOR THE
MIS MAJOR

If your company decides to develop its own software, the MIS function is responsible for managing this activity. If the company decides to buy software, the MIS function deals with software vendors in analyzing their products. The MIS function also is responsible for upgrading software as vendors release new versions.

SUMMARY

1. Discuss the strategic issues that link hardware design to business strategy.

   Strategic issues linking hardware design to business strategy include the following: How do organizations keep up with the rapid price/performance advancements in hardware? How often should an organization upgrade its computers and storage systems? How can organizations measure benefits gained from price/performance improvements in hardware?

2. Differentiate between the two major types of software.

   Software consists of computer programs (coded instructions) that control the functions of computer hardware.

There are two main categories of software: systems software and application software. Systems software manages the hardware resources of the computer system; it functions between the hardware and the application software. The major type of systems software is the operating system. Application software enables users to perform specific tasks and information-processing activities. Application software may be proprietary or off-the-shelf.

>>>GLOSSARY

application software The class of computer instructions that directs a computer system to perform specific processing activities and provide functionality for users.

arithmetic logic unit (ALU) Portion of the CPU that performs the mathematical calculations and makes logical comparisons.

augmented reality A live, direct or indirect, view of a physical, real-world environment whose elements are enhanced by computer-generated sensory input such as sound, video, graphics, or GPS data.

binary form The form in which data and instructions can be read by the CPU—only 0s and 1s.

bit Short for *binary digit* (0s and 1s), the only data that a CPU can process.

byte An 8-bit string of data, needed to represent any one alphanumeric character or simple mathematical operation.

cache memory A type of high-speed memory that enables the computer to temporarily store blocks of data that are used more often and that a processor can access more rapidly than main memory (RAM).

central processing unit (CPU) Hardware that performs the actual computation or "number crunching" inside any computer.

computer programs The sequences of instructions for the computer, which comprise software.

control unit Portion of the CPU that controls the flow of information.

documentation Written description of the functions of a software program.

fat clients Desktop computer systems that offer full functionality.

flash memory devices Nonvolatile electronic storage devices that are compact, are portable, require little power, and contain no moving parts.

gesture recognition An input method that interprets human gestures, in an attempt for computers to begin to understand human body language.

graphical user interface (GUI) Systems software that allows users to have direct control of the hardware by manipulating visible objects (such as icons) and actions, which replace command syntax.

laptop computers (notebook computers) Small, easily transportable, lightweight microcomputers.

magnetic disks (or **hard drives** or **fixed disk drives**) A form of secondary storage on a magnetized disk divided into tracks and sectors that provide addresses for various pieces of data.

magnetic tape A secondary storage medium on a large open reel or in a smaller cartridge or cassette.

mainframes Relatively large computers used in large enterprises for extensive computing applications that are accessed by thousands of users.

microcomputers The smallest and least expensive category of general-purpose computers, also called micros, personal computers, or PCs.

microprocessor The CPU, made up of millions of transistors embedded in a circuit on a silicon wafer or chip.

minicomputers Relatively small, inexpensive, and compact mid-range computers that perform the same functions as mainframe computers, but to a more limited extent.

Moore's law Prediction by Gordon Moore, an Intel cofounder, that microprocessor complexity would double approximately every 2 years.

multimedia technology Computer-based integration of text, sound, still images, animation, and digitized full-motion video.

netbook A very small, lightweight, low-cost, energy-efficient, portable computer, typically optimized for Internet-based services such as Web browsing and e-mailing.

notebook computer See **laptop computers**.

open-source software Software made available in source-code form at no cost to developers.

open systems Computing products that work together by using the same operating system with compatible software on all the computers that interact in an organization.

operating system (OS) The main system control program, which supervises the overall operations of the computer, allocates CPU time and main memory to programs, and provides an interface between the user and the hardware.

optical storage devices A form of secondary storage in which a laser reads the surface of a reflective plastic platter.

package Common term for an integrated group of computer programs developed by a vendor and available for purchase in prepackaged form.

personal application software General-purpose, off-the-shelf application programs that support general types of processing, rather than being linked to any specific business function.

primary storage (also called **main memory**) High-speed storage located directly on the motherboard that stores data to be processed by the CPU, instructions telling the CPU how to process the data, and operating system programs.

programming The process of writing or coding programs.

proprietary software Software that has been developed by a company and has restrictions on its use, copying, and modification.

random access memory (RAM) The part of primary storage that holds a software program and small amounts of data when they are brought from secondary storage.

read-only memory (ROM) Type of primary storage where certain critical instructions are safeguarded; the storage is nonvolatile and retains the instructions when the power to the computer is turned off.

registers High-speed storage areas in the CPU that store very small amounts of data and instructions for short periods.

secondary storage Technology that can store very large amounts of data for extended periods.

sequential access Data access in which the computer system must run through data in sequence to locate a particular piece.

server Smaller midrange computers that support networks, enabling users to share files, software, and other network devices.

social interface A user interface that guides the user through computer applications by using cartoon-like characters, graphics, animation, and voice commands.

software A set of computer programs that enable the hardware to process data.

software suite See **package**.

solid-state drives (SSDs) Data storage devices that serve the same purpose as a hard drive and store data in memory chips.

speech-recognition software Software that recognizes and interprets human speech, either one word at a time (discrete speech) or in a stream (continuous speech).

supercomputer Computers with the most processing power available; used primarily in scientific and military work for computationally demanding tasks on very large datasets.

systems software The class of computer instructions that serve primarily as an intermediary between computer hardware and application programs; provides important self-regulatory functions for computer systems.

tablet computer (or **tablet**) A complete computer contained entirely in a flat touchscreen that uses a stylus, digital pen, or fingertip as an input device instead of a keyboard or mouse.

thin-client systems Desktop computer systems that do not offer the full functionality of a PC.

thumb drive Storage device that fits into the USB port of a personal computer and is used for portable storage.

wearable computer A miniature computer worn by a person allowing the user to multitask.

>>>DISCUSSION QUESTIONS

1. What factors affect the speed of a microprocessor?

2. If you were the CIO of a firm, what factors would you consider when selecting secondary storage media for your company's records (files)?

3. Given that Moore's law has proved itself over the past two decades, speculate on what chip capabilities will be in 10 years. What might your desktop PC be able to do?

4. If you were the CIO of a firm, how would you explain the workings, benefits, and limitations of using thin clients as opposed to fat clients?

5. Where might you find embedded computers at home, at school, and/or at work?

6. You are the CIO of your company, and you have to develop an application of strategic importance to your firm. What are the advantages and disadvantages of using open-source software?

7. What does this statement mean: "Hardware is useless without software."

>>>PROBLEM-SOLVING ACTIVITIES

1. Access the Web sites of the major chip manufacturers—for example, Intel (www.intel.com), Motorola (www.motorola.com), and Advanced Micro Devices (www.amd.com)—and obtain the latest information regarding new and planned chips. Compare performance and costs across these vendors. Be sure to take a close look at the various multicore chips.

2. Access "The Journey Inside" on Intel's Web site at http://www.intel.com/content/www/us/en/education/k12/the-journey-inside.html. Prepare a presentation of each step in the machine instruction cycle.

3. A great deal of free software is available over the Internet. Go to http://www.pcmag.com/article2/0,2817,2381528,00.asp, and observe all the software available for free. Choose a software program, and download it to your computer. Prepare a brief discussion about the software for your class.

4. Enter the IBM Web site (www.ibm.com), and perform a search on the term "software." Click on the drop box for Products, and notice how many software products IBM produces. Is IBM only a hardware company?

5. Compare the following proprietary software packages with their open-source software counterparts. Prepare your comparison for the class.

Proprietary	Open Source
Microsoft Office	Google Docs, OpenOffice
Adobe Photoshop	Picnik.com, Google Picasa

6. Compare the Microsoft Surface interface with Oblong Industries' (www.oblong.com/g-speak) g-speak spatial operating environment. Demonstrate examples of both interfaces to the class. What are the advantages and disadvantages of each one?

>>> COLLABORATION EXERCISE

STEP 1 – Background

Upgrading hardware is a difficult task. The initial step is to decide to upgrade. This is not an easy first step, however. A company has several alternatives to upgrading; specifically, it can extend its current maintenance, upgrade its existing hardware, purchase service contracts, or even virtualize its entire hardware infrastructure. In this activity, you will work toward a decision with a team where members adopt different perspectives on the upgrade process.

Imagine that you are a supplier of auto parts for a very innovative auto manufacturer. Your customer is currently upgrading its systems, though this upgrade is not projected to be completed for two more years.

STEP 2 – Activity

Visit http://www.wiley.com/go/rainer/MIS3e/collaboration, and click on the link provided for Collaboration Exercise PI2. This link will take you to a Web site that reviews the basic issues to consider when you are investigating a mainframe upgrade. Create a team, and divide your members into three approaches: maintain the status quo, upgrade completely, and move to a virtualized platform. Finally, have one or two people on the team serve as the "decision makers" who will review the arguments proposed by the other members.

Next, create a shared Google Doc where each team member presents his or her perspective for the decision makers to review.

STEP 3 – Deliverable

The decision makers should read all of the arguments concerning the best upgrade strategy. Based on the information presented, they should then determine the best route and defend it. Submit your shared Google Doc to your professor.

Banking

One challenge that all businesses face is deciding when to upgrade their standard desktop units. Hardware and software improvements are produced at differing paces, and they have very different impacts on the organization. Hardware improvements often enable employees to be more productive, whereas software improvements allow for greater security and an improved user experience.

There are, however, many disadvantages to upgrading hardware and software. Because hardware is always improving, better technology is always just over the horizon. Should you wait for it to become available? Should you buy the best equipment that is available today? Or, should you purchase something that just meets your current needs, with the idea that you will upgrade in the future? Similarly, software improvements may bring an improved user experience, but a time-tested, solid, secure environment is hard to give up.

This is the dilemma that Jeremy Farr is facing at First Noble Bank. He is the Director of IT, and he needs advice on how and when to upgrade the bank's desktop computers and, eventually, the operating systems that run them. Below is an e-mail message from Jeremy.

To:	IT Intern
From:	Jeremy Farr
Subject:	Hardware and Software Upgrades

Hi again!

Our desktop computers might be a bit out of date. They work just fine, but they are four years old, and the warranty is about to expire. I need to decide whether to upgrade our hardware and software or simply purchase an extended warranty. I would greatly appreciate your assistance in determining the right questions to ask.

Your assignment is to search the Web for a few articles related to this topic. There has to be something out there. Maybe you can read three or four articles on the subject and see if you can identify any common suggestions. If you do, please make some notes, and provide me with a list of the advantages and disadvantages of upgrading hardware and software.

Thanks for all of your work!

Jeremy

Note: Any links or Web sites mentioned in this e-mail are available at http://www.wiley.com/go/rainer/MIS3e/internship.

Fundamentals of Relational Database Operations

PLUG IT IN LEARNING OBJECTIVES >>>

PI3.1 Understand the process of querying a relational database.

PI3.2 Understand the process of entity–relationship modeling.

PI3.3 Understand the process of normalization and the process of joins.

Introduction

There are many operations possible with relational databases. In this Plug IT In, we discuss three of these operations: query languages, normalization, and joins.

As you saw in Chapter 3, a relational database is a collection of interrelated two-dimensional tables, consisting of rows and columns. Each row represents a record, and each column (or field) represents an attribute (or characteristic) of that record. Every record in the database must contain at least one field that uniquely identifies that record so that it can be retrieved, updated, and sorted. This identifier field, or group of fields, is called the *primary key*. In some cases, locating a particular record requires the use of secondary keys. A *secondary key* is another field that has some identifying information, but typically does not uniquely identify the record. A *foreign key* is a field (or group of fields) in one table that matches the primary key value in a row of another table. A foreign key is used to establish and enforce a link between two tables.

These related tables can be joined when they contain common columns. The uniqueness of the primary key tells the DBMS which records are joined with others in related tables. This feature allows users great flexibility in the variety of queries they can make. Despite these features, however, the relational database model has some disadvantages. Because large-scale databases can be composed of many interrelated tables, the overall design can be complex, leading to slow search and access times.

PI3.1 Query Languages

The most commonly performed database operation is searching for information. **Structured query language (SQL)** is the most popular query language used for interacting with a database. SQL allows people to perform complicated searches by using relatively simple statements or key words. Typical key words are SELECT (to choose a desired attribute), FROM (to specify the table or tables to be used), and WHERE (to specify conditions to apply in the query).

To understand how SQL works, imagine that a university wants to know the names of students who will graduate cum laude (but not magna or summa cum laude) in May 2014. (Refer to FIGURE 3.3 in Chapter 3.) The university IT staff would query the student relational database with an SQL statement such as

```
SELECT Student_Name
FROM Student_Database
WHERE Grade_Point_Average >= 3.40 and Grade_
       Point_Average < 3.60;
```

The SQL query would return John Jones and Juan Rodriguez.

Another way to find information in a database is to use *query by example* (QBE). In QBE, the user fills out a grid or template—also known as a *form*—to construct a sample or a description of the data desired. Users can construct a query quickly and easily by using drag-and-drop features in a DBMS such as Microsoft Access. Conducting queries in this manner is simpler than keying in SQL commands.

┌─ BEFORE *YOU GO ON....* ─────────┐
1. What is structured query language?
2. What is query by example?
└──────────────────────────────────┘

Apply The Concept PI3.1

LEARNING OBJECTIVE PI3.1 Understand the process of querying a relational database.

STEP 1 – Background (Here is what you are learning.)

Structured query language is a computer code that allows you to ask questions of a database, much as you would ask a question in a library. Somewhere in that library is the answer you are seeking. To find it, however, you have to know how to look. Perhaps the correct area, row, call number, or author would help you locate what you are looking for. Working with SQL is much the same. SQL is the key to unlocking many "data doors," and you must learn how to use it.

STEP 2 – Activity (Here is what you are doing.)

Imagine that you have access to a database that contains data on the number of traffic accidents in Panama City, FL. There are four tables in this database: Accidentinfo, Driverinfo, Accidentcauses, and Injuries.

STEP 3 – Deliverable (Here is what you will turn in.)

Write the SQL code that will answer the following questions.

- How many accidents were caused by DUI during the summer months (May–August) of 2014?
- How many one-car accidents occurred that involved drivers who are only 16 years old?

To write these SQL queries correctly, you will need to use your imagination as to the data that could be contained in each table. However, you should be able to determine which tables contain the appropriate data.

Submit your SQL code to your instructor.

PI3.2 Entity–Relationship Modeling

Designers plan and create databases through the process of **entity–relationship modeling**, using an **entity–relationship (ER) diagram**. There are many approaches to ER diagramming. You will see one particular approach here, but there are others. The good news is that if you are familiar with one version of ER diagramming, then you will be able to easily adapt to any other version.

ER diagrams consist of entities, attributes, and relationships. To properly identify entities, attributes, and relationships, database designers first identify the business rules for the particular data model. **Business rules** are precise descriptions of policies, procedures, or principles in any organization that stores and uses data to generate information. Business rules are derived from a description of an organization's operations, and help to create and enforce business processes in that organization. Keep in mind that *you* determine these business rules, not the MIS department.

Entities are pictured in rectangles, and relationships are described on the line between two entities. The attributes for each entity are listed, and the primary key is underlined. The **data dictionary** provides information on each attribute, such as its name, if it is a key, part of a key, or a non-key attribute, the type of data expected (alphanumeric, numeric, dates, etc.), and valid values. Data dictionaries can also provide information on why the attribute is needed in the database; which business functions, applications, forms, and reports use the attribute; and how often the attribute should be updated.

ER modeling is valuable because it allows database designers to communicate with users throughout the organization to ensure that all entities and the relationships among the entities are represented. This process underscores the importance of taking all users into account when designing organizational databases. Notice that all entities and relationships in our example are labeled in terms that users can understand.

Relationships illustrate an association between entities. The *degree of a relationship* indicates the number of entities associated with a relationship. A **unary relationship** exists when an association is maintained within a single entity. A **binary relationship** exists when two entities are associated. A **ternary relationship** exists when three entities are associated. In this Plug IT In, we discuss only binary relationships because they are the most common. Entity relationships may be classified as one-to-one, one-to-many, or many-to-many. The term, **connectivity**, describes the relationship classification.

Connectivity and cardinality are established by the business rules of a relationship. **Cardinality** refers to the maximum number of times an instance of one entity can be associated with an instance in the related entity. Cardinality can be mandatory single, optional single, mandatory many, or optional many. FIGURE PI3.1 displays the cardinality symbols. Note that we have four possible cardinality symbols: mandatory single, optional single, mandatory many, and optional many.

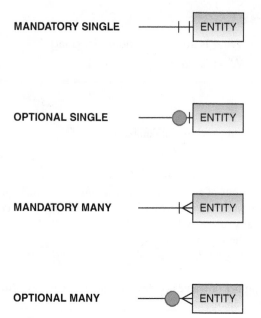

Figure PI3.1 Cardinality symbols.

STUDENT	PARKING PERMIT
Student Identification Number	Permit Number
Student Name	Student Identification Number
Student Address	Car Type

Figure PI3.2 One-to-one relationship.

Let's look at an example from a university. An *entity* is a person, place, or thing that can be identified in the users' work environment. For example, consider student registration at a university. Students register for courses, and they also register their cars for parking permits. In this example, STUDENT, PARKING PERMIT, CLASS, and PROFESSOR are entities. Recall that an instance of an entity represents a particular student, parking permit, class, or professor. Therefore, a particular STUDENT (James Smythe, 8023445) is an instance of the STUDENT entity; a particular parking permit (91778) is an instance of the PARKING PERMIT entity; a particular class (76890) is an instance of the CLASS entity; and a particular professor (Margaret Wilson, 390567) is an instance of the PROFESSOR entity.

Entity instances have *identifiers,* or *primary keys*, which are attributes (attributes and identifiers are synonymous) that are unique to that entity instance. For example, STUDENT instances can be identified with Student Identification Number; PARKING PERMIT instances can be identified with Permit Number; CLASS instances can be identified with Class Number; and PROFESSOR instances can be identified with Professor Identification Number.

Entities have **attributes**, or properties, that describe the entity's characteristics. In our example, examples of attributes for STUDENT are Student Name and Student Address. Examples of attributes for PARKING PERMIT are Student Identification Number and Car Type. Examples of attributes for CLASS are Class Name, Class Time, and Class Place. Examples of attributes for PROFESSOR are Professor Name and Professor Department. (Note that each course at this university has one professor—no team teaching.)

Why is Student Identification Number an attribute of both the STUDENT and PARKING PERMIT entity classes? That is, why do we need the PARKING PERMIT entity class? If you consider all of the interlinked university systems, the

PARKING PERMIT entity class is needed for other applications, such as fee payments, parking tickets, and external links to the state Department of Motor Vehicles.

Let's consider the three types of binary relationships in our example.

In a *one-to-one (1:1)* relationship, a single-entity instance of one type is related to a single-entity instance of another type. In our university example, STUDENT–PARKING PERMIT is a 1:1 relationship. The business rule at this university represented by this relationship is: Students may register only one car at this university. Of course, students do not have to register a car at all. That is, a student can have only one parking permit but does not need to have one.

Note that the relationship line on the PARKING PERMIT side shows a cardinality of optional single. A student can have, but does not have to have, a parking permit. On the STUDENT side of the relationship, only one parking permit can be assigned to one student, resulting in a cardinality of mandatory single. See FIGURE PI3.2.

The second type of relationship, *one-to-many (1:M),* is represented by the CLASS–PROFESSOR relationship in FIGURE PI3.3. The business rule at this university represented by this relationship is: At this university, there is no team teaching. Therefore, each class must have only one professor. On the other hand, professors may teach more than one class. Note that the relationship line on the PROFESSOR side shows a cardinality of mandatory single. In contrast, the relationship line on the CLASS side shows a cardinality of optional many.

The third type of relationship, *many-to-many (M:M),* is represented by the STUDENT–CLASS relationship. Most database management systems do not support many-to-many relationships. Therefore, we use *junction* (or *bridge*) *tables*, so that we have two one-to-many relationships. The business

PROFESSOR	CLASS
Professor Identification Number	Class ID
Professor Name	Class Name
Professor Department	Class Time
	Class Place

Figure PI3.3 One-to-many relationship.

Figure PI3.4 Many-to-many relationship.

rule at this university represented by this relationship is: Students can register for one or more classes, and each class can have one or more students (see FIGURE PI3.4). In this example, we create the REGISTRATION table as our junction table. Note that Student ID and Class ID are foreign keys in the REGISTRATION table.

Let's examine the relationships:

- The relationship line on the STUDENT side of the STUDENT–REGISTRATION relationship shows a cardinality of optional single.

- The relationship line on the REGISTRATION side of the STUDENT–REGISTRATION relationship shows a cardinality of optional many.

- The relationship line on the CLASS side of the CLASS–REGISTRATION relationship shows a cardinality of optional single.

- The relationship line on the REGISTRATION side of the CLASS–REGISTRATION relationship shows a cardinality of optional many.

— **BEFORE** *YOU GO ON....* —

1. What is an entity? An attribute? A relationship?

2. Describe one-to-one, one-to-many, and many-to-many relationships.

Apply The Concept PI3.2

LEARNING OBJECTIVE PI3.2 Understand the process of entity–relationship modeling.

STEP 1 – Background

It is very important that you understand the connections among entities, attributes, and relationships. This section has defined each of these terms for you. Typically, entities are described by their attributes, and they are related to other entities. For example, if "student name" is the entity, then age, gender, country of origin, marital status, and other demographic data are the attributes (characteristics) of that particular student. That student is also related to other entities such as financial information, major, and course information.

STEP 2 – Activity

An entity–relationship model is one of the most challenging aspects of designing a database because you have to (1) understand the rules that govern how things work and (2) be able to define and describe these rules in a picture. This section has provided you with the necessary tools to draw a basic ER model.

Imagine the following scenario. You are designing a database for your local police department to keep track of traffic violations. The department has provided you with the following rules:

- Each officer can write multiple tickets.
- Each ticket will list only one officer.
- Each ticket will list only one driver.
- Drivers can receive multiple tickets.

STEP 3 – Deliverable

Using the tools described in this section, demonstrate you understand the process of ER modeling by drawing and submitting an ER model for the scenario provided in Step 2.

PI3.3 Normalization and Joins

To use a relational database management system efficiently and effectively, the data must be analyzed to eliminate redundant data elements. **Normalization** is a method for analyzing and reducing a relational database to its most streamlined form to ensure minimum redundancy, maximum data integrity, and optimal processing performance. Data normalization is a methodology for organizing attributes into tables so that redundancy among the non-key attributes is eliminated. The result of the data normalization process is a properly structured relational database.

Data normalization requires a list of all the attributes that must be incorporated into the database and a list of all of the defining associations, or functional dependencies, among the attributes. **Functional dependencies** are a means of expressing that the value of one particular attribute is associated with a specific single value of another attribute. For example, for a Student Number 05345 at a university, there is exactly one Student Name, John C. Jones, associated with it. That is, Student Number is referred to as the determinant because its value *determines* the value of the other attribute. We can also say that Student Name is functionally dependent on Student Number.

As an example of normalization, consider a pizza shop. This shop takes orders from customers on a form. FIGURE PI3.5 shows a table of nonnormalized data gathered by the pizza shop. This table has two records, one for each order being placed. Because there are several pizzas on each order, the order number and customer information appear in multiple rows. Several attributes of each record have null values. A null value is an attribute with no data in it. For example, Order Number has four null values. Therefore, this table is not in first normal form. The data drawn from that form is shown in FIGURE PI3.5.

In our example, ORDER, CUSTOMER, and PIZZA are entities. The first step in normalization is to determine the functional dependencies among the attributes. The functional dependencies in our example are shown in FIGURE PI3.6.

Figure PI3.6 Functional dependencies in pizza shop example.

In the normalization process, we will proceed from nonnormalized data, to first normal form, to second normal form, and then to third normal form. (There are additional normal forms, but they are beyond the scope of this book.)

FIGURE PI3.7 demonstrates the data in *first normal form*. The attributes under consideration are listed in one table and primary keys have been established. Our primary keys are Order Number, Customer ID, and Pizza Code. In first normal form, each ORDER has to repeat the order number, order date, customer first name, customer last name, customer address, and customer zip code. This data file contains repeating groups and describes multiple entities. That is, this relation has data redundancy, a lack of data integrity, and the flat file would be difficult to use in various applications that the pizza shop might need.

Consider the table in FIGURE PI3.7, and notice the very first column (labeled Order Number). This column contains multiple entries for each order—three rows for Order Number 1116 and three rows for Order Number 1117. These multiple rows for an order are called *repeating groups*. The table in FIGURE PI3.6 also contains multiple entities: ORDER, CUSTOMER, and PIZZA. Therefore, we move on to second normal form.

To produce second normal form, we break the table in FIGURE PI3.6 into smaller tables to eliminate some of its

Order Number	Order Date	Customer ID	Customer F Name	Customer L Name	Customer Address	Zip Code	Pizza Code	Pizza Name	Quantity	Price	Total Price
1116	9/1/14	16421	Rob	Penny	123 Main St.	37411	P	Pepperoni	1	$11.00	$41.00
							MF	Meat Feast	1	$12.00	
							V	Vegetarian	2	$9.00	
1117	9/2/14	17221	Beth	Jones	41 Oak St.	29416	HM	Ham and Mushroom	3	$10.00	$56.00
							MF	Meat Feast	1	$12.00	
							TH	The Hawaiian	1	$14.00	

Figure PI3.5 Raw data gathered from orders at the pizza shop.

Order Number	Order Date	Customer ID	Customer F Name	Customer L Name	Customer Address	Zip Code	Pizza Code	Pizza Name	Quantity	Price	Total Price
1116	9/1/14	16421	Rob	Penny	123 Main St.	37411	P	Pepperoni	1	$11.00	$41.00
1116	9/1/14	16421	Rob	Penny	123 Main St.	37411	MF	Meat Feast	1	$12.00	$41.00
1116	9/1/14	16421	Rob	Penny	123 Main St.	37411	V	Vegetarian	2	$9.00	$41.00
1117	9/2/14	17221	Beth	Jones	41 Oak St.	29416	HM	Ham and Mushroom	3	$10.00	$56.00
1117	9/2/14	17221	Beth	Jones	41 Oak St.	29416	MF	Meat Feast	1	$12.00	$56.00
1117	9/2/14	17221	Beth	Jones	41 Oak St.	29416	TH	The Hawaiian	1	$14.00	$56.00

Figure PI3.7 First normal form for data from pizza shop.

data redundancy. Second normal form does not allow partial functional dependencies. That is, in a table in second normal form, every non-key attribute must be functionally dependent on the entire primary key of that table. FIGURE PI3.8 shows the data from the pizza shop in second normal form.

If you examine FIGURE PI3.8, you will see that second normal form has not eliminated all the data redundancy. For example, each Order Number is duplicated three times, as are all customer data. In *third normal form*, non-key attributes are not allowed to define other non-key attributes. That is, third normal form does not allow transitive dependencies in which one non-key attribute is functionally dependent on another. In our example, customer information depends both on Customer ID and Order Number. FIGURE PI3.9 shows the data

Order Number	Order Date	Customer ID	Customer F Name	Customer L Name	Customer Address	Zip Code	Total Price
1116	9/1/14	16421	Rob	Penny	123 Main St.	37411	$41.00
1116	9/1/14	16421	Rob	Penny	123 Main St.	37411	$41.00
1116	9/1/14	16421	Rob	Penny	123 Main St.	37411	$41.00
1117	9/2/14	17221	Beth	Jones	41 Oak St.	29416	$56.00
1117	9/2/14	17221	Beth	Jones	41 Oak St.	29416	$56.00
1117	9/2/14	17221	Beth	Jones	41 Oak St.	29416	$56.00

Order Number	Pizza Code	Quantity
1116	P	1
1116	MF	1
1116	V	2
1117	HM	3
1117	MF	1
1117	TH	1

Pizza Code	Pizza Name	Price
P	Pepperoni	$11.00
MF	Meat Feast	$12.00
V	Vegetarian	$9.00
HM	Ham and Mushroom	$10.00
TH	The Hawaiian	$14.00

Figure PI3.8 Second normal form for data from pizza shop.

ORDER

Order Number	Order Date	Customer ID	Total Price
1116	9/1/14	16421	$41.00
1117	9/2/14	17221	$56.00

CUSTOMER

Customer ID	Customer F Name	Customer L Name	Customer Address	Zip Code
16421	Rob	Penny	123 Main St.	37411
17221	Beth	Jones	41 Oak St.	29416

ORDER-PIZZA

Order Number	Pizza Code	Quantity
1116	P	1
1116	MF	1
1116	V	2
1117	HM	3
1117	MF	1
1117	TH	1

PIZZA

Pizza Code	Pizza Name	Price
P	Pepperoni	$11.00
MF	Meat Feast	$12.00
V	Vegetarian	$9.00
HM	Ham and Mushroom	$10.00
TH	The Hawaiian	$14.00

Figure PI3.9 Third normal form for data from pizza shop.

from the pizza shop in third normal form. Third normal form structure has these important points:

- It is completely free of data redundancy.
- All foreign keys appear where needed to link related tables.

Let's look at the primary and foreign keys for the tables in third normal form:

- The ORDER relation: the primary key is Order Number and the foreign key is Customer ID.
- The CUSTOMER relation: the primary key is Customer ID.
- The PIZZA relation: the primary key is Pizza Code.
- The ORDER–PIZZA relation: the primary key is a composite key, consisting of two foreign keys, Order Number and Pizza Code.

Now consider an order at the pizza shop. The tables in third normal form can produce the order in the following manner by using the join operation (see FIGURE PI3.10). The **join operation** combines records from two or more tables in a database to obtain information that is located in different tables. In our example, the join operation combines records from the four normalized tables to produce an ORDER. Here is how the join operation works:

- The ORDER relation provides the Order Number (the primary key), Order Date, and Total Price.

- The primary key of the ORDER relation (Order Number) provides a link to the ORDER–PIZZA relation (the link numbered 1 in FIGURE PI3.10).

Figure PI3.10 The join process with the tables of third normal form to produce an order.

- The ORDER–PIZZA relation supplies the Quantity to ORDER.
- The primary key of the ORDER–PIZZA relation is a composite key that consists of Order Number and Pizza Code. Therefore, the Pizza Code component of the primary key provides a link to the PIZZA relation (the link numbered 2 in FIGURE PI3.10).
- The PIZZA relation supplies the Pizza Name and Price to ORDER.
- The Customer ID in ORDER (a foreign key) provides a link to the CUSTOMER relation (the link numbered 3 in FIGURE PI3.10).
- The CUSTOMER relation supplies the Customer FName, Customer LName, Customer Address, and Zip Code to ORDER.

At the end of this join process, we have a complete ORDER. Normalization is beneficial when maintaining databases over a period of time. One example is the likelihood of having to change the price of each pizza. If the pizza shop increases the price of the Meat Feast from $12.00 to $12.50, this process is one easy step in FIGURE PI3.10. The price field is changed to $12.50 and the ORDER is automatically updated with the current value of the price.

Apply The Concept PI3.3

LEARNING OBJECTIVE PI3.3 Understand the process of normalization and the process of joins.

STEP 1 – Background

Normalization, as described in this section, breaks a flat data file into multiple tables to eliminate redundancy by creating redundancy in the form of keys that tie the tables together. In the example provided in the text, the normalized database allows for a pizza order to contain multiple pizzas without having to repeat the order number and leave blank (null) values.

Joins are very important because they take the data from multiple locations and tie things together with relationships. Repeating and relating the order number on the pizza table as a primary key in the order table enables you to maintain a cleaner set of data without null values.

STEP 2 – Activity

Normalize the following student table into first, second, and third normal forms.

Student	Age	Subject
Juan	19	English, History, College Algebra, Intro to Business
Anita	18	English, Public Speaking, French, Biology
Jason	19	History, Intro to MIS, Intro to Business, Business Communications

STEP 3 – Deliverable

Demonstrate that you understand the normalization process by working with the table provided in Step 2 to the second form of normalization. For additional practice, imagine that in the second form a "student information" table is added that contains student name, street address, city, state, and zip code. How might this table be normalized further?

What's in **IT** for ME?

FOR ALL BUSINESS MAJORS

As you see from the What's in IT for Me? section in Chapter 3, all business majors will have to manage data in their professional work. One way to manage data is through the use of databases and database management systems. First, it is likely that you will need to obtain information from your organization's databases. You will probably use structured query language to obtain this information. Second, as your organization plans and designs its databases, it will most likely use entity–relationship diagrams. You will provide much of the input to these ER diagrams. For example, you will describe the entities that you use in your work, the attributes of those entities, and the relationships among them. You will also help database designers as they normalize database tables, by describing how the normalized tables relate to each other (e.g., through the use of primary and foreign keys). Finally, you will help database designers as they plan their join operations to give you the information that you need when that information is stored in multiple tables.

SUMMARY

1. Understand the process of querying a relational database.

   The most commonly performed database operation is requesting information. *Structured query language* is the most popular query language used for this operation. SQL allows people to perform complicated searches by using relatively simple statements or key words. Typical key words are SELECT (to specify a desired attribute), FROM (to specify the table to be used), and WHERE (to specify conditions to apply in the query).

   Another way to find information in a database is to use *query by example*. In QBE, the user fills out a grid or template—also known as a *form*—to construct a sample or a description of the data desired. Users can construct a query quickly and easily by using drag-and-drop features in a DBMS such as Microsoft Access. Conducting queries in this manner is simpler than keying in SQL commands.

2. Understand the process of entity–relationship modeling.

   Designers plan and create databases through the process of **entity–relationship modeling**, using an **entity–relationship diagram**. ER diagrams consist of entities, attributes, and relationships. Entities are pictured in boxes, and relationships are represented as diamonds. The attributes for each entity are listed, and the primary key is underlined.

   ER modeling is valuable because it allows database designers to communicate with users throughout the organization to ensure that all entities and the relationships among the entities are represented. This process underscores the importance of taking all users into account when designing organizational databases. Notice that all entities and relationships in our example are labeled in terms that users can understand.

3. Understand the process of normalization and the process of joins.

   Normalization is a method for analyzing and reducing a relational database to its most streamlined form to ensure minimum redundancy, maximum data integrity, and optimal processing performance. When data are *normalized*, attributes in each table depend only on the primary key.

   The *join operation* combines records from two or more tables in a database to produce information that is located in different tables.

>>>GLOSSARY

attribute Each characteristic or quality describing a particular entity.

binary relationship A relationship that exists when two entities are associated.

business rules Precise descriptions of policies, procedures, or principles in any organization that stores and uses data to generate information.

connectivity Describes the classification of a relationship: one-to-one, one-to-many, or many-to-many.

data dictionary A collection of definitions of data elements; data characteristics that use the data elements; and the individuals, business functions, applications, and reports that use these data elements.

entity–relationship (ER) diagram Document that shows data entities and attributes and relationships among them.

entity–relationship (ER) modeling The process of designing a database by organizing data entities to be used and identifying the relationships among them.

functional dependency A means of expressing that the value of one particular attribute is associated with, or determines, a specific single value of another attribute.

join operation A database operation that combines records from two or more tables in a database.

normalization A method for analyzing and reducing a relational database to its most streamlined form to ensure minimum redundancy, maximum data integrity, and optimal processing performance.

query by example To obtain information from a relational database, a user fills out a grid or template—also known as a *form*—to construct a sample or a description of the data desired.

relationships Operators that illustrate an association between two entities.

structured query language The most popular query language for requesting information from a relational database.

ternary relationship A relationship that exists when three entities are associated.

unary relationship A relationship that exists when an association is maintained within a single entity.

>>>DISCUSSION QUESTIONS

1. Draw the entity–relationship diagram for a company that has departments and employees. In this company, a department must have at least one employee, and company employees may work in only one department.

2. Draw the entity–relationship diagram for library patrons and the process of checking out books.

3. You are working at a doctor's office. You gather data on the following entities: PATIENT, PHYSICIAN, PATIENT DIAGNOSIS, and TREATMENT. Develop a table for the entity, PATIENT VISIT. Decide on the primary keys and/ or foreign keys that you want to use for each entity.

>>> COLLABORATION EXERCISE

STEP 1 – Background

A database is the heart of a computer-based information system. It is vital to the collection, analysis, and distribution of data to users of the IS. Simply put, a well-designed database is the key to a successful IS.

STEP 2 – Activity

Join with a few of your classmates to create a team for this activity. Imagine that you are a startup company that is going to supply carabiner clips for climbers. You manufacture five specialized models that serve different purposes, and you produce each model for four different weight categories. You need to design a database to contain your customer, product, inventory, and sales information.

Collaborate with your team to create a plan for your database. Make certain that your design is normalized, relationships are established, and rules are stated.

STEP 3 – Deliverable

Use Google Drive to create a series of documents that outline the above information. Use Google Sheets to model the normalized tables. (Use multiple sheets to show the different sheets). Create a Google Doc to explain the relationships among the tables and to define the primary keys. Use Google Draw to draw an ER model for your database.

When you have completed all of these tasks, save all of these files in a single folder in Google Drive, and share that folder with your instructor.

Banking

Mapping business processes in an entity–relationship model is no easy task. Not only is this process difficult to understand, but also it is difficult to describe in a drawing. Fortunately, several tools are available that utilize drag-and-drop functionality to make the process easier to execute. One of these is tools is the draw.io app on Google Drive. For more information on this app, visit http://www.wiley.com/go/rainer/MIS3e/internship.

The difficulty mentioned above is exactly the challenge facing Jeremy Farr at First Noble Bank. He is the Director of IT, and he needs assistance creating an ER model to help his database company complete a new project. Below is an e-mail message from Jeremy.

To:	IT Intern
From:	Jeremy Farr
Subject:	ER Modeling

Hi again!

Recently, our company decided to upgrade our database so that it better reflects our current (and desired) business practices. Consider the following pieces of information.

1. We offer multiple types of accounts.
2. Each type of account can have many customers.
3. We have multiple types of customers (business, personal).
4. There are many customers in each type.
5. Customers can have multiple types of accounts.
6. Customers can have multiple accounts of the same type.

Trust me, I know how confusing this sounds. Will you work on an ER model for me that would help to get these relationships straight? If you find that you need more information, please make a list of questions, and I will try to find an answer.

I discovered that Google Drive has an app called draw.io that will allow you to build this model using the proper ER model symbols. Perhaps this will be helpful to you.

Thanks for all of your work!

Jeremy

Note: Any links or Web sites mentioned in this e-mail are available at http://www.wiley.com/go/rainer/MIS3e/internship.

Cloud Computing

LEARNING OBJECTIVES >>>

PI4.1 Describe the problems that modern information technology departments face.

PI4.2 Describe the key characteristics and advantages of cloud computing.

PI4.3 Identify a use case scenario for each of the four types of clouds.

PI4.4 Explain the operational model of each of the three types of cloud services.

PI4.5 Identify the key benefits of cloud computing.

PI4.6 Discuss the concerns and risks associated with cloud computing.

PI4.7 Explain the role of Web services in building a firm's IT applications, providing examples.

Because the overall goal of this book is for you to be an informed user of information technology, we devote this Plug IT In to a vital and cutting-edge topic: cloud computing. A working knowledge of cloud computing will enhance your appreciation of what technology can and cannot do for a business. In addition, it will enable you to make an immediate contribution by analyzing how your organization manages its IT assets. Going further, you will be using these computing resources in your career, and you will have input into decisions about how your department and organization can best utilize them. Additionally, cloud computing can be extremely valuable if you decide to start your own business.

This Plug IT In defines **cloud computing** as a type of computing that delivers convenient, on-demand, pay-as-you-go access for multiple customers to a shared pool of configurable computing resources (e.g., servers, networks, storage, applications, and services) that can be rapidly and easily accessed over the Internet. Cloud computing allows customers to acquire resources at any time and then delete them the instant they are no longer needed. We present many examples of how the cloud can be used for business purposes. In addition, the cloud provides you with personal applications. Therefore, this guide can help you plan for your own use of the cloud. For a more detailed discussion of how you can utilize the cloud, see the section titled IT's Personal: "The Cloud."

PI4.1 Introduction

You were introduced to the concept of IT infrastructure in Chapter 1. Recall that an organization's *IT infrastructure* consists of IT components—hardware, software, networks, and databases—and IT services—developing information systems, managing security and risk, and managing data. (It is helpful to review FIGURE 1.3 here.) The organization's IT infrastructure is the foundation for all of the information systems that the organization uses.

Modern IT infrastructure has evolved through several stages since the early 1950s, when firms first began to apply information technology to business applications. These stages are as follows:

- *Stand-alone mainframes.* Organizations initially used mainframe computers in their engineering and accounting departments. The mainframe was typically housed in a secure area, and only MIS personnel had access to it.

- *Mainframe and dumb terminals.* Forcing users to go to wherever the mainframe was located was time consuming and inefficient. As a result, firms began placing so-called "dumb terminals"—essentially electronic typewriters with limited processing power—in user departments. This arrangement enabled users to input computer programs into the mainframe from their departments, a process called *remote job entry*.

- *Stand-alone personal computers.* In the late 1970s, the first personal computers appeared. The IBM PC's debut in 1981 legitimized the entire personal computer market. Users began bringing personal computers to the workplace to improve their productivity—for example, by using spreadsheet and word processing applications. These computers were not initially supported by the firm's MIS department. However, as the number of personal computers increased dramatically, organizations decided to support these devices, and they established policies as to which PCs and software they would support.

- *Local area networks (client/server computing).* When personal computers are networked, individual productivity is substantially increased. For this reason, organizations began to connect personal computers into local area networks (LANs) and then connect these LANs to the mainframe, a type of processing known as *client/server computing*.

- *Enterprise computing.* In the early 1990s, organizations began to use networking standards to integrate different kinds of networks throughout the firm, thereby creating enterprise computing. As the Internet became widespread after 1995, organizations began using the TCP/IP networking protocol to integrate different types of networks. All types of hardware were networked, from mainframes to personal computers to smartphones. Software applications and data could now flow seamlessly throughout the enterprise and between organizations.

- *Cloud computing and mobile computing.* Today, organizations and individuals can use the power of cloud computing. As you will see in this Plug IT In, cloud computing provides access to a shared pool of computing resources, including computers, storage, applications, and services, over a network, typically the Internet.

Keep in mind that the computing resources in each stage can be cumulative. For instance, most large firms still use mainframe computers (in addition to all the other types of computing resources) as large servers to manage operations that involve millions of transactions per day.

As you have learned from our discussion of the evolution of IT infrastructures, the world is experiencing a digital and mobile transformation, with more information becoming available more quickly from more sources than ever before. As a result, businesspeople increasingly rely on IT-enabled services to manage this transformation and envision new opportunities.

To appreciate the transformative effects of cloud computing, you first need to understand traditional IT departments in organizations and the challenges they face. Today, most companies own their IT infrastructure (their software, hardware, networks, and data management) and maintain it "on premise" in their data centers. On-premise software, then, is the traditional model of the IT function in organizations.

Traditional IT departments spend huge amounts on both the IT infrastructure and the expert staffs they need to build and maintain complex IT systems. These expenses include physical facilities, software licenses, hardware, and staff training and salaries. Despite all of this spending, however, organizations typically do not use their infrastructure to its full capacity. The majority of these expenses are typically applied to maintaining the existing IT infrastructure, with the remainder being allocated to developing new systems. In addition, traditional IT departments are struggling to capture, store, manage, and analyze vast amounts of data. As a result of these problems, traditional IT infrastructures can actually inhibit an organization's ability to respond quickly and appropriately to today's rapidly changing business environments.

Large organizations can implement comprehensive enterprise software and hire top IT talent, but only at significant costs. These companies can buy or build software and install these systems in their data centers. They can also enable their applications to be used on different devices—desktops, laptops, tablets, and smartphones—and make them accessible to employees regardless of their location, as well as to people outside the organization, such as consultants, contractors, suppliers, customers, and other business partners. In addition, the companies' IT departments are often overtaxed and therefore unable to execute all of these functions effectively. This problem is even more acute for smaller organizations, which typically do not have the resources required to execute these functions.

As you will see in the next section, cloud computing can help organizations manage the problems that traditional IT departments face. The next section defines cloud computing and describes its essential characteristics.

--- BEFORE *YOU GO ON....* ---

1. Describe the stages in the evolution of today's IT infrastructure.

2. Describe the challenges that traditional IT departments face.

Apply The Concept PI4.1

LEARNING OBJECTIVE PI4.1 Describe the problems that modern information technology departments face.

STEP 1 – Background (This is what you are learning.)

This section has discussed the evolution of computer infrastructure over time. Early computing models were called "terminal to host"; today we have "cloud" or "distributed computing" models available. A knowledge of how infrastructure models have changed can help you understand the challenges confronting modern IT departments.

Review the evolution of IT infrastructure as presented in this section. It is likely that all businesses today have some form of a local area network (LAN) in the client/server model of computing. Beginning with that stage, consider the problems that modern IT departments face as their systems evolve.

Imagine that your boss has asked your advice on moving from traditional LAN computing, in which each department operates a separate network, toward enterprise or cloud computing. What type of challenges could you help your boss anticipate?

Write a letter to your boss (your instructor) that describes the problems that modern IT departments must address as they evolve toward enterprise and cloud computing.

PI4.2 What Is Cloud Computing?

Information technology departments have always been tasked to deliver useful IT applications to business users. For a variety of reasons, today's IT departments are facing increased challenges in delivering useful applications. As you study cloud computing, you will learn how it can help organizations manage the problems that occur in traditional IT departments. You will also discover why so many organizations are utilizing cloud computing. A survey conducted by the Open Data Center Alliance—which includes companies such as Lockheed Martin, BMW, Deutsche Bank, China Unicom, and Terremark—found that more than half of the survey respondents expect to utilize some form of cloud computing by 2015.

Cloud Computing Characteristics

The cloud computing phenomenon has several important characteristics. We take a closer look at them in this section.

Cloud Computing Provides On-Demand Self-Service. A customer can access needed computing resources automatically.

Cloud Computing Encompasses the Characteristics of Grid Computing. **Grid computing** pools various hardware and software components to create a single IT environment with shared resources. Grid computing shares the processing resources of many geographically dispersed computers across a network.

- Grid computing enables organizations to utilize their computing resources more efficiently.

- Grid computing provides fault tolerance and redundancy, meaning that there is no single point of failure, so the failure of one computer will not stop an application from executing.

- Grid computing makes it easy to *scale up*—that is, to access increased computing resources (i.e., add more servers)—to meet the processing demands of complex applications.

- Grid computing makes it easy to *scale down* (remove computers) if extensive processing is not needed.

Consider Dell Computing (www.dell.com). After years of database proliferation, Dell began to run out of physical space in its data center for its databases. The company deployed each new database on its own server. It ended up with roughly 10,000 databases, each of which ran on individual servers and spread across multiple data centers. In addition to occupying physical space, this system resulted in high costs for power, cooling, and management. Furthermore, it was taking Dell as long as two to three months to launch a new database project. The company needed to speed up the process so that it could respond more quickly to changes in its business environment.

Dell chose a grid computing solution to its problem. The solution reduced the physical database environment by 30 percent, accelerated new database project launches to less than five days, and saved the company more than $20 million.

Cloud Computing Encompasses the Characteristics of Utility Computing. In **utility computing**, a service provider makes computing resources and infrastructure management available to a customer as needed. The provider then charges the customer for its specific usage rather than a flat rate. Utility computing enables companies to efficiently meet fluctuating demands for computing power by lowering the costs of owning the hardware infrastructure.

Cloud Computing Utilizes Broad Network Access. The cloud provider's computing resources are available over a network, accessed with a Web browser, and they are configured so that they can be used with any computing device.

Cloud Computing Pools Computing Resources. The provider's computing resources are available to serve multiple customers. These resources are dynamically assigned and reassigned according to customer demand.

Cloud Computing Often Occurs on Virtualized Servers. Cloud computing providers have placed hundreds or thousands of networked servers inside massive data centers called **server farms** (see FIGURE PI4.1). Recall that a *server* is a computer that supports networks, thus enabling users to share files, software, and other network devices. Server farms require massive amounts of electrical power, air-conditioning, backup generators, and security. They also need to be located fairly closely to fiber-optic communications links (FIGURE PI4.2).

Going further, Gartner estimates that typical utilization rates on servers are very low, generally from 5 to 10 percent. That is, most of the time, organizations are utilizing only a

Media Bakery

Figure PI4.1 A server farm. Notice the ventilation in the racks and ceiling.

small percentage of their total computing capacity. CIOs tolerate this inefficiency to make certain that they can supply sufficient computing resources to users in case demand should spike. To alleviate this problem, companies and cloud computing providers are turning to virtualization.

Server virtualization uses software-based partitions to create multiple virtual servers—called *virtual machines*—on a single physical server. The major benefit of this system is that each server no longer has to be dedicated to a particular task. Instead, multiple applications can run on a single physical server, with each application running within its own software environment. As a result, virtualization enables companies to increase server utilization. In addition, companies realize cost savings in two areas. First, they do not have to buy additional servers to meet peak demand. Second, they reduce their utility costs because they are using less energy. The following example illustrates the benefits of virtualization for Amerijet International (www.amerijet.com).

When commercial and personal shippers need to move cargo quickly and reliably, they often turn to Amerijet International. The company carries more than 200 million pounds of freight annually to more than 550 destinations worldwide. Amerijet is experiencing continued global growth, but the firm's existing information systems were inadequate to support that growth. Amerijet's current systems could not provide maximum availability for critical applications. Moreover, the company had run out of space in its data center to add additional hardware.

Amerijet's worldwide cargo transportation services depend on a reliable IT infrastructure. Furthermore, the carrier needed to change its approach to IT management to support both new application development and its rapid business growth. In short, Amerijet had to turn its IT infrastructure into a business enabler.

Amerijet decided to virtualize the servers in its data center. As a result, the carrier was able to run more than 120 virtual machines on just 14 physical servers. The entire conversion process to virtualized servers took a total of just 10 hours. The benefits were compelling:

- Amerijet is able to file a flight plan for a particular aircraft in 2 minutes versus 45 minutes prior to virtualization. This faster process enables the firm to get planes in the air faster and to meet more customs cutoff times for international freight clearance. As a result, Amerijet's customers do not have to wait an extra day to receive their shipments.

- Amerijet has realized a 60 percent reduction in data center energy costs.

- Amerijet managers receive cargo inventory reports in seconds versus 30–40 minutes prior to virtualization.

- Amerijet has experienced no unplanned downtime since deployment of its virtualized servers.

With cloud computing, setting up and maintaining an IT infrastructure need no longer be a challenge for an organization. Businesses do not have to scramble to meet the evolving needs of developing applications. In addition, cloud computing reduces upfront capital expenses and

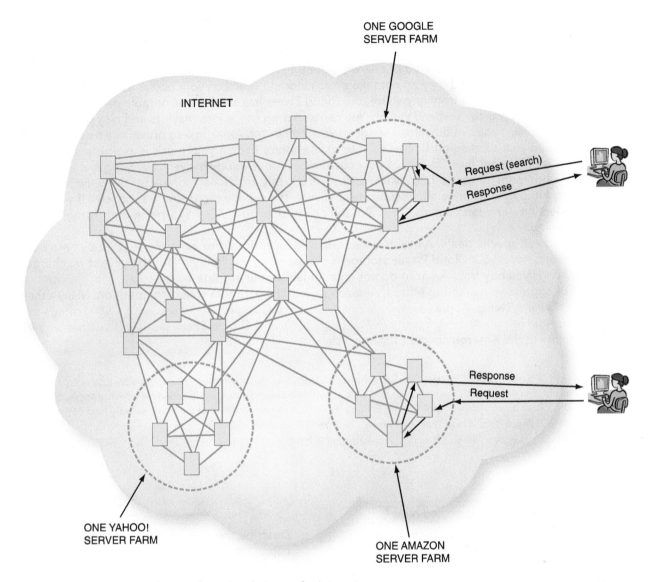

Figure PI4.2 Organizational server farms in relation to the Internet.

operational costs, and it enables businesses to better utilize their infrastructure and to share it from one project to the next. In general, cloud computing eases the difficult tasks of procuring, configuring, and maintaining hardware and software environments. In addition, it allows enterprises to get their applications up and run faster, with easier manageability and less maintenance. It also enables IT to adjust IT resources (e.g., servers, storage, and networking) more rapidly to meet fluctuating and unpredictable business demand.

EXAMPLE

Amazon, whose online music store competes with Apple's (www.apple.com/icloud), has "moved music into its cloud" to solve two problems. The first problem is that music libraries have typically been scattered. For example, when you bought a new song at home, you could not listen to it at work, at least not without copying it manually. You could buy a song on your phone, but you had to perform a sync to download it onto your computer. Moreover, if your music library was large, then you could fit only a portion of it onto your phone. The second problem is that Amazon wants more people to buy music from its proprietary store instead of from iTunes.

In March 2011, Amazon released a package of software and services that solved both problems. The fundamental idea behind the new package is that your music collection will reside in the cloud. That way, you can conveniently listen to it from any computer—at home, at work, at a friend's home—by logging into a special Web page called the Amazon Cloud Player (www.amazon.com/clouddrive). You can also listen to any of the songs in your music collection on an Android phone without having to copy or sync the music. All of your songs are always available everywhere, and they do not take up any storage space on your phone itself.

In addition to being accessible from anywhere, the Cloud Player has some other notable perks. It contains a list of your songs, which you can sort and search. You can also drag songs into playlists and play back a song, an album, or a playlist. Plus, you can download songs to your computer. Amazon also provides a free Uploader app that lets you send your existing music files to your online library so that your music is available anywhere.

The Cloud Player is almost free. To attract new customers, Amazon offers everyone 5 gigabytes of free space online—enough room for about 1,200 MP3 songs. You can buy additional storage for the price of $1 per gigabyte per year. Although this price might seem insignificant, the service can become expensive if you have a huge music collection—enough to make sites like Rhapsody that offer "pay $15 per month for unlimited music" look appealing.

In addition to these special deals, Amazon is also offering incentives. For example, if you buy an album from Amazon's music store, your Cloud Player storage is increased to 20 gigabytes for the year at no charge. In addition, any songs you buy from Amazon do not count against your storage limit.

Despite these aggressive marketing efforts, Amazon's Cloud Player faces tough competition. Many other companies offer similar systems. Apple (www.apple.com/icloud) and Google (http://music.google.com) offer similar services. Also, Rdio (www.rdio.com), Spotify (www.spotify.com), and GrooveShark (www.grooveshark.com) all offer some elements of the Amazon concept for less money.

Sources: Compiled from D. Sung, "Apple iCloud vs. Google vs. Amazon Cloud Drive vs. Dropbox vs. Microsoft SkyDrive," *Pocket Lint,* April 26, 2012; A. Kingsley-Hughes, "The Dangerous Side of Apple's iCloud," *Forbes,* August 4, 2012; L. Bedigian, "What Apple, Google Need to Beat Amazon's Cloud Drive," *Forbes,* April 1, 2011; E. Bott, "How Amazon Has Outsmarted the Music Industry (and Apple)," *ZDNet,* March 30, 2011; D. Pogue, "The Cloud That Rains Music," *New York Times,* March 30, 2011; www.amazon.com/clouddrive, www.apple.com/icloud, http://music.google.com, accessed April 1, 2014.

Businesses are increasingly employing cloud computing for important and innovative work. The next example illustrates how Amazon has successfully "moved music into the cloud."

In the next section, you learn about the various ways in which customers (individuals and organizations) can implement cloud computing. Specifically, you will read about public clouds, private clouds, hybrid clouds, and vertical clouds.

> ┌─ BEFORE *YOU GO ON....* ─┐
> 1. Describe the characteristics of cloud computing.
> 2. Define server virtualization.

Apply The Concept PI4.2

LEARNING OBJECTIVE PI4.2 Describe the key characteristics and advantages of cloud computing.

STEP 1 – Background

One of the more popular virtual servers is a virtual Web server offered by Web hosting companies. Historically, someone would simply purchase and share space on a server that would host his or her files. However, many people today need dedicated servers that guarantee performance for their consumers.

STEP 2 – Activity

Visit http://www.wiley.com/go/rainer/MIS3e/applytheconcept, and click on the link provided for Apply the Concept PI4.2. This link will take you to a case study on an offshore drilling company, Seadrill, that migrated from in-house data centers to a virtual private cloud data center.

As you review the site, focus carefully on the advantages and concerns mentioned in the case study.

STEP 3 – Deliverable

In a Word document, describe the key characteristics and advantages of cloud computing for Seadrill. Submit your document to your instructor.

PI4.3 Different Types of Clouds

There are three major types of cloud computing that companies provide to customers or groups of customers: public clouds, private clouds, and hybrid clouds. A fourth type of cloud computing is called vertical clouds (FIGURE PI4.3).

Public Cloud

Public clouds are shared, easily accessible, multicustomer IT infrastructures that are available nonexclusively to any entity in the general public (individuals, groups, and/or organizations). Public cloud vendors provide applications, storage, and other computing resources as services over the Internet. These services may be free or offered on a pay-per-usage model.

Movirtu, a private technology company, is an example of a public cloud. Significantly, it is playing a major role in addressing a widespread global problem. In the developing world, people commonly share their mobile phones. They frequently use their own SIM card, which they switch in and out when they borrow a mobile device. This practice can compromise privacy, however. In addition, SIM cards are easy to lose.

Now, millions of impoverished citizens in Africa and Asia will receive mobile phone numbers under a plan developed by the United Nations. Movirtu (www.movirtu.com) is a cloud-based phone service that allows people to manage their own mobile network accounts—phone number, voice mail, texting, etc.—without ever owning a phone or a SIM card. Movirtu prices its service with lower-income users in mind, and it shares its profits with the mobile network carriers.

Under the UN plan, Movirtu will supply low-cost mobile phone numbers to participants, who can use any mobile device to log in with their own number to make and receive calls and to access information and services. The primary beneficiaries

will be women in rural communities in South Asia and sub-Saharan Africa, because they are far less likely than men to own their own phones.

Movirtu had deployed this technology to 12 or more markets in the selected regions by early 2014, thereby improving the lives and expanding the earning potential of at least 50 million people. The company selected Madagascar, an island nation off Africa's east coast, as a starting point. This country has an extensive network, but many of its citizens cannot afford their own phone. The service became available throughout the island via a local carrier in August 2011.

Private Cloud

Private clouds (also known as *internal clouds* or *corporate clouds*) are IT infrastructures that can be accessed only by a single entity or by an exclusive group of related entities that share the same purpose and requirements, such as all of the business units within a single organization. Private clouds provide IT activities and applications as a service over an intranet within an enterprise. Enterprises adopt private clouds to ensure system and data security. For this reason these systems are implemented behind the corporate firewall. As an example of a private cloud, let's take a look at Credit Agricole.

Credit Agricole (www.credit-agricole.com), the largest retail bank in France and one of the largest financial services groups in Europe, serves 25 million customers every day. The bank is undergoing a business transformation. Its objective is to redefine its business processes to ensure that it can deliver the best possible customer service while simultaneously enhancing its profitability. IT transformation is a key pillar of that transformation.

The bank's IT group recognized that a private cloud strategy would deliver both the agility needed to support a rapidly changing business environment and the efficiency needed to

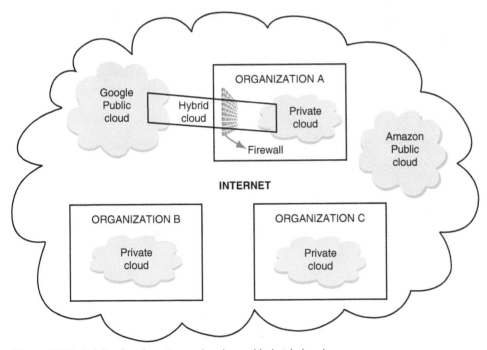

Figure PI4.3 Public clouds, private clouds, and hybrid clouds.

make the bank more profitable. Their solution was to simplify the bank's IT operations by utilizing the private cloud to run a broad array of critical production systems on a standardized infrastructure. An additional goal was to minimize the deployment risk because so much was at stake for the bank and its business transformation.

After deploying its private cloud, the bank realized its immediate and significant benefits. The bank's applications now run much faster, and the costs of its IT operations have dropped. As one example, one of the bank's business units realized a 25 percent savings after it moved to the private cloud. The primary benefit, however, has been the increased agility. The bank now possesses the flexibility to adjust to rapidly changing business conditions.

Hybrid Cloud

Hybrid clouds are composed of public and private clouds that remain unique entities, but are nevertheless tightly integrated. This arrangement offers users the benefits of multiple deployment models. Hybrid clouds deliver services based on security requirements, the mission-critical nature of the applications, and other company-established policies. For example, customers may need to maintain some of their data in a private cloud for security and privacy reasons while storing other, less-sensitive data in a public cloud because it is less expensive. Let's examine two examples of hybrid cloud computing.

Boeing (www.boeing.com) is among the world's largest aircraft manufacturers. The company has developed two hybrid cloud-computing applications.

The first application enables Boeing to track all of the flight paths that planes take around the world. Boeing's sales staff uses the app to help sell aircraft by demonstrating how a newer, faster plane could improve operations. The app incorporates both historical and real-time data, which creates some computationally heavy workloads. Therefore, the app requires huge amounts of processing power to collect the data, analyze them, and present them in a user-friendly format.

The application was running on five connected, synchronized laptop computers. When Boeing's IT team wanted to migrate the app to the cloud, they needed approval from Boeing's internal security and legal teams.

In order to protect proprietary data in the app, Boeing uses a process it calls "shred and scatter." Boeing takes the data it plans to put in the cloud and breaks them up into the equivalent of puzzle pieces. Those pieces are then encrypted and sent to Microsoft's Azure Cloud, where they are stored and processed. To gather any actionable information, however, the user must reassemble the data on Boeing's cloud behind the company's firewall.

In the second application, Boeing uses Amazon's Web Services cloud along with on-premise Boeing software to create a hybrid application. The app is essentially a Digital Toolbox that allows mechanics around the world to research, conduct, and verify maintenance and repairs performed on Boeing aircraft. It combines data that Boeing hosts itself about its own planes with repair information from other aircraft manufacturers. The app automatically and seamlessly routes users to information inside Boeing's data centers if it is stored there, or to Amazon's Web Services cloud if the information is from another airline. The app has been a success because many of the large airlines work with multiple aircraft manufacturers (e.g., Boeing and Airbus), but they can go to Boeing to get the Digital Toolbox information from a variety of manufacturers.

Vertical Clouds

It is now possible to build cloud infrastructure and applications for different businesses—the construction, finance, or insurance businesses, for example—thus building vertical clouds (see www.vertical-cloud.com).

BEFORE YOU GO ON....

1. What is a public cloud?
2. What is a private cloud?
3. What is a hybrid cloud?
4. What is a vertical cloud?

Apply The Concept PI4.3

LEARNING OBJECTIVE PI4.3 Identify a use case scenario for each of the four types of clouds.

STEP 1 – Background

This section describes four types of clouds: public, private, hybrid, and vertical. The common feature among all four types is that resources are hosted remotely and made available to a wide range of devices over high-speed Internet connections. All four types display the basic features of the cloud that were presented in earlier sections. However, the applications of these features differ for each type.

STEP 2 – Activity

Refer to the Boeing example presented in this section. Boeing employs a hybrid cloud. As you have seen, there are many possible strategies for utilizing the cloud. Imagine a use case scenario for Boeing for each type of cloud.

STEP 3 – Deliverable

Build a table that identifies a use case scenario for each of the four types of clouds for Boeing.

PI4.4 Cloud Computing Services

Cloud computing services are based on three models: infrastructure-as-a-service (IaaS), platform-as-a-service (PaaS), and software-as-a-service (SaaS). These models represent the three types of computing generally required by consumers: infrastructure to run software and store data (IaaS), platforms to develop applications (PaaS), and software applications to process their data (SaaS). FIGURE PI4.4 illustrates the differences among the three models.

As you examine the figure from left to right, note that the customer manages the service less and less, and the vendor manages it more and more.

Although each model has its distinctive features, all three share certain characteristics. First, customers rent them instead of buying them. This arrangement shifts IT from a capital expense to an operating expense. Second, vendors are responsible for maintenance, administration, capacity planning, troubleshooting, and backups. Finally, obtaining additional computing resources—that is, scale from the cloud—is usually fast and easy. Examples are more storage from an IaaS vendor, the ability to handle more PaaS projects, and more users of a SaaS application.

Infrastructure as a Service

With the **infrastructure-as-a-service** (IaaS) model, cloud computing providers offer remotely accessible servers, networks, and storage capacity. They supply these resources on demand from their large resource pools, which are located in their data centers.

IaaS customers are often technology companies with IT expertise. These companies want access to computing power, but they do not want to be responsible for installing or maintaining it. Companies use the infrastructure to run software or simply to store data.

To deploy their applications, IaaS users install their operating system and their application software on the cloud computing provider's computers. They can deploy any software on this infrastructure, including different operating systems, applications, and development platforms. Each user is responsible for maintaining their operating system and application software. Cloud providers typically bill IaaS services on a utility computing basis—that is, the cost reflects the amount of resources the user consumes.

Amazon is a well-known IaaS provider. The company sells the spare capacity of its vast IT infrastructure to its customers in a cloud environment. These services include its Simple Storage Service (S3) for storing their customers' data and its Elastic Compute Cloud (EC2) service for operating their customers' applications. Customers pay only for the amount of storage and computing they use.

To illustrate IaaS, let's examine Courtagen Life Sciences (www.courtagen.com). This firm operates a DNA sequencing laboratory. To analyze one person's genome, Courtagen runs a workload that is computationally intensive for two to three hours, requiring 15–16 Amazon virtualized server instances or virtual machines. (A server instance, or virtual machine, is a software partition of a physical server. Recall our discussion of virtualization in PI4.2). The analysis employs Courtagen's Ziphyr bioinformatics software to examine the patient's genome sequence and search medical journals and online patient forums. The software then integrates the results and creates a report for doctors that combines an individual's genomic information with the most relevant, recent research. Courtagen's goal is to find subtle inferences in the data that are currently missing from the medical system.

ON-PREMISE SOFTWARE	INFRASTRUCTURE-AS-A-SERVICE	PLATFORM-AS-A-SERVICE	SOFTWARE-AS-A-SERVICE
CUSTOMER MANAGES: Applications, Data, Operating system, Servers, Virtualization, Storage, Networking	CUSTOMER MANAGES: Applications, Data, Operating system. VENDOR MANAGES: Servers, Virtualization, Storage, Networking	CUSTOMER MANAGES: Applications, Data. VENDOR MANAGES: Operating system, Servers, Virtualization, Storage, Networking	VENDOR MANAGES: Applications, Data, Operating system, Servers, Virtualization, Storage, Networking
Examples	Amazon, IBM, Google, Microsoft, Rackspace	Mircosoft Windows Azure, Google App Engine, Force.com	Salesforce.com, Google Apps, Dropbox, Apple iCloud, Box.net

Figure PI4.4 Comparison of on-premise software, infrastructure-as-a-service, platform-as-a-service, and software-as-a-service.

Courtagen operates without a supporting data center. Instead, the company relies on Amazon Web Services (AWS) infrastructure-as-a-service. (We discuss Web services later in this Plug IT In.) One critical feature that influenced Courtagen's decision to select Amazon was the option to buy cloud computing at bargain rates in the middle of the night or on weekends, when demand is lower. Amazon offers set prices for on-demand services, set prices for reserved virtual machines, and spot prices for virtual machines that vary with demand. Amazon's spot marketplace allows companies to bid a rate at which they would run a computing job, and Amazon decides if it has the capacity to perform the operation at that price. Courtagen's staff watches for dropping prices on Amazon Spot Instances to find the right price to bid.

Courtagen asserts that Amazon meets its business IT needs–the capacity to handle effectively computationally intensive tasks, adequate security to safely handle personal information, and minimal operating costs. In mid-2014, Courtagen was analyzing about 200 people's genomes per month, and the company was growing roughly 20 percent per month.

Platform as a Service

In the **platform-as-a-service** (PaaS) model, customers rent servers, operating systems, storage, a database, software development technologies such as Java and .NET, and network capacity over the Internet. The PaaS model allows the customer both to run existing applications and to develop and test new applications.

PaaS offers customers several advantages, which include the following:

- Application developers can develop and run their software solutions on a cloud platform without the cost and complexity of buying and managing the underlying hardware and software layers.

- Underlying computing and storage resources automatically scale to match application demand.

- Operating system features can be upgraded frequently.

- Geographically distributed development teams can work together on software development projects.

- PaaS services can be provided by diverse sources located throughout the world.

- Initial and ongoing costs can be reduced by the use of infrastructure services from a single vendor rather than maintaining multiple hardware facilities that often perform duplicate functions or suffer from incompatibility problems.

As an example of an entity that employed PaaS to improve its performance, consider the city of Miami (www.miamigov.com). Miami has created a service that monitors nonemergency 311 requests. City officials and local residents can access a Web site that pulls up a map of the city with pins in every spot that is tied to a 311 complaint. Before cloud computing became available, the city needed three months to develop the concept, purchase new hardware (including backups in case of a hurricane), hire a team to install the necessary software, and then build the application. In contrast, by utilizing PaaS, Miami created a working prototype within eight days, and it deployed the application shortly thereafter.

Software as a Service

With the **software-as-a-service (SaaS)** delivery model, cloud computing vendors provide software that is specific to their customers' requirements. SaaS is the most widely utilized service model, and it provides a broad range of software applications. SaaS providers typically charge their customers a monthly or yearly subscription fee.

SaaS applications reside in the cloud instead of on a user's hard drive or in a data center. The host manages the software and the infrastructure that runs this software and stores the customer's data. The customers do not control either the software, beyond the usual configuration settings, or the infrastructure, beyond changing the resources they use, such as the amount of disk space required for their data. This process eliminates the need to install and run the application on the user's computers, thereby simplifying maintenance and support.

What differentiates SaaS applications from other applications is their ability to scale. As a result, applications can run on as many servers as is necessary to meet changing demands. This process is transparent to the user.

To reduce the risk of an infrastructure outage, SaaS providers regularly back up all of their customers' data. Customers can also back up their data on their storage hardware.

To understand how SaaS operates, consider the case of AAA Northern California, Nevada, and Utah (AAA NCNU) (http://calstate.aaa.com), formerly known as the California State Automobile Association, which is one of the largest motor clubs in the American Automobile Association (AAA) National Federation. The club needed to replace its old human resource (HR) management and financial management (FM) systems. For example, the FM system alone contained 6,000 charts of accounts. Furthermore, the club had overcustomized its HR and FM systems, which made them difficult to maintain and enhance in order to respond to changing business conditions.

The club chose Workday (www.workday.com) for its new IT platform for its FM and HR systems. Workday provides software-as-a-service offerings for enterprisewide HR and FM systems. In addition to the benefits of SaaS offerings, the Workday system tightly integrates the HR and FM systems, thereby enhancing real-time visibility into the business. For instance, the ability to immediately identify how a change in the number of employees at any of the nearly 100 field offices might affect that location's profit-and-loss statement has taken managerial capabilities to a new level.

IT'S PERSONAL: "THE CLOUD"

This Plug IT In defines the cloud as distributed computing services, and it presents many examples of how the cloud can be used for both personal and business purposes. This IT's Personal is intended to help you differentiate between the business and personal applications of the cloud and to help you plan for your own use of the cloud.

First, you need to understand that there is no single "cloud." Rather, almost all businesses refer to their Internet-based services as "cloud services." Basically, anything you do over the Internet that you used to do on a local computer is a form of cloud computing. When you store files on Dropbox, create a document using Google Docs, use iCloud to store purchases or sync documents, or use OnLive on your iPad, you are using cloud-based services that are intended for personal use.

Infrastructure-as-a-service is an important application of the cloud for personal purposes. Dropbox is one of the most prominent companies in this area. In the past, users had to carry around a USB drive, a CD, an external hard drive, or (way back in the day) floppy discs to store their personal information. Today, users can employ Dropbox for this purpose. At the time of this writing, a free Dropbox account offered 2 GB of online storage. Not only does Dropbox offer you a place to store your files (eliminating the need for a personal infrastructure of removable storage), but it also provides synchronization across computers and access from mobile devices!

Virtualization is gaining ground. If you have an iPad, you should look up the app called "OnLive" and give it a test run. OnLive allows you to log into a virtual computer that is running Windows 7 or Windows 8. Here, your iPad is simply providing the input/output, and the server is "serving up" a virtual operating system. It is very likely that one day your home computer will be virtual as well.

Software-as-a-service has been a popular option for quite some time. For example, Google Docs offers Internet-based word processing, spreadsheet, presentation, forms, and drawing tools. Recently, Microsoft has moved into the game with their Microsoft Office 365 product. Basically, each of these services allows you to use a computer program without having to install it on your computer or mobile device. You simply access the entire program (and your saved files) over the Internet.

Google recently combined a couple of these cloud services with Google Drive, a service that offers the same services as Dropbox in addition to Google Docs' online editing and file-sharing capabilities. This also crosses over with SaaS because of the added benefit of Google Docs. It is very likely that one day Google will merge virtualization, infrastructure, and software into a single cloud-based service. If this technology becomes available, then all you will need as a consumer is an Internet-connected device, and you will be able to store, access, edit, and share your files from the cloud. You will also be able to choose apps to run on your "virtual machine" much the way you currently purchase applications for your mobile devices from a vendor-approved store.

So, what is the point? Simply, cloud-based services are here to stay. The rise of ubiquitous Internet access has engendered a new world of possibilities.

A word of caution, however. Along with its seemingly endless possibilities, cloud computing raises many critical security and privacy issues. Because your files, apps, and editing capability will no longer be stored on a local machine, they are only as safe as the company to which you have entrusted them makes them. So, when you select a cloud provider, make sure you choose wisely!

After one year, the club has reduced the total cost of ownership of its FM and HR systems—including IT support, maintenance, and licensing—by 60 percent. Additionally, those 6,000 charts of accounts now number just 80. This dramatic reduction has greatly simplified administrative tasks while improving reporting and analysis.

As we previously discussed, a major concern related to cloud computing is security. In the case of AAA NCNU, the company's CIO realized she was taking risks as she handed over her company's HR and FM computing tasks to Workday. What would happen, for example, if Workday lost sensitive employee and/or financial data? Fortunately, the company's employee information has remained secure.

A subset of SaaS is the *desktop-as-a-service* (DaaS) model, also known as a *cloud desktop* or *desktop in the cloud*. In this model, a SaaS provider hosts a software environment for a desktop personal computer, including productivity and collaboration software—spreadsheets, word processing programs, and so on—such as Google Apps, Microsoft 365, and other products. Significantly, in DaaS only a thin client (discussed in Plug IT In 2) can access all the required software. The DaaS model can be financially advantageous for consumers because they do need to purchase a fully configured personal computer, or fat client. In addition, this model makes the PC environment simpler to deploy and administer.

BEFORE *YOU GO ON....*

1. Describe infrastructure-as-a-service.
2. Describe platform-as-a-service.
3. Describe software-as-a-service.

Apply The Concept PI4.4

STEP 1 – Background

Infrastructure-as-a-service (IaaS), platform-as-a-service (PaaS), and software-as-a-service (SaaS) are relatively new processing models made available by the rise in dependable, high-speed Internet access and powerful "host-computer" processing capabilities. The three cloud models are differentiated by how users employ them and which services providers offer with each one.

STEP 2 – Activity

Review the material in this section. For each operational model, consider who owns the infrastructure, the operating systems, and the applications.

STEP 3 – Deliverable

In a Word document, explain the operational model for each of the three types of cloud services by highlighting the differences in who is responsible for the infrastructure, the operating systems, and the applications for each model. Submit your document to your instructor.

PI 4.5 The Benefits of Cloud Computing

Cloud computing offers benefits for both individuals and organizations. It allows companies to increase the scale and power of their IT and the speed at which it can be deployed and accessed. It eliminates administrative problems and it operates across locations, devices, and organizational boundaries.

Nearly half of the respondents in a recent CIO Economic Impact survey indicated that they evaluate cloud computing options first—before traditional IT approaches—before making any new IT investments. IBM predicts that the global cloud computing market will grow 22 percent annually to $241 billion by 2020. Next we examine three major benefits that cloud computing provides to individuals and organizations.

Benefit 1: Cloud Computing Has a Positive Impact on Employees

Cloud computing enables companies to provide their employees with access to all the information they need no matter where they are, what device they are using, or with whom they are working. Consider this example.

The attorneys of one multistate law firm needed to access documents and data on a constant basis. Since 2000, the firm's data volume had expanded from 30 gigabytes to more than 40 terabytes. Moreover, all of these data have to be stored and accessed securely. In the past, attorneys often had to manually copy case-relevant data onto external hard drives and USB devices, and then ship these devices back and forth among themselves and the firm's headquarters. These processes were nonsecure, time-consuming, and expensive.

To address these needs, the law firm turned to cloud computing for data storage, offsite disaster recovery, and multisite access within a highly secure public cloud. Rather than maintaining a massive inventory of extra storage as required by its old IT infrastructure, the firm can now increase storage capacity on demand. The cloud provides attorneys with constant access via encrypted communication channels. Furthermore, the cloud facilitates collaboration among distributed teams of attorneys, thereby increasing their overall productivity. The cloud environment has made the firm's attorneys much more efficient and the firm's IT expenses have declined by 60 percent.

Benefit 2: Cloud Computing Can Save Money

Over time, the cost of building and operating an on-premise IT infrastructure will typically be more expensive than implementing the cloud computing. Cloud providers purchase massive amounts of IT infrastructure (e.g., hardware and bandwidth) and gain cost savings by buying in large quantity. As a result, these providers continually take advantage of Moore's law (discussed in Plug IT In 2). For example, the Amazon cloud, known as Amazon Web Services, reduced its prices a dozen times between 2008 and 2012.

As a result, cloud computing can reduce or eliminate the need to purchase hardware, build and install software, and pay software licensing fees. The organization pays only for the computing resources it needs, and then only when it needs them. This pay-for-use model provides greater flexibility and it eliminates or reduces the need for significant capital expenditures.

For example, State Street Bank (www.statestreet.com) in Boston creates its own highly customized software to manage its assets. In fact, the bank spends some 25 percent of its annual IT budget on software development. In addition, State Street's data center contains a broad array of best-of-breed systems. Integrating these systems, a job the State Street traditionally has performed in-house, is quite expensive.

Consequently, State Street is implementing a private cloud to achieve approximately $600 million in cost savings from reduced amounts of software development and a reduced need for systems integration.

Benefit 3: Cloud Computing Can Improve Organizational Flexibility and Competitiveness

Cloud computing allows organizations to use only the amount of computing resources they need at a given time. Therefore, companies can efficiently scale their operations up or down as needed to meet rapidly changing business conditions. Cloud computing is also able to deliver computing services faster than the on-premise computing.

Consider College Hunks Hauling Junk (CHHJ) (www .collegehunkshaulingjunk.com), a moving junk removal company with 43 franchises around the country. CHHJ was experiencing numerous issues with the proprietary software system it was using to run its scheduling and franchising operations. When CHHJ first deployed this system, it was exclusively a junk removal company. Over time, however, it had added new and more complex operations, such as moving customers' goods. The original system did not easily support these new lines of business. In addition, CHHJ needed a system that could collect different types of data and

produce necessary reports based on an analysis of those data. Essentially, CHHJ needed a system that could accommodate all of its service lines while providing flexibility for continued growth, in both new areas of business and new franchises.

CHHJ turned to Waterstreet Technology Group (www .waterstreet.net) to develop an entirely new system. Waterstreet developed the software and housed it on its own servers. CHHJ uses the software as a SaaS product. The software supports CHHJ's junk removal and moving businesses as well as its franchise operations and call center.

The new software provides much improved reporting on data gathered from CHHJ customers and franchisees. This capability enables CHHJ to provide better customer service and to support its expanding franchise business more effectively. In addition, the software allows CHHJ to expand its lines of business and its franchises.

BEFORE YOU GO ON....

1. Describe how cloud computing can help organizations expand the scope of their business operations.

2. Describe how cloud computing can help organizations respond quickly to market changes.

Apply The Concept PI4.5

LEARNING OBJECTIVE PI4.5 Identify the key benefits of cloud computing.

STEP 1 – Background

This section has outlined the benefits that are driving many organizations to transition to cloud computing. Productivity, cost reductions, collaboration, more robust data mining, flexibility, and scope expansion are just the beginning. Cloud computing is a powerful tool that is changing the ways we do business.

STEP 2 – Activity

Visit http://www.wiley.com/go/rainer/MIS3e/applytheconcept, and click on the link provided for Apply the Concept PI4.5. This link will take you to the amazon.com site that describes Amazon's business cloud services. This site contains several customer testimonials. As you watch them, look for common benefits the various customers receive from cloud computing.

STEP 3 – Deliverable

Based on the video and the material in this section, identify the key benefits of cloud computing that amazon.com offers its business customers.

PI4.6 Concerns and Risks with Cloud Computing

Gartner predicts that cloud computing will grow at an annual rate of 19 percent through the year 2015. Even if this prediction is accurate, however, cloud computing will still account for less than 5 percent of total worldwide IT spending that year. Why is this percentage so low? The reason is that there are serious concerns with cloud computing. These concerns fall into six categories: legacy IT systems, reliability, privacy, security, the legal and regulatory environment, and criminal use of cloud computing.

Concern 1: Legacy IT Systems

Historically, organizational IT systems have accumulated a diversity of hardware, operating systems, and applications. When bundled together, these systems are called "legacy spaghetti." These systems cannot easily be transferred to the cloud because they must first be untangled and simplified. Furthermore, many IT professionals have vested interests in various legacy systems, and they resist efforts to exchange these systems for cloud computing.

Concern 2: Reliability

Many skeptics contend that cloud computing is not as reliable as a well-managed, on-premise IT infrastructure. The cloud's reliability was called into question in April 2011 when large parts of Amazon's Web Services infrastructure went down for as long as three days (see the example below). This outage created serious problems for many companies that used the service. Although the outage was serious, however, it affected only one of Amazon's U.S. data centers. Amazon had also explicitly advised its customers to design their IT architectures to withstand a service interruption. Other cloud companies have learned from Amazon's experience, and they are improving the redundancy and reliability of their offerings.

Concern 3: Privacy

Privacy advocates have criticized cloud computing for posing a major threat to privacy because the providers control, and thus lawfully or unlawfully monitor, the data and

EXAMPLE

Amazon Web Services (AWS) (http://aws.amazon.com) is designed with backups to the backups' backups to prevent its hosted Web sites and applications from failing. Despite all of these safety measures, however, in April 2011 Amazon's cloud crashed, taking with it Reddit (www.reddit.com), Quora (www.quora.com), FourSquare (www.foursquare.com), ProPublica (www.propublica.org), parts of *The New York Times* (www.nytimes.com), and about 70 other Web sites. The massive outage raised questions about the reliability of Amazon Web Services and about the cloud itself.

Thousands of companies use Amazon Web Services to run their Web sites through a service called Elastic Compute Cloud (EC2). Rather than hosting their sites on their own servers, these customers essentially rent some of Amazon's unused server capacity. EC2 is hosted in five regions: Virginia, California, Ireland, Tokyo, and Singapore. Within each region are multiple "availability zones," and within each availability zone are multiple "locations" or data centers.

Amazon assured its customers that its method of linking together many different data centers would protect them from isolated failures. It promised to keep customers' sites up and running 99.95 percent of the year, or it would reduce their monthly bills by 10 percent. Based on these claims, customers could be down a maximum of just 4.4 hours in a year. In fact, during the outage, some customers' Web sites were down for days.

The crash occurred at Amazon's Virginia data center, located in one of the company's East Coast availability zones. Amazon claimed that a "networking event" caused a domino effect across other availability zones in that region, which in turn caused many of its storage volumes to create backups of themselves. That process filled up Amazon's available storage capacity, and it prevented some Web sites from accessing their data. Amazon did not reveal what the "networking event" was.

Web sites like Quora and Reddit were able to come back online in "read-only" mode, but users were not able to post new content for many hours. Many experts blamed Amazon's customers themselves, asserting that their Web sites should have spread out their processing among multiple geographical regions to take full advantage of Amazon's backup systems. In fact, sites like Reddit were simply following the instructions that Amazon provided in its service agreement, which states that hosting in a single region should be sufficient. Furthermore, some smaller companies could not afford the resources needed to duplicate their infrastructure in data centers all over the world.

One company that experienced an Amazon outage was able to put a dollar figure on the resulting damage. Amazon outages completely took down the online dating site WhatsYourPrice (www.whatsyourprice.com). Men and women create profiles on the site, featuring the basic information a person would find on most dating sites. However, women also include the amount of money they would accept from someone to go on a date with him. Men browse the profiles and make offers to women who "catch their eye." After a man makes an offer, the woman checks his profile. She then can choose to accept the offer, reject it, or come up with a different price.

During a two-hour outage, the WhatsYour Price staff fielded nearly 1,000 complaints from users who were trying to make a date. The outage did more than simply tarnish the reputation of WhatsYourPrice.com and leave its customers without dates. The company estimates that the two hours during which it was unable to operate cost it almost $8,000 in lost commissions.

Sources: Compiled from M. Boisvert, "Still Single? Blame the Recent Amazon EC2 Outages," *SearchCloudComputing.com*, July 13, 2012; S. Johnston, "Cloud Outage Report of 13 Providers Reveals Downtime Costs," *SearchCloudComputing.com*, June 22, 2012; S. Johnston, "Will Amazon's Outage Cause Would-Be Cloud Adopters to Run Screaming?" *SearchCloudComputing.com*, June 20, 2012; C. Brooks, "A Crack in the Cloud: Why the Amazon Outage Caught So Many by Surprise," *SearchCloudComputing.com*, April 27, 2011; D. Goldman, "Why Amazon's Cloud Titanic Went Down," *CNN Money*, April 22, 2011; J. Brodkin, "Amazon EC2 Outage Calls 'Availability Zones' into Question," *CIO*, April 21, 2011; http://aws.amazon.com, accessed March 19, 2014.

communication stored between the user and the host company. For example, AT&T and Verizon collaborated with NSA to use cloud computing to record more than 10 million phone calls between American citizens. In addition, providers could accidentally or deliberately alter or even delete some information.

Using a cloud computing, provider also complicates data privacy because of the extent to which cloud processing and cloud storage are used to implement cloud services. The point is that customer data may not remain on the same system or in the same data center. This situation can lead to legal concerns over jurisdiction.

There have been efforts to address this problem by integrating the legal environment. One example is the US-EU Safe Harbor, a streamlined process for U.S. companies to comply with the European Union directive on the protection of personal data.

Concern 4: Security

Critics also question how secure cloud computing really is. Because the characteristics of cloud computing can differ widely from those of traditional IT architectures, providers need to reconsider the effectiveness and efficiency of traditional security mechanisms. Security issues include access to sensitive data, data segregation (among customers), privacy, error exploitation, recovery, accountability, malicious insiders, and account control.

The security of cloud computing services is a contentious issue that may be delaying the adoption of this technology. Security issues arise primarily from the unease of both the private and public sectors with the external management of security-based services. The fact that providers manage these services provides great incentive for them to prioritize building and maintaining strong security services.

Another security issue involves the control over who is able to access and utilize the information stored in the cloud. (Recall our discussion of least privilege in Chapter 7.) Many organizations exercise least privilege controls effectively with their on-premise IT infrastructures. Some cloud computing environments, in contrast, cannot exercise least privilege controls effectively. This problem occurs because cloud computing environments were originally designed for individuals or groups, not for hierarchical organizations in which some people have both the right and the responsibility to exercise control over other people's private information. To address this problem, cloud computing vendors are working to incorporate administrative, least-privilege functionality into their products. In fact, many have already done so.

Security experts note that the best strategies to achieve excellent security are to constantly monitor the threat landscape, to buy or build the best technologies to protect devices and networks, and to hire and retain top digital security specialists. Cloud computing vendors are better able to do these things than all but the very largest and most security-conscious organizations.

Concern 5: The Regulatory and Legal Environment

There are numerous legal and regulatory barriers to cloud computing, many of which involve data access and transport. For example, the European Union prohibits consumer data from being transferred to nonmember countries without the consumers' prior consent and approval. Companies located outside the European Union can overcome this restriction by demonstrating that they provide a "safe harbor" for the data. Some countries, such as Germany, have enacted even more restrictive data export laws. Cloud computing vendors are aware of these regulations and laws, and they are working to modify their offerings so that they can assure customers and regulators that data entrusted to them are secure enough to meet all of these requirements.

To obtain compliance with regulations such as the Federal Information Security Management Act (FISMA), the Health Insurance Portability and Accountability Act (HIPAA), and the Sarbanes-Oxley Act in the United States, the Data Protection Directive in the European Union, and the credit card industry's Payment Card Industry's Data Security Standard (PCI DSS), cloud computing customers may have to adopt hybrid deployment modes that are typically more expensive and may offer restricted benefits. This process is how, for example, Google is able to "manage and meet additional government policy requirements beyond FISMA," and Rackspace (www.rackspace.com) is able to claim PCI compliance. FISMA requires each federal agency to develop, document, and implement a program to provide information security for the infor- mation and information systems that support the operations of the agency, including those provided by contractors. PCI DSS is a set of requirements designed to ensure that all companies that process, store, or transmit credit card information maintain a secure environment.

Concern 6: Criminal Use of Cloud Computing

The cloud opens up a world of possibilities for criminal computing. Cloud computing makes available a well-managed, generally reliable, scalable global infrastructure that is, unfortunately, as well suited to illegal computing activities as it is to legitimate business activities.

The huge amount of information stored in the cloud—including, most likely, your credit card and Social Security numbers—makes it an attractive target for data thieves. Additionally, the very nature of cloud computing makes it difficult to catch criminals.

The biggest problem, however, is that the cloud puts immense computing power at the disposal of anyone. Cloud criminals have access to easy-to-use encryption technology and anonymous communication channels that make it less likely that their activities will be intelligible to, or intercepted by, authorities. When law enforcement pursues criminals, the wrongdoers can rapidly shut down computing resources in the cloud, thus greatly decreasing the chances that there will be any clues left for forensic analysis.

One of the most straightforward options criminals are employing is simply to register for an account (with an assumed name, of course) and "legitimately" procure services for illegal purposes. Criminals are using Gmail or the text-sharing Web site Pastebin (www.pastebin.com) to plan crimes and share stolen information with near impunity. Although such uses are prohibited by most company's terms-of-service agreements, policing the cloud is expensive and not very rewarding for cloud providers.

Criminals with greater computing needs are using stolen credit cards to purchase access to computers and storage in the cloud. One emerging criminal use of cloud computing is brute-force password cracking. To break into encrypted files, attackers run programs that repeatedly try different passwords until the program finds the correct one. Today, attackers can rent time on hundreds of servers at once by employing services such as Amazon's Elastic Computing Cloud. German security specialist Thomas Roth calculated that he could use Amazon's cloud to crack the encryption keys used to protect Wi-Fi networks in six minutes. The cost of doing so would be $1.68.

In addition to creating opportunities for cybercriminals, the cloud can make it difficult for authorities or companies to track digital crimes. One reason is the rise of server virtualization, where users rent instances or virtual machines from cloud vendors. When users no longer need the virtual machine and shut it down, other clients of the cloud vendor immediately reuse the storage and computational capacity allocated to that machine. Therefore, the criminal information is overwritten by data from legitimate customers. Although incident response and law enforcement officials can forensically recover useful data from an operating virtual machine, it is nearly impossible to recover any data after the machine has been "de-provisioned." In a real sense, that virtual machine no longer exists, nor does any evidence that it may have held.

Criminals may also disappear in another way. Many cloud vendors offer geographical diversity—that is, virtual machines that are located in different physical locations. Criminals can use this feature to attack computers in the United States from computers in, say, Asia, or vice versa. Such transnational attacks typically place political and technical obstacles in the way of authorities seeking to trace a cyberattack back to its source.

Another weakness exploited by criminals arises from the Web-based applications, or SaaS offerings, provided by cloud vendors. With millions of users commingling on tens of thousands of servers, a criminal can easily mix in among legitimate users.

Even more complicated for authorities and victims, cyberattacks can originate within cloud programs that we use and trust. For instance, researchers at the security firm F-Secure reported that they had detected several phishing sites hosted within Google Docs. What made the attacks possible is a feature within Google's spreadsheet system that lets users create Web-based forms, with titles such as "Webmail Account Upgrade" and "Report a Bug." These forms, located on a Google server, were authenticated with Google's encryption certificate. Significantly, they requested sensitive information such as the user's full name, username, Google password, and so on, according to the F-Secure researchers.

BEFORE *YOU GO ON....*

1. Discuss the various risks of cloud computing.
2. In your opinion, which risk is the greatest? Support your answer.

Apply The Concept PI4.6

LEARNING OBJECTIVE PI4.6 Discuss the concerns and risks associated with cloud computing.

STEP 1 – Background

This section has discussed why the risks associated with cloud computing outweigh the benefits for some organizations. The statistics provided early on that cloud computing will remain a small portion of IT spending reflect concerns regarding these risks.

Visit http://www.wiley.com/go/rainer/MIS3e/applytheconcept, and click on the link provided for Plug IT In 4.6. This link will take you to an article that addresses some of the risks of cloud computing that senior managers need to consider. As you read the article, try to organize the managers' thoughts according to the concerns presented in this section: legacy systems, costs, reliability, security, privacy, and regulatory and legal environment.

Imagine you have just overheard a conversation about how wonderful cloud computing is that mentioned all of the positives and none of the negatives. How would you respond?

Based on the material contained in this section and the information conveyed in the article, write a response to the above scenario that discusses the concerns and risks associated with cloud computing.

PI4.7 Web Services and Service-Oriented Architecture

Thus far we have explained how cloud computing can deliver a variety of functionality to users in the form of services (think IaaS, PaaS, and SaaS). We conclude by examining Web services and service-oriented architecture.

Web services are applications delivered over the Internet (the cloud) that MIS professionals can select and combine through almost any device, from personal computers to mobile phones. By using a set of shared standards, or protocols, these applications permit different systems to "talk" with one another—that is, to share data and services—without requiring human beings to translate the conversations. Web services have enormous potential because they can be employed in a variety of environments: over the Internet, on an intranet inside a corporate firewall, on an extranet set up by business partners. In addition, they perform a wide variety of tasks, from automating business processes to integrating components of an enterprise-wide system to streamlining online buying and selling.

Web services provide numerous benefits for organizations:

- The organization can utilize the existing Internet infrastructure without having to implement any new technologies.
- Organizational personnel can access remote or local data without having to understand the complexities of this process.
- The organization can create new applications quickly and easily.

The collection of Web services that are used to build a firm's IT applications constitutes a **service-oriented architecture**. Businesses accomplish their processes by executing a series of these services. One of the major benefits of Web services is that they can be reused across an organization in other applications. For example, a Web service that checks a consumer's credit could be used with a service that processes a mortgage application or a credit card application.

Web services are based on four key protocols: XML, SOAP, WSDL, and UDDI.

Extensible markup language (XML) is a computer language that makes it easier to exchange data among a variety of applications and to validate and interpret these data. XML is a more powerful and flexible markup language than **hypertext markup language (HTML)**. HTML is a page-description language for specifying how text, graphics, video, and sound are placed on a Web page document. HTML was originally designed to create and link static documents composed primarily of text (FIGURE PI4.5). Today, however, the Web is much more social and interactive, and many Web pages have multimedia elements, such as images, audio, and video. To integrate these rich media into Web pages, users had to rely on third-party plug-in applications such as Flash, Silverlight, and Java. Unfortunately for users, these add-ons require both additional programming and extensive computer processing.

The next evolution of HTML, called **HTML5**, solves this problem by enabling users to embed images, audio, and video directly into a document without the add-ons. HTML5 also makes it easier for Web pages to function across different display devices, including mobile devices and desktops. HTML5 also supports offline data storage for apps that run over the Web. Web pages will execute more quickly, and they will resemble smartphone apps. HTML5 is used in a number of Internet platforms, including Apple's Safari browsers, Google Chrome, and Firefox browsers. Google's Gmail and Google Reader also use HTML5. Web sites listed as "iPad ready" are using HTML5 extensively. Examples of such sites are CNN, *The New York Times*, and CBS.

Whereas HTML is limited to describing how data should be presented in the form of Web pages, XML can present, communicate, and store data. For example, in XML a number is not simply a number. The XML tag also specifies whether the number represents a price, a date, or a ZIP code. Consider this example of XML, which identifies the contact information for Jane Smith.

```
<contact-info>
<name>Jane Smith</name>
<company>AT&amp;T</company>
<phone>(212) 555-4567</phone>
</contact-info>
```

(a) html

```html
<!DOCTYPE HTML PUBLIC "-//W3C//DTD XHTML 1.0 Transitional//EN" http://www.wiley.com/college/gisslen/0470179961/video/
video111
<html xmlns="http://www.wiley.com/college/rainer/0470179061/video/video111.html"><head>
<meta http-equiv="content-Type" content="text/html; charset=ISO-8859-1">
<title>CSS Text Wrapper</title>
<link type="text/css" rel="stylesheet" href="css/stylesheet.css">
</head><body id="examples">

<div id="container">
        <div class="wrapper">
                <div class="ex">
                        <script type="text/javascript">shapewrapp
er("15","7.5,141,145|22.5,89,89|37.5,68,69|52.5,46,50|67.5,3
height: 15px; width: 39px;"></div><div style="float: left; clear: left; height: 15px; width: 27px;"></div><div style="float:
15px; width: 4px;"></div><div style="float: left; clear: left; height: 15px; width: 6px;"></div><div style="float:
right; cle
width: 43px;"></div><div style="float: left; clear: left; height: 15px; width: 57px;"></div><div style="float: right; clear:
                        <span style="font-size: 13px;" class=c">
```

(b) XML

```xml
<feature numbered="no" xml:id="c08-fea-0001">
    <titleGroup>
        <title type="featureName">OPENING CASE</title>
        <title type="main">Tiger Tans and Gifts</title>
    </titleGroup>
    <section xml:id="c08-sec-0002">
        <p>
            <blockFixed onlyChannels="print" type="graphic">
                <mediaResource alt="p0310" copyright="John Wiley &amp; Sons, Inc." eRights="yes"
                    href="urn:x-wiley:9781118443590:media:rainer9781118443590c08:p0310" pRights="yes"/>
            </blockFixed>
            Lisa Keiling owns & tanning salon in Wedowee, Alabama, that does very well from January to May....
        </p>
    </section>
</feature>
```

Figure PI4.5 (a) Screenshot of an HTML wrapper. This wrapper gives instructions on how to open a video associated with this book. (b) Example of XML tagging done on Chapter 8 of this book.

Simple object access protocol (*SOAP*) is a set of rules that define how messages can be exchanged among different network systems and applications through the use of XML. These rules essentially establish a common protocol that allows different Web services to interoperate. For example, Visual Basic clients can use SOAP to access a Java server. SOAP runs on all hardware and software systems.

The *Web services description language* (*WSDL*) is used to create the XML document that describes the tasks performed by the various Web services. Tools such as VisualStudio.Net automate the process of accessing the WSDL, reading it, and coding the application to reference the specific Web service.

Universal description, discovery, and integration (*UDDI*) allows MIS professionals to search for needed Web services by creating public or private searchable directories of these services. In other words, UDDI is the registry of descriptions of Web services.

Examples of Web services abound. As one example, the Food and Nutrition Service (FNS) within the U.S. Department of Agriculture (USDA) uses Amazon Web Services successfully. The FNS administers the department's nutrition assistance programs. Its mission is to provide children and needy families with improved access to food and a healthier diet through its food assistance programs and comprehensive nutrition education efforts.

The Supplemental Nutrition Assistance Program, or SNAP, is the cornerstone of the USDA's nutrition assistance mission. More than 47 million people—most of them children—receive SNAP benefits each month. To help recipients, in 2010 the FNS created a Web application called the SNAP Retail Locator. Faced with limited budget and time to implement the solution, the FNS selected Amazon Web Services to host the application. As its name suggests, the SNAP Retail Locator, which receives 30,000 visitors per month, helps SNAP recipients find the closest SNAP-authorized store and also provides driving directions to the store. The application has been available 100 percent of the time since it was launched. In addition, by employing Amazon, the FNS saved 90 percent of the cost it would have incurred had it hosted the application on-premises.

BEFORE *YOU GO ON....*

1. What are Web services?
2. What is a service-oriented architecture?

Apply The Concept PI4.7

LEARNING OBJECTIVE PI4.7 Explain the role of Web services in building a firm's IT applications, providing examples.

STEP 1 – Background

Web services allow companies to increase functionality with minimal effort by using standard protocols to access and share data. The advantage of using Web services is that it standardizes the Web platform. Using the same Web protocols that allow you to access any Web site makes sharing data much easier.

STEP 2 – Activity

Imagine you work for a bank and you want to display some financial data on your intranet to keep your employees up-to-date on major market trends. One option is to gather data, perform an analysis, build and share charts and graphs, and then keep everything current. This probably sounds like a lot of work. But, suppose someone else had done all of the work for you?

Visit http://www.wiley.com/go/rainer/MIS3e/applytheconcept, and click on the link provided for Apply the Concept PI4.7. This link will take you to a Web site that discusses the available "widgets" (another name for an embeddable Web service) that businesses can select to display on their sites. Review the available information, and consider how it would help you add content to your bank's intranet with minimal effort.

STEP 3 – Deliverable

Write a summary that explains the role of Web services in building a firm's IT applications. Include a few examples based on the options you viewed in Step 2.

 What's in **IT** for ME?

FOR ALL BUSINESS MAJORS

As with hardware (Plug IT In 2), the design of enterprise IT architectures has profound impacts for businesspeople. Personal and organizational success can depend on an understanding of cloud computing and a commitment to knowing the opportunities and challenges they will bring.

At the organizational level, cloud computing has the potential to make the organization function more efficiently and effectively, while saving the organization money. Web services and SOA make the organization more flexible when deploying new IT applications.

At the individual level, you might utilize cloud computing yourself if you start your own business. Remember that cloud computing provides startup companies with world-class IT capabilities at a very low cost.

SUMMARY

1. Describe the problems that modern information technology departments face.

Traditional IT departments face many problems:
- They spend huge amounts on IT infrastructure and expert staffs to build and maintain complex IT systems. These expenses include software licenses, hardware, and staff training and salaries.

- They must manage an infrastructure that often is not used to its full capacity.
- They spend the majority of their budgets on maintaining existing IT infrastructure, with the remainder being spent on developing new systems.
- They have difficulty capturing, storing, managing, and analyzing all these data.

- They can actually inhibit an organization's ability to respond quickly and appropriately to rapidly changing dynamic environments.
- They are expensive.

2. Describe the key characteristics and advantages of cloud computing.

Cloud computing is a type of computing that delivers convenient, on-demand, pay-as-you-go access for multiple customers to a shared pool of configurable computing resources (e.g., servers, networks, storage, applications, and services) that can be rapidly and easily accessed over the Internet. The essential *characteristics* of cloud computing include the following:

- Cloud computing provides on-demand self-service.
- Cloud computing includes the characteristics of grid computing.
- Cloud computing includes the characteristics of utility computing.
- Cloud computing utilizes broad network access.
- Cloud computing pools computing resources.
- Cloud computing typically occurs on virtualized servers.

3. Identify a use case scenario for each of the four types of clouds.

Public clouds are shared, easily accessible, multicustomer IT infrastructures that are available nonexclusively to any entity in the public (individuals, groups, and/or organizations). *Private clouds* (also known as *internal clouds* or *corporate clouds*) are IT infrastructures that are accessible only by a single entity, or by an exclusive group of related entities that share the same purpose and requirements, such as all the business units within a single organization. *Hybrid clouds* are composed of public and private clouds that remain unique entities but are bound together, offering the benefits of multiple deployment models. *Vertical clouds* serve specific industries.

4. Explain the operational model of each of the three types of cloud services.

With the *infrastructure-as-a-service* (IaaS) model, cloud computing providers offer remotely accessible servers, networks, and storage capacity. In the *platform-as-a-service* (PaaS) model, customers rent servers, operating systems, storage, a database, software development technologies such as Java and .NET, and network capacity over the Internet. With the *software-as-a-service* (SaaS) delivery model, cloud computing vendors provide software that is specific to their customers' requirements.

5. Identify the key benefits of cloud computing.

The benefits of cloud computing include making individuals more productive; facilitating collaboration; mining insights from data; developing and hosting applications; cost flexibility; business scalability; improved utilization of hardware; market adaptability; and product and service customization.

6. Discuss the concerns and risks associated with cloud computing.

Cloud computing does raise concerns and have risks, which include legacy spaghetti, cost, reliability, privacy, security, and the regulatory and legal environment.

7. Explain the role of Web services in building a firm's IT applications, providing examples.

Web services are applications delivered over the Internet that MIS professionals can select and combine through almost any device, from personal computers to mobile phones. A service-*oriented architecture* makes it possible for MIS professionals to construct business applications using Web services.

>>>GLOSSARY

cloud computing A technology in which tasks are performed by computers physically removed from the user and accessed over a network, in particular the Internet.

extensible markup language (XML) A computer language that makes it easier to exchange data among a variety of applications and to validate and interpret these data.

grid computing A technology that applies the unused processing resources of many geographically dispersed computers in a network to form a virtual supercomputer.

HTML5 A page-description language that makes it possible to embed images, audio, and video directly into a document without add-ons. Also makes it easier for Web pages to function across different display devices, including mobile devices as well as desktops. Supports the storage of data offline.

hybrid clouds Clouds composed of public and private clouds that remain unique entities but are bound together, offering the benefits of multiple deployment models.

hypertext markup language (HTML) A page-description language for specifying how text, graphics, video, and sound are placed on a Web page document.

infrastructure-as-a-service (IaaS) A model with which cloud computing providers offer remotely accessible servers, networks, and storage capacity.

platform-as-a-service (PaaS) A model with which customers rent servers, operating systems, storage, a database, software development technologies such as Java and .NET, and network capacity over the Internet.

private clouds (also known as *internal clouds* or *corporate clouds*) IT infrastructures that are accessible only by a single entity or by an exclusive group of related entities that share the same purpose and requirements, such as all the business units within a single organization.

public clouds Shared, easily accessible, multicustomer IT infrastructures that are available nonexclusively to any entity in the general public (individuals, groups, and/or organizations).

server farms Massive data centers, which may contain hundreds of thousands of networked computer servers.

server virtualization A technology that uses software-based partitions to create multiple virtual servers (called *virtual machines*) on a single physical server.

service-oriented architecture An IT architecture that makes it possible to construct business applications using Web services.

software-as-a-service (SaaS) A delivery model with which cloud computing vendors provide software that is specific to their customers' requirements.

utility computing A technology whereby a service provider makes computing resources and infrastructure management available to a customer as needed.

Web services Applications delivered over the Internet that IT developers can select and combine through almost any device, from personal computers to mobile phones.

>>>DISCUSSION QUESTIONS

1. What is the value of server farms and virtualization to any large organization?

2. If you were the chief information officer (CIO) of a firm, how would you explain the workings, benefits, and limitations of cloud computing?

3. What is the value of cloud computing to a small organization?

4. What is the value of cloud computing to an entrepreneur who is starting a business?

>>>PROBLEM-SOLVING ACTIVITIES

1. Investigate the status of cloud computing by researching the offerings of the following leading vendors. Note any inhibitors to cloud computing.

   - Dell (see, for example, http://www.wiley.com/go/rainer/MIS3e/problemsolving)
   - Oracle (see, for example, http://www.wiley.com/go/rainer/MIS3e/problemsolving)
   - IBM (see, for example, http://www.wiley.com/go/rainer/MIS3e/problemsolving)
   - Amazon (see, for example, http://www.wiley.com/go/rainer/MIS3e/problemsolving)
   - Microsoft (see, for example, http://www.wiley.com/go/rainer/MIS3e/problemsolving)
   - Google (see, for example, http://www.wiley.com/go/rainer/MIS3e/problemsolving)

>>> COLLABORATION EXERCISE

STEP 1 – Background

Cloud technology has fundamentally transformed the ways we communicate; conduct business transactions; store, analyze, and share information; and much more. If you have performed any of the Collaboration Exercises thus far, then you have used cloud technologies to complete part of your education!

STEP 2 – Activity

Google Drive is valuable for performing many activities. Its default package offers documents, spreadsheets, presentations, drawings, forms, and other capabilities. In addition, because it is a cloud-based tool, it enables users to collaborate on projects and to share their materials.

Google Drive also allows for Web services! For this activity, work with a team of colleagues to find the best

Web service for working with PDF files within Google Drive. To complete this activity, create a new spreadsheet (or document), and share it with your team as a way to take notes.

Have each team member open Google Drive and click on "Create." You will see "Connect More Apps" at the bottom of the box that opens up. Clicking on this link will display numerous Web services that integrate with Google Drive. Have each team member review two PDF apps.

STEP 3 – Deliverable

After each team member has taken notes on the capabilities of the various apps, as a team select the app that offers the most functionality to Google Drive. Explain your choice to your professor.

INTERNSHIP ACTIVITY> OXFORD ORTHOPAEDICS

Healthcare

In the Chapter 4 Internship Activity you helped Chad Prince and Oxford Orthopaedics develop criteria for measuring latency in the cloud. The company now needs to determine how they can print from the cloud. When they print from a local network, they rely on a print server that is physically connected to each of the available computers and printers. Software then is programmed to manage the printing in the office.

Suppose, however, that all of the company's data are stored in the cloud. How will the cloud-based print servers interact with the local print servers? Although this issue may sound trivial, in a healthcare industry the ability to print records quickly and easily is vital!

Below is a letter from Chad about this project.

To:	IT Intern
From:	Chad Prince
Subject:	Cloud Printing

Hello!

As you recall from a previous assignment, we recently migrated to a cloud-based environment for our Practice Management/Electronic Health Records (PM/EHR) system. One issue that recently came up in a meeting was the ability to print our documents. Though we are using digital files, we still print a large number of documents, such as receipts, appointments, and prescriptions.

Will you research this issue for me? A couple of names popped up when I looked into it. Google Cloud Print enables businesses to print from the Web, and Lantronix offers hardware that may be compatible with Google's service.

Let me know what you find regarding the compatibility of these technologies with Windows, Linux, and other server types.

Thanks for your help!

Chad

Note: Any links or Web sites mentioned in this e-mail are available at http://www.wiley.com/go/rainer/MIS3e/internship.

PLUG IT IN 5

Intelligent Systems

LEARNING OBJECTIVES >>>

PI5.1 Explain the potential value and the potential limitations of artificial intelligence.

PI5.2 Provide examples of the benefits, applications, and limitations of expert systems.

PI5.3 Provide examples of the use of neural networks.

PI5.4 Provide examples of the use of fuzzy logic.

PI5.5 Describe the situations in which genetic algorithms would be most useful.

PI5.6 Describe the use case for several major types of intelligent agents.

PI5.1 Introduction to Intelligent Systems

This Plug IT In focuses on information systems that can make decisions by themselves. These systems are called **intelligent systems**. The major categories of intelligent systems are expert systems, neural networks, fuzzy logic, genetic algorithms, and intelligent agents. You will learn about each of these systems in the following sections.

The term intelligent systems describes the various commercial applications of artificial intelligence (AI). Artificial intelligence is a subfield of computer science that studies the thought processes of humans and re-creates the effects of those processes via machines, such as computers and robots.

One well-publicized definition of AI is "behavior by a machine that, if performed by a human being, would be considered intelligent." This definition raises the question, "What is *intelligent behavior*?" The following capabilities are considered to be signs of intelligence: learning or understanding from experience, making sense of ambiguous or contradictory messages, and responding quickly and successfully to new situations.

The ultimate goal of AI is to build machines that mimic human intelligence. A widely used test to determine whether a computer exhibits intelligent behavior was designed by Alan Turing, a British AI pioneer. The Turing test proposes a scenario in which a man and a computer both pretend to be women or men, and a human interviewer has to identify which is the real human. Based on this standard, the intelligent systems exemplified in commercial AI products are far from exhibiting any significant intelligence.

We can better understand the potential value of AI by contrasting it with *natural (human) intelligence*. AI has several important commercial advantages over natural intelligence, but it also displays some limitations, as outlined in Table PI5.1.

Intelligent systems show up in a number of places, some of them surprising, as the following examples illustrate:

- A good session player is hard to find, but ujam (www.ujam.com) is always ready to rock. This Web app doubles as a studio band and a recording studio. It analyzes a melody and then produces sophisticated harmonies, bass lines, drum tracks, horn parts, and more.

Before ujam can produce accompaniment, the app must figure out which notes the user is singing or playing. Once ujam recognizes these notes, its algorithms (an **algorithm** is a problem-solving method expressed as a finite sequence of steps) use a mix of statistical techniques and programmed musical rules to search for chords to match the tune.

© Luis Alonso Ocana/Age Fotostock

- To the human eye, an X-ray is a murky puzzle. But to a machine, an X-ray—or a CT scan or MRI scan—is a dense data field that can be assessed down to the pixel level. AI techniques currently are being applied aggressively in the field of medical imaging.

New software gathers high-resolution image data from multiple sources—X-rays, MRI scans, ultrasounds, CT scans—and then groups together biological structures that share hard-to-detect similarities. For instance, the software can examine several images of the same breast to measure tissue density. The software then color-codes tissues of similar densities so that humans can observe the pattern as well.

The software finds and indexes pixels that share certain properties, even pixels that are far apart in one image or in a different image altogether. This process enables medical personnel to identify hidden features of diffuse structures as well as features within a region of tissue.

- For years, electric utilities manually collected data from meters in homes and businesses. The companies analyzed that data to bill their customers for usage. Utility planners analyzed that data to better estimate future usage and plan new facilities. This system has always had problems. For instance, many regions of the United States are subject to brownouts when the utilities cannot meet peak power demands during heat waves. The utilities typically appealed to customers over the radio and television to try and get them to lower their use of air-conditioning.

The shortcomings of that system highlight the benefits of intelligent systems. A developing solution is to use an intelligent meter's real-time information about each customer's usage during peak times, share details about temperature conditions with customers, and try to entice them to take action. Ideally, utilities would like to be able to send a message to each customer telling them that the utility will charge more per kilowatt hour in those periods of peak demand. The customer could then decide whether to pay more or use less. With such an intelligent system, a utility would be able to save the cost of buying electricity on the spot market at a much higher rate to meet peak demands, thereby reducing the number of brownouts and delivering better customer service.

- Building a model to run a major railroad is a complex task. One of the nation's largest freight carriers, Norfolk Southern (www.nscorp.com), uses an intelligent system, the Princeton Locomotive and Shop Management System (PLASMA), to manage its huge operation. PLASMA uses algorithms to analyze the railroad's operations by tracking thousands of variables to predict the impact of changes in fleet size, maintenance policies, transit time, and other factors. The key breakthrough was refining PLASMA so that it could mimic the complex behavior of the company's dispatch center in Atlanta, Georgia. PLASMA examines vast amounts of historical data contained in the railroad's databases. It then uses this analysis to model the dispatch center's collective human decision making and suggest improvements.

TABLE PI5.1 Comparison of the Capabilities of Natural Versus Artificial Intelligence

Capabilities	Natural Intelligence	Artificial Intelligence
Preservation of knowledge	Perishable from an organizational point of view	Permanent
Duplication and dissemination	Difficult, expensive, takes time	Easy, fast, and inexpensive of knowledge in a computer
Total cost of knowledge	Can be erratic and inconsistent, incomplete at times	Consistent and thorough
Documentability of process and knowledge	Difficult, expensive	Fairly easy, inexpensive
Creativity	Can be very high	Low, uninspired
Use of sensory experiences	Direct and rich in possibilities	Must be interpreted first; limited
Recognizing patterns and relationships	Fast, easy to explain	Machine learning still not as good as people in most cases, but in some cases better than people
Reasoning	Making use of wide context of experiences	Good only in narrow, focused, and stable domains

- South Jersey Healthcare (www.inspirahealthnetwork .org) deployed an intelligent medication distribution system, which provides easy access to its pharmaceutical inventory, medical records, and patient billing. The system is managing over 700,000 doses of medication per month and has delivered quantifiable benefits. With the system, the healthcare company has been able to make more effective ordering decisions based on real-time inventory information. As a result, the firm has reduced medication inventory by almost 40 percent. Furthermore, the system helps nurses and pharmacists deliver medicine to patients faster. Medication distribution time has been cut from 2 hours to 18 minutes, on average.

- Nakajima USA (www.nakajimausa.com) is a manufacturer of licensed plush, collectible, and seasonal toys, lifestyle goods, and trendy character merchandise. The firm has developed an intelligent, real-time inventory control system, instead of relying on periodic inventory reports. This process is critical for the firm because its products come from overseas and have a long replenishment cycle. (A replenishment cycle is the time between when an order for inventory is placed until the time the next order for inventory is placed.) The intelligent system gives the company faster and better visibility into which of its core products are selling and need to be restocked, therefore allowing more efficiency in managing inventory in stores. The system also allows the company to capture more customer information at checkout.

- Vertical, or topic-specific, search is gaining popularity in areas from travel and electronics to books, films, and more. Vertical search occurs when a person goes directly to a site such as IMDB or Kayak rather than through a general search engine such as Google or Bing. Vertical search uses semantic analysis, text classification, feature extraction, and advanced big data analytics, combined with other artificial intelligence algorithms. Google has noted the threat and is putting a lot of effort into vertical search in an effort to deliver more relevant, focused, tailored search results. However, vertical search does present an opportunity to get an edge on Google by incorporating human logic and knowledge into specific vertical topics. An example is Zite (www.zite.com), an app that offers relevant news articles by learning behavior. The app uses several AI technologies to make news delivery much more intelligent than a simple Google News feed.

BEFORE *YOU GO ON....*

1. What is artificial intelligence?
2. Differentiate between artificial and human intelligence.

Apply The Concept PI5.1

LEARNING OBJECTIVE PI5.1 Explain the potential value and the potential limitations of artificial intelligence.

STEP 1 – Background (Here is what you are learning.)

This section introduced you to several applications of artificial intelligence. One of these applications was the Google self-driving car. This innovation presents a scenario where technology could potentially greatly enhance the safety of motorists, pedestrians, and passengers. However, there are also significant risks posed by turning over the keys to the computer.

STEP 2 – Activity (Here is what you are doing.)

Visit http://www.wiley.com/go/rainer/MIS3e/applytheconcept, and click on the link provided for Plug IT In 5.1. This link will take you to a YouTube video that introduces the Google self-driving car. Although this innovation is very exciting, it can also be very scary! While you are watching the video, imagine the advantages and disadvantages of this type of intelligent system. Would it function best as a "pilot" or a very helpful "copilot"?

STEP 3 – Deliverable (Here is what you submit.)

Build a table that displays both the potential value (advantages) and the potential limitations (disadvantages) of artificial intelligence for different scenarios illustrated in the example below.

	Advantages	Disadvantages
Tired driver		
Distracted driver (texting)		
Sick/stressed driver		
Ambulance driver		
School bus driver		
Soccer mom, mini van driver		

PI5.2 Expert Systems

When an organization has to make a complex decision or solve a problem, it often turns to experts for advice. These experts possess specific knowledge and experience in the problem area. They can offer alternative solutions and predict whether the proposed solutions will succeed. At the same time, they can calculate the costs that the organization may incur if it does not resolve the problem. Companies engage experts for advice on such matters as mergers and acquisitions, advertising strategy, and purchasing equipment. The more unstructured the situation, the more specialized and expensive is the advice.

Expertise refers to the extensive, task-specific knowledge acquired from training, reading, and experience. This knowledge enables experts to make better and faster decisions than nonexperts in solving complex problems. Expertise takes a long time (often many years) to acquire, and it is distributed unevenly across organizations.

Expert systems (ESs) are computer systems that attempt to mimic human experts by applying expertise in a specific domain. Expert systems can either *support* decision makers or completely *replace* them. Expert systems are the most widely applied and commercially successful intelligent systems. A fascinating example of an expert system is IBM's Watson (see closing case 1 in Chapter 2).

HRM Human resources management uses expert systems to analyze applicants for available positions. These systems assign "scores" to candidates, lessening the workload for HR managers in the hiring process. HR managers still make the final decision, but the expert system provides useful information and recommendations.

An ES is typically decision-making software that can perform at a level comparable to a human expert in certain specialized problem areas. Essentially, an ES transfers expertise from a domain expert (or other source) to the computer. This knowledge is then stored in the computer, which users can call on for specific advice as needed. The computer can make inferences and arrive at conclusions. Then, like a human expert, it offers advice or recommendations. In addition, it can explain the logic behind the advice. Because ESs can integrate and manipulate enormous amounts of data, they sometimes perform better than any single expert can.

An often overlooked benefit of expert systems is that they can be embedded in larger systems. For example, credit card issuers use expert systems to process credit card applications.

The transfer of expertise from an expert to a computer and then to the user involves four activities:

1. *Knowledge acquisition.* Knowledge is acquired from domain experts or from documented sources.
2. *Knowledge representation.* Acquired knowledge is organized as rules or frames (object-oriented) and stored electronically in a knowledge base.
3. *Knowledge inferencing.* The computer is programmed so that it can make inferences based on the stored knowledge.

4. *Knowledge transfer.* The inferenced expertise is transferred to the user in the form of a recommendation.

The above examples demonstrate the usefulness of expert systems in a relatively narrow domain. Overall, however, expert systems may not be as useful as users would like. Consider the Microsoft® Windows troubleshooting software located in the Help section in the taskbar menu. Microsoft has designed this expert system to provide solutions, advice, and suggestions for common errors that users encounter in the operating system. We have all found however that in some cases the Help section does not provide particularly useful advice.

The Components of Expert Systems

An expert system contains the following components: knowledge base, inference engine, user interface, blackboard (workplace), and explanation subsystem (justifier). In the future, ESs will include a knowledge-refining component as well. You will learn about all these components below. In addition, FIGURE PI5.1 shows the relationships among these components.

The *knowledge base* contains knowledge necessary for understanding, formulating, and solving problems. It comprises two basic elements: (1) *facts*, such as the problem situation, and (2) *rules* that direct the use of knowledge to solve specific problems in a particular domain.

The *inference engine* is essentially a computer program that provides a methodology for reasoning and formulating conclusions. It enables the system to make inferences based on the stored knowledge. The inference engine is considered the "brain" of the ES.

Here is an example of the inference engine for a medical expert system for lung cancer treatment:

> IF lung capacity is high
>
> AND X-ray results are positive
>
> AND patient has fever
>
> AND patient has coughing
>
> THEN surgery is necessary.
>
> IF tumor has spread
>
> OR contraindications to surgery exist
>
> THEN surgery cannot be performed.

The *user interface* enables users to communicate with the computer. The communication is carried out in a natural language, usually a question-and-answer format, and in some cases is supplemented by graphics. The dialogue between the user and the computer triggers the inference engine to match the problem symptoms with the knowledge contained in the knowledge base and then generate advice.

The *blackboard* is an area of working memory set aside for the description of a current problem, as specified by the input data. Thus, it is a kind of database.

Unique to an ES is its ability to *explain* its recommendations. This function is performed in a subsystem called the *explanation subsystem* or *justifier*. The explanation subsystem

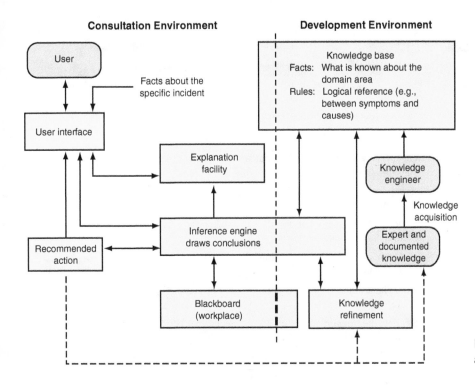

Consultation Environment

Development Environment

Figure PI5.1 Structure and process of an expert system.

interactively answers questions such as the following: *Why* did the ES ask a certain question? *How* did the ES reach a particular conclusion? *What* is the plan to reach the solution?

Human experts have a *knowledge-refining* system; that is, they can analyze their own performance, learn from it, and improve it for future consultations. This type of evaluation is necessary in computerized learning as well so that the program can be improved by analyzing the reasons for its success or failure. Unfortunately, such a component is not available in commercial expert systems at the moment; however, it is being developed in experimental systems.

Applications, Benefits, and Limitations of Expert Systems

Today, expert systems are found in all types of organizations. They are especially useful in the 10 generic categories shown in Table PI5.2.

During the past few years, thousands of organizations worldwide have successfully applied ES technology to problems ranging from researching AIDS to analyzing dust in mines. Why have ESs become so popular? The answer is, because they provide such a large number of capabilities and benefits. Table PI5.3 lists the major benefits of ESs.

Despite all of these benefits, expert systems present some problems as well. The following difficulties are involved with using expert systems:

- Transferring domain expertise from human experts to the expert system can be difficult because people cannot always explain *how* they know what they know. Often they are not aware of their complete reasoning process.

- Even if the domain experts can explain their entire reasoning process, automating that process may not be

possible. The process might be either too complex or too vague, or it might require too many rules.

- In some contexts, there is a potential liability from the use of expert systems. Humans make errors occasionally, but they are generally "let off the hook" if they took reasonable care and applied generally accepted methods. An organization that uses an expert system, however, may lack this legal protection if problems arise later. The usual example of this issue is medical treatment, but it

TABLE PI5.2 Ten Generic Categories of Expert Systems

Category	Problem Addressed
Interpretation	Inferring situation descriptions from observations
Prediction	Inferring likely consequences of given situations
Diagnosis	Inferring system malfunctions from observations
Design	Configuring objects under constraints
Planning	Developing plans to achieve goal(s)
Monitoring	Comparing observations to plans, flagging exceptions
Debugging	Prescribing remedies for malfunctions
Repair	Executing a plan to administer a prescribed remedy
Instruction	Diagnosing, debugging, and correcting student performance
Control	Interpreting, predicting, repairing, and monitoring systems behavior

TABLE PI5.3 Benefits of Expert Systems

Benefit	Description
Increased output and productivity	ESs can configure components for each custom order, increasing production capabilities.
Increased quality	ESs can provide consistent advice and reduce error rates.
Capture and dissemination of scarce expertise	Expertise from anywhere in the world can be obtained and used.
Operation in hazardous environments	Sensors can collect information that an ES interprets, enabling human workers to avoid hot, humid, or toxic environments.
Accessibility to knowledge and help desks	ESs can increase the productivity of help desk employees, or even automate this function.
Reliability	ESs do not become tired or bored, call in sick, or go on strike. They consistently pay attention to details.
Ability to work with incomplete or uncertain information	Even with an answer of "don't know," an ES can produce an answer, although it may not be a definite one.
Provision of training	The explanation facility of an ES can serve as a teaching device and a knowledge base for novices.
Enhancement of decision-making and problem-solving capabilities	ESs allow the integration of expert judgment into analysis (e.g., diagnosis of machine malfunction and even medical diagnosis).
Decreased decision-making time	ESs usually can make faster decisions than humans working alone.
Reduced downtime	ESs can quickly diagnose machine malfunctions and prescribe repairs.

can also arise if a business decision driven by an expert system harms someone financially.

In the case of medical treatment, consider a physician who consults with a medical expert system when treating a patient. If the patient's care goes poorly, then the question arises, who is liable? The physician? The expert system? The vendor of the expert system?

┌─ **BEFORE** *YOU GO ON....* ─┐
1. What is an expert system?
2. Describe the benefits and limitations of using expert systems.

Apply The Concept PI5.2

LEARNING OBJECTIVE PI5.2 Provide examples of the benefits, applications, and limitations of expert systems.

STEP 1 – Background

Throughout much of human history, expertise was transferred from a master to an apprentice through years of training. Only after the apprentice had mastered all of the "tricks of the trade" was he or she considered ready to perform on his or her own. We still employ a similar system for doctors, who must participate in a residency program under the guidance of the resident doctor before they can begin their own practice.

This approach is not appropriate, however, for many non-life-threatening situations. In some cases, being able to make an expert decision is simply a matter of having access to the experts' knowledge and experiences. If this knowledge can be captured in a computer-based information system, then it can be distributed for other people to use in similar scenarios.

Although this sounds great, there are many challenges to developing this type of system.

STEP 2 – Activity

Visit http://www.wiley.com/go/rainer/MIS3e/applytheconcept, and watch the YouTube video linked for Apply the Concept PI5.2. This video will show you a short demonstration of an expert cooking system. The video mentions that you are responsible for building and testing an expert system, but that is not part of this activity. As you watch the video, pay particular attention to the miscommunication between the cook and the computer. You will find this interaction to be quite comical.

STEP 3 – Deliverable

Based on the video and the material in this section, provide examples of the benefits, applications, and limitations of using expert systems within the world of cooking. Create a Word document and submit it to your instructor.

PI5.3 Neural Networks

A **neural network** is a system of programs and data structures that simulates the underlying functions of the biological brain. A neural network usually involves a large number of processors operating in parallel, each with its own small sphere of knowledge and access to data in its local memory (see FIGURE PI5.2). Typically, a neural network is initially "trained" or fed large amounts of data and rules about data relationships.

Neural networks are particularly adept at recognizing subtle, hidden, and newly emerging patterns within complex data, as well as interpreting incomplete inputs. Neural networks can help users solve a wide range of problems, from airline security to infectious disease control. They are the standard for combating fraud in the credit card, healthcare, and telecom industries, and they are becoming increasingly important in today's stepped-up international efforts to prevent money laundering.

Neural networks are used in a variety of ways, as illustrated by the following examples.

- The Bruce nuclear facility in Ontario, Canada, has eight nuclear reactors, making it the largest facility in North America and the second largest in the world. The plant uses a neural network in its checkpoint X-ray screening system to detect weapons concealed in personal belongings. The system also identifies biologically dangerous liquids.

- Neural networks are used in research into diseases like Alzheimer's, Parkinson's, and epilepsy. Researchers build robots with simulated rat brains that mimic the rats' neural activity. The researchers then can study the brain's function and its reaction to stimuli.

- Investors employ neural networks to forecast the performance of stock index futures, currencies, natural gas, and oil stocks, T-bond futures, gold stocks, and other major investments.

- In banking systems, neural networks help detect fraud in credit card transactions and insurance claims, fight crime, and gauge customer satisfaction.

FIGURE PI5.2 illustrates how a neural network might process a typical mortgage application. Note that the network has three levels of interconnected nodes (similar to the human brain): an input layer; a middle, or hidden, layer; and an output layer. When the neural network is trained, the strengths, or *weights*, of its connections change. In our example, the input nodes are age, income, occupation, marital status, employer, length of time with that employer, the desired amount of the mortgage, and the current interest rate. The neural network has already been trained with data input from many mortgage applications, successful and unsuccessful. That is, the neural network has established a pattern as to which input variables are necessary for a

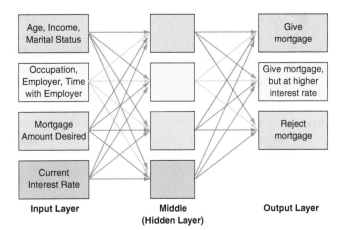

Figure PI5.2 Neural network.

successful mortgage application. Interestingly, the neural network can adjust as both mortgage amounts and interest rates increase or decrease.

Machine learning systems often use neural networks. **Machine learning systems** are artificial intelligence systems that learn from data. For instance, a machine learning system can be trained on e-mail messages to learn to distinguish between spam and nonspam messages. After learning, the system can then be used to classify new e-mail messages into spam and nonspam folders. The following are other examples of machine learning:

- *Optical character recognition.* Printed, handwritten characters are recognized automatically based on previous examples.

- *Face recognition.* Identify faces in images.

- *Topic identification.* Categorize news articles as to whether they are about politics, sports, entertainment, and so on.

- *Fraud detection.* Identify credit card transactions that may be fraudulent.

- *Customer segmentation.* Identify which customers may respond positively to a particular promotion.

Because neural networks are difficult to set up and use, two researchers at the University of Vienna (Austria) have created a system called N2Sky. N2Sky helps to set up neural networks in the cloud so that their services can be shared. The two researchers want to make neural networks available as a shared resource so that anyone, anywhere can use them easily for the problem that they have at hand.

BEFORE YOU GO ON....

1. What are neural networks?
2. Describe how neural networks function.

Apply The Concept PI5.3

STEP 1 – Background

This section describes a neural network as one that operates much like a human brain. Our minds are able to analyze and sometimes predict and make decisions much more quickly than computers. Neural networks also resemble our learning processes. Imagine yourself as a child learning to walk. Each time you stood and each time you fell, your brain generated new connections that ultimately helped you learn to walk.

STEP 2 – Activity

Visit http://www.wiley.com/go/rainer/MIS3e/applytheconcept, and click on the link for Plug IT In 5.3. This link will take you to a YouTube video that demonstrates a neural network in which a car learns to drive itself around a road. Watch this demo, and be amazed at how this system learns over time. It appears as though the car is constantly crashing, and then all of a sudden it successfully navigates the entire track.

Imagine other applications that could utilize neural network systems to learn to navigate problematic scenarios like predicting the stock market and gold futures and even predicting crime!

STEP 3 – Deliverable

Build a list of possible uses for neural networks. Research the Web if you need help. For example, imagine the trial and error we have gone through to learn modern medical care and the treatment of various diseases. Submit your list of possible applications to your professor.

PI5.4 Fuzzy Logic

Fuzzy logic is a branch of mathematics that deals with uncertainties by simulating the processes of human reasoning. The rationale behind fuzzy logic is that decision making is not always a matter of black or white, or true or false. Rather, it frequently involves gray areas where the term *maybe* is more appropriate.

A computer programmed to use fuzzy logic precisely defines subjective concepts that humans do not define precisely. For example, for the concept "income," descriptive terms such as "high" and "moderate" are subjective and imprecise. Using fuzzy logic, however, a computer could define "high" incomes as those exceeding $200,000 per year, and "moderate" incomes as those ranging from $150,000 to $200,000 per year. A loan officer at a bank might then use these values when considering a loan application.

Fuzzy logic has also been used in financial analysis and Internet searches. In accounting and finance, fuzzy logic allows you to analyze assets expressed in imprecise values (e.g., intangible ones like goodwill). As an example, Google uses fuzzy logic to locate answers to your search terms, based on your perception of the topic as reflected in how you phrase your query, which determines the relevance of the Web pages that Google delivers to you.

> ## BEFORE YOU GO ON....
> 1. What is fuzzy logic?
> 2. Give some examples where fuzzy logic is used.

Apply The Concept PI5.4

STEP 1 – Background

Fuzzy logic allows computers to use our vague descriptions as data points. Although we may describe a house in poorly defined terms such as big or small, the computer will assign specific data ranges to "big" houses and "small" houses so that, for example, a house under 1000 square feet is "small" and anything larger is "big." Fuzzy logic, then, enables computer systems to analyze and consider options where "fuzzy" descriptions are the best we can come up with.

STEP 2 – Activity

Imagine that you are going to use fuzzy logic to design a formula to determine whether people who are texting while they drive are at risk for having an accident. What variables would you use? What categories would you create for each variable? Come up with at least five variables, where each variable has three categories. For example, you may use "comfort with texting" as a variable and have measurements such as the following:

"Uncomfortable" (sends less than 100 messages per month)

"Somewhat comfortable" (sends 101–500 messages per month)

"Very comfortable" (sends more than 501 messages per month)

STEP 3 – Deliverable

Based on your experience developing the foundations of fuzzy logic in Step 2, provide other examples of the use of fuzzy logic. Submit your examples to your instructor.

PI5.5 Genetic Algorithms

Recall that an algorithm is a problem-solving method expressed as a finite sequence of steps. A genetic algorithm mimics the evolutionary "survival-of-the-fittest" process to generate increasingly better solutions to a problem. That is, a genetic algorithm is an optimizing method that finds the combination of inputs that produces the best outputs. Genetic algorithms have three functional characteristics:

- *Selection (survival of the fittest)*. The key to selection is to give preference to better and better outcomes.
- *Crossover*. Combining portions of good outcomes in the hope of creating an even better outcome.
- *Mutation*. Randomly trying combinations and evaluating the success (or failure) of an outcome.

Genetic algorithms are best suited to decision-making environments in which thousands or millions of solutions are possible. Genetic algorithms can find and evaluate solutions intelligently, and they can process many more possibilities more thoroughly and quickly than a human can. (Users do have to tell the genetic algorithm what constitutes a "good" solution, which could be low cost or high return, or any number of other results.) Let's look at some examples:

- Boeing uses genetic algorithms to design aircraft parts such as the fan blades on its 777 jet. Rolls Royce and Honda also use genetic algorithms in their design processes.
- Retailers such as Marks and Spencer, a British chain with 320 stores, use genetic algorithms to manage their inventories more effectively and to optimize their store displays.
- Air Liquide, a producer of industrial gases, uses genetic algorithms to find optimal production schedules and distribution points in its supply chain. The company, which has 40 plants and 8,000 client sites, must consider factors such as power prices and projections of customer demand, as well as the power costs and efficiency of each plant.

BEFORE YOU GO ON....

1. What is a genetic algorithm?
2. Give examples of the use of genetic algorithms.

Apply The Concept PI5.5

LEARNING OBJECTIVE PI5.5 Describe the situations in which genetic algorithms would be most useful.

STEP 1 – Background

Genetic algorithms are used to calculate possible outcomes of hundreds (or thousands) of scenarios over time. These algorithms attempt to predict how things will change in the long term based on criteria set forth within the algorithm.

STEP 2 – Activity

Visit http://www.wiley.com/go/rainer/MIS3e/applytheconcept, and click on the links provided for Plug IT In 5.5. These links will take you to a page where you can observe a genetic algorithm in action. Specifically, you get to change variables on "plants" and "eaters" and observe how things evolve differently over time. The first link provides basic information about the algorithm, and the second link takes you to the actual demonstration.

Run this algorithm with different variables at least five times. Write down your initial settings and the outcome.

STEP 3 – Deliverable

Put your results into a table, and submit the table to your professor along with a description of how this exercise has helped you to better understand genetic algorithms and the effects of variance in initial settings. Also, describe a few real-life situations in which genetic algorithms would be most useful.

PI5.6 Intelligent Agents

An intelligent agent is a software program that assists you, or acts on your behalf, in performing repetitive computer-related tasks. Intelligent agents often use expert systems and fuzzy logic behind the scenes to create their seemingly intelligent behavior.

You may be familiar with an early type of intelligent agent—the paper clip (Clippy) that popped up in early versions of Microsoft Word. For example, if your document appeared as though it was going to be a business letter—that is, if you typed in a date, name, and address—the animated paper clip would offer helpful suggestions on how to proceed. Users objected so strenuously to this primitive intelligent agent that Microsoft eliminated it from subsequent versions.

There are many intelligent agents (also called *bots*) used for a wide variety of tasks. You can view the many different types of available agents by visiting BotSpot (www.botspot .com) and SmartBot (www.smartbot.com). The following sections examine three types of agents: information agents, monitoring and surveillance agents, and user or personal agents.

Information Agents

Information agents search for information and display it to users. The best known information agents are buyer agents. A buyer agent, also called a shopping bot, helps customers find the products and services they need on a Web site. There are many examples of information agents. We present here a few illustrative cases.

- The information agents for Amazon.com display lists of books and other products that customers might like, based on past purchases.

- Google and Ask.com use information agents to find information, and not just when you request it. Google, for example, sends out Googlebots to surf all the Web sites in Google's index. These bots copy individual pages to Google's repository, where Google's software indexes them. Therefore, whenever you perform a Google search, the search engine builds a list of all the pages that have the keywords you specify, and it presents them to you in PageRank order. Google's PageRank algorithm sorts Web pages based on the number of links on the Web that point to each page. That is, the more the Web links that point to a particular page, the higher that page will be on the list.

- The Federal Electronic Research and Review Extraction Tool (FERRET) was developed jointly by the Census Bureau and the Bureau of Labor Statistics. You can use FERRET to find information on employment, healthcare, education, race and ethnicity, health insurance, housing, income and poverty, aging, and marriage and the family.

Monitoring and Surveillance Agents

Monitoring and surveillance agents, also called predictive agents, constantly observe and report on some item of interest. There are many examples of predictive agents. Consider the following:

- Allstate uses monitoring and surveillance agents to manage its large computer networks 24/7/365. Every five seconds, the agent measures 1,200 data points. It can predict a system crash 45 minutes before it happens. The agent also watches to detect electronic attacks early so that they can be prevented.

- Monitoring and surveillance agents can watch your competitors and notify you of price changes and special offers.

- Predictive agents can monitor Internet sites, discussion groups, and mailing lists for stock manipulations, insider trading, and rumors that might affect stock prices. **FIN**

- These agents can search Web sites for updated information on topics of your choice, such as price changes on desired products (e.g., airline tickets).

User Agents

User agents, also called personal agents, take action on your behalf. Let's look at what these agents can do (or will be able to do shortly).

- Check your e-mail, sort it according to your priority rules, and alert you when high-value e-mails appear in your in-box.

- Automatically fill out forms on the Web for you. They will also store your information for future use.

Apply The Concept PI5.6

LEARNING OBJECTIVE PI5.6 Describe the use case for several major types of intelligent agents.

STEP 1 – Background

Information agents are a type of intelligent agent that searches for information or products and displays the results to the users. The best-known information agents are buyer agents.

STEP 2 – Activity

Let us assume the big game is coming up this weekend, and you have invited a group of friends over to watch it at your apartment. However, last evening, your TV died! So, you need to shop for a new TV quickly. You have heard about Web sites that can help you find the best deals, so you decide to try one out. You have at most about $450 to spend.

Because a lot of people are coming, you would like a big screen, at least 50 inches, so that everybody can see. In addition, you are partial to LCD screens. Visit http://www.wiley.com/go/rainer/MIS3e/applytheconcept and click on the link provided for Plug IT In 5.6. This link will take you to Shopzilla's Web site, where you can input the criteria described above and shop multiple sites at one time. When you are finished, compare your results with those you find on Google's shopping site (or any other shopping site you choose).

STEP 3 – Deliverable

After you work through the activity described above, submit your top five choices to your professor. Also, in addition to describing your experiences, discuss the use case for several major types of intelligent agents.

What's in for ME?

 FOR THE
ACCOUNTING MAJOR

Intelligent systems are used extensively in auditing to uncover irregularities. They are also used to uncover and prevent fraud. Today's CPAs use intelligent systems for many of their duties, ranging from risk analysis to cost control. Accounting personnel also use intelligent agents for mundane tasks such as managing accounts and monitoring employees' Internet use.

 FOR THE FINANCE MAJOR

People have been using computers for decades to solve financial problems. Innovative intelligent applications have been developed for activities such as making stock market decisions, refinancing bonds, assessing debt risks, analyzing financial conditions, predicting business failures, forecasting financial trends, and investing in global markets. Often, intelligent systems can facilitate the use of spreadsheets and other computerized systems used in finance. Finally, intelligent systems can help reduce fraud in credit cards, stocks, and other financial services.

FOR THE MARKETING MAJOR

Marketing personnel use intelligent systems in many applications, from allocating advertising budgets to evaluating alternative routings of salespeople. New marketing approaches such as targeted marketing and marketing transaction databases are heavily dependent on IT in general and on intelligent systems in particular. Intelligent systems are especially useful for mining customer databases and predicting customer behavior. Successful applications appear in almost every area of marketing and sales, from analyzing the success of one-to-one advertising to supporting customer help desks. With customer service becoming increasingly important, the use of intelligent agents is critical for providing fast response.

 FOR THE PRODUCTION/ OPERATIONS MANAGEMENT MAJOR

Intelligent systems support complex operations and production decisions, from inventory to production planning. Many of the early expert systems in the production/operations management field were developed for tasks ranging from diagnosing machine failures and prescribing repairs to complex production scheduling and inventory control. Some companies, such as DuPont and Kodak, have deployed hundreds of ESs in the planning, organizing, and control of their operational systems.

FOR THE HUMAN RESOURCES MANAGEMENT MAJOR

Human resources personnel employ intelligent systems for many applications. For example, recruiters use these systems to find applicants' resumes on the Web and sort them to match needed skills. Expert systems are also used in evaluating candidates (tests, interviews). HR personnel use intelligent systems to train and support employees in managing their fringe benefits. In addition, they use neural networks to predict employee job performance and future labor needs.

FOR THE MIS MAJOR

The MIS function develops (or acquires) and maintains the organization's various intelligent systems, as well as the data and models that these systems use. In addition, MIS staffers sometimes interact with subject area experts to capture the expertise used in expert systems.

SUMMARY

1. Explain the potential value and the potential limitations of artificial intelligence.

   Table PI5.1 differentiates between artificial and human intelligence on a number of characteristics.

2. Provide examples of the benefits, applications, and limitations of expert systems.

   Expert systems are computer systems that attempt to mimic human experts by applying expertise in a specific domain. Tables PI5.2 and PI5.3 offer examples of expert systems.

3. Provide examples of the use of neural networks.

   A neural network is a system of programs and data structures that simulate the underlying concepts of the human brain. Neural networks are used to detect weapons concealed in personal belongings, in research on various diseases, for financial forecasting, to detect fraud in credit card transactions, to fight crime, and many other applications.

4. Provide examples of the use of fuzzy logic.

   Fuzzy logic is a branch of mathematics that deals with uncertainties by simulating the process of human reasoning. Fuzzy logic is used in financial analysis, the manufacture of antilock brakes, measuring intangible assets like goodwill, and finding responses to search terms in Google.

5. Describe the situations in which genetic algorithms would be most useful.

   A genetic algorithm is an intelligent system that mimics the evolutionary, survival-of-the-fittest process to generate increasingly better solutions to a problem. Genetic algorithms are used to design aircraft parts such as fan blades to manage inventories more effectively, to optimize store displays, and to find optimal production schedules and distribution points.

6. Describe the use case for several major types of intelligent agents.

   An intelligent agent is a software program that assists you, or acts on your behalf, in performing repetitive, computer-related tasks. Intelligent agents are used to display lists of books or other products that customers might like, based on past purchases; to find information; to manage and monitor large computer networks 24/7/365; to detect electronic attacks early so that they can be stopped; to watch competitors and send notices of price changes and special offers; to monitor Internet sites, discussion groups, and mailing lists for stock manipulations, insider trading, and rumors that might impact stock prices; to check e-mail, sort it according to established priority rules, and alert recipients when high-value e-mails appear in their inbox; and to automatically fill out forms on the Web.

>>> CHAPTER GLOSSARY

algorithm A problem-solving method expressed as a finite sequence of steps.

artificial intelligence (**AI**) A subfield of computer science that is concerned with studying the thought processes of humans and re-creating the effects of those processes via machines, such as computers.

buyer agent (or **shopping bot**) An intelligent agent on a Web site that helps customers find products and services that they need.

expert systems (**ESs**) Computer systems that attempt to mimic human experts by applying expertise in a specific domain.

fuzzy logic A branch of mathematics that deals with uncertainties by simulating the processes of human reasoning.

genetic algorithm An approach that mimics the evolutionary, "survival-of-the-fittest" process to generate increasingly better solutions to a problem.

information agent A type of intelligent agent that searches for information and displays it to users.

intelligent agent A software program that assists you, or acts on your behalf, in performing repetitive, computer-related tasks.

intelligent systems A term that describes the various commercial applications of artificial intelligence.

machine learning systems Artificial intelligence systems that learn from data.

monitoring and surveillance agents (or **predictive agents**) Intelligent agents that constantly observe and report on some item of interest.

neural network A system of programs and data structures that simulates the underlying concepts of the human brain.

personal agents See **user agents**.

predictive agents See **monitoring and surveillance agents**.

shopping bot See **buyer agent**.

Turing test A test in which a man and a computer both pretend to be women (or men), and the human interviewer has to decide which is the real human.

user agents (or **personal agents**) Intelligent agents that take action on your behalf.

>>>DISCUSSION QUESTIONS

1. Explain how your university could employ an expert system in its admission process. Could it use a neural network?

   What might happen if a student were denied admission to the university and his parents discovered that an expert system was involved in the admissions process?

2. One difference between a conventional business intelligence system and an expert system is that the former can explain *how* questions, whereas the latter can explain both *how* and *why* questions. Discuss the implications of this statement.

>>>PROBLEM-SOLVING ACTIVITIES

1. You have decided to purchase a new video camcorder. To purchase it as inexpensively as possible and still get the features you want, you use a shopping bot. Visit several of the shopping bot Web sites that perform price comparisons for you. Begin with MySimon (www.mysimon.com), BizRate.com (www.bizrate.com), and Google Product Search.

   Compare these shopping bots in terms of ease of use, number of product offerings, speed in obtaining information, thoroughness of information offered about products and sellers, and price selection. Which site or sites would you use, and why? Which camcorder would you select and buy? How helpful were these sites in making your decision?

2. Access the MyMajors Web site (www.mymajors.com). This site contains a rule-based expert system to help

   students find majors. The expert system has more than 300 rules and 15,000 possible conclusions. The site ranks majors according to the likelihood that a student will succeed in them, and it provides 6 possible majors from among 60 alternative majors that a student might consider.

   Take the quiz, and see if you are in the "right major" as defined by the expert system. You must register to take the quiz.

3. Access Exsys (www.exsys.com), and click on the Corvid Demo (www.exsyssoftware.com/CORVID52/corvidsr?KBNAME=../Download2/DownloadForm.cvR). Provide your e-mail address, and click on the link for "Student— Needed for Class." Try the various demos, and report your results to the class.

>>> COLLABORATION EXERCISE

STEP 1 – Background

Intelligent agents help make us "experts" by thinking like the experts we are not. These agents are moving into our homes. In many cases, they may already be in your home without your even realizing it! One example is the Nest thermostat (www.nest.com) that will learn your patterns and automatically create a schedule, program itself, and keep the program. It also makes modifications, notices when you are not at home, and makes changes accordingly.

STEP 2 – Activity

Visit http://www.wiley.com/go/rainer/MIS3e/collaboration, and click on the link provided for Collaboration Exercise PI5. This link will take you to HowStuffWorks.com, where you will read an article about rice cookers that use fuzzy logic to prepare perfect rice.

Near the bottom of the page you find links to other appliances that use fuzzy logic such as washing machines,

dryers, and dishwashers. Assign one example to each team member to learn about.

Next, read about the particular example of fuzzy logic you have been assigned by your team, and report on the following:

- How does the system learn?
- How does it make decisions?
- Is there a significant level of human interaction?

Then, meet with your team to discuss the implications of fuzzy logic (and artificial intelligence) over the next 10 years.

STEP 3 – Deliverable

Create and share a single Google Doc that summarizes your findings. Based on your findings, can you identify potential problems with using fuzzy logic in a home security (or business security) system?

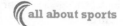

Retail

Amazon.com has huge advantage over brick-and-mortar retailers due to the intelligent systems they have developed. All you have to do is get close to a product category, and their intelligent systems will provide links to products other customers shopped for or purchased after they viewed that particular item. Often, in a few clicks you have found a top-rated product you were not aware of just a few minutes earlier.

For Harrison Kirby, owner of All About Sports sporting goods store from the Internship Activity for Chapters 1, 7, 8,

and 9, Amazon presents a real problem. Harrison has a tough time competing with online sporting goods stores because he is not able to carry a comparable inventory selection and he does not have sufficient data to create similar intelligent systems. Harrison is interested in creating a system that would allow his customers to tap into the intelligent systems that are available online but at the same time would keep his customers in his store for purchases.

Below is an e-mail from Harrison about this project.

To: IT Intern

From: Harrison Kirby

Subject: Intelligent Systems

Hello!!

I am at a bit of a disadvantage. Too often I see customers come into my store, scan a product on the shelf, tap on their phone, and then leave without buying anything. I never know for certain what they are doing, but I am afraid they are shopping online with barcode reader apps, looking up reviews, finding cheaper pricing, and ultimately purchasing from someone else. Basically, I often feel like a window shop for Amazon.com!

I need to know how I can handle this situation. I would like to offer my customers a price match with companies like Amazon.com and GolfSmith.com. However, I need to be able to analyze how much money I would lose by implementing this type of policy. What I need is some business intelligence.

Search the Web for a spreadsheet-based BI tool. It can be an add-on, or something where you upload your spreadsheet data into the system for analysis. Let me know what you find in terms of how the system runs: as a spreadsheet, an add-on, a stand-alone system that accepts spreadsheets, or a cloud-based spreadsheet analysis tool. Of course, the cost is also very important to us

Thanks for your help!

Harrison

Note: Any links or Web sites mentioned in this e-mail are available at http://www.wiley.com/go/rainer/MIS3e/internship.

Project Management

LEARNING OBJECTIVES

PI6.1 Explain the relationship between the triple constraints on projects.

PI6.2 Describe the five phases of the project management process.

PI6.3 Review how each of the nine processes of the Project Management Body of Knowledge is necessary in order to ensure smooth project deployment.

PI6.1 Project Management for Information Systems Projects

Projects are short-term efforts to create a specific business-related outcome. These outcomes may take the form of products or services. In the context of information systems (IS), many of the resource investments made by organizations are in the form of projects. For example, Home Depot (www.homedepot.com) recently engaged in an IS project to develop an inventory management system. The objectives of the project were to improve inventory turnover, reduce product stock-outs, and integrate more tightly with supply chain partners. The outcome was to lower companywide costs by carrying less physical inventory.

Almost every organization that utilizes information technology to support business processes engages in some form of IS project management. **IS project management** is a directed effort to plan, organize, and manage resources to bring about the successful achievement of specific IS goals. All projects, whether they are IS projects or not, are constrained by the same three factors, known as the **triple constraints of project management**: time, cost, and scope. *Time* refers to the window of opportunity in which a project must be completed to provide a benefit to the organization. *Cost* is the actual amount of resources, including cash and labor, that an organization can commit to completing a project. *Scope* refers to the processes that ensure that the project includes all the work required—and only the work required—to complete the project successfully. For an IS project to be successful, the organization must allow an adequate amount of time, provide an appropriate amount of resources, and carefully define what is and is not included in the project.

The triple constraints are related and involve trade-offs. For example, scope can often be increased by using additional time and incurring increased costs. Cost and/or time can often be saved by reducing scope. For a given scope, time can sometimes be saved by increasing cost. The following example illustrates just how complex projects can be.

EXAMPLE

Building a Natural Gas Pipeline to Hong Kong

As one of the world's most populous cities, Hong Kong needs energy to supply its 7.1 million residents with electricity. The city relies on a mix of fuels, chosen for reliability, sustainability, and efficiency.

One of these energy sources is natural gas. Since 1996, Hong Kong's Black Point Power Station has drawn natural gas from the reserves of a gas field in Hainan, a nearby Chinese province. However, these reserves had begun to deplete, and it was clear that Hong Kong needed a new plan to maintain a consistent supply of natural gas and to comply with tightened emission caps that will be required by the government of Hong Kong in 2015.

In 2008, the governments of Hong Kong and the People's Republic of China signed a memorandum of understanding on energy cooperation, which identified three new gas sources from which mainland China could supply gas to Hong Kong.

One of the sources was the second West–East Gas Pipeline (WEPII), which is the world's longest natural gas pipeline. Building a natural gas pipeline from the existing WEPII network to Hong Kong is an incredibly complex project, presenting numerous challenges:

Regulations. Because it crossed the border between mainland China and Hong Kong, the project team had to acquire permits from both jurisdictions. The project also had to obtain different statutory approval processes between the jurisdictions.

Communications. The various project team members spoke different languages, and the parties involved had different requirements for documentation and reporting. The teams predominantly used English, Putonghua, and Cantonese. However, they used English and Cantonese for documents and PowerPoint presentations. The project team also had to manage a multitude of stakeholders, including over 30 government departments in both jurisdictions.

Environmental requirements. The project had to fulfill stringent environmental requirements for the two jurisdictions. Project managers instituted a robust monitoring and audit program during the project's execution phase, with intensive water quality monitoring, marine mammal monitoring, and site inspections. Mitigation measures also included the deployment of silt curtains and limitations of working speed during marine dredging operations.

Physical restraints. The actual laying of the pipeline was subject to many physical constraints. The project required a 12-mile undersea pipeline through three shipping channels. There were also challenges involving shallow water with a dredged marine channel, anchorage areas, and an existing subsea pipeline and cables.

Before laying the pipeline, the project team conducted an extensive marine traffic impact assessment. They also coordinated closely with local marine and port control authorities to successfully work around channel traffic, laying the entire 12-mile undersea pipeline in only 6–7 months.

To handle a complex project of this magnitude and to finish on time and on budget, the project team needed careful planning. Before project initiation, the team thoroughly planned, scheduled, and engineered the project to ensure that the pipeline would function properly and, more importantly, that it would be safe.

The project had a tight schedule. To meet the deadlines, project managers implemented elements of the waterfall approach, where certain milestones had to be completed before the next tasks could begin. For example, the channel dredging had to be finished before the pipeline could be laid. Proper planning, critical path monitoring, and close coordination between Hong Kong and China helped ensure that the project finished on time.

The project team tightly controlled the scope of the project. Any changes had to go through a rigorous change management process, which kept the project on track.

The team also realized that communication was a key component to successfully completing the pipeline. Project managers made special efforts to build effective teams. They established processes to always engage the right person for the right task and to encourage teamwork. For instance, given the different nationalities involved, all materials and discussions were in multiple languages.

Project managers focused on quality and safety. They performed daily site visits, as well as scheduled and nonscheduled management walkthroughs. There were also third-party inspections done on critical tasks, such as the pipe welding.

As a result of excellent project management, the pipeline was finished on time, and it began supplying Hong Kong with natural gas in 2013. The project also had a minimal impact of heavy marine traffic in the area, especially on the container ships that are vital to that area's economy.

Sources: Compiled from "Hong Kong Natural Gas Pipeline," *Project Management Institute Case Study*, 2014; "Hong Kong Branch of Second West–East Gas Pipeline Completed and Operational," *Penn Energy*, October 21, 2103; J. Cullen, "Second West–East Gas Pipeline Set to Start Hong Kong Supplies This Summer," *South China Morning Post*, June 16, 2013.

Questions

1. What were the drivers of the new natural gas pipeline to Hong Kong?
2. Describe the key factors contributing to the success of the pipeline project.
3. Describe the triple constraints of Hong Kong's pipeline project.

Apply The Concept PI6.1

LEARNING OBJECTIVE PI6.1 Explain the relationship between the triple constraints on projects.

STEP 1 – Background (This is what you are learning.)

This section describes how companies employ software to support project management. Project management software offers tools such as planning, communication, coordination, measurement, and data collection to help companies navigate the triple constraints on projects: time, cost, and scope.

STEP 2 – Activity (This is what you are doing.)

Visit http://www.wiley.com/go/rainer/MIS3e/applytheconcept, and click on the link provided for Plug IT In 6.1. This link will take you to a Web site that sells project management software. At this site you can click on links that will show you tours, customer success stores, pictures, and demos of the software. As you explore the site, look for the ways different products are marketed to help companies deal with the triple constraints.

STEP 3 – Deliverable (This is what you turn in.)

From the site you looked at in Step 2, choose one software package, and explain how it helps companies deal with the relationships among time, cost, and scope of projects. Submit your explanation to your instructor.

PI6.2 The Project Management Process

The traditional approach to project management divides every project into five distinct phases: initiation, planning, execution, monitoring and control, and completion (FIGURE PI6.1). These phases are sequential, and we discuss them in order.

Project Initiation

The first phase in the management of a process is to clearly define the problem that the project is intended to solve and the goals that it is to achieve. In this phase, it is also necessary to identify and secure the resources necessary for the project, analyze the costs and benefits of the project, and identify potential risks.

In an IS project, a user's business problem or need typically initiates a project that can solve the problem and meet the need. The user must clearly define the problem so that the IS team can understand it. The user must also define the benefits he or she expects to gain from successful completion of the IS project.

Project Planning

As the term *planning* suggests, in this phase, every project objective and every activity associated with that objective must be identified and sequenced. This phase is critically important to avoid scope creep once the project gets underway. **Scope creep** refers to uncontrolled changes in a project's scope. This phenomenon can occur when the scope of a project is not properly defined, documented, or controlled. It is generally considered a negative occurrence that is to be avoided.

In an IS project, users often contribute to scope creep when they ask for additional features or functionality after the project is underway. This situation often leads to the project being over time and over budget.

Many tools assist developers in sequencing these activities, including dependence diagrams, such as the program evaluation and review technique (PERT), the critical path method (CPM), and a timeline diagram called the Gantt chart. Project managers use these tools to ensure that activities are performed in a logical sequence. As the project progresses,

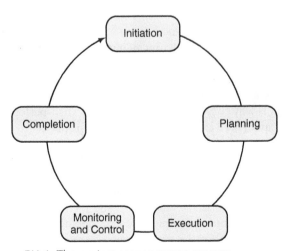

Figure PI6.1 The project management process.

project managers also employ these tools to evaluate whether the project is on schedule and, if not, where the delays are occurring and what the managers must do to correct them.

Project Execution

In this phase, the work defined in the project management plan is performed to accomplish the project's requirements. Execution coordinates people and resources, and it integrates and performs project activities in accordance with the plan.

Users may be involved in project execution. For example, in an IS project, users often evaluate prototypes so that they can provide meaningful feedback to the IS team.

Project Monitoring and Control

The purpose of monitoring and control is to determine whether the project is progressing as planned. This phase consists of three steps: (1) monitoring ongoing project activities (where we are); (2) comparing project variables (cost, effort, time, resources, etc.) with the actual plan (where we should be); and (3) identifying corrective actions (how do we get on track again).

Project Completion

The project is completed when it is formally accepted by the organization. All activities are finalized and all contracts are fulfilled and settled. In addition, all files are archived and all lessons learned are documented.

Project Management Failure

As IT systems have become an important competitive necessity in modern organizations, IT projects are getting larger, involve more parts of the organization, and pose a risk to the company if something goes wrong. Research by McKinsey and the University of Oxford suggest that half of all large IT projects—defined as those with initial price tags exceeding $15 million—go far over their budgets. Their research also shows that, on average, large IT projects run 45 percent over budget and 7 percent over time, while delivering 56 percent less value than predicted. Such projects are called *runaway projects*, meaning they are so far over budget and past deadline that they must be abandoned, typically with large monetary loss. Even worse, the researchers found that 17 percent of large IT projects are so bad that they threaten the very existence of a company.

The researchers found that four groups of issues caused most IT project failures:

- A lack of focus, including unclear objectives and lack of business focus
- Content issues, such as shifting requirements (e.g., scope creep) and technical complexity)
- Skill issues, such as a team not aligned with business objectives and a general lack of skills
- Execution issues, such as an unrealistic schedule and reactive planning (on the fly, as opposed to sufficient planning at the start of a project)

Enabling Project Management Success

The research findings bring up the crucial question: How do companies maximize the chance that their IT projects deliver the expected value on time and within budget? The findings indicated that the key to project management success is in mastering four broad dimensions of project management:

- Focusing on managing strategy and stakeholders instead of exclusively concentrating on budgeting and scheduling
- Mastering technology and project content by securing critical internal and external talent
- Building effective teams by aligning their incentives with the overall goals of projects
- Excelling at core project management practices, such as short delivery cycles and rigorous quality checks

Let's discuss each of these in turn.

Manage Strategy and Stakeholders. IT projects often pay little attention to strategy and stakeholders and manage projects only according to budget and schedule targets. These problems are illustrated by one bank's IT transformation effort, in which its finance department became involved only a few months before the system was due to become operational. This problem led to several complex changes in the accounting software modules as a result of a recently introduced performance management system. Occurring so late in the project, the changes delayed the launch by more than three months, at a cost of more than $8 million.

Top-performing projects, on the other hand, establish a clear view of the project's strategic value—one that goes beyond technical content. By building a robust, well-understood business case and maintaining focus on business objectives along the entire project timeline, success teams can avoid cost and time overruns.

These teams ensure that the project aligns with the company's business strategy and undertake detailed analyses of stakeholder positions. Team leaders continually engage with all business unit and functional area heads to ensure consistent alignment.

Secure Critical Talent. Drawing on expert help as needed, high-performance teams integrate all technical aspects of the project, including IT architecture and infrastructure, functionality trade-offs, quality assurance, migration and rollout plans, and project scope. The excellent team will understand both business and technical concerns, which is why companies must assign a few high-performing and experienced experts for the length of the project.

One common problem occurs when teams focus too much on technology issues and targets. For instance, a large retailer wanted to create a central data warehouse to overcome inconsistencies that occurred among its business unit financial data, centralized financial data, and risk data. However, the project team focused purely on developing the IT architecture solution for the data warehouse instead of addressing the end goal, which was to manage data inconsistencies.

As a result, the project budget increased as the team pursued architectural "perfection," which involved the inclusion of unnecessary data from other systems. The bank finally had to halt the project after 18 months and several million dollars.

Build Effective Teams.

Large projects can take a life of their own in an organization. Project teams need a common vision, shared team processes, and a high-performance culture. Members must have a common incentive structure that is aligned with the overall project goal, in contrast with individual goals.

For example, to ensure the smooth startup of new front-end and core systems that more than 8,000 people would use, one company project team launched a massive, and successful, change management program. This program included a regular newsletter, desktop calendars that highlighted key changes and milestones, and quarterly town hall meetings with the CEO. The team made sure that all business unit leaders were involved during the user acceptance phase of the project.

Excel at Project Management Practices.

To achieve excellent project management, there is no substitute for tested practices. These practices include having a strategic and disciplined project management office and establishing rigorous processes for managing project requirements and change requests.

BEFORE *YOU GO ON....*

1. What are the five phases of the project management process?

2. What are the major causes of project failure?

3. Describe how to best ensure the success of projects.

Apply The Concept PI6.2

LEARNING OBJECTIVE PI6.2 Describe the five phases of the project management process.

STEP 1 – Background

As you have seen in this section, project management is a complicated task. Multiple people, multiple activities, and multiple opinions about the "right" way to handle the project always make it difficult for the individuals who are actually managing the operation.

STEP 2 – Activity

Visit http://www.wiley.com/go/rainer/MIS3e/applytheconcept, and click on the link provided for Plug IT In 6.2. The link will take you to an article that discusses the difficulties that Hershey's experienced when it implemented a new IT system. In fact, this project cost the company more than $100 million in sales because the ordering system did not function properly.

After reading the article, search the Web for additional information on this story.

STEP 3 – Deliverable

Based on what you read in Step 2, describe the five phases of the project management process at Hershey's. Try to determine in which step (or steps) Hershey's made its mistakes. Submit your description to your instructor.

PI6.3 The Project Management Body of Knowledge

The **Project Management Body of Knowledge (PMBOK)** is a collection of processes and knowledge areas generally accepted as best practice within the project management discipline. As an internationally recognized standard, it provides the fundamentals of project management, regardless of the type of project (e.g., construction, software, engineering, automotive, etc.). The purpose of the PMBOK is to provide and promote a common vocabulary within the project management profession for discussing, writing, and applying project management concepts.

The PMBOK recognizes five basic process groups and nine knowledge areas typical of almost all projects. You learned about the five basic process groups in the previous section:

- Initiation
- Planning
- Execution
- Monitoring and control
- Completion

Processes overlap and interact throughout a project. Processes are described in terms of inputs (documents, plans, designs), tools and techniques, and outputs (documents, products).

The nine knowledge areas of the PMBOK are as follows:

- *Project Integration Management.* Project integration management includes those processes required to ensure that all the project's components are properly coordinated. The project plan development processes, project plan execution processes, and integrated change control processes are all included in this area of knowledge. Each process has expected inputs and outputs and plus the appropriate tools and techniques to support the change of inputs to outputs.

- *Project Scope Management.* Project scope management defines the processes that limit and control the work included in a project. Scope creep is a serious problem that often causes projects to go over time and over budget. These processes ensure that all the work of the project is included and properly accounted for.

- *Project Time Management.* Proper sequencing is vital to timely project completion. When the amount of time needed is established, it takes excellent scheduling skills and tools to manage the activities to complete project milestones and the project itself within the allotted time. Different tools are available to assist with this process, such as Gantt charts, milestone charts, and network charts. Each tool helps managers see the big picture and stay in control of the project's progression.

- *Project Cost Management.* Resource planning and cost estimation are equally vital to time management. These two processes cannot exist independent of each other. Resource cost management is difficult to estimate and even more difficult to manage when unforeseen events take place. Early in a project, managers may project a budget range and then fine-tune it as the project progresses.

- *Project Quality Management.* Every project needs a set of processes ensuring that project outcomes meet the needs for which the project was executed. Quality planning, assurance, and control are included in this area. There are many quality management models to consider, such as the Deming Prize, TQM, and Six Sigma. All of these aim to help organizations produce quality products the first time they try. There are also many paradigms applicable to this area of knowledge, such as "Zero Defects" and "DTRTRTFT" (Do the right thing right the first time). These paradigms are meant to inspire organizations to operate at higher quality levels.

- *Project Human Resource Management.* People can be the major headache or the major asset of any project.

People with differing skill sets are required at various times during a project and their individual skills have to be used effectively for the project to succeed. This area of knowledge includes concepts such as staffing decisions; team management; and organizational culture, style, and structure.

HRM

- *Project Communications Management.* A vast amount of communication is necessary in successful projects. Information must be collected, disseminated, stored, and destroyed at the appropriate time. This area of knowledge contains the processes to perform these functions. Often, organizations investigate personality styles to determine their most effective communicators. Choosing the right person to be a leader can make all the difference in the success of a project.

- *Project Risk Management.* All projects face risk. With organizational success, jobs, careers, and livelihoods on the line, it is a good idea to minimize the risk of projects as much as feasible. Therefore, risk management must be an integral part of any project because things do not always happen as planned. The risk management process includes identification of risks, quantitative and qualitative analyses, risk response planning, and risk monitoring.

- *Project Procurement Management.* No matter how good the idea behind a project, without funding it will never be more than a good idea. The accumulated knowledge related to project procurement management encompasses processes of solicitation, selection, contractual agreements, and closeout processes.

BEFORE *YOU GO ON....*

1. What is the Project Management Body of Knowledge and why is it important to organizations?

2. What part of the PMBOK do you think is most important? Can a project succeed without all the parts?

Apply The Concept PI6.3

LEARNING OBJECTIVE PI6.3 Review how each of the nine processes of the Project Management Body of Knowledge is necessary in order to ensure smooth project deployment.

STEP 1 – Background

Project management is critical to the successful implementation of any new system. As you saw from the Hershey's case in Plug IT In 6.2, projects can get out of hand very quickly. (If you did not complete this activity, visit http://www.wiley.com/go/rainer/MIS3e/applytheconcept and click on the link for Plug IT In 6.2 to read the article). There are many stories you could read that would demonstrate just how quickly projects go awry.

STEP 2 – Activity

Visit http://www.wiley.com/go/rainer/MIS3e/applytheconcept, and click on the link provided for Plug IT In 6.3. This link will take you to an article about a failure of the Denver Airport Baggage System. As you review this story, consider the nine processes of the Project Management Body of Knowledge, and try to determine which ones could have helped the project succeed.

Within the context of the Denver Airport Baggage story you read in Step 2, review how each of the nine processes of the Project Management Body of Knowledge is necessary to ensure smooth project deployment.

What's in for ME?

FOR ALL BUSINESS MAJORS

Regardless of the functional area in organizations, each of you will be on project teams beginning very early in your careers. These projects will be critical to your organization's success. Therefore, it is critical that all majors understand the project management process so that you can make immediate contributions to your project teams.

SUMMARY

1. Explain the relationship between the triple constraints on projects.

   Projects are short-term efforts to create a specific business-related outcome. *IS project management* is a directed effort to plan, organize, and manage resources to bring about the successful achievement of specific IS goals. All projects, whether they are IS projects or not, are constrained by the same three factors, known as the *triple constraints of project management*: time, cost, and scope. *Time* refers to the window of opportunity in which a project must be completed to provide a benefit to the organization. *Cost* is the actual amount of resources, including cash and labor, that an organization can commit to completing a project. *Scope* refers to the processes that ensure that the project includes all the work required—and only the work required—to complete the project successfully.

2. Describe the five phases of the project management process.

   Project initiation clearly defines the problem that the project is intended to solve and the goals that it is to achieve.

   In *project planning*, every project objective and every activity associated with that objective must be identified and sequenced. In the *project execution* phase, the work defined in the project management plan is performed to accomplish the project's requirements. The purpose of the *monitoring and control phase* is to determine whether the progress is progressing as planned. The *project completion* phase is when the project is formally accepted by the organization.

3. Review how each of the nine processes of the Project Management Body of Knowledge is necessary in order to ensure smooth project deployment.

   IS projects do not deliver their potential value for a number of reasons, including lack of sufficient planning at the start of a project; difficulties with technology compatibility (i.e., new technology may not work with existing technology); lack of commitment by management in providing the necessary resources; poorly defined project scope; and lack of sufficient time to complete the project.

>>>GLOSSARY

IS project management A directed effort to plan, organize, and manage resources to bring about the successful achievement of specific IS goals.

project Short-term effort to create a specific business-related outcome.

Project Management Body of Knowledge (PMBOK) A collection of processes and knowledge areas generally accepted as best practice within the project management discipline.

scope creep Uncontrolled changes in a project's scope.

triple constraints of project management Time, cost, and scope.

>>>DISCUSSION QUESTIONS

1. You manage the department that will use a system being developed on a large project. After carefully reviewing the requirements definition document, you are positive that there are missing, ambiguous, inaccurate, and unclear requirements. The project manager is pressuring you for your sign-off because he has already received sign-offs from all of your coworkers. If you fail to sign off on the requirements, you are going to put the entire project at risk because the time frame is not negotiable. What should you do? Why? Support your answer.

2. You have been hired as a consultant to build an employee payroll system for a startup restaurant. Before you even have a chance to interview them, the two owners decided to independently come up with a list of their business requirements. When you combine their two lists, you have the following list:

   - All employees must have a unique employee ID.

   - The system must track employee hours worked based on employees' last names.
   - Employees must be scheduled to work a minimum of 8 hours per day.
   - Employee payroll is calculated by multiplying the employees' hours worked by $7.25.
   - Managers must be scheduled to work morning shifts.
   - Employees cannot be scheduled to work more than 8 hours per day.
   - Servers cannot be scheduled to work morning, afternoon, or evening shifts.
   - The system must allow managers to change and delete employees from the system.
     a. Highlight potential issues with the list.
     b. Add requirements that you think should be there but are not.
     c. What do you tell the owners when you derive your new list?

>>> COLLABORATION EXERCISE

STEP 1 – Background

One key element of Project Management is dealing with people. In fact, effective interaction skills are listed as one of the nine knowledge areas of the Project Management Body of Knowledge. To help their employees develop these skills, many companies use personality profiles to develop teams that have the best chance of success.

STEP 2 – Activity

Visit http://www.wiley.com/go/rainer/MIS3e/collaboration, and click on the link provided for the Collaboration Exercise for Plug IT In 6. This link will take you to a Web site where you can complete a free personality profile. This profile, known as the Jung Typology Test, is based on the

Meyers-Briggs personality test that is widely used by HR departments.

Complete this activity as an individual, and print a copy of your results. Then, build a Google Document with your team that includes everyone's results. Determine whether you have a good balance on all four criteria.

STEP 3 – Deliverable

As a team, determine whether you have a good mix of personalities that would work well together. If there is an area where you do not have good balance, it can pose a problem. Submit your team document that includes both your individual responses and your team's thoughts.

Apply each of the five project management processes of the PMBOK to the following massive project. Then, discuss each process with regard to that project. Finally, use a search engine to find out where the project stands now. Would this be considered a runaway project? Why or why not?

Established in 1948, the National Health Service (NHS) in the United Kingdom is the largest healthcare organization in Europe. Controlled by the British government, it is also a vast bureaucracy, employing more than 1 million workers and providing a full range of healthcare services to the country's 60 million citizens.

The inspiration to digitize this huge bureaucracy first surfaced in 2001. At that time, much of the NHS was paper based and severely lagging in its use of technology, largely because of years of underinvestment. Hospitals throughout the United Kingdom were dealing with multiple vendors, many of them small to mid-size UK software companies. Predictably, the NHS had become a hodgepodge of incompatible systems from different suppliers, with differing levels of functionality. The NHS had created silos of information that were not shared, or even sharable.

In an attempt to resolve these problems, in 2002 the British government initiated the National Program for Information Technology (NPIT), which includes England, Northern Ireland, and Wales (but not Scotland). The overall objective of the NPIT was to build a single, electronic healthcare record for every individual. In effect, this record would be a comprehensive, lifelong history of a patient's healthcare information, regardless of where, when, and by whom he or she was treated. In addition, the NPIT would provide healthcare professionals with access to a national data repository. Finally, it would support the NHS in collecting and analyzing information and monitoring health trends to make the best use of clinical and other resources.

A major obstacle for the NPIT was the sheer size of England's healthcare system. For example, in one year, the system served some 52 million people; it dealt with 325 million consultations in primary care, 13 million outpatient consultations, and 4 million emergency admissions; and it issued 617 million prescriptions.

The NPIT is a 10-year project designed to build new information systems to (1) connect more than 100,000 doctors, 380,000 nurses, and 50,000 other healthcare professionals; (2) allow for the electronic storage and retrieval of patient medical records; (3) permit patients to set up appointments via their computers; and (4) let doctors electronically transmit prescriptions to local pharmacies.

Specifically, the information systems that the NHS is attempting to deliver include the following:

- *The National Spine.* The National Spine is a database at the heart of the NPIT. The Spine encompasses individual electronic NHS lifelong care records for every patient in England, securely accessible by the patients and their health providers. The Spine will enable patients and providers to securely access integrated patient data, prescription ordering, proactive decision support, and best-practice reference data.

- *Choose and Book.* Choose and Book provides convenience for patients in electronically selecting the date, place, and time of their appointments.

- *N3.* The N3 national network is a massive, secure, broadband, virtual private network that provides the IT infrastructure and broadband connectivity for the NHS so that it can share patient information with various organizations. The N3 supports Choose and Book, electronic prescriptions, and electronic transfer of patient information.

The NHS first had McKinsey & Company conduct a study of the UK healthcare system. McKinsey concluded that the project was too large for any one vendor to act as prime contractor for all of it. Consequently, the NHS divided England into five regions—London, Eastern, Northeast, Northwest, and Southern—each with about 12 million people. Each of the five regions would be serviced by a prime IT vendor, known as a Local Service Provider (LSP).

The vendor selection process was conducted with great secrecy. Unfortunately, the secrecy led to most frontline healthcare providers being excluded from the vendor selection process. The NHS offered 10-year service contracts to the LSPs for the five regions, each worth about $2 billion.

The LSPs are responsible for developing and integrating information systems at a local level. The LSPs are also responsible for implementing clinical and administrative applications, which support the delivery of patient care and enable trusts to exchange data with the National Spine. (A trust is a regional healthcare agency that administers England's national healthcare programs). In addition, the LSPs provide the data centers to run all the applications.

Significantly, all of the NHS's contracts with the LSPs stipulated that vendors would not be paid until they delivered working systems. Because the vendors were the prime contractors, this stipulation also meant that the subcontractors would not be paid until they delivered working systems.

Accenture was named LSP for two regions. Computer Sciences Corporation (CSC), British Telecom (BT), and a Fujitsu-led alliance were named LSPs for the other three regions. BT was also given the contract to build both the N3 network and the National Spine. Atos Origin was chosen to provide Choose and Book.

As previously explained, the LSPs were to act as prime contractors for their respective regions, and they were able to choose their own software vendors and subcontractors. BT and the Fujitsu group selected IDX (now part of GE Healthcare), an established healthcare services and software provider, to develop health records software. Accenture and CSC chose iSoft, a UK-based supplier of healthcare software, for that function.

Developing this software presented many challenges. Both iSoft and IDX had to write some of the software from scratch. The difficulty was that the programmers and systems developers did not comprehend some of the terminology used by the British health system and, more important, how the British health system actually operated.

Compounding these problems was the decision by Accenture and CSC to select iSoft as its clinical and administrative software vendor. These companies were depending on iSoft's Lorenzo application suite, which at that time was still in development. However, iSoft seriously underestimated the time and effort necessary to develop the Lorenzo suite. As a result, under the collect-on-implementation contract that the LSPs had signed with the NHS, neither Accenture nor iSoft could generate revenue. In a catch-22 situation, this lack of revenue left iSoft short of the cash it needed to finish developmental work on Lorenzo.

The ongoing delay of Lorenzo left Accenture and CSC in a quandary. Should they continue to wait for Lorenzo, or should they lock into older, existing applications? Accenture opted to wait and use Lorenzo. In contrast, CSC chose to implement iSoft's existing line of products.

While waiting for Lorenzo, Accenture worked with general practitioners, as opposed to CSC, which focused almost entirely on hospitals. Accenture's problem was that the general practitioner implementation was extremely difficult because there are so many of them and the NHS had given them an option called GP Systems of Choice. This option stipulated that the doctors did not have to follow Accenture's lead in selecting a system but could, instead, choose on their own. This choice, in turn, further complicated the transfer of more than 10 years of data from old systems to the Spine compliant systems being provided by Accenture. Typically, it cost about $9,000 and took six months to transfer the data of each practitioner.

Meanwhile, there were concerns with GE Healthcare's IDX as well. Fujitsu and BT had agreed to develop a Common Solution Program, meaning that the two LSPs would develop common applications for two of England's regions. Because of time delays at IDX, Fujitsu and BT replaced the firm with Cerner, a U.S. healthcare IT company. This replacement caused additional time delays for the project.

The NPIT was originally budgeted at $12 billion, but that figure has risen to $24 billion as a result of the many problems encountered in developing the NPIT. By mid-2007, the NHS had delivered some of the program's key elements. For example, 1 million patient referrals to specialist care were made through Choose and Book and 97 percent of doctors' offices were connected to the N3 network.

However, many deliverables of the project have been delayed. In addition, the N3 network experienced more than a hundred failures in 2006. One network outage disrupted mission-critical computer services such as patient administration systems for three days.

Another problem was that the project has little support among healthcare workers. This problem stemmed from excluding frontline healthcare professionals in the early phases of the project. Therefore, it fell largely to the vendors and the bureaucrats to create the system. Physicians complained that the system focused too much on administrative needs and not enough on clinicians' concerns. A survey conducted in 2006 showed that only 38 percent of British general practitioners and nurses believed that the project was an important priority for the NHS, and only 13 percent believed that the project represented a good use of NHS resources.

The NHS policy to pay vendors only on delivery of working systems was shortsighted because the policy provided no flexibility to deal with vendors that encountered unexpected problems. In late 2006, Accenture announced that it was walking away from its contract with the NHS. Accenture did not say why it was exiting the project, but the company had set aside some $500 million to cover losses from its work in England.

As of mid-2007, the NHS itself had run short of funding, resulting in huge layoffs, possible closings of hospitals, and reductions in services. These problems were so serious that they prompted the British government to initiate an effort to bring costs under control. Some experts estimate that it will take another $15 billion (over the $24 billion already spent) to get the NPIT initiative fully functional.

The NHS is an incredibly political system. On the one hand, in mid-2014, the NHS continues to operate chronically short of funds. British analysts predict that by 2020, the largest healthcare system in the world will be operating a deficit six times larger than its annual operating budget, forcing the closure of up to 20 percent of Britain's hospitals, which are already inundated with patients.

On the other hand, proponents of the NHS say that it operates efficiently, delivering better health outcomes than the United States at half the cost. In fact, proponents state that NHS physicians and patients are more humble about their expectations of what their healthcare system should provide than physicians and patients in the United States.

INTERNSHIP ACTIVITY> southwest wire A PRODUCTION COMPANY

Manufacturing

Southwest Wire is preparing to roll out a new system for managing the paperwork associated with their R&D processes. Getting a new wire product ready for market involves numerous steps and reams of paperwork. Multiple labs, technicians, tests, and results are required for a product to meet government regulations.

Above and beyond these considerations are the many users who will need the information generated by this new system. Sales representatives benefit from knowing how long it will take to have a product ready for market. Production needs to know the projected sales. The accountants need to know the costs of certification as well as the cost per linear foot to produce the product.

To achieve any of these objectives, Southwest Wire needs a well-planned rollout. So, once again, CIO Halle Smith is in need of your help. Below is an e-mail from Halle about this project.

To:	IT Intern
From:	Halle Smith
Subject:	Managing the Development and Implementation of Our New R&D System

Hello!

I am very much interested in learning about some industry standard practices on managing projects. I have plans to implement a new system in our R&D Department to manage the paperwork involved in their processes. I need some idea of what other project managers plan for at this stage of the game.

There appear to be some best practices in our industry regarding Information Technology Project Management. One practice that I recall from my undergrad days was COBIT, thought I do not remember anything about it. Search the Web for any training material that can provide me with an overview of COBIT and perhaps some alternative project management practices as well.

Thanks for your help!

Halle

Note: Any links or Web sites mentioned in this e-mail are available at http://www.wiley.com/go/rainer/MIS3e/internship.

Protecting Your Information Assets

LEARNING OBJECTIVES

PI7.1 Explain why it is critical that you protect your information assets.

PI7.2 Identify the various behavioral actions you can take to protect your information assets.

PI7.3 Identify the various computer-based actions you can take to protect your information assets.

PI7.1 How to Protect Your Assets: The Basics

We travel on our jobs, we work from home, and we access the Internet from home and from our favorite hotspots for any number of reasons—shopping, ordering products, planning trips, gathering information, and staying in touch with friends and family via e-mail. Unfortunately, every time we use our computers or access the Internet, we risk exposing both professional and personal information to people intent on stealing or exploiting that information. Therefore, we have prepared this Plug IT In to explain how you can protect your information assets when you are computing at home or while you are traveling.

Hopefully, when you are at work or when you access your university's network from home or on the road, you have the advantage of "industrial-strength" information security that your company or university's IS department has implemented. In all other cases, however, you are on your own, so it is *your* responsibility to protect yourself. Maintaining proper security is becoming even more critical because organized crime is increasingly turning its attention to home users. As businesses improve their information security, consumers become the next logical target. According to Symantec (www.symantec.com), which manufactures the Norton Internet security products, if you connected an unprotected personal computer to the Internet in 2003, it would have been attacked within 15 minutes. Today, that same computer will be attacked within seconds.

You can take two types of actions to protect your information assets: behavioral actions and computer-based actions (see FIGURE PI7.1). Behavioral actions are those actions that do not specifically involve a computer. Computer-based actions relate to safe computing. If you take both types of actions, you will protect your information and greatly reduce your exposure to fraud and identity theft.

BEFORE *YOU GO ON....*

1. Why is it so important that you take the responsibility for the security of your information assets?

2. Differentiate between behavioral and computer-based actions taken to protect your information assets.

Figure PI7.1 Two types of actions can protect your information assets.

Apply The Concept PI7.1

LEARNING OBJECTIVE PI7.1 Explain why it is critical that you protect your information assets.

STEP 1 – Background (This is what you are learning.)

If you knew all the tricks the thieves would use at a department store, you would know how to fend them off. The same is true online, although it is often much more difficult to know when you have left yourself vulnerable. Sometimes, the best strategy to assess your security is a simple tracking activity.

STEP 2 – Activity (This is what you are doing.)

Spend one hour online. Keep track of every bit of information you put on the computer: usernames, passwords, preferences you complete, Web sites to which you submit your e-mail address, and so on. If you visit a site that can identify you, make note of that. Visit your junk mail at the end of the hour, and see how many messages have been sent to that folder since you began the activity.

STEP 3 – Deliverable (This is what you turn in.)

Review your diary of events, and write a summary to your professor that explains why it is critical that you protect your information assets. Make certain to include specific references to your online activities.

PI7.2 Behavioral Actions to Protect Your Information Assets

You should take certain behavioral actions to protect your information assets. We discuss these actions in this section.

General Behavioral Actions

You should never provide personal information to anyone in any format—physical, verbal, or electronic. As discussed in Chapter 7, you are vulnerable to social engineering attacks at home as well as at work. Therefore, it is critical to be on your guard at all times. For example, always verify that you are talking to authorized personnel before you provide personal information over the telephone. To accomplish this, you should hang up and call back the person or company, at a number that you obtain independently of the phone call. If the call is fraudulent, then the number the caller gives you will also be fraudulent. Credit card companies usually print their numbers on the back of their cards and/or on every statement. Further, you can find telephone numbers on your credit card company's Web site. Similarly, you should never click on a link received in an e-mail. If your bank e-mails you for an account update, then open your Web browser and go directly to the bank's Web site to complete this activity. If you click through the e-mail, you could fall victim to identity theft by giving your information to someone using a fake Web site.

One critical behavioral action you should take is to protect your Social Security number. Unfortunately, far too many organizations use this number to uniquely identify you. When you are requested to provide this number, ask why you cannot substitute some other combination of nine numbers and letters. If the person asking for your Social Security number—for example, someone at your physician's office—is not responsive, then ask to speak with a supervisor. *Remember:* You have to take the initiative here.

The good news is that the use of Social Security numbers for identification has rapidly decreased. For example, the federal Social Security Number Protection Act of 2007 places restrictions on the use of Social Security numbers for identification purposes. The bad news is that you might have to remember many more identifiers. However, your information will become more secure.

Another critical consideration involves your use of credit cards. Securing your credit cards is important because fraudulent credit card use is so widespread. One security measure you can take is to use credit cards with your picture on them. Although cashiers probably cannot read your signature on the back of your card, they can certainly compare your picture to your face. For example, Bank of America will place your picture on several of its credit cards for free. To access this service, visit www.bankofamerica.com/creditcards, click on "Manage Your Account" on the top menu, and then click on "Protect Your Account." Also, do not sign the back of your credit cards. Instead, write "Photo ID Required" on the back.

You may also want to use virtual credit cards, which offer you the option of shopping online with a disposable credit card number. For no extra charge, you sign up at your credit card provider's Web site and typically download software onto your computer. When you are ready to shop, you receive a randomly generated substitute 16-digit number that you can use at the online store. The number can be used only once or, in some cases, repeatedly, but only at the same store. It can also be used to purchase goods and services over the phone and through the mail, although it cannot be used for in-store purchases that require a traditional plastic card. Several companies offer virtual credit cards, but the major ones are Citibank and Discover. (Recall our discussion of virtual credit cards in Chapter 9.)

Also, pay very close attention to your credit card billing cycles. You should know, to within a day or two, when your credit card bills are due. If a bill does not arrive when expected, call your credit card company immediately. If your credit card is stolen and is being used fraudulently, the first thing the thief does is change the address on the account so that you do not receive the bill. Fortunately, you can view your credit card bills online and on most mobile devices. Further, most credit card issuers offer the option to receive your credit card bills via e-mail. This process eliminates postal mail theft as a problem. In addition, when you write checks to pay any of your accounts, particularly your credit card accounts, do not write your complete card number on the "For" line of your check. Instead, write only the last four digits.

Another important action is to limit your use of debit cards. Debit cards are linked to your bank account, meaning that a person who steals your debit card and personal identification number (PIN) can clean out your bank account. In contrast, your liability with credit cards is usually zero (or a small amount). Instead, your credit card company bears the liability for fraudulent charges, provided that you notify the company within 60 days of the theft.

Do not use a personal mailbox at your home or apartment for anything other than catalogs and magazines. Use a private mailbox or a P.O. (Post Office) box. It is far too easy for thieves to steal mail from home mailboxes when no one is at home for much of the day. Think about the wealth of information that could be stolen from your mailbox: credit card statements, bank statements, investment statements, and so on.

When you discard mail or old records, use a cross-cut, or confetti, shredder to cut them up. Recall our discussion of dumpster diving in Chapter 7. A single-cut shredder is not sufficient because, with enough time, a thief can reassemble the strips.

Another security option is to sign up with a company that provides proactive protection of your personal information. Examples of such companies are LifeLock (www .lifelock.com), TrustedID (www.trustedid.com), and Card-Cops (www.cardcops.com).

LifeLock and TrustedID allow customers to lock their credit files so that new lines of credit cannot be opened unless customers first unlock their existing files. When credit files are locked, merchants and banks must have verbal or written permission from the customer before opening new credit in

A paper shredder is a simple, but effective tool to use to protect your identity.

the customer's name. Ordinarily, the locking process involves sending registered mail every 90 days to each of the three major credit agencies: Equifax (www.equifax.com), Experian (www.experian.com), and TransUnion (www.transunion .com). LifeLock and TrustedID perform this service for you and thus proactively monitor your various credit files.

CardCops provides an early warning service that notifies its customers that the company has found their personal information circulating on the Internet. It also collects compromised data on the Internet and makes them available to its customers and to merchants.

What to Do in the Event of Identity Theft

Identity theft is on the rise, with more than 12.5 million victims reported in the United States in 2012. If you follow the behavioral and computer-based actions recommended in this Plug IT In, you will greatly reduce, but not eliminate, the chances that your identity will be stolen.

The Federal Trade Commission (FTC) provides the following instructions of what to do if your identity is stolen. You can review these instructions at www.consumer.ftc.gov/ articles/pdf-0009-taking-charge.pdf. The recommended immediate steps are the following:

1. Place an Initial Fraud Alert by contacting one of the three nationwide credit reporting companies: Equifax, Experian, or TransUnion. Report that you are a victim of identity theft, and request that the company put a fraud alert on your file. Also, make certain the company will contact the other two credit companies. Finally, keep a record of every phone call, letter, e-mail, or other forms of communication for your files.

2. Order your credit reports from each of the three credit reporting companies listed above. Inform them that you have placed an initial fraud alert, and request a free copy of your credit that lists only the last four digits of your Social Security number. Again, keep detailed records of everything you requested and received.

3. Create an Identity Theft Report that includes an Identity Theft Affidavit (you can find examples of this online) and a Police Report.

4. Finally, get in the habit of regularly reviewing your credit report. Pay particular attention to medical benefit explanations from your insurance company, and respond quickly to notices from the Internal Revenue Service (IRS). It is not necessary to obtain legal counsel to report identity theft, but it is a good idea. A lawyer who is experienced in this type of crime will be able to help you get back on your feet more quickly.

┌─ **BEFORE** *YOU GO ON....* ─┐

1. Describe three behavioral actions you can take to thwart social engineering attacks.
2. Describe the steps you should take if you think your identity is stolen.

Apply The Concept PI7.2

LEARNING OBJECTIVE PI7.2 Identify the various behavioral actions you can take to protect your information assets.

STEP 1 – Background

Education is extremely important in being able to determine whether something on the Web is legitimate. This section teaches you how to respond if your identity has been stolen. One way this could happen is via phishing, the process whereby a thief sends an e-mail that looks legitimate and requests your username and login information so that he or she can update it. Once you send that information, your account—and possibly your identity—is no longer secure. (Recall our discussion of phishing in Chapter 7.)

STEP 2 – Activity

Visit http://www.wiley.com/go/rainer/MIS3e/applytheconcept, and click on the link provided for Plug IT In 7.2. This link will take you to a page on the Chase Web site that provides examples of false e-mails. Read over these e-mails, and develop five clues that suggest these messages may be fraudulent. Also, prepare a statement of best practices to pursue when you receive phishing e-mails.

STEP 3 – Deliverable

Based on what you learned by reading this section and reviewing the Chase Web site in Step 2, identify the various behavioral actions you can take to protect your information assets.

PI7.3 Computer-Based Actions to Protect Your Information Assets

You can take many computer-based actions to increase the security of your information. We first discuss how to determine where persons who use your computer have visited on the Internet. Next, we briefly explain how to access social networking sites safely. We then consider how to determine if your computer is infected with malicious software (malware) and what actions you can take to prevent such infections. Next, we discuss how to protect your portable devices—for example, laptops and flash drives—and the information they contain. We follow with discussions of other valuable computer-based actions, how to protect your privacy when using the Internet and e-mail, how to recover from a disaster, and how to protect yourself when you are computing wirelessly.

Determining Where People Have Visited on the Internet Using Your Computer

At home, you may have a single computer or several computers connected to a network. Although you may practice "safe computing," other people who use your computer might not. For example, you might have roommates who use your computer. Their friends could be using your computer as well. You cannot be certain that these individuals take the same safety precautions that you do. You can, however, identify the Internet sites that anyone who uses your computer has visited. To accomplish this task, check the browser history. It is important to note that all modern browsers have a "private browsing" mode in which the viewing history is not recorded. If someone uses private browsing on your computer, then you will not be able to check that person's browser history. The better practice is to keep your computer password protected so that users must enter the correct password to use it. Also, allow only people you trust to access your computer. If you are paying for the Internet connection, then you are responsible for the actions taken on your computer.

The Dangers of Social Networking Sites

You should never post personal information about yourself or your family in chat rooms or on social networking sites. In fact, you should access these Web sites and review any entries that you have made. Although you may never be able to recover all of your entries because someone could have saved copies of pictures you posted or took screen shots of your posts, you can take positive steps to remove them from

© Jure Porenta/Shutterstock

Social Media operates on openness, but safety is in maintaining some privacy.

the main host. The reason for these precautions is that potential employers are now searching these Web sites for information about you. Well-known social networking sites include MySpace, Friendster, Xanga, YouTube, Facebook, and Flickr. Additionally, several people have been robbed when they posted pictures on social networks that let criminals know they were not home.

The good news is that social networking Web sites have added features to give us more control over our information. The bad news is that the privacy settings are not always easy to find and use. Your first decision is whether to make your profile publicly available or to keep it more private. More than one-third of adult users allow everyone to see their profiles. In contrast, some two-thirds restrict access in some way.

On Facebook the default is a private profile, where users decide what information to make publicly available. To make privacy adjustments on Facebook, follow these steps:

- Click on "Settings."
- Click on "Privacy Settings."
- Work with the options you find there.

If you want to keep a low profile on Facebook, it is a good idea to look at the "Applications" section in Privacy Settings. You may have shielded parts of your profile from public access, but that does not mean that you have done the same for Facebook applications that have access to much of the same data by default. For a full explanation of Facebook's privacy settings, see www.facebook.com/privacy/explanation.php.

On LinkedIn, most people want their profiles to be public, and that is the default. The information that LinkedIn users share tends to be professional credentials, not details of their social lives, so there is less need for privacy. If you want additional privacy on LinkedIn, follow these steps:

- Click on "Account & Settings" from your home page.
- Scroll down to adjust your privacy settings.

One company, Reputation Defender (www.reputation defender.com), will search out all information about you on the Internet and present it to you in the form of a report. Then, at your command, it will "destroy all inaccurate, inappropriate, hurtful, and slanderous information about you."

Determining if Your Computer Is Infected

There are several signs to look for if you think your computer system is infected with malicious software or malware (discussed in Chapter 7), including the following:

- Your computer shuts down unexpectedly by itself.
- Your computer does not start normally.
- Your computer exhibits erratic behavior, displaying some or all of these characteristics:
  - Your system unexpectedly runs out of memory on your computer's hard drive.
  - Your system continually runs out of main memory (RAM).
  - Programs take longer to load than normal.
  - Programs act erratically.
  - Your monitor displays strange graphics or messages.
  - Your system displays an unusually high number of error messages.
  - Your e-mail program sends messages to all the contacts in your address book without your knowledge or permission.

If you note any or all of these signs, then your computer might be infected with malware. You can then take the computer-based actions discussed later in this chapter to rid your computer of this software. However, taking the actions discussed in the next section will reduce your chances of being infected in the first place.

Computer Actions to Prevent Malware Infections

Many of the actions we discuss in this section are common sense, but surprisingly large numbers of people do not pay attention to them. Taking these steps will help you prevent a malware infection of your computer system. We begin by considering actions that you must *never* take with your computer.

Never open unrequested attachments to e-mail files, even if they are from people you know and trust. Their computers may have been compromised without their knowledge, in which case the e-mail could be a phishing attack. Never open attachments or Web links in e-mails from people you do not know. These attachments can infect your system with a worm or virus. Similarly, these Web links can be a phishing attack that can infect your system with a Trojan horse, turning your computer into a zombie or bot (short for robot). As we saw in Chapter 7, when this occurs your computer is no longer under your control.

Never accept files transferred to you during Internet chat or instant messaging sessions. These files are usually not from people you know, and they can infect your system.

Never download any files or software over the Internet from Web sites that you do not know. Never download files or software that you have not requested.

Test Your System.
It is a good idea to test your system. Several Web sites provide free security tests. These tests send different types of messages to your computer to evaluate how well your system is protected from a variety of attacks. Free testing Web sites include Shields Up! (www.grc.com), Symantec Security Check (http://security.norton.com), and McAfee My SecurityStatus (search "McAfee My SecurityStatus" on the Web).

Microsoft provides a valuable scanning tool called the Microsoft Baseline Analyzer. This tool scans Windows-based computers for common security problems and generates individual security reports for each computer that it scans. The Baseline Analyzer can be downloaded for free. You can also run free malware scans on your computer. Several companies, including the following, will scan your computer to identify viruses, worms, and other malware, and offer suggestions about how to clean up your system if it is infected:

- Trend Micro (search the Web for "Trend Micro HouseCall")
- Panda Software (http://www.pandasecurity.com/usa)

Install a Security Suite on Your Computer.
Security suites are software packages that contain a variety of security products, such as anti-malware software, spam protection, e-mail fraud protection, spyware detection, intrusion detection, and monitoring software. These suites provide a great deal of functionality in one package. There is a question of whether the individual functions in a security suite can match the combined functions of a group of individual products. Therefore, we discuss individual products in the next sections.

Well-known security suites include the following, but there are many others:

- ZoneAlarm Security Suite (www.zonelabs.com)
- McAfee Internet Security Suite (www.mcafee.com)
- Norton Internet Security (www.symantec.com)
- PC-cillin Internet Security (www.trendmicro.com)

Install an Anti-malware Product on Your Computer.
You should install an anti-malware product on your computer and use it, ideally at least once per week. Remember that every time you scan your computer for malware with your anti-malware product, you must update your malware definitions before you scan. Typically, anti-malware product vendors automatically update your malware definitions over the Web.

There are free anti-malware products and commercial anti-malware products. In general, the free products are adequate, but the commercial products offer more functionality. An excellent resource that offers a great deal of information on free anti-malware products, as well as many other security products, is www.thefreecountry.com. Go to Security > Free Antivirus Software to access their list of anti-malware products.

Well-known commercial anti-malware products include the following, but there are many others:

- Norton Anti-malware (www.symantec.com)
- PC-cillin (www.trendmicro.com)
- VirusScan (www.mcafee.com)

Install a Firewall on Your Computer.
A personal firewall is software installed on your home computer that controls communications to and from your computer by permitting or denying communications based on your security settings. A personal firewall usually will protect only the computer on which the software is installed. Nevertheless, firewalls perform essential functions.

Essentially, firewalls should make your computer invisible. This means that your firewall should not respond to Internet requests to ports (i.e., communications links to your computer) that are not used for common Internet use. In effect, your computer operates in stealth mode on the Internet.

Firewalls also should alert you to suspicious behavior. They should tell you when a program or connection is attempting to do something you have not instructed it to do, such as download software or run a program such as ActiveX. ActiveX (by Microsoft), which can execute programs downloaded from Internet Explorer, can be exploited by attackers trying to compromise your computer. It can be managed on all Windows computers. Search the Web to find instructions on managing ActiveX on your particular operating system and Internet browser.

Firewalls should block outbound connections that you do not initiate. Your firewall should not let your computer access the Internet on its own. If your computer tries to access the Internet by itself, this is a sure sign that it is infected with malware.

As with anti-malware programs, firewall products can be either free or commercially produced. Again, the free products are adequate, but the commercial products offer more functionality. For a list of free firewall software, search "about.com free firewalls".

Many companies offer commercial firewall software. These are some of the best-known commercial firewall products:

- ZoneAlarm Security Suite (www.zonelabs.com)
- Norton Internet Security (www.symantec.com)
- PC-cillin Internet Security (www.trendmicro.com)
- McAfee Internet Security (www.mcafee.com)
- F-Secure Internet Security (www.f-secure.com)
- Panda Platinum Internet Security (www.pandasoftware.com)

It is a good idea to test your firewall. However, it is best to use only those test Web sites that are run by actual firewall or security software companies. A good firewall test site is the

McAfee HackerWatch site at www.hackerwatch.org/probe. The HackerWatch site allows you to perform a basic probe test on your computer to determine whether your firewall is blocking ports that may be vulnerable.

Install an Antispyware Product on Your Computer. As with anti-malware products and firewalls, free antispyware products are adequate, but commercial antispyware products offer greater functionality. Free antispyware products include the following:

- Ad-Aware SE Personal (www.lavasoft.com)
- Spybot Search&Destroy (www.safer-networking.org)

Well-known commercial antispyware products include the following, but there are many others:

- CounterSpy (www.sunbeltsoftware.com)
- Spy Sweeper (www.webroot.com)
- Ad-Aware (www.lavasoft.com)
- SpyCatcher (www.tenebril.com)

In addition, several companies offer free spyware scans:

- Spy Audit (www.webroot.com)
- Zonelabs (www.zonelabs.com)
- Norton (www.symantec.com)

Install Monitoring Software on Your Computer. Monitoring software logs keystrokes, e-mails, applications, windows, Web sites, Internet connections, passwords, chat conversations, Web cams, and even screenshots. Companies that offer monitoring software include the following:

- SpyAgent (www.spytech-Web.com)
- SpyBuddy (www.exploreanywhere.com)
- WinSpy (www.win-spy.com)
- SpectorSoft (www.spectorsoft.com)

Install Content-Filtering Software on Your Computer. Content-filtering software performs many functions. It can block access to undesirable Web sites, and it can record and view all of the Web sites that you or other users have visited. It can also record both sides of chat conversations from AOL Instant Messenger (AIM and AIM Triton), Yahoo! Messenger, and MSN Messenger.

Content-filtering software provides many filter categories, thus enabling you to selectively filter content. Companies that offer this software include the following:

- Cybersitter (www.cybersitter.com)
- NetNanny (www.netnanny.com)
- CyberSpy (www.cyberspyware.com)

Internet Explorer's Content Advisor utility allows you to block access to Web sites that meet specified criteria and to set your own tolerance levels for various types of Internet content. To activate and configure Content Advisor, search the Web for instructions specific to your version of Windows and Internet Explorer.

Install Antispam Software on Your Computer. Antispam software helps you to control spam. Well-known commercial antispam products include the following, but there are many others:

- Cloudmark (www.cloudmark.com)
- MailFrontier Desktop (www.sonicwall.com/)
- SpamKiller (www.mcafee.com)
- Norton Antispam (www.symantec.com)
- SpamGourmet (www.spamgourmet.com)
- SpamAssassin (http://spamassassin.org)

You might also want to set up multiple free e-mail accounts, such as accounts on Hotmail and Gmail. Then, as you surf the Internet and are asked for your e-mail address, you can use one of these accounts rather than your home or business e-mail account. When your free e-mail accounts are full of spam, you can close them and open new accounts.

Manage Patches. Companies typically release software patches to repair security problems. You should download and install all patches immediately—for example, patches for Windows. If you do not, then your computer will be extremely vulnerable to attack. Both Microsoft and Apple provide automatic downloads for updates and patches. It is recommended that you configure your system to automatically download and install these updates so that your computer is not left vulnerable.

Use a Browser Other Than Internet Explorer. You might consider using a browser other than Internet Explorer, such as Firefox (www.mozilla.org), Opera (www.opera.com), Safari from Apple (www.apple.com/safari/download), or Google Chrome (www.google.com/chrome). These browsers are not impregnable, but they are less prominent, and hackers, at least so far, have paid less attention to them.

Use an Operating System Other Than Windows. The two main alternatives to Windows 7 and Windows 8 are Apple's Mac OS X and Linux. These two operating systems are not invulnerable, but they are both based on UNIX, which makes them inherently more secure than any version of Windows. (UNIX is an operating system developed by AT&T in the 1960s and 1970s that usually runs on servers rather than on desktops.) In addition, Linux and Mac OS X have smaller market shares than Windows and thus are less attractive targets for malware.

Protecting Your Portable Devices and Information

Theft or loss of laptops, notebook computers, tablets, thumb drives, and smartphones, as well as the data contained on these devices, is a significant problem. You can take many proactive steps to protect portable devices and their data, including preventing the theft, using two-factor authentication, and encrypting your data. You can also take reactive steps after a theft or loss has occurred. We consider all of these actions in this section.

Before we discuss these steps, there are two commonsense precautions that many people forget. First, keep your laptop in an inconspicuous container. Laptop cases with your company logo simply draw the attention of thieves. Second, do not leave your laptop unattended in plain view—for example, in your car where it can be seen. Instead, lock it in the trunk.

One strategy to prevent the theft of a portable device is to use alarms. Laptop security systems operate by detecting motion, analyzing the motion to determine whether a threat exists, and, if it does, implementing responses. These alarms are battery powered, they are independent of the computer operating system, and they operate whether the laptop is on or off. If a laptop armed with a security system is carried beyond a perimeter specified by the user, then the alarm assumes the laptop is being stolen. In these cases, it can prevent access to the operating system, secure passwords, and encryption keys, and it can sound an audible alarm. One laptop security system is Absolute Software's LoJack for Laptops (www.absolute.com).

Two-factor authentication (discussed in Chapter 7) requires two forms of identification to access your computing device. The first authentication factor uses a token or biometrics. The second factor is your personal password. A token generates a one-time password that you must enter within a specified time limit. This password typically consists of six digits, which appear on the token's LCD screen. Companies offering tokens for two-factor authentication include Authenex (www.authenex.com), Kensington (www.kensington.com), and SecuriKey (www.securikey.com).

Fingerprints are the biometric used for two-factor authentication, by incorporating fingerprint readers into the laptop itself. See IBM (www.ibm.com) and Microsoft (www.microsoft.com). You can also use fingerprint authentication on your thumb drive with the SanDisk Cruzer (www.sandisk.com), the Lexar JumpDrive TouchGuard (www.lexar.com), the Sony MicroVault (www.sony.net), and the Kanguru Bio Slider (www.kanguru.com).

Data encryption provides additional protection by turning data into meaningless symbols that can be deciphered only by an authorized person. You can encrypt some or all of the data on your computer by using built-in encryption, folder-based encryption, or full-disk encryption. If you are not certain how to encrypt files on your particular operating system, search the Web for instructions on how to complete this task. Alternatively, you can purchase a third-party product from firms such as Beachhead Solutions (www.beachheadsolutions.com) and Credant (www.credant.com), which provide applications that allow you to encrypt files and folders.

Another step you can take to improve your security is to encrypt your entire hard drive, including your applications. See Mobile Armor (www.mobilearmor.com), the Kanguru Wizard (www.kanguru.com), and the PCKey (www.kensington.com).

If your laptop is lost or stolen, then you can use laptop-tracing tools or device reset/remote kill tools. For example, the XTool Computer Tracker (www.computersecurity.com), PC PhoneHome (www.pcphonehome.com), and LaptopLocate (www.laptoplocate.net) provide transmitters that secretly send a signal to their respective company control centers via telephone or the Internet. This signal enables the company to track your computer's location, with the help of the local authorities, Internet service providers, and telephone companies.

You can also use device reset/remote kill tools to automatically eliminate specified data on a lost or stolen laptop to prevent it from being compromised or misused. The solution works even when other security software or encryption methods fail. Examples of companies providing these solutions are McAfee (www.trustdigital.com) and Beachhead Solutions (www.beachheadsolutions.com).

Other Actions That You Can Take on Your Computer

Other actions you can perform on your computer to increase your protection include detecting worms and Trojan horses, turning off peer-to-peer file sharing, searching for new and unusual files, detecting spoofed (fake) Web sites, and adjusting the privacy settings on your computer. Often, Microsoft provides tips on how to handle problems on a Windows computer. Mac computers have built-in software to protect, detect, and remove malware automatically. If you are interested in learning how these features work, look up XProtect, Gatekeeper, and Malware Removal Tool (MRT) for Mac.

How to Detect a Worm. Worms are malicious programs that perform unwanted actions on your computer (see Chapter 7). They exhibit several characteristics you can watch for:

- Your system exhibits unexplained hard disk activity.
- Your system connects to the Internet by itself without any action on your part.
- Your system seems to be short on available memory.
- Your family, friends, or colleagues notify you that they have received an odd e-mail message from you that they are certain you did not send.

Ordinarily, your anti-malware software should detect and remove worms. However, if your Windows-based computer is currently infected with a worm, you may not be able to delete that file. In this case, you will have to reboot (start up) your system from a bootable disk and then delete the worm file from the Command Prompt. Then normally, when you reboot your system, the worm file should no longer be present.

How to Detect a Trojan Horse. Trojan horses are malicious programs disguised as, or embedded within, legitimate software (see Chapter 7). On a Windows computer, you can determine if your computer is infected with a Trojan horse by using a DOS-based utility program called Netstat. The steps to use Netstat will vary depending on the version of Windows you are running. However, it is easy to find instructions online.

© Popovici Ioan/Shutterstock

The Trojan horse virus is named for the Trojan Horse offered to Troy by Greece during the Trojan War. It was part of a plan to destroy the city.

(Source: Travel Library Limited/SuperStock)

How to Detect Fake Web Sites. A fake Web site is typically created to mimic a well-known, legitimate site with a slightly different or confusing URL. The attacker tries to trick people into going to the spoofed site and providing valuable information by sending out e-mail messages and hoping that some users will not notice the incorrect URL. (We discussed this attack, known as phishing, in Chapter 7.) Products that help detect fake Web sites include the SpoofStick, the Verification Engine, and McAfee's SiteAdvisor. These products are not definitive solutions, but they are helpful.

The SpoofStick (www.spoofstick.com) helps users detect fake Web sites by prominently displaying a new toolbar in your browser that indicates which site you are actually surfing. For example, if you go to Amazon's Web site, the SpoofStick toolbar says, "You're on amazon.com." However, if you go to a fake Web site that pretends to be Amazon, the SpoofStick toolbar displays the actual IP address of the Web site you are surfing; for example, "You're on 137.65.23.117."

Similarly, the Verification Engine (www.vengine .com) enables you to verify that the site you are visiting or are directed to via e-mail can be trusted. If you move your mouse to the logo brand or image you want to verify, the Verification Engine will authenticate the trust credentials of the site you are surfing. In addition, during a secure communications session with Internet Explorer, you can move your mouse over the padlock to verify that (1) the padlock is genuine and not a fraudulent graphic and (2) the site uses a transport layer security (TLS) certificate (discussed in Chapter 7) that contains the correct information about the company to which you are connected. McAfee's SiteAdvisor (www.siteadvisor. com) sticks a green, yellow, or red safety logo next to search results on Google, Yahoo!, and MSN. It also puts a color-coded button in the Internet Explorer toolbar. Mousing over the button displays details as to why the Web site is good or bad. SiteAdvisor also scores Web sites based on the excessive use of pop-up advertisements, how much spam the Web site will generate if you reveal your e-mail address, and whether the site spreads spyware and adware.

Protecting Your Privacy

In today's hostile Internet environment, you must use strong passwords (discussed in Chapter 7) and adjust the privacy settings on your computer. You may also wish to protect your privacy by surfing the Web and e-mailing anonymously. In this section, we discuss these actions.

Use Strong Passwords. You can use the Secure Password Generator at PCTools to create strong passwords. The Generator lets you select the number and type of characters in your password.

Remembering multiple passwords is difficult. You can use free software such as Password Safe or Roboform (www .roboform.com) to help you remember your passwords and maintain them securely.

How to Adjust Your Privacy Settings on Your Computer. Both Windows and Mac allow you to set personal privacy settings on your computer. Because this process is different for each operating system and space is limited, it is recommended that you visit their respective Web sites for specifics. We do, however, want to make a note about cookies.

Note: A first-party cookie either originates on, or is sent to, the Web site you are currently viewing. These cookies are commonly used to store information, such as your preferences when visiting that site. In contrast, a third-party cookie either originates on, or is sent to, a different Web site from the one you are currently viewing. Third-party Web sites usually provide some content on the Web site you are viewing. For example, many sites rely on advertising from third-party Web sites, which frequently use cookies. A common use for third-party cookies is to track your browsing history for advertising or other marketing purposes.

How to Surf the Web Anonymously. Many users worry that knowledge of their IP addresses is enough for outsiders to connect their online activities to their "real-world" identities. Depending on his or her technical, physical, and legal access, a determined party (such as a government prosecutor) may be able to do so, especially if he or she is assisted by the records of the ISP that has assigned the Internet Protocol (IP) address. To protect their privacy against this type of activity, many people surf the Web and e-mail anonymously.

Surfing the Web anonymously means that you do not make your IP address or any other personally identifiable information available to the Web sites that you are visiting. There are two ways to surf the Web anonymously: You can use an anonymizer Web site as a proxy server, or you can use an anonymizer as a permanent proxy server in your Web browser.

A *proxy server* is a computer to which you connect, which in turn connects to the Web site you wish to visit. You remain anonymous because only the information on the proxy server is visible to outsiders.

For example, consider Anonymouse (http://anonymouse .org). When you access this site, you can click on a link called "Your calling card without Anonymouse." You will see the information that is available to any Web site you visit when you surf normally.

If you want to surf anonymously, enter the URL of the site you want to visit on the Anonymouse Web site where it says "Enter URL." For example, suppose you wish to visit www .amazon.com. You enter this URL where indicated on the Anonymouse Web site. When the Amazon Web site opens on your computer, the URL will look like this: http://anonymouse .org/cgi-bin/anon-www.cgi/http://www.amazon.com/gp/ homepage.html/102-8701104-7307331. You are now anonymous at Amazon because Anonymouse is a proxy server for you, so Amazon sees only the information from Anonymouse. Keep in mind that although anonymous surfing is more secure than regular surfing, it is also typically slower. Other anonymizers include Anonymize (www.anonymize.net), Anonymizer (www.anonymizer.com), IDZap (www.idzap.com), Ultimate Privacy (www.ultimate-anonymity.com), and GhostSurf Platinum. These sites allow you to surf the Web anonymously because the anonymizer acts as a permanent proxy server on your computer.

How to E-Mail Anonymously. The reasons for anonymous e-mail are the same as those for surfing the Web anonymously. Basically, you want to protect your privacy. When you e-mail anonymously, your e-mail messages cannot be tracked back to you personally, to your location, or to your computer. Essentially, your e-mail messages are sent through another server belonging to a company—known as a *re-mailer*—that provides anonymous e-mail services. The recipient of your e-mail sees only the re-mailer's header on your message. In addition, the re-mailer encrypts your messages so that if they are intercepted, they cannot be read. One possible drawback to utilizing a re-mailer is that your intended recipients might not open your e-mail because they will not know it is from you.

Leading commercial re-mailers include CryptoHeaven (www.cryptoheaven.com), Ultimate Privacy (www .ultimate-anonymity.com), and Hushmail (www .hushmail.com). The commercial version of Pretty Good Privacy (PGP) is available at www.pgp.com.

In addition, several free products for anonymous e-mailing and encryption are widely available. For example, the free, open-source version of Pretty Good Privacy, called Open PGP, is available at www.pgpi.org. For a list of these free products and a review of each one, visit http://netsecurity.about .com/. The Outlook e-mail client that comes with Microsoft Office also allows you to encrypt outgoing e-mail messages. This product is based on public key technology (discussed in Chapter 7), so you must download and purchase a digital certificate. The first time you send an encrypted message, Microsoft takes you through the steps necessary to obtain your certificate. Thawte (www.thawte.com) is a company that offers a free personal digital e-mail certificate.

It is a good idea to periodically check the trusted certificate authorities that are configured in your browser and verify

that those companies can be trusted. Again, this process will vary depending on the browser you use. Most browsers make these settings easy to review, so you should be able to find instructions through a simple Web search.

Erasing Your Google Search History. If you have signed up for Google's Personalized Search, then you can follow these steps to erase your search history. First you sign in to your Google account at www.google.com/psearch. You can examine the Search History page and choose days on the calendar to see every search you have made since you created your Google account. Click on the Remove Items button. Remember, however, that even after you remove items from your computer, logs and backups will still exist on Google's servers. To prevent Google from collecting this information in the future, select items such as "Web," "Images," and "News" about which you do not want data collected, and then press the "Pause" button.

Preparing for Personal Disasters

Disasters are not limited to businesses. You can experience disasters at home, such as fires and floods. Therefore, you should take certain steps to protect your information assets, whether they are stored on your computer (digital form) or in another form (hard copy). First and foremost, you should have a safety deposit box at your bank for your important papers. You should also have a fireproof safe at home where you can store other important papers. You should make a regular backup of your key files and keep these backups in the safe as well. You might also want to encrypt your backup files if they contain sensitive information.

Both Windows and Mac have fairly easy processes for restoring backup files. Mac computers use a built-in program called Time Machine; in Windows this program is named System Restore. It is important to have a backup of your files in the event that you need to restore them.

Several third-party companies offer external backup drives that include their own backup and restore systems. Before you purchase one, make certain it is compatible with the operating system you are using.

In recent years, the cloud (see Plug IT In 4) has also become a viable backup alternative. You do not necessarily need to back up your entire computer; rather, you might want to save only your important documents. Dropbox.com, Box .com, Google Drive, Apple's iCloud, Microsoft SkyDrive, and many other companies offer substantial cloud storage space where you can back up photos, videos, and other important files.

Wireless Security

Many home users have implemented a wireless local area network (LAN). The security considerations for wireless networks are greater than those for wired networks. The reason for this is simple. If you are wirelessly computing and communicating, then you are broadcasting, and therefore, by definition, you are nonsecure. The most common reason for intruders to connect to a nonsecure wireless network is to gain access to the Internet. Intruders might also connect in order to use your network as a base for spamming or for other unethical or illegal activities. Finally, they may do so to gain access to your sensitive personal information.

Unfortunately, recent studies have indicated that three-fourths of all home wireless users have not activated any security features to protect their information. Unless you take the steps we discuss here, your information assets are extremely vulnerable.

Hide Your Service Set Identifier (SSID).
Your wireless router, which connects your home network with your ISP, comes with a default SSID that is the same for thousands or millions of routers made by the manufacturer. Therefore, an attacker can search for wireless networks by looking for a relatively small number of default SSIDs. For this reason, you should (1) change your default SSID to a unique SSID and (2) configure your wireless home network to stop broadcasting the SSID. A step-by-step guide to perform these security measures is available online: Simply search "about.com change default SSID."

Use Encryption.
To avoid broadcasting in the clear, you must use encryption with your wireless home network. Wireless equivalent protocol (WEP) is an old protocol that is now very easy to crack and therefore should *not* be used. Instead, you should use Wi-Fi Protected Access (WPA2), which is the second generation of WPA. WPA2 is much stronger than WEP and will protect your encryption against attackers. (*Note:* Your wireless router must support WPA2. Otherwise, use WPA rather than WEP.) In addition, you should use a strong passphrase of at least 20 random characters on your router. (Chapter 7 provides specific instructions for creating strong passphrases.)

Filter Out Media Access Control Addresses.
Every piece of networking hardware has a unique identification number called a media access control (MAC) address that looks like this: 00-00-00-00-00-00. (This MAC address is only an example.) You should compile the MAC address of all computers on your home wireless network. Then, instruct your router to connect only with those computers, and deny access to all other computers that attempt to connect with your network.

Limit Internet Protocol Addresses.
You should instruct your router to allow only a certain number of IP addresses to connect to your network. Ideally, the number of IP addresses will be the same as the number of computers on your network.

Sniff Out Intruders.
A variety of wireless intrusion detection systems will monitor your wireless network for intruders, alert you when intruders are on your network, display their IP addresses and their activity, and even inform them that you know that they are there. Commercial products include the Internet Security Systems (www.iss.net) wireless scanner and AirDefense Personal (www.airdefense.net). AirSnare is a free wireless intrusion detection system.

Using a Public Hotspot.
When you travel, keep in mind that most public wireless providers and hotspots employ *no security measures at all*. As a result, everything you send and receive is in the clear and is not encrypted. Many intruders go to public hotspots specifically to listen in on the wireless computing and communications taking place there. If you must compute wirelessly at a public hotspot, you should take several precautions before you connect.

- Use virtual private networking (VPN) technology to connect to your organization's network (discussed in Chapter 7).
- Use Remote Desktop to connect to a computer that is running at your home.
- Configure the Windows firewall to be "on with no exceptions."
- Only use Web sites that use secure sockets layer (SSL) for any financial or personal transactions.

Test Your Wireless Network.
After you have finished all of the necessary steps to protect your wireless home network, it is a good idea to test the network for vulnerabilities. A free Wi-Fi vulnerability scanner has been created by eEye and is available for download (just search "eEye download" for the link). This tool scans your vicinity looking for wireless devices to test. When you run it, it generates a detailed report that outlines all of the security problems it finds.

Wireless Security Software.
For extra security, you can purchase wireless security programs. Trend Micro (www .trendmicro.com) has added Wi-Fi Intrusion Detection to PC-cillin, which also includes a personal firewall, antivirus software, and antispyware software. The software warns you when an unknown user tries to access your wireless network. Zonelabs (www.zonelabs.com) has a product called ZoneAlarm Wireless Security that automatically detects wireless networks and helps secure them.

McAfee (www.mcafee.com) provides a free scan to check the security of the wireless network connection that you are using. The scan works only with Internet Explorer. Go to www.mcafee.com, click the section for home users, and look under Free Services for McAfee Wi-Fi scan.

Mobile Security

In recent years, technology has created a highly mobile computing market that previously was almost unimaginable. Several basic features of modern information technologies made these innovations possible. First, computer processors have become physically smaller and computationally more powerful, thus enabling small devices to operate at amazing speeds. Second, computer memory has become physically smaller while dramatically expanding its capacity. Consequently, small computers can now store and manipulate massive amounts of data. Third, the rise in high-speed Internet access over multiple channels (cellular and Wi-Fi) allows for near ubiquitous connectivity and distributed processing (cloud computing). Finally, input methodologies have migrated to touchscreens. As a result, smaller and lighter devices now have larger useful screens. Together, these factors have created the rapidly expanding mobile smartphone/tablet market. Today, that market is dominated by two operating systems: Apple's iOS and Google's Android.

As with all new technologies, issues have arisen concerning how people utilize and secure (or don't secure) their mobile devices. Below we discuss some general principles that apply to securing all mobile devices.

Mobile Best Practices. There are a few habits you should develop no matter what mobile device you are using. First, always use a strong password. Your e-mail, contacts, photos, billing information, and other personal data are stored on your mobile device, and a strong password can help protect your information. A strong password is one that is longer and more difficult to crack than the simple four-digit password that some devices allow. Your settings will allow you to create a password that is much more difficult to figure out. Avoid using common words, names (including your name!), birthdays, and other information that is easy to guess.

In addition, you should keep an encrypted backup all of the information on your device. Most of us use our devices to store pictures, music, videos, contacts, files, e-mails, text messages, calendars, and account information. With so much personal information, it is imperative that you regularly back it up. Fortunately, you have quite a few choices here. If you have an Apple iOS device, your backup will either remain on your personal computer or in iCloud (Apple's proprietary cloud product). Both methods are acceptable, and users have different reasons for choosing one over the other. The local backup keeps a complete copy of your data on your computer, which it can restore to your device. The iCloud backup maintains information about settings and apps, but this information has to be re-downloaded from the app store.

In contrast to iOS, Android devices do not offer a built-in backup system. However, there are several apps on the market that perform this task for you. Various apps will back up your photos, text messages, settings, and other key data. MyBackup Pro (www.rerware.com/Android-Backup/) will keep a complete backup of everything.

Also, make use of the auto-lock feature on your device. We all lay down our devices momentarily, and sometimes they are still on and unlocked. Therefore, you want your device to lock itself as quickly as possible so that an unauthorized user cannot gain access to your information.

Currently, mobile devices allow only one user account. Therefore, a device should be used only by the individual whose account is on the device. Perhaps one day you will be able to create multiple user accounts on mobile devices. Until then, do not share or loan any personal device that contains your personal information. If you have an unused device that you loan, make certain to restore it to factory settings so that none of your personal information is still on the device when the borrower uses it.

Today, most smartphones have a global positioning system (GPS) chip to receive location signals from the GPS satellites. (Recall our discussion of GPS in Chapter 10.) This information was originally intended exclusively for navigation purposes. Today, however, many apps use your position to offer location-based advertising, tags within social apps, and other commercial purposes. To prevent every app you download from sharing your location, access your privacy settings, and select the apps you want to share this information with.

As with your computers, you should keep your operating systems updated. All smartphones have a feature to autodownload and install recent apps and security features. Although you may want to wait a day or two to see if there are problems with the latest update, in general you want to update your mobile device as soon as possible. Many updates offer critical patches to vulnerabilities of the operating systems that hackers could exploit.

Be careful with the apps you download. Both Apple and Google offer virtual stores for you to find and purchase apps, but the clearing procedure is not the same with each system. Apple reviews and clears each app before allowing it to be posted on its store. In contrast, Google's Android system allows users to download apps from any Web site and install them. To be safe, follow these tips:

- Download only from a reputable app store such as Google Play or Amazon Appstore where you can read user reviews. Typically, if people have experienced problems with a particular app, it will be obvious in the ratings.

- Do not download apps that do not have ratings!

- Download only official apps. Unfortunately, it is fairly easy to create a fraudulent app that appears to be from a legitimate company. In addition to using a reputable store and reading reviews, try to determine who developed and owns the app before you download it.

- Use an antivirus program such as Lookout Mobile Security (www.lookout.com), Symantec (www.symantec.com/mobility), or AVG (www.avg.com/us-en/for-mobile).

BEFORE *YOU GO ON....*

1. Describe two actions you should take to prevent malware infections.

2. Describe two actions you should take to protect the information on your mobile devices.

3. Describe two actions that you can take to protect your privacy.

4. Describe two mobile best practices for information security.

Apply The Concept PI7.3

LEARNING OBJECTIVE PI7.3

STEP 1 – Background

Computer-based actions are vital to computer security. Significantly, all of these actions begin with the decision to protect your information assets. A vast array of tools is available to help you protect your information. Try to become familiar with these tools, many of which are presented in this chapter.

STEP 2 – Activity

Visit http://www.wiley.com/go/rainer/MIS3e/applytheconcept, and click on the link provided for Plug IT In 7.3. This link will take you to a McAfee product Web site called "Site Advisor." Look for the "How It Works" link at the top of the page. You will see that this simple tool makes it easy for you to be more aware of the security level of the sites you are visiting.

Download and install this tool, and browse the Web for 30 minutes or so. Visit the sites you routinely go to, and write down the security rating McAfee gives each one. Does this activity make you want to change any of your browsing behaviors?

STEP 3 – Deliverable

Considering what you learned in Step 2, identify at least five computer-based actions you can take to protect your information assets. Submit those actions to your instructor in a Word document.

SUMMARY

1. Explain why it is critical that you protect your information assets.

   We live in a digital world. Unfortunately, every time we use our computers or access the Internet, we risk exposing both professional and personal information to people looking to steal or exploit that information. It is your responsibility to protect yourself in our hostile digital environment. Protecting yourself is becoming even more critical because organized crime is increasingly turning its attention to home users. As businesses improve their information security, consumers become the next logical target.

2. Identify the various behavioral actions you can take to protect your information assets.

   - Do not provide personal information to strangers in any format (physical, verbal, or electronic).
   - Protect your Social Security number.
   - Use credit cards with your picture on them.
   - Do not sign the back of your credit cards. Instead, write "Photo ID Required."
   - Pay very close attention to your credit card billing cycles.
   - Limit your use of debit cards.
   - Do not use a personal mailbox at your home for anything other than catalogs and magazines.
   - Use a cross-cut, or confetti, shredder.
   - Sign up with a company that provides proactive protection of your personal information.

3. Identify the various computer-based actions you can take to protect your information assets.

   - Identify the Internet sites that anyone who used your computer visited.
   - Never post personal information about yourself or your family in chat rooms or on social networking sites. Use the privacy features provided by social networking sites to limit public access to your profile.
   - Never open unrequested attachments to e-mail files, even from people you know and trust.
   - Never open attachments or Web links in e-mails from people you do not know.
   - Never accept files transferred to you during Internet chat or instant messaging sessions.
   - Never download any files or software over the Internet from Web sites that you do not know.
   - Never download files or software that you have not requested.
   - Test your system.
   - Run free malware scans on your computer.
   - Install an anti-malware product on your computer, and use it (ideally at least once per week).
   - Install a firewall on your computer.
   - Install an antispyware product on your computer.
   - Install monitoring software on your computer.
   - Install content-filtering software on your computer.
   - Install antispam software on your computer.

- Install proactive intrusion detection and prevention software on your computer.
- Manage patches.
- Use a browser other than Internet Explorer.
- Use a laptop security system.
- Use two-factor authentication.
- Use encryption.
- Use laptop-tracing tools or device reset/remote kill tools.
- Look for new and unusual files.
- Detect fake Web sites.
- Use strong passwords.
- Surf the Web anonymously.
- E-mail anonymously.
- Adjust the privacy settings on your computer.
- Erase your Google search history.
- Personal disaster preparation: back up, back up, back up!
- Wireless security
    - Hide your service set identifier.
    - Use encryption.
    - Filter out media access control addresses.
    - Limit IP addresses.
    - Sniff out intruders.
    - Change the default administrator password on your wireless router to something not easily guessed.
    - Use VPN technology to connect to your organization's network.
    - Use Remote Desktop to connect to a computer that is running at your home.
    - Configure Windows firewall to be "on with no exceptions."
    - Visit only those Web sites that use SSL for any financial or personal transactions.
    - Use wireless security programs.
- Mobile security
    - Use a strong password.
    - Keep an encrypted backup.
    - Use your device's auto-lock feature.
    - Do not share your device.
    - Be careful with whom you share your location.
    - Keep your operating system updated.
    - Use caution with the apps you download.

>>>DISCUSSION QUESTIONS

1. Why is it so important for you to protect your information assets? Can you assume that your organization's MIS department will do it for you?

2. Discuss the differences between behavioral actions that you should take and computer-based actions that you should take.

>>>PROBLEM-SOLVING ACTIVITIES

1. Using one product suggested in this Plug IT In or a product you find, do the following:

    a. Test or scan your computer for malware.

    b. Test your firewall.

    c. Scan your computer for spyware.

2. Follow the steps in this Plug IT In to see if you have a Trojan horse on your computer.

BEFORE YOU GO ON....

1. Why is it so important for you to protect yourself?

2. What are the two types of action that you can take to protect yourself?

INTERNSHIP ACTIVITY>

Hannah Shaw has a friend whose home was recently destroyed by a tornado. Unfortunately, the friend had not backed up her personal information, and she lost years of family photos and important documents. After hearing about this tragedy, Hannah decided to create a backup plan for her personal materials. Below you will find an e-mail from her requesting your assistance with this project

To:	IT Intern
From:	Hannah Shaw
Subject:	Help with a personal protection plan

Hello!

I have a lot to ask of you for this project. Unfortunately, it is a completely personal request. A close friend recently lost all of her computer's and personal data in a tornado. Thankfully, her life was spared, but all of her personal possessions are gone.

I have decided to take the necessary precautions to prevent such a tragedy from happening to me. To do this, I will require your help in several areas. First, I need to learn more about the types of threats—both physical and digital—to which I am susceptible. Also, for the digital threats (malware), please recommend an Internet security package as well any other software you feel would be beneficial. Finally, I want to put a plan in place that will help me to know what to do in the event of a problem. What should a plan like that cover?

Thank you for all of your help on the various projects!

Hannah

Note: Any links or Web sites mentioned in this e-mail are available at http://www.wiley.com/go/rainer/MIS3e/internship.

Index

Page numbers in **bold** indicate end of chapter glossary terms.
Page number in *italics* indicate figures.
Page numbers followed by "t" indicate tables.

A Guide to Icons in This Book

As you read this book, you will notice a variety of icons interspersed throughout the chapters. These icons fall into two groups which highlight different types of content:

The first group of icons highlights material relating to different functional areas. MIS concepts are relevant to all business careers, not just careers in IT. The functional area icons help students of different majors quickly pick out concepts and examples of particular relevance to them. Below is a quick reference of these icons.

 FOR THE ACCOUNTING MAJOR highlights content relevant to the functional area of accounting.

 FOR THE FINANCE MAJOR highlights content relevant to the functional area of finance.

 FOR THE MARKETING MAJOR highlights content relevant to the functional area of marketing.

 FOR THE PRODUCTION/OPERATIONS MANAGEMENT MAJOR highlights content relevant to the functional area of production/operations management.

 FOR THE HUMAN RESOURCES MAJOR highlights content relevant to the functional area of human resources.

 FOR THE MIS MAJOR highlights content relevant to the functional area of MIS.

The second group of icons highlights a general focus of the material. Below is a quick reference of these icons.

 GLOBAL FOCUS appears next to content with a global focus.

 ETHICS FOCUS appears next to content that focuses on business ethics.

 MISUSE OF IS ICON appears next to content that focuses on an IS failure or a misuse of IS.

 GOVERNMENT ICON appears next to content that focuses on IS in government or the public sector.

 SOCIAL ICON appears next to content that focuses on IS that meet a social need.

For full Internship Activities and additional online-only content, please visit the book companion site at www.wiley.com/college/rainer